AF779546

S CORPORATION TAXATION GUIDE

2000 S CORPORATION TAXATION GUIDE

Planning and Compliance for Today's Practitioner

ROBERT W. JAMISON, CPA, Ph.D.

Harcourt Professional Publishing

SAN DIEGO NEW YORK CHICAGO LONDON

In memory of
C. Allen Bock
1943–1999

This publication is designed to provide accurate and authoritative information in regard to the subject matter covered. It is sold with the understanding that the publisher is not engaged in rendering legal, accounting, or other professional service. The publisher has not sought nor obtained approval of this publication from any other organization, profit or non-profit, and is solely responsible for its contents.

Copyright © 2000 by Harcourt, Inc.

All rights reserved. No part of this publication may be reproduced or transmitted in any form or by any means, electronic or mechanical, including photocopy, recording, or any information storage and retrieval system, without permission in writing from the publisher.

Permission is hereby granted to reproduce the CPE Answer Sheet in this publication in complete pages, with the copyright notice, for professional use and not for resale.

Portions of this work were published in previous editions.

HARCOURT and logo are a trademark of Harcourt, Inc.

Printed in the United States of America

ISBN: 0-15-607022-7

99 00 01 02 VG 4 3 2 1

CONTENTS

CONTENTS

PREFACE

The Small Business Job Protection Act of 1996 contains the most important amendments to Subchapter S since 1982, and its effects are being felt by S corporations now more than ever. The 2000 *S Corporation Taxation Guide* covers the Act and its resulting regulatory authority in depth. In addition, the Guide includes:

- Coverage of recent court cases, including important new case law on shareholder basis, corporate bankruptcy basis, and other issues
- Concise guidance on the "fix it" provisions relating to shareholder consents, invalid elections, late elections, and loss of S corporation status, plus analysis of the numerous rulings issued to date in these areas, including major developments from late 1998
- Major restructuring of Chapter 11 for thorough coverage of the important aspects of the built-in gains tax, plus new examples for easier research
- Thorough discussions and citations to the Internal Revenue Code, income tax Regulations, and other primary authority affecting S corporations through June 30, 1999

You'll find clear and concise explanations of the key new rules, including:

- Revenue Procedure 98-55 for late election rules
- Reversal of the *Winn* decision on pass-through of cancellation-of-debt income to shareholders

The Guide uses extensive examples to illustrate both simple and complex situations. In areas where authorities do not provide clear guidance, the author constructs plausible courses of action, with appropriate analysis. Although this Guide focuses primarily on the rules of Subchapter S of the Internal Revenue Code, it also integrates these rules with other portions of the tax law, which can have important effects on S corporations and their shareholders.

At the end of each chapter are pertinent checklists, worksheets, and sample election letters. These are also contained on a disc in versions for both Microsoft Word for Windows and WordPerfect formats. The disc also contains the complete Internal Revenue Code and Regulations for S corporations through July 31, 1999.

The section of the Guide titled "Statutory Authority" contains all the Code sections referenced in the book, so that practitioners can easily review the original language of cited Code sections. In addition, the accompanying CD-ROM contains the full text of significant, recent cases and IRS letter rulings referenced in the book.

Acknowledgments

The author gratefully acknowledges the support of those who encouraged him to undertake the early project, especially James H. Boyd of Arizona State University, Deborah D. Bradly of Anchorage, Alaska, C. Allen Bock of the University of Illinois, Barbara Berry of Davenport, Iowa, and Rod L. Foster of Washington, D.C. Special thanks go to Tracey A. Anderson of Indiana University at South Bend, William A. Duncan of Arizona State University—West, Robert L. Gardner of Brigham Young University, and William N. Kulsrud of Indiana University for their technical review of portions of the earlier drafts. Maryann Gavenda, David Knutte, Norma Bonser Hadley, Susan McClellan, Melissa Y. Schmink, Sally Talarico, and Richard W. Wilberg provided technical assistance.

Over the years, this book has also been enhanced by input from Jim Eisenmenger, Michelle Engle, Brian Fischmar, Catlin Haggerty, Richard Heineke, Myoung Im, Jon Davis, Ellen Nuss, James Pumphret, Andrew Schmidt, Brenda Sharp, Robert Stampf, Tricia Su, John Sulga, and Kevin Walsh. Thanks are due David Berenson, Herbert Lerner, and their partners at Ernst & Young's Washington National Tax Department for their assistance and encouragement on the initial version. The author also thanks his wife, Sharon, his son, Robert, and his daughter, Mary, for proofreading drafts of chapters. The final product would not have been possible without the editorial assistance of Bill Teague, Jon Koschei, Cate DaPron, and Katie Michelmore of Harcourt Professional Publishing.

The author acknowledges the contributions of two outstanding teachers. Without the encouragement of Hjalmar J. Rathe of Portland State University and Ray M. Sommerfeld of the University of Texas at Austin, he would never have had the educational and consulting experience necessary to complete the project.

Finally, the author is saddened by the loss of two of his friends and mentors. Ray Sommerfeld passed away in Austin, Texas, in 1995. Al Bock died at his home in Fisher, Illinois, in 1999. These wonderful gentlemen are sorely missed.

Robert W. Jamison
Professor of Accounting
Indiana University, Indianapolis

ABOUT THE AUTHOR

Robert W. Jamison, CPA, Ph.D., is Professor of Accounting at Indiana University, Indianapolis. In addition to the *S Corporation Taxation Guide*, published annually by Harcourt Professional Publishing, he is the author of *S Corporation, CEA Tax 4*, published by the AICPA. His professional experience has included employment with the University of Illinois, San Diego State University, Portland State University, Ernst & Young, and other national and local CPA firms. His articles have appeared in *The Tax Adviser, Journal of S Corporation Taxation, The Journal of Accountancy*, and various other publications. Jamison has taught many professional education programs for national and local accounting firms and has developed material used in their continuing education programs. He has been a lecturer in AICPA programs and has developed and presented training material for several large accounting firms.

ABOUT THE ELECTRONIC FILES

The CD-ROM provided with the 2000 *S Corporation Taxation Guide* contains electronic versions of all text-based letters, worksheets, and checklists. In addition, it contains the Internal Revenue Code and Regulations for S corporations, current through August 31, 1999; a brief history of the S Corporation business entity, and full text of significant, recent cases and letter rulings.

Note: While every effort has been made to be as complete and as current as possible, these files are included for convenience only. The reader is counseled to check with the appropriate state jurisdiction for the most complete and current information.

Subject to the conditions in the license agreement and the limited warranty, which is displayed onscreen when the disc is installed and is reproduced at the end of the book, you may duplicate the files on this disc, modify them as necessary, and create your own customized versions. Installing the disc contents and/or using the disc in any way indicates that you accept the terms of the license agreement.

The data disc is intended to be used in conjunction with your word processing software. There are versions of each document in WordPerfect® 6.0 and Microsoft Word® 6.0, both for Windows™. If you do not own either of these programs, your word processing package may be able to convert the documents into a usable format. Check your owner's manual for information on the conversion of documents.

Installing the Templates

To install the files on the disc using Windows 95 or above, select the Control Panel from the Start menu. Then choose Add/Remove Programs and select Install. You may also choose Run from the File menu and type Install.exe. You will be asked a series of questions. Read each question carefully and answer as indicated.

First, the installation program will ask you to specify which drive you want to install to. You will then be instructed to specify the complete path where you would like the files installed. The installation program will suggest a directory for you, but you can name the directory anything you like. If the directory does not exist, the program will create it for you.

You can choose to install either Word or WordPerfect files. The program will automatically install the files in Word and/or WordPerfect subdirectories.

Opening the Files

Open your word processing program. If you are using Microsoft Word or WordPerfect 6.0, choose Open from the File menu. Select the subdirectory that contains the loaded files to list the names of the files. Highlight the name of the file you want to open and click OK or press ENTER. You can also open a document in the Windows Explorer (in Windows 95 or above) or from the File Manager (in Windows 3.1) by highlighting the name of the file you want to use and double-clicking your left mouse button.

Refer to the Disc Contents section of the book to find the filename of the document you want to use. The Disc Contents section is also available on your disc in a file called "Contents." You can open this file and view it on your screen or print a hard copy to use for reference.

Word Processing Tips

Wherever possible, the text of the documents has been formatted as tables so that you can modify the text without altering the format of the documents. To maneuver within a table, press TAB to move to the next cell, and SHIFT + TAB to move backward one cell. If you want to move to a tab stop within a cell, press CTRL + TAB. For additional tips on working within tables, consult your word processor's manual. It might be helpful to turn on the invisible table lines in Microsoft Word while modifying the document by selecting Gridlines from the Table menu. In WordPerfect, select Reveal Codes from the View menu to reveal all formatting codes at the bottom of the screen; this will help you to determine the shape of the table.

Microsoft Word and WordPerfect are equipped with search capabilities to help you locate specific words or phrases within a document. The Find option listed under the Edit menu performs a search in both Microsoft Word and in WordPerfect 6.0.

Important: When you are finished using a file you will be asked to save it. If you have modified the file, you may want to save the modified file under a different name rather than the name of the original file. (Your word processing program will prompt you for a file name.) This will enable you to reuse the original file without your modifications. If you want to replace the original file with your modified file, save but do not change the name of the file.

Print Troubleshooting

If you are having difficulty printing your document, the following suggestions may correct the problem:

Microsoft Word

- Select Print from the Microsoft Word File menu. Then choose the Printer function.
- Ensure that the correct printer is selected.
- From this window, choose Options.
- In the media box, make sure that the paper size is correct and that the proper paper tray is selected.
- Check your network connections if applicable.
- If you still have trouble printing successfully, it may be because your printer does not recognize the font Times New Roman. At this point, you should change the font of the document to your default font by selecting the document (CTRL + A) and then choosing Font from the Format menu and highlighting the name of the font you normally use. Changing the font of the document may require additional adjustments to the document format, such as margins, tab stops, and table cell height and width. Select Page Layout from the View menu to view the appearance of the pages before you try to print again.

WordPerfect

- Select Print from the WordPerfect 6.0 File menu. Then choose Select.
- Make sure the correct printer is selected.

- From this menu, press Setup.
- Ensure the correct paper size and paper source are selected.
- You may be having difficulty because your printer does not recognize the selected font. You can correct this problem by changing the base font of the document to your default font. From the Edit menu choose Select All (or press CTRL+A). The entire text of the document should be highlighted. Then choose Font from the Layout menu and highlight the font you normally use. Changing the font of the document may require additional adjustments to the document format, such as margins, tab stops, and table cell height and width. Select Two Page from the View menu to view the appearance of the pages before you try to print again.

DISC CONTENTS

File Name	*Title*
C0201	Checklist 2-1: Shareholder Eligibility
C0202	Checklist 2-2: Trust Eligibility
C0203	Checklist 2-3: Stock Eligibility
C0204	Checklist 2-4: Debt Eligibility
C0205	Checklist 2-5: List of Agreements
C0301	Checklist 3-1: Feasibility of S Election
W0301	Worksheet 3-1: LIFO Recapture
C0501	Checklist 5-1: S Corporation Eligibility
C0502	Checklist 5-2: S Election Procedures
L0501	Sample Letter 5-1: Consent for Shareholder
L0502	Sample Letter 5-2: Consent for Joint or Community Interest Holder
L0503	Sample Letter 5-3: Request for Extension of Shareholder Consent
L0504	Sample Letter 5-4: Resubmission of Form 2553 and Delayed Shareholder Consent
L0505	Sample Letter 5-5: Sample QSST Election
L0506	Sample Letter 5-6: Sample ESBT Election
L0601	Sample Letter 6-1: Election to Reduce Basis for Deductible Items
L0602	Sample Letter 6-2: Election to Terminate Taxable Year under §1377(a)(2)
L0603	Sample Letter 6-3: Election to Terminate Taxable Year for Disposition of Stock
L0604	Sample Letter 6-4: Election to Terminate Taxable Year for Issuance of New Stock
L0701	Sample Letter 7-1: Election to Distribute AEP before AAA
L0702	Sample Letter 7-2: Election to Distribute AEP before PTI
L0703	Sample Letter 7-3: Election to Distribute Deemed Dividend
W0701	Worksheet 7-1: Distributions by Source—No Bypass Election
W0702	Worksheet 7-2: Distributions by Source—AAA Bypass Election
W0703	Worksheet 7-3: Distributions by Source—AAA and PTI Bypass Election or Deemed Dividend Election
W0704	Worksheet 7 - 4: Distributions by Source—No Bypass
W0705	Worksheet 7 - 5: Distributions by Source—AAA Bypass
W0706	Worksheet 7 - 6: Distributions by Source—AAA and PTI
C0801	Checklist 8-1: Agreements between the Corporation and Each Shareholder
C0901	Checklist 9-1: Year-End Basis Planning
W0901	Worksheet 9-1: Stock Basis
W0902	Worksheet 9-2: Stock Basis in Post-1997 Net Loss Year
W0903	Worksheet 9-3: Debt Basis
W0904	Worksheet 9-4: Open Account Debt Basis
C1001	Checklist 10-1: Year-End Amount-at-Risk Planning
W1001	Worksheet 10-1: Stock Amount at Risk

File Name	*Title*
C1703	Checklist 17-3: Divisive Reorganization Considerations
C1801	Checklist 18-1: Premortem Corporate Succession Plan
C1802	Checklist 18-2: Postmortem Corporate Succession Plan
C1803	Checklist 18-3: Premortem Shareholder Succession Plan
history	History of the S Corporation

Subchapter S Code and Regulations through August 31, 1999

FREG	Final Regulations under Subchapter S as of August 31, 1999
PREG	Proposed Regulations under Subchapter S as of August 31, 1999
TREG	Temporary Regulations under Subchapter S as of August 31, 1999
Code	Subchapter S as Amended by the Small Business Job Protection Act of 1996, as in Effect for Taxable Years Beginning after 1997

Cases

CAS01	Bergman v. U.S., 83 AFTR 2d 99-1882 (8th Cir.)
CAS02	Boatner, TC Memo 1997-379
CAS03	Bolding v. Comm., 80 AFTR 2d 97-5481 (5th Cir.)
CAS04	Buda, TC Memo 1999-132
CAS05	Carlins, TC Memo 1988-79, 59 TCM 228
CAS06	Catalano, TC Memo 1998-447
CAS07	Chesapeake Outdoor Enterprises, Inc., TC Memo 1998-175
CAS08	Chesterton v. Chesterton, 80 AFTR 2d 97-7280
CAS09	Conviser, TC Memo 1999-47
CAS10	Cronin, TC Memo 1999-22
CAS11	Custom Chrome, Inc., TC Memo 1998-317
CAS12	Davis, TC Memo 1997-80, aff'd in Davis v. Comm., 82 AFTR 2d 98-5488
CAS13	Ding, TC Memo 1997-435
CAS14	Doe v. Comm., 80 AFTR 2d 97-5535 (10th Cir.)
CAS15	Dugan, TC Memo 1997-458
CAS16	Fankhauser, TC Memo 1998-328
CAS17	Farley, 83 AFTR 2d 99-1641 (DC PA)
CAS18	Foust, TC Memo 1997-446
CAS19	Frederick, 101 TC 35 (1993)
CAS20	Friedman, TC Memo 1998-196
CAS21	Gaudiano, TC Memo 1998-408
CAS22	Green, TC Memo 1998-361
CAS23	Hafiz, TC Memo 1998-104
CAS24	Haymond, TC Memo 1997-289
CAS25	Hillsboro National Bank v. Comm., 460 US 370, 51 AFTR 2d 83-874 (1983)
CAS26	Johnson, Jr., TC Memo 1997-558
CAS27	Joly, TC Memo 1998-361
CAS28	Jones, TC Memo 1997-400
CAS29	LaFavor, TC Memo 1998-366
CAS30	Liberty Vending, Inc., TC Memo 1998-177

File Name	*Title*
CAS31	Mclane Land and Timber Co. v. U.S., 80 AFTR2d 97-6248
CAS32	Miller v. U.S., 83 AFTR 2d 99-1559 (DC WV)
CAS33	Moye, TC Memo 1997-554
CAS34	Musgrave, TC Memo 1997-19, 73 TCM 1721
CAS35	Nahey, 111 TC No. 13
CAS36	Nelson, 110 TC No. 12 (1998)
CAS37	Ng, TC Memo 1997-248
CAS38	Parrish v. Comm., 99-1 USTC Para. 50,293 (8th Cir.)
CAS39	Pahl v. Comm., 82 AFTR 2d 98-5418
CAS40	Payne, TC Memo 1998-227
CAS41	Pugh, TC Memo 1999-38
CAS42	Reed, TC Memo 1997-533
CAS43	Rosenberg, 96 TC 451 (1991)
CAS44	Roy, TC Memo 1998-125
CAS45	Ruckman, TC Memo 1998-83
CAS46	Salem, TC Memo 1998-63
CAS47	Scallen, TC Memo 1987-412
CAS48	Sleiman, TC Memo 1997-530
CAS49	Spencer, 110 TC No. 7 (1997)
CAS50	St. Charles Investment Co., 110 TC No 6 (1998)
CAS51	Streck, TC Memo 1997-407
CAS52	Thurman, TC Memo 1998-233
CAS53	Wagner, TC Memo 1998-338
CAS54	Westbrook, TC Memo 1993-634
CAS55	Williams, 110 TC No. 4 (1998)
CAS56	Witzel, TC Memo 1999-64
CAS57	Wysong, TC Memo 1998-128

Private Letter Rulings

File Name	*Title*
LR01	PLR 9652016
LR02	PLR 9701015
LR03	PLR 9701016
LR04	PLR 9701017
LR05	PLR 9701019
LR06	PLR 9701019
LR07	PLR 9703028
LR08	PLR 9707018
LR09	PLR 9719016
LR10	PLR 9721010
LR11	PLR 9731028
LR12	PLR 9733009
LR13	PLR 9734005
LR14	PLR 9734024
LR15	PLR 9734031
LR16	PLR 9735005
LR17	PLR 9735006
LR18	PLR 9735008
LR19	PLR 9735020
LR20	PLR 9735022
LR21	PLR 9735026
LR22	PLR 9736022
LR23	PLR 9736024
LR24	PLR 9739012
LR25	PLR 9739029
LR26	PLR 9741005

File Name	Title
LR27	PLR 9741006
LR28	PLR 9741008
LR29	PLR 9741024
LR30	PLR 9741028
LR31	PLR 9742034
LR32	PLR 9743005
LR33	PLR 9743008
LR34	PLR 9743009
LR35	PLR 9743014
LR36	PLR 9743036
LR37	PLR 9745011
LR38	PLR 9745017
LR39	PLR 9746012
LR40	PLR 9746037
LR41	PLR 9746038
LR42	PLR 9746046
LR43	PLR 9748022
LR44	PLR 9748024
LR45	PLR 9750026
LR46	PLR 9751009
LR47	PLR 9751027
LR48	PLR 9752041
LR49	PLR 9752054
LR50	PLR 9801008
LR51	PLR 9801029
LR52	PLR 9801029
LR53	PLR 9802041
LR54	PLR 9803008
LR55	PLR 9803008
LR56	PLR 9803023
LR57	PLR 9804008
LR58	PLR 9804018
LR59	PLR 9807002
LR60	PLR 9807003
LR61	PLR 9808013
LR62	PLR 9808021
LR63	PLR 9808028
LR64	PLR 9812008
LR65	PLR 9812033
LR66	PLR 9814003
LR67	PLR 9814009
LR68	PLR 9814013
LR69	PLR 9814017

File Name	Title
LR70	PLR 9814024
LR71	PLR 9815026
LR72	PLR 9815030
LR73	PLR 9815031
LR74	PLR 9815037
LR75	PLR 9816004
LR76	PLR 9816011
LR77	PLR 9817015
LR78	PLR 9818018
LR79	PLR 9818062
LR80	PLR 9820013
LR81	PLR 9821006
LR82	PLR 9823032
LR83	PLR 9825028
LR84	PLR 9826009
LR85	PLR 9827013
LR86	PLR 9827029
LR87	PLR 9828001
LR88	PLR 9828005
LR89	PLR 9828006
LR90	PLR 9828025
LR91	PLR 9829020
LR92	PLR 9829044
LR93	PLR 9830009
LR94	PLR 9830024
LR95	PLR 9831027
LR96	PLR 9832003
LR97	PLR 9832015
LR98	PLR 9832038
LR99	PLR 9833027
LR100	PLR 9834010
LR101	PLR 9834031
LR102	PLR 9837035
LR103	PLR 9838015
LR104	PLR 9839007
LR105	PLR 9839012
LR106	PLR 9839013
LR107	PLR 9839013
LR108	PLR 9840027
LR109	PLR 9840035
LR110	PLR 9841028
LR111	PLR 9841029
LR112	PLR 9842011

File Name	*Title*
LR113	PLR 9842021
LR114	PLR 9842022
LR115	PLR 9842043
LR116	PLR 9843027
LR117	PLR 9843029
LR118	PLR 9846013
LR119	PLR 9847007
LR120	PLR 9852005
LR121	TAM 199908039
LR122	PLR 199904005
LR123	PLR 199905011
LR124	PLR 199906027
LR125	PLR 199906044
LR126	PLR 199907009
LR127	PLR 199908002
LR128	PLR 199908046
LR129	PLR 199909010
LR130	PLR 199909023
LR131	PLR 199909026
LR132	PLR 199920007

Part I

Preparation and the Election

BACKGROUND AND ENVIRONMENT

Contents

100. Overview.

S corporation is a federal income tax concept that allows certain corporations to avoid some or all of the federal corporate income tax. The term has little significance outside of the tax consequences. It is not a unique form of business entity. An S corporation is a corporation for all purposes other than its treatment under tax law. As such, it offers the owners the advantage of limited liability for obligations of the business.

100.1. Types of business entities. There are three basic classifications of business entities, from a tax point of view: Proprietorship, Partnership, and Corporation.

For the most part, the type, or form, of business enterprise is determined by local law. For example, a single-owner business that has not incorporated is a *proprietorship*. A business with two or more owners that has not incorporated is a *partnership*. A business, regardless of its number of owners, may become a *corporation* under local law.

The form of operation of a business entity has significant federal income tax consequences. In general, unincorporated enterprises such as proprietorships or partnerships pay no separate income tax on business profits. Their profits or losses flow through to the owners, who must include these items on their personal income tax returns. In general, owners of unincorporated businesses can transfer property to, or from, the business without recognition of a taxable event. An unincorporated business, however, may have two significant disadvantages, not directly related to taxation:

1. One or more of the owners generally must have unlimited personal liability for all claims against the business. When there is only one owner, there is no realistic way to escape unlimited liability without incorporating.
2. The unincorporated business generally is not well suited to raising large amounts of capital from diverse investors.

In an increasingly litigious society, the limitation of an individual's personal liability may be one of the most important factors to consider in planning and operating a business. Incorporation offers investors limited liability from claims against the business. Accordingly, the corporation has become the most popular method of organizing business ventures. For a widely held business enterprise, incorporation offers the additional advantage of obtaining financing, because investors can readily trade the corporation's shares on established markets. Corporations can issue various classes of debt and equity securities to give individual investors a choice between fixed return securities with low risk and riskier securities that may yield high rates of return.

Incorporation, however, introduces unpleasant tax consequences. Corporate earnings, including earnings distributed as dividends, are subject to the federal income tax. If a corporation incurs losses, the tax benefit may only inure to the corporation itself and not reduce the tax liabilities of its owners. In the realm of the publicly held corporation, the tax factors are undoubtedly reflected in the market price of securities. Investors are aware of the tax structure, and they plan their investments accordingly.

In the case of a closely held corporation, however, the business is likely to be a significant, or even the only, source of income for the owners. Accordingly, the tax cost of incorporation is an extremely important aspect of business planning for these enterprises. The entrepreneur must consider all of the tax aspects of incorporation, in addition to the important feature of limited liability. As contrasted with a proprietorship or partnership, transfers of property to and from the business generally are taxable events. Although there are simple methods for structuring contributions of property to a corporation that do not result in taxation, the reverse is rarely true. Withdrawals of business income may result in tax to both the corporation and its shareholders.

All 50 states and the District of Columbia now recognize a form of business known as the *limited liability company*. An LLC is, in essence, a partnership in which there is no general partner. An LLC can provide valuable nontax benefits, in that its owners bear no personal liability for debts of the business enterprise. Federal tax law does not recognize the LLCs as a separate type of tax entity and most are structured so that they are treated as partnerships for federal tax purposes. An LLC will provide an advantage over the S corporation in terms of flexibility, because these enterprises will not be subject to the same rigid ownership requirements as S corporations. They may have considerably more flexibility in the allocation of profits and losses among the owners. An S corporation, by contrast, has its own advantages. First, it will be much more difficult to convert an existing C corporation to a limited liability company than to convert it to an S corporation. Second, an S corporation's status is certain, even if it has only one shareholder. In some states, an LLC must have more than one owner. (For additional information on limited liability companies, refer to the *Limited Liability Companies Guide* published by Harcourt, Inc.)

100.2. The S corporation, in general. The S corporation offers a reasonable compromise between the nontax benefits and the tax drawbacks of a corporation. The underlying principle of Subchapter S is to shift the burden of taxation from the corporation to its individual shareholders. An S corporation generally pays no income tax on its earnings. This exemption extends to the regular income tax, the alternative minimum tax, the environmental income tax, the accumulated earnings tax, and the personal holding company tax. Routine distributions are also exempt from tax, at least to the extent that shareholders have been required to include the corporation's income on their own returns.

SUMMARY OF AUTHORITY: CODE SECTION 1363(a)

- An S corporation is exempt from any tax imposed by Chapter 1 of Subtitle A of the Internal Revenue Code, including the regular corporate income tax, the alternative minimum tax, the environmental income tax, the personal holding company tax, and the accumulated earnings tax.
- By its wording, §1363(a) allows for exceptions, which are discussed later in this book.

Shareholders include their portions of income and deductions from the corporation on their own returns. [§1366(a)(1)] Shareholders are also able to withdraw their portions of the corporation's income without a second round of taxation. [§1368(b)] There is an important exception to this rule for distributions from former C corporations (see Chapter 7). [§1368(c)(2)]

100.3. Requirements. A corporation must elect to be an S corporation. There are rigid procedural requirements for the election, including time limits and shareholder consent. See Chapter 5.

100.4. Qualifications. To qualify for the S election, a corporation must meet several requirements (discussed in Chapter 2). For tax years beginning after 1996, a corporation must meet the following requirements to qualify as an S corporation:

- The corporation must be a domestic corporation.
- The corporation must have no more than 75 shareholders (35 shareholders before 1997).
- Generally, each shareholder must be an individual U.S. citizen or resident, an estate, or one of a few types of trusts, most of which are specially designed to qualify as shareholders in S corporations. For tax years after 1996, eligible shareholders include a new type of electing small business trust, qualified retirement plan trusts, and charitable organizations.

- The corporation must have only a single class of stock.
- For tax years beginning before 1997, an S corporation was not permitted to be a member of an affiliated group of corporations. That restriction effectively prevented an S corporation from owning more than 80% of another S corporation or a C corporation. For tax years beginning after 1996, S corporations can own 80% or more of a C corporation subsidiary. In addition, an S corporation may now own 100% of the stock of a "qualified Subchapter S subsidiary." (See Chapter 2 and Chapter 14.)

Certain corporations that qualify for other special tax rules cannot be S corporations, even if they meet the qualifications listed above. However, for tax years beginning after 1996, banks (except for those that use the reserve method of accounting for bad debts) can elect S status.

100.5. Popularity of the entity. The Subchapter S election has been extremely popular with owners of closely held corporations. As of 1994, over 2 million corporations, nearly half of the total, were filing as S corporations. [Statistics of Income Bulletin, Spring 1997, page 38]

110. Background.

110.1 Before the Subchapter S Revision Act of 1982. Although the original version of Subchapter S was enacted in 1958, it had its genesis in two 1940s studies that provided concepts that are in Subchapter S even today, and some that are not. [Richard B. Goode, *The Postwar Corporation Tax Structure,* U.S. Treasury Department (1946), and U.S. Treasury Department, Division of Tax Research, *Taxation of Small Business: Hearings Before the House Committee on Ways and Means,* 80th Congress., 1st Sess., part 5 (1947)]

The Revenue Act of 1954 added §1361, which allowed unincorporated associations to be treated like corporations for tax purposes, as part of new Subchapter R. The new Subchapter did not provide any of the nontax benefits of corporations, such as limited liability, was ignored by taxpayers, and was repealed in 1966.

For more details on the early sources and history of Subchapter S, see the author's article, *The History of Subchapter S,* reproduced on the accompanying disk.

110.2. Subchapter S Revision Act of 1982. The Subchapter S Revision Act of 1982 is the basis of the current law governing S corporations. In form, it completely rewrote Subchapter S. It took effect in taxable years beginning after 1982. The new law cleared up many of the problems from the 1958 legislation, but removed some planning opportunities. It also retained most of the eligibility restrictions from the 1958 legislation, although some of the provisions were modified.

Certain "qualified electing casualty insurance corporations" and "qualified oil corporations," which do not meet the eligibility requirements of current law, were allowed to retain their S corporation status under §6(c) of the Subchapter S Revision Act of 1982. These corporations are subject to all of the Subchapter S rules that existed prior to the Subchapter S Revision Act of 1982. This book does not cover the rules applicable to these corporations.

110.3. Amendments to the Subchapter S Revision Act of 1982. Amendments to the Subchapter S Revision Act of 1982 have been frequent, although most have been technical in nature. There were minor revisions and technical corrections in the Technical Corrections Act of 1982 and the Tax Reform Act of 1984.

The Tax Reform Act of 1986, with its reversal of the historic relationships between individual and corporate rates, caused a massive switch to the S election. By electing, corporations could effectively be subject to the individual rates rather than the corporate rates. There were also substantive revisions to Subchapter S in 1986. These changes were significant and generally detrimental to S corporations. The most important were the tax on built-in gains and the restrictions on taxable years allowed to S corporations.

There were further substantive revisions in 1987. The Revenue Act of 1987 added a tax on LIFO reserves of existing corporations making S elections. This provision is a major obstacle to the S election for businesses that have large LIFO reserves. This also provided a new opportunity for S corporations that wanted to keep fiscal years. It allowed a fiscal year election under §444, which requires payment of a tax deposit.

Amendments continued in 1988 and 1989. The Technical and Miscellaneous Revenue Act of 1988 made the built-in gains tax more pervasive, but it provided better coordination with the passive income tax. The Revenue Reconciliation Act of 1989 subjected the built-in gains, passive investment income, capital gains, and investment tax credit recapture tax to estimated payments. There were other minor revisions in these two Acts. The Revenue Reconciliation Act of 1990 made only one technical amendment to Subchapter S, which was a cross-reference to another Code section.

While the Revenue Reconciliation Act of 1993 did not amend Subchapter S, there are some indirect effects on S corporations that relate to the changes in individual and corporate tax-rate brackets. For example, the cost of electing or retaining a fiscal year under §444, discussed in Chapter 4 at 415., increased dramatically. Some S corporations may have converted to the calendar year as a result. The change in the top corporate rate—from 34% to 35%—affects the tax liability of S corporations that are subject to the built-in gains tax, discussed in Chapter 11, or the passive investment income tax, discussed in Chapter 12. There were also changes that affected all taxpayers, including S corporations. These changes are discussed in context throughout the book.

110.4. The Small Business Job Protection Act of 1996. The Small Business Job Protection Act of 1996 contains the most significant amendments to Subchapter S since the Subchapter S Revision Act of 1982. The Act eases the qualification requirements for S corporation status by increasing the limit on the number of shareholder from 35 to 75, allowing new types of S corporation shareholders, and permitting S corporations to own both C corporation and S corporation subsidiaries. In addition, the Act made a number of technical changes.

110.5. The Taxpayer Relief Act of 1997. This Act made only minor technical changes that directly affect S corporations. It specifies that an electing small business trust cannot be a charitable remainder trust (see Chapter 2). It provides that S corporation income passing through to an employee stock ownership plan is not taxable to the plan as unrelated business taxable income. This Act also made some changes that increase the attractiveness of the S corporation vis-à-vis other entities. For instance, gain on the disposition of small business (§1202) corporation stock is taxed at a rate of 28%, whereas gain on the sale of S corporation stock is taxed at 20%, if the stock is held for more than 18 months. A minor change to partnerships makes it more likely that partners will report ordinary income on a portion of gain recognized on a disposition of a partnership interest. This rule also applies to dispositions of interests in limited liability companies. By contrast, certain small C corporations are now exempt from the alternative minimum tax. Therefore, the S corporation will be less attractive than the C corporation where alternative minimum tax is a major factor.

115. Authorities for S corporation tax rules.

The authorities in the Code and regulations are found in §1361 through §1379.

115.1. Statutory authority for S corporations. The statutory authority governing S corporations is found in Title 26 U.S. Code, Subtitle A, Chapter 1, Subchapter S, §§1361–1379. The provisions are reproduced in the Appendix.

115.2. Final Regulations. The IRS has been slow to issue Final Regulations under the Subchapter S Revision Act of 1982. As of this writing, the following Final Regulations have been adopted:

§1.1361-0	Table of contents [of §1361 Regulations]
§1.1361-1	S corporation defined
§1.1362-0	Table of contents [of §1362 Regulations]
§1.1362-1	Election to be S corporation
§1.1362-2	Termination of election
§1.1362-3	Treatment of S termination year
§1.1362-4	Inadvertent termination
§1.1362-5	Election after termination
§1.1362-6	Elections and consents
§1.1362-7	Effective date [of §1362 Regulations]
§1.1363-1	Effect of election on corporation
§1.1363-2	Recapture of LIFO benefits
§1.1366-2	Special rules on requirement to separately state meal, travel, and entertainment expenses
§1.1367-0	Table of contents [of §1367 Regulations]
§1.1367-1	Adjustments to basis of shareholder's stock in an S corporation
§1.1367-2	Adjustments to basis of indebtedness to shareholder
§1.1367-3	Effective date [of §1367 Regulations]
§1.1368-0	Table of contents [of §1368 Regulations]
§1.1368-1	Distributions by S corporations
§1.1368-2	Accumulated adjustments account (AAA)
§1.1368-3	Examples [of §1368 Regulations]
§1.1368-4	Effective date [of §1368 Regulations]
§1.1374-0	Table of contents [of §1374 Regulations]
§1.1374-1	General rules and definitions
§1.1374-2	Net recognized built-in gain
§1.1374-3	Net unrealized built-in gain
§1.1374-4	Recognized built-in gain and loss
§1.1374-5	Deduction carryforwards
§1.1374-6	Credits and credit carryforwards
§1.1374-7	Inventory
§1.1374-8	Section 1374(d)(8) transactions
§1.1374-9	Anti-stuffing rules
§1.1374-10	Effective dates [of §1374 Regulations]
§1.1374-1A	Tax imposed on certain capital gains
§1.1375-1	Tax imposed when passive investment income of corporation having Subchapter C earnings and profits exceeds 25 percent of gross receipts
§1.1377-0	Table of contents [to §137 Regulations]
§1.1377-1	Pro rata share
§1.1377-2	Post-termination transition period
§1.1377-3	Effective date [of §1377 Regulations]

115.3. Temporary Regulations. The IRS issued Temporary Regulations in 1982 that dealt with problems of immediate importance, such as procedures for filing and terminating S elections. Temporary Regulations under the Subchapter S Revision Act of 1982 in effect at the time of writing are as follows:

§18.0	Effective date of temporary regulations under the Subchapter S Revision Act of 1982
§18.1371-1	Election to treat distributions as dividends during certain post-termination transition periods

§18.1378-1	Taxable year of S corporation
§18.1379-1	Transitional rules on enactment
§18.1379-2	Special rules for all elections, consents, and refusals

All of these Temporary Regulations were issued before November 20, 1988. Accordingly, they are not subject to the automatic expiration period of three years, and continue to have the force and effect of law.

115.4. Proposed Regulations. Proposed Regulations under Subchapter S that are outstanding at the time of this writing are as follows:

§1.1361-0	Table of contents [to §1361 Regulations] (Amendment)
§1.1361-1	S corporation defined (Amendment)
§1.1361-2	Definitions relating to S corporation subsidiaries
§1.1361-3	QSSS (QSub) election
§1.1361-4	Effect of QSSS (QSub) election
§1.1361-5	Termination of QSSS (QSub) election
§1.1361-6	Effective date
§1.1362-0	Table of contents [to §1362 Regulations] (Amendment)
§1.1362-2	Termination of election (Amendment)
§1.1362-3	Treatment of S termination year (Amendment)
§1.1362-8	Dividends received from affiliated subsidiaries
§1.1366-0	Table of contents [to §1366 Regulations]
§1.1366-1	Shareholder's share of items of an S corporation
§1.1366-2	Limitations on deduction of pass-through items of an S corporation to its shareholders
§1.1366-3	Treatment of family groups
§1.1366-4	Special rules limiting the pass-through of certain items of an S corporation to its shareholders
§1.1366-5	Effective date [of §1366 Regulations]
§1.1367-0	Table of contents [to §1367 Regulations] (Amendment)
§1.1367-1	Adjustments to basis of shareholder's stock in an S corporation (Amendment)
§1.1368-0	Table of contents [to §1368 Regulations] (2 Amendments)
§1.1368-1	Distributions by S corporations (2 Amendments)
§1.1368-2	Accumulated adjustments account (AAA)
§1.1368-3	Examples (Amendment)
§1.1368-4	Effective date [of §1368 Regulations] and transition rule (Amendment)

115.5. Interpreting Regulations under Subchapter S. The fast pace of legislation in the 1980s outpaced the IRS's ability to write Regulations in many areas, including Subchapter S. Some Final Regulations have become obsolete due to subsequent legislation, although Regulations §1.1375-1 still covers some current law. Some portions of the Temporary Regulations have also been rendered obsolete by legislation enacted since the Subchapter S Revision Act of 1982. The Small Business Job Protection Act of 1996 also renders some portions of existing Regulations obsolete. These authorities must be interpreted with care.

Until the IRS issues comprehensive Final Regulations dealing with all of the general rules of Subchapter S, taxpayers will need to rely on less authoritative pronouncements.

120. Definitions.

Subchapter S begins with two important definitions. This book consistently follows the terms adopted by the Code.

SUMMARY OF AUTHORITY: CODE SECTION 1361(a)

- A corporation that has an S election in effect is termed an *S corporation.*
- Any other corporation is termed a *C corporation.*
- These two definitions are the exclusive meanings of these terms for all tax purposes.

Note that only a *small business corporation* can be an S corporation (covered in detail in Chapter 2). And an S corporation is subject to all the rules of a regular corporation when Subchapter S does not specifically address an issue. Transactions such as contribution of property by a shareholder, stock redemptions, partial and complete liquidations, and tax-free reorganizations are subject to most of the rules in Subchapter C (§§301–386). When there are no specific modifications of these provisions within Subchapter S, the transactions are subject to the Subchapter C rules.

Section 1361 refers to an *election*. Merely complying with all of the requirements of a small business corporation is not enough; the corporation must also follow rigorous rules for making the election. Once filed, the election is effective until it is revoked or terminated. There are restrictions on re-electing S status.

125. Advantages of S corporations over C corporations.

Because each business is unique, the advantages of an S election must be evaluated with respect to the tax situation of that business. The characteristics of each corporation will determine which of these potential advantages are expected to provide tax benefits. Advantages of an S election include:

- The corporation is exempt from the §11 regular income tax, the §§55–59 alternative minimum tax, the §59A environmental income tax, the §§531–537 accumulated earnings tax, and the §541 personal holding company tax.
- The effective rate of tax savings on the S corporation's losses is governed by the individual, rather than by the corporate, rate structure.
- Corporate distributions to shareholders are exempt from a second round of taxation.
- The general exemption applies to both routine operations and distributions of property, such as distribution in liquidation of the business.
- The risk of disallowance of excessive compensation to a shareholder is minimized.
- A corporation that cannot benefit from net operating losses, net capital losses, and credits passes those tax benefits through to its shareholders.
- An S corporation may provide opportunities for family income shifting.
- An S election may allow a leveraged shareholder to deduct acquisition interest without being subject to the investment interest limits.
- A corporation may revoke its S election if the election is no longer advantageous.
- The corporation becomes subject to the individual charitable contribution rules.
- The corporation may use the cash method of accounting, regardless of its gross receipts.
- A corporate-level capital gain will retain its character to the shareholders, subject to a maximum rate of tax of 20%, 25% or 28%.

- An S corporation may invest in certain small business stock and pass the preferential gain treatment to its shareholders.
- S corporations and their shareholders may be subject to better tax treatment on cancellation of corporate debt.

Most of these advantages receive further discussion later in this book. These advantages must be weighed against some of the disadvantages of the S election, (discussed below), and evaluated in light of a particular corporation's circumstances.

130. Disadvantages of S corporations compared to C corporations.

Although the S election is often advantageous, there are drawbacks. Some of the disadvantages, such as the election requirement, are really little more than nuisance provisions. Others may be so significant that a business may find it desirable, or necessary, to forgo S status. Like the advantages, each of the disadvantages must be weighed in light of the situation of a particular business.

The Small Business Job Protection Act of 1996 eases some of the qualification requirements and restrictions on S corporations. Nonetheless, even the more lenient restrictions will pose problems for some corporations. Some of the disadvantages of an S election are:

- Rigid election procedures
- Limitation on number of shareholders
- Limitation on types of eligible shareholders
- Restriction to a single class of stock
- Restrictions on subsidiary corporations
- Inability to file consolidated returns
- Loss of the corporate graduated rate schedule
- Immediate shareholder taxation regardless of distribution
- Inability to utilize carryovers generated in Subchapter C years
- Inability to carry S corporation losses to Subchapter C years
- Restrictions on taxable years
- Inability to shelter fringe benefits on behalf of shareholder-employees
- Prohibition of shareholder-employees to borrow from a qualified retirement plan
- Application of the individual, as opposed to corporate, loss limits of §469
- Disallowance of the dividends-received deduction available to C corporations
- Shareholders subject to the investment interest limits if the corporation has investment interest in excess of investment income
- Corporation subject to the hobby loss deduction limits if the profit motive of any corporate activity is questionable
- The exclusion of up to 50% of the gain from certain small business stock is not available to S corporation shareholders.

135. Special considerations for personal service corporations.

Personal service corporations are subject to special rules. However, there is no single or uniform statutory definition of what constitutes a PSC. Below, the various definitions are briefly described in the context of the tax treatment to which they are subject. The discussion then compares the advantage, disadvantage, or neutrality of the entity's status as an S corporation, as opposed to its treatment as a C corporation.

For most tax rules, including computation of taxable income, distributions, redemptions of stock, liquidations, and reorganizations, a PSC is subject to all of the C corporation rules. A PSC that meets the qualifications to be an S corporation can make an S election. If it becomes an S corporation, its status as a personal service corporation retains little, if any, significance. Unless stated otherwise, a PSC is treated like any other C corporation. In brief, the special tax rules applicable to personal service corporations are as follows:

- The IRS has the power to reallocate items between the owners and the corporation.
- PSCs are subject to restrictions on taxable years.
- PSCs are subject to a flat rate of 35% on taxable income.
- PSCs may use the cash method of accounting.
- PSCs are subject to the same rules as are individuals on passive activity losses.
- PSCs may take advantages of fringe benefits on behalf of shareholder-employees (see Chapter 8, at 825.).

140. Comparison of S corporations to partnerships.

An S corporation is not the same as an incorporated partnership. Although the pass-through of income and losses in an incorporated partnership is similar to the pass-through of income and losses in an S corporation, there are several substantive differences. Among the more important areas of distinction are:

- Restrictions on ownership
- Need for a general partner
- Basis of an owner's interest in the business
- Contributions of property to the business
- Allocations of income among the owners
- Compensation of owner-employees
- Distributions of property to the owners
- Basis adjustments after change in ownership
- Liquidations of the business

A limited liability company generally is the same as a partnership for federal tax purposes. Therefore, all of the comparisons between partnerships and S corporations, except for the need for a general partner, are valid comparisons between S corporations and LLCs.

145. Comparison of S corporations to small business stock corporations.

As an incentive to invest in small business, the Revenue Reconciliation Act of 1993 added a provision whereby investors may exclude 50% of gain from the disposition of *certain small business stock.* [§1202] This investment incentive does not apply to S corporations, since the issuer of the qualified stock must be a C corporation. [§1202(c)(1) & (2)] Some tax advisors may prefer the §1202 small business provision over the S election and may advise clients to not make an S election to qualify stock for this special exclusion. The S election will usually be preferred over the §1202 qualification.

The §1202 exclusion applies only to stock issued after enactment of the Revenue Reconciliation Act of 1993 [§1202(c)(1)] (August 11, 1993) and held by the investor for at least five years. [§1202(a)] Thus, no taxpayer will actually exclude any such gain before 1998. The tax rate applied to the included portion of the gain is 28%, rather than the reduced rate of 20%. [§1(h)(7)]

The corporation may have no more than $50,000,000 aggregate assets at the time of (and immediately after) the issue of the qualified small business stock. In general, the corporation must use substantially all of its assets in the conduct of an active trade or business. [§1202(c)(2)] Certain professional services, rents, and some other sources of income are not treated as an active trade or business for this purpose. [§1202(e)(3)]

The issuing corporation may have no more than $50,000,000 invested capital at the time the qualified small business stock is issued. [§1202(d)(1)(A)] The investor's cumulative exclusion cannot exceed $5,000,000 for any given issue of stock. (Code §1202(b)(1)(A) limits the amount of gain to be taken into account to $10,000,000.) Furthermore, the eligible gain cannot exceed 10 times the investor's aggregate basis in stock of the same issuer that is sold in any given year. [§1202(b)(1)(B)] Any gain that is taxable is treated as a capital gain and is taxed at the 28% maximum rate applicable to capital gains. (This provision appears in the House Committee Report to the Revenue Reconciliation Act of 1993.) Forty-two percent of the excluded gain is treated as a tax preference for alternative minimum tax purposes. [§57(a)(7)] The excluded gain cannot be offset by other capital losses or investment interest.

Only individuals may exclude the gain on the stock. [§1202(a)] Therefore a C corporation cannot qualify as an investor. An individual, however, may exclude his or her proportionate share of gain recognized by an S corporation, when the S corporation is the actual investor. [§1202(g)] The portion of gain excluded by any shareholder is limited to the shareholder's percentage ownership of the S corporation stock at the time the qualified small business stock was acquired.

EXAMPLE 1 - 1: In 1993, Invco invests in qualified small business stock of Issco. In 1998 Invco sold the stock and recognized a gain of $4,000,000. If Invco were a C corporation, the tax would be 35% of $4,000,000, or $1,400,000. If Invco were an S corporation and passed the gain to the shareholders, the total tax at the shareholder level would be:

Gain	$4,000,000
Excluded portion	(2,000,000)
Taxable portion	$2,000,000
Tax at 28%	$ 560,000

Superficially, the combination of a 50% exclusion and a gain taxable at the individual's capital gain rate (currently 28%) would yield an effective rate of tax of 14% on the gain, as opposed to 28% on capital gains generally. Thus an investor could pay more tax on the gain on disposition of S corporation stock than on the same amount of gain on stock that would qualify for the exclusion without an S election.

EXAMPLE 1 - 2: In 1997, Gary invests $1,000,000 in stock of Linco. Five years later he sells the stock for $5,000,000. If the stock is qualified small business stock, Gary's tax would be:

Gain	$ 4,000,000
Excluded portion	(2,000,000)
Taxable portion	2,000,000
Tax at 28%	$ 560,000

If the stock is not qualified small business stock, the tax would be 20% of $4,000,000, or $800,000. There appears to be a tax savings of $240,000 resulting from the §1202 status.

The tax savings from a gain on the sale of qualified small business stock may be reduced for a taxpayer who is subject to the alternative minimum tax (AMT). Forty-two percent of the excluded gain is treated as a tax preference. [§57(a)(7)] Since the highest AMT rate on individuals has been increased to 28%, a taxpayer with AMT considerations may find the tax savings from the qualified small business stock exclusion reduced. The AMT imposes no additional tax on any other capital gain, since the rates of tax are equal.

EXAMPLE 1 - 3: Refer to Example 1 - 2. If Gary were subject to the alternative minimum tax in the year of sale, he would incur additional tax as follows:

42% of excluded gain	$840,000
Alternative minimum tax at 28%	$235,200
Income tax (from Example 1 - 2)	560,000
Total tax from gain	$795,200

If the stock is not qualified small business stock, the tax would be 20% of $4,000,000, or $800,000. Therefore, considering the alternative minimum tax, the tax savings from the §1202 status appears to be only $4,800 ($800,000 – $795,200).

As Examples 1 - 2 and 1 - 3 indicate, some tax savings may result from the disposition of qualified small business stock. Since that provision is not available for stock in an S corporation, the S election may be a disadvantage. There are some mitigating factors, however. For one, the requirements for qualified small business stock are somewhat rigorous and are not applicable to S corporations. The tax treatment of qualified small business stock is available only to an original investor in the corporation. [§1202(c)(1)(B)] Therefore, a subsequent purchaser would be taxed on all of the gain from the sale of such stock.

Second, and perhaps more important, is that there are no basis adjustments permitted for the holder of qualified small business stock. [§1202(b)(1)] See Chapter 9, at 925.1, for discussion of basis adjustments to stock in a C corporation. The basis adjustments on S corporation stock, by contrast, are likely to considerable if the stock is sold at a substantial gain.

The benefits of qualified small business stock treatment apply only to gains. It is unlikely that any investor will profit from this provision unless the corporation has been profitable for the required five-year ownership period.[1] If the corporation is an S corporation, the gains would have passed through to the shareholder, increasing his or her basis and reducing the ultimate taxable gain on the sale.

EXAMPLE 1 - 4: Refer to Examples 1 - 2 and 1 - 3. Assume that Linco was an S corporation and thus that Gary was not entitled to the special qualified small business stock treatment. Also assume that Gary's share of the corporation's taxable income had been $4,000,000 over the five-year period. The corporation had distributed $1,600,000 to Gary over this period in order to allow him to pay his income tax on his share of the corporation's taxable income. Therefore, Gary's basis at the time of sale would be:

Initial investment	$ 1,000,000
Add income from S corporation	4,000,000
Less distributions	(1,600,000)
Basis on date of sale	$ 3,400,000

Gary's gain from the sale would be $1,600,000, which would result in a tax of $320,000 (20% of $1,600,000). This tax is considerably less than Gary would pay under the best possible treatment of qualified small business stock, illustrated in Examples 1 - 2 and

[1] In rare circumstances, the corporation's stock might have appreciated in value with little or no taxable income over the five-year period in which the investor held the stock.

1 - 3. If Gary were subject to the alternative minimum tax, had capital losses from other sources, or both, the sale of S corporation stock would yield far better results than the sale of qualified small business stock.

When evaluating an S election for a corporation whose stock might be qualified small business stock, it is important to consider the basis adjustments allowed to shareholders by Subchapter S. It will be unusual for a corporation that qualifies for an S election to be able to benefit its shareholders by avoiding S status due to the qualified small business stock rules.

150. Other considerations.

Other considerations include special character of income and deductions, among others. For instance, one party may have net capital gains and the other may have net capital losses. Without the S election, the party with the gains would treat them as ordinary income and the other party would receive little, if any, benefit from the capital losses. In this instance, an S election would be advantageous, since the income and losses would be offset at the shareholder level.

150.1. Minimum tax considerations. The corporation might be subject to a book income (1989 and earlier) or adjusted current earnings (1990 and later) alternative minimum tax problem. This adjustment would disappear with an S election.

With an S election in effect, preferences and adjustments (other than book income or adjusted current earnings) as well as taxable income of the two parties would be combined. This could have the effect of reducing or eliminating the alternative minimum tax exemption. In this respect, the S election would be a disadvantage.

150.2. Collateral effects on shareholders. Any increment in adjusted gross income might cause the shareholder to lose tax benefits from medical expenses, personal casualty losses, or miscellaneous itemized deductions. If the corporation is profitable, the shareholder's inclusion of the corporation's income would cost the shareholder certain deductions. If the corporation had a loss, however, the S election would reduce the shareholder's adjusted gross income, and it might give the shareholder additional tax benefits.

The shareholder might have an active rental property outside the corporation. If the S election caused the shareholder's adjusted gross income to exceed $150,000, the shareholder would lose his or her active real estate deduction. In this respect, the S election would be a disadvantage.

OBSERVATION: In some cases, the benefits or drawbacks of the S election are so obvious that the tax advisor will have an easy decision advising the client to make or avoid an S election. In other cases, there may be enough trade-offs that there is a split decision. When in doubt, it is probably better to make the election as soon as the corporation is eligible, rather than waiting until some later date. If the corporation is newly formed, it is probably better off having the election in effect from its inception than waiting until it is a former C corporation. There can be built-in gains and earnings and profits problems with former C corporations that are absent for corporations that have always been S corporations. Chapter 3 discusses problems of former C corporations that can be avoided by corporations making S elections for their initial taxable years.

155. Proposals for change.

Proposals for change must always be considered in evaluating any tax strategy. From 1982 through 1996 there were various proposals for change to Subchapter S and to other Code sections relevant to S corporations. Some of the provisions that had been suggested were included in the Small Business Job Protection Act of 1996 (H.R. 3448). Some of the other changes may be enacted in the future. Table 1-1 shows amendments that have received serious consideration, and the chapters that would be affected if these changes were enacted.

The last provision would be particularly onerous. If enacted, it would impose a prohibitive toll charge on an S election for profitable C corporations.

> **OBSERVATION:** Many amendments have had effective dates applicable to corporations that file S elections on or after a certain date, usually the date that a provision is introduced as legislation that is ultimately enacted. Therefore, there may be some incentive for eligible corporations to file S elections before the constructive liquidation provision is formally introduced.

TABLE 1-1: Proposed Amendments Not Enacted

Proposed Provision	*Affected Chapters*
In testing for the 50-shareholder limit, the S corporation could elect to have the family attribution rules of §267 apply.	2
Nonresident aliens could own shares in S corporations.	2
S corporations could issue preferred stock.	2
Excessive passive investment income would no longer terminate an S election. The tax on excess net passive income would be increased.	12
The limitations on tax-deductible fringe benefits would conform to C corporation rules.	8
S corporations would be allowed to claim a deduction in excess of basis for contributions of inventory and scientific property to certain charitable organizations.	6
Certain losses realized by shareholders on liquidations of S corporations would be ordinary.	16
Certain distributed and undistributed income of S corporations would be taxed to shareholders as self-employment income.	8
An election by an existing C corporation would be treated as a constructive liquidation, resulting in full double taxation as of the effective date of the S election	3, 11, 12

In 1998 and 1999, there have been various proposals to allow Individual Retirement Arrangements to be shareholders in S corporations. A more comprehensive set of changes is included in H.R. 689, which has several sponsors in the House of Representatives. Some of the more important provisions of this bill are listed in Table 1-2.

TABLE 1-2: Proposed Amendments in H.R. 689

Proposed Provision	*Affected Chapters*
Nonresident aliens would be permitted shareholders, subject to withholding of U.S. income tax.	2, 6
S Corporations would be allowed to issue preferred stock	2
Convertible debt would be within the straight debt safe harbor	2
Passive investment income rules would change	12
C corporation rules would apply for charitable contributions	6
C corporation rules would apply for fringe benefits	6
Certain losses realized by shareholders on liquidations of S corporations would be ordinary.	16

2

200. Overview.

To elect and maintain S corporation status, an entity must be a *small business corporation*. The requirements were amended in August 1996 by the passage of the Small Business Job Protection Act of 1996.

SUMMARY OF AUTHORITY (AFTER DECEMBER 31, 1996): CODE SECTION 1361(b)

- A small business corporation must be a domestic corporation.
- It cannot have more than 75 shareholders.
- All shareholders must be individuals, estates, or certain trusts. Certain exempt organizations may become shareholders after December 31, 1997.
- No shareholder may be a nonresident alien.
- A small business corporation cannot have more than one class of stock.
- A bank is allowed to be an eligible small business corporation unless such institution uses a reserve method of accounting for bad debts.
- The corporation cannot be an insurance corporation and cannot elect a possessions tax credit or be a former domestic international sales corporation (DISC).

The S corporation must comply with all of the requirements on the date it files its election, and it must continue to meet the requirements to keep its election in effect.

210. Domestic corporation requirement.

To make an S election, a small business corporation must be a domestic corporation, as defined in Regulations §301.7701-5. An association taxable as a corporation under Regulations §301.7701-2 may elect S corporation status. [Regs. §1.1361-1(c)]

An entity that was a valid corporation under state law, but would not be recognized for federal income tax purposes, could not make a valid S election. [Rev. Rul. 77-440, 1977-2 CB 317] The IRS has also held that associations that were not corporations per se under state law, but were treated as corporations under §7701(a)(3), were eligible to make S elections.[1] In most cases, an entity that desires S corporation status should incorporate under local law and make a timely S election. (See Chapter 5, at 520, for the problems in determining when the first tax year of a new corporation begins.)

In earlier years, the IRS attempted to disallow an S election by a corporation that was not engaged in any active trade or business. The Tax Court held otherwise. [*Buono*, 74 TC 187 (1980)] Thus, an inactive corporation can elect S status. The IRS has recently held that a corporation that had dissolved under state law had not been liquidated for tax purposes. The corporation's charter was retroactively reinstated. The IRS ruled that the S election remained in effect during the period in which the corporation had no valid charter. [PLR 9411040]

> **OBSERVATION:** A limited liability company can qualify for S status, if it elects to be classified as a corporation for federal income tax purposes under Regulations §301.7701-3 (the "check-the-box" regulation for limited liability companies). See PLR 9636007, and discussion in Chapter 17, at 1730.36. The association must meet all of the other eligibility requirements in Subchapter S, and filed a proper and timely S election. In most cases, however, LLCs will probably prefer partnership status. See discussion in Chapter 14, at 1435.2.

---

[1] See PLR 7918056, allowing an Arizona close corporation to make an S election, and PLR 8342088, which permitted an S election for a Massachusetts business trust. Also see PLR 9636007, in which a limited liability

2

A corporation organized under the laws of a foreign country and domesticated in the United States by the filing of certificates of domestication and incorporation qualified as a small business corporation. [PLR 9512001]

215. Eligible shareholders.

The tax classification of shareholders is an important qualification for the S corporation.

SUMMARY OF AUTHORITY: CODE SECTION 1361(b)(1)

- No person other than an individual, an estate, or a trust (but only if the trust meets special qualifications) may be a shareholder.
- Exempt organizations may become shareholders after December 31, 1997.
- No nonresident alien may be a shareholder in an S corporation.

215.1. Individuals. The term *individual* includes U.S. citizens and residents who can be taxed by the United States on their worldwide income. For Subchapter S, this term does not include estates and trusts.

215.11. Identity of true owner. On occasion, the IRS will examine the beneficial, or true, ownership of shares to determine whether or not a shareholder qualifies. For example, Regulation §1.1361(g)(1) provides that if a nonresident alien spouse has a current ownership interest in the stock of the S corporation, by reason of any applicable law (such as community property laws), the corporation has an ineligible shareholder from the time the nonresident alien acquires the interest. According to the Regulations, a survivorship interest does not have the same effect. The person with the survivorship interest would not be treated as a shareholder until the person with the current interest dies, and the survivorship interest becomes a current interest.

215.12. Non–U.S. persons. Generally, a nonresident alien is ineligible to be a shareholder in an S corporation. An exception exists, however, when the nonresident alien is married to a U.S. citizen or resident. [§6013(g)] The nonresident alien spouse may elect to report all of his or her worldwide income on a joint return with the U.S. citizen or resident. [§6013(h)] A spouse who makes such an election becomes a U.S. resident for tax purposes, and thus becomes eligible to hold shares in an S corporation. Such an election may benefit taxpayers in situations similar to that of *Ward v. U.S., 81-2 USTC 9519 (Ct. Cls.),* reviewed in *Ward v. U.S.,* 81-2 USTC 9674 (Ct. Cls.). In another instance a resident alien shareholder returned to his home but continued U.S. resident status. He was an eligible shareholder. [PLR 9018045]

215.13. Dual residence. Certain citizens of other countries are entitled to claim dual resident status. This status allows the dual resident to be treated as a U.S. resident for several purposes. The IRS holds that such a person is treated as a U.S. resident, and thus an eligible shareholder in an S corporation, if he or she does not claim any reduced tax rate due to a treaty between the United States and the country of his or her citizenship. [Proposed Regs. §301.7701(b)-7(a)(4)(ii)] If a dual status resident claims a reduced tax rate under a treaty, he or she is ineligible to be a shareholder in an S corporation. The ineligibility occurs on the first day of the resident's taxable year in which he or she claims the treaty benefit. [Proposed Regs. §301.7701(b)-7(a)(4)(iii)] A dual resident with a treaty benefit, however, may take some steps to become eligible.

1. The person must treat all items of income or loss from the S corporation as pass through items from a U.S. trade or business. [Proposed Regs. §301.7701(b)-7(a)(4)(iv)(A)] By doing so, the resident waives treaty privileges for such income.

2. The resident must treat any gain or loss on the sale of his or her S corporation stock as if it were an interest in a partnership, thereby subjecting such sale to U.S. taxation. [Proposed Regs. §301.7701(b)-7(a)(4)(iv)(A)]
3. The shareholder and the corporation must agree that the corporation will withhold U.S. tax from the income of the S corporation allocated to the dual status resident and also withhold tax attributable to any gain on the disposition of the shareholder's stock. [Proposed Regs. §301.7701(b)-7(a)(4)(iv)(A)]
4. The dual status resident must file Form 1040NR with the Philadelphia Internal Revenue Service Center and indicate on the form that he or she understands that failure to comply with these provisions will cause the corporation to lose its S election. [Regs. §301.7701(b)-7(b) and (c); Proposed Regs. §301.7701(b)-7(c)(3)]

> **OBSERVATION:** If a nonresident alien qualifies to be a shareholder under §6013(g), or if a dual status alien qualifies to be a shareholder, a grantor trust established by one of these persons should also be a qualified shareholder. Similarly, a qualified Subchapter S trust should not fail to be an eligible shareholder if the income beneficiary qualifies under one of these provisions.

Taxpayers have been similarly unsuccessful in trying to preserve S elections when shares were held by ineligible taxpayers, even though beneficial ownership clearly reverted to individuals who were eligible. [See *W & W Fertilizer Corp. v. U.S.*, 76-1 USTC 9130 (Ct. Cls.); *Fulk & Needham, Inc., v. U.S.*, 69-2 USTC 9452 (4th Cir.); and *American Nurseryman Publishing Co.*, 75 TC 271 (1980).]

215.2. Estates. Estates are eligible shareholders; if they were not, an S corporation would lose its election whenever any shareholder died or declared bankruptcy.

215.21. Estates of decedents. An estate of a U.S. citizen or resident may be a shareholder. No special elections or restrictions apply to decedents' estates. They can have multiple beneficiaries, and the executor or administrator may have flexibility with respect to distributions of S corporation income and other property. This is in marked contrast to the restrictions placed on trusts, as explained below.

When the administration of a decedent's estate is unduly prolonged, the estate may be reclassified as a trust. [*Old Virginia Brick Co.*, 44 TC 724 (1965), aff'd *Old Virginia Brick Co.*, 66-2 USTC 9708 (4th Cir.)] If an estate is reclassified as a trust, the S election may be in danger, since it may not meet all of the conditions necessary for a trust to qualify.

215.22. Bankruptcy estates. When a person declares bankruptcy, his or her property is transferred to a bankruptcy estate. Prior to the Bankruptcy Tax Act of 1980, a transfer of S corporation shares to a bankruptcy estate terminated an S election. That Act made a bankruptcy estate an eligible shareholder. [§1361(c)(3)] There is a danger, however, that a bankruptcy court would distribute the bankrupt shareholder's stock to an ineligible person, in which case the S election would be terminated.

215.3. Trusts. For many years, only individuals and estates could be shareholders, with some trusts temporarily allowed to hold shares following the death of a shareholder. Between 1976 and 1981, Congress gradually relaxed this rule and permitted certain trusts to be shareholders. The features of these allowable trusts, discussed below, have created an interesting paradox: Although a trust has the most steeply graduated tax rate of any U.S. tax entity, it is generally not permitted to be an S corporation shareholder. The enforcement of these requirements has been the greatest single source of Subchapter S private letter rulings.

The only trusts that can safely be assumed to qualify as shareholders with no further action on the part of the beneficiaries are grantor trusts (including trusts over which the beneficiary has sufficient powers to be treated as the grantor. Certain voting trusts are also eligible shareholders. See discussion at 215.38. Other trusts will require a careful review of their terms, to see if they qualify as a Qualified Subchapter S Trust (QSST) or an Electing Small Business Trust (ESBT). No foreign trust may be an eligible shareholder, even if it otherwise qualifies under one of these definitions. [§1361(c)(2)(A)]

This section covers grantor trusts, QSSTs, ESBTs, testamentary trusts, and voting trusts.

215.31. Grantor trusts. A grantor trust exists when a person (the grantor) transfers property to a trust but retains rights to use trust property, or to have the property revert to him or her. A trust with these features is not a separate entity for income tax purposes. Among the powers that will cause a trust to be treated as a grantor trust are:

- A reversionary interest, whereby trust property may revert to the grantor [§673(a)]
- Power to control beneficial enjoyment of trust income or property (corpus) [§674(a)]
- Power to borrow trust property without approval of an adverse party, or to borrow without adequate interest or security [§675]
- Power to revoke the trust [§676; PLR 9308006]
- Power to receive distributions of income or corpus [§677; PLR 9309007, clarified in PLR 9323040]

All of the taxable income, deductions, and other tax attributes of the trust pass through to the grantor and are reported directly on his or her tax return. [§671] Although transferring property to a grantor trust serves no tax planning purpose, it may have some other objectives. For instance, property held by a grantor trust may pass directly to designated persons on the death of the grantor without probate. A grantor trust may also be useful in separating property pursuant to a prenuptial agreement, especially in community property states.

A grantor trust is a permitted shareholder in an S corporation, if the grantor is a U.S. citizen or resident. The grantor is treated as the owner. [§1361(c)(2)(A)(i)] The relevant period for making the determination of whether the trust meets the requirements of §1361(c)(2)(A)(i) is the period during which the trust holds S corporation stock. [Regs. §1.1361-1(i)] A trust also qualifies as a shareholder if the beneficiary has sufficient control over trust property to be treated as the recipient of all of the trust's income under §678.

> **EXAMPLE 2 - 1:** George owns all of the shares of S, Inc., an S corporation. In order to ease passage of title at death, and to protect assets from creditors, George transfers 50 shares to GT1 (a trust) and GT2 (also a trust). Income from trust GT1 will be used to support George's son. Income from trust GT2 will be used to support George's daughter. George retains discretion over distributions and retains reversionary interest in both trusts. Both trusts are eligible shareholders.

The IRS occasionally rules that a trust has one or more of the features that causes it to be treated as a grantor trust and thus is eligible to be a shareholder in an S corporation. Many of these rulings merely recognize the existence of one or more of the grantor trust criteria. [e.g., PLRs 9335028, 9404017, 9446008]

Some of the rulings, however, give clues to some hazards and planning opportunities. For example, the IRS has ruled that the mere retention of the power to vote stock is not sufficient to guarantee that the trust will be treated as a grantor trust. The status of the trust, and thus its eligibility to be a shareholder in an S corporation, may depend on the actual exercise of the vote. [PLR 9418024] One power that deserves special mention is the retention by the grantor of a right to substitute property of equal value to the S corporation stock in a nonfiduciary capacity. This power is specified as a power that causes a trust to be a grantor trust. [§675(4); PLRs 9337011, 9648045] Note, however, that the determination of whether the grantor is acting in a nonfiduciary capacity is a question of fact; all circumstances surrounding trust administration will be considered. [PLR 9437022] This power, however, does not exempt the transfer of the stock into trust from the federal gift tax. Thus a grantor may transfer S corporation stock into a grantor retained annuity trust (GRAT) without endangering the corporation's S election. [PLR 9352004]

215.32. Beneficiary controlled trusts, including Crummey trusts. When a grantor transfers property to a trust, and the beneficiary has sufficient control over the property to convert the property to his or her own use, there is a legal fiction that the beneficiary has withdrawn all of the property and contributed it back to the trust. Under §678, when the beneficiary of the trust has the power to remove property from the trust, the beneficiary is taxable on the trust's income, just as if the beneficiary were the grantor. [§678(a); PLRs 9320018, 9311021] If those events actually happened, the beneficiary would have become the grantor. In view of the theoretical transfers, a beneficiary with the power to control trust property is treated in the same manner as a grantor. [§678] A trust of this nature is often known as a *deemed grantor trust*, a *beneficiary controlled trust*, or a *§678 trust*. Any trust that is controlled by the beneficiary, whether the beneficiary is the actual grantor or a deemed grantor, is also known as a *Subpart E trust*. (Code §§671 through 678 are found in Subpart E, Part I, of Subchapter J.) As long as the deemed grantor is a U.S. citizen or resident, a Subpart E trust is eligible to hold shares in an S corporation. [§1361(c)(2)(A)(i)]

When a parent creates a trust for a child, the child may have a reasonable time (usually 30 days after the property is contributed to the trust) to withdraw the contributed property. The reason for such a provision is to make sure that the contribution is a present interest (as opposed to a future interest) in property. Gift of a present interest qualifies for the annual gift tax exclusion of §2503(b). [*Crummey v. Comm'r*, 397 F.2d 82 (9th Cir. 1968). See also Rev. Rul. 73-405, 1973-2 CB 321.] This temporary power to withdraw trust property is often termed a "Crummey Power." The power to direct a trust to distribute income or property to oneself, or to accumulate income or property, is one of the powers that cause a trust to be treated as a grantor trust. [§677(a)] Similarly, the relinquishment of this power is one of the indicia of a grantor trust. When this power has been held by a person other than the grantor, the person who held the power is treated as a grantor. [§678(a)(2)] Thus, vesting a Crummey power in a trust beneficiary causes the trust to be treated as a deemed grantor (or beneficiary-controlled) trust. (See PLRs 9745010, 9809004, 9809005, 9809006, 9809007, 9809008, 9810006, 9810007, and 9810008.) In one instance, a Crummey power was granted to beneficiaries of trusts that had received S corporation shares as part sale, part gift. The withdrawal power required assumption of the purchase money note. [PLR 9801025]

Granting a Crummey power to a child (or other beneficiary) will cause the trust to be a qualifying shareholder in an S corporation under §678, without requiring that the trust meet the rules applicable to the QSST or the ESBT. The grantor must be careful to allow this power on the entire value of the S corporation shares contributed by the trust, rather than on just enough value to qualify for the annual exclusion. If less than the entire value of the shares is subject to the withdrawal power, only the subject portion will qualify as a shareholder. (See PLRs 9739026, 9811028, and 9812006.)

215.33. Grantor trusts, after death of grantor. A grantor trust (or 678 trust) remains an eligible shareholder for a limited time after the death of the grantor (or deemed grantor). The estate of the decedent is treated as the owner for all purposes, including the shareholder limit and any necessary consents that may be required for the various corporate elections. If the entire corpus is included in decedent's estate, the estate must transfer the shares within two years of decedent's death. [§1361(c)(2)(A)(ii)]

EXAMPLE 2 - 2: Susan transfers her shares in Suco, an S corporation, into a trust. The trust property will pass directly to her son, Steve, upon her death, if she dies within 10 years of the transfer. If she does not die within 10 years, the trust assets will revert to Susan. In the meantime, Susan has complete power over distributions of income and corpus. If Susan dies within the 10-year period, the entire trust corpus will be included in her estate. The trustee has two years to distribute the shares from the trust to Steve without causing the trust to be an ineligible shareholder.

If less than the entire corpus is included in the decedent's estate, the period of ownership was much more restrictive before January 1, 1997. The trust was required to transfer all shares out to qualified shareholders within 60 days after the prior owner's death. [§1361(c)(2)(A)(ii)] The IRS has ruled that a grantor trust established by a U.S. resident alien could hold the S corporation stock for 60 days following the grantor's death. [PLR 9301020] The Small Business Job Protection Act of 1996 expanded the post-death holding period to two years for these trusts, for tax years beginning after December 31, 1996.

EXAMPLE 2 - 3: Owen died in 1992, leaving his shares in Owco, an S corporation, to his two daughters, with a life interest to his widow, Martha. Martha has the right to receive income for life and to invade corpus as she desires. During Martha's lifetime, the trust income will be taxed to Martha, pursuant to §678.

If Martha dies, the trust corpus will not be included in her estate. If her death occurs before November 2, 1996, the trust has only 60 days following Martha's death to distribute the S corporation shares to the surviving beneficiaries. However, if Martha dies on or after November 2, 1996, the trust would have two years to distribute the S corporation shares.

In community-property states, the husband and wife may establish a community-property grantor trust. The IRS has ruled that such a trust may continue to hold stock for two years following the death of one spouse, even though the community interest of the surviving spouse is not included in the decedent's gross estate. [PLR 9311036]

A grantor trust can be drafted so that after the death of the grantor, the trust will retain the property in separate shares for various descendants. In such a case, the original trust need not distribute the S corporation stock within two years, provided the terms of the trust that take effect after the grantor's death qualify the trust for QSST status. The beneficiary of each of the shares must make a timely QSST election. [See, for example, PLRs 9311020, 9319025, and 9548013.]

215.34. Qualified Subchapter S trusts. Although QSSTs are not listed in §1361(c) as eligible shareholders, they are indirectly permitted by §1361(d).

SUMMARY OF AUTHORITY: CODE SECTION 1361(d)

- A QSST is treated as a trust controlled by the beneficiary (i.e., a grantor trust), which qualifies it as a shareholder in an S corporation.
- The beneficiary is treated as the owner of the shares.
- The beneficiary must make an election for the trust to be a QSST.

As long as the beneficiary of the QSST is a U.S. citizen or resident, the trust can qualify as a shareholder. However, the trust instrument must contain important restrictions on the powers of the trustee.

SUMMARY OF AUTHORITY: CODE SECTION 1361(d)(3)

- The trust instrument must provide that there is only one current income beneficiary during the life of the current income beneficiary.

- The trust instrument must provide that all current distributions of trust property be made only to the income beneficiary.
- The trust instrument must provide that the income beneficiary's interest in the trust cannot terminate during his or her lifetime.
- The trust instrument must provide that all trust property be distributed to the income beneficiary, if the trust terminates during his or her lifetime.
- The trust instrument may require that all trust income be distributed annually, or the trustee must make annual distributions of income, if the trust instrument does not require these distributions.

A husband and wife who file a joint return, are both U.S. citizens or residents, and are both designated beneficiaries of a trust, are treated as one beneficiary for purposes of meeting the requirement of §1361(d)(3)(A)(i). [Regs. §1.1361-1(j)(2)(i)]

A trust instrument may provide for more than one current income beneficiary, if the rights of the various beneficiaries are so segregated that they constitute separate shares of the trust. In this case, each share is treated as a separate trust. [§1361(d)(3); PLRs 9317016, 9344020, 9627010, 9640010, 9643021, 199922052]

The IRS has allowed a QSST to make distributions to another trust. An individual who was legally incompetent was the beneficiary of a trust that held shares in an S corporation. The individual's guardian set up a disability trust to be used solely for the health, support, and best interests of the individual. Distributions from the first trust were to be paid to the disability trust. The IRS ruled that the individual would be treated as the current income beneficiary of the first, so the trust could make an election to be a QSST. [PLR 9444059]

If any distribution from the trust satisfies the grantor's legal obligation to support the income beneficiary, the trust ceases to qualify as a QSST. The rationale for this rule is that a distribution in satisfaction of the grantor's legal support obligation is a distribution on behalf of the grantor, and not the beneficiary. [Regs. §1.1361-1(j)(2)(ii)(B)] In this case, the grantor is treated either as the owner of the ordinary income portion of the trust or as a beneficiary. As a consequence, it is common to see language in a trust instrument that forbids any distributions from the trust in satisfaction of a grantor's legal support obligation. [PLR 9627010]

The required distributable income is determined by trust accounting rules, rather than taxable income rules. [§643(b)] Under trust accounting rules, for example, the distributions from the S corporation are likely to constitute all of the trust's accounting income, as opposed to the taxable income items that pass through from the S corporation.

EXAMPLE 2-4: Trust Q is a QSST that owns shares in the XYZ Corporation, an S corporation. In the current year, Q's share of the corporation's taxable income is $100,000. XYZ distributes $40,000 to Q. Under the trust accounting rules, Q's income is $40,000, so Q must distribute $40,000 to the beneficiary. For federal tax purposes, however, the trust is treated as a pure pass-through entity, so the beneficiary must report $100,000 on his or her tax return for the current year.

Trust instruments frequently provide that capital gains are not considered trust accounting income. In one ruling, an S corporation distributed cash and cavity storage rights to its shareholders. Two shareholders were QSSTs that distributed cash but retained storage rights. The IRS held that the trusts complied with QSST distribution requirements because storage rights did not constitute trust accounting income. [PLR 8952014]

OBSERVATION: There is no provision in the Code stating that the trustee cannot distribute trust corpus to the beneficiary. The rules merely state that all trust income must be distributed currently and that no person other than the income beneficiary may receive any distribution of trust income or property during that person's lifetime. When one trust has separate shares for two or more individuals, it is a good idea to specify that a distribution of corpus to one beneficiary will not affect the distribution of current or future income to the other beneficiaries. [PLR 9627010]

A trust may have a provision that requires annual income distributions as long as the trust holds shares in an S corporation. The trust instrument may provide that the trustee has discretion to distribute or accumulate income in the event that the corporation no longer holds S corporation stock. [Rev. Rul. 92-20, 1992-1 CB 301, PLR 9649038]

An S corporation redeemed stock from a QSST. The trust was not required to distribute corpus received from the stock redemption. Regular S corporation rules determine how much of a redemption distribution is income and how much is corpus. [PLR 9710026]

Any gain or loss resulting from sale of the S corporation stock must be recognized by the trust, rather than by the current income beneficiary. [Regs. §1.1361-1(j)(8)]

Finally, the beneficiary of the trust must make an election to treat the trust as a Qualified Subchapter S Trust. This election is separate from that filed by the corporation to be an S corporation (details of both elections are covered in Chapter 5). By making the election, the beneficiary agrees to treat the trust as a 678 trust, but only with respect to the stock of the S corporation whose stock is held by the trust.

EXAMPLE 2 - 5: Jerry transfers property to a trust for the benefit of his daughter Carrie. The trust property includes some blue-chip stock, some bonds, and shares in Jerco, an S corporation. Carrie files the appropriate QSST election. By doing so, she agrees to treat the income and other items that pass through from Jerco as if they were received by her 678 trust, and she must include all of the trust's share of Jerco's taxable items on her return each year. This election, however, does not extend to the income from the blue-chip stocks and bonds.

If the QSST holds property other than stock in an S corporation, it must distribute all of its accounting income annually. This requirement extends to income realized from sources other than the S corporation. If a trust holds stock in more than one S corporation, the beneficiary must file a QSST election for each S corporation in which the trust holds stock.

Continued eligibility of the trust as a QSST is necessary for the S corporation to keep its S election in force. There is a dichotomous treatment of a trust's failure to retain its qualifications. If the terms of the trust are amended, so that the trust instrument no longer meets the requisite distribution rules, the S corporation will have an ineligible shareholder as of the day that the trust no longer qualifies. [§1361(d)(4)(A)] However, if the trust no longer distributes income, or is no longer required to distribute income, the trust is an ineligible shareholder as of the first day of the taxable year following the failure to meet the distribution requirement. [§1361(d)(4)(B)]

OBSERVATION: Although the percentage of S corporations that have trusts as shareholders is probably low, the trust qualifications and terms have been the greatest single source of confusion in all of Subchapter S. (See Chapter 13, at 1350., for discussion of trusts and inadvertent terminations of S elections.) Since the trust cannot accumulate any income, it provides little, if any, income tax saving strategies. There are, however, several uses for the QSST as a financial planning device.

EXAMPLE 2 - 6: Dan owns all shares of Danco. He has two minor children, Elaine and Frank. He transfers one-third of Danco's stock to trusts for the benefit of each child. He wants all of the income from the shares to go to the children, and he wants the children to pay the taxes. (Note: Under to the Tax Reform Act of 1986 "Kiddie Tax" rules, there are no potential income tax savings if the children are under age 14.)

He is willing to give up control of the trust assets, so that the trusts will not be treated as grantor trusts. He retains no reversionary interest (except as local law may dictate). The trusts will be eligible shareholders if each child (or guardian) files a QSST election.

The IRS often issues rulings approving the status of QSSTs and grantor trusts as shareholders in S corporations. These rulings typically present no new interpretations of the law. [See, for example, PLRs 9127035, 9133017, 9140055, 9140058, 9141037, 9142005, 9142023, 9142024, 9144028, 9148004, 9152034, 9152043, 9314015, 9314022 (replaced by PLR 9319020), 9338007, 9410032, 9419035, 9440024, 9545004, 9544009, 9543024, 9543028, 9739009, 9815021, 9736017, and 9746036.] The IRS has held that a share of a trust cannot qualify as a QSST if there is even a remote possibility that trust corpus could be distributed to any person other than the current income beneficiary during the beneficiary's lifetime. [Rev. Rul. 93-31, 1993-1 CB 186] However, in one case, the IRS ignored terms in a trust agreement that provided that the assets of one trust, including S corporation stock, would pass to a second trust under certain circumstances. The second trust was never funded and was terminated shortly after it was set up. Because there was no practical possibility that the assets of the first trust would pass to the second trust, the first trust met the requirement for a QSST. [PLR 9437021]

In one instance a trust was required to distribute trust income to its beneficiary until age 25. The trustee had discretion to distribute corpus if needed. The trust terminated when the beneficiary turned 25, at which time he received all of the trust corpus. The IRS ruled that there was a valid QSST. [PLR 9710024]

Under QSST distribution rules, no distribution has to be made for a beneficiary's support when another person is legally obligated to support the beneficiary. Such a distribution would be for the benefit of the obligated person (e.g., the parent of the beneficiary when the beneficiary is a minor) and would not be a distribution to the beneficiary per se. See PLR 9808020.

215.35. Death of a QSST beneficiary. Subchapter S contains no special rules for the successor in interest of the current income beneficiary of a QSST. While this omission allows flexibility when establishing the QSST, it may prove burdensome in the long run. There may be more than one successive beneficiary, or the successive beneficiary may be an ineligible shareholder. In either of these cases, the corporation's S election would terminate upon the death of the current income beneficiary.

If there is only one successive income beneficiary, and that person is eligible to hold shares in an S corporation, the qualification of the trust continues beyond the death of the current income beneficiary. In the event of the current beneficiary's death, the surviving beneficiary need not make a new QSST election. A final hazard in QSSTs, however, exists with the power of a successive income beneficiary to unilaterally revoke the QSST election. [§1361(d)(2)(B)(ii)]

A trust that had qualified as a QSST held stock in an S corporation at the time of the beneficiary's death. The entire trust corpus was included in the beneficiary's gross estate. The trust was treated as an eligible shareholder for two years following the beneficiary's death. After the two-year period, it could no longer qualify as a shareholder, even though the trust had to be maintained for several more years. [PLR 9311025]

> **PLANNING TIP:** The Small Business Job Protection Act of 1996 allows stock in an S corporation to be held by an "Electing Small Business Trust." If it becomes necessary for a testamentary trust to remain an S corporation shareholder after the two-year period has expired, it could possibly look to this provision for temporary relief.

In the year in which a beneficiary of a QSST dies, the income attributable to the shares owned by the trust must be apportioned between the decedent and the successor. The allocation mechanics are discussed in detail in Chapter 6, at 630. These rules, however, do not govern the distributions from the trust to the beneficiaries in the year of death. A carefully drafted trust instrument may provide that all undistributed income at the date of the beneficiary's death must be distributed to the beneficiary's estate. If the trust instrument is silent on distributions in the year of death, the IRS has ruled that the trust must distribute all income received up to the date of death to the beneficiary's estate, and only amounts received after death would be distributed to the new beneficiary. [Rev. Rul. 92-64, 1992-2 CB 214; PLR 9315030]

> **EXAMPLE 2 - 7:** Tom was the current income beneficiary of the Jolly Trust, which owned shares in Annco, an S corporation. Annco, Tom, and the Jolly Trust all used the calendar year. Tom died on September 2, 1995. Jolly Trust was a QSST. Upon Tom's death, Doug became the current income beneficiary of the Jolly Trust. The Jolly Trust's share of Annco's income for 1995 was $36,500. Of this, $24,500 was allocated to Tom and $12,000 was allocated to Doug. (See Chapter 6, at 630.)
>
> The Jolly Trust distributes all income on June 30 and December 31 of each year. On August 1, 1995, Annco made a distribution of $10,000 to the Jolly Trust. On October 1, 1995, Annco made a distribution of $6,000 to the Jolly Trust. The Jolly Trust received no other items of income between July 1 and December 31, 1995. On December 31, 1995, the Jolly Trust must distribute $10,000 to Tom's estate and $6,000 to Doug.

As discussed above, at 215.33., a grantor trust can continue to be a shareholder for two years following the grantor's death, if the entire trust corpus is included in the grantor's gross estate. The IRS has held that a QSST can also continue to hold shares for two years after the beneficiary's death, if the entire trust corpus is included in the deceased beneficiary's gross estate. [PLR 9311025]

215.36. Electing Small Business Trusts. The Small Business Job Protection Act of 1996 allows stock in an S corporation to be held by a new type of shareholder—the "Electing Small Business Trust" (ESBT). The statutory description is brief, and is found in §1361(e).

SUMMARY OF AUTHORITY: CODE SECTION 1361(e)

- An ESBT is an eligible shareholder for S corporation's taxable years beginning after 1996.
- An ESBT may have more than one potential current income beneficiary.
- An ESBT may only have an individual, an estate, or a charitable organization as a potential current income beneficiary.
- An ESBT may not be an exempt trust, a QSST, or a charitable remainder trust.
- A potential current income beneficiary is a person or organization who may receive distributions from the principal or income of the trust, at the discretion of the trustee.
- No person may acquire an interest in the trust by purchase, which includes any transaction for which the basis of acquired property is cost.
- A trust must elect ESBT status.

There are numerous additional rules governing ESBTs. Unlike most trusts, an ESBT must pay tax on its share of the S corporation's income, and may not allocate this income to any beneficiary. [§614(d)(2)] The trust must pay the highest individual rate on all income, except for capital gains. The trust must include any gain or loss on the disposition of S corporation stock in its own income. The trust does not deduct any distribution to its beneficiaries.

The statute is quite brief on certain problems. For instance, it requires that there must be a proper election, but it does not give any specifics as to the time frame for making the election. The IRS has issued the appropriate rules in Notice 97-12, 1997-3 IRB. For election procedures see Chapter 5, at 540.2.

There are other problems with the statue as written. On its face, it appears to offer no possibility that any of a beneficiary's interest can be transferred to another trust. This could make these trusts impossible to use. For example, a grantor might want to provide a contingency that upon the death of a beneficiary, the decedent's interest should be transferred to a QSST for the benefit of the decedent's children. The seeming prohibition against any possibility of any contingent use of a trust beneficiary would cause the trust to violate the ESBT rules. This prohibition would render the ESBT useless. Fortunately, the IRS has clarified the issue, in Notice 97-49, 1997-36 IRB.

This Notice provides that when an ESBT has a provision requiring the stock to be distributed to a trust, upon some event such as the death of a current beneficiary, the beneficiaries of the distributee trust will be treated as the contingent beneficiaries of the ESBT. Thus the successor trust is not treated as a beneficiary of the ESBT. Further, no person who has only a contingent beneficial interest in the trust is treated as a potential current income beneficiary.

> **EXAMPLE 2 - 8:** Fred is a potential current income beneficiary of the FB Trust, which intends to acquire stock in an S corporation. The terms of the trust provide that, in the event of Fred's death, his interest in the trust will be divided and given to two trusts for the benefit of his minor children. According to Notice 97-49, neither the children nor either of the trusts that would be created upon Fred's death is to be treated as a potential income beneficiary of the FB Trust during Fred's lifetime. The contingent beneficiaries would be the children, and not the trusts that would be created upon Fred's death. Nothing in this arrangement would disqualify the FB Trust from being an eligible ESBT. However, at the time of Fred's death, the trusts created for the benefit of the children must meet one of the S corporation qualifications, such as ESBT or QSST eligibility, or the S corporation could be lost at that time.

Notice 97-49 also clarifies the treatment of certain distributions from ESBTs. A distribution received by the trust from the S corporation does not enter into the calculation of distributable net income (DNI) of the trust. It is to be treated in the same manner as income allocated to corpus when the trust calculates the tax effect of its distributions to beneficiaries.

Each potential current beneficiary of the trust is counted as a shareholder for purposes of the 75-shareholder limitation. A *potential current income beneficiary* is any person, with respect to the applicable period, who is entitled to receive, at the discretion of any person, a distribution from the principal or income of the trust. If there are no potential current income beneficiaries, the trust is to be treated as the shareholder.

Recently, the IRS issued rulings on the ESBT problems. In one instance, a trustee had power to apportion distributions between a beneficiary and her children. The trust qualified as an ESBT. [PLR 9809037] However, the IRS refused to rule as to the qualification as an ESBT where a trust would establish a separate share for each afterborn grandchild of the grantor. [PLR 9738021]

215.37. Testamentary trusts. A testamentary trust is created by the terms of a shareholder's will. It may protect a person's assets after his or her death and ease passage of title to a desired beneficiary.

> **EXAMPLE 2 - 9:** Jay, age 46, and Kay, age 38, are husband and wife with two children. Jay realizes that if he should die within the next few years, Kay would probably remarry. He understands that if these events happen, Kay's next husband would have certain rights under local law to all of Kay's property, including what Kay might have inherited from Jay. Jay's will provides that in the event of his death, all of his property will transfer to a trust for the benefit of his two children. This planning may protect his children's rights to his property in the event of his death. This trust, which does not exist in Jay's lifetime, is a testamentary trust.

If a testamentary trust gives sufficient powers to one person so that the trust constitutes a 678 trust, the trust will be an eligible shareholder (if the person with the powers is an eligible shareholder). In that case, the trust need not take any special action.

EXAMPLE 2 - 10: Refer to Example 2 - 9. If Jay dies, Kay can withdraw any property from the trust without approval from any adverse party. This trust will be eligible to hold shares in an S corporation, since Kay is treated as if she were the grantor under §678.

Alternatively, a testamentary trust may contain all of the features defined in the requirements for a QSST. In this case, the trust qualifies as a permanent shareholder, provided the beneficiary makes the appropriate QSST election. [PLR 9348036]

EXAMPLE 2 - 11: Mary, age 64, is the sole shareholder of an S corporation. Her husband Roy, age 76, is not active in the corporation. Her daughter Jean, age 42, is active in the business. Mary's will provides that in the event of her death, all of her shares will be transferred to a trust for the benefit of Roy and Jean. Jean will be the trustee. The trust, however, must annually distribute all of its income to Roy during his lifetime. If the trust terminates during Roy's lifetime, or makes any distribution of corpus, it must all go to Roy. If Roy dies and Jean survives him, all of the trust property will be distributed to Jean.

If Mary dies, and both Roy and Jean survive, the trust will meet the requirements of a QSST. If Roy files an election to treat the trust as a QSST, the trust will be an eligible shareholder. He must file the election within 2 months and 15 days after the date the trust receives the stock.

PLANNING TIP: Example 2 - 10 demonstrates two aspects of estate planning for S corporation shareholders. First, a testamentary trust instrument can be drafted so that the trust is eligible to hold shares in an S corporation. Second, a trust that may qualify as a QSST is eligible only if the beneficiary makes a QSST election for the trust. This procedural aspect is often overlooked and has been a source of numerous ruling requests. To date, the IRS has been lenient in enforcing the deadline for the QSST election. The cost of leniency, however, is the necessity of requesting a private letter ruling.

If a testamentary trust does not qualify as a 678 trust and does not contain all of the features of a QSST, it is still an eligible shareholder, but only for two years after it receives the stock. [§1361(c)(2)(A)(iii)] During this period, the estate was treated as the owner for purposes of the 75-shareholder limit and any necessary consents to corporate elections. The estate must transfer the stock to eligible shareholder(s) within two years of receipt of the stock, or the corporation's S election is lost.

215.38. Voting trusts. A voting trust holds title to shares but has no power other than the right to vote. The right must be temporary, since a voting trust must terminate at a specific time or on the occurrence of some event. The trust document must require that all distributions of the stock be delivered to the beneficial owners, and it must provide that title to the certificates returns to the beneficial owners upon termination of the trust. [Regs. §1.1361-1(h)(1)(v)] In addition, the final version of this Regulation states that a voting trust must be a Subpart E trust (one for which the beneficial owners are treated as the owners of their respective portions of the trust) to qualify as an S corporation shareholder.

A voting trust that meets all of these criteria is an eligible shareholder. Voting trusts were allowed to be shareholders for a few years prior to the Subchapter S Revision Act of 1982. At that time, an S corporation could not issue nonvoting shares. The Subchapter S Revision Act of 1982 permitted nonvoting shares (see discussion below). The principal use of a voting trust under current law is to divert voting power.

EXAMPLE 2 - 12: A and B each own 50 shares of Stirfry Corporation. Each transfers one share to a trustee, who has rights to vote. All distributions and other rights remain with A and B.

2

The nominal ownership of the two shares by the trustee does not create an ineligible shareholder. A and B are considered to be the two sole shareholders for all tax purposes.

A voting trust with a set term can be extended, with the consent of all beneficial owners. [PLR 9410010] Any money or other property received by the trustee from the corporation must be distributed pro rata to each beneficiary, in proportion to his or her percentage of shares held by the trust. [PLR 9311026]

215.39. Other trust problems. It is possible for a trust to be classified as both at QSST and a grantor trust. [PLR 9422041] Ordinarily, this dual qualification would be redundant, since a grantor trust does not need to meet all of the QSST rules. It may, however, be useful to make a QSST election in order to ensure that the trust will continue to qualify as a shareholder after the death of the grantor. As is discussed above, a grantor trust may be limited to a 2-year eligibility period. A QSST, by contrast, is permanently eligible, even after the death of the current income beneficiary.

On occasion, a trust may be retroactively reformed in order to qualify as an eligible S corporation shareholder. The IRS has ruled that it will not give retroactive tax effect to a trust that has been reformed. [Rev. Rul. 93-79, 1993-36 IRB 5] Accordingly, a trust that is retroactively amended to become a QSST after it has received shares will not prevent the corporation from losing its S status. In this situation, the only course of action that will keep the S election in place is an application for inadvertent termination relief. See discussion in Chapter 13, at 1350. A testamentary trust that held stock in a C corporation was required to distribute all of its income to another testamentary trust, pursuant to the terms of the decedent's will. Thus the shareholder was ineligible to hold stock in an S corporation. The shareholder trust was reformed so that the distributions were to be made directly to the beneficiaries of the second trust. After reformation, the trust qualified to be an ESBT. [PLR 9823032]

One way to convert a nonqualifying trust into a qualifying shareholder is to merge the nonqualifying trust into another trust, where the survivor will meet one of the *S corporation shareholder* definitions. [See PLR 9739008.]

Sometimes an arrangement may create a de facto trust under state law. In this event, the trustee may need to file an appropriate election for the trust to be a QSST or an ESBT. [See PLR 9801018.]

Finally, it is possible for one trust to simultaneously meet the definition of both a QSST and an ESBT. As a matter of fact, most QSSTs probably qualify as ESBTs. The IRS has agreed to allow some flexibility to convert between the two trust types. [See Rev. Proc. 98-23, 1998-10 IRB 30.] Also see discussion of the election mechanics in Chapter 5.

215.4. Charitable organizations and pension trusts. These organizations were not permitted as shareholders before the Small Business Job Protection Act of 1996. That Act, however, allowed these organizations to be shareholders, effective for the corporation's first taxable years beginning after 1997. The legislative history is scanty.

SUMMARY OF AUTHORITY: CODE SECTION 1361(c)(6)

- After 1997, a qualified pension, profit-sharing, or stock bonus plan trust (described in §401) may be a shareholder in an S corporation.
- After 1997, a charitable organization (described in §501(c)(3)) may be a shareholder in an S corporation.

There are several complications when one of these entities becomes a shareholder. First, when an individual contributes stock to a charitable organization, the contribution deduction may be less than the fair market value of the stock. The deduction will be reduced by the

2

amount that would be ordinary income of the contributing shareholder if it sold all of its assets at fair market value.[2]

Another complication arises with the entity that holds the S corporation stock. A charitable or pension trust (other than an Employee Stock Ownership Plan) must treat its income flowing through from the S corporation as unrelated business taxable income (UBTI) and pay income tax on this income. [§512(e)] Any gain from disposition of the stock is also UBTI to the trust or charity. [§512(e)(1)(B)(I)] However, it is not UBTI to an ESOP. [§512(e)(3)]

> **OBSERVATION:** A charitably inclined shareholder could benefit the charity by giving a debt security, rather than stock, to the organization. The interest on the security would not be UBTI. After 1997, the debt security would qualify for the straight-debt safe harbor rules, since the charity is eligible to hold shares in the S corporation.

An Employee Stock Ownership Plan (ESOP) has several interesting and unusual tax rules. However, some of those rules do not apply when the stock in question is S corporation stock. For instance, an employer may deduct principal payments on a loan used by the ESOP to acquire employer securities, if the employer is a C corporation, but not if the employer is an S corporation. [§404(a)(9)] In a similar vein, a corporation may deduct dividend payments made to shares held by the ESOP if the corporation is a C corporation, but not if it is an S corporation. [§404(k)] Also, a shareholder who sells stock to an ESOP may, under certain circumstances, defer gain by investing in other securities. This provision also applies only when the stock involved is stock in a C corporation. [§1042(c)(1)(A)] The Small Business Job Protection Act of 1996 also provided that income passing through to the ESOP would be taxable as UBTI. The Taxpayer Relief Act of 1997, however, repealed this rule, so that such income is not UBTI.

In conclusion, although the expansion of the categories of permitted shareholders may provide some benefits to an occasional closely held corporation, it is not likely to cause widespread changes. It is unlikely that a great number of corporations will change to S status merely to take advantage of these new rules.

215.5. Ineligible shareholders. The shareholder eligibility requirements ensure that all of an S corporation's income will be taxed by the U.S. government at individual rates. The S corporation's income cannot be shifted or reallocated by any means other than an outright transfer of shares.

Persons and entities who are ineligible to hold shares in an S corporation are:

- Any individual who is not a U.S. citizen or resident
- Any partnership
- Any C corporation
- Any trust, except for a grantor trust, QSST, Electing Small Business Trust, testamentary trust, or voting trust discussed earlier in this chapter

> **PLANNING TIP:** An S corporation may want to restrict all stock so that any transfer to an ineligible shareholder is null and void. See discussion of the class-of-stock

[2] Section 170(e)(1) states that a rule similar to §751 shall apply. Section 751 applies to partnership interests, and it classifies the amount that would be ordinary income separately from unrealized receivables and inventory items if the partnership sold its assets at fair market value.

problem at 225.4. The IRS has recently ruled that a transfer to an ineligible shareholder, which was null and void under local law, did not terminate the corporation's S election. [PLR 9409023] In a civil non-tax case, a defendant was barred from transferring shares in an S corporation when there was a transfer restriction. The court held that the transfer restriction was valid even though the shareholder claimed to have no knowledge of the restriction. [*Chesterton, Inc. v. Chesterton,* 951 F.Supp. 291 (D. Mass., 1997)] Also see PLR 9733002, where the IRS treated the transfer of stock to an ineligible person as null and void, when the transfer violated restrictions.

Partnerships can formulate ingenious income allocation schemes. The prohibition of these entities as shareholders is consistent with the general focus on administrative simplicity for S corporations. Mere ownership of stock by persons as tenants in common does not rise to the level of being a partnership. Therefore, if the co-owners are all eligible persons, the arrangement does not invalidate an S election. [PLR 9803008]

Similarly, a limited liability company generally would be an ineligible shareholder in an S corporation. However, a single-member limited liability company generally will be disregarded as a tax entity, pursuant to Regulations §301.7701-3(b)(1)(ii). If such an organization's sole owner is an individual, or other eligible S corporation shareholder, the IRS allows the limited liability company to be a shareholder in an S corporation. [See PLR 9745017.]

There is, however, no prohibition against an S corporation being a partner in a partnership.

The ban on C corporations as shareholders in S corporations was enacted when the corporate top rates were considerably lower than those on individuals. Recently, the IRS has been merciful when shares in an S corporation have mistakenly fallen into the hands of a disqualified shareholder. See the discussion in Chapter 13, at 1350.

An employee stock ownership plan (ESOP) was ineligible to hold shares in an S corporation in taxable years beginning before January 1, 1998. An ESOP is a tax-exempt trust; it did not meet any definition of an *eligible shareholder* before the passage of the Small Business Job Protection Act of 1996. The same prohibition extended to pension trusts. The IRS had specifically ruled that an IRA trust cannot be a shareholder in an S corporation. [Rev. Rul. 92-73, 1992-2 CB 224] The results of this ruling are not surprising, since an IRA trust must accumulate income and cannot pass its income and deductions through to a beneficiary. The IRS has also held that a charitable remainder trust cannot be an eligible shareholder in an S corporation.[3] [Rev. Rul. 92-48, 1992-1 CB 301] However, the recently enacted provisions relating to electing small business trusts provide that charitable organizations may hold contingent remainder interests in such trusts beginning in 1997. Charitable organizations have been eligible to be shareholders since 1998, they may be potential current income beneficiaries of ESBTs.

215.6. Nominal and beneficial shareholders. In some cases there is both a nominal and a beneficial owner of stock. Perhaps the most obvious example is a trustee, or fiduciary, who holds title to stock, but may have no beneficial, or economic, attributes of ownership. Recent Regulations specifically hold that a nominal holder need not be one of the eligible types of shareholders, as long as the beneficial owner is eligible. (Regs. §1.1361-1(e)(1) provides that a partnership may hold S corporation stock as nominee for a person who qualifies as an S corporation shareholder.)

This position is consistent with IRS ruling policy for several years. For example, see PLR 9044003, in which shares of an S corporation were owned by several QSSTs. The beneficiary of each trust was a minor. The mother of the children was their legal guardian, and she

---

[3] This denial is based largely on procedural grounds, even though the ruling admits that a trust could meet both the *charitable remainder trust* definition and the definition of a *grantor trust* or *QSST*.

signed all necessary consents on behalf of the children. The mother, however, was a nonresident alien. The IRS accepted the trusts as eligible.

When there is both a nominal and a beneficial owner, the corporation must be careful to establish the identity and role of each person. The IRS will not likely be persuaded that an ineligible person was a nominal owner, unless the corporation has clearly defined the relationships among the parties.

In one case, the taxpayers attempted to persuade the IRS and the Tax Court that a partnership should be able to hold title to shares in an S corporation. Even though all of the partners were individual U.S. citizens, the Tax Court sustained the IRS's disallowance of the S election. [*Kling*, 41 TCM 1133, TC Memo 1981-133] Taxpayers have been similarly unsuccessful in trying to preserve S elections when shares were held by ineligible taxpayers, even though beneficial ownership clearly reverted to individuals who were eligible. [See *W & W Fertilizer Corp. v. U.S.*, 76-1 USTC 9130 (Ct. Cls.); *Fulk & Needham, Inc., v. U.S.*, 69-2 USTC 9452 (4th Cir.); *American Nurseryman Publishing Co.*, 75 TC 271 (1980); and *Kates*, TC Memo, 1968-264.]

> **OBSERVATION:** Whenever there are both nominal and beneficial owners at the time the corporation files an S election, the corporation should be sure that the beneficial owner, as opposed to the nominal owner, consents to the S election. See Chapter 5, at 530.1. [*Kean*, 51 TC 337 (1968); *Cabintaxi Corporation*, 68 TC 49 (1994), TC Memo 1994-316]

220. Limit on number of shareholders.

The maximum number of shareholders allowed for an S corporation is 75. Before January 1, 1997, was 35. There are some planning considerations, discussed below.

220.1. Applying the limit. The shareholder limit is applicable at a given moment in time. There can be more than 35 shareholders (taxable years beginning before January 1, 1997) or 75 shareholders (taxable years beginning after December 31, 1996) in a tax year if purchases and sales keep the number of shareholders to the 35 or 75 limit at any time. [Rev. Rul. 78-390, 1978-2 CB 220] Although the shareholder limit is generally straightforward, a few situations require special analysis:

- Ownership by husband and wife (and their estates)
- Ownership by a testamentary trust
- Ownership by a grantor trust or QSST
- Ownership by an Electing Small Business Trust

There is no combination of related-party ownership, except for the special rules discussed in this section. [Rev. Rul. 59-187, 1959-1 CB 224]

220.11. Husband and wife attribution. When husband and wife own shares, they are counted as one owner.

SUMMARY OF AUTHORITY: CODE SECTION 1361(c)(1)

- Husband and wife are treated as one shareholder.
- When one or both of the spouses dies, this attribution extends to the estate(s).
- This attribution applies only to the 35- or the 75-shareholder limit.

Any form of ownership (community property, separate blocks, joint tenancy, etc.) will not affect the count. [Regs. §1.1361-1(e)(2)]

This exception continues after the death of either or both spouses, as long as the estate(s) of the decedent(s) continues to own the shares. As soon as the estate distributes the shares to a beneficiary (other than the surviving spouse), there would be another owner. If any shares are jointly owned by persons other than husband and wife, each person is counted as a separate owner.

EXAMPLE 2 - 13: Harry and Wilma (husband and wife) each own 100 shares of an S corporation. Harry dies, and stock is transferred to his estate. Harry's estate and Wilma continue to be counted as one owner. If Harry's estate transfers stock to Sammy, Wilma and Sammy are two owners.

If spouses each own stock and are divorced, there will be two owners. If the S corporation is already at the maximum 35- or 75-shareholder limit, the corporation will lose its eligibility.

EXAMPLE 2 - 14: Pursuant to a divorce decree, Warren is awarded half of Helga's shares. If the transfer occurs after the divorce, there are two shareholders as of the date of transfer. If the transfer occurs before the divorce, there are two shareholders at the date of divorce.

PLANNING TIP: If a divorce endangers S status, the corporation or other current shareholder should purchase shares from one of the parties prior to the divorce or the property division.

OBSERVATION: Note that this special treatment of husband and wife as one shareholder is limited to the 35-shareholder or 75-shareholder count. It does not extend to the consent to the S election. See Chapter 5, which deals with the mechanics of election and consent.

220.12. Trust disregarded as owner. Stock owned through artificial entities (estates and trusts) is subject to some special rules. There is no attribution through estates. The estate per se is considered to be the owner, even if it has multiple beneficiaries. Stock owned by a trust, however, is treated as if it were owned by its beneficiaries. This counting rule is consistent with the treatment of grantor trusts and QSSTs as pure pass-through entities. Since these trusts cannot retain any of the income from the S corporation, they are not treated as shareholders for the limit. For example, in PLR 9526021, the IRS ruled that 19 individuals who were the income beneficiaries of a total of 33 QSSTs would be treated as 19 shareholders for purposes of applying the shareholder limit.

If shares are owned by a grantor trust, the grantor is treated as the owner; the same treatment is true for the deemed owner of a 678 trust. The current income beneficiary of a QSST is counted as the holder of all shares owned by the trust. When a testamentary trust owns stock, the estate is treated as the owner for counting purposes. The estate is also treated as the owner of any shares held by a grantor trust or 678 trust after the death of the deemed owner. When a QSST has separate shares for separate beneficiaries, each beneficiary is counted as an owner. A voting trust may also have multiple beneficiaries, and each beneficiary is counted as a separate owner. These are the only instances in which one entity can hold stock and represent more than one owner.

220.13. Beneficiaries of Electing Small Business Trusts. Each potential current income beneficiary of an Electing Small Business Trust is counted as a shareholder for purposes of the 75-shareholder limit. If there are no current beneficiaries, the trust would be treated as the shareholder. [§1361(c)(2)(B)(v)]

220.2. Attempts to circumvent the limit. The IRS has enforced the maximum shareholder limits principally when two or more corporations are associated with each other through a partnership.

2

In Revenue Ruling 77-220 [Rev. Rul. 77-220, 1977-1 CB 263], a group of 30 individuals attempted to form three S corporations to conduct a single business. (The limit was 10 shareholders at the time of the ruling.) The business was to be conducted as a joint venture among the three corporations. The IRS held that the substance of the transaction was an attempt to circumvent the maximum limit on shareholders, and it stated that each corporation would be treated as having 30 shareholders and the S election would be disallowed. In this ruling, the IRS stated that the substance of the arrangement dominated the form.

In 1994, however, the IRS revoked Revenue Ruling 77-220. In Revenue Ruling 94-43, the IRS stated that the only reason for the limit on the number of shareholders was to reduce the administrative complexity with respect to an S corporation's tax matters. [Rev. Rul. 94-43, 1994-27 IRB 8] Since membership in a partnership has no effect on the administrative complexity of the corporation, per se, the IRS will no longer challenge an S election when a corporation conducts its operations as a member of a partnership. For further discussion, see Chapter 14, at 1435.13.

225. One class of stock.

An S corporation must have a *single class of stock*. [§1361(b)(1)(D)] The Code is brief on this issue and does not even define the term.

SUMMARY OF AUTHORITY: CODE SECTION 1361(b)(1)(D)

- A small business corporation may not have more than one class of stock.
- The Code does not define the term *class of stock*.

OBSERVATION: If an S corporation could issue a second class of stock, shareholders could temporarily maneuver income between each other by raising or lowering dividends on different classes of stock. Although the term *class of stock* is not defined within Subchapter S, or in any other place in the Code, the Regulations address a variety of financing instruments to see if a second class of stock exists. Instruments that are not denominated as stock per se may be subject to challenge if they could confer future rights to a corporation's assets on persons who are not currently subject to taxation on the corporation's earnings. Such rights may be conferred by corporate debt or options. An S corporation should pursue a cautious strategy if it contemplates the use of any financing instruments that could entitle the holder to potential equity in the corporation.

The Code does not state whether the single class requirement applies to all stock (including treasury and unissued shares), or merely to outstanding stock. Regulations under prior Subchapter S, as well as the more recently adopted Final Regulations, limit the test to outstanding stock. [Regs. §1.1361-l(2)(i)] Unissued or treasury shares have no rights to vote, are afforded no interest in the corporation's assets, and thus are disregarded.

Final Regulations §1.1361-1 gives a general effective date of application to taxable years beginning after May 28, 1992. Any corporation may elect to have its provisions apply retroactively. [Regs. §1.1361-1(l)(7)] The rules of this Regulation are so inherently reasonable that most corporations will probably want retroactive application.

225.1. General rules for issued stock. More than one class of stock may exist if all shares do not have equal rights to all current and liquidating distributions. [Regs. §1.1361-1(l)(1)] Unequal rights may be created by:

- Laws of the state of incorporation [Regs. §1.1361-1(l)(2)(v), Example 1]

2

- The corporate charter or bylaws
- A binding shareholder agreement to give preference to some shares, but only if the agreement has a principal purpose of circumventing the single class of stock requirement [Regs. §1.1361-1(l)(2)]

EXAMPLE 2 - 15: A corporation issues shares to some shareholders in return for cash and to others in exchange for contributions of property. State law provides that in the event the corporation is liquidated, the shareholders who contributed cash must be repaid their original contributions before the other shareholders can receive any liquidation proceeds. The IRS may contend that state law has created a second class of stock, and the corporation cannot be an S corporation.[4]

OBSERVATION: A state charter may provide for two classes of stock. In this situation, the shareholders could not override the provisions of the charter by bylaws or any other agreement. If, by contrast, a corporation issued only one class of stock, the shareholders could create a second class by binding agreement. If a corporation intends to do business in a state that will require more than one class of stock, it should establish its charter in another state that has no such requirement.

Pursuant to the Regulations, a binding agreement to alter the rights of shareholders does not include an employment or lease agreement. [Regs. §1.1361-1(l)(2)(i)] (Also see Regulations §1.1361-1(l)(2)(v), Example 2, and PLR 9442007.) See Chapter 8 for discussions of these arrangements between S corporations and their shareholders.

225.2. Voting rights. Voting stock has the ability to elect directors, whereas nonvoting stock has no such power. In some cases, all shares have the right to elect directors, but some shares (often called *super voting stock*) have more votes than other shares. State law may confer certain voting rights on all shares. The state may, for instance, require that each share have equal votes on the merger or dissolution of the corporation.

An S corporation may issue shares with different voting rights and not be in violation of the single-class-of-stock requirement.

SUMMARY OF AUTHORITY: CODE SECTION 1361(c)(4)

- The Code specifically permits an S corporation to issue shares with different voting rights.
- This allowance does not permit any other differences in the rights of shareholders.

This exception to the single class requirement, adopted by the Subchapter S Revision Act of 1982, has important implications for family financial planning and for maintenance of control.

EXAMPLE 2 - 16: Gordon owns all of the stock of Gorco, an S corporation. He would like to give some of the stock to his children. According to his plan, he might want to give more than 50% of the value of his stock to the children. Gordon's children are minors. Gordon is divorced, and the children's mother is their legal guardian. If Gordon gives the children voting shares, his ex-wife might be able to have substantial influence on his corporation's affairs. If he gives nonvoting shares, he will be able to retain complete control.

225.3. Distributions. The safest distribution policy for any S corporation is to make only equal distributions to each share and to make those distributions at the exact same time.

---

[4] This situation is based on the facts in *Paige v. U.S.*, 78-2 USTC 9702 (9th Cir.), in which the court held the corporation ineligible for an S election.

2

Business considerations and shareholder cash needs, however, do not always permit adherence to such a policy. The Regulations provide that any differences in timing or amount must be given *appropriate tax effect*. [Regs. §1.1361-1(l)(2)(i)] For instance, a shareholder who did not receive his or her proportionate distribution may have a claim against the corporation or against other shareholders. Alternatively, an uneven distribution might be indicative of an imputed transfer among the shareholders. [Regs. §1.351-1(b)(1); Rev. Rul. 76-454, 1976-2 CB 102; Rev. Rul. 79-10, 1979-1 CB 140; Rev. Rul. 73-233, 1973-1 CB 179; Rev. Rul. 58-614, 1958-2 CB 920] If a shareholder receives a distribution that is disproportionate, the IRS may apply §7872 or other recharacterization provisions. [Regs. §1.1361-1(l)(2)(i)] (See Chapter 8 for discussion and examples of §7872.)

OBSERVATION: Regulations under prior Subchapter S stated that each share of stock should have equal rights to the corporation's profits and assets, but they did not mention distributions. [Regs. §1.1371-1(g)] One Regulation held that shareholders in a family-owned S corporation could waive their rights to dividends, without causing the corporation to have a second class of stock. [Regs. §1.1375-3(d)] The current Regulations do not contain any similar provision. Under current law, however, it is possible to receive a distribution, and then loan the money back to the corporation, without creating a second class of stock. [PLR 9746038]

Since the distribution rules are important focal points for S corporations, any rules regarding distributions must have a significant effect on all S corporations. The distribution rules are discussed in detail in Chapter 7. Certain transactions between closely held corporations and their shareholders may be treated as constructive distributions by the IRS. Chapter 8 discusses transactions, other than actual distributions, between an S corporation and its shareholders.

225.31. Disproportionate distributions. As discussed above, a disproportionate distribution does not create a second class of stock per se. A binding agreement to circumvent the single-class-of-stock rule, however, may create two classes of stock. One possible pitfall could be an agreement to provide shareholders with an equal after-tax rate of return. [Regs. §1.1361-1(l)(2)(v), Example 6] Such a plan could be a binding plan to alter the intersts of each share's rights to current and liquidating distributions

EXAMPLE 2 - 17: Stateco is an S corporation with two equal shareholders, Sam and Terry. Sam is in the 31% federal income tax bracket and lives in a state that imposes a 9% income tax rate on personal income. Terry is in the 28% federal income tax bracket and lives in a state that imposes no personal income tax. For the current year, each shareholder's portion of Stateco's taxable income is $100,000. Stateco would like to distribute $40,000 to Sam and $28,000 to Terry. Stateco does not plan to give Terry any rights to receive $12,000 as a compensatory distribution. Both shareholders plan to retain equal rights to all current and liquidating distributions after the current year's distributions. The corporation would have two classes of stock if it follows this plan.

225.32. Distributions based on varying interests. Many S corporations have a policy of making sufficient distributions to compensate shareholders for their tax liability resulting from the S corporation's taxable income. As long as the corporation assumes that each shareholder will have an equal marginal tax rate, including federal, state, and local income taxes, such a policy will not be tantamount to a binding agreement that creates a second class of stock.

EXAMPLE 2 - 18: Assume the same facts as in Example 2 - 17 except that Stateco distributes $40,00 to each shareholder. If Terry does not need more than $28,000 cash, the corporation may distribute $28,000 cash and a note or other property with a fair market value of $12,000.

The distributions would be equal per share, and the distribution would not cause a problem with the stock classes.

As is discussed in Chapter 6, the amount of S corporation income included on a shareholder's individual tax return depends on the shareholder's weighted average of ownership of the stock for the year.[5] [§1377(a)(2)] In most cases, a shareholder cannot determine his or her taxable income from an S corporation until after the S corporation's year has closed. Since many S corporations use the calendar year for tax reporting, many shareholders cannot determine their liability for tax on an S corporation's taxable income until some time after the shareholder's year has also closed. (See Chapter 4 for a discussion of taxable years used by S corporations.)

In order to allow an S corporation to distribute money to its shareholders in proportion to the income reported by each, the Regulations allow distributions to be based on varying interests. The corporation may distribute proportionately to a shareholder's average ownership in the current or immediately prior year. [Regs. §1.1361-1(l)(2)(iv)]

EXAMPLE 2 - 19: Varco is an S corporation that uses the calendar year. Varco's policy is to distribute 40% of its income to each shareholder in order to compensate for the shareholder's state and federal income tax liabilities with respect to the corporation's income. The distribution is to be made by April 15 of the following year.

Throughout 1995, Michelle was Varco's sole shareholder. In January 1996, Varco issued new shares to Ned, who became a 50% shareholder. On March 1, 1996, Varco computed Michelle's portion of the corporation's 1995 taxable income as $100,000. On that date Varco distributed $40,000 to Michelle and none to Ned. Even though the distributions are disproportionate, the corporation does not have a second class of stock.

An S corporation had a policy of distributing a portion of its taxable income to each shareholder in order to enable each shareholder to pay his or her taxes attributable to S corporation income. The corporation declared bankruptcy. The court ordered the trustee not to make distributions to shareholders, when it was known that the shareholders had suspended losses in excess of basis, and thus could not be liable for taxes on their current portions of the S corporation's income. [*In re Cumberland Farms, Inc.*, 162 BR 62 (Bankr. D.Mass., 1993)]

225.33. Constructive distributions. Constructive distributions, as well as actual distributions of cash or property, are included in determining a shareholder's rights to current and liquidating distributions. Constructive distributions are likely to arise in the case of:

- Unreasonable compensation (see Chapter 8, at 820.2.)
- Disallowed travel and entertainment (see Chapter 8, at 830.)
- Interest-free loans (see property distributions) (see Chapter 8, at 845.2.)
- Bargain rents or purchases by the shareholder of corporate property (see Chapter 8, at 810., and 840.12.)
- Any other payment by the corporation to a shareholder or for a shareholder's benefit (see Chapter 8, at 810.)

If a constructive distribution is disproportionate to a shareholder's interest, it could be pursuant to a plan to alter the shareholders' rights. In that case, it could indicate that there are two classes of stock.

---

[5] There are special rules for shareholders who terminate their entire interests or dispose of a substantial portion of stock. These rules are discussed in Chapter 6.

2

EXAMPLE 2-20: Shareholder A owns 90% of the shares in AB, an S corporation. Shareholder B owns the remaining 10%. In 1996, shareholder A drives the company car 50,000 miles for personal use. AB does not collect rent from A and does not include the value of the use of the car in A's compensation. AB has two classes of stock, if the use of the car is part of a binding agreement to alter the shareholders' rights. If the use of the car is not pursuant to such a plan, the corporation can make a proportionate distribution of cash or property to shareholder B, and there will be only one class of stock.

One form of constructive distribution is the payment of state taxes on behalf of shareholders by the S corporation. Some states require an S corporation to withhold taxes on the portion of the income allocated to nonresident shareholders but do not require such withholding on behalf of resident shareholders. The Regulations anticipate the possibility that such unequal distributions may exist. Accordingly, state laws that require withholding taxes on nonresident shareholders do not create a second class of stock, provided that other shareholders have rights to equivalent distributions. [Regs. §1.1361-1(l)(2)(ii)]

EXAMPLE 2-21: M Corporation is an S corporation incorporated in State M. State M requires that all S corporations deposit a 6% withholding tax on the portion of income allocated to nonresident shareholders. M Corporation has two equal shareholders, R and N. R is a resident of State M, but N is a resident of another state. In the current year, M's taxable income is $200,000. Therefore, M must deposit $6,000 on behalf of N, but does not make a deposit on behalf of R. The deposit requirement does not create a second class of stock, provided that R has a right to receive a $6,000 compensatory distribution.

PLANNING TIP: An S corporation might want to formalize agreements between the corporation and all shareholders to provide evidence that there is no binding agreement to alter the rights of any share with respect to current and liquidating distributions. To achieve this result, each shareholder might want to agree to repay any amount of compensation, expense reimbursement, or other corporate payment in the event that the payment to the shareholder is disallowed as a corporate expense. This type of agreement is popularly known as an "Oswald clause," derived from the name of a case in which a taxpayer used a similar agreement to ameliorate certain compensation problems. [*Oswald, Vincent E.*, 49 TC 645 (1968)] The Oswald technique receives further discussion in Chapter 8, at 820.34.

225.34. Stock redemptions. A stock redemption occurs when a corporation buys its own stock from a shareholder. Redemptions of stock may be treated as exchanges or distributions. (Redemption tests are contained in §§302 and 303.) See Chapter 15 for descriptions and examples of the rules. A redemption that does qualify as an exchange will not be treated as a nonconforming distribution, and does not indicate the existence of a second class of stock. Even if a redemption does not qualify as an exchange, it generally does not result in a second class of stock. [PLRs 9124009, 9308006, 9710026]

Shares in an S corporation may be subject to transfer restrictions, discussed below. If a shareholder is obligated to buy stock from another shareholder, the arrangement is termed a *buy–sell* agreement, or *cross-purchase* agreement. If the corporation must purchase its own shares back from a shareholder, there is a *redemption* agreement. These arrangements are often used in anticipation of a shareholder's death, disability, or becoming ineligible to hold shares in an S corporation.

Under Regulations §1.1361-1, buy–sell agreements do not create a second class of stock. Also see PLR 9649039. Often a cross-purchase agreement takes the form of an option. If the corporation is not party to the option arrangement, a second class of stock is not possible. Thus, options can be used to give current shareholders the income and distributions from the S corporation, whereas the option holder could participate in the long-term growth.

OBSERVATION: For a creative use of options see the case of *Estate of Paul E. Brown*, TC Memo 1997-195. Paul Brown, the controlling shareholder of the Cincinnati Bengals football team, died in 1991. Cincinnati Bengals was an S corporation. There was only one share (out of 330 outstanding shares) of Bengals stock in Brown's estate. All the remaining 329 shares were held by another owner. Brown's two sons held options to purchase all of those outstanding shares. This scheme allowed the other owner to report virtually all of the corporation's taxable income on his return, and it enabled him to receive all of the distributions during his period of ownership. After Paul Brown's death, his sons exercised the options, which had a relatively low exercise price.

Redemption agreements do not create a second class of stock unless the agreement is an attempt to circumvent the class-of-stock rule and the redemption price differs significantly from the stock's fair market value. [Regs. §1.1361-1(l)(2)(iii). See also PLRs 8506114, 8908069, 8927027, 8937034, 9011055, 9425027.] An S corporation's redemption agreement that provided for redemption of minority shares at a discount was disregarded in determining whether the corporation had a second class of stock. [PLR 9433024] Another S corporation entered into an agreement providing for annual redemption of shares held in a voting trust; the IRS disregarded this agreement as well. [PLR 9508022] A redemption price that is between fair market value and book value is not a price that differs significantly from the fair market value of the stock. [Regs. §1.1361-1(l)(2)(iii)]. In one ruling, an agreement to redeem shares from certain shareholders at fair market value did not create a second class of stock. [PLR 9814003] Similarly, a plan to redeem all of the shares owned by a father, when the remaining shares were owned by his children, did not create a second class of stock. [PLR 9807002]

EXAMPLE 2 - 22: Bob and Mary are equal shareholders in the GJ Corporation, an S corporation. In 1996, GJ redeems all of Bob's stock for $1,000,000. The value of Bob's stock at the time of the redemption was $500,000. The variation between the stock's true value and the amount paid gives the appearance that the parties had intended to give Bob a preferred investment. If the IRS can demonstrate that such a plan existed, the corporation would have had two classes of stock.

The corporation's determination of fair market value is respected unless it was substantially in error and not performed with reasonable diligence. [Regs. §1.1361-1(l)(2)(iii)(A)] Book value is respected if it was determined in accordance with generally accepted accounting principles (GAAP) or is used for any substantial nontax purpose. [Regs. §1.1361-1(l)(2)(iii)(C)] The IRS may expand (not contract) the types of agreements that do not create a second class of stock.

225.4. Problems relating to transfers of shares. In several instances, S corporations have been concerned about the transferability of stock. Often, there are restrictions on transferability. On occasion, there are call arrangements and special sales agreements.

225.41. Transfer restrictions. An S corporation may impose transfer restrictions on its shares. One purpose may be to ensure continued eligibility of the corporation for S status. With unrestricted transferability of shares, a shareholder could transfer shares to an ineligible person or transfer blocks of shares to enough holders that the corporation would be in violation of the shareholder limit. Accordingly, the IRS has consistently ruled that restrictions on transferability do not create a second class of stock. [PLR 9308006]

Buy–sell agreements and redemption agreements may be necessary to prohibit the shares from falling into the hands of disqualified shareholders. The IRS has consistently ruled that

2

these restrictions do not constitute a second class of stock. For example, a requirement to surrender shares on termination of employment does not create a second class of stock. [PLRs 8927027, 9425027, 9445019] In a similar ruling, a corporation's right of first refusal to buy back stock intended for sale or gift, or at the death of a shareholder, does not create a second class of stock. [PLR 8908069]

The favorable rulings cited above, as well as the position of the Regulations, hold that transfer restrictions do not create a second class of stock if the surrender price is reasonably close to fair market value. If the surrender price is set by an arbitrary formula, not based on the fair market value of the stock, a second class of stock may exist. [PLRs 8407082, 8528049] An agreement to purchase at death, divorce, disability, or termination of employment cannot create a second class of stock. [Regs. §1.1361-1(l)(2)(iii)(B). Also see Regulations §1.1361-1(l)(2)(v), Examples 8, 9.]

OBSERVATION: The IRS has allowed S corporations to place transfer restrictions on some shares, but not on others. For example, a corporation was permitted to selectively impose stock transfer restrictions on stock issued to employees but was not required to place the same restrictions on the principal shareholder.[PLR 8506114. See also PLR 8907016.] In another situation a corporation's right of first refusal to buy stock from most shareholders, subject to a lifetime exemption for one shareholder, did not create a second class of stock. [PLR 8937034] Employment agreements affecting shareholder-employee rights, with a lifetime exemption for the founding shareholder, did not creae a second class of stock. [PLR 9011055] This policy could provide some valuable opportunities for controlling shareholders who want to cement employee commitments but intend to tie employee ownership to a continued commitment.

EXAMPLE 2 - 23: Brenda is the principal shareholder of Brenco, an S corporation. She has certain key employees who are interested in equity ownership in Brenco. She knows that some of the employees are highly marketable and are likely to leave if she does not grant them stock ownership. She wants to be sure, however, that no employees of competing firms will ever own shares in Brenco. To serve these purposes, she may issue stock to employees subject to the restriction that all such shares must be offered back to Brenda, or to Brenco, if an employee terminates employment. Brenco should be able to secure a favorable letter ruling that this arrangement will not constitute a second class of stock.

EXAMPLE 2 - 24: CY Corporation is an S corporation. The stock is owned by C and his two children. One daughter lives in France and is married to a French citizen. If the daughter died, her husband would become the owner of her CY shares under the laws of France. If the corporation issued all stock subject to a right of first refusal upon the death of any shareholder, her husband would have no rights to stock ownership. He would be entitled to receive the fair market value of the shares in cash. This strategy would allow the corporation to keep its S election intact by repurchasing the shares. The corporation might want the daughter to put her shares into a grantor trust or QSST to ensure the result.

OBSERVATION: An S corporation limited transferability of shares, so that no ineligible person could be a shareholder. This restriction was enforced after the corporation declared bankruptcy. The bankruptcy court noted that the restriction applied to heirs and assigns, including the trustee in bankruptcy. The court prohibited the transfer of stock to any ineligible person, and thus allowed the current shareholders to continue holding stock. [*In re Cumberland Farms, Inc.*, 162 BR 62 (Bankr. D.Mass., 1993)]

225.42. Other transfer problems. Call arrangements to repurchase shares at book value do not create a second class of stock. The same ruling stated that agreements allowing shareholders to participate in sales of jointly owned shares were not indicators of multiple classes of stock. [PLR 9803008]

In another instance, the question came up with respect to a selling arrangement. A corporation purchased all of the stock of an S corporation. The agreement contained a contingent price, or "earnout" clause, whereby some selling shareholders would receive additional consideration based upon the performance of the target corporation. Other shareholders received additional cash. Therefore, not all prices per share were equal to the selling shareholders. The IRS ruled that there was no second class of stock immediately before the sale. [PLR 9821006]

225.5. Stock and other equity-flavored compensation arrangements. Corporations may use a variety of equity interests in employee compensation plans. Among these are outright grants of stock, issuance of restricted stock, stock options, and *equity-flavored* plans, known as "stock appreciation rights," "phantom stock plans," and "incentive units." S corporations have considerable flexibility in using these arrangements, but must observe three precautions:

- The plans must not result in issuance of stock to an ineligible shareholder.
- The plans must not cause the total number of shareholders to exceed the shareholder limit.
- No instrument issued under any of these plans can be treated as a second class of stock.

The general rule governing the taxability of noncash compensation to the recipient is §83. Under that provision, property recipients are taxed on the fair market value of noncash compensation. The employer gets a deduction of the same amount of employee income, at the same time it is recognized by the employee. If an employee receives property subject to a substantial risk of forfeiture, he or she defers the income until the risk lapses, and the rights are fully vested. An employee may elect to report the gross income on receipt of the property, before it is vested. The election is irrevocable and must be filed within 30 days of receipt of the property.

225.51. Restricted stock. A corporation may issue an employee stock in which the employee has no vested interest until the occurrence of some event. For example, a corporation may issue stock to an employee, but retain actual ownership until the employee had completed five years of service. Stock issued subject to a risk of forfeiture is commonly known as *restricted stock*. The IRS has held that the risk of forfeiture does not create a second class of stock. [PLRs 8819041, 9119041, 9121037] Restricted stock, which could only vest upon a merger, liquidation, or change in control of the corporation, did not constitute a second class of stock. [PLRs 9308022, 9839007] It is customary, but not necessary, for the restricted stock to be nonvoting.

225.52. No Section 83(b) election. According to Regulations §1.83-2, restricted stock for which the recipient has not made an election under §83(b) is not treated as outstanding stock until the risk of forfeiture expires. [Regs. §1.1361-1(b)(3) provides consistent treatment.] Accordingly, no part of the corporation's income or deductions should be allocated to this stock. Some S corporations may need to amend returns to reallocate to unrestricted shareholders. Any distributions with respect to restricted stock should be deducted as employee compensation. Such distribution would be subject to all withholding and payroll taxes on compensation.

2

225.53. Immediate recognition. An employee may elect to include stock in income on the date of receipt. [§83(b)] The election, which is irrevocable, must be filed within 30 days of receipt of the property.

Immediate recognition of income by the recipient changes the treatment. If the recipient elected immediate recognition under §83(b), the stock is treated as outstanding. [Regs. §1.1361-1(b)(3)] The shares should receive income, deduction, and loss allocations in the same manner as any other outstanding stock. The forfeiture potential per se should not be construed as evidence of a second class of stock.

EXAMPLE 2 - 25: Janet is an employee of Marco, an S corporation. The corporation is willing to issue Janet some equity ownership but wants to receive the stock back if Janet resigns within five years of issuance. The corporation issues the stock on February 8, 1991, with the proviso that Janet will not receive a vested ownership interest in the stock unless she is still employed on February 8, 1996. The value of the stock issued to Janet on February 8, 1991, is $50,000.

Under §83(b), Janet may elect to treat the stock as having been received on February 8, 1991. She would report $50,000 as gross income in 1991. The corporation would be allowed a compensation deduction in the amount of $50,000 in 1991. The corporation would need to be certain that Janet's shares received the same distributions and rights to liquidation proceeds as any other shares.

If Janet did not make the election under §83(b), she would not be considered a shareholder, within the meaning of §83, until February 8, 1996. Until that time, according to Regulations §1.1361-1, the corporation would not need to provide Janet with the same distribution and liquidation rights as other shareholders. Any distributions that the corporation does make to Janet will be treated as compensation. They should be subjected to the same payroll and withholding taxes as any other form of compensation.

OBSERVATION: A corporation that issues restricted stock should not treat that stock as outstanding. However, if a corporation issued such stock on or before May 28, 1992, and treated that stock as outstanding, it may continue to do so. [Regs. §1.1361-1(b)(6)] Some restricted stock issues may require that the employee not make a §83(b) election. [PLR 9317009]

PLANNING TIP: There are two serious risks associated with the §83(b) election that usually discourage taxpayers from the election:

1. The income from the compensation is immediately taxable, even though the employee receives no cash.
2. There is no loss allowed to the employee upon forfeiture. Only if the stock is expected to appreciate substantially in value should the recipient opt for immediate recognition.

225.54. Stock options issued to employees. A stock option allows the holder to purchase stock at a predetermined price. The holder exercises the option by purchasing the stock at the price given. Although stock options probably are not widely used in closely held corporations (which include most all S corporations), an S corporation should be able to issue options. If an S corporation uses stock options, it should observe all necessary precautions to prevent the exercise of an option from causing ineligibility for S status. By restricting the transferability of options, no ineligible shareholder will ever hold stock and the number of shareholders will not exceed the shareholder limit when the option is exercised. The two varieties of options, from the tax point of view, are:

- Nonqualified stock options
- Incentive stock options

Nonqualified stock options have the advantage of flexibility. They can be issued at any price, to any actual or potential shareholders, and can be exercised at any time. When exercised, any difference between the exercise price and the fair market value of the stock is income to the holder. An employee who already holds stock may "pyramid" holdings by trading in old stock to acquire new. To the extent the old stock has appreciated, the employee will not recognize gain when the old stock is exchanged for new stock. [§1036] A nonqualified profit-sharing plan did not create a second class of stock, and did not result in constructive receipt. [PLR 9840035]

Incentive stock options will not result in taxable income when exercised. The incentive stock option may not have an exercise period of more than 10 years. The option price must not be less than the fair market value of the stock on the date the option is granted. If the optionee owns more than 10% of the stock on the date the option is granted, the price must be at least 110% of the fair market value of the stock on grant date, and the exercise period cannot exceed five years. The option may not be transferable. The employee must hold the stock for at least two years after the option is granted and one year after it is exercised. [§422] The difference between fair market value and exercise price is an alternative minimum tax adjustment. [§56(b)(3)]

There is a concern, if only in theory, that an option may create a second class of stock when it is issued. The rationale for this concern is that the holder of the option may be able to share in the long-term growth of the corporation by exercising the option at a future date, when the stock value exceeds the option price (also known as the *exercise price* or *strike price*). Although the holder would receive equity in the future, he or she is not subject to tax on the corporation's current income (or is not subject to a tax benefit for current losses).

Under the Regulations, an option issued to an employee or independent contractor in connection with performance of services is not treated as stock if the option is nontransferable and has no readily ascertainable fair market value. [Regs. §1.1361-1(l)(4)(iii)(B)(2)] Thus, S corporations may use nonqualified and incentive stock options without creating a second class of stock.

Employee stock option plans (ESOPs) are now specifically allowed to own S corporation stock. An ESOP owning shares in an S corporation does not create a second class of stock. The ESOP itself, and not the employees, is treated as the owner of the S corporation stock for all Subchapter S purposes. [PLR 199906044]

225.55. Other equity-flavored compensation. There are compensation arrangements, known as *phantom stock plans* and *stock appreciation rights* (SARs), which base some portion of employee compensation on the value of the corporation's stock. These plans probably are not widely used with privately held corporations, due to the problems associated with valuation of stock. In several rulings, the IRS has allowed S corporations to use these plans without creating a second class of stock. [See PLRs 9817015, 9840035]

An S corporation may use a phantom stock plan to provide incentive to key employees. Under such a plan, each eligible employee is credited with a bookkeeping entry for a number of imaginary shares. Future appreciation and dividend payments are then credited to the employee as they occur. On some future event, such as death, disability, or termination of employment, the corporation pays cash to the employee for his or her share of appreciation and dividends. The IRS has held that there is no constructive receipt when the employee's account is credited. The employee, or beneficiary, has income when the cash is transferred, and the employer gets a deduction at that time. Since there is no actual issue of stock, there is no possible second class and no danger of exceeding the limit on the maximum number of

2

shareholders. [Rev. Rul. 67-269, 1967-2 CB 298, GCM 39750; PLRs 8834085, 8838049, 807032] A "stock equivalency plan," which is the same as a phantom stock plan, does not constitute a second class of stock.[6] [PLR 9317021]

SARs may be used in lieu of, or in combination with, nonqualified stock options. Instead of issuing stock, the employer pays the employee in cash for the difference between the fair market value of the stock on the payment date and the fair market value when the SAR was granted. Since this plan involves no actual issue of stock, it avoids the class and shareholder limit problems. [PLRs 8828029, 9119041, 9317009. This last letter ruling provides a thorough description of a stock appreciation right plan. See also PLRs 9406017, 9406018, 9406019, 9406020.]

According to the Regulations, deferred compensation arrangements are not classes of stock if they are unfunded, do not have voting rights, and are issued to individuals in connection with performance of services. [Regs. §1.1361-1(b)(4)] The Final Regulations specifically permit dividend equivalency payments to holders, even if included in holder's current income. [Regs. §1.1361-1(b)(4)] The IRS follows the spirit of the Regulations in its ruling policy. [PLRs 9421011, 9626033, 9817015] The IRS has also ruled on some varieties of the usual phantom stock plan. A contributory plan, whereby employees purchase their units, does not create a second class of stock. [PLR 9803023] Similarly, a phantom stock plan issued by a subsidiary corporation, when the subsidiary was treated as a QSub, did not create a second class of stock with respect to the parent corporation. [PLR 9803008]

225.56. Split-dollar life insurance arrangements. A split-dollar life insurance arrangement exists when the employer and the employee jointly purchase a term insurance policy. The employer receives all of the cash surrender value, and the employee receives the life insurance protection. In the early years, when the increase in cash surrender value is less than the premium, the employee pays the excess of the premium over the increase in cash surrender value. In later years, when the increase in cash surrender value equals or exceeds the premium, the employer pays the entire premium. If the employee does not pay the premiums, the value of the insurance must be included in the employee's gross income. [Rev. Rul. 79-50, 1979-1 CB 138] If the employee receiving the benefit of the split-dollar life insurance is also a shareholder, the arrangement could constitute a benefit conferred on that particular shareholder that is not conferred proportionately on all outstanding shares. The IRS has ruled that a split-dollar life insurance arrangement does not constitute a second class of stock. [PLRs 9309046, 9318007, 9331009, 9413023, 9651017, 9709027, 9735006, 9803008]

225.57. Other fringe benefit plans. On occasion, a closely held corporation may be nervous about any item that is paid to one shareholder, but not to all. Accordingly, one corporation requested a ruling as to the effect of paying health insurance on behalf of shareholder-employees. The IRS ruled that an employment agreement to pay health insurance premiums is a fringe benefit, not a vehicle to circumvent the one-class-of-stock requirement. [PLR 9803008]

225.6. Options issued to nonemployees. Warrants, options, and other rights to acquire stock are often used to create incentives for persons to len money or provide services to a corporation. Generally, options are not stock per se. [Rev. Rul. 67-269, 1967-2 CB 298; Regs. §1.1361-1(l)(4)(iii)(A)] Even though an option is not considered to be stock, however, the owner of the option may be treated as the owner of stock. The holders of options, for instance, have been treated as the owners of stock for the constructive ownership rules of §318, that has important effects on stock redemptions and other transactions within Sub-

---

[6] This ruling was conditioned upon the representation that the value of the participants' units was reasonable compensation for services performed.

chapter C.[7] The principal importance of this rule relates to tests for exchange treatment of a stock redemption, in which the shareholder's ownership of shares after the redemption is an important factor. If, for example, a shareholder sells shares back to a corporation but retains an option to purchase an equal number of shares, he or she is treated as having sold no shares and is not afforded exchange treatment. See Chapter 15 for a comprehensive discussion of stock redemptions.

There have also been "deep in the money" options where the owner of the option is treated as the owner of the stock. [Rev. Rul. 80-238, 1980-2 CB 96; Rev. Rul. 82-150, 1982-2 CB 110; and Rev. Rul. 85-57, 1985-1 CB 182] A deep-in-the-money option exists when the option holder has already paid a substantial portion of the stock's fair market value in order to acquire the option. Such an arrangement is equivalent to having made a large down payment on the stock itself. The Supreme Court has respected the treatment of an option holder as holding an option, rather than the stock itself, when the option price was 25% of the stock's value. [*Lobue v. U.S.*, 56-2 USTC 9607 (S.Ct.)] In the *Lobue* case, the option holder needed to pay only 25% of the stock's value to acquire the stock in exchange for the option. The IRS treated the option holder as the holder of the shares, since the holder needed to pay a relatively small portion of the stock's value to acquire the shares. The Court, however, did not treat the option holder as a shareholder.

> **EXAMPLE 2 - 26:** The value of XYZ Corporation's stock is currently $100 per share. The corporation issues an option to Q, whereby she may purchase 200 shares at a price of $30 per share at any time within the next two years. The IRS might contend that Q is constructively, the owner of the 200 shares on the date she receives the option. The rationale would be that the value of the stock would need to drop by 70% within the next two years in order for Q not to exercise her option. Therefore, in all likelihood Q has all of the benefits of ownership of the stock on the day she receives the option, since all she needs to do is pay a relatively low price to obtain all 200 shares on any date she wishes, within the time period allowed. Under the rule of the *Lobue* case, as long as the option price is at least $25, Q would not be treated as a shareholder until she actually exercised the option.

There are three possible consequences to S corporations of having option holders treated as stockholders, any of which could disqualify a corporation's S election:

1. If an option holder were ineligible to hold shares directly, treatment of the option holder as a shareholder would disqualify the S election. This would be a serious problem for S corporations that had warrants, options, or other "equity kickers" outstanding to banks or other commercial lenders. Often, lenders grant a reduced interest rate if they have the potential to acquire equity in the corporation.
2. If the option holders would bring the number of shareholders above the maximum-shareholder limit, the corporation would be disqualified from S corporation status.
3. An option could itself be a second class of stock. Treating an option as a second class of stock would be accomplished by showing that the option holder, if treated as the shareholder, would have rights and interests different from those of any other shareholder. In effect, this result is not entirely unreasonable. An option holder could fail to exercise its option and could thereby avoid pass-through of the corporation's income or loss. Then, by exercising an option in a later year, the holder would be entitled to distributions or proceeds in liquidation, only if the option price were less than or equal to the fair market value of the stock.

---

[7] Code §318(a)(4) treats the holder of an option as the holder of the stock to which the option could be converted.

2

EXAMPLE 2 - 27: Ann and Brenda are establishing the AB Corporation. Ann will provide capital and no services. If the business is successful, they will become 50–50 shareholders. Until the corporation arrives at the measure of success, however, Ann intends to have all of the rights to the corporation's property in liquidation. Brenda will be entitled to only 50% of the stock after Ann has received a rate of return of 8% per annum on her investment.

The two parties could accomplish this effect by issuing two classes of stock, giving Ann a cumulative dividend of 8% and rights to the par value of her stock on liquidation. With a participation feature, which would allocate some of the profits to preferred stock, Ann could keep a 50% economic interest even after the business becomes successful, and Brenda's stock ownership would gain value only when the corporation is successful. An S Corporation cannot use this scheme, since there can be only one class of stock.

In an S corporation, however, they might issue Ann all of the stock. The corporation could then issue Brenda an option to buy stock at a certain price that would be based on the value of Ann's stock. If the agreement is carefully worked out, they could duplicate the economic effect of a second class of stock by using options.

Regulations §1.1361-1 treats options issued by the corporation as stock, under certain circumstances. Such instruments are a second class of stock if the option is *substantially certain to be exercised* and if the option was issued with a principal purpose of avoiding the class-of-stock rule. When the exercise, or "strike," price is substantially below the market price on the date of issue, an option is treated as substantially certain to be exercised. [Regs. §1.1361-1(l)(4)(iii)(A)] Thus, the Regulations under §1361 do not follow the *Lobue* case. They do, however, provide additional protection from reclassification of an option, by stating that avoidance of the single-class-of-stock rule must be a principal purpose, or the option is not treated as stock.

The Regulation does not define when an option is substantially certain to be exercised. There is, however, a safe harbor for options. They are not substantially certain to be exercised if the exercise price is at least 90% of fair market value. [Regs. §1.1361-1(l)(4)(iii)(C)] The Regulations provide that the safe-harbor test is to be applied when an option is issued, materially modified, or transferred to a person ineligible to be a shareholder in an S corporation (other than an employee or a lender). If an ineligible person transfers an option to another ineligible person, there is no need to test the option as of the date of such transfer. [Regs. §1.1361-1(l)(4)(v), Examples 1, 2]

There are two exceptions to the option rule, whereby an option is not treated as a second class of stock even if it fails to meet the 90%-of-value safe-harbor test:

1. An option issued to an employee, as discussed above, is not treated as substantially certain to be exercised and is therefore not treated as a second class of stock.
2. An option issued to an active lender, in connection with a loan with commercially reasonable terms, is not substantially certain to be exercise, without regard to the general safe harbor. [Regs. §1.1361-1(l)(4)(iii)(B)] If the lender transfers the loan to a new holder and transfers the option along with the loan, the transfer does not create a second class of stock. [Regs. §1.1361-1(l)(4)(iii)(B)(1)]

225.7. Debt reclassified as equity. Debt reclassified as equity was a major concern under prior Subchapter S. The IRS frequently argued that debts from S corporations should be considered a second class of stock. The rationale is that the debt holder may have rights different from those of a shareholder. Under prior Subchapter S, several courts determined that debt from S corporations would not constitute a second class of stock. The Subchapter S Revision Act of 1982 enacted a straight-debt safe harbor, in an effort to prevent a resurgence of litigation on this issue.

225.71. Background. Controversy over debt and equity with respect to S corporations began soon after the 1958 law required that an S corporation must have only a single class of stock.

In the first two cases heard under this Regulation, the IRS was successful. Taxpayers in *Catalina Homes, Inc.* [*Catalina Homes, Inc.*, 23 TCM 1361, TC Memo 1964-225], and *Henderson v. U.S.* [*Henderson v. U.S.*, 65-2 USTC 9598 (Mid.D. Ala.)] did not contest the Regulation.

The Tax Court found the Regulation invalid in *Gamman* [*W.C. Gamman*, 46 TC 1 (1966), appeal dismissed (9th Cir., 1967)], and the corporation was entitled to retain its S election.

In later cases, taxpayers were able to challenge the new version of the Regulation. Debts that were not proportionate from the shareholders were not treated as a disqualifying second class of stock. In some cases, the court respected the form of the debt. Since the debt was not equity, it could not create a second class of stock. [*Alfred N. Hoffman*, 47 TC 218 (1966); *Milton T. Raynor*, 50 TC 762 (1968); and *Sam Novell*, 28 TCM 1307, TC Memo 1969-255]

In other cases, the courts agreed with the IRS that the purported debt was in fact equity, but they agreed with the taxpayer that there was no second class of stock. Even though the debt was equity, it was a contribution to capital.

In *August F. Nielsen Co.* [*August F. Nielsen Co.*, 27 TCM 44, TC Memo 196-11], debt was reclassified as equity. In that case, the Tax Court stated that the reclassified debt "did not confer . . . any rights or interests which they did not already have by virtue of their nominal stock holdings." Accordingly, the corporation had only one class of stock. Courts reached similar conclusions—that reclassified debt was a contribution to capital—in *Lewis Building Supplies, Inc.* [*Lewis Building Supplies, Inc.*, 25 TCM 844, TC Memo 1966-159], *Brennan v. O'Donnell* [*Brennan v. O'Donnell*, 71-1 USTC 9399 (N.D. Ala.)], and *Amory Cotton Oil v. U.S.* [*Amory Cotton Oil v. U.S.*, 72-2 USTC 9714 (5th Cir.)]

In other cases, the courts did not decide how purported debt should be classified under general debt equity principles. The reasoning was that, regardless of classification, it would not create a second class of stock. [*Stinnett*, 54 TC 221 (1970); *Spinner Corporation*, 29 TCM 462, TC Memo 1970-99; *Estate of Allison*, 57 TC 174 (1971); *Shores Realty*, 72-2 USTC 9715 (5th Cir.); *Portage Plastics v. U.S.*, 73-1 USTC 9261 (7th Cir.); and *Brutsche* 65 TC 1034 (1976)] In *Portage Plastics*, the purported loans were made by persons who had never been shareholders in the corporation. The loans in *Portage Plastics* had no fixed repayment schedule.

Portage Plastics became the most famous of all of the cases under prior Subchapter S. After losing this case, the IRS decided it would not litigate the issue further.[8] [TIR 1248 (July 27 1973)] This case was cited in the legislative history to the Subchapter S Revision Act of 1982, when Congress decided to enact the straight debt safe harbor. [Senate Report No. 97-640; 97th Cong., 2d Sess., H.R. 6055, page 6]

As late as 1990, the IRS was still not raising the class of stock issue in cases involving S corporations. In the case of *Georgia Cold Storage Company v. U.S.* [*Georgia Cold Storage Company v. U.S.*, 90-2 USTC 50,450 (M.D. Ga.)], an S corporation had borrowed money from another corporation, which was owned in part by shareholders of the borrower. The S corporation deducted interest paid on the loan. The IRS reclassified the debt as equity, in order to disallow the interest deduction. The court upheld the IRS's classification and disallowed the interest deduction to the S corporation. In this case, the IRS did not even raise the question as to whether there were two classes of stock. The court treated the loan as a contribution to capital.

225.72. Straight-debt safe harbor. The straight-debt safe-harbor rules of §1361(c)(5) provide that reclassification of some debt obligations as equity will not result in a second class of stock. [§1361(c)(5)(A)] The Congressional intent was to avoid the litigation that had occurred under prior law. The safe harbor, however, does not cover all debt that might be susceptible to reclassification. The debt covered must meet four requirements:

---

[8]In *Brutsche*, which was decided three years later, there were other issues involved.

2

1. There must be a written unconditional promise to repay the loan.
2. The interest rate and payment dates must not be subject to discretion of the corporation.
3. The debt must not be convertible into stock.
4. The holder must be eligible to own stock in an S corporation. For taxable years beginning after 1996, a person or an institution regularly engaged in the lending business may be a holder of qualified straight debt. [§1361(c)(5)(B)(iii)]

EXAMPLE 2 - 28: Sierra Corporation is capitalized with $1,000 stock and $9,000 securities. Both the stock and the securities are held by one individual. If the IRS reclassifies the debt as equity, Sierra's S election will not be jeopardized.

If the debt were held by a person not qualified to be an S corporation shareholder, the debt would be outside the safe harbor, and reclassification could cause the debt to be a second class of stock.

Subordination does not cause a debt instrument to fall outside the safe harbor. [Regs. §1.1361-1(l)(5)(ii)] The IRS is not prohibited from reclassifying straight debt as equity. For instance, reclassification of straight debt as equity may disallow a bad debt deduction to the holder, if such debt becomes uncollectible.[9] Straight debt, however, cannot become a second class of stock, even if it is reclassified as equity. If the straight-debt safe harbor is reclassified while the S election is in effect, payments of "interest" will be deductible by the corporation and included in the income of the holder. [Senate Report No. 97-640, 97th Cong., 2d Sess., H.R. 6055, page 6] There may be adverse consequences when the corporation repays the debt, as discussed in Chapter 9. There may also be adverse effects after the S corporation terminates its S election. See Chapter 13 for discussion.

OBSERVATION: The legislative history to the Subchapter S Revision Act of 1982 explains that the straight-debt safe harbor indicates that Congress wanted to make sure that the litigation under old Subchapter S was not repeated under new law. The safe harbor, however, did not include the situations of several of the cases that had been decided in the taxpayer's favor.

Before the issuance of Final Regs. §1.1361-1 in May 1992, the IRS was reluctant to rule on the qualification of straight debt. Recently, the IRS ruled that nonconvertible debts to shareholders of an S corporation did not constitute a second class of stock. [PLR 9308006] The IRS has also ruled that a debt could be within the safe harbor when the interest rate was set to vary in accordance with the prime rate. [PLR 9342019]

If a straight debt is materially modified so that it no longer meets the safe harbor, or if it is transferred to a person who is ineligible to hold a straight debt instrument, it could constitute a second class of stock. The corporation would lose its S election at the time of such an event.

225.73. General principles and Section 385. Under §385, the IRS has the authority to write Regulations that differentiate between debt and equity in borderline cases. The problem usually arises in the context of closely held corporations. Often these corporations are thinly capitalized, with little or no owners' equity, and shareholders have loaned money to the corporation. See Chapter 14, at 1425., for further discussion.

225.74. Reasonable interest rate. There is no express requirement that a safe harbor debt bear a reasonable rate of interest. If the interest rate is lower than the applicable federal rate, however, the loan may be subject to imputed interest. See Chapter 8 for a description of these

---

[9] See *Miles Production Company*, 28 TCM 1387, TC Memo 1969-274, aff'd *Miles Production Company*, 72-1 USTC 9331 (5th Cir.), for this particular effect of reclassifying debt. That case dealt with years before there was a straight debt safe harbor, but the results should be the same under new law.

rules. The IRS has stated that a loan with an unreasonably high interest rate does not automatically fall outside of the safe harbor. If a straight debt instrument bears interest that is significantly higher than the applicable federal rate, the excess interest may be recharacterized as a payment other than interest. It does not, however, create a second class of stock. [Regs. §1.1361-1(l)(5)(iv)]

225.75. Debt outside the safe harbor. The Regulations address several possibilities for treatment of debt as a second class of stock. Convertible debt (which is not within the safe harbor) may be a second class of stock (1) if it constitutes equity under general tax law or (2) if it embodies characteristics of an option that would be a second class of stock, but only if avoidance of the single-class-of-stock rule is a principal purpose of the debt. [Regs. §1.1361-1(l)(4)(iv)]

Treatment of debt outside the safe harbor depends upon the treatment of the debt obligation as equity, rather than debt, under general principles of federal tax law. [Regs. §1.1361-1(l)(5)] (See Chapter 14 for a discussion of debt and equity principles.) In issues unrelated to the rules of Subchapter S per se, courts have applied the debt and equity principles to S corporations in the same way that those principles govern C corporations.

For example, in the *Georgia Cold Storage Company* case [*Georgia Cold Storage Company v. U.S.*, 90-2 USTC 50,450 (M.D. Ga.)], the court disallowed an interest deduction to the borrowing S corporation on debt that was reclassified as a contribution to capital. In an earlier case, the court denied a bad debt deduction to a shareholder whose loans to an S corporation were reclassified as contributions to capital of the S corporation. [*Miles Production Company*, 28 TCM 1387, TC Memo 1969-274 28 TCM 1387, TC Memo 1969-274 TCM 1969-274, aff'd *Miles Production Company*, 72-1 USTC 9331 (5th Cir.)]

Under current Regulations, such debt instruments may be reclassified as a second class of stock, but only if they were issued with a principal purpose of avoiding the single class rule.

The IRS has ruled that a debt to an ineligible shareholder was not a second class of stock. The debt was nonconvertible, bore interest at a fixed rate, and had a regular payment schedule. [PLR 9308006]

225.76. Loans by shareholders. In many cases, a loan from a shareholder will fall within the safe harbor and cannot become a second class of stock under any circumstance, unless it is transferred to an ineligible person or its terms are modified. Frequently, however, the shareholders may not observe the formalities necessary to keep a debt within the safe harbor. For instance, a shareholder may advance money to a corporation without taking back a written debt instrument. The Regulations provide two instances where loans from shareholders will not be treated as a second class of stock, even though the debt is not within the statutory safe harbor.

Short-term unwritten advances that do not exceed $10,000 from any shareholder will not constitute a second class of stock. [Regs. §1.1361-1(l)(4)(ii)(B)(1)] Obligations held by the sole shareholder, or proportionately by all shareholders, will not create a second class of stock. [Regs. §1.1361-1(l)(4)(ii)(B)(2)]

225.8. Miscellaneous problems. In one situation, a former public company was the subject of a leveraged buyout through subsidiary bonds. After the buyout, the subsidiary was merged into a parent S corporation, which assumed the debt. Assumption of the debt did not create a second class of stock. [PLR 8842005] In another situation, the payment by an S corporation of federal and state estimated taxes on part of beneficiaries of a QSST did not create a second class of stock. [PLR 9142029]

225.9. Summary of class-of-stock rules. Figure 2 - 1 illustrates the class-of-stock rules as they apply to actual stock. Figure 2 - 2 illustrates the application of these rules to debt and options.

Figure 2 - 1: Class of stock rules applied to actual stock.

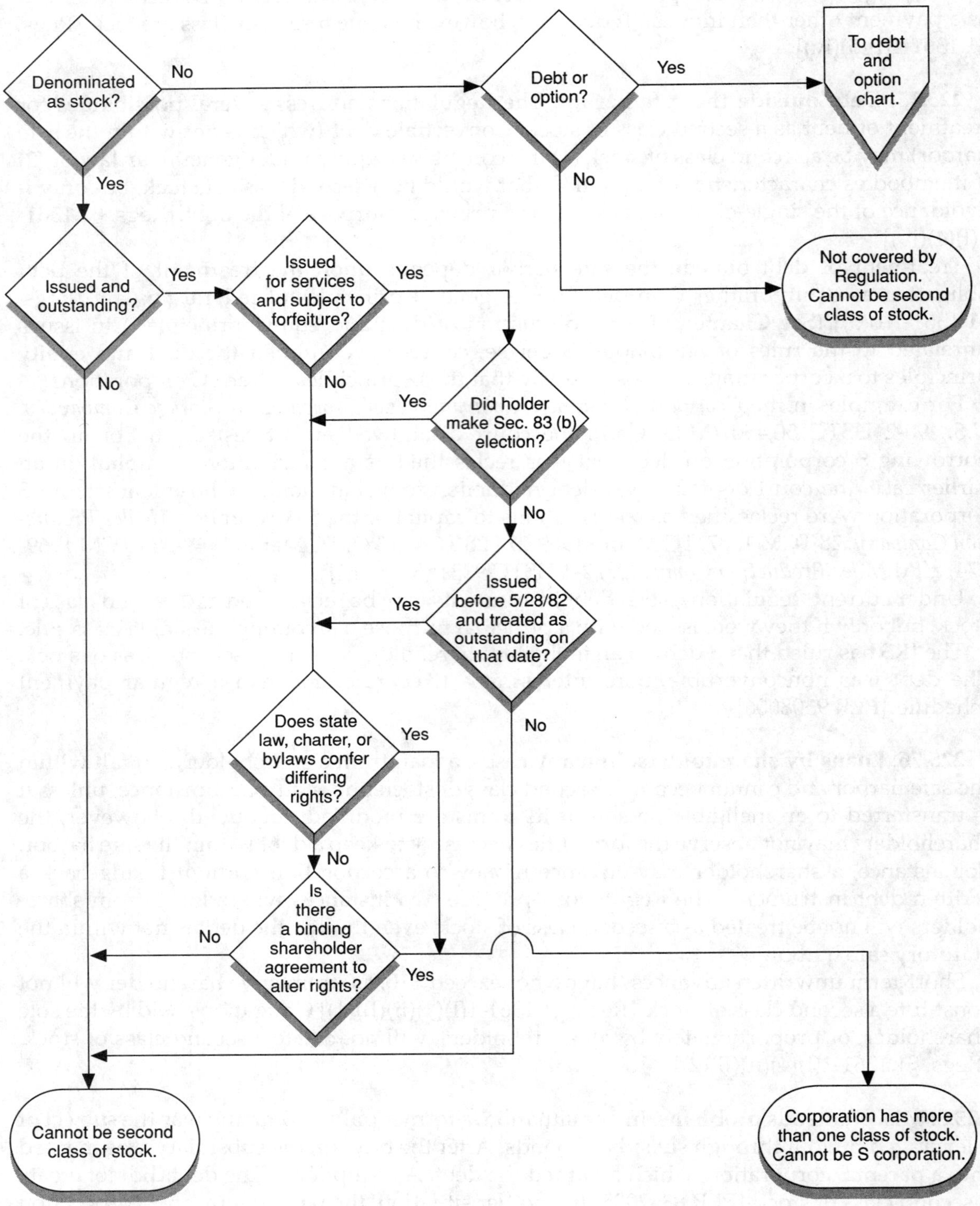

***Figure 2 - 2:** Class of stock rules applied to debt and options.*

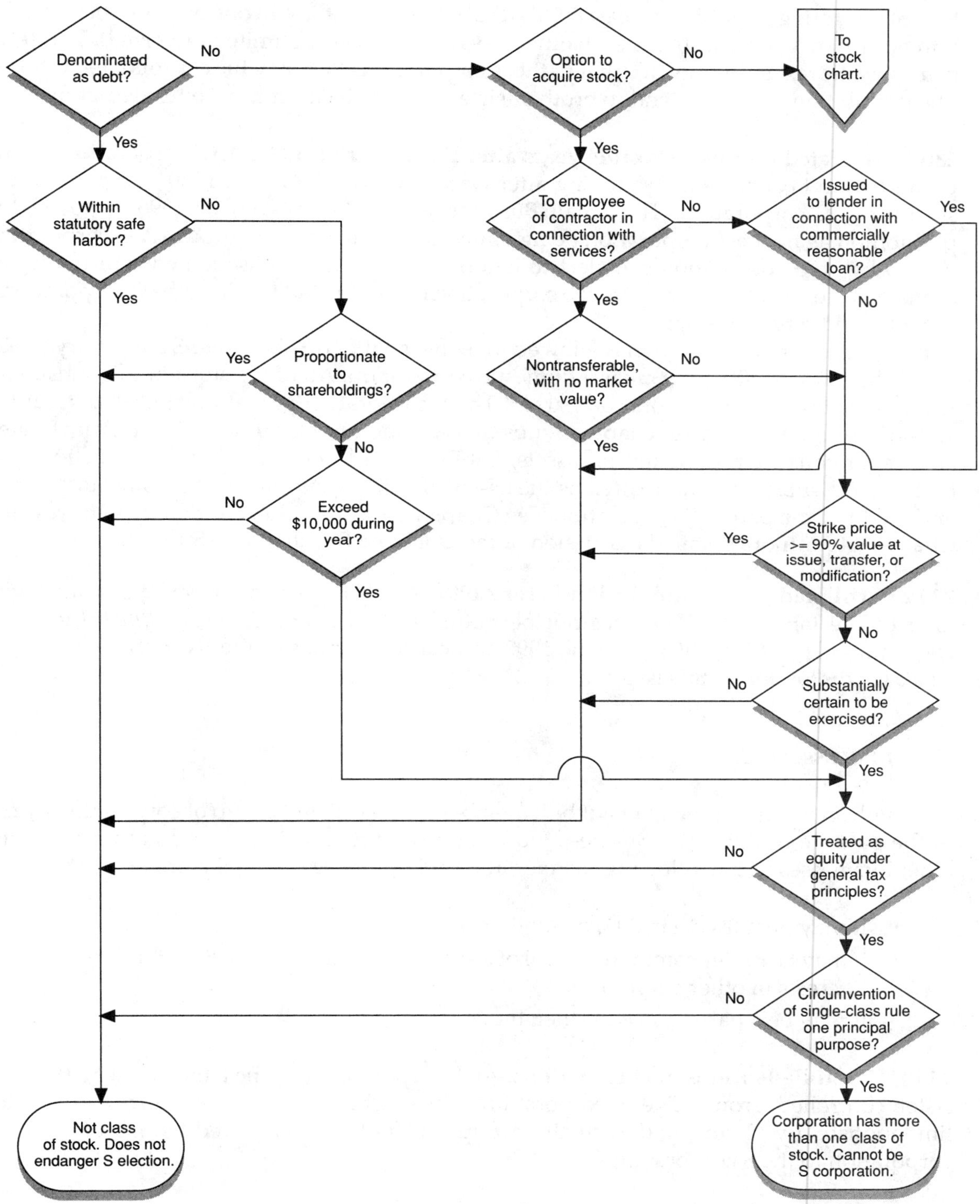

230. Affiliated groups.

Section 1504(a) defines an *affiliated group* as one in which a parent corporation owns at least 80% of the voting stock, and at least 80% of the value of the stock, in one or more subsidiaries. It must also own at least 80% of each other class of stock (except limited preferred). This term has a specific tax definition, peculiar to those corporations that may file consolidated returns. The prohibition did not extend to brother–sister or parent–subsidiary controlled groups.

230.1. Affiliated groups in taxable years after December 31, 1996. An S corporation is now permitted, in taxable years beginning after December 31, 1996, to own 80% or more of the stock of a C corporation. The Small Business Job Protection Act of 1996 removed the prohibition against a S corporation being a member of an affiliated group. A C corporation owned by an S corporation can elect to join in the filing of a consolidated return with its affiliated C corporations. The parent S corporation is not allowed to join in the C corporation's consolidated return election.

In addition, an S corporation is allowed to own a qualified Subchapter S subsidiary (QSSS or QSub). [§1361(b)(3)] A QSub is a domestic corporation. All of the stock of this subsidiary must be held by the S corporation parent. The S corporation parent must elect to treat the subsidiary as a qualified Subchapter S subsidiary. Under the election, the QSub is not treated as a separate corporation, and all assets, liabilities, and items of income, deduction, and credit of the subsidiary are treated as the assets, liabilities, and items of income, deduction, and credit of the parent S corporation. See Chapter 5 for the QSub election procedures, and Chapter 14 for more detailed discussion of the Qualified Subchapter S Subsidiary.

230.2. Affiliated group prohibition before 1997. An S corporation in taxable years beginning before January 1, 1997, was not permitted to be a member of an *affiliated group* of corporations. [§1361(b)(2)(A)] See the 1997 and earlier editions of the *S Corporation Taxation Guide* for discussion of this issue.

235. Other associations.

Although an S corporation may not be a member of an affiliated group of corporations, prior to the passage of the Small Business Job Protection Act of 1996 it may be associated with other businesses in the following manner in taxable years beginning before January 1, 1997:

- It may own less than 80% of another corporation.
- It may be under common control of a shareholder or group of shareholders who own interests in other corporations.
- It may be a partner in a partnership.

235.1. Controlled groups of corporations. An S corporation may be a member of a brother–sister controlled group. The S corporation will not be subject to the surtax exemption limitations. Any C corporation in the group will not be considered as a brother–sister corporation to the S corporation.

> **OBSERVATION:** The owners of a closely held business may want to divide the activities between a C corporation and an S corporation. The C corporation may take advantage of the graduated rate schedule and deductible fringe benefits that are not available to an S corporation. The shareholders should be aware of §482, which gives the IRS discretion to reallocate income among businesses under common control.

235.2. Partnerships and limited liability companies. An S corporation may own an interest in a partnership. Presumably any percentage of interest is allowed. Before 1994, there was a danger that the IRS would challenge the substance of such an arrangement and disallow an S election. However, the IRS has now stated that such arrangements do not endanger the S election. [Rev. Rul. 94-43, 1994-27 IRB 8] An S corporation may also own any percentage of interest in a limited liability company that is treated as a partnership for tax purposes, because such an association does not form an affiliated group. However, ownership by an S corporation of at least 80% of a limited liability company classified as an association for tax purposes will result in termination of the S election in taxable years beginning before January 1, 1997. [PLR 9433008]

On occasion, corporations have attempted to invalidate their S elections through a variety of means. In one case, an S corporation tried to use its association with other corporations through several partnerships to disavow its S election. It claimed, in essence, that the partnership should be disregarded and the corporation should have been a member in an affiliated group. The statute on affiliated groups, however, provides only for direct ownership, and the court refused to let the corporation disregard its S election. [*Michael G. Jolin*, 50 TCM 140, TC Memo 1985-287]

OBSERVATION: The owners of an S corporation will find it more difficult to attempt to invalidate an S election now that the permissible number of shareholders has been increased to 75 and the affiliated group limitation has been eliminated.

EXAMPLE 2 - 29: Corporation A has two equal shareholders, and Corporation B has three equal shareholders. Each of the two corporations contributes equal amounts of cash to partnership P, and each of the two corporations will receive equal allocations of the partnership's profits and losses. The two corporations are both S corporations. Indirectly, the shareholders of Corporation A will receive 25% of the partnership's profits and losses. The shareholders of B will each receive $16^2/_3$ of the partnership's profits and losses. Under the rationale of Revenue Ruling 77-220, the IRS might have contended that the entire arrangement was in fact a single corporation with two classes of stock. Under the recent holding of Revenue Ruling 94-43, however, the IRS is no longer likely to challenge the eligibility of either corporation for an S election as a result of the partnership arrangement.

Another issue that should be considered is whether or not membership in a partnership will create an ineligible shareholder. This could be the case if the IRS were to combine the entities. In one instance, a ruling stated that each member of the partnership was eligible to be an S corporation and that no corporations ineligible to be S corporations would become members in the partnership. [PLR 8823027] In another ruling, the IRS held that no other member of the partnership was considered to be a shareholder in one of the partners that was an S corporation. [PLR 8916057]

When an S corporation is a member of a partnership, its choice of taxable years will probably be restricted. See Chapter 4 for discussion of both the natural business year end and the §444 year.

240. Other ineligible corporations.

The final statutory restriction covers prohibited entities. Former DISCs, banks that use the reserve method of accounting for bad debts, insurance companies, and corporations availing themselves of the possessions tax credit all have their own special deferral rules or other tax benefits. Congress decided that these corporations did not need the opportunity for an additional tax break by making an S election. This set of restrictions will not receive further discussion in this book.

245. Banks and bank holding companies.

Through December 31, 1996, banks were ineligible to be S corporations. [§1361(b)(2)(B)], prior to amendment by the Small Business Job Protection Act of 1996] The affiliated group prohibition made bank holding companies ineligible to be S corporations. [PLRs 9211027, 9551032, 9602029, 9603009]

For taxable years beginning after 1996, banks will become eligible to be S corporations, unless they use the reserve method of bad debt deduction. [§1361(b)(2)(A)], after amendment by the Small Business Job Protection Act of 1996] There are a number of cautions to be observed by banks and bank holding companies that are considering this strategy.

1. The change from the reserve method of bad debt deduction to the direct charge-off method is a change in accounting method. [Regs. §1.446-1] A taxpayer may change a method of accounting only with permission from the IRS. [§446(e)] In order to change to the direct charge-off method, the bank will need to file Form 3115 within 180 days of the beginning of its taxable years. [Rev. Proc. 92-20, 1992-1 CB 685] The bank may file this form within the last 186 days of 1996. For the 1997 tax year, banks may follow a similar procedure. See Revenue Procedure 97-18 [1997-10 IRB 53]. The Service has granted a bank an extension to change its method of accounting for bad debts from the reserve method to the specific charge-off method. [PLR 199908021]
2. In the case of a bank owned by a holding company, the bank will need to be a qualified Subchapter S subsidiary, owned 100% by the parent S corporation. In some cases there may be a statutory requirement that the bank's directors hold some shares of the bank directly. Thus these shares would appear to make it impossible for the bank to qualify as a qualified Subchapter S subsidiary.

   CAUTION: At the time of this writing, there is no sure and easy answer to the dilemma of a bank that has directors' shares outstanding and must continue to do so. An old Revenue Ruling may be relevant. Revenue Ruling 64-309 [1964-2 CB 333] held that certain shares held by the Federal Housing Administration in certain corporations were not treated as outstanding stock for purposes of Subchapter S. Although Revenue Ruling 64-309 does not deal with bank directors' shares, and may not be relied upon to qualify a bank for qualified Subchapter S subsidiary status, it may be useful as a precedent if a bank intends to request a private letter ruling.

3. A bank may have a substantial portfolio of interest-bearing securities. The interest on these instruments will be treated as passive investment income, although the interest from loans made in the active course of the banking business will not be passive investment income. If passive investment income exceeds 25% of the bank's gross receipts in any given year, and the banks has accumulated earning and profits at the end of that year, the bank will be subject to a tax on its excess net passive income. If the situation continues for three consecutive years, the bank will lose its S election at the beginning of the next taxable year. See Chapter 12.

250. Other restrictions on eligibility.

An otherwise eligible corporation that has terminated an S election generally may not make a new S election until it has been a C corporation for five taxable years. [§1361(g)] The Small

Business Job Protection Act of 1996 provided a limited relief from this restriction. For the purposes of the five-year rule, any termination of Subchapter S status occurring in a taxable year beginning before January 1, 1997, will not be taken into account. This topic receives thorough discussion in Chapter 5, at 525.

Generally, a corporation that has been a QSub of an S corporation may not elect to be an S corporation for five years following the termination of its QSub status. [§1361(b)(3)(D)(ii)] The IRS has granted exceptions in several cases, and has issued a Proposed Regulation to allow an immediate S corporation election for a corporation that has been a QSub, as long as the corporation spends no time as a C corporation. [Prop. Regs. §1.1361-5(d)(2)] See Chapter 5, at 525.7.

An S corporation that has accumulated earnings and profits from years in which it was a C corporation may lose its S election if its gross receipts from passive investment income exceed 25% of its total gross receipts for three consecutive years. See Chapter 3 for a discussion of earnings and profits and Chapter 12 for coverage of the passive investment income problems.

255. Practice aids.

The following checklists help determine the eligibility of shareholders, trusts, stock, debt, and affiliated groups.

Checklist 2-1: Shareholder eligibility

	Applicable (Yes/No)	*Completed (Date)*
1. Determine number of shareholders: Husband, wife, estate attribution	________	________
2. Determine eligibility of all shareholders:	________	________
a. Are all individuals U.S. citizens?	________	________
b. If any shareholders are not U.S. citizens, check for residence status, Green Card Election under §6013(g)	________	________
Dual status: Check status of Regulations. If necessary, seek ruling.	________	________
c. Any estates?	________	________
Unduly prolonged?	________	________
Check for intended transferees. Are beneficiaries eligible? If trust, see Checklist 2-2.	________	________
d. Any trusts, complete Checklist 2-2.	________	________

Copyright © 2000 by Harcourt, Inc. All rights reserved.

2

Checklist 2-2: Trust eligibility

	Applicable (Yes/No)	Completed (Date)
1. Review trust instrument.		
2. For *inter vivos* trust:		
a. Does grantor have power to receive income or corpus?		
i. If yes, and grantor is U.S. citizen or resident, no election is necessary.		
ii. If no, check for beneficiary's power.		
b. Does beneficiary have power to receive income or corpus without consent of adverse party?		
i. If yes, and beneficiary is U.S. citizen or resident, no election is necessary.		
ii. If no, check for QSST eligibility.		
c. Voting trust: No separate election necessary.		
i. Each beneficiary must be U.S. citizen or resident.		
ii. Each will be included in 75-shareholder count.		
d. Other trust: Separate election necessary to be QSST or Electing Small Business Trust—verify all other provisions of trust instrument for qualification as QSST or Electing Small Business Trust.		
i. One current income beneficiary, who is U.S. citizen or resident		
ii. No other person can receive income or corpus during beneficiary's lifetime.		
iii. No other person can receive income or corpus during beneficiary's lifetime if trust terminates.		
iv. Requirement or trustee's acknowledged responsibility to distribute all income currently.		
v. Trustee may accumulate or distribute corpus.		
vi. Election to be QSST:		
(1) Must be filed by beneficiary, parent, or legal guardian—not by trustee.		
(2) Must be filed within 2 months and 5 days of Form 2553; if held at time of election, may file with Form 2553.		
(3) Must be filed within 2 months and 15 days of acquisition of shares, if stock is received after corporation files Form 2553.		
vii. Election to be Electing Small Business Trust:		
(1) Must be filed by fiduciary.		
3. For testamentary trust:		
a. Honor 2-year limit, unless trust is qualified as beneficiary-controlled trust (no election necessary) or QSST or ESBT (election necessary).		

Copyright © 2000 by Harcourt, Inc. All rights reserved.

2

b. Review item 2 (*inter vivos* trust, above) to see if trust qualifies permanently. ________ ________

c. If trust does not qualify, distribute shares within 2 years after receipt. ________ ________

d. If judicial interference is necessary, keep shares in estate. ________ ________

4. For grantor trust after death of deemed grantor:

a. Review item 2 (*inter vivos* trust, above) to see if trust qualifies permanently. ________ ________

b. If all corpus was included in decedent's gross estate, distribute stock to eligible shareholder within two years. ________ ________

Checklist 2-3: Stock eligibility

	Applicable (Yes/No)	*Completed (Date)*
1. Are all shares of identical class?	________	________
2. If not of same class, are there any differences other than vote?	________	________
3. Do any state laws create different rights?	________	________
If so, consider moving charter.	________	________
4. Examine all the following, and rectify if necessary:		
Charter	________	________
Bylaws	________	________
Binding agreements	________	________
5. Does the corporation have any restricted stock outstanding?		
If yes, did holder make §83(b) election?	________	________
If no, will vesting create eligibility violation?	________	________
6. Are any options outstanding?		
To lender, in ordinary business?	________	________
Nontransferable?	________	________
To employee or contractor?	________	________
Nontransferable?	________	________
To any other party?	________	________
Substantially certain to exercise?	________	________

Copyright © 2000 by Harcourt, Inc. All rights reserved.

2

Checklist 2-4: Debt eligibility

	Applicable (Yes/No)	Completed (Date)
1. Does all debt to shareholders meet the safe harbor?		
Written?		
Nonconvertible?		
Payment terms and interest not discretionary?		
2. Unwritten debt to shareholders:		
Proportional?		
Under $10,000?		
3. Debt to nonshareholders:		
If lender is eligible, does the debt meet other safe harbor conditions?		
4. Debt to ineligible persons:		
(See Chapter 14 for debt–equity reclassifications risks.)		

Checklist 2-5: List of agreements

(Also see Agreement Checklist in Chapter 8.)

	Applicable (Yes/No)	Completed (Date)
1. Nontransferability agreement binding on all shares, giving right of first refusal to corporation or controlling shareholder		
2. Procedures to monitor changes in ownership, upon death or bankruptcy of shareholder		
3. Special agreement applicable to alien: Immediate transfer upon ineligibility		
4. Bylaws nullifying any transfer to ineligible person or person in excess of shareholder limit		
5. Provision for mandatory redemption in event of shareholder divorce		
6. Inform all shareholders of estate planning constraints		

Copyright © 2000 by Harcourt, Inc. All rights reserved.

C CORPORATIONS CONSIDERING THE S ELECTION: ADVANTAGES, DISADVANTAGES, AND SOLUTIONS

3

Contents

3

3

300. Overview.

When a corporation makes an S election for its first year of operations, the impact of the eligibility requirements is easy to assess. It must comply with all of the rules or it will not be eligible. The various restrictions can be considered in the initial meetings among the corporation's investors, their accountants, and attorneys. When a corporation is already in existence, however, matters may become more complicated.

There are several reasons why a C corporation may consider electing S status. The most important of these reasons were listed in Chapter 1, at 125. There are also a variety of reasons why a corporation that desires an S election has not had one in effect. First, it may not have qualified for the election in past years, but has now met the qualifications or intends to meet the qualifications. Second, the disadvantages of the S election in the past may have outweighed the advantages, but circumstances have changed and this is no longer the case for a particular corporation. Third, a corporation may have had poor tax advice, and not made the election when it should have, or the corporation may have made an invalid election.

Assuming that the corporation now qualifies for S status, the election itself is a simple matter, as discussed in Chapter 5. In general, a corporation must file its S election within 2 months and 15 days of the beginning of its taxable year. And while the beginning of the taxable year may be somewhat difficult to ascertain for a new corporation, the date is already known for an existing corporation. Any new corporation must make certain elections for accounting methods, inventories, etc., and must make all of these in a timely fashion. An existing corporation already has these elections in place, and does not need to worry about start-up problems.

In other respects, however, the decision to make an S election is more complicated and potentially more costly for an existing C corporation than it is for a new corporation. (See 310.)

Before an existing corporation makes an S election, it should anticipate the collateral effects of the S election. The LIFO and foreign loss recapture income will add to the tax liability of the last year as a C corporation. The pension and profit-sharing plans should be reviewed for any loans to shareholder-employees. These loans should be paid back before the S election takes effect. A study of the corporation's accumulated earnings and profits may be advisable. Some corporations have been surprised to find that their shareholders have received dividend income from distributions after the S election has been in effect (see Chapter 7). Others have faced the even more unpleasant surprise that they have lost their S elections due to the combination of accumulated earnings and profits and excessive passive investment income (see Chapters 12 and 13).

310. Possible secondary costs of making S election.

Once a corporation has determined that it is eligible for the S election, or has determined that the cost of becoming eligible is not prohibitive, it must be aware of some costs that make the S election less attractive than it would be for a newly formed corporation:

- It may find out that some of its unrealized gains and accumulations of income may not escape double taxation.
- If the corporation maintains qualified pension and profit-sharing plans, the plan trustees should scrutinize loans to shareholder-employees. (See at 315.)
- If the corporation uses the LIFO inventory method, it may be taxed as if it had liquidated its inventory. (See at 320.)

- Future distributions may be subject to double taxation as dividends, if the corporation has accumulated earnings and profits. (See Chapter 7, at 720.)
- A corporation that has sustained foreign losses may need to recapture those losses as income in its final year as a C corporation. (See at 330.)

Each of these situations presents tax problems. The pension plan loans, LIFO recapture, calculation of accumulated earnings and profits and foreign loss recapture are the subjects of the remainder of this chapter.

In addition, the corporation may face some corporate-level taxes when it begins operating as an S corporation. These taxes, like the corporate income tax on a C corporation, may subject the corporation and its shareholders to double taxation. In some cases, the double taxation of an S corporation and its shareholders may result in a greater tax liability than would have been the case if it had remained a C corporation. The most important taxes an S corporation may face on its own income are:

- The tax on built-in gains (discussed in Chapter 11)
- The tax on excess net passive income (discussed in Chapter 12)

Exposure to these taxes can have a significant effect on the corporation's decision to make an S election, or to remain a C corporation. The built-in gains tax and passive investment income tax do not result in immediate tax liability, but they are affected by events that occur after the S election takes effect. The problems discussed in this chapter, by contrast, have an immediate effect on the corporation when it files its S election.

315. Pension and profit-sharing considerations.

Employers may establish qualified pension and profit-sharing plans on behalf of their employees. Tax qualification of pension and profit-sharing plans is beyond the scope of this book. A few simple definitions and the general rules, however, will serve to put the problems of S corporations in perspective.

The essence of a qualified plan is that the employer receives an immediate deduction for the contributions to the plan, whereas the employees report no immediate income. The employer contributes the annual amounts to a trust, which is exempt from tax on its earnings. When an employee retires, he or she reports taxable income on the distributions received from the plan. The opportunities for tax deferral and the ability to invest in reasonably safe assets make the pension and profit-sharing plan area one of the most important tax-planning arenas.

Until 1962, corporations were the only entities that could take advantage of tax-deferred retirement savings plans. When the original version of Subchapter S was enacted in 1958, there was no distinction between a C corporation and an S corporation with respect to qualified plans. The rules changed several times over the years. In 1962, Congress allowed unincorporated enterprises to establish qualified plans, known as *Keogh* plans or *H.R. 10* plans[1], but they could contribute only $2,500 per year for each of its owners. In 1969, plans maintained by S corporations became subject to the Keogh limits.[2] [§1379] The Keogh limits were raised to $7,500 per year in 1974 and to $15,000 per year in 1981. In 1982, the Tax Equity and Fiscal Responsibility Act of 1982 (TEFRA) brought the limits of Keogh plans into general conformity with those of plans maintained by corporations. TEFRA, which was signed into

---

[1] Congressman Keogh sponsored H. R. 10, the law that enabled unincorporated businesses to establish qualified plans. Hence the terms *Keogh* and *H.R. 10* plans for the self-employed taxpayers.

[2] This provision remains in the Code, even though it has been inoperative since 1984.

law approximately two months before the Subchapter S Revision Act of 1982, kept the old Keogh limits in effect through 1983. The Subchapter S Revision Act of 1982 did not amend TEFRA rules for S corporations. Therefore, there have been few differences between C corporation rules and S corporation rules since 1984.

A pension plan may be one of two basic types—the defined benefit plan and the defined contribution (also known as money purchase) plan. A *defined benefit plan* guarantees each participating employee a certain level of income at normal retirement age, usually based on the level of compensation and years of service.

> **EXAMPLE 3 - 1:** XYZ Corporation establishes a pension plan whereby each employee is guaranteed 2% of his or her highest level of compensation for each year of service. If an employee retires at age 65 with 40 years of service, he or she will receive 80% of the highest annual salary as a pension.

The employer's annual contribution to the plan is deductible, although there are certain maximum limits on pensions that the plan cannot exceed. Because the contribution is based on the life expectancy of each employee, the employees' current ages, expected turnover, current market value of plan assets, and expected earnings of the plan's assets, the current year's contributions must be determined by actuaries. In a defined benefit plan, the risk of the plan's investments is ultimately borne by the employer, who must make an annual contribution sufficient to keep the plan funded.

A *defined contribution plan* is a much simpler form of pension plan. The formula requires that the employer contribute a given percentage of each employee's current compensation to the plan. The trustee of the plan must observe fiduciary standards in managing the plan's investments. When the employee retires, he or she will receive all of the employer's contributions made on his or her behalf, plus all of the earnings attributable to those contributions. The employer makes no warranty as to what the balance might be at the time of the employee's retirement. A defined contribution plan, therefore, shifts the risk of the plan's earnings from the employer to the employee. In order for a plan to qualify as a pension plan, the employer must contribute a constant percentage of each participating employee's compensation to the plan each year. The percentage may not exceed 25%, and the annual contribution may not exceed $30,000 per year for each employee.

A *qualified profit-sharing plan* is a defined contribution plan. It is based on all of the same principles as a defined contribution plan, except that the employer may vary the percentage of compensation contributed to the plan each year. The percentage of compensation may vary from almost nothing to 15% of the employee's compensation.

> **PLANNING TIP:** An employer may maintain a pension plan and a profit-sharing plan simultaneously. The pension plan may be either a defined benefit or a defined contribution plan. A profit-sharing plan may only be a defined contribution plan. If both plans are defined contributions, the total contributions to both plans on behalf of one employee cannot exceed the lesser of $30,000 or 25% of the employee's compensation in any one year.[3] A reasonable strategy for an employer who wants to maintain both types of defined contribution plans is to set the pension plan contributions at 10% of compensation and the maximum contribution to the profit-sharing plan at 15% of compensation, with contributions to both plans based on the employee's compensation that does not exceed $120,000. This approach allows the employer to contribute the maximum allowable contribution of $30,000 or 25% of the compensation to the plans in the years in which funds are available to do so. In years when money is tight, the employer must contribute 10% (but no more than 10%) of each

[3] The limitations are more complicated when the employer maintains a defined benefit pension plan and a profit-sharing plan.

3

employee's compensation to the pension plan, in which the contribution percentage must be constant from year to year. The contributions to the profit-sharing plan, however, may be extremely low.

Many employers maintain both pension plans and profit-sharing plans. Aside from the contribution formulas, these two types of plans are identical. The term *qualified plans* includes both pension plans and profit-sharing plans.

315.1. Prohibited transactions. Qualified plans are subject to strict fiduciary standards. Penalties for engaging in "prohibited transactions" include penalty taxes and a loss of plan qualification. Among the prohibited transactions are certain dealings between the plan trust and any "disqualified person."[4]

Disqualified persons include the corporate employer sponsoring the plan, significant shareholders, and highly compensated employees.

The prohibited dealings include purchases of property, sales of property, and loans.

Under no circumstances may an employer borrow from the plan's assets, unless the employer receives specific permission from the IRS to do so.

315.11. C corporations' plans. A brief discussion of the rules applicable to plans maintained by C corporations will suggest some potential problems for the tax professional to examine before making the S election.

A plan sponsored by a C corporation may not make loans to the employer. It also cannot make a loan to an officer, a person who owns more than 10% of the shares of the employer, or a person who receives more than 10% of the corporation's total compensation for the taxable year, unless loans are available to all plan participants on the same terms. [§4975(e)(2)(H)] In addition, the loans must bear a reasonable rate of interest, and must be adequately secured. [§4975(d)(1)] In practice, many C corporations' plans have loan provisions that meet these criteria. Therefore, shareholder-employees, including controlling shareholders, may be able to borrow from their corporations' qualified plans, without causing the plan to engage in a prohibited transaction.

Employees need to be concerned with certain limits on plan loans. If the total amount of loans to any one employee exceeds the limits, the loan may be characterized as a distribution and result in taxable income to the borrower.[5] A loan is not treated as a distribution if the total of the loans to the participant does not exceed $50,000 or one-half of the participant's nonforfeitable accrued benefit, whichever is less.[6] [§72(p)(2)] A *de minimis* rule allows loans up to $10,000, without regard to the borrower's nonforfeitable accrued benefit. As a general rule, the participant's rights to distributions from the plan constitute adequate security for the loan. The loan agreement must require repayment within five years, unless the loan proceeds are used to acquire a residence. [§72(p)(2)(B)]

EXAMPLE 3 - 2: Mel is the sole shareholder in Melco, a C corporation. Melco maintains a qualified pension plan. At a time when Mel's accrued nonforfeitable benefit is $90,000, he borrows $45,000 from the plan trust. Assuming that loans are available to other participants on equivalent terms, that the loan bears a reasonable rate of interest, and that it meets the required repayment schedule, Mel's loan is not treated as a distribution or as a prohibited transaction.

---

[4] Code §4975(c)(1) lists the prohibited transactions, and §4975(e)(2) lists the disqualified persons.

[5] A distribution from a plan before the employee retires may have other serious consequences, which are beyond the scope of this book.

[6] The nonforfeitable accrued benefit is the amount to which the employee would be entitled if he or she retired immediately.

315.12. S corporations' plans. S corporations' qualified plans have very few differences from those of C corporation. Exception: Any loan to a shareholder who owns more than 5% of the stock is a prohibited transaction. [§4975] When a plan trust engages in a prohibited transaction, the participant is subject to a 15% excise tax on the fair market value of the "amount involved" in the prohibited transaction. (This penalty was 5% before amendment by §1074 of the Taxpayer Relief Act of 1997.) In the case of a loan, the "amount involved" is the fair market value of the use of the money, which constitutes a reasonable rate of interest. [Regs. §53.4941(e)(1)(1)(b)(4), Example 4] The tax is imposed during the "taxable period" of the prohibited transaction, which begins when the transaction commences. It ends on the earliest of the following:

1. The date on which the IRS sends a notice of deficiency
2. The date on which the IRS assesses the tax
3. The date on which the prohibited transaction is corrected [§4975(f)(2)]

> **EXAMPLE 3 - 3:** Assume that the loan in Example 3 - 2 is a prohibited transaction. Mel discovers that the loan is prohibited and immediately repays the loan, after it has been outstanding for one year. A reasonable rate of interest at the time is 10% per annum. The 15% excise tax imposed on Mel is $675 ($45,000 x .1 x .15).

If the transaction is not corrected within the taxable period, there is an additional 100% excise tax. [§4975(b)] This is ample reason for a taxpayer to correct a prohibited transaction before the IRS assesses a penalty.

> **EXAMPLE 3 - 4:** Assume that the loan in Examples 3 - 2 and 3 - 3 was a prohibited transaction. After the loan had been outstanding for three years, the IRS sent the trust a notice of deficiency. The taxes imposed would be as follows:

Amount involved ($45,000 x .1 x 3)	$13,500	
Excise tax at 15%		$ 2,025
Additional tax for failure to correct	13,500	
Total		$15,525

315.2. Effect of S election. Dealings between a qualified plan and its participants have absolutely no effect on the employer's ability to make an S election. There is, however, a special trap for the plan and certain borrowers when a C corporation makes an S election. If a loan to a shareholder is outstanding at the time the election takes effect, the loan immediately becomes a prohibited transaction. [Dept. of Labor Opinion No. 84-44A (11/9/84]

The IRS has indicated that plan loans to shareholder-employees may be granted exemption from prohibited transaction status. Such exemption is granted on a case-by-case basis, and typically requires the borrower to pledge property as security. [Ann. 92-182, 1992-52 IRB 45]

> **EXAMPLE 3 - 5:** Assume that the loan in the previous examples was not a prohibited transaction. On January 1, 1996, when the loan balance was $40,000, Melco became an S corporation. The plan would be engaging in a prohibited transaction as of January 1, 1996. Mel should repay the loan as soon as possible, in order to minimize the excise tax.

> **PLANNING TIP:** An existing corporation making an S election should review the status of qualified plans. Any loans to shareholders will not appear on the corporation's books and records, since all plan assets are owned by trusts. The plan administrator may be able to secure from the IRS a waiver of prohibited transaction status for the loan. A plan that continues to engage in prohibited transactions may lose its qualified status, so the parties involved should take prompt action to correct the situation.

If the borrowing employees cannot immediately repay the loans, the corporation should seriously consider postponing its S election until the shareholders can make the repayments. In many cases, if the corporation has been in operation for several years, the assets held by the plan trusts may exceed the assets held by the corporation. In these cases, the corporate tax savings from the S election may be insignificant compared to the risk of disqualifying the plan.

320. LIFO recapture.

The built-in gains tax has become one of the major problems of Subchapter S. A former C corporation is subject to the built-in gains tax on certain recognized gains in its first 10 years as an S corporation. The built-in gains tax was an important provision of the Tax Reform Act of 1986. It was enacted as a portion of the General Utilities doctrine repeal,[7] so that C corporations could not avoid the tax on liquidation by making an S election. The built-in gains tax results in double taxation of S corporations, to the extent that unrealized gains were accrued before the S election took effect. In late 1986 and most of 1987, it appeared that a corporation could avoid the built-in gains tax on its inventory gains by using the LIFO method.

A corporation using the LIFO inventory assumption would not recognize gain on any of its opening inventory in the first 10 years as an S corporation unless it depleted its inventory level. LIFO recapture was added by the Revenue Act of 1987 to close this "loophole" left by the built-in gains tax imposed by the Tax Reform Act of 1986. The LIFO recapture rules were incorporated into the bill that became the Revenue Act of 1987 on December 17, 1987. To protect corporations from retroactivity, there were two important transitional rules:

1. A corporation that had filed its S election on or before December 17, 1987, was exempt from the LIFO recapture tax.
2. A corporation whose board of directors had adopted a resolution on or before December 17, 1987, to make an S election was exempt from the LIFO recapture if the corporation filed its S election before January 1, 1989. (The Revenue Act of 1987, §10227(b)(2), contains both transitional rules.)

SUMMARY OF AUTHORITY: CODE SECTION 1363(d)(1)

- LIFO recapture applies only to former C corporations.
- The LIFO recapture amount is included in the corporation's taxable income in its last year as a C corporation.

The LIFO recapture tax is imposed on the corporation's income in its last year as a C corporation, as if the corporation had liquidated its LIFO reserve on the last day of the year. Since the tax is determined by reference to the C corporation's taxable income, it operates differently from the taxes on built-in gains or excess net passive income, discussed in Chapters 11 and 12.

OBSERVATION: As of this writing, the LIFO recapture rules have not received much attention. This tax may be so onerous that it effectively prevents a C corporation with a significant LIFO reserve from becoming an S corporation. To date, the IRS has issued one Regulation dealing with LIFO recapture. [Regs. §1.1363-2] This Regulation is extremely limited in scope. It does not amplify the Internal Revenue Code,

[7] See Chapter 7 for the derivation of the term and Chapter 16 for an explanation of the corporate liquidation rules adopted by the Tax Reform Act of 1986.

except that it extends the LIFO recapture rule to C corporations that transfer assets to S corporations in tax-free reorganizations or liquidations. The reorganization rules are discussed in Chapter 17 at 1710., and tax-free liquidations are discussed in Chapter 15 at 1525.7. It was not until late 1994, nearly seven years after enactment of the LIFO recapture statute, that the IRS issued any operating rules on the proper accounting for inventories after LIFO recapture. [Rev. Proc. 94-61, 1994-38 IRB 56]

The IRS has ruled that LIFO recapture does not apply when a proprietorship is incorporated and immediately makes an S election. [PLR 9039005] This ruling is hardly revolutionary, since the tax applies only to former C corporations.

Similarly, the IRS has ruled that no LIFO recapture results from the divisive reorganization of an S corporation. [PLR 9424046] See Chapter 17, at 1735., for discussion of divisive reorganizations.

320.1. Calculation of LIFO recapture amount. The rules for the LIFO recapture amount are prescribed in §1363(d)(3) and (4).

SUMMARY OF AUTHORITY: CODE SECTION 1363(d)(3) AND (4)

- The LIFO recapture amount is the excess of the corporation's FIFO carrying value over its LIFO carrying value.
- The LIFO recapture is determined at the end of the corporation's final Subchapter C year.
- The corporation must include all of its inventory, or stock in trade, in calculating LIFO recapture.
- A retailer may use retail LIFO in valuing its inventories.
- Corporations that do not use the retail method may use the lower of cost or market method.

Calculation of the LIFO recapture amount involves the following steps:

1. Determine the corporation's FIFO cost from the corporation's books and records.
2. Adjust FIFO cost for any uniform capitalization adjustments.
3. Compare FIFO cost with market value. See Chapter 11, at 1110.85, for a discussion of inventory valuation techniques.
4. Determine LIFO cost with appropriate uniform capitalization adjustments. [§263A]
5. Compare the lower of FIFO cost or market with LIFO cost. The difference is the LIFO recapture amount.[8]

See Worksheet 3-1, at 340.

The starting point is FIFO inventory.[9] The FIFO inventory cost data should be readily ascertainable from the corporation's books and records, since most businesses use FIFO for books even though they might use LIFO for tax. To arrive at the tax FIFO cost, the corporation must adjust for uniform capitalization costs applicable to the closing inventory.[10]

OBSERVATION: Changes in inventory methods may result in certain adjustments to taxable income. The inventory carrying values are adjusted immediately, but the taxable income adjustments are phased in over several years. [§481] Any inventory adjustments that have not been completely phased in at the end of the last Subchapter C year are not subject to the LIFO recapture tax. However, they may be treated as built-in gains (see Chapter 11).

---

[8] In the unusual, but possible, situation where LIFO cost exceeds the lower of FIFO cost or market, the corporation would not be allowed to recognize a loss. [Rev. Proc. 94-61, 1994-38 IRB 56, Sec. 3, A-4]

[9] The Code makes no allowance for taxpayers who use specific identification or any of the averaging conventions. Future Regulations may clarify this issue.

[10] Uniform capitalization rules require complex accounting calculations that are beyond the scope of this book. Code §263A and the Regulations thereunder provide the rules necessary to calculate these adjustments.

Although LIFO is a cost-based method, a relief provision allows the FIFO value to be calculated at the lower of FIFO cost or market. [§1363(d)(4)(c)(ii)]

EXAMPLE 3 - 6: XYZ Corporation was a calendar-year C corporation through 1995. In February 1996, it filed an S election effective for calendar year 1996. Using LIFO, it had taxable income of $70,000 for 1995. Its books and records as of December 31, 1995, showed the following inventory values:

FIFO (cost)		$160,000
FIFO (LOCOM)	$150,000	
LIFO (cost)	$110,000	

XYZ is treated as having sold its inventory at the lower of FIFO cost or market. The market value is lower than cost in this case, so XYZ is treated as if it had sold its inventory for its market value of $150,000. The difference between that amount and LIFO cost is $40,000. Therefore, the LIFO recapture amount is $40,000.

The LIFO recapture amount is not treated as anything other than ordinary income. Thus, the corporation may use any allowable deductions, including net operating loss carryforwards, to offset this income. [Rev. Proc. 94-61, 1994-38 IRB 56, Sec. 3, A-5]

320.2. Calculation of LIFO recapture tax. The corporation computes the tax by comparing its income tax with the LIFO recapture to the tax that would result without the recapture.

EXAMPLE 3 - 7: XYZ, from Example 3 - 6, computes its LIFO recapture tax as follows:

Taxable income including LIFO recapture	$110,000	
Tax on $110,000		$26,150
Taxable income excluding LIFO recapture	70,000	
Tax on $70,000		(12,500)
LIFO recapture tax		$13,650

320.3. Payment of LIFO recapture tax. Although all the income from the LIFO recapture is treated as arising in the final year before the S election takes effect, the actual tax liability is not immediate. Code §1363(d)(2) allows a deferred payment schedule on the tax resulting from the recapture.

SUMMARY OF AUTHORITY: CODE SECTION 1363(d)(2)

- The LIFO recapture tax is payable in four equal installments.
- The first installment is due on the due date (without extension) for the corporation's final return as a C corporation.
- The remaining installments are payable on the due dates for the corporation's next three tax returns (without extension).
- Estimated tax payments are not required. [Rev. Proc. 94-61, 1994-38 IRB 56, Sec. 3, A-7]
- The installments do not bear interest.

EXAMPLE 3 - 8: XYZ, from Examples 3 - 6 and 3 - 7, has a total 1995 income tax liability of $26,150. It must make its tax payments by the following rules:

Normal rules (estimates or exceptions)	$12,500
Payable March 15, 1996 [(1/4) x 13,650]	3,412
Payable March 15, 1997	3,413
Payable March 15, 1998	3,412
Payable March 15, 1999	3,413
	$26,150

320.4. Accounting for inventory after the S election. The IRS has provided for blanket permission to discontinue LIFO. [Rev. Proc. 88-15, 1988-1 CB 683] The change takes place after the LIFO recapture and offers no immediate savings for most taxpayers. If the LIFO method no longer serves a valid tax planning objective, the new S corporation may want to consider discontinuing it. If, however, the corporation chooses to continue LIFO, it will need to recast its inventory layers.

320.41. Basis of inventory. The corporation is allowed a basis adjustment to its inventory, so that the recaptured LIFO layer is not again included in income if the corporation depletes its inventory. [§1363(d)(1)] The appropriate accounting treatment depends on whether the corporation switches to FIFO or continues to use LIFO. If the corporation changes to FIFO, the basis for the first year of the S election is the inventory value after restatement for the LIFO recapture. This inventory will be presumed sold in the first year, under normal circumstances, and will present no future accounting complications.

EXAMPLE 3 - 9: XYZ Corporation, from Example 3 - 6, changes its inventory method to FIFO. Its FIFO value at January 1, 1996, is $150,000.

320.42. Basis adjustment following adjustment to FIFO cost. In theory, the corporation has sold all of its inventory at its FIFO cost and has repurchased at the current price level. The corporation is allowed a basis adjustment to reflect the hypothetical repurchase. Accordingly, the corporation restates its inventory as if it consisted of one layer, purchased at the end of the year of the LIFO recapture. [Rev. Proc. 94-61, 1994-38 IRB 56, Sec. 3, A-2]

EXAMPLE 3 - 10: Barco makes an S election, effective January 1, 1996. It has used the LIFO inventory method since 1990. Its inventory carrying value, before LIFO recapture:

FIFO cost	$54,400
Less LIFO reserve	(12,400)
LIFO carrying value	$42,000

Its layers as they were computed before the LIFO recapture from the corporation's books and records are shown below. The data are borrowed from Regulations §1.263A-1T.

Layer	*Base Year Costs*	*Index*	*LIFO Carrying Value*
Base	$14,000	1.00	$ 14,000
1990	4,000	1.20	4,800
1991	5,000	1.30	6,500
1992	2,000	1.35	2,700
1993	0	1.40	0
1994	4,000	1.50	6,000
1995	5,000	1.60	8,000
Total	$34,000		$ 42,000

Barco's FIFO cost is $54,400, computed by restating all layers to the current year index. The details are shown in the next part of the example.

If the market value of the inventory is at least $54,400, Barco will recapture all of its LIFO reserve of $12,400. Barco would now account for its inventory as one layer in the amount of $54,400. To create an audit trail, it may restate each of its layers to the current index, as follows:

Layer	*LIFO Carrying Value*	*Base Index*	*Current Index*	*Basis Adjustment*	*Carrying Value*
Base	$14,000	1.00	1.60	$ 8,400	$22,400
1990	4,800	1.20	1.60	1,600	6,400
1991	6,500	1.30	1.60	1,500	8,000
1992	2,700	1.35	1.60	500	3,200
1993	0	1.40	1.60	0	0
1994	6,000	1.50	1.60	400	6,400
1995	8,000	1.60	1.60	0	8,000
Total	$42,000			$12,400	$54,400

Note that these calculations are equivalent to replacing all of the earlier layers with one layer, at an index value of 1.60. Barco could choose to keep its layers separate, although all of its layers now have a carrying value based on an index of 1.60 as follows:

Layer	*Base Year Costs**	*Index*	*LIFO Carrying Value*
Base	$22,400	1.60	$22,400
1990	6,400	1.60	6,400
1991	8,000	1.60	8,000
1992	3,200	1.60	3,200
1993	0	1.60	0
1994	6,400	1.60	6,400
1995	8,000	1.60	8,000
Total	$54,400		$54,400

*After basis adjustment for LIFO recapture.

Maintenance of the above schedule is now redundant for tax purposes, since all layers are computed with the same index. In essence, the corporation now has one layer, all of which is carried at the year-end 1995 price index. This is the exact same value as its FIFO cost, and is the same computation Barco would use if it were changing from FIFO to LIFO. Its inventory carrying value, after LIFO recapture, is summarized as follows:

FIFO cost	$54,400
Less LIFO reserve	(0)
LIFO carrying value	$54,400

OBSERVATION: The single layer method, as shown above, is the method prescribed for accounting in Revenue Procedure 94-61 [1994-38 IRB 56, Sec. 3, A-2]. If a corporation is not able to reflect the LIFO basis adjustment on its financial statements, the corporation would need to maintain its historical layers, at their historical price levels. The IRS has held that this procedure will not violate the financial statement conformity requirement to §472(c). [Rev. Proc. 94-61, 1994-38 IRB 56, Sec. 3, A-3] When the corporation must maintain separate historical levels for financial statement purposes, it should be able to maintain those same layers, albeit at a different price level, for tax.

320.43. Continued use of LIFO. Unless a corporation changes inventory methods in its first year as an S corporation, it must continue to use LIFO in accounting for its next year's increment or decrement. A decrement will be relatively simple to handle, since all of the layers are now at the same index value. [Rev. Proc. 94-61, 1994-38 IRB 56, Sec. 3, A-2]

There are two methods for accounting for increments to LIFO inventory—the double extension method and the link-chain method. The double extension method, which is preferred by the IRS, requires that each year's inventory be converted to base price levels for comparison to the prior year's balance. [Regs. §1.472-8(e)(2)] If the taxpayer can demonstrate that the double extension method is impractical, the IRS may give permission to use the link-chain method. [Regs. §1.472-8(e)(1)] The link-chain method applies a rolling index, whereby each year's inventory is stated at the prior-year price level rather than a base-year level.

EXAMPLE 3-11: Refer to Example 3-10. For tax purposes, Barco would now show one layer of $54,000. Its index for future increases and decreases would depend upon whether it used the double extension method or the link-chain method of accounting for future increments. Assuming that Barco uses the double extension method, it must continue to restate each year's inventory at the base-year (1989) price. Thus the layer immediately after the recapture would be stated as:

Layer	*Base Year Costs*	*Index*	*LIFO Carrying Value*
Base	$34,000	1.60	$54,400

Assume that the price level at the end of 1996 is 1.70. Also assume that the inventory, at current year price, is $ 61,200 at the end of 1996. The LIFO layers at the end of that year are:

Layer	*Base Year Costs*	*Index*	*LIFO Carrying Value*
Base	$34,000	1.60	$54,400
1996	2,000	1.70	3,400
Total	$36,000		$58,800

Alternatively, assume that Barco used the link-chain method. Barco's price level at the time of LIFO recapture would be 1.60. Since this method is so rarely encountered in practice, this book does not provide any examples of its use.

320.44. Basis adjustment following adjustment to FIFO market. Although there are many calculations involved in LIFO, the concept is simple when the corporation uses FIFO cost in determining the recapture. LIFO requires that all inventory values be based on actual cost rather than market values. The recapture is treated as a phantom disposition of all of the corporation's LIFO inventory, followed by a replacement at the current FIFO cost.

Section 1363(d) allows the corporation to compute LIFO recapture by using the lower of FIFO cost or market at the date of the recapture. If market is less than FIFO cost, the corporation should use the market value, since it will result in less LIFO recapture tax. There will be complications, however, since the corporation will be deemed to have disposed of less than its entire inventory. According to Revenue Procedure 94-61 (1994-38 IRB 56), the new base layer is computed by dividing the new basis by the pre-recapture historical base-year cost to create a new special layer. This layer will be relevant only in case of a future decrement.

EXAMPLE 3-12: Tovco makes an S election, effective January 1, 1996. It has used the LIFO inventory method since 1990. Tovco has exactly the same inventory amounts as did Barco in Example 3-10. Its inventory, at lower of FIFO cost or market, however, is only $50,000. Tovco's inventory carrying value before LIFO recapture is summarized as follows:

FIFO cost	$ 54,400
Less LIFO reserve	(12,400)
LIFO carrying value	$ 42,000

Its layers are shown below. The data are borrowed from Regulations §1.263A-1T.

Layer	*Base Year Costs*	*Index*	*LIFO Carrying Value*
Base	$14,000	1.00	$14,000
1990	4,000	1.20	4,800
1991	5,000	1.30	6,500
1992	2,000	1.35	2,700
1993	0	1.40	0
1994	4,000	1.50	6,000
1995	5,000	1.60	8,000
Total	$34,000		$42,000

Having arrived at the proof of the ending inventory before LIFO recapture and the ending inventory after the LIFO recapture, Tovco may now calculate the LIFO recapture amount:

Inventory at lower of FIFO cost or market	$50,000
Inventory at LIFO	(42,000)
Recapture	$ 8,000

Tovco computes its new adjusted index as follows:

Basis after recapture	$50,000	
Divide by inventory at historical base cost	34,000	
New index (50,000/34,000)		1.47

Thus, for future calculations, the inventory as of the beginning of 1996 would be:

Layer	*Base Year Costs*	*Index*	*LIFO Carrying Value*
Base	$34,000	1.47	$50,000

If an S corporation is liquidated or extinguished in a reorganization before it has paid all of its LIFO recapture tax installments, the remaining tax is immediately due and payable. [Rev. Proc. 94-61, 1994-38 IRB 56, Sec. 3, A-8] See discussion at 320.5., below, of the LIFO recapture problems that result from a tax-free reorganization or liquidation of a C corporation into an S corporation.

OBSERVATION: Several problems result from a lack of guidance and specific rules from the IRS. Among these are the effects of future events, such as liquidation, reorganization, or termination of the S election. Presumably, the corporation would still be liable for tax on LIFO recapture if the S election is terminated or revoked.

320.45. Other operational problems. There are several collateral problems resulting from the LIFO recapture rules. The scant legislative history and limited guidance offered by the IRS leave the tax professional with several gray areas. The discussions that follow are based on general understanding of the tax laws, and thus they have few authoritative citations.

One problem that a corporation may face is revocation of the S election before the corporation has completed payment of all of the LIFO recapture tax installments. There is no provision that would allow the corporation to reduce its tax payments and, in essence, "reverse" any of its LIFO recapture.

EXAMPLE 3-13: Tovco, from the preceding examples, revokes its S election on June 30, 1996, after only six months as an S corporation. Although it is a C corporation for the last half of 1996 and all succeeding years, it must pay the remaining installments of the LIFO recapture tax.

PLANNING TIP: There are few opportunities to avoid or minimize the LIFO recapture tax. Reducing inventory levels before year-end would be the worst possible strategy, since the decrement would be assigned to the current year's income, which is payable according to the normal rules rather than the four-year installment plan. The only possibilities would be to reduce the corporation's taxable income for its final Subchapter C year. The corporation should consider measures such as paying the controlling shareholders any bonuses or other items that normally would accrue to them, thereby accelerating the deductions.

If the corporation is able to substantially reduce its income by accelerating deductions or postponing delivery of sales in its final year as a C corporation, it could reduce its taxable income for that year to a point where the LIFO recapture tax is relatively inexpensive. If it discovers that the S election has been a mistake, it may be able to rescind the election and continue its status as a C corporation. Rescission of an S election must be made within the first 2 months and 15 days of the year for which it would have taken effect. The means for rescission are discussed in Chapter 13.

The LIFO recapture tax may be the most serious obstacle to an S election. It is imposed at the marginal rate for the C corporation, which may be as high as 39%. There is some benefit from the time value of money, since the tax is payable over four years. A corporation will minimize the impact if it has net operating loss carryforwards, which it could not use as an S corporation. It might also want to declare a large employee bonus. If there is a controlling shareholder, his or her bonus must be paid before the end of the final C year, even though the corporation is on the accrual method. [§267(a)(2)] The bonus must withstand tests of reasonable compensation, and it will have the indirect effect of imposing the LIFO recapture tax at the individual rate.

Although LIFO recapture may be so costly as to make an S election infeasible in some circumstances, this is not necessarily the case. If a C corporation has a significant loss in the year of LIFO recapture or has loss carryforwards from prior years, these losses will be able to offset the income from the LIFO recapture. The losses could not be carried forward to S corporation years generally, and they may best serve the corporation as a reduction or elimination of the LIFO recapture income. Thus a C corporation should not automatically shy away from an S election merely because it uses the LIFO inventory method.

PLANNING TIP: There is one instance in which the LIFO recapture rule may actually benefit a corporation. If a C corporation intends to liquidate or to substantially reduce LIFO layers in one tax year, it might incur a large incremental tax liability in that year. If it made an S election for the beginning of that year, it could spread the tax payments over four years.

The effect of LIFO recapture on the corporation's current earnings and profits for its final year as a C corporation is not entirely clear. There is no doubt that the tax itself will reduce the corporation's current earnings and profits. The installments of this tax should be treated as a payment of a corporate liability, rather than as a payment of a nondeductible expense.

The inclusion of the recapture income in the corporation's earnings and profits depends upon when the LIFO layers were created. As is discussed below, at 325.44., corporations have generally been required to use the FIFO inventory method in computing their current earnings and profits for all years beginning after September 30, 1984. Thus the recapture of any layers that had accumulated after September 30, 1984, would not be included in the corporation's current earnings and profits in the year of recapture. The recapture of any earlier LIFO layers, however, would result in an increase in the corporation's current earnings and profits for the year of the recapture.

> **PLANNING TIP:** When the LIFO recapture is prohibitive, a C corporation may want to establish different corporate shells for other aspects of its business. For example, an automobile dealer may establish new corporations for servicing, leasing, and other activities, in order to bring these operations into S corporations.

The IRS has ruled that LIFO recapture is required when the inventory is held by a partnership (including a limited liability company) in which the C corporation converting to S status is a partner. The corporation must compute its recapture tax as if it held its portion of the partnership's inventory directly. [TAM 9716003]

The IRS also has held that a C corporation that has discontinued the use of LIFO before the year of conversion is subject to a special problem. If it has not completed its required adjustment under §482 to restore the LFIO reserve, it must recognize all remaining §481 adjustments in its final year as a C corporation. [Rev. Proc. 97-27 1997-21 IRB, §7.03(3)(c)(ii), (iii)]

The LIFO recapture tax does not apply to any inventory transferred from an S corporation. Thus there is no reason to believe that this tax would be triggered if an S corporation transferred its LIFO inventory to a subsidiary in a nonrecognition transaction, such as a §351 transfer or a contribution to capital. (See Chapter 14.) However, the IRS was asked to rule that the recapture tax did not apply to transfer of inventory from a parent S corporation to several QSSS subsidiaries (see Chapter 14). The IRS has ruled that there is no LIFO recapture on the transfer of LIFO inventory from an S corporation to a wholly owned subsidiary in a nonrecognition transaction. [PLRs 9746011, 9746015, 9746016, 9746017, 9746018, 9746019, 9746020, 9746021, 9746022, 9746023, 9746024, 9746025, 9746026, 9746027, 9746028, 9807023, 9746028]

320.5. Applicability to reorganizations and liquidations. The statute is silent on the applicability of the LIFO recapture rules to a C corporation that is acquired by an S corporation in a tax-free reorganization or liquidation. See Chapter 15, at 1525.74., and Chapter 17, at 1710., for discussion of these transactions. In either of these transactions, an S corporation may acquire all of the assets of a C corporation, and the C corporation reports no gain or loss on the transfer. Following the reorganization or liquidation, the asset basis and accounting methods are retained. [§381] See Chapter 17, at 1730.3.

The Regulations under §1363 provide that if the extinguished C corporation had LIFO inventory, it must recapture the LIFO reserve in its final year of existence. [Regs. §1.1363-2(a)(2)] This rule is effective for transactions that occur after August 18, 1993.

> **EXAMPLE 3 - 14:** On September 1, 1996, Essco, an S corporation, acquires all of the assets of Ceeco, a C corporation, in a tax-free reorganization. Both corporations had used the calendar year before the reorganization. Ceeco had used the LIFO inventory method, and must recapture its LIFO reserve. Ceeco's final tax return covers its year beginning January 1, 1996, and ending September 1, 1996, and must include the LIFO recapture.

The extinguished corporation's LIFO recapture tax is calculated in the same manner as that of a C corporation making an S election, and it is payable in four equal installments. The first installment is payable on the due date for the extinguished corporation's final return (without extension). [Regs. §1.1363-2(b)] The next three installments must be paid on the due dates for the surviving corporation's tax returns for the "three succeeding years." The Regulations are silent as to whether the "succeeding years" of the surviving corporation include the year of the reorganization or liquidation. Presumably, the year of the reorganization or liquidation is treated as a succeeding year.

> **EXAMPLE 3-15:** Refer to Example 3-14. The first installment of Ceeco's LIFO recapture tax will be paid by Essco, the surviving corporation, along with the final tax return for Ceeco, which is due on December 15, 1996.[11] The remaining installments would become due on March 15, 1997, on March 15, 1998, and on March 15, 1999.

325. Earnings and profits.

Before a C corporation makes an S election, it should consider the implications of its accumulated earnings and profits. Under current law an S corporation cannot generate, and therefore cannot accumulate, any earnings and profits. Any earnings and profits accumulated by the corporation before it becomes an S corporation, however, remain in place when the S election takes effect. The accumulated earnings and profits from prior C corporation years may cause complications when an S corporation distributes money or property to its shareholders. They may cause even more serious problems if the corporation receives substantial *passive investment income*. See Chapter 7 for discussion of distributions and Chapter 12 for complete coverage of the passive investment income problems.

Although the distribution rules governing S corporations are discussed in full in Chapter 7, a brief summary of the rules applicable to both C corporations and S corporations is in order. A distribution from a C corporation is a dividend, and it is included in the recipient shareholder's gross income to the extent of the C corporation's current and accumulated earnings and profits. The calculation of earnings and profits is quite complex.

In contrast, an S corporation's distributions are generally not taxed to the shareholders, subject to two important limitations:

1. A distribution that exceeds the shareholder's stock basis immediately before the distribution may be a taxable gain.
2. If an S corporation has any accumulated earnings and profits from its prior C corporation status or from having acquired another corporation as a shareholder, any distributions from that balance are treated as dividends and are included in the shareholder's gross income.[12]

Although a corporation does not generate any earnings and profits while an S election is in effect, it may have accumulated earnings and profits from its years as a C corporation. The balance in that account does not disappear when the S election takes effect. When this account has a positive balance as of the close of the last Subchapter C year, some or all of the distributions made by the S corporation may be taxed to the shareholders as dividends. See Chapter 7 for a complete discussion of the accounting rules that the corporation must follow after the S election is in effect. For now, an example is needed in order to put the distribution problem into perspective.

---

[11] A corporation's tax return is due on the 15th day of the third month after the month in which its year closes.

[12] Code §1368(c) treats distributions as coming from accumulated earnings and profits after the S corporation exhausts its accumulated adjustments account, which is in essence a surrogate for earnings and profits of an S corporation. The rules for computation of the accumulated adjustments account are contained in Chapter 7.

3

EXAMPLE 3 - 16: A C corporation makes an S election at the beginning of 1996. At the end of 1995, its accumulated earnings and profits were $100,000. In 1996, the corporation reports taxable income of $50,000, all of which is taxable to the shareholders under the rules of Subchapter S. In 1995, the corporation distributes $120,000 to its shareholders. Under the Subchapter S accounting rules, only $50,000 will be treated as tax-free distributions, and the remainder will be taxed as dividend income to the shareholders. If the corporation had no accumulated earnings and profits from its years as a C corporation, none of the distribution would be treated as a dividend.

A former C corporation with an S election in effect may also find that accumulated earnings and profits limit its ability to generate *passive investment income.* This term, which receives comprehensive discussion in Chapter 12, generally includes dividends, interest, rents, and royalties received by the S corporation. An S corporation with no accumulated earnings and profits can have unlimited passive investment income with no adverse effects. However, if an S corporation has any accumulated earnings and profits from its Subchapter C years, and its passive investment income exceeds 25% of its gross receipts, it faces two problems:

1. It may be required to pay a corporate-level tax, which in some cases may exceed the income tax it would have paid if it had remained a C corporation.
2. If the corporation's passive investment income exceeds 25% of its gross income for three consecutive years, it will lose its S election.

This book has already mentioned inadvertent termination relief in several contexts. See Chapter 13.

The Code does not define *earnings and profits,* although §312 provides some of the rules necessary for the computation. The primary reference is §316, which merely states that distributions from a corporation are dividends to the extent of the corporation's current and accumulated earnings and profits. There are some specific adjustments required for earnings and profits elsewhere in the Code, mostly in §312. These specific items are cited in this book when appropriate. Earnings and profits may have been generated in any year after March 1, 1913, in which an S election was not in effect. They could also have arisen in any year from 1958 through 1982 in which S election was in effect. After 1982, however, an S corporation does not generate any earnings and profits.

325.1. Earnings and profits study. The context in which earnings and profits were first developed was measurement of a corporation's ability to pay dividends. Distributions that do not exceed a corporation's earnings and profits are taxable as dividends. Distributions that do exceed earnings and profits are not dividends, but are treated instead as a reduction of the receiving shareholder's stock basis. If distributions exceed earnings and profits and the shareholder's basis, the excess is treated as a gain from the sale of stock. [§301(c)] Most recently, earnings and profits received attention in calculating a corporation's adjusted current earnings (ACE) for the corporate alternative minimum tax. (See §56(g) and Regulations §1.56(g)-1 for the lengthy rules governing the computation of ACE.) Until ACE took effect (taxable years beginning January 1, 1990), it was rarely necessary for a corporation to compute its earnings and profits. In practice, few corporations distribute enough of their earnings to invite the possibility that any distributions could exceed earnings and profits. By merely reporting all distributions to shareholders as dividends, a corporation could avoid calculating its earnings and profits. If a corporation liquidated under §333, each individual shareholder reported dividend income to the extent of his or her portion of the corporation's accumulated earnings and profits.[13] The only other reason that a corporation needed to

[13] Code §333 was repealed by the Tax Reform Act of 1986. There were a few transitional corporations that could use this method through calendar year 1988. It receives no further mention in this book.

calculate earnings and profits was to assess its distribution and passive investment income problems when it filed an S election.

Until the ACE adjustment took effect, many corporations never made a calculation of earnings and profits. It was necessary to do so only when distributions exceeded earnings and profits, or when a corporation liquidated under §333 (prior law). Since the first instance rarely happens, and since the second could happen only in the corporation's final act, there are rarely complete records available.

The earnings and profits study is a recording of the tax history of the corporation up to the present, and includes any predecessor corporation if there has been a tax-free reorganization. Conceptually, the calculation is achieved by beginning with each year's taxable income. This figure must be adjusted for tax-free income, nondeductible expenses, and other items discussed in this chapter. The result is some theoretical measure of the corporation's income that can be distributed to its shareholders without impairing capital.

The best method to determine earnings and profits is to work forward from the first year of the corporation's existence. (If the corporation was in existence before March 1, 1913, work forward from that date.) Earnings and profits can be generated by income. They can be reduced by losses and distributions. The distributions can be dividends, stock redemptions, partial liquidations, split-offs, or spin-offs. These transactions are discussed in Chapters 7, 16, and 17. The IRS provides Form 5452 for the calculation of earnings and profits. This form includes a worksheet that provides columns for comparison of book income and taxable income. It lists some of the adjustments, but has not been updated for the economic income rules of the Tax Reform Act of 1984.

The general concept is to determine what amount of income is distributable, rather than taxable. There is no inclusive definition of *earnings and profits* in the Code or Regulations. There have been several statutory changes, however. The most important occurred in 1972 and 1984. Since many corporations now in existence were formed before 1972, it is important to be familiar with all of the rules.

325.2. Earnings and profits before July 1, 1972. For all taxable years beginning before July 1, 1972, there were relatively few adjustments between taxable income and current earnings and profits. Most, if not all, of the adjustments can be quickly compiled by reference to Schedule M-1 of the corporation's tax return. For these years there are no adjustments for depreciation or economic income (as that term is defined in §312(n) and discussed below).

325.21. Upward adjustments. The starting point is taxable income, as reported on the year's tax return. There are upward adjustments for items of tax-exempt income and for statutory deductions that required no economic outlay. The rationale is that even though these items are not taxable, they are economic increments of wealth that are fully distributable to the shareholders. The most likely adjustments of this type are:

- Municipal bond interest
- Proceeds of life insurance
- Discharge of indebtedness for insolvent corporations
- Dividends received deduction
- Carryovers deducted in current year, such as net operating losses, capital losses, and charitable contributions that are incurred in some other year

325.22. Downward adjustments. Consistent with the theory that the distributable income can be measured by reference to a corporation's taxable income, there also were downward adjustments. Certain items that are not deductible are nevertheless dispositions of wealth that are no longer available for distribution. These include:

- The federal income tax, including minimum tax, investment tax credit recapture tax, personal holding company and accumulated earnings taxes, minus any credits
- Other nondeductible expenditures, including fines and penalties, punitive damages, illegal bribes and kickbacks, expenses to carry tax-exempt interest, life insurance premiums, and disallowed expenses that were accrued to shareholders under prior §267
- Items not deductible because of limits, for example, capital losses and charitable contributions that exceeded the statutory deduction limit

325.23. Items requiring no adjustments. There were, and still are, no adjustments between taxable income and current earnings and profits for certain excluded income and gain items, such as contributions to capital, deferred gain on like-kind exchange or involuntary conversion, and gains from dealing in the corporation's own stock.

EXAMPLE 3 - 17: In calendar year 1972, Y corporation has the following:

Taxable income	$50,000
Dividends-received deduction	8,500
Capital losses (not carried back)	(12,000)
Income tax	$17,500

Its current earnings and profits are:

Taxable income	$50,000
Add:	
Dividends-received deduction	8,500
Less:	
Capital losses	(12,000)
Income tax	(17,500)
Current earnings and profits	$29,000

325.3. Depreciation adjustment after June 30, 1972. Congress was concerned with corporations, primarily public utilities, that were able to eliminate earnings and profits through accelerated depreciation. These corporations would have financial accounting net income that allowed them to pay "dividends." These distributions were not dividends for tax purposes, since there were no earnings and profits. Accordingly, Congress added the requirement that earnings and profits must be computed using the straight-line depreciation method. The rule was modified in 1981 and 1986, to reflect the new statutory depreciation methods on the following items. For 1987 and all later years, there are three principal types of depreciable property, for which earnings and profits adjustments vary:

1. Property placed in service before 1981 was not covered by the rules of the 1981 changes to depreciation. The 1981 rules were the accelerated cost recovery system, which was known as *ACRS*. Property that had been placed in service before this law has become known as *pre-ACRS property*.
2. Property placed in service during the years 1981 through 1986 was subject to rules enacted in 1981. Depreciation for those years was governed under the 1981 version of ACRS. Property that was placed in service in these years is known as *ACRS property*. Some commentators use the term *original ACRS property*.
3. Property placed in service after 1986 is depreciable under rules enacted by the Tax Reform Act of 1986. The depreciation system under that law is known as modified ACRS. Property placed in service under these rules is known as *modified ACRS*, or *MACRS property*.

325.31. Pre-ACRS personal property. For pre-ACRS property, corporations use the straight-line method and the same life as used on the tax return.

325.32. ACRS personal property. For original ACRS property placed in service between 1981 and 1986, corporations use the straight-line method with an extended life, depending on the ACRS recovery period. [§312(k)] For all property except real property, corporations use the half-year convention in computing earnings and profits depreciation. The recovery period for earnings and profits is determined according to the period allowed for income tax.

ACRS Class	*Extended Life*
3	5
5	12
10	25
15	35
18, 19	40

EXAMPLE 3 - 18: Q corporation reports the following for calendar year 1984:

Long-term capital gain	$ 30,000
Capital loss carryforward from 1983	35,000
Used in 1984	(30,000)
Ordinary income (except depreciation)	160,000
Depreciation (5-year ACRS)	(60,000)
Taxable income	$100,000

Q's income tax was $25,750 under the rates in effect for 1984. Q's depreciation, using the 12-year straight-line method, was $16,667.

Earnings and profits:	
Taxable income	$100,000
Add capital loss used in 1984	30,000
Add tax depreciation	60,000
Less earnings and profits depreciation	(16,667)
Less income tax	(25,750)
Current earnings and profits	$147,583

325.33. MACRS personal property. Depreciation of MACRS property uses the "alternative depreciation system." [§312(k)] Note that earnings and profits depreciation is the same as alternative minimum tax depreciation for long-lived assets, but differs for short-lived property. The Code permits the 150% declining balance method for alternative minimum tax, but requires straight-line for earnings and profits. MACRS depreciation governs all property placed in service after 1986. Corporations could elect to depreciate property placed in service in the latter half of 1986 under the new MACRS rather than the old ACRS.[14]

Personal property subject to MACRS must be depreciated using straight-line method over the Asset Depreciation Range midpoint in computing earnings and profits. If the midpoint is not listed, use 12 years. A corporation uses the same conventions for earnings and profits it uses on its tax return (half-year, mid-quarter, or mid-month).

[14] There were few instances when this election was beneficial. Nevertheless, the tax planner conducting the earnings and profits study should examine the records for 1986 depreciation to determine whether or not the corporation made this election.

3

325.34. Buildings. Buildings have been subject to slightly different rules than personal property. Buildings placed in service before 1981 are depreciated for earnings and profits using the same life reported on the tax return, but the corporation must use the straight-line method.

Buildings placed in service between January 1, 1981, and September 30, 1984, are depreciated using the straight-line method and a 35-year life. Buildings placed in service after September 30, 1984, must be depreciated using 40-year straight-line. This rule applies to both old (18- or 19-year) and new (27.5-, 31.5-, or 39-year) ACRS.

325.4. Economic income after September 30, 1984. In the Tax Reform Act of 1984, Congress attacked other accounting methods that allowed corporations to reduce earnings and profits. It added §312(n) to make earnings and profits conform to a corporation's "economic income." Note that many of these changes have since been enacted in broader contexts. For example, some of the accounting methods that first applied only to earnings and profits were later extended to become the rules for taxable income, such as construction period interest and taxes. Other methods first used for earnings and profits, such as accounting for circulation expenses, later became the rules for alternative minimum tax.

325.41. Construction period interest and taxes. Under early law, construction period interest, carrying charges, and taxes were deductible in the year incurred. They became subject to a 10-year amortization period in the early 1980s. In 1984, however, Congress decided that such costs should be capitalized, and the cost should be recovered through depreciation on the constructed property. [§312(n)(1)] The 1984 change affected only the computation of earnings and profits. Later changes required the same treatment for computation of taxable income. Therefore, a corporation that incurred such costs between September 30, 1984, and December 31, 1986, must make a special adjustment in computing earnings and profits.

325.42. Intangible drilling costs. Intangible drilling costs (IDC) and mineral exploration and development costs also receive special treatment. Both types of costs may be expensed in the year incurred, from a corporation's computation of its taxable income. For computation of earnings and profits, however, the corporation must capitalize these costs in the year incurred. The amortization period depends on the nature of the cost. IDC are capitalized and amortized over 60 months. Mineral exploration and development costs are capitalized and amortized over 120 months. [§312(n)(2)]

325.43. Rapid amortization of circulation expenses. Rapid amortization of circulation expenses, trademark, and tradename expenses, as well as organizational expenses, requires another adjustment. These costs may be expensed for computing taxable income. For measurement of earnings and profits, however, they must be capitalized and considered part of the basis of the asset. [§312(n)(3)]

325.44. LIFO inventories. LIFO inventories are subject to a special adjustment. Calculation of earnings and profits requires the corporation to use the FIFO method of accounting, although any LIFO reserve for the end of the last taxable year that began before September 30, 1984, requires no adjustment. Inventory changes in years beginning after September 30, 1984, must be restated in terms of FIFO, so any increase in the LIFO reserve must be added to taxable income, when the corporation computes its earnings and profits. [§312(n)(4)]

EXAMPLE 3 - 19: R Corporation uses the LIFO inventory method and the calendar year. Its inventories were:

3

Date	FIFO Value	LIFO Reserve	Balance Sheet Amount
1/1/84	$60,000	$10,000	$50,000
1/1/85	$75,000	$12,000	$63,000
1/1/86	$85,000	$15,000	$70,000
1/1/87	$80,000	$14,000	$64,000

Earnings and profits adjustments:

1984	None (Year began before 9/30/84)
1985	+$3,000
1986	–$1,000

325.45. Installment sales. In 1984, taxpayers could use the installment sale method to account for deferred payment sales of most types of property. (The installment method has become much more limited by subsequent legislation.) Congress believed that the installment method did not truly reflect economic income. Therefore, the 1984 legislation provided that a corporation that used the installment method to report its taxable income should be required to use the accrual method to calculate its earnings and profits. Therefore, the gain on an installment sale is treated as recognized in the year of sale for the calculation of earnings and profits. Later collections, which cause the taxpayer to report gain for income tax purposes, do not cause increases in earnings and profits. [§312(n)(5)]

EXAMPLE 3 - 20: Q Corporation uses the calendar year. It makes the following installment sales and collections thereon:

Year	Collections on Installment Sale	1984 Sale	1985 Sale
1984	$60,000	$ 0	$ 0
1985	$80,000	$10,000	$ 0
1986	$75,000	$12,000	$20,000

Its earnings and profits adjustments are:

Year	Sale	Collection	Explanation
1984	$ 0	$ 0	Began before 9/30/84
1985	+$80,000	$ 0	Include 1985 sale
1986	+$75,000	–$20,000	Include 1986 sale, but reduce for collection on 1985 sale

Installment sales have created $135,000 accumulated earnings and profits as of December 31, 1986.

325.46. Completed-contract method. Corporations using the completed-contract method of accounting for long-term construction projects report no income from a contract until the year of completion. Under post-1986 law, this method of accounting is available only to certain home builders and other small companies. In 1984, however, this method was available to most businesses with projects that took more than one year to complete. Another method for calculating the income from long-term contracts is the percentage-of-completion method. Under the percentage-of-completion method, the contractor reports income proportionately as the customer makes progress payments.

In 1984, Congress believed that the percentage-of-completion method was a better reflection of economic income than the completed-contract method. Therefore, it required all corporations with long-term contracts to use the percentage-of-completion method when computing earnings and profits. [§312(n)(6)]

The percentage-of-completion method of accounting requires certain estimates of each year's profit. These estimates may be revised as future costs are incurred. The Tax Court has held that the pre-election accumulated earnings and profits are in effect "frozen" when an S election takes effect, and may not be revised based on hindsight. [*Cameron*, 105 TC No. 25 (1995); *Broadway v. Comm'r*, 97-1 USTC 50,355 (8th Cir.)] Thus an S corporation cannot reduce its pre-election earnings and profits based on hindsight without filing an amended return for its final C corporation year.

325.47. Stock redemptions. A stock redemption occurs when a corporation buys some of its own shares from a shareholder. The effect of a stock redemption on a corporation's earnings and profits is discussed in Chapter 15. The general rule, however, is that the corporation must reduce its earnings and profits to correspond with the percentage of shares redeemed. [§312(n)(7)]

325.5. Computation of accumulated earnings and profits of C corporations. Current earnings and profits are the first measure of a corporation's ability to pay dividends. In any year in which a corporation does not distribute its current earnings and profits, the undistributed earnings and profits are closed to accumulated earnings and profits.

The calculations for accumulated earnings and profits parallel the financial accounting for retained earnings. Accumulated earnings and profits are available for distribution as dividends, after current earnings and profits have been exhausted. In general, the accumulated earnings and profits balance remains with the corporation forever, or until the corporation pays out dividends or liquidates. In special cases, such as stock redemptions or tax-free reorganizations, there may be adjustments to the accumulated earnings and profits balance that are not run through current earnings and profits. These concepts are discussed in later chapters.

In the discussion of current earnings and profits there has been no mention of the effects of corporate distributions on the earnings and profits calculation. Current earnings and profits are measured without regard to any distributions. Current earnings and profits can be positive or negative, depending on the taxable income and adjustments for the year in question. Current earnings and profits, however, are not affected by any distributions.

Accumulated earnings and profits *are* affected by dividends. Each year's addition to accumulated earnings and profits is determined by subtracting any distributions, to the extent of either current earnings and profits or accumulated earnings and profits, as they existed at the end of the prior year, from the current earnings and profits of the year. Distributions, however, cannot create or add to a negative earnings and profits balance.

> **EXAMPLE 3 - 21:** MNO Corporation calculates current earnings and profits of $35,000 in its first year of existence. It distributes $20,000 as a dividend to its shareholders in that year. Its accumulated earnings and profits, at the beginning of its second year, are $15,000.
>
> In its second year, MNO Corporation has $30,000 of current earnings and profits and distributes $40,000 to its shareholders as dividends. Its accumulated earnings and profits are $5,000 ($15,000 + $30,000 – $40,000) at the beginning of its third year.

As a general rule, distributions are dividends to the extent of current earnings and profits that are not offset by negative accumulated earnings and profits. Conversely, the Regulations under §316 give allocation rules for distributions made in a year in which there are negative current earnings and profits and a positive balance in accumulated earnings and profits. [Regs. §1.316-2(b)]

3

325.6. Effect of an S election on earnings and profits. The S election has no effect on a C corporation's accumulated earnings and profits. This balance remains available for distributions. As demonstrated in Chapter 7, there are specific rules for distribution of this account. Distributions of this balance will be treated as dividends, after a corporation exhausts its Accumulated Adjustments Account, which was briefly introduced above. [§1368(b)] Distributions from an S corporation's accumulated earnings and profits are treated as dividends and included in the shareholders' gross income in the same manner as dividends from C corporations.

In years beginning after 1982, there are no current earnings and profits generated when an S election is in effect. [§1371(c)(1)] There are no reductions of accumulated earnings and profits due to reversals (installment sales, depreciation, etc.) after the S election takes effect. This can create a double trap, since the first adjustment, which creates earnings and profits, eventually reverses. The following example illustrates the effect/ of an installment sale that takes place when the corporation is a C corporation, but for which the gain is included in income after the corporation is an S corporation.

> **EXAMPLE 3 - 22:** XYZ Corporation is a C corporation in 1995. In that year, it makes an installment sale of investment land and defers $100,000 of gain. Its taxable income is zero for the year. Pursuant to §312(n)(5), the corporation has $100,000 earnings and profits from the installment sale.
>
> In 1996, the corporation makes an S election and collects the installment receivable. Its shareholders report $100,000 of taxable income from the installment sale in 1996, under the rules of Subchapter S. If the corporation had been a C corporation in 1996, it would have reported a negative adjustment to its current earnings and profits for the installment collection, which created $100,000 current earnings and profits in 1995. Once the S election takes effect, however, the corporation has no opportunity to make any adjustments to earnings and profits. Therefore, the corporation still has $100,000 earnings and profits from 1995 that will be taxed as dividends if the corporation's distributions exceed its Accumulated Adjustments Account. See Chapter 7 for an explanation of the Accumulated Adjustments Account. Accordingly, the shareholders would have to take the same installment sale into income twice. First, they report the income from the installment sale when it is collected, since the S corporation passes all of its income through to the shareholders. Second, the shareholders will treat the $100,000 earnings and profits as dividends if the corporation ever exhausts its accumulated adjustments account.

To add further insult to injury, the corporation may be subject to a corporate-level tax on an item that originally created earnings and profits. In the above example, collection of the installment receivable would create a recognized built-in gain to the corporation [§1374],[15] which may be taxable to the corporation even though the corporation now has S status. It would also pass through as taxable income to the shareholders, but the shareholders' taxable income would be reduced for any built-in gains tax the corporation pays. Even the corporate built-in gains tax would not reduce the earnings and profits accumulated while the corporation was a C corporation, so the shareholders would still realize dividend income if the balance were ever distributed.

There are exceptions to the no-reduction rule. In some cases, accumulated earnings and profits are reduced for investment tax credit recapture tax imposed on the corporation. [§1371(d)(3)] This tax, discussed in Chapter 11, is rapidly disappearing.

Accumulated earnings and profits are also changed for audit adjustments of the S corporation's taxable income for years when it was a C corporation. This possibility requires no specific S corporation rules, since an adjustment of an earlier year's return is essentially a correction of what should have been reported. Accumulated earnings and profits can be

[15] The built-in gains tax is the subject of Chapter 11.

reduced for dividend distributions (see Chapter 7). [§1371(c)(2)] Accumulated earnings and profits can also be reduced for stock redemptions (see Chapter 15). [§1371(c)(3)]

Occasionally, an S corporation can acquire or increase its accumulated earnings and profits balance after the S election takes effect. This can happen only when an S corporation engages in a tax-free reorganization and emerges as the surviving entity. [§381(c)(2)] See Chapter 17 for discussion of tax-free reorganizations involving S corporations.

From 1958 through 1982, S corporations could accumulate earnings and profits. They followed the same general rules as C corporations, with some exceptions. In those years, an S corporation began its earnings and profits calculation with its taxable income, adding exempt income and other upward adjustments to its taxable income to determine its current earnings and profits. It decreased its addition to current earnings and profits for dividends.

Under rules in effect at that time, an S corporation could not distribute less than its taxable income as a dividend distribution. Chapter 7 contains an explanation of the pre-1983 rules to the extent they have continuing significance. Current earnings and profits could not be negative [§1377(c)], or less than the corporation's current taxable income. [§1377(b)] There were certain adjustments that bypassed current earnings and profits and went directly to accumulated earnings and profits. These included the depreciation adjustment [§1377(d)] and nondeductible items such as officers' life insurance premiums. [§1377(b)] Although the assignment of certain items directly to accumulated earnings and profits had some significance in those years, these special rules have had no lasting effect. The important thing to remember in post-1982 years is that an S corporation could have accumulated earnings and profits prior to the Subchapter S Revision Act of 1982.

From 1983 through 1996, these accumulations were treated in the same manner as earnings and profits accumulated in Subchapter C years, and were dividends if the S corporation exhausted its Accumulated Adjustments Account in those years. The Small Business Job Protection Act of 1996, in a non-Code provision, states that S corporations' earnings and profits from pre-1983 years are to be eliminated. [Small Business Job Protection Act of 1996 §1311] That Act also replaced all references to Subchapter C earnings and profits with references to accumulated earnings and profits, implying that all earnings and profits arose when the corporation was a C corporation. Neither the Code nor the Small Business Job Protection Act of 1996 supplied any information as to the procedures for eliminating the accumulated earnings and profits from pre-1983 Subchapter S years.

330. Foreign loss recapture.

Although an S corporation must be incorporated in the U.S., [§1361(b)(1)] it may engage in foreign operations. Any U.S. corporation is subject to U.S. tax on its worldwide income. U.S. taxpayers with foreign losses may offset these losses against U.S. taxable income.

Foreign loss recapture occurs when a corporation has used foreign source losses to offset U.S. source income and then disposed of its foreign operations that created the loss. [§904(f)(3)(A)] The corporation must also recapture 50% of its foreign losses when the foreign operations produce taxable income. When a C corporation has used foreign source losses to offset U.S. income, and the C corporation then makes an S election, its foreign losses are recaptured. [§1373(b)] As a general rule, the recapture amount is the lesser of (1) the realized gain on the disposition and (2) the foreign losses that had been deducted. Since there is no actual disposition when a C corporation makes an S election, the corporation calculates the pro forma gain on a hypothetical disposition.

EXAMPLE 3 - 23: Hayco is an Illinois corporation with significant operations in England. Through 1995, it was a C corporation. As of the end of 1995 its English operations had accumulated losses of $50,000. The fair market value of the property used in England is $250,000 and its adjusted basis is $175,000.

Hayco makes an S election effective January 1, 1996. The hypothetical disposition occurs on December 31, 1995. Hayco must include its foreign loss recapture on its 1995 tax return. The amount included is the lesser of the accumulated foreign losses ($50,000) or the gain on the hypothetical distribution ($75,000). Thus, Hayco reports $50,000 in 1995, its last year as a C corporation.

335. Analysis of alternatives.

An S election is not the only method to save taxes. Any corporation considering the election should evaluate alternative strategies for tax savings, if these are not already in use. These could include a LIFO election, adoption of fringe benefit and tax-deferred retirement plans, rental of business property from the shareholders, and compensation of shareholder-employees. Another alternative would be to liquidate the corporation.

335.1. LIFO election. A business may be able to reduce its taxable income by electing the LIFO inventory method. Under this assumption, the most recently purchased goods are assigned to the current year's cost of goods sold. In industries where prices increase, such as automobile dealerships, this method can substantially reduce taxable income. In industries where prices are decreasing, such as computers and other electronic goods, however, this method may actually increase taxable income. LIFO requires detailed inventory calculations each year. Every business enterprise needs to evaluate the possible payoff of using the LIFO method, as well as its drawbacks. LIFO can be used in conjunction with an S election, and the combination of the two elections may result in dramatic tax savings.

335.2. Fringe benefit and retirement plans. A corporation may establish fringe benefit plans, such as accident and health insurance programs. If the corporation is not an S corporation, the corporation deducts the payments into these plans, and the employees never include the benefits in gross income. These plans do not provide as great a tax benefit to the S corporation, since the shareholder-employees cannot exclude the value of the fringe benefits from gross income. This problem was listed in Chapter 1 as one of the disadvantages of an S election. The specific rules receive more thorough discussion in Chapter 8.

A corporation may establish qualified pension and profit-sharing plans, discussed earlier in this chapter. This option is not mutually exclusive from an S election, but it may be a less costly way to reduce taxes than making an S election, especially if the corporation would incur considerable expense in meeting the S corporation requirements.

In considering both fringe benefit plans and qualified retirement plans, the corporation should be cognizant of various nondiscrimination rules. Although these requirements are extremely detailed and are beyond the scope of this book, the corporation that is considering these plans should be aware that it may be quite costly to cover all employees.

335.3. Payment of deductible expenses to shareholders. Compensation, interest, and rent receive extensive discussion in Chapter 8. That discussion centers around the problems of S corporation shareholders, but also discusses the tax treatment of C corporations that make these payments to their shareholders. In general, if a C corporation can employ its shareholders, rent property from shareholders, or borrow money from shareholders, it can deduct the payments of these expenses to its shareholders. If the payments are sufficiently high to exhaust the C corporation's taxable income, the corporation and its shareholders will be able to escape double taxation.

335.4. Liquidation of the corporation. Another alternative to the S election is to liquidate the corporation and operate the business as a proprietorship or partnership. The major disadvantage to liquidation is that it is a fully taxable event to both the corporation and the shareholders. If the corporation has experienced significant appreciation in asset value, and the shareholders' stock basis is less than its value, the immediate tax consequences may be prohibitive. If the corporation and the shareholders would undergo tax losses, they may be caught by nondeductibility. In a few situations, however, liquidation could be advantageous. The attributes pointing toward liquidation are:

- The corporation's gain on liquidation could be largely or completely offset by loss carryforwards.
- The corporation's loss on liquidation could be carried back against taxable income from the last three years.
- The shareholders' capital gain on the liquidating distribution could be offset by capital losses from other sources.
- The shareholders' capital loss on the liquidating distribution could offset capital gains from other sources.

Before considering liquidation of the corporation, the tax advisor should consult carefully with the corporation's shareholders and counsel regarding the nontax aspects of liquidation. There are likely to be good reasons, such as limited liability, why the business should continue to operate in corporate solution. Corporate liquidation rules are discussed in Chapter 15.

If a business is too profitable to effectively eliminate the double taxation, an S election still may not provide the answer. A corporation that needs to retain income will probably find little difference in paying the corporate tax as a C corporation and distributing an amount to the shareholders that will reimburse them for their personal tax liabilities if the corporation elects S status. If the corporation's anticipated taxable income exceeds any foreseeable business needs, it may find that the S election is the most appropriate tax saving device. Ironically, it may not be the income tax, per se, that the corporation is seeking to avoid. The S election will prevent imposition of the personal holding company or accumulated earnings tax on the undistributed corporate earnings. The avoidance of these taxes is probably the most important tax saving offered by the S election.

340. Practice aids.

Following are checklists that may be useful when a corporation is contemplating an S election and has already met the qualifications and a worksheet for calculating the LIFO recapture tax and adjustment to the inventory.

Checklist 3-1: Feasibility of S election

	Applicable (Yes/No)	*Completed (Date)*
1. Cost to qualify		
a. Eliminate ineligible shareholders.		
b. Recapitalize or redeem shares to eliminate multiple classes of stock.		

Copyright © 2000 by Harcourt, Inc. All rights reserved.

2. Cost of election
   a. Calculate LIFO recapture. ________ ________
   b. Determine foreign loss recapture. ________ ________
   c. Determine cost of loss of sheltered fringe benefits. ________ ________
   d. Evaluate exposure to passive investment income tax: ________ ________
      i. Anticipated passive investment income. ________ ________
      ii. Study of accumulated earnings and profits. ________ ________
   e. Evaluate exposure to built-in gains tax. ________ ________
   f. Have 5% shareholders repay pension plan loans, or request waiver. ________ ________
3. Advantages of election
   a. Minimize reasonable compensation exposure. ________ ________
   b. Avoid potential tax from ACE. ________ ________
   c. Avoid potential accumulated earnings tax or personal holding company tax. ________________

Worksheet 3-1: LIFO recapture

Complete for each LIFO inventory pool.

1. Determine FIFO cost from books and records. $ __________
2. Add uniform capitalization adjustment. $ __________
3. Determine FIFO cost basis. (1 + 2) $ __________
4. Determine market value of inventory. (See Rev. Proc. 77-12.) $ __________
5. Lower of 3 or 4 is FIFO inventory amount. $ __________
6. Determine LIFO cost, including uniform capitalization adjustments. $ __________
7. Result is LIFO recapture income. $ __________
8. Determine federal income tax, including LIFO recapture. $ __________
9. Determine federal income tax, excluding LIFO recapture. $ __________
10. LIFO recapture tax (8 – 9)
    Pay 1/4 on due date with final Form 1120 without extension) $ __________
    Pay 1/4 on due date of next three corporate returns (without extension) $ __________
11. Add LIFO recapture income to basis of inventory. (See at 325.4.) $ __________

Copyright © 2000 by Harcourt, Inc. All rights reserved.

TAX YEARS OF S CORPORATIONS

4

CONTENTS

4

400. Overview.

A corporation must select a tax year when it files its S election. A C corporation is generally allowed to select a fiscal year.[1] An S corporation, by contrast, has limited choices on fiscal years. The reason is that the shareholders in an S corporation report the corporation's income in the year in which the corporation's taxable year ends. Most S corporation shareholders are individuals, and most individuals use the calendar year.

Restrictions on taxable years limit the deferral opportunities for shareholders in S corporations. In many respects, the accounting is simplest when the corporation's taxable year coincides with that of the shareholder. A shareholder benefits from the deferral afforded by a natural business year end, with no required deposit. The natural business year end, however, may be difficult to obtain. A §444 year is easy to obtain, but requires a deposit, which removes some of the economic benefit from the deferral.

400.1. Background. The rules governing taxable years of S corporations generally have followed those applicable to partnerships. With both entities, the income or loss from the business passes through to the owners on the last day of the business taxable year. If an S corporation is allowed to claim a fiscal year, and that year differs from the shareholders' taxable year, there are possibilities for deferral of income.

If a corporation sustains losses, there is no benefit, and there is some detriment, from the deferral. Most businesses, however, anticipate profits in the long term. Therefore, the shareholders might be willing to have the corporation elect a fiscal year with long-run profits in mind.

400.11. General requirements of Subchapter S. Under §1378, an S corporation must use a *permitted year* to report its taxable income and other information.

SUMMARY OF AUTHORITY: CODE SECTION 1378

- An S corporation must use a permitted year.
- A calendar year is permitted for any S corporation.
- An S corporation may use another year, if it has a business purpose.
- The IRS must approve the use of a year other than the calendar year.
- Deferral of income to the shareholders is not a business purpose.

400.12. History. Subchapter S was enacted in its original form by the Technical Corrections Act of 1958. That legislation made no distinction between an S corporation and a C corporation in the matter of taxable years. Any corporation could establish its initial taxable year by filing a proper return.

The Treasury Department soon realized that an S corporation could benefit from the deferral. Although the Treasury Department had no control over the adoption of a taxable year by an S corporation, it did have power to approve or disapprove changes. An early Regulation placed S corporations under the same rules as partnerships for changes in taxable years. [Regs. §1.442-1 (1959 amendment)]

The Subchapter S Revision Act of 1982 required the calendar year, as a general rule. [§1378(b)(1)] It permitted a corporation to use another year with a valid business purpose. [§1378(b)(2)] Corporations that had filed S elections prior to October 19, 1982, were allowed to keep fiscal year ends.

The IRS issued Revenue Procedure 83-25 [Rev. Proc. 83-25, 1983-1 CB 689], which listed three valid purposes for which it would automatically grant a fiscal year. The corporation

---

[1] If a C corporation is classified as a personal service corporation, it is subject to the same restrictions as an S corporation. See Chapter 1, at 150.2., for discussion.

could use the same year as the year of holders of more than 50% of its shares. It could use a year that caused deferment of no more than three months to holders of more than 50% of shares. This Revenue Procedure also invented the natural business year end.

The Tax Reform Act of 1986 expressly overruled the three-month deferment, but expressly continues natural business year end, unless the year end was September, October, or November. [Conference Report to accompany H.R. 3838, page II-319] The natural business year ends allowed were those granted under Revenue Procedures 72-51, 74-33, and 83-25.

The IRS issued Revenue Procedure 87-32 [Rev. Proc. 87-32, 1987-2 CB 396] in the middle of 1987. This Revenue Procedure allowed S corporations to adopt, retain, or change to a shareholder year. It also allowed S corporations to adopt, retain, or change to a natural business year end, in most circumstances. If an S corporation had qualified under one of the earlier Revenue Procedures for any year ending between January 31 and August 31, it could keep that year. Since these years were retained without any new action by the taxpayers, they were called *grandfathered years*. Any S corporation that had a natural business year end of September, October, or November, as well as any S corporation that had automatically received a fiscal year before the Subchapter S Revision Act of 1982, however, was required to change to the calendar year or persuade the IRS to grant it a natural business year end.

The Revenue Act of 1987 added §444, which allowed certain S corporations to use a fiscal year even though they did not qualify for a natural business year end. This rule allowed S corporations to retain any fiscal year if the corporation had used that taxable year in 1986. These years were also known as *grandfathered years*. A corporation filing a new S election, whether it is a newly formed corporation or an existing C corporation, can have a fiscal year, but only if it ends in September, October, or November. The use of a fiscal year under §444 requires that the S corporation make a federal tax deposit to compensate the government for the approximate revenue loss from the deferral.

The natural business year end has rigid qualifications, which may be difficult to meet. If a corporation does qualify, there is no required deposit. A corporation may qualify for any month's year end. By contrast, the §444 election year has the advantage that no qualification is necessary. The selection of tax years is limited, and the corporation must make the required deposit.

400.13. Years now available. As of 1999, an S corporation may have any of several limited options for taxable years:

- The calendar year
- A fiscal year if it has majority shareholders on the same year
- A natural business year
- A newly elected fiscal year under §444
- A grandfathered fiscal year under §444 (any year end)

Only the first four possibilities are available after 1988. Some corporations, however, were able to retain other years.

> **OBSERVATION:** A fiscal year may allow a tax saving through deferral. A natural business year end requires no deposit, but qualification is difficult. A §444 year is freely allowed, but requires tax deposits. It can still result in savings, especially if the corporation's income is steadily growing. Any year other than the calendar year, however, can cause complexity when shareholders sell stock or the corporation distributes more than its profits.

Any C corporation that has been using a fiscal year and then makes an S election is allowed to switch to the calendar year when its S election takes effect. See Chapter 5, at 535.

There are special limitations on changes to C corporation years in contemplation of an S election. See Chapter 5, at 520.2.

410. Natural business years.

Revenue Procedure 87-32 [Rev. Proc. 87-32, 1987-2 CB 396], the current authority on the natural business year, allows a new corporation filing an S election to adopt a fiscal year. It allows existing C corporations making S elections to retain or change to a fiscal year if it is a shareholder year or a natural business year. It also gives guidance for corporations that are close to meeting the natural business year end test.

The most important provision in Revenue Procedure 87-32 is the *automatic approval* of a natural business year end. To qualify, the corporation must meet all of the tests outlined in §4.01(1) of the Revenue Procedure:

- Gross receipts from the last 2 months of the most recent fiscal 12-month period must exceed 25% of the gross receipts for the 12 months.
- The corporation must meet the same test for each of the 2 next most recent 12-month periods.
- No other 2-month period can yield a greater average percentage.
- All computations use the corporation's tax accounting method.
- If the corporation is an outgrowth of another business, it uses the gross receipts of the predecessor organization.
- An S corporation with no previous operating history in any form, or with a history of less than 47 months, may not qualify for expeditious approval of a natural business year end. The business must have at least 36 months of experience in which it meets the required pattern of receipts. It must also have 11 earlier months of activity in order to perform all of the required tests.

EXAMPLE 4 - 1: Vera has owned and operated a boutique for several years. Her peak sales usually fall in December and January. She has used the calendar year. She wants to incorporate the boutique and make an S election. She plans to incorporate on November 1, 1996, and would like to use a January 31 fiscal year. As a first step, she should compile her gross receipts for the three 12-month periods ended January 31, 1996, 1995, and 1994. She must then calculate the percentages that fall within December and January.

She must also calculate the percentages that fall within the 11 other 2-month periods, from February through December. This will necessitate compiling all of the gross receipts from March 1992 through January 1996, so that every 2-month period can be tested.

Assume her data on gross receipts are as follows:

	Years			
Month	*92–93*	*93–94*	*94–95*	*95–96*
February	n/a	2,000	2,000	3,000
March	4,000	4,000	3,000	4,000
April	2,000	5,000	2,000	6,000
May	6,000	7,000	6,000	5,000
June	7,000	9,000	9,000	12,000
July	9,000	8,000	10,000	11,000
August	8,000	4,000	7,000	8,000
September	6,000	7,000	9,000	9,000
October	1,000	9,000	10,000	12,000
November	14,000	11,000	12,000	13,000
December	15,000	18,000	19,000	21,000
January	11,000	12,000	13,000	15,000

Beginning with February 1992, she must calculate the last 2 months' receipts as a percentage of the last 12 months' receipts. For example, in February 1993, the last 2 months' receipts are $13,000, and the last 12 months' receipts are $85,000. Thus the January and February percentage is 15.29% of the February through January total. Repeating this calculation for the last three columns in the table yields the following:

4

	Years		
Month	*93–94*	*94–95*	*95–96*
February	15.29%	14.58%	15.53%
March	7.06%	5.26%	6.73%
April	10.23%	5.43%	9.26%
May	13.48%	8.79%	10.28%
June	17.58%	16.48%	15.45%
July	18.89%	20.43%	20.72%
August	13.95%	17.71%	16.96%
September	12.64%	16.33%	15.18%
October	16.84%	19.19%	18.42%
November	21.74%	22.00%	21.74%
December	30.53%	30.69%	29.06%
January	31.25%	31.37%	30.25%

Notice that Vera qualifies for both a December and a January year end, since the gross receipts for these 2-month periods consistently exceed 25% of the total for the 12-month period. Now she must calculate which 2-month period has the higher average. Since December averages 30.09% of the gross receipts and January averages 30.96%, her corporation will qualify for a January 31 year end.

410.1. Exceptions to automatic approval. Revenue Procedure 87-32 lists several exceptions to automatic approval. [Rev. Proc. 87-32, 1987-2 CB 396, §4.01(2)]

- A fiscal year is not granted if the corporation has changed to a natural business year by this Revenue Procedure within six years.
- A fiscal year is also denied for personal service corporations making an S election immediately following a short tax year.
- An S corporation that is a partner in a partnership, the beneficiary of an estate or a trust, or a U.S. shareholder in a domestic international sales corporation (DISC) or former DISC cannot use the natural business year end.

410.2. Ownership tax year. Since the majority of individuals use the calendar year, and since most S corporation shareholders are individuals, the shareholder year is not of widespread importance. Section 4.01(2) of Revenue Procedure 87-32 states that the owners of more than 50% of shares must have, or must concurrently change to, the fiscal year. The corporation must change to another year if the shareholders sell their shares, or if the shareholders change years again.

It is not easy for an individual to change his or her taxable year. The individual must request permission for the change from the IRS. The request for change must demonstrate a substantial business purpose. [Regs. §1.442-1(b)(1)] The IRS has denied requests for change when the individual is a shareholder in an S corporation. [See Rev. Rul. 66-50, 1966-1 CB 40; Rev. Rul. 76-407, 1976-2 CB 127; Rev. Proc. 81-40, 1981-2 CB 604.] As a practical matter, therefore, the ability of an S corporation to use an ownership year is limited to situations where a majority shareholder is already using a fiscal year.

Under current law, an estate is the only eligible shareholder that is likely to use a fiscal year. Therefore, if an estate owns the majority of the stock when a corporation files an S election, the corporation may qualify for the ownership year. If the estate then transfers its shares to one or more shareholders who use the calendar year, the S corporation will be required to change to the calendar year.

> **EXAMPLE 4 - 2:** An estate owns all of the shares of Zeeco, a C corporation. The estate uses a January fiscal year. If Zeeco files an S election while the estate owns all of the shares, it can use a January year. As soon as the estate's ownership drops to 50% or less, the corporation will need to change its year if the new shareholders have a different year.

In one situation, an S corporation had been using an ownership year. Based on information provided by the corporation, the accountant believed that the corporation no longer qualified for the year. Upon later discovery that the corporation could have retained its ownership year, the accountant requested a ruling allowing the corporation to retain its fiscal year. The IRS declined to allow the corporation to retain the fiscal year, since the corporation had not made a timely request. [PLR 9314040]

410.3. Request for natural business year. Revenue Procedure 87-32 gives instructions to a corporation that does not meet the automatic 25% test but wants to apply for a fiscal year. [Rev. Proc. 87-32, 1987-2 CB 396, §4.03] In this case, approval is not automatically granted. The Revenue Procedure refers to Revenue Ruling 87-57 [Rev. Rul. 87-57, 1987-2 CB 117], which lists four situations where the IRS normally will not grant approval and four situations where the IRS normally will grant approval.

The four situations for which the IRS will *not* approve a natural business year end are:

- The taxpayer uses January 31, suggested as a natural business year end by the AICPA in *Journal of Accountancy*, December 1955. The taxpayer uses this year for financial reporting.
- The taxpayer's accountant is busy after the calendar year and will reduce accounting fees if the taxpayer uses September 30.
- The taxpayer has used November 30 since the inception of business 15 years ago. Change would ruin financial reporting consistency.
- The taxpayer wants September 30 to issue a timely Form 1065 K-1 so that the owners can file timely returns.

The situations where the IRS *will* grant approval are:

- The taxpayer wants to use November 30, and has more than 25% of gross receipts in October–November but a higher average in December–January.
- The taxpayer requests June 30 and would meet a June 30 natural business year except that a strike interrupted normal work flow.
- The taxpayer wants May 31. Weather keeps operations closed between June 1 and August 31. There is no other use of the facilities during down time.
- The taxpayer wants to retain March 31. The taxpayer uses the cash method for tax returns and does not meet the 25% test. On the taxpayer's audited accrual method statements, the 25% test is met for March. The taxpayer agrees to change to the accrual method for tax returns.

410.4. Additional conditions. There are additional conditions of the natural business year end. [Rev. Proc. 87-32, 1987-2 CB 396, §4.02(2)] To qualify for the natural business year end, the corporation must file a timely return (including extensions) for any short period, which begins on the day after the last day of old tax year and ends on the day before the new tax year.

EXAMPLE 4 - 3: XYZ qualifies for a natural business year end. It files the proper statement when it elects S status but it neglects to file a timely Form 1120S or extend its return. As a consequence, it loses its privilege to use the natural business year end.

The books must be closed as of the last day of the short period. Subsequent books and statements must be maintained on the new fiscal year. Any annual statement to shareholders or creditors that uses a period other than the fiscal year claimed for tax purposes would cause the corporation to violate this condition.

OBSERVATION: Revenue Procedure 87-32, §11, also warns that the IRS may monitor the 25% test. It may, in the future, modify the business year end test. It may require documentation of continued eligibility to keep the year end granted under Revenue Procedure 87-32.

The Revenue Act of 1987 gave the IRS authority to charge user fees for rulings, determinations, and other procedural assistance. Revenue Procedure 90-17[Rev. Proc. 90-17, 1990-1 CB 479] sets the fee at $200. This fee does not apply when a corporation qualifies for the automatic grant of a natural business year end, but only when the year is subject to IRS approval.

An S corporation may elect a natural business year end only when it files its election to become an S corporation. If a corporation automatically qualifies for the natural business year end, it merely indicates its year end, with reference to the appropriate part of Revenue Procedure 87-32, on Form 2553. The request for a natural business year end for a corporation that does not automatically qualify is somewhat more burdensome. The corporation sends all required information to the IRS along with Form 2553. It also needs to indicate what it intends to do if the IRS does not grant the request for the desired fiscal year. See Chapter 5 for further discussion of the election procedures.

415. Section 444 years.

Section 444 allows an S corporation to elect a fiscal year other than a required taxable year. The qualification for this type of fiscal year is much simpler than for the natural business year end.

SUMMARY OF AUTHORITY: CODE SECTION 444(a) and (e)

- Section 444 provides rules for electing a taxable year other than the calendar year that is required within Subchapter S.
- Section 444 provides elective taxable years for partnerships and personal service corporations.

Under §444, the maximum deferral for new elections is three months. [§444(b)(1)] If a corporation is changing from another fiscal year, however, the deferral cannot exceed the deferral period of the prior fiscal year.

SUMMARY OF AUTHORITY: CODE SECTION 444(b)

- An S corporation may elect to use a taxable year that does not result in a deferral of more than three months from its required year.
- Since an S corporation's required year is the calendar year, an S corporation may use only a September, October, or November fiscal year under §444.
- If a corporation that files an S election is already using a fiscal year, it cannot change to a fiscal year that ends before its current fiscal year.

EXAMPLE 4 - 4: Monty Corporation is a C corporation that files an S election. Monty has been using a November 30 year end as a C corporation. Monty does not qualify for a natural business year end under Revenue Procedure 87-32. Monty can change to the calendar year, or it may retain its November year under §444. It cannot use a September or October fiscal year, because these exceed the deferral period of the prior fiscal year.

The procedures for making the §444 election are discussed in Chapter 5. The S corporation makes the election and is responsible for making the required tax deposit described below. [§444(c)] The deposit is the cost of using the deferral privilege. The election remains in effect for all future years, unless the corporation terminates the election. The S corporation may terminate the §444 election, but it can never re-elect §444 after this termination. Section 444 states, in part:

SUMMARY OF AUTHORITY: CODE SECTION 444(c) and (d)

- An S corporation that elects a §444 year must make a payment.
- The election to use a fiscal year is made at the corporate, rather than the shareholder, level.
- Once the corporation makes the election to use a §444 year, it keeps this year.
- An S corporation may change from a §444 year to the calendar year without receiving consent from the Internal Revenue Service.

If the corporation was a personal service corporation and made a §444 election, the election is continued when it becomes an S corporation. The reverse is also true: If a corporation terminates an S election and becomes a personal service corporation, it may keep a §444 fiscal year.

Code §280H applies to personal service corporations that are not S corporations. It limits the corporation's deduction of applicable payments. A personal service corporation cannot carry a loss back from, or forward to, a §444 year. A personal service corporation receives harsher treatment than an S corporation under §444.

415.1. The required tax deposit. Code §7519, *Required Payments for Entities Electing Not to Have a Required Tax Year,* states the cost of making a §444 election: a tax deposit, which approximately compensates the government for the time value of deferrals. The deposit is calculated as if it were a cumulative tax on the deferral from the current and all previous §444 years. A *de minimis* exemption excuses payment if the cumulative total deposit is less than $500. The essential terms relating to the deposit are as follows (Definitions of these terms, which are scattered throughout the Regulations, are presented below at 415.11.–415.17.):

- Deferral period
- Deferral ratio
- Base year
- Net income for the base year
- Applicable payments
- Net base-year income
- Adjusted highest section 1 rate

The payment is due on May 15 of the year following the beginning of the deferral year (or end of base year). [Temporary Regs. §1.7519-2T(a)(4)(ii)]

Some of the terminology may be best illustrated by a time line.

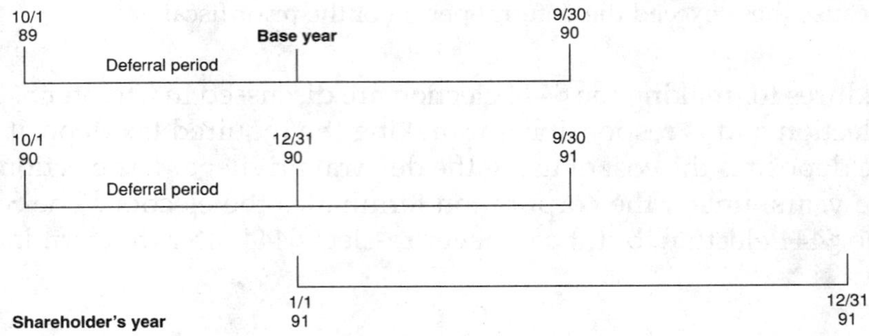

EXAMPLE 4 - 5: Assume that an S corporation has a taxable year ending September 30 and that the shareholders use the calendar year. For its year ended September 30, 1996, its base year is the year ended September 30, 1995. Although both its 1995 and 1996 years have deferral periods, the deferral period that will be referred to for the current year deposit is the period of October, November, and December 1995.

415.11. Deferral period. The *deferral period* is the months between the beginning of the fiscal year and the end of the required [calendar] year. The rule is stated in §444(a)(4).

SUMMARY OF AUTHORITY: CODE SECTION 444(a)(4)

The deferral period is the number of months between the end of the corporation's fiscal year and December 31.

Note that each §444 year will have a deferral period. [Regs. §1.444-1T(b)(4)]

EXAMPLE 4 - 6: XYZ Corporation uses an October year end under §444. Its deferral period is November and December.

415.12. Deferral ratio. The *deferral ratio* is the number of months in the deferral period divided by 12. [Regs. §1.7519-1T(b)(5)]

415.13. Base year. The *base year* is the corporation's taxable year preceding the taxable year for which the calculations are made. [Regs. §1.7519-1T(b)(3)] If an S corporation makes a §444 election for its first taxable year in existence, it has no base year until its second year of existence. Thus the corporation is not required to make a deposit for its first fiscal year. If an S corporation makes a §444 election, but was a C corporation, its first base year is its final year as a C corporation. Thus the corporation must make a deposit for its first year as an S corporation if it had net income in its final C year.

EXAMPLE 4 - 7: ABC Corporation is an S corporation that has been using a September 30 year end. For its year ended September 30, 1996, its base year is the year ended September 30, 1995.

415.14. Net income for the base year. *Net income for the base year* (not to be confused with "net base-year income") is the sum of all items of income and deduction that pass through to the shareholders from the corporation's base year. These income and deduction items, discussed in full in Chapter 6, include capital gains, passive income or loss, and other items that require special treatment at the shareholder level, as well as the corporation's ordinary income or loss for a given year. In calculating an S corporation's net income for the base year, separate classification of income and deduction items, as well as any limitations applicable to shareholders, are ignored. [Regs. §1.7519-1T(b)(5)(iii)]

> **EXAMPLE 4 - 8:** QRS Corporation is an S corporation with a §444 year. In its base year it reported ordinary income of $20,000 and a capital loss of $12,000. Its net income for the base year is $8,000, in spite of the fact that it must report the ordinary income and the capital loss separately to its shareholders. This calculation also disregards the possibility that one or more of the shareholders are not able to use all of the capital loss in computing taxable income.

4

415.15. Applicable payments. *Applicable payments* are payments—such as compensation, interest, and rent—from the corporation to any shareholder that are included in the shareholder's gross income in the corporation's base year. [Regs. §1.7519-1T(b)(5)(iv)] As the examples demonstrate, the corporation must keep track of the total applicable payments made in any base year, as well as the applicable payments made during the deferral period of the base year.

There are some interpretive problems with the term *applicable payments*. Applicable payments do not include any gains resulting from the sale of property from the shareholder to the corporation, even though the gain would be included in the shareholder's gross income.[2] [§7519(d)(3)(B)(i)]

Applicable payments also do not include dividends paid to the shareholders. [§7519(d)(3)(B)(ii)] As explained in Chapter 7, most but not all distributions from S corporations are *not* treated as dividends. The language of the Code seems broad enough to exclude all distributions to shareholders from treatment as applicable payments.[3]

Certain payments to related parties are also treated as applicable payments. These include payments to a shareholder's spouse or minor child and payments to other corporations, partnerships, and trusts in which the shareholders (who own more than 50% of the stock in the S corporation with the §444 year) own an aggregate interest of more than 50%. [Regs. §1.7519(b)(5)(D)] The primary sources of applicable payments are wages, salaries, rents, and interest.

415.16. Net base-year income. *Net base-year income* is the base for the calculation of the required tax deposit. It is calculated by multiplying the net income for the base year times the deferral ratio, plus the excess of the deferral ratio times the applicable payments for the base year, less the applicable payments actually made within the deferral period of the base year. The literal definition from Regulations §1.7519-1T(b)(5)(i) follows:

SUMMARY OF AUTHORITY: REGULATIONS SECTION 1.7519-1T(b)(5)(i)

The calculation of net base-year income requires four steps:

- First, the corporation must multiply the net base-year income by the deferral ratio.
- Second, the corporation must multiply the applicable payments within the entire base year by the deferral ratio.
- Third, the corporation must subtract the applicable payments actually made during the deferral ratio from the amount computed in step 2.
- Finally, the corporation adds the result in step 1 to the result in step 3.

---

[2] As explained in Chapter 8, sales of property between an S corporation and its shareholders may be subject to some special limitations.

[3] As explained in Chapter 7, the only distributions from an S corporation that are included in a shareholder's gross income are actual dividends and distributions in excess of basis. The former are clearly excluded by §7519, and the latter are treated as gains from the sale of property.

EXAMPLE 4 - 9: RAM Corporation is an S corporation that makes a §444 election to retain a September 30 taxable year. Its deferral period is three months and its deferral ratio is 25%. For its base year ended September 30, 1995, it had the following:

Taxable income	$50,000
Compensation to shareholders	$80,000
Interest to shareholders	$10,000

From October 1 through December 31, 1995 (the deferral period within the base year), it paid $20,000 in compensation, and no interest, to its shareholders. Its excess applicable payments are:

Payments in base year (FYE 9/30/96)	$90,000
Multiplied by deferral ratio	.25
	22,500
Less payments in October–December	(20,000)
Excess payments	$ 2,500

Its net income for the deferral period is:

Taxable income for base year	$50,000
Multiplied by deferral ratio	.25
	12,500
Add excess applicable payments	2,500
Net base-year income	$15,000

415.17. Adjusted highest Section 1 rate. This payment rate is the highest individual tax rate plus one percentage point. [§7519(b)] When tax rates change, the rate used for a payment is the rate in effect for the calendar year in which the base year ends. [§7519(b)]

EXAMPLE 4 - 10: GAV Corporation began operations in October 1988 and immediately filed an S election. Pursuant to §444, it adopted a September 30 year end. Its first taxable year ended September 30, 1989. For that year, its net base-year income was zero, since it had no previous taxable year. For its year ended September 30, 1989, it had $480,000 net income and no excess applicable payments. The net base-year income for its taxable year ended September 30, 1990, was $120,000 [$480,000 x (3/12)]. The highest rate of tax specified for individuals in 1990 was 28%.

The shareholders accounted for their shares of the $120,000 in calendar year 1991. In addition, the corporation had to make a deposit, computed as follows:

(3/12) x $120,000 x .29 = $8,700

415.18. Effect of prior years' deposits. The S corporation is given credit for prior years' deposits. If the required deposit increases, the entity must make up the difference. [§7519(b), as amended by the Technical and Miscellaneous Revenue Act of 1988] If the required deposit decreases, the entity may claim a refund (without interest). The required payment is refundable 90 days after the claim is filed, or on April 15 of the year following the tax year of the reduced income. [§7519(b)]

EXAMPLE 4 - 11: Assume that GAV from Example 4 - 10 reported $320,000 net income and $80,000 net base-year income in its year ended September 30, 1991. In 1991, the highest individual rate was 31%. GAV's required deposit for 1995 was:

(3/12) x $80,000 x .32 = $6,400

Since GAV had deposited $8,700 for its year ended September 30, 1990, it was entitled to a refund of $2,300. GAV could file for the refund when it reported a required deposit of $6,400.

OBSERVATION: The Revenue Reconciliation Act of 1993 increased the maximum rate on individuals to 39.6%, effective for all taxable years beginning after 1992. By reference, the adjusted highest Section 1 rate, as used in §7519, became 40.6%. As a consequence of this rate increase, many S corporations terminated their §444 years. See discussion, below, at 425., for termination procedures.

EXAMPLE 4 - 12: Fyco used a September §444 year from 1987 through 1993. For its taxable year ended September 30, 1992, its net base-year income was $100,000. It had made a timely deposit of $32,000 on May 15, 1993. Assume that Fyco's net base-year income for its fiscal year ended September 30, 1993, was also $100,000. Its required deposit for May 15, 1994, would be $40,600. It could have avoided this increase, and received a refund of its $32,000, by terminating its §444 year.

415.19. Administrative provisions. Administrative provisions for §444 years are primarily contained in Regulations §1.7519-2T.

- Deposits are due on May 15 following the fiscal year end.
- Required payments in 1990 and earlier years were sent with Form 720.
- Beginning in 1991, deposit payments and refund claims are made with Form 8752.
- Any late payment is subject to a 10% penalty. [Regs. §1.7519-2T(a)(5)]
- The required payment is treated in the same administrative manner as a tax. [Regs. §1.7519-2T(b)] Accordingly, it is subject to all negligence and fraud penalties.
- In case of willful failure to make the deposit, the S corporation loses its tax year. [Regs. §1.7519-2T(c)]

PLANNING TIP: In spite of the cost and inconvenience of the tax deposit, the §444 year may make sense. If the corporation is new, its *first year* deposit will be zero. It will need to make a deposit after the second year, but its shareholders will have had one year's use of the funds. As long as the income is growing steadily, the advantage will be continued.

In the case of a corporation with erratic income, the §444 election may be more trouble than it is worth. Its deposit might be based on a high base year when it is in the middle of a low year. Each taxpayer will need to evaluate the facts and circumstances unique to the situation.

415.110. Special rules for certain corporations. There are two special rules for the first year of an S election. If the corporation was not in existence for the prior year, its net base-year income is zero. If the corporation was a C corporation in the prior year, its net base-year income is the taxable income when it was a C corporation.

A former C corporation may change its taxable year in order to become an S corporation. If it does so, its first year as an S corporation will consist of less than 12 months. In order to keep the net base-period income on a level monthly basis, the corporation must annualize its net income from the short year when it computes its net base-period income for its second year as an S corporation. [Regs. §1.7519-2T(b)(5)(v)]

There is no expressed treatment of successor corporations in §444. The IRS recently ruled, however, that a personal service corporation that had adopted a January 31 year under §444 (during the period in 1988 when certain corporations were allowed to retain their 1986 fiscal years) would not lose that year as a result of a tax-free reorganization. [PLR 9304023] The reorganization was a "Type F" change in location. See Chapter 17, at 1740.38, for a discussion of Type F reorganizations. Generally, in this type of reorganization, the old corporation and the new corporation maintain a single taxable year. Therefore, the ruling that the §444 year could be retained is consistent with other rules governing these transactions.

420. Restrictions on tiered structures.

An S corporation may be a member in a partnership. If it is a partner, it will be a member of a "tiered structure." In general, a tiered structure exists when a partnership has another partnership or an S corporation as a partner. Example 4 - 13 illustrates the potential tax savings of an S corporation that uses a fiscal year owning an interest in a partnership that uses the calendar year.

> **EXAMPLE 4 - 13:** Jay is a 50% partner in the JK partnership. He contributes his partnership interest to Jayco, an S corporation in which Jay is the 100% shareholder. Assume that JK and Jay use the calendar year and that Jayco is allowed to use a November taxable year. For the year ending December 31, 19X1, Jayco's share of JK's taxable income is $100,000. The following time line illustrates the potential deferral:
>
> 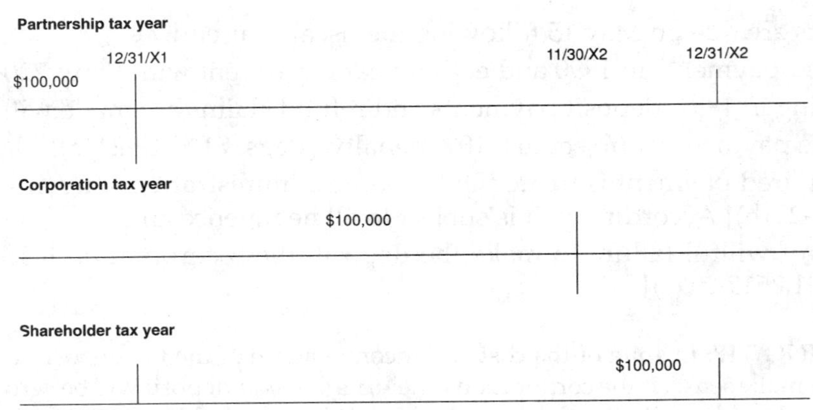
>
>
> Jay's share of the partnership income for the 19X1 partnership year would be reported on his 19X2 individual tax return.

As a consequence of this saving potential, there are two important restrictions on the availability of fiscal years:

1. An S corporation that is a partner in a partnership may not use a natural business year end. [Rev. Proc. 87-32, 1987-2 CB 396, §3.01(2)(c)] This Revenue Procedure allows for no *de minimis* exceptions.
2. As a general rule, an S corporation cannot make a §444 election if it is a member of a *tiered structure.* The rule is stated in §444(d)(3).

SUMMARY OF AUTHORITY: CODE SECTION 444(d)(3)

- Any partnership or S corporation that is a member of a tiered structure may not use a fiscal year under §444 unless all members of the tiered structure use the same taxable year.
- If any S corporation or partnership becomes a member of a tiered structure, any §444 election that is already in effect is terminated.

This definition includes membership in a partnership, as does Revenue Procedure 87-32, but the §444 Regulations go into great detail to expand the definition. A *tiered structure* is defined in Regulations §1.444-2T:

SUMMARY OF AUTHORITY: REGULATIONS SECTION 1.444-2T(b)(1) AND (2)

- Partnerships, S corporations, personal service corporations, and many trusts are defined as *deferral entities*.
- Grantor trusts and QSSTs are not deferral entities.
- A tiered structure exists when any deferral entity owns an interest in any other deferral entity.

An S corporation that is a member of a partnership or is a beneficiary of a trust cannot make or continue a §444 election. Nor can it make a §444 election if it owns any stock in a personal service corporation.

The fact that a grantor trust or QSST owns shares in an S corporation does not make it a member of a tiered structure. An estate is not listed as a deferral entity. As a consequence, the only permitted shareholders that could cause an S corporation to be ineligible for a §444 election are testamentary trusts, grantor trusts following the death of the grantor (provided that they do not meet another S corporation shareholder qualification), and ESBTs.

There are several arrangements that could cause the S corporation to be treated as a member of a tiered structure under the anti-abuse rule of Regulations §1.444-2T(b)(3), which provides:

SUMMARY OF AUTHORITY: REGULATIONS SECTION 1.444-2T(b)(3)

- A tiered structure may exist when a deferral entity has the opportunity to shift income to another deferral entity with common ownership.
- In these situations it is not necessary for one deferral entity to directly own any interest in another deferral entity.

The rationale behind this rather broad definition of a tiered structure should not be viewed as unwarranted authority on the part of the IRS. It is intended to prevent situations such as the following:

> **EXAMPLE 4 - 14:** Norman owns all of the shares in Norco, an S corporation that uses the calendar year. He also owns all of the shares in Manco, another S corporation. If Manco could make an election to use a September 30 year, Norco could shift substantial income to Manco in Manco's deferral period. The income from the deferral period would not be reported on the shareholder's tax return until the following calendar year.

There are two *de minimis* rules that permit minor ownership by deferral entities:

1. Regulations §1.444-2T(c)(2) states the "downstream rule," which allows the S corporation to own an interest in a partnership or trust, if it meets either of the following tests for the immediate preceding taxable year:
   - No more than 5% of the S corporation's taxable income (aggregation of all separately reported items) is from its interest in all partnerships and trusts.
   - No more than 2% of the S corporation's gross income is from its interest in all partnerships and trusts.

   If an S corporation increases its ownership in a partnership during a taxable year, it must apply a special calculation to see if it still meets the *de minimis* exception. It must calculate its hypothetical share of taxable income and gross income from the partnership for the prior year, as if it had owned its current percentage interest in the partnership. [Regs. §1.444-2T(c)(2)(iv)(A)]

4

EXAMPLE 4 - 15: Tierco is an S corporation that uses a §444 taxable year. In its year ended September 30, 1995, it owned 10% of the FY Partnership, which uses the calendar year. For that year, Tierco's gross income from all sources was $600,000, and Tierco's taxable income was $50,000. FY had gross income of $100,000, of which Tierco's share was $10,000. FY's taxable income was $20,000 and Tierco's portion was $2,000. Tierco owns no interest in any other deferral entity. In applying the tests for the year ended September 30, 1995, Tierco makes the following calculations:

Gross income from all sources	$600,000
Maximum allowable from deferral entities for *de minimis* exception (2%)	$ 12,000
Actual gross income from deferral entities	$ 10,000
Taxable income from all sources	$ 50,000
Maximum allowable from deferral entities for *de minimis* exception (5%)	$ 2,500
Actual taxable income from deferral entities	$ 2,000

For 1995, Tierco meets both *de minimis* exceptions and may continue to use its fiscal year. In early 1996, Tierco acquires an additional 5% interest in FY. To see if Tierco may continue to use its fiscal year, it must perform the same tests, using last year's income and the current year's ownership percentage. Its test would be:

Gross income from all sources	$600,000
Maximum allowable from deferral entities for *de minimis* exception (2%)	$ 12,000
Hypothetical gross income from deferral entities	$ 15,000
Taxable income from all sources	$ 50,000
Maximum allowable from deferral entities for *de minimis* exception (5%)	$ 2,500
Hypothetical taxable income from deferral entities	$ 3,000

Since Tierco fails to meet either of the *de minimis* tests, it can no longer use a §444 year.

2. Regulations §1.444-2T(c)(3) states the "upstream rule," which allows the S corporation to have a deferral entity as a shareholder if all deferral entities own less than 5% of the S corporation's stock. If all deferral entities have the same taxable year, they are allowed to make or continue a §444 election. [Regs. §1.444-2T(e)]

425. Changing taxable years after the S election takes effect.

The rules for changing taxable years after an S election depend on which type of fiscal year the corporation is using. Changing to or from a natural business year end requires consent of the IRS. [Rev. Proc. 87-32, 1987-2 CB 396, §4.03(1)] The corporation must file Form 1128 by the 15th day of the second month following the desired short year. The change is subject to IRS approval, and will not be granted automatically. [Regs. §1.442-1(c)(4)] An S corporation must file Form 1128, even if it is changing from an improper year to a permissible year. There is a ruling request fee of $250 for changing a taxable year. [Rev. Proc. 98-1, 1998-1 IRB 7, Appendix A.]

The IRS has the authority to grant relief for a late Form 1128, under Regulations §301.9100-1. The IRS has granted such relief, for S corporations that demonstrated unusual and compelling circumstances for failure to file a timely form. [PLRs 9348057, 9516044, 9516045, 9830009] The IRS has also denied the request when an S corporation did not demonstrate unusual and compelling circumstances. [PLR 9337032] Unfortunately, these rulings do not give sufficient information to determine the nature of the circumstances, so they provide little guidance as to the proper strategy for formulating a request for relief.

A §444 election may be terminated by operation of law or voluntarily. It will terminate by operation of law if the corporation becomes ineligible (such as by becoming a member of a tiered structure) or voluntarily if a corporation willfully fails to make timely deposits under §7519.

Regulations §1.444-1T(a)(5)(i)(C) refers to willful failure to comply with §7519. An IRS audit adjustment that creates a deposit liability should not terminate the election, but the IRS could terminate the §444 election if it finds other instances of willful failure in its audit. The IRS has discretion in determining the effective date of the termination in the case of willful failure. [Regs. §1.444-1T(a)(5)(ii)(C)] The IRS will not allow a taxpayer to claim willful failure and thus retroactively terminate a §444 year. [PLR 9419002]

If an S corporation becomes a member of a tiered structure, the change is effective on the first day of the taxable year in which the corporation becomes a member. [Regs. §1.444-1T(a)(5)(ii)(D)] The District Director has discretion in administering this rule, which could work some hardships. As of this writing, the IRS has not specified any hardships for which this rule might be waived. Example 4 - 16 illustrates a situation that should constitute such a hardship.

EXAMPLE 4 - 16: JKL Corporation is an S corporation that has been using a September year end. On June 30, 1995, JKL becomes a partner in a partnership. Under the rule stated in the Regulation, the §444 year is terminated as of October 1, 1994. JKL should have filed Form 1120S for its short year ended December 31. It should request permission to retain its §444 year through September 30, 1995, and switch to the calendar year as of December 31, 1995.

A termination of a §444 year also happens when an S corporation's S election is terminated. [Regs. §1.444-1T(a)(5)(i)(E)] Note that the corporation will never be allowed to make another §444 election if it becomes an S corporation in some future year. (See the special rule, above, for cases in which the corporation is a personal service corporation after terminating the S election.)

An S corporation may retain its S election but voluntarily revoke its §444 election. If it does so, it may never make another §444 election. [§444(d)(2)(B)]

To terminate a §444 election, the corporation must file a short year return, with the following statement at the top of page 1 [Regs. §1.444-1T(a)(5)(ii)(F)]:

SECTION 444 ELECTION TERMINATED

There are no other procedures necessary. The corporation may not change to a natural business year end or shareholder year without filing Form 1128 and obtaining IRS approval for the change. [Regs. §1.444-1T(a)(4)] The corporation may file a completed return, or an extension, by March 15 following the intended short year. [Ann. 94-5, 1994-2 IRB 39] The IRS will not allow an S corporation to terminate a §444 year by filing a late return for the short period. [PLR 9419002]

The required payment is refundable on April 15 following the termination of a §444 election. [§7519(c)] The IRS is not required to pay interest on late refunds. [§7519(f)(3); PLR 9430001]

PLANNING TIP: Many corporations elected §444 years during a transitional period in 1988. At that time, they could retain any fiscal year. One of the reasons for such an election was to shift shareholder income from the 1987 rates to the 1988 rates. If the individual rate increases, as it did for 1991, it would be a good idea to evaluate the strategy of terminating the §444 election. By doing so, the corporation could accelerate income into a year when the shareholders are at their lowest foreseeable rate.

As a result of the increase in the required deposit rate to 40.6% for 1993 and later years, many S corporations will consider termination of their §444 years and adopt the calendar year. Before doing so, all parties should be aware that this change in the corporation's fiscal year will accelerate the reporting of income to the shareholders. The shareholders will need to cover the additional income with estimated tax payments. By contrast, the required deposit is not subject to estimated tax payments. Interest and penalties on shareholders, especially those in the top tax bracket, may make it more expensive for the corporation to terminate the §444 year than to make a deposit under §7519.

430. Loss of S election for failure to change taxable year.

The Subchapter S Revision Act of 1982 allowed certain S corporations to keep their fiscal years under old law. [§1378(c), repealed by the Tax Reform Act of 1986] These corporations were required to change to a permitted year after the year in which more than 50% of the stock changed hands. The Tax Court recently rendered a decision on the results of a failure to follow this rule. In *Farmers Gin, Inc.* [TC Memo 1995-25, 69 TCM (CCH) 1696], an S corporation had retained a pre-1982 fiscal year. Its stock had changed ownership and the corporation had failed to change its taxable year. The IRS held that the corporation's S election had terminated. The corporation, by contrast, insisted that the IRS should allow it to recompute its income and other items on basis of the calendar year and to file amended returns. In this manner the corporation was hoping to keep its S election intact. The court held for the IRS, and the corporation lost its S election.

> **OBSERVATION:** *Farmers Gin, Inc.*, dealt with a provision of the tax law that was in effect only between 1982 and 1986. At any rate, the corporation would have been required to change to a permitted year in 1987. The only provision under current law that requires an S corporation to change its year end upon a change of ownership in stock relates to the ownership tax year. See 410.2.

The rationale of *Farmers Gin, Inc.*, does not apply to any fiscal year retained under one of the allowable exceptions to the permitted year rules of the Tax Reform Act of 1986. Thus, if an S corporation had received permission to use a fiscal year under Revenue Procedure 74-33 or Revenue Procedure 83-25, it would not be required to change to the calendar year if a majority of its stock changed hands. Similarly, any corporation that retained or changed to a fiscal year (other than an ownership year) under any of the transition rules allowed by the Tax Reform Act of 1986 would not be required to change its fiscal year upon the change in holdings of it shares. The following examples illustrate the very limited application of the holding of *Farmers Gin, Inc.*

> **EXAMPLE 4-17:** Firstco elected S status before 1982. It continued to use a March 31 year end after the Subchapter S Revision Act of 1982. It had never applied for permission for a fiscal year, but based its year on the rule of §1378(c), as in effect from 1982 through 1986. In 1985, more than 50% of Firstco's outstanding shares were sold to new owners Firstco would lose its S election if it did not change to a permitted year.

> **EXAMPLE 4-18:** Secondco elected S status before 1982. It retained a March 31 year end after the Subchapter S Revision Act of 1982. There were no changes in holdings of Secondco's shares from 1982 through 1986. In 1987, Secondco was granted permission to keep its fiscal year under Revenue Procedure 87-32. In 1996, more than 50% of Secondco's outstanding shares were sold to new owners. Secondco is not required to change its year end.

EXAMPLE 4 - 19: Thirdco elected S status before 1982. It retained a March 31 year end after the Subchapter S Revision Act of 1982. There were no changes in holdings of Thirdco's shares from 1982 through 1986. In 1988, Thirdco elected to keep its fiscal year under §444. In 1996, more than 50% of Thirdco's outstanding shares were sold to new owners. Thirdco is not required to change its year end.

435. Decision flowcharts.

Figure 4-1 illustrates the process of selecting a taxable year at the time a corporation makes an S election.

Figure 4-2 illustrates the year-end planning for making a required deposit under §7519 for a §444 year.

Figure 4-1. Selecting a taxable year when making an S election.

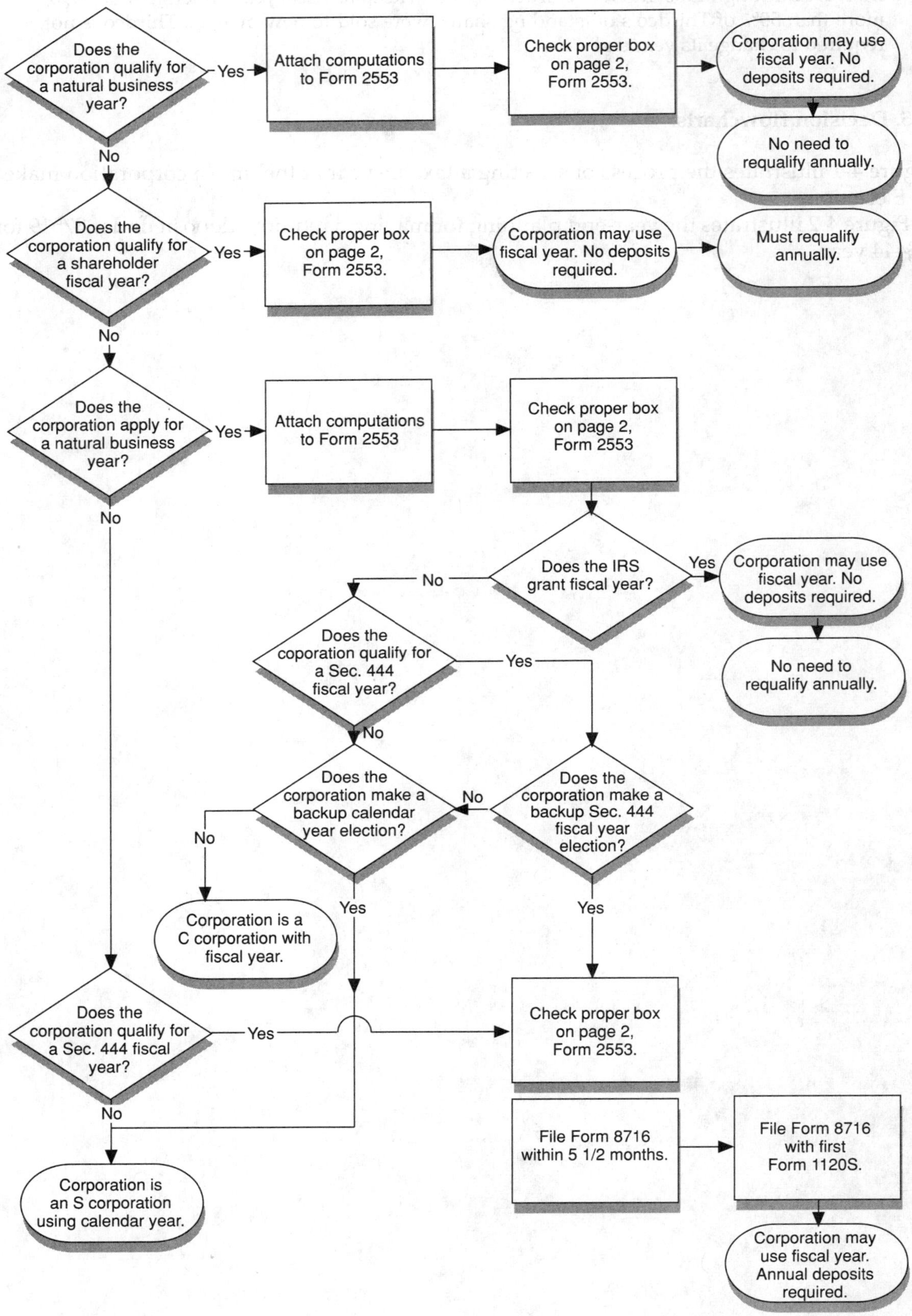

Figure 4-2. *Required deposit under §7519.*

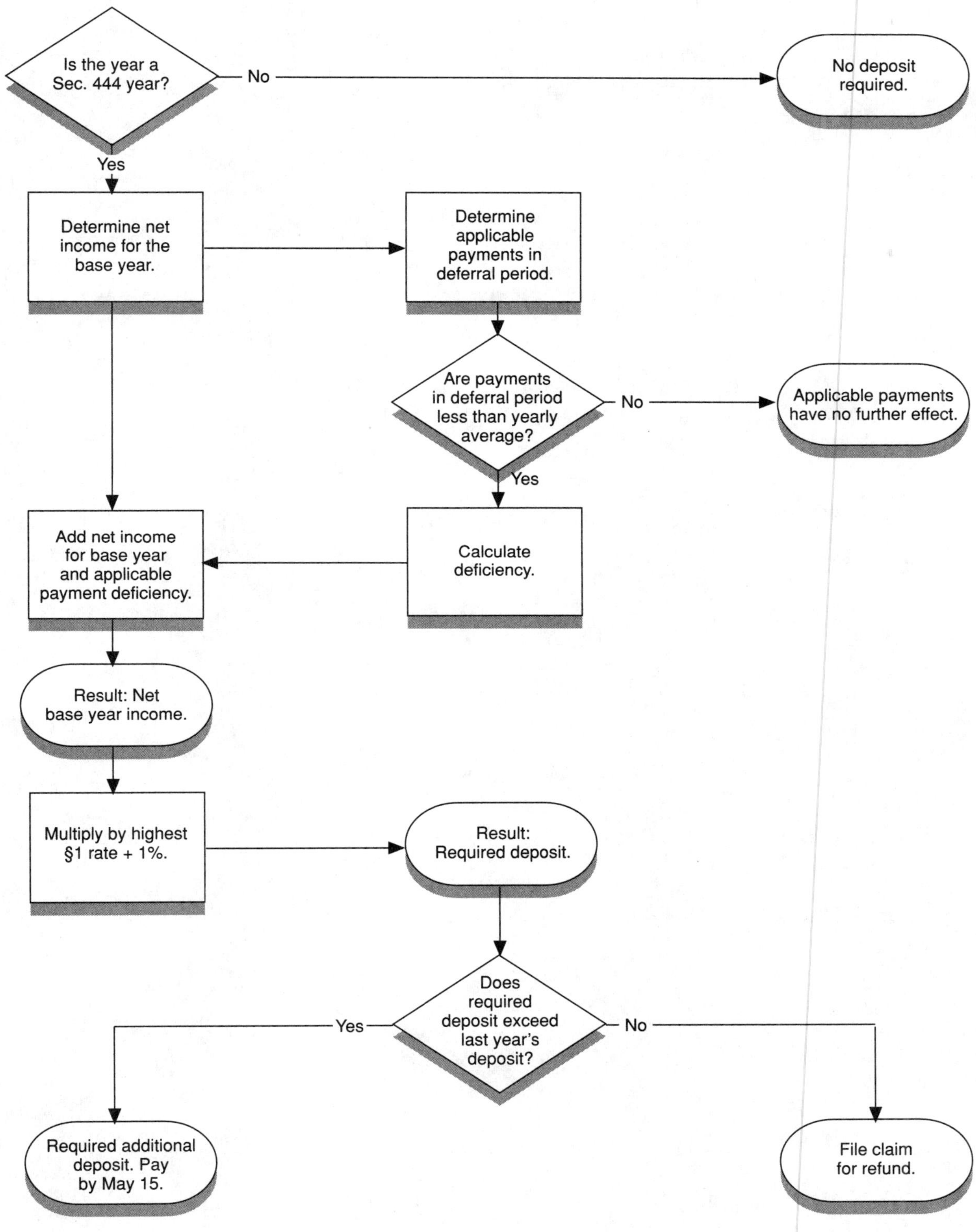

CORPORATE AND SHAREHOLDER ELECTIONS

Contents

5

500. Overview.

To be an S corporation, a corporation must file an election. Before it can file a valid election, it must meet all of the eligibility requirements. (See Chapter 2.) The rules are statutory, and the IRS has only limited flexibility in enforcement. The Service has generally refused to honor the argument that the substance of the election dominates the form. In this case, the form and the substance have equal importance. The IRS has occasionally been merciful and allowed an election despite some minor defect.

Corporations that file defective elections are caught in the uncomfortable position of being C corporations that have acted as if they were S corporations. Reliance on counsel may not provide any relief. The corporation must first qualify, and then take all necessary steps.

> **OBSERVATION:** In August 1996, President Clinton signed the Small Business Job Protection Act of 1996 into law. Among the more important provisions of that Act are provisions that allow the IRS to waive inadvertently defective or late elections by S corporations. [§1362(f), as amended by the Small Business Job Protection Act of 1996, and §1362(b)(5), added by the Small Business Job Protection Act of 1996] These rules are in effect for all years beginning after 1982.

An S election remains in effect until it is terminated. Termination is discussed in Chapter 13. Re-election of S status following a termination of an earlier S election is subject to a restriction: As a general rule, a former S corporation must operate for five years as a C corporation before it can again become an S corporation. There are certain circumstances under which this period may be reduced.

There are two dates of importance:

- The filing date
- The effective date

The filing date is the day on which Form 2553 is delivered to the government, generally the postmark date. The effective date is the first day that the corporation actually becomes subject to the rules of Subchapter S.

Since the shareholders will have personal liability for tax on the S corporation's income, the law provides that they must consent to the election. Occasionally, the identity of the shareholder, and the person whose consent is required, present problems.

At the time of the election of S corporation status, the corporation must also choose its taxable year. A new corporation must adopt one of the required or permitted years. An existing corporation may be able to retain its taxable year, or it may be required to change to a new taxable year. The actions that the corporation takes when filing its S election are critical to the determination of its taxable year. (See Chapter 4.)

Perhaps no rule within Subchapter S has caused more confusion than the ownership of shares by trusts. In addition to meeting the rigid qualification requirements (described in Chapter 2), the beneficiary of a QSST must file a separate election on behalf of the trust. Failure to comply with this requirement has led to numerous Private Letter Rulings, which have allowed an S election to take effect, or continue in effect. These rulings are cited in Chapter 13, at 1350.

Revisions to Subchapter S during 1996 permit Electing Small Business Trusts to be shareholders in S corporations. Each potential current beneficiary of the trust is counted as a shareholder—or if there are no potential current beneficiaries, the trust itself is treated as the shareholder.

> **OBSERVATION:** At present, no Regulations have been issued to provide guidance on handling consents by potential current beneficiaries of an Electing Small Business

5

Trust. The tax professional should anticipate some initial problems in this area—judging from the number of Private Letter Rulings generated on the topic of consents by the beneficiary of a QSST—and should to look to these QSST rulings for precedent-setting situations that could be applied to Electing Small Business Trusts.

In summary, to elect S status, the corporation must meet the following requirements:

1. Must be eligible
2. Must make the election within the proper time frame, accompanied by the consent of all shareholders
3. Must select a taxable year at the same time as the election
4. Must ensure that any trusts that own shares file their own QSST elections or Electing Small Business Trust elections

In late 1992, the IRS issued Final Regulations governing the S election and related matters. S corporations are subject to rules contained in these Final Regulations for years beginning after December 31, 1992. For all earlier years, refer to the 1993 edition of the *S Corporation Tax Guide*.

The most important change in election procedures was in the Small Business Job Protection Act of 1996. This law allows the IRS to grant relief for late or defective elections. Its provisions receive substantial discussion in this chapter, at 550.

OBSERVATION: Although the IRS now grants relief for late or defective elections, it is best to follow the election rules, to the letter. Even though relief provisions are available, they may be expensive. Also, there may be delays, during which time the corporation is unsure of its S corporation status.

510. Relationship of eligibility rules and the election.

Only a "small business corporation" may be an S corporation. The term *small business corporation* means a corporation that meets all of the eligibility requirements (discussed in Chapter 2) for each day of each taxable year for which the election is in effect. The election rules also state that "a small business corporation may elect" to be an S corporation. [§1362(a)(1)] The corporation must meet all of the eligibility requirements on the date that it files the S election.

510.1. Eligibility on filing date. The corporation must be eligible for the S election on the date the election is filed. If the corporation did not meet all of those requirements, it was not a small business corporation within the meaning of the law. Much of the confusion in this area relates to trusts that own shares in the corporation on the filing date.[1] See the discussion of the QSST election, below, at 540.2.

EXAMPLE 5 - 1: WXY Corporation has a nonresident alien shareholder in 1995. The corporation wants to make an S election for its year to begin on January 1, 1996. On December 1, 1995, it files Form 2553. On December 20, 1995, all of the nonresident alien's stock is redeemed. Since the corporation was not eligible on the day the election was filed, the election will not be effective for any tax year.

If the election had been filed after the nonresident alien's shares were redeemed, it would have been effective for 1996. The corporation may cure the defect by filing another election on or before March 15, 1996.

---

[1] A corporation filed Form 2553, but on the date of filing it had trusts that could not meet the definition of an *eligible shareholder*. The IRS held that the S election was not valid. [PLR 9016087]

In one ruling, shareholders apparently relied on counsel when the corporation issued a second class of stock. The attorney advised that there would be no problems qualifying the corporation as an S corporation, since the only apparent differences between the classes were voting rights. Upon review by an independent accountant, however, it was discovered that there were possible differences in dividend rights between the two classes. The corporation amended its certificate of incorporation to eliminate the differences. The corporation then applied for inadvertent termination relief. Unfortunately, however, the two classes of stock had been outstanding when the corporation filed Form 2553. In the ruling, the IRS pointed out that for inadvertent termination relief to apply, there must have been a valid S election, that had then terminated. Since the corporation in question had never had a valid S election, the IRS could not grant inadvertent termination relief under §1362 (f), as it was in effect at the time. [PLR 9115003]

510.2. Continued eligibility. The corporation must remain eligible on each day of the tax year during that the election is effective. As discussed in Chapter 13, the corporation may lose its S election if it becomes ineligible at any time after the S election takes effect.

If the corporation files an S election in the taxable year before its effective date, it must be a small business corporation on the date it files the election. It must also be a small business corporation on the first day of the taxable year for which the election is effective. It is possible, however, to become disqualified during the period after the filing date and before the effective date. If the corporation cures the disqualification before the effective date, the S election will be effective. Therefore, it is important to monitor all events that occur after the filing date in order to determine their effect on the S election.

Perhaps the most likely cause of temporary ineligibility is transfer of stock to a trust. The trust must qualify as either a grantor trust or a QSST. An otherwise eligible QSST must be certain to file the QSST election within 2 months and 15 days after the date it acquires stock in an S corporation. See discussion at 540.2., below.

> **EXAMPLE 5 - 2:** On September 1, 1995, GHI Corporation files an S election, effective for calendar year 1996. Some of its shares are owned by trust T1, which meets all of the requirements of a QSST. T1 must file its QSST election on or before November 15, 1995, or GHI's S election will be invalid.
>
> On October 1, 1995, shares in GHI are transferred to trust T2, which also meets all of the requirements of a QSST. Note that the S election that was filed on September 1, 1995, is not invalidated (assuming that T1 makes a timely QSST election), because there were no ineligible shareholders on September 1. The S election will not be effective in 1996, however, if there are any ineligible shareholders on January 1. Trust T2 may become an eligible shareholder by filing a QSST election on or before March 15, 1996.
>
> Note that T2 does not need to be an eligible shareholder on October 1, 1995, the date it acquired the stock. The corporation was not an S corporation at that time and was not filing Form 2553 on that date. T2 did not need to be eligible on September 1, 1995, since it was not a shareholder. T2 must be eligible on January 1, 1996, and has 2 months and 15 days thereafter to file its election.

515. Election procedures.

The corporation must file Form 2553 with the appropriate IRS service center. The appropriate service center is the one to which the corporation sends all its tax returns. [Regs. §1.1362-6(a)(2)(i)] The form can filed by hand delivery, or through the U.S. Postal Service. [§7502(a)]

SUMMARY OF AUTHORITY: CODE SECTION 1362(b)

- The corporation must meet the eligibility requirements of a "small business corporation" in order to file an S election.

- The election may be filed (1) at any time in the year immediately before it is to take effect or (2) within 2 months and 15 days after the beginning of the year in which it is to take effect.

EXAMPLE 5 - 3: GHI Corporation was a C corporation. On October 23, 1995, it decides that an S election would be advantageous. It has passed the deadline for an election to be effective for 1995. It may file any time between October 23, 1995, and March 15, 1996, for the election to be effective for the calendar year 1996.

5 Form 2553 requires that the corporation state the tax year for which it is to be effective. This statement should be made with care to avoid confusion regarding the effective date.

EXAMPLE 5 - 4: QRS Corporation is a personal service corporation that has not had an S election in effect. It has been using a November 30 fiscal year. Pursuant to §1378 it changes to the calendar year. It must file a tax return for the short year beginning December 1 and ending December 31, 1996.

QRS decides that an S election would be advantageous for the calendar year 1988. On November 30, 1996, it files Form 2553, specifying January 1, 1997, as the effective date. Since the election was not filed in the year immediately preceding the effective date (i.e., in the short year December 1–December 31), it is not a valid election. A routine letter from the IRS acknowledging the election will not cause the election to be valid. The corporation must file another election, or request relief, for an inadvertently defective or untimely election. It may be filed in the short year ending December 31, 1996, or any time up to March 15, 1997.[2]

The Regulations explicitly provide that a corporation must file Form 2553. In one case, a corporation attempted to secure S status by having its shareholders sign and attach a consent statement to Form 1120S. The Tax Court found that the corporation was not in substantial compliance, and refused to allow the election. [*Rockwell Inn, Ltd.*, 65 TCM 2374, TC Memo 1993-158] (Note: In PLR 8835011, misstatement of the tax year was not fatal. The form was correct in every other respect.) Therefore, the corporation was a C corporation for all years under consideration. In another case, the corporation attempted to elect S status by filing Form 1120S as its election and Form 1040 as a valid consent by the shareholder. The Tax Court found this to be an invalid election and consent, because it did not establish a clear intent to elect S status or show unequivocal consent by the shareholder. [*Elbaum*, 68 TCM 638 1994, TC Memo 1994-439]

OBSERVATION: Under the new provision allowing the IRS to accept a late election with reasonable cause, the invalidity of the elections in cases similar to those cited above may be avoided. However, in order to accept a late election the corporation may need to request a ruling and pay a ruling fee. See 550, below. Thus it is always safest to play by the rules, and submit a timely Form 2553 for the first year in which S status is desired.

515.1. Year of less than $2\frac{1}{2}$ months. If the first tax year in which the S election is to be effective is less than $2\frac{1}{2}$ months long, the election may be filed after the year ends.

SUMMARY OF AUTHORITY: CODE SECTION 1362(b)(4)

- A corporation with a taxable year of less than 2 months and 15 days may file its S election after the end of the short year, as long as it is filed within 2 months and 15 days of the beginning of the short taxable year.

---

[2] There is no record of the IRS granting relief for an S election that was filed too early. In one case, under prior law, a court granted an S election that was filed prematurely. See *McClelland Farm Equipment Co. v. U.S.*, 79-2 USTC 9472 (8th Cir.).

515.2. Beginning of taxable year. The beginning of the taxable year is an important date, since it measures the deadline for the Form 2553. There are differing considerations for a new business and for an existing C corporation.

515.21. New corporations. There are some special definitions for a new corporation. The IRS states that the taxable year starts on the earliest date that the corporation:

- Issues shares
- Acquires property
- Commences business [Form 2553 and Regs. §1.1362-6(a)(2)(ii)(C)]

The interpretation of this rule has caused some confusion. If state law provides that a corporation has issued shares when the charter is finalized, the IRS may look to that date, rather than the date of physical issue. [*William C. Lyle*, 30 TCM 1412, TC Memo 1971-324]

> **OBSERVATION:** This book could not purport to give up-to-date and accurate advice on the legal status of incorporation. To do so would be an attempt to analyze the constantly changing corporate statutes in every jurisdiction. Accordingly, the user is advised to consult competent counsel to determine when a corporation is deemed to have shareholders under local law.

> **PLANNING TIP:** If entrepreneurs are planning to establish an empty corporation (often called a "shelf corporation") in anticipation of an active business venture, they may want to assure that an S election will be in effect from the first day of the corporation's existence. See discussion at 520., for some of the reasons that this could be important. Also see discussion in Chapter 14, at 1415.7. One technique to accomplish this objective might be to issue shares to one person at the corporation's inception. This person could then consent to the S election, and it would not be necessary to obtain consent from subsequent shareholders.

The corporation must be in existence as a corporation before it may file the S election. [*Frentz v. Commissioner*, 67-1 USTC 9363 (6th Cir.), aff'g 44 TC 485 (1965); *Ratcliff*, TC Memo 1980-12, 39 TCM 886] A corporation that filed within the proper time after beginning business, but had shareholders at an earlier date, was denied the election. [*Brutsche v. Commissioner*, 78-2 USTC 9745 (10th Cir), aff'g 65 TC 1034 (1976)]

An association may be taxable as a corporation under §7701(a)(3). Since it meets the federal income tax definition of a *corporation*, it should be able to make an S election if it also meets all of the other S corporation eligibility requirements. [PLRs 8534099, 9543017]

> **OBSERVATION:** In late 1996, the IRS issued Regulations that adopt the "check the box" entity classification approach, allowing an unincorporated enterprise to choose its tax classification. Regulations §301.7701-3 treats a domestic unincorporated entity as a partnership if it has more than one owner, or as a nonentity if it has only one owner. The organization may elect out of its default classification and opt to be treated as a corporation for tax purposes. It is expected that few associations will elect to be treated as corporations. Any such association that desires S status must be careful to note the event that causes it to begin is first taxable year as a corporation, so that it can observe the filing deadline.

When a corporation's first taxable year begins on a day other than the first day of the month, the day count is not rolled back. [Regs. §1.1362-6(a)(2)(iii)]

EXAMPLE 5 - 5: JKL Corporation was formed on November 5, 1995, and uses the calendar year. It may file an S election anytime on or before January 19, 1996, in order for the S election to be effective for the year ended December 31, 1995.

515.22. Existing corporations. The beginning of a taxable year for an existing corporation usually poses no special problems. If the corporation has been a member of an affiliated group, however, and has filed consolidated returns, it may be able to accelerate the end of the current taxable year and thus begin a new year before the normal date.

If a parent corporation disposes of a subsidiary corporation, the subsidiary's taxable year ends on the date of the disposition. [Regs. §1.1502-76(b)(2)] Therefore, a corporation that has been a subsidiary of another corporation may find itself immediately eligible to become an S corporation.

EXAMPLE 5 - 6: Gencor was the parent corporation of Harcor. The group filed a consolidated return and used the calendar year. On July 21, 1993, Gencor sold all of the stock in Harcor to persons eligible to be S corporation shareholders. Harcor met all of the other requirements for S status. Harcor's taxable year would end on July 21, 1993. It would be eligible for S status for its taxable year beginning July 22, 1993.

The parent's year could also be terminated prematurely, but this step would require additional planning. If the parent corporation disposes of all of its stock in all subsidiaries, or sufficient stock to destroy the affiliated group in its entirety, the parent's year would not automatically end. However, if the parent corporation became a member of a new affiliated group, it would begin a new tax year. [Regs. §1.1502-76(b)(3), Example 3]

EXAMPLE 5 - 7: Refer to Example 5-6. If Gencor terminated its affiliated group status on July 21, 1993, its taxable year would end on December 31, 1993. Gencor would not be eligible for S status until January 1, 1994. However, if Gencor formed a new subsidiary in which it owned at least 80% of the stock on July 22, 1993, it would become a member of a new affiliated group on that date, and its taxable year would end on July 21, 1993. It would be eligible to make an S election for its taxable year beginning July 22, 1993, if it met all of the other requirements of Subchapter S on that date. If the newly formed subsidiary were an inactive subsidiary, the existence of the new affiliated group would not disqualify Gencor from S status.

There are alternative ways to structure an early end of a taxable year, and thus accelerate the effective date of an S election. In some cases, a parent corporation that had been filing consolidated returns merged into its sole remaining subsidiary.[3] The taxable year of the old consolidated group ended on the date of the merger. Therefore, the taxable year of the former subsidiary began on the day after the merger. The IRS has ruled that the surviving corporation was immediately eligible for S status in this situation. [PLRs 9303015, 9707018, 9833027, 9852005]

EXAMPLE 5 - 8: Parco owns 100% of the stock of Subco. Both are C corporations. On September 11, 1997, Parco merges into Subco. Subco now has a taxable year beginning on September 12, 1997. Parco may file its election any time through November 27, 1997.

CAUTION: As is discussed in Chapter 17, there are several different types of tax-free reorganizations. In many of these, the corporation that goes out of existence loses its taxable year, as was the case in the Letter Rulings discussed above. However, there could be a hazard if a corporation set up a dummy subsidiary and then immediately merged itself into the subsidiary. The IRS could treat this merger as a "Type F"

[3] This transaction is commonly referred to as a "downstream merger." See Chapter 17 for discussion of mergers and other tax-free reorganizations.

reorganization, in which the prior corporation survives intact and does not terminate its old year. See Chapter 17, at 1720.8.

515.3. Importance of deadline. Historically, the IRS had no authority to extend the deadline for filing the S election. However, the Small Business Job Protection Act of 1996 changed the law to allow relief for late elections.

515.31. Before enactment of the Small Business Job Protection Act of 1996. The deadline was rigid, and the IRS had no flexibility in its enforcement. [Rev. Rul. 60-183, 1960-1 CB 625] If the 2.5 month period ends on a weekend or holiday, general tax rules allow the corporation to file Form 2553 on the next working day. [7503]

Regulations §301.9100-1 permits extensions for filing elections, but it is limited to cases where the Code does not specify a deadline. It was inapplicable to S elections, therefore, since the Code specified the deadline, at least before the Small Business Job Protection Act of 1996. In one case, a corporation applied for an extension of time to file Form 2553. Apparently, the corporation believed it had good cause for the failure to file within the statutory period. The IRS, however, denied the extension. Good cause is not an admissible argument, since the time is rigid and is prescribed in the statute. [PLRs 9025021, 9049009]

The courts generally enforced the deadline. [*Pestcoe*, 40 TC 195 (1963); *Feldman*, 47 TC 329 (1966)] A postmark indicating a late mailing dominated a private postmark from a postal meter showing timely mailing. [*Leslie Combs II*, 57 TCM 288 (1989), aff'd sub. nom.; *Nally v. Commissioner*, 907 F.2d 151 (6th Cir., 1990)] A Form 2553 hand-delivered one day late was not accepted. [*Simons v. U.S.*, 62-2 USTC 9838 (DC Conn.)] In one case, there was limited relief for a premature election. [*McClelland Farm Equipment Co. v. U.S.*, 79-2 USTC 9472 (8th Cir.)]

515.32. After enactment of the Small Business Job Protection Act of 1996. The law specifically allows the IRS to accept late elections. See discussion below, at 550.1.

515.4. Importance of accuracy. Form 2553 is filed with the IRS service center where the corporation files its tax returns. The form must be mechanically correct and signed (under penalties of perjury) by a corporate officer. A paid preparer may not sign the form.

515.41. Before enactment of the Small Business Job Protection Act of 1996. In general, the IRS had no specific authority to overlook defects in the election, other than its usual administrative powers. The IRS was often willing to accept a form with minor deficiencies. For example, a minor error in listing shares owned on Form 2553 did not invalidate the corporation's S election. [PLR 8822046] Similarly, an error in specifying the effective date on Form 2553 did not invalidate the corporation's S election. The form was filed by March 15, 1987, but specified January 1, 1988. The IRS allowed the election to take effect on January 1, 1987. [PLR 8836031, citing *Thompson*, 66 TC 737 (1976)] Failure to specify an effective date did not invalidate the corporation's S election. The corporation stated the proper date in later correspondence. [PLR 8835011] The IRS also allowed an S election to take effect when Form 2553 contained an erroneous effective date, which was corrected by later filing a correct Form 2553.[4] [PLR 9040040] In another ruling, the IRS allowed a valid S election even though Form 2553 contained incorrect dates of incorporation, incorrect first date of the taxable year, and incorrect date on which the corporation's sole shareholder acquired his shares. [PLR 9424022] Improper identity of the shareholders, especially when shares are owned by a trust, can also be overlooked by the IRS,[5] as can a corporation's issuing a lesser number of shares of

[4] The significance of this ruling is that the IRS accepted the filing of the erroneous Form 2553 before January 1, 1987. This date has considerable significance with respect to the built-in gains tax, discussed in Chapter 11.

[5] The IRS allowed S elections to be effective under these circumstances in PLRs 9038019, 9047027, 9047026, and 9047025.

stock than was set both in a timely filed election on Form 2553. [Rev. Rul. 74-150, 1974-1 CB 241] In a family-owned corporation, the IRS has been willing to allow the corporation to correct a misstatement of the number of shares owned by a specific family member. [PLR 9626035]

If the IRS did not accept an improperly filed Form 2553, the courts are unlikely to validate the S election. For example, failure to reconcile total outstanding shares with those listed, by shareholder, invalidated an S election. [*Fratantonio*, 55 TCM 611 (1988)]

A corporation filed Form 2553, leaving all of the information about issued and outstanding shares blank, because the officers thought "it was none of respondent's [IRS] business." When the IRS returned the form for correction, the corporation completed some of the items, but left the total issued shares box blank. The IRS accepted the second form. On subsequent audit, however, the IRS determined that the S election was invalid. The Tax Court held the election invalid. [*Garrett & Garrett, PC*, TC Memo 1993-453, 66 TCM 905]

In an extreme case, a taxpayer wanted to retroactively terminate an S election. The IRS had accepted an unsigned Form 2553. At the taxpayer's request, however, the Tax Court held that the election was not valid, because the signature on the transmittal accompanying the unsigned form did not subject the corporation's president to penalties of perjury. [*Jon P. Smith*, 54 TCM 1535 (1988)] In contrast, a shareholder was not allowed to disavow S election based on his contention that his Form 2553 contained invalid signatures, was late, and was incomplete. [*Johnson*, TC Memo 1997-558]

A corporation bankruptcy proceedings is not precluded from filing an S election. For the election to be valid, Form 2553 should be signed by the trustee. [*Levy*, 46 TC 531 (1966)]

> **OBSERVATION:** The election process is not inherently complicated. There have been many cases and rulings that could have been avoided by careful preparation of Form 2553. Where the errors were material, corporations discovered that they had never been S corporations. As discussed in Chapter 18, there is no statute of limitations that mitigates the failure to file a proper Form 2553. Corporations and their shareholders might be protected for years that are barred by the statute if they have filed as S corporations, but the IRS is not bound to accept an invalid S election as effective for any open year. The IRS has been reasonable in allowing taxpayers to correct errors on improperly prepared Forms 2553, and will continue to do so after the inadvertent defective election rules adopted in the Small Business Job Protection Act of 1996. Even in these cases, however, the taxpayers may have had to expend considerable sums in securing favorable rulings. A ruling request must be accompanied by a $3,650 filing fee. In addition, it takes a competent tax advisor several hours to properly complete the request. Sometimes direct conferences with the IRS national office are necessary before a favorable ruling is granted. Therefore, while a favorable ruling is preferred to a loss of S status, it is far less expensive and troublesome to be sure that the form is filed properly in the first place. A corporation in this situation is also faced with a period of uncertainty. While a taxpayer is waiting for a response from the IRS on a ruling request, neither the corporation nor the shareholders will know whether there is a valid S election in effect. This uncertainty during the interim may make compliance difficult and intelligent planning impossible.

There may be a burden on the taxpayer to sustain the fact that a Form 2553 was filed. In one recent case, the court did not award the taxpayer attorney's fees from the IRS in connection with an examination of this issue, even after the IRS had conceded that a Form 2553 was timely filed. [*Dugan*, TC Memo 1997-458]

515.42. After enactment of the Small Business Job Protection Act of 1996. The law specifically allows the IRS to accept defective elections as valid. See discussion below, at 550.4.

515.5. Importance of evidence. When the IRS audits an S corporation, the examiner often will want to inspect records to confirm that the corporation is an S corporation. Clearly, it is a good idea for the corporation to have evidence to that effect in its files.

Filing of Form 1120S does not by itself ensure that a corporation is an S corporation. The corporation needs proof that it also filed Form 2553. [*William C. Lyle*, 30 TCM 1412, TC Memo 1971-324] The corporation should retain evidence that the S election was accepted. Three basic types of evidence can be used to show that the corporation has filed Form 2553:

1. Receipt of a letter from the IRS accepting the S election
2. Proof of delivery, such as a stamped, receipted duplicate copy of the form, or a registered or certified mail receipt
3. All other forms of evidence

The first type is the most desirable, since it shows that the IRS acknowledges having processed the form. The second type is prima facie evidence of delivery to the IRS, and thus shifts the burden of proof of receipt to the IRS. The third type is the least reliable and does not always accomplish its purpose.

515.51. Receipt of letter from IRS. Under normal circumstances, the IRS receives Form 2553 and examines it for facial accuracy. The IRS then sends the corporation a letter acknowledging and accepting the S election. The IRS instructs taxpayers to contact the service center if the IRS does not respond within 90 days. It is the taxpayer's responsibility, however, to follow up on the status of the election.

In one case, a taxpayer was unsuccessful in claiming monetary damages from the IRS for a failure to respond to Form 2553. [*Girling Health Systems, Inc., v. U.S.*, 90-2 USTC 50,576 (Cls. Ct.), aff'd in *Girling Health Systems v. U.S.*, 92-1 USTC 50,570 (F. Cir.)] Girling Health Systems, Inc., had filed Form 2553 on October 15, 1986. The IRS did not respond to the election request for over a year. On December 15, 1987, the IRS informed Girling that its election request had been denied. Girling then sued the IRS for monetary damages. The corporation's argument was that the instructions to Form 2553 state that the IRS would generally respond to an election request within 60 days of filing. In 1990, the U.S. Claims Court heard the taxpayer's claim for monetary damages based on breach of contract by the IRS. The claims court decision for the IRS was appealed by Girling to the U.S. Court of Appeals for the Federal Circuit, which reached its decision on this case in November 1991. The appellate court upheld the lower court's decision. Therefore, a statement in instructions to a form apparently does not contractually bind the government, and does not give a taxpayer a right to sue for monetary damages.

515.52. Registered or certified mail receipt. As the foregoing discussion indicates, there is a risk that the IRS will lose or otherwise fail to properly process a corporation's Form 2553. An extra precaution, strongly advised, is to obtain a copy of Form 2553 stamped by the IRS acknowledging its receipt. As an alternative, the corporation or its tax advisor should be able to produce a registered or certified mail receipt (although the receipt would give no evidence of what was actually mailed). This receipt is prima facie evidence of delivery to the IRS. [§7502(c)]

515.53. Other evidence. When evidence of filing Form 2553 is missing, the taxpayer may be able to establish that the form was filed on time. Establishing this fact requires substantiation. Testimony by witnesses who actually saw the form deposited in the mail seems to be the only acceptable proof. However, this can be rebutted by the IRS offering credible evidence of nonreceipt. [*Zaretsky*, 26 TCM 1283 (1967); *Leve*, 49 TCM 1575 (1985)] Such uncontroverted testimony, however, may not meet the same standard as a registered or certified mail receipt.

> **CAUTION:** Most circuit courts appear willing to accept reliable testimony in lieu of a registered or certified mail receipt. That is not the case, however, in the Sixth Circuit. [See *Carroll*, TC Memo, 1994-229, 67 TCM (CCH) 2995, aff'd in *Carroll v. C.I.R.*, 71 F.3d 1228, 76 AFTR 2d 95 8115, 96-1 USTC P 50,010.]

> **OBSERVATION:** The IRS now accepts certain private couriers for delivery of tax returns. A receipt from one of these firms probably will be viewed as equivalent to a certified mail receipt. As of this writing, there have been no cases on this particular issue.

Unsubstantiated testimony by tax advisors and attorneys has been held as insufficient evidence [See *Thaddeus J. Zalewski*, 55 TCM 1430, TC Memo 1988-340; *T v. U.S.* (N.D. Ohio, 1990); and *Helen S. Leather*, TC Memo 1991-534.] In another case there was incontrovertible testimony that Form 2553 was mailed, but the IRS had not received the form. The corporation did not use registered or certified mail, however, and thus was unable to prove that it had mailed the form. The Tax Court upheld the IRS's disallowance of the S election. [*Smith*, TC Memo 1994-270; also see *Rudd*, TC Memo 1995-350] Courts have found that uncontroverted testimony was not proof of filing Form 2553. The corporation had no election in place. [*McLane Land & Timber Co. v. U.S.*, 80 AFTR 2d 97-6248, *Fankhauser*, TC Memo 1998-328, CCH Dec. 52,872(M)] In *Fankhauser*, the shareholder was not liable for a negligence penalty that the IRS had imposed.

> **OBSERVATION:** Some of the cases cited above should now be able to qualify for late election relief under §1361(b)(5). See section 550 of this chapter for a description of the extensive activity of this rule since its enactment in 1996.

None of the above provides proof that the corporation was eligible for S status. The corporation's records should clearly demonstrate that it met all of the qualifications on the date it filed Form 2553. The IRS is not bound by its letter accepting the S election, if the corporation did not file the election properly.[6] Similarly, a taxpayer argued that equitable estoppel applied where the corporation had never filed Form 2553, but the IRS had accepted Form 1120S for several years. On a later audit, the IRS determined that the corporation had never been an S corporation. Thus the IRS was allowed to adjust the tax of the corporation and its shareholders for all open years. [*Smith, S., Inc.*, 93-2 USTC 50, 514 (E.D. NC)]

> **PLANNING TIP:** The corporation should retain a permanent file that demonstrates that it met all of the eligibility requirements when it filed its S election. It should be able to demonstrate that its stock ledger showed the same holders and numbers of shares as shown on Form 2553. It should have a statement signed by each shareholder that he or she is a U.S. citizen or resident. If any shares were held by trusts, the corporation would be wise to retain a copy of the trust's governing instrument on file. The file should show that the trust has been reviewed for eligibility as a grantor trust, a beneficiary-controlled trust, an Electing Small Business Trust, or a QSST. The file should also indicate that any stock investments have been examined to demonstrate that the corporation was not a member of an affiliated group if the election was made prior to January 1, 1997.

---

[6] For example, *Combs* [57 TCM 288 (1989)] had a letter from the IRS acknowledging the election.

OBSERVATION: The burden of noncompliance has been lessened considerably by the Small Business Job Protection Act of 1996. See 550.2, below, for a discussion of relief provisions applicable to inadvertently defective S elections.

515.6. Substantial compliance. The IRS presumably has the option of enforcing the letter of the law in all instances. As some of the cases discussed in this chapter demonstrate, the courts are unlikely to overrule the IRS when it denies a corporation S status due to a defective election. However, the IRS often overlooks a minor defect under the doctrine of "substantial compliance."

5

This doctrine appears to be used most often when a QSST is a shareholder in an S corporation. See the discussion under 540.1., below. It has also been used in other contexts. For example, a recent ruling described a situation in which some stock was held by QSSTs, whereas other shares were held by the beneficiaries outright. The beneficiaries had consented to the corporation's S election in their capacities as individual shareholders, but not in their roles as QSST beneficiaries. The IRS was willing to accept the election, on the grounds that the corporation was in substantial compliance with the law. [PLR 9626035]

When evidence of filing Form 2553 is missing, the taxpayer may be able to establish that the form was filed on time. Establishment of this fact requires substantiation. Testimony by actual witnesses who have seen the form deposited in the mail seems to be the only acceptable proof. However, this can be rebutted by the IRS offering credible evidence of nonreceipt. [*Zaretsky*, 26 TCM 1283 (1967); *Leve*, 49 TCM 1575 (1985)] Unsubstantiated testimony by tax advisors and attorneys has been held as insufficient evidence. [See *Thaddeus J. Zalewski*, 55 TCM 1430, TC Memo 1988-340; *Trimarco v. U.S.* (N.D. Ohio, 1990); and *Helen S. Leather*, TC Memo 1991-534.]

520. Timing of the S election for a new corporation

In most situations, a corporation that has decided to become an S corporation will want to do so as soon as possible. In the case of a new corporation, an effective S election for its first taxable year may allow the corporation to avoid problems such as built-in gains tax (Chapter 11), complex distribution problems (Chapter 7), passive investment income problems (Chapter 12), and LIFO recapture (Chapter 3). In the case of an existing C corporation, the parties may want to begin the ten-year recognition period for built-in gains at the earliest possible date. They may also want to minimize excessive compensation problems, or allow shareholder deduction of corporate losses at the earliest possible time. Thus both newly formed and pre-existing corporations must be cognizant of the rules regarding taxable years at the time of an intended S election.

520.1. Considerations for a new corporation. As discussed above, the S election will be effective for the taxable year in which it is filed only if it is filed within 2 months and 15 days after the beginning of the taxable year. The first taxable year begins on the earliest date that the corporation (1) acquires assets, (2) issues shares, or (3) commences business.

A new corporation that has already missed its deadline for filing the S election may file for its second taxable year. For its first year it will be a C corporation. A new corporation can accelerate its S election by selecting the earliest possible taxable year as its first year. It can then elect S status for its second year.

EXAMPLE 5 - 9: AGM Corporation begins business on June 23, 1995. Its deadline for filing an S election for its first year is September 7, 1995. On September 14, 1995, it realizes that it should have made an S election. It can file a return on September 15 for its year ended June 30. It can file Form 2553 on September 15, which will take effect for the taxable year beginning July 1, 1995.

PLANNING TIP: Selection of a fiscal year in order to accelerate a new corporation's first year end is an excellent rescue technique and may compensate, at least in part, for a failure to make a timely S election for the first year of the corporation's existence. There are some hazards, if the corporation is unable to have an S election take effect before one or more of the shareholders have transferred appreciated property. See Chapter 14, at 1415.7., for additional discussion of this topic.

5

In order to use a fiscal year, a taxpayer must keep books and records based on that year. If a taxpayer keeps no books or records, the calendar year must be used. [Regs. §1.441-1T(g)] Thus a corporation that arbitrarily selected a taxable year solely in order to make a timely S election for its second year was denied S status. [*Columbia Steak House II, Inc.*, TC Memo 1981-142, 41 TCM 1163]

EXAMPLE 5 - 10: AGM, from Example 5 - 8, would need to produce books and records for its fiscal year ended June 30, 1995, if the IRS were ever to challenge the effective date of its S election. If the corporation had no books or records for the fiscal year, the IRS could assert that the corporation had used the calendar year. If the IRS were successful on this point, the corporation would be a C corporation through December 31, 1995.

520.2. Considerations for an existing C corporation. When a corporation has been a C corporation for any length of time, it will face some problems, such as corporate-level taxes, in making the selection. The LIFO recapture and passive income tax will probably not be serious, since the corporation has had little time to accumulate earnings and profits or build up a LIFO reserve. The built-in gains tax, however, may be significant. See Chapter 11 for further discussion of this tax. A corporation's net unrealized built-in gain is measured by the fair market value of its assets, less the aggregate adjusted basis of its assets. A corporation that has always been an S corporation is generally exempt from the built-in gains tax; a single taxable year as a C corporation will subject it to this tax.

EXAMPLE 5 - 11: AGM, from Example 5 - 8, was capitalized by one shareholder, Hubert. He transferred to the corporation property with a basis of $100,000 and fair market value of $1,000,000. The transfer was covered by §351 and no gain was recognized. See Chapter 14 for discussion of §351 and its related rules. If AGM had filed its S election in time for it to take effect on June 23, AGM would not be subject to the built-in gains tax.

If AGM filed as a C corporation, with an 8-day short-period taxable year, it would be subject to the built-in gains tax. Up to $900,000 of its gains will be subject to double taxation for 10 years.

OBSERVATION: Although the built-in gains tax is intended to subject corporations to the double tax on appreciation realized in Subchapter C years, it is not limited to appreciation in value during those years. A gain realized by an individual shareholder that was not recognized in a §351 transfer or any other tax-free exchange is not exempt from the built-in gains tax, if the corporation was ever a C corporation. A gain realized by an individual shareholder on property transferred to the corporation will be exempt from the built-in gains tax only if the corporation files an effective S election for its first taxable year.

Under certain circumstances, a C corporation may change its taxable year without prior permission. [Regs. §1.442-1(c)] This change requires filing Form 1128 within 1 month and 15 days of the end of the short period following the last full 12-month year. [Regs. §1.442-1(b)(1)] A C corporation, however, may not use this provision if it makes an S election for the year following the short period. [Regs. §1.442-1(c)(2)(v)] Therefore, an existing C corporation cannot use an automatic-year change to accelerate its S election.

EXAMPLE 5 - 12: Yearco is a C corporation that has been using a June 30 fiscal year. On November 5, 1996, the corporation decides to make an S election, and wants to have its S status commence as soon as possible. It is too late to make an election for the year beginning July 1, 1996. The corporation could file Form 1128 on or before November 15, 1996, and change to a year ending September 30 or October 31. This change would not be valid, however, if Yearco made an S election for its next taxable year. Therefore, the corporation cannot have an S election take effect before the beginning of its next regular year—July 1, 1997.

OBSERVATION: The IRS changed its position, and allowed several C corporations to change to a short period immediately before they made an S election. [Notice 97-3, 1997-1 IRB 8; Notice 97-20, 1997-10 IRB 5] In these cases, it was necessary for the short year to end December 31, 1996, and the S corporation year to begin on January 1, 1997. This provision has not been extended to any later year, and Regulations §1.442-1(c)(2)(v) is again in force. Recently, the IRS has issued rulings allowing late requests for changes in years by C corporations that intend to become S corporations. Curiously, the IRS is willing to allow a late election to change taxable years, but it comments that will not rule on a corporation's eligibility to make an S election for its next taxable year. [See PLRs 9842025, 9840023, 9840022, 9845007, 9845006, 199906048, 199906043, 199906041, 199909055.]

There are some other techniques to accelerate eligibility. For example, a parent corporation merged into a wholly owned subsidiary (downstream merger). See discussion at 515.22. If a corporation is unable to close its C corporation year early, it may wait for the start of its next fiscal year and become an S corporation on that date. The corporation will be allowed an automatic change to the calendar year in its first year as an S corporation. [Temporary Regs. §18.1378-1(b)(2)(i)]

525. Election after prior termination.

Corporations that have terminated their S elections are subject to a waiting period before they may again elect S corporation status, even though they may still meet all of the other requirements of a small business corporation. Chapter 13 discusses the methods by which an S election may be terminated.

525.1. General rule. As a general rule, there is a five-year waiting period to re-elect S corporation status after termination. [§1362(g)]

SUMMARY OF AUTHORITY: CODE SECTION 1362(g)

- A corporation that has terminated a prior S election must wait five years before making a new S election.
- The five-year wait applies to certain successor corporations.
- The IRS may waive the five-year period.

In counting the five-year period, the IRS accepts a short year in the same manner as a 12-month year. [PLR 9033041]

525.2. Certain elections under prior law. The Small Business Job Protection Act of 1996 made substantial changes to Subchapter S of the Internal Revenue Code. Because of the magnitude of these changes, §1317(b) of the Act provided a relief provision for former S corporations with terminated elections. It states that for purposes of §1362(g) (relating to election after termination), any termination under §1362(d) of such Code in a tax year beginning before January 1, 1997, will not be taken into account.

SUMMARY OF AUTHORITY: SECTION 1317(b)
THE SMALL BUSINESS JOB PROTECTION ACT OF 1996

- There is no waiting period to re-elect S status if the termination took place before January 1, 1996.
- There is no need to request that the IRS consent to such re-elections.
- For purposes of the five-year rule in §1362(g), any termination of Subchapter S status in effect before January 1, 1997, is not taken into account. Thus, any small business corporation that had terminated its S corporation election within the five-year period from December 31, 1992, to December 31, 1996, may re-elect Subchapter S status without having to apply for a ruling from the IRS.

525.3. Reduced waiting period. For the near future, the relief provisions described at 525.2. will serve to mitigate most corporate re-election problems after a prior termination. However, the existing body of case law and rulings is still applicable and should be looked to for possible sources of relief when a corporation's S election has been terminated in a taxable year beginning after January 1, 1997.

The IRS has the power to reduce the period to one year. The IRS position on reducing the waiting period is that it will allow early re-election if the corporation meets two criteria:

1. There must have been a change in ownership of more than 50% of the corporation's shares since termination of the prior election.
2. The prior termination must have been beyond the control of the current shareholders. [Regs. §1.1362-5(a)]

The key factor appears to be the change in ownership since the prior termination. The IRS appears to require little, if any, further justification. The change in ownership is most often accomplished by a sale of a majority of the corporation's stock. [PLRs 8847004, 8930010, 9003057, 9014059, 9014062, 9015015, 9025029, 9027015, 9045006, 9050050, 9302004, 9308011, 9432016, 9848014, 199916032, 199918031] It can also be accomplished by a combination of redemption and sale of stock to new shareholders. [PLRs 8825023, 8910076, 9133020, 9139010, 9135029, 9149020, 9344008, 9626024, 9644064, 9709011, 9714013, 9825021, 9825022]

If at least half of the corporation's shares are still owned by the same persons who owned them when the prior S election terminated, the IRS has been unwilling to shorten the waiting period. For example, the IRS refused to shorten the period when exactly one-half of the corporation's shares had changed hands since it had terminated an S election. [PLR 8823036] However, in a more recent ruling, the IRS reduced the waiting period for a corporation that had inadvertently issued shares to an ineligible shareholder and thus terminated its S election. The shares were subsequently reacquired and, at the same time, exactly 50% of the outstanding stock was issued to an unrelated party. [PLR 9436034] In another recent ruling, the IRS allowed the reduced waiting period when only 25% of shares changed hands, but remaining shareholders were not in a position to prevent the earlier termination. [PLR 199904008]

The reason for termination of an S election seems to have no relevance in attempting to persuade the IRS to reduce the period. Some corporations have tried, but failed, to receive permission for an early re-election, if their elections had been terminated due to other changes in the tax law. [PLRs 8511016, 8524024, 8547048, 8541078, 8537050, 8536009] A corporation that had terminated its S election in order to maintain its fiscal year was denied permission to reduce the waiting period. [PLR 8922087] Even when there is a good business purpose for terminating an S election, the IRS looks only to a change in ownership. For instance, a corporation's bonding company had insisted that the corporation revoke its S election. The IRS denied permission for an early re-election, because the decision to terminate was within the control of the current shareholders. [PLR 9047010] There have been other Letter Rulings with similar holdings.[7]

Two recent rulings indicate the firmness of the IRS's position that there is no reason for which it allows early re-election, if the old shareholders are still in control. In one situation the six persons who had owned all of the stock in a domestic S corporation sold their shares to a foreign corporation, at which point the domestic corporation's S election was terminated. In October 1990, the foreign corporation sold all of the shares to a domestic holding company, in which two of the former shareholders owned 46.7% and in which the spouse of another of the former shareholders owned 21.7%. The reacquired corporation was then merged into the holding company, which then requested permission to make an S election. Although the former shareholders directly owned only 46.7% of the successor corporation, the IRS attributed the current ownership of the former shareholder's spouse to the former shareholder, and denied the corporation's request. [PLR 9144015]

In another circumstance, the shareholders of an S corporation had contributed all of their stock to another corporation, which caused the acquired corporation to lose its S election. For valid business reasons, the shareholders then reacquired their stock, slightly more than two years later. The IRS denied permission for the corporation to re-elect S status before the five-year waiting period expired. [PLR 9149020]

> **OBSERVATION:** It appears futile to request a waiver of the five-year waiting period for re-election, unless more than 50% of the stock is owned by persons who did not own any shares when the corporation terminated its prior S election. The business purposes for the prior termination seem to have no impact on the ruling policy. The IRS apparently has adopted an attribution rule, whereby former shareholders are treated as owning what related parties now own. A transfer of a controlling interest to family members apparently will not enable a corporation to make a new S election without waiting five years.

The IRS recently appears to have softened its position that it will grant no early reelection of S status when the corporation is controlled by the same persons who controlled the corporation at the date of the prior termination. In one situation, a sole shareholder sold all of her stock in an S corporation to another corporation. That event terminated the S corporation's election. Shortly thereafter, the parent corporation was merged into the former S corporation. The owners (who did not include the seller of the stock) applied for early re-election. The IRS granted the early re-election. [PLR 9323032] This ruling also points out some of the problems that can result from poor planning and procedural compliance errors.

The IRS allowed early re-election when a minority shareholder had transferred stock to an ineligible shareholder with the express intention of terminating the S election and then reacquired the stock. The IRS held that the persons in control of the corporation had not intended to terminate the S election. [PLR 9340047]

In another recent ruling, a minority shareholder had transferred stock to an ineligible person, thus terminating the corporation's S election. The minority shareholder then reacquired the shares, and the corporation redeemed them. The corporation was allowed to reelect S status within the five-year period. [PLR 9628006]

---

[7] See PLR 8511014, in which a corporation did not attempt to explain any reason for a voluntary termination. The request was denied. In contrast, in PLR 9030009, the IRS reduced the waiting period for no apparent reason.

OBSERVATION: It appears that several of the terminations could have been prevented if the corporation had enforceable transfer restrictions on its stock. See Chapter 2, at 225.4.

As is discussed in Chapter 12, an S election may terminate when the corporation has accumulated earnings and profits from C corporation years and also has excessive passive investment income. In November 1992, the IRS issued Final Regulations that adopted new definitions of *passive investment income* that were more favorable to the taxpayers than previous cases and rulings had been. Thus, corporations that believed they had passive investment income found out that the income no longer met the new rules. In one situation, an S corporation had revoked its S election because it believed that the election would be terminated due to excessive passive investment income. After it had revoked the election, it determined that its income would not be passive investment income. It applied for an early re-election. Although none of the shares had changed hands since the revocation, the IRS granted permission for the corporation to make an early re-election. [PLR 9418005]

525.4. Successor corporations. The waiting period also applies to successor corporations. [§1362(g)] A successor corporation is one in which at least 50% of shares are owned (directly or indirectly) by persons who owned at least 50% of another corporation that had terminated its S election. The successor corporation must have a substantial portion of the assets of the corporation that had terminated its S election. [Regs. §1.1362-5(b)] There is no definition of "direct or indirect" ownership, or "substantial portion" of assets. The law is clearly part of an attempt to stop corporations from undergoing simple Type F reorganizations (explained in Chapter 16) in order to change identity. It would frustrate a variety of other attempts as well. Consider the following example:

EXAMPLE 5 - 13: ABC Corporation was an S corporation until it terminated its S election in 1996. At the end of 1996, its shareholders decide they would like to have the S election back in force. Accordingly, they contribute all of the stock of XYZ to a holding company, then liquidate XYZ into the new holding company on December 31, 1996. On January 1, 1997, they decide to have the new corporation file an S election. It would be barred from electing until five years after ABC had terminated its S election. Note that it would not matter whether the transfers of property were taxable or tax-deferred. The new corporation would be a successor corporation.

The IRS has dealt with successor corporations in the same manner as it has dealt with the original corporations. For example, a split-off subsidiary of a former S corporation did not need to wait five years to make an S election, because the controlling shareholders of the new corporation had not controlled the old corporation. [PLR 8932065] (See Chapter 17 for a discussion of split-offs and other corporate divisions.)

OBSERVATION: The Code does not give the IRS specific regulatory authority to define a successor corporation. Nor does the Code define a successor corporation. The Regulations do not give any well-defined mechanical test, or safe harbor, as to what constitutes a successor corporation. The Code does, however, give the IRS the power to approve or disapprove S elections of successor corporations. As a consequence of the language of the Code, any corporation that has acquired assets from a former S corporation and is controlled by the same shareholders who controlled the former S corporation will more than likely fall within the special re-election provision of S corporation status provided by the Small Business Job Protection Act of 1996. If the termination occurs in a taxable year beginning after January 1, 1997, the former S corporation should apply for a ruling if it intends to make an S election within five years of the termination of the former S corporation's election.

At certain times, either the Congress or the IRS has granted blanket permission to waive the five-year period. Blanket permission to re-elect before the five-year period was mandated by Committee Reports to Subchapter S Revision Act of 1982. The IRS acknowledged this rule in several Letter Rulings. [PLRs 8306016 and 8306041]

The IRS granted blanket waivers of the five-year period in late 1986 for corporations that had terminated their elections before October 22, 1986. These corporations could re-elect any time before January 1, 1987. [Rev. Rul. 86-141, 1986-2 CB 151] One corporation revoked its S election on October 31, 1986, ten days after the period specified by the IRS for which immediate re-election would be allowed. The corporation filed an S election on December 31, 1986, and the election was disallowed by the IRS. The corporation filed its return for 1987 as a C corporation and sued the IRS for the additional tax liability that resulted from denial of S status. A district court awarded the corporation damages, stating that the IRS had arbitrarily exceeded its powers by refusing to grant the corporation's new S election. [*White Rubber Corporation v. U.S.*, 92-1 USTC 50,101 (N.D. Ohio)]

5

525.5. Relationship to inadvertent terminations. The provision governing inadvertent termination relief has been one of the most important, and most widely used, rules since it was enacted in 1982. [§1362(f)] (The rules are discussed in detail in Chapter 14.) When a corporation has accidentally become ineligible, it may request relief to avoid losing its S election. The IRS generally grants this relief, although it may require certain conditions. If the corporation meets the conditions, the IRS generally grants inadvertent termination relief. Since the inadvertent termination relief provision treats the corporation as if its S election had continued uninterrupted, the waiting period has no relevance to the corporation's status as an S corporation.

525.6. Effect of former ineffective S election. A corporation may file Form 2553 but never become an S corporation. This can happen for a number of reasons:

1. There may have been an error in the Form 2553 the corporation submitted. In this case, the IRS may grant the election under the doctrine of "substantial compliance." Substantial compliance appears most frequently with respect to QSST elections and is discussed in that context below.
2. A corporation might have filed Form 2553 at a time when the corporation was ineligible. Unless the ineligibility is related to a trust's ownership of shares, which is the most frequent application of substantial compliance, the S election would be ineffective.
3. Occasionally, a corporation files an S election that could be valid, but revokes the election before it ever takes effect. Procedures for revocation are discussed in full in Chapter 14. This phenomenon occurred frequently in late 1986 and early 1987 when many corporations rushed S elections to avoid the built-in gains tax. Some of the corporations were ineligible, and others immediately revoked their elections due to unforeseen problems.

A concern that occasionally surfaces is whether the five-year waiting period applies to a corporation that has filed Form 2553 but has never become an S corporation. The Regulations state that these corporations do not need to wait five years before filing a new election, since they never have been S corporations. [Regs. §1.1362-5(c)] The IRS policy has been consistent with §1.1362-5 in three different types of factual situations:

1. The IRS has held that there is no waiting period to refile when a corporation originally filed a defective S election. [PLR 8925077]

2. Corporations that have revoked S elections before they ever became effective have also been given permission to make S elections in any future year. [PLRs 8828050, 8909044, 8918090, 8922016, 8923016, 8924083, 8933010, 8943052, 9001059, 9013025, 9017041, 9019007, 9023032, 9030022, 9034036, 9036021, 9036035, 9040033, 9044023, 9044041, 9049014, 9104030, 9139010, 9141047, 9305004]
3. Corporations that have filed apparently valid S elections, but were ineligible on the date the election was filed, have been allowed to immediately file valid S elections. [PLRs 8835007, 8842007, 8918090, 8925077, 9022023]

5

EXAMPLE 5 - 14: King Corporation filed an S election in 1996 to take effect on January 1, 1997. At the time it filed its S election, it had an ineligible shareholder. In early 1997, it discovers that it has been ineligible, and it terminates the interest of the ineligible shareholder. If it meets all of the other criteria, it can now file a new election immediately.

OBSERVATION: For years beginning after December 31, 1992, the Final Regulations provide sufficient authority for filing a new S election without permission, and without seeking a ruling, when a corporation has filed Form 2553 but its S election was never in effect.

525.7. Effect of former QSub status. A corporation may be treated as a QSub if all of its stock is owned by an S corporation. See discussion in Chapter 14, at 1435.4. If the corporation then loses its QSub status, it is treated as coming into existence as a new corporation on the day of the disqualifying event. [§1361(b)(3)(C), Proposed Regs. §1.1361-5(a)(1)(iii)]

A corporation that loses its status as a QSub generally is not permitted to become an S corporation or another QSub for five years from the date of the terminating event. [§1361(b)(3)(D)] The legislative history is for this is scant, although the rule appears to be a measure to prevent a corporation from using QSub status to circumvent the general five-year waiting period of §1362(g).

The Proposed Regulations issued in 1998 provide a sensible interpretation of this rule. In general, while a corporation that loses its QSub status may not become a QSub or make an S election for five years without permission from the IRS [Proposed Regs. §1.1361-5(d)(1)], the corporation can move freely between QSub status and stand-alone S corporation status, as long as there is no period in which the corporation is a C corporation. [Proposed Regs. §1.1361-5(d)(2)]

EXAMPLE 5 - 15: Q Corporation is a QSub, owned entirely by PS Corporation, an S corporation, until July 16, 1998. On that date PS sells all of the stock of Q. If the buyers include any ineligible person, Q will become a C corporation as of July 17, 1998. It will then be ineligible to become an S corporation or a QSub before July 17, 2003. If the buyer is an S corporation, however, it may elect to treat Q as a QSub beginning July 17, 1998. Similarly, if the buyers are eligible to hold shares in an S corporation, they may cause Q to elect to be an S corporation beginning July 17, 1998.

Administratively, the IRS has been issuing rulings that are entirely consistent with the Proposed Regulations position. The five-year re-election period was waived for a former QSub after shares were distributed to parent S corporation's shareholders as a result of divisive reorganization. [PLR 9823016] Similarly, a QSub of one S corporation was immediately allowed to become a QSub of another S corporation when the first corporation sold the stock of the subsidiary to the second S corporation. [PLR 199909011] Also, the IRS has allowed S corporations to acquire the stock of an S corporation and make QSub elections, with no mention of the five-year waiting period. [See PLRs 9827029, 9828025, 9842022, 9843029, 9843034.]

530. Shareholder consent.

All shareholders must consent to the corporation's S election.

SUMMARY OF AUTHORITY: CODE SECTION 1362(a)(2)

- All shareholders must consent to a corporation's election to be an S corporation.
- Consent is required only from persons who hold shares on the date the corporation files its S election.
- A corporation that does not obtain consent to the election from all shareholders will not have a valid S election in effect.

Form 2553 provides spaces for shareholder names and consent signatures. All shareholders at the date the election is filed must consent to the S election. [Regs. §1.1362-6(b)(2)] They may sign on the face of the form or attach a separate consent statement. [Regs. §1.1362-6(b)(3)(i)]

OBSERVATION: In a non-tax case, a court held that consenting to an S election imposes a fiduciary duty to one's fellow shareholders to refrain from any action that would devalue the corporation. [*Chesterton, Inc. v. Chesterton*, 80 AFTR 2d 97-7280 (1997)]

530.1. Persons required to consent. Any person who is treated as a part-owner or co-owner must also sign his or her consent. [Regs. §1.1362-6(b)(2)(i)] These persons include spouses, if the shares are held in joint tenancy, tenancy in common, or community property.

EXAMPLE 5 - 16: Mary and Gary (who are married, but not to each other) are equal shareholders in the MG Corporation. The corporation is located in Illinois, a separate property state. Mary is a resident of Illinois. Gary is a resident of Washington, a community property state. The corporation files Form 2553, making an S election. The shares are issued to Mary and Gary, as individual holders. Mary and Gary must consent to the election. Mary's husband need not sign a consent. Gary's wife, however, must sign the consent.

When the actual shareholder is an estate or a trust or a person not legally able to sign, another person is required to sign on behalf of that shareholder. [Regs. §1.1362-6(b)(2)] The corporation must be careful to ascertain all persons who are considered to be shareholders under state law. In some cases, corporations have been denied S status for failure to include persons who did not actually received stock certificates but who had legal standing as shareholders under state law. [*Thomas E. Bone*, 52 TC 913 (1969); *Murray R. Denemark*, 35 TCM 1170, TC Memo 1967-267; *Cabintaxi Corporation*, 68 TC 49 (1994), TC Memo 1994-316; Rev. Rul. 74-150, 1974-1 CB 241; Rev. Rul. 72-257, 1972-1 CB 270]

If shares are held by	*The person who must sign is*
Estate	Executor or administrator
Grantor trust	Deemed owner
QSST	Beneficiary
Electing Small Business Trust	Trustee
Certain tax-exempt organizations	Chief Executive Officer or administrator
Minor	Self or legal representative

OBSERVATION: The Small Business Job Protection Act of 1996 permits Electing Small Business Trusts to become shareholders in an S corporation. Certain tax-exempt organizations may also become S corporation shareholders in taxable years beginning after December 31, 1997. No Regulations have been issued describing how these organizations will consent to the S election. The tax-exempt organization will be

> regarded as one shareholder. It seems logical that the organization's Chief Executive Office or administrator would sign the consent. Electing Small Business Trusts present a more complex situation. The trust must elect to be treated as an Electing Small Business Trust. This election is made by the trustee. Each potential current beneficiary is counted as one shareholder. If there are no potential current beneficiaries, the trust will be treated as the shareholder. The IRS has provided no guidance at this time on the handling of consents by potential current beneficiaries.

As is discussed briefly in Chapter 2, at 215.6., there may be a nominal shareholder and a beneficial shareholder, in which case it is important that the beneficial owner consent to the S election. S elections were found invalid when beneficial owners did not consent, even when the nominal owners did consent. [*Cabintaxi*, TC Memo 1994-261; *Payne*, TC Memo 1998-227]

When a shareholder dies before the S election is filed, the executor or administrator of the shareholder's estate is the proper party to give consent. [Rev. Rul. 92-82, 1992-2 CB 238]

EXAMPLE 5 - 17: Panco was a calendar-year C corporation through December 31, 1995. On March 1, 1996, one of its shareholders, Rich, died. The other shareholders, including the executor of Rich's estate, decided to convert Panco to S status. They filed the S election on March 10, 1996. On that date, Rich's stock was held by his estate. If the election is to be effective for Panco's taxable year beginning January 1, 1996, all of the shareholders who have owned stock from January 1, 1996, through March 10, 1996, must consent to the corporation's S election. The executor of Rich's estate will consent to the election in two capacities:

1. On behalf of Rich, who owned the shares from January 1, 1996, through February 28, 1996
2. On behalf of Rich's estate, which owned the shares from March 1, 1996, through March 10, 1996

In most cases, the person required to sign is the same person who signs other legal documents on behalf of the entity or person who owns the shares. Accordingly, there apparently have been few problems with obtaining proper signatures. Occasionally, there may be some problems when a spouse who has joint ownership is unwilling to sign. There have probably been some instances where the parties are unaware of the joint ownership, although there has been no noticeable ruling activity on this situation.

In one instance, shares in an S corporation were owned by several QSSTs. The beneficiary of each trust was a minor. The mother of the children was their legal guardian, and she signed all necessary consents on behalf of the children. The mother, however, was a nonresident alien. The IRS accepted the trusts as eligible shareholders and accepted the mother's signature as valid consent. [PLR 9044023] In another instance, the sole shareholder of a corporation had died. His widow had community interest in one-half of the shares and a usufructuary interest in the remainder of the shares. The IRS treated the widow as the sole shareholder. Her consent was all that was necessary for the S election to take effect. [PLR 9018048]

The most frequently encountered problem is the absence of consent by the beneficiary of a QSST. The tax advisor should be aware that it is the beneficiary (or guardian), rather than the trustee, who must sign the consent to the S election. This problem receives more discussion under the QSST consent, below.

530.2. Time for filing consent. Although the Code is specific on the deadline for filing the election, it is silent on the time for filing the consent. Rulings cited above demonstrate that there is no extension for filing the election, but the IRS is willing to grant an extension for filing a shareholder consent. [Regs. §1.1362-6(b)(3)(iii)] The IRS requires the taxpayer to demonstrate that there was reasonable cause for the delay and that the interests of the government will not be jeopardized. The consent must be filed within the period granted by the IRS, and it must be accompanied by consent statements of all shareholders who have not previously consented to the S election. The IRS has not extended the time for a shareholder consent, if there were other flaws in the election. [*Thomas E. Bone*, 52 TC 913 (1969)] However, this case was decided before late or defective elections could be accepted by the IRS. See discussion of relief provisions at 550.4.

530.3. Change of shareholders during the year the election is filed. There are special rules when shares change hands in the same year in which a corporation files its election:

1. Persons who initially acquired shares after the corporation has filed its S election do not need to consent. [§1362(a)(2)]
2. If the S election is to take effect for the taxable year after the corporation files the election, persons who have already terminated their interests in the corporation will not need to consent.

However, if the election is filed by the corporation within 2 months and 15 days of the beginning of the taxable year, the former shareholders may have a significant impact on the effective date of the S election. If there was an ineligible shareholder during the tax year but before the election was filed, the election is effective for the next tax year. If there was an eligible shareholder during the year, but that person sold his or her shares before the S election was filed, the S election is effective for the next tax year, unless a consent is obtained from the former shareholder. [§1362(b)(2)]

EXAMPLE 5 - 18: On January 1, 1996, Carrie owned 49% of the stock of Union Corporation. On February 1, 1996, she sold all of her stock to Jerry. Gary, Harry, and Mary each owned 17% of the stock for the entire year. The corporation uses the calendar year for tax purposes.

The corporation makes an S election by filing Form 2553 on March 3, 1996. Assuming that the corporation meets all of the requirements of a small business corporation on March 3, 1996, the election is valid. There may, however, be some question as to its effective date. If Carrie was ineligible to hold shares in an S corporation, the election could not take effect until January 1, 1997. If Carrie was eligible to hold shares in an S corporation, the election still could not take effect until January 1, 1997, unless Carrie also consented to the election.

OBSERVATION: When a corporation discovers that it is missing a consent, it should immediately attempt to secure an extension of time for filing the consent. There is no rule that the corporation must apply for the extension at the time it files Form 2553. It should be prepared to demonstrate, however, that there has been no tax avoidance motive, and no actual tax avoidance caused by the missing consent. As an extra precaution, it may file a protective Form 2553 at the time it requests the extension. If the extension of time is granted for the original Form 2553, the corporation will need to file a new Form 2553, with the consent of all persons who hold shares at the time the new form is filed.

This approach is not without some risk, and it should not be undertaken without full knowledge of the IRS. The corporation might want to request a Letter Ruling to assure the result. There could be considerable trouble if there have been changes in shareholders since the original Form 2553 was filed. The taxpayer should base its request on the doctrine of substantial compliance.

EXAMPLE 5 - 19: PRI Tech, Inc., files Form 2553 in January 1994. One of its shareholders lives in Texas, a community property state. That shareholder's spouse was not a shareholder in the corporation, and did not consent to the election. In 1996, the corporation discovers the error. It should file a protective Form 2553, for which the S election will take effect at the earliest possible date, and request an extension for consent on the original Form 2553. PRI should include the consent of all persons, including the Texas spouse, on the new Form 2553.

The IRS may accept the protective Form 2553 as the extended version of the original form, or it may require filing of a new Form 2553. As long as all of the shareholders had properly reported their shares of income or loss for the corporation, there should be a strong argument for acceptance of the S election under the doctrine of substantial compliance.

535. Taxable year election.

The taxable year election must be filed, or at least anticipated, when the corporation files Form 2553. The rules are somewhat disjointed. On Form 2553, the corporation must indicate whether it is adopting, retaining, or changing its taxable year. [Form 2553, item O] A new corporation would be adopting a taxable year. An existing corporation would either retain or change to a permitted year. Any corporation making an S election can adopt the calendar year, with no special permission or special election.

If an existing corporation has been using a fiscal year, filing Form 2553 constitutes an automatic change to the calendar year. The corporation does not need to file Form 1128 or request permission. (See Chapter 4 for discussion of the years available to S corporations.)

535.1. Automatic fiscal year election. A new or existing corporation that qualifies for automatic approval of a natural business year end (or the shareholder year end) should elect its year on Form 2553. [Form 2553, item P] The corporation must attach the gross receipts schedule for its last 47 months, so that the IRS can verify the calculation. No other form needs to be filed to select the natural business year end or shareholder year end. As discussed in Chapter 4, a corporation that meets one of these two automatic years is not requesting permission, and needs no response from the IRS in order to use one of these years. There is no ruling fee for election of a year that is automatically granted.

535.2. Requested fiscal years and backup elections. A corporation that requests a fiscal year but does not qualify for automatic approval must request the year end with its Form 2553. [Form 2553, Part Q, box 1] It will be sent a bill for a processing fee (see Chapter 4). The corporation must then decide what its options are, if the IRS denies the request for the fiscal year. If the corporation uses the fiscal year without IRS approval, it is not using a permitted year and cannot be an S corporation. However, the IRS gives the corporation two options for obtaining a valid S election in case the request for the fiscal year is denied:

1. It can make a backup calendar-year election. [Form 2553, Part Q, box 3]
2. It can make a backup §444 election. [Form 2553, Part Q, box 2] If it makes a backup §444 election, it can also make a secondary backup calendar-year election.

EXAMPLE 5 - 20: RWJ Corporation is a C corporation that has been using a June fiscal year. In July 1996, it files an S election. It has a four-year operating history, but it does not quite meet the 25% test for a natural business year end. It requests permission to continue its June year end under Revenue Ruling 87-57. [Rev. Rul. 87-57, 1987-2 CB 117] It checks the backup §444 and backup calendar-year elections on Form 2553. It has assured the validity of its S election, and now it has three possibilities open to it for its taxable year:

- If the IRS approves its request for a June year end, it will be an S corporation with a June fiscal year.
- If the IRS disapproves the June fiscal year, it may make a §444 election to use a September, October, or November year end.
- If the IRS disapproves the June fiscal year, and RWJ decides not to make a §444 election, fails to make a proper §444 election, or becomes disqualified to make a §444

election (e.g., it becomes a member of a tiered structure), it will be a calendar-year S corporation.

If RWJ had not made any of the backup elections, and the IRS denied the fiscal-year request, presumably the corporation would continue to use its June year end, although it would not be an S corporation.

535.3. Section 444 election and backup. A corporation that wants to elect a §444 year should indicate its intention to do so when it files Form 2553. [Form 2553, Part R, box 1] Without this indication it cannot make a §444 election. Unlike a natural business year end election, however, a valid §444 election has additional requirements:

1. To actually make the election, the corporation must also fill out Form 8716. Form 8716 is filed with the service center where the corporation files its tax returns. (Form 8716 is used by partnerships and personal service corporations as well as S corporations. Aside from this fact, there is no reason for the additional paperwork.)
2. The deadline for filing Form 8716 is "the 15th day of the fifth month following the month that includes the 1st day of the tax year for which the election will be effective" [Regs. §1.444-3T(b)(1)(i)] (in other words, the 15th day of the sixth month) or the due date (without extensions) for the tax year for which the §444 election is to take effect. As a matter of convenience, Form 8716 can be filed along with Form 2553.
3. There must be a duplicate filing of Form 8716 with the first Form 1120S. It will not be necessary to file this form again in future years.

EXAMPLE 5 - 21: AAA Corporation begins its first taxable year on March 5, 1996. It immediately files Form 2553, effective for its first taxable year. It elects a September 30 year end under §444. It must file Form 8716 on or before August 15, 1996 (the fifteenth day of the sixth month of its year).

If the corporation began business on September 1, 1996, and adopted a September 30 year end, it would need to file Form 8716 on or before December 15, 1996 (the due date for its first return, without extension). It could extend its return, but not Form 8716.

When the corporation files Form 2553, it may make a backup election to use December 31, in case it is unable to make a §444 election. [Form 2553, Part R, box 2]

535.4. Election of 52–53-week taxable year. In general, taxpayers can adopt a year that consistently ends on the same weekday. [§441(f)] The weekday may be the date that is the last such day in one calendar month or falls nearest the end of the calendar month.

EXAMPLE 5 - 22: Fifty-Two Corporation intends to close its taxable year on a Saturday in December. It could select the last Saturday in December, or the Saturday that falls nearest December 31. Under the latter option, the actual closing would occasionally take place in January.

An S corporation may elect a 52–53-week year, by reference to the taxable year that the corporation may otherwise use. For example, an S corporation could use a December 52–53-week year without permission. However, it must indicate that it is doing so when it files Form 2553. [Form 2553, Part I]

The IRS has indicated a willingness to accept late requests for changes to the 52–53-week year. [PLR 9316030] Perhaps this leniency is due to the extremely limited tax deferral opportunity of this type of year.

The 52–53-week year presents no tax deferral opportunities to the shareholders. The shareholders must report all of their income or loss items in the year that is the reference point of the 52–53-week year. [Regs. §1.441-2T(e)(2)(ii)]

EXAMPLE 5 - 23: ROM Corporation is an S corporation that elected to use a 52–53-week taxable year. It selected the Friday closest to December 31 as the close of its year. In 1992, December 31 fell on a Thursday. The corporation closed its year on January 1, 1993. The shareholders use the calendar year. They had to report all of the S corporation items for the year ending January 1, 1993, on their returns for calendar 1992.

An S corporation can use a 52–53-week year that corresponds to its natural business year. [Regs. §1.442-2T(c)(3)(ii)] If an S corporation makes a §444 year election, it can use a 52–53-week year that uses the otherwise allowable §444 year as its reference date. [Regs. §1.444-1T(b)(iv)(B)]

540. Separate trust elections.

Certain trusts that are allowed as shareholders may need to make their own separate elections to qualify as shareholders in S corporations. Not all qualifying trusts need to make special elections. For example, a grantor trust (or a trust treated as a grantor trust under §678) qualifies as a shareholder if the grantor (or deemed grantor) is a U.S. citizen or resident. This type of trust needs to make no special election. Similarly, a voting trust or a testamentary trust needs no election. Nor does a grantor trust after the death of the grantor, at least for the two-year period in which this trust will qualify as a shareholder in its own right. See Chapter 2, at 215.3., for discussions of the various types of trusts that qualify as S corporation shareholders. The two trusts that need to make elections in order to be qualified shareholders are the QSST and the ESBT. The election procedures for the QSST differ slightly from those of the ESBT. Moreover, in 1998 the IRS issued a Revenue Procedure that allows any trust that simultaneously meets the definitions of both a QSST and an ESBT to switch from one type to the other. This part of the chapter discusses these elections.

540.1. Separate QSST election. The QSST election is a separate election that is made by the beneficiaries of a QSST. As a matter of convenience, Form 2553 provides space on page 2 for one such election. Beneficiaries must file separate statements if there is more than one trust owning shares at the time the corporation files the S election. QSSTs that acquire stock after the corporation files Form 2553 must also file separate statements. The separate statements should duplicate the language given on Form 2553, Part III.

Trusts that own stock prior to the date on which the corporation files the S election must meet all of the QSST conditions (see Chapter 2) on the date the S election is filed. Each trust must file a QSST election within $2^1/_2$ months of the date on which eligibility is needed or face ineligibility as shareholders when the corporation filed its S election. If it had an ineligible shareholder, the corporation would not be a small business corporation, and the S election would not be valid for any year.

EXAMPLE 5 - 24: RST Corporation uses the calendar year. It is owned equally by R (an individual), S (also an individual), and T (a trust that meets the QSST qualifications). On February 2, 1996, RST files an S election. If T's beneficiary does not file the QSST election by March 15, the S election will not be valid for any tax year. The corporation will have had an ineligible shareholder on the date the election is made. If the trust files a timely QSST election, the S election will be valid for 1996 or 1997, whichever is specified on Form 2553.

If a trust receives stock after the S election is effective, the QSST election must be filed within $2^1/_2$ months after the stock is received. The QSST election must not predate the S election. [Regs. §1.1361-1(j)(6)(iii)]

EXAMPLE 5 - 25: In Example 5 - 23, T's beneficiary may not file the QSST election before February 2, 1996, the date that the corporation filed its S election.

If a trust has disposed of its shares early in a taxable year, and the corporation wants to file an S election to take effect as of the beginning of the taxable year, there are two potential problems:

1. If the trust, by its very terms, cannot qualify as either a grantor trust or a QSST, the corporation's S election cannot take effect until the next taxable year. (See the discussion in 510.2., above.)
2. If the trust qualifies as a grantor trust, it need not file any election. If the trust meets the requirements of a QSST, it would need to consent to the corporation's S election as a former shareholder. In addition, its beneficiary would need to consent to treatment of the trust as a QSST.

EXAMPLE 5 - 26: On January 1, 1998, the stock of the XYT Corporation was owned by eligible individuals X and Y and trust T. On February 2, 1998, X purchased all of T's shares. On February 3, XYT filed an S election, obtaining the consent of X and Y. Assuming that T was an ineligible shareholder, XYT's S election would be ineffective for 1998, although it would be effective for 1999.

Assume, however, that T was a grantor trust and that individual Z was the deemed owner of the trust. If Z consented to the S election, XYT would be an S corporation for 1998. Z would include his share of the corporation's income or loss (from January 1 through February 2) for 1998.

Assume finally that T was a trust that met the requirements of a QSST or an ESBT. Presumably, T could file an election to be a QSST or an ESBT, even though it is no longer a shareholder. It could then consent to the S election, which would be in effect for 1998.

Confusion over the requirements governing QSSTs has been one of the most significant causes of Private Letter Rulings. In most cases, the IRS appears to interpret the rules somewhat liberally. There are two contexts in which the requirement of the separate QSST election seems to be observed in the breach. The first context is inadvertent terminations, which occur when a corporation has a valid S election in effect but then transfers shares to one or more trusts. (See Chapter 13, at 1350., for reference to several Letter Rulings in which the IRS has approved the eligibility of trusts as shareholders, in spite of failure to file a QSST election.) The second context is when one or more trusts own stock at the time the corporation files its S election.

If a corporation files an S election and some of its shares are owned by trusts that purport to be QSSTs, the beneficiaries must consent to the corporation's S election and must separately consent to the treatment of the trusts as QSSTs. If one beneficiary fails to file a consent, the corporation's S election is not valid. The same problem could result from the failure of a trust to file an election to be an ESBT. Therefore, the corporation has never had a valid S election in effect, and it cannot apply for inadvertent termination relief, although the corporation may file for relief from an inadvertently defective election. See at 550.4., and note the relief requests granted on these issues. In several 1994 Private Letter Rulings, the IRS held that an extension of time for filing shareholder consents to the S election also extended the time for making the QSST election. [PLRs 9424060, 9424061, 9427013]

To resolve some of the complexities and oversights that may result when a trust owns shares of a small business corporation, taxpayers and the IRS have turned to the doctrine of "substantial compliance." The doctrine of substantial compliance has been cited frequently in Letter Rulings when the beneficiary of a trust consented to the S election but failed to file a separate QSST consent. [PLRs 9015039, 9017049, 9018008, 9021036, 9027016, 9027017, 9030043, 9032036, 9040020, 9042015, 9047025, 9047026, 9047027, 9052006] The key element seems to be that the beneficiary did consent to the S election. If the beneficiary did not consent to the corporation's S election, however, the IRS has not found the corporation to be in substantial compliance. [PLRs 9048025, 9048026, 9048030] The most frequent mistake appears to have been that the fiduciary, rather than the beneficiary, signed the Form 2553.

A grantor trust, testamentary trust, voting trust, decedent's estate, or estate of an individual in bankruptcy does not file a QSST election. Accordingly, these entities have encountered few problems as S corporation shareholders.

540.2. Separate ESBT election. Internal Revenue Code §1361(c)(2) (relating to certain trusts permitted as shareholders) was amended in 1996 to include electing small business trusts. Status as an electing small business trust must be elected by the trustee.

SUMMARY OF AUTHORITY: CODE SECTION 1361(e)(3)

- Status as an electing small business trust must be elected.
- The election is made by the trustee.
- Once made, the election cannot be unilaterally revoked by the trust.

The IRS has the authority to describe the times and places for filing the election. The trustee files the election for the trust to be treated as an ESBT. [Notice 97-12, 1997-3 IRB] The trustee gives the following information:

1. Provides names, addresses, and taxpayer identification numbers of all potential current beneficiaries, the trust, and the corporation;
2. Identifies of the election as an election made under §1361(e)(3);
3. Specifies the date on which the election is to become effective (not earlier than 15 days and two months before the date on which the election is filed);
4. Specifies the date (or dates) on which the stock of the corporation was transferred to the trust.

The election statement must also provide all information and representations necessary to show that all potential current beneficiaries meet the shareholder requirements of §1361(b)(1). In other words, the ESBT election must affirm the status of each potential income beneficiary as an individual or a charitable organization. It must also state that the trust instrument corresponds with all of the requirements for an ESBT. See Chapter 2, at 215.36.

The trustee of the ESBT must file the ESBT election within the 2 month and 15-day period that would govern a QSST. In the case of newly electing S corporations, the trustee may attach the ESBT election to the Form 2553. [See PLR 9823032]

540.3. Election to convert between QSST and ESBT status. A trust may fit the definition of both a QSST and an ESBT; for example, a trust with only one beneficiary, who is a U.S. citizen or resident, could qualify to be either type of trust. However, no trust can be both types simultaneously, so the trustee and beneficiary will need to make one type of election or the other.

In general, the election by a beneficiary to treat a trust as a QSST is irrevocable. [§1361(d)(2)(C)] Similarly, an election by the trustee to treat a trust as an ESBT is irrevocable. [§1361(e)(3)] The IRS has the power, however, to grant permission to revoke either election.

In 1998, the IRS promulgated a Revenue Procedure that allows a trust that meets both sets of qualifications to change its status without specific permission by the IRS. [Rev. Proc. 98-23, 1998-10 IRB 30] This Revenue Procedure is effective for taxable years beginning after December 31, 1996. An election can be made effective as of any date on or after January 1, 1997, and before March 9, 1998, if it is filed not more than 15 days and 2 months after March 9, 1998.

540.31. Change from QSST to ESBT. Technically, the conversion involves the beneficiary revoking the QSST election and the fiduciary making the ESBT election simultaneously. The IRS will allow these events to take place without specific permission, if there has not been a previous conversion within 36 months. In order to bring about the conversion, both the current income beneficiary and the fiduciary must sign the ESBT election, which then constitutes a valid revocation of the QSST election. The effective date of the conversion may be not more than 2 months and 15 days before the filing of the election; nor may it be more than 12 months after the date on which the election to convert is filed. Any date outside of the limit will be changed to make the conversion effective on the nearest date within the limit.

> **EXAMPLE 5 - 27:** On July 15, 1998, the beneficiary and the fiduciary of the ABC trust decide to convert from QSST status to ESBT status. They file a conversion statement on that date. If the effective date stated in the conversion is earlier than May 1, 1998, the conversion will take place on May 1, 1998. If the election specifies a date after July 15, 1999, the conversion will take effect on July 15, 1999.

The conversion need not take effect at the beginning of the corporation's taxable year. If it takes place in mid-year, it is treated as a termination of interest of the prior shareholder and an acquisition by a new shareholder. Thus for allocation purposes the corporation can elect to close its year as of the conversion date. See Chapter 6, at 630.2. Unlike all other transfers of interest, this transfer ends the beneficiary's ownership on the date before the conversion.

The procedural aspects are simple. The election contains all necessary information discussed at 540.2., above, and must state at the top:

ATTENTION ENTITY CONTROL—
CONVERSION OF A QSST TO AN ESBT PURSUANT TO REV. PROC. 98-23

> **EXAMPLE 5 - 28:** Assume the same facts as in Example 5 - 27, except that the conversion takes place on July 15, 1998. The beneficiary is treated as the owner through July 14, 1998, and the trust is treated as the owner beginning on July 15, 1998.

Revenue Procedure 98-23 does not allow any conversion within a 36-month period after a prior conversion. Therefore, the parties must request a ruling. Ironically, the IRS has declined to rule on this issue, other than to guide the parties to Revenue Procedure 98-23. [PLRs 9824011, 9824010, 9824008, 9824007, 9823038, 9823036, 9823035, 9823034]

540.32. Change from ESBT to QSST. The rules for this type of conversion mirror the rules for conversion from QSST to ESBT. The election procedures are practically identical, except that the fiduciary and the beneficiary file a QSST election. The election contains all necessary information discussed at 540.1., above, and must state at the top:

ATTENTION ENTITY CONTROL—
CONVERSION OF AN ESBT TO A QSST PURSUANT TO REV. PROC. 98-23

The effective date rules are identical, as is the treatment of the conversion as a termination of the trust's interest as a shareholder and the acquisition of the interest by the beneficiary. The corporation may be able to elect to split the taxable year for allocation purposes.

545. Election for qualified Subchapter S subsidiary.

An S corporation is permitted to own a qualified Subchapter S subsidiary in taxable years beginning after December 31, 1996. The term *qualified Subchapter S subsidiary* means a domestic corporation that would be eligible to be an S corporation if the stock of the corporation were held directly by the shareholders of its parent S corporation. The parent S corporation must hold 100% of this subsidiary's stock. The parent S corporation must elect to treat the subsidiary as a qualified Subchapter S subsidiary. The Code leaves the task of prescribing the details of the election to the IRS.

5

545.1. Before Final Regulations are issued. In 1997 the IRS issued its first procedural rules. These aspects are given in Notice 97-4, 1997-2 IRB. The parent S corporation files Form 966, "Corporate Liquidation or Dissolution," with the following modifications:

1. At the top of the Form 966, print "FILED PURSUANT TO 97-4."
2. In the box labeled "Employer identification number" (EIN), enter the subsidiary's EIN (if applicable). If the subsidiary did not exist before the time of election and does not have an EIN, there will be no need to obtain a taxpayer identification number for the subsidiary. In this case, insert "QSSS" in the box. (If the parent corporation chooses to obtain an EIN for the newly formed QSub, the parent should check "Other" at "Type of entity" on the SS-4 and should specify that the entity is a QSub.)
3. In Box 4 on Form 966, enter the desired effective date for the election. The election may be effective on the date Form 966 is filed or up to 75 days before the filing of Form 966, provided that the date is not before the effective date of §1308 of the Act and that the subsidiary otherwise qualified as a QSub for the entire period for which the retroactive election is in effect. For these purposes, the requirement that Form 966 be filed within 30 days of the date in Box 4 is ignored.
4. In Box 7c on Form 966, enter the name of the parent. The parent's EIN should be included in Box 7d.
5. In Box 10 on Form 966, enter "§1361(b)(3)(B)."
6. Form 966 must be signed by a corporate officer authorized to sign the parent's tax return. Banks and bank holding companies should consult Notice 97-5, 1997-2 IRB, before filing an election under the procedures listed above.

545.2. Proposed Regulations. In 1998, the IRS issued Proposed Regulations dealing with various aspects of the QSub, including the election procedures. These Regulations will be prospective, from the time the IRS issues Final Regulations covering these matters. Therefore, practitioners should be on the alert. Until these Regulations are issued, S corporations will follow the rules from Notice 97-5.

The rules adopted in the Proposed Regulations are generally sensible. The effective date of the QSub election cannot be more than 2 months and 15 days before the filing of the election, nor can it be more than 12 months after the date on which the election to convert is filed. Any date outside of the limit will be effective on the nearest date within the limit. [Proposed Regs. §1.1361-3(a)(3)] The Qualified Subchapter S Subsidiary election need not be made as of the beginning of the taxable year of the QSub.

> **EXAMPLE 5 - 29:** On July 15, 1998, PS Corporation, an S corporation, acquires all of the stock of Q Corporation. Q Corporation has used the calendar year. The QSub election may take effect on July 15, 1998, or any later date.

If the subsidiary corporation has had any prior existence, the election is filed with the corporation's IRS service center. The parent S corporation files Form 966, "Corporate Liquidation or Dissolution," with the modifications discussed above.

If the QSub is a new entity, the election to be a QSub is filed with the service center of the parent corporation. [Proposed Regs. §1.1361-3(a)(1)] The election form is to be prescribed by the IRS.

550. Relief for late and defective elections.

The various elections discussed in this chapter have specified procedures and time horizons. However, in practice, these rules are not always strictly observed. In the era of a "kinder and gentler" IRS, Congress has enabled several statutory relief provisions, the most important being the inadvertent termination relief rules, enacted in 1982. These are discussed in Chapter 13, at 1350.

In 1996, the Small Business Job Protection Act of 1996 expanded inadvertent termination relief to situations in which the corporation had never filed a proper S election. The new extensions of that relief are discussed below. That same Act added §1361(b)(5), which specifically allows the IRS to accept late elections. Since its enactment, this rule has been one of the busiest ruling areas in all of Subchapter S. 5

SUMMARY OF AUTHORITY: CODE SECTION 1362(b)(5)

- The IRS is authorized to accept late elections as having been filed on time.
- For the entity to qualify for this relief, there must be reasonable cause for the failure to file a timely election.

> **OBSERVATION:** Contrast the language of the late election relief with that of the defective election relief, discussed below at 550.4. For late election relief, there must be "reasonable cause," whereas for defective election relief the defect must have been "inadvertent." Reasonable cause is an easier test to meet than inadvertence. Thus the two relief provisions operate differently.

Because the law does not specify how the IRS is to administer this provision, the IRS has the authority to decide if it is a service center issue or a national office issue. The initial rule was that late requests for the 1996 taxable year would be dealt with by the district director's office for the location of the corporation. [Ann. 97-4, 1997-3 IRB] These requests could only be for elections that should have been filed for the corporation's 1996 taxable year, and they needed to be filed by February 15, 1997. Later in 1997, the IRS issued some permanent rules for untimely elections. [Rev. Proc. 97-40, 1997-33 IRB 50] In late 1998, the IRS issued a more comprehensive set of rules in Revenue Procedure 98-55, 1998-46 IRB 1, which rendered Revenue Procedure 97-40 obsolete. In situations specified in Revenue Procedure 98-55, the corporation may file for relief with the service center or district director, and it does not need to file a ruling request with the national office of the IRS. In all other cases, the corporation must file a ruling request with the national office and must pay the user fee for ruling requests, which at the time of this writing is generally $5,000. [Rev. Proc. 99-1, 1999-1 IRB 6, Appendix A, (3)(c)]

> **OBSERVATION:** The relief rules that do not require the filing of a ruling request are limited to extremely disjointed circumstances. In some cases they will apply to taxpayers who have been extremely sloppy or negligent, whereas persons who attempt to comply with the rules under less fortuitous circumstances will be forced to pay for rulings. The expeditious relief provisions that the IRS promulgated through mid-1998 do not follow any sort of pattern. As a result, most corporations that find that they have not made a timely S election will be forced to apply for rulings from the IRS national office.

550.1. Relief for late election within one year—Revenue Procedure 98-55. In 1998, the IRS issued Revenue Procedure 98-55, 1998-46 IRB 1. This pronouncement, which is much more comprehensive than the earlier procedures, covers all of the following:

- Late S corporation elections, discussed here
- Late QSub and ESBT elections, discussed at 550.5.
- Late QSST elections, discussed at 550.6.

5

550.11. Late 2553 only. If a corporation qualifies for relief under this provision, the relief is granted by the IRS service center, and it does not require payment of the ruling fee. [Rev. Proc. 98-55, §3.05] In order to qualify for this relief, the corporation must file Form 2553 within one year of the due date. Another requirement to qualify under this rule is redundant: The deadline for filing the corporation's tax return for the year in question must not have passed. Finally, the corporation must state the reasonable cause for the lateness of the election.

EXAMPLE 5 - 30: Careco Corporation commences business on November 5, 1998. On March 1, 1999, the corporation's office manager brings its books and records to a CPA for preparation of the 1997 tax return. The CPA queries management as to whether Careco is a C corporation or an S corporation. The president, who is the sole shareholder, has no idea, but likes the concept of the S corporation. Careco meets all of the eligibility requirements for S status.

The deadline for Careco to file Form 2553 was January 20, 1999. Therefore, if the CPA or Careco prepares Form 2553 now and files it with the service center, it will not be more than twelve months late.

The corporation files a Form 2553 with the IRS service center where it normally files tax returns, and attaches consents of all persons who have owned stock in the corporation from the date that the election is to be effective until the date of filing. At the top of Form 2553 the corporation notes the following:

FILED PURSUANT TO REV. PROC. 98-55

The corporation also attaches a letter explaining the cause for the delinquency. If the IRS approves the cause as reasonable, it grants the election. The IRS service center has the authority to accept or reject the explanation for the cause.

EXAMPLE 5 - 31: On August 18, 1998, Lico, a new corporation, had three shareholders: Marcia, Andy, and Doug. Lico intended to be an S corporation, but did not file a timely Form 2553 on or before November 2, 1998. On March 1, 1999, Lico's tax advisor, Jay, became aware that no such form had been filed. Jay believed that the cause for not filing Form 2553 was reasonable.

In the meantime, there had been some activity with respect to Lico's shares. The corporation issued new shares to Marianne on January 10, 1999. On February 2, 1999, Marcia sold all of her shares to Glenn. Jay must prepare a Form 2553, and the corporation must file this form on or before March 15, 1999 (if Lico uses the calendar year). The request must be signed by Marcia, Andy, Doug, Marianne, and Glenn.

OBSERVATION: It is never advisable to make a false statement to the IRS, and this principle certainly applies to the explanation that must accompany Form 2553 under Revenue Procedure 98-55. However, the citations at 550.14., below, regarding Letter Rulings issued under §1362(b)(5) make it evident that the IRS is extremely lenient in finding that the cause is reasonable in nearly every failure to file a timely 2553.

EXAMPLE 5 - 32: Refer to Example 5 - 31, above. Lico must attach an explanation of its reasonable cause for not filing a timely Form 2553. Any true statement, such as that management was unaware of the deadline, would probably suffice.

550.12. Late 2553 and late QSST or ESBT. Relief under Revenue Procedure 98-55 is available when a trust that could qualify as a QSST or an ESBT (1) owned stock in a corporation that intended to be an S corporation but did not file a timely Form 2553 and (2) did not file a timely election to qualify as an S corporation shareholder. [Rev. Proc. 98-55, §4.02(1)] In such a case, the corporation files the late Form 2553, and the appropriate parties attach the required trust elections, with the IRS service center where the corporation files its returns. Note that both the late S corporation election and the late trust elections must be filed with the corporation's service center, even if the trust or beneficiary files its returns at another location. [Regs. §1.1361-1(j)(6)(ii)]

The corporation must qualify for late relief under Rev. Proc. 98-55. Accordingly, the unextended due date for the parent's first intended S corporation year must not have expired when the corporation and other parties file the elections under this procedure.

The corporation explains the reasonable cause for the late election. If the service center accepts the late 2553, it will automatically accept the trust election as being made for the first day of the parent S corporation's first S corporation year. [Rev. Proc. 98-55, §4.04]

> **EXAMPLE 5 - 33:** Kaayco intended to be an S corporation for its initial taxable year beginning March 31, 1999. On that date, some of its shares were held in trust for the benefit of Kelly, a minor. The corporation did not file a timely S election. The trust was drafted to qualify as a QSST, but Kelly did not file a timely QSST election. On or before March 15, 2000, the corporation may file for relief under Revenue Procedure 98-55. In order to qualify, the corporation must file Form 2553 with the explanation for the filing delay, and Kelly must simultaneously file the QSST election at the same service center. If the IRS accepts the corporation's reasonable cause for the late Form 2553 it will automatically approve the trust's status as a QSST, beginning on March 31, 1999.

550.13. Late 2553 and late QSub election. Revenue Procedure 98-55 applies when a parent corporation owned all of the stock of a subsidiary corporation on the date it intended an S election to take effect, but did not file a timely Form 2553 or a timely QSub election. Thus, the corporation will not need to file separate applications for the S corporation election and the QSub election relief. Again, the unextended due date for the parent's first intended S corporation year must not have expired. [Rev. Proc. 98-55, §4.02(2)]

The corporation files the late Form 2553 and the QSub election simultaneously, with the appropriate IRS service center(s). The corporation explains the reasonable cause for the late Form 2553. If the service center accepts the late 2553, it will automatically accept the QSub election as being made for the first day of the parent S corporation's first S corporation year. [Rev. Proc. 98-55, §4.04]

> **EXAMPLE 5 - 34:** Paayco intended to be an S corporation for its taxable year beginning January 1, 1999. On that date it owned 100% of the stock of Zaayco. Paayco intended for Zaayco to be a QSub beginning January 1, 1999. Paayco did not file a timely S election, and it did not file a QSub election for Zaayco.
>
> On or before March 15, 2000, Paayco may file for relief under Revenue Procedure 98-55. In order to qualify, the corporation must file Form 2553 with the explanation for the filing delay. Paayco must simultaneously file the QSub election at the appropriate service center. (If Zaayco had been filing returns, the QSub election would be filed at Zaayco's service center.)
>
> If the IRS accepts Paayco's reasonable cause for the late Form 2553, it will automatically approve Zaayco's status as a QSub, beginning on January 1, 1999.

550.2. Relief under Revenue Procedure 97-48. In 1997, the IRS issued several Revenue Procedures and other pronouncements dealing with late S elections. The only one that has survived into 1999 is Revenue Procedure 97-48, 1997-43 IRB 19. This procedure is useful only under very narrow circumstances, but retains some viability. Specifically, it is limited to two fact patterns:

- The corporation did not file a timely Form 2553, but was **not** notified by the IRS within six months after filing its first Form 1120S that it should not have filed as an S corporation. More than six months have elapsed since the corporation filed its first Form 1120S (Situation 1, discussed at 550.21).
- The corporation did not file a timely Form 2553, but **was** notified by the IRS within six months after filing its first Form 1120S that it should not have filed as an S corporation (Situation 2, discussed below at 550.22).

The primary benefit of relief under Revenue Procedure 97-48 is that it is automatic. The corporation does not need to wait for approval from the IRS in order to be an S corporation.

550.21. No notification from the IRS within 6 months of filing 1120S. Under Revenue Procedure 97-48, §4.01(1), there are four basic requirements to qualify for relief in Situation 1:

1. The corporation fails to qualify as an S corporation solely because Form 2553 was not timely filed;
2. The corporation and all of its shareholders reported their income consistent with S corporation status for the year the S corporation election should have been made, and for every subsequent taxable year (if any);
3. At least six months have elapsed since the date on which the corporation filed its tax return for the first year the corporation intended to be an S corporation; and
4. Neither the corporation nor any of its shareholders was notified by the IRS of any problem regarding the S corporation status within six months of the date on which the Form 1120S for the first year was timely filed.

In short, for the corporation to qualify for this relief provision everyone involved—including the corporation, its tax advisors, and the IRS—must have overlooked the filing requirements for Form 2553, and the first Form 1120S must have been filed at least six months ago. Thus, this particular relief provision will not be available if there is prompt action by a competent and ethical tax professional but the discovery comes too late to qualify for relief under Revenue Procedure 98-55.

EXAMPLE 5-35: Sunshine Corporation commences business on April 10, 1997. The due date for its Form 2553 is June 25, 1997. By March 15, 1998, Form 1120S is due, and the corporation files a timely Form 1120S. In 1999, Sunshine engages a new CPA, who discovers that the corporation never filed Form 2553. Note that if the corporation's tax preparer does not determine whether the S election is valid, and prepares all returns as if the S election is in effect, the corporation may qualify for relief under Situation 1 of Revenue Procedure 97-48. In order for the corporation to qualify for this provision, however, the IRS must fail to notify the corporation that it has no election on file within six months of the filing of Form 1120S for 1997.

However, the corporation has engaged a competent CPA, who determines that the corporation has not filed Form 2553, and the parties are in a quandary: If the CPA discovers that Sunshine Corporation does not qualify as an S corporation, he or she cannot prepare Form 1120S for the corporation. Nor may the CPA include income or loss from the corporation on the shareholder's personal return. The CPA must prepare Form 1120 for the C corporation and advise the shareholders to file their returns excluding any income or loss items that would pass through from an S corporation. Having filed Form 1120, the corporation would not qualify for the automatic relief of Revenue Procedure 97-48, Situation 1.

EXAMPLE 5 - 36: Slopco, Inc., commences business in 1996 and files Form 1120S for its taxable year ending December 31, 1996. It never files Form 2553. Seven months after it files Form 1120S it receives a notice from the IRS that there is no S election on file. At this point, Slopco engages a competent Enrolled Agent, who advises Slopco to prepare and file Form 2553 under Revenue Procedure 97-48. That action will be sufficient to qualify the corporation as an S corporation. There will be no need to amend the corporation's returns or any shareholder's tax returns for 1996.

The procedural requirements are simple. The corporation must file Form 2553 with the IRS service center. If the corporation is under examination by the IRS, it files Form 2553 with the district director. This form must be accompanied by the consent of every person who was a shareholder during the entire period that the S election is intended to be in effect. In addition, the corporation and each shareholder must state under penalty of perjury that the returns have been filed as stated in the communication. Thus any owner of any number of shares during that period may block the relief.

Once a corporation qualifies under this provision, the relief is automatic. The corporation does not need to file a ruling request, and does not need to wait for further communications from the IRS acknowledging the validity of the S election. The corporation and its shareholders are now assured that the election will be accepted as timely for the first year for which the corporation was intended to be an S corporation. The corporation notes the following at the top of Form 2553:

FILED PURSUANT TO REV. PROC. 97-48

550.22. Notification from IRS, and no closed years. Situation 2 of Revenue Procedure 97-48, §401.2, differs considerably from Situation 1. There are six specified requirements, as follows:

1. The corporation failed to qualify as an S corporation solely becuase Form 2553 was not filed timely for a taxable year that began prior to January 1, 1997;
2. The corporation received notification from the IRS that the Form 2553 was not timely filed, that the corporation must file as a C corporation for the first taxable year the corporation intended to be an S corporation, and that the election would be treated as an S corporation election for the following taxable year;
3. The corporation and all of its shareholders reported their income (if any) properly for treating the corporation as a C corporation for the first taxable year the corporation had intended to be an S corporation;
4. The corporation and all of its shareholders reported their income consistent with S corporation status for all subsequent years;
5. The period of limitations on assessment under §6501(a) has not lapsed for any of the taxable years of the corporation beginning on or after the date the corporation intended to be taxable as an S corporation; and
6. The period of limitations on assessment under §6501(a) has not lapsed for any taxable year of any of the corporation's shareholders in which any intended S corporation year ends.

The most obvious requirement for Situation 2 is that the corporation had filed Form 2553, but not in time for the first intended year as an S corporation. The IRS had accepted the election, but for years subsequent to the first intended S corporation year. Perhaps less obvious is the requirement (not present in Situation 1) that the first intended S year must have begun before 1997. Perhaps equally important is than no taxable year of the corporation or of any shareholder may be closed under the statute of limitations (generally three years from the due date for the return, or the filing date if later). Thus, this provision will be relatively short-lived and will expire when the 1996 taxable years are closed under the statute.

EXAMPLE 5 - 37: Assume the same facts as in Example 5 - 36, except that Slopco filed Form 2553, but not within the 2-month and 15-day period for it to take effect in 1996. Assume further that the IRS notified Slopco of this, within 6 months of the filing of its first Form 1120S. Subsequently, Slopco amended its 1996 return by filing Form 1120, and its shareholders amended their returns accordingly. Slopco may qualify for automatic relief under Revenue Procedure 97-48, Situation 2.

5

The procedural requirements are simple. The corporation must file a new Form 2553 with the IRS service center (even though it had already filed a Form 2553). The new form must be accompanied by the consent of every person who was a shareholder during the entire period that the S election was intended to be in effect. In addition, the corporation and each shareholder must state under penalties of perjury that the returns have been filed as stated in the communication. Thus, any owner of any number of shares during that period may block the relief. Since the form is filed with the service center, and not with the national office, there is no reason to submit a ruling request or the processing fee of $3,650. The corporation and all affected shareholders must then amend their returns for the initial year, in which the corporation filed as a C corporation. At the top of Form 2553 the corporation notes the following:

FILED PURSUANT TO REV. PROC. 97-48

OBSERVATION: If the first year for which the S election was to be in effect was the first year of the corporation's existence, the relief afforded by Revenue Procedure 97-48 may be substantial. This Revenue Procedure will give the corporation justification to claim that it has always been an S corporation, and the corporation will not be subject to the LIFO recapture tax (Chapter 3), the built-in gains tax (Chapter 11), or the passive investment income tax (Chapter 12).

550.3. Rulings issued allowing late elections. Although the Revenue Procedures discussed above provide substantial relief, they cover only three narrow fact patterns. As a consequence, there have been many requests for rulings granting relief in instances where the corporation does not qualify under either Revenue Procedure 97-48 or Revenue Procedure 98-55. Beginning in 1997, the IRS issued rulings for late S elections. Table 5-1 gives a sample of rulings, with the causes accepted as being reasonable.

OBSERVATION: Throughout 1997, 1998, and early 1999, there were literally hundreds of rulings accepting late S elections. In many, if not most, of these cases, no reason was stated for rulings involving the failure to file a timely Form 2553. Thus, it has become counterproductive to sift through the hundreds of substantially identical rulings in an attempt to determine some sort of pattern. Table 5-1 gives only a small sampling of the reasonable causes that have been accepted. Numerous other rulings (approximately 700) are listed in an appendix at the end of this chapter.

5

Table 5-1: Rulings Granting Late Election Relief

Reasonable cause	*Citation*
Employee filed Form 2553 in filing cabinet	PLR 9752041
Reliance on employees, who had failed to file 2553	PLR 9733009
Corporation delayed Form 2553 due to problems in obtaining consent from shareholders	PLR 9752054
Erroneously filed by corporate officer prior to formal incorporation	PLR 9816004
No election received by service center	PLR 9748022
"In the confusion of Company's start up period, the form was filed internally rather than mailed to the appropriate Service Center."	PLR 9750026
Shareholder purchased a "corporate kit"; for personal reasons was unable to consult an attorney or accountant	PLR 9746012
Shareholder(s) believed that the corporation was an S corporation	PLR 9802041
Sole shareholder believed that filing the articles of incorporation was in itself sufficient for X to become an S corporation	PLR 9815037
Misunderstanding between attorney and bookkeeper	PLR 9814024
Paid professional had death in family, and other stress	PLR 9736024
Shareholder "attempted to file Form 2553," but IRS never received it	PLR 9736022
Corporate president did not file Form 2553	PLR 9735026
Neither attorney nor accountant advised shareholder of need to file Form 2553	PLR 9735020
CPA did not inform shareholder of deadline	PLR 9735008
Shareholder believed that original 2553 was copy, and that original had been filed	PLR 9735005
Prior shareholder represented that the corporation was an S corporation; purchasing shareholder had already dissolved corporation when election was accepted under §1362(b)(5)	PLR 9734024
Sole shareholder had hired new accounting firm and was engaged in acrimonious divorce	PLR 9734005
Unaware of need for new 2553 after merging S corporation into sister C corporation	PLR 9731028
Unaware of need for new 2553 after spin-off from S corporation	PLR 9814013
Reliance on corporate officer	PLR 9731028
Reliance on bookkeeper	PLR 9808013
Shareholders believed Form SS-4 was sufficient for the S election	PLR 9751009
Shareholders intended to file Form 2553, but were preoccupied with other business matters	PLR 9741024
Reliance on contract management firm	PLR 9735022
Reliance on treasurer	PLR 9812033
Reliance on attorney and accountant	PLR 9743009
Reliance on accountant	PLR 9801008
Reliance on paid professional	PLR 9743014
Accountant advised that Form 2553 and Form 1120S were unnecessary and that all information could be filed on Schedule C	PLR 9743036
Accountant failed to file timely 2553	PLR 9741005
"Reasons stated in the ruling request"	PLR 9746037
Form 2553 was neglected during transition of accounting services	PLR 9742034
Mis-routing of documents	PLR 9743005
Miscommunication with accountant	PLR 9746046

5

Reasonable cause	Citation
Miscommunication with accountant and attorney	PLR 9743008
Miscommunication with attorney and advisor	PLR 9808021
Miscommunication with attorney	PLR 9802029
Misunderstanding	PLR 9815031
Reliance on corporate treasurer and attorney	PLR 9812033
Miscommunication with attorney and financial consultant	PLR 9751027
Shareholder expected corporation to be S corporation, but did not file Form 2553	PLR 9739029
Unaware of need for 2553	PLR 9652016
Client did not follow attorney's advice to sign and file Form 2553	PLR 9739012
Corporation intended to be an S corporation	PLR 9802029
Corporation believed it had filed timely, but IRS had no evidence	PLR 9734031
Reliance on attorney	PLR 9719016
Timely election not filed—no reason stated	PLR 9717016

550.4. Defective elections. Before passage of the Small Business Job Protection Act of 1996, there was no official relief for defective elections. Thus any error, or breach of the eligibility rules of Subchapter S, would cause a Form 2553, even if timely filed, to be invalid. There was a provision to allow the IRS to waive an inadvertent termination, but for this waiver to occur, the corporation must have had a valid S election in effect before the eligibility violation. [§1362(f)] This rule had been in effect since 1982, and has been the source of frequent rulings from the IRS. See Chapter 13, at 1350., for discussion of this provision.

It may be paradoxical, but relief is easier for a late election than for a defective election. For the IRS to accept a late election, there must only be *reasonable cause*, which is correctable by the service center within certain time frames, principally those outlined in Rev. Proc. 98-55, 1998-46 IRB 1. For the IRS to accept a defective election, the defect must be inadvertent. Only the national office can rule on inadvertence, and the only way to apply is in the form of a ruling request, complete with the user fee. Thus it is better to be careful and late (but not too late) than timely but improper in filing an S election.

550.41. Eligible corporation with faulty election. The Small Business Job Protection Act of 1996 expanded the scope of §1362(f) to include inadvertently invalid S elections. Thus, the IRS is now specifically authorized to allow corporations to remedy defective S elections. Congress has directed the IRS to apply the same standards to late or defective elections that it had applied in granting inadvertent termination relief. [H.R. Conf. Rep. 104-737, p. 204]

CODE SECTION 1362(f): SUMMARY OF AUTHORITY

- The IRS is authorized to accept defective elections as valid.
- For an entity to qualify for this relief, it must convince the IRS that the defect was inadvertent, which is a stricter standard than reasonable cause.
- The corporation and its shareholders must have taken corrective action within a reasonable time after discovery of the problem.

This rule is in effect for all years beginning after 1982. To qualify for relief for a defective election, the corporation must request a ruling, even if the corporation is under examination. [Ann. 97-4, 1997-3 IRB] In rulings issued to date, the IRS has granted elections when the corporation had not been eligible to be an S corporation when it filed Form 2553. See discussion below at 550.3. Also see Chapter 13, at 1350., for a history of the rulings under

Table 5-2: Rulings Granting Defective Election Relief

Defect of Election	*Corrective Action*	*Citation*
Election timely filed but lacking consent of some shareholders	Obtained proper consents	PLR 199909010

§1362(f) as it has been applied to inadvertent terminations.Table 5-2 shows some rulings that have been specifically issued for corporations that were eligible to be S corporations and filed timely elections, but had one or more defects in the election.

550.42. Corporation ineligible when election is filed. Before the Small Business Job Protection Act of 1996, there was no relief for a corporation that had not met all of the definitions of a *small business corporation* when it filed Form 2553. As earlier editions of this book advised, the only safe course of action was to file another Form 2553 once the corporation was eligible, and to hope that the earlier years would disappear under the statute of limitations. The broadened scope of §1362(f), relating to inadvertent termination and invalid elections, has also been applied to corporations that filed Form 2553 at a time when they did not meet all of the eligibility criteria to be S corporations.

In 1997, the IRS began to issue rulings under the provision for inadvertent defective election, holding that corporations that technically were not eligible to file would qualify under this provision. The corrective actions required for a corporation to obtain the ruling have been reasonable and have been limited to curing the defect that existed at the time the corporation filed its original Form 2553. The rulings to date are shown in Table 5-3.

Table 5-3: Rulings Granting Inadvertent Defective Election Relief for Corporations Ineligible to File Form 2553

Eligibility Problems	*Corrective Action*	*Citation*
Corporation had two classes of stock when it filed Form 2553	Modified share rights so that there was one class and filed for relief	PLR 9701015
Filed when ineligible person held stock	Ineligible person transferred shares to eligible holders	PLRs 9816011, 9832015, 9839013, 9848012, 199917013
Filed when preferred stock was outstanding	Recalled preferred shares	PLRs 9815026, 9745011, 9829020
Filed with no valid QSST election on one or more shareholders	Filed QSST election	PLRs 9815030, 9843027, 9848020, 9843027, 199917058
Filed with no valid ESBT election on one shareholder	Filed ESBT election	PLRs 9808028, 9814017, 9820013
Trust was ineligible to be ESBT, but filed ESBT election, when corporation filed Form 2553	Trustee relinquished certain powers, and trust became eligible as ESBT	PLR 9832003
Shares were owned by IRAs	Transferred shares to eligible holder	PLR 9741028
Shares were owned by IRAs	Corporation redeemed stock	PLR 199918045
Affiliated group status on date Form 2553 filed (pre-1/1/97).	Amended merger to be effective on earliest possible date, or liquidated subsidiary	PLRs 9717019, 9741006, 9741008, 9804018, 9830024, 9851025, 199922016

OBSERVATION: To qualify for relief from a defective election (including an election by an ineligible corporation), the corporation must demonstrate that the cause of the defect was inadvertent. The standard for proving inadvertence is more stringent than that of showing reasonable cause, for which the IRS can accept a late election. Although it may seem paradoxical, to not file an election at all is better than to do so improperly. At 550.3., above, there are cites to many rulings issued for late elections when there seemed to be no cause at all, except that the corporation did not file the form. It is difficult to imagine that the IRS would be quite as tolerant in accepting a defective election.

550.5. Late QSST and ESBT elections. Late QSST elections have been a persistent compliance problem since the QSST became a permitted shareholder in 1981. Beginning in 1983, the late QSST election became a frequent cause of inadvertent terminations of S elections (discussed in Chapter 13, at 1350). Since 1996, they have also been frequent causes of inadvertently defective S elections (discussed above at 550.42).

Although the ESBT is a newcomer to the S corporation scene, it is beginning to exhibit many of the same problems as the QSST. Namely, the trustees are not filing timely ESBT elections. As a consequence, the IRS has begun to issue rulings on late ESBT elections. In addition, the IRS has coordinated certain relief rules for these trusts with those that apply to QSSTs. Moreover, it is likely that a corporation that does not file a timely S election may also neglect to have a beneficiary file a timely QSST election, or a trustee may neglect to file a timely ESBT election. Each of these particular situations is discussed below.

550.51. With late S corporation election. If the corporation's late election qualifies for relief under Rev. Proc. 98-55, the QSST or ESBT may obtain automatic relief if the election is filed simultaneously with the late 2553. See discussion at 550.12.

If the corporation's late election does not qualify under Rev. Proc. 98-55, the trust may still qualify for a late election under Rev. Proc. 98-55, 1998-46 IRB 1. This apparent paradox is due to the different time horizons permitted by Rev. Proc. 98-55. A late election can only qualify if the due date for the corporation's first Form 1120S has not expired. However, Rev. Proc. 98-55 extends relief to QSSTs for two full years after their elections are due (26 months and 15 days). There is an identical time horizon for ESBTs.

Finally, if the late S corporation and the late trust election are beyond both of the time horizons in Rev. Proc. 98-55, there will be two ruling requests: one by the corporation itself and one by the QSST beneficiary or by the ESBT fiduciary (or one request with two issues).

Table 5-4 summarizes the various possibilities for a late QSST or ESBT election with a late Subchapter S election.

Table 5-4: Late S corporation election and late QSST or ESBT election

Situation	*Remedy*
Both 2553 and QSST or ESBT election are not beyond the due date for first 1120S.	File both relief requests under Rev. Proc. 98-55. If the IRS approves the 2553, it will automatically grant retroactive QSST or ESBT status.
Both 2553 and QSST or ESBT election are beyond the due date for first 1120S, but not beyond 26 months and 15 days late.	File ruling request for late 2553 (unless the corporation qualifies under Rev. Proc. 97-48). File with service center for late QSST or ESBT.
Both 2553 and QSST or ESBT election are beyond 26 months and 15 days late.	File ruling requests for both relief provisions.

550.52. Inadvertent defective election or termination—no QSST or ESBT ruling. The QSST and ESBT election procedures are often overlooked in practice. When a beneficiary fails to file the proper election, it causes an inadvertent termination, or an inadvertently defective election. See this chapter at 550.42. and Chapter 13 at 1350. for discussion of these topics. If the trust's election is filed within two years of its due date (26 months and 15 days after the S corporation's election or after the trust acquires S corporation stock), then the election qualifies for relief under Revenue Procedure 98-55, 1998-46 IRB 1. The trust's election must be filed by the beneficiary in the case of a QSST, and by the trustee in the case of an ESTB. See Chapter 13, at 1350.22., for the details on this relief provision. Relief is granted by the service center, and no ruling is necessary.

> **OBSERVATION:** Through either a strange paradox or an oversight, the IRS will allow the service center to approve inadvertent termination or inadvertent defective election relief if the only cause is a late QSST or ESBT election that is not more than two years delinquent. However, the service center can grant a late S election with a late trust election only if it is not more than one year late. In this respect, it may be easier to qualify for inadvertent defective election or inadvertent termination relief than for late election relief.

550.53. Inadvertent defective election or termination—ruling required. If a QSST or ESBT election is more than two years late, the IRS national office must rule on the inadvertent defective election or inadvertent termination relief. There have been numerous rulings allowing relief under these circumstances—see this chapter at 550.42. and Chapter 13, at 1350. Table 13-1 lists rulings that have been granted on this issue in the five years preceding this edition of the *S Corporation Taxation Guide*. Also see PLRs 9832038, 9841029, 9842011, and 9842022 for situations in which the IRS has permitted a late ESBT election along with a late S corporation election. Relief has been granted under Regulations §§301.9100-1 and 301.9100-3.

550.54. Extension of shareholder consent and QSST or ESBT election. The Code specifies a rigid time limit for the consent to QSST treatment, so the IRS cannot waive the deadline under Regulations §301.9100-1. In several 1994 Private Letter Rulings, however, the IRS held that an extension of time for filing consents to the S election also extended the time for making the QSST election. [PLRs 9424060, 9424061, 9427013] Since extensions for consent to the S election are administered at the service center level [Regs. §1.1362-6(b)(3)(iii)], the service center should be the logical place to request an extension for a trust election along with an extension for consent.

550.6. Late QSub Elections. The deadline for filing the QSub election is not specified in the Code, so the IRS can grant relief from the deadline under Regulations §301.9100-1. The IRS has included late QSub elections as being subject to relief under the provisions of Revenue Procedure 98-55, 1998-46 IRB 1. Note that a late QSub election cannot be a cause of inadvertent termination or inadvertent defective election of the parent corporation, as is the case with a QSST or an ESBT. Therefore, the treatment of late QSub elections does not parallel the treatment of late trust elections.

550.61. With late S corporation election. If a corporation owns 100% of the stock of a subsidiary corporation, but neglects to file a timely Form 2553, it is also likely to neglect to file a timely QSub election. The rules of Revenue Procedure 98-55 are extended to this situation. If the unextended due date for the parent's first intended S corporation year has not expired, then the corporation may file a consolidated relief request with the service center. This rule applies when a parent corporation owned all of the stock of a subsidiary corporation on the date it intended for an S election to take effect, but did not file a timely Form 2553 or a timely QSub election.

5

The procedures are quite simple: The corporation files the late Form 2553 and the QSub election simultaneously, with the appropriate IRS service center(s). The corporation explains the reasonable cause. The corporation must note at the top of each request:

FILED PURSUANT TO REVENUE PROCEDURE 98-55

If the service center accepts the late 2553, it will automatically accept the QSub election as being made for the first day of the parent S corporation's first S corporation year. [Rev. Proc. 98-55, §4.04]

When the late S corporation election and the late QSub election do not qualify under Revenue Procedure 98-55, 1998-46 IRB 1, the corporation may file a single ruling request with two issues. It may request that the S election be accepted as of the desired date, and that the QSub election also be accepted at the same date. The IRS has granted dual relief for both late elections. [PLR 199917067]

550.62. Late QSub election only—no ruling. Revenue Procedure 98-55 provides expeditious relief when a parent S corporation owns a subsidiary that could have qualified as a Qsub, but the parent failed to file a timely QSub election. [Rev. Proc. 98-55, §5] As is the case with other provisions in Revenue Procedure 98-55, the parent corporation files for relief with the service center rather than with the national office of the IRS. Consequently, there is no ruling application and no user fee.

In order for the corporation to qualify for this relief, the due date for the parent corporation's return for the first intended year of QSub status must not have expired. The parent S corporation must file a completed QSub election with the applicable service center. Attached to the form must be a statement explaining why the corporation failed to file a QSub election within the time period required for the desired effective date. The QSub election must state at the top of the form:

FILED PURSUANT TO REVENUE PROCEDURE 98-55

If the service center accepts the reason, the QSub election is valid for the desired date. [Rev. Proc. 98-55, §4.04]

550.63 Late QSub election only—ruling required. Proposed Regulations issued in 1998 specifically address the problem of late QSub elections. There is a terse statement in Proposed Regulations §1.1361-3(a)(5): "An extension of time to make a QSub election may be available under the procedures applicable under §§301.9100-1 and 301.9100-3 of this chapter." The Regulation offers no further guidance, such as a specific time period or procedure. Therefore, if this rule is adopted in a Final Regulation without further amplification, it will merely be as permission to request relief by means of a Private Letter Ruling.

The IRS has granted late QSub elections in several cases, under Regulations §301.9100-3. [PLRs 9748024, 9814009, 9825028, 9826009, 9834010, 9837035, 9838015, 9839012, 9839012, 9839013, 9839013, 9840027, 9840027, 9841029, 9842011, 9842022, 9843029, 9843029, 9843034, 9845025, 9847019, 9851027, 9852021, 9853046, 9853060, 199901020, 199906005, 199906019, 199906022, 199908030, 199909053, 199912025, 199913027, 199915055, 199916015, 199916019, 199917021, 199917067, 199918045] In some cases, the IRS has used Temporary Regulations §301.9100-3T as the source of its rulings. [PLRs 9827013, 9827029, 9828025]

550.7. Relief for other late or defective elections. Under its general authority to enforce the tax laws, the IRS is empowered to grant extensions for various actions. In general, the IRS may grant extensions of time for an election when (1) the time is not expressly prescribed in a statute, (2) the request is made within a reasonable time, and (3) the IRS is satisfied that the extension will not jeopardize the interests of the government. [Regs. §301.9100-1(a)] The IRS has applied this rule to some situations of special concern to the S corporation.

550.71. Late §444 taxable year elections. The deadline for filing the §444 election is not specified in the Code. Accordingly, the IRS can grant relief from the deadline under Regulations §301.9100-1. The §444 election has been specified as eligible for an automatic 12-month extension. [Regs. §301.9100-2T(a)(2)(i)]

The IRS has allowed extensions for filing §444 elections when the failure to file has been on the part of the tax advisor. [PLRs 9025017, 9025019, 9025020, 9025026, 9025063, 9125070, 9138018, 9253033] The client must have instructed the advisor to file for the fiscal year. If the client has not discussed the possibility with the tax advisor, then the IRS appears not to grant relief from the deadline. [PLRs 9025043, 9139019]

550.72. Other late elections. The IRS has granted late elections for several other purposes. For example, there are several rulings granting late requests for year-end changes. See this chapter, at 520.2. Also popular is the §338 election to treat a stock purchase as an asset purchase. See Chapter 15, at 1525.84.

550.8. Relief provisions summarized. Table 5-5 identifies some potential problems and cures for defective elections and inadvertent terminations.

Table 5-5: Cures for Procedural Errors in Elections and Inadvertent Terminations

Error	*Action to be taken*	*IRS Office*	*User fee*	*Citation*	*For discussion of rules, refer to:*
Late S election, not more than 12 months	File 2553 with letter of explanation.	Service Center	No	§1362(b)(5); Rev. Proc. 98-55	Chapter 5, 550.1.
Late S election, no notification within 6 months of first 1120S	File 2553 with letter of affidavit.	Service Center	No	§1362(b)(5); Rev. Proc. 97-48	Chapter 5, 550.21.
Late S election, notification within 6 months of first 1120S; pre-1997, no closed years	File 2553 with letter of affidavit.	Service Center	No	§1362(b)(5); Rev. Proc. 97-48	Chapter 5, 550.22.
Late S election, more than 12 months, not eligible for Rev. Proc. 97-48	Ruling Request	National	Yes	§1362(b)(5); Rev. Proc. 98-55	Chapter 5, 550.3.
Inadvertent defective election	Ruling Request	National	Yes	Regulations §1.1362-4(c)	Chapter 5, 550.4., 550.4.
Late shareholder consent	Request permission for late consent.	District	No	Regulations §1.1362-6(b)(3)(iii)	Chapter 5, 530.2.
Inadvertent termination, other than QSST or ESBT election, less than 2 years late	Ruling Request	National	Yes	Regulations §1.1362-4(c)	Chapter 13, 1350.21.

Error	*Action to be taken*	*IRS Office*	*User fee*	*Citation*	*For discussion of rules, refer to:*
Inadvertent termination, sole cause is QSST or ESBT election, less than 2 years late	File QSST consent with affidavit by corporation and all shareholders.	District	No	Rev. Proc. 98-55	Chapter 13, 1350.22. 1350.23.
Late taxable-year election under §444	File late request.	National	Yes	Regulations §301.9100-1, §301.9100-3	Chapter 5, 550.71.
Late QSub election, not more than 1 year late	File late QSub election with letter of explanation.	Service Center	No	Rev. Proc. 98-55; Proposed Regs. §1.1361-3(a)(5) §301.9100-1, §301.9100-3	Chapter 5, 550.62.
Late QSub election, more than 1 year late	No specific action prescribed. Request relief under general rules for late elections.	National	Yes	Regulations §301.9100-1, §301.9100-3	Chapter 5, 550.63

5

555. Practice aids.

The election rules are summarized in Figure 5-1. There are several practice aids that should help the tax professional to advise his or her client on the procedural aspects of the S election.

555.1. Form 2553. The first page of Form 2553 is shown in Tax Form 5 - 1. An S corporation that has no QSST or Electing Small Business Trust as a shareholder and uses the calendar year needs to complete only page 1. Page 2 of Form 2553, shown in Tax Form 5 - 2, is necessary if the corporation uses a fiscal year or has a QSST or Electing Small Business Trust as a shareholder.

Form 2553 must be signed, under penalties of perjury, by a corporate officer who has the authority to sign the corporation's tax returns. Failure to sign the form may render the S election invalid. [*Jon P. Smith,* 54 TCM 1535 TC Memo 1988-18]

A corporation must meet all of the eligibility requirements when it files Form 2553. If it does not, the filing of the form does not constitute a valid S election. Checklist 5 - 1 provides a checklist to review a corporation's eligibility. It should be completed immediately before Form 2553 is filed.

When a corporation files Form 2553, it should be certain that the form is properly prepared. Checklist 5-2 provides a convenient checklist of the filing requirements.

555.2. Shareholder consents. As discussed above, at 530., each shareholder must consent to the corporation's consent. The Regulations also permit any shareholder to sign a separate letter of consent that properly identifies the corporation and on which the shareholder states the number of shares he or she holds, and the date the shares were acquired. [Regs. §1.1362-6(b)(3)] Sample Letter 5 - 1 illustrates an acceptable consent form.

If it is convenient to gather all shareholders together at one time in one place, they could all sign their consents on the face of Form 2553. If the shareholders are geographically dispersed, however, it is usually best for the tax advisor to keep Form 2553 in his or her possession, and send out a separate consent letter to be signed by each shareholder. In this

***Figure 5-1:** Flowchart for S election requirements and procedures.*

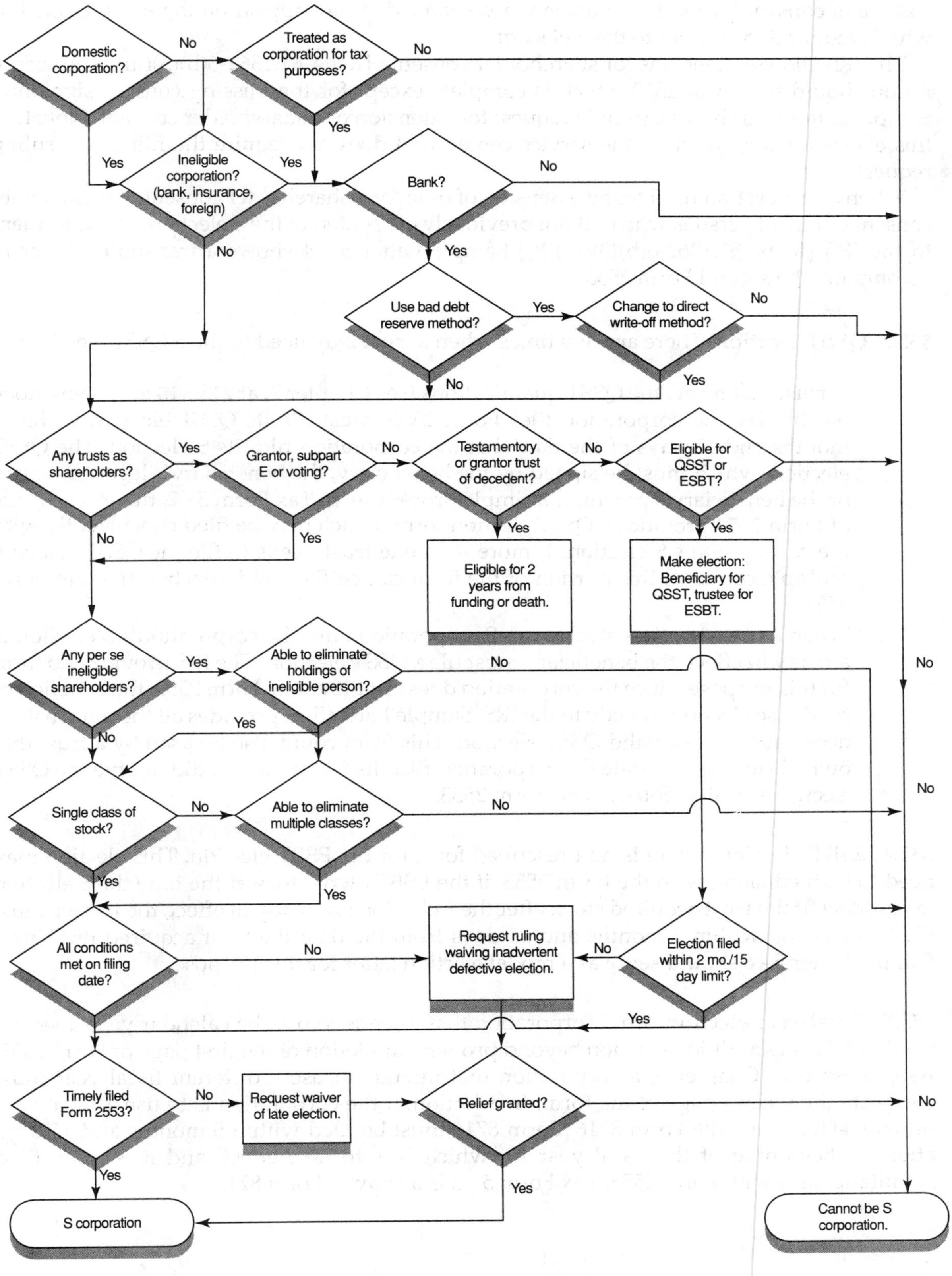

manner, the form is unlikely to be lost or temporarily diverted. In some situations, a person with an ownership interest in shares may not be listed as a shareholder. This is most likely to occur in the community property states. [Regs. §1.1362-6(b)(2)(i)] Sample Letter 5 - 2 illustrates a of consent for use by a person whose name does not appear on the stock ledger but who is required to consent to the S election.

The IRS allows extensions for shareholder consents. [Regs. §1.1362-6(b)(3)(iii)] The corporation should file Form 2553 which is complete except for the missing consent signature. Sample Letter 5 - 3 shows a sample request for extension of a shareholder consent. Note that this extension is granted by the service center, and does not require the filing of a ruling request.

When a corporation receives an extension of time for a shareholder consent, it must obtain consents from all persons who had not previously consented to the S election and send them to the IRS. [Regs. §1.1362-6(b)(3)(iii)(B)] Sample Letter 5 - 4 shows a transmittal letter to accompany the second Form 2553.

555.3. QSST election. There are two times when a trust may need to file a QSST election:

1. A trust that meets the QSST qualifications (see Chapter 2, at 215.34.) and owns stock on the day the corporation files Form 2553, must file its QSST election within 2 months and 15 days of the date that the corporation files its S election. The QSST election, which must be signed by the beneficiary, the beneficiary's legal guardian, or the beneficiary's parent, is a simple procedure. In Tax Form 5 - 2, the second page of Form 2553 provides a QSST election form, which may be filed concurrently with the corporation's S election. If more than one trust needs to file the QSST election, multiple copies of this portion of the form can be filed and attached them to Form 2553.
2. When a trust acquires stock in an S corporation after the corporation's S election is already in effect, the beneficiary must file a QSST election. The IRS provides no form for this purpose. Since the corporation does not file a new Form 2553, the beneficiary sends the election directly to the IRS. Sample Letter 5 - 5 provides all the information necessary to file a valid QSST election. This form could also be used by a trust that owned stock on the date the corporation filed its S election but did not file the QSST election simultaneously with Form 2553.

555.4. ESBT election. There is no prescribed form for the ESBT election. This election may need to be filed along with the Form 2553, if the ESBT owns stock at the time the S election takes effect. If the trust acquired stock after the S election is already in effect, the trustee must file this election within 2 months and 15 days from the date the trust acquired its shares. Sample Letter 5 - 6 should serve as a model election letter for this purpose.

555.5. Fiscal-year election. An S corporation that intends to use the calendar year does not need to take any additional action beyond proper completion of the first page of Form 2553. As discussed in Chapter 5, a corporation that intends to use a different fiscal year must complete the second page of the form. In addition, if the corporation is to use a fiscal year under §444, it must file Form 8716. Form 8716 must be filed within 5 months and 15 days after the beginning of the fiscal year for which it is to take effect, and it is often filed simultaneously with Form 2553. Tax Form 5 - 3 is a copy of Form 8716.

Checklist 5 - 1: S corporation eligibility

	Applicable (Yes/No)	Completed (Date)
1. Verify ownership of all outstanding stock.	______	______
2. Number of shareholders—no more than 75		
a. Husband and wife count as one.	______	______
b. Widow and deceased husband's estate count as one.	______	______
c. Widower and deceased wife's estate count as one.	______	______
d. Estates of deceased husband and wife count as one.		
3. Identity of each shareholder		
a. Individuals must be U.S. citizens or residents.	______	______
b. Estates are eligible.	______	______
c. Exempt organizations (yrs. beginning after 12/31/97)	______	______
d. If trusts, verify status—see Trust Eligibility checklist (Checklist 2 - 2)	______	______
4. Ownership of stock in other corporations (before 1997) If 100% stock owned, consider QSUB	______	______
5. Domestic corporation		
a. Must be incorporated in state or D.C.	______	______
b. If chartered as business trust, verify federal tax status as corporation.	______	______
c. Cannot be ineligible corporation.	______	______
6. Classes of stock		
a. Voting rights may differ.	______	______
b. Confirm that state law, charter, or bylaws create no differences.	______	______
c. Options and warrants:		
i. Can be issued to lenders.	______	______
ii. Can be issued to employees or independent contractors for services.	______	______
iii. Not substantially certain to be exercised.	______	______
7. Prior S elections		
a. Never resulted in S corporation status?	______	______
b. Not terminated within 5 years?	______	______
c. Termination occurred in a taxable year beginning before January 1, 1997.	______	______
d. If more than 50% shares have changed ownership, may request permission to reelect.	______	______
e. If prior inadvertent termination occurred, may request relief.	______	______

Copyright © 2000 by Harcourt, Inc. All rights reserved.

5

Checklist 5 - 2: S election procedures

	Applicable (Yes/No)	*Completed (Date)*
1. Have all eligibility requirements been met?	______	______
2. Identify year S election is to take effect.		
a. If new corporation, file Form 2553 within 2 months, 15 days of earliest of the following:		
i. Date corporation issued shares (check with applicable state law)	______	______
ii. Date corporation acquired assets	______	______
iii. Date corporation commenced business	______	______
b. If existing corporation, file Form 2553:		
i. In tax year before election is to be effective, or	______	______
ii. Within 2 months and 15 days of start of year.	______	______
iii. Must have been eligible all year.	______	______
3. Identify and list all shares and shareholders.		
a. Verify all outstanding shares from stock records.	______	______
b. Ascertain any unrecorded transfers.	______	______
i. Are all new shareholders eligible?	______	______
ii. Prepare any necessary QSST elections.	______	______
iii. Prepare necessary Electing Small Business Trust elections.	______	______
4. Obtain consent from each shareholder—sign on face of Form 2553 or attached letter.		
a. If minor, parent or guardian must sign.	______	______
b. If grantor trust, grantor must sign.	______	______
c. If not grantor trust, beneficiary must sign.	______	______
d. If estate, executor must sign.	______	______
e. Identify potential current beneficiaries of Electing Small Business Trusts. Obtain signatures.	______	______
f. If no potential current beneficiaries, Electing Small Business Trust is shareholder. Trust must consent.	______	______
g. Need signature of each joint or community-property holder.	______	______
h. Need signatures of prior eligible shareholders, if they held stock this year.	______	______
i. If any shareholder is unavailable, prepare consent extension request—will need to file second Form 2553 with original signatures for consent.	______	______
5. Have Form 2553 signed by president, vice president, or treasurer.	______	______
6. Identify type of tax year desired.		
a. If calendar year, enter year end on face of Form 2553.	______	______
b. If natural business year end automatic:		
i. Check box on part II.	______	______
ii. Attach computations.	______	______
iii. Sign computations under penalties of perjury.	______	______

Copyright © 2000 by Harcourt, Inc. All rights reserved.

c. If natural business year end requested:
   i. Check box on part II. ________ ________
   ii. Attach computations, cite Rev. Rul. 87-57. ________ ________
   iii. Make backup §444 election, if desired. ________ ________
   iv. Make backup calendar-year election, if desired. ________ ________

d. If §444 election:
   i. Check box in part II. ________ ________
   ii. Fill out and attach Form 8716. ________ ________
   iii. Make backup calendar-year election, if desired. ________ ________

7. Send via registered mail and retain receipt in file. ________ ________
8. When response arrives from IRS:
   a. If positive, retain in files. ________ ________
   b. Ascertain any necessary corrections. ________ ________
   c. If natural business year end was requested but was denied by IRS, file Form 8716 if backup §444 election is desired. ________ ________
   d. If extension was requested for consent, note time period granted by IRS. ________ ________
      i. Keep original consent signatures on file. ________ ________
      ii. File new complete Form 2553 within extension period granted. ________ ________
9. Inquire with IRS if no response within 60 days of first filing. ________ ________

Sample Letter 5 - 1: Consent for shareholder

Consent to S election under Internal Revenue Code §1362(a)(2)

[Date]

[Name]
[Address]
[City, State ZIP Code]

I, [Name], am the owner of [number] shares in [Company], FEIN [number], located at [address] [City, State, ZIP Code]. I acquired these shares on [date]. I hereby consent to the election by [Company] to be an S corporation for its taxable year beginning [date].

Corporation	*Shareholder*
[Company] [Address] [City, State, ZIP Code] [FEIN]	[Company] [Address] [City, State, ZIP Code] [Social Security number]

[Name]
[Social Security number]

Copyright © 2000 by Harcourt, Inc. All rights reserved.

5

Sample Letter 5 - 2: Consent for joint or community interest holder

Consent to S election under Internal Revenue Code §1362(a)(2)

[Date]

[Name]
[Address]
[City, State ZIP Code]

I, [Name], own a community-property interest in [number] shares in [Company], FEIN [number], located at [address]. The shares are held in the name of [Name], and were acquired by [him/her] on [date]. I hereby consent to the election by [Company] to be an S corporation for its taxable year beginning [date].

Corporation	*Actual shareholder*	*Owner of community-property interest*
[Company] [Address] [City, State ZIP Code]	[Name] [Address] [City, State ZIP Code]	[Name] [Address] [City, State ZIP Code]
[FEIN]	[Social Security number]	[Social Security number]

[Name]
[Social Security number]

Sample Letter 5 - 3: Request for extension of shareholder consent

[Company]
[Address]
[City, State ZIP Code]
[FEIN]

[Date]

Internal Revenue Service Center
[City, State ZIP Code]

Form 2553 and request for extension of consent.

Copyright © 2000 by Harcourt, Inc. All rights reserved.

Attached is Form 2553 on which [Company] elects under §1362(a) to be an S corporation for its taxable year beginning [date]. The form is complete except for consent by shareholder [Name]. [Name] is [reason for inability to make contact]. Pursuant to Regulations §1.1362-6(b)(3(iii), the corporation requests an extension of time until [date], to obtain [Name]'s consent.

Sincerely,

[Name]
President, [Company]

Encl: Form 2553

Sample Letter 5 - 4: Resubmission of Form 2553 and delayed shareholder consent

[Company]
[Address]
[City, State ZIP Code]
[FEIN]

[Date]

Internal Revenue Service Center
[City, State ZIP Code]

Form 2553 and request for extension of consent.

Attached is Form 2553 on which [Company] elects under §1362(a) to be an S corporation for its taxable year beginning [date]. The corporation filed Form 2553 on [date], but at that time had no consent by shareholder [Name]. On [date], your office granted our request for an extension of [Name]'s consent until [date], pursuant to Regulations §1.1362-6(b)(3)(iii)(B).

Sincerely,

[Name]
President, [Company]

Encl: Form 2553, with consent of [Name]
Letter from IRS, dated [date], granting extension.

Copyright © 2000 by Harcourt, Inc. All rights reserved.

Sample Letter 5 - 5: Sample QSST election

Qualified Subchapter S Trust Election
Under Internal Revenue Code §1361(d)(2)

[Date]

5 On [date], [Name of Trust] acquired [number] shares in [Company], an S corporation. The [Name of Trust] has only one income beneficiary, [Name], a minor. The provisions of the trust do not allow any distribution of income or corpus to any person other than [Name] during [his/her] lifetime. Should the trust terminate during [Name]'s lifetime, [he/she] will receive all of the trust's corpus. The terms of the trust require that all of the trust accounting income, as defined in Internal Revenue Code §643(b), must be distributed no less frequently than annually, to [Name].

Identification of all parties:

Current Income Corporation	*Beneficiary*	*Trust*
[Company] [Address] [City, State ZIP Code] [FEIN]	[Name] [Address] [City, State ZIP Code] [Social Security number]	[Name] [Address] [City, State ZIP Code] [number]

I, [Name], [self or parent or guardian] of [Name], file an election under Internal Revenue Code §1361(d)(2) to treat the [Name of Trust] as a Qualified Subchapter S Trust, described in Internal Revenue Code §1361(c)(2)(A)(i).

____

[Name]

Copyright © 2000 by Harcourt, Inc. All rights reserved.

Sample Letter 5 - 6: Sample ESBT Election

Electing Small Business Trust Election
Under Internal Revenue Code §1361(e)

[Date]

On [date], [Name of Trust] acquired [number] shares in [Company], an S corporation. The [Name of Trust] has only the following potential current income beneficiaries:

[Name], [a U.S. citizen] [a minor]

[Name], [a charitable organization described in paragraph (2), (3), (4), or (5) of §170(c)]

[Name],

[Name],

This trust is not exempt from tax, is not a qualified Subchapter S trust, and is not a charitable annuity trust or a charitable unitrust.

Identification of all parties:

Current Income *Corporation*	*Beneficiary*	*Trust*
[Company] [Address] [City, State ZIP Code] [FEIN]	[Name] [Address] [City, State ZIP Code] [Social Security number]	[Name] [Address] [City, State ZIP Code] [number]

I, [Name], [trustee] of [Name], file an election under Internal Revenue Code §1361(d)(2) to treat the [Name of Trust] as an Electing Small Business Trust, described in Internal Revenue Code §1361(e).

____

[Name]

Copyright © 2000 by Harcourt, Inc. All rights reserved.

5

Tax Form 5 - 1: Form 2553, page 1

Form **2553** (Rev. July 1999) Department of the Treasury Internal Revenue Service

Election by a Small Business Corporation

(Under section 1362 of the Internal Revenue Code)

▶ See Parts II and III on back and the separate instructions.

▶ The corporation may either send or fax this form to the IRS. See page 1 of the instructions.

OMB No. 1545-0146

Notes: 1. *This election to be an S corporation can be accepted only if all the tests are met under* **Who may elect** *on page 1 of the instructions; all signatures in Parts I and III are originals (no photocopies); and the exact name and address of the corporation and other required form information are provided.*

2. *Do not file* **Form 1120S,** *U.S. Income Tax Return for an S Corporation, for any tax year before the year the election takes effect.*

3. *If the corporation was in existence before the effective date of this election, see* **Taxes an S corporation may owe** *on page 1 of the instructions.*

Part I Election Information

Please Type or Print	Name of corporation (see instructions)	**A** Employer identification number
	Number, street, and room or suite no. (If a P.O. box, see instructions.)	**B** Date incorporated
	City or town, state, and ZIP code	**C** State of incorporation

D Election is to be effective for tax year beginning (month, day, year) . . . . ▶ / /

E Name and title of officer or legal representative who the IRS may call for more information

F Telephone number of officer or legal representative ( )

G If the corporation changed its name or address after applying for the EIN shown in **A** above, check this box . . . . ▶ ☐

H If this election takes effect for the first tax year the corporation exists, enter month, day, and year of the **earliest** of the following: (1) date the corporation first had shareholders, (2) date the corporation first had assets, or (3) date the corporation began doing business . . . . ▶ / /

I Selected tax year: Annual return will be filed for tax year ending (month and day) ▶..................

If the tax year ends on any date other than December 31, except for an automatic 52-53-week tax year ending with reference to t he month of December, you **must** complete Part II on the back. If the date you enter is the ending date of an automatic 52-53-week tax year, write ™52-53-week year⌡ to the right of the date. See Temporary Regulations section 1.441-2T(e)(3).

J Name and address of each shareholder; shareholder's spouse having a community property interest in the corporation's stock; and each tenant in common, joint tenant, and tenant by the entirety. (A husband and wife (and their estates) are counted as one shareholder in determining the number of shareholders without regard to the manner in which the stock is owned.)	**K** Shareholders' Consent Statement. Under penalties of perjury, we declare that we consent to the election of the above-named corporation to be an S corporation under section 1362(a) and that we have examined this consent statement, including accompanying schedules and statements, and to the best of our knowledge and belief, it is true, correct, and complete. We understand our consent is binding and may not be withdrawn after the corporation has made a valid election. (Shareholders sign and date below.)		**L** Stock owned		**M** Social security number or employer identification number (see instructions)	**N** Share-holder's tax year ends (month and day)
	Signature	Date	Number of shares	Dates acquired		

Under penalties of perjury, I declare that I have examined this election, including accompanying schedules and statements, and to the best of my knowledge and belief, it is true, correct, and complete.

Signature of officer ▶ **Title ▶** **Date ▶**

For Paperwork Reduction Act Notice, see page 2 of the instructions. Cat. No. 18629R Form **2553** (Rev. 7-99)

5

Tax Form 5 - 2: Form 2553, page 2

Form 2553 (Rev. 7-99) Page 2

Part II Selection of Fiscal Tax Year (All corporations using this part must complete item O and item P, Q, or R.)

O Check the applicable box to indicate whether the corporation is:

1. ☐ A new corporation adopting the tax year entered in item I, Part I.
2. ☐ An existing corporation retaining the tax year entered in item I, Part I.
3. ☐ An existing corporation changing to the tax year entered in item I, Part I.

P Complete item P if the corporation is using the expeditious approval provisions of Rev. Proc. 87-32, 1987-2 C.B. 396, to request **(1)** a natural business year (as defined in section 4.01(1) of Rev. Proc. 87-32) or **(2)** a year that satisfies the ownership tax year test in section 4.01(2) of Rev. Proc. 87-32. Check the applicable box below to indicate the representation statement the corporation is making as required under section 4 of Rev. Proc. 87-32.

1. Natural Business Year ▶ ☐ I represent that the corporation is retaining or changing to a tax year that coincides with its natural business year as defined in section 4.01(1) of Rev. Proc. 87-32 and as verified by its satisfaction of the requirements of section 4.02(1) of Rev. Proc. 87-32. In addition, if the corporation is changing to a natural business year as defined in section 4.01(1), I further represent that such tax year results in less deferral of income to the owners than the corporation's present tax year. I also represent that the corporation is not described in section 3.01(2) of Rev. Proc. 87-32. (See instructions for additional information that must be attached.)

2. Ownership Tax Year ▶ ☐ I represent that shareholders holding more than half of the shares of the stock (as of the first day of the tax year to which the request relates) of the corporation have the same tax year or are concurrently changing to the tax year that the corporation adopts, retains, or changes to per item I, Part I. I also represent that the corporation is not described in section 3.01(2) of Rev. Proc. 87-32.

Note: *If you do not use item P and the corporation wants a fiscal tax year, complete either item Q or R below. Item Q is used to request a fiscal tax year based on a business purpose and to make a back-up section 444 election. Item R is used to make a regular section 444 election.*

Q Business Purpose–To request a fiscal tax year based on a business purpose, you must check box Q1 and pay a user fee. See instructions for details. You may also check box Q2 and/or box Q3.

1. Check here ▶ ☐ if the fiscal year entered in item I, Part I, is requested under the provisions of section 6.03 of Rev. Proc. 87-32. Attach to Form 2553 a statement showing the business purpose for the requested fiscal year. See instructions for additional information that must be attached.

2. Check here ▶ ☐ to show that the corporation intends to make a back-up section 444 election in the event the corporation's business purpose request is not approved by the IRS. (See instructions for more information.)

3. Check here ▶ ☐ to show that the corporation agrees to adopt or change to a tax year ending December 31 if necessary for the IRS to accept this election for S corporation status in the event (1) the corporation's business purpose request is not approved and the corporation makes a back-up section 444 election, but is ultimately not qualified to make a section 444 election, or (2) the corporation's business purpose request is not approved and the corporation did not make a back-up section 444 election.

R Section 444 Election–To make a section 444 election, you must check box R1 and you may also check box R2.

1. Check here ▶ ☐ to show the corporation will make, if qualified, a section 444 election to have the fiscal tax year shown in item I, Part I. To make the election, you must complete **Form 8716,** Election To Have a Tax Year Other Than a Required Tax Year, and either attach it to Form 2553 or file it separately.

2. Check here ▶ ☐ to show that the corporation agrees to adopt or change to a tax year ending December 31 if necessary for the IRS to accept this election for S corporation status in the event the corporation is ultimately not qualified to make a section 444 election.

Part III Qualified Subchapter S Trust (QSST) Election Under Section 1361(d)(2)*

Income beneficiary's name and address	Social security number
Trust's name and address	Employer identification number

Date on which stock of the corporation was transferred to the trust (month, day, year) . . . . ▶ / /

In order for the trust named above to be a QSST and thus a qualifying shareholder of the S corporation for which this Form 2553 is filed, I hereby make the election under section 1361(d)(2). Under penalties of perjury, I certify that the trust meets the definitional requirements of section 1361(d)(3) and that all other information provided in Part III is true, correct, and complete.

Signature of income beneficiary or signature and title of legal representative or other qualified person making the election — Date

*Use Part III to make the QSST election only if stock of the corporation has been transferred to the trust on or before the date on which the corporation makes its election to be an S corporation. The QSST election must be made and filed separately if stock of the corporation is transferred to the trust after the date on which the corporation makes the S election.

Form 2553 (Rev. 7-99)

5

Tax Form 5 - 3: Form 8716

Form **8716**
(Rev. July 1997)
Department of the Treasury
Internal Revenue Service

Election To Have a Tax Year Other Than a Required Tax Year

OMB No. 1545-1036

Please Type or Print	Name	Employer identification number
	Number, street, and room or suite no. (or P.O. box number if mail is not delivered to street address)	
	City or town, state, and ZIP code	

1 Check applicable box to show type of entity:
☐ Partnership
☐ S corporation (or C corporation electing to be an S corporation)
☐ Personal service corporation (PSC)

2 Name and telephone number (including area code) of person who may be called for information:

3 Enter ending date of the tax year for the entity's last filed return. A new entity should enter the ending date of the tax year it is adopting. . . . . Month | Day | Year

4 Enter ending date of required tax year determined under section 441(i), 706(b), or 1378 . . . Month | Day

5 Section 444(a) Election.–Check the applicable box and enter the ending date of the first tax year for which the election will be effective that the entity is (see instructions): Month | Day | Year
☐ Adopting ☐ Retaining ☐ Changing to

Under penalties of perjury, I declare that the entity named above has authorized me to make this election under section 444(a), and that the statements made are, to the best of my knowledge and belief, true, correct, and complete.

▶ Signature and title (see instructions) ▶ Date

General Instructions

Section references are to the Internal Revenue Code unless otherwise noted.

Purpose of Form

Form 8716 is filed by partnerships, S corporations, and personal service corporations (as defined in section 441(i)(2)) to elect under section 444 to have a tax year other than a required tax year.

Attach a copy of the Form 8716 you file to Form 1065 or a Form 1120 series form (1120, 1120-A, 1120S, etc.), whichever is applicable, for the first tax year for which the election is made.

When To File

Form 8716 must be filed by the earlier of:

1. The 15th day of the 5th month following the month that includes the 1st day of the tax year the election will be effective, or

2. The due date (not including extensions) of the income tax return for the tax year resulting from the section 444 election.

Items **1** and **2** relate to the tax year, or the return for the tax year, for which the ending date is entered on line 5 above.

Under Temporary Regulations section 301.9100-2T, the entity is automatically granted a 12-month extension to make an election on Form 8716. To obtain an extension, type or legibly print ™FILED PURSUANT TO SECTION 301.9100-2T∫ at the top of a properly prepared Form 8716, and file the form within 12 months of the original due date.

Where To File

File the election with the Internal Revenue Service Center where the entity will file its return. See the instructions for Form 1065 or a Form 1120 series form for service center addresses. For a foreign entity, file Form 8716 with the Internal Revenue Service Center, Philadelphia, PA 19255.

Effect of Section 444 Election

Partnerships and S corporations.– An electing partnership or S corporation must file **Form 8752,** Required Payment or Refund Under Section 7519, for each year the election is in effect. Form 8752 is used to figure and make the payment required under section 7519 or to obtain a refund of net prior year payments. Form 8752 must be filed by May 15 following the calendar year in which each applicable election year begins.

The section 444 election will end if the partnership or S corporation is penalized for willfully failing to make the required payments.

Personal service corporations.– An electing personal service corporation (PSC) should not file Form 8752. Instead, it must comply with the minimum distribution requirements of section 280H for each year the election is in effect. If the PSC does not meet these requirements, the applicable amounts it may deduct for payments made to its employee-owners may be limited.

Use **Schedule H (Form 1120),** Section 280H Limitations for a Personal Service Corporation (PSC), to figure the required minimum distribution and the maximum deductible amount. Attach Schedule H to the income tax return of the PSC for each tax year the PSC does not meet the minimum distribution requirements.

The section 444 election will end if the PSC is penalized for willfully failing to comply with the requirements of section 280H.

Members of Certain Tiered Structures May Not Make Election

No election may be made under section 444(a) by an entity that is part of a tiered structure other than a tiered structure that consists entirely of partnerships and/or S corporations all of which have the same tax year. An election previously made will be terminated if an entity later becomes part of a tiered structure that is not allowed to make the election. See Temporary Regulations section 1.444-2T for other details.

For Paperwork Reduction Act Notice, see back of form. Cat. No. 64725S Form **8716** (Rev. 7-97)

Appendix:
Late S corporation elections permitted, 1997 through mid-1999

9715021, 9716024, 9717020, 9719009, 9734056, 9735019, 9737002, 9737004, 9737022, 9737033, 9740012, 9740021, 9741003, 9741012, 9741015, 9741023, 9741027, 9741031, 9741045, 9742017, 9742032, 9743038, 9744010, 9744018, 9745006, 9745014, 9745015, 9746008, 9746009, 9746030, 9746041, 9746042, 9746043, 9746044, 9746047, 9746054, 9747007, 9747008, 9747009, 9747010, 9747013, 9747015, 9747016, 9747018, 9747019, 9747026, 9748011, 9748012, 9748013, 9748014, 9748015, 9748016, 9748017, 9748018, 9748019, 9748027, 9748030, 9748031, 9748032, 9748033, 9749003, 9749004, 9749005, 9749006, 9749011, 9750003, 9750023, 9750035, 9750046, 9750050, 9750051, 9750052, 9750060, 9751005, 9751011, 9751013, 9751018, 9751023, 9751025, 9752010, 9752012, 9752013, 9752020, 9752021, 9752028, 9752037, 9752040, 9752044, 9752046, 9752048, 9752053, 9752055, 9801006, 9801034, 9801040, 9801044, 9801045, 9801046, 9802003, 9802008, 9802009, 9802010, 9802011, 9802015, 9802020, 9802022, 9802025, 9802028, 9803007, 9803011, 9803014, 9803016, 9804002, 9804003, 9804004, 9804005, 9804010, 9804015, 9804016, 9804017, 9804025, 9804032, 9804041, 9804048, 9805005, 9805006, 9805011, 9805012, 9805013, 9805014, 9805022, 9805024, 9805026, 9805027, 9805028, 9805029, 9805035, 9807006, 9807011, 9807014, 9807016, 9807022, 9808004, 9808017, 9808019, 9808023, 9808025, 9808026, 9808027, 9808029, 9808030, 9808033, 9808042, 9809028, 9809033, 9809039, 9809040, 9809042, 9809044, 9809047, 9809048, 9809050, 9810014, 9810023, 9811007, 9811009, 9811012, 9811013, 9811014, 9811031, 9811032, 9811034, 9811035, 9811040, 9811043, 9811046, 9812009, 9812010, 9812011, 9812016, 9812017, 9812020, 9812021, 9812023, 9812024, 9812024, 9812029, 9812029, 9813005, 9813006, 9814004, 9814005, 9814012, 9814014, 9814016, 9814022, 9814027, 9814033, 9815025, 9815028, 9815032, 9815033, 9815034, 9815038, 9815042, 9815043, 9815045, 9815047, 9815055, 9816005, 9816006, 9816009, 9816012, 9816013, 9816016, 9816019, 9816026, 9817005, 9817009, 9817016, 9817017, 9817020, 9817021, 9817023, 9817024, 9817025, 9817026, 9818007, 9818010, 9818018, 9818019, 9818038, 9818039, 9818040, 9818041, 9818043, 9818045, 9818047, 9818049, 9819002, 9819024, 9819025, 9819027, 9819028, 9819032, 9819039, 9820001, 9820002, 9820003, 9820006, 9820007, 9820008, 9820012, 9820014, 9821004, 9821007, 9821008, 9821010, 9821011, 9821014, 9821019, 9821020, 9821027, 9821028, 9821035, 9821039, 9821040, 9821041, 9821046, 9821047, 9821048, 9821050, 9822010, 9822010, 9822015, 9822022, 9822023, 9822027, 9822028, 9822032, 9822033, 9822036, 9822040, 9822049, 9822050, 9822051, 9823001, 9823020, 9823021, 9823022, 9823026, 9823027, 9823031, 9823033, 9823054, 9823055, 9824003, 9824004, 9824005, 9824006, 9824009, 9824012, 9824013, 9824013, 9824016, 9824017, 9824020, 9824021, 9824022, 9824024, 9824025, 9824025, 9824027, 9824027, 9824033, 9824035, 9824037, 9824039, 9824040, 9824044, 9824046, 9825023, 9825027, 9825029, 9825032, 9826003, 9826004, 9826011, 9826012, 9826013, 9826014, 9826020, 9826024, 9826026, 9826027, 9827003, 9827004, 9827005, 9827009, 9827012, 9827019, 9827022, 9827023, 9827024, 9827025, 9827026, 9828007, 9828008, 9828009, 9828010, 9828011, 9828013, 9828022, 9828027, 9829010, 9829013, 9829022, 9829028, 9829029, 9829032, 9829037, 9829038, 9829039, 9829040, 9829043, 9829054, 9829055, 9829058, 9830010, 9830011, 9830012, 9830014, 9830020, 9830026, 9830038, 9831014, 9831015, 9831016, 9831017, 9831019, 9831021, 9831022, 9831029, 9832004, 9832010, 9832013, 9832018, 9832019, 9832032, 9833018, 9833021, 9833022, 9833026, 9833028, 9833029, 9833031, 9834006, 9834008, 9834009, 9834016, 9834025, 9834029, 9834030, 9837024, 9837025, 9837026, 9837027, 9838001, 9838013, 9838021, 9838022, 9838023, 9839010, 9839011, 9840013, 9840014, 9840017, 9840021, 9840028, 9840034, 9840037, 9840045, 9840047, 9841018, 9841022, 9841032, 9841033, 9841036, 9842012, 9842013, 9842014, 9842015, 9842016, 9842017, 9842020, 9842026, 9842039, 9842041, 9842042, 9842044, 9842045, 9842049, 9842052, 9842053, 9842061, 9843013, 9843025, 9843032, 9844018, 9844023, 9844024, 9844025, 9844026, 9844028, 9844030, 9844035, 9845017, 9845029, 9846011,

9846012, 9846014, 9846017, 9846020, 9846023, 9846024, 9846026, 9846036, 9847015, 9847020, 9847021, 9848013, 9848015, 9848036, 9848037, 9848039, 9848040, 9849008, 9849009, 9849011, 9849015, 9849016, 9849017, 9849018, 9849019, 9849020, 9849021, 9849022, 9850006, 9850007, 9850008, 9850012, 9850013, 9851003, 9851004, 9851008, 9851009, 9851021, 9851028, 9851029, 9851034, 9852003, 9852006, 9852007, 9852008, 9852009, 9852010, 9852014, 9852017, 9852029, 9852032, 9853019, 9853032, 9853043, 9853045, 9853047, 9853056, 9853057, 9853059, 199901010, 199901011, 199901012, 199901022, 199901035, 199902006, 199902012, 199902015, 199903002, 199903003, 199903006, 199903007, 199903008, 199903009, 199903012, 199903016, 199903021, 199903022, 199903041, 199903043, 199903044, 199904003, 199904006, 199904007, 199904011, 199904024, 199904030, 199905006, 199905013, 199905016, 199906009, 199906013, 199906020, 199906040, 199907010, 199908011, 199908012, 199908025, 199908034, 199908035, 199908047, 199908048, 199908049, 199908050, 199908051, 199909017, 199909019, 199909035, 199909036, 199909041, 199909047, 199909049, 199909050, 199909051, 199909052, 199909057, 199910017, 199910018, 199910023, 199910024, 199910027, 199910028, 199910030, 199910031, 199910032, 199910034, 199910035, 199910036, 199910037, 199910039, 199910065, 199911017, 199911018, 199911020, 199911022, 199911023, 199911024, 199911032, 199911034, 199911036, 199911037, 199911052, 199912006, 199912031, 199913005, 199913008, 199913013, 199913015, 199913017, 199913019, 199913024, 199913038, 199913039, 199914004, 199914005, 199914008, 199914014, 199914015, 199914016, 199914019, 199914020, 199914021, 199914023, 199914026, 199914039, 199915016, 199915019, 199915029, 199915032, 199915033, 199915034, 199915047, 199915051, 199916018, 199916021, 199916022, 199916024, 199916027, 199916029, 199916034, 199916036, 199916048, 199916052, 199917014, 199917018, 199917030, 199917032, 199917053, 199917057, 199917067, 199917073, 199917074, 199918037, 199918041, 199919026, 199919036, 199920006, 199920008, 199920018, 199920021, 199920022, 199920025, 199920033, 199921013, 199921020, 199921023, 199921026, 199921028, 199921031, 199921038, 199921039, 199921040, 199922026, 199922035, 199922043, 199923019, 199923024, 199923031, 199923033, 199923036, 199923038, 199923039, 199923042

Part II

Operating the S Corporation

INCOME MEASUREMENT AND REPORTING

CONTENTS

6

6

6

600. Overview.

An S corporation acts as a conduit entity and must report its income, deductions, and other relevant items to its shareholders. As a general rule, the corporation pays no income tax. There are exceptions for the LIFO recapture tax (Chapter 3), the passive income tax (Chapter 12), the investment tax credit recapture tax (Chapter 12), and the built-in gains tax (Chapter 11). This chapter covers the measurement problems of corporations that are not subject to tax at the corporate level.

The primary role of the S corporation is that of a reporting entity, rather than a tax-paying entity. The fact that the corporation does not pay taxes does not mean that its duties are trivial. S corporations must report all of the information necessary for the shareholders to compute their personal income tax liabilities properly. The information needed by shareholders can become extremely complex.

In one case, an individual who was a minority shareholder in an S corporation failed to include his portion of the S corporation's income on his personal return. He claimed that he had no knowledge of the corporation's S election and that he had never consented to the election. (He was not a shareholder at the time the election was filed, and therefore was not required to consent to the election.) The judge upheld the IRS's assessment and stated that it is a taxpayer's responsibility to ascertain the tax consequences of his business dealings. [*Knott*, TC Memo 1991-352] In a more recent case, shareholders of an S corporation were assessed fraud penalties for understating an S corporation's gross receipts. [*Olbres*, TC Memo 1997-437]

In some cases, the corporation cannot anticipate all of the information needed by shareholders. It may not know, for example, a shareholder's basis, amount at risk, or whether the shareholder participates materially in the corporation's business activities. It cannot know the ultimate utilization of separately reported income or loss items by the shareholders.

In many cases, a shareholder may "wear several hats" in his or her relationship with the corporation. The shareholder may also be an employee, debtor, creditor, lessor, lessee, purchaser of property from, or seller of property to, the corporation. Chapter 8 deals with these different relationships and their impact on corporate and shareholder income.

In all cases, the corporation must focus on the individual rules for computation of the items that flow through to the shareholders. When the corporation is subject to one of the corporate-level taxes, however, it must also make a computation of taxable income under corporate rules. S corporations share some special accounting rules with partnerships. Finally, there are some rules for the computation of taxable income that are unique to S corporations.

The focus of this chapter is on getting the essential information to the shareholder in his or her role as a shareholder. The entire process can be defined by asking three simple questions:

- *What items* at the corporate level must be reported to the shareholders?
- *How much* of each item is reported to each shareholder?
- *When* does the shareholder report the items on his or her tax return?

Tax professionals should be aware that not all of the accounting rules for S corporations are well defined. The major tax revisions of the 1980s developed new rules that have not been addressed by Regulations. Accordingly, there are many issues for which there is no firm answer. This chapter explains some of the more common problems of tax accounting as they relate to S corporations and their shareholders. Figure 6-1 gives an overview of the process.

610. Measurement of income and deductions.

Measurement of income and deductions by the corporation is the first essential task in the reporting process. The basic rule is found in §1363.

6

***Figure 6 - 1:** Flowchart of S corporation's income and deductions.*

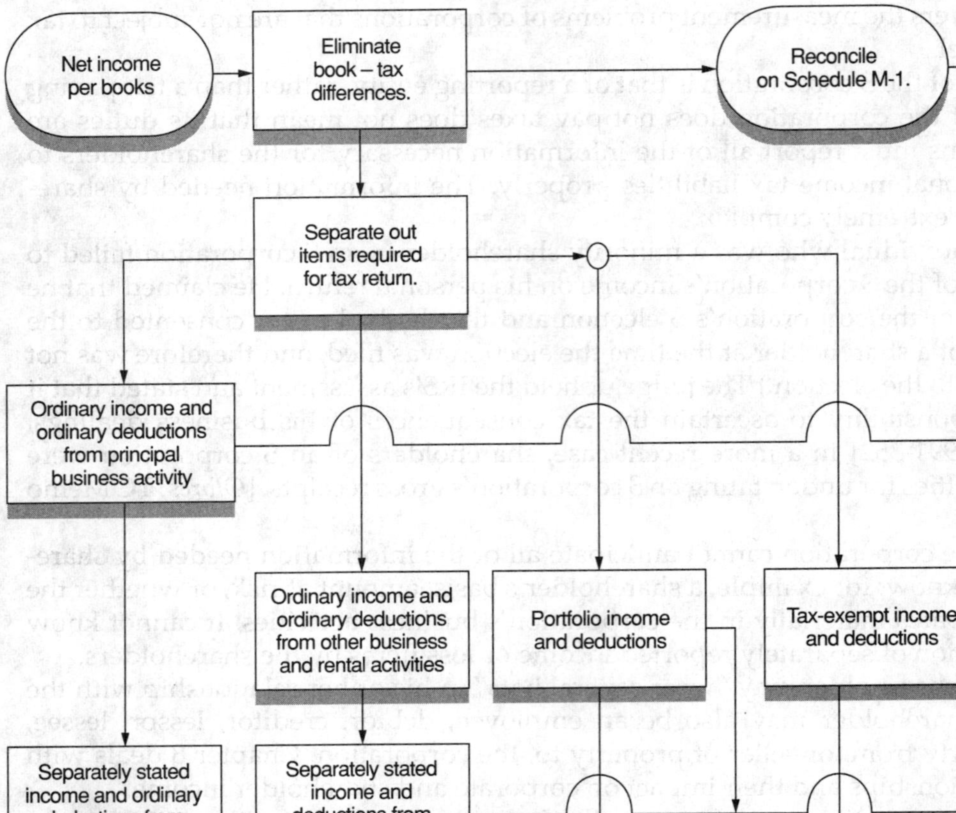

SUMMARY OF AUTHORITY: CODE SECTION 1363(a) AND (b)

- An S corporation follows the individual, rather than corporate, rules for computation of taxable income.
- Section 1363 refers to §1366(a)(1)(a) and requires the S corporation to state separately certain items that require separate reporting by the shareholders.
- By reference to §703, Subchapter S follows partnership rules for modifications of the individual rules for the computation of taxable income.
- S corporations are allowed to amortize organizational expenses in the same manner as any other corporation.
- Section 291, which restricts certain tax benefits to C corporations, applies to a former C corporation in its first three taxable years as an S corporation.

Note that one of the key phrases is that the S corporation shall compute its taxable income "in the same manner as in the case of an individual." The reason for this rule is that the shareholders are individuals (including estates) and will include their portions of the corporation's income, loss, and deduction items as if they had received the income, or sustained the deductions and losses, personally. There are numerous instances, however, where the impact of this rule is unclear. There are also some specific exceptions, listed in other provisions of Subchapter S and elsewhere in the tax law, that develop special rules for S corporations. In some instances, the special Subchapter S rules are derived from partnerships. In a few cases, there are rules that apply uniquely to S corporations.

Among the cross-references in §1363, §1366(a)(1)(A) and §703(a)(2) are the most important. Section 1366(a)(1)(A) and (B) state that the shareholder must report:

SUMMARY OF AUTHORITY: CODE SECTION 1366(a)(1)(A) AND (B)

- Section 1366(a)(1)(A) requires each shareholder of an S corporation to report his or her portion of any corporate item, if the separate reporting could affect the shareholder's tax liability.
- Section 1366(a)(1)(B) requires shareholders to include the corporation's ordinary, or nonseparately [sic] computed income or loss on their returns.
- Section 1366 refers to shareholders rather than to S corporations, per se.
- Section 1363, which prescribes the taxable income rules for S corporations, refers directly to §1366.
- Since the shareholders rather than the corporation bear the ultimate liability for the income tax, the reporting needs of the shareholders control the reporting requirements of S corporations.

As stated above, §1363 requires each S corporation to use the individual, rather than the corporate, rules for determining taxable income. Section 1363, however, also refers to a partnership provision, §703(a)(2), Subchapter K, for the disallowance of certain items. It states some deductions that are not allowed at the entity level.

SUMMARY OF AUTHORITY: CODE SECTION 703(a)(2)

- Partnerships are not allowed to deduct personal exemptions, foreign taxes, charitable contributions, certain other itemized deductions, or oil and gas depletion, according to §703(a)(2).
- The direct reference in §1363 to §703(a)(2) applies these same disallowance rules to S corporations.
- Nothing in §703 or §1363 prohibits an individual partner or shareholder from claiming these deductions on his or her own tax return.

An S corporation may be required to compute its taxable income in the same manner as a corporation if the corporation is subject to the tax on excess net passive income, built-in gains, or capital gains. There are certain other instances when the corporation engages in transactions—such as contributions to capital, stock redemptions, liquidations, and reorganizations—that have no counterparts in the scheme of individual taxation. In these instances, the corporation usually follows the regular corporate rules, although there may be some modifications. [§1371(a)(1)] Chapters 14, 15, and 16 demonstrate the application of corporate taxation rules to S corporations.

In some instances, the wording of the law has not been entirely clear when different rules apply to individuals and to corporations. For example, it may not have been entirely clear whether the individual rules or the corporate rules applied when an S corporation subdivided certain real estate for sale. Section 1237 has long provided that certain real estate sales could qualify for capital gain treatment if an individual had held the property and subdivided it. In contrast, a corporation that had subdivided real property would be treated as a dealer, and no property sold from the tract could qualify for capital gain treatment. Starting with corporate taxable years beginning after 1996, it is clear that an S corporation is subject to the same rules as an individual. [Small Business Job Protection Act of 1996, §1314, amending IRC §1237]

610.1. Corporate and shareholder elections. Any taxpayer may need to make certain elections in computing its taxable income. Some of these elections are permanent; others deal with specific transactions. Generally, any elections that affect the calculation or timing of taxable income are made by the corporation. [§1362(c)(1)]

Most of the necessary elections are made at the corporate level and are indirectly binding on all of the shareholders. Code §1363(c)(1) states the rule.

SUMMARY OF AUTHORITY: CODE SECTION 1363(c)(1)

- With few exceptions, most of the elections necessary to determine taxable income are made by the S corporation, rather than by the individual shareholders.
- Accordingly, most of the corporate elections are indirectly binding on all of the shareholders.
- Most of the corporation's routine elections do not require consent by shareholders.

Among the permanent elections made by the corporation are the overall accounting method (cash or accrual) and the inventory method (FIFO, LIFO, etc.). The S corporation is treated in the same manner as any other taxpayer and generally is not allowed to change accounting methods without permission from the IRS.

From year to year, there are other elections that any taxpayer must make. These include electing out of the installment method on applicable sales, deferral of gain on involuntary conversions, and treatment of income from discharge of indebtedness.

Other elections are made by each shareholder in accordance with §1363(c)(2).

SUMMARY OF AUTHORITY: CODE SECTION 1363(c)(2)

- Each shareholder elects separately whether to deduct or capitalize certain mining expenditures incurred by the S corporation.
- Each shareholder elects separately to take a deduction or a credit for foreign income taxes paid by the S corporation.

In addition to these two items, shareholders individually make certain alternative minimum tax elections. Each shareholder can elect the optional 10-year write-off of tax preferences.[1]

610.2. Exclusion of S corporation from membership in controlled group of corporations. Code §1563 requires that component members of controlled groups of corporations be treated as one single taxpayer for certain limits. Most of the limits, such as apportionment of the graduated rate schedule and alternative minimum tax exemption, have no application to S corporations.

Some rules, such as the required apportionment of a §179 election, may affect the taxable income of an S corporation, as well as other corporations controlled by the same shareholders. Unfortunately, neither §1563 nor any provision in Subchapter S explicitly includes or excludes S corporations from treatment as component members.

6

It may be important to distinguish a "member" of a controlled group of corporations from a "component member" of such a group. Certain rules are applicable to members, and other rules are applicable only to component members. All members are subject to certain rules for related party dealings. See Chapter 8, at 835., for examples of related party dealings that may be applied to members of controlled groups. Similarly, the IRS held that acquisition of one S corporation's debt by another S corporation, when the two S corporations were controlled by the same family, fell within certain controlled group dealing rules. [TAM 9541006]

The Regulations under §1563 state that an S corporation is generally not subject to inclusion as a component member of a controlled group. [Regs. §1.1563-1(b)(2)(ii)(c)] This particular reference has not been updated since the Subchapter S Revision Act of 1982. It refers to an electing small business corporation as defined in §1371(b) (the pre-Subchapter S Revision Act of 1982 election provision).[2] The Regulation implies, however, that an S corporation is to be included as a component member in a controlled group if it is subject to the corporate-level capital gains tax (the only corporate-level tax imposed on S corporations before the Subchapter S Revision Act of 1982).[3]

OBSERVATION: The omission of S corporations as component members from controlled groups appears to have even stronger justification under the Subchapter S Revision Act of 1982 than it did in years before that legislation. Under old Subchapter S, an S corporation used most of the corporate rules in computing its taxable income. Under current law, however, an S corporation computes its taxable income in the same manner as an individual. [§1363(b)] Since there are no "controlled groups" of individuals, there should be no apportionment among S corporations and other corporations that have common ownership. Therefore, any item (such as the §179 expensing deduction, discussed at 610.43.) that is required to be allocated among members of a controlled group of corporations should not be allocated to an S corporation. The IRS instructs D corporations to check Item 5 on Schedule B, other information to indicate membership in a controlled group. There are no instructions or other directives from the IRS on the significance of this item, except for the possible alert to the possibility of dealing with related parties.

EXAMPLE 6 - 1: Carol Sims owns all of the stock in Essco, an S corporation, and all of the stock in Ceeco, a C corporation. Essco and Ceeco may each claim a full §179 expensing deduction, assuming that each corporation independently meets all the other requirements

---

[1] Code §59(e)(4) allows individuals to elect a 3-year amortization period for circulation expenses and a 10-year period for research, intangible drilling, development, and mining exploration expenditures.

[2] The definition of *small business corporation* was moved to §1361(b) by the Subchapter S Revision Act of 1982.

[3] Regulations §1.1563-1(b)(2)(ii)(c) refers to the tax imposed by §1378. That section was redesignated as §1374 by the Subchapter S Revision Act of 1982.

pertaining to the deduction. In addition, Ceeco will not be required to reduce its graduated rate brackets, alternative minimum tax exemption, or any other tax attributes that would be required if Ceeco were a member of a controlled group of corporations.

610.3. Disallowance of carryovers between C corporation and S corporation years. An S corporation is not subject to most of the loss limitations contained in the Code. Such items as net operating losses, net capital losses, deductions in excess of amounts at risk, and passive activity loss limits are all measured at the shareholder level. The shareholder limits are discussed in detail in Chapters 9 and 10. Section 1371(b)(2) states that an S corporation does not generate corporate-level carryovers.

SUMMARY OF AUTHORITY: CODE SECTION 1371(b)(2)

- A C corporation cannot use any carryover generated when an S election was in effect.
- Since most deductions and losses of S corporations pass through to the shareholders, this provision seems to have little practical impact.
- The legislative history of Subchapter S is silent on the inclusiveness of the terms *carryforward* and *carryback.*

The S corporation cannot use any carryovers generated in a prior (or future) Subchapter C year. Section 1371(b)(1) states:

STATUTORY AUTHORITY: CODE SECTION 1371(b)(1)

(b) No carryover between C year and S year.—

(1) From C year to S year.—No carryforward, and no carryback, arising from a taxable year for which a corporation is a C corporation may be carried into a taxable year for which such corporation is an S corporation.

From the language of the Code, it can be inferred that an S corporation cannot use a net operating loss or net capital loss that was incurred in a year when the corporation did not have an S election in effect. In some cases, this prohibition can make electing S corporation status more costly than remaining a C corporation.

EXAMPLE 6 - 2: XYZ Corporation was a C corporation through 1990. At the end of 1990, it had generated net operating loss (NOL) carryforwards of $50,000. It makes an S election in 1991 and reports $50,000 taxable income in that year. Its shareholders must include $50,000 in their taxable incomes for 1991. If it had remained a C corporation, the shareholders would have paid no tax in 1991.

A corporation with corporate-level carryforwards faces one more hazard from making an S election: The calendar continues to run while the S election is in effect.

SUMMARY OF AUTHORITY: CODE SECTION 1371(b)(3)

- A former C corporation treats each S corporation year as an elapsed year for the utilization of any C corporation carryforwards or carrybacks, even though it cannot deduct these carryovers while the S election is in effect.

A corporation with loss carryforwards may benefit from an S election, if it has the effect of accelerating the tax benefit of near-term losses. If the corporation makes an election for this purpose, it should watch the running of the statute on the carryforwards it generated while it was a C corporation.

EXAMPLE 6 - 3: Talco was a C corporation in 1990, its first year of operations. In that year, it incurred a $60,000 NOL. It anticipates losses for its next two or three years. If it remains a

C corporation, it will not receive any tax benefit from the losses until it generates income. If it makes an S election, it might be able to provide a tax benefit to its shareholders for future losses. Assume that the corporation makes an S election for 1991 and loses $50,000 in that year. The loss would flow through to the shareholders. Deductibility at the shareholder level would be subject to the basis limits, discussed in Chapter 9, and some other limits, such as the at-risk or passive loss rules, covered in Chapter 10. The corporation could revoke its S election at some future date in order to use the loss generated in 1990. It would need to do so before 2005, since the S election does not suspend the running of limitations.

When an S corporation is subject to the built-in gains tax, it is required to compute its taxable income like other corporations do. For that measurement purpose only, an S corporation is allowed to use NOL, capital loss, and general business credit carryforwards from Subchapter C years. See Chapter 11 for further discussion.

The legislative history of this provision is minimal. Accordingly, it may be difficult to interpret the term *carryover*, which is used in only a few instances. Over the years, the IRS and the courts have given *carryover* a rather broad definition and have held that it includes such items as disallowed passive activity losses. [*St. Charles Investment Co.*, 110 TC 6 (1998)] The courts have taken a dim view of any creative uses of prior C corporation carryforwards, such as to add to basis of property sold after the S election takes effect. [*Rosenberg*, 96 TC 451 (1991)]

In one situation an S corporation tried to use the carryforward prohibition to its advantage, claiming that it should not report income from a refund of a previously deducted amount, since the deduction had been claimed before the S election took effect. [*Frederick*, 101 TC 35, (1993)] The Court responded by pointing out a Supreme Court decision that specifically allows the IRS to require a shareholder to include income from a liquidated corporation as an assignee, and that the S election is analogous to this situation. [See *Hillsboro Natl. Bank v. Comm'r*, 460 U.S. 370, 51 AFTR2d 83-874 (1983).]

610.4. General methods of accounting. In computing its taxable income, a taxpayer must select a general accounting method. The two most popular methods are cash and accrual. In general, C corporations must use the accrual method of accounting. [§448(a)] There is an exception for corporations with average gross receipts of $5,000,000 or less in their past three years. [§448(b)(3)] The statute requiring the accrual method refers specifically to C corporations. By this omission, the statute does not require S corporations to use the accrual method.

OBSERVATION: Exempting S corporations from the general requirement of the accrual method does not mean, however, that all S corporations are free to use the cash method. For instance, a C corporation that has been using the accrual method would not be allowed to change to the cash method when it files an S election. [§446(e)]

If the S corporation is engaged in a business that involves production or sale of goods, it will be required to take its beginning and ending inventories into account in determining taxable income. [Regs. §1.446-1(a)(i)] Any taxpayer that is required to inventory goods must use the accrual method in accounting for the sale and purchase of its goods. [Regs. §1.446-1(c)(2)(i)] Finally, all taxpayers must use a method of accounting that clearly reflects income. [§446(b)] In summary, an S corporation is not completely free to use the cash method of accounting. If it must take inventory to clearly reflect its income, it must use the accrual method, as must any other taxpayer.

In one situation, a corporation had failed to file a timely S election for its first taxable year. That year was before the Small Business Job Protection Act of 1996 allowed relief for late elections. Due to a sister corporation's gross receipts, the aggregate amount of the controlled group's gross receipts exceeded $5,000,000. Accordingly, when the new corporation failed to immediately qualify for S status it was required to use the accrual method of accounting. When the IRS granted relief under §1362(b)(5), the relief was granted for the new corporation's first taxable year. The IRS allowed the corporation to retroactively change to the cash method. [PLR 9824037]

610.5. Accounting for specific transactions. The Code has special accounting rules for various transactions and for other items crucial to determining income. Some are related only to special industries and are not covered in this text. In other instances, this text explains the more important specific transactions and their effect on S corporations and their shareholders. The topics covered in this chapter are those with special rules for S corporations.

610.51. Uniform capitalization rules. Any taxpayer engaged in the production or sale of property is subject to the uniform capitalization rules of §263A. The uniform capitalization rules are extremely long and complex. In brief, they require any taxpayer to add certain costs to the basis of property. The property may be created by the taxpayer for use in its business, such as a building or equipment. Taxpayers who produce or acquire inventory for resale are also required to add certain costs to the inventory, rather than deducting those costs when they are incurred. The major impact of the uniform capitalization rules is to defer a deduction until the property is depreciated, in the case of self-constructed assets, or until the property is sold, in the case of inventory. This provision contains some of the most lengthy and complicated rules of the entire tax law. There are two types of capitalized costs of immediate concern:

1. Indirect production costs
2. Interest costs

Indirect Production Costs. Since the uniform capitalization rules apply to both individuals and corporations, an S corporation is subject to these provisions. Organizations engaged in resale with average gross receipts that do not exceed $10,000,000 for the past three years are exempt from the uniform capitalization rules. [§263A(b)(2)(B)] This exemption, however, is subject to some aggregation rules. [§263A(b)(2)(C) refers to §448(c), which refers to §52(a), §52(b), §414(m), and §414(o) for the aggregation rules.] The aggregation rules take two different approaches. First, businesses under common control must be aggregated to see if their total receipts exceed $10,000,000. The common-control rules resemble those of controlled groups of corporations, but they have a lower threshold of common ownership. The controlled-group rules generally require that five or fewer persons own at least 80% of two or more corporations and that these individuals must have minimum identical ownership of more than 50% in the two or more corporations. [§1563(a)] For purposes of the uniform capitalization exemption, however, the five or fewer persons must own at least 50% of the stock of each corporation. [§52(a)] The aggregation rules extend to unincorporated, as well as incorporated, enterprises. [§52(b)] Accordingly, an S corporation's gross receipts must be aggregated with those of other businesses controlled by the majority shareholders, including proprietorships, partnerships, C corporations, and other S corporations.

The second type of aggregation rule applies to affiliated service groups. [§414(m), §414(o)] Under these rules, an S corporation that is a partner in a partnership and provides services to the partnership must aggregate its gross receipts with those of the partnership. There are no special rules regarding S corporations' uniform capitalization of direct production costs.

Interest Costs. Capitalization of interest has special application to S corporations and partnerships. [§263A(f)(3)] As a general rule, any taxpayer must capitalize interest on produced property that has (1) a "long" useful life, (2) an estimated production period exceeding two years, or (3) an estimated production period exceeding one year and a cost exceeding $1,000,000. [§263A(f)(1)(B)] Any interest paid or incurred during the production period must be capitalized. The capitalized interest includes that which is directly attributable to the production period and any interest costs that would have been avoided if the taxpayer had not undertaken the production. [§263A(f)(2)] The rules are to be applied at the entity level for partnerships and S corporations. Specific applications and examples are presented in Notice 88-99. [Notice 88-99, 1988-2 CB 422] The first interest to be capitalized is the interest on debt directly traceable to production expenditures. If such debt does not at least equal the production expenditures themselves, the taxpayer must capitalize interest costs on other debts. Examples 6 - 4 and 6 - 5 are based on Notice 88-99.

EXAMPLE 6 - 4: UC Corporation is an S corporation that uses the calendar year. In July 1991 it commences construction of a boat that will be used in its business. The cost of the boat is estimated to be $5,000,000. From July through December 1991, the corporation incurs $1,500,000 in construction costs. During this period it borrows $1,000,000, which is traced directly to the construction project. It pays $45,000 interest on the $1,000,000 loan.

Since the loan directly identified with the construction is less than the construction cost, the corporation must capitalize certain other interest costs, under the "avoided cost" rule. Assume that the corporation has $4,000,000 average outstanding debt throughout 1991, in addition to the $1,000,000 borrowed for the construction project. It pays $480,000 interest on this debt during the year. It would allocate $500,000 of this debt to production (total production costs incurred is $1,500,000, less traceable debt of $1,000,000). The shortfall of $500,000 is equivalent to one-eighth of the corporation's other debt. Therefore it must capitalize one-eighth of its interest on the other debt. The corporation's total interest costs capitalized would be:

From directly traced debt	$45,000
From other debt	6,000
Total	$51,000

A corporation recovers the capitalized interest costs by adding it to the basis of the property, and it recovers the cost in its depreciation deduction for future years. If the entity has insufficient debt to absorb the required capitalization, the "beneficiary" (shareholder in the S corporation or partner in the partnership) may be required to capitalize certain outside interest costs. When the production period ends, the taxpayer may begin to amortize the capitalized interest costs. Not all of the shareholder's interest expense must be capitalized, but only that on eligible debt. *Eligible debt* is all indebtedness other than that which is:

- Permanently nondeductible (e.g., §265)
- Personal interest
- Qualified residence interest [Notice 88-99, 1988-2 CB 422, II(A)]

EXAMPLE 6 - 5: Refer to Example 6 - 4. Assume that the corporation has no debt other than the $1,000,000 directly connected to construction. The corporation would allocate $500,000 of avoided cost to the shareholders, who would be required to capitalize interest costs on up to $500,000 of their other debts. The corporation would then notify the shareholders when the production is complete and would begin to depreciate the property. The shareholders would begin to amortize their capitalized costs at that time.

OBSERVATION: There are no guidelines as to the method of reporting any interest capitalization requirements to the shareholders under this rule. Similarly, there are no rules governing the effect of such capitalization, or the amortization thereof, on a shareholder's basis in S corporation stock or debt.

610.52. Installment sales. When an S corporation makes a sale that is subject to the installment method, the corporation may elect to report all of the income in the year of sale. In addition, certain installment sales are subject to interest charges. These include installment sales of time-shares and residential lots. [§453(l)(3)] The seller is also required to pay interest on the tax savings from the installment method, if the selling price of any of the installment receivables exceeds $150,000 and the total outstanding installment obligations at the end of the year exceeds $5,000,000.

There are no Regulations explaining or amplifying the installment sale rules with respect to S corporations and their shareholders. Until and unless any Regulations or other pronouncements are issued to deal with the interest charges, the following observations should assure that neither the S corporation nor any of its shareholders is subject to a penalty for failure to comply.

1. The aggregate sale price of any specific sale of property should be determined at the corporate level. If the aggregate sale price of any specific item exceeds $150,000, the corporation should report to each shareholder the amount of sales subject to installment receivable interest.
2. The $5,000,000 minimum installment receivable balance that requires payment of interest should be computed at the shareholder level, since it is the shareholder who is liable for the interest. The shareholder may have installment receivables from transactions outside the S corporation and would need to compute his or her interest charges.

EXAMPLE 6 - 6: Alru Corporation, an S corporation, has two equal shareholders, Al and Ruth. In 1993, Alru sells property on the installment method to an unrelated party. The aggregate sales price is $350,000, which includes $50,000 of cash and $300,000 of an installment receivable. The basis of the property before the sale was $175,000. The gross profit ratio is 50%. In addition to the other reporting requirements for the year, Alru must report to Al and Ruth that each shareholder's portion of the installment receivable is $150,000 and that the gain thereon is $75,000.

Assume that Al has no other outstanding installment receivables at the end of 1993. Ruth has $6,000,000 of outstanding installment receivables at the end of that year. Al is not required to pay any interest on the portion of the installment gain that he was allocated from Alru. Ruth must include her $150,000 of Alru's installment sale in her total and include this amount in her installment gain subject to interest.

A taxpayer who makes an installment sale may elect to report the entire gain in the year of sale. When the seller is an S corporation, this option is a corporate-level election and will be binding on all shareholders. The interest would be charged at the shareholder level and is treated as personal interest. [Notice 88-81, 1988-2 CB 397; Notice 89-33, 1989-1 CB 674] The S corporation should aggregate its total installment obligations with those of other businesses under common control.[4]

There are special installment rules dealing with liquidations of S corporations. [§453(h) and §453B(h)] See Chapter 16 for a discussion of liquidations.

610.53. Expensing of depreciable property. An individual, corporation, or partnership may elect to deduct the cost in the year of acquisition of property that would otherwise be depreciable. [§179] The Small Business Job Protection Act of 1996 enacted a phased in increase in the dollar limit, which was $17,500 in 1996. [Small Business Job Protection Act of 1996, §1111(b)] Under current law, the phased in amounts are shown in Table 6-1.

---

[4] The aggregation rules refer to the same attribution sections as did some of the uniform capitalization rules discussed above. They use the modified controlled-group rules of §52(a) and §52(b).

Table 6-1: Phase-in of Expensing Limitations under §179

If the taxable year begins in:	*The applicable amount is:*
1997	$18,000
1998	18,500
1999	19,000
2000	20,000
2001 or 2002	24,000
2003 or thereafter	25,000

6

When the purchaser of the qualifying property is an S corporation, this election is made at the S corporation level. [Regs. §1.179-1(h)]

To qualify for the expensing election, the property must be acquired by purchase, rather than by a tax-free transaction [§179(d)(1)], and it must not be acquired from a related person.[5] [§179(d)(2)(A)] The expensing deduction may be elected only in the year in which property is actually placed in service. [§179(a)] An S corporation was precluded from claiming a §179 deduction on property that had actually been purchased by the shareholder. [*Green*, TC Memo 1998-356]

The property must be depreciable personal property and must be used in an active trade or business. [§179(d)(1)] Leasing is not considered an active trade or business for an individual or an S corporation. [Regs. §1.179-1(a)] An active trade or business would not include any activity that would be subject to the hobby loss disallowance rules. [Regulations §1.179-2(c)(6)(i)] See at 625.1. for a discussion of the hobby loss rules. The determination of the active trade or business is made at the corporate level. [Regs. §1.179-1(h)]

The $17,500 to $25,000 limit is reduced for any taxpayer that places more than $200,000 of qualifying property in service in any taxable year. [§179(b)(2)] Therefore, if a taxpayer placed more than $219,000 of qualified property in service (in 1999, when the statutory maximum is $19,000) there is no expensing allowable. If the taxpayer places more than $200,000, but less than $219,000, of qualified property in service, the limit is reduced accordingly. The qualifying property placed in service by an S corporation is not aggregated with that placed in service by the shareholders, for determination of the limit applicable to either. [Regs. §1.179-2(b)(4)]

> **EXAMPLE 6 - 7:** Bill and Barbara are equal shareholders in BB, an S corporation. All parties use the calendar year. In 1999, BB placed in service qualified §179 property worth $200,000. Bill operates a proprietorship, and he placed in service $150,000 of qualified §179 property in 1999. Barbara also operates a proprietorship, and she placed in service $180,000 of qualified §179 property in 1999. None of the parties, standing alone, has placed in service more than $200,000 of qualified §179 property in 1999. Therefore, any or all of the three parties may claim the maximum expensing election of $19,000. The parties should be careful, however, not to exceed the maximum deduction limit that will be applied at the shareholder level.

The statutory limit applies at both the corporate level and the shareholder level. The simultaneous application of the limit to the S corporation and each of its shareholders may seem redundant, since no person can own more than 100% of an S corporation's stock. If, however, any of an S corporation's shareholders also owns interests in other pass-through entities, the expensing election by an S corporation may create a trap.

[5] For an S corporation, a *related person* is a shareholder who owns more than 50% of the stock, directly or indirectly, using the constructive ownership rules of §267. See Chapter 8, at 835.1.

EXAMPLE 6 - 8: Refer to Example 6 - 7. If the corporation elected to assume the maximum amount possible for 1999, it would pass $19,000 through to its shareholders, or $9,500 to each. If either Bill or Barbara unwittingly expensed $19,000 of his or her own asset purchases in the same year, he or she would have claimed $28,500 ($19,000 + $9,500) expensing. Each shareholder could only deduct $19,000, and the remaining expensing would produce no tax benefit in any year.

OBSERVATION: An S corporation should not make a §179 election unless it is reasonably certain that the shareholders will be able to deduct their allocated shares of the expense. As discussed at 630., below, an S corporation cannot specifically allocate any deduction among the shareholders, apart from the shareholder's normal share of the corporation's income and deductions for the year. In some situations, a shareholder may be allocated §179 expense from partnerships or other S corporations and may inadvertently exceed the statutory limit. There is no carryover, or any other favorable tax treatment of expensing in excess of this limit.

6

After the statutory maximum limit of $17,500 to $25,000 (depending on the year) and the phaseout for taxpayers with excess investments in qualified §179 property, there is a further limit based on taxable income. The §179 deduction cannot exceed a taxpayer's taxable income from trades or businesses in the year. [§179(b)(3)] This limitation applies to both the S corporation and each shareholder. [§179(d)(8)] There are some special rules, however, that apply to both.

At the corporate level, the corporation's taxable income limit is computed before any deduction for compensation to shareholders. [Regs. §1.179-2(c)(3)(ii)] The shareholder may include wages and salaries from all sources, including those from the S corporation, along with his or her share of the corporation's net income, in determining this limit for the §179 deduction. [Regs. §1.179-2(c)(7)(iv)]

EXAMPLE 6 - 9: Patsy owns all of the stock in Patco, an S corporation. Both Patsy and Patco use the calendar year. In 1999, before the corporation decides to expense any property, Patco's taxable income would be $1,000, after deducting $45,000 of compensation to Patsy. Patsy has no active trade or business income other than her salary and profits from the S corporation. Patco placed in service $50,000 of qualifying §179 property in 1999. Patsy did not place any qualifying §179 property in service in 1999 outside of Patco. The corporation and the shareholder compute their taxable income limitations as follows:

Patco:

Taxable income before §179 deduction	$ 1,000
Add deduction for Patsy's compensation	45,000
Taxable income limitation for §179	$46,000

Patco is able to claim a $19,000 §179 deduction, and pass it through to the shareholder in its entirety.

Patsy:

Taxable income before §179 deduction	$46,000

Patsy may deduct the entire §179 deduction on her 1999 income tax return.

A taxpayer may actually claim an expensing election in excess of the taxable income limit. In this case, the excess expensing is carried forward to the next taxable year. This is one of the few carryforwards that is retained at the corporate level by an S corporation. [Regs. §1.179-3(g)]

EXAMPLE 6 - 10: Assume the same facts as in Example 6 - 9, except that the corporation would report a $43,000 loss after deducting Patsy's compensation. Patco would compute its taxable income limitation for §179 as follows:

Taxable income before §179 deduction	$(43,000)
Add deduction for Patsy's compensation	45,000
Taxable income limitation for §179	$ 2,000

Patco is able to claim $19,000 §179 deduction, but it could pass only $2,000 through to Patsy. Patsy would be able to deduct the $2,000 in full in 1999.

Patco would claim the remaining $17,000 of its 1999 expensing as a 2000 deduction, assuming that it would otherwise be eligible to claim an expensing election.

When a §179 allowance in excess of the taxable income limit is carried forward, it may be treated as a deduction in the next year, subject to the limitations in the next year. The total amount claimed as a §179 deduction, however, cannot exceed the statutory maximum in any single taxable year. [Regs. §1.179-3(b)]

EXAMPLE 6 - 11: Refer to Example 6 - 10. In 2000, Patco reports taxable income of $80,000. In 2000, Patco places $150,000 of qualifying §179 property in service. Patco can expense $20,000 in 2000. The maximum amount that Patco can allocate to its shareholder this year, however, is $20,000. If Patco expenses $3,000 in 2000, it would pass $20,000 to the shareholder, which would include the $3,000 of the 2000 deduction and $17,000 carried forward from 1999. If Patco expensed $20,000 in 2000, it would carry $17,000 (20,000 + 17,000 - 20,000) into 2001.

If a taxpayer carries forward any §179 expensing in excess of its taxable income, it will be subject to the maximum property limit in each succeeding year. Therefore, a §179 carryforward could continue indefinitely.

EXAMPLE 6 - 12: Refer to Example 6 - 10. In 2000, Patco reports taxable income of $80,000. In 2000, Patco places $250,000 of qualifying §179 property in service. Patco cannot claim any §179 deduction for 2000. Therefore the carryforward from 1999 is carried to 2001.

An S corporation that claims §179 expensing must reduce the basis of the qualifying property. The basis reduction is required even if the taxpayer cannot use the entire §179 deduction. [Regs. §1.179-3(g)(1)] If the S corporation later disposes of the property, any expensing that has actually been deducted is treated as ordinary income under the depreciation recapture rules of §1245. [§1245(a)(2)(C)] If the owner of §179 property on which an expensing allowance has been claimed, but not deducted, disposes of the property in a tax-free transaction, the unused expensing allowance is added to the property's basis at the time of transfer. [Regs. §1.179-3(f)(1)]

EXAMPLE 6 - 13: Refer to Example 6 - 10. Patco was required to reduce basis of its §179 property by $19,000 in 1999, even though it could pass only $2,000 through to the shareholder.

In 2000, Patco contributes the §179 property it acquired in 1993 to a partnership in a tax-free transfer. (See Chapter 14, at 1435.11., for a brief discussion of transfers of property to partnerships.) Patco will add $17,000 (the unused §179 deduction) to its basis of the property, immediately before the transfer to the partnership.

OBSERVATION: There are no provisions in the Code or Regulations dealing with a corporate-level §179 carryforward when the expensing was claimed by a C corporation and the corporation makes an S election before deducting the carryover. Similarly, there are no rules dealing with a suspended §179 deduction that was claimed by an S corporation that then terminates its S election. Probably the safest route is to add the suspended deduction back to the property's basis when the corporation's status changes, since there is a general rule prohibiting an S corporation from utilizing carryovers from a C corporation year and vice versa.

The shareholders in an S corporation must adjust basis in their stock to correspond to the corporation's required basis adjustments in the §179 property. [Regs. §1.179-1(f)(2)] The shareholder must reduce his or her stock basis, even if the corporation was subject to the taxable income limitation on the §179 deduction. [Regs. §1.179-3(g)(2)]

6

EXAMPLE 6 - 14: Refer to Example 6 - 10. Patsy must reduce the basis in her stock by $19,000 in 1999, even though the corporation could allocate only $2,000 of expensing to her in that year.

A shareholder's portion of the §179 deduction may not reduce a shareholder's stock basis below zero. If the shareholder's §179 deduction exceeds the shareholder's stock basis, it may reduce the shareholder's debt basis. See at 630.6., below.

If a shareholder disposes of the stock after deducting his or her portion of the corporation's §179 allowance, the gain attributable to a basis adjustment is not treated as depreciation recapture, since the stock itself is not depreciable property. If a shareholder disposes of stock but has not been able to fully utilize the §179 deduction, due to the taxable income limitation, the amount not deducted is added back to the shareholder's basis at the time of disposition. [Regs. §1.179-3(h)(2)]

The §179 deduction is not allowed for estates or trusts. [§179(d)(4)] When one or more of these entities owns stock in an S corporation, there could be some major obstacles to claiming an expensing deduction, since there is no means of allocating the deduction except on a per-share per-day basis. See discussion at 630. There is, however, a relief provision for S corporations that might otherwise be forced to waste a §179 allocation, or be unable to make the expensing election. When an estate or trust owns shares in an S corporation, the corporation does not claim §179 expense on the portion of the qualified property attributable to the ownership of these entities. [Regs. §1.179-1(f)(3)]

EXAMPLE 6 - 15: XYZ Corporation is an S corporation. Of its shares, 70% are owned by an individual, and the remaining 30% are owned by an estate. XYZ wants to make a maximum §179 election for 1993. XYZ is limited to expensing $12,250 (0.7 x $17,500), all of which flows through to the individual shareholder. XYZ reduces basis in its §179 property by $12,250.

OBSERVATION: The Code and Regulations make no distinction between an estate or trust that is treated as a taxable entity and one whose existence is disregarded for federal income tax purposes, such as a grantor trust or QSST. The law should probably allow an S corporation to pass the allocable share of an expensing election to these trusts, since all income and deductions must be reported on individuals' tax returns. If any shares of an S corporation are owned by an estate, or an otherwise nonqualified trust, such as an ESBT or testamentary trust, the S corporation clearly could not allocate any §179 expense to these entities, and it must reduce the corporate-level election to reflect the percentage of shares held by these entities.

There is adequate authority under current law for an S corporation to allocate §179 expensing to grantor trusts or QSSTs. Revenue Ruling 85-13, 1985-1 CB 184, holds that if a grantor is treated as the owner of an entire trust, the grantor is the owner of the trust's assets for federal income tax purposes. Thus the stock of the S corporation is treated as if it were owned by the grantor or the beneficiary, as the case may be.

There is no reduction to the §179 deduction based on the length of time that the property is actually in service during the taxable year. [Regs. §1.179-1(c)(1)(i)] Similarly, there is no reduction of the §179 deduction for a taxpayer that places qualifying property in service in a short taxable year. [Regs. §1.179-1(c)(1)(ii)] In the S corporation context a short taxable year might occur with a newly formed corporation, a corporation that liquidates and prematurely terminates its S election, or a corporation that terminates its S election during a taxable year. See Chapter 13, at 1335.51. In these situations, the corporation should be able to claim the entire allowance in any short year. The treatment of an interim closing when a shareholder terminates his or her interest in the S corporation and the S election continues, however, is less clear. See discussion at 630.2. In that situation, the Code does not specify that each accounting period constitutes a short year for any purpose other than the percentage allocation of the S corporation's income and deductions among the shareholders.

OBSERVATION: An S corporation may terminate a §444 year. See Chapter 4, at 425. The short period of the termination would qualify as a short year for §179 expensing purposes. A §179 election in this situation might ease the burden on the shareholders of reporting income from two S corporation years on one return. In this situation, however, it is especially important to remember that the statutory limit applies at the shareholder level, for the shareholder's taxable year.

The election to expense depreciable property is made by the S corporation on Form 4562, with other depreciation elections. The return need not be filed in a timely manner for the election to be valid, and the corporation may claim an expensing election on an amended return for the year in which the property is placed in service. [Regs. §1.179-5(a)] The election may not be revoked without permission of the National Office of the IRS.[6] [Regs. §1.179-5(b)]

OBSERVATION: There is no doubt that the §179 election may be beneficial to small businesses. When an S corporation is faced with this election, however, it should be certain that all of the shareholders, other than estates and trusts, can utilize their shares of the deduction. If the corporation makes the election, which is irrevocable, and a shareholder's portion of §179 expensing from other sources, such as partnerships or other S corporations, would exceed the statutory maximum allowance, there is no relief provision. Similarly, there would be no relief for a shareholder who received an allocation of an S corporation's §179 deduction and had placed in service more than $217,500 to $225,000 (depending on the year) of §179 property outside of the corporation. The only relief allowed for excess expensing is when the deduction exceeds the shareholder's taxable income limitation.

As was discussed in Chapter 3, at 325.3., there are special depreciation rules that apply to determine a C corporation's earnings and profits. Any amount expensed under §179 is amortized ratably over a five-year period for calculating earnings and profits. [§312(k)(3)(B)] Therefore, although a corporation might benefit from a §179 election in its last year as a C corporation, if the election reduces its tax for that year, the corporation would still have accumulated earnings and profits to contend with after the S election took effect.

610.54. Deduction for bad debts. In general, a corporation is allowed an ordinary deduction for any bad debt written off in a taxable year. [§166] A taxpayer other than a corporation, however, must determine whether the bad debt is a business bad debt or a nonbusiness bad debt. If the receivable was generated in the ordinary course of the taxpayer's business, it is a

---

[6] The Regulations give no indication as to what circumstances (if any) would influence the IRS to allow revocation of the election.

business bad debt, and the taxpayer is allowed an ordinary deduction. If the loan was made in any context other than the corporation's ordinary course of business, however, it is a nonbusiness bad debt. A nonbusiness bad debt is deductible in the same manner as a short-term capital loss. [§166(d)]

An S corporation that sustains a bad debt is subject to the same business and nonbusiness bad debt rules as an individual. Accordingly, if an S corporation writes off a nonbusiness bad debt, it is not entitled to an ordinary deduction. It must state the bad debt as a short-term capital loss under §166(d) and report it separately to the shareholders. [Rev. Rul. 93-36, 1993-1 CB 187]

610.55. Charitable contributions. An S corporation does not deduct its contributions to qualified charitable organizations. See discussion at 610., above, which demonstrates that §702 disallows charitable contributions to partnerships and that §1363 incorporates the rules of §702 and §703. Accordingly, an S corporation is not entitled to the special corporate rules regarding charitable contributions. For instance, an S corporation that uses the accrual method of accounting is not entitled to deduct accrued contributions in the year accrued, under §170(a)(2). [PLRs 9703028, 199908039] It is not entitled to deduct the fair market value of inventory contributed to an organization for the care of the needy, the ill, or infants. [IRC §170(e)(3)(A) specifically disallows this deduction to S corporations.] A charitable contribution made by an S corporation is one of the items separately reported to shareholders, who are subject to the individual charitable contribution rules.

When an S corporation contributes capital gain property to a qualifying organization, the amount of the contribution is the fair market value of the property. [Regs. §170A-1(c), PLR 9828001] When a taxpayer donates property to a private foundation or donates tangible property to an organization that will sell the property, rather than using it in its exempt function, the amount of the contribution is limited to the property's basis. [§170(e)(1)(B)]

An S corporation that makes a charitable contribution does not claim a deduction, but passes the contribution through to its shareholders. The shareholders are then subject to the individual taxpayer limits on claiming the deduction. When an S corporation makes a charitable contribution of capital gain property, the amount of the contribution claimed by the shareholders is the property's fair market value. [PLR 9340043] See Chapter 10, at 1040., for some special rules applicable to charitable contributions by S corporations.

610.56. Cutback of tax preferences. Code §291 provides a cutback in tax preferences for C corporations in determining taxable income. For example, rules relating to depletion of iron ore and coal provide that 20% depletion in excess of basis is disallowed. Pollution control facilities are also subject to preference reduction. Amortization of costs over a 60-month period is permitted (by election), but §291 permits such amortization on only 80% of the facility's basis. The remainder of the basis is subject to MACRS deduction. Intangible drilling and mineral exploration and development costs are subject to another reduction, in which 30% of the cost cannot be expensed immediately but may be amortized over a 60-month period. Since S corporation taxable income is computed by reference to individuals' rules, §291 generally does not apply. [§1363(b)] There is an exception, however, for the first three years of the S election of a former C corporation. [§1363(b)(4)] The most widely encountered aspect of §291 is the characterization of gains on the sale of depreciated realty. Under §1250, 20% of gain attributable to straight-line depreciation is treated as ordinary income.

610.6. Cancellation of debt. In times of financial hardship, many creditors find it necessary to work out a reduction of debt with borrowers. The unique blend of corporate and partnership attributes, combined with somewhat ill-defined laws, has created some interesting and controversial tax treatments for S corporations that have debt canceled.

In some cases, the debt is reduced through a foreclosure or other transfer of mortgaged property. In other situations, the debtor keeps the property, and the creditor, who realizes that the original arrangement will not work, modifies the terms of the debt. In either situation, the debtor's obligation is reduced or eliminated. The tax treatment of debt cancellation in connection with a transfer of property, however, may be markedly different from the cancellation of debt where the debtor transfers no property.

A debt reduction may occur when a creditor agrees to a reduction of the debt, or when the creditor accepts stock of the debtor and the value of the stock is less than the principal amount of the debt. [108(e)(8)] Cancellation of debt may also occur when the creditor makes no attempt to enforce the debt and it is evident from the facts that the debt will not be repaid. [*Salva*, TC Memo 1993-90, 65 TCM 2080] There are special rules for S corporations, if shareholders cancel the corporation's debt by making a contribution to capital. See Chapter 9, at 935.4.

610.61. Debt reduction income illustrated. When debt is reduced or cancelled in connection with a transfer of property, the amount of debt transferred to the new owner is generally treated as an amount realized on the sale of the property. If the borrower is not personally liable and the lender's only remedy for enforcement is foreclosure on the property, the debt is termed a *nonrecourse liability*. When the borrower is personally liable for repayment of the debt and the creditor may enforce payment in full, even if the property transferred has insufficient value to satisfy the debt, the obligation is termed a *recourse liability*.

If a nonrecourse liability is satisfied by foreclosure of property, the entire amount of the debt is treated as an amount realized on the sale of the property. The fair market value of the property is irrelevant in this situation. [*Commissioner v. Tufts*, 83-1 USTC 9328 (S Ct.)] The difference between the total amount realized and the property's adjusted basis is treated as a gain or loss on the sale. The character of the gain or loss is determined by the usual tax rules. Accordingly, it may be capital, §1231, or ordinary.

> **EXAMPLE 6 - 16:** BR Corporation owes $250,000, on a nonrecourse basis, to First National Bank. The property pledged as security for the loan has a basis of $180,000 to BR and fair market value of $200,000. BR deeds the property to the lender, who takes no further action against BR. BR is treated as having sold the property for the amount of the debt, or $250,000. Therefore, BR recognizes a gain of $70,000. This gain is not discharge of debt, and it may be capital, ordinary or §1231, depending upon the character of the property transferred. It is included in BR's gross income and is not subject to any of the rules discussed below for cancellation of debt.

> **OBSERVATION:** Nonrecourse financing was popular during the heyday of tax shelters in the 1970s and early 1980s. Since the demise of the savings and loan industry, nonrecourse financing has become difficult, if not impossible, to obtain except in unusual circumstances.

In general, the same principles apply to a foreclosure or other transfer of property involving a recourse debt. In this circumstance, however, if the fair market value of the property does not satisfy the obligation, the mortgagor still has a claim against the debtor. If the creditor pursues no other remedies and accepts the property in cancellation of the debt, the liability is bifurcated into two parts:

1. The amount of debt canceled that does not exceed the fair market value of the property is treated as an amount realized on the sale of the property. The character of the gain or loss is determined by the usual tax rules. Accordingly, it may be capital, §1231, or ordinary.

2. The amount of debt that exceeds the property's fair market value is income from cancellation of debt. [Regs. §1.1001-2(a)(2); *Bressi*, TC Memo 1991-651] This portion of the debt cancellation may only be ordinary income, but it is subject to some special exclusion rules. This portion of the debt is treated in the exact same manner as cancellation of debt where there is no property transferred.

EXAMPLE 6 - 17: Assume the same facts as in Example 6 - 16, except that the liability was recourse debt, and that First National Bank canceled the entire debt. The excess of the fair market value of the property over its adjusted basis, or $20,000, would be a gain on the disposition of the property. It is not subject to any of the rules discussed below for cancellation of debt. The excess of the liability over the property's fair market value, however, is income from cancellation of debt. It is subject to the bankruptcy or insolvency exceptions to inclusion in gross income.

6

610.62. Exclusions from gross income. If a creditor forgives or reduces debt and there is no transfer of property, the debt reduction is generally included in gross income. [§61(a)(12)] Since there is no transfer of property on which a gain or loss may be realized, this income can only be ordinary income. There are, however, several special rules that may allow the debtor to exclude all, or a portion, of the debt cancellation.

1. There is no gross income from discharge of debt in a federal or state bankruptcy proceeding. [§108(a)(1)(A)]
2. A taxpayer who is insolvent after the cancellation of debt recognizes no gross income from the debt cancellation. [§108(a)(1)(B)]
3. When a seller of property finances the purchase and later reduces the debt balance, there is no gross income to the borrower. (§108 contains the rules for nonrecognition of income when debt is discharged.)
4. If the borrower is a farmer and the debt is related to the farming business, the lender's forgiveness may be a reduction of qualified farm indebtedness and excluded from gross income. [§108(a)(1)(C)] This rule apples to discharge of indebtedness after April 9, 1986.
5. If the debt is discharged after December 31, 1992, it may not be included in gross income if it is *qualified real property business indebtedness*. [§108(a)(1)(D)] This rule applies to discharge of indebtedness after December 31, 1992.

Each of these rules needs some further explanation. The precedence is in the order shown above. For instance, if the debt is discharged by a person other than the seller, and the discharge occurs in a bankruptcy proceeding, it is immaterial whether the debtor is solvent (although this condition would probably preclude bankruptcy). In this situation, it does not matter that the creditor is the seller of the property or whether the debt is qualified farm indebtedness or qualified real property business indebtedness. [§108(a)(1)(B)]

Similarly, if a seller of property later reduces the debt, unless the borrower is bankrupt or insolvent it is irrelevant whether the debt meets the definition of *qualified farm indebtedness* or of *qualified real property business indebtedness*. If the debtor is solvent and the debt is qualified farm indebtedness, the debt does not need to qualify as qualified real property business indebtedness. [§108(c)(3)]

610.63. S corporations and other tax entities contrasted. The tax status of the debtor may have an important effect on the application of the debt cancellation rules, as well as on the collateral consequences thereof. Individuals, estates, trusts, and corporations are all treated as separate entities that stand alone in meeting the tests. For instance, if a corporation is bankrupt, any cancellation of debt at the corporate level is excluded from the corporation's gross income. The financial status of its shareholders is irrelevant. By contrast, a partnership does not in and of itself qualify for any of the exclusions, except for the purchase price reduction when a seller later reduces debt. For a partnership, all of the relevant tests for insolvency, bankruptcy, qualified farm indebtedness, or qualified real property business indebtedness are made at the partner level. [§108(d)(6)]

If the debtor is an S corporation, the tests are all made at the corporate level. [§108(d)(7)(A)] In this respect, an S corporation is treated in the same manner as a C corporation and differently from a partnership.

OBSERVATION: The divergent treatment of cancellation of indebtedness for a partnership and an S corporation is in accordance with the specific intent of Congress. The Subchapter S Revision Act of 1982 included provisions that applied the bankruptcy and insolvency tests, as well as certain elections relating to bankrupt or insolvent taxpayers, at the shareholder level. [§1363(c)(2)(A) and §108(d)(6) prior to amendment by the Deficit Reduction Act of 1984] In 1984, however, Congress apparently recognized that the treatment of partnership debt, which is fundamentally different from the treatment of S corporation debt for all income tax purposes, was not appropriate to S corporations when debts were canceled or reduced.[7] Therefore, Congress enacted the current provisions, that all cancellation of debt rules for obligations of S corporations were applied at the corporate level. [Deficit Reduction Act of 1984, §721(b)] The amendments were retroactive to January 1, 1981, and thus applied even to S corporations before the Subchapter S Revision Act of 1982. [Deficit Reduction Act of 1984, §721(y)(2)]

6

610.64. Purchase money debt reduction. When the seller of property subsequently agrees to a reduction of a purchase money debt, there is no gross income to the debtor. The debtor, however, must reduce the basis of the property secured by the debt. [§108(e)(5)] There is no election required and no other tax treatment permitted.

EXAMPLE 6 - 18: Borco, an S corporation, buys some property from Lenco in 1990. The purchase price was $1,000,000. Borco gave Lenco $200,000 cash as a down payment, and Lenco financed the remaining $800,000. In 1993, when the value of the property had declined substantially, the principal balance was $750,000. Lenco agreed to reduce the balance to $650,000. Borco has no gross income from the debt reduction, and it reduces its basis in the property by $100,000.

This exception from income recognition applies only when the creditor is the seller of the property. Thus, it is not available to a debtor when the financing has been provided by any person other than the seller. [See *Bressi*, TC Memo 1991-651.] When the borrower is an S corporation, there is no requirement that the shareholders reduce stock or debt basis to correspond to the corporation's reduction in basis of the purchased property. Accordingly, the reduction of debt has no effect on the S corporation's AAA or OAA. See Chapter 7 for discussion of these accounts.

610.65. Qualified farming and business real property exceptions. For a taxpayer who is not bankrupt or insolvent, the Code provides special treatment for the cancellation of qualified farm indebtedness. To qualify for this treatment, 50% or more of the debtor's aggregate gross receipts in its three taxable years preceding the year of discharge must have

---

[7] In general, partnership debts are allocated among partners for basis purposes, according to §752. Increases in partnership debts are treated as cash contributions made by the partners, and decreases in partnership debts are treated as cash distributions received by the partners. There are no parallels to these rules for S corporations and their shareholders.

come from an active farming trade or business. [§108(g)(2)(B)] If the taxpayer is an individual or a C corporation, the test for the gross receipts is made at the entity level and does not include the receipts of any related parties. If the taxpayer is an S corporation, the test is made at the corporate level. [§108(d)(7)] In the case of a partnership, however, the test is made at the partner level. [§108(d)(6)] This divergence between the treatment of S corporations and the treatment of partnerships is by design of Congress.

The debt reduced under the qualified farm indebtedness rules must have been incurred in the farming business. [§108(g)(2)(A)] The lender must be a person or an institution that lends money in the ordinary course of its business, such as a bank or other commercial lender. The lender must not be related to the borrower. The amount of debt reduction excluded under these provisions may not exceed the "adjusted tax attributes of the debtor" [§108(g)(3)(B)], plus the adjusted basis of "qualified property." The attributes are those listed above that a bankrupt or insolvent taxpayer must reduce (after reduction for any prior insolvency or bankruptcy of the same taxpayer). Where the debtor is an S corporation, the shareholder-level loss carryforwards are treated as part of the adjusted tax attributes. The debtor must reduce these attributes at the beginning of the next taxable year in the same manner as required for a bankrupt or insolvent taxpayer.

The qualified property is any property used in the farming business. Any amount of debt reduction in excess of the attributes and qualified property is included in the debtor's gross income.

The Revenue Reconciliation Act of 1993 added a new exception to income recognition, for reduction of qualified real property business indebtedness. [§108(c)] In general, this rule allows a solvent debtor to exclude reduction of debt from gross income. Any taxpayer other than a C corporation may qualify for this exclusion. [§108(a)(1)(D)] This exclusion applies to discharges of debt that occur after December 31, 1992. Accordingly, an S corporation with a fiscal year that ends in 1993 may elect to have this exclusion apply, if the actual discharge of debt occurred within calendar year 1993.

The debt must have been incurred in connection with an active trade or business and must be secured by real property used in the trade or business. [§108(c)(3)(A)] If the debt was originally incurred after December 31, 1992, it must have been incurred in order to acquire, improve, or rehabilitate real property used in the taxpayer's business. [§108(c)(3)(B)]

This exclusion does not apply to bankrupt or insolvent taxpayers, and it must be elected by the taxpayer. [§108(c)(3)(C)] When the taxpayer involved is an S corporation, the election is made by the corporation. [§108(d)(7)(A)] The corporation makes the election by filing a statement with its tax return for the year of the discharge. [§108(d)(9)] In general, the election to exclude cancellation-of-debt income under this rule must be made on the tax return of the debtor for the year of the discharge, on Form 982. [Regs. §1.108(c)-1(b)] The IRS has, however, granted extensions of time under its general powers of §301.9100-3T. [PLR 9738033]

The debtor does not reduce the tax attributes, such as net operating losses, that are required for bankrupt or insolvent taxpayers. When the debtor is an S corporation, there is no reduction of any shareholder attributes [§108(d)(7)(B)], but the cancellation-of-debt income does not flow through to any shareholder as tax-exempt income.[8] The only required attribute reduction is the basis of depreciable real property. [§108(c)(1)(A)] Accordingly, an S corporation's exclusion under the qualified real property business indebtedness rule has no effect on the corporation's AAA or OAA. See Chapter 7 for discussion of these accounts.

In this respect, the accounting treatment is identical to the purchase price reduction when a seller reduces debt, as discussed above.

---

[8] The Code is less than specific on this point, but the Committee Reports to the Revenue Reconciliation Act of 1993 mandate this result.

There are two important limitations on the amount of income that can be excluded as qualified real property business indebtedness. First, the exclusion is limited to the amount of debt reduced in excess of the fair market value of the property securing the debt. [§108(c)(2)(A)]

> **EXAMPLE 6 - 19:** Debco, an S corporation, owned real estate used in its trade or business. Debco uses the calendar year. On September 9, 1993, when the fair market value of the property was $200,000, Debco worked out an arrangement with the mortgagor, reducing the mortgage on the property from $220,000 to $190,000. The debt met all the requirements of qualified real property business indebtedness. Debco was not bankrupt or insolvent at the time of the reduction. Debco may elect to exclude $20,000 of the discharge from gross income as qualified real property business indebtedness. The remaining $10,000 must be included in Debco's gross income. Debco's shareholders will include $10,000 of the debt reduction that exceeded the limit on qualified real property business indebtedness in their shares of taxable income for the year. They will not adjust basis in their stock or any other tax attributes, such as losses in excess of basis, for the $20,000 that was within the limit for qualified real property business indebtedness.

Moreover, the debt excludable under the qualified real property business indebtedness rule cannot exceed the taxpayer's basis of all depreciable real property at the time of discharge. The basis limitation uses all of the taxpayer's depreciable real property and is not limited to the property secured by the discharged debt. [§108(c)(2)(B)] Any real property acquired solely for the purpose of absorbing debt discharge is disregarded.

> **EXAMPLE 6 - 20:** Refer to Example 6 - 19. If Debco's depreciable real property is at least $20,000, Debco may exclude $20,000. If Debco's aggregate adjusted basis in such depreciable property is less than $20,000, the exclusion from gross income would be limited to Debco's basis.

The basis reduction takes place on the first day of the corporation's taxable year following the discharge. [§1071(a)] If the taxpayer sells the property during the year of discharge, the basis is reduced at the date of sale. [§1017(b)(3)(F)] Any reduction of basis due to debt discharge is treated as depreciation and is thus recaptured as ordinary income on the sale of the property. [§1017(d)]

> **CAUTION:** When a taxpayer reduces the basis of property under the §108 rules, the entire reduction is treated as depreciation. Therefore, if the taxpayer sells the property later on the installment method, the entire basis reduction must be recaptured in the year of sale. [§453(i)(2)]

610.66. Reduction of tax attributes. The bankruptcy and insolvency exceptions are somewhat more complicated than the purchase money debt reduction rule, in that they require reduction of certain tax attributes in exchange for the nonrecognition of gross income. A taxpayer who is discharged of debt in a bankruptcy proceeding recognizes no income from discharge of indebtedness. [§108(a)(1)(A)]

There is a somewhat more limited exception for taxpayers who are not in bankruptcy but are insolvent before the discharge. [§108(a)(1)(B)] A taxpayer is *insolvent* when its liabilities exceed the fair market value of its assets. [§108(a)(3)] When a taxpayer is insolvent but not in a bankruptcy case, the exclusion is limited to the amount of the insolvency (the amount by which liabilities exceed assets). [§108(d)(3)]

Any taxpayer who excludes cancellation of debt under the bankruptcy or insolvency rules must reduce certain tax attributes, which could otherwise reduce its tax liability in future years. The Revenue Reconciliation Act of 1993 added some items that must be reduced. For discharges of indebtedness in taxable years beginning after 1993, the attributes, in the order in which they should be reduced, are as follows [§108(b)(2)], as amended by the Revenue Reconciliation Act of 1993]:

1. Net operating loss of the year of discharge
2. Net operating loss carryover to that year
3. General business credit carryforward
4. Alternative minimum tax credit carryforward from years prior to discharge
5. Capital loss of the year of discharge
6. Capital loss carryover to the year of discharge
7. Reduction of basis of all property held by the taxpayer
8. Passive activity loss and credit carryforwards from the year of the discharge
9. Foreign tax credit carryover

The reduction of loss attributes (or basis) is dollar for dollar, corresponding to the cancellation of debt. The credit reduction, however, is only one-third of the debt reduction. [§108(b)(2)(B)] The reduction of the attributes takes place at the beginning of the year following the discharge of debt. The taxpayer is allowed to use any of those attributes during the year of discharge to offset any taxable income or tax liability from that particular year. [§108(b)(4)]

The unique nature of the S corporation requires some special calculations. The required reduction of tax attributes is generally applied at the corporate level. [§108(d)(7)(A)] There is one shareholder-level attribute, however, for which reduction is required. The net operating loss for the year of discharge is the loss for the year that is disallowed to the shareholders under their basis limitations. [§108(d)(7)(B)]

The shareholder-level loss carryforward that must be reduced under this rule includes all losses from previous years, as well as the current year's loss. As discussed at 630.6., any loss that exceeds a shareholder's stock and debt basis is treated as a loss sustained by the shareholder in the corporation's next taxable year. Therefore, all cumulative losses that have exceeded a shareholder's basis in years prior to the discharge or reduction of debt are treated as if they were losses incurred in the year of discharge.

The IRS has recently addressed the proper treatment of the corporate- and shareholder-level attribute reduction when an S corporation has excludable §108 income. [TAM 9541001] A central point to the reasoning of the IRS is that an S corporation cannot utilize any carryover generated in a C corporation year, and so cannot reduce any attributes. Thus, the only attributes really open to reduction are the following:

1. Corporate losses of the year of discharge, in excess of the shareholder's basis
2. Corporate losses carried over to the year of discharge, in excess of the shareholder's basis
3. Reduction of basis of all property held by the corporation

Note that of all of the attributes listed for taxpayers in general, the only attribute that can be reduced directly by an S corporation is the basis of property held after the cancellation of debt.

EXAMPLE 6 - 21: Brokeco, an S corporation, declares bankruptcy and has $100,000 of debt reduced in 1996. Brokeco sustained a loss of $80,000 for 1996. Its sole shareholder had no basis in his stock or debt, and he had $15,000 of losses in excess of basis from 1995. According to TAM 9541001, Brokeco's shareholder would reduce his loss carryforward with respect to Brokeco stock to zero, as of the beginning of 1997. This reduction would utilize only $95,000 of Brokeco's $100,000 excluded cancellation-of-debt income. Therefore, Brokeco must reduce basis in any property it still owns by $5,000.

CAUTION: Example 6 - 21 did not comment on the tax treatment of the $100,000 cancellation-of-debt income. See discussion below, at 610.67. and 610.68., of the controversy with respect to this income.

610.67. Treatment of cancellation-of-debt income. Another problem that the IRS has faced in recent years is the treatment of the income under §108 itself. If the income is taxable (that is, it does not meet one of the §108 exclusionary rules), it would seem clear that the income would flow through to the shareholders and increase their basis, in the manner described in this chapter at 630. If the cancellation-of-debt income is excluded under §108, the income could also be treated as a flow-through item to the shareholders under §1366(a)(1)(A), which specifically instructs each shareholder to take into account his or her share of the corporation's tax-exempt income. If income excluded under §108 is taken into account by each shareholder, it would then add to the shareholder's basis as of the end of the corporation's taxable year. If this is the case, there could be some opportunities to mismatch tax-exempt income with suspended deductions at the shareholder level.

EXAMPLE 6 - 22: Rupco, an S corporation, declares bankruptcy in 1993. Rupco and all of its shareholders use the calendar year. The aggregate amount of debt canceled in the bankruptcy is $500,000. The shareholders would not be precluded from deducting their portions of the corporation's losses from current or prior years on their 1993 returns. They would, however, be required to reduce any carryforwards of unused losses for 1994.

Assume that the shareholders, in the aggregate, had $600,000 of disallowed losses from the corporation at the beginning of 1993 and that the corporation had no items of income and loss during 1993. Also assume that the corporation had $150,000 of unexpired NOL carryforwards from years prior to its S election and $75,000 of general business credit carryovers from those years, at the beginning of 1993.

The corporation's discharge of debt income would receive the following tax treatment:

1993 (year of discharge)	
Tax-exempt income to shareholders	$500,000
Shareholders' deduction of prior losses	(500,000)
1994 (assuming corporation is still in existence)	
Cancellation-of-debt income from 1993	$500,000
Absorbed in the following order:	
1. Shareholder loss carryover after 1993	(100,000)
Amount remaining after 1.	400,000
2. Corporation's loss carryforward from prior years	(150,000)
Amount remaining after 2.	250,000
3. Corporation's general business credit carryforward from prior years [(1/3) x 75,000)]	(25,000)
Amount remaining after 3.	$225,000

If Rupco had none of the other attributes for which reduction is required, and if it owned no property, there would be no further consequences to the corporation. In this situation, it is quite likely that Rupco will not even be in existence after 1993.

OBSERVATION: As a practical matter, the year in which an S corporation's debts are discharged in bankruptcy is likely to be the final year of the S corporation's existence. If the corporation survives the bankruptcy, it is unlikely that the former shareholders will have any substantial continuing interest in the corporation. The ability to use the corporation's income from discharge of debt to offset loss carryforwards of the shareholders that would otherwise be nondeductible is a major benefit to the shareholders, and the reduction of any loss carryforwards at the shareholder level is not likely to cause the shareholders any tax disadvantage.

610.68. IRS positions on cancellation-of-debt income. The IRS has become aware that the ability of a shareholder to increase stock basis for his or her share of the corporation's cancellation-of-debt income may provide unwarranted tax benefits. Accordingly, the IRS has issued several Technical Advice Memoranda holding that income excluded under §108 is not "tax-exempt income" within the meaning of §1366. [TAM 9423003, 9541001, 9541006] The rationale behind this opinion is that the attribute reduction required for taxpayers who exclude income under §108 makes this particular exclusion a timing difference, as opposed to true tax-exempt income.

6

610.69. Tax Court position on cancellation-of-debt income. In 1997, the Tax Court has ruled that cancellation-of-debt income excluded under §108 is, in fact, tax-exempt income within the meaning of §1366. Thus, a shareholder was allowed to increase basis for excluded §108 income and to use that basis to deduct previously suspended losses. [*Winn*, TC Memo 1997-286]

The *Winn* victory in 1997 turned out to be illusionary. The Tax Court revisited the issue several times in 1998, and has now decided that the language of §108(d)(7) precludes the pass-through of cancellation-of-debt income from S corporation to shareholder. Therefore, shareholders are not permitted to increase basis for corporate-level cancellation-of-debt income. [*Nelson*, 110 TC 12 (1998)] On the same day, the Court withdrew its 1997 *Winn* decision [TC Memo 1997-286] and held that cancellation-of-debt income could not increase a shareholder's basis in S corporation stock. [*Winn*, TC Memo 1998-71] The courts have reached the same result in *Chesapeake Outdoor Enterprises Inc.* [TC Memo 1998-175], *Friedman* [TC Memo 1998-196], *Gaudiano* [TC Memo 1998-408], *Cronin* [TC Memo 1999-22], *Pugh* [TC Memo 1999-38], *Witzel* [TC Memo 1999-64], *Convisor* [TC Memo 1999-47], and *Farley* [83 AFTR 2d 99-1641 (DC PA)].

In an ironic and asymmetrical twist on this rule, a shareholder attempted to exclude cancellation-of-debt income of an S corporation when the corporation itself was solvent and no other exception applied. The Tax Court held that this income must be included on the shareholder's return as ordinary income. [*Foust*, TC Memo 1997-446]

610.610. Elective basis reduction. Any taxpayer who excluded cancellation-of-debt income under the bankruptcy or insolvency rules may elect to reduce basis of depreciable property before reduction of net operating loss. [§108(a)(5)] After August 1993, a taxpayer's depreciable property includes goodwill and other intangible assets. [§1245(a)(3)] Therefore, these assets should be available for reduction of basis under the same election. See Chapter 16, at 1620., for discussion of amortization of intangible assets. In the case of an S corporation, it would be unlikely that the election to reduce basis of depreciable property, rather than loss carryforwards, would be beneficial. The reduction of basis takes place at the beginning of the year of discharge. Therefore, the reduction of basis would create additional gain on any property transferred to creditors in connection with the debt cancellation. This gain would not be income from discharge of debt, but would be treated as a gain on the sale of property. As such, it would pass through to the shareholders and would result in taxable income at the shareholder level. Since the shareholders are unlikely to have any continuing interest in the corporation after the year of discharge, they will probably lose little if any tax benefit by reducing or eliminating their carryforwards from the S corporation for use in years after the discharge. There are, of course, fact patterns where the election to reduce the basis of depreciable property may be beneficial.

610.7. Character of income passing through to shareholders. As a general rule, the character of income remains constant from the corporation to the shareholder. There are some special rules for capital gain and loss treatment of S corporations and their shareholders.

610.71. Damages awarded to the corporation. The impact of this rule was exemplified when a new shareholder purchased the stock of two S corporations. The S corporations were plaintiffs in a lawsuit and were awarded damages. The damages received were clearly in relation to the corporations' historic business, and should have been treated as ordinary income to the S corporations. [*Hudson v. Commissioner*, 20 TC 734 (1953), aff'd per curiam sub nom. *Ogilvie v. Commissioner*, 216 F.2d 748 (6th Cir. 1954)] However, the new shareholder asserted that the settlement of the lawsuits constituted an exchange of property (the claim against the defendant) and should be capital gain. The court held that the settlement awards were ordinary income to the corporation and must be treated as ordinary income to the shareholders. [*Nahey*, 111 TC No. 13]

610.72. Special rules for dispositions of contributed assets. In general, the nature of gain or loss on the disposition of property depends on the characterization of property to the selling party. Thus, if an asset is a capital asset to the seller, any gain or loss is capital. However, there are two rules in the Proposed Regulations that deal with contributions of property to the corporation by a shareholder, followed by a disposition of the property by the corporation.

One anti-avoidance rule treats certain capital gains as ordinary income, if the assets were contributed by a shareholder that would recognize ordinary income on the disposition. [Proposed Regs. §1.1366-1(b)(2)] This recharacterization applies if the conversion from ordinary income to capital gain was a "principal purpose" of the contribution of the property by the shareholder.

> **EXAMPLE 6 - 22a:** Amanda is a dealer in real estate. She contributes land with a basis of $40,000 and fair market value of $250,000 to Amanco, an S corporation. The contribution is tax-free under §351. Amanda is the sole shareholder of Amanco. The corporation is not a dealer in real estate and then sells the property for a gain of $210,000. Under general tax principles, the corporation would report capital gain from the sale of the property. However, if the conversion of ordinary income to capital gain was a principal purpose of Amanda's contribution of the property, then she must report the $210,000 gain as ordinary income.

A similar rule applies when a shareholder has contributed a high-basis, low-value capital asset to the corporation in order to convert the loss to an ordinary loss. [Proposed Regs. §1.1366-1(b)(3)] If the corporation sells the contributed asset, the loss will be treated as a capital loss, even if the asset is not a capital asset to the S corporation.

610.73. Other gain and loss problems. In a recent case, the requirement that an S corporation follow the individual rules led to the treatment of certain securities losses as capital losses, rather than as ordinary deductions. Corporate-level losses from trading in securities were capital losses when passed through to the shareholder. [*Boatner*, TC Memo 1997-379]

An S corporation was not able to pass through loss to shareholders until the year that the loss was finally determined. [*Wagner*, TC Memo 1998-338] Similarly, an S corporation could not pass through an abandonment loss in a year other than that in which the abandoned property became worthless. [*Buda*, TC Memo 1999-132] In addition, in order to claim an abandonment loss, a taxpayer must prove an intent to abandon, coupled with an act of abandonment. [*Massey-Ferguson, Inc. v. Commissioner*, 59 TC 220, 225 (1972)]

When a U.S. citizen sells certain foreign corporation stock, a portion of the gain may be treated as dividend income under §1248. The IRS has ruled that the sale of such stock by an S corporation requires the shareholders to report §1248 ordinary income. [PLRs 199908044, 199908045]

610.74. Disregard of a QSub. After an involuntary conversion of property held by the parent, an S corporation decided to put replacement property directly into a QSub. The IRS ruled that the replacement property would be treated as owned by the parent S corporation because the QSub is disregarded for all federal income tax purposes. [PLR 199909054]

615. Line-item classification and reporting.

6

As discussed at 610., an S corporation must calculate its taxable income. It must, however, separate any items that could affect the tax liability of any shareholder. As far as the classification of items is concerned, S corporation rules are close to partnership rules, with one major exception: An S corporation does not generate self-employment income. The allocation rules for an S corporation differ materially from those for partnerships. The S corporation allocation rules are discussed at 630., which deals with the separately reported items, as distinguished from ordinary income or loss.

615.1. Two-dimensional classification. The role of any reporting entity (including S corporations) is to give the ultimate taxpayers—in the case of S corporations, the shareholders—all the information they need to properly compute their personal tax returns, insofar as the *entity's* transactions are concerned. The S corporation cannot provide all of the information shareholders need to compute tax liabilities, since the shareholders may have income, losses, or limits that do not relate directly to the corporation's operations.

Since the amendments made by the Subchapter S Revision Act of 1982, S corporations have been required to separate items such as capital gains from ordinary income. These rules are found in §1363 and §1366. More recently, reporting entities have had to cope with the passive, portfolio, and active income classifications required by the Tax Reform Act of 1986. The responsibility for identification of activities and the status of income as rent or other trade or business income falls upon the corporation. The participation rules generally apply at the shareholder level, as do the limitations on income, deductions, and credits from the various activities.

615.2. Traditional line-item classification. The S corporation must compute combined (bottom-line) taxable income or loss, which consists of everything except separately stated items.

Gross (ordinary) income excludes gains and income that require special treatment at the shareholder level. [§1363(b)(1), §1366(a)(1)(A)] Examples of items requiring special treatment are capital and §1231 gains, interest, dividends, charitable contributions, and any other item that may be subject to a limitation for any shareholder.

> **EXAMPLE 6 - 23:** AB Corporation sells machinery in 1987 for $12,000. It had purchased the property for $10,000 and claimed $7,000 depreciation. Under §1245, $7,000 of the gain will be ordinary income. The remaining $2,000 gain will generally be §1231 gain. The §1245 gain is an ordinary item and should be combined with other ordinary income. The §1231 gain will be separately reported, since a shareholder might need to offset this gain with §1231 losses or treat it as a capital gain.

The corporation should also be able to demonstrate the allocation of gross income to a shareholder, in case that shareholder may be subject to a six-year statute of limitations. [§1366(c). Also see *Gmelin*, TC Memo 1988-338, 55 TCM 1410.] The corporation must reduce ordinary gross income by ordinary deductions. [§1366(a)(2)] Consistent with the gross income reporting, the corporation does not include deductions, expenses, and losses that require separate reporting by any shareholder.

An S corporation must report separately any items that could affect the tax liability of any shareholder. [§702(a), §1366(a)(1)(A)] For income tax purposes, the separately reported items include the following:

- Long-term capital gain or loss
- Short-term capital gain or loss
- Gain from the sale of certain small business stock, which qualifies for exclusion at shareholder level (beginning in 1998)
- Gain or loss from sale of §1231 property
- §1231 casualty and theft gain or loss
- §179 expensing
- Nonbusiness bad debts
- Any interest expense subject to shareholder limits, such as investment interest or interest expense attributable to a passive activity
- Charitable contributions
- Qualified investment in §38 property
- Disposition of §38 property
- Jobs credit
- Research credit
- Other credits
- Taxes on investment property that are deductible as itemized deductions by the shareholders under §164

The S corporation must also report tax-exempt income and nondeductible expenses to its shareholders. These items need not be separated out, except for a few of those items that have special tax treatment at the shareholder level, such as tax-exempt interest (which may affect taxability of a shareholder's social security benefits) and income from a private activity bond.[9] The items that require no separate reporting at the shareholder level, such as exempt income from cancellation of debt or receipt by the corporation of life insurance proceeds, must be reported to the shareholders so that they can make appropriate basis adjustments. See Chapter 9.

615.3. Alternative minimum tax considerations. The S corporation must also separately state any item necessary to compute shareholders' alternative minimum tax. Some of these items are:

- Accelerated depreciation on buildings placed in service before 1987
- Accelerated depreciation on leased personal property placed in service before 1987
- Accelerated depreciation on all property placed in service after 1986
- Depletion on mineral (other than oil and gas) property
- Income from completed contract method of accounting (and income from percentage of completion/capitalized cost method of accounting)
- Income from installment method of accounting (and collection on prior years, post-1986 installments; sales originating in 1987 only)

---

[9] This item is a tax preference, and may affect a shareholder's alternative minimum tax.

- Losses from passive farming activities
- Charitable contributions of appreciated property
- Tax-exempt interest on private activity bonds issued after August 7, 1986

620. Reporting for passive activity loss rules.

Section 469 limits deductions and losses from passive activities to income from passive activities. Credits from passive activities are limited to tax from passive activities. These rules, adopted by the Tax Reform Act of 1986, have had a significant impact on both tax preparation and investment strategies.

The §469 limitations apply to shareholders of S corporations in two instances:

1. If a shareholder does not materially participate in the corporation's business, then that shareholder's portion of the corporation's income or loss will be classified as passive.
2. If any of the corporation's income is from rent, that income and its related deductions will be classified as passive to any shareholder, regardless of the degree of his or her participation in the corporation's endeavors.

An S corporation that has no rental income and whose shareholders all participate in the business will have little, if any, immediate concern with the passive loss rules.

An S corporation that has either rental income or inactive shareholders must be concerned with these limits. The primary burden on the corporation is the proper reporting of income and deductions. As this chapter indicates, the reporting burden is not trivial. The principal roles of the corporation are:

- Classifying the corporation's income as portfolio, rent, professional service, oil and gas, or other type
- Deciding whether the corporation has a single activity or multiple activities

The economic limitations are felt at the shareholder level. Shareholders must first understand the nature of the information the corporation provides. They must also determine their degree of participation in the corporation's ventures.

620.1. Relationship of the S corporation to activities. Regulations §1.469-4T (issued May 1989) contains extensive definitions of *separate* and *combined* activities. It has separate applications to S corporations and to shareholders of S corporations. The tendency is to combine operations into one activity, rather than to treat operations separately. Regulations §1.469-5T refers to activities conducted by partnerships and S corporations. Similar references in Temporary Regulations §1.469-1T, §1.469-2T, and §1.469-4T and Proposed Regulations §1.469-4 demonstrate that an S corporation is not the same as an activity. See Chapter 10 for further discussion.

> **OBSERVATION:** The distinction between an activity and an S corporation has little impact when the corporation is engaged in a single business. When a corporation has multiple lines of business, and several shareholders, the problems could become quite complex.

An S corporation may own several activities. In contrast, an S corporation may be a component of a larger activity, with respect to one or more of its shareholders. An S corporation may represent the entire interest in an activity for one shareholder and be part of an activity to another.

The primary burdens on the S corporation in this situation are reporting income, deductions, gains, losses, etc., to shareholders and accounting for separate and combined lines of business. The burdens of disallowance, and the benefits of deducting suspended losses, fall entirely on the shareholders.

620.11. Multiple activities. S corporations engaged in multiple activities need to segregate income and deductions from each activity. The corporation must separately state income and deductions related to each rental real estate activity in which one or more shareholders actively participate in management. The S corporation will need to separately report items of income and loss from each farming activity (which requires special alternative minimum tax treatment at the shareholder level) and from each trade or business activity other than rental real estate or farming. From 1987 through 1990, the corporation was also required to distinguish any activities it acquired before October 23, 1986 (which were subject to a transitional disallowance rule), from those it acquired on or after that date.

620.12. Activities and non-activities. Although the classification rules for activities defy *simple* explanation, one logical place to begin is to determine whether an investment constitutes (1) an activity, (2) a component of an activity, or (3) a non-activity. An *activity* must be a trade or business for which there is a profit motive, production of income, and regularity of entrepreneurial activity. (Temporary Regs. §1.469-1T(e)(2) excludes operations that are merely incidental to holding property for investment.) A *non-activity* is an investment that produces purely passive or portfolio income.

Thus any interest, annuities, royalties, dividends on C corporation stock, income from a real estate investment trust, a regulated investment company, etc., cannot be included as income from an activity. [Temporary Regs. §1.469-2T(c)(3)(i)(A)] Certain interest income is not considered to be portfolio income and is treated as trade or business income. [Temporary Regs. §1.469-2T(c)(3)(ii)] For example, interest income on loans and investments made in the ordinary course of business and interest on accounts receivable are treated as business income.

Deductions must also be classified as activity or portfolio. An S corporation must allocate interest expense according to the interest tracing rules of Regulations §1.163-8T. Thus, if an S corporation incurs a debt and identifies the debt with an activity, the interest expense would be allocated to that activity. [Temporary Regs. §1.469-2T(d)(3)] Expenses other than interest are associated with portfolio income only if they are "clearly and directly allocable to portfolio income" and "incurred as a result of, or incident to," portfolio property. [Temporary Regs. §1.469-2T(d)(4)]

620.13. Line items within activities. The line item, or traditional, classification must coexist with the activity classification. For each identifiable activity, the S corporation must decide if any item of income or expense needs separate classification. One of the most important deductions to watch is a casualty loss. Casualty losses are generally deductible, without regard to the classification of the activity. (§165(c) takes precedence over §469. See Temporary Regs. §1.469-2T(d)(2)(x).)

If all or any portion of a loss from an activity is disallowed, a ratable portion of each passive activity deduction (other than an excluded deduction) is disallowed. This portion is calculated by dividing the deduction by the sum of all passive activity deductions from the activity.

Separately identified deductions include (but are not limited to) the following:

- Deductions that arise in a rental real estate activity in which the taxpayer actively participates

- Deductions that arise in a rental real estate activity in which the taxpayer does not actively participate
- Deductions that are taken into account under §1211 or §1231
- Income and deductions related to activities acquired by the corporation prior to October 23, 1986

To comply with alternative minimum tax rules, the corporation must segregate income and deduction from any passive farming venture and must also identify the tax preferences and adjustments with each activity.

6

Casualty and theft losses, other than those regularly incurred in a business (such as shoplifting), are not treated as passive activity deductions, even if the taxpayer does not materially participate or the losses are incurred in connection with a rental operation.

620.2. Definition of a rental activity. *Rental activities* are defined in Regulations §1.469-1T(e)(3). If an activity is "rental," it is, by definition, passive. If it is not rental, the degree of participation by any shareholder affects treatment as active or passive, at the shareholder level.

620.3. Special rules for oil and gas working interests. In general, oil and gas investments do not produce passive income or loss if they are held directly or through a working interest. [§469(c)(3)(A)] A working interest can exist only when the taxpayer subject to §469 (the shareholder, when S corporations are involved) holds the interest in the property through an entity that does not limit the taxpayer's liability.

Since an S corporation is a form of entity that limits shareholder liability, oil and gas interests held in an S corporation will create passive income or loss to shareholders. There are special rules, however, for former working interests. Once a taxpayer has any loss from a working interest, that same holder will not be able to create passive income or loss from that interest in any subsequent year. [§469(c)(3)(B)]

620.4. Other recharacterization rules. An activity of trading personal property such as stocks and securities for the account of owners is not passive. Thus, an investment club will not realize passive income on sales. This rule prevents conversion of gains from investments into passive activity income. In a similar vein, income from an equity-financed lending operation is not passive.

620.5. Sales of property and activities by an S corporation. The S corporation must inform its shareholders of sales of corporate passive activities and sales of property used in the corporation's activities. In the case of a disposition of the corporation's entire interest in an activity, some shareholders may be able to deduct suspended losses from earlier years. The S corporation may be required to identify the person who purchased the activity, in case the purchaser is a related party to any of the shareholders.

> **EXAMPLE 6 - 24:** Grayco is an S corporation in the service business. It has also owned an interest in a rental partnership for several years. In 1991, it disposes of its interest in the rental property. It must report the gain or loss on the sale of the property. It must inform shareholders that the gain or loss results from a complete disposition of its interest in the rental property. Grayco should identify the purchaser, so that any of Grayco's shareholders can determine if they are related to the purchaser.

620.51. Dispositions to related parties. At the time of this writing, there are no Regulations issued or proposed on the disposition of an activity. [Temporary Regs. §1.469-6T is reserved for disposition rules.] It is important to note, however, that a taxpayer can use all suspended losses identified with an activity in the year of disposition. [§469(g)] If the disposition is not a fully taxable transaction (e.g., a partially like-kind exchange, contribution to a corporation, or contribution to a partnership), the taxpayer is not permitted to use suspended losses in the year of the disposition. [§469(g)(1)] Whether the sale is a fully taxable disposition should be determined at the corporate level.

> **EXAMPLE 6 - 25:** Grayco, from Example 6 - 24, disposes of its rental property by contributing it to a partnership, in which Grayco receives a partnership interest. Since this type of disposition is not fully taxable under §721, none of Grayco's shareholders would be able to use suspended losses in the year of the transfer.

After a nontaxable disposition, the S corporation should keep track of the ownership of the property. Presumably, disposition of the original activity by the buyer, or disposition of the remaining interest in the property, would allow the shareholders to use their suspended losses.

> **EXAMPLE 6 - 26:** In 1992, Grayco, from Examples 6 - 24 and 6 - 25, disposes of its interest in the partnership to which it contributed the rental property. It must inform its shareholders of the gain or loss recognized on the disposition of the partnership interest. It should also inform them that it has now completely disposed of its interest in the rental property.

> **EXAMPLE 6 - 27:** In 1992, Grayco, from Examples 6 - 24 and 6 - 25, retains its interest in the partnership to which it contributed the rental property. The partnership, however, disposes of the rental property that had been contributed by Grayco in 1991. Grayco must allocate its income or loss from the partnership to its shareholders under the general requirements of Subchapter S. It should also inform them that it has now indirectly disposed of its interest in the rental property.

A seller is not allowed to recognize all suspended losses if the disposition is to a related party [within the meaning of §267(b) or §707(b)(1)]. See Chapter 8, at 835.1., for discussion of related parties. Since the restrictions of §469 apply to the individual shareholders, rather than to the S corporation itself, it is reasonable to assume that the related-party test is made at the shareholder level. However, the corporation might not know if the buyer of property is related to one of the selling corporation's shareholders. Accordingly, it should inform its shareholders of the identity of the purchaser.

> **EXAMPLE 6 - 28:** Jeco is an S corporation that conducts two separate activities. It has two shareholders, Jay and Jeanne, who are not related to each other. In 1991, Jeco sells one of the activities to Jeanne's brother. At the shareholder level, this would probably constitute a complete disposition to Jay, but not to Jeanne.

An S corporation that disposes of an activity must provide all of the necessary information to each shareholder so that he or she may evaluate whether or not suspended losses may be recognized in the year of disposition. The above examples provided some illustration that the shareholders might receive divergent treatment when an S corporation disposes of its interest in an activity. The required aggregation of undertakings might also cause asymmetrical effects to the shareholders.

620.52. Identity of property sold by the S corporation. The S corporation must identify sales of property with the activity in which the property was used. If property is sold at a gain, the corporation will report the gain as gross income from the activity to which the property relates. [Temporary Regs. §1.469-2T(c)(2)(i)] There are additional allocations if an S corporation sells property that has been used in more than one activity. Pursuant to §1.469-2T(c)(2)(ii), the amount realized from the disposition and the adjusted basis of such interest must be allocated. Sole allocation to one activity is permitted if:

1. The property has been used in a single activity for the past 12 months, *and*
2. The fair market value of the property does not exceed the lesser of $10,000 or 10% of fair market value of all property used in the activity.

The following examples, all taken from Temporary Regs. §1.469-2T(c)(2)(ii), illustrate the computations that the S corporation may be required to make on the disposition of property.

6

620.53. Recharacterization of gains from property sales. In some cases, gains from sales of property will be characterized as portfolio income. This rule applies to the disposition of property that produces portfolio income [Temporary Regs. §1.469-2T(c)(3)(i)(C)] and the disposition of property held for investment. [Temporary Regs. §1.469-2T(c)(3)(i)(D)] A gain that is not passive is portfolio income only if the property was held "for investment" more than 50% of the time it was used in nonpassive activities. Otherwise, it must be classified as "active" gain. [Temporary Regs. §1.469-2T(c)(2)(iii)(E)]

620.6. Conversion from C status to S status. Under some circumstances, a C corporation may be subject to the passive activity loss limits. A personal service corporation is subject to the same rules as an individual. [§469(a)(2)(C)] A closely held corporation is subject to loss limits, but is allowed to offset "net active income" with losses from passive activities. [§469(e)(2)] When a C corporation that has been subject to the passive activity loss limits makes an S election, there is no prescribed treatment in the Code or legislative history for any of the suspended losses from the Subchapter C years. However, the IRS has been of the opinion that a disallowed deduction under the passive activity loss rules is to be treated as a carryover and is subject to the disallowance of carryovers from C corporation years. The Tax Court has agreed. [*St. Charles Investment Co.*, 110 TC 6 (1998)] See discussion of carryovers at 610.3.

EXAMPLE 6 - 29: In 1997, Z Corporation was a closely held C corporation that invested in equipment that was seven-year ACRS property. The cost was $140,000. The 1997 depreciation was $20,000. Z Corporation leased the property out and collected $4,000 rent during 1997. It had no active gross income in 1997. Therefore, $16,000 of the depreciation deduction was disallowed as a passive loss in 1997. The basis in the equipment was reduced by the full $20,000.

In 1998, Z filed an S election. It claimed depreciation of $34,286 in 1998. It collected $40,000 rents in 1998. Its 1998 depreciation deduction is allowed in full, since it has passive income in excess of the deduction. The suspended loss from 1997 would be treated as a carryover from a C corporation year, and would not be allowed as a deduction in 1997, or in any later year in which Z was an S corporation.

OBSERVATION: There is no comprehensive guidance on the ultimate disposition of a suspended loss under §469 from C corporation years. Presumably, the loss would be freed up if the corporation revoked its S election and became a C corporation again, as is the case with a net operating loss. The suspended passive activity loss has no expiration in terms of years, so it could be important to keep the record of this loss for decades. Also see discussion of §469 suspended losses in relation to the built-in gains tax in Chapter 11, at 1125.18.

620.7. Transitional rules. From 1987 through 1990, taxpayers were allowed to deduct a certain portion of passive losses.[10] This transitional rule applied at the shareholder level. To take a transitional deduction for a loss from an activity held through an S corporation, there were three criteria:

1. The corporation must have acquired its interest in the activity before October 23, 1986.
2. The shareholder must have acquired his or her stock in the corporation before October 23, 1986.
3. The corporation must have had its S election in effect before October 23, 1986. [Temporary Regs. §1.469-11T(c)(2)(ii)]

An activity not owned by the corporation on October 22, 1986, qualifies for the transitional deduction under certain binding contract exceptions. (Temporary Regs. §1.469-11T(c)(3)(i) explains the exceptions, which have little relevance after 1990.) The responsibility of the corporation is to inform the shareholders of the date on which the corporation acquired an activity. The shareholders themselves must determine whether they owned their stock on the date of enactment of the Tax Reform Act of 1986.

625. Special income and loss problems.

Since most S corporations are closely held, there may be a gray area of dealing between an S corporation and its shareholders. In some instances an S corporation may be an alter ego for shareholders. It may be difficult to determine whether the income and deductions of an S corporation are truly business related, or are more appropriately treated as shareholder-level items. There have been several cases dealing with S corporations that are paying expenses on behalf of their shareholders, collecting income on behalf of shareholders or vice versa.

Loss limitations require some shuffling between individual and corporate rules. Some losses are subject to limits at the shareholder level as discussed in Chapter 9, on shareholder basis, and in Chapter 10, on the hierarchy of basis, at-risk, and passive losses.

Other losses may be limited at the corporate level. These include disallowed losses on sales to related parties and denial of the accrual method to amounts accrued to shareholders. The accounting rules governing transactions with shareholders are covered in Chapter 8.

625.1. Improper identification of income. Confusion can arise when a party deals with a corporation and also has business dealings with one or more of the shareholders. In one recent situation, a vendor issued Form 1099 to an S corporation for payments it had made to the corporation, but reported one of the shareholders' Social Security numbers on the form. The IRS then audited the shareholder, who had apparently underreported his gross income. The IRS was apparently willing to concede the issue, but requested certain information from the corporation. The corporation was not prompt in providing the IRS with all of the information it requested. The shareholder incurred substantial legal expenses in dealing with the IRS. The shareholder then sued the IRS for $9,502 in administrative costs, on the

---

[10] Code §469(m)(2) provides the following schedule:

Year Beginning in	*Loss Allowed (%)*
1987	65
1988	40
1989	20
1990	10
1991	0

grounds that the IRS was not substantially justified in continuing its audit. [§7430] The Tax Court held that the taxpayer's delays in providing requested information precluded the award. [*Miller*, TC Memo 1994-142] Therefore, it is important to check all tax information reported on Form 1099.

> **OBSERVATION:** The S corporation and shareholder in this case could have avoided a great deal of trouble if they had discovered the problem and acted quickly. First, they should have contacted the vendor and requested that a revised Form 1099 be issued to the shareholder, with a zero payment reported. Another option would have been for the shareholder to have issued a 1099 reporting the income back to the vendor. A third would have been for the shareholder to issue a 1099 to the S corporation. The third option would have left a clean audit trail for the IRS, and would have avoided the administrative cost.

In another recent case, a shareholder attempted to assign his earned income to an S corporation in order to avoid the self-employment tax. The Tax Court upheld the imposition of the self-employment tax. [*Ruckman*, TC Memo 1998-83] In other cases, taxpayers have attempted to disregard the corporate entity entirely, and in each of these the Tax Court has forced the corporation and its shareholders to abide by the structure of separate entities. [*Moye*, TC Memo 1997-554; *Reed*, TC Memo 1997-533]

625.2. Hobby loss limits. The hobby loss rules of §183 disallow any net loss from an activity without a profit motive. The IRS may test for the hobby loss disallowance at the corporate level. If losses are disallowed at the corporate level, they will not pass through to the shareholders. A profit motive is presumed based on the number of years the activity has produced income. The nine factors listed below are subjective: Any one of them, if sufficiently strong, may be an indication of the motive. If there is no one factor or combination of factors that is decisive, there is one objective presumption: Code §183(d) states that the profit motive is presumed when the activity has shown a profit in three of the last five years. In the case of horse breeding, training, racing, or showing, there must have been profits in two of the last seven years. The Regulations list nine tests to be used as indicators [Temporary Regs. §1.183-2]:

1. The manner in which the taxpayer carries on the activity: A taxpayer who does not keep books or records, or engage in normal business practices, will not likely be treated as having a profit motive.
2. The expertise of the taxpayer or his advisors: A taxpayer with little background and training may fail this test. This problem can be overcome if the taxpayer has recently shifted substantial time and effort into learning the business.
3. The time and effort expended by the taxpayer in carrying on the activity: Devotion of substantial time to the activity is evidence that the taxpayer has the requisite profit motive. Occasional attention to the activity is evidence that the profit motive is lacking.
4. Expectation that assets used in the activity may appreciate in value: A long-term, rather than current, profit expectation may be acceptable. This factor, by itself, gives little support to the deduction of current expenses, unless the taxpayer can meet the presumption described below.
5. The success of the taxpayer in carrying on other similar or dissimilar activities: A taxpayer who has a history of turning losing enterprises into profitable ventures will be likely to demonstrate the profit motive.
6. The taxpayer's history of income and losses with respect to the activity: If the taxpayer has been engaged in the activity for many years, and has suffered a series of misfortunes, the profit motive may be present.

7. The amount of occasional profits which are earned: An occasional large profit indicates that there is a realistic profit motive.
8. The financial status of the taxpayer: A taxpayer who has little financial means other than the enterprise in question may demonstrate the profit motive.
9. Elements of personal pleasure or recreation: Those activities, such as a collection of valuables, a country estate, raising animals, music, or artistic creation, which many persons engage in as hobbies, are ripe for suspicion as to a genuine profit motive.

The disallowance is permanent. Deductions which are disallowed under §183 cannot be carried into any other tax year. This rule makes documentation of the profit motive extremely important. If possible, the activity should not show a loss for more than two consecutive years. If the taxpayer is able to prepay or postpone expenses, elect slower depreciation, or implement any other legitimate device to help the activity show a profit, the activity may meet the profit presumption.

If an S corporation lacks a profit motive, or does not meet the criteria listed above, the IRS has the ability to disallow the loss. There has not been extensive activity in this area, although the IRS was upheld in one recent disallowance case. [*Upton*, 59 TCM 653 (1990)] In another recent case, an S corporation with certain farming activities was subjected to the hobby loss limits, and the loss was disallowed at the corporate level. [*Westbrook*, TC Memo 1993-634, 66 TCM 1823, aff'd *Westbrook v. CIR*, 68 F.3d 868, 76 AFTR 2d 95-7397, 95-2 USTC P 50,587 (5th Cir.)] Other recent cases held that the requisite tests were missing from the S corporation's activities, and denied S corporations deductible losses, based on the hobby loss rules. [*Ballard*, TC Memo 1996-68; *Hilliard*, TC Memo 1995-473, 70 TCM (CCH) 898, *Lucid*, TC Memo 1997-247]

Similarly, an S corporation was not able to claim research and experimentation expenses as deductible items. The S corporation was not involved in any trade or business and was thus disallowed a deduction for any expenses. [*Cook*, TC Memo 1993-581, 66 TCM 1523].

An attempt to deduct hobby losses, in which part of the deduction was rent paid to the shareholder, landed the shareholder in double jeopardy. An S corporation was prohibited from claiming a deduction for rent paid on pleasure boats to the sole shareholder. However, the shareholder was required to claim the rent received from the corporation as income. Note that the shareholder was claiming deductions with respect to the boats. [*Catalano*, TC Memo 1998-447]

625.3. Other disallowances of corporate-level expenses. An S corporation should keep careful records which separate the corporation's business activities from those of its shareholders. In a recent case, a corporation was disallowed deductions for payment of certain expenses which were personal to the shareholder. [*Westbrook*, TC Memo 1993-634, 66 TCM 1823, aff'd *Westbrook v. CIR*, 68 F.3d 868, 76 AFTR 2d 95-7397, 95-2 USTC P 50,587 (5th Cir.)] Some of the expenses paid by the corporation would have been deductible on the shareholder's tax return. The Tax Court, however, disallowed even these expenses, since they were not legitimate expenses of the corporation, per se. In other cases, the corporation's payment of shareholder expenses may be characterized as compensation, or as a distribution. [*Gerald D. Handke*, 59 TCM 766, TC Memo 1990-273] See Chapter 8, at 810., for further discussion.

> **OBSERVATION:** The courts are not always consistent in their disallowance of deductions for personal expenses of shareholders paid by controlled corporations. See Chapter 8, at 810. Note especially the discussion of Prewitt. [TC Memo 1995-487, 70 TCM (CCH) 962]

In another recent case, an S corporation was allowed to deduct the cost of a settlement of a lawsuit by a client. An employee of the corporation had embezzled funds from the client.

The IRS tried to impute some sort of matching principle, and it denied the deduction for the settlement, since the corporation had never reported the embezzlement income. The court held for the taxpayer. In the same case, the court divided legal fees between those incurred for the client lawsuit from other legal expenses in connection with recovery of life insurance proceeds. The portion allocated to the insurance recovery was nondeductible under §265(a)(1). [*Musgrave*, TC Memo 1997-19, 73 TCM 1721]

Legal expenses can often be on the edge between business and personal. Legal fees paid by an S corporation were allowed as deductions when a shareholder fought successfully to retain control of corporate assets; such fees were incidental to a divorce of the controlling shareholder, but they were definitely tied to the corporation's business purpose. [*Liberty Vending Inc.*, TC Memo 1998-177]

630. Allocation of items to shareholders.

As stated earlier, allocation of items to shareholders has three dimensions:

- Which items?
- How much to each shareholder?
- When?

The first question was covered at 615. The next task is to focus on the allocations to the individual shareholders.

630.1. Pro rata allocation. Pro rata allocation is the general rule for allocating income, deductions, credits, and any other corporate-level items to shareholders. Code §1377(a)(1) provides that each item shall be allocated on a per-share, per-day basis.

SUMMARY OF AUTHORITY: CODE SECTION 1377(a)(1)

- An S corporation must apportion each item of income, deduction, etc., to its shareholders on a per-share, per-day basis.

If there is no change in share ownership, there is no reason to ever deviate from this formula. Each shareholder includes his or her share of income, loss, deduction, credit, etc., based on a weighted average. By inference, there are no special allocations, as is permitted with partnerships. This rule also precludes special allocations for contributed property. Such allocations are required for partnerships by §704.

> **EXAMPLE 6 - 30:** An S corporation has a 60% shareholder and a 40% shareholder. It has $70,000 ordinary income, $20,000 long-term capital gains, and $5,000 dividend income. The long-term capital gain arose from a gain that had accrued before the 60% shareholder contributed the property to the corporation. The 60% shareholder will report 60% of each item, and the 40% shareholder will report 40% of each.

As a general rule, the pro rata allocation is required when there is a change in shareholdings within the taxable year. This formula completely disregards the timing of actual transactions at the corporate level.

> **EXAMPLE 6 - 31:** On January 1, 1987, J owns all of the shares of the GJ Corporation. On May 26, 1987, he sells 45% of the shares to G. G is considered to be the *owner* for all of May 26, but all items occurring on that date are allocated to J, the seller. May 26 is exactly 40% of the way through the year. The allocation of each item will be:

To J [(.4 x 1)+(.6 x .55)]	73%
To G (.6 x .45)	27%

630.2. Interim closing. If a shareholder terminates his or her interest in an S corporation, the corporation may elect separate accounting periods, before and after the termination. [§1377(a)(2)] A similar rule allows an election to close the books as of the date of a substantial disposition of stock, or substantial issuance of new shares to new shareholders. [Regs. §1.1368-1(g)] By making this election, the corporation accounts for all items that are required to be reported to shareholders from the beginning of the taxable year to the date of the closing, and it reports those items on a weighted average daily basis to persons who were shareholders during that period. It makes similar allocations for the portion of the year that begins after the closing.

6

SUMMARY OF AUTHORITY: CODE SECTION 1377(a)(2), IN EFFECT FOR S CORPORATION TAXABLE YEARS BEGINNING ON OR AFTER JANUARY 1, 1997

- When a shareholder terminates his or her interest in an S corporation, the corporation may close its books on the date of the termination. It accounts for the subsequent portion of the year as if it were a separate taxable year.
- The Code does not define termination of a shareholder's interest, but delegates that authority to the IRS.
- This provision requires consent of all "affected" shareholders, for transfers made in S corporations' taxable years beginning after 1996. This provision no longer requires consent of any person whose tax situation would not be affected by the election.
- Any person who owns shares at any time during the year must consent, even if he or she owns no shares on the date of the termination.
- Within each portion of the taxable year, the corporation must apportion all items of income, deduction, etc., on a per-share, per-day basis.
- The only effect of such an election is to allocate income among the various shareholders.

The IRS has issued two different Regulations dealing with the interim closing election. Regulations §1.1368-1(g) allows a corporation to elect an interim closing upon certain dispositions that otherwise would not qualify as a termination of a shareholder's entire interest. Regulations §1.1377-1, issued in late 1996, governs the termination of a shareholder's entire interest.

630.21. Termination of a shareholder's interest. A termination of a shareholder's interest occurs when a shareholder disposes of all of his or her shares. [§1377(a)(2); Regs. §1.1377-1(b)(4)] The Code gives no amplification of the term *disposition*. The Regulations permit an interim closing upon any of the following events [Regs. §1.1377-1(b)(4)]:

- Sales of stock
- Gifts of stock
- Transfer at death
- Redemptions of stock, whether treated as exchanges or distributions (See Chapter 15 for discussion.)
- Divisive reorganizations, where some shareholders exchange stock in the distributing corporation (See Chapter 17 for discussion.)
- A conversion of a trust from a QSST to an ESBT, or vice versa. See Chapter 5, at 540.3.

The disposition of all of the stock of any shareholder allows the corporation to elect to treat the year as separate accounting periods. In this instance, the percentage of the corporation's shares is irrelevant.

EXAMPLE 6 - 32: Beverly owned 15% of the outstanding shares in Bevco, an S corporation that uses the calendar year. On October 29, 1992, Beverly sold all of her stock. The corporation may elect to treat January 1 through October 29, 1992, as one accounting period and October 30, 1992, through December 31, 1992, as a second accounting period.

The election to close the year is not available if the shareholder does not dispose of all of his or her shares, if the total shares transferred are less than 20% of the corporation's outstanding stock. Accordingly, a shareholder who owns no more than 20% of the stock must dispose of his or her entire interest.

EXAMPLE 6 - 33: Refer to Example 6 - 32. If Beverly had retained even one share in Bevco, the corporation could not elect to close its books on October 29, 1992. Beverly's disposition would not have met either of the criteria for separate accounting periods, since she did not dispose of all of her shares or dispose of 20% of the corporation's outstanding stock.

630.22. Substantial disposition or issuance of stock. The Regulations under §1368 allow an S corporation to elect an interim closing whenever one of the following occurs. [Regs. §1.1368-1(g)]

- One shareholder disposes of 20% or more of the outstanding and issued stock of an S corporation in one or more transactions in a 30-day period.
- The corporation issues stock to new shareholders, and the number of shares issued exceeds 25% of the shares that were outstanding before the issue.

When a shareholder owns at least 20% of the corporation's outstanding stock, that shareholder does not need to dispose of his or her entire interest, as long as the shares relinquished by the shareholder are at least 20% of the corporation's issued stock. [Regs. §1.1368-1(g)(2)(i)] The disposition may be in a single transaction or in two or more transactions within a 30-day period within the corporation's taxable year.

EXAMPLE 6 - 34: On January 1, 1992, Mary owns all 100 outstanding shares of Marrco, an S corporation. On April 17, 1992, she sells 20 shares to Bob. The corporation may elect, with the consent of the shareholders, to close the books as of April 17, 1992.

EXAMPLE 6 - 35: Assume the same facts as in Example 6 - 34, except that Mary had sold only 19 shares to Bob. The corporation could not close its books on the date of transfer.

EXAMPLE 6 - 36: Assume the same facts as in Example 6 - 34, except that Mary had sold only 19 shares to Bob. On April 30, Mary sold 3 shares to Bill. The corporation may elect, with the consent of the shareholders, to close the books as of April 30, 1992.

OBSERVATION: The Proposed Regulations under §1377 address the situation when a termination of a shareholder's entire interest is also a substantial disposition of stock, within the meaning of Regulations §1.1368-1(g). In this instance, the corporation should file an election under §1377(a)(2), and not under Regulations §1.1368-(1)(g). [Regs. §1.1377-1(b)(1)]

It appears that there must be a direct disposition of shares, rather than an indirect reduction of a shareholder's ownership, to be within the substantial disposition rule. Similarly, it appears that one sole shareholder must dispose of 20% of the stock. Apparently, dispositions by two or more persons are not aggregated for this test. When an S corporation intends to admit a new shareholder, it should be aware of the rules for an interim closing.

EXAMPLE 6 - 37: Changeco has two shareholders, Charlie and Delta. Each owns 600 shares. The parties have agreed to sell a one-third interest to Earl, who will provide cash. The corporation is authorized by its charter to issue 1,000 additional shares. If the corporation issues 600 new shares to Earl, none of the shareholders will have disposed of any of the outstanding shares. If Charlie and Delta each sell 200 of their shares to Earl, or have the corporation redeem those shares, there will be a disposition. In this case, however, neither Charlie nor Delta will have disposed of the required percentage of stock. However, if the corporation redeemed 240 each of Charlie and Delta's shares, each would have a disposition of the required 20%. Changeco would be allowed to close its books as of the date of Charlie and Delta's disposition. The corporation could then issue 360 shares to Earl and achieve the desired percentage ownership.

PLANNING TIP: When a new shareholder intends to increase percentage ownership during a corporation's taxable year, the parties may want to allocate to that person a portion of the post-change income or loss of the corporation that corresponds with his or her percentage ownership for that portion of the year. This objective is attained by making an election under Regulations §1.1368-1(g).

It also appears that a disposition to a related person, such as a family member, allows the corporation to make the interim closing election. Conversely, there is no rule that allows any shareholders, including related parties, to aggregate their ownership.

630.23. Accounting for the year of termination. There are two requirements that the corporation must observe:

1. One or more shareholders must have terminated their interest in the corporation.
2. All "affected" shareholders must consent to split the year into separate periods. For taxable years beginning before January 1, 1997, the affected shareholders include any person who holds shares at any time during the entire tax year of the corporation. For taxable years beginning after December 31, 1996, the affected shareholders include any person whose tax liability could be affected by the election to split the year. In any year, if the shareholder who terminates his or her interest does so by having the shares redeemed by the corporation, all persons who are shareholders at any time during the taxable year of the redemption must consent.

EXAMPLE 6 - 38: On January 1, 1987, Rex owns 70% and Mavis owns 30% of the shares in RM Corporation. On August 6 (60% of the year), Mavis sells all of her shares to Percy. The corporation showed the following items for the year:

	Period		
	1/1–8/6	*8/7–12/31*	*Total*
Ordinary income	$20,000	$80,000	$100,000
§1231 gain	15,000	0	15,000
Short-term capital loss	0	30,000	30,000

Using the general allocation rule, the shareholders would report the following:

	Shareholder		
Percentage	*Rex*	*Mavis*	*Percy*
.7 x 1	.70		
.3 x .6		.18	
.3 x .4			.12
Ordinary income	$70,000	$18,000	$12,000
§1231 gain	10,500	2,700	1,800
Short-term capital loss	21,000	5,400	3,600

Under the separate period election, the shareholders would report:

	Shareholder		
	Rex	*Mavis*	*Percy*
Ordinary income	$70,000[a]	$6,000[d]	$24,000[g]
§1231 gain	10,500[b]	4,500[e]	0[h]
Short-term capital loss	21,000[c]	0[f]	9,000[i]

[a]70% of $100,000
[b]70% of $15,000
[c]70% of $30,000
[d]30% of $20,000
[e]30% of $15,000
[f]30% of $0
[g]30% of $80,000
[h]30% of $0
[i]30% of $30,000

The election to use separate periods would not be available if Mavis had retained any of her shares. The election also would be invalidated if any person acquired shares later in the taxable year and did not consent to the election.

If multiple terminations occur within one tax year of a corporation, there could be more than two accounting periods. The Regulations allow one single election to cover all elections to close the books for one taxable year. [Regs. §1.1368-1(g)(2)(ii); Regulations §1.1377-1(b)(5)(i)] There is no express requirement, however, that the corporation elect to close its books for each termination of a shareholder's interest.

EXAMPLE 6 - 39: Shiftco is an S corporation that uses the calendar year. On January 1, 1997, its shares were held in equal portions by Steven, Teresa, and Ulysses. On April 17, 1997, Steven sold all of his stock to Vera. On October 17, 1997, Ulysses sold all of his stock to Wilma. Both the sale from Steven to Vera and the sale from Ulysses to Wilma qualify the corporation to elect to close its books. The corporation has four options for allocating income and losses for the taxable year:

1. The corporation may prorate all of its income and other items on a daily basis from January 1, 1997, through December 31, 1997.
2. The corporation may prorate all of its income and other items on a daily basis from January 1, 1997, through April 17, 1997, and prorate all of its income and other items on a daily basis from April 18, 1997, through December 31, 1997.
3. The corporation may prorate all of its income and other items on a daily basis from January 1, 1997, through October 17, 1997, and prorate all of its income and other items on a daily basis from October 18, 1997, through December 31, 1997.
4. The corporation may prorate all of its income and other items on a daily basis from January 1, 1997, through April 17, 1997; prorate all of its income and other items on a daily basis from April 18, 1997, through October 17, 1997; and prorate all of its income and other items on a daily basis from October 18, 1997, through December 31, 1997.

If a shareholder who terminated his or her interest early in the year has already consented to an interim closing, the same shareholder need not consent to a later interim closing. [Regs. §1.1377-1(b)(4)(iii)] Thus, in the above example, all five shareholders must consent to close the year on April 17, 1997. If all of the shareholders agree to this interim closing, Steven need not consent to an interim closing on October 17, 1997.

OBSERVATION: Regulations §1.1368-1(f)(5) and Regs. §1.1377-1 contain cryptic statements that "a shareholder of the corporation for the taxable year is a shareholder as described in section 1362(a)(2)." The cross-reference refers to persons who are shareholders on the date that a corporation files its S election. Common sense would indicate that the persons who owned shares on the date the corporation filed its S election may not be the same persons who owned shares during the year of termination of a shareholder's interest. Although the author may only speculate as to the exact meaning of that phrase, it is probably intended to include all persons who have ownership interests, such as community property interests, in any shares during the year for which the corporation is electing to split its taxable year into two portions.

630.24. Scope and limitations of election. The election to close the books on the date of termination of a shareholder's interest serves primarily as a means to allocate income to shareholders. It does not cause the corporation's year to end for most other purposes.

EXAMPLE 6 - 40: Aprico is an S corporation with an April 30 fiscal year. All of its shareholders use the calendar year. On October 17, 1993, one shareholder disposes of his stock, and the corporation elects to close the books. The corporation's income and other items from May 1 through October 17, 1993, are allocated to the shareholders in proportion to their stock ownership through that date. The shareholders, however, do not report any of these items on their 1993 returns, since the corporation's taxable year ends on April 30, 1994.

The various Regs. have taken somewhat spotty and inconsistent positions on the effects of an election to close a year under each rule. Table 6-2 highlights the known, as well as the probable, effects of these elections. Where there is no guidance in either Regulation, the table advises that any reasonable position may be taken.

630.25. Procedural aspects of the elections. The two separate elections have slightly different procedural requirements. First, the requirements for filing the election due to the termination of a shareholder's interest in a corporation are found in Regs. §1.1377-1(b)(5). In brief, the requirements are:

1. The corporation must attach a statement to its Form 1120S for the year of the termination.
2. The statement must affirm that the corporation is electing under §1377(a)(2) and Regs. §1.1377-1(b) to treat the year as if it consisted of two taxable years.
3. The statement must give the details on the terminating event.
4. The statement must declare that all affected shareholders have consented to the split of the taxable year.
5. The statement must be signed by an officer of the corporation who is authorized to sign the corporation's tax returns.
6. A statement from each affected shareholder, consenting to the split year election, must be included.

The election to split the year under §1377(a)(2) is irrevocable. [Regs. §1.1377-1(b)(1)] It may be made on a timely filed, extended or amended Form 1120S for the year of the terminating event. [Regs. §1.1377-1(b)(5)(i)] A single election may cover all terminations of shareholder interests during one year. Note, however, that the regulations do not explicitly permit an election to split the year under §1377(a)(2) to also cover a substantial disposition or new issue under Regulations §1.1368-1(g).

The election to split a taxable year due to a substantial disposition or issue of new shares has almost identical rules to the election described above. The requirements are:

7. The corporation must attach a statement to its Form 1120S for the year of the termination.
8. The statement must affirm that the corporation is electing under Regulations §1.1368-1(g) to treat the year as if it consisted of two taxable years.
9. The statement must give the details on the terminating event.

6

Table 6-2: Effects of Interim Closings under §1377(a)(2) and Regs. §1.1368-1(g)

	Citation for termination of shareholder interest	*Citation for substantial disposition or acquisition*
Does affect		
Allocation to transferors	Regs. §1.1377-1(b)(3)(i)	Regs. §1.1368-1(g)(2)(ii)
Allocation to transferees	Regs. §1.1377-1(b)(3)(i)	Regs. §1.1368-1(g)(2)(ii)
AAA on closing date	Regs. §1.1368-2(e)	Regs. §1.1368-2(e)
Character of distributions in each portion of year	Regs. §1.1368-1(g)(2)(ii)	Regs. §1.1368-1(g)(2)(ii)
Proration of income passing through from partnerships	Regs. §1.1377-1(b)(3)(iv)	Could take any reasonable position
Does not affect		
Closing of corporation's taxable year	Regs. §1.1377-1(b)(3)(ii)	Regs. §1.1368-1(g)(2)(ii)
Due date for filing 1120S	Regs. §1.1377-1(b)(3)(ii)	Regs. §1.1368-1(g)(2)(ii)
Timing of shareholder reporting	Regs. §1.1377-1(b)(3)(iii)	Regs. §1.1368-1(g)(2)(ii)
Elections to bypass AAA and PTI	Regs. §1.1368-1(f)(5)(iv)	Regs. §1.1368-1(f)(5)(iv)
Deemed dividend election	Regs. §1.1368-1(f)(5)(iv)	Regs. §1.1368-1(f)(5)(iv)
Should not affect		
Timing of §482 adjustments		
§179 expensing limit		
Depreciation on property held throughout year		
Running of years for any carryover		
Running of years for application of §291		
Could take any reasonable position		
Depreciation on property acquired in either portion of the year		
Built-in gains tax attributable to identifiable parts of year		
Passive investment income tax attributable to identifiable parts of year		

10. The statement must declare that all persons who were shareholders, at any time during the year, have consented to the split of the taxable year.
11. The statement must be signed by an officer of the corporation who is authorized to sign the corporation's tax returns.
12. A statement from each shareholder, consenting to the split year election, must be included.

The election to split the year under §1.1368-1(g) is irrevocable. It may be made on a timely filed, extended or amended Form 1120S for the year of the terminating event. [Regs. §1.1368-1(g)(2)(iii)] A single election may cover all substantial dispositions and/or new issues during one year. Note, however, that the Regulations do not explicitly permit an election to split the year under Regulations §1.1368-1(g) to also cover a termination of a shareholder's interest under §1377(a)(2).

Either election to terminate the corporation's accounting year has certain implications for distributions. See Chapter 7 for discussion of these issues. Although the Code and Regulations require that a signed formal election be attached to the corporation's return, the most important aspect is consistent reporting by all shareholders. The IRS has held that an S corporation that split its year into two portions, and all of whose shareholders reported their income and deductions consistently with the corporation's accounting, was in substantial compliance with the rule, even though it had not filed the proper election to split its year. [TAM 9303005] The IRS granted an extension of time for good cause to make an election to split the corporation's taxable year under §1377(a)(2). [PLR 9341022. The ruling did not specify the cause.]

630.3. Ownership on the date of transfer. The Code is silent on allocation of items between a previous owner and a new owner on the date of transfer of shares. Regulations under the pre-1983 version of Subchapter S held that the transferee, or new owner, was the owner on the date of transfer. [Regs. §1.1374-1(b)(3), prior law] The IRS followed this rule on instructions to Form 1120S through 1993.

In 1994, when the IRS issued Final Regulations under §1367 and §1368, the Regulations adopted the opposite rule, and allocated all items occurring on the date of transfer to the prior owner. [Regs. §1.1367-1(d)(3)] In 1995, the IRS issued Proposed Regulations under §1377. Proposed Regulations §1.1377-1 also treats the transferor, or seller, as the owner of the stock on the date of transfer. [Proposed Regs. §1.1377-1(a)(2)(ii)] Similarly, a deceased shareholder is treated as the owner of stock for allocation of all items on the date of death.

> **OBSERVATION:** All discussion and examples in earlier editions of the *S Corporation Taxation Guide* assumed that the transferee would be treated as the owner of stock on the day of transfer. All examples in this edition have been revised to reflect the changed rules.

630.4. Income and loss items occurring on the date of transfer. As discussed above, the seller is usually considered to be the owner of stock on the date of a transfer. In some situations, a corporation will engage in an unusual transaction on the same day that a shareholder transfer occurs. For instance, a buyer of stock may not want all of the corporation's assets. The corporation might transfer the unwanted assets to the seller. The seller and buyer of the stock can negotiate the sales price based on a reduced asset base of the corporation.

630.41. Allocation when there is no interim closing. If an S corporation does not elect to close its books on the date of a transfer, there are no special rules to cover any transactions that occur on that date. The corporation allocates all of those items, along with any other income and loss items for that year, in the normal pro rata manner.

EXAMPLE 6 - 41: On October 8, 1992, Moe sells all of the stock in MJ Corporation, a calendar-year S corporation, to Joe. MJ had a capital asset that it distributed to Moe on the date of sale, since Joe did not need the asset to continue the business. The capital asset had a basis to MJ of $10,000 and a fair market value of $60,000. MJ's ordinary income for 1992 was $100,000.

Under general rules, Moe is considered the owner through October 7, 1992, but he is allocated all items occurring through October 8. He was the owner for 281 days of the corporation's 1992 taxable year, and Joe is the owner for the remaining 85 days. The corporation does not elect to close the books as a result of the termination of Moe's interest. Therefore, Moe receives approximately 77% (282/366) and Joe receives approximately 23% (84/366) of both the ordinary income and the capital gain.

6

630.42. Allocation when there is an interim closing. The Code provides no special rules governing the allocation of items occurring on the date of transfer, even when the corporation close its books on that date. The Temporary Regulations are similarly silent on this issue. The Regulations, however, require allocation of all items through the close of the day of transfer to the old owner. [Regs. §1.1367-1(d)(3)]

EXAMPLE 6 - 42: Refer to Example 6 - 41. MJ's ordinary income was $66,000 through October 9, 1992, and $34,000 thereafter. The corporation, with the consent of Moe and Joe, elects to close its books when Moe terminates his interest. The $66,000 ordinary income occurring up to the date of the transfer, as well as the entire capital gain, would be allocated to Moe. Joe would be allocated only $34,000 of ordinary income for the year.

The Regulations do not provide any different rules when a transaction that occurs on the date of transfer is the result of dealings between the corporation and the new shareholder.

EXAMPLE 6 - 43: Refer to Examples 6 - 41 and 6 - 42. Assume the same facts, except that the corporation distributed the capital asset to Joe (the purchaser) on October 9, 1992. The gain on the distribution would still be allocated to Joe (the seller).

PLANNING TIP: The purchaser and seller should be careful to negotiate the timing of any transactions that are expected to occur on or near the date of the transfer of shares. If they intend for the seller to include the tax effect of any of these transactions on his or her return, the transaction should be consummated on or before the day of the transfer. If they intend for the buyer to bear the burden or receive the benefit of the transaction, the corporation should wait until the day after the transfer of shares to complete the transaction. The timing of any such transactions should be clearly described in the agreement between the seller and the buyer.

630.5. Timing of shareholder reporting. Each shareholder reports his or her share of income and loss items on the last day of the corporation's taxable year, in accordance with §1366(a)(1).

SUMMARY OF AUTHORITY: CODE SECTION 1366(a)(1)

- Each shareholder must take into account his or her portion of every item of income, deduction, etc., which the S corporation must report.
- The time for inclusion is on the last day of the corporation's taxable year.

When the corporation's taxable year coincides with that of the shareholder, there are no special reporting problems. When the corporation's taxable year differs from that of a shareholder, there are some special considerations.

The shareholders should treat the income from the corporation as regularly recurring and should cover it by estimated tax payments. This particular issue has not been addressed in Regulations since the Subchapter S Revision Act of 1982. There are some old rulings that held otherwise, but they were peculiar to old law. (Rev. Ruls. 62-202, 1962-2 CB 344, and 81-144, 1981-1 CB 588, should no longer be valid.) In private letter rulings the IRS has held the shareholders liable for estimated tax payments. [PLRs 8542034, 8544011]

630.51. Termination of a shareholder's interest. When the corporation's year ends after the shareholder's interest is terminated, the shareholder reports income and loss on the last day of the corporation's year end. Disposition of stock before the corporate year end does not accelerate income to the shareholder.

EXAMPLE 6 - 44: RV Corporation is an S corporation with a September year end. R and V, the two shareholders, both use the calendar year. On December 1, 1989, shareholder R sells all of her shares. She will report her share of the corporation's income or loss, as well as all separate items, for the 1989–1990 taxable year in 1990.

Note one complicating factor: She will not be able to determine her basis as of December 1, 1989, until she receives Schedule K-1 for the 1990 taxable year. She will have no choice but to make a reasonable estimate of the gain or loss on the sale and amend her 1989 return at a later date.

630.52. Death of a shareholder. When a shareholder dies during an S corporation's taxable year, the estate must report all of his or her portion the corporation's income or loss, up to the date of death, on his or her final tax return. [§1366(a)(1)] When the S corporation uses a fiscal year, this rule may force the decedents income or loss to be reported one year earlier than that of the other shareholders.

EXAMPLE 6 - 45: VW Corporation is an S corporation with a September year end. W, one of the two shareholders, uses the calendar year. On December 1, 1989, shareholder W dies. His estate then becomes the owner. W's share of the corporation's income or loss, as well as all separate items, is included on his final return in 1989.

Note one complicating factor: W's executor will not be able to determine W's income as of December 1, 1989, until he receives Form 1120S, Schedule K-1, for the 1990 taxable year. The executor will have no choice but to make a reasonable estimate of the income to that date and amend the 1989 return at a later date.

630.6. Shareholder loss limitations. Although each shareholder is allocated his or her share of an S corporation's loss by the pro rata method (except in the case of termination of a shareholder's interest), the losses are not necessarily deductible in the year incurred. Section 1366(d)(1) limits the deductible portion of a shareholder's loss to his or her basis in stock and debt. When a loss passes through to a shareholder, it reduces his or her stock basis, but not below zero. See Chapter 9, at 925.22. A loss that exceeds a shareholder's stock basis may reduce debt basis, but not below zero. See Chapter 9, at 930.22.

SUMMARY OF AUTHORITY: CODE SECTION 1366(d)(1)

- A shareholder's potentially deductible share of an S corporation's losses is limited to his or her stock basis.
- If a shareholder's loss from an S corporation exceeds stock basis, the shareholder may deduct losses to the extent of his or her debt basis.

OBSERVATION: The basis rules and loss limitations in general are much more complicated than §1366(d)(1) indicates, for two reasons:

1. Basis is a highly complicated and often litigated problem.
2. There are several other limitations that may prevent or postpone deductibility of a shareholder's losses from S corporations.

Deductible losses may be subject to several restrictions. The first limit on a potentially deductible loss is the shareholder's basis in his or her stock. [§1366(d)(1)(A)] The second limit is basis in debt. [§1366(d)(1)(B)] Chapter 9 describes both stock and debt basis in detail. Section 1366(d)(2) provides that losses suspended under these rules are carried forward indefinitely.

SUMMARY OF AUTHORITY: CODE SECTION 1366(d)(2)

- Losses that exceed a shareholder's basis in stock and debt are carried forward to the next taxable year.
- The carryforward continues until the shareholder has sufficient basis to absorb the losses.
- By inference, the suspended losses are not transferable to any other property or to any other person.

EXAMPLE 6 - 46: A owns 40% and D owns 60% of the L Corporation. At the beginning of 1987, A's stock basis is $12,000 and D's stock basis is $30,000. In 1987, D loans L $40,000. In 1987, L reports a loss of $100,000. D's share of the loss—$60,000—is deductible in full, since it does not exceed the shareholder's basis in stock and debt. A's share of the loss is $40,000. Since her basis is only $12,000, she will deduct $12,000 in 1987. The remaining $28,000 will be treated as a loss incurred in 1988.

630.61. Stock basis—general rules. The Code provides a basis adjustment ordering rule, which allows a shareholder to increase basis for income items, including tax-exempt income. The IRS has not issued any Regulations on the meaning of the term *tax-exempt income*, as of this writing. Most of the controversy has arisen in connection with cancellation of debt, discussed above, at 610.6.

Recent Proposed Regulations are consistent with the prior IRS position that certain items are not income, per se. In general, tax-exempt income does not include items that are of a timing, rather than an exclusionary, nature. Thus, income from cancellation of debt (excluded under §108) and improvements made by a lessee on a lessor's property (excluded under §109) are not treated as pass-through items of income. [Proposed Regs. §1.1366-1(a)(2)(viii)]

There are also some cautions from the partnership area that should be observed. In general, partners are not allowed to increase basis for income that has not yet been reported on the partnership's tax return. See Revenue Ruling 81-241, 1981-2 CB 146, holding that a partner does not receive basis in a partnership when the partnership has received cash that is not yet included in income under the completed contract method of accounting. See Revenue Ruling 81-242, 1981-2 CB 147, for a similar application of this principle to gain deferred by virtue of the involuntary conversion rule of §1033. More recently, the IRS has ruled that there is no basis adjustment permitted for S corporation shareholders due to unrealized income on product warranty contracts. [Rev. Proc. 97-38, 1997-33 IRB 43]

Occurrence of multiple types of losses in the same tax year may pose problems. Losses may be ordinary, capital, from active business, from rental activities, etc. Since the general income and loss concept of S corporations was borrowed from the partnership rules, the partnership formula provides some useful examples of application of basis limits. [Regs. §1.704-1(d)(2)] The partnership rules have long provided that allocation of the basis limit shall be apportioned to each loss. Proposed Regulations under Subchapter S have adopted an identical rule for losses passing through to S corporation shareholders. [Proposed Regs. §1.1366-2(b)(3)]

See Chapter 10, at 1015., for further discussion of these problems, and examples of the loss limit applied to losses of different characters.

Expenses that are not deductible must also pass through to the shareholders, who are required to reduce basis for these items. See Chapter 9, at 925.22. Examples include disallowed meal and entertainment expense and also insurance premiums on employees' lives when the employer is the beneficiary on the policies. If these nondeductible expenditures exceed a shareholder's basis, there is no requirement that the shareholder carry these forward and reduce basis in future years. Also see Chapter 9, at 935.3., for discussion of the inapplicability of any tax benefit rule to shareholder basis.

After a loss clears the shareholder basis limits, it may be subject to the at-risk and passive loss limits. Chapter 10 discusses these and other important limitations on deductibility of losses and expenses. Chapter 10 also demonstrates the multiplicity of carryovers that can result from a single year's corporate transactions. Also see Chapter 13, at 1340., for the ability of a shareholder to deduct certain losses after an S election terminates, during the post-termination transition period.

630.62. Effect of income in the same year as a loss. The Code provides a basis adjustment ordering rule, which allows a shareholder to increase basis for any income items before calculating basis for loss purposes. The language is not entirely clear, and it requires some careful attention to some cross-references.

SUMMARY OF AUTHORITY: CODE SECTIONS 1366(d)(1) AND 1367(a)(1)

- A shareholder may take into account losses from the S corporation that do not exceed his or her stock basis.
- The basis for loss limitations is calculated by including any basis adjustment for income items that occur in the same year.

When a loss in excess of basis is carried forward to a future year, it will be deductible if the shareholder's basis at the end of the subsequent year is sufficient. The shareholder's basis at the end of the subsequent year is determined after taking into account the corporation's income, deductions, and nondeductible expenses for that year. [TAM 9304004]

EXAMPLE 6 - 47: Losco, an S corporation, has one shareholder, Louie. At the beginning of 1993, Louie's basis was $10,000. In 1993, Losco reported a $50,000 loss. Louie deducts $10,000 of the loss in 1993 and carries the remaining $40,000 forward to 1994. In 1994, the corporation reports $75,000 of taxable income to Louie. Assuming that Louie had no other adjustments to basis, his basis at the end of 1994, before considering the loss carried forward from 1993, is $75,000. Accordingly, Louie may deduct the $40,000 loss suspended from 1993 in 1994.

The discussion of basis in this chapter serves only to illustrate the loss limitation rules. Basis is such an important and complicated issue for S corporation shareholders that Chapter 9 is devoted to this topic.

A shareholder adjusts his or her basis for income items that pass through from the corporation and are reported on the shareholder's Schedule K-1. However, the income allowable as a basis adjustment does not include any gain from the disposition of the shareholder's stock. [*Miller v. U.S.*, 83 AFTR 2d 99-1559 (DC WV)]

OBSERVATION: In the *Miller* case, the taxpayer claimed to have relied on commercial software to calculate basis, which included the shareholder's gain from a stock redemption. The case is slightly more complicated due to the fact that the shareholder did not materially participate in the corporation's business activities, so the gain did create income for §469 purposes. However, the purported reliance on software was not a valid defense of the basis calculations.

630.63. Ordering rules, pre-1977. A discussion of shareholder basis adjustments cannot be complete without taking distributions into account, even though most of this topic is not covered until Chapter 7. In general, distributions and losses may "compete" for basis. The rationale for this competition is that both loss deductions and tax-free distributions are limited to a shareholder's basis, and both losses and tax-free distributions reduce a shareholder's basis.

Basis is provided by amounts left over from the prior year, plus any income items of the current year. As long as the total of losses and distributions does not exceed all available basis, there is little room for confusion. In some situations, however, there need to be well-established rules for the calculation of basis. In brief, from 1982 through 1996 the hypothetical ordering was as follows:

6

- Sources of basis in a taxable year
  1. Basis left from prior year (or initial basis for newly acquired shares)
  2. Additions from all income and depletion sources
- Absorptions of basis in a taxable year
  1. Reductions for losses and depletion
  2. Reductions for distributions

EXAMPLE 6 - 48: Terrence is a sole shareholder in T Corporation. At the beginning of 1996, his basis in stock is $2,000. During 1996, he withdraws $50,000 from the corporation. In 1996, the corporation reports tax-exempt income of $6,000, ordinary taxable income of $82,000, and capital losses of $30,000. At the end of 1996, Terrence's basis in his stock (before the distribution) is:

Beginning basis	$2,000
Tax exempt income	6,000
Taxable income	82,000
Capital loss	(30,000)
Basis before distributions	$60,000

Terrence's distributions exceeded the beginning-of-year basis. Since they did not exceed the year-end basis, he reports no gain from his distributions in 1996. He would start 1997 with a basis of $10,000. Note that the corporate capital losses, which flow through to Terrence, reduce his basis. The reduction takes effect, even if he receives no tax benefit on his personal return for the capital losses.

Note two key points in the above example. First, the taxable year of concern is before 1997. Second, the corporation's income items (the tax-exempt income and the taxable income) exceed the loss items. Under either of these conditions, the analysis shown would be correct.

Before the Small Business Job Protection Act of 1996, a shareholder was required to reduce his or her basis for losses, before reducing basis for distributions. [§1366(d)(1)(A), before amendment by the Small Business Job Protection Act of 1996]

Accordingly, some shareholders could find themselves in a paradox. An S corporation might not want to distribute its income for the year until it had been able to close its books and determine the final amount of taxable income. If it did so, however, the nature of the distributions could not be determined with complete accuracy until it had closed its books for the year of the distribution. As is discussed in Chapter 7, a distribution is generally tax-free to a shareholder, unless the distribution exceeds the shareholder's stock basis at the close of the year of the distribution.

EXAMPLE 6 - 49: Erratico, Inc., is an S corporation that experiences considerable fluctuation in its income from year to year. It wants to distribute half of its income each year to its sole shareholder and retain the remainder of its income to finance future operations. For 1994, its shareholder's basis, before considering any distributions, would be as follows:

Beginning basis	$ 12,000
Taxable income	88,000
Basis before distributions	$100,000

Erratico would like to distribute $44,000 to its shareholder. Assume that it does so on April 1, 1995. The shareholder will report no gain form the distribution, unless the corporation has a loss in 1995 that reduces or eliminates the shareholder's basis. For example, if Erratico sustains a loss of $70,000 in 1995, the results of 1995 operations and distribution to the shareholder would be:

Beginning basis	$100,000
Taxable loss	(70,000)
Basis before distributions	$ 30,000

Of the $44,000 distributed, only $30,000 would be tax-free to the shareholder, since $30,000 is the shareholder's basis before distributions. The remaining $14,000 would be treated as a gain at the shareholder level. See Chapter 7, at 715.

Example 6 - 49 illustrates how losses took priority over distributions in a year in which basis was insufficient to accommodate both. As a result, the shareholder in the prior example would have had sufficient basis to deduct the loss for 1995.

630.64. Ordering rules, post-1996. The basis ordering rules in effect through taxable years beginning before 1997 had been adopted by the Subchapter S Revision Act of 1982. Although the rule that losses must precede distributions in the calculation was arbitrary, it did not appear to be unreasonable. Indeed, one shareholder in this situation simply did not have sufficient basis to get the full tax benefit of a deductible loss and a tax-free distribution. This ordering rule had become the target of several requests for change by various study groups over the years. The Small Business Job Protection Act of 1996 changed the ordering rules so that, in loss years, distributions reduce basis before losses. [§1366(d)(1)(A), after amendment by the Small Business Job Protection Act of 1996]

The following examples illustrate the workings of the post-1996 rules and the benefit of the new rules to shareholders.

EXAMPLE 6 - 50: Updown, Inc., is an S corporation that experiences considerable fluctuation in its income from year to year. Each year it wants to distribute half of its income to its sole shareholder, and retain the remainder of its income to finance future operations. For 1996, its shareholder's basis, before considering any distributions, would be as follows:

Beginning basis	$ 12,000
Taxable income	88,000
Basis before distributions	$100,000

Updown would like to distribute $44,000 to its shareholder. Assume that it does so on April 1, 1997. If Updown sustains a loss of $70,000 in 1997, the results of 1997 operations and distribution to the shareholder would be:

Beginning basis	$100,000
Distribution	(44,000)
Basis before loss	$ 56,000

Since the distribution occurred in a taxable year beginning after 1996, all of it would be tax-free to the shareholder. See Chapter 7, at 715. The loss deduction, however, would be limited to the $56,000 remaining after the shareholder's basis is reduced for the distribution. The remaining $14,000 of the loss would be carried forward to 1998.

The change in the rules from 1996 to 1997 may have little impact on many shareholders. After all, under either rule, the total tax benefit of distributions and corporate losses is limited to the shareholder's basis. In some cases, the old rules may have worked to the shareholders' advantage, if the corporation's loss was ordinary. The old rules provided for a more generous allowance of the ordinary loss passing through from the corporation, at the cost of a capital gain from the distribution.

EXAMPLE 6 - 51: Examples 6 - 49 and 6 - 50 used the exact same amounts for beginning basis, losses, and distributions. The shareholders would have received the following tax benefits for the year of the distribution:

Example	6 - 50	6 - 51
Tax-free distribution	$ 30,000	$ 44,000
Deduction for loss	70,000	56,000
Total tax benefit	$100,000	$100,000

To understand the tax benefit of the new rules as opposed to the old, it is necessary to see the tax effects of a subsequent year. The benefit of the change is most easily illustrated if the corporation has income after the loss and distribution year.

EXAMPLE 6 - 52: Refer to Examples 6 - 49 and 6 - 50. Assume that in the next year (1996 for Example 6 - 49 and 1998 for Example 6 - 50) the corporation has taxable income of $50,000 and makes no distributions. The results to the shareholder in each situation in the subsequent year would be:

Example	6 - 50	6 - 51
Taxable income of current year	$50,000	$50,000
Less deduction for prior-year loss	0	(14,000)
Shareholder income of current year	$50,000	$36,000

Thus the shareholder covered by the new rules would only temporarily lose the tax benefit of the loss in excess of basis. The shareholder covered by the old rules would have no way of recovering any sort of tax benefit for the taxable distribution, except for increased basis in his or her stock. The basis of each shareholder after reporting the $50,000 income would be:

Example	6 - 50	6 - 51
Beginning basis	$ 0	$ 0
Taxable income of current year	$50,000	$50,000
Less deduction for prior-year loss	0	(14,000)
Ending basis	$ 50,000	$36,000

630.65. Basis of different shares. A shareholder may have acquired different shares for different prices. Accordingly, a shareholder may need to adjust basis of separate blocks of shares. When a shareholder acquires different shares at different times, the basis allocation for income or loss is made in accordance with the portion of the year during which the shareholder owned the stock. [Regs. §1.1367-1(b)(2). See also Regulations §1.1367-1(f), Example 1.]

EXAMPLE 6 - 53: On December 31, 1992, Boyd owns 100 shares of Rebecca, Inc., an S corporation, which has 1,000 outstanding shares. Boyd's basis on January 1, 1993, is $3,000. On May 26, 1993 (40% of Rebecca's year has elapsed), Boyd purchases 200 other shares for a total of $5,000. For the calendar year 1993, Rebecca's taxable income is $100,000. Rebecca has no separately reported losses, and makes no distributions, in 1993. Rebecca does not elect to terminate its taxable year on May 26, 1993. Boyd's basis adjustment for 1993 is:

	Date Block Acquired	
	Before 12/92	*As of 5/26/93*
Percent of outstanding shares	10%	20%
Percent of 1993 shares held by Boyd	100%	60%
Weighted average of income allocated	10%	12%
Income allocated to each block	$10,000	$12,000
Add basis prior to income	3,000	5,000
Basis at end of 1993	$13,000	$17,000

In general, basis is computed for each shareholder as of the close of business on the last day of the corporation's taxable year. If a shareholder sells stock during a taxable year, his or her basis must be calculated as of the last day of ownership. If a shareholder's losses allocated to one block exceed basis in that block, the losses may be measured against the basis of other shares owned by the same person.

EXAMPLE 6 - 54: Ann owned 200 shares in Annco, an S corporation. She had purchased the shares in two blocks of 100 at different times, for different prices. At the beginning of 1993, her basis in one block was $20 per share ($2,000 total block basis) and her basis in the other block was $30 per share ($3,000 total block basis). Her portion of Annco's loss for 1993 was $4,400. She is able to deduct the entire loss, since it does not exceed her total stock basis. Her allocation to the shares would be:

	Block	
	$20/share	*$30/share*
Beginning basis	$2,000	$3,000
Loss allocated for year	(2,200)	(2,200)
Excess or (deficiency) in basis	(200)	800
Reallocation of excess loss	200	(200)
Ending basis	$ 0	$ 600

630.66. General ordering rule for disallowed items. The Code provides no specific rules governing the sequence of basis reduction when an S corporation has both deductible and nondeductible expenses and the total of these items allocated to a shareholder exceeds the shareholder's stock and debt basis. The Proposed Regulations issued in 1992 required a shareholder to reduce his or her basis for nondeductible items in order to compute the basis remaining for deductible losses and expenses. [Proposed Regs. §1.1367-1(e)] The Final Regulations issued in January 1994 retain this priority as a general ordering rule. [Regs. §1.1367-1(e)]

EXAMPLE 6 - 55: In 1994, an S corporation has a single shareholder, Gail. Gail's basis at the beginning of 1994 is $30,000. In 1994, the corporation has nondeductible meal and entertainment expense of $10,000, premiums on officer's life insurance of $5,000, and an ordinary loss of $35,000. The corporation has no income items and makes no distributions during 1994. According to Regulations §1.1367-1(e), Gail would make the following basis adjustments at the end of 1994:

Basis before loss	$ 30,000
Less meal, entertainment and insurance	(15,000)
Basis remaining for ordinary loss	$ 15,000

In the preamble to the Final Regulations, the IRS stated that it had received several complaints about this ordering rule. The Final Regulations retained this rule, but also added an elective ordering rule.

630.67. Elective ordering rule for disallowed items. As an alternative to the general ordering rule, the Final Regulations provide an elective ordering rule. Under this election, a shareholder may reduce basis for deductible items, before reducing basis for nondeductible expenditures. [Regs. §1.1367-1(f)] Although it might appear at first glance that this election would always be advantageous, there are two possible drawbacks:

6

- The election is irrevocable.
- As a condition of this election, the shareholder must agree to carry forward any disallowed expenses that exceed basis and to reduce basis in future years.

Absent the agreement in the elective ordering rule, there is no provision in the Code or Regulations that requires a shareholder to carry forward any portion of nondeductible losses and expenses that exceeds his or her basis for the year in which such items are sustained by the corporation.[11]

EXAMPLE 6 - 56: Mary is a shareholder in Maco, an S corporation. At the beginning of 1994, Mary's basis in her stock was $5,000. In 1994, Maco sustains an ordinary loss and also incurs some meal and entertainment expenses. Mary's share of the ordinary loss is $4,500, and her share of the disallowed portion of the meal and entertainment expense is $1,500. The corporation has no income items for 1994, and Mary receives no distributions. Under the general rule, Mary would reduce her basis from $5,000 to $3,500 as a result of the disallowed meal and entertainment expenses. She would then be allowed to deduct $3,500 of her $4,500 share of the corporation's ordinary loss. The $1,000 portion of the loss that exceeds her basis would be carried forward to 1994.

Under the elective rule, Mary would reduce her basis by her $4,500 portion of the ordinary loss. She would then be able to deduct all of the $4,500 loss in 1994 (subject to the at-risk and passive activity loss limitations). She would then reduce her basis to zero, with $500 of the disallowed meal and entertainment expenses, and would carry the remaining $1,000 of these expenses forward.

PLANNING TIP: When a shareholder's total of deductible and nondeductible losses and expenses exceeds his or her basis, the elective ordering rule usually would be beneficial. It allows a current, rather than a deferred, deduction to the shareholder. Sometimes, however, the general ordering rule may work to the shareholder's advantage. The general ordering rule will be advantageous when the shareholder's basis is less than the amount of the disallowed losses and deductions, and the tax benefit of a deduction might be greater in a future year than in the year in which the losses and deductions are sustained. The election may be made on a timely or amended return.

EXAMPLE 6 - 57: Assume the same facts as in Example 6 - 56, except that Mary's stock basis was only $500 at the beginning of 1994. Under the elective ordering rule, Mary would claim

[11] Code §1366(d)(2) requires a carryforward of losses and deductions that were disallowed due to the basis limitation of §1366(d)(1). Losses and expenses that are disallowed by other Code provisions are not subject to the carryforward rule.

a $500 deduction in 1994 and carry $4,000 of deductible loss forward to 1994. She would also carry $1,500 of the nondeductible items forward to 1995. She would thus be required to reduce her basis for $5,500 of items carried forward from 1994, concurrent with any future basis increases.

Under the general ordering rule, Mary would receive no deduction in 1994. She would reduce her basis to zero for $500 of the $1,500 disallowed meal and entertainment expenses. She would carry the $4,500 of deductible losses forward to 1995. The $1,000 of disallowed meal and entertainment expenses that exceeded her basis in 1994 would never be treated as a reduction in basis of her stock.

Further assume that Mary's share of the corporation's income in 1995 was $6,000 and that Mary received a distribution of $1,000 in 1995. If she had elected to take deductible items into account first in 1994, her consequences for 1995 would be:

Basis at the beginning of 1995	$ 0
Add 1995 income	6,000
Basis before losses and distributions	6,000
Less:	
Ordinary loss carried forward from 1994	(4,500)
Meal and entertainment carried forward from 1994	(1,000)
Basis before distribution	$ 500

In this instance, Mary would claim $4,500 as an ordinary loss deduction in 1995. She would treat $500 of the distribution as a return of capital and report the remaining $500 as a gain from the sale of her stock. If Mary had not elected to take the deductible loss before the nondeductible items in 1994, her results for 1995 would be:

Basis at the beginning of 1995	$ 0
Add 1995 income	6,000
Basis before losses and distributions	6,000
Less:	
Ordinary loss carried forward from 1994	(5,000)
Basis before distribution	$1,000

Mary would treat her entire distribution as a return of capital. Comparing the two options:

	Claiming Ordinary Loss	
	First	*Last*
Taxable income 1994	$ (500)	$ 0
Taxable income 1995		
Pass-through from corporation	6,000	6,000
Loss from 1994	(4,500)	(5,000)
Capital gain distribution	500	0
Total taxable income	$1,500	$1,000

Although the Regulations are not specific on this point, it would appear that any nondeductible expenses carried forward under the elective basis reduction rule would apply in the succeeding year, after reduction for any deductible losses of that year. The elective ordering rule does not change the general rule that all losses and nondeductible items reduce basis before distributions.

PLANNING TIP: The distinction between nondeductible items and separately stated deductions is sometimes hazy. In particular, tax professionals must be aware that charitable contributions made by an S corporation are nondeductible items to the corporation. In a year in which an S corporation makes a large charitable contribution and also has ordinary losses, a shareholder would probably be well advised not to make the election to put deductible items first. See Chapter 10, at 1040., for additional discussion of the unique treatment of S corporations' charitable contributions.

630.68. Basis of debt. When a shareholder's loss exceeds the basis of all of his or her shares, and the shareholder has also loaned money to the corporation, the loss is allowed to the extent of the debt basis. In general, the debt must be a direct loan of money from the shareholder to the corporation. When a shareholder uses debt basis to sustain the deduction of losses, the basis of debt is reduced for the amount of loss. Debt basis receives extensive discussion in Chapter 9.

630.7. Special rules for inheritances and gifts. Recent statutory changes and Proposed Regulations have adopted some new basis rules for inherited stock and for stock received as a gift. The inheritance rules can be somewhat complicated.

630.71. Special basis rule for inherited stock. Before the Small Business Job Protection Act of 1996, a shareholder who inherited stock from a deceased shareholder would claim a basis of fair market value as of the decedent's death (or alternate valuation date). See Chapter 9, at 910.2. There were no other special rules for a deceased shareholder's successor in interest. The Small Business Job Protection Act of 1996 made two important changes, however, effective for persons who receive stock due to the death of a shareholder after August 20, 1996.

1. Any corporate-level items properly characterized as "income in respect of a decedent" (IRD) will retain their character to the shareholder who owns the deceased shareholder's stock when these items are realized at the corporate level.
2. The new shareholder will reduce basis (from fair market value) by the amount of net IRD in the corporation at the date of death of the prior shareholder.

SUMMARY OF AUTHORITY: CODE SECTION 1367(b)(4)

- A shareholder who inherits stock after August 20, 1996, will need to reduce basis for his or her share of the corporation's income in respect of a decedent.
- A shareholder who is subject to these new rules will need to take into account his or her share of the corporation's income in respect of a decedent.

CAUTION: Note that the effective date of this rule is immediate upon enactment of the Small Business Job Protection Act of 1996. Thus it will affect shareholders' 1996 reporting years.

In general, IRD includes items that had been economically realized, but not yet reported, by a cash-method taxpayer. This categorization can extend to installment receivables of any taxpayer. [§691(a)] The general thrust of §691(a) is that a deceased shareholder's successor in interest cannot avoid treatment of certain income items as taxable income merely because these items had been earned, but not reported, by a decedent.

OBSERVATION: The characterization of S corporation items as IRD, per se, has little effect on the reporting of these income items by subsequent shareholders. The treatment of these items is determined by the method of accounting of the S corporation, rather than by the shareholders. The major effects of the new rules will be in the basis reductions and in the allowance of the estate tax deduction under §691(c). The new basis rules will deprive the new shareholders of some tax benefit in the event of a pass-through loss or a large distribution in relation to basis, or upon the sale of the stock. The estate tax deduction will provide a benefit to shareholders, including shareholders who are not burdened by the basis reductions.

EXAMPLE 6 - 58: David died in August 1996. He left his stock in Davco, an S corporation, to his son, Keith. The corporation used the cash method of accounting. It had uncollected accounts receivable of $6,000,000 as of the date of David's death. David had owned one-third of the stock. Thus one-third of the accounts receivable, or $2,000,000, will be IRD to Keith, when it is reported by Davco. Note that whether David died before August 21 or after August 20, the accounts receivable, including the $2,000,000 attributable to David's stock, would be reported as income by the corporation and allocated to the shareholders. If the corporation used an interim closing at the date of David's death, the collection of the $2,000,000 accounts receivable would be income to Keith, regardless of the date of David's death.

If the corporation used pro rata allocation of the 1996 income, it might be difficult to determine exactly when the $2,000,000 of IRD was allocated to Keith. As a practical matter, as long as the corporation reports the first $2,000,000 of gross income allocated to Keith as IRD, it will probably be in substantial compliance with the new law.

OBSERVATION: Classification of an item as IRD must be accompanied by a way to trace the receipt of the item to the decedent's successor. Where the item of IRD is held by an S corporation, the tracing will be relatively easy, if the corporation elects to split its year under §1377(a)(2) as of the date of death. If the corporation allocates its income by the pro rata method for the year of death, there may be some problems in actually tracing the income items to a specific shareholder.

There are two correlative provisions. First, §691(b) allows a successor in interest to deduct certain deductions in respect of a decedent. These are generally the trade accounts payable of a cash-method taxpayer. Second, §691(c) allows the person who reports IRD to claim a deduction for the portion of the decedent's federal estate tax attributable to the IRD.

EXAMPLE 6 - 59: Refer to Example 6 - 58. Assume that David died after August 20, 1996, and that David's estate tax attributable to the $2,000,000 of IRD was $800,000. When Keith reports the $2,000,000 of income, he will be able to claim an itemized deduction for $800,000 under §691(c).

The most significant drawback of the new law, as far as shareholders are concerned, is the new basis rule of §1367(b)(4)(B). The impact of the new law is illustrated in the next example.

EXAMPLE 6 - 60: Refer to Example 6 - 58. Assume that David died before August 21, 1996. The value of his stock on the date of death was $5,500,000, including his share of the accounts receivable. Keith's basis in the Davco stock would be $5,500,000.

Alternatively, assume that David died on August 21, 1996. Keith's basis in the Davco stock would be $3,500,000 (fair market value less value of IRD).

630.72. Special basis rule for stock received as a gift. There is a statutory limit on losses that can be claimed on sales or dispositions of property that had been received as a gift. Although the basis is generally the donor's basis, the transferee's basis for loss purposes cannot exceed the property's fair market value at the date of the gift. [§1015(a)] Recent Proposed Regulations have applied this principle to the pass-through loss limitation of shareholders. [Proposed Regs. §1.1366-2(a)(6)] Presumably, this rule would apply even after the stock basis had been adjusted for subsequent activity.

6

EXAMPLE 6 - 61: Cate give shares in Caco, an S corporation, to Katie on July 12, 1999. Caco uses the calendar year. At the date of the gift, Cate's basis was $40,000 and the fair market value was $25,000. Katie's basis (generally) at this point in time is $40,000. However, if she disposed of the shares for less than $25,000, she would use the $25,000 fair market value as her basis. Under Proposed Regulations §1.1366-2(a)(6), her limit on losses for 1999 would be $25,000.

630.8. Treatment of suspended losses on disposition. Disposition of stock when a shareholder has suspended losses may cause some confusion. Transferability of suspended losses had never been explicitly addressed until 1995. As noted above, however, there is implicit authority that the losses are nontransferable.

6

The Code implies that only the shareholder who owned the stock when the losses were sustained may utilize the suspended losses. Section 1366(d)(2) provides that "Any loss or deduction which is disallowed for any taxable year by reason of paragraph (d)(1) is treated as incurred by the corporation in the succeeding taxable year with respect to *that* shareholder." [Emphasis added.] The Proposed Regulations clarify this statement, and specifically deny any deduction for a loss that passed through to a prior shareholder. [Proposed Regs. §1.1366-2(a)(5)]

In one recent situation, a former spouse transferred stock to the other former spouse pursuant to a divorce. At the time of the transfer, the spouse who relinquished shares had sustained losses in excess of his or her basis. The IRS held that the recipient spouse could not claim the losses that had been allocated to the other spouse in an earlier year. [TAM 9552001]

OBSERVATION: A shareholder was able to legally rescind a transfer of stock for which there had been suspended losses. This rescission enabled the shareholder to deduct suspended losses. [PLR 9829044] The transfer was made to a person who was ineligible to hold shares in an S corporation. The rescission also reserved the corporation's S status.

Another potential problem is the deductibility of suspended losses after the shares are sold. Because the suspended losses did not reduce basis, they will reduce gain on ultimate sale. Gain from the sale of stock is not an item that would permit deduction of a suspended loss. [*Miller v. U.S.*, 83 AFTR 2d 99-1559 (DC WV)]

EXAMPLE 6 - 62: X acquired her shares in Z, Inc., an S corporation, for $50,000. While she owned the shares, her portion of the corporation's losses was $60,000. She then sold the shares for $40,000, and reported a gain of $40,000. She cannot deduct the $10,000 at the time of sale. The result is sensible from an accounting point of view:

Sale price of shares	$ 40,000
Purchase price of shares	(50,000)
Net economic loss	$(10,000)
Taxable gain on sale	$ 40,000
Deductible losses while she owned shares	(50,000)
Net tax loss	$(10,000)

Allowing any of X's suspended losses to the purchaser would be a form of retroactive allocation. Allocations among shareholders are on a per-day, per-share basis only.

OBSERVATION: A transfer of property between spouses or between former spouses incident to a divorce is subject to some special rules. [§1041] In general, the transferred property's basis carries to the recipient. Thus, it should be arguable that other tax attributes, such as suspended losses, will carry to the recipient. [Temporary Regs. §1.1041-1T] It would probably be a good idea to specify the ownership of loss carryovers and other favorable attributes in the divorce decree or property settlement.

635. Reporting requirements.

Each S corporation must file Form 1120S with the appropriate Internal Revenue Service Center. The due date of the return is the 15th day of the third month following the close of the taxable year (March 15 for calendar-year corporations).

The S corporation's ordinary income and deductions from the corporation's principal business activity are netted on Form 1120S, page 1. Other items are reported on Schedule K. All income loss, deduction, and credit information is reported to the shareholders on Schedule K-1.

The S corporation must provide Schedule K-1 to each shareholder. This schedule is really the most important portion of the S corporation's return, since it gives the shareholders the information necessary to compute their tax liabilities.

The corporation must report the weighted average of the shares owned by each shareholder on the Schedule K-1. In most cases, these averages will correspond to the portion of each line item allocated to the shareholders. If the corporation elects to split its year due to a termination of one or more shareholders' interests, these average ownership percentages will not necessarily correspond to the percentage of income and other items allocated to a shareholder.

After 1996, there will be qualified Subchapter S subsidiaries, which will be separate corporations under state law. These corporations will not file separate tax returns of any kind, but will combine all assets, liabilities, and items of income, deduction, and credit with those of the parent corporation, and will join in a combined return. [§1361(b)(3)(A)(ii)] Thus these corporations will not issue Schedule K-1 or any other federal income tax return.

OBSERVATION: The IRS will need to issue some rules for computing taxable income of the parent corporation. It remains to be seen whether these rules will parallel the consolidated return Regulations or be a simpler form of combined accounting. In particular, tax preparers will need to be on the alert for treatment of intercompany sales and other self-dealings. Tax professionals will also need to be aware of state and local reporting requirements, payroll taxes, and other types of reports that might treat the parent corporation and its subsidiary corporation as separate or combined corporations.

640. Practice aids.

The areas of concern for Chapter 6 are the shareholder election to take deductible items into account before nondeductible items, a substantial disposition of stock, or issuance of new shares.

Sample Letter 6 - 1 is a model of the shareholder's election to reduce basis for deductions and deductible losses before nondeductible expenses. It should be filed with the shareholder's Form 1040 (for individuals) or Form 1041 (for estates and for trusts other than grantor trusts, Subpart E trusts, and QSSTs). A shareholder should make certain that an election was never made with respect to the same S corporation for any prior year. If the shareholder has made the election, he or she will be bound by the prior election and will not need to make a new election. Note that this statement is an attachment to the shareholder's return for the year and does not require a separate signature. See the worksheets in Chapter 9 for the impact of this election on the shareholder's basis.

A corporation that intends to close its books on the date of termination of a shareholder's interest must file a statement with its Form 1120S for the year of the transfer. The statement must disclose the manner of the shareholder's termination, such as a sale, a gift, a transfer at death, or a stock redemption. Even though the statement is attached to the corporation's tax return, and the return must be signed by an appropriate corporate officer, the statement itself must also be signed by a corporate officer. The consent of each person who was a shareholder during any time of the year must also be attached to the return. The Regulations do not require that the corporation explicitly identify the number of shares held by each person throughout the year, but only the shares transferred. Sample Letters 6 - 2, 6 - 3, and 6 - 4 contain sample statements of election by the corporation to terminate its taxable year and a statement of consent by each shareholder.

Sample Letter 6 - 1: Election to reduce basis for deductible items

Election to reduce basis under Regulations §1.1367(f)

[Name]
[Tax ID]

Attachment to Form 1040 (Form 1041)

I elect to reduce basis in my stock and debt from [Corporation], an S corporation, for items deductible before reducing basis for nondeductible items. I agree to carry forward any nondeductible items in excess of my basis and to reduce basis for those items in future years.

[Name]
Shareholder, [Corporation]

Sample Letter 6 - 2: Election to terminate taxable year

Election to terminate taxable year under Internal Revenue Code §1377(a)(2) and Regulations §1.1377-1(b)

[Corporation]
[FEIN]

Attachment to Form 1120S

[Corporation] elects to treat its taxable year beginning [date] and ending [date] as two taxable years under Internal Revenue Code §1377(a)(2) and Regulations §1.1377-1(b). The first taxable year termi-

Copyright © 2000 by Harcourt, Inc. All rights reserved.

nated on [date], within the meaning of §1377(a)(2). On that date, [Name] sold all of [his/her] shares to [Name]. The second taxable year, within the meaning of §1377(a)(2), begins on [date] and ends on [date].

[Name]
[Title]

As a shareholder in [Corporation] during the corporation's taxable year beginning [date] and ending [date], I consent to the corporation's election under Internal Revenue Code §1377(a)(2) and Regulations §1.1377-1(b) to treat that year as two taxable years.

[Name]
Shareholder, [Corporation]

Sample Letter 6 - 3: Election to terminate taxable year

Election to terminate taxable year under Regulations §1.1368-1(g), for substantial disposition of stock

[Corporation]
[FEIN]

Attachment to Form 1120S

[Corporation] elects to treat its taxable year beginning [date] and ending [date] as two taxable years under Regulations §1.1368-1(g). The first taxable year terminated on [date], within the meaning of Regulations §1.1368-1(g). During a 30-day period ending on that date, [Name] transferred [number of shares] of [his/her] shares to [Name]. The specific details of the transfer were [sale/gift/stock redemption/other].

The shares transferred in that period were equal to or greater than 20% of the outstanding shares outstanding during that period. The second taxable year, within the meaning of §1377(a)(2), begins on [date] and ends on [date].

[Name]
[Title]

As a shareholder in [Corporation] during the corporation's taxable year beginning [date] and ending [date], I consent to the corporation's election under Regulations §1.1368-1(g) to treat that year as two taxable years.

[Name]
Shareholder, [Corporation]

Copyright © 2000 by Harcourt, Inc. All rights reserved.

Sample Letter 6 - 4: Election to terminate taxable year

Election to terminate taxable year under Regulations §1.1368-1(g), for issuance of new stock

[Corporation]
[FEIN]

Attachment to Form 1120S

6

[Corporation] elects to treat its taxable year beginning [date] and ending [date] as two taxable years under Regulations §1.1368-1(g). The first taxable year terminated on [date], within the meaning of Regulations §1.1368-1(g). During a 30-day period ending on that date, the corporation issued new shares to:

[Name]
[Name]
[Name]

who were not shareholder's in [Corporation] before the issuance of the shares.

The shares issued in that period were equal to or greater than 25% of the outstanding shares outstanding before that period. The second taxable year, within the meaning of §1377(a)(2), begins on [date] and ends on [date].

[Name]
[Title]

As a shareholder in [Corporation] during the corporation's taxable year beginning [date] and ending [date], I consent to the corporation's election under Regulations §1.1368-1(g) to treat that year as two taxable years.

[Name]
Shareholder, [Corporation]

Copyright © 2000 by Harcourt, Inc. All rights reserved.

DISTRIBUTIONS OF INCOME

7

CONTENTS

7

7

700. Overview.

The application of individual tax rates to corporate income is only one of the benefits of the S election. Without special rules for distributions, however, Subchapter S would be almost useless for profitable corporations. The reduction in tax rates to the individual level would be cold comfort to a shareholder who was liable for tax on corporate income, if the only way to get cash out were to treat it as a dividend.

The full benefit of a Subchapter S election is attained by avoiding double taxation on the distribution of income to the shareholders. To this end, §1368 provides for tax-free distribution of S corporation earnings. The rationale is to give a shareholder free access to corporate income if it has already been subject to taxation. It is irrelevant whether any tax has actually been paid on that income. For instance, an S corporation may have realized capital gains and the shareholder(s) may have had sufficient capital losses to result in a partial or complete offset. The corporation's income resulting from the capital gain may be distributed tax-free. The potential shareholder taxability is the important factor.

It is also unimportant whether the potential shareholder tax liability arises in the same taxable year in which the corporation makes the distribution or had arisen in some prior taxable year. In other words, there is no need to match a distribution with income earned in any specific year. 7

The identity of the particular shareholder who bore the potential tax liability of the corporation's income is also insignificant. For instance, if one shareholder owned the corporation's stock when it recognized the income but sold his or her shares before the corporation distributed cash or property, the new shareholder will receive the same tax treatment as the prior shareholder would have.

There are three important exceptions to the freedom of an S corporation to distribute its current or accumulated income:

1. If the S corporation existed previously as a C corporation, any income accumulated prior to its becoming an S corporation is subject to the C corporation distribution rules. Distributions of a former C corporation's accumulated earnings and profits (AEP) are treated as dividends, subject to a second round of taxation to the receiving shareholder. (See Chapter 3 for a discussion of the measurement of earnings and profits by a C corporation.) Distributions of a former C corporation's earnings and profits will be discussed further in this chapter.
2. The distribution rules for a corporation that accumulated income under old Subchapter S between 1958 and 1982 are considerably different from those adopted by the Subchapter S Revision Act of 1982. Any income accumulated in those years is still subject to the rules of old Subchapter S when it is distributed. These accumulations may be distributed tax-free if they were characterized as previously taxed income (PTI) under prior law. If they were classified as AEP, which was possible under old law, they will be treated as dividends when distributed, in years beginning before 1996. These accumulations, if not distributed in 1996, are eliminated at the beginning of the corporation's taxable years beginning after 1996. [Small Business Job Protection Act of 1996, §1311]
3. When a shareholder lacks basis in his or her stock, distributions in excess of basis are taxable as if the shareholder had sold the stock.

The policy underlying the current rules is mostly fair and logical. The law allows tax-free distributions of income by profitable S corporations. Since taxable income gives shareholders basis, it will be unusual for a distribution to a shareholder to exceed basis. A shareholder's basis is the sum of amounts contributed to the corporation, amounts paid for stock, and accumulated income allocated to that shareholder. Only when a distribution exceeds the sum total of these amounts will a distribution create a taxable gain.

The rules covering a former C corporation's distributions are similarly logical. Double taxation is an integral part of the tax law of C corporations. A C corporation accumulates earnings and profits by failing to distribute its income. It would frustrate this policy to allow any C corporation to eliminate its earnings and profits merely by making an S election.

The logic breaks down when a corporation distributes income accumulated under old Subchapter S. An awkward transitional rule (rendered even more confusing by a duplicate Code section number) preserves the pre-1983 rules for these accumulations, even though Congress completely rejected the old rationale when it adopted new Subchapter S. The old rules have been subject to selective IRS interpretation.

There is a special election by which a corporation may disburse dividends to shareholders before they receive tax-free distributions. Although a voluntary round of double taxation may seem counter-intuitive, there are situations in which it is useful. These situations receive special attention in this chapter, and they relate closely to planning opportunities discussed elsewhere in the book.

The distribution rules work quite well in routine situations. The Subchapter S Revision Act of 1982 and the legislation that preceded it, however, did not give specific accounting guidance to cover many transactions. For several years, the instructions to Form 1120S and Publication 589 (this publication is now out of print) were the only sources of information. They were not comprehensive and did not provide the accounting rules necessary for many specific transactions. In June 1992, the IRS issued Proposed Regulations under §1367 and §1368 that dealt with basis and distribution problems. In January 1994 the IRS issued the same Regulations, with some modification, as Final Regulations. The Regulations under these Code sections clarify many of the issues that had been unresolved since the Subchapter S Revision Act of 1982.

In 1998, the IRS issued proposed amendments to the Regulations under §1367 and §1368. This chapter takes issue with some of the provisions in these Regulations, which do not seem to follow the Small Business Job Protection Act of 1996 rules accurately.

This chapter points out the problems in reconciling the intent of the law with the accounting rules. By studying the text and examples, the tax professional should develop the skills necessary to work out a reasonable solution to any distribution situation.

When Subchapter S is silent, the rules of Subchapter C govern. As important as the distribution rules of Subchapter S may be, they do not encompass all of the problems that an S corporation may face. It is often necessary to refer to the Subchapter C rules to fully understand the tax treatment of a distribution by an S corporation. Accordingly, brief coverage of the Subchapter C distribution rules is appropriate for this overview.

> **OBSERVATION:** The Regulations issued under §1367 and §1368 are binding on all S corporation tax years beginning after December 31, 1993. The Regulations state that all S corporations and their shareholders must treat basis and distribution problems in prior years in a "reasonable manner." [Regs. §1.1367-3, §1.1368-4] All of the rules contained in the Regulations, which are covered in this chapter and in Chapter 9, are reasonable positions, with one exception. The deemed dividend election, discussed at 740.5., is not a reasonable position for years beginning before 1994. Therefore, an S corporation and its shareholders could not make this election without permission from the IRS.

700.1. Corporate distributions, in general. Corporate distributions are subject to three different classifications, depending on the property distributed, the transaction in which a distribution occurs, and, occasionally, the relationship of the shareholder to the corporation.

Depending on the context of the distribution, it may be taxable as ordinary income, treated as an amount realized in an exchange, or treated as an amount realized in a nontaxable transaction. A distribution may be in the form of cash, other property, or stock.

700.2. Types of distributions, and their effects on shareholders. For several important transactions, S corporations have unique rules, some of which are derived from partnership tax law. When Subchapter S is silent with respect to a given transaction, however, the tax professional needs to know where to look for guidance. The general rule is stated in §1371(a)(1).

SUMMARY OF AUTHORITY: CODE SECTION 1371(a)

- When an S corporation engages in any transaction for which Subchapter S provides no rules, Subchapter C should govern the tax consequences.
- If a rule of Subchapter C is deemed inconsistent with Subchapter S, Subchapter C should not govern the transaction.
- The legislative history offers little guidance on what Subchapter C rules might be inconsistent with Subchapter S.
- *As of this writing there are no regulations, rulings, or other pronouncements that interpret this general statement.*

When a corporation engages in a distribution outside the normal course of business, Subchapter S may offer little or no guidance. In private letter rulings, the IRS has exercised discretion in applying this rule. This chapter confines the discussion to current, or nonliquidating, distributions that are commonly referred to as *dividends*; later chapters describe unusual distributions.

To set the stage for complete understanding of the Subchapter S distribution rules, however, it is necessary to discuss briefly several types of corporate distributions. A quick overview of the Subchapter C rules is in order first, since these rules may also apply to S corporations.

700.21. Dividends. Under Subchapter C, a distribution may be a periodic distribution of profits. This transaction is commonly known as a *dividend*. The tax rules governing dividends are included in §301, which provides that a distribution is a dividend to the extent of a corporation's current and AEP. Such a dividend is included in the gross income of the recipient, pursuant to §301(c)(1) and §61.

700.22. Stock redemptions. Under Subchapter C, a distribution may also be a stock redemption. In form, a stock redemption occurs when a corporation purchases its own stock. For tax purposes, a stock redemption may be treated as either a dividend or an exchange. A redemption is treated as an exchange if it meets certain tests, described in Chapter 15, at 1510.1.

700.23. Corporate liquidations. A third form of distribution allowed under Subchapter C is the complete liquidation of a corporation. A complete liquidation results in exchange treatment for *all* shareholders. It is a fully taxable transaction, and each shareholder reports his or her gain or loss as if the stock had been sold, pursuant to §331. Liquidations are discussed in Chapter 16.

700.24. Reorganizations. Finally, Subchapter C permits distributions in connection with a tax-free reorganization of a corporation. In many cases, the property distributed is stock in the reorganized corporation or a successor corporation. The recipient recognizes no gain or loss, pursuant to §354. A reorganization may involve a corporate acquisition, a division of the business, or an internal restructuring. As a general rule, stock received in a reorganization is tax-free. Other property received in a reorganization may be taxable as a capital gain or as ordinary income. [§356] Reorganizations are discussed in Chapter 17.

700.25. Effect of the S election on distributions. The primary section dealing with distributions of S corporations is §1368. Subsection (a) sets forth a rule that limits the applicability of Subchapter S.

SUMMARY OF AUTHORITY: CODE SECTION 1368(a)

- Subchapter S prescribes special rules for S corporations' distributions, only if they would be covered by §301(c).
- Section 301(c) is the provision that treats C corporations' distributions as dividends to shareholders, to the extent of the corporation's current earnings and profits and AEP.
- Section 301(c) governs distributions that are not related to stock redemptions, complete liquidations, or tax-free reorganizations.
- The stock redemption and tax-free reorganization rules may divert the treatment of some or all of a distribution to §301.
- *If a transaction is not covered by §301, it is not covered by §1368. In these cases, Subchapter S may not provide any special treatment of the distribution.*

7

Unlike C corporations, S corporations are not required to use any earnings and profits calculations in determining the taxability of distributions to shareholders.

SUMMARY OF AUTHORITY: CODE SECTION 1371(c)(1)

- An S corporation does not calculate earnings and profits for purposes of measuring distributions to shareholders.
- In general, distributions from S corporations do not reduce the corporation's earnings and profits.
- There is an important exception for former C corporations.
- *There are exceptions for distributions that are made in the context of a stock redemption or tax-free reorganization.*

The major distribution rule is that shareholders are not treated as receiving dividends from S corporations, at least to the extent the distribution is attributable to the earnings of the corporation while the S election is in effect. This rule covers many distributions that are not stock redemptions, complete liquidations, or distributions in connection with tax-free reorganizations. These last three types of transactions are not governed by Subchapter S, unless one of the rules in Subchapter C would treat a portion of the distribution as a dividend. For instance, Subchapter S has no rules on how to treat a shareholder who receives a distribution in the form of a redemption of stock. Subchapter S is silent on complete liquidations and tax-free reorganizations. For these provisions, an S corporation is subject to Subchapter C. These transactions may have results for S corporations and their shareholders that are not fully covered by the C corporation rules. Chapter 17 contains detailed descriptions of these transactions, as well as their implications for S corporations and their shareholders.

700.3. Type of property distributed. Probably the most common form of distribution, at least in the routine context, is cash. Cash is certainly the simplest to account for, since there are no problems in determining basis or fair market value and there is generally no gain or loss incurred on the distribution.

Distributions may take other forms, however. A corporation may distribute property other than cash—for example, corporate assets such as inventory or investment property. A corporation may also distribute its own debt obligations, a useful technique when the corporation wants to make a distribution but has a cash flow problem. For C corporations, §301 applies to distributions of both cash and other property. Therefore, the special rules of Subchapter S will apply to both cash and property distributions.

Distributions of stock may be taxable or nontaxable. These distributions are covered by §305. In general, §305 provides that a distribution of stock with respect to common stock is not taxable if it gives no shareholder the opportunity to alter his or her interest in the corporation. If a stock distribution does give any shareholder the potential to alter his or her overall interest, or if a stock dividend is issued on preferred stock, the stock dividend is taxable, subject to the rules of §301. Subchapter S is silent on stock dividends. Therefore, it is a reasonable interpretation of the law to say that an S corporation can make a nontaxable stock dividend under the rules of §305. If a stock dividend were taxable under the rules of §305, it would become subject to §301. Section 1368 would then treat a stock distribution in the same manner as a property or cash distribution. As a practical matter, probably only a few S corporations issue stock dividends. These devices could be useful, however, in shifting control.

700.4. Constructive distributions. A constructive distribution may result when a shareholder who has effective control of a corporation receives something of benefit from the corporation—for example, use of a company car, an interest-free loan, or excessive compensation. When a shareholder in a C corporation receives a constructive distribution, the IRS typically reclassifies the value received by the shareholder as a dividend, thereby including it in the shareholder's gross income.

A shareholder in an S corporation may receive a constructive distribution, and in many cases such a distribution will not result in dividend income. It could, however, result in the corporation being treated as having two classes of stock, thereby disallowing the S election. The problems of constructive distributions are discussed in Chapter 8.

700.5. Effects of distributions on the corporation. Except for a nontaxable stock dividend, each type of distribution has an effect on the distributing corporation's equity accounts. A dividend from a C corporation reduces the distributing corporation's earnings and profits by the amount of the dividend. [§312(a)] Stock redemptions from C corporations also reduce earnings and profits, based on the percentage of shares redeemed. [§312(n)(7)] A distribution in complete liquidation is a step in terminating the corporation's existence, so the accounting treatment at the corporate level is moot. In a tax-free reorganization, there are rules providing that earnings and profits of all corporations that existed before the reorganization survive intact. [§381]

If a corporation distributes property other than cash, it must determine the relationship between the fair market value and the basis of the distributed property immediately before the distribution. For many years, a corporation did not recognize gain or loss on the distribution of property. [§311(a)] This rule was originally promulgated in a Supreme Court decision [*General Utilities & Operating Co. v. Helvering*, 36-1 USTC 9012 (S.Ct.)] known as the "General Utilities" rule. Over the years, the rule was gradually eroded by specific exceptions and varying rules depending on whether the distribution was a dividend, a stock redemption, a complete liquidation, or a tax-free reorganization. The Tax Reform Act of 1986, which repealed the General Utilities rule (or at least parts of the rule), leaves corporations with the following recognition provisions on distributions:

- Gain or loss is never recognized on a stock dividend. [§311(a)]
- Loss is never recognized on a distribution of property in a nonliquidating distribution, including a distribution in redemption of stock. [§311(a)]

- Gain is recognized on a distribution of property in a nonliquidating distribution, including a distribution in redemption of stock. [§311(b)]
- Gain or loss is recognized on a distribution in complete liquidation of a corporation. [§336(a)] (See Chapter 15, at 1525.2., for comprehensive discussion of the recognition of gain or loss, as well as several exceptions to this general rule.)
- Gain or loss is not recognized on a distribution of qualifying stock or securities in connection with a tax-free reorganization. [§361] (See Chapter 17.)

Subchapter S is completely silent on the recognition or nonrecognition of gains and losses upon the distribution of property. Therefore, an S corporation must determine the C corporation rules that would apply to the corporation in the context of a specific distribution of property. In brief, an S corporation recognizes gain, but not loss, on the distribution of property in a nonliquidating distribution or a stock redemption. It recognizes no gain or loss on the distribution of stock, if the distribution passes the test as a tax-free stock dividend. An S corporation recognizes all gains and losses on distributions in complete liquidation, subject to some limitations discussed in Chapter 15. Finally, an S corporation recognizes no gains and losses on the distribution of qualifying stock or securities in a tax-free reorganization. This rule is also subject to some limitations.

700.6. Distributions and classes of stock. As was discussed at length in Chapter 2, an S corporation may have only one class of stock. In general, it would be safest for an S corporation with more than one shareholder to make sure that all distributions are exactly proportionate, per share, and are all paid on the same date. Any variation on this payment scheme could raise the possibility that some shares have a preference over others for current distributions. See Chapter 2, at 225.3., for a discussion of permitted variations in distributions, which will not be indicative of a second class of stock. Also see Chapter 8, 820.34., for a discussion of compensation issues and classes of stock.

710. Background.

Under prior law, an S corporation was only partially a pass-through entity. Income did not pass through to the shareholders directly. Taxation of income at the shareholder level was accomplished through a complex set of dividend rules, which were adapted from C corporation taxation. Taxable income was computed at the corporate level in a manner similar to C corporations' computations. As a general rule, since income did not pass through to the shareholders, it could not retain its character. Dividends to the shareholders were treated as capital gains, to the extent that an S corporation's taxable income was attributable to a net capital gain.

These rules were discussed in some detail in the 1998 and earlier editions of the *S Corporation Tax Guide.* Table 7 - 1 shows the hierarchy of distributions after the Subchapter S Revision Act of 1982.

715. Corporations with no AEP.

S corporations with no accumulated earnings and profits have the simplest set of distribution rules. The presence of any AEP, regardless of how small the amount, will subject the corporation to the more complex accounting rules discussed in the next portion of the chapter.

In several situations, no AEP exist. A newly formed corporation, or one that has been an S corporation since its inception, has no earnings and profits. Pursuant to §1371(c)(1), no

Table 7 - 1: Hierarchy of Distributions of Cash and Property as in Effect after the Subchapter S Revision Act of 1982

Order	*Description of Distribution*	*Source of Distribution*	*Taxability*	*Effect on Basis*
1.	To all shareholders to the extent of AAA (See discussion at 720.)	AAA, as adjusted for current year's income and loss items	Not taxable unless in excess of shareholder's basis	Reduce basis to the extent thereof
2.	To shareholders who have pre-1983 PTI accumulations	PTI	Not taxable unless in excess of shareholder's basis	Reduce basis to the extent thereof
3.	To all shareholders in S corporations that have AEP	AEP	Ordinary income	No effect on basis
4.	All remaining distributions		Not taxable unless in excess of shareholder's basis	Reduce basis to the extent thereof

earnings and profits are generated in a post-1983 year in which an S election is in effect. Therefore, no earnings and profits exist in a corporation that was formed in a year beginning after 1982 and that has had an S election in effect continuously since formation.

A pre-existing C corporation may or may not have earnings and profits. Determination of the earnings and profits may necessitate a detailed study (see Chapter 3). Due to differences between tax and accounting income, the retained earnings account is only an indicator of the earnings and profits. AEP are likely if the corporate records show a retained earnings account, and they are unlikely if the corporation has no book retained earnings. As pointed out in Chapter 3, however, a quick glance at the retained earnings account is no substitute for a careful study of the corporation's tax history. As discussed in Chapter 13, at 1350., several corporations have discovered the unpleasant surprises that result from failure to carefully examine earnings and profits.

Earnings and profits accumulated in old Subchapter S years were preserved under the Subchapter S Revision Act of 1982, which gave no instructions for dealing with them separately from C corporation accumulated earnings and profits. Regulations issued in 1993 treated the accumulations under old Subchapter S as being in line behind earnings and profits accumulated in C corporation years. [Regs. §1.1368-1(f)(2)(iii)] Finally, the Small Business Job Protection Act of 1996 allows all S corporations to eliminate this earnings and profits layer at the opening of the first taxable years beginning after 1996. [Small Business Job Protection Act of 1996, §1311] Therefore, a corporation that has always been an S corporation, even in pre-1983 years, will have no accumulated earnings and profits unless it has acquired a C corporation (or a former C corporation) in a tax-free reorganization or liquidation. See Chapter 16 for discussion of corporate liquidations and Chapter 17 for discussion of corporate reorganizations.

715.1. Stock basis governs. When an S corporation has no AEP, the distribution rules look strictly to shareholder basis, and not to any accounts on the corporation's books, for determination of taxability.

SUMMARY OF AUTHORITY: CODE SECTION 1368(b)

- When an S corporation has no AEP, any distributions are excluded from the shareholder's gross income, to the extent they do not exceed the shareholder's stock basis.
- Distributions in excess of a shareholder's stock basis are treated as gains from the sale of stock.
- As indicated earlier, the distributions governed by Subchapter S do not necessarily include distributions in stock redemptions, complete liquidations, or tax-free reorganizations.

7

Stock basis is an extremely important issue in Subchapter S. As pointed out in Chapter 6, at 630.6, basis may be the primary limitation on the deductibility of losses. It is also critical in determining taxability of distributions, as indicated above. In fact, stock basis is such an important topic that it will receive a comprehensive discussion in Chapter 9. For the time being, however, some fundamental related concepts must be covered.

To calculate a shareholder's stock basis correctly at any point in time, it is necessary to know the entire history of the stock in the hands of the shareholder: when the stock was acquired, the consideration paid for the stock, and the nature of the transaction in which the stock was acquired. Some of the more common acquisitions and basis rules are discussed in Chapter 9.

It is also necessary to know of any adjustments that may have been made to the stock basis since acquisition. These rules are also discussed in Chapter 9, but at this point the relationship of the corporation's income, losses, and distribution to basis must be considered.

Income of the corporation is allocated to the shareholders in proportion to each person's weighted average stock ownership during the year. Losses are allocated by the same formula. A shareholder's loans to a corporation could absorb losses.[1] Distributions are governed by stock basis, which is only occasionally, and indirectly, affected by debt basis.

715.11. General ordering of basis adjustments. There is a potential circularity problem, since a shareholder's stock basis is affected by income, losses, and distributions. Fortunately, the Code provides reasonable ordering rules. Basis is computed at the close of the tax year in which the distributions are made. [§1368(d)] It is adjusted first for income of the year, before being measured for distributions. [§1368(d)(1)]

EXAMPLE 7 - 1: Ty is the sole shareholder in T Corporation. At the beginning of 1996, his basis in stock is $2,000. During 1996, he withdraws $50,000. In 1996, the corporation reports tax-exempt income of $6,000, and ordinary taxable income of $82,000. At the end of 1996, T's basis in his stock (before the distribution) is:

Beginning basis	$ 2,000
Tax exempt income	6,000
Taxable income	82,000
Basis before distributions	$90,000

Ty's distributions exceeded the beginning-of-year basis. Since they did not exceed the year-end basis, he reports no gain from his distributions in 1996. He would start 1997 with a basis of $40,000 ($90,000 basis before distributions less $50,000 distribution).

As of this writing, there have been no Final Regulations that define *tax-exempt income* in the context of shareholder basis. Thus, there could be some confusion as to what is truly tax-exempt

[1] Chapter 9 contains a thorough discussion of problems related to debt basis, which has been litigated frequently.

income, and what increments to wealth may not be treated as income in the economic sense. In short, not all exclusions from gross income will be allowed as increases to shareholder basis. For instance, contributions to the corporation's capital would add to the basis of the contributing shareholder, but not to the basis of any other shareholder. Proposed Regulations §1.1366-1(a)(2)(viii) gives a workable, but less than comprehensive, definition of *tax-exempt income* for this purpose. As is discussed in Chapter 6, this Regulation does not treat amounts excluded under §108 (cancellation of debt) or §109 (improvements made to property by a lessee) as flow-through items that would increase a shareholder's basis. See Chapter 6 for discussion.

As is discussed in Chapter 6, at 630.66., each shareholder must reduce basis for his or her portion of the corporation's nondeductible losses and expenses, before determining the basis available for deduction of allowable losses and expenses. Also see 630.67. for discussion of the elective rule, whereby a shareholder may claim his or her share of allowable losses and expenses before reducing basis for nondeductible items.

715.12. Income and loss years, post-1996. The hypothetical ordering of basis adjustments does not depend on whether a corporation has net positive or net negative adjustments in taxable years beginning after 1996. Refer to Chapter 6, at 630.64., for discussion of the new rules. In some cases these rules have a significant impact on distributions. In general, the rules provide that the basis for a shareholder's allowable losses is determined by adding the income items to the beginning-of-year basis and reducing for distributions (other than distributions of AEP, discussed below at 720.12.). [§1366(d)(1)(A)] In contrast, the basis for distributions is determined by taking into account the current year's income items, but no loss items. [§1368(d), §1367(a)(1)]

EXAMPLE 7-2: Cheryl is the sole shareholder of Cherco, an S corporation that uses the calendar year. On January 1, 1998, Cheryl's basis in her stock is $120,000. During 1998 the corporation has $150,000 of income items and $151,000 of loss items ($1,000 net loss). Cheryl receives $250,000 of distributions in 1998. Assuming Cherco has no accumulated earnings and profits, her distributions would be entirely tax-free, as follows:

Beginning basis	$120,000
Income items	150,000
Basis before distributions	$270,000
Distributions	(250,000)
Basis before loss items	$ 20,000

She could take into account $20,000 of the loss items and reduce her basis to zero. The remaining $131,000 of loss items would be carried forward to 1999. The treatment would be almost the same in 1998 if the loss items were $149,000, with overall net income of $1,000. She would have losses of $129,000 to carry forward.

The result of having distributions and losses in the same year was quite different under pre-1997 rules, and there is also a significant difference with respect to the AAA measurement rules, discussed below at 720.14. Example 7 - 3, below, illustrates some subtle but important differences.

715.13. Income and loss years, pre-1997. Before 1997, a shareholder was required to reduce basis for losses before considering distributions. Refer to Chapter 6, at 630.63., for discussion of the prior rules.

EXAMPLE 7 - 3: Cheryl is the sole shareholder of Cherco, an S corporation that uses the calendar year. On January 1, 1996, Cheryl's basis in her stock is $120,000. During 1998 the corporation has $150,000 of income items, and $151,000 of loss items ($1,000 net loss). Cheryl receives $250,000 of distributions in 1996. Assuming Cherco has no accumulated earnings and profits, her distributions would be partially taxable, as follows:

Beginning basis	$120,000
Income items	150,000
Less loss items	(151,000)
Basis before distributions	$119,000
Less tax free distributions	(119,000)
Basis before loss items	$ 0

She could take into account all of the loss items, and would reduce her basis to zero for $119,000 of the distributions. The remaining $131,000 of the distribution would be taxable as a gain form the sale of her stock.

If the year were 1997 or later, the order of basis adjustments would be:

7

Beginning basis	$120,000
Income items	150,000
Basis before distributions	$270,000
Less tax free distributions	(250,000)
Basis before loss items	$ 20,000
Less loss items	(20,000)
Basis at end of year	$ 0

She could take into account only $20,0000 of the loss items as potential deductions for the year. The remaining $131,000 of the distribution would be carried forward.

In one case, a shareholder neglected to reduce his basis for losses and treated the distributions as tax-free. This calculation would have been correct in a post-1996 year. The year in question was before the changes in ordering, however, and the Tax Court required the shareholder to reduce basis for losses and report distributions as taxable. [*Williams*, 110 TC 4 (1998)] Similarly, the IRS was precluded from reducing shareholders' bases for distributions before it allowed losses. [*Joly*, TC Memo 1998-361]

OBSERVATION: The 1998 proposed amendments to the Regulations under §1367 state that the new ordering rules are applicable to years beginning on or after August 18, 1998. The prior rules are in effect for years beginning before January 1, 1997. This leaves an unexplained gap for all years beginning from January 1, 1997, through August 17, 1998. The Small Business Job Protection Act of 1996 clearly applied the new rules to all years beginning after 1996. Any reason for the gap in the Regulations, as well as any significance thereto, is completely obscure.

715.14. Timing of basis adjustments. If a shareholder owns stock at the end of the corporation's taxable year, all basis adjustments occur on the last day of the corporation's taxable year. If a shareholder has disposed of his or her stock, the basis adjustments occur on the last day of ownership. [Regs. §1.1367-1(d)(3)]

EXAMPLE 7 - 4: Patsy owned shares in Patsco, an S corporation that uses the calendar year. On November 9, 1996, Patsy sold all of her Patsco stock. Her basis at the beginning of 1996 was $50,000. Her portion of the corporation's income for 1996 was $20,000. She received distributions of $38,000 between January 1, 1996, and November 9, 1996. Her basis was $32,000 ($50,000 + $20,000 – $38,000) at the time of sale.

715.15. Allocation of distributions to different blocks of shares. A shareholder who owns more than one block of shares must keep track of the different basis of each. When the shareholder receives a distribution, he or she must allocate the distribution proportionately among the shares owned at the time. Each share's basis is reduced by its allocable portion of the distribution. [Regs. §1.1367-1(c)(3)] If the amount allocated to one share exceeds the basis of that share, the excess may be used to reduce basis of other shares. [Regs. §1.1367-1(f), Example 2]

EXAMPLE 7 - 5: Donn owned 200 shares in Donco, an S corporation. He had purchased the shares in two blocks of 100 at different times, for different prices. At the end of 1996, his basis in one block was $20 per share ($2,000 total block basis), and his basis in the other block was $30 per share ($3,000 total block basis). In 1996, Donn received $4,400 in distributions. His entire distribution is a reduction of basis, since it does not exceed his basis in all of his shares. It is allocated to the two blocks of stock in the following manner:

	Block	
	$20/share	*$30/share*
Pre-distribution basis	$2,000	$3,000
Allocation of distributions	(2,200)	(2,200)
Excess or (deficiency) in basis	(200)	800
Reallocation of excess distribution	200	(200)
Ending basis	$ 0	$ 600

7

715.16. Effect of election to close year. As was discussed in Chapter 6, at 630.2., a corporation may elect to close its year when a shareholder terminates his or her interest in a corporation. [§1377(a)(2), Regs. §1.1368-1(g)] When a corporation makes this election, each shareholder must determine his or her basis at each closing date. [Regs. §1.1367-1(d)(3)] The basis calculation rules apply to any shareholder who continues his or her interest, as well as to the terminating shareholder. [See Regs. §1.1367-1(f), Example 3]

EXAMPLE 7 - 6: On December 31, 1996, Eagle Corporation, a calendar-year S corporation, had two equal shareholders, Mike and Eva. Eagle's 1996 taxable income was $200,000. Eagle's AAA was $200,000 on December 31, 1996. Each shareholder's basis, after 1996 activity, was $110,000. In January 1997, Eagle distributed $100,000 to each shareholder.

On May 26, 1997 (40% of Eagle's taxable year had elapsed), Eva bought all of Mike's shares for $20,000. Eagle's 1997 taxable income was as follows:

Loss from January 1 through May 26	($180,000)
Income from May 27 through December 31	400,000
Total for year	$220,000

If Eagle does not elect to close the books when Mike terminates his interest, the treatment of the distributions will be as follows:

	Eva	*Mike*
Stock basis, January 1, 1997	$110,000	$110,000
Adjustment for 1997 income:		
Eva [50% + (50% x 60%)]	176,000	
Mike (50% x 40%)		44,000
Basis before distribution	286,000	154,000
Reduce for distribution	(100,000)	(100,000)
Basis after distribution	$186,000	$ 54,000

Each shareholder would report no gain from the distribution, since it did not exceed his or her basis.

If Eagle does elect to close the books when Mike terminates his interest, the treatment of the distributions will be as follows:

	Eva	*Mike*
Stock basis, January 1, 1997	$110,000	$110,000
Basis before distribution	110,000	110,000
Reduce for distribution	(100,000)	(100,000)
Basis after distribution	$10,000	$10,000
Adjustment for early 1997 loss	($10,000)	($10,000)

At this point, each shareholder would have a suspended loss of $80,000. Mike would not be able to use his loss in the future, since he is no longer a shareholder. Eva would carry her $80,000 to the next "year," which begins the next day.

7

Neither shareholder reports a gain from the distribution. If the corporation had accumulated earnings and profits, a portion of the distribution could be treated as dividend income to both shareholders, due to the differences between basis and AAA computations.

Comparing the two methods of allocating income for the year, the results are as follows:

To Mike:

	With Closing Election		*Without Closing Election*	
	Basis	*Income*	*Basis*	*Income*
Beginning of year	$110,000		$110,000	
Pass-through income	0	0	44,000	$ 44,000
Distribution	(100,000)		(100,000)	0
Pass-through loss	(10,000)*	$ (10,000)	0	0
Basis before sale	$ 0		$ 54,000	
Sale price	20,000		20,000	
Gain or loss on sale		20,000		(34,000)
Total income for year		$10,000		$10,000

* $80,000 of Mike's loss is not deductible due to basis limits.

To Eva:

	With Closing Election		*Without Closing Election*	
	Basis	*Income*	*Basis*	*Income*
Beginning of year	$110,000		$110,000	
Distribution	(100,000)		(100,000)	0
First period income	(90,000)	$ (90,000)	176,000	$176,000
Purchased stock	20,000		20,000	
Second period income	400,000	400,000	n/a	n/a
Basis at end of year	$340,000		$206,000	
Total income for year	$310,000		$176,000	

715.17. Treatment of distributions to former shareholders. As is discussed in Chapter 2, at 225.32., a corporation may base distributions on each shareholder's varying percentage interest of stock ownership for the current or immediate prior year. A distribution of this nature may cause distributions to differ markedly from the percentage of shares held on the distribution date, but this difference will not be evidence that the corporation has a second class of stock. [See Regulations §1.1361-1(l)(2)(iv).] If a shareholder has disposed of all of his or her stock, but receives a distribution after the disposition, there may be some confusion as to the proper tax treatment of the distribution. The Code and Regulations give no guidance on the proper treatment of a distribution to a former shareholder.

There would seem to be only one logical treatment of a distribution from the former shareholder's point of view. The shareholder should treat the distribution as a distribution with respect to stock in which he or she has no basis. Thus the shareholder would treat the entire distribution as a capital gain.

> **EXAMPLE 7 - 7:** On December 31, 1996, Kevin sold all of his stock in Walco. Walco based its distributions on each shareholder's percentage interest throughout the prior year. On March 1, 1997, Kevin received a distribution of $20,000 from Walco. Under general tax rules, Kevin would have determined his basis as of December 31, 1996, and would have reported his gain or loss from the sale of his Walco stock on his 1996 tax return. Thus, as of March 1, 1997, he would have no remaining basis in his stock. The distribution should be treated as a gain from the sale of stock. Note that this treatment gives exactly the same result as if Kevin had received the distribution on December 31, 1996, and reduced his basis by $20,000 on that date. The timing of the gain reporting would be different, since Kevin sold the stock in 1996 and received the distribution in 1997. Note also that the 1997 distribution could be characterized, in whole or in part, as a dividend, if Walco had accumulated earnings and profits. See discussion of distributions by corporations with accumulated earnings and profits at 720.
>
> Although there is no statutory or regulatory authority to justify the treatment recommended, it is consistent with the treatment afforded payment of corporate expenses by a former shareholder. [*F. D. Arrowsmith*, 52-2 USTC 9527 (S.Ct.)]

7

715.2. Complications caused by debt basis. The basis for distributions is limited to the shareholder's basis in stock. [§1368(b)(1)] Contrast this rule with the basis limit for losses (see Chapter 6), where a shareholder can deduct losses to the extent of stock and debt basis.

Unless a shareholder receives a loss allocation that exceeds his or her stock basis, there is no reason to adjust debt basis. If a shareholder's portion of an S corporation's loss exceeds his or her stock basis, the shareholder reduces debt basis. In no case can either stock or debt basis be reduced below zero.

Generally, there is no reason to adjust debt basis upward, unless the shareholder actually loans more money to the corporation. The one exception to this rule occurs after a shareholder has reduced debt basis. If the corporation has income in a future year, the income will restore debt basis before it adds to stock basis. In this case, the normal ordering rules for basis calculations are interrupted, because the stock basis rules and debt basis rules are not quite identical with respect to income and distributions. A brief discussion of the contrasting rules is in order.

When there has been no prior reduction to debt basis, income, losses, and distributions affect stock basis, in that order. When there has been a prior reduction in debt basis due to a shareholder's losses in prior years, any distributions of the current year are netted against income of the current year to measure the increase to debt basis. [§1367(b)(1)(B)] See Table 7 - 2.

> **CAUTION:** It would be a mistake to view the distribution basis rules and the loss limitation basis rules as identical. As is discussed in Chapter 6, at 630.6., a shareholder may deduct his or her share of corporate losses, to the extent the losses do not exceed his or her stock and debt basis. A distribution on stock is tax-free only to the extent of stock basis. Thus a shareholder may have debt basis and assume that he or she may receive distributions tax-free.

TABLE 7 - 2: Stock and Debt Basis Ordering

Stock Basis	*Debt Basis*
Income in excess of restoration of debt basis	Loss in excess of stock basis
Loss to the extent of stock basis	Income in excess of distributions

715.3. Distributions in excess of stock basis. The excess of a distribution over shareholder stock basis is treated as a gain from the sale of property (stock). [§1368(b)(2)] Except in the rare case of a collapsible corporation, or a dealer who happens to be holding the stock in inventory, the gain is treated as a capital gain.[2] The holding period of the stock determines the long- or short-term character of the gain.

7

As is discussed in Chapter 6, at 630.63. and 630.64., the Small Business Job Protection Act of 1996 revised the order of basis adjustments for a year in which an S corporation has both losses and distributions and the total of those two items exceeds a shareholder's basis.

EXAMPLE 7 - 8: In 1997, Ty from Example 7 - 1 again withdraws $50,000. In 1997, the corporation has tax-exempt income of $6,000 but has negative taxable income of $50,000. Thus there is a net loss, for purposes of the basis adjustment rules, of $44,000. Anticipating that losses will exceed basis, Ty loans the corporation $45,000. His 1997 basis adjustments are:

Item	*Basis in Stock*	*Debt*	*Total*
Beginning basis	$ 10,000	$ 0	$ 10,000
Add tax exempt income	6,000	0	6,000
Add loan	0	45,000	45,000
Basis before distribution	$ 16,000	$ 45,000	$ 65,000
Less distribution	(16,000)	(0)	(16,000)
Basis before loss	$ 0	$ 45,000	$ 45,000
Less taxable loss	(0)	(45,000)	(45,000)
Basis after loss	$ 0	$ 0	$ 0

Since Ty has only $10,000 stock basis before adjustment for current-year income, $34,000 of the $50,000 distributed to him in 1997 will be treated as a gain on the sale of stock.

If these facts had occurred in 1996 or an earlier year, the results would have been different. Since Ty would have had no stock basis after adjustment for current-year losses, the entire $50,000 distributed to him in 1997 would have been treated as a gain on the sale of stock.

The next example illustrates the interactive effects of income and distributions in a year that follows debt basis reduction. First consider a situation in which the corporation has income and makes no distributions.

EXAMPLE 7 - 9: In 1998, T Corporation from Examples 7 - 1 and 7 - 8 has taxable income of $46,000. Ty receives no distributions in 1998. The tax consequences are:

---

[2] A *collapsible corporation* is defined in §341. This is a complicated rule, which causes long-term capital gain to be classified as ordinary income. Since TRA '86 imposed a tax on corporate liquidations, collapsible corporation status is unusual, if not impossible, in years after 1988.

Item	*Stock*	*Basis in Debt*	*Total*
Beginning basis	$ 0	$ 0	$ 0
Add 1998 taxable income	1,000[b]	45,000[a]	46,000
Basis before distribution	$1,000	$45,000	$46,000

[a]Lesser amount of current year's income or debt basis reduction in prior years.
[b]Income remaining after amount applied to restoration of debt basis.

Ty could now withdraw all of his debt basis in the form of debt repayment. He would also have $1,000 stock basis to withdraw, although the treatment of distributions in 1999 would depend on the corporation's 1999 income or loss.

OBSERVATION: If Ty had contributed the $45,000 to capital in 1997, rather than making a loan to the corporation, his gain from the 1997 and 1998 distributions would have been reduced. His tax consequences would have been:

Year	*Item*	*Effect on Basis*
1997	Beginning basis	$10,000
	Add contribution	45,000
	Add tax-exempt income	6,000
	Basis before 1997 distribution	61,000
	Less nontaxable distribution	(50,000)
	Basis before net loss	11,000
	Less taxable loss	(11,000)
1998	Beginning basis	$ 0

Under this strategy none of his distributions would be taxable as gains. Of his losses, $11,000 would have been deductible, whereas the remainder would have exceeded basis and been carried forward.

OBSERVATION: Shareholders who find that they have debt basis but lack stock basis and intend to take a distribution may wish that they had contributed to the corporation's capital, rather than made a loan to the corporation. Even if the debt basis has been reduced, it is not too late to contribute the debt instrument to the corporation and convert debt basis to stock basis. See Chapter 14, at 1420.3, for further discussion.

715.4. Fiscal year problems. There are special problems when the tax year of the corporation differs from that of the shareholder. The shareholder's basis, which limits tax-free distributions, is determined at the end of the corporation's tax year. [§1366(a)(1), §1367(a)(1), §1368(d)(1)] A shareholder might have distributions from two corporate years in one individual year. The Code and Regulations are silent on whether to use FIFO or pro rata accounting for the tax-free and taxable distributions. Pro rata accounting for distributions is probably the proper method. It conforms to the required accounting for the Accumulated Adjustments Account (AAA), described at 720. Consequently, the tax status of any distribution may not be known until the close of the corporation's year end.

EXAMPLE 7 - 10: H Corporation, which owns and operates a turkey farm, uses a fiscal year ending November 30. It justifies retaining the year end after the Tax Reform Act of 1986 by showing that it is a natural business year. In December 1995, H Corporation makes a distribution to its calendar-year shareholder. The distribution is made in the corporate fiscal year ending November 30, 1996. On August 15, 1997, when the corporation files its extended

7

return, it determines that distributions for its 1996 year exceeded the shareholder's basis on November 30, 1996. It must report the distribution to the shareholder, who must then amend his or her 1995 tax return.

715.5. Corporate accounting for distributions. The Code and Regulations give no guidance on the proper accounting for distributions by the corporation if the corporation has no accumulated earnings and profits (AEP). As is discussed below at 720.12., there is no express requirement that a corporation with no AEP must maintain an Accumulated Adjustments Account (AAA). If the corporation does not maintain the AAA, it should reduce book retained earnings by the amount of the distribution, and it would not be required to adjust any tax account.

If the corporation does maintain the AAA, it should reduce the AAA, but not below zero, by the amount of any distribution to a current or former shareholder. If a distribution would cause the AAA to become negative, the Other Adjustments Account (OAA) would be a logical account for the excess.

EXAMPLE 7-11: Newco began business in January 1996. It used the calendar year and filed a valid S election for its first taxable year. In 1996, Newco had taxable income of $40,000 and made distributions of $45,000. The proper financial accounting entry for the income and distributions would be:

	Debit	Credit
Income summary	$40,000	
Retained earnings		$40,000
(To post the current year's income to retained earnings)		
Retained earnings	$45,000	
Cash		$45,000
(To reduce retained earnings for the distribution)		

The proper tax accounting, if the corporation maintained the AAA, would be:

	Debit	Credit
Income summary	$40,000	
AAA		$40,000
(To post the current year's income to retained earnings)		
AAA	$40,000	
OAA	5,000	
Cash		$45,000
(To reduce retained earnings for the distribution)		

720. Corporations with AEP.

S corporations with AEP are governed by a more complex set of rules than corporations without them. The complications arise because the earnings and profits would have been dividends if they had been distributed to the shareholders when the corporation was a C corporation. When the Subchapter S Revision Act of 1982 was enacted, Congress did not want the election of S status to allow a corporation and its shareholders to escape from dividend treatment for the earnings and profits that had already accumulated. At the same time, Congress explicitly rejected the idea of treating an S election as a constructive liquidation. The scheme devised for taxing AEP is a reasonable compromise that allows shareholders to treat the distribution of income taxable under Subchapter S rules as tax-free reductions of basis but does not allow them to make tax-free withdrawals of corporate income that had been accumulated before the S election took effect. The means used to accomplish this involve a special corporate-level account for taxable income accumulated while the S election is in effect. That account, the AAA, is the buffer zone for tax-free distributions.

SUMMARY OF AUTHORITY: CODE SECTION 1368(c)

- Code §1368(c) provides a three-tiered hierarchy of distribution rules.
- The corporation's AAA is the first source of distributions.
- Distributions that do not exceed the AAA are treated like those of corporations with no AEP (i.e., they are tax-free to extent of basis, then are treated as gain).
- Once the AAA is exhausted, distributions are treated as dividends to the extent of the corporation's AEP.
- After AEP are exhausted, the corporation becomes subject to the rules for S corporations with no AEP (i.e., distributions are tax-free reductions of shareholder basis to the extent thereof, with any excess treated as a gain from the sale of stock).

Code §1368(c) does not mention PTI accumulated before 1983. This account is distributed before AEP, but it requires some further analysis. See 725., below. Distributions of PTI are partly based on new Subchapter S and partly determined by old Subchapter S. It is unlikely that many S corporations still have balances in PTI, but the topic will be discussed later in this chapter.

720.1. Distributions from the AAA. Distributions up to the balance in the AAA are subject to the same rules as corporations with no AEP. These distributions reduce each shareholder's stock basis to the extent thereof. Any distribution in excess of basis is treated as a gain from the sale of stock. In concept, the rule is quite simple. The AAA, however, has some special rules that deserve further explanation. There are also gaps in the law and the legislative history that can cause some confusion.

720.11. AAA defined. Defining the *Accumulated Adjustments Account* is critical for corporations that have AEP. It sets the limit on distributions that are not treated as dividends.

SUMMARY OF AUTHORITY: CODE SECTION 1368(e)(1)

- The AAA is an equity account on the corporation's balance sheet.
- The account has no balance until there is a post-1982 S corporation year.
- The account reflects, but may not exactly duplicate, shareholder basis adjustments for income and distributions.
- The account is reduced for all losses that pass through to shareholders, whether they reduce stock basis, reduce debt basis, or are suspended due to lack of shareholder basis.
- There is no adjustment for tax-exempt income or expenses attributable to tax-exempt income (even though these items do affect shareholder basis).
- There are no specific portions of the account that are identified with individual taxable years or individual shareholders.
- Unusual distributions, such as stock redemptions, may have additional rules (see Chapters 15 and 16).
- There are several gaps in this subsection of the Code.

720.12. Relationship to shareholder basis and pass-through. The accounting rules for the AAA are derived from the basis rules, which are in turn derived from the income and deduction rules. Table 7 - 3 clarifies the differences and similarities.

TABLE 7 - 3: Relationship of Income and Expenditures to Shareholder Basis and Corporation's AAA

Type of Income or Expenditure	*Effect on Shareholder Income*	*Effect on Shareholder Basis*	*Effect on AAA*
Ordinary income	Increase	Increase	Increase
Other taxable gains	Increase	Increase	Increase
Ordinary loss	Decrease, to extent of basis, amount at risk, §469, or other limits	Decrease, but not below zero, regardless of deductibility	Decrease for entire amount
Other deductible items	Same as ordinary loss	Same as ordinary loss	Same as ordinary loss
Tax-exempt income	No effect	Increase	No effect
Expenses related to tax-exempt income	No effect	Questionable	No effect
Other nondeductible expenses	Questionable	Questionable	Questionable

7

As the table indicates, the effect of nondeductible expenses on the AAA is less than clear. Under the Subchapter S Revision Act of 1982, §1368(e)(1)(A) stated that nondeductible items would not reduce the AAA. The Tax Reform Act of 1984 changed the wording so that the only nondeductible expenditures that are specifically not charged against the AAA are those related to the production of tax-exempt income. [Tax Reform Act of 1984, §721(r)] The legislative history of the 1984 Act suggests that Congress intended nondeductible items to reduce the AAA. [Joint Committee on Taxation, *Tax Reform Act of 1984—General Explanation*, page 1024]

Requiring a shareholder to reduce his or her basis for nondeductible items would also be consistent with the general objective of the Subchapter S Revision Act of 1982 in conforming S corporations to partnerships. Subchapter S refers directly to the partnership statutes governing separate reporting of income, deductions, and other items at the corporate level and allocation of such line items to shareholders. (See extensive discussion in Chapter 6). Partners are required to reduce basis for their portions of partnership nondeductible items. [Regs. §1.705-1(a)(3)(ii)] Nondeductible expenses, however, are not mentioned as specific pass-through items of partnerships.[3] The IRS instructs shareholders in S corporations to reduce basis for nondeductible expenses. [See *Instructions for Form 1120S* (1998), page 23.] The Regulations state that shareholders must decrease basis for nondeductible corporate expenditures. Such items include, but are not limited to:

- Illegal bribes, kickbacks, and other payments not deductible under §162(c)
- Fines and penalties not deductible under §162(f)
- Expenses and interest relating to tax-exempt income under §265
- Losses for which the deduction is disallowed under §267(a)(1)
- The portion of meals and entertainment expenses disallowed under §274
- Two-thirds of treble damages paid for violating antitrust laws not deductible under §162 [Regs. §1.1367-1(c)(2)]

[3] The Regulations under §§702 and 703 are silent on this issue.

OBSERVATION: The actual wording of the statute leads to confusion. The AAA rules are derived from the basis rules, which are in turn derived from the income rules. Section 1368(e), which defines the AAA, states that the account shall be adjusted "in a manner similar to . . . section 1367," which defines the basis rules. Section 1367 requires that shareholders decrease basis for "loss and deduction described in . . . section 1366(a)(1)," which in turn requires reporting of items that "could affect the liability for tax of any shareholder." Since a permanently disallowed expense could not affect the tax liability of any shareholder, the statutory requirement for reducing AAA by nondeductible losses is questionable. The apparent intent of Congress, however, is that S corporations must reduce the AAA for nondeductible expenses, except those related to the production of tax-exempt income. The IRS instructs S corporations to reduce AAA for these items. [Instructions for Form 1120S (1998), page 24]

The Code does not state directly whether the AAA is computed at the end of the shareholders' years or at the end of the corporation's year. The only sensible rule would be for the corporation to determine the AAA at the end of its own taxable year. The IRS agrees with this position. [PLRs 8712049, 8842024, 8908016] When a corporation closes its books due to the termination of a shareholder's interest, the AAA is measured at the end of each of the two short periods. [Regs. §1.1368-2(e)]

Section 1368 mentions the AAA only in connection with corporations that have AEP. It can be questioned whether corporations with no AEP should maintain this account, since its balance has no apparent effect on the taxability of distributions to the shareholders. The IRS has held consistently in Publication 589 (no longer in print), as well as in the instructions for Form 1120S, that all S corporations are required to maintain this account. It has implied the necessity of the account in several private letter rulings, and it specifically required one corporation with no earnings and profits to maintain the AAA. [PLR 9046036]

OBSERVATION: There are two instances in which the AAA can be an important measure of distributions, even for an S corporation with no AEP: the post-termination transition period (discussed later in this chapter) and the period following a tax-free reorganization (discussed in Chapter 16). It is doubtful that a positive AAA balance could be a disadvantage.

EXAMPLE 7 - 12: M Corporation is an S corporation that has AEP at the beginning of 1997. Its first S year is 1997. Its sole shareholder, A, has a basis in her stock of $12,000 as of January 1, 1997.

In 1997, M has taxable income of $40,000 and tax-exempt income of $7,000. It makes a distribution of $35,000 to A, its sole shareholder. The effects of the year's activities on shareholder income and basis and the corporation's AAA are:

Item	*Basis*	*Taxable Income*	*AAA*
Beginning balance	$12,000	$ 0	$ 0
1997 taxable income	40,000	40,000	40,000
1997 exempt income	7,000	0	0
Distribution	(35,000)		(35,000)
Ending balance	$24,000	$40,000	$ 5,000

In most cases, the AAA will not exceed the total basis to all shareholders. To begin with, no shareholder may have a basis of less than zero. The next example illustrates why the adjustments to basis and adjustments to the AAA will usually cause the aggregate shareholders' basis to be at least as high as the AAA.

EXAMPLE 7 - 13: Individual R forms Corporation Y by a contribution to capital in 1996. R's basis in the property contributed to Y is $41,753. Y immediately files an S election. At the beginning of the first taxable year, R's basis is $41,753 and Y's AAA is $0. Note the effects of the following on R's basis and Y's AAA:

1. Any taxable income that Y earns will add to basis and AAA in equal amounts. R's basis will exceed the AAA by $41,753.
2. Any tax-exempt income will add to R's basis. It will not add to Y's AAA.
3. Potentially deductible losses will reduce both Y's AAA and R's basis. A net loss up to $41,753 will reduce R's basis and Y's AAA by equal amounts. If a loss exceeds $41,753, it will reduce the AAA in full but will reduce basis only to $0. In this case, the AAA will be less than basis. There is no way that a potentially deductible loss can reduce basis by an amount greater than the reduction to AAA.
4. The only way that routine operations might create basis less than AAA is for expenses associated with tax-exempt income to exceed all income (taxable and exempt), plus $41,753.

7

There are situations, however, where the AAA may exceed shareholders' total basis. A shareholder's unadjusted basis is not determined by reference to the AAA. For example, a shareholder may have inherited stock at a time when the value was low, even though after-tax profits had accumulated in Subchapter S years. Or a shareholder may have purchased shares from a former shareholder who was in distress. An example would be a legal dispute settled out of court, such as a property settlement in a divorce.

EXAMPLE 7 - 14: In 1996, individual A buys all of the stock in Corporation N, an S corporation. The corporation has an AAA balance of $500,000. N invested heavily in real estate in Anchorage, Alaska, in 1990. Its investments have declined in value by $400,000, but it has no recognized losses for tax purposes. Individual A pays $100,000 for the stock and takes a cost basis of $100,000. The corporation's AAA is unaffected by a shareholder transfer, and it remains at $500,000.

720.13. Timing problems. The additions and reductions to an S corporation's AAA are determined by reference to the corporation's taxable income. Therefore, certain items of deferral permitted or required by the tax law will not affect the AAA until they are reported on the corporation's tax return. For instance, the deferral of gain or loss under the involuntary conversion or like-kind exchange rules will not have an immediate effect on the corporation's AAA. (See Revenue Ruling 81-242, 1981 CB 147, for application of this rule in a partnership context.)

EXAMPLE 7 - 15: Gerco is an S corporation. In 1997, Gerco's warehouse was destroyed by fire. Gerco's adjusted basis in the building was $220,000 at the time of the fire, and Gerco received $300,000 in insurance proceeds. Gerco replaced the building within the time period prescribed by §1033 and elected to defer the gain. The $80,000 deferred gain does not increase the shareholders' basis or the corporation's AAA.

Similarly, the temporary disallowance of amounts accrued to shareholders or related parties requires coordination between the corporation's taxable income and its AAA. [§267(a)(2)] See Chapter 8, at 815., for further discussion of this rule. The expense reduces the AAA at the same time it is deducted on the corporation's tax return.

EXAMPLE 7 - 16: Ronico has one shareholder, Veronica. Ronico is an accrual-method, calendar-year taxpayer, whereas Veronica uses the cash method and a calendar year. On December 31, 1996, Ronico has accrued $10,000 of salary to Veronica. Veronica receives the salary in January 1997. Under the rules of §267(a)(2), Ronico deducts the $10,000 in 1997. The

$10,000 has no effect on Ronico's AAA at the end of 1996, but will reduce it, along with the other ordinary deductions, in 1997.

The IRS has recently allowed sellers of durable goods to defer income from warranty contracts. [Rev. Proc. 92-97, 1992-2 CB 510, and Rev. Proc. 92-98, 1992-2 CB 512] These Revenue Procedures specifically provide that the deferred income has no effects on a shareholder's basis or on an S corporation's AAA.

As of this writing, the IRS has not specified any accounting rules for the AAA when the S corporation makes an accounting method change and the impact of the change is phased in over more than one year under §481 or §472(d). Presumably, the increment or decrement to the AAA is calculated at the same time the adjustment is reported on Form 1120S.

EXAMPLE 7 - 17: Johnny Corporation is an S corporation that used the cash method of accounting through its year ending December 31, 1995. In 1996, Johnny voluntarily changed to the accrual method, and the IRS allowed Johnny to spread the impact of the change over a six-year period beginning in 1996. The cumulative impact of the change was a $120,000 increase in taxable income. Johnny will report $20,000 under §481 for six years, beginning in 1996. Therefore, Johnny's AAA should be adjusted to reflect its taxable income for each of those years, which will include $20,000 from the §481 adjustment in each year.

7

720.14. Income and loss years, post-1996. The Small Business Job Protection Act of 1996 amended the rules of ordering from the AAA. Before 1997, the ordering rules for the AAA were exactly same as the basis ordering rules. In other words, the corporation's loss items for the year reduced the AAA before distributions.The basis rules for income and loss years were discussed in Chapter 6, at 630.6., and above at 715.12. and 715.13.

The Small Business Job Protection Act of 1996 amended the AAA rules and the basis, but not in an identical manner. There are some subtle and strange differences between the basis adjustments and the AAA accounting rules. While basis for distributions is calculated by taking the income items into account, but ignoring the loss items, there are different rules for the AAA. In general, the corporation must account for all income and loss items before calculating the AAA balance available for distributions. However, in the case of a year in which there are "net negative adjustments," the Code allows the AAA to be calculated without any net negative adjustment being taken into account. [§1368(e)(1)(C)] A net negative adjustment occurs when loss items exceed income items. Contrast this treatment with that of basis, in the following example.

EXAMPLE 7 - 18: The facts in Example 7 - 2 were as follows: Cheryl is the sole shareholder of Cherco, an S corporation that uses the calendar year. On January 1, 1998, Cheryl's basis in her stock is $120,000. During 1998 the corporation has $150,000 of income items, and $151,000 of loss items ($1,000 net loss). Cheryl receives $250,000 of distributions in 1998. Now assume that Cherco has accumulated earnings and profits. Cheryl's basis would be computed in the same manner as it was in Example 7-2, as follows:

Beginning basis	$120,000
Income items	150,000
Basis before distributions	$270,000

She could not complete her basis calculation without knowing the character of the distributions, since distributions from AEP have no effect on basis. Note, however, that the basis limit, per se, would not cause her to recognize any gain, since her basis exceeds the distributions by $20,000.

Assuming that the corporation has a beginning AAA balance of $120,000, the year's activities would affect the AAA as follows:

Beginning balance	$120,000
Income items	150,000
Less loss items (limit to zero net negative adjustment)	(150,000)
Balance before distributions	$120,000
Distributions from AAA	(120,000)
Balance before net negative adjustment	$ 0
Net negative adjustment	(1,000)
Balance after loss items	$ (1,000)

The basis and AAA in Example 7 - 2 were calculated in entirely different manners, due to the special rule of §1361(e) that disregards any net negative adjustment. A slight change in facts gives slightly different results.

7

EXAMPLE 7 - 19: Assume the same facts as in Example 7 - 18, except that the corporation has $150,000 of income items and $149,000 of loss items ($1,000 net income). Cheryl receives $250,000 of distributions in 1998. Now assume that Cherco has accumulated earnings and profits. Cheryl's basis would be computed in the same manner as in Example 7-2, as follows:

Beginning basis	$120,000
Income items	150,000
Basis before distributions	$270,000

She could not complete her basis calculation without knowing the character of the distributions, since distributions from AEP have no effect on basis. Note, however, that the basis limit, per se, would not cause her to recognize any gain, since her basis exceeds the distributions by $20,000.

Assuming that the corporation has a beginning AAA balance of $120,000, the year's activities would affect the AAA as follows:

Beginning balance	$120,000
Income items	150,000
Less loss items	(149,000)
Balance before distributions	$ 21,000
Distributions from AAA	(21,000)
Balance of AAA	$ 0
Distributions not from AAA	$231,000

Thus, up to $231,000 would be taxable as dividends, if the corporation's accumulated earnings and profits were at least that high.

> **OBSERVATION:** The proposed amendments to Regulations §11368-2 inexplicably ignore the net negative adjustment rules shown above. The amended version would allow all distributions to come from AAA before any of the year's losses and nondeductible items are taken into account for taxable years beginning on or after August 18, 1988. [Proposed Regs. §1.1368-2(a)(5).] In either of the two examples above, the AAA would be $270,000 (beginning balance of $120,000 plus income of $150,000) before the distribution. Practitioners should be on the alert to changes in Final Regulations from this rule.

720.15. Special accounting rules for the AAA. The Code gives little guidance on the accounting rules for the AAA. From 1983 through 1991, the instructions given by the IRS were somewhat sketchy, and the arrangement of Form 1120S made interpretation difficult. The Regulations issued in January 1994 provide some amplification. The account is increased for each year's taxable income, including separately reported income and gains and combined taxable income. [Regs. §1.1368-2(a)(2)]

An S corporation posts a net loss for the year, as well as nondeductible expenses, as reductions to the AAA. It does not, however, reduce AAA for any federal taxes attributable to the corporation from a C year or for any expense related to tax-exempt income. [Regs. §1.1368-2(a)(3)]

There are also some special rules for S corporations that have oil and gas interests. In this case, each shareholder calculates his or her depletion allowance separately. The shareholder must report the depletion deduction to the corporation, which in turn reduces the AAA for the depletion claimed by the shareholder. [Regs. §1.1368-2(a)(3)(i)(D)] If a shareholder's depletion deduction exceeds his or her portion of the corporation's basis in the depletable property, the corporation adds the excess depletion back to the AAA. [Regs. §1.1368-2(a)(2)(iii)]

> **OBSERVATION:** There is no ordering rule for deductible and nondeductible loss and expense items when computing the AAA, as there is for basis adjustments. Thus, both the nondeductible and deductible losses are lumped together and compared with the year's income items to determine any net negative adjustment.

An S corporation must also reduce the AAA for certain distributions. The Code requires that the AAA be reduced for any distribution other than a distribution included in a shareholder's gross income. [Regs. §1368(d)(1), §1367(a)(2)(A)] Under current law, two types of distributions can be included in a shareholder's gross income and therefore not reduce the AAA: dividends from the corporation's AEP and distributions that exceed the shareholder's basis for the year of the distribution.

The Regulations provide a slightly different interpretation of this rule. They require that the corporation decrease its AAA for distributions other than distributions of AEP and PTI. [Regs. §1.1368-2(b) (last paragraph)] The distributions that reduce AAA are limited to those not included in the shareholder's gross income.[4] Therefore, a distribution that exceeds a shareholder's basis could reduce the AAA, under the Regulations.

> **OBSERVATION:** Between 1983 and 1991, the IRS instructions for the AAA for corporations with no accumulated earnings and profits departed from the language of the Code. The IRS instructed these corporations to increase the AAA for all items of income, including tax-exempt income. Any expenses relating to the production of tax-exempt income were to be charged against the AAA. Regulations §1.1368-2 provides no special instructions for corporations with **no** accumulated earnings and profits, so these corporations should now follow the same rules as corporations **with** accumulated earnings and profits.

If a corporation's distributions exceed its AAA, after adjustment for the year's income and loss items, the excess does not create a negative balance in the AAA. [Regs. §1.1368-2(a)(3)(iii)] The Code and the Regulations do not give complete guidance on what happens when a corporation's distributions exceed its AAA. If the distributions exceed AAA, they would reduce each shareholder's PTI to the extent thereof, and any remaining excess distribution would reduce the corporation's AEP. Once these accounts are exhausted, there is no accounting guidance. Presumably, book retained earnings would be the appropriate account. It would do no harm to use the Other Adjustments Account (OAA), since this account has no independent tax significance.

---

[4] Regulations §1.1368-2(a)(3)(iii) refers only to a distribution to which §1368(b) or (c)(1) applies. A distribution under either subsection could be taxable as a gain, if it exceeds the shareholder's basis.

EXAMPLE 7 - 20: An S corporation has $8,000 AAA, no PTI, and no AEP at the end of its taxable year before considering its distributions. The corporation distributes $11,000 in the same taxable year. The corporation's AAA balance, after all current year adjustments, would be zero. The $3,000 of distributions in excess of the AAA could be posted to book retained earnings or to the OAA.

If distributions exceed the AAA, the corporation must allocate the AAA to each distribution made during the tax year in proportion to the percentage of total distributions made during the year. This rule would have little significance if the corporation has no AEP. When a corporation does have AEP, however, this rule could lead to some surprises. The two instances that should be of greatest significance are a termination of a shareholder's interest and an S corporation's use of a fiscal year.

EXAMPLE 7 - 21: P Corporation is an S corporation with a fiscal year ending May 31. As of May 31, 1995, it has an AAA of $4,000 and AEP of $6,000. In its fiscal year ended May 31, 1996, it has taxable income of $3,000. It makes the following distributions to its sole shareholder:

Date	*Amount*
11/1/95	$ 8,000
4/15/96	2,000
	$10,000

AAA is only $7,000, after the May 1996 income adjustment. There have been distributions of AEP. The AAA is 70% of the total distributions, so 70% of each distribution is from the AAA. The proper accounting would be:

Date	*AAA*	*AEP*	*Total*
11/1/95	$5,600	$2,400	$ 8,000
4/15/96	1,400	600	2,000
	$7,000	$3,000	$10,000

At the end of fiscal 1996, the corporation's tax basis balance sheet would show the following accounts:

AAA	$ 0
AEP	$3,000

As discussed below, the dividend distributions must be reported according to the calendar year of distribution. When an S corporation uses a fiscal year, the corporation may not be able to determine the amount of dividend distribution until it closes its books for the fiscal year. This will undoubtedly result in delinquent information returns of the corporation and amended returns for the shareholders.

720.16. Year in which a shareholder's interest terminates. The election to split the tax year when a shareholder terminates his or her entire interest was discussed in Chapter 6. This election can have some interesting side effects on the distributions made in one of these years, and thus can even affect continuing shareholders. If the corporation elects to treat the year as two separate accounting periods, the corporation must calculate its AAA at the end of each of the short periods. [Regs. §1.1368-2(e), Regulations §1.1368-3, Example 3]

EXAMPLE 7 - 22: ALW Corporation is an S corporation with $25,000 in its AAA and $30,000 of AEP at the beginning of 1996. At the beginning of the year, shareholders A and L each own 50% of the outstanding stock. On May 26, L sells all of his shares to W. The S election remains in effect. The corporation shows the following income and loss for the year, all of which is ordinary:

Dates	*Amount*
1/1–5/26	$(15,000)
5/27–12/31	75,000
Total for entire year	$ 60,000

On March 31, it distributed $20,000 to each shareholder. It made no other distribution during 1996. If the corporation does not elect to cut off its accounting period on May 26, the accounting for the distributions will be:

Beginning AAA balance	$25,000
Income through December 31	60,000
AAA before distributions	85,000
Less distributions (all from AAA)	(40,000)
Final AAA	$45,000

The distribution is treated as a return of capital and a reduction of basis by both A and L. The corporation—with the consent of A, L, and W—may elect to split the year into two accounting periods. If it does so, the distribution would be made in the first short period. The consequences would be:

Beginning AAA balance	$25,000
Income through May 26	(15,000)
AAA before distributions	10,000
Less distributions (from AAA)	(10,000)
Final AAA (5/26)	$ 0

Allocation of distributions:

	Source		
Shareholder	*AAA*	*AEP*	*Total*
A	$ 5,000	$15,000	$20,000
L	5,000	15,000	20,000
Total	$10,000	$30,000	$40,000

Each shareholder would report $15,000 of dividend income and reduce his basis by $5,000.

Assume that shareholder L had basis of $30,000 at the beginning of the year and sold his shares for $50,000. The tax treatment of his entire transactions with the corporation, including the sale, would be:

	Without §1377(a)(2) Election		*With §1377(a)(2) Election*	
Income from corporation		$12,000[a]		$ (7,500)[b]
Dividend		0		15,000
Realized on sale		50,000		50,000
Basis, beginning	$30,000		$30,000	
Income or loss	12,000		(7,500)	
Less distribution	(20,000)		(5,000)	
Basis at sale	$22,000	(22,000)	$17,500	(17,500)
Total for year		$40,000		$40,000

[a] $60,000 x .5 x .4

[b] $(15,000) x .5

Note that there is no difference, under either option, between the total income and the gain realized by L in the taxable year. There could be a difference in the taxability of capital gain and ordinary income, depending on the circumstances of L and the congressional treatment of capital gains. There could, however, be a significant difference to the other shareholders.

	Without §1377(a)(2) Election		*With §1377(a)(2) Election*	
	A	*W*	*A*	*W*
Income from corporation	$30,000	$18,000[a]	$30,000	$37,500[b]
Dividend	0	0	15,000	0
Total income	$30,000	$18,000	$45,000	$37,500

[a] $60,000 x .5 x .6

[b] $75,000 x .5

Total income and gain to all three shareholders:

Shareholder	*Without §1377(a)(2) Election*	*With §1377(a)(2) Election*
A	$30,000	$ 45,000
L	40,000	40,000
W	18,000	37,500
Total	$88,000	$122,500

The rules discussed in this chapter are limited to situations that do not involve stock redemptions, complete liquidations, or tax-free reorganizations. The special accounting rules for those transactions are discussed in later chapters.

720.17. Significance of negative AAA. If a corporation has negative AAA and positive AEP, there could be some unpleasant surprises. If the corporation is profitable in the current year, the shareholders will not be able to receive distributions, except for taxable dividends, until the AAA has a cumulative positive balance.

EXAMPLE 7-23: Rundown, Inc., is an S corporation with AEP of $200,000. At the beginning of 1997, Rundown's AAA was negative $300,000. In early 1997, Ms. Rainmaker purchased all of Rundown's stock. Rundown reported $160,000 of taxable income in 1997. If the corporation were to make no distribution in 1997, the negative AAA would be reduced to $140,000. Ms. Rainmaker is liable for tax on Rundown's $160,000 taxable income. If she attempts to take any distributions from Rundown, the distributions would be characterized as dividends. Thus, in order to compensate for her taxes, Ms. Rainmaker would need to take sufficient distributions to cover the tax on the $150,000 and the tax on the distributions.

720.2. Distributions from AEP. Distributions come from AEP after the AAA is exhausted.[5] Earnings and profits may have been generated only in a year prior to the S election, or in Subchapter S years 1958 through 1982. Accumulations under old Subchapter S, before 1983, are treated as earnings and profits if distributed in 1996 or an earlier year. After 1996, they are eliminated. [Small Business Job Protection Act of 1996, §1311] Currently, an S corporation may acquire earnings and profits only if it emerges as the survivor in a tax-free reorganization with a C corporation and the mergee had AEP. [§381(c)(2)] See discussion in Chapter 17.

AEP may be reduced in several ways while the S election is in effect:

- If the corporation pays a dividend during an S year [§301(c)(1), §1371(c)(3)]
- Proportionately, if a stock redemption is treated as a sale or an exchange during an S year or a C year [§312(n)(7), §1371(c)(2)] (See Chapter 15.)

---

[5] If any of the shareholders has a PTI account, explained below, PTI is sandwiched between AAA and AEP.

- By payment of investment tax credit recapture tax by the corporation during a post-1982 S year [§1371(d)(3)] (See Chapter 11.)
- By adjustment of a prior year's corporate income tax during a year in which an S election is in effect[6] [§1368(e)(1)(A)]

The effect of treating such distributions as dividends is to put the corporation in the same position it would have been in if dividends were paid before S status was elected.

EXAMPLE 7 - 24: N Corporation was a C corporation through 1996 and had AEP of $14,000 as of December 31, 1996. In 1997, it makes an S election. As of January 1, 1997, its sole shareholder's stock basis is $35,000. In 1997 it has tax-exempt income of $3,000 and taxable income of $18,000. It distributes $22,000 to its shareholder in 1997. The effects of the 1997 activities on the corporation and the shareholder are:

	Shareholder		*Corporation*	
Item	*Basis*	*Taxable Income*	*AAA*	*AEP*
Beginning balance	$35,000	$ 0	$ 0	$14,000
Taxable income	18,000	18,000	18,000	0
Exempt income	3,000	0	0	0
Balance before distributions	56,000	18,000	18,000	14,000
Distributions:				
From AAA	(18,000)	0	(18,000)	0
From AEP	0	4,000	0	(4,000)
Final balance	$38,000	$22,000	$ 0	$10,000

There are no rules in Subchapter S for distribution of AEP. Subchapter C provides the ground rules, all of which predate Subchapter S. Distributions from AEP are allocated in order of the distributions made during the corporation's tax year (FIFO ordering rule). [Regs. §1.316-2(b)] The Regulations under §1368 create two layers of AEP for any corporation that has both Subchapter C AEP and Subchapter S AEP. [Regs. §1.1368-1(f)(2)(iii)] Any distribution of AEP is treated as coming first from Subchapter C AEP.

EXAMPLE 7 - 25: G Corporation was formed in 1988, and it accumulated $3,000 of earnings and profits through 1990. In 1991, it made a Subchapter S election. In 1991 and 1992, it accumulated $1,400 of earnings and profits. From 1993 through 1997, it generated an AAA (before 1997 distributions) of $4,500. In 1997, it paid its sole shareholder a distribution of $6,000. The proper accounting for the distribution would be:

From AAA	$4,500
From AEP	
Accumulated 1991–1992 (Subchapter S AEP)	0
Accumulated 1988–1990 (Subchapter C AEP)	1,500
	$6,000

At the close of 1997, it has AEP of $2,900, $1,500 of which was accumulated between 1988 and 1990, when the S election was not in effect. The distinction between accumulated Subchapter C earnings and profits and accumulated Subchapter S earnings and profits becomes important for a corporation with passive investment income.

6 Code §1368(e)(1)(A) states that such an adjustment does not reduce the AAA. By inference, the corporation's taxable income in a C year is being finally determined, and the current earnings and profits for that year would be reduced.

7

720.3. Distributions in excess of AEP. Distributions in excess of the AAA and AEP are again subject to the same rules as distributions for corporations that have no AEP. This rule is actually redundant. At this point the corporation has no AEP, by definition. A distribution from any corporation with no earnings and profits is treated as a reduction of shareholder basis to the extent thereof, and as a gain from the sale of stock thereafter.[7] [§301(c)(2) and (3)]

Under normal circumstances, an S corporation would completely exhaust its AEP only once in its existence, since it will not generate any future earnings and profits while its S election is in effect. At this point the corporation will be subject to the rules for S corporations with no AEP. All distributions will reduce shareholder basis, to the extent thereof, with any excess being taxed as a gain from the sale of stock.

EXAMPLE 7 - 26: G Corporation has a zero AAA balance and AEP of $4,000 at the beginning of 1997. The sole shareholder, A, has a stock basis of $12,000. In 1997, G has taxable income of $15,000 and distributes $20,000. The distribution would be treated as follows:

7

From AAA	$15,000
From AEP	4,000
Excess	1,000
Total	$20,000

	Shareholder		*Corporation*	
Item	*Basis*	*Taxable Income*	*AAA*	*AEP*
Beginning balance	$12,000	$ 0	$ 0	$ 4,000
1997 taxable income	15,000	15,000	15,000	0
Balance before distribution	27,000	15,000	15,000	4,000
Distribution from AAA	(15,000)		(15,000)	
Distribution from AEP		4,000		(4,000)
Remaining distribution	(1,000)[a]	0	0	0
Ending balance	$11,000	$19,000	$ 0	$ 0

[a]To OAA, book retained earnings, or paid-in capital.

720.4. The Other Adjustments Account. Subchapter S provides no accounting rules for distributions that exceed AEP. Nor is there any statutory rule regarding the accounting treatment of tax-exempt income or related expenses, which cannot be posted to the AAA and cannot add to (or reduce) the S corporation's AEP. The IRS adopts the term *Other Adjustments Account* (OAA) to account for tax-exempt income and related expenses.

According to the IRS instructions, the OAA is reduced by distributions after AEP are exhausted. [Instructions to Form 1120S (1998, page 24)]

OBSERVATION: In and of itself, the OAA has no tax significance. Whereas AAA governs the maximum distributions available before dividend treatment, and AEP sets the maximum distributions that may be treated as dividends, the OAA does not provide any limit. Any corporation, with or without an OAA or an election in effect, that over-distributes its earnings and profits must report the distribution to the shareholders as a return of capital. The only governing factor at this point is the shareholder's basis in his or her stock.

[7] There is an exception in §301(c)(4), which relates to distributions of earnings that a corporation had accumulated before March 1, 1913. For obvious reasons, such distributions rarely occur.

725. Previously taxed income.

As discussed at 710., the accumulation rules for S corporations before the Subchapter S Revision Act of 1982 were considerably different from those in effect today. Such accumulations were posted to *previously taxed income* (PTI) accounts, many of which survived the transition from old Subchapter S to new Subchapter S. [§1379]

725.1. Creation of PTI. Under Subchapter S as it existed before 1983, corporate distributions were dividends, to the extent of current and AEP. If a Subchapter S corporation distributed less than its taxable income, each shareholder received a deemed dividend on the last day of the corporation's taxable year. This deemed dividend was assigned to an account called *undistributed taxable income* (UTI). Each shareholder's deemed dividend was included on his or her return as income received on the last day of the corporation's taxable year.

Distributions within $2^1/_2$ months after the end of the tax year were from UTI, if paid to the same shareholder to whom UTI was taxed. [§1375(f)] If the prior year's UTI was not distributed to the shareholders within $2^1/_2$ months, the balance in each shareholder's UTI account became PTI. Although PTI appeared as an equity account in the corporation's balance sheet, there was actually a separate PTI account for each shareholder. [Regs. §1.1375-4(e) (prior law)] 7

PTI was reduced by the shareholder's portion of corporate losses for years prior to 1983. [Regs. §1.1375-4(d) (prior law)] Although a negative PTI account affects a shareholder's basis, it has no other ramifications under current law. It is not affected by any item of corporate income or loss after 1982.

725.2. Distributions of PTI. The Subchapter S Revision Act of 1982 enacted a cryptic rule stating that any previously taxed income still in existence could be distributed under rules of prior law. Since the creation of PTI (as UTI) was a dividend to the shareholder, he or she would not be taxed on the withdrawal of PTI. It was a reduction of the shareholder's basis. (In rare cases, it was possible for a shareholder's PTI account to exceed the shareholder's basis. In this case, the distribution of PTI was a capital gain.)

Distributions of PTI were any distributions after current earnings and profits and before AEP. [Regs. §1.1375-4(d) (prior law)] The Subchapter S Revision Act of 1982 allowed S corporations to distribute PTI in post-1982 years, but neither the Subchapter S Revision Act of 1982 nor its legislative history provided any clearly defined operating rules. The sole reference to distributions of PTI under current law is §1379. [Transitional Rules on Enactment]

SUMMARY OF AUTHORITY: CODE SECTION 1379(c)

- S corporations that had accumulated taxable income under prior Subchapter S are allowed to distribute those accumulations in post-1982 years.
- Current law states that old law shall govern the distributions.
- The old law referred to in §1379 placed PTI between current earnings and profits and AEP.

The transitional rule is, to say the least, vague. The old law required S corporations to compute current earnings and profits, which was the source of distributions before PTI. Under new Subchapter S, however, S corporations do not calculate current earnings and profits.

The IRS was forced to devise the rules, which first appeared on the 1983 Form 1120S and have not been changed. Under current law, PTI is distributed after AAA. If AAA is zero or negative, PTI is the first source of distributions for the tax year.

Distributions of PTI are made from the earliest distributions in the tax year, when total distributions exceed the AAA (FIFO accounting). [Regs. §1.1375-4(d) (prior law)]

EXAMPLE 7 - 27: K Corporation retains a fiscal year ending May 31 under the new law. As of May 31, 1996, it has an AAA of $4,000, PTI of $1,500, and AEP of $6,000. In its fiscal year ended May 31, 1997, it has taxable income of $3,000. It makes the following distributions to its sole shareholder:

Date	*Amount*
11/1/96	$ 8,000
4/15/97	2,000
	$10,000

AAA is only $7,000 after the May 1997 income adjustment. There have been distributions of AEP. The AAA is 70% of the total distributions, so 70% of each distribution is from the AAA. The first $1,500 of distributions in excess of AAA would be from PTI, and the remainder from AEP. The proper accounting would be:

Date	*AAA*	*PTI*	*AEP*	*Total*
11/1/96	$5,600	$1,500	$ 900	$ 8,000
4/15/97	1,400		600	2,000
	$7,000	$1,500	$1,500	$10,000

At the end of fiscal 1997, the corporation's tax basis balance sheet would show the following accounts:

AAA	$ 0
PTI	0
AEP	4,500

725.3. Peculiarities of PTI. As stated at 710., the distribution rules in existence before 1983 were some of the complications Congress sought to remedy in the new law. There are still major problems, however, for corporations that have PTI.

Under prior law, only cash distributions could come from PTI. The IRS now may allow property distributions to come from PTI.[8] Previously, each shareholder maintained a personal PTI account, and that particular shareholder was the only person who could withdraw the PTI. According to the IRS, this limitation is still in effect. Under prior law, PTI was extinguished upon the termination of the S election. The IRS is silent on this issue under present law. Further, it does not state that PTI may be withdrawn during the post-termination period discussed below.

EXAMPLE 7 - 28: V and E each own 50% of the stock in N Corporation, which has been an S corporation since 1980. Until 1994, shareholder V had owned all of N Corporation's stock. In 1991, N Corporation had undistributed taxable income of $6,000, which was not paid within the first $2^{1}/_{2}$ months of 1992 and had not been paid out as of the end of 1996. As of the end of 1992, the corporation had AEP of $8,000. From 1993 through 1996, it had generated an AAA of $12,000.

In 1997, N Corporation had taxable income of $15,000, and it distributed cash of $18,000 to each of the two shareholders. Before adjusting for any distributions, the equity accounts on N Corporation's balance sheet are:

AAA	$27,000
PTI (shareholder V)	6,000
AEP	8,000

[8] Instructions to Form 1120S (1998, page 25) have consistently allowed property distributions as reductions of PTI. However, the Regulations treat distributions of *money* that exceed AAA as reductions of PTI. See Regulations §1.1368-1(d)(2). The Regulations offer no explanation of this change in policy.

The distribution will be treated as follows:

	Treatment		
Source	*To V*	*To E*	*Total*
AAA	$13,500	$13,500	$27,000
PTI	4,500	0	4,500
AEP	0	4,500	4,500
Total	$18,000	$18,000	$36,000

The final balances of the equity accounts on N Corporation's balance sheet are:

AAA	$ 0
PTI (shareholder V)	1,500
AEP	3,500

Shareholder V reports no income as a result of the distributions, and she reduces stock basis by $18,000. Shareholder E reports $4,500 of dividend income from the distribution, and he reduces basis by $13,500. (Explaining to clients the divergent treatments of identical cash distributions to equal shareholders may present a challenge to the tax advisor.)

7

If the S election terminates, PTI may never again be distributed. [Regs. §1.1375-4(a) (prior law)] The corporation is now a C corporation. The Code and Regulations are silent on corporate accounting for PTI that can never be reached. PTI should not be closed to AEP. It was taxed as a constructive dividend out of current earnings and profits when it was created. Paid-in capital would seem to be the most appropriate placement, since PTI is, in substance, a dividend that was contributed back to the corporation. Similar treatment is afforded consent dividends. [Regs. §1.565-3(a)]

Thus, whenever a shareholder with a PTI account disposes of his or her entire interest, the corporation should make a journal entry removing that shareholder's PTI account from the books. A sample entry would be:

PTI, shareholder X	$xxx	
Paid-in capital		$xxx

In summary, PTI may still be withdrawn. Consistent with the rules of prior law, it is treated as a reduction of shareholder basis. If a shareholder's PTI account exceeds his or her basis, the distribution is taxable as a gain from the sale of stock. The consequences to a shareholder of a distribution from PTI are no different than the consequences of a distribution from AAA. Either classification results in reduction of basis and is taxable only if the total distributions for a taxable year exceed the shareholder's basis.

OBSERVATION: Before 1983, a distribution of noncash property could not reduce PTI, due to some unique quirks in the distribution rules in those years. In the early years after the Subchapter S Revision Act of 1982, the IRS took the position that cash and noncash distributions could reduce PTI. In the 1994 Regulations, the IRS inexplicably returned to the prior law rule that noncash distributions could not reduce PTI.

730. Property distributions.

Property distributions are subject to most of the cash distribution rules, with some additional complications. For property distributions, the rules of Subchapter S and Subchapter C combine. According to Subchapter S, distributions up to the AAA (or shareholder basis, if the corporation has no AEP) are returns of basis. When total distributions exceed basis, the remainder is a gain from the deemed sale of stock. If a property distribution combined with other distributions in the same taxable year exceeds the AAA, the distribution may be treated as a dividend (if the corporation has AEP). In these respects, a distribution of property is identical to a cash distribution. However, the rules of Subchapter C must be considered before a corporation makes a distribution of property. When an S corporation cancels a debt from a shareholder, the cancellation is treated as a property distribution. [*Haber*, 52 TC 255 (1969)]

Under old Subchapter S, property distributions were subject to entirely different rules than were cash distributions. [See Regs. §1.1373-1(d) (prior law)] Those rules were also completely different from the distribution scheme adopted by the Subchapter S Revision Act of 1982. Accordingly, the Regulations, rulings, and other pronouncements under old Subchapter S have no relevance to property distribution problems under new law.

730.1. C corporation property distribution rules. When a corporation distributes property in a nonliquidating distribution, it must determine its adjusted basis and the fair market value of the property. In some cases, the corporation realizes no gain or loss. For example, a corporation may distribute a note with an adequate stated rate of interest. It may also distribute stock in a transaction that fails to qualify as a tax-free stock dividend. In other cases, however, the fair market value and adjusted basis will usually be different. It is sometimes misstated that in 1986 Congress repealed the General Utilities rule [*General Utilities & Operating Co. v. Helvering*, 36-1 USTC 9012 (S.Ct.)], which permitted corporations to distribute property without recognition of gain or loss. Actually, Congress repealed only half of the General Utilities rule. Corporations that distribute appreciated property must recognize gains on such distributions as if the property had been sold "to the distributee." [§311(b)] This recognition provision does not cover property that has depreciated in value. Such distributions still come under the other half of the General Utilities rule. Corporations are not allowed to recognize losses on the distribution of property. [§311(a)]

When a C corporation distributes property, it reduces its earnings and profits (but not below zero) for the adjusted basis of the property distributed. If a corporation recognizes gain on the distribution of appreciated property, it steps up the basis immediately before the distribution, so that the basis is now fair market value.

730.2. Adaptations to S corporations. An S corporation follows the same gain recognition and loss nonrecognition rules on the distribution of property as does a C corporation. The incidence of taxation is shifted from the corporation to the shareholder, so that a recognized gain on the distribution of property is taxable in the same manner as any other gain. It is combined with the bottom line income or loss if the gain is ordinary income, and it is reported separately if it is a capital or §1231 gain. (See Chapter 8 on the possible treatment of an otherwise §1231 gain as ordinary income, due to the rules of §1239.) Since the gain is passed through to the shareholders, it increases the basis of all shareholders, and accordingly it increases the AAA.

Pursuant to the general rule regarding an S corporation's earnings and profits, the distribution of property will not reduce the corporation's earnings and profits, unless the fair market value of the property causes the total distributions for the taxable year to exceed the AAA.

730.3. Effects on the shareholders. A shareholder who receives a property distribution from a C corporation treats the fair market value of property as the amount distributed. [§301(b)] Subchapter S does not modify this rule. Under the language of §1368, a distribution to which §301 applies is treated as a reduction of basis, gain, or dividend as discussed at 715. and 720.

730.4. Distributions of gain property. When combined, the rules for distributions of appreciated property are exactly the same as if the corporation had sold the property to the shareholder for its fair market value, received cash as consideration, and then distributed the cash to the shareholder.[9]

EXAMPLE 7 - 29: D Corporation is an S corporation with one shareholder, A. At the beginning of 1996, A has a basis of $10,000 in her D stock. D has an AAA balance of $3,000 and AEP of $5,000. In 1996, D distributes property to A. The property had a basis to D of $8,000 and fair market value of $15,000. D made no other distributions in 1996. Its taxable income, exclusive of the distribution, was $3,000. The property distribution is treated as follows:

	Shareholder		*Corporation*	
Item	*Taxable Income*	*Basis*	*AAA*	*AEP*
Beginning balance		$10,000	$ 3,000	$ 5,000
1996 taxable income[a]	$10,000	10,000	10,000	0
Distribution[b]	2,000	(13,000)	(13,000)	(2,000)
Ending balance	$12,000	$ 7,000	$ 0	$ 3,000

[a] $3,000 ordinary income plus $7,000 gain on distribution.
[b] $13,000 from AAA, $2,000 dividend from AEP.

7

730.5. Distributions of loss property. No loss is recognized by a corporation on the distribution of economically depreciated property. [§311(a)]

Although the distribution of gain property is equivalent to a sale of the property followed by a distribution of the proceeds, a distribution of loss property yields much worse results than a sale of loss property.

Consider the following:

- A loss may be allowed to the corporation on the *sale* of property to a person who does not own more than 50% of the corporation's stock. [§267(a)(1)]
- On a *sale* of loss property to a shareholder, the shareholder may be able to use the loss disallowed to the corporation to reduce a gain on a later sale of property. [§267(d)]

Neither of these possible benefits is available on a *distribution* of loss property. Chapter 8 discusses the specific loss provisions on sales of property between S corporations and their shareholders.

A C corporation that distributes loss property must reduce its earnings and profits in the amount of the adjusted basis of the property distributed. An S corporation that has AEP would not be able to reduce earnings and profits for any portion of the distribution, including the disallowed loss. [§1371(c)(1)] Accordingly, the S corporation must reduce its AAA.

The Code provides reasonable, but not specific, guidance on the effect of a property distribution on the corporation's AAA. As discussed at 720.11, the AAA is defined by reference to shareholder basis adjustment, with limited exceptions. The shareholder distribution rules under §1368 are defined by reference to §301. [§1368(a)] Therefore, no reference is made, directly or indirectly, to the rules governing a corporation's earnings and profits for the treatment of the AAA in case of a property distribution. Since shareholders must account for all distributions from any C or S corporation at fair market value [§301(b)], the impact of the S corporation rules is that the shareholder who receives a distribution of property must reduce his or her basis in stock by the fair market value of the property received. Thus the corporation must reduce its AAA in the same amount as the shareholder's basis reduction—the fair market value of the property distributed.

[9] Distribution of securities resulted in gain, but not loss, to an S corporation. [PLR 8908016]

EXAMPLE 7 - 30: SharCo is an S corporation that owns some real estate with a fair market value of $150,000 and a basis of $250,000. SharCo distributes this property to Sharon, SharCo's 100% shareholder. Sharon's basis in SharCo is $280,000 before any effects of the distribution are considered. Additionally, SharCo has AAA of $200,000 and AEP of $500,000 before the distribution is considered.

The results of this transaction are as follows:

	Shareholder		*Corporation*	
Item	*Taxable Income*	*Basis*	*AAA*	*AEP*
Pre-distribution balance		$280,000	$200,000	$500,000
Distribution[a]	$0[b]	(150,000)[c]	(150,000)[c]	0
Ending balance	$0	$130,000	$ 50,000	$500,000

[a] The distribution is accounted for at fair market value pursuant to §301.

[b] None of the distribution is included in Sharon's taxable income, because it does not exceed the corporation's AAA or Sharon's stock basis.

[c] The disallowed loss of $100,000 does not reduce stock basis or AAA.

The Regulations offer limited, but reasonable, guidance on the distribution of loss property. The Regulations state that the corporation reduces its AAA by the fair market value of the property distributed. [Regs. §1.1368-2(c)(2)] This rule is equitable, in that it reduces the AAA by no more than the shareholder's new basis in the property distributed. It is overly constrained, however, in that it applies only when the corporation meets three criteria:

1. The corporation must have AEP at the end of the taxable year of the distribution. [Regs. §1.1368-2(c)(1), Regulations §1.1368-1(d)(2)]
2. The corporation must make both cash and property distributions in one taxable year. [Regs. §1.1368-2(c)]
3. The distribution of money and property must exceed the corporation's AAA, which would *otherwise* be properly allocated to the distribution. [Regs. §1.1368-2(c)(1)(iii)] The Regulation offers no explanation on whether the fair market value or the adjusted basis of the property is used in this test.[10]

If any of these conditions is absent, the Regulations provide no guidance on the proper accounting at the corporate level. Similarly, the Regulations offer no accounting rules for the loss disallowed at the corporate level on the distribution of property to a shareholder. The loss is omitted from the list of items for which the shareholder must reduce basis. (See Regulations §1.1367-1(e), discussed in Chapter 6 at 630.63. and 630.64.)

OBSERVATION: The Regulations could clarify distributions of loss property merely by stating that the corporation reduces the AAA by the fair market value of the property distributed. Any loss disallowed by reason of §311(a) should be posted to the Other Adjustments Account.

PLANNING TIP: In most circumstances, a distribution of loss property to a shareholder yields extremely poor tax results. The shareholder receives a step down in basis, whereas the corporation may not recognize any loss. If the parties were to structure the transaction as a sale, the shareholder would at least be able to benefit from the corporation's disallowed loss on a later sale of the property. See Chapter 8, at 835.1.

The Regulations are completely silent as to the treatment of a distribution of loss property when the corporation makes a bypass or deemed dividend election to rid itself of its earnings and profits. However, see 740.4. for discussion of a private letter ruling that provides sensible guidance on this problem.

---

[10] The term *otherwise* refers to an undefined situation.

730.6. Other problems related to property distributions. When there are two or more shareholders, there are some additional considerations for property distributions. First, the corporation should take care in measuring the value of property distributed. If the values of all distributions, per share, are not equal, the corporation could run the risk of having a second class of stock. (See the discussion of nonconforming distributions in Chapter 2. For a related topic, see the discussion of constructive distributions in Chapter 8.)

When a corporation distributes gain property, there is no method to allocate the gain recognized except on a per-share, per-day basis. Thus, even though only the receiving shareholder gets the fair market value basis in the distributed property, all shareholders will be allocated portions of the recognized gain. These rules make it extremely important that the corporation take great care to properly value the distributed property and to adequately compensate other shareholders in distributions that are proportionate.

EXAMPLE 7 - 31: G Corporation has two shareholders. One owns 30% of the stock and the other owns 70%. In 1997, G distributes $3,000 cash to the 30% shareholder and property valued at $7,000 to the 70% shareholder. Shortly thereafter, the 70% shareholder sells the property for $45,000. Based on the facts and circumstances, the distributions were disproportionate with respect to the stock. The consequences could be:

1. On the date of the distribution, there were two classes of stock.
2. The S election was terminated as of the date of the distribution.
3. Gain was recognized to the resulting C corporation, which created taxable income and current earnings and profits.
4. The distribution was a dividend to both shareholders, included in full in gross income.
5. The corporation is liable for corporate income taxes.

If the property distribution occurs in the same year that a shareholder terminates his or her interest, there may be some unforeseen consequences.

EXAMPLE 7 - 32: C held all of the stock in H Corporation from January 1 through December 9, 1997. On December 9, C sold all of his stock to E. As of that date, the corporation was very close to zero taxable income for the year. It had made no distributions of cash or property.

At the time of sale, H held the following two properties:

Description	*Basis*	*FMV*
Inventory	$10,000	$90,000
Securities	$85,000	$ 5,000

When C sold the H Corporation stock, he had a basis of $95,000, which was also its fair market value. He believed that he would have no recognized gain or loss on the sale.

On December 30, E causes the corporation to distribute all of the inventory, which results in the recognition of $80,000 of ordinary income. Under the general allocation rule, the income would be allocated as follows:

To C [(343/365) x 80,000]	$ 75,179
To E [(22/365) x 80,000]	4,821
	$ 80,000

Results:		
E's basis in inventory		$ 90,000
E's basis in stock:		
Purchase price	$ 95,000	
Income to E	4,821	
Less distribution	$(90,000)	$ 9,821

C's final basis in stock:		
Basis before adjustment	$ 95,000	
Income to C	75,179	$170,179
Amount realized on sale		(95,000)
C's capital loss on sale		$ 75,179

If the corporation filed an S election under §1377(a)(2) to use separate accounting periods, all of the $80,000 income on the distribution would have been allocated to E, the purchaser. The seller would have had no gain or loss on the sale of his stock. However, if E had sold even one share of his stock to a new shareholder before year end, the new shareholder could invalidate the §1377(a)(2) election by refusing to consent.

After any gain is recognized, the property distribution is treated the same as a cash distribution. [§1368(a)] If distributions exceed AAA, then AAA is allocated proportionately to each distribution made during the year. [§1368(c)]

7

EXAMPLE 7 - 33: Refer to Example 7 - 32, and assume all of the same facts except that up to December 9, the date of sale, H Corporation had taxable income of $5,000. H Corporation had AEP of $5,000 and no AAA at the end of 1986. On December 8, the corporation distributed $5,000 (representing taxable income to date) to C. After December 9, the corporation had no taxable income, except for the gain caused by the distribution of inventory. The end results would be:

Calculation of corporation's taxable income:

Income to 12/9	$ 5,000
Income after 12/9	80,000
	$85,000

Calculation of AAA:

Beginning balance	$ 0
Add income	85,000
	$85,000

The distributions would be treated as follows:

Shareholder	*AAA*	*AEP*	*Other*	*Total*
C	$ 4,473[a]	$500	$ 37	$ 5,000
E	80,527[b]	0	9,473	90,000
	$85,000	$500	$9,500	$95,000

[a][(5/95) x 85,000]
[b][(90/95) x 85,000]

To add insult to injury, C received a $500 dividend in addition to his portion of the ordinary income realized by the corporation.

A former C corporation may be subject to the built-in gains tax or the tax on passive investment income, described in Chapters 11 and 12, respectively. A gain on distributed property may subject the corporation to one (or in some cases both) of these taxes. As murky as the rules are with respect to disallowed losses on property distributions alone (as discussed above), the potential confusion involved in determining the treatment of such distributions is compounded when a corporation is subject to the built-in gains tax in a year in which it distributes loss property.

730.7. Effect of property distributions on PTI. Distributions of property also affect previously taxed income. Under pre-1983 law, a distribution of property other than cash could not reduce PTI. Therefore, prior law is of little use in determining the effect of property distributions on PTI. The IRS could have used the language of §1379 to continue to prohibit property distributions from PTI. With the new rules requiring recognition of gains on property distributions (equivalent to a sale of the property followed by a distribution of the proceeds), the IRS apparently saw no policy objective in continuing the rules of prior law on this situation. (See, however, Regulations §1.1368-1(d)(2), which appears, without explanation, to permit only distributions of money to reduce PTI.) Under current IRS instructions, property and cash distributions reduce PTI. The gain on the distribution of property recognized by the corporation will create additional AAA, and not increase PTI, even if the distribution comes from PTI.

> **EXAMPLE 7 - 34:** In 1997, D Corporation's taxable income from routine operations is $5,000. It has no AAA at the start of the year, so its ending AAA balance, before distributions, is $5,000. Its sole shareholder, A, has a PTI account of $8,000. D distributes property with a basis and fair market value of $12,000. The distribution is a tax-free return of capital, with $5,000 from the AAA. It would seem reasonable to take $7,000 from PTI, although the Regulations do not expressly permit this result. A will take a basis of $12,000 in the property received.
>
> To be assured that this distribution would reduce PTI, the corporation should distribute $12,000 cash to the shareholder, who would then immediately use the $12,000 to purchase the property from the corporation. This could be a good strategy for a corporation considering termination of its S election.

7

Like cash distributions, a shareholder's PTI account comes between the AAA and AEP. All other rules regarding property distributions from PTI were discussed above under cash distributions from PTI, at 725.

735. Accounting and reporting of distributions.

Reporting of distributions on the S corporation's tax return has been a source of confusion for many tax professionals. From 1983 through 1989, the IRS required each S corporation to maintain book and tax schedules for the AAA and OAA. There was no reconciling schedule on Form 1120S; taxpayers were instructed to attach their own schedule explaining the differences. In 1990, the book AAA and OAA accounts were replaced with a single book retained earnings account. The 1990 and later Form 1120S provides Schedule M-1, for reconciliation of book and taxable income, including separately reported income items.

Schedule M-2 provides a worksheet for reconciling the beginning and ending tax balances for the Accumulated Adjustments Account, previously taxed income (in total), and the Other Adjustments Account. As long as an S corporation has no accumulated earnings and profits, M-2 should be a convenient tool for computing the balances of these accounts.

Schedule M-2 **Analysis of Accumulated Adjustments Account, Other Adjustments Account, and Shareholders' Undistributed Taxable Income Previously Taxed** (see page 24 of the instructions)

	(a) Accumulated adjustments account	**(b)** Other adjustments account	**(c)** Shareholders' undistributed taxable income previously taxed
1 Balance at beginning of tax year			
2 Ordinary income from page 1, line 21			
3 Other additions			
4 Loss from page 1, line 21	( )		
5 Other reductions	( )	( )	
6 Combine lines 1 through 5			
7 Distributions other than dividend distributions			
8 Balance at end of tax year. Subtract line 7 from line 6			

There is no place on Form 1120S (or on Form 1120 for C corporations) that requires disclosure of earnings and profits. Distributions from AEP are dividends, and they must be reported to the shareholders on Form 1099DIV on a calendar-year basis. They are also disclosed on each shareholder's Form 1120S, Schedule K-1.

Distributions from the Accumulated Adjustments Account, previously taxed income, and the Other Adjustments Account are reported to the shareholders on Form 1120S, Schedule K-1. Since Schedule K-1 is prepared concurrently with the remainder of Form 1120S, these distributions are reported on the basis of the corporation's fiscal year.

EXAMPLE 7 - 35: M Corporation has two equal shareholders, G and A. M uses the calendar year. At the beginning of 1996, M had AEP of $5,000 and a balance in AAA of $8,000. Shareholder G had a PTI balance of $4,000 and shareholder A had a PTI balance of $1,500. In 1996, the corporation had tax-exempt income of $2,000, capital gains of $3,000, and ordinary taxable income of $11,000. It made charitable contributions of $1,800 and distributed $13,000 to each shareholder. The corporation's equity accounts, before the distributions for the year, would have the following balances:

Account	*AAA*	*PTI*	*AEP*	*OAA*
Beginning	$ 8,000	$5,500	$5,000	$ 0
1996 items:				
Ordinary income	11,000	0	0	0
Exempt income	0	0	0	2,000
Capital gain	3,000	0	0	0
Contributions	(1,800)	0	0	0
Pre-distribution balance	$20,200	$5,500	$5,000	$ 2,000

The proper tax treatment of the distributions would be:

Shareholder	*AAA*	*PTI*	*AEP*	*Total*
G	$10,100	$2,900	$ 0	$13,000
A	10,100	1,500	1,400	13,000
	$20,200	$4,400	$1,400	$26,000

The corporation reports the distributions and account balances on Schedule M-2:

Schedule M-2 **Analysis of Accumulated Adjustments Account, Other Adjustments Account, and Shareholders' Undistributed Taxable Income Previously Taxed** (see page 24 of the instructions)

	(a) Accumulated adjustments account	(b) Other adjustments account	(c) Shareholders' undistributed taxable income previously taxed
1 Balance at beginning of tax year	8,000	0	5,500
2 Ordinary income from page 1, line 21	11,000		
3 Other additions	3,000	2,000	
4 Loss from page 1, line 21	( )		
5 Other reductions	(1,800)	( )	
6 Combine lines 1 through 5	20,000	2,000	5,500
7 Distributions other than dividend distributions	20,000		4,400
8 Balance at end of tax year. Subtract line 7 from line 6	0	2,000	1,100

Note that the dividend distribution of $1,400 to shareholder A does not appear on the Schedule M-2. It would be reported on Form 1099DIV. The other distributions would be reported to each shareholder on Schedule K-1.

The corporation's equity accounts, after the distributions for the year, would have the following balances:

Account	*AAA*	*PTI*	*AEP*	*OAA*
Pre-distribution balance	$20,200	$5,500	$5,000	$2,000
Less distributions	(20,200)	(4,400)	(1,400)	(0)
Final balance	$ 0	$1,100	$3,600	$2,000

740. Elections with respect to distributions.

There are two elections—commonly called *bypass* elections—that alter the normal sequence of distributions. Since AAA is the first source of distributions, and a distribution from AAA is tax-free to the shareholders, no election is necessary to secure favorable tax treatment for the first distributions in a taxable year. In most cases, S corporations and their shareholders would not want to depart from the normal sequence of distributions. Under some circumstances, however, the corporation or its shareholders may actually benefit from treating an S corporation's distributions as dividends. Dividends may be desirable if:

- The corporation faces passive income problems, as described in Chapter 12.
- A shareholder has excess investment interest, or expiring NOL carryforwards, and a dividend would be essentially tax-free.
- A shareholder is subject to the alternative minimum tax in the current year, and wants to accelerate income into the alternative minimum tax year because of the unusually low rates.

Avoiding the passive investment income problems is probably the most important reason for making the bypass election. Tax practitioners should be on the alert for other situations in which the bypass election would be beneficial, as described in the next three subsections.

740.1. Election to bypass AAA. With the consent of all shareholders who receive distributions during a taxable year, an S corporation may elect to distribute AEP before AAA. [§1368(e)(3)]

SUMMARY OF AUTHORITY: CODE SECTION 1368(E)(3)

- An S corporation may elect to bypass the AAA and instead treat AEP as the first source of distributions during the taxable year.
- The election is for one year at a time, and it does not affect any other taxable year.
- Any shareholder who receives a distribution during the taxable year must consent to the election to distribute earnings and profits before AAA.

The statute leaves open the possibility that not all shareholders will receive distributions during the taxable year. Ordinarily, if one shareholder receives a distribution, all other shareholders must receive a proportionate distribution, or the corporation may be treated as having a second class of stock. When shareholdings change hands, however, not all shareholders might receive distributions.

EXAMPLE 7-36: Jayco is an S corporation. At the beginning of 1997, all of its shares were owned by J, A, and Y. In June 1997, J sold all of his shares to K. The corporation made no distributions between January and July of 1997. In July, the corporation distributed cash to each shareholder in proportion to his or her stock ownership. K, A, and Y must consent if the corporation makes a bypass election. J need not consent, because he received no distributions in 1997.

7

The Regulations provide some additional guidance on the election to bypass AAA. They also deal with the election to bypass PTI, discussed at 740.2. For a corporation that has no PTI, the rules are straightforward. The corporation elects to treat its distributions as coming first from AEP. The election is binding on all shareholders who actually receive distributions from the corporation during the year. A corporation cannot set some arbitrary amount as a distribution from earnings and profits and limit the dividend treatment. [Regs. §1.1368-1(f)(2)(i); PLR 8935013]

EXAMPLE 7 - 37: Veeco is an S corporation with $300,000 AEP and $500,000 AAA at the beginning of 1996. Its sole shareholder, Virgil, has $200,000 investment interest that he could not otherwise deduct. He would like to withdraw $300,000 in 1996 and treat only $200,000 as a dividend. Section 1368(e)(3) would not allow him to segregate distributions between earnings and profits and AAA. If Veeco makes the bypass election, the first $300,000 of distributions will be dividends. If Veeco does not make the bypass election, the corporation cannot distribute any dividends until total distributions exceed $500,000, plus the corporation's income for 1996.

PLANNING TIP: The creative tax planner can find ways to limit the amount paid out as a dividend to less than the total AEP. Perhaps the simplest way is to make the bypass election and limit the total distributions to the desired level of dividends. The year-by-year nature of the bypass election is helpful in this regard. In the above example, for instance, any distribution made immediately before or immediately after the tax year for which the bypass election was effective would not be considered a dividend. Another alternative is to not make the bypass election and to overshoot the AAA by the desired amount of dividend income. In the example above, if the corporation had distributed all of its AAA, plus $200,000, and not made a bypass election, the dividend to the shareholder would have been $200,000. This strategy requires careful recordkeeping, so that the corporation has a close estimate of the annual adjustments to AAA before the year ends.

In many cases, the corporation would not want to limit the dividend distribution to less than the total AEP. Probably the most popular instance of the bypass election is to eliminate the corporation's earnings and profits completely—to avoid the corporate-level passive investment income tax and possibly to avert a termination of the S election if the S corporation has excessive passive investment income. (See Chapters 12 and 13 for further discussion of these problems.)

There is one other use of the bypass election that, though probably not relevant to many S corporations, can be a valuable source of tax planning for those to which it does apply. The corporations whose shareholders will benefit from the election are those in which shareholders still have a positive PTI balance.

The election under §1368(e)(3) refers only to the order of distributions under new law. Therefore, AEP are placed before the AAA. Under old law, a distribution of PTI was not a dividend. [prior §1375(d)(1)] Distributions were dividends from AEP only when the PTI account was exhausted. Since the election under §1368(e)(3) does not affect the ordering under prior law, PTI would come before AEP. Current §1379(c) preserves the old ordering when there is PTI present. Therefore, an election under §1368(e)(3) places PTI first in the hierarchy. [Regs. §1.1368-1(f)(2)(ii)] This situation can be beneficial when all of the current shareholders have PTI accounts and want to plan for a transfer of shares.

EXAMPLE 7 - 38: Alvin owns all of the shares of Alco, an S corporation. Alco has the following account balances:

AAA	$50,000
PTI	20,000
AEP	30,000

Alvin has decided to sell all of his shares to Beulah. Alvin will withdraw $50,000 from the corporation before he sells his shares. If Alco makes no election under §1368(e)(3), Alvin will exhaust the AAA. Beulah will not be able to receive any of Alvin's PTI, and her first source of distributions will be AEP. If Alco makes the election under §1368(e)(3), however, the distribution will be from Alvin's PTI account. The AAA will be left intact for Beulah.

Note, however, that the election to place AEP before AAA will be binding on both Alvin and Beulah for the year of sale. Beulah will not be able to withdraw any of the AAA until the year following the sale.

740.2. Election to bypass PTI. When an S corporation has PTI and needs to exhaust its AEP, the election under §1368(e)(3) is not sufficient to exhaust AEP. The S corporation must also make an election to distribute AEP before PTI. [Regs. §1.1368-1(f)(4)]

An election to distribute AEP before PTI continues from old Subchapter S. The election is filed with a timely Form 1120S for the tax year of the distributions. [Regs. §1.1375-4(c)] All shareholders must consent. When combined with an election to bypass AAA, this election will assure that the corporation may exhaust its AEP. It may also allow for equalization of tax treatment between shareholders.

7

EXAMPLE 7-39: Q Corporation has two shareholders, R and S. R had owned all of the shares until 1995, at which time he sold half of the shares to S. The two shareholders agreed that they will split any dividend distributions equally. As of the close of 1997, before accounting for 1997 distributions, Q has an AAA of $20,000, PTI (all belonging to R) of $15,000, and AEP of $30,000. Q distributes $15,000 to each shareholder in 1987. Without making the §1.1375-4(c) election to bypass PTI, the distributions would be:

Shareholder	*AAA*	*PTI*	*AEP*	*Total*
R	$10,000	$5,000	$ 0	$15,000
S	10,000	0	5,000	15,000
	$20,000	$5,000	$5,000	$30,000

Note that R would receive a $15,000 tax-free distribution, whereas S would receive a $10,000 tax-free distribution and a dividend of $5,000.

If the corporation elected to distribute AEP before AAA, all of the distributions in 1997 would be taxable to both the shareholders. If the corporation elected to distribute AEP before PTI (but after AAA), the results would be:

Shareholder	*AAA*	*PTI*	*AEP*	*Capital*	*Total*
R	$10,000	$0	$ 5,000	$0	$15,000
S	10,000	0	5,000	0	15,000
Total	$20,000	$0	$10,000	$0	$30,000

Each shareholder has received a tax-free distribution of $10,000 and a taxable distribution of $10,000. To achieve this result, the corporation would make an election to bypass PTI but would not make an election to bypass AAA.

740.3. Other aspects of the bypass elections. The elections should be attached to the corporation's return for the year, and consent should be signed under penalty of perjury by each shareholder and attached to the same return. [Regs. §1.1368-1(f)(5)] In one case, however, the IRS was lenient in allowing a corporation to make a bypass election without observing all of the procedures. A corporation made a defective election to distribute its AEP. The shareholders did report the distribution as dividend income, but the corporation failed to attach the required election statement under §1368(e)(3). In this situation, the corporation needed to exhaust all of its earnings and profits to avoid termination due to excessive passive investment income. (See Chapters 12 and 13.) The IRS held that the corporation had substantially complied with the statute, and allowed the defective bypass election. [PLR 8952047]

740.4. Relationships of noncash distributions to bypass elections. The bypass election can apply to noncash as well as cash distributions. The IRS has issued several letter rulings that have allowed S corporations to distribute notes and eliminate earnings and profits. [PLRs 8917025, 9003042, 9149030]

When a corporation distributes property and makes a bypass election, there is no clear guidance on the effect on its earnings and profits. If the property has appreciated, or its basis is exactly the same as its fair market value, the reduction should be the fair market value. If a corporation distributes property with a basis that exceeds its fair market value, the sensible result would be to reduce its earnings and profits by the basis of the property. This is the same treatment as for a C corporation that distributes depreciated property. [§312(a)(3)] The IRS has agreed with this result in a private letter ruling. [PLR 9221011]

EXAMPLE 7 - 40: KW Corporation has one shareholder, Kevin. KW is an S corporation that uses the calendar year. At the beginning of 1996, the corporation has $50,000 AEP. KW also owned land that had a basis of $50,000 and fair market value of $30,000. In 1996, with Kevin's consent, KW makes an election under §1368(e)(3) to distribute its AEP before its AAA. In 1996, KW distributes the land to Kevin. The *amount* of the distribution, which Kevin must include in his gross income, is $30,000, the fair market value of the property. The corporation, however, reduces its AEP by the property's adjusted basis of $50,000.

740.5. Deemed dividend election. There are no rules in the Code covering the deemed dividend election for S corporations, although there are statutory rules permitting the election for corporations with personal holding company or accumulated earnings tax problems. The Regulations, however, provide a deemed dividend election, which may be useful if an S corporation wants to eliminate its earnings and profits but has not made sufficient distributions to accomplish this objective.

An S corporation that makes a bypass election may also make a deemed dividend election. The election allows a corporation to be treated as if it distributed all of its Subchapter C earnings and profits on the last day of its taxable year. All persons who own shares on the last day of the corporation's taxable year must attach consent to the deemed dividend election (under penalties of perjury) and agree to consistent treatment on their own tax returns. [Regs. §1.1368-1(f)(2)(iii)]

EXAMPLE 7 - 41: Pasco, Inc., an S corporation, discovers that it had excessive passive investment income in calendar year 1997. It also had $5,000 accumulated earnings and profits at the end of 1997. If Pasco had made at least $5,000 of distributions in 1997, it could have made (with the consent of its shareholders) a bypass election to treat the first $5,000 as a dividend. It would avoid any passive investment income problems for 1997, since it would have no AEP at the end of the year. However, Pasco made no distributions during 1997. Therefore, apparently Pasco still had $5,000 AEP at the end of 1997.

With the consent of all of its shareholders, Pasco may make the deemed dividend election. The shareholders could agree to report $5,000 of dividend income on their 1997 tax returns, and thus rid Pasco of its AEP. The corporation and its shareholders would treat the deemed dividend as an actual distribution, followed by a contribution to capital.

The income reported by the shareholders under the deemed dividend election is limited to an S corporation's C corporation earnings and profits in years beginning before 1997. After 1996, the deemed dividend election will apply to all earnings and profits, since the old Subchapter S accumulated earnings and profits will have been eliminated. See Chapter 12 for further discussion.

EXAMPLE 7 - 42: Refer to Example 7 - 41. Assume that Pasco made no distributions in 1997 and that only $1,000 of the AEP were generated while the corporation was a C corporation. The remaining $4,000 was accumulated before 1983, when Pasco was an S corporation. Pasco could make a deemed dividend election of only $1,000 and rid itself of its passive investment income problems.

CAUTION: The deemed dividend election is available only for S corporation taxable years that begin after 1993. It is the only rule adopted by the January 1994 Regulations that is not a reasonable position for earlier taxable years. [Regs. §1.1368-4] The deemed dividend election was first introduced in the Proposed Regulations issued in June 1992. [Regs. §1.1368-1(f)(3)(i)] In several recent rulings, the IRS has permitted inadvertent termination relief for excessive passive investment income, if the corporation and its shareholders would make a deemed dividend election. Thus, in these situations the IRS has permitted deemed dividend elections for years beginning before 1994, in contrast to the general effective date of the deemed dividend election. [PLRs 9342034, 9342035, 9342036, 9342040]

The primary use of the deemed dividend election will most likely be to rid the corporation of its AEP, in order to avoid the passive investment income problems discussed in Chapter 12. However, there may be other uses for this election. For instance, it may be useful in a year in which the corporation has losses and the shareholder has insufficient basis to deduct the loss. The deemed dividend election will give the shareholders basis, in proportion to the dividend imputed on the last day of the taxable year, since it is treated as a contribution to capital. Thus the shareholder will have sufficient basis from the deemed dividend to offset losses that would otherwise be suspended.

The deemed dividend election may also be useful when shareholders have excess investment interest, which would be suspended under §163(d). The dividend income created by the deemed dividend election is treated as portfolio income, and it relaxes the limit on deductibility of investment interest. (See Chapter 10, at 1030., for further discussion of investment interest.) When a shareholder has both situations—losses in excess of basis and excess investment interest—the deemed dividend election may provide substantial tax savings.

EXAMPLE 7 - 43: Leo is the sole shareholder in Lecor, a calendar-year S corporation. At the end of 1997, Leo has no basis in stock or debts. Lecor has an ordinary loss of $30,000 for 1997. Lecor also has AEP of $25,000 from prior C corporation years. In addition, Leo has $15,000 of investment interest for 1997 and no investment income. Leo has received no distributions for Lecor in 1997. Absent a deemed dividend election, Leo will have no taxable income or loss from Lecor and will not be able to deduct his investment interest. The deemed dividend election would cause Leo to report $25,000 of dividend income. He would increase his year-end basis to $25,000 and would be able to deduct $25,000 of the corporation's loss. In addition, he would deduct $15,000 of investment interest. Thus the deemed dividend election creates a net $15,000 deduction for Leo in 1997.

740.6. Effect of election to split a taxable year. As discussed in Chapter 6, at 630.3. an S corporation may elect to treat a single year as two short years when a shareholder terminates his or her interest or disposes of a substantial portion of the corporation's stock. An election to terminate a year in this manner is disregarded for the bypass and deemed dividend elections. [Regs. §1.1368-1(f)(2)(i)] Accordingly, the corporation cannot make the election for one portion of the year and not for the other.

EXAMPLE 7 - 44: Kenneth Wick owned all of the shares in Richland, an S corporation, through October 10, 1996. On that date he sold all of his stock to Walter Wallace. Before October 10, 1996, Richland distributed $100,000 to Kenneth. After October 10, 1996, but before January 1, 1997, the corporation distributed $50,000 to Walter. The corporation elected to close its books on October 10, 1996.

Richland had AEP of $75,000 on December 31, 1995. If Richland made a bypass election for 1996, it could not separate the two portions of the year. Therefore, all of the dividend would go to Kenneth.

740.7. Revocation of a bypass election. The Code does not state that an election to bypass the AAA is irrevocable. [§1368(e)(3)] Similarly, the Final Regulations under old Subchapter S, which provided the election to distribute earnings and profits before PTI, did not state that the election was revocable. The Regulations state, however, that the elections (including elections to bypass PTI and make a deemed dividend) are irrevocable. [Regs. §1.1368-1(f)(5)] They offer no legislative history to support that position.

The IRS allows revocation of bypass elections, in limited circumstances. As discussed in Chapter 12, at 1200., the IRS issued new passive investment income regulations in 1992. The new rules are much more favorable to taxpayers than were the prior cases and rulings. Accordingly, S corporations that believed they had passive investment income can now determine that they did not. The new passive investment income Regulations were effective for all taxable years not closed by the statute of limitations. Therefore, S corporations were allowed to file amended returns in order to revoke bypass elections. [Regs. §1.1362-7]

In one situation, an S corporation believed that it would have excessive passive investment income from dealing in securities, so it wanted to distribute out all of its earnings and profits. Because it lacked sufficient funds to exhaust its earnings and profits, it made the distributions to the shareholders, who immediately contributed a large portion of the funds back to the corporation. When Regulations §1.1362-2 became final, the corporation discovered that its gross receipts would not be passive. (See Chapter 12, at 1200., for discussion of the retroactive effect of the 1992 Final Regulations under §1362.) Accordingly, it requested a ruling to allow it to revoke its bypass election. The IRS granted the revocation. [PLR 9312027. This ruling is also discussed in Chapter 12, at 1200.] In addition, the ruling allowed the corporation to limit its distribution to the amounts retained by the shareholders. Example 7-45 illustrates the principles involved in the ruling.[11]

EXAMPLE 7 - 45: Simmco was an S corporation with a March 31 fiscal year. Its principal source of income was derived from dealing in securities. For its taxable year ended March 31, 1996, it believed that its gains from dealing in securities would be passive investment income and would subject it to the passive investment income tax and possible eventual termination of its S election. Simmco's AEP were $100,000. It distributed $100,000 to its shareholders, who immediately contributed $90,000 to the corporation's capital. The shareholders reported the entire $100,000 as dividend income under the rules of §1368(e)(3).

In late 1996, after the IRS released Final Regulations §1.1362-2, Simmco determined that its income would not have been passive investment income. It requested permission to revoke the bypass election for its 1995 taxable year, and the IRS granted permission. The shareholders amended their 1995 returns to eliminate the dividend income. In addition, the IRS held that the shareholders had received distributions of only $10,000. The corporation's AAA and the shareholders' basis were reduced by only $10,000.

In a more recent ruling, the IRS refused to allow a corporation to rescind a dividend, although the IRS admitted that the corporation could revoke a bypass election. In this situation, the shareholders had withdrawn the money and had contributed it back to the corporation in a later year. The distribution was held to be a reduction of AAA, after revocation of the bypass election. [PLR 9341010]

OBSERVATION: The rulings described above were requested after the IRS issued Proposed Regulations §1.1368-1, but before it issued Final Regulations §1.1368-1, which states that the bypass election is irrevocable. The preamble to the Final Regula-

[11] The ruling does not state the dollar amounts or number of shareholders.

tions that included §1.1362-2, however, directed the IRS to allow revocation of the bypass election in connection with passive investment income problems. [57 FR 55445-01, page 6 (11/25/92)] The permission to revoke a bypass election appears to be limited to the passive investment income problem. The conflict between the two positions seems unwarranted. The Regulations regarding distributions would be more appropriate if they allowed revocation of a bypass election with the permission of the IRS, rather than flatly stating that such an election is irrevocable. When a corporation revokes a bypass election, solely because of the new passive investment income definitions, a ruling is not necessary. [See PLRs 9341010, 9342018.]

740.8. Treatment of a defective bypass election. A former C corporation adopted a resolution to bypass earnings and profits, believing that the accumulated earnings and profits were around $800,000. The corporation distributed over $2 million to shareholders, believing that part of it was from accumulated earnings and profits. The corporation never filed a proper election pursuant to the Regulations. The shareholders reported dividend income on their returns, but amended returns showed no dividend income and treated the distribution as being from the corporation's AAA. The IRS tried to force dividend income by asserting a doctrine of substantial compliance. The shareholders prevailed. [*Thurman*, TC Memo 1998-233, 52,767(M)]

745. Distributions during the post-termination transition period.

Cash distributions during the post-termination transition period will be deemed to come from the AAA, as it existed on the last day of the corporation's final year as an S corporation. [§1377(b)] Such distributions are tax-free returns of capital (or gains if they exceed a shareholder's basis). This treatment is limited to the corporation's balance in the AAA, and it does not extend to balances in PTI or the OAA. Note that Regulations provide that the pre-termination AAA can only be distributed to persons who were shareholders at the time of the termination. [Regs. §1.1377-2(b)]

This rule illustrates the importance of keeping careful track of the AAA balance for all S corporations, including those with no AEP. See Chapter 13 for a thorough discussion of the post-termination transition period.

750. Transitional rules from the Tax Reform Act of 1986.

A transitional election in the Tax Reform Act of 1986 required many S corporations to change their taxable years. [Tax Reform Act of 1986, §806] Thus, in 1987, there were two corporation taxable years ending in one shareholder year (see Chapter 6). Each shareholder was allowed to report the short-period income ratably over four years. Any shareholder may have elected to report both years' income in 1987. Although this four-year transition period has completely phased out of the law as of this writing, it is one of those rules that never completely disappears. A tax practitioner in any future year may need to evaluate the tax returns filed in these transitional years in order to determine the proper AAA balance, and possibly to determine a shareholder's basis. (See the 1996 and earlier editions of the *S Corporation Taxation Guide* for a detailed explanation of this rule.)

755. Summary flowcharts.

The following flowcharts summarize the distribution accounting rules. Figure 7 - 1 is for corporations with no AEP and corporations with AEP that do not elect to bypass AEP or PTI. Figure 7 - 2 is for corporations that have AEP and elect to bypass AAA but not PTI. Figure 7 - 3 is for corporations that have AEP and do make the election under §1368(e)(3) to distribute earnings and profits before the AAA and PTI.

7

Figure 7 - 1: Distribution sequence for corporation without AEP or corporation with AEP and no bypass election.

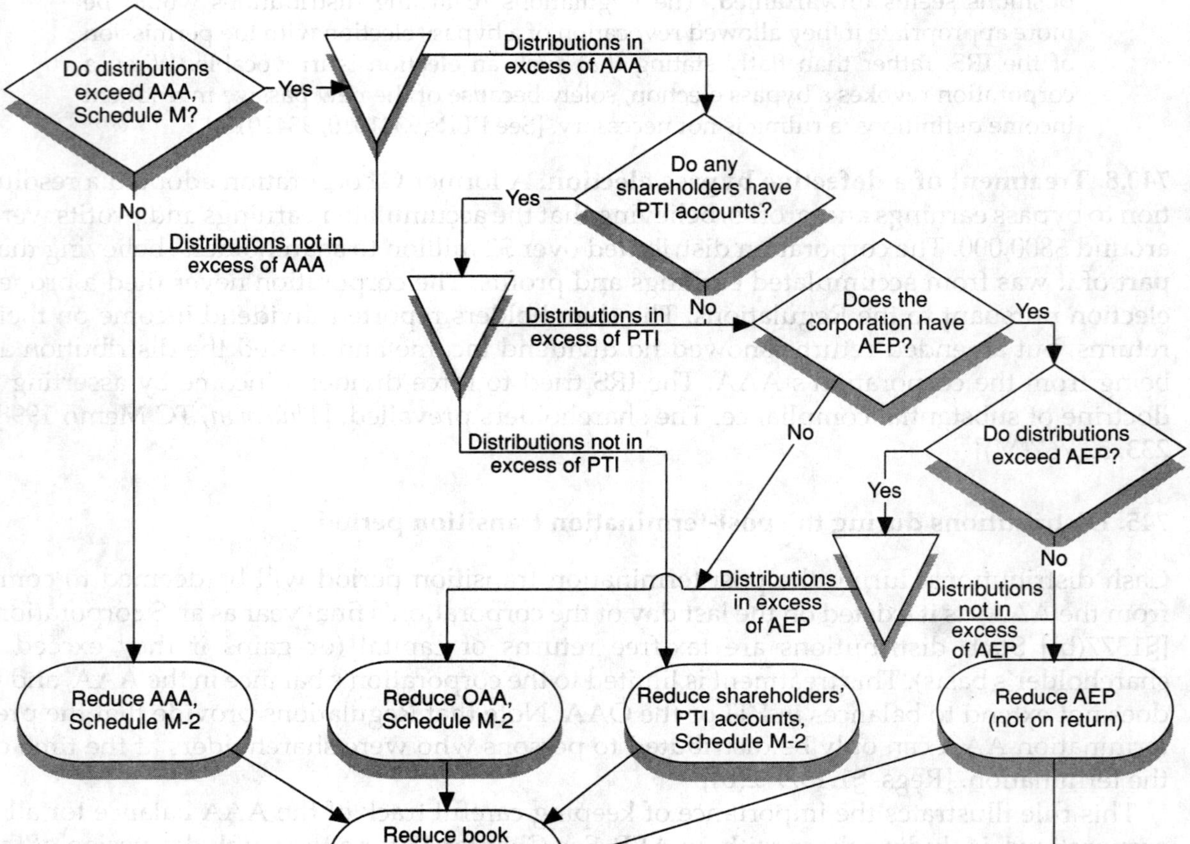

Figure 7 - 2: Distribution sequence with AAA bypass election.

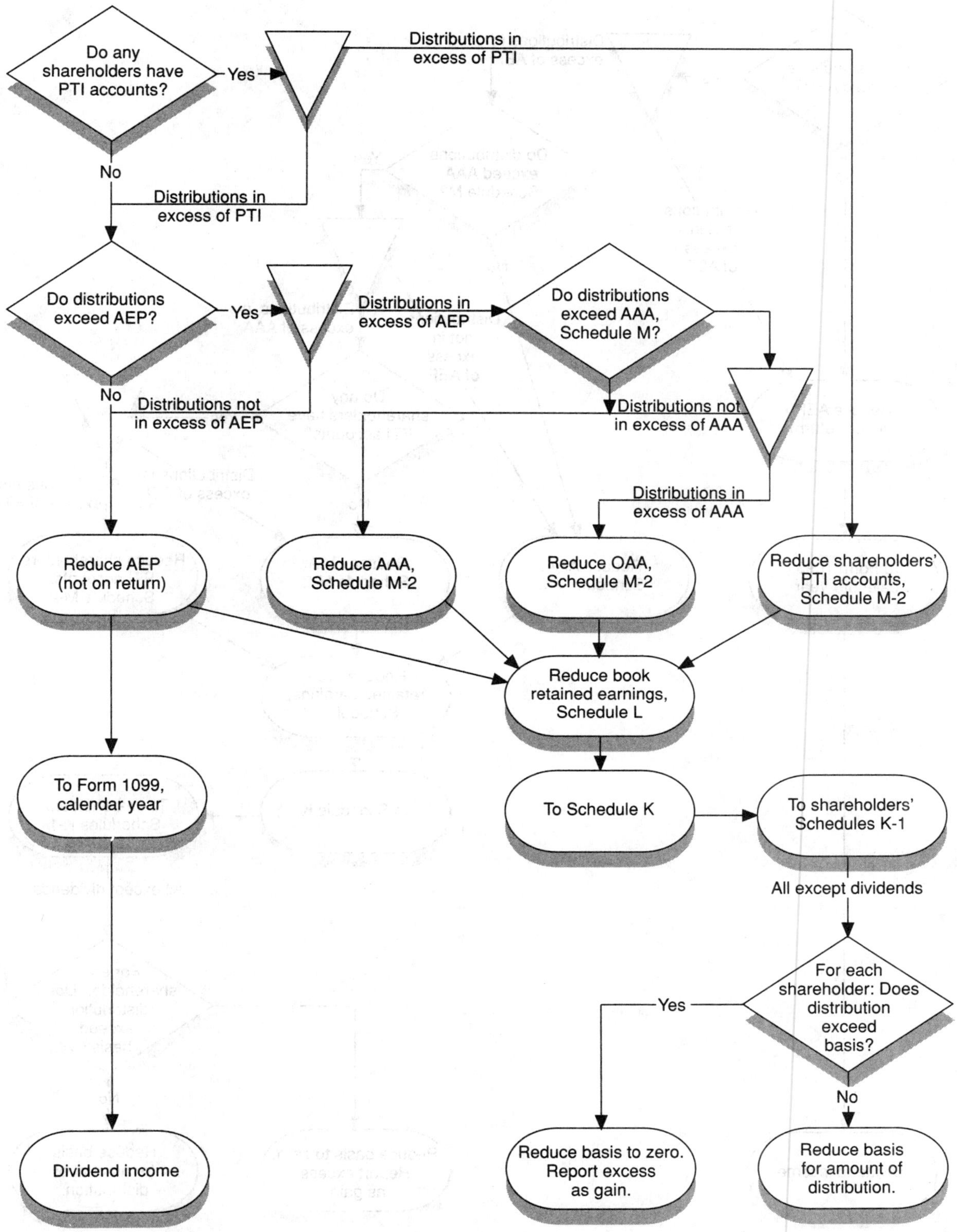

7

7

Figure 7 - 3: Distribution sequence with AAA and PTI bypass elections.

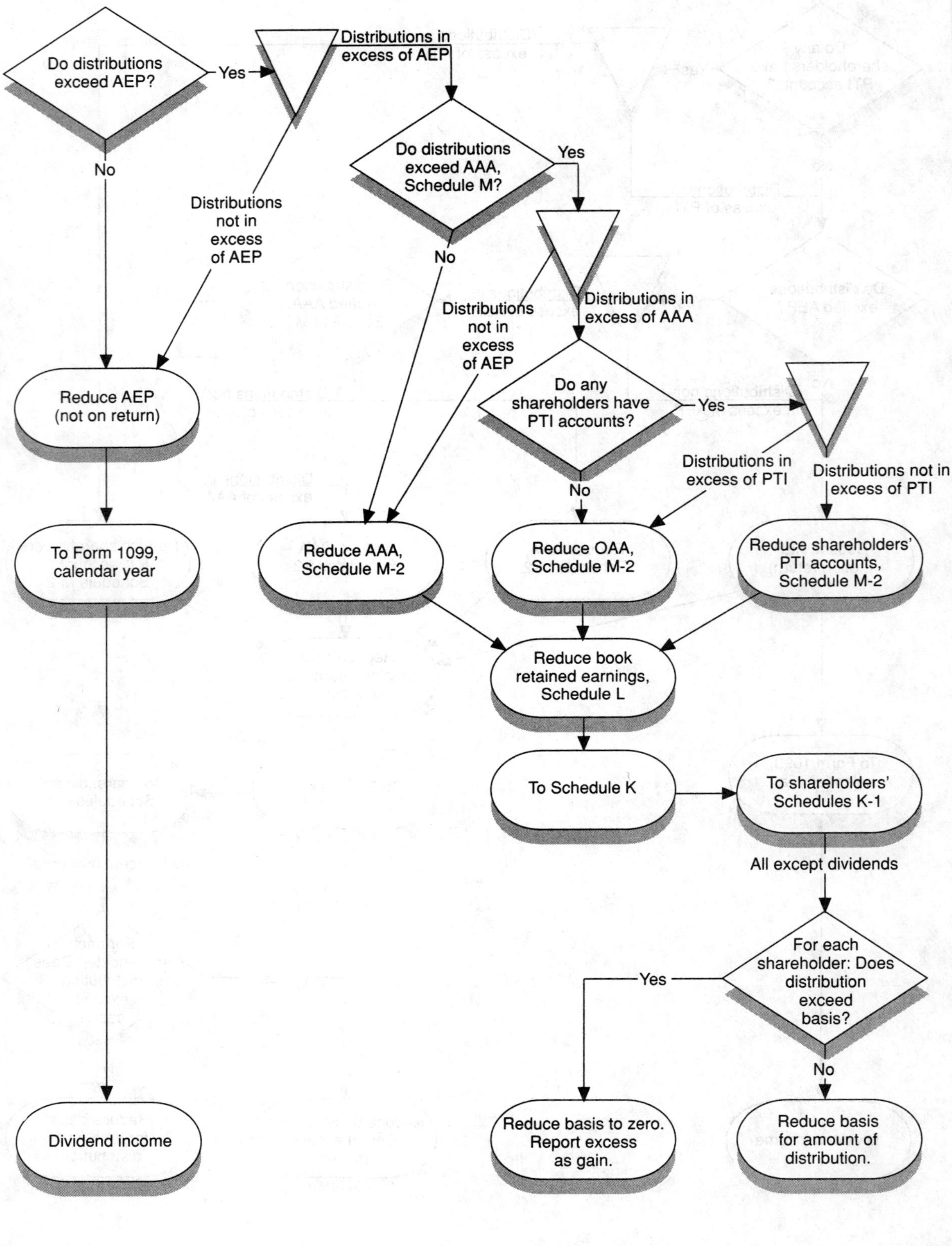

760. Practice aids.

A corporation that elects to distribute its AEP before its AAA must attach a statement to its Form 1120S for the taxable year of the distribution.

Sample Letter 7 - 1 contains a sample statement and shareholder consents for the AAA bypass election. Sample Letter 7 - 2 contains a sample statement and shareholder consents for the PTI bypass election. Sample Letter 7 - 3 contains a sample statement and shareholder consents for the deemed dividend election.

Worksheet 7-1 provides a means to analyze distributions at the corporate level. Worksheet 7-2 provides a similar analysis for a corporation that has an election in effect to bypass AAA, but no election to bypass PTI. Worksheet 7-3 provides a format for computations when a corporation has elections to bypass both AAA and PTI or a deemed dividend election. Worksheets 7-4 through 7-6 provide similar calculations for post-1996 years. In these years, it is necessary to know if there have been net income years or net loss years, under each of the possible scenarios. See discussion at 715.11., 715.12., and 715.13.

Also, see the basis worksheets in Chapter 9 for determination of basis and its effects on distributions to the shareholders.

Sample Letter 7 - 1: Election to distribute AEP before AAA

Election to distribute accumulated earnings and profits under
Internal Revenue Code §1368(e)(3)

[Company]
[FEIN]

[Company] elects to distribute its accumulated earnings and profits before its Accumulated Adjustments Account in its taxable year beginning January 1, 19XX, and ending December 31, 19XX.

Under penalties of perjury,

____
[Signature]
[Name]
President, [Company]

Under penalties of perjury, I consent to the election by [Company] to distribute its accumulated earnings and profits before its Accumulated Adjustments Account in its taxable year beginning January 1, 19XX, and ending December 31, 19XX.

____
[Signature]
[Name]
Shareholder, [Company]

Copyright © 2000 by Harcourt, Inc. All rights reserved.

Sample Letter 7 - 2: Election to distribute AEP before PTI

Election to distribute accumulated earnings and profits under Internal Revenue Code §1368(e)(3) and Regulations §1.1367-1(f)(2)(ii)

[Company]
[FEIN]

[Company] elects to distribute its accumulated earnings and profits before all shareholder's previously taxed income accounts in its taxable year beginning January 1, 19XX, and ending December 31, 19XX.

Under penalties of perjury,

[Signature]
[Name]
President, [Company]

7

Under penalties of perjury, I consent to the election by [Company] to distribute its accumulated earnings and profits before my previously taxed income Account in the corporation's taxable year beginning January 1, 19XX, and ending December 31, 19XX.

[Signature]
[Name]
Shareholder, [Company]

Sample Letter 7 - 3: Election to distribute deemed dividend

Election to distribute deemed dividend under Regulations §1.1367-1(f)(3)

[Company]
[FEIN]

[Company] elects to treat all of its Subchapter C accumulated earnings and profits as if they were distributed on the final day of its taxable year ended December 31, 19XX.

Under penalties of perjury,

[Signature]
[Name]
President, [Company]

Under penalties of perjury, I consent to the election by [Company] to treat its accumulated Subchapter C earnings and profits as if they were distributed on December 31, 19XX. I agree to report $[amount] on my form 1040 for the year ended December 31, 19XX, as dividend income.

[Signature]
[Name]
Shareholder, [Company]

Copyright © 2000 by Harcourt, Inc. All rights reserved.

Worksheet 7-1: Analysis of distributions by source

For years beginning before 1997
No bypass election in effect

1. Accumulated Adjustments Account
   a. Beginning balance $
   b. Add all taxable income items
   c. Add any increase (subtract any decrease) from tax-free reorganization (See Chapter 17.)
   d. Less all deductions and nondeductible expenses and losses ( )
   e. Maximum distributions from AAA
   f. Less distributions (not to exceed 1.e.) ( )
   g. Less allocated to stock redemption (See Chapter 15.) ( )
   h. Ending balance $ ______
2. Previously taxed income accounts
   a. Beginning balance (list separately for each shareholder) $
   b. Less distributions (list separately for each shareholder) ( )
   c. Ending balance $ ______
3. Accumulated earnings and profits
   a. Beginning balance $
      i. From Subchapter C years
      ii. From pre-1983 Subchapter S years
   b. Add any increase from tax-free reorganization (See Chapter 17.)
   c. Less any reduction for ITC recapture ( )
   d. Maximum distributions from AEP
   e. Less distributions ( )
   f. Less allocated to stock redemption (See Chapter 15.) ( )
   g. Ending balance $ ______
      i. From Subchapter C years
      ii. From pre-1983 Subchapter S years
4. Other Adjustments Account
   a. Beginning balance $
   b. Add exempt income items (CAUTION: See discussion at 715.11., if the corporation had income from cancellation of debt.)
   c. Add any increase (subtract any decrease) from tax-free reorganization (See Chapter 17.)
   d. Less nondeductible expenses connected with tax-exempt income ( )
   e. Maximum distributions from OAA
   f. Less distributions ( )
   g. Ending balance $ ______

7

Copyright © 2000 by Harcourt, Inc. All rights reserved.

7

Worksheet 7-2: Analysis of distributions by source

For years beginning before 1997
AAA bypass election in effect

1. Previously Taxed Income Accounts
   a. Beginning balance (list separately for each shareholder) — $
   b. Less distributions (list separately for each shareholder) — ( )
   c. Ending balance — $

2. Accumulated Earnings and Profits
   a. Beginning balance — $
      i. From Subchapter C years
      ii. From pre-1983 Subchapter S years
   b. Add any increase from tax-free reorganization (See Chapter 17.)
   c. Less any reduction for ITC recapture — ( )
   d. Maximum distributions from AEP
   e. Less distributions — ( )
   f. Less allocated to stock redemption (See Chapter 15.) — ( )
   g. Ending balance — $
      i. From Subchapter C years
      ii. From pre-1983 Subchapter S years

3. Accumulated Adjustments Account
   a. Beginning balance — $
   b. Add all taxable income items
   c. Add any increase from tax-free reorganization (See Chapter 17.)
   d. Less all deductions and nondeductible expenses and losses — ( )
   e. Maximum distributions from AAA
   f. Less distributions (not to exceed 3.e.)
   g. Less allocated to stock redemption (See Chapter 15.)
   h. Ending balance — $

4. Other Adjustments Account
   a. Beginning balance — $
   b. Add exempt income items (CAUTION: See discussion at 715.11., if the corporation had income from cancellation of debt.)
   c. Add any increase (subtract any decrease) from tax-free reorganization (See Chapter 17.)
   d. Less nondeductible expenses connected with tax-exempt income — ( )
   e. Maximum distributions from OAA
   f. Less distributions — ( )
   g. Ending balance — $

Copyright © 2000 by Harcourt, Inc. All rights reserved.

Worksheet 7-3: Analysis of distributions by source

For years beginning before 1997
AAA and PTI bypass election in effect or deemed dividend election in effect

1. Accumulated Earnings and Profits
   a. Beginning balance $
      i. From Subchapter C years
      ii. From pre-1983 Subchapter S years
   b. Add any increase (subtract any decrease) from tax-free reorganization (See Chapter 17.)
   c. Less any reduction for ITC recapture ( )
   d. Maximum distributions from AEP
   e. Less distributions (limit to a.i. for deemed dividend election) ( )
   f. Less allocated to stock redemption (See Chapter 15.) ( )
   g. Ending balance $ ________
      i. From Subchapter C years
      ii. From pre-1983 Subchapter S years
2. Accumulated Adjustments Account
   a. Beginning balance $
   b. Add all taxable income items
   c. Add any increase (subtract any decrease) from tax-free reorganization (See Chapter 17.)
   d. Less all deductions and nondeductible expenses and losses ( )
   e. Maximum distributions from AAA
   f. Less distributions (not to exceed 1.e.) ( )
   g. Less allocated to stock redemption (See Chapter 15.) ( )
   h. Ending balance $ ________
3. Previously Taxed Income Accounts
   a. Beginning balance (list separately for each shareholder) $
   b. Less distributions (list separately for each shareholder) ( )
   c. Ending balance $ ________
4. Other Adjustments Account
   a. Beginning balance $
   b. Add exempt income items (CAUTION: See discussion at 715.11., if the corporation had income from cancellation of debt.)
   c. Add any increase (subtract any decrease) from tax-free reorganization (See Chapter 17.)

7

Copyright © 2000 by Harcourt, Inc. All rights reserved.

d. Less nondeductible expenses connected with tax-exempt income ( )
e. Maximum distributions from AAA
f. Less distributions ( )
g. Ending balance $ ______

Worksheet 7-4: Analysis of distributions by source

For years beginning after 1996
No bypass election in effect

1. Accumulated Adjustments Account
   a. Beginning balance $
   b. Add all taxable income items
   c. Add any increase (subtract any decrease) from tax-free reorganization (See Chapter 17.)
   d. Less all deductions and nondeductible expenses and losses (not to exceed 1b) ( )
   e. Maximum distributions from AAA
   f. Less distributions ( )
   g. Net negative adjustment (excess, if any, of 1d over 1b)
   h. Less allocated to stock redemption (See Chapter 15.) ( )
   i. Ending balance $ ______
2. Previously taxed income accounts
   a. Beginning balance (list separately for each shareholder) $
   b. Less distributions (list separately for each shareholder) ( )
   c. Ending balance $ ______
3. Accumulated earnings and profits
   a. Beginning balance $
   b. Add any increase (subtract any decrease) from tax-free reorganization (See Chapter 17.)
   c. Less any reduction for ITC recapture ( )
   d. Maximum distributions from AEP
   e. Less distributions ( )
   f. Less allocated to stock redemption (See Chapter 15.) ( )
   g. Ending balance $ ______
4. Other Adjustments Account
   a. Beginning balance $
   b. Add exempt income items (CAUTION: See discussion at 715.11., if the corporation had income from cancellation of debt.)
   c. Add any increase (subtract any decrease) from tax-free reorganization (See Chapter 17.)

Copyright © 2000 by Harcourt, Inc. All rights reserved.

d. Less nondeductible expenses connected with tax-exempt income ( )
e. Maximum distributions from OAA
f. Less distributions ( )
g. Ending balance $ ______

Worksheet 7-5: Analysis of distributions by source

For years beginning after 1996;
AAA bypass election in effect

1. Previously Taxed Income Accounts
   a. Beginning balance (list separately for each shareholder) $
   b. Less distributions (list separately for each shareholder) ( )
   c. Ending balance $ ______
2. Accumulated Earnings and Profits
   a. Beginning balance $
   b. Add any increase (subtract any decrease) from tax-free reorganization (See Chapter 17.)
   c. Less any reduction for ITC recapture ( )
   d. Maximum distributions from AEP
   e. Less distributions ( )
   f. Less allocated to stock redemption (See Chapter 15.) ( )
   g. Ending balance $ ______
3. Accumulated Adjustments Account
   a. Beginning balance $
   b. Add all taxable income items
   c. Add any increase (subtract any decrease) from tax-free reorganization (See Chapter 17.)
   d. Less all deductions and nondeductible expenses and losses ( )
   e. Maximum distributions from AAA
   f. Less distributions (not to exceed 3.e.)
   g. Less allocated to stock redemption (See Chapter 15.)
   h. Ending balance $ ______
4. Other Adjustments Account
   a. Beginning balance $
   b. Add exempt income items (CAUTION: See discussion at 715.11., if the corporation had income from cancellation of debt.)
   c. Add any increase (subtract any decrease) from tax-free reorganization (See Chapter 17.)

7

Copyright © 2000 by Harcourt, Inc. All rights reserved.

d. Less nondeductible expenses connected with tax-exempt income ( )
e. Maximum distributions from OAA
f. Less distributions ( )
g. Ending balance $ ______

Worksheet 7-6: Analysis of distributions by source

For years beginning after 1996;
AAA and PTI bypass election in effect or deemed dividend election in effect

7

1. Accumulated Earnings and Profits
   a. Beginning balance $
   b. Add any increase (subtract any decrease) from tax-free reorganization (See Chapter 17.)
   c. Less any reduction for ITC recapture ( )
   d. Maximum distributions from AEP
   e. Less distributions ( )
   f. Less allocated to stock redemption (See Chapter 15.) ( )
   g. Ending balance $ ______
2. Accumulated Adjustments Account
   a. Beginning balance $
   b. Add all taxable income items
   c. Add any increase (subtract any decrease) from tax-free reorganization (See Chapter 17.)
   d. Less all deductions and nondeductible expenses and losses ( )
   e. Maximum distributions from AAA
   f. Less distributions (not to exceed 2.e.) ( )
   g. Net negative adjustment (excess, if any, of 2d over 2b)
   h. Less allocated to stock redemption (See Chapter 15.) ( )
   i. Ending balance $ ______
3. Previously Taxed Income Accounts
   a. Beginning balance (list separately for each shareholder) $
   b. Less distributions (list separately for each shareholder) ( )
   c. Ending balance $ ______
4. Other Adjustments Account
   a. Beginning balance $

Copyright © 2000 by Harcourt, Inc. All rights reserved.

b. Add exempt income items (CAUTION: See discussion at 715.11., if the corporation had income from cancellation of debt.)
c. Add any increase from tax-free reorganization (See Chapter 17.)
d. Less nondeductible expenses connected with tax-exempt income ( )
e. Maximum distributions from OAA
f. Less distributions ( )
g. Ending balance $ ______

7

Copyright © 2000 by Harcourt, Inc. All rights reserved.

CORPORATE–SHAREHOLDER TRANSACTIONS

Contents

8

800. Overview.

Chapter 6 dealt with the measurement and apportionment of the S corporation's taxable income and other items to the shareholders. Chapter 7 discussed the taxability of distributions to shareholders. These two concepts are the key factors in understanding the basic operations of S corporations. Chapter 8 expands the discussion of transactions between S corporations and their shareholders, beginning with a discussion of *constructive distributions*. These occur when a corporation pays excessive rent, interest, or salary to a shareholder. They may also occur when a shareholder receives a below-market loan or bargain use of corporate property. Perhaps the most serious potential problem is that when an S corporation has more than one shareholder, a constructive distribution may be viewed by the IRS as a second class of stock, which would terminate the S election.

There may be other transactions between an S corporation and its shareholders. Shareholders may "wear several hats," and have several economic relationships to closely held corporations. They may loan money to, borrow money from, sell or rent property to, buy or rent property from, and perform services as employees on behalf of, the corporate entity. The economic substance of these transactions may not vary significantly due to an S election. This chapter is concerned with the transactions that take place between an S corporation and its shareholders when the latter fulfill roles other than that of "shareholder."

Compensation of shareholder-employees is a major tax planning and compliance area for closely held corporations. Since the early years of the original Subchapter S, there have been some important issues that are unique to S corporations. An S corporation is truly separate from its employees, whether or not these employees are shareholders. A partner in a partnership is not an "employee" for federal income and employment tax purposes. However, a shareholder-employee of an S corporation, even a sole shareholder, is an employee for all purposes. A shareholder-employee receives compensation through wage or salary payments. These payments are not allocations of profits in the form of guaranteed payments. In form, the compensation of a shareholder-employee is the same for an S corporation as it is for a C corporation.

The unique characteristics of S corporations have led to some unusual tax problems in the shareholder compensation area. The IRS can challenge the reasonableness of compensation arrangements between any closely held corporation and its shareholders. In the context of a C corporation, the IRS frequently challenges the compensation as excessively high, and imputes constructive dividend treatment. This issue has arisen, and has been litigated, with respect to S corporations as well. The specific contexts, however, were the treatment of dividends (before the Subchapter S Revision Act of 1982) and the maximum tax on personal service income (before the Economic Recovery Tax Act of 1981). This second issue is not likely to appear in post-1981 years.

The reverse problem—unreasonably low compensation—is rarely, if ever, raised in the context of a C corporation; it has appeared in two circumstances with respect to S corporations:

1. A family S corporation in which one person has given stock to family members might be used to shift earned income from the primary earner to other family members. Both the 1958 and 1982 versions of Subchapter S have given the IRS the power to reallocate income to prevent this type of abuse.

2. There is no self-employment income of S corporations. Shareholders are not liable for any self-employment tax on their portions of an S corporation's profits. The corporation and its employees are subject, however, to all payroll-related taxes on compensation. The few cases and rulings on this point have arisen with respect to pre-1983 tax years, but they are still significant under current law.

Indirect compensation in the form of fringe benefits has some special rules for S corporations and their shareholders. The tax law is more permissive for C corporations than it is for S corporations. A shareholder in a C corporation can receive health insurance and other fringe benefit plans provided by the corporation without reporting the value of the benefit in gross income. A shareholder in an S corporation, however, must report the value of employer-provided health insurance in gross income. A *de minimis* rule excludes an employee who (actually and constructively) owns less than 2% of the corporation's stock. An awkwardly worded statute [§1372] has led to needless confusion, which has persisted due to the lack of any Regulations in this area. There are no reporting guidelines on the treatment of fringe benefits other than health insurance. This chapter suggests some alternative treatments.

Pension and profit-sharing plans are useful tax-saving devices for any taxpayer. There are few differences between plans maintained by S corporations and those established by C corporations. The most important difference is the general prohibition of plan loans to shareholders where the S corporation funds the retirement plan. In many closely held businesses, the protection of retirement plans is more important than the tax treatment of the business entity. S corporation shareholders and their tax advisors must be careful to observe the fiduciary requirements imposed on these plans.

8

The characteristics of S corporations pose some unusual problems in dealing with employee reimbursements. Changes made by the Tax Reform Act of 1986 and subsequent legislation have made the form of the treatment of employee business expenses as important as its substance. The divergent treatments of reimbursed and unreimbursed expenses necessitate careful planning and meticulous compliance.

Sales of property between S corporations and their shareholders are not subject to any special rules within Subchapter S. Since most S corporations are closely held, however, tax planners must deal with the rules governing sales of property between related parties. The flow-through aspect of S corporations, when coupled with the rules applicable to related party transactions, deserves special attention.

Shareholders may rent property to, or from, an S corporation, and there are many valid business and tax reasons for doing so. Unfortunately, the passive activity loss limits of §469 probably cannot be circumvented in this manner. Regulations issued to date (July 1998) and one as-yet-unissued Regulation may cause some serious tax traps. When taxpayers attempted to shift income from an S corporation to a sister C corporation via unreasonably high rental costs, the IRS was successful in limiting the deductions to reasonable amounts. [*Randy L. Wysong, et ux. v. Comm'r*, TC Memo 1998-128]

Loans between shareholders and S corporations also present peculiar problems. Perhaps the most significant is the effect on basis, to be discussed in Chapter 9. The analysis extends to the problems of "back-to-back" loans, where one party borrows money from a second party and lends, or contributes, the money to a third party. This chapter concentrates on the treatment of interest payments on such loans.

810. Constructive distributions.

A corporation may make a constructive distribution to a shareholder whenever it confers a benefit on the shareholder in his or her capacity as such. Probably the most frequent constructive distribution occurs when a C corporation makes some sort of payment to a controlling shareholder. Often the payment is classified as compensation, rent, or interest, all of which are deductible at the corporate level. However, the IRS may recharacterize the payment as a dividend distribution, which is not deductible to the corporation. Constructive distributions have been found in connection with the following types of transactions:

- Unreasonable compensation[1]
- Interest on a below-market loan[2]
- Forgiveness of shareholder debt[3]
- Payment of shareholder expense or debt (including personal travel and entertainment) [See *Gerald D. Handke*, 59 TCM 766, TC Memo 1990-273, for a case in which the shareholder of an S corporation was deemed to receive a constructive distribution under these circumstances. Also see *Old Colony Trust Co. v. CIR*, 1 USTC 408 (S.Ct.).]
- Bargain sale or lease of property to a shareholder (Regulations §1.301-2(j). Also see *Marcus W. Melvin*, 88 TC 63 (1987), for a constructive dividend due to a shareholder's personal use of a company car.)
- A transfer of corporate property to an escrow agent as consideration for a like-kind exchange, where the replacement property was deeded to the sole shareholder. [*Allen*, TC Memo 1993-612, 66 TCM 1690]

A corporation that is unable to avoid double taxation by making deductible payments to its shareholders is a good candidate for an S election. Under the single taxation model of Subchapter S, distributions of profits often have the same, or an even more advantageous, tax treatment for shareholders as do payments of other types. There are, however, reasons why the IRS might seek to reclassify a corporate expense as a constructive distribution:

- The S corporation may be subject to the tax on excess net passive income (Chapter 12), the tax on built-in gains (Chapter 11), or both. In these cases, a deductible corporate-level expense would reduce the corporate-level tax, but a distribution of profits would not reduce the tax.[4]
- The payments may be used to shift income to one shareholder at the expense of others. If the payment appears to circumvent the single-class-of-stock rule, the corporation may be found to have a second class of stock and the S election would be terminated.
- If an S corporation has significant accumulated earnings and profits (AEP) and little or no Accumulated Adjustments Account (AAA), payments of deductible expenses to shareholders may avoid dividend treatment.

EXAMPLE 8 - 1: Gavco is an S corporation that uses the calendar year. At the beginning of 1996, its AAA had a negative balance of $250,000. Gavco has AEP of $100,000. In 1996, its income before any bonus to the sole shareholder was $100,000. It had already paid the shareholder a salary of $60,000. If the corporation distributes $100,000, it will be a dividend, since the current year's income is insufficient to restore the AAA to a positive balance, even though the shareholder would include the $100,000 of corporate income in her taxable income for 1996. If Gavco pays $100,000 to its shareholder as compensation (or rent or interest), the corporation's taxable income will be zero. The shareholder will report the

---

[1] Regulations §1.162-8 describes the disallowance of excessive compensation. The relationship between the person being excessively compensated and the corporation claiming the deduction is usually that of a shareholder and a corporation controlled by that shareholder. Hence, it is logical to reclassify the excessive portion of the compensation as a distribution with respect to stock.

[2] The only reference to S corporations is found in Proposed Regulations §1.7872-4(d)(1), which states that when the corporation is the lender, foregone interest shall be treated "as a distribution of money (characterized according to section 301, or, in the case of an S corporation, section 1368) . . ."

[3] Regulations §1.301-1(m) states that cancellation of shareholder debt is a distribution of property. In the case of S corporations, §1368 takes precedence over §301 in defining the tax treatment of a distribution.

[4] As Chapters 11 and 12 demonstrate, an S corporation that is subject to one of these corporate-level taxes may employ the same tax strategies as a C corporation to minimize double taxation.

$100,000 as income, but she will not report any of the distribution as dividend income, and she will not report any flow-through income from the corporation. The advantages of a bonus can be illustrated as follows:

If the corporation does not pay a bonus, but distributes $100,000 to the shareholder, her income will be:

Salary	$ 60,000
Taxable income flowing through	100,000
Dividend income from distribution	100,000
Total taxable income	$260,000

If the corporation pays a bonus, but does not distribute $100,000 to the shareholder, her income will be:

Salary	$160,000
Taxable income flowing through	0
Dividend income from distribution	0
Total taxable income	$160,000

All of the constructive distribution cases concerning S corporations (at the date of this writing) were heard under Subchapter S as it existed before the Subchapter S Revision Act of 1982. They should, however, be valid precedents under the post-1982 law.

In several cases, the IRS tried to find a constructive dividend under the constructive receipt rule. Constructive receipt can occur when one party receives property with no substantial action. For instance, a sole shareholder in an S corporation may be able to receive a distribution merely by writing a check to himself or herself on the corporation's account, with no authorization or countersignature by an other party. In this situation, the IRS might argue that corporate funds were constructively received by the shareholder at the time they were deposited to the corporation's account. Under old Subchapter S, an actual distribution was dividend income when received by the shareholder. If the corporation did not distribute all of its taxable income, there was a deemed dividend on the last day of the corporation's taxable year. The IRS tried to use a constructive receipt argument to accelerate the dividend.

Various courts determined that the IRS could not use this logic to accelerate the timing of the deemed dividend that occurred under prior law on the last day of the S corporation's taxable year. [*McKelvy v. United States*, 73-1 USTC 9433 (Ct. Cl.); *Attebury v. U.S.*, 70-2 USTC 9538 (5th Cir.); *Estate of McWhorter*, 69 TC 650 (1978), aff'd 590 F.2d 340 (8th Cir. 1978)] These cases are not as important under new law since there is no longer a deemed dividend on the last day of the S corporation's taxable year, but they could be valuable defenses in certain situations.

EXAMPLE 8 - 2: Venco is an S corporation that uses a September 30 year end. Its sole shareholder uses the calendar year. At the end of the corporation's 1996 taxable year, the corporation has no AAA, but its accumulated earnings and profits exceeded $100,000. On October 1, 1996, the corporation distributed $100,000 to the shareholder. For the year ended September 30, 1997, the corporation had at least $100,000 AAA, before considering the effects of a distribution.

If the corporation had made the distribution one day earlier, the shareholder would have reported $100,000 of dividend income in her 1996 taxable year. By delaying the payment one day, however, the shareholder reports no income from the distribution in any year. The IRS might attempt to accelerate the distribution to September 30, 1996. The cases cited above, however, should give the shareholder substantial authority to prevail.

In one recent case, the Tax Court found that the payments of a shareholder's personal expenses were constructive dividends. [*Handke*, 59 TCM 766, TC Memo 1990-273] (The events occurred prior to 1983, when most distributions from S corporations were dividends.)

The taxpayer attempted to rely on the cases cited above, but the court limited the application of these cases on the basis of timing.

None of the constructive distribution cases dealt with a situation whereby the S corporation paid business expenses of a shareholder that were not related to the corporation's business. In general, in order to claim a deduction for a business expense, the payment must be made by the person claiming the deduction. In some cases, however, a taxpayer may claim a deduction for an expense paid by another person. [See *Lohrke*, 48 TC 679, 684-685 (1967).] The Tax Court confronted this situation when an S corporation had made payments of business expenses on behalf of its sole shareholder, and the corporation characterized the payments as loans to the shareholder. The IRS did not attempt to treat the loans as constructive distributions to the shareholder, but was not willing to allow the shareholder the deduction for the amount paid by the corporation. However, the Tax Court allowed the shareholder the deduction, as if the corporation had actually loaned the money to the shareholder and the shareholder had personally paid the expenses. [*Prewitt*, TC Memo 1995-487, 70 TCM (CCH) 962]

815. Expenses accrued to shareholders.

In general, a taxpayer (including an S corporation) that uses the accrual method of accounting deducts expenses when the liability for the expense is fixed and determinable in amount.[5] Even though an S corporation and its shareholders are considered to be separate entities, an S corporation cannot claim a deduction for an amount accrued to a shareholder until the day the shareholder takes the item into income.

This rule creates a disadvantage for S corporations, in comparison to most C corporations. A C corporation is prohibited from deducting accruals to shareholders who actually or constructively own more than 50% of the corporation's stock. [§267(a)(2) (See at 835.1. for discussion of the constructive ownership rules that govern such accruals.) An S corporation, however, may not deduct a payment to any person who actually or constructively owns any of the corporation's shares, until the day the shareholder takes the amount into income. [§267(e)] The same rule applies to personal service corporations. See Chapter 1 for a brief discussion of personal service corporations.

> **EXAMPLE 8 - 3:** ABC Corporation is a corporation with three equal shareholders, Alvin, Beulah, and Clyde. The three are unrelated, and all three use the cash method of accounting. The corporation uses the calendar year and the accrual method of accounting. On December 31, 1996, the corporation accrues bonuses to the three shareholders. The bonuses meet all of the other tests for deductibility.
>
> If the corporation is a C corporation, it may deduct the bonuses in 1996, since none of the shareholders owns more than 50% of the stock. If it is an S corporation, however, it cannot deduct the bonuses until it pays them to the shareholders.

In determining the constructive ownership of stock, the corporation must use the attribution rules of §267. These rules are discussed below, in connection with sales of property between an S corporation and its shareholders. It is important to point out that there are no *de minimis* rules for S corporation shareholders.

> **EXAMPLE 8 - 4:** West Corporation is an S corporation. Willie owns 90% of the stock. The remainder is owned by several of the employees. The corporation uses an August 31 natural business year end. It hires Tiffany, the daughter of one of the employees, as a summer

[5] Code §461(h) requires that the deduction may not be taken unless the economic performance for which the expense is incurred occurs within certain time periods.

employee in 1996. Tiffany's father owns one share of the corporation's stock. West hires many seasonal employees, and it accrues bonuses to all summer employees who work through August 31. Since Tiffany is a constructive owner of one share, the corporation may not deduct her bonus until she reports it as income.

This last example illustrates a special trap for fiscal-year S corporations. When an accrual is made to an actual shareholder, he or she will not get the benefit of the corporation's deduction until the taxable year in which the payment is made.

EXAMPLE 8 - 5: Baker is the sole shareholder of Roger Corporation, an S corporation that uses a June 30 natural business year. On June 30, 1996, Roger has accrued a $20,000 salary payment to Baker. It does not include the withholding or FICA tax payments in its Form 941 for the quarter ending June 30, 1996.

The corporation would have difficulty claiming the salary as a deduction for its year ended June 30, 1996, although it would be entitled to deduct the amount in its next tax year. Baker's share of Roger's income for the 1996 tax year would not be reduced for the salary payment. His gross income, however, would include the $20,000, since he received it in 1996.

OBSERVATION: A fiscal-year S corporation that accrues payments to significant shareholders is well advised to make the payments before the end of the taxable year of the accrual. It should take consistent positions on its payroll tax returns to substantiate the day that the shareholder is required to take the payment into income.

The limitation on accruals to shareholders is not limited to special payments, such as year-end bonuses. It applies equally to routine payments of salary, as well as to other payments such as rent or interest.

820. Direct compensation of shareholders.

Compensation of shareholders for services performed for an S corporation is subject to entirely different accounting rules than compensation of partners in partnerships. In a partnership, a partner cannot be an employee for federal tax purposes. Many local jurisdictions follow the same rule, and do not afford a partner the rights of employees for worker's compensation or unemployment insurance. If a partnership compensates a partner for services, it may structure the arrangement as a guaranteed payment, to ensure that the partner will receive some remuneration above his or her normal distributive share of profits.

A person who performs services for a corporation is an employee for federal tax purposes, as well as for most local employment statutes, even if the employee owns all of the stock in the corporation. For this treatment, it does not matter whether the employing corporation is a C corporation or an S corporation. The compensation is treated as wage or salary income to the employee and as a deduction to the corporation. The unique aspects of S corporations, however, create some planning opportunities and pitfalls for the shareholder-employee that are quite different from the problems faced by C corporations.

820.1. Employee status of shareholders. Shareholders are employees to the extent that they are compensated (reasonably) for services. Salary is income when received. [§451] Contrast this with the treatment of shares of income, which occur at the end of the corporation's taxable year. Salaries are subject to FICA, FUTA, etc., for withholding and employer payroll taxes. [§3121]

There is no self-employment income passing through from S corporations to shareholders for purposes of Keogh plans; nor is there self-employment tax. Code §1402 does not include a person's share of income from an S corporation as self-employment income. This rule has been in effect since 1958 and was unchanged by the Subchapter S Revision Act of 1982. [Rev. Rul. 59-221, 1959-1 CB 225; Rev. Rul. 66-327, 1966-2 CB 3547; PLR 8716060, *Durando*, 76 AFTR 2d 95-7464, 95-2 USTC 50,615 (9th. Cir.), (post-Subchapter S Revision Act of 1982)] Shareholders were not permitted to reduce self-employment income from other sources due to losses passing through from an S corporation. [*Ding*, TC Memo 1997-435]

PLANNING TIP: An S corporation may be attractive compared to an unincorporated enterprise because the earned income of a proprietorship or a partnership is taxable as self-employment income to the proprietor or partner. However, if the partner or proprietor has wage and salary income from other sources, a proprietorship or partnership may offer tax savings over an S corporation.

EXAMPLE 8 - 6: Nadine and Darrell are professors at the University of Utopia. They receive FICA salaries of $62,000 each from the University. They also have a consulting business that earns $60,000. The Social Security old-age tax ceiling is $8,400 for 1998.

If the business is incorporated, Nadine and Darrell should withdraw salaries of $30,000 each. The corporation would be liable for payroll and withholding tax on the entire amount of the salaries. Nadine and Darrell would receive a tax credit for overpayment of employee FICA, but there would be no relief for the corporation.

If the business were operated as a partnership, Nadine and Darrell could each receive a draw of $30,000. Their shares of partnership self-employment income would be $30,000 each. They would be exempt from at least part of the self-employment tax, however, since they each have wages subject to FICA in excess of the old-age tax ceiling. In this case the partnership offers an advantage.

OBSERVATION: An S corporation must treat at least some of its distributions to shareholders as compensation, if the shareholders are performing services for the corporation. See discussion below at 820.32. Beginning in 1994, the disadvantage of compensation in this situation is reduced. There is no ceiling on the portion of FICA or self-employment tax that covers Medicare.

On occasion, a payment from an S corporation may be self-employment income to the shareholder, although the usual classification of such a payment would be wage or salary payment. However, when the payments are clearly inconsistent with employee status, they may be classified as self-employment income. In one recent case, a shareholder who was blackmailing the corporation was required to treat the extortion payments as self-employment income. [*Parrish*, TC Memo 1997-474; aff'd *Parrish v. Comm'r*, CA-8, 99-1 USCT 50.293]

820.2. Excessive compensation problems. The Code allows deductions for compensation, but only to the extent to which the deduction is reasonable in amount. [§162(a)(1)] When the employer is a C corporation, the IRS's disallowance of excess compensation usually occurs when the recipient is a shareholder, and the compensation in excess of the deductible amount is usually treated as a dividend. The amount of reasonable compensation is inherently subjective, and it varies from case to case. There has been substantial litigation on this issue. One case that is often cited is *Mayson Manufacturing Co.* [*Mayson Manufacturing Co. v. Commissioner*, 49-2 USTC 9467 (6th Cir.)] The *Mayson* case lists several factors that may be used to assess the reasonableness of compensation. These factors include the following:

1. The employee's qualifications
2. The nature, extent, and scope of the employee's work
3. The size of the business
4. The complexities of the business

5. A comparison of the salaries with the employer's gross and net income
6. The prevailing general condition of the economy
7. A comparison of the salaries paid with dividends paid to the shareholders [Also see Rev. Rul. 79-8, 1979-1 CB 92.]
8. The salaries paid for similar positions in similar businesses
9. The salary policy of the corporation with respect to its employees, especially officers[6]
10. Compensation paid to employee in previous years (For example, a shareholder may have taken little or no salary during formative years when business was not profitable.)
11. Approval by the board of directors[7]

As discussed in Chapter 1, an S election reduces the risk that the IRS will disallow excessive compensation to a shareholder-employee. The rationale behind the advantage is that the shareholders report *all* their income from the corporation, either as wage or salary income, or as their share of the S corporation's profits. Therefore, classifying a shareholder's income as salary or as a share of the corporation's taxable income should make no difference.

8

In many cases this strategy works quite well, especially if a corporation is extremely profitable and is not able to avoid double taxation by paying all of its income to its shareholders as compensation. It would be erroneous to conclude, however, that an S election completely eliminates the risk of disallowance of compensation or completely neutralizes its effect. There are several instances, most importantly where the S corporation is subject to the built-in gains tax or the passive investment income tax, when it is beneficial to use compensation to drive the corporation's taxable income to zero. In such cases, the IRS could disallow compensation. To date, there are no cases on point that deal with S corporations for years after the Subchapter S Revision Act of 1982. There have been several cases decided under old Subchapter S in which the IRS was sustained in its attempts to limit the compensation deduction to a reasonable amount.

In *Estate of Wallace* [95 TC 37 (1990)], the Tax Court held that certain commissions and bonuses were excessive compensation and therefore were constructive distributions. The years under consideration were before the Economic Recovery Tax Act of 1981 and the Subchapter S Revision Act of 1982, and the motive of the service was to treat the income as unearned, in order to disallow the shareholder-employee the benefits of the maximum tax on personal service income, which was peculiar to prior law. This case does point out, however, that the IRS is still actively pursuing the classification of constructive distributions.

> **OBSERVATION:** If the IRS were to recharacterize excessive compensation as a distribution, the distribution would be made only to the shareholder who received the compensation. If there are other shareholders, the distribution would not be proportionate to all shares of stock. There is a remote possibility that this situation would create a second class of stock. Under Regulations §1.1361-1(l)(2)(i), an employment arrangement does not usually create a second class of stock, even if compensation is characterized as excessive. See Regulations §1.1361-1(l)(2)(v), Example 3.

Although excessive compensation occurs primarily when a shareholder is the direct recipient of salary, the doctrine can be applied to limit the deduction for compensation paid to other employees. In a recent case, excessive compensation to a family member of a sole shareholder was disallowed. [*Westbrook*, TC Memo 1993-634, 66 TCM 1823] In addition, the losses of the S corporation were disallowed as deductions under the hobby loss rules. The

---

[6] For example, are salaries determined in advance of the year? Are performance bonuses based on ascertainable standards? Do others receive bonuses based on the corporation's income?

[7] This may not be very helpful in a one-shareholder corporation, such as in *Radtke*.

son's personal return was not discussed in the case. It is quite likely, however, that the son was required to claim all of his salary, including the disallowed portion, as income on his personal return. Unless there was an Oswald clause (see at 820.34., below) in the employment agreement (which is unlikely given the facts of the case), the compensation arrangement would have worked to the tax detriment of the son, with no tax benefit to the parents.

Another recent case points out the importance of documentation of past services performed by a shareholder. A special bonus of $75,000 was challenged by the IRS but was upheld as reasonable compensation by the Tax Court. [*White's Ferry, Inc.*, TC Memo 1993-639, 66 TCM 1855]

> **PLANNING TIP:** An employment agreement such as the "Oswald clause," which specifies that an employee must repay any excessive compensation to the corporation, can be a valuable line of defense in case of IRS disallowance. At a minimum, it would allow the employee to claim a deduction for repayment. It could also avert a possible IRS claim that the excessive compensation was a binding agreement among the shareholders to alter the rights of certain shares and thus create a second class of stock. See Chapter 2, at 225.33. The corporation should also expand this agreement to cover any shareholder expenses that are paid or reimbursed by the corporation and are subsequently disallowed by the IRS.

820.3. Insufficient compensation. Unreasonably low compensation is an issue not often raised with C corporations.[8] It has been addressed in two S corporation contexts.

820.31. Family S corporations. Family income-shifting is one area addressed by the law. Section 1366(e) states that a family member who provides services or capital to the corporation should receive reasonable compensation, or the income of the corporation may be reallocated among the family members.

> **EXAMPLE 8 - 7:** Virgil is the sole shareholder of Virco Corporation, an S corporation. He has three college-age children and gives each of them 30% of the stock. He retains 10%. His stock votes, but the children's does not. In 1996, Virco Corporation has $300,000 taxable income. Virgil works full-time at the corporation, but takes only $30,000 salary. The children would each have $90,000 of profit and could withdraw that amount from the corporation's Accumulated Adjustments Account. The IRS could challenge the low salary paid to Virgil and adjust it up to a reasonable level.

The IRS has been successful in reallocating income to one family member when the services that person performed were substantial. [Cf. *Fundenburger*, 40 TCM 138, TC Memo 1980-113.] The Tax Court has held that the transfer of stock in an S corporation from a parent to children was invalid, when the parent continued to act as the shareholder, and the children received no dividends or other incidents of ownership. Accordingly, all of the income from the corporation was taxable on the parent's return. [*Duarte*, 44 TC 193 (1965); *Beirne*, 52 TC 210 (1969)]

The mere fact that there is a family S corporation, however, does not give the IRS the power to reallocate income to a family member who has performed only minimal services. [*Edwin Davis*, 64 TC 1034 (1975)]

> **OBSERVATION:** It is possible for a proprietorship or partnership to employ minor children of the owner or owners and for the payments to these children to be exempt from Social Security taxes. However, when these children are employed by a corpora-

---

[8] See *Gorrill*, TC Memo 1963-168, for an instance in which the IRS did find that a C corporation had paid too little compensation.

> tion, no such exemption exists. Nevertheless, the employment of the children can offer some tax savings. If any child is under age 14 and has sufficient income, he or she must pay tax on any unearned income at the parent's marginal rate. Salary paid to a child, however, would not be unearned income. Thus, the child could pay tax on this salary at the marginal rate based on the child's income. Similarly, employment of a child would allow the child to offset his or her earned income with a standard deduction. The standard deduction may not offset unearned income of any person who is claimed as another taxpayer's dependent. Finally, if the child's services and compensation are substantial, the child may not be a dependent of the parents, due to the child's gross income and ability to pay more than half of his or her own support. The parents' loss of the dependence exemption may not be costly if the parents' income is high enough that personal and dependency exemptions are completely or partially phased out.

Other corporations have tried a different approach to income shifting to the children. If a parent owns the stock, putting children on the corporation's payroll shifts income away from the parent to the child. The IRS has succeeded in disallowing compensation deductions under these circumstances when the children's salaries have been excessive in relation to the work performed. [*Carlins*, TC Memo, 1988-79, 55 TCM 228; *Westbrook*, TC Memo 1993-634, 66 TCM 1823]

820.32. Avoidance of payroll taxes. As mentioned above, no self-employment income passes from an S corporation to its shareholders. Several taxpayers have attempted to use this provision to avoid Social Security and other payroll taxes. The rationale is that if the shareholder-employee receives no salary, then the corporation is not liable for payroll taxes and is not obligated to withhold employee FICA or income tax. Although this scheme may work if the corporation makes no distributions, the IRS has long exercised its power to treat distributions from S corporations to shareholder-employees as salary, if the distributions are, in substance, compensation to the shareholder-employee. [*Joly*, TC Memo 1998-361; *Davis*, TC Memo 1997-80, aff'd *Davis v. Commissioner*, 82 AFTR 2d 98-5488 (10th Cir.)]

As a general rule, all compensation is subject to employment and withholding tax, regardless of the form of payment. [Regs. §31.3121(a)-1(b), Regs. §31.3306(b)-1(b)] Revenue Ruling 74-44 held that amounts paid to shareholders of a Subchapter S corporation as compensation for services are subject to withholding and payroll taxes. [Rev. Rul. 74-44, 1974-1 CB 287] That ruling addressed a situation where an S corporation paid its shareholders no salaries, but distributed profits. The IRS held that the distributions were really a disguised form of compensation and that the corporation was responsible for payroll taxes. Another S corporation's effort to enjoin the IRS from collecting payroll taxes was unsuccessful. [*C.D. Ulrich, Ltd., v. U.S.*, 88-1 USTC 9318 (D. Minn.)] Purported distributions were recharacterized as FICA wages to a shareholder-employee when the shareholder-employee reported only about $6,000 per year as wages. [*Eugene Ziobron Inc. v. U.S.*, 80 AFTR 2d 97-8202]

One S corporation paid no salary to its sole shareholder for several years. Each year, it would make a loan to its shareholder in the same amount as its undistributed taxable income. (See Chapter 7, at 725.1., for discussion of undistributed taxable income, which was the pre-1983 counterpart to AAA.) After several years, the shareholder anticipated a sale of half of his stock. At that time, he caused the corporation to distribute all of the loans. The court held that the distribution was in fact payment of salary and that the corporation was liable for FICA and FUTA taxes. [*Gale W. Greenlee, Inc., v. U.S.*, 87-1 USTC 9306 (DC Colo.)]

For many years, the IRS did not appear to aggressively pursue the holding of this ruling. In 1989, however, the IRS prevailed in a district court on this issue. In the case of *Radtke* [*Joseph Radtke, S.C., v. U.S.*, 89-2 USTC 9466 (E.D. Wis.), aff'd in *Joseph Radtke, S.C., v. U.S.*, 90-1 USTC 50,113 (7th Cir.)], an attorney had incorporated his law practice and was the sole shareholder. The corporation filed a valid S election. Mr. Radtke entered into an employment contract with his S corporation whereby he would receive no compensation for services. Instead, at various times during the year, the corporation declared and distributed dividends (state and prior law). The court held that the payments were taxable as compensation. The S corporation was required to pay back FICA and FUTA taxes, and was denied a claim for refund.[9]

In 1990, the IRS was successful in two other cases where the shareholders of S corporations had taken distributions rather than salary. In each case, the IRS was successful in converting the entire distributions to salary payments. [*Spicer Accounting, Inc., v. U.S.*, 91-1 USTC 50,103 (9th Cir.); *Esser v. U.S.*, 750 F.Supp. 421 (D. Ariz., 1990)]

In a 1994 case, Dunn and Clark were shareholders in an S corporation that was engaged in a part-time law practice. Both shareholders had other full-time employment. They claimed that the distributions from the law practice were not wage or salary income. The IRS held that all distributions were taxable as FICA income and assessed the corporation the payroll taxes and penalties. The district court did not distinguish this situation from the *Spicer* case, even though the shareholders were not engaged in the corporation's business on a full-time basis. The court upheld the determination of the IRS and subjected all distributions to payroll and withholding taxes. [*Dunn and Clark*, 73 AFTR 2d 94-1860]

Another district court has joined various circuits in holding that distributions to a shareholder who received no wage or salary from the S corporation could be recharacterized as FICA wages. [*Boles Trucking, Inc. v. U.S.*, 75 AFTR 95-799 (D. Neb., 1995)]

8

EXAMPLE 8 - 8: E, the sole shareholder of the E Corporation, is age 66. In 1996, the corporation's net income (before salary) is $60,000. E withdraws $4,000 as a salary and $56,000 as a distribution in stock.

If the salary were successfully challenged, the corporation would be liable for payroll taxes on the distribution. It could also face penalties for failure to withhold income tax. E might also lose Social Security benefits for 1996.

PLANNING TIP: The IRS has considerable powers in enforcement of payroll tax collection. The penalties for failure to comply may be quite severe and may be enforced against employees of the corporation. Accordingly, persons who provide services to an S corporation should receive wages or a salary. Care should be taken to document that the amounts paid as salary are *reasonable* compensation for the services performed. If the corporation pays no salary to a shareholder, it should be able to demonstrate that the shareholder performed no services to the corporation or that the shareholder received no distributions from the corporation in the taxable year. Another approach that might be useful to fend off an IRS attack recharacterizing distributions and compensation is to state the value of any property contributed by each shareholder and specify a policy that the corporation should provide a return on each shareholder's capital investment. Thus the corporation would have additional justification that distributions are a return on capital rather than compensation for services.

CAUTION: Several IRS Service Centers have launched major projects to collect employment taxes on distributions from S corporations to their shareholders. The most likely candidates for this adjustment are S corporations that show little or no officer's compensation on page 1 of Form 1120S and that are also reporting distributions to shareholders on Schedules K and K-1, Form 1120S. Thus every S corporation is advised to report compensation to officers on the face of its return. There can be complications if the corporation is required to capitalize substantial portions of

[9] The total compensation at issue was less than $20,000. This case dealt with a pre–Subchapter S Revision Act of 1982 year, but the results should still be valid under current law.

> compensation to officers as part of the Uniform Capitalization rules of §263A. In this situation, the corporation should show the compensation on page 1 and reverse the deduction elsewhere on the return. Similarly, a corporation that uses another employer as a common paymaster should report all of its payments to the paymaster as officer's compensation, to the extent that the paymaster compensates shareholders. See Chapter 14, at 1435.7., for discussion of the common paymaster arrangement.

Appeal of an employment tax penalty must be brought by the corporation, not the shareholders. [*Griffin*, TC Memo 1995-246, 69 TCM (CCH) 2821]

820.33. Social Security earnings. The Social Security administration has also examined distributions from S corporations to their shareholders. Distributions from S corporations to "retired" shareholders may be characterized as earned income, which reduces or eliminates Social Security payments for taxpayers at certain ages. The courts seem to make their determinations based on the facts of each case. For example, distributions to persons who actually performed services for S corporations were considered wages for purposes of the earned income ceiling. [*Ludeking v. Finch*, 421 F.2d 499 (8th Cir., 1970); *Somers v. Gardner*, 254 F.Supp. 35 (E.D. Va., 1966); *Weisenfeld v. Richardson*, 463 F.2d 670 (3rd Cir., 1972)]

8 In contrast, a court refused to reallocate salary from a wife to her husband, which would have denied the husband Social Security benefits. [*Gardner v. Hall*, 366 F.2d 132 (10th Cir., 1966)] Similarly, one court refused to find that constructive receipt of corporate profits should be treated as earned income, which would have denied the shareholder Social Security payments. [*Letz v. Weinberger*, 401 F.Supp. 598 (D. Co., 1975)]

> **OBSERVATION:** An elderly shareholder who intends to receive Social Security benefits should monitor his or her transactions with the S corporation carefully. The elderly shareholder should set the salary at a level that will not disqualify him or her for Social Security benefits. Other distributions should be avoided, if at all possible. Constructive distributions, such as loans to the shareholder, could also present the Social Security Administration with ammunition to disallow benefits.

Recently, the Social Security Administration has attempted to characterize income passed through from an S corporation to a shareholder as earned income, even though the corporation did not distribute the income to the shareholder. A district court held for the shareholder, and did not treat the undistributed income as earned income for purposes of the Social Security limit. [*Picha v. Shalala*, unreported decision, 1995 WL 387791 (N.D. Ill.)]

820.34. Collateral problems from recharacterization of compensation. Recharacterization of compensation may create problems unique to S corporations. If there is more than one shareholder, the recharacterization of distributions or compensation may result in unequal distributions per share. Regulations §1.1361-1 requires that such amounts be "given appropriate tax effect," but does not say that recharacterization automatically creates a second class of stock.

> **EXAMPLE 8 - 9:** MN Corporation is an S corporation with two equal shareholders, Norton and Michael. Norton is a passive investor who performs only minimal services for the corporation. Michael is a full-time employee. MN pays Michael a salary of $250,000 and pays no compensation to Norton.
>
> Assume that in an audit, the IRS determines that reasonable compensation for Michael is only $150,000. The other $100,000 would be treated as a constructive distribution to Michael. If the corporation did not make a corresponding distribution to Norton, the distributions would be disproportionate. The Regulations state that the disproportionate distribution must be given appropriate tax effect. The appropriate tax effect might be:

- To make a constructive loan from MN to Michael
- To make a constructive loan from Norton to MN
- To recognize a second class of stock

Either of the first two alternatives would require an imputation of interest under §7872. See the discussion of these problems at 845.3. Either of these alternatives, however, is probably better for all parties than the determination that the corporation has two classes of stock.

> **PLANNING TIP:** Any corporation that perceives a risk of excessive compensation should enter into an agreement with its employees that the employee must return any compensation found to be excessive. This provision is known as an "Oswald clause," from a well-known Tax Court case. [*Vincent E. Oswald*, 49 TC 645 (1968)] In the *Oswald* case, the corporation's bylaws required employees to repay excessive compensation. The court allowed the employee a deduction upon repayment.
>
> The *Oswald* case did not involve an S corporation and was not concerned with the possibility of a second class of stock. The holding in *Oswald*, however, should be useful authority as to the appropriate tax effect of excessive compensation, if the recipient is obligated to repay. The end result in *Oswald* was that the employee had no claim of right to excessive compensation.
>
> If an employee repays excess compensation, but the repayment is not required by express employment agreement or the corporate bylaws, the employee may not be allowed a deduction for the repayment. [*Pahl*, 67 TC 286 (1967)] Accordingly, it is important to prevent challenges to the employee's deduction by including an Oswald clause in employment agreements or bylaws. Therefore, a distribution for which the recipient has no claim of right should not be treated as creating a second class of stock. (See §1341 for the special deduction rules for restoration of amounts held under claim of right.)

8

In 1995, the Tax Court upheld the validity of an Oswald clause in a case that did not involve excessive compensation per se. An employment agreement required the shareholder-employee to repay compensation for any year in which the corporation suffered a loss. [*DeLorean*, TC Memo 1995-287]

820.35. Other effects of compensation of shareholders. There are several reasons why an S corporation may be well served to look beyond the immediate payroll tax savings and seek to raise the level of compensation of its shareholder-employees:

- Setting an unrealistically low level of compensation may create audit problems, whereby the corporation is assessed FICA and payroll taxes, as well as interest and penalties for failure to make timely deposits.
- The corporation may be well advised to establish qualified retirement plans. But in order for an S corporation to fund qualified pension and profit-sharing plans on behalf of its shareholders, it must compensate them as employees.
- An S corporation may be subject to the tax on built-in gains or on excess net passive income (both are discussed in Chapters 11 and 12). In some cases, the corporation may minimize the corporate-level tax by reducing its taxable income.
- If a shareholder incurs expenses on behalf of an S corporation, and attempts to deduct those expenses, status as an employee may be critical. In the *Russell* case, the Tax Court disallowed shareholders deductions for expenses incurred in relation to their employment. [*Richard R. Russell*, 57 TCM 292, TC Memo 1989-207] The individuals involved—a husband and wife—owned all of the shares in an S corporation. They incurred various out-of-pocket expenses on behalf of the corporation, but

received no reimbursement for the expenses and no compensation for the services performed.

> **OBSERVATION:** The taxpayers in the *Russell* case did not attempt to deduct the expenses under §212 as expenses for production of income. The case involved pre-1982 Subchapter S. It is not known whether the same rule would apply to new Subchapter S. Note that under current law, an employee expense and an investment expense receive the same tax treatment. They are both itemized deductions, subject to the 2% AGI floor and the 3% phaseout.
>
> The treatment of unreimbursed shareholder expenses of an S corporation is another example of a distinction between an S corporation and a partnership. A partner in a partnership is treated as a self-employed person. Therefore, any business expenses paid by a partner on behalf of the partnership are treated as deductions in arriving at adjusted gross income and are reported on Schedule E, Form 1040. The treatment of such expenses paid by a shareholder of an S corporation, as demonstrated in the *Russell* case, is not as beneficial. The best treatment that the shareholder could hope for is an itemized deduction as employment-related or investment-related expense.

Similarly, a shareholder in an S corporation attempted to claim certain farming deductions. The court disallowed the deductions on the shareholder's return, because the shareholder was not in the trade or business of farming. [*DeMoss*, TC Memo 1993-636, 66 TCM 1823] The shareholder was not entitled to claim the expenses as an employee deduction, since he was not an employee of the corporation. The IRS indicated it would permit deduction as investment expenses, provided the expenditures could be substantiated.

The IRS has also disallowed deductions when a shareholder paid a debt that was purported to be the corporation's obligation. [*Foust*, TC Memo 1997-446] The proper classification of such a payment would generally be a contribution to capital. See Chapter 14.

825. Fringe benefits.

The tax benefits of fringe benefits are severely limited for shareholder-employees of S corporations. In general, an S corporation is treated as an employer and so may deduct the cost of providing tax-favored fringe benefits to employees. The Code also provides statutory exclusions for employees, who thus do not have to include the value, or cost, of the fringe benefits in their reported income. When the S corporation pays for certain fringe benefits on behalf of persons owning more than 2% of the corporation's stock, however, the tax advantage disappears. Statutory authority is Code §1372(a) and (b), as discussed below.

SUMMARY OF AUTHORITY: CODE SECTION 1372(a) AND (b)

- Section 1372(a) applies partnership treatment of fringe benefits to S corporations and 2% shareholders.
- Section 1372(b) defines a *2% shareholder* as one who owns more than 2% of the corporation's stock on any day of the corporation's taxable year.
- Section 1372(a) does not define how a partnership treats fringe benefits paid on behalf of the partners.
- Section 1372(a) does not elaborate on the types of fringe benefits covered by this rule.

825.1. Fringe benefits defined. There are a variety of payments that an employer might make on behalf of its employees that are not direct wages or salaries. In the broadest sense, *fringe benefits* could cover contributions to retirement plans, insurance premiums, and anything else that might provide a direct or indirect benefit to an employee. The statute does not enumerate which benefits are subject to special treatment when paid by S corporations on behalf of 2% shareholders. The Subchapter S Revision Act of 1982 listed only five types of fringe benefits:

- Group term life insurance premium exclusion
- $5,000 death benefit exclusion
- Amounts received under accident and health plans
- Premiums on employer-paid accident and health insurance
- Exclusion of meals and lodging provided by the employer

The Committee report did not state that the list was to be inclusive, but it offered no further explanation. There is no provision in the partnership statutes that describes any fringe benefits or specifically states the tax treatment. Therefore, it is necessary to examine the statutory treatment of each fringe benefit individually and determine when a partner is considered to be an employee.

A study of the various Code sections indicates that a partner is not an employee and therefore is not entitled to an exclusion from gross income for the following fringe benefits:

8

- Group term life insurance premiums[10] [§79]
- Amounts received under accident and health plans [§105]
- Premiums on employer-paid accident and health insurance [§106]
- Meals and lodging provided by the employer [§119]
- Parking and transit passes provided by the employer [§132(f)(5)(E)]

The Committee reports did not claim that the above list is exhaustive, but there appear to be no other fringe benefits for which a partner is not entitled to an exclusion. The remaining fringe benefits, listed below, are available for exclusion at the partner level, and therefore a 2% shareholder in an S corporation should also be permitted to exclude them. The tax professional is advised to consult the cited Code section to determine whether a specific benefit is subject to nondiscrimination requirements. An S corporation should be able to claim a deduction, and the employee should report no gross income, for the following fringe benefits:

- Employee achievement awards [§74(c)]
- Educational assistance programs [§127] (not available after 1994)
- Dependent care assistance [§129]
- No-additional-cost benefits [§132(b)]
- Qualified employee discounts [§132(c)]
- Working-condition fringe benefits [§132(d)]
- *De minimis* fringe benefits [§132(e)]
- On-premises athletic facilities [§132(j)(4)]

OBSERVATION: S corporations should be able to deduct the cost of providing all of the above fringe benefits to any employee, including a 2% shareholder. The citation to

[10] Regulations §1.79-0 refers to Regulations §31.3401(c)-1 for the definition of *employee*, which may include a partner if the partner is in fact an employee. Until future Regulations amplify this position, it is safest to assume that a partner, and therefore a 2% shareholder in an S corporation, cannot exclude any premiums on a group term insurance policy paid by the employer.

each of these benefits treats a self-employed person as an "employee." Since partners are self-employed, any deduction allowed to a partnership for a benefit provided to a partner should not result in gross income to a 2% shareholder.

Cafeteria plans [§125] have become popular in recent years because they allow employees to select certain taxable and nontaxable benefits according to their specific needs. Partners are not eligible to receive tax-free benefits from cafeteria plans, so 2% shareholders are likewise ineligible.

Worker's compensation may be an issue as well. The IRS has held that it is not deductible to a partnership if it is paid on behalf of a partner. [Rev. Rul. 72-396, 1972-2 CB 312] Shareholder-employees, however, are employees under local law, whereas partners are not. If a corporation is required to provide worker's compensation for all employees, it should be allowed as a necessary business expense, rather than disallowed as a fringe benefit.

825.11. Controversy over meals and lodging. The exclusion of meals and lodging provided by the employer has been the subject of some controversy. An early case held that shareholder-employees were entitled to exclude the value of meals and lodging provided by an S corporation in which they owned all of the stock. [*Wilhelm v. U.S.*, 257 F.Supp. 167, 18 AFTR 2d 5563, 66-2 USTC 9637 (DC Wyo.)] That case, however, was decided before the Subchapter S Revision Act of 1982 enacted the fringe benefit restrictions of §1372.

8

Another case, in the partnership area, held that meals and lodging provided to a partner in a partnership could be excluded by the partner. [*Armstrong v. Phinney*, 68-1 USTC 9355 (5th Cir.), 21 AFTR 2d 1260] In that case, the partner owned only 5% of the partnership. In certain cases, a partner's dealings with a partnership may be treated in the same manner as dealings between the partnership and an outsider. [§707(a), §707(c)] In this case, the court found that the partner was acting in the same manner as an employee.

In a recent case involving a 100% shareholder who excluded meals and lodging provided by the S corporation, a district court found that the exclusion did not apply. [*Dilts v. U.S.*, 1994 F.Supp., 94-1 USTC 50,162 (DC Wyo.)] Therefore, the shareholder was required to include the value of the meals and lodging on his personal tax return. The decision did raise two possibilities that could mitigate the taxability of meals and lodging provided to shareholders:

- A shareholder in an S corporation could have dealings with the corporation that resemble nonpartner dealings with a partnership. In that situation, the exclusion of meals and lodging could apply to a shareholder.
- A shareholder who is unable to exclude employer-provided lodging could claim a deduction for the portion of the home used for business, under §280A. See discussion at 840.23.

OBSERVATION: The statute refers directly to the partnership rules for determining the tax treatment of 2% shareholders. Therefore, it appears that a shareholder could construct a case for excluding fringe benefits from gross income. The key would be to prove that the shareholder was acting in a capacity that would be a nonpartner role if the organization were a partnership. The legislative history to the Deficit Reduction Act of 1984 provides several criteria for distinguishing partner capacity from nonpartner capacity [Senate Finance Committee Explanation of Deficit Reduction Act of 1984, pp. 227, 228]:

- Risk as to receipt. If a partnership's cash flow is reasonably certain to be sufficient to cover the payment, the payment is more likely to be a nonpartner payment. If the payment is subject to business risks, it is more likely to be a payment in a partner's capacity as a partner.

- Period of allocation. A temporary payment is more likely to be a nonpartner payment, whereas a lengthy or indefinite payment tends to be in a capacity as a partner.
- Proximity in time to performance of services or transfer of property. If a partnership pays a partner for services shortly after performance, or pays for property shortly after the transfer of property, the payment is more likely to be in a nonpartner capacity. If the payment is to cover an extended period of time, it is more likely to be a payment in a partner capacity.
- Tax advantage of the arrangement. If a person appears to have become a partner to obtain tax advantages, the payment is likely to be a payment in a nonpartner capacity.
- Relationship of payment amount to value of partner's continuing interest. If a payment to a partner is relatively large and the partner's continuing interest is relatively small, the payment appears to be in a nonpartner capacity.
- In the case of a transfer of property and a payment by the partnership to the partner, an unfeasible income allocation makes it likely that a payment is in a nonpartner capacity.
- In addition to these factors, the legislative history to the Deficit Reduction Act of 1984 interprets two prior Revenue Rulings:
  —Management fees paid to general partners, based on gross income, are to be treated as nonpartner payments. [Rev. Rul. 81-300, 1981-2 CB 143, is modified. Senate Finance Committee Explanation of Deficit Reduction Act of 1984, p. 230.]
  —A professional fee paid to a general partner for managing a portion of the business, but not managing the partnership, is a payment in a nonpartner capacity. [Rev. Rul. 81-301, 1981-2 CB 144, is approved.]

825.12. Parking and transit passes. Until 1993, parking and transit passes provided by an employer were included in working condition fringe benefits. Accordingly, 2% shareholder-employees of S corporations could exclude the value of these items from gross income. In 1992, however, Congress amended the treatment of these benefits with respect to partners. [Energy Policy Act of 1992, §1911(b)] For taxable years beginning after 1992, a partner is no longer considered an "employee" with respect to transportation fringe benefits. [§132(e)(5)(E)] Therefore, a 2% shareholder in an S corporation must include the value of parking and transit provided by the S corporation in his or her gross income. [Notice 94-3, 1994-3 IRB 14 Q-5.b] There are, however, some special rules:

- If the value of transit passes provided by the employer does not exceed $21 per month, the shareholder-employee may exclude the benefit as a *de minimis* fringe benefit. [Notice 94-3, 1994-3 IRB 14 Q-7.a]
- The value of parking away from the principal place of business may be excluded. [Notice 94-3, 1994-3 IRB 14 Q-7.b]

825.2. 2% shareholder defined. The statute defines a *2% shareholder* as a person who owns more than 2% of the S corporation's stock at any time during the corporation's taxable year. It refers to the attribution rules of §318 for constructive ownership and subjects a constructive owner of more than 2% of the shares to the same treatment. This rule prevents any shareholder from employing a family member in order to provide tax-free fringe benefits from the corporation to the family unit.

EXAMPLE 8 - 10: Monty is the sole shareholder of Monco, an S corporation. Monty is not an employee of Monco. His wife Marilyn is the president of Monco and is employed full-time. Marilyn is the constructive owner of all of Monty's stock, and she cannot exclude any of the forbidden benefits from her gross income.

The constructive ownership rules of §318 treat a shareholder's spouse, children, parents, and grandchildren as constructive owners of his or her stock. They also treat beneficiaries of estates and trusts as constructive owners of stock owned by the fiduciary, but only to the extent of the beneficiary's interest in the entity. Since grantor trusts and QSSTs have only one current income beneficiary, stock owned through one of these entities would be attributed to the beneficiary in accordance with the actuarial value of the beneficiary's income interest. Stock owned by an estate would be attributed to each beneficiary. (Chapter 15 discusses the attribution rules of §318 in more detail at 1510.2.)

825.3. Tax treatment of disallowed fringe benefits. As noted at 825., §1372 does not expressly provide for the tax treatment of fringe benefits. The legislative history suggests that the S corporation should not be allowed a deduction for the fringes, but the statute merely requires treatment in a manner similar to that of partnerships and partners. In fact, many partnerships are able to deduct payments for fringe benefits as guaranteed payments to partners under §707(c).

Until 1991, the instructions to Form 1120S provided the only guidance on the tax treatment of any of the forbidden fringe benefits. Those instructions stated that each of the disallowed fringe benefits should be reported as a nondeductible expense.

8

EXAMPLE 8 - 11: Bob and Norma each own half of the shares of the BN Corporation, an S corporation. Bob is an investor who performs no services for the corporation. Norma is the full-time manager and chief executive officer. BN pays $10,000 to provide Norma with health and accident insurance. According to the IRS instructions, the corporation should report the $10,000 as a nondeductible expense on Form 1120S, for any year from 1983 through 1990.

As Chapter 6 demonstrated, the only means to allocate any item of income or expense among S corporation shareholders is proportionately—per-share, per-day.[11] [§1377(a)(1)] Treating fringe benefit costs as nondeductible corporate expenses spreads the tax disallowance among all of the shareholders in an S corporation, since disallowed expenses must be reported to shareholders in the same manner as any other corporate item. Each shareholder would be required to treat his or her portion of the corporation's nondeductible expenses as a reduction in basis. This would be the case even if the fringe benefit did not provide an advantage to a shareholder who was not an employee. In the past, many tax professionals believed that the most equitable treatment was to have the shareholders who received the fringe benefit bear the corporation's tax cost. It seemed that the logical way to accomplish this result was to report the fringe benefit coverage as noncash compensation on Form W-2. By accounting for the fringe benefits in this manner, each shareholder who received benefits would be required to report them in his or her gross income. The corporation would be allowed a deduction for the costs—not as fringe benefits, but as compensation.

In April 1991, the IRS adopted the compensation approach for accident and health insurance benefits provided to shareholder-employees. [Rev. Rul. 91-26, 1991-1 CB 184] Although this rule was effective for taxable years beginning after 1982, the IRS also stated that it would not adjust the treatment on any return for which the taxpayer had followed the IRS's previous instructions. Curiously, the new rule applied only to accident and health insurance costs, covering no other fringe benefits. It seems logical that the compensation approach should be used to account for all of the forbidden fringe benefits.

---

[11] Code §1377(a)(2) allows the corporation to allocate income to different time periods when a shareholder completely terminates his or her interest, and §1362(e) allows for separating income and deduction items between portions of a year when a corporation terminates its S election. Within the separate periods allowed by these two provisions, however, there is no means to allocate any item to any shareholder, except on a per-share, per-day basis.

EXAMPLE 8 - 12: Refer to Example 8 - 12. According to Revenue Ruling 91-26, BN should report $10,000 as noncash compensation on Norma's W-2 for the year.

> **OBSERVATION:** S corporations that use fiscal years and had been following the IRS approach of reporting fringe benefits as nondeductible expenses may have some problems converting to the new approach. The old method required that the corporation report the disallowed deductions based on its fiscal year. All compensation, however, is reported on a calendar-year basis. When an S corporation converts to the new method, it should take care to avoid double-counting the disallowed fringe benefits or failing to report some months' costs.

In January 1994, the IRS issued instructions on the proper reporting of transit passes and parking provided by the S corporation to the 2% shareholder. The value of these benefits is reported as noncash compensation on the employee's Form W-2. [Notice 94-3, 1994-3 IRB 14, Q-12.a]

825.4. Special rule for accident and health insurance. Self-employed persons may deduct a portion of their health and accident insurance costs in arriving at adjusted gross income. [§162(l)] This deduction is limited to the person's self-employment income. Although this provision does not cover employees, per se, a shareholder-employee of an S corporation is able to deduct the same percentage of the cost of insurance provided by the S corporation. Wage or salary income is treated as earned income for purposes of the limit. [§162(l)(5), amended by the Revenue Reconciliation Act of 1990] The remaining cost of the insurance may be deductible as an itemized deduction.

The Tax and Trade Relief Extension Act of 1998 amended the phase-in schedule of the percentage deduction allowable [PL 105-277, §2002; Code §162(ell1)(1)(B)]:

For taxable years beginning in calendar year	*The applicable percentage is*
1998	45 percent
1999, 2000, and 2001	60 percent
2002	70 percent
2003 and thereafter	100 percent

8

825.5. Withholding and payroll tax problems. In §3121(a)(2)(B), payments on behalf of an employee for medical and hospitalization expenses are excluded from the definition of *wages*. To qualify for the Social Security tax exclusion, the payment must be made in accordance with a plan to benefit all, or a class of, employees. Section 3121(a)(2)(B) does not discriminate between medical payments that might be *excluded* from an employee's gross income and medical payments *included* in gross income. Therefore, the language of §1372 has no effect on the treatment of accident and health insurance premiums as excluded from the definition of *wages* in §3121(a).

On January 17, 1992, the IRS issued Announcement 92-16, 1992-5 IRB 53, which clarifies the treatment of accident and health insurance premiums paid by S corporations on behalf of 2% shareholders. It states that any accident and health payments made under a plan to benefit employees are exempt from FICA tax, pursuant to §3121(a). There are two points worthy of attention:

- There are no nondiscrimination requirements under §3121(a)(2)(B). For instance, if a plan covered only officers, it would not be disqualified for the exemption from FICA.

- The exclusion is limited to the amount paid "on behalf of employees." Therefore, a plan that benefits shareholders who do not claim employee status would not be subject to this exclusion.

PLANNING TIP: S corporations that do not pay wages or salaries to shareholders are subject to scrutiny by the IRS, which may reclassify distributions as compensation. As stated above, the IRS has been successful in imposing taxes and penalties on S corporations that have understated compensation. [See *Gardner v. Hall* and *Letz v. Weinberger*.]

Announcement 92-16 should provide further incentive for S corporations to pay salaries to their shareholders. By affirmatively treating its shareholders as employees, the corporation could provide accident and health insurance benefits that would be exempt from FICA. On the shareholder's personal tax return, 30% of the cost of the premiums paid by the corporation may be deducted, as allowed by §162(l). The remaining 70% of the health insurance is allowable as an itemized deduction, subject to the general limitation on medical expenses.

8

Under some circumstances, a shareholder-employee may be able to avoid substantially all of the taxes on accident and health insurance premiums paid on his or her behalf by the S corporation. A C corporation, however, may pay accident and health insurance premiums without including any of the payments in the shareholder-employee's gross income or Social Security wages.

OBSERVATION: Many closely held corporations and personal service corporations are able to drain corporate taxable income by paying reasonable direct compensation, contributions to qualified retirement plans, and tax-favored fringe benefits. By doing so, they can avoid double taxation, even without an S election.

EXAMPLE 8 - 13: Jay operates a consulting business, Jayco. Jayco's annual income before any compensation is $110,000. Jayco pays Jay a salary of $80,000. It also contributes $20,000 to its qualified pension and profit-sharing plans. It provides Jay with medical reimbursement and accident and health insurance. The cost of these medical plans is $10,000 per year.

If Jayco is a C corporation, it has no taxable income. Jay's taxable income is his salary of $80,000. If Jayco makes an S election, Jay will still have his salary of $80,000, plus $10,000 from the now nondeductible health plan costs. The $10,000 should be reported on Jay's W-2, according to Revenue Ruling 91-26. The $10,000 is not subject to FICA, pursuant to Announcement 92-16.

825.6. Pension and profit-sharing plans. As discussed in Chapter 3, an S corporation may maintain qualified pension and profit-sharing plans on behalf of its owner-employees. There are few differences between plans maintained by a C corporation and those of an S corporation. The major distinction is that a shareholder-employee of a C corporation can borrow from plan assets, but any person who owns more than 5% of the stock of an S corporation cannot borrow from the plan.

As a practical matter, most S corporation plans will meet the "top-heavy" definition of §416. In order to qualify a top-heavy plan, the corporation must provide benefits on a nondiscriminatory basis to a broad range of employees and provide for rapid vesting of employer contributions. The top-heavy rules are complicated and beyond the scope of this book. They apply to plans of unincorporated businesses, C corporations, and S corporations, so the presence or absence of an S election has no effect on the requirements to qualify a plan.

OBSERVATION: Contributions to the plans should be treated as ordinary deductions to the corporation, rather than being specially allocated as fringe benefits. When

Congress was drafting the Subchapter S Revision Act of 1982, it considered a provision that would have treated contributions on behalf of shareholder-employees in the same manner as fringe benefits. [Joint Committee on Taxation, Description of H.R. 6055, June 8, 1982, pp. 20, 21] Shortly before passage of the Subchapter S Revision Act of 1982, however, the Tax Equity and Fiscal Responsibility Act of 1982 substantially revised many of the rules relating to qualified plans. The provision to treat contributions by S corporations as fringe benefits was dropped from the final version of the Subchapter S Revision Act of 1982.

Although qualified plans maintained by corporations are generally subject to the same rules as plans of unincorporated businesses (known as "Keogh" plans, in reference to the congressman who introduced the legislation), there are some important differences:

- The measurement of compensation
- The treatment for self-employment tax purposes

Contributions to plans of C or S corporations are based on the compensation to the employee. The current limit on contributions to defined contribution plans is 25% of compensation or $30,000, whichever is less. [§415(c); *Durando*, 76 AFTR 2d 95-7464, 95-2 USTC 50,615 (9th Cir.)]

8

Contributions to Keogh plans on behalf of owner-employees, however, are based on the person's allocable share of earned income from the business. [§404(a)(8)(D)] *Earned income* is defined as self-employment income less the deduction for Keogh contribution.[12] [§401(c)(2)(A)(v)] The effect is to reduce 25% of compensation to 20% of earned income as the limit on a defined contribution plan. Although this difference in measurement may have negligible effects on a business with steady earned income, it may result in a substantial advantage for a business with erratic income.

EXAMPLE 8 - 14: Debbie is an individual with investment income of $60,000 and active business income that varies between $50,000 and $150,000. She maintains a defined-contribution Keogh plan. In a year when her income is at a low point, the maximum Keogh deduction would be $10,000. In a high-income year, her maximum deduction would be $30,000.

Assume that she incorporates as the DE Corporation. She contributes both the active business assets and the investment assets to DE. The corporation could set a salary at $120,000 and make a $30,000 annual contribution to a money-purchase pension plan. This contribution would be at the maximum limit of $30,000 or 35% of compensation. In years when the active business income is low, the investment income of the business could provide a funding source for the pension contributions. The IRS could challenge the reasonableness of compensation, but the history of the business's income should be an adequate defense.

Of special interest to the moderate-income taxpayer is the treatment of contributions to qualified plans as FICA or self-employment income. Contributions to a plan maintained by a corporate employer are not wages, and thus they are exempt from FICA tax, unemployment taxes, and withholding. [§3121(a)(5)] By contrast, Keogh contributions are not deductible in computing self-employment income.[13] As the rates and wage bases continue to rise on FICA and self-employment income, this distinction offers advantages to incorporation.

---

[12] There is a similar effect on defined benefit plans, whereby the compensation covered must be reduced by the Keogh contribution.

[13] There is no Code cite for this rule, but it is a long-standing treatment on Form 1040. The IRS was sustained in disallowing the Keogh deduction in arriving at self-employment income in *Seymour Gale v. U.S.*, 91-2 USTC 50,356 (N.D. Ill.).

EXAMPLE 8 - 15: Brad is a self-employed marketing consultant. For 1996, he estimates that his net income from self-employment will be $40,000. He has other income to the extent of itemized deductions and personal exemptions. He wants to shelter the maximum possible earnings in a Keogh plan. His maximum Keogh contribution is $8,000 (20% of $40,000). His taxable income for 1996 is $32,000, but his self-employment income is $40,000.

If Brad incorporates, he could receive a salary of $32,000 and the corporation could contribute $8,000 to defined-contribution pension and profit-sharing plans on his behalf. His taxable income, for income tax purposes, would be $32,000, as it would be if he operated as a proprietorship. His FICA wages, however, would be only $32,000. He would save approximately $1,200 in self-employment tax on $8,000 by incorporating.

Pension and profit-sharing plans are among the most valuable tax-saving devices available. They should be considered for all businesses, regardless of the form of organization. An incorporated business can make better use of such plans to shelter income than can an unincorporated business. A C corporation offers more flexibility than an S corporation, because shareholder-employees are able to borrow from the plans, within certain limits. (See Chapter 3 for discussion at 315.) Aside from this one advantage, however, an S corporation offers all of the features of a C corporation. An S corporation is the only form of organization whereby a contribution to a qualified plan can actually create or augment a loss at the owner level.

8

EXAMPLE 8 - 16: Martha is the sole owner of an S corporation that carries on an active business. In 1995, the corporation breaks even on operations, before deducting Martha's salary or contributing to the pension plan. In 1996, the corporation pays Martha a salary of $50,000 and contributes $10,000 to its pension plan on Martha's behalf. The result is a loss of $60,000, which passes through to Martha. Martha also reports $50,000 of salary income for that year. Her complete taxable income from the corporation will be a loss of $10,000. There is no other form of organization that will allow her to deduct a business loss on her personal return, yet contribute to a qualified retirement plan.

830. Business expenses of shareholder-employees.

An S corporation and its shareholder-employees should be aware of special complications in the area of employee business expenses. First, in order for an employee to claim any deduction for a business expense, the expenditure must pass the general tests of deductibility. Given that an expense is potentially deductible, the corporation's reimbursement policy may determine the most beneficial tax treatment.

830.1. General requirements for deduction of a business expense. In order for an expense to be allowed as a deduction, it must pass the general test of being an ordinary and necessary business expense. [§162(a)] Certain limitations apply to expenses that might have mixed business and personal uses—for example, expenses relating to an office in the home, automotive expenses, travel, meals, and entertainment. There are no special rules applicable to an S corporation, per se, or its employees, including shareholder-employees. As mentioned above under the discussion of the *Russell* case, there must be an employer–employee relationship, evidenced by compensation to the employee, for a person to deduct an expense as an employee.

Generally, individuals are entitled to deduct trade or business expenses, although there are restrictions that apply to expenses of employees. Although an S corporation computes its taxable income in the same manner as an individual, the S corporation, per se, will not be classified as an employee. Therefore, an S corporation should be able to deduct its business expenses in the same manner as a self-employed individual. It should include all ordinary deductions, including those made in the form of reimbursements to shareholder-employees, as ordinary deductions, and it should reduce ordinary taxable income.

830.2. Alternative methods of payment. There are three basic approaches to the payment of the business expenses of an employee:

- Have the corporation pay all of the employee's business expenses directly.
- Have the corporation reimburse the employee for all employment-related expense.
- Make no provision to reimburse the employee for employment-related expenses.

The first two methods produce identical tax results; the major difference between the two is the burden of recordkeeping. The third approach—payment by the employee without reimbursement—will usually result in reduced deductions for the employee. Accordingly, an employer, including an S corporation, should adopt one of the first two approaches. In many situations, a mix of the two methods will be appropriate.

830.21. Direct payment by the corporation. Direct payment is probably the smoothest method from the tax point of view. The principal risk is that the shareholder-employee will be tempted to mix personal expenses with legitimate business deductions. In one recent case, the IRS held that an S corporation's purchases of liquor for consumption by the majority shareholder of an S corporation constituted a constructive distribution to the shareholder. [See *Handke*, at 810.] This risk is always present to the owner of a closely held business, regardless of the form in which the business is operated.

In this area, the rules for S corporations do not differ from those of any other employer-employee relationship. The major concern is that the corporation and its owners subject themselves to the self-discipline and recordkeeping necessary to substantiate business deductions. The direct payment of necessary business expenses qualifies as a working-condition fringe benefit. Therefore, the corporation is allowed a deduction, and the shareholder-employee does not report gross income. Note that even a shareholder-employee of an S corporation qualifies for this exclusion, since it is available to partners in partnerships. [§132(d)]

830.22. Reimbursement of employee expenses by the corporation. When it is not practical for the corporation to pay all employee expenses directly, the best option is for the corporation to reimburse the employee. Employee expenses are deductible in arriving at adjusted gross income only to the extent that they are reimbursed by the employer.[14] [§62(a)(2)(A)] This treatment of reimbursed employee expenses yields the same result as the direct payment of expenses by the corporation. The major precaution to be observed is that the payment made by the corporation to the employee qualifies as a reimbursement, rather than as additional compensation.

The most hazardous situation is an expense allowance, which is not tied directly to the employee's expenses. Code §62(c) treats an arrangement as compensation, rather than as expense reimbursement, if the employee is not required to substantiate expenses or to return any excess reimbursements. The Regulations stipulate three criteria for a reimbursement plan:

- There must be a business connection for the expense.
- The employee must substantiate the expense in a report to the employer.
- The employee must be obligated to return excess reimbursements or advances. [Regs. §1.162-2T]

Any advance must be no more than the reasonably anticipated expenses, and it must be made no more than 30 days in advance of the expenses. Excess advances must be returned within 120 days of the incurrence of the expense. Alternatively, the employer may use quarterly substantiation reports.

[14] Code §62(a)(2)(B) also allows a deduction in arriving at adjusted gross income for certain qualified performing artist expenses.

In general, an employer may provide per diem reimbursements without requiring specific accounting. If the employee owns more than 10% of the stock of the employer, however, a per diem arrangement does not qualify as a reimbursed plan. [Rev. Proc. 89-67, 1989-2 CB 795]

830.23. Employee expenses without reimbursement. Employee expenses that are not reimbursed by the employer are miscellaneous itemized deductions, and they do not produce a tax benefit unless they (when combined with other miscellaneous itemized deductions) exceed 2% of the employee's adjusted gross income. [§67(a) and (b)] In addition, if the employee's adjusted gross income exceeds $100,000, these itemized deductions are subject to a reduction of 3% of the excess.[15] [§68(a)] The less desirable treatment of unreimbursed expenses makes it extremely important for an S corporation to observe the formalities of a reimbursement plan.

EXAMPLE 8 - 17: Ted owns 100% of the stock in Tedco, an S corporation. Ted travels extensively on business in the current year, and he incurs $80,000 of employment-related expenses. Tedco reimburses Ted for the full $80,000. Ted's adjusted gross income from all sources other than the reimbursement is $90,000. His other itemized deductions equal $20,000, none of which is subject to the 2% floor on miscellaneous itemized deductions. If Ted observes the substantiation rules that qualify the $80,000 as reimbursements, Ted will be allowed a complete deduction for the $80,000. If Ted and Tedco do not comply with the reimbursement rules, the $80,000 received from Tedco will be gross income to Ted and the $80,000 expenses will be only partially deductible.

If the reimbursement plan meets the qualifications discussed above, Ted will have no gross income from the reimbursement, and he will claim no deduction for the expenses. His taxable income will be $70,000 (AGI of $90,000 less itemized deductions of $20,000). If the arrangement does not qualify as a reimbursed plan, the amounts received from Tedco will be gross income to Ted and the expenses will be itemized deductions. Due to the limitations on itemized deductions, the expenses will not completely offset his gross income. Ted's taxable income would be:

Adjusted gross income		$170,000
Less itemized deductions:		
Employee expenses	$80,000	
Less 2% AGI floor	(3,400)	
Subtotal	76,600	
Other itemized deductions	20,000	
Subtotal	96,600	
Less 3% of AGI over $100,000	$ (2,100)	
		(94,500)
Taxable income before exemptions		$ 75,500

In addition, Ted would lose some of the benefits of his otherwise allowable personal and dependency exemption deductions if the plan does not qualify as a reimbursement.

830.3. Recharacterization of itemized deductions. A partnership or an S corporation may attempt to circumvent the treatment of certain itemized deductions by paying the expenses directly. In anticipation of this possible abuse, the IRS is authorized to issue Regulations that prohibit such recharacterization. [§67(c)] This rule would prevent S corporations from claiming deductions for such items as employee moving expenses. Such expenses must be passed through to the employee, who may then claim an itemized deduction. Neither the Code provision nor the Regulations issued to date, however, have made any attempt to recharacterize employment-related expenses paid by the corporation as itemized deductions.

[15] If the employee is married and files a separate return, itemized deductions become subject to the 3% reduction when adjusted gross income exceeds $50,000.

830.4. Special rules for certain expenses. Because of the propensity of many taxpayers to mix personal and business expenses, two categories of expense are subject to special rules:

- Meal and entertainment expenses
- Expenses of owning automobiles and other listed property

Claiming a deduction for either of these expenses requires strict substantiation. In addition, some of the expenses may be subject to special dollar or percentage limitations.

830.41. Meal and entertainment expenses. To claim a deduction for meal and entertainment expenses, a taxpayer must provide strict substantiation that the event was directly related to, or associated with, the taxpayer's business. If an expense meets this requirement, 20% of the amount expended is deductible. The remaining 50% is a nondeductible expense. For taxable years beginning before 1994, the nondeductible portion of meal and entertainment expense was 50%. [§274(n), as amended by §13209 of the Revenue Reconciliation Act of 1993] The Revenue Reconciliation Act of 1993 also disallows a deduction for any club dues paid after 1993. [§274(a)(3), as amended by §13210 of the Revenue Reconciliation Act of 1993]

In the context of an S corporation, both the deductible and nondeductible portions of the meal and entertainment expense pass through to the shareholders. The deductible portion is claimed as an ordinary deduction and reduces the S corporation's taxable income. The nondeductible portion is stated separately and passes through to the shareholders. It reduces basis, and it also reduces the corporation's Accumulated Adjustments Account.

8

OBSERVATION: Regulations §1.1366-2 may wrongly give the impression that all meal and entertainment expenses must be treated as itemized deductions by shareholders in S corporations. This Regulation states that each shareholder must report his or her share of the corporation's travel, meal, and entertainment expense separately for corporate years that began in 1986 and ended in 1987.

Tax practitioners can expect an updated version of Regulations §1.1366-2 to reflect the reduction of the meal and entertainment expense and the disallowance of club dues. The IRS may provide that fiscal year S corporations (and partnerships) separate the portion of these expenditures paid in calendar year 1993 from those paid in calendar year 1994.

As worded, the Regulations do not convert trade or business expenses of S corporations into itemized deductions. Thus, while the deduction limitation applies to meal and entertainment expenses, the 2% adjusted gross income floor, as well as the reduction for 3% of itemized deductions when a taxpayer's adjusted gross income exceeds $100,000, does not apply to shareholders, unless the deductions are incurred in connection with a §212 activity. As a consequence, the allowable meal and entertainment expenses are ordinary deductions and are not passed through as itemized deductions. The next example illustrates the advantage of maintaining a reimbursement plan, even for a 100% shareholder-employee, as opposed to having nonreimbursed expenses.

EXAMPLE 8 - 18: Debbie is the sole shareholder and sole employee of the Echo Corporation, an electing S corporation that uses the calendar year. In 1998, the corporation pays her a salary of $60,000. It has net income (after deducting her salary) of $20,000. She has $8,500 of employment-related expenses, including $1,000 of meals and entertainment. All of the meal and entertainment expenses relate to the conduct of an active trade or business; none of the expenses would be classified as an investment expense. If Echo does not reimburse her for the expenses, the tax consequences will be:

Compensation income	$60,000
Income from S corporation	20,000
Adjusted gross income	80,000

Employee expenses:		
Meal and entertainment	$1,000	
Less nondeductible portion	(500)	
	500	
Other expenses	7,500	
	8,000	
Less 2% AGI	(1,600)	(6,400)
Contribution to taxable income		$73,600

However, if Echo reimburses Debbie for her expenses, the corporate income will be:

Net income before reimbursement	$20,000
Deductible reimbursement	(8,000)
Income from S corporation to Debbie	$12,000
Compensation income	60,000
Adjusted gross income to Debbie	$72,000

830.42. Automobile expenses. Automobile expenses are subject to the same rigid documentation rules as entertainment expenses. The taxpayer must be able to produce mileage logs showing the miles and nature of each business trip. In addition, there are several restrictions on deductions for owning an automobile:

- Although automobiles are classified as five-year property for depreciation purposes, the depreciation deductions are limited, so that automobiles that cost more than approximately $15,300 (indexed annually for inflation) are subject to slowed-down depreciation.
- Unless the business use exceeds 50% of the car's total mileage during a taxable year, the owner is not allowed to use accelerated depreciation. (The rules for calculation of depreciation, and recapture of depreciation if business use drops to 50% or less in a succeeding taxable year, are extremely complicated and are beyond the scope of this book.)

As far as depreciation limits are concerned, there is no advantage or disadvantage to having the corporation or the shareholder-employee own the automobile. There may be other advantages, however, to having the corporation own the automobile.

1. A self-employed taxpayer, or a business entity (including an S corporation), needs only to meet the substantiation requirements to claim the allowable depreciation, as well as all operating costs, as a business deduction. An employee must meet a stricter standard: The employee must use the vehicle for the employer's convenience and as a condition of employment.
2. The corporation may deduct all of the allowable depreciation, as well as insurance and operating costs. The employee's personal use of the vehicle will not be a business use if the employee owns more than 5% of the corporation's stock, but such use may be reported as noncash compensation to the employee. Alternatively, the corporation may charge the employee rent for the personal use. If the employee's personal use equals or exceeds 50% of the total mileage during the taxable year, the corporation may use only straight-line depreciation. The limits on automobile depreciation are so strict, however, that they have absolutely no impact on the deduction for the first five years when an automobile costs more than approximately $31,000.

In calculating the value of the employee's personal use of the automobile, the Regulations provide certain lease value tables, based on the value of the automobile at the time of its acquisition. [Regs. §1.61-21(d)(2)(iii)] The lease value includes all costs of maintenance and insurance, but does not include fuel. The lease value is multiplied by the percentage of an employee's personal use, to yield the value of an employer-furnished automobile for a taxable year. The value, which assumes a four-year lease term, is established by determining the fair market value of the automobile in the year that it first becomes available to the employee, and the same lease value is used for four years. The employer must report the value of the personal use as compensation, or require that the employee reimburse the employer for the rental value.

EXAMPLE 8 - 19: Rainco, an S corporation, provides Tina with an automobile that she is allowed to use for personal purposes as well as for business. In the current year, she drives the car 10,000 miles. She uses the car 60% on company business and 40% for her personal purposes. The corporation purchased the automobile for $20,000 on April 1. The personal use value for Tina is:

Lease value		*Percent personal*		*Percent of year owned*		*Value to employee*
$5,600*	x	.40*	x	.75	=	$1,680

* From Regulations §1.61-21(d)(2)(iii).

Rainco can either include $1,680 on Tina's W-2 or require her to pay the corporation rent for that amount.

8

If the employee is not a shareholder in the employing corporation, the employer may include the employee rent or compensation as business use. Treatment of the S corporation's deductions attributable to personal use by the employee are not clearly specified in the Code. If the corporation's actual cost of owning and operating the vehicle exceeds the amount that the corporation must charge the employee as compensation or rent, there is a tax benefit to having the corporation, as opposed to the employee, own the vehicle. Treatment of the personal use as compensation, rather than rent, would appear to affect the deductions.

EXAMPLE 8 - 20: Refer to Example 8 - 19. Tina is not a shareholder of Rainco. The corporation's actual costs of owning and operating the automobile in the current year are $7,500 (including the allowable depreciation on the vehicle). All of the use is treated as business use to the corporation, which deducts the $7,500. If the corporation treats Tina's personal use as compensation, the deduction of $7,500 is an ordinary business expense. If the corporation collects rent from Tina, the deductions attributable to the rental use are arguably passive activity deductions. The corporation would subtract the ownership costs of $3,000 (40% of $7,500) from the rent of $2,520 to report a passive activity loss of $480.

If Tina owned the vehicle directly, and her business use of it met the strict standards of convenience of employer and condition of employment, she could deduct the business-related expenses (60%) of owning and operating the car. However, she could not deduct any of the cost attributable to personal use (40%).

If the employee owns, directly or indirectly, 5% or more of the employer, the personal use by the employee does not count as business use by the employer. (See §280F(d)(6)(C). Indirect ownership is determined by the rules of §267.) The relevance of this provision, however, appears to be limited to the testing of business use for depreciation computations. If any taxpayer (including an S corporation) does not use an automobile more than 50% (in miles) for business use in any taxable year, the taxpayer is limited to straight-line depreciation.[16]

---

[16] There are also rules requiring recapture of excess depreciation if a taxpayer has claimed accelerated depreciation and business use drops to 50% or less in any succeeding taxable year.

EXAMPLE 8 - 21: Refer to Example 8 - 19. Assume that Tina owns more than 5% of the stock in Rainco, and that her business use of the automobile in the current year was only 40% of the mileage. The corporation is limited to straight-line depreciation, since its business use of the vehicle does not exceed 50% of the total mileage. The corporation would, however, be entitled to deduct depreciation on the entire cost of the vehicle by the straight-line method.

Another consideration in having the corporation, as opposed to the employee, own the vehicle is the treatment of the interest on any debt incurred with the purchase of the automobile. Interest incurred in the capacity as an employee is not deductible. [§163(h)(2)(A)] This provision appears to be applicable only to individuals, and not to S corporations, since an S corporation cannot be an "employee."

EXAMPLE 8 - 22: Refer to Example 8 - 19. Rainco financed the purchase of the automobile with a $16,000 loan, on which it paid $1,200 interest in the current year. The corporation should be able to deduct the interest. If Tina had acquired the automobile herself, she would not be entitled to deduct any interest, including any portion attributable to her qualified business use.

8

OBSERVATION: If an S corporation provided an automobile to a shareholder, and there was little or no business use of the automobile, the corporation could risk disallowance of interest. As mentioned above, §67(c) gives the IRS the authority to prevent recharacterization of itemized deductions through the use of pass-through entities.

835. Sales of property between corporations and shareholders.

The Code provides some special rules for sales of property between related parties. There are restrictions on deductibility of losses, characterizations of gains, and possible disallowance of the installment method. The most recent addition is a rule that might disallow deferral of gain on like-kind exchanges. The general rules, which are prescribed outside of Subchapter S, mostly apply to sales between corporations and their controlling shareholders; there are few special rules that relate to S corporations, per se.

835.1. Disallowance of losses. Losses are disallowed on sales of property between various related parties. [§267(a)(1)] The related parties are defined in §267(b) as:

- Family members (brothers, sisters, spouse, ancestors, lineal descendants)
- An individual and a corporation (including an S corporation) if that individual owns more than 50% in value of the outstanding stock in the corporation
- Two corporations with more than 50% common ownership
- A grantor and the fiduciary of a trust
- Fiduciaries of trusts with a common grantor
- The fiduciary and any beneficiary of a trust
- The fiduciary of a trust and a beneficiary of another trust with the same grantor
- The fiduciary of a trust and a corporation owned (more than 50%) by the grantor of the trust
- A person (including a corporation) and an exempt organization, when the person controls the exempt organization
- A corporation and a partnership with more than 50% common ownership
- An S corporation and another S corporation with more than 50% common ownership
- An S corporation and a C corporation with more than 50% common ownership

EXAMPLE 8 - 23: Greg owns all of the shares of Greco, Inc. A sale of property that has basis in excess of fair market value from Greg to Greco, or vice versa, will result in a disallowed loss.

The purchaser in a related-party sale takes a cost basis in the property. There is a relief provision that allows the purchaser to use the seller's disallowed loss, but only to the extent of a gain on a future sale.

EXAMPLE 8 - 24: Refer to Example 8 - 23. In 1995, Greco sells property to Greg. Greco's adjusted basis immediately before the sale was $75,000. The sale price was $50,000. Greco is not allowed to recognize the loss. Greg's basis in the property is its cost to him of $50,000. If Greg sells the property in the future, up to $25,000 of Greg's gain is offset by the loss that was disallowed to Greco.

OBSERVATION: Chapter 7 discussed the disallowance of losses on distributions from corporations to shareholders. The loss disallowance on a sale is not as harsh as the disallowance rule on distributions, for two reasons. First, the distribution rules disallow losses on property distributed to any shareholder, no matter how small the percentage of the shareholder's ownership. The sale rules, however, apply only to sales between corporations and majority shareholders. Second, the sale rules provide relief for future sales, by allowing the previously disallowed loss to offset gains. The distribution rules give no equivalent relief.

In determining the ownership of partnerships or corporations, there are certain attribution, or constructive ownership, rules to follow. [§267(c)]

- Stock owned by a partnership, corporation, estate, or trust is considered to be owned by the partners, shareholders, or beneficiaries.
- An individual is treated as owning any stock owned by a family member.
- A partner in a partnership is treated as the constructive owner of any stock held by another partner in the same partnership.

EXAMPLE 8 - 25: Ruth owns all of the stock in Ruco, an S corporation. Ruco sells property to Ruth's sister Corinne. The property, which had a basis to Ruco of $60,000, was sold for $40,000. The loss is disallowed to Ruco, but it may offset any gain on a future sale by Corinne.

When the constructive ownership is through a corporation, partnership, estate, or trust, the stock may again be attributed to another related party. If the constructive ownership is between family members or between partners, however, there is no further attribution. [§267(c)(5)]

The accounting treatment of a disallowed loss on a sale by an S corporation is not clear. As discussed in Chapter 6, at 630., an S corporation is required to report all items of income, losses, and deductions to its shareholders. The reporting includes nondeductible expenses—such as the disallowed portion of meal and entertainment costs to the shareholders, who must reduce basis for their portions of these costs. The corporation must mirror the shareholder adjustments by reducing the Accumulated Adjustments Account. Regulations specifically require that shareholders reduce basis for any loss disallowed under §267(a)(1). [Regs. §1.1367-1(c)(2)]

EXAMPLE 8 - 26: Refer to Example 8 - 25. Ruco's disallowed loss of $20,000 passes through to Ruth and reduces her basis in her stock.

835.2. Characterization of gains. Gains on sales of depreciable property and patents between related parties are treated as ordinary income under §1239. The related parties are:

- An individual and a corporation (including an S corporation) if the individual owns more than 50% in value of outstanding stock
- A partnership and a partner who owns more than 50% of capital and profits
- Two corporations with more than 50% common ownership
- A corporation and a partnership with more than 50% common ownership
- An S corporation and another S corporation with more than 50% common ownership
- An S corporation and a C corporation with more than 50% common ownership
- An employer and its welfare benefit fund

There are no special rules for S corporations, per se. The unique aspects of S corporation taxation, however, can provide a significant loophole for buying ordinary deductions with capital gains, when capital gain treatment is beneficial to a shareholder.

8

EXAMPLE 8 - 27: Phil owns all of the shares in Phico, an S corporation. The corporation owns land and a building with a basis of $50,000 and fair market value of $250,000. Phico has consistently used straight-line depreciation, so there would be no depreciation recapture and all gain would be §1231 gain to the corporation.

Phil has significant capital losses from other sources, and no §1231 losses. Accordingly, if the corporation were to sell the land and building to an unrelated party, any §1231 gain of the corporation would be offset by Phil's capital losses on his personal return. If the corporation were to sell the land and building to Phil, the corporation's gain would be ordinary income, and Phil would not be able to offset the gain with any capital losses.

835.3. Installment sale problems. A seller of depreciable property may not use the installment method if the sale is made to a related party and tax avoidance is one of the principal purposes of the sale. [§453(g)] Related parties are the same as those listed above under §1239. This rule prevents an immediate step up in basis without immediate recognition of gain.

EXAMPLE 8 - 28: MNO Corporation is owned equally by M, N, and O. N and O are brothers, and M is not related. In 1995, N sells the corporation a building for $250,000. N's basis in the building, after deducting straight-line depreciation of $80,000, is $120,000. N takes installment notes payable over a 10-year period.

Pursuant to §453(g), the gain is all reported in 1995. Absent this rule, the corporation would immediately begin to pass ordinary depreciation deductions through to the shareholders, but the gain would not be reported by the seller until the corporation paid the installments. In addition, all of N's gain on the building is ordinary under §1239.

The question of what is a tax avoidance purpose recently came up in the *Guenther* case. [*Guenther*, TC 1995-2801] A taxpayer sold two depreciable properties to an S corporation in which he owned a 25% interest and his four daughters owned the other 75%. The Tax Court ruled that he could not use the installment method to report his gain on the sale. The taxpayer argued that he did not have a tax avoidance purpose because his depreciation before the sale was larger than his share of the corporation's depreciation after the sale. But the Tax Court rejected the argument on the grounds that the tax benefits accruing to all parties, including his daughters, increased as a result of the sale.

835.4. Like-kind exchanges between related parties. When a taxpayer gives personal or real property held for use in a trade or business or for investment purposes, and receives property of a like kind in exchange, there is generally no gain or loss recognized on the exchange. [§1031(a)] In the context of an S corporation and its shareholders there were, before 1990, some potential planning opportunities to help avoid, or at least postpone, recognition of some gains.

EXAMPLE 8 - 29: Lisa owns all of the shares in Lico, an S corporation. Lisa owns an apartment building that she intends to sell. The fair market value of the apartment building is $300,000, and Lisa's basis is $100,000. Lico owns an office building with a fair market value of $300,000 and adjusted basis of $350,000. If Lisa were to exchange the apartment building for the office building, the like-kind exchange rules would provide that neither Lisa or Lico would recognize any gain or loss. Lisa would substitute the apartment building's basis of $100,000 as her basis in the office building. Lico would substitute its $350,000 office building basis as basis in the apartment building. If Lico were to sell the apartment building later, it would recognize a $50,000 loss.

A 1989 amendment to the Code disallows like-kind exchange treatment between related parties, if the property exchanged is sold within two years of the exchange. [§1031(f)] Related parties are the same as those defined at 835.1. under the loss disallowance rule.[17] [§1031(f)(3)]

EXAMPLE 8 - 30: Refer to Example 8 - 29. Under the 1989 amendments to the like-kind exchange rules, a sale of the apartment by Lico within two years of the exchange would invalidate the tax-deferred treatment of the original exchange. Lisa would have to recognize $200,000 gain on the exchange of the apartment with the corporation. Simultaneously, the corporation would be unable to recognize any loss on the sale of the office building to Lisa, under the loss disallowance rules discussed at 835.1.

8

840. Rentals of property between a shareholder and the corporation.

Corporations may rent property to their shareholders, and vice versa. When the corporation and its shareholders undertake a rental arrangement, all parties should make sure that the corporation charges a reasonable market rent, or there may be some tax problems.

840.1. Rental of corporate property by a shareholder. Perhaps the most common transaction of a shareholder renting property from the corporation involves a residence. If the corporation owns the residence, and rents it to a shareholder, the form of the transaction will usually be respected if the rent is paid at fair market value.

If a shareholder pays less than fair market rent, the IRS can recharacterize the savings as a distribution from the corporation to the shareholder. If a shareholder pays excessive rent, the IRS could treat the excessive portion as a contribution to capital.

840.11. Treatment as passive investment income. If the S corporation has accumulated earnings and profits from Subchapter C years, it may be subject to passive investment income problems, unless the corporation provides significant services.

EXAMPLE 8 - 31: Tiffany rents property from Tifco, an S corporation in which she owns all of the shares. The rent Tiffany pays to Tifco is passive investment income to Tifco. As such, it may cause Tifco to pay a corporate-level tax, and it may cause the corporation to terminate its S election.

When an S corporation owns property that shareholders might want to use for personal purposes, the corporation could avoid the passive investment income problem by selling the property to the shareholder. Sales of tangible property do not create passive investment income to an S corporation.

840.12. Bargain rentals. Rental of corporate property to a shareholder at less than a fair market rent could be treated as a bargain rent. Bargain rents can be characterized as constructive

[17] A partnership and any person who owns more than 50% of the capital or profits interest in the partnership are also related parties for this disallowance.

distributions, in the same manner as excessive compensation. If there is more than one shareholder, a constructive distribution to one shareholder may indicate a second class of stock.

840.13. Treatment as passive activity. Any net loss from the rental of property, including rental to a shareholder, would be a passive activity loss. As such, the net loss would be reported separately by the S corporation to the shareholders and would not be deductible, except within the limits of §469. See Chapters 6 and 10 for further discussion of these issues.

> **EXAMPLE 8 - 32:** Madison owns all of the shares of Madco, an S corporation. Madison rents property from Madco. Madco's rental income is less than Madco's expenses associated with the rented property. The net rental loss is a passive activity loss, which flows through to Madison in his capacity as a shareholder.

> **OBSERVATION:** If a shareholder rents property from an S corporation and the rental produces net income to the corporation, it is questionable whether the income would be passive. The IRS is empowered to write Regulations that characterize income or loss as passive or otherwise. [§469(l)] The next example describes a shareholder's attempt to create passive income.

> **EXAMPLE 8 - 33:** Johnson owns all of the shares of Orace, an S corporation. Johnson pays Orace rent of $10,000 for the use of some of Orace's property. Orace's cost of owning the property is only $8,000. The net income of $2,000 should be characterized as passive to Orace under the general rules of §469. If Johnson can properly claim the rental expense as a deduction, he has succeeded in creating passive activity income, which may be sheltered by passive losses from other activities. As of this writing, there is no direct prohibition against creating passive activity income in this manner. There is, however, a recharacterization rule, described below, that would treat income generated in the reverse situation—Orace renting from Johnson—as nonpassive.

840.14. Rent of a dwelling unit to a shareholder. S corporations are subject to the same limitations as individuals on rentals of vacation homes and other dwelling units. Under §280A, the expenses attributable to any dwelling used by the owner, including any shareholder if the S corporation owns the property, may not create a deductible loss. For the personal use test, the use by any shareholder is treated as a day of personal use by the S corporation. [§280A(f)(2)] In one case, an S corporation was not entitled to deductions for depreciation, insurance, and utilities when it provided a home to its shareholder-employees. [*Proskauer*, 46 TCM 679, TC Memo 1983-395]

> **OBSERVATION:** The disallowance of corporate-level expenses, plus the denial of tax-free fringe benefits for meals and lodging provided to the employee, may create a dangerous combination for S corporations and their employees. If an S corporation provides rent-free use of a home to a shareholder, the shareholder must include the fair value of the rental in income. The corporation is not allowed to deduct any expenses associated with the property, under the vacation home rules. As a consequence of the collision of these rules, an S corporation that provides a shareholder with a dwelling should either charge a fair market rent for all days used or report it as compensation to the shareholder-employee.

840.2. Rental of property from a shareholder. Rental of a shareholder's property by the corporation is common, especially with real estate used by the business.

> **PLANNING TIPS:** There are several reasons why a shareholder (or group of shareholders) may want to keep some business property out of corporate ownership and instead rent it to the corporation:

- If the property is expected to appreciate, and the shareholder plans to leave the property to his or her heirs, the property will receive a fresh start basis at the time of the current owner's death. This cannot be accomplished by transferring the property to the corporation.
- If the corporation is a C corporation, the shareholder may be able to transfer income from the corporation in the form of rent payments. Such payments are deductible by the corporation, and are exempt from the double tax. In general, rent payments are exempt from payroll or self-employment taxes.
- Before the Tax Reform Act of 1986, it was possible to use ACRS deductions—which were fully deductible by the shareholder—to help create a tax loss from the rental.
- If two or more individuals are planning to create a corporation, and one person has a disproportionate portion of the property that the business needs, it may be prudent to have the current owner retain ownership of the property and lease it to the corporation, rather than contribute the property to the corporation.

As of this writing, the first reason for keeping property out of a corporation is still valid, if the property has appreciated or is expected to appreciate before the current owner's death. There are also many arrangements that were consummated before the Tax Reform Act of 1986 or when the corporation was a C corporation.

840.21. Passive income and loss. There are both benefits and drawbacks to an S corporation renting property from a shareholder. The alternative is to have the corporation own the property. In general, rental income and expenses associated with property that a shareholder rents to a corporation will be subject to the passive activity loss rules of §469.

EXAMPLE 8 - 34: Tom owns all of the shares of Jolly, Inc., an S corporation. The corporation uses land and buildings in its business. The depreciation, interest, taxes, and insurance on the building total $65,000 for the current year. Due to depressed real estate conditions in the area, a fair market rent is only $50,000 per year. If the corporation owns the land and buildings, all of the deductions associated with the property are ordinary business deductions. If Tom owns the property and rents it to the corporation for $50,000, Tom will report a net loss of $15,000, which will be a passive activity loss. It will not be deductible in the current year unless Tom has other sources of passive income.

Assume that the corporation's income, without regard to the building costs or rent, is expected to be $80,000 per year. Also assume that Tom has no passive income from other sources. Compare the effect on Tom's income of having the corporation own or rent the property:

	If Jolly, Inc.,	
	Owns	*Rents*
Jolly's income		
Before building costs	$80,000	$80,000
Building costs	(65,000)	(50,000)
Net income to Tom	$15,000	$30,000
Tom's deductible rental loss	n/a	(0)*
Tom's income from the business	$15,000	$30,000

*Tom has a loss of $15,000 from the rent. Due to the limitations of §469, none of the loss is deductible.

If an S corporation can rent property from a shareholder, and the shareholder is not concerned with the passive activity loss limits, rental can provide some benefits.

EXAMPLE 8 - 35: Refer to Example 8 - 34. Assume the same facts except that Jolly, Inc., has income (before building costs or Tom's compensation) of $100,000. Also assume that the fair rental of the land and building is $75,000. If the corporation owns the building, its net income (before Tom's compensation) will be $35,000. If it rents the building, its net income (before Tom's compensation) is only $25,000. In either case, if it makes any distributions to Tom without providing a reasonable level of compensation, the IRS is likely to recharacterize the distributions as salary to Tom under the rationale of Revenue Ruling 74-44 and the *Radtke* case, cited earlier. By renting the building, Jolly, Inc., can direct cash toward Tom without the danger of constructive distributions. It also would decrease its exposure to payroll and FICA taxes.

840.22. Rents do not produce net passive income. A shareholder may be tempted to rent property to the corporation at a high rental rate in order to create passive activity income. Consider the following possibility.

EXAMPLE 8 - 36: Leon is the sole shareholder in Leco, an S corporation. Outside the corporation, he has several passive activities that produce losses. He owns real estate that Leco uses in its business. Leon materially participates in the corporation's business. His income from Leco, in the form of profits, compensation, or interest, cannot be offset by any of his other passive activity losses.

The market rates of rent are sufficiently broad that he can rent the property for $50,000 or $75,000 and withstand a test of reasonableness. At $50,000, Leon will break even on the rental property. At $75,000, he will show $25,000 net income from the rent and reduce his income from the S corporation by the same amount. By switching $25,000 from business income to rental income, he is attempting to alter the character of that income from active business to passive rent. If he is successful, he could offset $25,000 with his losses from other passive activities.

The U.S. Treasury has thwarted this strategy by recharacterizing certain net rental income (but not net loss) as "nonpassive." Property rented to a trade or business in which the taxpayer materially participates does not produce net passive income. [Regs. §1.469-2T(f)(6)] Accordingly, it is important to know what constitutes an activity in which the taxpayer materially participates.

According to the Regulations, a taxpayer's interest in an activity includes an interest held through a partnership or an S corporation. [Regs. §1.469-2T(e)(1)] Therefore, although the rental of property from a shareholder to an S corporation is generally considered a passive activity, such rental activity cannot create net passive income.

EXAMPLE 8 - 37: Merle, Henry, and Pauline are practicing dentists. Their corporation, MHP Co., PC, is a dental corporation. Merle, Henry, and Pauline also have a partnership that owns the building in which the dental practice is conducted. The partnership rents the building to the corporation. The rent income from the corporation exceeds the partnership's costs of owning and operating the building. The rental of the building does not result in net passive rent income to the partnership.

There is an exception for property rented to a business in which the taxpayer materially participates, if the rental agreement was signed before February 19, 1988. [Regs. §1.469-11T(a)(2)(ii)] In these cases, the rent charged to the S corporation may create net passive income.

840.23. Office-in-home expenses. In general, an individual or an S corporation may not claim expenses for an office in the home unless the office meets certain strict standards. [*LaFavor*, TC Memo 1998-336] (All tests referred to are contained in §280A(c)(1).) If the office is in the same physical structure as the residence, the office must be the principal place of business or must be used by the taxpayer to meet with customers, clients, or patients on a regular basis. A separate structure is subject to a less stringent standard and must merely be used in connection with the business. Whether the office is attached or separate, it must be used regularly and exclusively for business. If an office in the home is used by an employee, it must be for the convenience of the employer.

If a shareholder of an S corporation intends to use a portion of his or her home for office space, it may be advisable for the shareholder and the corporation to own the residence jointly. Otherwise, even though the office may meet the tests for deductibility, the shareholder's deductions would be miscellaneous itemized deductions, subject to the 2% adjusted gross income limit, the reduction for taxpayers whose adjusted gross income exceeds $100,000, and addition to income for alternative minimum tax purposes. By contrast, if the corporation actually owns the portion of the residence used for the office, the deductions—though subject to the same rigorous standards—would be ordinary business deductions to the corporation and would reduce the shareholder's adjusted gross income.

If an employee rents a portion of his or her home to the employer, the employee is not entitled to any deductions for the cost of owning and operating the office. [§280A(c)(6)] This rule is not limited to shareholder-employees of S corporations, but covers any employee of any employer. An employee is allowed to claim deductions for office-in-home if the office is not rented to the employer. The deductions, however, are miscellaneous itemized deductions, subject to the 2% adjusted gross income floor, the phaseout of 3% of itemized deductions when adjusted gross income exceeds $100,000, and the alternative minimum tax adjustment. In one situation, a shareholder disregarded $12,000 of rent paid by the S corporation for use of the office in the shareholder's home. The shareholder claimed that the $12,000 was *de minimis* and should excluded. The IRS and the Court held otherwise. [*Roy*, TC Memo 1998-125]

845. Interest on loans between the corporation and its shareholders.

Loans between an S corporation and its shareholders may occur in several contexts. Often, as discussed in Chapters 6 and 9, one or more of the shareholders loan money to the corporation to create basis for the pass-through of losses. In this situation, usually the corporation is experiencing cash flow problems, and the shareholder is trying to bolster the corporation. The reverse scenario, where the S corporation loans money to shareholders, may happen for a variety of reasons. Perhaps one or more shareholders have a cash flow problem and the corporation does not want to record taxable compensation or a taxable distribution.

845.1. Uses and hazards of loans to S corporations. Shareholders may loan money to an S corporation to create basis for losses. As discussed in detail in Chapter 9, a properly structured loan may provide a shareholder with sufficient basis to absorb his or her portion of an S corporation's losses. In the case of an S corporation with only one shareholder, however, a contribution to capital or a purchase of additional stock may be an easier way to establish basis. Loans for basis purposes are most useful when there is more than one shareholder and the contribution from each shareholder is not in accordance with the desired stock ownership.

EXAMPLE 8 - 38: Harry and Ray are equal shareholders in HR, an S corporation. In the current year, the corporation needs $100,000 in cash. Harry has no cash to contribute, but Ray is able to contribute or loan the corporation the full $100,000.

If Ray contributed $100,000 without taking back additional stock, the economics of the transaction might be questionable. If he received no additional rights to the corporation's profits or assets, he may have made a constructive gift to Harry. If he were given preference in current or liquidating distributions, the corporation would likely have a second class of stock. Therefore, the only alternatives seem to be for Ray to purchase additional stock or to loan the corporation the money.

If he could purchase additional stock, it could be nonvoting stock and would not disturb the current voting ratios. He would automatically be entitled to greater distributions than Harry, as well as a greater percentage allocation of the corporation's income or loss, by virtue of his increased equity. Again, however, he could not be given a preference without having the corporation violate the single-class-of-stock rule.

A valid loan would give Ray a legitimate preference over Harry, at least until the corporation retired the loan. Both HR and Ray should observe all of the formalities necessary to qualify the loan for the straight-debt safe harbor, discussed in Chapter 2. Ray would receive $100,000 in additional basis, which could provide for deductibility of his portion of HR's loss in the current and future years.

845.2. Loan from an S corporation to a shareholder. Sometimes an S corporation loans money to a shareholder. If there is only one shareholder, it is usually simpler to make a distribution. When there are two or more shareholders, however, and the corporation cannot afford to make sufficient distributions to satisfy all of the shareholders, loans may be useful.

EXAMPLE 8 - 39: Olive and Pamela are equal shareholders in the OP Corporation, an S corporation. In the current year, the corporation has taxable income of $200,000, but only $150,000 of available cash. Olive needs $100,000 of cash, whereas Pamela needs only $50,000. If the corporation distributes $100,000 to Olive and only $50,000 to Pamela, the corporation could risk having a second class of stock. The Regulations do not mandate this treatment automatically, but they do state that such distributions shall be given appropriate tax effect. [Regs. §1.1361-1(l)(2)] Note that there are two possible tax effects that the shareholders could record:

8

1. The corporation could distribute $50,000 to each shareholder, and make a $50,000 loan to Olive.
2. The corporation could distribute $100,000 to each shareholder, and have Pamela loan $50,000 back to the corporation.

The corporation would do well to record the distribution on its books in one of the two manners suggested, thereby minimizing the risk that the IRS would find two classes of stock.

There are risks to using loans rather than distributions or contributions to capital. When a corporation makes a loan to a substantial shareholder, there is always the risk that the IRS will question the validity of the loan. The IRS can recharacterize loans as distributions when there are no loan formalities. [*Jones*, TC Memo 1997-400]

If the loan is treated as a constructive distribution, this treatment could pose the following problems:

- If the corporation has more than one shareholder and the loans are not made in proportion to stock ownership, the constructive distributions could be seen as a second class of stock.
- If the corporation's Accumulated Adjustments Account is less than the total amount of the loans to shareholders, and the corporation has accumulated earnings and profits, the constructive distribution could create dividend income at the shareholder level.

Loans from shareholders to the corporation are also subject to some hazards. As discussed in Chapter 14, if the corporation needs additional funds and one or more of the shareholders purchase more stock, the stock may qualify for §1244 treatment. This provision allows shareholders to claim an ordinary loss on the sale or worthlessness of the stock. There is no corresponding provision for the loss on sale or worthlessness of a loan. A lender may be able to claim an ordinary loss deduction on a business bad debt, but the IRS often contests such treatment. Cancellation of purported loans from a corporation to its shareholder can be treated as compensation income to the shareholder—rather than as a bad debt and cancellation of debt income, which would have cancelled each other out at the shareholder level. [*Haber*, 52 TC 255 (1969)] Courts are willing to agree with the IRS that a loan to a troubled corporation may in fact be a capital contribution. [See *Miles Production Co. v. Commissioner*,

72-1 USTC 9331 (5th Cir.)] Nor do contributions to capital qualify for §1244 ordinary loss treatment. [Regs. §1.1244(d)-2] (See Chapter 14 for discussion of §1244.) Since a contribution to capital is not a debt, it does not qualify for a business bad debt deduction. Therefore, a shareholder who advances money to a troubled corporation should seriously consider the purchase of additional stock, which may qualify for §1244 ordinary loss treatment on its sale or worthlessness.

845.3. Requirement to charge interest. Loans between shareholders and corporations must also bear a reasonable rate of interest. A loan with a less than reasonable rate of interest is subject to the interest imputation rules of §7872, discussed below. Code §7872 requires that interest be imputed on loans where the interest charged is less than the applicable federal rate. The amount of interest not charged is treated as transferred from the lender to the borrower. The characterization of the transfer depends on the relationship between the lender and the borrower. The most likely contexts are gifts, compensation, dividends (or other corporate distributions), and contributions to capital.

The borrower is treated as repaying the interest to the lender, with the following results:

- Interest income is imputed to the lender.
- The imputed interest payment by the borrower is potentially deductible, but it must meet the tracing rules of Regulations §1.163-8T (discussed at 845.4.).
- The method of accounting of either party does not affect the transfer. It is treated as made "for purposes of this title [Internal Revenue Code]." [§7872(a)]

The rules for imputation of interest apply to both term and demand loans. The timing of transfers, however, differs between the two types of loans. With a *demand loan*, both transfers occur on the last day of the calendar year. The amount is based on the number of days the loan was outstanding and on the applicable federal rate.

By contrast, with a *term loan*, the two-way transfers are not mirror images. The lender's transfer of foregone interest to the borrower occurs at the time the loan is made. The borrower's repayment to the lender is computed by the original issue discount rules. The concept of *original issue discount* in connection with a below-market loan is illustrated in Example 8 - 42, in the context of a loan from an S corporation to a shareholder.

845.31. Loans from the S corporation to a shareholder. The interest imputation rules of §7872 expressly apply to loans between corporations and their shareholders. Regulations §1.7872-4(d) extends the provision to loans between S corporations and their shareholders. Interest foregone on loans from the corporation to the shareholder will be treated as a distribution made by the S corporation. Results of a demand loan to a sole shareholder are negligible.

Figure 8 - 1 depicts the fictional transfers of foregone interest when the S corporation is the lender and a shareholder is the borrower.

EXAMPLE 8 - 40: J Corporation, an S corporation, loans $100,000 to K, its sole shareholder, on March 14, 1996. The loan carries no interest and is payable on demand of the lender. Assume that the applicable federal rate is 12% per annum. By December 31, 1996, K has made no payment on the loan.

On December 31, 1996, there are two "transfers":

1. K to J [$100,000 x .12 x (292/365)]	$9,600
2. J to K [$100,000 x .12 x (292/365)]	$9,600

The transfer by K to J will be treated as a payment of interest. The statute states that the transfer is made "for purposes of this title." The fact that K and J are related parties (subject

Figure 8 - 1:
Foregone interest on a loan from an S corporation to a shareholder.

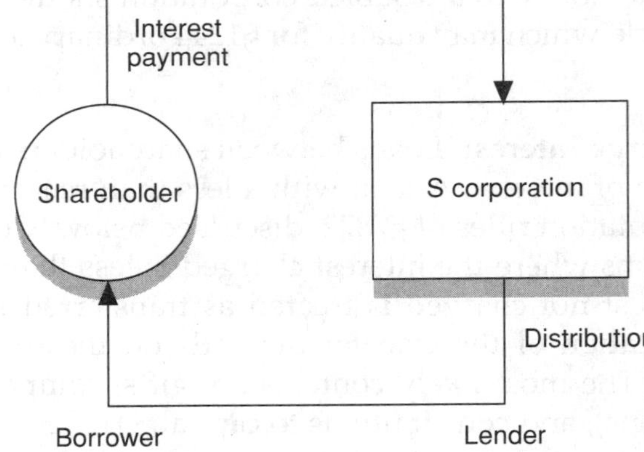

8

to the timing rules of §267) is irrelevant. The accounting method employed by both parties is likewise unimportant. K will be allowed a deduction for interest, assuming that the payment meets the general requirement of deductibility. J will report interest income from this transaction. Since K is the sole shareholder, there will be no net tax effect.

The transfer by J will be treated as a distribution. Note that J's AAA is augmented for the interest income received (for purposes of this title) on December 31, 1996. The distribution will be subject to all of the usual distribution rules. If there is a sufficient balance in the AAA, there will be no taxability to the shareholder.

If the borrower is not the sole shareholder, additional complications arise. Section 7872 will treat the borrower as receiving the distribution and paying the interest. The interest deemed paid to the corporation will be allocated among all of the shareholders in accordance with their weighted average ownership of shares. Therefore, each shareholder will potentially be liable for tax on a portion of phantom income. The single-class-of-stock rule will also require the corporation to take into account the constructive distribution to the borrowing shareholder. It should make corresponding distributions to all other shareholders.

EXAMPLE 8 - 41: Assume the same facts as in Example 8 - 40, except that K is a 50% shareholder. The two "transfers" on December 31, 1996, are exactly the same. The net result is quite different, due to two factors:

1. The $9,600 imputed interest income recognized by J Corporation will be divided among the shareholders in the usual allocation formula. Therefore, K will receive only $4,800 of the income, with the remainder going to the other shareholders.
2. K, however, receives an imputed distribution of $9,600, although he is taxable on only $4,800 income. Unless the corporation has made proportionate distributions to the other shareholders, the deemed distribution would be disproportionate. Regulations §1.1361-1 states that disproportionate distributions are to be given appropriate tax effect. Although it is possible that the corporation has a second class of stock, this is not the only proper treatment. Another possibility is that the corporation has made fictional distributions to all shareholders and the other shareholders have made fictional loans back to the corporation. These fictional loans would in turn be subject to the imputed interest rules of §7872. Aside from the bookkeeping complications in recording all of the fictional events over the life of the loans, each shareholder would be required to report certain amounts of income, which would exist only on paper.

Examples 8 - 40 and 8 - 41 demonstrate some of the potential problems involved when an S corporation makes a below-market loan to a shareholder. It would be far better for the corporation to require payment of interest, so it could record the interest payments with full knowledge of the shareholders.

The timing of the transfers for a term loan may be considerably different from the timing of the hypothetical transfers for a demand loan. Interest on a below-market term loan is calculated by the original issue discount rules. In brief, the original issue discount rule uses the accrual method to compute interest on the net present value of an obligation. The lender's transfer of interest to the borrower is the difference between the principal amount of the loan and its discounted present value, using the applicable federal rate of interest at the time the loan is made. The borrower's repayment to the lender is deemed to occur each year, by multiplying the applicable federal rate by the carrying value of the debt at the beginning of that year.

For the first year, the carrying value is the net present value. Each year's imputed interest is added to the carrying value for subsequent years.

EXAMPLE 8 - 42: Assume that Y, Inc., loans $100,000 to shareholder Z on January 1, 1996. The loan bears no interest and matures on January 1, 1999. Using a 6% interest rate, the net present value of $100,000 to be paid back three years in the future is $83,962.

The amount of interest to be foregone is $16,038. This amount is "transferred" from Z to Y on January 1, 1996. It is treated as a distribution. Using the original issue discount rules, the amount transferred from Y to Z is:

12/31/96 ($83,962 x .06)	$ 5,038
12/31/97 [($83,962 + $5,038) x .06]	5,340
12/31/98 [($83,962 + $5,038 + $5,340) x .06]	5,660
Total	$16,038

Note that Y's AAA for 1995 includes only $5,038 of income from interest "retransferred" from Z. If the total balance in AAA is not at least $16,038, any or all of the following could happen:

1. If the corporation has accumulated earnings and profits, the shareholder would receive a constructive dividend.
2. To the extent the distribution does not come from accumulated earnings and profits, the shareholder would reduce basis in his stock. This reduction would affect the deductibility of current and future losses.
3. If the distribution exceeds the sum of accumulated earnings and profits and the shareholder's adjusted basis in stock, the excess is taxable as a gain.
4. If the shareholder is not the sole shareholder, there may be a second class of stock. In the case of a term loan, the distribution would be on the date that the loan is made, and the S election may be terminated at that time.

845.32. Loans from a shareholder to the S corporation. Loans from shareholders to corporations are also governed by §7872. When a shareholder loans money to the corporation, the interest foregone by the shareholder will be treated as a contribution to capital.

Figure 8 - 2 depicts the fictional transfers of foregone interest when the S corporation is the borrower and a shareholder is the lender.

There is no essential difference between a C corporation and an S corporation in the treatment of foregone interest and the contribution to capital. An S election may, however, ameliorate the overall tax treatment. First, consider the case of a shareholder making a below-market loan to a C corporation:

Figure 8 - 2:
Foregone interest on a loan from a shareholder to an S corporation.

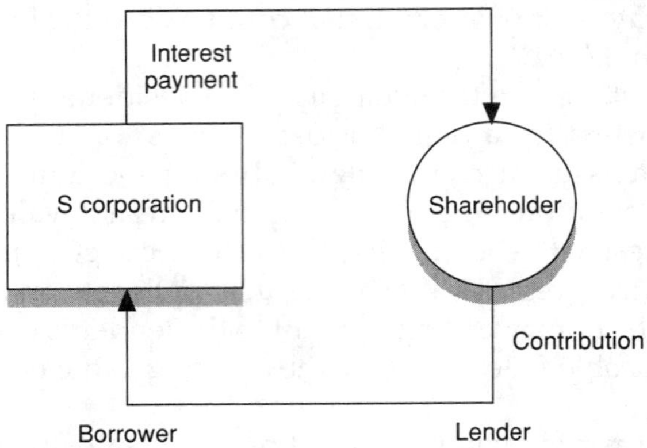

EXAMPLE 8 - 43: Maggie, the sole shareholder of Grand Corporation, loans $100,000 to the corporation on March 14, 1996. Grand is a C corporation. The loan carries no interest and is payable on demand of the lender. Assume that the applicable federal rate is 12% per annum. By December 31, 1996, no payment has been made on the loan.

On December 31, 1996, there are two "transfers":

1.	Grand to Maggie [$100,000 x .06 x (292/365)]	$4,800
2.	Maggie to Grand [$100,000 x .06 x (292/365)]	$4,800

Grand's transfer to Maggie will be treated as a payment of interest. Grand will be allowed a deduction for interest, but that deduction reduces corporate taxable income.

Maggie will report interest income from this transaction. Therefore, Maggie's taxable income is increased by the entire $9,600. Since a shareholder is most likely to loan money to a troubled corporation, the corporation is not likely to receive any tax benefit.

The transfer from Maggie to Grand will be a contribution to capital. It will increase Maggie's basis, but a basis increase is of little value to a shareholder in a C corporation.

If a shareholder makes a below-market loan to an S corporation, the shareholder will at least possibly get a tax benefit for the imputed interest paid by the corporation.

EXAMPLE 8 - 44: Assume the same facts in Example 8 - 43, except that an S election is in effect. The results would be the same, except that the shareholder gets the benefit of the interest deduction of the corporation.

The above examples and commentary serve to illustrate the operation of §7872, which applies only to foregone interest in a below-market loan. If a loan bears an adequate rate of interest, the economics of the transactions are exactly the same as those illustrated above. A below-market loan may be structured to fall within the safe-harbor debt requirements of §1361(c)(5), discussed in Chapter 2. Even a below-market loan that does not meet the straight-debt safe harbor (such as an unwritten obligation) should not be treated as a second class of stock if it is made by the sole shareholder or in proportion to the shareholders' stock ownership. [Regs. §1.1361-1(l)(4)(ii)(B)(2)]

OBSERVATION: A loan from a shareholder to a closely held corporation is always subject to the risk of recharacterization as equity. If the debt is reclassified, it should be redeemed while the S election is still in effect. If it is not, it will be treated as a stock redemption and may be treated as a dividend to the shareholder. See Chapter 15.

845.4. Interest tracing rules in general. S corporations are subject to the same interest tracing rules as any other taxpayer. Regulations §1.163-8T requires allocation of interest as trade or business, passive activities, portfolio, or consumer, depending on the use of the borrowed funds. Since the loan is "traced" to an expenditure, the Regulation requiring allocation of interest is known as the "tracing regulation." The Regulation provides that a partnership or an S corporation must determine the nature of its interest by tracing borrowed funds at the entity level. [Regs. §1.163-8T(n)(3)(ix)]

The tracing Regulation is lengthy and contains many complicated rules and examples. In brief, the tracing rules are:

- If borrowed funds are applied directly to an expenditure (such as a purchase money mortgage where the lender disburses directly to the seller), the interest is associated with the expenditure.

EXAMPLE 8 - 45: An S corporation secures a loan commitment from a bank to finance the purchase of a new pickup truck. The S corporation purchases the pickup from a local dealer, and the bank writes the check directly to the dealer. Any interest paid on the loan will be associated with the pickup truck. For instance, if the pickup is used directly in the S corporation's business, then the interest paid would be an ordinary business expense.

8

- If borrowed funds are deposited in an account and are commingled with other funds, the expenditures immediately following the deposit are treated as coming from the loan.

EXAMPLE 8 - 46: An S corporation draws $10,000 on its line of credit and puts the money in its general-purpose checking account. The next day it makes a portfolio investment of $10,000. The loan will be traced to the portfolio investment, and the interest on the loan will be treated as investment interest.

- The tracing rules depend almost entirely on the form, rather than the substance, of the transaction. A careful taxpayer may use separate accounts, and time any transactions carefully, to achieve desired results.

EXAMPLE 8 - 47: Refer to Example 8 - 46. If the borrowing corporation had used unborrowed funds to make the portfolio investment on the day before it drew the $10,000 on its line of credit, the interest on the $10,000 would not be traced to the portfolio investment.

- The Regulation allows a taxpayer to make any desired allocation to any expenditures within 15 days of the borrowing.

EXAMPLE 8 - 48: Refer to Example 8 - 46. Assume that the corporation expended $10,000 in ordinary and necessary business expenses within 15 days after drawing on its line of credit. In spite of the fact that the portfolio investment was the *first* expenditure made after the loan, the corporation could trace the loan to its first $10,000 of ordinary expenditures within the 15-day period following the loan.

Regulations 1.163-8T(f) is reserved for tracing interest on a loan incurred by an S corporation that distributes the borrowed funds to its shareholders. In the absence of any special provision, however, loans between S corporations and their shareholders should be traced in the same manner as any other loans.

EXAMPLE 8 - 49: Joann owns all of the stock in Joco, an S corporation. She borrows $100,000 from Joco. Within 15 days of the loan she invests the $100,000 in another active business venture. Under the tracing Regulation, she will characterize her interest payment to Joco as an active trade or business deduction.

Unless future Regulations require contrary treatment, the character of the interest income to a related lender will be portfolio income. Note in the last example that the shareholder was able to secure an active business interest deduction. The corporation, however, would pass the interest income to the shareholder as portfolio income. [Rev. Rul. 84-131, 1984-2 CB 37]

> **EXAMPLE 8 - 50:** Joann, in Example 8 - 49, pays $10,000 in interest to Joco. She also pays $10,000 of investment interest on a loan traced to a common stock investment. Under the general classification rules, the interest income to Joco is portfolio income, and it will retain that characteristic when it passes through to Joann. Joann could offset the interest income from Joco with interest she paid on the common stock investment.

Unless the shareholder is subject to the passive activity loss restrictions, currently there are no Regulations to combat the potential mismatching of income and deductions through the use of related party loans. The rules relating to mismatching of interest income and deductions in regard to a passive activity are stated at 845.51. As of this writing there are no Regulations dealing with the ability to create portfolio income. However, if the IRS were to decide that such characterization is abusive, it could pursue a course of action such as the following:

> **EXAMPLE 8 - 51:** Refer to Examples 8 - 49 and 8 - 50. The IRS might pursue one of two alternative recharacterization treatments:
>
> 1. Treat the interest paid by Joann to Joco as investment interest, to match the character of the income she receives from the corporation, or
> 2. Treat Joco's interest income as active trade or business income to Joann, to match the treatment of her interest deduction.

The problems would be compounded when the corporation has more than one shareholder but loans money to only one shareholder. The IRS might attempt partial reallocation. At this point, the actual treatment of such problems is pure conjecture.

845.5. Recharacterization of interest income or deductions in a passive activity. An S corporation's interest income is generally characterized as portfolio income. The S corporation must report its portfolio income separately to its shareholders. This source of income cannot be offset by passive activity losses, but it can be offset by investment interest. The next example illustrates a possible disadvantage of mismatching interest income and deductions.

> **EXAMPLE 8 - 52:** Alexis owns all of the shares of Lexico, an S corporation. In the current year she receives $10,000 of interest from a loan she has made to Lexico. Lexico is involved in a rental activity that produces a $25,000 loss for the current year. Lexico properly traces the use of its loan from Alexis to the passive activity. Alexis has no sources of passive income that would allow her to deduct her passive loss from Lexico.
>
> If there were no way to recharacterize either the interest income to Alexis or the interest expense to the corporation, there would be a mismatch. Alexis would report the following amounts from Lexico:

Portfolio income (taxable)	$ 10,000
Passive loss (not deductible)	$ (25,000)

845.51. General rules of Proposed Regulations §1.469-7T. In April 1991, in Proposed Regulations §1.469-7T, the IRS addressed this issue of mismatching. [P.S. 39-89, 4/5/91] Proposed Regulations §1.469-7T recharacterizes interest income from a passive activity as passive activity gross income, rather than portfolio income, when the loan is made between a pass-through entity and an owner. The borrowed funds must be used in a passive activity.

EXAMPLE 8 - 53: Refer to Example 8 - 52. Pursuant to Proposed Regulations §1.469-7T, Alexis would recharacterize her interest income from Lexico as passive activity gross income. She would be able to offset $10,000 of her passive activity loss with this income.

845.52. Required ownership. An *owner* is defined as a taxpayer who owns any direct interest, or a qualified indirect interest, in the pass-through entity. A *qualified indirect interest* occurs when one pass-through entity (either a partnership or an S corporation) owns an interest in another pass-through entity. [Proposed Regulations §1.469-7T(b)(2)] (Due to the ownership rules of S corporations, there can be no indirect interest in an S corporation.)

EXAMPLE 8 - 54: Boris owns 50% of the shares in Yelco, an S corporation. Yelco, in turn, owns 30% of the capital and profits in Rusco, a partnership. Rusco loans Boris $200,000, and Boris pays Rusco $20,000 interest in the current year. Boris properly traces the $200,000 loan to an interest in a passive activity, so his interest expense is treated as a passive activity deduction.

Boris has a qualifying indirect interest in Rusco, since he indirectly owns 15% (50% of 30%) of the capital and profits. Rusco treats the $20,000 interest income as portfolio income. Rusco allocates $6,000 of this income (30% of $20,000) to Yelco. Yelco in turn allocates $3,000 of the income to Boris (50% of $6,000). Under Proposed Regulations §1.469-7T, Boris treats the $3,000 interest income as passive activity gross income.

8

Although there is no minimum direct ownership requirement, there is a minimum qualifying indirect ownership. If the indirect ownership is less than 10% of capital and profits, Proposed Regulations §1.469-7T does not permit recharacterization of any of the interest income.

EXAMPLE 8 - 55: Refer to Example 8 - 54. Assume the same facts, except that Yelco owns only 16% of the capital and profits in Rusco. Rusco passes $3,200 of the interest received from Boris to Yelco, which in turn passes $1,600 of this interest through to Boris. Since Boris owns only an 8% indirect interest in Rusco, there is no recharacterization of this interest. Boris must treat his portion of the interest income as portfolio.

OBSERVATION: There is no apparent rationale to the minimum threshold of the qualifying indirect interest. Any direct interest, no matter how small, qualifies for the recharacterization. It appears that any direct interest, combined with any indirect interest, would allow recharacterization.

EXAMPLE 8 - 56: Refer to Example 8 - 55. Assume that in addition to his indirect interest in Rusco, Boris also owns a 1% direct interest in Rusco's capital and profits. Rusco would pass $200 of Boris' interest directly to Boris. Boris would also receive $1,600 via his ownership in Yelco. Note that Boris' total direct and indirect interest in Rusco is less than 10%. A literal reading of Proposed Regulations §1.469-7T allows Boris to recharacterize the entire $1,800 of interest as passive activity gross income.

845.53. Recharacterization limited to passive activities. In order to qualify for the recharacterization, the loan giving rise to the interest must be traced to a passive activity. To the extent that the borrowed funds are used for other purposes, there is no recharacterization.

EXAMPLE 8 - 57 [derived from Proposed Regulations §1.469-7T(g), Example (3)]: Earl owns 50% of the stock in X Corporation, an S corporation. Earl borrows $30,000 from X. Earl pays X $3,000 interest in the current year. Earl traces $15,000 of the loan to a passive activity and $15,000 to personal expenditures. Under the general tracing rules, half of Earl's interest expense is a passive activity deduction and half is personal interest.

X passes through $1,500 of interest income to Earl in the current year. Since half of X's interest income is attributable to a passive activity, Earl recharacterizes half of the interest income ($750) as passive activity gross income. The remaining interest income is portfolio.

845.54. Transactions with multiple owners. When more than one owner loans money to a pass-through entity, each will have a portion of self-charged interest. The recharacterization permitted to each lender is the lesser of:

- The lender's portion of the borrower's self-charged interest deductions attributable to passive activities
- The lender's self-charged interest income from the entity

The self-charged interest deductions used in the formula include interest paid to all owners. An example from the Proposed Regulation illustrates the computations for an entity with two owners:

EXAMPLE 8 - 58 [derived from Proposed Regulations §1.469-7T(g), Example (2)]: Clarence and Carla each own 50% of Hearings, Inc., an S corporation. Clarence lends $10,000 and Carla lends $20,000 to Hearings for use in a passive activity. In the current year, Hearings pays $1,000 interest to Clarence and $2,000 interest to Carla. The self-charged interest allocated to each of the shareholders is $1,500. The two shareholders will recharacterize their portions of interest income as passive activity gross income, as follows:

8

	Clarence	*Carla*
Share of self-charged interest deductions	$1,500	$1,500
Self-charged interest income	$1,000	$2,000
Passive activity gross income	$1,000	$1,500

845.55. Election out of recharacterization. If the taxpayers do not want to recharacterize any of the interest income as passive activity gross income, the Proposed Regulation provides for an election out. [Proposed Regulations §1.469-7T(f)] The election is filed by the entity and is binding upon all self-charged interest received by (or from) any owners. It is binding for all future years and cannot be revoked without permission of the IRS.

845.56. Differing taxable years of borrower and lender. When the borrower and the lender have different taxable years, the formula changes slightly. The recharacterized income is the lesser of:

- The lender's portion of the borrower's self-charged interest deductions attributable to passive activities *in the borrower's taxable year*, or
- The lender's self-charged interest income from the entity in the lender's taxable year.

The Proposed Regulation provides an example that illustrates this concept.

EXAMPLE 8 - 59 [derived from Proposed Regulations §1.469-7T(g), Example (4)]: Darrell, a calendar-year individual, is a 50% shareholder in an S corporation that uses a June 30 year end. On September 1, 1996, Darrell loans the corporation $50,000, all of which is traced to a passive activity. Interest is payable at the rate of $1,250 per quarter on December 1, March 1, June 1, and September 1. The loan is repaid in full on August 31, 1998. For each of the corporation's fiscal years, the interest deductions are as follows:

Year Ended	*Interest Deduction*	*Darrell's Portion*
6/30/96	$ 0	$ 0
6/30/97	$3,750	$1,875
6/30/98	$5,000	$2,500
6/30/99	$1,250	$ 675

Darrell's interest income from the transaction is:

Year Ended	*Income*
12/31/96	$1,250
12/31/97	$5,000
12/31/98	$3,750

The general flow-through rules (discussed in Chapter 6) of Subchapter S require that a shareholder take into account his or her portion of the S corporation's income in the shareholder's year in which the corporation's year ends. For recharacterization of interest income, Darrell must match his gross income with the corporation's self-charged interest expense in a single year. Darrell's income and expense from the transactions are matched as follows:

Year Ended	*Interest Income*	*Interest Deduction*	*Recharac-terized**
12/31/96	$1,250	$ 0	$ 0
12/31/97	$5,000	$1,875	$1,875
12/31/98	$3,750	$2,500	$2,500
12/31/99	$ 0	$ 675	$ 0

*Lesser of two amounts

8

845.57. Recharacterization limited to interest deductions. A person was a sole shareholder in an S corporation. He also owned interests in several partnerships, and he did not participate in those partnerships' activities. The S corporation charged management fees to the partnerships. The management fee income passed through from the S corporation as active income to the shareholder. However, the shareholder's portion of the management fee expense in the partnerships was passive. Therefore a mismatch occurred, where one transaction created both active income and passive loss. The IRS held that the self-charged interest rule did not extend to other types of charges, and the mismatch stood. [TAM 9718002]

845.6. Interest paid on debt-financed distributions. As of this writing there are no Regulations regarding the treatment of debt-financed distributions. Regulations §1.163-8T(f) is reserved for this issue but has not yet been completed. The treatment of such interest cannot be easily ascertained by merely looking at the S corporation's expenditure, since the loan would not be traced to a business expenditure, a passive activity, or a portfolio investment.

> **EXAMPLE 8 - 60:** Jaynie owns all of the shares in Jaynco, an S corporation. On November 10 of the current year, Jaynco borrows $50,000 from a local bank. The next day, Jaynco distributes $50,000 to Jaynie. Jaynco has one active business, no passive activities, and no portfolio investments. Making a distribution to a shareholder, however, is not likely to be treated as a valid business expenditure. Jaynco's treatment of the interest expense as a valid business deduction is questionable, to say the least.

A similar problem was addressed in the context of a partnership borrowing money and making distributions to partners who were investing the distribution in tax-exempt bonds. [Rev. Proc. 72-18, 1972-1 CB 740] In this situation, the IRS applied §265 (disallowance of interest on debt used to acquire tax-exempt investments) to the interest paid by the partnership on the loan that was taken out to finance the distribution. This instance occurred years before the tracing Regulation was issued, but it is conceptually consistent with tracing the distributions of a pass-through entity to the expenditures made by the recipients.

In a later notice, the IRS reaffirmed its position that interest paid on loans taken out by a partnership or an S corporation to finance distributions must be allocated to partners or shareholders and allocated by them according to the use they make of distribution proceeds. [Notice 88-37, 1988-1 CB 522]

EXAMPLE 8 - 61: Refer to Example 8 - 60. Assume that Jaynie used the $50,000 on personal expenditures. The IRS would contend that the interest paid by Jaynco would be personal interest, which would pass through to Jaynie as a nondeductible expenditure.

Careful attention to the tracing Regulation, however, can assure that an S corporation may allocate its loans to business expenditures rather than distributions. As discussed above, the S corporation could use separate accounts or could trace its loan proceeds to any desired expenditures within 15 days of borrowing the money.

EXAMPLE 8 - 62: Refer to Example 8 - 60. Between November 10 and November 25 of the current year, Jaynco pays $50,000 of ordinary business expenses, including Jaynie's salary. Pursuant to Regulations §1.163-8T, Jaynco could allocate the $50,000 to these expenditures. Since the loan would be treated as expended on ordinary business matters, the interests would be an ordinary business deduction.

If a distribution is in the form of a stock redemption, the treatment of the interest should be considerably different. As discussed in Chapter 14, the purchase of stock in an S corporation is treated like the purchase of the S corporation's assets. [Notice 88-20, 1988-1 CB 487, as updated by Notice 89-35, 1989-1 CB 917] See further discussion in Chapter 15, at 1525.8. In a stock redemption, the S corporation is purchasing its own stock. Therefore, the S corporation should allocate the interest as if it were purchasing a portion of its entire asset composition. The IRS has agreed to this treatment in a letter ruling. [PLR 9116008]

845.7. Interest paid by shareholders on income tax. Before 1987, interest paid by a shareholder due to the late payment of federal and state income tax was allowed as a deduction. After 1986, however, such interest is treated as personal interest and is not deductible. [§163(h)(2)(E)] A recent decision indicates that the IRS is still adjusting pre-1987 interest on S corporation items. Where the shareholder was a passive investor in the S corporation, the IRS held that the interest on a tax deficiency was an investment expense and was treated as an itemized deduction, rather than a trade or business deduction, in arriving at adjusted gross income. [*True v. U.S.* , 93-2 USTC 50,461 (D. Wyo.); *Carlson v. Commissioner*, 112 TC 17 (1999)]

850. Practice aids.

Many of the practice aids suggested in this chapter are legal documents, which are not filed with the corporation or shareholder's federal tax returns. This book cannot give models of agreements that might be effective under local law. The tax practitioner who is not an attorney should recommend that the client consult with competent local counsel to make sure that all of these agreements are valid. Checklist 8 - 1 provides a list of shareholder agreements that should be in place at the end of each year.

Checklist 8 - 1: Agreements between the corporation and each shareholder

Complete as necessary for all shareholders.

	Yes	*No*	*N/A*
1. Minimum compensation to avoid Revenue Ruling 74-44. For any shareholders who receive little or no compensation, the corporation should document that these persons are passive investors and serve little or no management or other employee functions.	___	___	___

Copyright © 2000 by Harcourt, Inc. All rights reserved.

	Yes	No	N/A
2. Maximum compensation agreement. The corporation should determine approximate amounts paid to persons in similar businesses or occupations. A controlling shareholder might serve several functions, such as management, sales, production, purchasing, and finance. It would also be helpful to document the lengthy hours spent on business activities. Each shareholder, and perhaps some other employees, should have an "Oswald clause" in his or her employment agreement so that any subsequent disallowed compensation would be repaid to the corporation.	___	___	___
3. When shareholders have contributed property to the corporation, the corporation should be careful to value the property and to document a reasonable return on capital. In this manner, the corporation and its shareholders may be able to refute an IRS claim that distributions that represent return on capital investments are in fact disguised compensation.	___	___	___
4. The corporation should document its policy to pay distributions to the shareholders in order to cover estimated federal and state income tax payments. The corporation might need to review and redraft any loan covenants to permit such distributions.	___	___	___
5. Reasonableness of rent on real property from the shareholders, or by partnerships under control of the shareholders, to the corporation should be ascertained. If the contract was signed before February, 1988, it will possible create passive activity income for the shareholders. In this situation, the parties may not wish to alter any terms as long as the original lease term is still in effect.	___	___	___
6. Loans to any shareholder from the corporation should be documented. In order to avoid a challenge by the IRS that such loans are disguised dividends or compensation, the loan agreements should specify the purpose, terms, and interest rates. The corporation should ascertain that the parties have all complied with the terms of past loan agreements.	___	___	___
7. Documentation policy for employee expenses and reimbursements must be in place. The accounting procedures for reimbursements should be clearly specified, so as to allow the employee to exclude reimbursements from gross income. Especially for an employee who is also a shareholder, there should be an "Oswald clause," in the event that any shareholder expenses that are paid or reimbursed by the corporation are subsequently disallowed as business expenses by the IRS.	___	___	___
8. Loans from the shareholders to the corporation should be documented. The loan agreements should specify the purpose of the loan, any property pledged as security, the interest rate to be charged, and any other important items. See Chapter 9 and Chapter 14.	___	___	___
9. For qualified deferred compensation agreements, consult with a specialist in deferred compensation to make sure that any qualified pension and profit-sharing plans are up to date. The requirements to keep these plans qualified can change frequently.	___	___	___
10. Be sure that the terms governing the rent of any property from the corporation to any shareholder are reasonable, so as to avoid challenge from the IRS as constructive dividends or constructive compensation.	___	___	___
11. Regarding documentation of any unusual transactions between the corporation and any shareholder, be sure to state the nature and purpose of any payment, and means used to determine the fair market value of the transaction.	___	___	___

8

Copyright © 2000 by Harcourt, Inc. All rights reserved.

SHAREHOLDER STOCK BASIS AND DEBT BASIS

Contents

9

900. Overview.

A shareholder's basis in his or her stock is an extremely important consideration in the context of Subchapter S. As Chapters 6 and 7 demonstrated, a shareholder may need to calculate basis for two special attributes of S corporations:

- An S corporation's loss that flows through to a shareholder may be limited to the shareholder's basis.
- A distribution from an S corporation to a shareholder may be tax-free to the extent of the shareholder's basis.

In addition, basis determines the gain or loss on the shareholder's disposition of stock.
Sometimes, as discussed in Chapter 8, a person loans money to a corporation in which he or she is a shareholder. Such loans may give shareholders basis to allow the deductibility of losses when stock basis is exhausted. The ability to obtain basis for loans has been one of the most frequently litigated aspects of Subchapter S.
This chapter explores the major issues concerning shareholders' stock and debt basis:

- Initial basis in stock and debt (see at 910.)
- Litigation of debt basis (see at 920.)
- Adjustments to stock and debt basis (see at 925.)

9

The material in this chapter gives an understanding of these fundamental, and often misunderstood, concepts. Tax advisors will be able to structure transactions so that S corporation shareholders can avoid problems that have plagued taxpayers since the initial version of Subchapter S was enacted.

910. Historical basis.

A shareholder who is concerned with basis needs to determine the tax history of his or her holding of the property, as well as when and how the shareholder acquired his or her stock or debt. This task may be difficult in some cases, especially when the shareholder has held stock for many years.

910.1. Initial contribution directly to the corporation. Often, the measurement of basis for loss purposes occurs in a newly formed corporation. In many cases, the shareholders who are concerned with basis are the founders of the corporation. A likely source of basis rules is §358, which deals with shareholder basis following the contribution of property in a tax-free exchange for stock under §351. Although Chapter 14 contains a detailed description of these rules, a brief statement is in order at this point. A shareholder determines his or her basis resulting from the contribution of property to a corporation by the following formula [§358(a)]:

	Basis of property contributed
+	Gain recognized
–	Boot (property other than stock) received
–	Liabilities taken by corporation
=	Basis of stock received

When a shareholder receives more than one class of stock in one exchange, he or she must allocate the total basis to each class in proportion to fair market value. [Regs. §1.358-2(a)(2)] When an S corporation is involved, shareholders should never receive more than one class of stock, unless it is a mixture of voting and nonvoting shares.

There is an important transition date in the law: October 2, 1989. On or before that date, a shareholder could receive both stock and debt securities without triggering the recognition of gain. For any exchange after that date, however, debt securities are treated as boot and will be assigned a basis equal to their fair market value at the time of transfer. At the time of this writing, many existing corporations were formed by contributions of property before October 3, 1989. The rules that existed on that date may continue to govern prior stock and debt basis adjustments for shareholders who held stock during those years.

EXAMPLE 9 - 1: Individual J formed JK Corporation in 1987. J transferred:

Property basis (Fair market value = $80,000)	$ 30,000
Subject to liabilities	20,000
J receives:	
Common stock valued at	$ 15,000
10-year securities valued at	45,000
Total basis in stock and securities:	
Basis of property transferred	$ 30,000
Less liabilities	(20,000)
Total basis	$ 10,000
J's basis allocation:	
Stock [$10,000 x ($15,000/$60,000)]	$ 2,500
Securities [$10,000 x ($45,000/$60,000)]	7,500
	$ 10,000

EXAMPLE 9 - 2: Refer to Example 9 - 1. If J had consummated the same transaction after October 2, 1989, the securities would have constituted boot. They would take a basis of $45,000, their fair market value at the date of transfer. J's basis computation would be:

Basis of property transferred	$ 30,000
Add gain recognized	45,000
Less boot received	(45,000)
Less liabilities	(20,000)
Stock basis	$ 10,000

910.2. Other sources of initial basis. When a shareholder has contributed property in exchange for stock, the corporation's records for paid-in capital should be approximately or exactly equal to the shareholder's basis in his or her stock. When a shareholder acquires stock from another shareholder, however, the corporation's records will have no necessary relationship to the current shareholder's basis. Table 9 - 1 contains some of the more commonly encountered rules for establishing initial basis.

PLANNING TIP: A shareholder might acquire a new block of stock after he or she has exhausted basis of all previously owned stock or debt. See discussion of reductions in Chapter 6, at 630.65. Basis in new stock could absorb excess losses from old stock. This windfall could happen when a shareholder inherits stock that has value, even if the basis of the stock had been reduced to zero by the deceased shareholder.

TABLE 9 - 1: Determination of Initial Basis

Acquisition Transaction	*Basis*	*Citation*
Purchase from another shareholder	Cost	§1012
Inheritance	Fair market value at prior owner's death (or alternate valuation date)	§1014
Gift before 1/1/77	Donor's basis, adjusted for gift tax paid by donor (may not exceed fair market value on date of gift)	§1015(d)(1)
Gift after 12/31/76	Donor's basis, adjusted for gift tax paid by donor, attributable to appreciation while property was held by donor	§1015(d)(6)
Tax-free reorganization	Basis of stock surrendered	§358(a)
Compensation	Fair market value on date taken into income	Regulations §1.83-4(b)*

*This principle was applied to S corporation stock in PLR 8752006.

EXAMPLE 9 - 3: Curtis and his son Dick were equal shareholders in CD Corporation, an S corporation that used the calendar year. In 1995 the losses were sufficient that each shareholder's basis was reduced to zero. In 1996, Curtis died and Dick inherited all of Curtis's stock. At the time of Curtis's death, his stock was worth $100,000. Thus, Dick receives an increase in basis of $100,000 in 1996, and he could use that basis to offset his suspended losses from 1995.

CAUTION: Any stock received due to the death of a shareholder after August 20, 1996, must be reduced for any corporate-level items that are properly characterized as income in respect of a decedent. See Chapter 6, at 630.7., for discussion.

915. Statutory provisions for debt basis.

A brief review of the statutory provisions and legislative history of debt basis is in order.

915.1. Rules of the 1958 version of Subchapter S. The 1958 version of Subchapter S, under which most cases to date have been argued, was perhaps more clearly worded than its present counterpart. Statutory authority is found in Code Section 1374(c)(2).

SUMMARY OF AUTHORITY: CODE SECTION §1374(c)(2)
AS IN EFFECT BEFORE REPEAL BY THE SUBCHAPTER S REVISION ACT OF 1982

- Prior law allowed a shareholder to deduct his or her portion of an S corporation's net operating loss.
- If the shareholder's portion of a net operating loss exceeded his or her stock basis, it was allowable to the extent of the indebtedness to the shareholder.
- Unlike present law, prior law held that a corporate net operating loss was the only type of loss that could pass through from an S corporation.
- Unlike present law, prior law held that a loss that exceeded a shareholder's stock and debt basis could not be carried to a future year.

The phrase "indebtedness to the shareholder" was a major cause of confusion. Most of the cases cited below deal with taxable years prior to the Subchapter S Revision Act of 1982. As the discussion at 920. demonstrates, however, these cases are still extremely important.

OBSERVATION: The rules governing basis of shareholders in S corporations are markedly different from those for partners. Generally, a partner is allowed basis for his or her share of the partnership's debts to outsiders. [§752(a)] A shareholder in an S corporation, however, must actually loan money to the corporation before he or she receives basis. The IRS and the courts apply this rule rigidly.

EXAMPLE 9 - 4: Martha and Debbie are equal partners in the MD Partnership. The partnership borrows $100,000 from an outside lender. Under the partnership rules, Martha and Debbie would each increase basis by $50,000.

If MD were an S corporation, Martha and Debbie would get no increase in basis if the corporation borrowed from an outside lender. In order to increase basis, they would each have to contribute capital, or loan the money to MD directly.

915.2. Effects of the Subchapter S Revision Act of 1982. Under current Code §1366(d)(1), losses in excess of basis are carried forward by the shareholder until basis is restored. [§1366(d)(2)] This provision is discussed in Chapter 6. This rule was added by the Subchapter S Revision Act of 1982 to remedy the harsh results obtained under old law.

9

EXAMPLE 9 - 5: Hans is a shareholder in Hansco, an S corporation. In a taxable year, the corporation records a loss of $50,000. Hans's basis at the end of the year is only $10,000. If the taxable year of the loss began before 1983, Hans would be allowed to deduct $10,000. The remaining $40,000 would not be deductible in any year. If the taxable year began after 1982, Hans's allowable loss for that taxable year would be $10,000. The remaining $40,000, however, would be carried forward, and Hans could deduct it when his basis increased.

SUMMARY OF AUTHORITY: CODE SECTION 1366(d)(1)

- Current law provides that the aggregated losses allowable to a shareholder cannot exceed stock basis and debt basis, respectively.
- Unlike prior law, current law holds that losses that pass through from S corporations retain their character as ordinary, capital, etc.
- The stock basis and debt basis have origins similar to those under prior law.
- The basis of stock and debt may be adjusted, as discussed at 925.2. and 930.2.

Are the cases under old Subchapter S still valid precedent for years governed by the Subchapter S Revision Act of 1982? On the particular issue of basis determination, there was a change in wording. The Senate Committee Report on the Subchapter S Revision Act of 1982, however, indicates that there is no change from prior law in the measurement of loss limits. [U.S. Congress, Senate Report on H.R. 6055 [the Subchapter S Revision Act of 1982], 1982-2 CB 726] Therefore, the phrase "indebtedness to the shareholder" remains the focus of the litigation.

920. Litigation of debt basis.

Debt basis litigation has been frequent since enactment of the original Subchapter S, and there have been few taxpayer victories. Although some of the cases cited in this portion of the chapter have unique aspects, the cases generally can be divided into three categories:

- Loans from related parties, in which shareholders have claimed basis by attribution

- Loans from third-party lenders to S corporations where shareholders have guaranteed or co-signed the notes
- Procedural problems where the IRS and the taxpayer disagreed over the form of the transaction

In most of the cases in the first two categories, the IRS has prevailed. In one notable case involving a guarantee, the taxpayer prevailed, but this case seems to have been an aberration. On the procedural issues, the victories have been mixed.

> **OBSERVATION:** Most of the cases litigated to date involved pre-1983 tax years. In those years, there was no relief provision for losses in excess of basis. If a shareholder had insufficient basis in the year the corporation sustained a loss, there was no carryforward. Consequently, a favorable court decision was the only way to gain any tax benefit from a corporate loss. Although many taxpayers had flimsy arguments, they had no hope of obtaining any tax deduction for an S corporation's loss unless they could win in court. Under post–Subchapter S Revision Act of 1982 rules, the outcome is not as drastic, and litigation of this issue can be expected to diminish.

As noted above, the statute allows losses to the extent that they do not exceed the shareholder's *adjusted basis* in stock and debt. [§1366(b)] The statute and Regulations are completely silent on the definition of *adjusted basis* for this purpose. The IRS bases most of its arguments on a requirement that the shareholder must have made an *economic outlay* to establish basis. As the following discussion indicates, the IRS has usually been successful in enforcing the condition to allow losses. *Economic outlay* occurs when a shareholder, using funds that are not obtained from the corporation, loans money to the corporation. There is no economic outlay when there is an indirect loan or when a shareholder has only potential economic risk at stake.

920.1. Loans from parties related to shareholders In several cases, taxpayers have argued that the phrase *indebtedness to the shareholder* should be applied by attribution. Figure 9 - 1 depicts the relationship.

However, the courts have been unwilling to give shareholders basis for loans made by related parties when the lender is:

- An estate of which the shareholder is a beneficiary
- A trust of which the shareholder is a beneficiary
- A partnership in which the shareholder is a partner
- A C corporation in which the S corporation shareholder is also a shareholder
- An S corporation in which the borrowing S corporation shareholder is also a shareholder

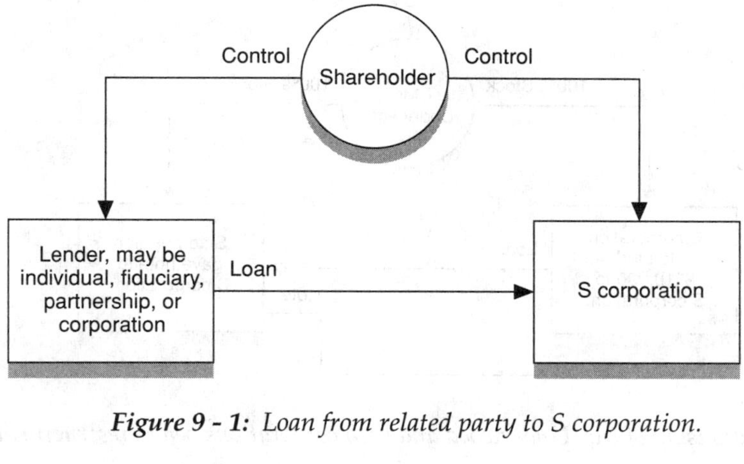

Figure 9 - 1: *Loan from related party to S corporation.*

In the case of *Prashker*, a widow was the beneficiary and executrix of an estate. [*Prashker, Ruth M.*, 59 TC 172 (1972)] She was also a shareholder in an S corporation, and she did not have sufficient stock basis to absorb the anticipated losses of the S corporation. The estate loaned the corporation funds. The shareholder treated these loans as if she had made them directly to the corporation. The court refused to ignore the existence of the estate as a separate entity. Since the estate was not a shareholder, and since the shareholder did not make the loans, there was insufficient basis for deduction of the corporation's loss.

In the *Robertson* case, the shareholder was a beneficiary of a trust and a shareholder in an S corporation. [*Robertson, James Y., v. U.S.*, 73-2 USTC 9645 (DC Nev.)] The trust had loaned the corporation $50,000. Robertson claimed that as a beneficiary in the trust, he had in substance made the loan to the corporation. The court held for the IRS in assessing a deficiency.

In *Frankel*, two shareholders of an S corporation were also partners in a partnership. [*Frankel*, 61 TC 343 (1973)] The partnership loaned money to the corporation, and the partner-shareholders tried to deduct the loss, again to no avail. [See also *Edward H. Allen*, 55 TCM 641, TC Memo 1988-166, and *Hill Blalock et al. v. U.S.*, 88-2 USTC 9495 (N. D. Miss.).] Shareholders in S corporations have found the same disallowance when they attempted to use loans from related C corporations, and S corporations, as indirect sources of debt basis. [*Gurda, Jr., Michael A.*, 54 TCM 104 (1987); *Meissner, Douglas W.*, 69 TCM 2505 (1995), TC Memo 1995-191]

OBSERVATION: Many taxpayers who have litigated this issue unsuccessfully indicate that they could have taken the money from the lender and loaned it directly to the S corporation, in which case they would have had basis. Their contentions are most likely correct. The IRS and courts, however, have placed extreme reliance on the form, as well as the substance, of the transactions.

EXAMPLE 9 - 6: Robert is a shareholder in an S corporation and also the sole beneficiary of an estate. If Robert withdraws some money from the estate and loans it to the S corporation, he will have basis in the S corporation. If, instead, the estate loans money to the S corporation, Robert will not be allowed to increase his basis in the S corporation.

In the cases cited above, the taxpayers made no attempt to restructure the transactions. Other shareholders restructured the loans so that they would become direct creditors of the S corporation. In *Underwood*, the taxpayer attempted to avoid the pitfalls of earlier cases by using a substitution. [*Underwood v. Commissioner*, 76-2 USTC 9557 (5th Cir.); aff'g 63 TC 468 (1975)] Mr. Underwood owned two corporations—one a C corporation with surplus cash, the other an S corporation with losses. The C corporation loaned the S corporation $110,000 in 1966. Figure 9-2 shows the relationships among Mr. Underwood and his two corporations after the C corporation made the loan to the S corporation.

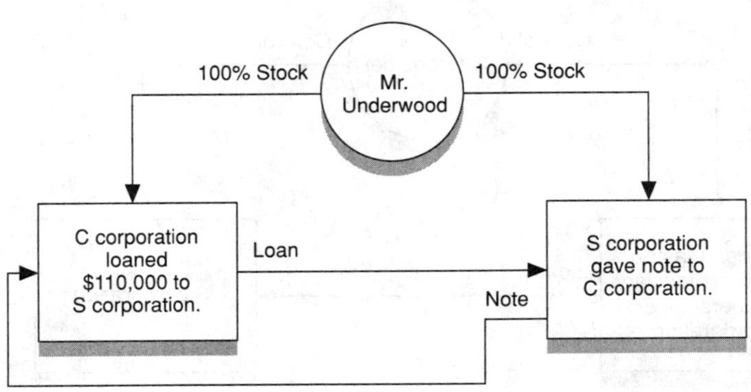

Figure 9 - 2: *Relationship of Mr. Underwood and both corporations before restructuring the loan.*

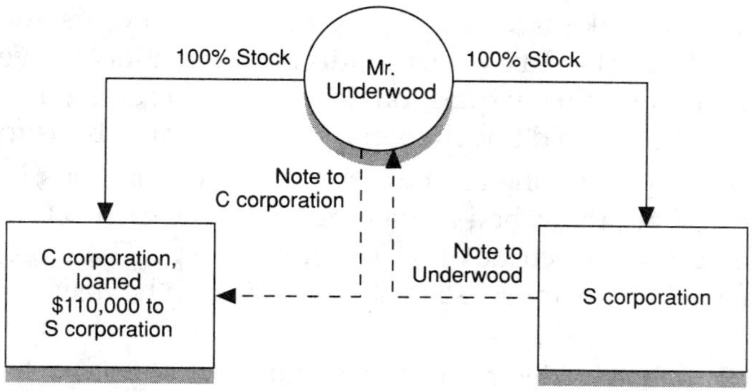

Figure 9 - 3: *Relationship of Mr. Underwood and both corporations after restructuring the loan.*

Mr. Underwood was much more careful than the taxpayers in *Prashker, Robertson,* and *Frankel.* In 1967, Mr. Underwood substituted his personal note to the C corporation for $110,000. The C corporation canceled the note from the S corporation. The S corporation wrote its note to the shareholder. In 1969, the S corporation's losses exceeded the shareholder's basis in his stock. He claimed all of the losses, due to his basis in the $110,000 loan. Figure 9-3 shows the relationships among Mr. Underwood and his two corporations after the new arrangement.

The court disallowed the loan basis because Mr. Underwood had not loaned the money directly to the S corporation. In *Underwood,* apparently, the S corporation was indebted to the shareholder. The lack of an actual, direct economic transfer from the shareholder to the corporation appears to have been fatal.

Loans from related S corporations have met the same dismal fate. In two cases, the Tax Court refused to recognize that the distribution of a loan from the S corporation to the shareholder provided the necessary economic outlay for basis. [*Shebester,* 57 TCM 824, TC Memo 1987-246; *Burnstein,* 47 TCM 1100, TC Memo 1984-74] In *Burnstein,* a profitable S corporation had loaned money to another S corporation with identical shareholders. The corporations' accountant had made adjusting entries to reclassify the loans as (1) loans from the profitable S corporation to the shareholders and (2) loans from the shareholders to the S corporation that sustained losses. In *Shebester,* which had similar facts, the controlling shareholder had assumed the loan of the borrowing S corporation by recording it to his "drawing account" in the lending S corporation. Neither *Burnstein* nor *Shebester* involved the actual transfer of funds between the shareholder and the borrowing corporation.

In one case, the Court refused to allow basis for a loan to an S corporation from a related S corporation and refused to allow basis when the shareholder guaranteed the loan. [*Spencer,* 110 TC 62 1998] In 1991, the Tax Court heard a case involving multiple S corporations under common control. In *Wilson,* a group of shareholders owned stock in two unprofitable S corporations and one profitable S corporation. [*Wilson,* TC Memo, 1991-544] The profitable corporation loaned funds to the unprofitable corporations. In 1982, 1983, and 1984, the profitable corporation distributed interests in the loans to the shareholders. The distributions were recorded on the lending corporation's books and were properly taken into account by the shareholders.[1] The Tax Court, following its decisions in *Burnstein* and *Shebester,* did not allow the shareholders basis. Again it emphasized that there must be an actual economic outlay on the part of the shareholders. In *Wilson,* the Tax Court also upheld the IRS's imposition of a penalty for taking a position without substantial authority and without disclosure on a return. There were two other noteworthy aspects of the *Wilson* decision:

---

[1] In 1982, the shareholders reported the distributions as dividends, in accordance with the rules in effect before the Subchapter S Revision Act of 1982. In the later years, they reported the value of the loans as reductions in basis, as required by the new law.

- The actions in *Wilson* took place one year before and two years after the Subchapter S Revision Act of 1982. The Tax Court made no distinction between the basis rules applicable to any of the years in question. It appears, therefore, that the Tax Court will follow its decisions under old Subchapter S in determining basis for years after 1982.
- The shareholders in *Wilson* loaned some cash to the S corporations, but they were unable to prove that the corporations had actually received the cash before year end. The Tax Court did not entertain a doctrine of constructive receipt. Therefore, shareholders who attempt to create debt basis must establish the timing of the delivery of funds.

> **OBSERVATION:** A shareholder in an S corporation should never rely on a loan to the S corporation from a related party to provide basis. Even if the shareholder takes possession of the loan, the IRS and Tax Court have been unwilling to grant basis. In the *Wilson* case, cited above, the shareholders should have planned more carefully. If the profitable corporation had distributed the cash to the shareholders, who would then have loaned it to the losing corporations, there probably would have been the requisite economic outlay. Considering the court's imposition of the negligence penalty in *Wilson*, tax professionals should advise their clients to adhere exactly to the correct form of a loan and not rely simply on the substance.

In a situation similar to the *Underwood* and *Wilson* cases, one shareholder owned all of the stock of three S corporations. One of the corporations (AF3) was indebted to one of the other corporations (AF2). On one day, the shareholder borrowed money from AF2, loaned the same money to AF3, and caused AF3 to repay its loan to AF2. The Eighth Circuit held that there was no true economic outlay by the shareholder and thus no increase in basis. The crux of the matter was the lack of demonstrable intent for the shareholder to ever pay back the loan to AF2, the lending corporation. [*Bergman v. U.S.*, 83 AFTR 2d 99-1882, (8th Cir.)]

920.2. Guarantees and similar arrangements. Generally, the IRS and the courts have denied shareholders basis for corporate debt to outside creditors. Guarantee of the corporation's debts by shareholders has not given basis until the shareholder is actually forced to pay some of the debt with his or her personal funds. This position was articulated in the often-cited *Raynor* case, as follows:

> No form of indirect borrowing, be it guaranty, surety, accommodation, comaking or otherwise, gives rise to indebtedness from the corporation to the shareholders until and unless the shareholders pay all or a part of the obligation. [*Raynor*, 50 TC 762 (1968)]

SUMMARY OF AUTHORITY: THE RAYNOR *CASE*

- The above quotation from *Raynor* is the most frequently cited judicial statement on the effect of guarantees on basis.
- The Tax Court and other courts generally uphold the IRS when it disallows basis for the guarantee or co-making of a corporation's loan by the shareholders.
- A shareholder receives basis for a guarantee of a corporation's debt only when the shareholder makes an actual payment on the corporation's behalf.

920.21. Cases decided before 1986. Before 1986, taxpayers repeatedly, and unsuccessfully, attempted to secure basis by guarantees in many cases. A partial list follows:

- *Perry, William H.*, 47 TC 159 (1966), aff'd 68-1 USTC 9297 (8th Cir.)
- *Borg, Joe E.*, 50 TC 257 (1968)
- *Neal, Estate of, v. U.S.*, 70-1 USTC 9306 (DC Cal.)

- *Blum*, 59 TC 436 (1972)
- *Cole*, 32 TCM 313 (1973)
- *Smalley*, 32 TCM 373 (1973)
- *Wheat v. U.S.*, 73-1 USTC 9221 (S. Dist. Tex.)
- *Mirow, Richard R.*, 34 TCM 628 (1975)
- *Duke, Albert D.*, 35 TCM 229 (1976)
- *Brown, J.W.*, 38 TCM 886 (1979)
- *Brown, Frederick G.*, 42 TCM 1460 (1981), aff'd 1983-1 USTC 9364 (6th Cir.)
- *Williams, Charles M.*, 41 TCM 844 (1981)
- *Calcutt*, 84 TC 716 (1985)
- *Harrington v. U.S.*, 85-1 USTC 9336 (Dist. Del.), where the loss was limited to $2.50

The *Williams* case used one of the flimsiest arguments: The shareholder claimed basis for a $2,200,000 loan made by a bank directly to the S corporation. The events were as follows: The shareholders co-signed for a loan. The bank applied $546,783 to pay off other loans to the shareholders and deposited the remaining $1,653,217 in the corporate account. The corporation used some of the funds to retire $840,333 of the shareholders' other debts. It made an accounting entry reducing the amount of loans from the shareholders. As if the substance of the argument weren't sufficiently capricious, on its audited financial statements the corporation treated the loan as a loan from a bank. Not surprisingly, the Tax Court held that the corporation had no valid indebtedness to the shareholders stemming from the bank loan.

9

920.22. IRS rulings. The IRS formally stated its position in several important Revenue Rulings. In 1970, the IRS ruled that a shareholder's guarantee of corporate debt gives basis to the shareholder only when the shareholder actually pays some or all of the note. [Rev. Rul. 70-50, 1970-1 CB 178] A 1971 ruling stated definitely that payment of an S corporation's note by a shareholder does not give the shareholder basis in any earlier year. [Rev. Rul. 71-288, 1971-2 CB 319] A pledge of personal assets did not create basis for a bank loan to a corporation guaranteed by a shareholder. [*Hafiz v. Commissioner*, TC Memo 1998-104]

In 1975, the IRS issued a ruling that advised taxpayers how to create basis by restructuring a third-party debt from an S corporation. [Rev. Rul. 75-144, 1975-1 CB 277] In this ruling, the S corporation had borrowed from a bank. The shareholder executed his personal note with the same lender, and the lender applied it to satisfy the corporation's obligation and the shareholder's guarantee thereof. Under the law of subrogation, the corporation's note to the bank becomes an obligation of the corporation to the shareholder.[2] When that occurs, the shareholder has basis.

> **EXAMPLE 9 - 7:** Allen owns all of the shares of Allco, an S corporation. Before the end of the current tax year, Allen discovers that he has insufficient basis to absorb the S corporation's losses. Allco is indebted to a bank, and Allen has given his personal guarantee for payment. According to the rulings and cases cited above, Allen has no basis resulting from his guarantee of the corporation's loan.
>
> Allen may negotiate with the bank to replace the corporation's note with his personal note. If the doctrine of subrogation applies, Allen will gain basis when the bank accepts his personal note in payment of the corporation's obligation. See discussion of *Gilday*, discussed at 920.34., for treatment of a substitution with no subrogation.

---

[2] *Black's Law Dictionary* defines *subrogation* as "The substitution of one person in the place of another with reference to a lawful claim, demand or right, so that he is substituted succeeds to the rights of the other in relation to the debt or claim, and its rights, remedies or securities." (6th ed., 1990, page 1427)

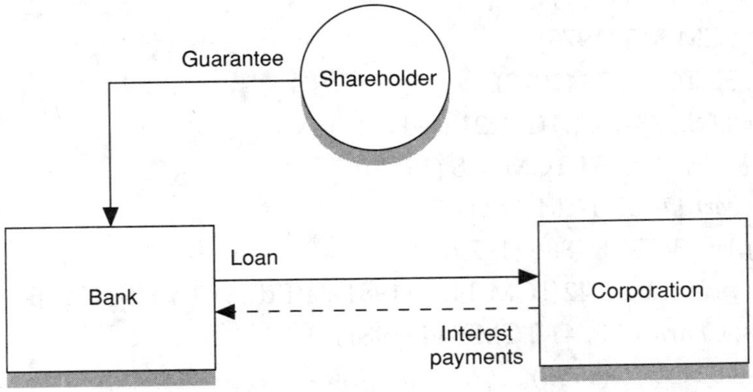

Figure 9 - 4: *Relationships of the parties in* ***Plantation Patterns*** *as the taxpayer characterized the loan.*

A later Revenue Ruling emphasizes actual economic outlay by the shareholder claiming basis. [Rev. Rul. 81-187, 1981-2 CB 167] A potential, or contingent, liability on behalf of the shareholder is not sufficient to create basis.

920.23. The *Selfe* decision. In December 1985, the Eleventh Circuit reviewed a district court decision that appeared to be so insignificant that it had not been reported. The circuit court heard a novel argument and allowed the shareholder a deduction attributable to basis created by guaranteed loans. The case, *Selfe v. U.S.*, created a resurgence of litigation on the subject of S corporation basis. [*Edward M. and Jane B. Selfe v. U.S.*, 86-1 USTC 9115 (11th Cir.)] The facts in *Selfe* were similar to those in many of the cases that taxpayers had argued unsuccessfully. The argument employed in this case, however, was creative.

Mr. Selfe, who represented himself before the Eleventh Circuit, cited an old case that did not involve an S corporation. In *Plantation Patterns, Inc., v. Commissioner,* on which Mr. Selfe relied, the IRS had prevailed in reclassifying debt as equity. [*Plantation Patterns, Inc., v. Commissioner,* 72-2 USTC 9494 (5th Cir.), cert. denied] There have been numerous cases in which debt from a C corporation has been reclassified as equity, but these cases involve loans from shareholders to the corporation. The *Plantation Patterns* case went one step further than the usual debt versus equity case. In it the IRS reclassified a debt from a third-party lender to the corporation as if the debt were a loan from the lender to the shareholder, followed by a contribution to the corporation's capital by the shareholder. Figure 9 - 4 shows the relationships of the lender, the corporation, and the shareholder according to the form of the loan arrangement.

Figure 9 - 5 shows the relationships of the lender, the corporation, and the shareholder according to the IRS's characterization of the substance.

In the *Plantation Patterns* case, in which the IRS prevailed, three of the apparently most important aspects were as follows:

- The corporation was extremely thinly capitalized.
- The shareholder who guaranteed the loan had substantial assets.
- The IRS secured a deposition from the loan officer that the lender was looking primarily to the shareholder, rather than to the corporation, for repayment.

Selfe was able to establish that his facts were practically identical to those in *Plantation Patterns.* His wife, Jane Selfe, was the sole shareholder. The corporation was thinly capitalized, and Jane had substantial assets. The Selfes secured a deposition from the lending officer that the bank was looking primarily to Mrs. Selfe, rather than to the corporation, for repayment of the loan. The Court looked to substance rather than form and treated the loan

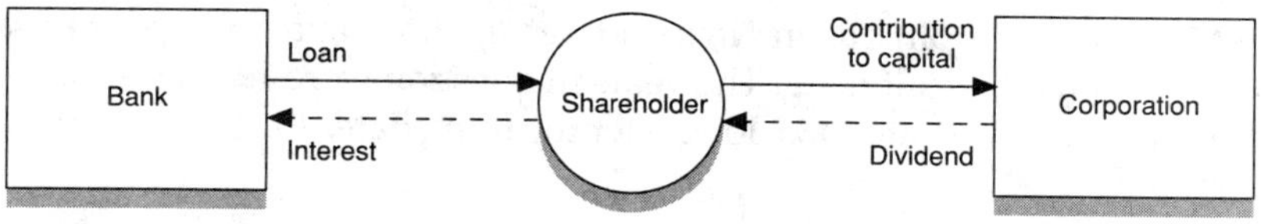

Figure 9 - 5: Relationships of the parties in ***Plantation Patterns*** *as the Tax Court characterized the loan.*

as equity contributions, in accordance with the precedent set in *Plantation Patterns*. Mrs. Selfe was allowed to deduct her loss.

920.24. Decisions after *Selfe*. Shortly after the *Selfe* decision was published, taxpayers began to litigate the issue with renewed vigor. To date, however, the courts other than the Eleventh Circuit have not been willing to follow the *Selfe* decision.

One of the first cases heard by the Tax Court after *Selfe* was *Estate of Leavitt* [*Leavitt, Daniel, Estate of*, 90 TC 206 (1988)], which the Tax Court could easily have rejected as being entirely different from *Selfe*. Several shareholders were involved, and the facts were quite different. The Tax Court went much farther, however. It stated its disagreement with the Eleventh Circuit decision in *Selfe*, holding that the *Plantation Patterns* doctrine was inappropriate for S corporations. It refused to accept a shareholder guarantee as the economic outlay necessary to create basis. One concurring opinion distinguished *Leavitt* from *Selfe* because the corporation in *Leavitt* had seven shareholders, each of whom claimed basis from guarantee.

9

The Tax Court has consistently followed the *Leavitt* decision and refused to allow basis for loan guarantees and similar arrangements in:

- *Schneiderman*, 54 TCM 1006, TC Memo 1987-551
- *Calcutt*, 91 TC 14 (1989)
- *Irwin, III*, 56 TCM 1343 (1989)
- *Fear*, 57 TCM 306 (1989)
- *Roesch*, 57 TCM 64 (1989)
- *Ellis*, 57 TCM 677 (1989)
- *Suisman*, 58 TCM 751 (1989) (negligence penalty imposed)
- *Uri, Lawrence R., Jr.*, 56 TCM 1217 (1989)
- *Russell, Dennis K.*, 59 TCM 217 (1990) (negligence penalty imposed)
- *Nigh*, 60 TCM 91, TC Memo 1990-349[3]
- *Keech*, 65 TCM 1986, TC Memo 1993-71
- *Walter*, TC Memo 1993-306
- *Allen*, 66 TCM 1690, TC Memo 1993-612
- *Doe*, 66 TCM 1376, TC Memo 1993-543
- *Sperl*, TC Memo 1993-515
- *Shaver*, TC Memo 1993-619
- *Reser*, TC Memo 1995-572, 70 TCM 1472

The Tax Court has been inconsistent, however, in upholding the IRS's imposition of negligence penalties. In *Suisman* and *Russell*, cited above, the IRS let the negligence penalty stand. In *Nigh*, *Keech*, and *Doe*, the court denied basis for guarantees by shareholders but held that the *Selfe* case was sufficient authority for avoidance of the negligence penalty.

---

[3] This case also contains an important decision on passive investment of an S corporation. See Chapter 12 for further discussion.

OBSERVATION: The opinions in *Nigh* and *Keech* allowing a taxpayer to use *Selfe* as substantial authority are confusing. The years in question were 1983 and 1984. The *Selfe* case was not decided until late 1985, long after the filing dates for 1983 and 1984 returns.

Recently, the IRS disallowed basis for transferee liability. The shareholder had actually made a cash loan to one corporation. A second corporation (the S corporation in question) had assumed that loan in dealing with the shareholder. The Tax Court held that the shareholder did not have basis. [*Hitchins*, 103 TC No. 40 (1994)] The Tax Court even suggested that a novation or round robin arrangement would have worked.

OBSERVATION: The Hitchins case seems to be an extremely rigid interpretation of someone's understanding of a statute that has some ambiguity already. The shareholder had made the requisite economic outlay, by loaning out-of pocket funds to a corporation. The S corporation had then assumed liability for the borrowing corporation's debts. This seems to be a similar situation to that of Hunt, discussed at 920.36., below, in which the borrowing corporation had merged into another corporation. The Hunt case held that the shareholder did have basis.

The rationale of *Hitchins* has been followed in a similar circumstance. In addition, the court upheld the IRS's imposition of the substantial understatement penalty of §6661. [*Bhatia*, TC Memo, 1996, 72 TCM 69]

9

A shareholder's pledge of personal assets to a lender as security for a corporate loan does not constitute the requisite economic outlay on the shareholder's part. The IRS will not allow basis, even when the pledge is in addition to the shareholder's guarantee. [*Shaver*, TC Memo 1993-619]

Various circuit courts have heard appeals on the issue. To date, none of the other circuits has agreed with the Eleventh Circuit's decision in *Selfe*. Decisions reported to date are:

- The Fourth Circuit sustained the Tax Court in *Leavitt*. [89-1 USTC 9332 (4th Cir.)]
- The Fifth Circuit agreed with the Tax Court and other circuit courts (except for the Eleventh Circuit) in denying shareholders basis for guarantee of corporate debt. [*Harris v. U.S.*, 90-2 USTC 50,341 (5th Cir.)]
- The Tenth Circuit has disallowed basis on the same grounds in *Goatcher v. U.S.* [91-2 USTC 50,450 (10th Cir.)] and also in *Uri v. Commissioner*.[4] [91-2 USTC 50,556 (10th Cir.)]

OBSERVATION: As of this writing, the *Selfe* opinion stands alone. Neither the Eleventh Circuit Court of Appeals nor any district court within that circuit has published a decision on shareholder basis in an S corporation. The Tax Court and several circuits disagree with the logic. *Selfe* is not likely to be useful in gaining basis through the guarantee of corporate loans. Accordingly, it is much better to structure transactions as direct loans. For existing corporate loans from third-party lenders, the tax planner should employ the technique stated by the IRS in Revenue Ruling 75-144. The shareholders should make arrangements with the lender to substitute themselves for debtors in the corporation's place.

In many cases, the lender will demand that certain corporate assets must be pledged as security. The IRS has privately ruled that using corporate property as collateral would not cause the corporation to be considered as a co-maker on the note.

---

[4] The *Goatcher* case was routine with respect to the basis issue. It also contains an important opinion with respect to the at-risk rules, discussed in Chapter 10. In *Uri*, the taxpayer pointed out the conflict among the circuit courts. Unfortunately, *Uri* was decided in the same circuit court as *Goatcher*.

TABLE 9 - 2: Opinions of the Circuit Courts on Loan Guarantees

Circuit	*Prevailing Party*	*Citation*
4	*Leavitt*, 89-1 USTC 9332	Government
5	*Harris*, 90-2 USTC 50,341	Government
6	*Brown, Frederick G.*, 83-1 USTC 9364	Government
8	*Perry, William H.*, 68-1 USTC 9297	Government
10	*Goatcher v. U.S.*, 91-2 USTC 50,450	Government
	Uri v. Commissioner, 91-2 USTC 50,556	Government
11	*Selfe v. U.S.*, 86-1 USTC 9115	Taxpayer

[PLR 8747013] An alternative would be for the corporation to assign a security interest in its assets to the shareholders, who could then collateralize their security instruments with the lender. Table 9 - 2 shows the opinions of the various circuit courts that have heard the issue to date.

920.3. Decisions involving procedural issues. Most of the cases involving shareholder basis have been concerned with the substantive arguments cited above. Some cases have been decided on procedures, however, when the form of the transaction was the issue. Shareholders have won some cases and lost others.

920.31. Carryback of losses. Under old Subchapter S rules, there was no opportunity to use one year's excess losses in any other year. One taxpayer questioned the clarity of the statute and attempted to carry back losses after he had restored basis. [*Plowden*, 48 TC 666 (1967)] Although the post-1982 rules now permit a carryforward of excess losses, there remains an implied prohibition against the carryback of any losses.

920.32. Failure to substantiate entitlement to loss deductions. The IRS may require extensive documentation of a shareholder's basis. The Tax Court has held that the expense involved in litigating this issue is not an unjustified expense, and it has refused to award taxpayers damages, even when the taxpayer has prevailed. [*Buxbaum*, 64 TCM 1376, TC Memo 1992-675; *Ellison*, 64 TCM 1684, TC Memo 1992-741] No loss was allowed where a shareholder could not establish basis. [*Scallen*, TC Memo 1987-412]

Occasionally, a shareholder fails to substantiate the existence of a loan. The courts will not accept mere bookkeeping entries as sufficient evidence of a loan to give a shareholder basis. [*Griffith, Leroy*, 56 TCM 220 (1988) (journal entries on the corporation's books had no economic substance); *Bronson*, 63 TCM 2225, TC Memo 1992-122] Transactions between a shareholder and his or her wholly owned S corporation may often be informal; however, there must be some bona fide evidence that the shareholder truly loaned money to the S corporation. [*Bolding*, TC Memo 1995-326] However, this case was reversed on appeal. The appellate court found that there was sufficient evidence that the shareholder, and not the corporation, was the true borrower, even though the bank loan was deposited directly into the corporation's account. [*Bolding v. Comm'r*, 80 AFTR 2d 97-5481 (5th Cir.)] No loss was allowed when taxpayers failed to properly substantiate basis or amount of corporate loss. [*Parrish v. Comm'r*, TC Memo 1997-474; *Streck v. Comm'r*, TC Memo 1197-407; *Ng v. Comm'r*, TC Memo 1997-248] Allowable losses were limited to basis that the shareholder could substantiate with loans and contributions. [*Williams v. Comm'r*, TC Memo 1997-326]

A taxpayer who fails to substantiate the existence of a valid S election may be denied a deduction for losses. (See *Dixon*, TC Memo 1991-614. This case is lengthy and provides little explanation of the taxpayer's argument.) In other instances, corporations have failed to substantiate the amount of a loss claimed in Form 1120S, and the shareholders have been disallowed a deduction for the loss. [*Westbrook*, TC Memo 1993-634, 66 TCM 1823; *DeMoss*, TC Memo 1993-636, 66 TCM 1834; also see *DeLorean*, TC Memo 1995-287.]

920.33. Back-to-back loans. It appears, from the cases cited above, that a shareholder could borrow money from a lender, and then lend it to the S corporation in order to create debt basis. In one instance, however, the IRS challenged such an arrangement.

In *Seven Sixty Ranch Co. v. Kennedy*, Mr. Earl P. Hanaway was the corporation's sole shareholder. [*Seven Sixty Ranch Co. v. Kennedy*, 66-1 USTC 9293 (Dist. Wyo.)] He personally borrowed money from banks, which disbursed the funds to his S corporation. The IRS attempted to disallow his loss deduction, but the taxpayer prevailed. In allowing Mr. Hanaway the deduction for corporate losses, the court noted that the corporation had properly drawn up promissory notes to Mr. Hanaway and that these notes were valid debt instruments. The success of the taxpayer in this case showed the importance of form, as well as economic substance. The shareholder was not merely *potentially* liable for the performance on a debt—he was *primarily* liable. The court found that the shareholder had made the requisite economic outlay. This arrangement is known as a "back-to-back" loan. (Also see dicta in *Burnstein*, TCM 1987-394, and PLR 8747013 for the judicial approval of back-to-back loans.)

Extreme cases of a back-to-back loan arrangement have not been successful in establishing basis. In one situation, a shareholder had borrowed money from the S corporation and then loaned the same funds back to the corporation. The Tax Court denied the shareholder basis. [*Bader*, 52 TCM 1398, TC Memo 1987-30]

9

In a more recent situation, one individual was in control of two S corporations. A bank loaned $780,000 to the first S corporation, which in turn loaned $780,000 to the second S corporation. The first corporation loaned an additional $910,000 of its own funds to the second S corporation. On one day, the second corporation repaid the entire $1,690,000 to the first corporation. On the same day, the first corporation distributed the entire $1,690,000 to the shareholder, who immediately loaned the same amount to the second corporation. The IRS ruled that the shareholder had not made any economic outlay and refused to allow the shareholder debt basis for this series of transactions. [PLR 9403003]

920.34. Substitution of personal note for corporate note. As stated above, Revenue Ruling 75-144 grants a shareholder basis when he or she is substituted for the corporation as payor on the note. The facts in *Gilday* were similar to those supporting the IRS's position in Revenue Ruling 75-144. [*Gilday, Donald S.*, 43 TCM 1295 (1982)] The only difference was that the state law doctrine of subrogation did not cover the transaction. The Tax Court held that the shareholder had complied with the position of the IRS in all material economic respects, and it allowed the loss deduction.

920.35. Character of payment on a guarantee. When a shareholder guarantees a debt and pays on the guarantee, the IRS treats the payment as a contribution to capital, rather than a loan to the corporation. Thus one shareholder was denied a bad debt deduction for payment on a guarantee. [*In re Lane*, 84-2 USTC 9817 (11th Cir.)]

920.36. Applicability to successor corporation. As will be discussed in Chapter 17, an S corporation may engage in a tax-free reorganization. Under general corporate reorganization rules, a shareholder who receives stock in a reorganization substitutes the basis of the stock surrendered for the basis in the stock received. In a case involving mergers of S corporations, a shareholder had paid liabilities on behalf of one corporation, then merged it into another S corporation. The same shareholder had paid debts on behalf of the merged S corporation, which allowed him basis in that corporation, pursuant to Revenue Ruling 70-50. The shareholder then merged that corporation into another S corporation. The shareholder was able to include basis from the extinguished corporation's debts in his basis of the surviving S corporation. [*Hunt*, 59 TCM 635 (1990)]

920.37. Unpaid wages from the corporation. Occasionally, shareholders have attempted to claim debt basis for wages owed to them from the corporation. Apparently the taxpayer's rationale is that the unpaid wages are debts from the corporation to the shareholder. The IRS has been successful in holding that the shareholder has no basis for any amount that he or she has not already claimed as taxable income. [*Borg*, 50 TC 257 (1968); *Leavitt*, 90 TC 206 (1988); *Sperl*, TC Memo 1993-515]

920.38. Indirect adjustment to debt basis. A corporation's dealings with the shareholder may indicate that debt has been informally repaid. [*Silverman*, 28 TC 1061 (1957); aff'd (8th Cir., 1958); *Jerkins*, TC Memo 1991-571, aff'd (11th Cir.)] A recent case held that services provided by the corporation to a member of the taxpayer's family constituted a constructive repayment.[5] [*Sperl*, TC Memo 1993-515] In these situations, the taxpayer is not allowed to claim basis, since the basis does not exist at the end of the corporation's taxable year.

920.39. Attempt to treat corporation as a partnership. In general, partners are allowed to claim basis for their portions of partnership debts to outside lenders. [§752(a), §722] Thus, in one case, the shareholder attempted to disavow the corporate form entirely and claim that the corporation was in fact a partnership. The court determined that the partnership in question had been terminated when the partners incorporated the business. The shareholders were not allowed to treat the corporation as nonexistent. [*Doe*, TC Memo 1993-543, 66 TCM 1376, aff'd in *Doe v. Commissioner*, 80 AFTR 2d 97-553]

9

920.4. Shareholder participation in other creditor's loans. In some situations, a shareholder may purchase a participation agreement in a loan from a third party to the corporation. This arrangement may be used when the parties want to accomplish one or more of the following objectives:

1. The shareholder may not want his or her name to appear on the corporation's financial statements as a creditor.
2. The lender may want the added security of having the shareholder deposit funds directly with the lending institution.
3. Usually, a commercial lender will demand that loans from shareholders be subordinated, so that none of the shareholder loan may be repaid before the bank loan is paid in full. A participation agreement may allow the corporation to pay both the bank and the shareholder in installments.

Example 9 - 8 illustrates a typical participation agreement.

> **EXAMPLE 9 - 8**: Partco has several shareholders. Mr. Parker is the principal shareholder, and he wants to lend the corporation $500,000. The corporation intends to borrow an additional $1,000,000 from Third National Bank. Mr. Parker and the bank agree that Mr. Parker will deposit $500,000 with Third National, and Third National will loan Partco $1,500,000. The bank will service both the loans and will remit one-third of each installment to Mr. Parker. If the corporation defaults on any payment, the balance owing to the bank becomes immediately due and payable. In this event, the bank will recover all of its investment on the loan.

As of this writing, there have been no cases or rulings that address a shareholder's debt basis in the context of a participation. It would seem that the shareholder should be able to obtain basis for the amount of his or her participation in the loan, since the shareholder has

---

[5] In *Sperl*, the IRS could have alternatively treated the rent-free use of corporate property by a member of the shareholder's family as a constructive distribution.

made the requisite economic outlay that has been the focus of the IRS disputes with taxpayers. Nevertheless, the taxpayer who participates in a loan from a third party to the corporation may want to take extra precautions.

The corporation should show the shareholder's portion of the loan as a shareholder loan on its books and tax return. In some cases, filing a return that is completely consistent with the taxpayer's desired position has been critical in attaining the desired result in court. (See *Weinert's Estate v. Commissioner*, 61-2 USTC 9644 (5th Cir.), and *Comdisco, Inc., v. U.S.*, 85-1 USTC 9245 (7th Cir.), for examples where consistent reporting was crucial to a favorable decision.) In other cases, the courts have looked to inconsistent reporting by the taxpayer in deciding for the IRS. (See *Illinois Power*, 87 TC 1417 (1986), and *Doe*, TC Memo 1993-543, 66 TCM 1376, in which improper reporting was probably fatal to the taxpayer's position.)

925. Adjustments to stock basis.

Stock basis may have been adjusted under several sets of rules:

- The corporation may have been a C corporation.
- The corporation may have been a Subchapter S corporation between 1958 and 1982.
- The corporation may have been an S corporation after 1982.

9

925.1. Adjustments to basis of stock in a C corporation. Adjustments to C corporation stock basis are rare, but not impossible. It is necessary to begin with the starting point (cost, substituted, etc.). If a shareholder has acquired different blocks of stock, he or she must compute the basis in each block separately.

After determining initial basis, the shareholder must:

- Increase basis for any contribution to capital
- Decrease the aggregate basis for any stock redeemed, if redemption is treated as an exchange under §302 (See Chapter 15, at 1510., for further discussion.)
- Decrease basis for any distribution in excess of earnings and profits

EXAMPLE 9-9: ISR Corporation, a C corporation, distributes $18,000 to its sole shareholder, Igor. At the close of the year of the distribution, ISR's current and accumulated earnings and profits are $13,000. Igor will report $13,000 as gross income and reduce basis of his shares by $5,000. If his basis were less than $5,000 he would reduce his basis to zero, treating the remainder of the distribution as if it were a gain from the sale of his stock.

925.2. Adjustments to basis of stock in an S corporation. A shareholder may have owned his or her stock in the S corporation in years before, and in years after, the Subchapter S Revision Act of 1982. He or she could have been required to adjust stock basis under both sets of rules.

925.21. Adjustments from 1958 through 1982. During this time, the shareholder's basis adjustments were subject to a unique set of rules. A Subchapter S corporation computed its taxable income and current earnings and profits in much the same way as a C corporation. (See Chapter 3 for additional discussion.) The corporation's taxable income and current earnings and profits had little effect, if any, on the shareholder's basis. There were some exceptions:

1. If the corporation had a net operating loss, it was allowed as a shareholder deduction, but limited to the shareholder's basis. Each shareholder would decrease basis for his or her allowable share of corporate losses. [prior §1376(b)] In computing the loss at the corporate level, there was no allowance of a net capital loss, a net capital loss carryback,

or a dividends-received deduction, in the same manner as income and losses are allocated under current law. The net operating loss flowed through to shareholders, computed per-share, per-day. The loss could not reduce the basis of any shareholder's stock below zero. [§1376(b)(1) (prior law), §1016(a)(18) (prior law)]

2. If the corporation had positive taxable income, the next step was to examine the corporation's distributions in the taxable year. If the corporation distributed all of its taxable income, there was no effect on shareholder basis. If it distributed less than its taxable income, shareholders were deemed to receive a dividend on the last day of the taxable year. [prior §1373(c)] This deemed dividend was an increase to basis. [prior §1376(a)] If a deemed dividend were withdrawn in a subsequent taxable year, there was a decrease in shareholder basis. [prior §1375(d) and §1375(f); §301(c)(2)] (See Chapter 7 for a discussion of distributions under old Subchapter S.)

EXAMPLE 9 - 10: QRS Corporation was an electing small business ("Subchapter S") corporation before 1983. In 1981, QRS reported taxable income of $75,000 and made distributions to its shareholders of $60,000. As a result, QRS had undistributed taxable income of $15,000.

Quinn owned one-third of the shares, so Quinn's share of the undistributed taxable income for 1981 was $5,000. Quinn's basis at the end of 1981 is increased by $5,000. In a later year, Quinn may withdraw the $5,000 without including the distribution in gross income. Such a distribution will reduce Quinn's basis in his stock.

9

OBSERVATION: As discussed in Chapter 7, S corporations maintained shareholder equity accounts known as previously taxed income (PTI) between 1958 and 1982. Any shareholder who was allocated a portion of an S corporation's loss would reduce his or her PTI account for the loss. If an S corporation still has PTI accounts on its balance sheet, they provide reasonable clues for the basis adjustments between 1958 and 1982. If a shareholder has no PTI account balance, then it is likely that the shareholder had no overall basis adjustments between 1958 and 1982. A positive PTI balance strongly indicates that the shareholder had an upward adjustment to basis by the same amount. A negative PTI balance indicates a downward adjustment for that shareholder. A negative PTI balance would not necessarily be the same as the shareholder's basis adjustment, since shareholders could reduce basis only to zero, and a negative adjustment to PTI could have included losses that the shareholder could not deduct.

925.22. Adjustments in 1983 and later years. A shareholder in an S corporation adjusts stock basis for his or her portion of the income and losses that flow through from the S corporation. A shareholder reduces basis for distributions received from the S corporation, unless the distribution is treated as a dividend or a gain. [§1016(a)(17). See also §1367(a), discussed below.] (See Chapter 7 for discussion of effects of distributions on basis.)

SUMMARY OF AUTHORITY: CODE SECTION 1367(a)

- A shareholder increases basis in stock for income items, including tax-exempt income, that flow through from the S corporation.
- A shareholder decreases basis in stock for loss and deduction items that flow through from the S corporation.
- There are special rules for oil and gas depletion on properties owned by an S corporation.
- A shareholder reduces stock basis for any distributions from the S corporation, unless the distributions are treated as income to the shareholder.
- A shareholder reduces stock basis for nondeductible expenses that flow through from the S corporation.
- In no event may losses or distributions reduce the shareholder's stock basis below zero.

As discussed in Chapter 7, at 715.14., each shareholder adjusts his or her basis on the last day of the S corporation's taxable year. The technical ordering of the basis adjustments is:

- In any taxable year beginning before 1997:
  —Income items before loss and deduction items [§1366(d)(1)(A)]
  —Distributions after income and loss items [§1368(d)(1)]
- In any taxable year beginning after 1997, if the corporation has a net loss:
  —Income items before loss and deduction items [§1366(d)(1)(A)]
  —Distributions before income and loss items [§1368(d)(1)]

The specific allowance of an upward adjustment to basis for tax-exempt income may provide a windfall of opportunity for certain taxpayers. For instance, a corporation that has held life insurance on a key employee or shareholder may collect a large sum of money upon the death of the insured. The insurance proceeds are tax-exempt income. [§101(a)(1)] As discussed in Chapter 6, at 630.8., a loss that is nondeductible due to basis limitations is carried forward to the next taxable year. If the surviving shareholders had losses in excess of basis in prior years, they would be allowed to deduct the loss in the year in which the corporation received the insurance, even though the shareholders would report no taxable income from the receipt of the insurance. Similarly, an S corporation that is insolvent or bankrupt may receive cancellation of indebtedness income that is exempt from tax. [§108] See discussion in Chapter 6, at 610.63. In this situation, the shareholders may have suspended losses due to prior years' basis limitations. The income from cancellation of debt would not be taxable to the shareholders, since the taxability of this income is determined at the corporate level. [§108(d)(7)(A)] Arguably, this income would, however, increase the shareholders' basis in stock or debt, and would provide an opportunity to deduct the losses suspended from prior years. The IRS has held recently, in a Technical Advice Memorandum, that income excluded under §108 by a bankrupt or insolvent S corporation does not result in an increase in basis, and thus does not allow shareholders to deduct previously suspended losses. [PLR 9423003 (TAM)] See additional discussion in Chapter 6, at 610.68.

9

Other adjustments to a shareholder's basis, not reflected in §1367(a), include the following:

- A shareholder increases his or her basis for any contributions to capital. [§358]
- Investment tax credit and recapture also require basis adjustments. These adjustments, at the shareholder level, mirror the corporation's adjustments upon acquisition or disposition of property. [§48(q)(6), repealed by the Tax Reform Act of 1986]

EXAMPLE 9 - 11: YX Corporation is an S corporation. In 1984, it acquired five-year ACRS property at a cost of $100,000. It claimed the full investment tax credit of $10,000, reducing basis in the property by $5,000. Xavier owned 50% of the shares in YX. He reduced basis in his shares by $2,500.

In 1985, YX sold the property after holding it for one full year. YX recaptured $8,000 of the credit and increased basis by $4,000. Xavier increased his basis by $2,000.

OBSERVATION: The investment tax credit was repealed by the Tax Reform Act of 1986. However, the rules requiring basis adjustment for the credit remain in effect, since shareholders need to take into account all adjustments to stock and debt basis during each shareholder's entire holding period.

OBSERVATION: A shareholder adjusts basis for only the income and losses that flow through from the S corporation to a shareholder in his or her capacity as such. There are no adjustments to basis for other items of income or deduction that a shareholder may realize in other capacities, such as:

- Salary from the S corporation [Byrne, John E., 45 TC 151 (1965), aff'd 66-2 USTC 9483 (7th Cir.)]
- Interest received from the S corporation
- Interest paid to the S corporation
- Rent received from the S corporation
- Rent paid to the S corporation
- Gains or losses on sales of property between the shareholder and the S corporation
- Distributions from the S corporation that are treated as gains or dividends
- Expenses paid on behalf of the S corporation by the shareholder, such as unreimbursed employee expenses
- Interest paid by the shareholder on a debt used to finance the purchase of his or her shares in the S corporation
- Gain from disposition of stock in the S corporation [*Miller v. U.S.*, 83 AFTR 2d 99-1559 (DCWV)]

PLANNING TIP: A shareholder who faces basis limitations should review his or her salary arrangement with the corporation carefully. By foregoing salary, the shareholder may reduce the corporation's loss, which would not be deductible, and decrease his or her gross income from the salary. (Of course, reduction to an unreasonably low level may create other problems, as discussed in Chapter 8, at 820.3.)

9

EXAMPLE 9 - 12: In 1996, a shareholder has no basis in S corporation stock or debt. She has been receiving a salary of $5,000 per month. As of September it appears that the corporation will realize a loss of $10,000, after deducting her salary of $60,000 for the year. She will be required to take the entire salary into income when she receives it, but she will not be able to deduct any of the loss, because she has no basis. By reducing her salary for the remainder of the year so that the total salary will be only $50,000, she will be able to eliminate the corporation's loss. She will report only $50,000 from her salary, and she will not forego any loss deduction from the corporation.

SPECIAL NOTE ON DEPLETION: Basis in an S corporation's depletable oil and gas properties is allocated to shareholders. Each shareholder then computes cost or percentage depletion. The shareholder then reduces basis (not below zero) in stock for depletion claimed. [§1367(a)(2)(E)] No adjustment is made directly to the shareholder's basis in stock for depletion on property other than oil and gas. Such depletion is a corporate deduction.

930. Adjustments to debt basis.

Adjustments to debt basis do not occur as frequently as adjustments to stock basis. In most cases, the shareholder's basis in any loan will be the amount of money he or she has lent to the corporation. Like stock basis, however, debt basis may have been subject to three different sets of rules. The corporation may have been a C corporation, an S corporation between 1958 and 1982, or an S corporation after 1982. Therefore, it is necessary to review the rules for all three situations.

930.1. Adjustments to basis of C corporation debt. Barring an extremely unusual transaction, debt basis is not adjusted when a corporation does not have an S election in effect. In some cases, however, a shareholder's basis in a debt from a C corporation will be less than the face amount of the loan. This situation is most likely to occur when the shareholder contributed property to the corporation in a §351 exchange before October 2, 1989. (Section

351 was discussed briefly at 910.1.) It receives extensive discussion in Chapter 14. Under the rules then in effect, a shareholder could receive stock and debt securities as nonrecognition property. The aggregate basis was allocated between the stock and debt securities in proportion to the fair market value of each. See additional discussion at 910.1. and 910.2. in this chapter. Refer to Chapter 14 for a more comprehensive discussion.

930.2. Adjustments to basis of S corporation debt. A shareholder in an S corporation may have made a loan to an S corporation before the Subchapter S Revision Act of 1982. Many shareholders have made loans to S corporations since the effective date of the new law. Therefore, it is important to discuss rules applicable to both eras in the history of Subchapter S.

930.21. Debt basis adjustments from 1958 through 1982. In this time period, the only possible adjustments to debt basis occurred when a shareholder's portion of the S corporation's losses exceeded his or her stock basis. The loss could not reduce the basis of any shareholder's debt below zero. [§1376(b)(2) (prior law), §1016(a)(18) (prior law)] If the corporation earned income in subsequent years, there was no provision allowing restoration of basis.

> **EXAMPLE 9 - 13:** Ann owned all of the stock in Annco, an S corporation. In the corporation's 1981 taxable year, Annco reported a $50,000 loss. Ann had stock basis of $15,000 and had loaned the corporation $60,000. She would reduce her stock basis to zero, and would also reduce her debt basis to $25,000. The corporation's subsequent income would have no effect on her debt basis. When the loan was repaid she would report $35,000 of gain.

9

The Subchapter S Revision Act of 1982 did not provide any means by which debt basis could be restored if it had been reduced for losses under old Subchapter S. Therefore, to the extent that any of these debts is outstanding, the shareholders will recognize gain upon repayment.

> **EXAMPLE 9 - 14:** Refer to Example 9 - 13. By 1990, Annco had accumulated $250,000 of taxable income, all of which had increased Ann's stock basis. In 1990, Annco repays Ann the $60,000 debt. Ann reports $35,000 gain.

930.22. Debt basis reductions after 1982. As a general rule, there is no adjustment to debt basis at any time when the shareholder has basis in his or her stock. However, when losses pass through to the shareholder, and the losses exceed stock basis, debt basis is reduced. [§1016(a)(17). See also §1367(b)(2)(A), discussed below.]

SUMMARY OF AUTHORITY: CODE SECTION 1367(b)(2)(A)

- When a shareholder's portion of an S corporation's losses exceed his or her stock basis, the shareholder reduces debt basis.
- The shareholder cannot reduce debt basis below zero.

> **OBSERVATION:** The debt basis reduction rule has been in existence since 1958. It was not changed by the Subchapter S Revision Act of 1982. Therefore, old Regulations and cases are still applicable to such reductions.

930.23. Debt basis restoration after 1982. After debt basis has been reduced, there may be subsequent income. Such income will first restore debt basis. See Code §1367(b)(2)(B) as discussed below.

SUMMARY OF AUTHORITY: CODE SECTION 1367(b)(2)(B)

- If debt basis has been reduced after 1982, the shareholder's portion of subsequent income (less distributions) of the corporation restores debt basis.
- The debt basis restoration occurs before any income adds to stock basis.

EXAMPLE 9 - 15: SMJ Corporation was formed in 1982. Its sole shareholder, S, contributed property with an adjusted basis of $40,000. She took back stock worth $25,000 and a debt security worth $75,000. The corporation immediately elected Subchapter S status. In calendar year 1982 (governed by prior Subchapter S), the corporation had a net operating loss of $15,000. In calendar year 1983 (governed by current Subchapter S), the corporation reported a net operating loss (no separately stated items) of $20,000. In 1984, the corporation had taxable income of $45,000. S took no distributions in any of the three years. The resultant basis computations to S would be:

	Basis of		
Item	*Stock*	*Security*	*Total*
Initial contribution			
(allocated per FMV)	$10,000	$30,000	$40,000
1982 loss	(10,000)	(5,000)	(15,000)
Basis, end of 1982	0	25,000	25,000
1983 loss	(0)	(20,000)	(20,000)
Basis, end of 1983	$ 0	$ 5,000	5,000
1984 income:			
To debt		20,000	20,000
To stock	25,000		25,000
Basis, end of 1984	$25,000	$25,000	$50,000

Note that the 1984 income first restores basis to debt. That restoration, however, is limited to the debt basis reduction that occurred after 1982. The remainder of the income adds basis to stock. Note further that any distributions to S would be tax-free, up to her stock basis of $25,000.

EXAMPLE 9 - 16: Refer to Example 9 - 15. Assume the same facts in 1984 except that the corporation distributed $37,000 to the shareholder. The 1984 results would be:

	Basis of		
Item	*Stock*	*Security*	*Total*
Basis, end of 1983 $ 5,000	$ 0	$ 5,000	
1984 income to stock basis 37,000	37,000		
1984 distribution (37,000)	(37,000)		
1984 income to debt basis 8,000		8,000	
Basis, end of 1984	$ 0	$13,000	$13,000

The rules governing basis adjustments to stock and debt require careful attention to the corporation's prior history of income and losses, as well as the current year's situation. Figure 9 - 6 diagrams the relationships.

930.3. Confusion in the statute. The rules governing basis adjustments to stock and debt require careful attention to the corporation's prior history of income and losses, as well as the current year's situation. Because of somewhat curious wording that serves no apparent purpose, the debt basis deduction limit is calculated before any income or loss adjustment for the current year. See Code §1366(d)(1), as discussed below.

Figure 9 - 6: Basis adjustments for income and losses.

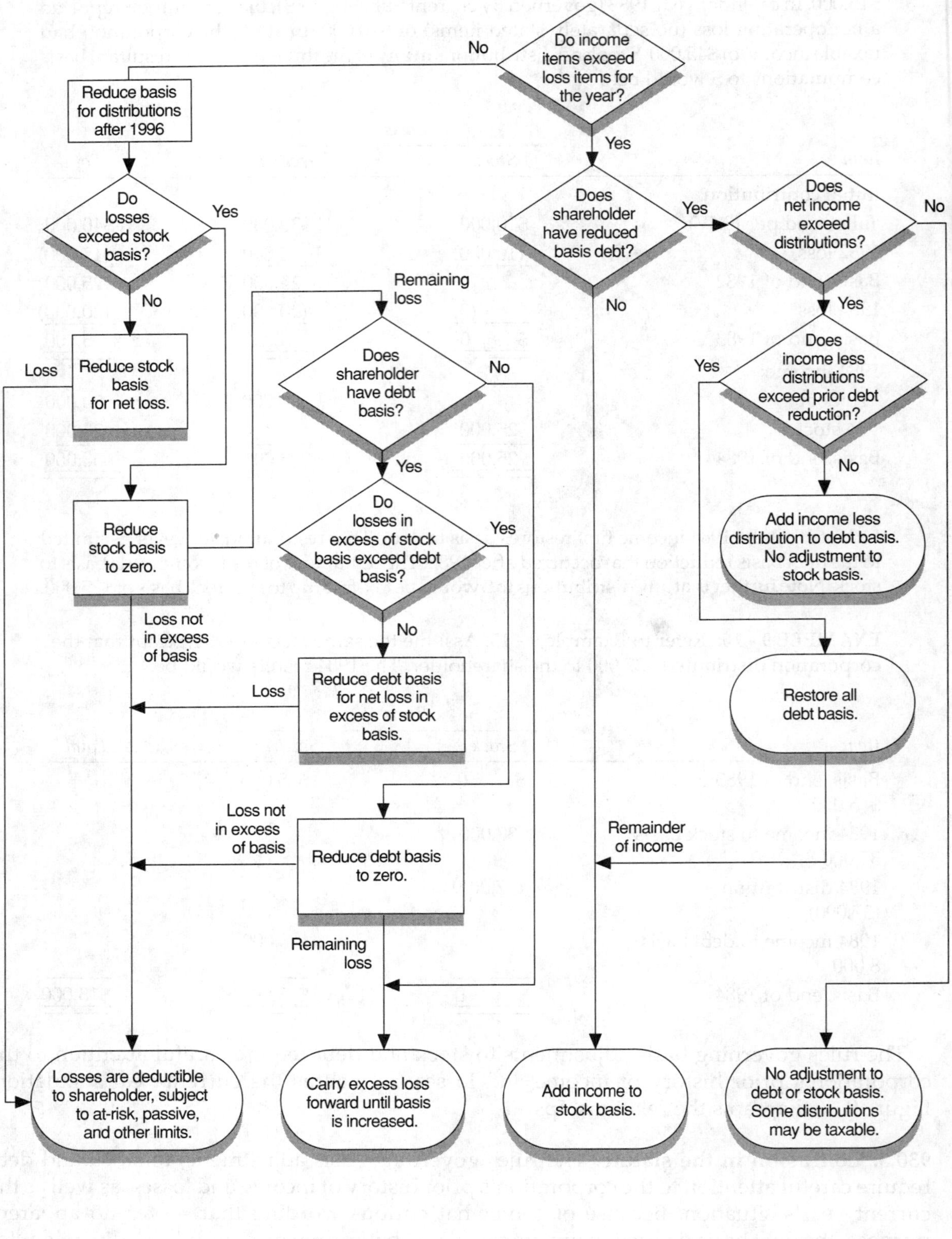

9

SUMMARY OF AUTHORITY: CODE SECTION 1366(d)(1)

- The adjusted basis of stock (for allowance of losses) includes all income items for the taxable year, but no distributions.
- The adjusted basis of debt (for allowance of losses) includes no income items for the taxable year.

As long as the next year has only income and no losses, there would be no cause for confusion. If the next year has both income and losses, the ordering rules would have a strange result.

When an S corporation and its shareholder report income and losses in the same year:

1. There may be separately reported income and losses (e.g., a capital gain and an ordinary loss) that flow through from the corporation to the shareholder in one year.
2. The corporation may have income in the current year, and the shareholder may have suspended losses from the immediate prior year.

OBSERVATION: The basis restoration rule does not seem to be in accordance with the intent of the statute. The legislative history states: "The loss carried forward can be deducted only by that shareholder if and when the basis in his or her stock of, **or loans to,** the corporation is restored." [Senate Report No. 97-640, 97th Cong., 2d Sess., H.R. 6055, page 3] [emphasis added]

Only a simple change to the statute is needed to get the proper results. If §1366(d)(1)(B) were changed to read ". . . (determined without regard to any adjustment under paragraph 2(A) of 1367(b) for the taxable year)," it would allow restoration of basis to be taken into account before the limitation on deductibility of loss would apply. By allowing adjustment for the next succeeding year's income, the statute would better serve its intended purpose.

930.4. Repayment of a reduced-basis loan. A shareholder reduces basis of a loan to an S corporation when he or she uses that loan to absorb losses from the S corporation. Under prior Subchapter S, there was no opportunity to restore basis in a loan once it had been reduced for losses. Under new law, basis may be restored when the corporation earns income in the future. There are, however, three events in which a corporation repays a loan from a shareholder after its basis had been reduced, but before basis is restored:

- The shareholder used the loan to absorb his or her portion of the S corporation's loss in a year that began before 1983.
- The corporation repays the loan before it passes through sufficient income to the shareholder to restore his or her debt basis.
- The shareholder disposes of his or her stock in the corporation, and the corporation repays the loan at a later date.

If the loan is evidenced by a note, the note becomes a capital asset. If the shareholder makes more than one loan, and each loan is formalized by a separate note, the shareholder must account for each loan separately. If the shareholder does not receive a note for a loan, all such unwritten loans are treated as a single note for basis purposes. (For recent cases in which a shareholder was denied basis due to failure to substantiate loans to the S corporation, see *Sperl*, TC Memo 1993-515, and *Shaver*, TC Memo 1993-619.)

OBSERVATION: The differential between current tax rates on ordinary income and capital gains should make it imperative that all shareholder loans to S corporations be documented as notes, so that repayment before basis is restored will result in capital gains, rather than ordinary income. Drafting each loan as a note will also facilitate the following Planning Tip.

PLANNING TIP: A shareholder who has reduced basis debt may want to consider giving the debt to a lower-tax-bracket family member or to a charity. A gift to the lower-bracket family member would cause the repayment of the gain to be taxed to the lower-bracket taxpayer. If the loan is evidenced by a note and the note is given to a charity, the shareholder who makes the gift will be able to claim a charitable contribution of the fair market value of the note. See Chapter 6, at 610.55., and Chapter 10, at 1040., for discussion of the unique charitable contribution rules applicable to S corporations.

The shareholder (or former shareholder) who receives payment on a reduced-basis loan will report a gain. The gain may be ordinary or capital, depending upon the structure of the loan arrangement. Repayment of an open account loan is treated as ordinary income to the creditor. [Rev. Rul. 64-162, 1964-1 CB (Part I) 304] If the loan is evidenced by a note, the note may be a capital asset to the holder. Repayment of a reduced-basis note creates capital gain. [Rev. Rul. 64-162, 1964-1 CB (Part I) 304] If part of the loan is repaid, the lender must prorate between basis and gain (analogous to an installment sale). [Rev. Rul. 64-162, 1964-1 CB (Part I) 304; *Smith, Joe M.*, 48 TC 872 (1967), aff'd 70-1 USTC 9327 (9th Cir.)]

9

EXAMPLE 9 - 17: In 1996, George loans $50,000 to Geoco, an S corporation. Geoco passes losses to George, who reduces his basis in the loan to $20,000. In 1997, Geoco has no income, so George does not restore any basis to his loan to Geoco. In 1997, Geoco repays $10,000 of the loan. George must allocate the repayment between basis and gain as follows:

Basis	$20,000
Face amount	50,000
Basis as percentage of face	40%
Repayment	$10,000
Repayment allocated to basis	4,000
Repayment treated as gain	6,000
Basis in remaining loan:	
Basis before repayment	20,000
Less basis allocated to repaid portion	(4,000)
Basis in remaining loan	$16,000

A shareholder may make several loans to an S corporation and use them to absorb losses of the corporation over more than one year. In this situation, prior case law held that each loan received a separate basis adjustment. [*Novell*, 28 TCM 1307, TC Memo 1969-255; *Cornelius*, 58 TC 417, aff'd *Cornelius v. U.S.*, 74-1 USTC 9449 (5th Cir.)] Regulations issued in 1994 continue this treatment under current law.

When a shareholder has made multiple loans to a corporation, any basis reduction for losses is prorated among the various loans. [Regs. §1.1367-2(b)(3)] If the shareholder owns stock at the end of the loss year, the basis reduction is allocated in proportion to the debts outstanding from the corporation to the shareholder at year end. [Regs. §1.1367-2(b)(1), §1367-2(b)(2)] The measure used for allocation is the shareholder's basis in each loan, after adjustment for prior years' losses.

EXAMPLE 9 - 18: Waylon is a shareholder in Willico, an S corporation. In 1995, Waylon loaned the corporation $10,000. In that year, Waylon's portion of Willico's losses exceeded his basis by $8,000. Therefore, Waylon reduced his basis in the loan to $2,000. In 1996, Waylon loaned Willico an additional $6,000. In 1996, Waylon's share of Willico's losses was $5,000. Waylon's basis adjustments to the two debts is as follows:

	Date of Loan		
	1995	*1996*	*Total*
Basis before 1996 loss	$2,000	$ 6,000	$ 8,000
Percent of total debt basis	25%	75%	
Apportioned percent of 1996 loss	(1,250)	(3,750)	(5,000)
Basis after 1996 loss	$ 750	$ 2,250	$ 3,000

If the shareholder has disposed of his or her stock during the loss year, the allocation of loss to debt is based on the loans outstanding from the corporation to the shareholder on the last date the person owns shares. [Regs. §1.1367-2(b)(2)]

930.5. Basis restoration when there are multiple loans. As discussed at 930.23., any income in a year subsequent to basis reduction goes first to debt, and then to stock. When the income is insufficient to restore all debt basis, and there are multiple loans outstanding from one shareholder, Regulations issued in January 1994 provide a formula for allocating basis restoration. [Regs. §1.1367-2(c)(2), §1.1367-2(e), Example 2] Generally, basis restoration is to be made to debts that are outstanding at the beginning of the corporation's taxable year. The restoration is allocated to the different debts in proportion to the amount of all previous basis reductions. 9

EXAMPLE 9 - 19: Refer to Example 9 - 18. In 1997, Waylon's share of Willico's income is $10,000. Both the 1995 loan and the 1996 loan are still outstanding at the end of 1997. Waylon restores basis of each debt in proportion to the total prior reductions. The computation of the percentage of income to each debt is:

	Date of Loan		
	1995	*1996*	*Total*
Original amount of each debt	$10,000	$6,000	$16,000
1995 reductions	$ 8,000	$ 0	$ 8,000
1996 basis reductions	1,250	3,750	5,000
Total reductions before 1997	$ 9,250	$3,750	$13,000

	Date of Loan		
	1995	*1996*	*Total*
Percent of total reduction applied to each	.7115	.2885	1.0000
Amount applied to each	$ 7,115	$2,885	$10,000
Basis after 1996 loss	750	2,250	3,000
Basis after 1997 income	$ 7,865	$5,135	$13,000

930.6. Basis adjustments in the year of repayment. The Code is completely silent on the adjustment to basis of a loan in the year in which it is repaid. Since losses pass through at the end of the corporation's taxable year, there could not be any basis reduction to debt that has been repaid before the end of the year. But the Code also provides that income passes through and adjusts a shareholder's stock and debt basis at the end of the S corporation's taxable year. When a debt has been repaid in a year in which the corporation also has income, there are two possible results:

1. The repayment of the debt could result in gain or income, if the basis of that debt is not adjusted upwards for the corporation's income.

2. The corporation's income could restore the basis of debt that has been repaid during the year, reducing or eliminating the gain on repayment.

Example 9 - 20 illustrates the dilemma that arose from the lack of a specific rule.

EXAMPLE 9 - 20: RC Corporation has one shareholder, Ray. In 1995, RC lost $150,000. Ray's stock basis at the beginning of 1995 was $60,000. He loaned the corporation $90,000, which gave him sufficient basis to deduct the 1995 loss in full. That loss reduced both his stock basis and his debt basis to zero.

In 1996, the corporation earned $100,000 net income and repaid Ray's $90,000 loan in full. If the income could add only to stock basis, since there is no debt outstanding at the end of 1996, Ray would report a gain of $90,000 on the repayment of the debt. By contrast, if the corporation's 1996 income restored the basis of the debt, Ray would have no gain on repayment.

For several years, the IRS appeared to vacillate on the treatment of income in a year of debt repayment. According to the 1988 version of Publication 589, income of the corporation in the year that the debt is repaid is added to basis. [IRS Publication 589 (1988), page 10] Later editions of Publication 589 eliminated this language, but they offer no direct contradiction of the rule.

Fortunately, the Regulations allow basis restoration to debt in the year of repayment. Regulations §1.1367-2 provides that restoration of debt basis is made in proportion to the basis of debt outstanding at the beginning of the year. [Regs. §1.1367-2(d)(1)] Example 9 - 21 illustrates the tax treatment when the entire debt is repaid in a year in which a corporation has income.

9

EXAMPLE 9 - 21: Refer to Example 9 - 20. According to Regulations §1.1367-2(d)(1), Ray adjusts the debt basis up to $90,000 at the time of repayment. He reports no gain on the repayment, and he adjusts his stock basis from zero to $10,000.

OBSERVATION: The result given in the Regulations is sensible. Adjusting debt basis for income in the year of repayment yields no different tax treatment than would a cash distribution in lieu of repayment. Refer to Chapter 7, at 715.2., for the effects of distributions on debt basis.

EXAMPLE 9 - 22: Refer to Example 9 - 20. If RC had not repaid the debt, but had distributed $90,000 to Ray in 1994, the distribution would have been tax-free. Ray would have increased his debt basis to $10,000. Therefore, the debt basis adjustment rule allows Ray to withdraw $90,000 tax-free, either as a distribution or as repayment of debt.

The Regulations also provide guidance for a shareholder who receives a repayment of part, but not all, of the reduced basis debt. In this situation, the corporation's income restores basis to a repaid debt before basis is added to other debt or stock. [Regs. §1.1367-2(d)(1)]

EXAMPLE 9 - 23: Loretta is a shareholder in Ward Corporation, an S corporation. At the beginning of the corporation's 1995 taxable year, Loretta had no basis in her stock in Ward. In 1995, she loaned Ward $50,000. Her share of Ward's 1995 losses reduced her basis in that loan to zero. In 1996, Loretta loaned Ward an additional $30,000. Her share of Ward's 1996 losses reduced her basis in that loan to zero.

In 1997, Ward was profitable. Loretta's share of Ward's 1997 income was $60,000. If Ward did not repay either of the loans, the income would be allocated proportionately between the two debts. In 1997, however, Ward repays Loretta's 1995 loan of $50,000 in full. It does not repay any of the 1996 loan. Loretta's portion of Ward's 1997 income would increase the basis of her 1995 loan back to its original $50,000. The remaining $10,000 of income would increase basis of the 1996 loan to $10,000.

930.7. Effect of termination of any shareholder's interest. As is discussed in Chapter 6, at 630.2., and Chapter 7, at 715.4. and 740.6., an S corporation may elect to account for its taxable year as two separate years when a shareholder terminates his or her interest or disposes of a substantial portion of the corporation's stock. [§1377(a)(2); Regs. §1.1368-1(g)] When a corporation makes this election, each shareholder must make separate basis calculations for each of the two portions of the corporation's taxable year. [Regs. §1.1367-2(d)(2)] This election could have some unpleasant side effects when a loan is repaid in the early part of the year and the corporation does not have sufficient income to restore the loan's basis until the later part of the year.

EXAMPLE 9 - 24: Throughout 1996 Jay and Jeannie were equal shareholders in JJ Corporation, a calendar-year S corporation. In 1996, Jay had no stock basis, but he loaned JJ $140,000. On March 1, 1997, JJ repaid Jay the entire $140,000. On May 26, 1997 (40% of the year had elapsed), Jay bought all of Jeannie's shares. JJ's 1997 taxable income was:

Loss from January 1 through May 26	$(180,000)
Income from May 27 through December 31	400,000
Total for year	$ 220,000

If JJ does not elect to close the books when Jeannie terminates her interest, the repayment of Jay's loan will be treated as occurring in the same year as the corporation's income. Adjustments to Jay's stock and debt basis will be as follows:

	Stock	*Debt*
Basis, January 1, 1997	$ 0	$ 0
Jay's adjustment for 1997 income [50% + (50% x 60%)]:	36,000	140,000
Basis before debt repayment	$36,000	$140,000

If JJ does elect to close the books when Jeannie terminates her interest, the repayment of Jay's loan will be treated as occurring in the year before the corporation's income. Adjustments to Jay's stock and debt basis will be as follows:

	Stock	*Debt*
Basis, January 1, 1997	$ 0	$ 0
Jay's adjustment for early 1997 loss ($90,000, no adjustment, since there is no basis)	0	0
Basis before debt repayment	$ 0	$ 0

Jay will report a gain of $140,000 on repayment. The adjustments for the latter part of the year will go solely to stock, since Jay has no indebtedness outstanding at the beginning of the second part of the year.

930.8. Disposition of stock by person who continues to hold debt. When a shareholder has loaned money to an S corporation and sells all of his or her stock, the stock and debt adjustments occur on the last day on which the person holds shares. [Regs. §§1.1367-1(d)(1) and 1.1367-2(d)(1)] If the shareholder continues to hold the debt after the disposition of the stock, there will be no opportunity to ever restore basis.

EXAMPLE 9 - 25: Ivan was a shareholder in Ivco, an S corporation. In 1996, he loaned $50,000 to the corporation. His share of the corporation's losses for 1996 reduced his stock basis to zero and his debt basis to $5,000. In 1997, Ivan sold all of his shares, but kept his note receivable from Ivco. Ivan's share of the corporation's 1997 income was $20,000. For 1997, Ivan will increase his basis in the loan to $25,000. There will be no opportunity for any future increase, since Ivan is no longer a shareholder. Therefore, repayment of the loan at any time will result in a taxable gain to Ivan.

9

930.9. Other dispositions of reduced basis debt. A shareholder may dispose of his or her debt instrument before the corporation has generated sufficient income so that the shareholder can restore basis. Most dispositions create no special tax problems. If the disposition is taxable, such as a sale of the debt or liquidation of the corporation, the gain will be taxed under the usual rules. When the debt is evidenced by a note, the note will generally be a capital asset, and the disposition will usually result in capital gain or loss. (See Chapter 14, at 1425.12., for discussion of bad debt deduction upon the worthlessness of a debt.) The sale of a reduced basis debt may qualify for installment sale treatment, if the proceeds are received in more than one taxable year of the seller. (See Chapter 16, at 1630.24., for discussion of installment sales of stock. The same rules apply to installment sales of debt.)

On one occasion, the IRS attempted to characterize a gain on disposition of debt as ordinary income. The IRS reasoned that the debt basis had been reduced due to the passthrough of ordinary losses, and attempted to impute ordinary income recapture. The Tax Court, however, held that since the asset was a capital asset to the holder, the gain on the disposition must be capital. [*Klein*, 75 TC 298 (1980)]

If the disposition is nontaxable, such as a disposition at death or by gift, no gain or loss will be reported as a result of the disposition. When the disposition occurs at death, the new owner will receive a fair market value basis in the debt. [§1014] If a debt instrument is transferred by gift, the recipient generally takes the donor's basis. [§1015] (See at 910.2. for possible adjustments to reflect the donor's gift tax.) When the recipient is not a shareholder in the corporation, he or she will have no opportunity to increase the basis in the debt. Thus, if the corporation eventually repaid the debt, the new creditor would report capital gain or ordinary income, depending upon whether the debt was written or informal.

9

> **OBSERVATION:** The Code and Regulations are completely silent on a transferee creditor's ability to restore debt basis if the transferee is also a shareholder in the corporation. Thus, a shareholder who has received reduced basis debt as a gift should be able to restore debt basis. The case for doing so would be especially strong if the debt were transferred to a spouse, or a former spouse, if the transfer were incident to a divorce. [§1041; Regs. §1.1041-1T]

935. Miscellaneous basis problems.

Given the importance of basis throughout the history of both versions of Subchapter S, it is not surprising that there have been a considerable number of cases and rulings. A few of these that do not fit neatly into any of the preceding categories are discussed below.

935.1. Basis adjustments after erroneous S election. Shareholders had deducted losses and reduced stock basis, believing that the corporation was an S corporation. On later audit, it was determined that the corporation had never filed Form 2553, so the S election was never effective. When the shareholders sold stock at a loss, they attempted to claim a §1244 deduction for the full basis. See Chapter 14, at 1430., for discussion of §1244. Some of the loss years, however, were barred by the statute of limitations. The court held that the shareholders' bases were reduced by the losses they had claimed in closed years. [*Coldiron*, 54 TCM 1084, TC Memo 1987-569]

935.2. Effect of excess deductions in closed years. In *Byrne*, the shareholder had deducted losses in excess of basis for a year that was closed when the IRS performed its audit. The IRS did not attempt to impute negative basis. [*Byrne, John E.*, 45 TC 151 (1965), aff'd 66-2 USTC 9483 (7th Cir.)]

> **EXAMPLE 9 - 26:** Glenn owns all of the shares in Glennco, an S corporation. At the beginning of 1984, Glenn's stock basis was $15,000. In that year, unaware of the basis limitation, Glenn claimed $35,000 of losses. The IRS later audited his 1985, 1986, and 1987 returns, after the statute had closed for 1984. The IRS would most likely give him zero basis at the beginning of 1985.

935.3. Inapplicability of any tax benefit rule. Shareholders must reduce debt basis for losses that do not result in any tax benefit. The IRS denied the taxpayer the opportunity to eliminate the gain by use of the tax benefit rule. [*Hudspeth v. Commissioner*, 90-2 USTC 50,501 (9th Cir.)]

EXAMPLE 9 - 27: Louise owns all of the shares in Louco, an S corporation. In 1996, before deducting any of Louco's losses, Louise had basis of $100,000 in her stock and debt. In that year, Louco posted a loss of $80,000. In that same year, Louise had $85,000 income from other sources and $25,000 itemized deductions and personal exemptions. Louco's loss would reduce Louise's adjusted gross income to $5,000. The itemized deductions and personal exemptions would eliminate her entire taxable income but would not result in a loss carryover. Louise receives a tax benefit of only $50,000 from the $80,000 loss from Louco. She would, however, be required to reduce her basis in Louco from $100,000 to $20,000.

OBSERVATION: A shareholder who anticipates a loss in excess of tax benefit may employ a reverse planning strategy. For example, a shareholder who has made loans to the S corporation in a manner that creates basis might want to substitute bank loans and have the corporation use the proceeds to repay all or a part of the loans to the shareholder.

EXAMPLE 9 - 28: Refer to Example 9 - 27. Assume that Louise's stock basis was $40,000 and her debt basis was $60,000. If Louco would borrow $50,000 from a third party before the end of 1996 and repay $50,000 of the loan from Louise, her basis would be $50,000. Her loss for that year would be limited to $50,000. Combining this loss with her other income of $75,000 would result in adjusted gross income of $25,000, which would be entirely absorbed by itemized deductions and personal exemptions, resulting in zero taxable income. The taxable income would be no different than was the case in Example 9 - 27. Louise would, however, be able to carry $50,000 of Louco's loss forward to 1989.

9

935.4. Contribution of reduced basis debt to capital. As a general rule, contribution of debt to capital may give rise to forgiveness of debt income under §108. A corporation is deemed to have satisfied the face amount of the obligation for an amount equal to the shareholder's adjusted basis in the debt. [§108(e)(6)] If the shareholder's basis is less than the face amount, the corporation reports income.

A special rule for S corporations provides that the shareholder's basis in debt that is contributed to capital is computed without regard to any basis adjustments for the pass-through of losses from an S corporation. [§108(d)(7)(C)] One letter ruling held that this rule applied when the contribution to capital was disproportionate to stock ownership. [PLR 8927051]

PLANNING TIP: When a shareholder has loaned money to an S corporation and has reduced basis for the pass-through of S corporation losses, contribution of the debt to the corporation's capital may provide a means for reducing or eliminating taxability of distributions. When debt basis has been reduced, there is no remaining stock basis. A repayment of reduced basis debt, in whole or in part, requires proration of basis and gain.

EXAMPLE 9 - 29: Mary owns all of the shares in M Corporation, an S corporation. In 1996, she loaned the corporation $50,000. The corporation's 1996 losses eliminated her stock basis and reduced her debt basis to $20,000. In 1997, she anticipates that the corporation will break even, but she wants to withdraw $10,000 of cash. A distribution on stock will be entirely taxable as a gain, whereas a partial repayment of debt will be 60% taxable. If she contributes the debt to the corporation's capital, she will increase her stock basis to $20,000. The corporation will realize no forgiveness of debt income. Mary will be able to withdraw up to $20,000 tax-free.

935.5. Aggregate or block basis of stock. When the shareholder has acquired different blocks of stock, there is an unresolved question: Does the shareholder use aggregate or block-by-block basis? Aggregate seems to be more consistent with the purposes of Subchapter S under current law. If the corporation has ever been a C corporation, and the shareholder received distributions in excess of earnings and profits and basis, block-by-block basis adjustment is required. Block-by-block was also used for distributions in excess of basis in pre-1982 Subchapter S. [Regs. §1.1376-2(a)(2) (prior law)] The Regulations apply this rule to post-1982 years. [Regs. §1.1367-1(c)(3)] See discussion at 715.15.

935.6. Special problems on dispositions. The disposition could include a distribution in partial or complete liquidation of the corporation. A loss may be ordinary if the stock is §1244 stock. A loss may be disallowed if the stock is sold to a related party. If the stock becomes worthless, it is treated as if it is sold for zero. The basis at the time of disposition is determined after all other basis adjustments are made. (See Chapter 14, at 1430., for a complete discussion of §1244 as it relates to S corporations' shareholders.)

935.7. Basis cannot be determined by an audit of the S corporation. The IRS may adjust certain items at the corporate level. In general, such adjustments apply to all shareholders. When the IRS challenges a shareholder's loss deductions due to the basis limitations, it must adjust the *shareholder's* return. Accordingly, basis limitations cannot be adjusted by reference
9 to the corporation's tax return. [See *Dial USA*, 95 TC 1 (1990).]

935.8. Alternative minimum tax basis. An S corporation is required to report tax preferences and adjustments to its shareholders. However, the limitations on losses may be somewhat different for alternative minimum tax purposes than they are for regular income tax, for two reasons:

- A loss pass-through to a shareholder must be calculated using the minimum tax rule. [§59(h)]
- Each shareholder must calculate a separate basis in his or her stock for alternative minimum tax purposes. [See *General Explanation of the Tax Reform Act of 1986*, page 438.]

EXAMPLE 9 - 30: Vinnie owns all of the stock in Vinco, an S corporation. In 1996, the corporation reports a loss of $50,000 for regular income tax. The corporation has tax adjustments of $10,000 for depreciation of assets placed in service after 1986. Therefore, the alternative minimum tax loss that Vinnie may report is only $40,000 in 1996.

At the beginning of 1996, Vinnie's adjusted basis in his stock was $70,000. The 1996 loss reduces his basis to $20,000 for regular income tax and to $30,000 for alternative minimum tax.

In 1997, the corporation has a loss of $35,000 for regular tax and $28,000 for alternative minimum tax. Vinnie's loss limitations and basis adjustments for 1996 and 1997 are:

	Regular Income Tax	*Alternative Minimum Tax*
Basis, 1/1/96	$70,000	$70,000
1996 loss	(50,000)	(40,000)
Basis, 1/1/97	20,000	30,000
1997 loss allowed	(20,000)	(28,000)
Basis, 1/1/98	$ 0	$ 2,000
Loss carried forward from 1997	$15,000	$ 0

OBSERVATION: The mechanics of alternative minimum tax basis are not articulated in any statute or any Regulation. Presumably, the alternative minimum tax adjustments to stock and debt basis should parallel those required for income tax. The following examples illustrate some of the problems that may be encountered; the solutions presented in the examples are not specifically mandated by any authoritative pronouncement, however, since none exists at the time of this writing. They should provide at least a reasonable basis for reporting transactions. Since they do not depart from any statute, they also should have a realistic possibility of being sustained in an IRS examination.

EXAMPLE 9 - 31: Refer to Example 9 - 30. Assume the same facts except that Vinnie's stock basis was $25,000 and his debt basis was $45,000 at the beginning of 1996. His 1996 computations should be:

	Regular Income Tax	*Alternative Minimum Tax*
Basis, 1/1/96		
Stock	$25,000	$25,000
Debt	45,000	45,000
1996 loss	(50,000)	(40,000)
Basis, 1/1/97		
Stock	$ 0	$ 0
Debt	20,000	30,000
Total	$20,000	$30,000

Assume that the corporation repays the full $45,000 debt in 1997. Since there is no net income to the corporation in 1997, there is no restoration of debt basis. Vinnie would report a gain of $25,000 for income tax. He would reduce the gain by $10,000 for alternative minimum tax.

OBSERVATION: Each shareholder should track stock and debt basis adjustments separately for income tax and alternative minimum tax. Failure to do so will deprive the shareholder of possible reversing adjustments.

In some circumstances, the combination of loss limitations (for income tax) and tax adjustments (for AMT) can have some strange side effects. The general rule that shareholders must include their allocable portions of tax preferences and adjustments in determining their tentative AMT liability could put shareholders in double jeopardy, if the law were to be enforced literally.

EXAMPLE 9 - 32: Minco is an S corporation with one shareholder, Greg. For 1997, the corporation has a loss of $100,00 for regular tax purposes and $75,000 of tax preferences. Thus, Minco's loss, for alternative minimum tax purposes, is $25,000.

If Greg's basis were sufficient for him to claim the entire $100,000 loss for regular income tax purposes, he would need to add the $75,000 adjustment from Minco to determine his alternative minimum taxable income. He should not be required to double-count the tax preferences by both adding $75,000 to his taxable income for preferences and adjusting his loss downward by the same $75,000.

Unfortunately, the Regulations and other authorities dealing with the entire AMT are scanty. There is only one reference in the Code to the coordination of the alternative minimum tax adjustment with the basis limitations. [§59(e)] This provision implies that no adjustment or preference is included in the shareholder's alternative minimum taxable income for any S corporation item when the shareholder's basis does not allow any current tax benefit. The instructions to Form 6251 provide that any AMT adjustment or preference taken into account to recompute a loss from a passive activity or a flow-through entity is not entered twice on the form. (See additional discussion on this issue with respect to passive activity losses in Chapter 10 at 1025.102.)

> **EXAMPLE 9 - 33:** Refer to Example 9 - 32. Greg would report a $75,000 adjustment on his AMT Form 6251 to reduce his reported loss from Minco for the year. He would not enter a tax preference of $75,000 in addition to his loss reduction.

The rule against double-counting should provide additional relief when a shareholder's basis limits the amount of loss deduction claimed for regular income tax purposes. Since the tax preferences and adjustments that flow through from the S corporation are used solely to recalculate the reported loss, they would not be treated as preferences or adjustments on any other part of Form 6251.

> **EXAMPLE 9 - 34:** Assume the same facts as in Example 9 - 32, except that Greg's income tax basis in his stock and debt was only $10,000 at the beginning of 1997. He would be allowed to deduct only $10,000 in computing his taxable income. Thus he would have received no tax benefit from the $75,000 of the corporation's tax preferences. He would claim the $10,000 for both income tax and AMT, and thus he would make no adjustment on his Form 6251. He would carry forward $90,000 of the loss for income tax purposes and $15,000 of the loss for AMT.

940. Additional loss limit concerns.

Other loss limits coexist with the Subchapter S basis rules. Depending on the taxpayer's degree of financial commitment and degree of involvement with the corporation's activities, there may be several hurdles to overcome before a portion of the corporation's losses can be deducted on the shareholder's return. The important shareholder limitations are listed below in their order of priority.

1. The loss must not be suspended within the corporation (such as a related-party accrual). (See Chapter 8.)
2. The hobby loss rules of §183 disallow any net loss from an activity without a profit motive. (See Chapter 6.)
3. Losses may be limited to the shareholder's amount at risk. (Chapter 10 discusses the at-risk rules of §465.)
4. Unless the shareholder materially participates in the corporation's business activity(ies), losses may be limited to the shareholder's passive income from other sources. (Chapter 10 discusses the passive activity loss limits of §469.)
5. If any portion of a loss is capital, it will be limited to the shareholder's net capital gains from other sources, subject to the allowance of a $3,000 net capital loss in any taxable year.
6. If a loss is characterized as an itemized deduction, it may be subject to several limitations at the shareholder level.

945. Practice aids.

Checklist 9 - 1 provides some overall considerations for evaluating a shareholder's basis in stock and debt. This checklist should be completed as near as possible to the end of the corporation's taxable year, so that there is time to take corrective action if needed.

Worksheets 9 - 1, 9 - 2, 9 - 3, and 9 - 4 should be useful in determining a shareholder's stock and debt basis after the year end. Both Worksheet 9-1 and Worksheet 9 - 2 are necessary for post- 1996 years, because the ordering rules differ depending on whether the corporation has net income or net loss for the year. See Chapter 6, at 630.6., for discussion.

As Worksheets 9 - 1 and 9 - 2 indicate, a shareholder who owns more than one block of stock should keep a worksheet for each block. Similarly, a shareholder who has made more than one loan to the corporation should keep a separate worksheet for each loan. Worksheet 9 - 4 should be useful if a shareholder has made any open account advances to the corporation.

Each shareholder should also keep separate schedules for the alternative minimum tax basis of each block of stock and for each debt instrument. The same worksheets can be used for this purpose, except that the beginning basis, income, and losses should be calculated separately by the alternative minimum tax rules.

Note that these worksheets must be maintained for each portion of the year if the corporation elects to terminate its taxable year upon the termination of a shareholder's interest, a substantial disposition of stock, or the issue of substantial amounts of new stock. See Chapter 6, at 630.22., for discussion of the techniques, as well as benefits and pitfalls, to be observed.

Checklist 9 - 1: Year-end basis planning

	Applicable (Yes/No)	*Completed (Date)*
1. Shareholder considerations (complete for each shareholder)		
a. Basis for potential losses	________	________
i. If insufficient, consider increasing basis by:	________	________
(1) Contributing to capital	________	________
(2) Making loan to corporation	________	________
(3) Substituting on bank loan	________	________
(4) Postponing payment of salary, rent, or interest—be wary of insufficient salary, effects on pension funding, debt reclassification problems.	________	________
ii. If basis is sufficient, consider reducing basis to suspend loss.	________	________
(1) Anticipated losses might overshoot personal exemptions and itemized or standard deduction.	________	________
(2) Losses may yield better tax result next year.	________	________
b. Basis for distributions	________	________
i. If basis after losses is insufficient to absorb distributions, consider increasing basis.	________	________
ii. Loan to corporation will not help.	________	________
iii. If unable to increase basis, consider AAA bypass election.	________	________
c. Possible benefits of corporate actions	________	________
i. Charitable contributions	________	________
ii. Recognized corporate level capital losses	________	________
iii. Other items	________	________

Copyright © 2000 by Harcourt, Inc. All rights reserved.

2. Corporate considerations
   a. Ascertain any new shareholders or anticipated transfers.
      i. Verify eligibility.
      ii. If already transferred to ineligible shareholder, prepare to take corrective action and prepare to request inadvertent termination relief.
   b. Record bonus, compensation, and borrowing resolutions in minutes of corporate meeting.
   c. Adopt or fund qualified pension and profit-sharing plans.
   d. If corporation has Section 444 year, consider any benefit from terminating year.
      i. Refund of deposit
      ii. Acceleration of income or loss to shareholders

Worksheet 9 - 1: Stock basis

Keep a separate worksheet for each block of stock.

If the corporation has terminated a year under §1377(a)(2) or Regs. §1.1368-1(g), complete a separate worksheet for each portion of the year.)

1. Basis at beginning of year, or at acquisition date if acquired during year $ ______
2. Additions to basis
   (CAUTION: Make sure that any debt basis has been restored to extent of prior reductions.)
   a. Add all taxable items from shareholder's K-1 (to the extent allocated to this block) $ ______
   b. Add all tax-exempt income (CAUTION: If including corporate cancellation of debt income, review current IRS position and consider disclosure.) See discussion at 925.22. $ ______
   c. Add any deemed dividend allocated to this block. (See Chapter 7, at 740.5.) $ ______
3. Subtotal (1 + 2a + 2b + 2c) $ ______
4. Reductions of basis
   (CAUTION: Determine if prior or current election to reduce for deductible expenses under Regs. §1.1367-1(f) is in effect. If such election is in effect, skip line 4a and go directly to line 4c.)
   a. Nondeductible expenses, not capitalized
      (Include any spillovers from other blocks of stock.)
      (Do not reduce basis below zero.)
      (Check to see if other block of stock has sufficient basis to absorb excess.)

Copyright © 2000 by Harcourt, Inc. All rights reserved.

(Check to see if shareholder debt has sufficient basis to absorb excess.)
(Do not carry forward any excess expense to next year.) $ ______________

b. Subtotal (3 – 4a) $ ______________

c. Deductible expenses and losses
(Include any spillovers from other blocks of stock.)
(Include any amounts carried forward from last year.)
(Do not reduce basis below zero.)
(Check to see if other block of stock has sufficient basis to absorb excess.)
(Check to see if shareholder debt has sufficient basis to absorb excess.)
(Carry forward any excess expense to next year.) $ ______________

d. Subtotal (4b – 4c)
(CAUTION: If prior or current election to reduce for deductible expenses under Regulations §1.1367-1(f) is not in effect, skip line 4e and go directly to line 4f.) $ ______________

e. Nondeductible expenses, not capitalized
(Include any spillovers from other blocks of stock.)
(Include any amounts carried forward from last year.)
(Do not reduce basis below zero.)
(Check to see if other block of stock has sufficient basis to absorb excess.)
(Check to see if shareholder debt has sufficient basis to absorb excess.)
(Carry forward any excess expense to next year.) $ ______________

f. Subtotal (4d – 4e) $ ______________

g. Distributions received by shareholder during year
(Do not include any dividend from earnings and profits or deemed dividend.)
(Do not reduce basis below zero. If distributions exceed basis, check to see if other block of stock has sufficient basis to absorb excess.) $ ______________

5. Ending basis (4f – 4g) $ ______________

Worksheet 9 - 2: Stock basis in post-1997 year

Keep a separate worksheet for each block of stock.

If the corporation has terminated a year under §1377(a)(2) or Regs. §1.1368-1(g), complete a separate worksheet for each portion of the year.)

1. Basis at beginning of year, or at acquisition date if acquired during year $ ______________

Copyright © 2000 by Harcourt, Inc. All rights reserved.

9

2. Additions to basis
(CAUTION: Make sure that any debt basis has been restored to extent of prior reductions.) ____________
   a. Add all taxable items from shareholder's K-1 (to the extent allocated to this block) $ ____________
   b. Add all tax-exempt income (CAUTION: If including corporate cancellation of debt income, review current IRS position and consider disclosure.) See discussion at 925.22. $ ____________
   c. Add any deemed dividend allocated to this block. (See Chapter 7, at 740.5.) $ ____________
3. Subtotal (1 + 2a + 2b + 2c) $ ____________
4. Reductions of basis
   a. Distributions received by shareholder during year (Do not include any dividend from earnings and profits or deemed dividend.) (Do not reduce basis below zero. If distributions exceed basis, check to see if other block of stock has sufficient basis to absorb excess.) $ ____________
   b. Subtotal (3 – 4a) $ ____________
   (CAUTION: Determine if prior or current election to reduce for deductible expenses under Regs. §1.1367-1(f) is in effect. If such election is in effect, skip line 4c and go directly to line 4d.) ____________
   c. Nondeductible expenses, not capitalized (Include any spillovers from other blocks of stock.) (Do not reduce basis below zero.) (Check to see if other block of stock has sufficient basis to absorb excess.) (Check to see if shareholder debt has sufficient basis to absorb excess.) (Do not carry forward any excess expense to next year.) $ ____________
   d. Deductible expenses and losses (Include any spillovers from other blocks of stock.) (Include any amounts carried forward from last year.) (Do not reduce basis below zero.) (Check to see if other block of stock has sufficient basis to absorb excess.) (Check to see if shareholder debt has sufficient basis to absorb excess.) (Carry forward any excess expense to next year.) $ ____________
   e. Subtotal (4b – 4c – 4d) ____________

Copyright © 2000 by Harcourt, Inc. All rights reserved.

(CAUTION: If prior or current election to reduce for deductible expenses under Regulations §1.1367-1(f) is not in effect, skip line 4f and go directly to line 4g.) $ ________

f. Nondeductible expenses, not capitalized
(Include any spillovers from other blocks of stock.)
(Include any amounts carried forward from last year.)
(Do not reduce basis below zero.)
(Check to see if other block of stock has sufficient basis to absorb excess.)
(Check to see if shareholder debt has sufficient basis to absorb excess.)

(Carry forward any excess expense to next year.) $ ________

g. Subtotal (4e – 4f) $ ________

5. Ending basis (4f – 4g) $ ________

Worksheet 9 - 3: Debt basis

Keep a separate worksheet for each debt instrument.

9

If the corporation has terminated a year under §1377(a)(2) or Regs. §1.1368-1(g), complete a separate worksheet for each portion of the year.

1. Basis at beginning of year, or at loan date if loaned during year $ ________

2. Additions to basis
(CAUTION: Limit to extent of prior reductions. If debt basis has never been reduced, skip to line 3.)

   a. Add all taxable items from shareholder's K-1 (to the extent allocated to this block) $ ________

   b. Add all tax exempt income
   (CAUTION: If including corporate cancellation of debt income, review current IRS position and consider disclosure.)
   See discussion at 925.22. $ ________

   c. Less distributions received by shareholder during year (do not include any dividend from earnings and profits or deemed dividend), limit to 2a + 2b (________)

3. Subtotal (1 + 2a + 2b – 2c) $ ________

4. Reductions of basis
(CAUTION: Determine if prior or current election to reduce for deductible expenses under Regs. §1.1367-1(f) is in effect.
If such election is in effect, skip line 4a and go directly to line 4c.)

Copyright © 2000 by Harcourt, Inc. All rights reserved.

a. Nondeductible expenses, not capitalized (to extent expenses exceed basis of stock) (Do not reduce basis below zero.) (Do not carry forward any excess expense to next year.) $ ________

b. Subtotal (3 – 4a) $ ________

c. Deductible expenses and losses (to extent expenses exceed basis of stock) (Include any amounts carried forward from last year.) (Do not reduce basis below zero.) (Carry forward any excess expense to next year.) $ ________

d. Subtotal (4b – 4c) (CAUTION: If prior or current election to reduce for deductible expenses under Regs. §1.1367-1(f) is not in effect, skip line 4e and go directly to line 4f.) $ ________

e. Nondeductible expenses, not capitalized (to extent expenses exceed basis of stock) (Include any amounts carried forward from last year.) (Do not reduce basis below zero.) (Carry forward any excess expense to next year.) $ ________

9

f. Subtotal (4d – 4e) $ ________

g. Partial repayments received by shareholder during year $ ________

5. Ending basis (4f – 4g) $ ________

Worksheet 9 - 4: Open account debt basis

If the corporation has terminated a year under §1377(a)(2) or Regulations §1.1368-1(g), complete a separate worksheet for each portion of the year.

1. Basis at beginning of year, or at loan date (If loaned during year, add new loans made during year.) $ ________
2. Additions to basis (CAUTION: Limit to extent of prior reductions. If debt basis has never been reduced, skip to line 3.)

   a. Add all taxable items from shareholder's K-1 (to the extent allocated to this block) $ ________

   b. Add all tax-exempt income (CAUTION: If including corporate cancellation of debt income, review current IRS position and consider disclosure.) See discussion at 925.22. $ ________

Copyright © 2000 by Harcourt, Inc. All rights reserved.

c. Less distributions received by shareholder during year (do not include any dividend from earnings and profits or deemed dividend), limit to 2a + 2b (________)

3. Subtotal (1 + 2a + 2b – 2c) $ ________
4. Reductions of basis
(CAUTION: Determine if prior or current election to reduce for deductible expenses under Regs. §1.1367-1(f) is in effect. If such election is in effect, skip line 4a and go directly to line 4c.)
   a. Nondeductible expenses, not capitalized (to extent expenses exceed basis of stock) (Do not reduce basis below zero.) (Do not carry forward any excess expense to next year.) $ ________
   b. Subtotal (3 – 4a) $ ________
   c. Deductible expenses and losses (to extent expenses exceed basis of stock) (Include any amounts carried forward from last year.) (Do not reduce basis below zero.) (Carry forward any excess expense to next year.) $ ________
   d. Subtotal (4b – 4c) (CAUTION: If prior or current election to reduce for deductible expenses under Regs. §1.1367-1(f) is not in effect, skip line 4e and go directly to line 4f.) $ ________
   e. Nondeductible expenses, not capitalized (to extent expenses exceed basis of stock) (Include any amounts carried forward from last year.) (Do not reduce basis below zero.) (Carry forward any excess expense to next year.) $ ________
   f. Subtotal (4d – 4e) $ ________
   g. Partial repayments received by shareholder during year $ ________
5. Ending basis (4f – 4g) $ ________

Copyright © 2000 by Harcourt, Inc. All rights reserved.

INTEGRATION OF LOSS LIMITS

CONTENTS

10

1000. Overview.

Certain losses and deductions may be subject to limits at the S corporation level. Others are subject to suspension or disallowance at the shareholder level. Chapter 9 dealt with basis, a subject sufficiently complicated to warrant a separate chapter. This chapter discusses some other shareholder limits, such as the hobby loss, at-risk, passive loss, and investment interest restrictions.

After a loss has cleared the basis limit, the shareholder may face two additional obstacles before he or she can actually deduct the loss:

- The shareholder must have a sufficient *amount at risk* to claim a deduction.
- The shareholder must clear the *passive activity loss* restrictions.

Each of these provisions has its own set of rules, discussed in this chapter, at 1020. and 1025., respectively.

This chapter also covers some items that have their own special limitations. Primary examples are charitable contributions, at 1040., and casualty losses, at 1025.8.

1005. Background.

Since the adoption of the Internal Revenue Code of 1954, Congress has enacted several limitations to curb deductions for various types of losses. The multiplicity of limits, together with the lack of any consistent rules for allocation and carryovers, can create some complexities in calculating a shareholder's deductions for losses and expenses from the S corporation. The first step is to determine deductibility at the corporate level. Figure 10 - 1 demonstrates the principal obstacles the S corporation faces in determining the amount of loss to pass through to its shareholders.

As formidable as the corporate loss limits may seem, they pale in comparison to those faced by shareholders. Figure 10 - 2 illustrates shareholder loss limits.

The remainder of this chapter deals with the specific limits. Table 10 - 1 lists the various limits applicable to some of the more commonly encountered loss and deduction categories that flow through to shareholders from S corporations.

TABLE 10 - 1: Limits Applicable to Various Categories of Losses and Deductions

Description	*Basis Limit*	*At-Risk Limit*	*Passive Income Limit*	*Other Limits*
Casualty loss on rental or business property	Yes	Yes	No	Subject to offset by casualty gains
Capital loss on rental or business property	Yes	Yes	Yes	Subject to offset by capital gains
§1231 loss on rental or business property	Yes	Yes	Yes	Subject to offset by capital gains
Ordinary loss on rental or business property	Yes	Yes	Yes	No
Investment interest	Yes	Yes	No	Shareholder's investment income
Charitable contributions	No	No	No	50%, 30%, or 20% AGI
Other itemized deductions	Yes	Yes	Yes, if connected with rent or business	Other limits, at shareholder level
State taxes	No	No	No	Shareholder limits

Figure 10 - 1: Corporate-level loss limits.

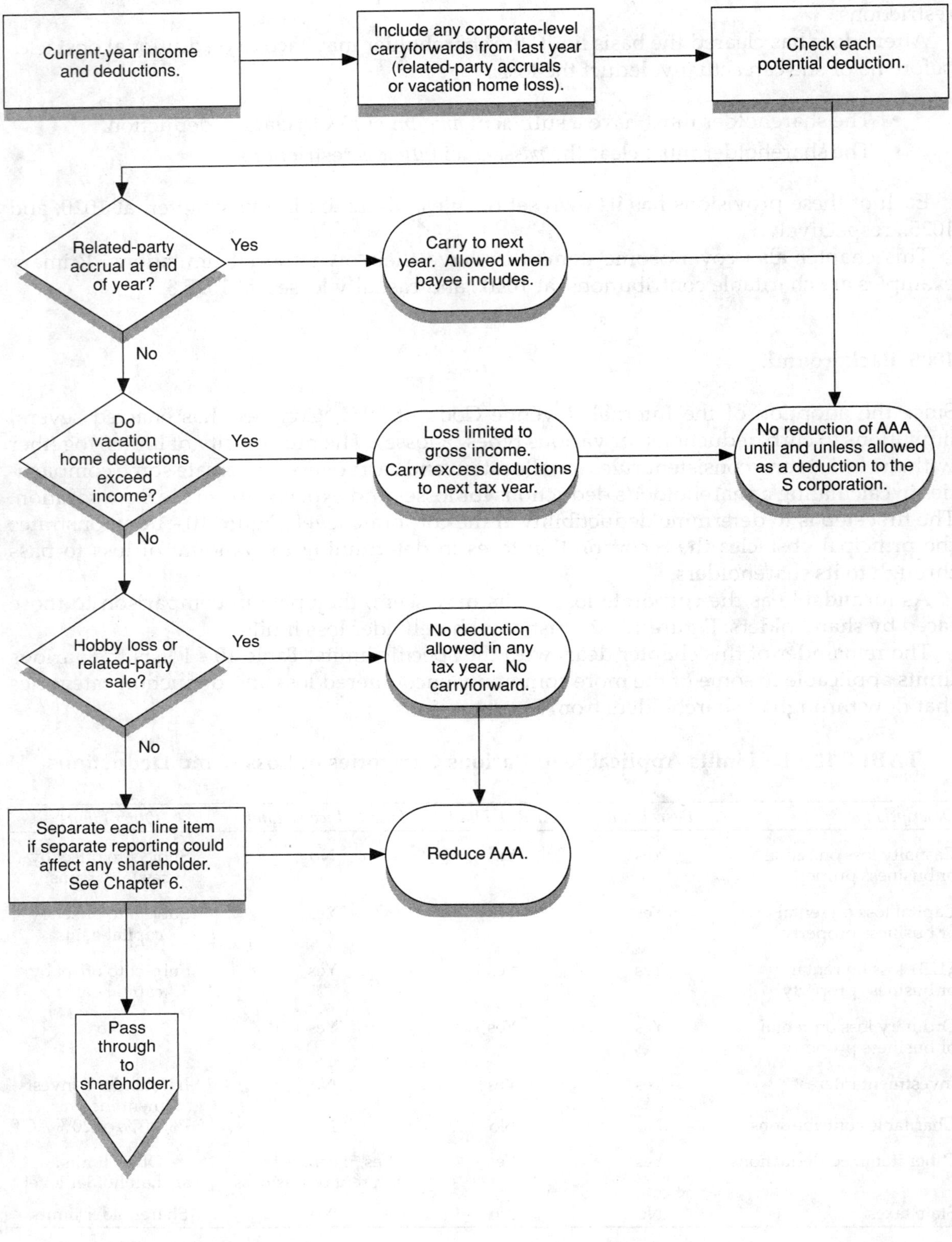

10

Figure 10 - 2: *Shareholder-level loss limits.*

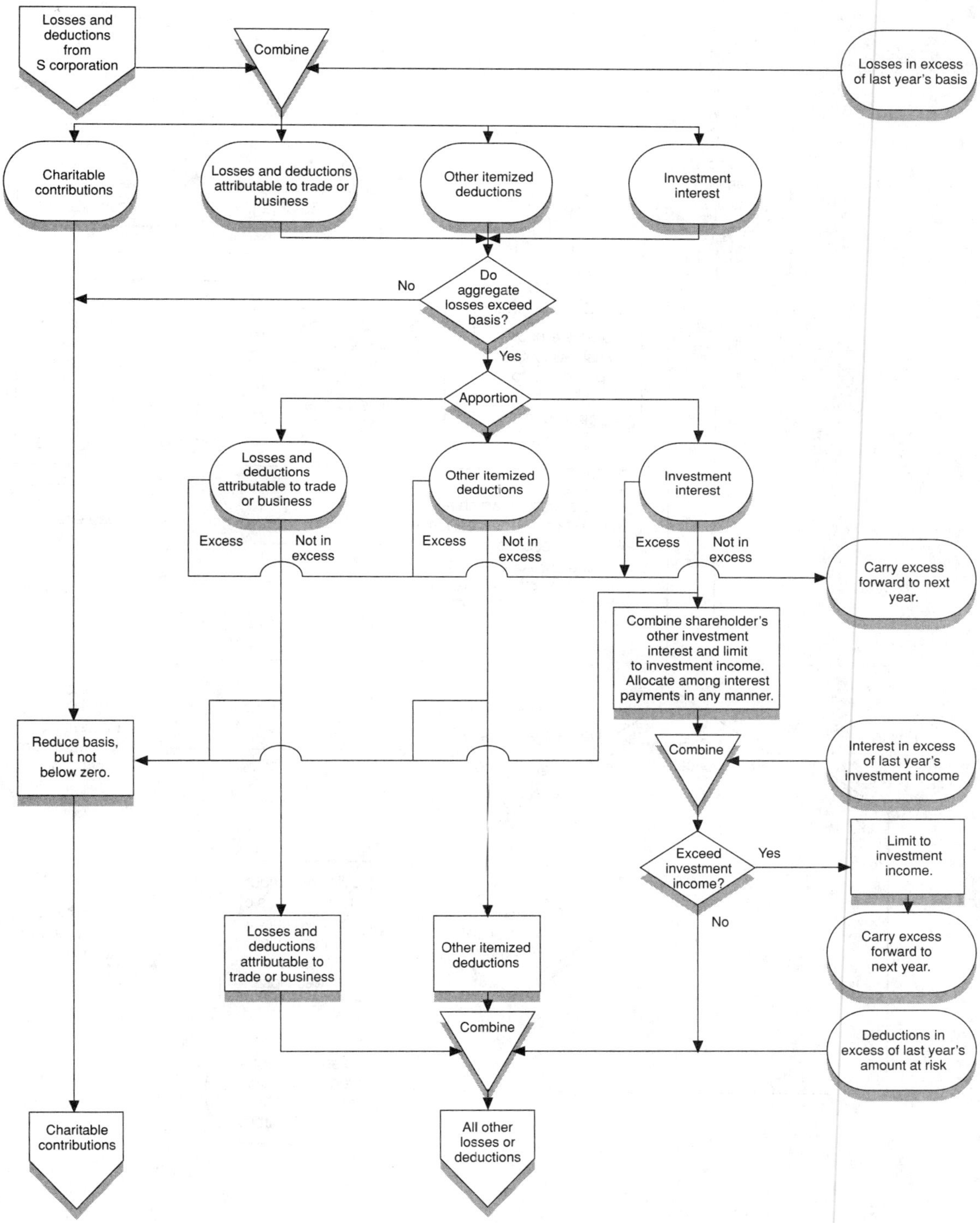

Figure 10 - 2 (continued): Shareholder-level loss limits.

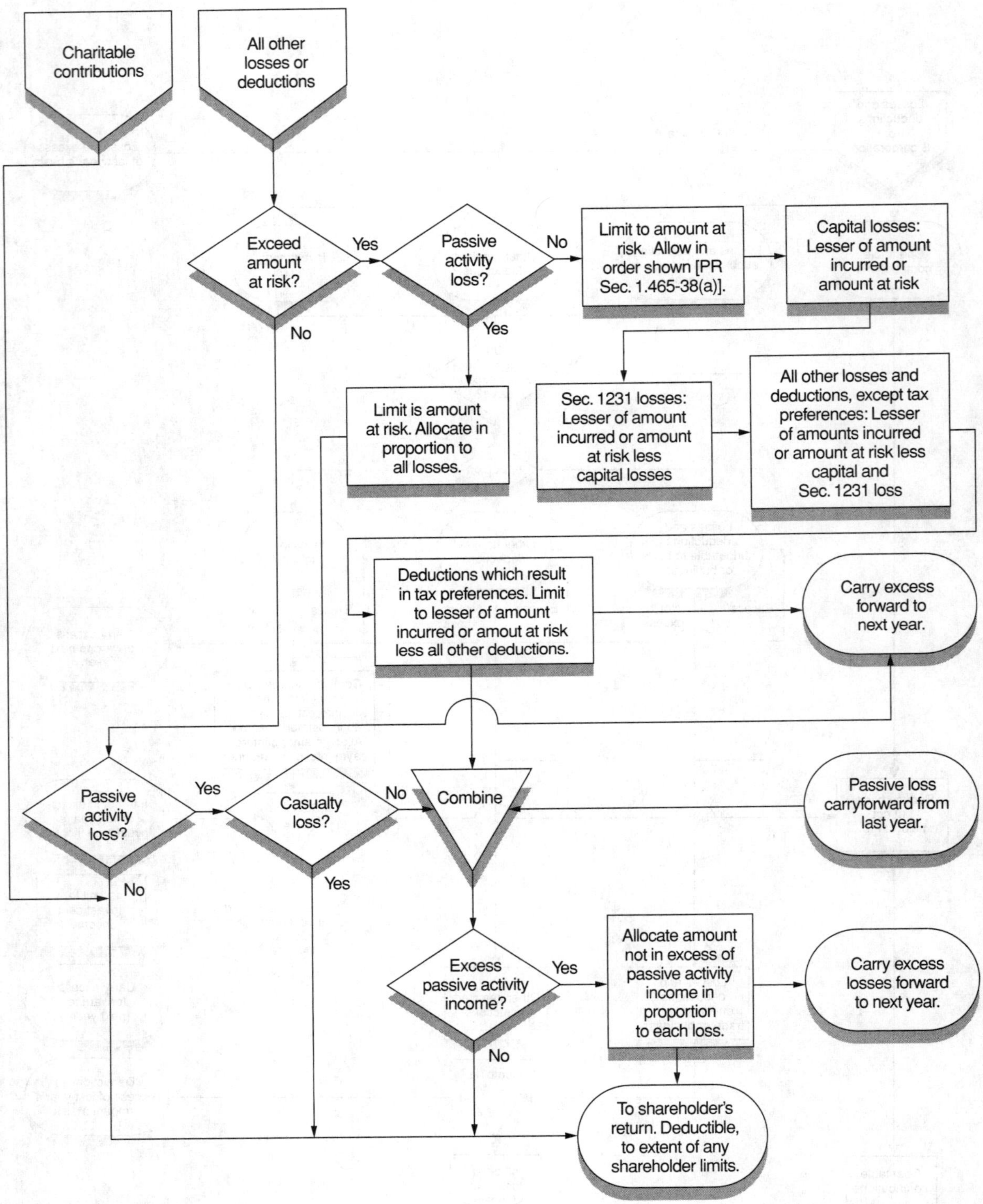

10

1010. Corporate-level limits.

Losses incurred in connection with an S corporation's trade or business activities are subject to loss limitations at both the corporate level and the shareholder level. The corporate-level limitations must be applied first. Therefore, before any loss can pass through to a shareholder, it must meet the following tests:

- It must not be subject to the general disallowance rules, such as related-party sales or hobby losses.
- If it is subject to the vacation home rules, the excess of deductions over gross income is not deductible in the current year but must be carried forward.
- Any portion of a book accounting loss that is attributable to an accrued expense to any shareholder must be carried forward and can be deducted only in the year in which it is paid.

EXAMPLE 10 - 1: Hobco is an accrual-method corporation that operates a business and owns a farm. The farm is located in a distant state and has never operated at a profit. It is used by the corporation's controlling shareholder primarily for vacations. In the current year, the corporation's book loss is $55,000. Included in this loss is $5,000 accrued salary to the controlling shareholder and $10,000 in deductions attributable to the farm. The farm produced no gross income in the current year. Therefore, the corporation has little, if any, defense against the hobby loss limitation on the farm loss.

The loss that will flow through to the shareholders is:

Loss per books	$55,000
Less accrual to shareholder	(5,000)
Less farm loss	(10,000)
Loss potentially available to shareholders	$40,000

If the shareholders meet all of the other tests discussed in this chapter, they will be able to deduct $40,000 in the current year. The $5,000 accrual to the shareholder will be deductible in a future year, when it is paid by the corporation. The farm loss will not be deductible by any shareholder in any taxable year.

Each of these limits has been discussed in Chapters 6 and 9. The remainder of this chapter is devoted to the discussion of shareholder limits.

10

1015. Limitations imposed within Subchapter S.

As discussed in Chapters 6 and 9, all losses and deductions arising from an S corporation (with the possible exception of charitable contributions, discussed below) are limited by the following:

- The first limit on a potentially deductible loss is the shareholder's basis in stock [§1366(d)(1)(A)]; and
- The second limit is the shareholder's basis in debt. [§1366(d)(1)(B)]

Losses that exceed these limits are carried forward to the next taxable year. [§1366(d)(2)] As discussed in Chapter 6, Proposed Regulations deal with the following three areas:

- Transferability of a suspended loss is not allowed. Thus, when a shareholder incurs losses in excess of his or her basis and then disposes of all of his or her stock, there is a specific rule that prevents a new owner from deducting a prior holder's losses. [Proposed Regulations §1.1366-2(a)(5)]

- A former shareholder loses his or her suspended loss after a sale or other disposition of all of his or her stock in the S corporation. [Proposed Regulations §1.1366-2(a)(5).]
- When an S corporation reports more than one category of loss (such as ordinary and capital), and the total of those losses allocated to a shareholder exceeds that shareholder's total basis, Proposed Regulations require proration.[1] [Proposed Regulations §1.1366-2(b)(3). Also see Regs. §1.704-1(d)(2), §1.704-1(d)(4), Example 3.]

EXAMPLE 10 - 2: An S corporation has one shareholder, whose basis in stock and debt is $20,000 before adjustment for the current year's losses. In the current year, the corporation reports an ordinary loss of $15,000 and a capital loss of $10,000. Neither type of loss in and of itself exceeds the shareholder's basis. The two losses in total, however, do exceed the shareholder's basis.

Using the proportionate allocation of Proposed Regulations §1.1366-2(b)(3), the shareholder would make the following computations:

Percent deductible in the current year:

Basis ($20,000) / All losses ($25,000) = 80%

	Deductible in Current Year (80%)	*Carried to Next Year (20%)*
Ordinary loss (total $15,000)	$12,000	$3,000
Capital loss (total $10,000)	8,000	2,000
Total	$20,000	$5,000

10

The ordinary loss of $12,000 would be deductible in full, subject to any at-risk or passive activity loss limits that the shareholder might face. The capital loss of $8,000 would also be subject to any at-risk or passive activity loss limits. In addition, it would need to pass the deduction rules for capital losses.

OBSERVATION: Until Final Regulations are issued on the allocation of multiple losses, a taxpayer may take a reasonable position without defying authority. For instance, the shareholder in Example 10-2 would prefer to treat the entire $15,000 of ordinary loss, and only $5,000 of the capital loss, as deductible in the current year. At present, the taxpayer could take this position on the return without facing any fraud or special negligence penalties. The solution shown above is the allocation method, which, in the author's opinion, is the most defensible position.

The problem of allocation of multiple types of losses can be compounded when suspended losses are partially allowed in future years. A shareholder might have several years' losses that are partially allowed in a later taxable year. Probably the best way to handle this situation is to allocate losses by type, rather than by year of origin.

EXAMPLE 10 - 3: Refer to Example 10-2. In the next year, the shareholder loans $10,000 to the corporation and receives additional basis for that amount. In that year, the corporation sustains $10,000 of ordinary loss and no losses of any other character. At this point, the character of the shareholder's potentially deductible losses is:

	Sustained in Current Year	*Carried from Last Year*	*Total*
Ordinary loss	$10,000	$3,000	$13,000
Capital loss	0	2,000	2,000
Total	$10,000	$5,000	$15,000

[1] Such allocation would also be required if the shareholder were subject to the passive activity loss limits of §469.

The probable treatment is:

Percent deductible in the current year:

Basis ($10,000)/All losses ($15,000) = 66²/₃%

Applied to each loss:

	Current Year (²/₃)	Deductible in Carried to Next Year (¹/₃)
Ordinary loss (total $13,000)	$ 8,667	$4,333
Capital loss (total $2,000)	1,333	667
Total	$10,000	$5,000

1020. Effects of the at-risk rules.

In general, losses from an activity are deductible only to the extent the investor has amounts at risk. [§465(a)(1)] The at-risk rules are meant to cover any trade or business activity or investment activity. The authority is found in §465(a)(1).

SUMMARY OF AUTHORITY: CODE SECTION 465(a)(1)

- The at-risk limits apply to individuals and certain closely held C corporations.
- The at-risk rules limit a taxpayer's allowable deduction for losses sustained in an activity.
- Although the at-risk rules do not govern S corporations, they do apply to shareholders in S corporations.

10

The at-risk limits are applied to otherwise deductible amounts. [Proposed Regs. §1.465-13] Therefore, at-risk limits with respect to ownership in an S corporation apply after the limits imposed by Subchapter S.

EXAMPLE 10 - 4: Kermit is a shareholder in an S corporation. At the end of the current year his basis, before accounting for current year losses, is zero. The amount at risk is irrelevant for this year, because Kermit has no basis to allow deductibility of losses.

Assume, alternatively, that Kermit had $10,000 basis in his stock, but had no amount at risk at the end of the year. He could not deduct the loss, since it exceeds his amount at risk.

Any losses in excess of that amount are suspended until there is an increase in the amount at risk. The suspended losses cannot be carried back. The suspension is another form of carryforward.

SUMMARY OF AUTHORITY: CODE SECTION 465(a)(2)

- A loss that is not deductible due to the at-risk limits is allocated to the same activity in the next taxable year.
- The deduction carried to the next taxable year shall be subject to the at-risk limits in the next taxable year.
- There is no set term of years to which such loss can be carried.
- No such deduction may be carried back to a prior taxable year.

EXAMPLE 10 - 5: Lorraine's basis in her S corporation stock and debt, before deducting any current year losses, is $5,000. Her share of S corporation losses for the current year is $7,000. Her amount at risk, however, is only $4,000. Her treatment of the S corporation loss will be:

Loss, before basis limit	$7,000
Limit to basis	(5,000)

Carryforward until basis is increased		$2,000
Loss after basis limitation	$5,000	
Limit to amount at risk	(4,000)	
Carryforward until amount at risk is increased		$1,000

OBSERVATION: There are substantial interpretive problems with the at-risk rules. Section 465 was enacted by the Tax Reform Act of 1976. Temporary Regulations issued in 1977, as well as Regulations proposed in 1979, do not reflect important changes made by the Revenue Act of 1978 or any subsequent legislation. Since the Subchapter S Revision Act of 1982 changed the entire relationship of S corporations and the at-risk rules, guidance on the detailed operation is limited. The Regulations do provide valuable guidance on aspects of the law that have not been amended since 1976. Selective reading and interpretation are necessary.

Perhaps the most confusing aspect of the Proposed Regulations under §465 as they affect S corporations and their shareholders is that they have not been updated for the Subchapter S Revision Act of 1982. Before that Act, S corporations were subject to the at-risk rules at the corporate level. In 1982, however, the rules were changed to apply only at the shareholder level. Thus, in these Proposed Regulations, the explanations and examples concerning S corporations are irrelevant to today's law. The provisions relating to partners, by contrast, are now applicable to shareholders in S corporations.[2]

1020.1. Taxpayers subject to the rules. The at-risk limits cover individuals, estates, and trusts, as well as certain closely held corporations. A corporation comes under the rules if five or fewer individuals own more than 50% of the outstanding stock at any time during the last half of the corporation's taxable year. [§465(a)(1)(B), §542(a)(2), §544(a)] An individual is considered to own any stock held by a family member or by a partnership in which the individual owns an interest. The least number of shareholders allowed for a corporation to be exempt from the limits would be 10 equal unrelated persons. There are exemptions for closely held corporations regularly engaged in equipment leasing and for other active businesses. [§465(c)(4), (5), (6)] The rules regarding equipment leases by closely held C corporations are beyond the scope of this discussion.

The at-risk rules, contained in §465, limit a shareholder's deduction for losses. These rules do not apply to S corporations, per se. They do apply, however, to individuals in their capacity as shareholders in S corporations. [§465(a)(1)]

1020.2. Amounts treated as at-risk. Amounts at risk include money and basis of other property contributed to the corporation. For an investment in *stock*, amounts at risk do not include money contributed if the money was borrowed from a related party or co-venturer. The Tax Court has given a broad interpretation to borrowing from a related party. In *Riggs*, a 50% shareholder in an S corporation borrowed money from another corporation that was wholly owned by the other 50% shareholder. The relationship between the two shareholders, who were not apparently husband and wife but shared a residence, as well as the understanding regarding Ms. Riggs' repayment obligations, led the court to believe that the debt to the lending corporation would be repaid only from the profits of the S corporation, which were not amounts at risk. (*Riggs*, 63 TCM 3107, TC Memo 1992-323. The IRS did not claim that the taxpayer lacked basis in her stock.)

---

[2] Proposed Regulations §1.465-10 deals with the at-risk rules as they relate to S corporations and their shareholders. Subsections (a) and (b) deal with the limitations imposed on S corporations. These portions of the Proposed Regulation are completely obsolete. By contrast, Proposed Regulations §1.465-10(c), which deals with the limitations imposed on shareholders, was not affected by the Subchapter S Revision Act of 1982 and still provides useful guidance. The statutory references in that subsection, however, are to the old Subchapter S provisions.

In general, amounts at risk do not include nonrecourse liabilities.[3] Nonrecourse financing can be used as basis if property (other than the interest in the S corporation) is pledged as security. The amount of risk is limited to the basis of the property less any senior liens. [§465(b)(2)(B)]

> **EXAMPLE 10 - 6:** In 1995, Jack buys 50% of J Corporation's stock, using $40,000 of his own funds. He pledges the stock to the bank for a loan of $42,000, which he uses to purchase the other 50% of the shares. Jack's basis in J Corporation is $82,000. His amount at risk, however, is only $40,000.

For *debt* basis, the amount at risk can include money borrowed from a related party or from another shareholder. [§465(b)(3)(B)] In this respect, the at-risk rules are more liberal for loans to S corporations than they are for contributions to S corporation capital.

> **EXAMPLE 10 - 7:** Refer to Example 10 - 6. After purchasing his stock, Jack borrows $20,000 from his father and loans the amount to J Corporation. His debt basis is $20,000. Since he has loaned the money to the corporation, rather than contributing it to capital, his amount at risk is increased by the $20,000 loan. Jack's total amount at risk in the J Corporation is $60,000, consisting of the $40,000 cash paid for the stock and the $20,000 loaned directly to the S corporation.

In the case of S corporations, a shareholder's amount at risk does not include any portion of corporate debt to other parties. This rule may appear to be redundant, since a shareholder would not receive basis for the guarantee of a loan and the basis limit would dominate the at-risk limit. In some situations, however, the at-risk rules could be important.

10

> **EXAMPLE 10 - 8:** Vern is a 50% shareholder in the VZ Corporation, an S corporation. Vern purchased half of his stock for $50,000 cash. He purchased the remainder of the stock from the corporation by means of a $50,000 nonrecourse note. Although Vern's stock basis is arguably $100,000, his amount at risk for the stock is only $50,000. Vern guarantees a bank loan to the corporation in the amount of $80,000. Vern's share of VZ's loss for the current year is $180,000.
>
> According to the rules of Subchapter S, $100,000 of the loss would be allowed as a deduction to Vern, since that amount does not exceed his stock basis. The remaining $80,000 would be carried forward to the next year under §1366(d)(2). Vern could not support the deduction by claiming that the guarantee of the bank loan gave him basis. That claim (aside from the apparent fluke of the *Selfe* case) has been unanimously rejected by the courts. See Chapter 9.
>
> The $100,000 allowable under Subchapter S, however, would not be deductible to the extent it exceeds Vern's amount at risk. The principal question is whether Vern's guarantee of the bank loan would increase his amount at risk, even though it does not give him basis.
>
> Due to the $50,000 cash Vern paid for half of his stock, $50,000 of the loss should be allowed. The deduction of the remaining $50,000 is questionable.

The Tenth Circuit recently addressed this issue in *Goatcher v. U.S.* [*Goatcher v. U.S.*, 91-2 USTC 50,450 (10th Cir.)] In this case, Mr. and Mrs. Goatcher invested $1,000 in an S corporation and personally guaranteed a series of loans in the aggregate amount of approximately $1,000,000. In 1982 and 1983, they deducted the S corporation's losses of approximately $50,000 and $41,000. The Court held that the losses could not pass through, due to the basis limitations.

---

[3] A nonrecourse debt is secured only by pledged property. The borrower has no obligation to pay the debt, other than to transfer the pledged property on default.

There was another aspect to this case, however. Mr. and Mrs. Goatcher had claimed investment tax credit from the corporation's asset purchases. For the years in question, investment tax credit was not limited to basis. It was allowed, however, only on property for which the taxpayer had an amount at risk. One of the rules contained in §465 is that amounts that are protected through a stop-loss agreement or similar arrangement are not considered to be at risk. [§465(b)(4)] In *Goatcher*, the court reasoned that the shareholders would have a claim against the corporation if they were required to perform on their guarantee. Therefore, they were protected by a stop-loss agreement and were not at risk with respect to their guarantee.

EXAMPLE 10 - 9: Refer to Example 10 - 8. In light of the *Goatcher* decision, Vern would be unable to claim an amount at risk for his guarantee of the bank loan. Therefore, his loss would be limited to $50,000 in the current year.

OBSERVATION: The Tenth Circuit's decision in *Goatcher* is an extremely literal interpretation of the Code provision. The finding that a corporation with only $1,000 capital could protect a shareholder with approximately $1,000,000 potential liability makes little economic sense. If the Goatchers had borrowed the money personally and then loaned or contributed it to the corporation, their economic situation would not have been significantly different. They would, however, have received basis and an amount at risk. In the area of the at-risk rules, as well as basis problems, the form of a transaction seems to be as important as its substance.

10

Recently the IRS ruled that a restructuring of debt in a multiple-shareholder corporation would give shareholders amounts at risk. The conversion of the debt was made in direct proportion to the shareholdings. This arrangement also gives each shareholder basis with respect to the loan. [See Rev. Rul. 75-144, 1975-1 CB 277; PLRs 9811016, 9811017, 9811018, 9811019] Also see Chapter 9, at 920.22.

1020.3. Activities subject to the rules. The at-risk rules limit the deductibility of losses from any business or investment activity. There are, however, three different sets of activities, each with its own special rules:

1. The "separate activities," which consist of any:
   a. Film or videotape
   b. §1245 property held for leasing
   c. Farm
   d. Oil and gas property
   e. Geothermal property
2. Any real estate activity
3. Any business or investment not classified in (1) or (2)

Because each of the three categories has its own special rules, it is important to properly classify an activity under one of the three categories.

1020.31. Rules for separate activities. The original at-risk rule, adopted in 1976, applied only to films and videotapes, leased §1245 property, farms, and oil and gas properties. It required that the loss from each individual activity be measured against the amount at risk for each individual activity. For these activities, as well as for geothermal properties, which were added in 1978, the non-aggregation rule still applies.

EXAMPLE 10 - 10: Oliver, an individual, owns two farms. In the current year, Farm 1 produces a loss of $40,000, and Oliver's amount at risk is $30,000. Farm 2 shows a loss of

$35,000 in the current year, and Oliver's amount at risk is $100,000. The at-risk rules limit Oliver's deduction to $65,000 ($30,000 from Farm 1 and $35,000 from Farm 2).

1020.32. Aggregation of amounts at risk. The same non-aggregation rule applies to other activities that the taxpayer owns outright. However, if a partnership or an S corporation owns activities in categories other than the "separate activities" category, each partner or shareholder may aggregate his or her amounts at risk for all of the activities. To come under the aggregation rule, the partnership or S corporation must allocate at least 65% of the losses to persons who actively participate in the entity's management. Otherwise, the shareholder must determine an amount at risk with respect to each activity.[4]

Partnerships and S corporations are also allowed to aggregate the separate items of leased §1245 property. [§465(c)(2)(B)(i)] As a practical matter, allocation of amounts at risk to separate oil and gas properties has proved so cumbersome that the IRS allows partnerships and S corporations to aggregate income, losses, and amounts at risk from all oil and gas investments. [Temporary Regs. §1.465-1T. Advance Notice 89-39, 1989-14 IRB 16, extends the rule until further notice.] This aggregation rule has only been allowed by temporary notices, and it may not continue into the future.

> **OBSERVATION:** Since a shareholder's amount at risk is determined with respect to his or her entire stock and debt holdings, rather than with respect to each activity that might be carried on by the corporation, the distinction between aggregation and separate accounting is blurred. For example, if an S corporation holds two motion pictures for distribution, the two properties must be reported separately. But the shareholders do not have a specific amount at risk with respect to each motion picture. Apparently, the amount at risk with respect to the stock and debt of the entire corporation would be the limiting factor on deductibility of losses from either picture.

10

1020.33. Special rule for real estate. Until 1987, real estate operations were exempt from the at-risk rules. Any real estate placed in service before 1987 continues to be exempt. For real estate placed in service after 1986, the at-risk rules apply, but with a significant modification. A nonrecourse loan gives the taxpayer an amount at risk, if it is "qualified nonrecourse financing."

A nonrecourse loan qualifies as an amount at risk if it is made by a commercial lender. The lender can be related to the borrower, if the terms of the loan are commercially reasonable. The lender cannot, however, be the seller of the property or any party related to the seller.

> **EXAMPLE 10 - 11:** XYZ National Bank repossesses an apartment building. It offers to finance the building on a nonrecourse basis. If a buyer accepts the terms offered by the bank, the buyer will not be at risk and cannot deduct any losses from the property.

1020.4. Adjustments to amounts at risk. The rules for adjusting a shareholder's amount at risk in an S corporation are not completely defined in any statute or Regulations. In general, these rules apply to shareholders of S corporations in the same manner as partners in partnerships. A taxpayer's amount at risk in any given activity is increased for any contributions of cash or property. The amount at risk is decreased for any withdrawals or distributions of cash or property.

A taxpayer's amount at risk may also be affected by refinancing of his or her interest in the activity. In general, a change from nonrecourse to recourse financing causes an increase in the taxpayer's amount at risk. Conversely, a conversion from recourse to nonrecourse financing is treated as a reduction of the taxpayer's amount at risk.

---

[4] See *John L. Jackson*, 86 TC 492 (1986), for an example of separate activities, and amounts at risk with respect to each, in a partnership context.

A taxpayer's amount at risk is increased for income from the activity and is decreased for losses from the activity. This rule is essentially the same as the basis increase rules for S corporation shareholders. Thus any income from an activity, including tax-exempt income, would increase a shareholder's amount at risk in the same way it increases his or her basis. [Temporary Regs. §7.465-2(b)] In one case, the Tax Court held that the increase in amount at risk was limited to net undistributed income, rather than gross income. [*Leonard Lansburgh*, 92 TC 448 (1989)]

The amount at risk is decreased by an investor's withdrawal of cash or property. It is also decreased by an investor's share of losses. If a recourse loan is refinanced with a nonrecourse loan, the borrower's amount at risk is decreased accordingly. The amount at risk cannot be decreased below zero. If a decrease in the amount at risk would create a deficit, the taxpayer must recapture losses deducted in earlier years, to bring the amount at risk back up to zero.

EXAMPLE 10 - 12: In prior years, G had deducted $40,000 losses on a farm. He had $50,000 at risk, which included a $10,000 cash contribution and a $40,000 note with full recourse. The losses had reduced his amount at risk to $10,000. In the current year he refinanced the loan with a $40,000 nonrecourse note. If it were not for the recapture rule, his amount at risk would be minus $30,000. He must recapture $30,000 of his previously deducted losses as income and bring the amount at risk back up to zero.

1020.5. Multiple losses and the at-risk rules. As discussed in Chapter 6, there are no rules under Subchapter S for the allocation of differing types of losses when the total exceeds a shareholder's basis, except for Proposed Regulations issued in 1998. [Proposed Regs. §1.1366-2(a)(4)] These Regulations are consistent with partnership Regulations, which prorate each loss in proportion to the total allowed to the shareholder.

EXAMPLE 10 - 13: In 1995, Sam's basis in his shares in Samco, an S corporation, is $40,000, before the deduction for any current-year losses. In that same year, the corporation reports a capital loss of $8,000, a §1231 loss of $12,000, and an ordinary loss of $30,000. The total of these losses is $50,000. It is most likely that Sam should claim 80% ($40,000/$50,000) of each loss and suspend the remainder until he has more basis. The likely result is:

	Claim on Current Return	*Carry to Next Year*
Capital loss	$ 6,400	$ 1,600
§1231 loss	9,600	2,400
Ordinary loss	24,000	6,000
Total	$40,000	$10,000

In contrast to the above rules (which also apply to activities subject to §469), the Proposed Regulations under the at-risk rules provide for a different allocation. The ordering of allowed losses under the at-risk rules is:

1. Capital losses
2. §1231 losses
3. Ordinary losses that do not receive preferential tax treatment
4. Deductions treated as tax preferences [Proposed Regs. §1.465-38(a)]

EXAMPLE 10 - 14: Refer to Example 10 - 13. Sam materially participates in Samco's business activities (which are not rental activities). Therefore, Sam is not subject to the passive activity loss limits with respect to Samco. If Sam's amount at risk at the end of 1995 was $25,000, under the at-risk Proposed Regulations, his losses reported and suspended would be:

	Claim on Current Return	*Carry to Next Year*
Capital loss	$ 6,400	$ 0
§1231 loss	9,600	0
Ordinary loss	9,000	15,000
Total	$25,000	$15,000

OBSERVATION: The Proposed Regulations under §465 contain a unique set of ordering rules, when compared to other loss limitations. As of this writing, they have existed in proposed form for almost 15 years. They were obsolete when issued, in that they did not reflect changes made by the Revenue Act of 1978. They need to be updated, and they should conform with the other rules governing loss limitations.

The arbitrary ordering of losses under the at-risk Proposed Regulations is entirely different from treatment of losses under the partnership rules and the rules in Proposed Regulations §1.1366-2(a)(4). It is also different from the rules required under the passive activity loss limits discussed below. The Temporary Regulations under §469 provide that a taxpayer who sustains deductions or losses of different types, when the overall loss from that activity is limited by the at-risk rules, must prorate such deductions and claim a ratable portion of each type of loss or deduction. [Temporary Regs. §1.469-2T(d)(6)(iii)] The Temporary Regulations under §469 are authoritative, whereas the Proposed Regulations under §465 merely indicate the position of the IRS at the time the Regulations were written. Therefore, a taxpayer should follow the §469 Temporary Regulations (which were issued in 1988), rather than the §465 Proposed Regulations (which were issued in 1979), if an activity is subject to both the at-risk rules and the passive activity loss limits.

EXAMPLE 10-15: Refer to Example 10-14. Assume the same facts, except that Sam is subject to the passive activity loss limits with respect to Samco. In calculating the pass-through of deductions from the at-risk rules, Sam would prorate the capital loss, §1231 loss, and ordinary loss as follows: 10

	Claim on Current Return	*Carry to Next Year*
Capital loss [(25/40) x $6,400]	$ 4,000	$ 2,400
§1231 loss [(25/40) x $9,600]	6,000	3,600
Ordinary loss [(25/40) x $24,000]	15,000	9,000
Total	$25,000	$15,000

1020.6. Consequences of disposition of an activity. The disposition of an interest in an activity does not give a taxpayer authority to deduct all of the previously suspended losses. There is a certain amount of relief available, however.

Any recognized gain from the sale of an interest in an activity is treated as income from the activity, and increases the seller's amount at risk. [Proposed Regs. §1.465-12(a), Proposed Regs. §1.465-66(a)] This rule is different from the rules governing losses suspended under Subchapter S.

EXAMPLE 10 - 16: In 1996, Gavco, an S corporation, reports a loss of $80,000. The sole shareholder's basis is $55,000, and her amount at risk is $35,000. She makes the following calculations for 1996:

Loss, before limits	$80,000
Loss in excess of basis, suspended	(25,000)
Loss allowable under basis rules	55,000
Loss in excess of amount at risk, suspended	(20,000)
Loss allowed for 1996	$35,000

On January 1, 1997, she sells her stock for $70,000. Since her basis was reduced to zero by the 1996 loss, the gain on the sale is $70,000. There is no provision that allows the deduction of the $25,000 loss suspended under the basis rules.[5] According to the at-risk rules, the shareholder increases her amount at risk on January 1, 1997, by the $70,000 gain. She may, therefore, deduct the loss of $20,000 from 1996, which was suspended due to the at-risk rules. The year of deduction would be 1997, the year in which she increases her amount at risk.

If an activity with suspended at-risk losses is exchanged in a carryover basis transaction, any suspended loss attaches to the basis in the replacement property. [Proposed Regs. §1.465-67(b)] In the case of an S corporation's stock, this is most likely to occur when the corporation is a party to a tax-free reorganization. See Chapter 17 for further discussion.

1025. Passive activity loss limits.

As part of the 1986 effort to broaden the tax base, Congress enacted §469, which limits an individual's deduction for losses incurred in connection with certain passive activities:

SUMMARY OF AUTHORITY: CODE SECTION 469

- Taxpayers covered by the passive loss limits shall not be allowed a net loss deduction for losses sustained in connection with passive activities.
- The covered taxpayers include individuals, estates, trusts, and certain corporations.
- The passive loss limits are extremely important to many shareholders in S corporations.
- The passive activity rules also limit certain credits, which are not discussed in this book.

10

Although S corporations are not directly covered by the passive activity loss limits, their shareholders are subject to these restrictions, for three reasons:

- Only individuals, estates, and trusts can hold shares in an S corporation. See Chapter 2.
- All individuals, estates, and trusts are subject to the passive activity loss rules.
- Any item of income or loss that passes through from an S corporation to its shareholders has the potential to be characterized as passive. [Temporary Regs. §1.469-2T(e)(1)]

The passive loss limits affect losses that have already met the tests for deductibility under the basis and at-risk rules. [Temporary Regs. §1.469-2T(d)(6)(i)] The important role of the S corporation in complying with these rules is to characterize its income and losses properly in reporting to the shareholders (see Chapter 6). This portion of the chapter deals with the rules applicable to the shareholders once they have received the information from the S corporation.

As discussed in Chapter 6, the S corporation is not subject to the passive activity loss rules at the corporate level. It must, however, report to the shareholders all of the information about its own business activities, so that the shareholders can comply with the passive activity loss rules. The corporation provides the shareholder with all of the information necessary to determine which of the corporation's activities are rental, which are not rental, and what is the nature of income and deductions from each activity. Shareholders in S corporations are subject to the passive activity loss limits of §469 in two circumstances:

---

[5] As explained in Chapter 6, however, the suspended loss indirectly gives her a tax benefit. If she were allowed to deduct the loss, she would have a negative basis, and the gain on the sale would be increased by that amount.

- The S corporation operates one or more rental activities.
- The S corporation operates a trade or business in which the shareholder does not materially participate.

If the corporation's activity is rental in nature, any income or loss that passes through to the shareholder is passive, by definition. If the corporation's activity is rental real estate, any shareholder who actively participates may be allowed a loss deduction, not to exceed $25,000 in any given year. (See at 1025.42. for further discussion.)

If the corporation's activity is not rental, the shareholder's participation in the activity determines whether the income from the activity is active or passive. A shareholder who materially participates in the corporation's business activity will report active income or loss.

1025.1. Application of limits on shareholders. A shareholder will receive information from the S corporation that should be sufficient to determine the extent of the corporation's income or loss from rental activities. If an S corporation operates more than one rental activity, it should give the shareholder information about each activity. The corporation should also provide information about income and deductions that are not associated with any activity, such as investment interest, portfolio income, and charitable contributions that are not included as passive activity gross income or subject to the passive activity loss limits.

The shareholder must then determine whether he or she:

- Materially participates in any of the corporation's business activities.
- Actively participates in any of the corporation's real estate rental activities.
- Owns any other interest in the corporation's activities. This final point is especially important in a year in which the corporation, the shareholder, or both dispose of any activities.

The passive activity loss rules govern the nature of the shareholder's profit or loss from the S corporation's activities. These rules apply only to the portion allocated to the shareholder, per se. They have no impact on a shareholder's compensation, fringe benefits, director's fees, or most other items received from the corporation. The passive activity loss rules may apply to interest received by a shareholder from the corporation, if it is treated as self-charged interest, as discussed in Chapter 8. The passive activity loss limits may also apply to any rent charged by the shareholder to the corporation, although there are some special applications of this rule. (See Chapter 8 for the discussion of rental of property by a shareholder to an S corporation.) In addition, a distribution in excess of the shareholder's basis in the corporation, which is treated as gain from the sale or exchange of stock, will be characterized as active or passive income depending on whether the underlying activities of the corporation are passive or active with respect to the taxpayer. [Rev. Rul. 95-5, 1995-2 IRB 5] Material participation in an S corporation's activities made income from the S corporation ordinary, and the shareholder was not permitted to offset it against a loss from a passive partnership interest. [*Carlstedt v. Comm'r*, TC Memo 1997-331] However, this part of Chapter 10 is concerned with the shareholder's portion of taxable income or loss (whether separately stated or ordinary).

1025.2. Aggregation vs. separation of activities. As discussed in Chapter 6, an S corporation that is involved in more than one business needs to determine if it is also involved in more than one activity and then report income and losses to the shareholders accordingly. Each shareholder may use this information to determine whether he or she materially participated in one or more of the corporation's business activities.

Once the shareholders have received this information, they may need to undertake a second round of the same process, determining whether the interest of each person in the S corporation represented his or her entire interest in an activity. A shareholder could aggregate his interest in one S corporation with interests in other business enterprises. The aggregation may be important for two reasons:

- It could be used in connection with one of the material participation tests, discussed below, to determine the degree of shareholder participation.
- It could determine whether a shareholder disposed of his or her entire interest in an activity.

As is the case with the corporate-level determinations, discussed in Chapter 6, there have been two separate sets of rules to govern aggregation and separation. In May 1989, the IRS issued Temporary Regulations §1.469-4T, approximately 50 pages long, which developed extensive tests requiring that certain business components (called "undertakings" in that Regulation) be separated and others be aggregated into a single activity. The Temporary Regulation expired three years later, under a 1988 law that gave all Temporary Regulations a three-year sunset.[6]

In October 1994, the IRS finalized a Regulation to replace the expired Temporary Regulation. In contrast to its predecessor, Regulations §1.469-4 is brief and contains only a few general rules. The Temporary Regulation was in effect between May 12, 1989, and May 11, 1992. The new Regulation is generally effective for all years ending after May 10, 1992. However, a taxpayer may elect to continue to apply the rules in the Temporary Regulation to its first tax year that ends after May 10, 1992, but begins before that date. [Regs. §1.469-11(b)(2)(i)(2)(i)]

1025.21. Rules in effect from 1989 through 1991. As discussed in Chapter 6, Regulations §1.469-4T provided some detailed rules requiring separation or aggregation of certain undertakings. In general, undertakings may not be combined into a single activity with another undertaking of a different type of business. The four types, which cannot be combined, are:

- Oil and gas ventures
- Rental properties
- Professional service activities
- Other businesses

An S corporation needed to determine the nature of its various undertakings to see if they were required to be separated. This rule may also have applied at the shareholder level.

Temporary Regulations §1.469-4T generally required undertakings to be aggregated into a single activity if they were:

- Under common control, and
- Either in similar business lines or vertically integrated

The shareholder may have been required to aggregate undertakings held through different entities (other than through a C corporation), if they met these criteria.

A taxpayer could elect to treat two or more undertakings as separate activities, even though they would generally be required to be aggregated. [Temporary Regs. §1.469-4T(o)(3),

---

[6] Temporary Regulations issued after November 20, 1988, remain in effect for only three years after issuance, according to §7805(e)(2), with the effective date stated in the Technical and Miscellaneous Revenue Act of 1988, §6232(a).

(4), and (5)] This election, however, was limited to taxpayers who do not materially or significantly participate in the activities. Several of the examples that follow illustrate the limitations of this election.

Separation of activities may free suspended losses when the corporation disposes of an undertaking or the shareholder disposes of his or her stock. Since a shareholder may intend to dispose of his or her interest in some, but not all, of the undertakings, the election was probably advisable.

The problems of disposition of an interest in a passive activity are discussed in Chapter 16, which deals with purchase and sale considerations. The discussion in this chapter is limited to situations where the shareholder continues his or her ownership in the S corporation, and the principal focus is the shareholder's material participation in the activities of the S corporation.

1025.22. Rules in effect beginning in 1992. For years ending after May 10, 1992, Regulations §1.469-4 suggests a much more flexible approach. One or more activities may be treated as a single activity if they constitute an appropriate economic unit for measuring gain or loss. Whether activities constitute an appropriate economic unit depends on all of the facts and circumstances, including the following:

- Similarities and differences in types of business
- Extent of common control
- Extent of common ownership
- Geographical location
- Interdependencies among the activities (e.g., purchases and sales of goods between activities, common customers, common employees, or accounting with a single set of books and records) [Regs. §1.469-4(c)(2)]

Once an S corporation groups its activities, the Regulation allows (or requires) shareholders to group those activities with each other, with activities conducted directly by the taxpayer, or with activities conducted through other S corporations or partnerships, in accordance with the same criteria. [Regs. §1.469-4(d)(5)(i)] A shareholder may not treat activities that are grouped together by the S corporation as separate activities. An activity conducted through a closely held C corporation may be grouped with another activity only for purposes of determining whether the taxpayer materially or significantly participates in the other activity. [Regs. §1.469-4(d)(5)(ii)]

> **EXAMPLE 10 - 17:** Paul is a shareholder in Pasco, an S corporation that operates three shoe stores in the same city, which it treats as a single activity. Paul also owns shares in Cloco, another S corporation, that owns and operates a clothing store in the same city as Pasco's shoe stores. Both S corporations have several shareholders in common. Paul can treat his interests in Pasco and Cloco as an interest in one activity, or interests in two activities, as he chooses.

The Regulation provides that rental income and expenses generally cannot be aggregated with income and expenses from nonrental operations unless the rental or nonrental operations are insubstantial in relation to the operations as a whole. Therefore, a person who owns shares in various S corporations, and also owns interests in partnerships, may not combine any interests in rental companies with interests in nonrental organizations with the intention of treating those interests as a single activity. Exception: If a rental activity and a nonrental activity are owned by the same owners in the same proportions, the portion of the rental activity that involves rental of items of property for use in the nonrental activity may be grouped with the nonrental activity. [Regs. §1.469-4(d)(1)(C)]

EXAMPLE 10 - 18: Jane and John are married and file a joint return. John is the sole shareholder of John's Market, an S corporation that operates a grocery store. Jane is the sole shareholder of J Co., which owns a building and rents it to John's Market. Because Jane and John file a joint return, they are treated as one taxpayer for purposes of the passive loss rules. [Regs. §1.469-1T(j)]. Therefore, the sole owner of John's Market is also the sole owner of J Co. As a result, Jane's rental activity and John's grocery store activity may be treated as a single activity.

Personal property rental activities can never be aggregated with real estate rental operations. Thus, a person cannot combine an interest in a partnership or S corporation that has real estate rents with one that rents out personal property.

As illustrated in the preceding section, it may be extremely important to keep certain activities separate, in the event that the taxpayer disposes of his or her interest in one venture but retains interests in others. The Regulation offers some flexibility in the event of partial dispositions of an activity. The Code states that a taxpayer may deduct all suspended losses with respect to an activity when he or she disposes of the entire interest in that activity. The Regulation allows a taxpayer to treat a partial disposition of substantially all of an interest in an activity as if it were a complete disposition. [Regs. §1.469-4(g)] The taxpayer must be able to demonstrate that the losses are attributable to the disposed interest.

The IRS reserves the right to change a taxpayer's grouping of different interests in an abusive situation. The next example demonstrates a situation in which a shareholder's classification is likely to be readjusted.

10

EXAMPLE 10 - 19: Clyde is a shareholder in Blazer, Inc., an S corporation that performs consulting services. He is also a shareholder in Trail, Inc., another S corporation. Trail rents certain equipment to Blazer, and the rental agreements are arranged so that Trail always shows a profit. Clyde is also a partner in an equipment leasing tax shelter that consistently produces tax losses. Under general rules, it would appear that Clyde could aggregate his interest in Trail with his partnership interest, since both are in the same line of business. However, the IRS reserves the right to reclassify these two economic interests so that the profits from Trail cannot offset the losses from the partnership.

1025.3. Shareholder participation in activities of S corporation. The Code does not define *material participation*. Temporary Regulations issued in 1988 give several definitions, most of which are purely mechanical tests. The Regulations do not offer any rules that are specifically designed to guide shareholders in S corporations. Instead, they treat all taxpayers who own interests in any activities, whether they be proprietorships, general partnerships, or S corporations, in the same manner. A taxpayer must measure his or her participation with respect to individual activities. When the S corporation is involved in one trade or business, a shareholder's participation in the corporation may be identical to his or her participation in the corporation's business activity. If an S corporation has more than one activity, however, it appears that the shareholder must determine his or her participation with each of the corporation's separate activities. Thus it would be possible for a shareholder to materially participate on one of an S corporation's business activities, but not materially participate in another.

If an S corporation has different functions that are not clearly a single activity, the rules for aggregating and separating activities may be extremely important. Under the final Regulations, it is most likely that S corporations will want to treat all business operations as a single activity. By doing so, any shareholder who meets one of the material participation tests discussed below, with respect to all involvement in the corporation, will not be required to separately prove participation in each of the corporation's business undertakings.

OBSERVATION: The tests in the Regulations are probably weighted to mandate material participation for activities that are likely to be profitable, or at least for which there would be a strong presumption of a profit motive. For example, several of the tests are based on time spent in a particular activity. A person with a profit motive is not likely to devote a good deal of time and energy to a venture unless he or she has a bona fide expectation of profits.

As of this writing, no portion of the Regulations has been challenged in court. Although some of the tests appear to be arbitrary, any person attempting to challenge the Regulations should recall the broad authority granted to the IRS by Congress under Code §469(1).

SUMMARY OF AUTHORITY: CODE SECTION 469(l)

- Under §469, the IRS has the power to write legislative Regulations.
- Participation in an activity is one area of specific regulatory authority.

1025.31. Participation exceeds 500 hours. A shareholder who participates for more than 500 hours in the corporation's business activity in one year is a material participant. [Temporary Regs. §1.469-5T(a)(1)] There are no interpretive problems for a shareholder if the S corporation engages in only one business activity. If an S corporation has multiple shareholder-employees and engages in more than one business, shareholders must focus on participation in each activity.

EXAMPLE 10 - 20: Bob and John are equal shareholders in the BJ Corporation, an S corporation that has two separate and distinct activities. Bob works more than 500 hours in the corporation's publishing branch, which is located in San Diego. John works more than 500 hours in the company's software development and sales branch, located in Seattle. Bob is occasionally consulted on software development, and he occasionally asks John's opinion on publishing ventures. The characterization of the corporation's income or loss from each activity will be:

	To Bob	*To John*
Publishing	Active	Passive
Software	Passive	Active

OBSERVATION: The 500-hour test is reasonable and objective. The participation would average about 10 hours per week, equivalent to a quarter-time position of employment. As of this writing, there have been no rulings or court cases involving this test.

EXAMPLE 10 - 21: An individual owns interests in 10 S corporations, all of which operate quick auto maintenance facilities. Each of the corporations is located in a different city. The individual participates approximately 60 hours per year in each of the facilities. Given the grouping rules of Regulations §1.469-4, he could treat his interests in the 10 S corporations as an interest in a single activity. He would then meet the 500-hour standard of material participation. The income and losses from each of the corporations would not be subject to the passive activity loss rules.

Alternatively, the shareholder could treat his interest in each corporation as an interest in a separate activity. He would then not be treated as materially participating in any of the activities.

1025.32. Substantially all participation is in the activity. If a shareholder-employee is the sole participant in an activity, that person's participation is material. [Temporary Regs. §1.469-5T(a)(2)] This criterion will be difficult to establish if there are any other co-owners or any other employees.

EXAMPLE 10 - 22: Everett is the sole shareholder and sole employee of E Corporation, an S corporation. The corporation's only activity is snow removal in a rural area of Virginia. In

10

a year in which there is no snow, Everett spends 50 hours maintaining the equipment and contacting new neighbors to solicit business for next year. Since Everett is the sole participant, his participation is deemed material no matter how few hours he put in that year. The income or loss for that year is not passive.

OBSERVATION: A taxpayer may be motivated to deduct losses from activities that require little participation. If there are no other participants, the test described here at 1025.32. might allow an individual to deduct such losses. Such activities may, however, be subject to the hobby loss restrictions, whereby no losses are allowed and none may be carried to any other year. Alternatively, the IRS might claim that such an activity is not a trade or business, but merely an investment, in which case the deductions would be miscellaneous itemized deductions.

1025.33. Greatest amount of time spent, and more than 100 hours. A third test of material participation requires that the taxpayer participate more than 100 hours, and not less than any other individual, during the year. [Temporary Regs. §1.469-5T(a)(3)] The participation by employees, as well as owners, must be considered.

EXAMPLE 10 - 23: Gene is the sole shareholder of the G Corporation, an S corporation. In 1996, he spends 200 hours on G Corporation business. He has a full-time employee who works 400 hours in 1996. Gene is not a material participant in 1996.

OBSERVATION: This test seems somewhat arbitrary. It would seem reasonable that a taxpayer should be treated as a material participant if he or she participates in an activity more than any other person. The additional requirement that the person spend more than 100 hours, however, places a minimum threshold. If it appears that this rule might be a way to generate passive income by participating only slightly more than 100 hours in an activity that has other participants who spend more time than the owner, the next test is a trap.

10

1025.34. Significant participation activities. Any trade or business activity in which a taxpayer participates for more than 100 but less than 500 hours in a taxable year is a *significant participation activity* (SPA). [Temporary Regs. §1.469-5T(c)(2)] The term *significant participation* is not used in the Code; it was an invention of the Regulations. This type of participation has some unique aspects, and it can have some strange effects.

First, the taxpayer must be careful to properly identify the particular activity in which he or she is seeking to determine the degree of participation. From 1989 through 1991, inclusive, there were some extremely complex mechanical tests, contained in Temporary Regulations §1.469-4T.

Under the Final Regulations, taxpayers have much more flexibility in aggregating or separating their interests. [Regs. §1.469-4] This could be of some importance when a taxpayer is engaged in a SPA.

When an activity is classified as a SPA, a taxpayer may be considered a material participant, even if he or she does not meet one of the other tests. The reason is that a taxpayer is required to aggregate his or her participation in all SPAs to determine material participation. *If the taxpayer's participation in all SPAs exceeds 500 hours, he or she is treated as a material participant in each.* [Temporary Regs. §1.469-5T(a)(4)]

EXAMPLE 10 - 24: Bart owns shares in three S corporations. Each S corporation owns a video rental store. Since the average period of customer use of the tapes and players is less than 7 days, none of the stores is treated as a rental activity. Bart participated in each of the three corporations' activities for 40 hours in 1991. Bart was considered a significant participant, since his hours spent on the three totaled 120 and exceeded the 100 hours required for treatment as a SPA. In addition to his interests in the video stores, Bart owns an interest in a restaurant. The restaurant is not in the same line of business as the video stores and is not controlled by common interests. Bart participates in the management of the restaurant for 400 hours in the current year. Therefore, the restaurant is a SPA to Bart. In 1992 and later years, Bart would be able to aggregate his interests in the video stores, and treat the three stores as one SPA.

Bart's total participation in SPAs for the current year is 520 hours (the 120 spent on the video stores and the 400 hours of participation in the restaurant). Therefore, Bart is considered a material participant in the three video stores as well as the restaurant. His income or loss from each of these ventures is active rather than passive.

The unusual treatment of SPAs extends to situations where a taxpayer meets the significant, but not the material, participation test in all of the activities. In these cases, the income or loss for that particular year from all SPAs must be combined and treated as income or loss from one activity. If the net amount is a loss, the loss is treated as passive. If the net result is income, the income is treated as active.

EXAMPLE 10 - 25: Jim and Roy own all of the stock in the JR Corporation, an S corporation. In 1995, Jim participates in JR's business 101 hours and Roy participates 499 hours. There are full-time employees who participate more than 500 hours. Jim is involved in three partnerships, in which he participates 200 hours each. Roy has no other trade or business activities. The categorization of JR's income or loss to each of the shareholders for 1995 is:

	To Jim	*To Roy*
Net income	Active	Active
Net loss	Active	Passive

1025.35. Participation in prior years. A taxpayer's participation in prior years may determine his or her participation in the current year. If a taxpayer materially participated in an activity (by one of the four tests listed above) in any 5 of the preceding 10 years, he or she will be treated as a material participant for the current year. [Temporary Regs. §1.469-5T(a)(5)] This rule can prohibit taxpayers from turning what is effectively retirement income into passive income. 10

EXAMPLE 10 - 26: Dale owns all of the stock of DM Corporation, an S corporation that owns an automobile dealership. In 1995, he retires. His son Mark operates the business, and Dale keeps all of his shares. Dale will be deemed a material participant through the year 2000.

This rule may also provide a windfall when a taxpayer has several SPAs and reduces participation or ownership. In these cases, some taxpayers may essentially retire from a business and generate active losses.

EXAMPLE 10 - 27: Al is the sole shareholder in an S corporation that owns a bar and restaurant. In 1995, he considered selling his business. A potential purchaser intended to expand Al's current operation into a much larger facility. The purchaser would need considerable amounts of capital to expand the operation. Al agreed to retain his interest in the S corporation and issue some new shares to the purchaser. The purchaser will receive a substantial salary, but the business as a whole is expected to lose money for the next five years. Al retires from the business entirely. The business passes through its losses to Al, who is still a shareholder. Al's losses for the next five years will be active and will not be subject to the passive activity loss limitations.

1025.36. Prior participation in personal service activity. If a taxpayer materially participated in an personal service activity for any three years, he or she will be considered a material participant *for life* if some interest in the activity is retained. [Temporary Regs. §1.469-5T(a)(6)] The material participation for the three years in question will be determined by one of the tests other than prior participation.

EXAMPLE 10 - 28: Rodney and Roger are dentists. Each owns half of the shares of RR Corporation, an S corporation whose activity is the practice of dentistry. In 1996, after 20 years of practice, Rodney retires. He retains his half interest in RR. Rodney will be deemed a material participant in RR for his lifetime.

OBSERVATION: Personal service activities are likely to produce net income, rather than losses. Therefore, retention of an interest in a personal service activity by a person retired from the business through a continued interest in a partnership, or retention of shares in an S corporation, should never generate any passive income.

1025.37. Facts and circumstances. The Regulations provide a final, somewhat nebulous test. A taxpayer is considered a material participant when he or she participates on a regular, continuous, and substantial basis. The Regulations are mostly silent on this test, except to say that there must be no other paid manager. [Temporary Regs. §1.469-5T(a)(7)] As of this writing, there are no examples in the Regulations. This test could, however, be used to create an arguable position for material participation in some instances.

EXAMPLE 10 - 29: Mary and Ann decided to embark on an interior design consulting business in December 1996. In 1996, each of the two spent approximately 75 hours on the project. Neither of the individuals meets any of the objective material participation tests. They would, however, be able to assert that they have materially participated by the facts and circumstances criterion.

10

1025.38. Participation by a spouse. When one spouse owns an interest in an activity, his or her participation includes the participation of the non-owner spouse. [Temporary Regs. §1.469-5T(f)(3)] Therefore, a husband and wife cannot create passive income by vesting the ownership of an activity to the spouse who does not participate.

EXAMPLE 10 - 30: Paul and Jane are husband and wife, living in a "separate property" state. Paul owns all of the stock of P Corporation, an S corporation. Jane is the sole employee of P Corporation. All of Paul's stock is held as separate property. Any income or loss from P Corporation will be treated as active to Paul, since Jane satisfies the material participation test. Therefore, Paul cannot treat his income from the S corporation as passive income.

1025.4. Special rules for real estate rental income and losses. Since its enactment, §469 has provided one special deduction to low- and moderate-income taxpayers who invested in real estate. Until the Revenue Reconciliation Act of 1993, however, there was no provision for any other person to deduct a rental loss, even if the taxpayer's full-time trade or business involved real estate. The Revenue Reconciliation Act of 1993 enacted a new provision that allows persons engaged in active real estate trades or businesses to deduct rental real estate losses. An S corporation should specifically identify any losses from rental real estate, so that any shareholder who qualifies for one of these two provisions may claim an appropriate deduction.

1025.41. Active real estate trade or business. Beginning in 1994, taxpayers who materially participate in active real estate trades or businesses do not treat losses from rental real estate as passive, per se.[7] [§469(c)(7)] This rule applies at the shareholder, rather than the corporate, level. To qualify for this deduction, the taxpayer must meet two criteria:

1. More than 50% of the personal services performed by the taxpayer in all trades or businesses must be in active real estate. [§469(c)(7)(B)(i)]

---

[7] The effective date is not in the Internal Revenue Code, but is found in Revenue Reconciliation Act of 1993, §13143.

2. The taxpayer must have participated in active real estate trades or businesses for at least 750 hours in the year. [§469(c)(7)(B)(ii)]

An active real estate trade or business includes development or redevelopment of real estate, as well as construction, reconstruction, acquisition conversion, rental or leasing, operation, management, or brokerage. [§469(c)(7)(C)]

Regulations finalized in 1995 make it clear that a taxpayer must materially participate in a real property trade or business in order for personal services performed by the taxpayer to count toward the 50% and 750-hour tests. [Regs. §1.469-9(c)(2)]

The shareholder must not perform the services in his or her capacity as an employee, unless the shareholder is treated as a "5% owner" of the business at all times during the tax year. [§469(c)(7)(D)(ii); Regs. §1.469-9(c)(4)] The term "5% owner" is imprecise. It actually means ownership of more than 5% of the stock, but it considers the attribution rules of §318 in determining the ownership. [§416(i)(1)(B)(i)(I)] See Chapter 15, at 1510.2.

Under the newly finalized Regulations, spouses filing a joint return will qualify only if one spouse separately meets both the 50% test and the 750-hour test. That is, each spouse's personal services are counted separately. However, both spouses' services can be taken into account in determining if the activity is a material participation activity. [Regs. §1.469-9(c)(3)]

Once a taxpayer has met the qualification test, any rental real estate activity *in which the taxpayer materially participates* is treated as an active trade or business. Thus, the taxpayer can write off current losses from the activity against any kind of income, including active business or investment income. On the other hand, if a material participation rental real estate activity throws off income, it is treated as active business income. Any rental real estate activity in which the taxpayer does not materially participate for the year remains passive. [Proposed Regs. §1.469-9(e)(1)]

10

If any losses from prior years that remain suspended at the beginning of 1994 are not freed up, the taxpayer must carry them forward as if they were incurred in connection with a former passive activity.[8] The Regulations make it clear that the suspended losses may qualify for the special $25,000 writeoff for active participation rental activities (see below). [Regs. §1.469-9(e)(2)(j)]

In general, each real estate investment is treated as a separate activity. [§469(c)(7)(A)(ii)] The Proposed Regulations provide that if rental real estate is owned through an S corporation, the number of activities held by the taxpayer generally depends on how the S corporation grouped its interests. If the S corporation grouped all of its rental real estate into a single activity, the taxpayer's share is treated as a single activity. On the other hand, if the S corporation treated each of its rental properties as a separate activity, the taxpayer is treated as having several activities. [Proposed Regs. §1.469-9(h)(1)] There is, however, an important exception to the general rule. If the taxpayer holds a 50% or greater interest in the S corporation, each interest in rental real estate held by the S corporation will be treated as a separate interest of the taxpayer, regardless of the S corporation's grouping.

Any taxpayer, however, may aggregate all of his or her real estate holdings into one activity. [§469(c)(7)(A)] The grouping of a taxpayer's activities can make a big difference in whether the taxpayer qualifies for current write-offs. For example, a taxpayer may materially participate in only some of his or her rental real estate holdings. If the taxpayer treats the activities as separate activities, only those in which the taxpayer materially participates will be treated as active trades or businesses. However, if the taxpayer groups the activities, the taxpayer will be treated as materially participating in the combined activity—and the combined activity will be treated as an active business. Grouping of activities should be

---

[8] The Code does not specify this result. The House Committee report to the Revenue Reconciliation Act of 1993 provides for this treatment.

considered carefully, however. The final Regulations make it clear that the election to combine rental real estate activities is binding until there is a material change in the taxpayer's circumstances. The fact that the election is less advantageous in a future year is not a material change, nor is the fact that the taxpayer does not qualify for the rental real estate break in a future year. [Regs. §1.469-9(g)]

1025.42. Losses in real estate rental where owner actively participates. An S corporation may own and operate real estate rental activities. Individual taxpayers who actively participate in real estate rentals may be entitled to a loss deduction of up to $25,000, notwithstanding the passive categorization of such loss. This deduction is allowed at the shareholder level, rather than at the S corporation level. In order to qualify for this deduction, the shareholder must meet certain tests:

10

- The shareholder must meet an "active participation" standard (not defined in Regulations as of August 1995).
- The shareholder may not have more than $150,000 adjusted gross income, before any passive activity loss deduction (including any real estate deduction allowed by §469(c)(7)), IRA deduction, or Social Security inclusion.
- The deduction is limited to the least amount of:
  - — The net loss from real estate in which the taxpayer actively participates,
  - — The net loss from all passive activities, or
  - — $25,000 less one-half of excess of the shareholder's adjusted gross income in excess of $100,000.
- The deduction is reduced to half of the above limits for a married taxpayer filing a separate return if the taxpayer lived apart from his or her spouse throughout the entire year.
- The deduction is not allowed for any married taxpayer filing a separate return, if the taxpayer lived with his or her spouse at any time during the taxable year.

1025.5. Proof of participation. The burden of proof is on the taxpayer to establish the degree of participation. Exactly what proof the taxpayer must provide is not entirely clear.

SUMMARY OF AUTHORITY: REGULATIONS SECTION 1.469-5T(f)(4)

- A shareholder must record his or her participation in the activities of an S corporation.
- The safest method is probably the maintenance of a daily diary, but other records are presumably acceptable.

Figure 10 - 3 may be useful in keeping track of the material participation tests.

1025.6. Rent of shareholder property to the S corporation. When a shareholder rents property to any other person, the gross income is passive and the associated expenses are passive activity deductions. There is a special recharacterization rule, however, whereby income from property a shareholder rents to an S corporation in which the shareholder owns an interest and materially participates is not passive and may not be offset by passive activity losses. [Temporary Regs. §1.469-2T(f)(6); *Schwalbach et ux. v. Commissioner, 111 TC 9 (1998)*] See discussion in Chapter 8. There is no effective way to use the election to separate activities (discussed at 1025.2.) to combat this recharacterization, since the election applies only to taxpayers who would not be considered material or significant participants if the undertakings were aggregated.

Figure 10 - 3: Material participation rules.

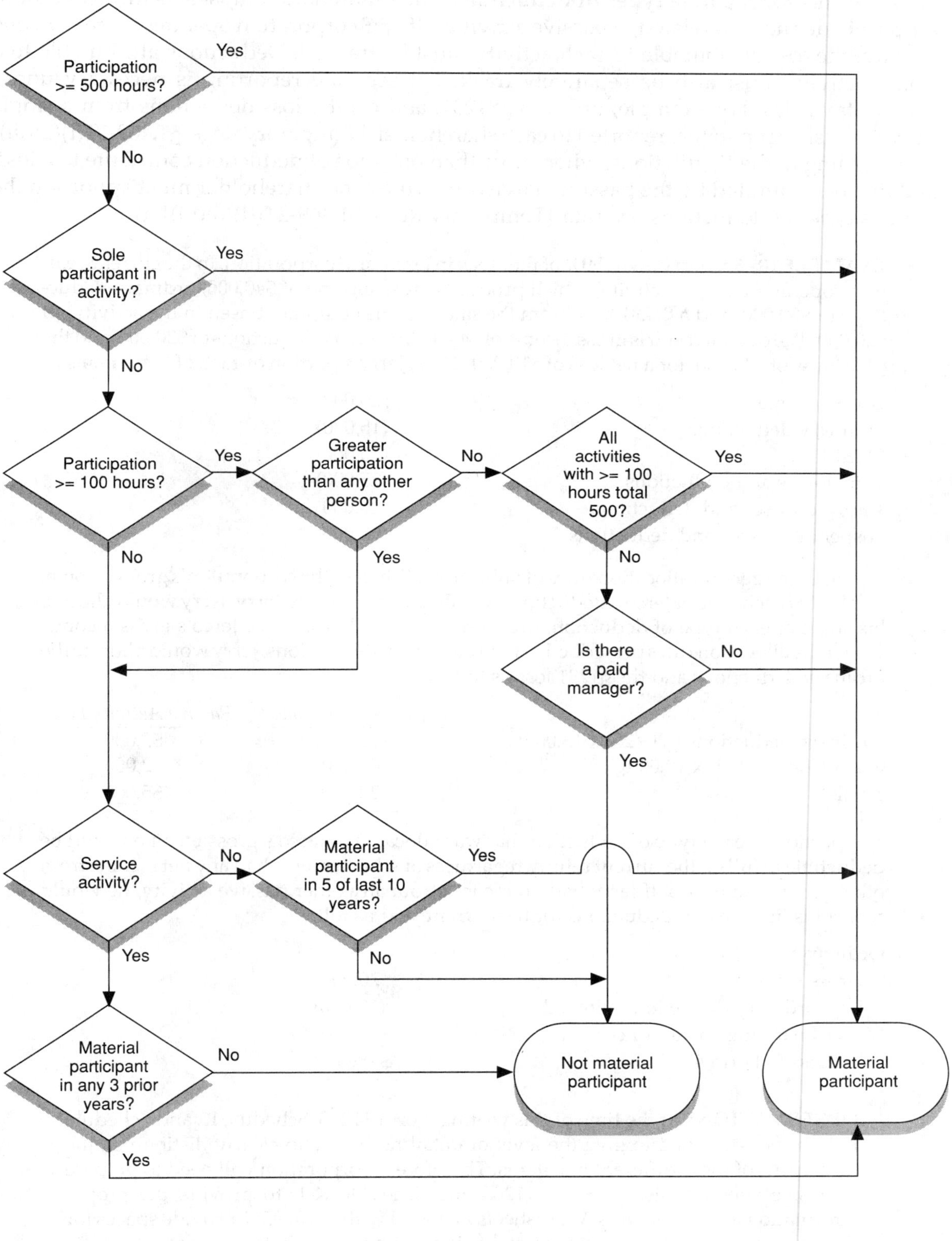

EXAMPLE 10 - 31: Mike owns land and a building that he rents to Miko, Inc., an S corporation in which he owns stock. If the rental produces a net loss, that loss will be passive. Any gross income in excess of the deductions, however, cannot produce net passive income. See additional discussion in Chapter 8, at 840.22.

1025.7. Rules for separate types of deductions. Each shareholder must specifically account for certain deductions related to passive activities. If an S corporation operates more than one activity, the loss attributable to each activity must be tracked. Deductions attributable to a single activity must also be separately tracked if separate reporting is necessary under general tax rules. For example, ordinary, §1231, and capital loss deductions from a single activity must be separately reported to each shareholder. [Temporary Regs. §1.469-1T(f)(2)(iii)]

According to the Regulations, when more than one type of deduction contribute to a loss, and the loss is limited by the passive activity loss rules, the shareholder must apportion the various types of deductions pro rata. [Temporary Regs. §1.469-2T(d)(6)(iii)]

EXAMPLE 10 - 32: Jerry owns 50% of the stock in Jerco, an S corporation. In the current year, Jerco operates a single activity, which produces gross income of $40,000, ordinary deductions of $30,000, and a §1231 loss (from the sale of some equipment used in the activity) of $20,000. The overall result is gross income of $40,000, ordinary deductions of $30,000, and the §1231 loss of $20,000, for a net loss of $10,000. Thus, Jerry's portion of each of these items is:

Gross income	$20,000
Ordinary deductions	(15,000)
§1231 loss	(10,000)
Total losses and deductions	(25,000)
Allowed losses and deductions	$20,000
Suspended losses and deductions	$ 5,000

10

Under the general allocation rules of Subchapter S, half of the corporation's gross income, and half of each type of Jerco's deductions, would pass through to Jerry. Jerry would allocate his share of each type of deduction, proportionately, to his share of Jerco's gross income. Under the allocation rules prescribed in the Temporary Regulations, Jerry would allocate the ordinary deductions and the §1231 loss as follows:

	Offset Gross Income	*Passive Activity Loss*
Ordinary deductions [(20/25) x 15,000]	$12,000	$3,000
§1231 loss [(20/25) x 10,000]	8,000	2,000
Totals	$20,000	$5,000

The portion of each type of deduction that was allocated to Jerco's gross income would be deductible in full on the current return, regardless of whether Jerry had any net income from other passive activities. If Jerry had no income from any other passive activity, he would report his income and deductions for the current year as follows:

Ordinary:	
Gross income	$20,000
Less ordinary deductions allowed	(12,000)
Net ordinary income to Schedule E	$ 8,000
§1231 loss to Form 4797	$ (8,000)

OBSERVATION: At the time of this writing, Form 1120S, Schedule K, and Schedule K-1 are not designed to give the level of detail necessary to clearly distinguish the treatments of these different line items. Therefore, a corporation will need to prepare extensive subschedules to Form 1120S and Schedule K-1, to provide the proper information to shareholders. Worksheets included with Form 8582 provide spaces for the separation of different types of deductions within an activity.

Any tax professional who prepares Form 1120S for passive investors should evaluate the ability of the 1120S software packages. It may be important to purchase a product that will allow the Form 1120S to separate line items among different activities.

1025.8. Special rule for casualty losses. Casualty losses are stated separately by the corporation to its shareholders. Casualty losses are subject to the limits on deductibility imposed by the basis and at-risk rules. They are exempt, however, from the limitation on passive activities. (Code §165(c) takes precedence over §469. See Temporary Regulations §1.469-2T(d)(2)(x).)

EXAMPLE 10 - 33: Refer to Example 10 - 32. Assume that the §1231 loss was a casualty loss rather than a loss from the sale of equipment. The casualty loss is not allocated to Jerco's gross income, but is deductible in full for the current year. Since Jerco's ordinary deductions do not exceed its gross income, Jerco would produce net passive income for the year.

Jerry would report his income and loss from Jerco as follows:

Ordinary:	
Gross income	$ 20,000
Less ordinary deductions allowed	(15,000)
To Schedule E	$ 5,000
§1231 casualty loss to Form 4797	$(10,000)

The Schedule E income could absorb $5,000 of losses from other passive activities or from deductions suspended from prior years.

1025.9. Transitional rules. For taxable years beginning before 1991, taxpayers were allowed to deduct a percentage of certain passive activity losses from activities that they had owned before October 23, 1986. For a shareholder in an S corporation to claim this transitional deduction, there were three conditions:

- The corporation must have owned its interest in the activity on October 22, 1986.
- The corporation must have been an S corporation on October 22, 1986.
- The shareholder must have owned his or her stock on October 22, 1986.

The transitional rules allowed a certain percentage of loss for the years 1987 through 1990, as follows:

Year Beginning in	*Loss Allowed (%)*
1987	65
1988	40
1989	20
1990	10
1991	0

Since this transitional rule has now been completely phased out, it receives no comprehensive discussion in this book. Operating rules are provided in Regulations §1.469-11T. It may be necessary, however, to keep track of the losses allowed for purposes of basis adjustments, especially when a taxpayer is faced with alternative minimum tax calculations.

1025.10. Alternative minimum tax considerations. An S corporation is exempt from the alternative minimum tax at the corporate level. However, the S corporation must report tax preferences and adjustments to each shareholder in the same manner as it reports all income tax items. As discussed in Chapter 9, the shareholder's portion of tax preferences and adjustments may create basis for alternative minimum tax that differs from the basis for income tax purposes. There can also be some differences in the passive activity loss calculations for alternative minimum tax purposes. In general, the alternative minimum tax rules require separate tracking of the passive activity loss limits. [§58(b)]

1025.101. Separate computation of income or loss. As discussed in Chapter 9, each shareholder's income or loss must be computed separately for income tax and alternative minimum tax purposes. When a shareholder's interest in an S corporation is subject to the passive activity loss rules, the separate tracking becomes more complex. The complexity compounds geometrically when a shareholder owns an interest in two or more passive activities.

EXAMPLE 10 - 34: In 1996, Debbie acquired shares in two S corporations, Deb1 and Deb2. She paid $50,000 for each block of shares, and did not materially participate in the activities of either corporation. For 1996, the information from each corporation was:

	Deb1	*Deb2*
Income tax income or loss	$30,000	$(75,000)
Alternative minimum tax adjustments	+10,000	+14,000
Alternative minimum tax income or loss	$40,000	$(61,000)

Her tax treatment of the income from Deb1 for 1996 was:

	Alternative Income Tax	*Minimum Tax*
Income	$30,000	$40,000

Her tax treatment of the loss from Deb2 for 1996 was:

10

	Minimum Tax	*Alternative Income Tax*
Allowable deduction	$30,000	$40,000
Carryforward	45,000	21,000

Her basis at the end of 1996 for each corporation would be:

	Deb1	*Deb2*
Income tax:		
Original cost	$50,000	$50,000
1996 income or loss	30,000	(30,000)
Basis	$80,000	$20,000
Suspended loss in Deb2		$25,000
Minimum tax:		
Original cost	$50,000	$50,000
1996 income or loss	40,000	(40,000)
Basis	$90,000	$10,000
Suspended loss in Deb2		$21,000

1025.102. Tax benefit rule for tax preferences and passive activities. A shareholder is generally required to report all tax preferences and adjustments that flow through from an S corporation. If the tax preferences and adjustments arise in a year when the shareholder also reports a loss from the S corporation, the separate computation of the passive activity loss limits for alternative minimum tax could put the taxpayer in double jeopardy.

EXAMPLE 10 - 35: Fred owns stock in Freco, an S corporation. Fred does not materially participate in Freco's business activities. In 1996, Freco reported a loss, and Fred's share was $40,000. Freco also claimed income tax depreciation in excess of the amount allowed for alternative minimum tax. Fred's share of Freco's depreciation adjustment for 1996 was

$12,000. Under the general rules, Fred would be required to add the $12,000 depreciation adjustment to his taxable income in arriving at his alternative minimum taxable income. Under the passive activity loss rules, however, Fred would calculate a loss of $28,000 for alternative minimum tax purposes, compared to his loss of $40,000 for income tax. Consider the possible double jeopardy under two scenarios. First, assume that he had passive income of $50,000 for both income tax and alternative minimum tax purposes.

	Income Tax	*Alternative Minimum Tax*
Passive income	$50,000	$50,000
Depreciation adjustment from Freco	0	12,000
Passive loss from Freco	(40,000)	(28,000)
Net passive income	$10,000	$34,000
Increase of alternative minimum taxable income over taxable income		$24,000

Note that Fred would report $24,000 alternative minimum taxable income if he were required to report both the depreciation adjustment and the separate application of the passive activity loss rules.

Assume the same facts except that Fred had no passive income for the year. If he were required to report the depreciation adjustment of $12,000, there would be an inequity, because he received no tax benefit from his portion of Freco's loss.

OBSERVATION: Fortunately, the IRS does not require the double counting. It instructs taxpayers not to report an adjustment when they are also subject to limitation by the passive activity loss rules. [Ann. 88-45, 1988-12 IRB 54. Also see Instructions to Form 6251, page 1 (1993).]

10

EXAMPLE 10 - 36: Refer to Example 10 - 35. According to the IRS position, Fred would not report a depreciation adjustment of $12,000, under either set of circumstances. If he had $50,000 passive income from other sources, his calculations would be:

	Income Tax	*Alternative Minimum Tax*
Passive income	$50,000	$50,000
Passive loss from Freco	(40,000)	(28,000)
Net passive income	$10,000	$22,000
Increase of alternative minimum taxable income over taxable income		$12,000

If he had no passive income from other sources, he would not be able to claim a deduction in the current year for his portion of Freco's loss. He would carry $40,000 of that loss forward for income tax and $28,000 forward for alternative minimum tax. He would not report the $12,000 depreciation adjustment since it produced no income tax benefit.

1025.103. Disallowance of the transitional deduction. The transitional deduction discussed above at 1025.9. was allowed for income tax from 1987 through 1990. It was not allowed for alternative minimum tax, and it became a tax adjustment for many taxpayers. [§58(b)(3)] Although the transitional deduction has been phased out of the law, it has important implications for suspended losses and basis calculations.

EXAMPLE 10 - 37: Martha owns stock in Marco, an S corporation. She does not participate in Marco's activities. She purchased her Marco stock before October 23, 1986. Marco's S election was in effect for 1986. As of January 1, 1987, Martha's basis in her Marco stock was $500,000.

Through 1990, Martha owned no other passive activities. From 1987 through 1990, Martha's Schedule K-1 from Marco reported the following:

Year	Income Tax Loss	Minimum Tax Adjustments
1987	$100,000	+$20,000
1988	$ 90,000	+$18,000
1989	$ 80,000	+$16,000
1990	$ 70,000	+$14,000

Her deduction for income tax purposes, and carryovers into future years, would be:

Year	Income Tax Loss	Transition Percentage	Deductible Loss	Suspended
1987	$100,000	.65	$ 65,000	$ 35,000
1988	90,000	.40	36,000	54,000
1989	80,000	.20	16,000	64,000
1990	70,000	.10	7,000	63,000
Totals	$340,000		$124,000	$216,000

As of the beginning of 1991, Martha has a carryover of $216,000 suspended losses from Marco. Those losses would be allowed to the extent of any future passive income, from Marco or any other passive activity. These losses would also be allowed in full if she should completely dispose of her interest in Marco's activity. Note that her basis in her Marco stock would be $160,000.

For alternative minimum tax purposes, Martha would have completely separate computations. Her losses for each year would be:

Year	Income Tax Loss	Minimum Tax Adjustments	Minimum Tax Loss
1987	$100,000	+$20,000	$ 80,000
1988	$ 90,000	+$18,000	$ 72,000
1989	$ 80,000	+$16,000	$ 64,000
1990	$ 70,000	+$14,000	$ 56,000
Total alternative minimum tax loss			$272,000

None of the losses would be allowed as a deduction for 1987 through 1990. As discussed above, Martha would not be required to report the alternative minimum tax adjustments, since the separate application of the passive activity loss rules for alternative minimum tax denies her the tax benefit of those adjustments.

As of the beginning of 1991, Martha has a carryover of suspended losses of $272,000 for alternative minimum tax, in contrast to her $216,000 carryover for income tax. Her basis in her Marco stock would be $228,000 for alternative minimum tax, as opposed to her $160,000 income tax basis.

1025.104. Passive farming activities. A taxpayer is not allowed to claim any deduction from a passive farming activity for alternative minimum tax, even to the extent of income from other passive activities. [§58(a)] If an S corporation owns a farm, any shareholder who does not materially participate in the farming activity will not be allowed to deduct any of his or her losses with respect to that activity for alternative minimum tax. This rule creates another situation where the suspended losses, and basis, will differ for income tax and alternative minimum tax.

1025.11. Disposition of shares in S corporation. A shareholder who disposes of his or her stock in an S corporation may need to cope with several passive activity loss rules. First, he or she must determine if there is an entire disposition to an unrelated party in a fully taxable transaction. If the disposition meets all of these tests, the shareholder will be able to deduct any losses suspended with respect to that activity under the passive loss disallowance provisions. If the disposition does not meet all of these tests, the losses may remain with the shareholder or be transferred to the recipient. These problems are discussed in Chapter 16 and 17, which relate to dispositions by sale or reorganization.

1030. Investment interest.

Individuals, including shareholders in S corporations, are subject to the investment interest limitations. These limitations provide that a taxpayer may deduct interest incurred to acquire or hold investments to the extent of the taxpayer's investment income. [§163(d)] An S corporation must report its investment income and investment interest to its shareholders under the general reporting rules of §1366. The income and interest will be combined at the shareholder level.

Under prior law, distributions from S corporations were dividends. As such, they were investment income. (See *Gordon*, 47 TCM 989, TC Memo 1984-49, and *Crook*, 80 TC 27 (1983), for a discussion of prior law.) The Tax Court held that undistributed taxable income (UTI) of S corporations was also investment income, since it was treated as a dividend to each shareholder. [*Crook*, 80 TC 27 (1983)] Under current law, however, distributions from S corporations are generally reductions of basis. Shareholders may receive a dividend from an S corporation, from its accumulated earnings and profits. A distribution of this nature is investment income.

The situation is less clear for a shareholder who receives a distribution that is not from the corporation's accumulated earnings and profits but exceeds the shareholder's basis. Arguably, such a distribution should be investment income, since it is treated as a gain from the sale of stock. A strict reading of the statute, however, limits gains that are treated as investment income to "gains attributable to the sale of property held for investment." [§163(d)(4)(B)(ii)] The term is further refined to include only property that is not a passive activity and with respect to which the taxpayer does not materially participate. [§163(d)(5)(A)(ii)] By reference, stock in an S corporation could be property held for investment only to the extent that it produces gross income from interest, dividends, annuities, or royalties other than royalties derived in the course of a trade or business. [§163(d)(5)(A)(i), §469(e)(1)]

1030.1. Interaction with the basis limits. Any investment interest paid or incurred by the corporation is treated as a loss or deduction subject to the general limits of stock and debt basis. (Code §1366(d)(1) applies the limits to the "aggregate amount of losses and deductions taken into account by a shareholder. . . .") Therefore, an S corporation's investment interest expense that is not deductible to a shareholder who lacks basis will not enter into that shareholder's calculation of deductible investment interest.

1030.2. Interaction with passive activity rules. The investment interest and passive activity loss rules provide that no item of income or interest expense is subject to both limits. In brief, the investment interest and passive activity loss limits never cross paths.[9] The Regulations under §469 exclude portfolio income from the definition of passive activity gross income. [Temporary Regs. §1.469-2T(c)(3)] They also exclude interest expense attributable to investments from treatment as a passive activity deduction. [Temporary Regs. §1.469-2T(d)(2)(iii)] Therefore, classification of interest as attributable to investment property or as attributable to a passive activity determines which set of loss limits govern deductibility.

---

[9] From 1987 through 1990, the transitional deduction allowed for certain passive activities was treated as a reduction of investment income when calculating the investment interest deduction. [§163(d)(4)(E)] This crossover has no effect for 1991 and later years.

1030.3. Interaction with the at-risk rules. The at-risk limits of §465 may limit the deductibility of investment interest. There are no Final, Temporary, or Proposed Regulations that coordinate the two limits. According to the most recent IRS instructions, which are consistent with those in prior years, a taxpayer must determine his or her deductible interest under the investment interest limits before applying the at-risk limit. [Instructions to Form 6198 (line 4), 1994]

EXAMPLE 10 - 38: Mary owns stock in Resources, Inc., an S corporation. Resources pays investment interest in the current year, of which Mary's portion is $15,000. Mary has $9,000 of investment income. If she has sufficient basis and amount at risk in her Resources stock to absorb $9,000 of the investment interest, she will be able to deduct $9,000 on her current year's income tax return, since she has investment income of $9,000.

Assume Mary has $15,000 or more basis and amount at risk in her Resources stock for the current year. She would deduct $9,000 investment interest on her current-year return and carry $6,000 forward to the next taxable year. The $6,000 would be deductible if she had at least $6,000 investment interest in her next taxable year, and it would not depend on her amount at risk or basis in Resources.

Alternatively, assume that Mary had only $10,000 at risk in Resources for the current year. She would deduct $9,000 investment interest in the current year. She would carry forward $1,000 to the next year, which would be allowed as a deduction if she had at least $1,000 investment income in that year. She would also carry forward $5,000, which would be deductible only if she increased her amount at risk and had investment income.

10

Finally, assume that Mary had only $7,000 at risk in her Resources stock for the current year. She would deduct $7,000 investment interest in the current year. She would carry $8,000 investment interest forward. In order to claim a deduction, she would need to report investment income and increase her amount at risk.

OBSERVATION: The hierarchy of the investment income and at-risk limits with respect to investment interest is counterintuitive. The at-risk limits, which apply to individual activities, should really limit the deduction before applying the investment income limit, which applies to a taxpayer's overall investment interest expense. Perhaps the rationale for the limits is chronological. The investment interest limits were enacted by the Tax Reform Act of 1969, whereas the at-risk limits were included in the Tax Reform Act of 1976. (Both provisions have been substantially modified by subsequent legislation.)

When a taxpayer makes investment interest payments with respect to more than one activity, he or she must determine the interest allocable to each activity. [Instructions to Form 6198 (line 4), 1994] There are no rules specifying any allocation method. Therefore, a taxpayer should be able to apply the investment interest limit to interest that is not limited by the at-risk rules.

EXAMPLE 10 - 39: Karl owns shares in Karco, an S corporation. Karl's share of Karco's investment interest for the current year is $12,000. Karl's amount at risk in Karco is $3,000 at the end of the current year. Karl also pays $8,000 in investment interest on a loan traced to bond investments. Karl is completely at risk on that loan. Karl's investment income for the current year is $9,000. It would seem reasonable that Karl should deduct $9,000 investment interest. Therefore, Karl should claim $8,000 interest on his loan related to bond investments and $1,000 of his investment interest passed through from Karco.

If future rules should require proration of interest attributable to various debts, Karl would be faced with the following limitations:

Investment interest limit:

Investment Interest Attributable to	*Amount Paid*	*Percent of Total*	*Current Year*	*Carry Forward*
Karco	$12,000	60	$5,400	$ 6,600
Bonds	8,000	40	3,600	4,400
Total	$20,000	100	$9,000	$11,000

At-risk limit:

		Amount Allowed After		
Investment Interest Attributable to	*Investment Interest Limit*	*At-Risk Limit*	*Allowed in Current Year*	*Carry Forward*
Karco	$5,400	$3,000	$3,000	$2,400
Bonds	3,600	3,600	3,600	0
Total	$9,000	$6,600	$6,600	$2,400

1030.4. Alternative minimum tax considerations. Like the passive activity loss limits, the investment interest limits must be calculated separately for the alternative minimum tax. The principal differences are that private activity bonds are taxable as a preference for the alternative minimum tax. [§57(a)(5)] These bonds are those issued by state and local governments after August 7, 1986, the proceeds of which were used for any purpose other than strict governmental use. The principal example of a private activity bond is an industrial development bond. Since interest on a private activity bond can be included in alternative minimum taxable income, interest paid to acquire or hold such bonds is allowable as deductible investment interest for the alternative minimum tax. [§56(b)(1)(C)(iii)] An S corporation must report to its shareholders any private activity bond interest income and any interest paid by the corporation that is attributable to its holding of private activity bond investments.

10

1035. Capital loss limits.

An individual's deduction for capital losses in any taxable year is limited to $3,000 plus the taxpayer's capital gains recognized in the same year. [§1211(b)] When an individual has both short-term and long-term capital losses in excess of his or her capital gains, the short-term loss is deducted first. Any capital loss not deductible in the taxable year is carried forward as if it were a capital loss sustained in the next taxable year. [§1212(b)]

If an S corporation sustains capital losses, such losses pass through to the shareholders and are subject to all of the other loss restrictions before they are potentially allowed as deductions on the shareholder's tax return. A capital loss is not subject to the investment interest limit, since it is not interest, per se. It may, however, reduce the shareholder's net investment income, if the loss is sustained on property held primarily for investment.

A capital loss is subject to basis limits and at-risk restrictions. It may also be subject to the passive activity loss rules, if the loss is incurred in connection with a passive activity. A capital loss sustained by an S corporation must pass each of these barriers before a shareholder may claim a deduction.

> **EXAMPLE 10 - 40:** Jayne owns all of the shares in Jaynco, an S corporation. At the beginning of the current year, Jaynco held an interest in a partnership that operated a rental property. In the current year, Jaynco disposed of a portion of its interest in the partnership and reported a capital loss of $20,000 on the disposition. Jaynco's share of the partnership's ordinary operating loss for the current year was $10,000. Jaynco had no other items of income or loss in the current year. Jaynco made no distributions to Jayne in the current year.

Jayne's basis in her Jaynco stock was $18,000, and her amount at risk in her Jaynco stock was $15,000, before she claimed any of the current year's losses. She had $9,000 of income from other passive activities and $2,000 of capital gains for the current year. In reporting her losses from Jaynco, she will be subject to the following allocation limits:

1. Basis limitation:

	Capital	*Ordinary*
Losses sustained in year	$20,000	$10,000
Percent of total losses	$^{2}/_{3}$	$^{1}/_{3}$
Allowed up to $18,000 basis	12,000	6,000
Carried forward	8,000	4,000

Authority for allocation: No Regulations exist for this under Subchapter S, except for Proposed Regulations §1.1366-2(a)(4). Partnership Regulations at §1.704-1(d)(2) would require this allocation for a partnership, and §§1363 and 1366 refer to partnership rules. Temporary Regulations §1.469-2T(d)(6)(ii)(B) adopts the identical rule for any pass-through item from an S corporation that could be subject to the passive activity loss rules.

2. Amount-at-risk limitation:

	Capital	*Ordinary*
Losses allowed to extent of basis	$12,000	$6,000
Percent of total losses	$^{2}/_{3}$	$^{1}/_{3}$
Allowed up to $15,000 at risk	10,000	5,000
Carried forward	2,000	1,000

10

Authority for allocation: Temporary Regulations §1.469-2T(d)(6)(iii), which requires pro rata allocation of each loss associated with an activity.

Note: Proposed Regulations §1.465-38(a), as discussed at 1020.5., would treat the capital loss as allowable in full, whereas the ordinary loss would be limited to the amount at risk remaining after the capital loss. However, since in this case the activity is subject to the passive loss rules, the Regulations under §469 would override the Proposed Regulations under §465.

3. Passive income limitation:

	Capital	*Ordinary*
Losses allowed to extent of amount at risk	$10,000	$5,000
Percent of total losses	$^{2}/_{3}$	$^{1}/_{3}$
Limited to $9,000 passive income	6,000	3,000
Carried forward	4,000	2,000

Authority for allocation: Temporary Regulations §1.469-2T(d)(6)(iii).

4. Capital loss limitation:

Loss allowed after passive activity loss limit	$ 6,000
Allowed to extent of capital gains	2,000
Allowed as ordinary deduction	3,000
Carried forward	1,000

Jayne's treatment of her losses from the corporation can be summarized as follows:

Ordinary loss:	
Deductible in current year	$ 3,000
Carried forward until Jayne has:	
Future basis, amount at risk, and passive income	4,000
Future amount at risk and passive income	1,000
Future passive income	2,000
Total	$10,000

Capital loss:	
Deductible in current year	$ 5,000
Carried forward until Jayne has:	
Future basis, amount at risk, passive income, and capital gain	8,000*
Future amount at risk, passive income, and capital gain2,000*	
Future passive income and capital gain	4,000*
Future capital gain	1,000*
Total	$20,000

*Up to $3,000 could be deducted against ordinary income in a future year.

1040. Charitable contributions.

For pass-through of income, losses, deductions, and any other items to shareholders, Subchapter S adopts the same rules as have been established for partnerships and partners. [§1366(a)(1)] Charitable contributions must be reported to partners, and they retain their identity at the partner level. [§702(a)(4)] Therefore, at least until Regulations issued under Subchapter S specify otherwise, an S corporation and its shareholders are subject to the same charitable contribution rules as are partnerships and partners.[10] At first glance, this may appear to be a distinction without a difference. Upon further examination, however, the difference may be significant. 10

Unlike other losses or deductions that pass through from an S corporation to its shareholders, charitable contributions appear to be subject to no limitations other than the individual shareholder's percentage of adjusted gross income. Under the partnership rules, charitable contributions are "disallowed," rather than treated as separately stated deductions, at the partnership level. [§703(a)(2)(C)] Since Subchapter S adopts the same disallowances as partnerships, such contributions are likewise disallowed (rather than treated as separately stated deductions) for an S corporation. [§1363(b)(2)] The Final Regulations and Proposed Regulations under Subchapter S are silent on this issue.

The partnership Regulations require that a partner reduce basis in his or her partnership interest for the pass-through of charitable contributions from the partnership, but they do not limit the partner's deduction to basis in the partnership interest. (Regulations §1.704-1(d)(2) limits losses to basis for all items except charitable contributions and foreign taxes.) Since Subchapter S has no Regulations regarding the pass-through of charitable contributions to shareholders, the partnership rules are probably valid. Therefore, the partnership Regulations provide the only reasonable authority for S corporations, and they should be followed.

The at-risk rules are limited to deductions and losses incurred in a trade or business or for production of income. [Proposed Regs. §1.465-13(a)] Since charitable contributions do not fit into either of these categories, they are exempt from application of the at-risk rules.

Charitable contributions are explicitly excluded from the limitations on passive activity losses. [Temporary Regs. §1.469-2T(d)(2)(viii)] Therefore, this type of expenditure is subject

[10] Regulations under Subchapter S, as it existed prior to the Subchapter S Revision Act of 1982, offer no guidance. Under that law, the S corporation was subject to the corporate charitable deduction limits. Contributions made by the corporation did not flow through to the shareholders.

to none of the loss limits discussed in this chapter or Chapter 9. The only limitation on the deductibility of a charitable contribution appears to be the shareholder limit to a portion of adjusted gross income. [§170(b)]

OBSERVATION: When a shareholder in an S corporation wants to donate to a charity, there could be two advantages to having the corporation, rather than the shareholder, make the contributions to the charitable organization:

- The shareholder would not be burdened with any of the deduction limits (other than the limitation based on adjusted gross income).
- The contributions would not be wage or salary income, so the shareholder would not be subject to FICA or withholding tax.

EXAMPLE 10-41: Whit Corporation, an S corporation, has two equal shareholders, Wallace and Caroline. Both shareholders are graduates of Whitman College and are charitably inclined toward that institution. Each of the two intends to give the university $10,000 in the current year.

Wallace materially participates in the corporation's business and usually receives a salary, although he has no compensation in the current year. Caroline is a passive investor and receives no compensation from the corporation. Neither shareholder has any basis in stock or debt of the corporation. The corporation has $20,000 positive cash flow but anticipates a loss of $10,000 for the current year.

10

Each shareholder intended to take $10,000 from the corporation in the form of a distribution. Upon further analysis, however, it is likely that the $10,000 received by Wallace could be recharacterized as compensation. (See the discussion in Chapter 8 of the cases of *Joseph S.C. Radtke v. U.S.*, 89-2 USTC 9466 (E.D. Wis.), aff'd in *Joseph S.C. Radtke v. U.S.*, 90-1 USTC 50,113 (7th Cir.), as well as cases that have followed.) In that event, the distribution of $10,000 to Caroline would be disproportionate, since Wallace would have received no distribution with respect to his stock. Although the distribution would probably not cause the corporation to have a second class of stock, it would need to be given appropriate tax effect in accordance with Regulations §1.1361-1. This Regulation is discussed in detail in Chapter 2. Some of the problems that relate specifically to employee compensation are also discussed in Chapter 8. The appropriate tax effect would probably be a constructive distribution of $10,000 to Wallace in the form of a corporate obligation. The tax problems from this plan would include the following:

- The corporation would be liable for payment of employer and employee FICA taxes of approximately $1,600.
- Wallace would have gross income of $10,000.
- The compensation and FICA taxes would increase the corporation's loss, which is not deductible to either shareholder since both lack basis.
- Caroline would also be subject to the passive activity loss limits, since she does not materially participate in the corporation's business activities.
- Each shareholder would be required to report the distribution as a capital gain, since the distribution would exceed each shareholder's stock basis.

A better alternative might be to have the corporation directly contribute $20,000 to Whitman College. The contribution would be allocated to each shareholder in accordance with his or her ownership, or 50% to each. Wallace and Caroline would each claim a $10,000 deduction, subject to the limits of 50% of each individual's adjusted gross income.

A charitable contribution from an S corporation may provide an even greater tax benefit to the shareholders if the contribution is made in the form of appreciated capital assets. When a taxpayer contributes capital gain property to a qualified organization, the donor claims the fair market value as a charitable deduction. [Regs. §170A-1(c)(1), Regs. §1.170A-6(b)(2)] Since the charitable deduction is disallowed to the S corporation, the shareholders are treated as if they had made the contribution directly to the organization at its fair market value. [PLR 9340043] A contribution is not treated as a constructive distribution to the shareholders. [PLR 9340043]

The shareholders should reduce basis, but not below zero, for their ratable shares of the fair market value of the contributed property. [PLR 9340043] If a shareholder's portion of the fair market value of the contributed property exceeds his or her basis, the shareholder would nevertheless be able to claim the entire value as a deduction in the year of the contribution. (See at 1040. for discussion of the inapplicability of basis limitations to charitable contributions.)

A shareholder cannot reduce his or her stock and debt basis below zero for a charitable contribution, even though the shareholder is allowed to claim the entire fair market value of the property contributed as an itemized deduction. The corporation should also reduce its AAA for the fair market value of the contributed property. The contribution could create a negative AAA.

In a year in which the S corporation has a net loss, as well as a charitable contribution, the total of these items may exceed a shareholder's basis. In this situation, there are two possible ordering rules for the deductible and nondeductible items. As is discussed in Chapter 6, at 630.66., the general ordering rule requires that a shareholder reduce his or her basis by nondeductible items in order to determine the basis limitation for deductible losses and expenses. [Regs. §1.1367-1(e)] An elective ordering rule, discussed in Chapter 6, at 630.67., allows a shareholder to reduce basis for deductible items before nondeductible expenditures. [Regs. §1.1367-1(f)] The trade-off for the elective ordering rule is that the shareholder must carry forward any nondeductible items in excess of basis and use these items to reduce basis in future years.

When the charitable contribution is all, or a substantial portion, of the corporation's nondeductible losses and expenses, the shareholder would be wise not to elect the special ordering rule and to stay with the general rule.

EXAMPLE 10-42: Charco, an S corporation, has one shareholder, Charles. Both Charco and Charles use the calendar year. In 1996, Charco donates a conservation easement to the state government. The value of the easement is $150,000. The corporation reports an ordinary loss of $20,000 for 1996. At the beginning of 1996, Charles's basis in his Charco stock was $30,000. Charles took no distributions from Charco in 1996, and there were no other nondeductible expenses or other items that would affect his stock basis. It appears that Charles may claim the entire $150,000 charitable deduction on his personal tax return, subject to the 50% AGI limit. This personal deduction would not be limited to his basis. [Regs. §1.704-2(d)(2)] Thus, the general or special ordering rule of Regulations §1.1367-1(e) would not affect his charitable deduction. Under the general ordering rule, Charles would reduce his basis to zero for the charitable contribution and would be unable to deduct any of the corporation's ordinary loss in 1996.

Charles may be tempted to use the special ordering rule, under which he would deduct $20,000 as an ordinary loss and reduce his stock basis to $10,000. He would then be able to deduct the entire charitable contribution in 1996, since charitable contributions are not limited to basis. Most likely, however, Charles would be better off, in the long run, not to make the special ordering election, for either of two reasons:

- The special ordering rule would require him to carry the charitable contribution in excess of basis forward and reduce stock basis in future years. By contrast, there is no requirement to carry nondeductible expenses forward as basis reduction under the general ordering rule.
- The deductible loss would reduce Charles's AGI and could possibly result in a reduced charitable deduction limit for 1996.

To illustrate the effects of the ordering rules further, assume that Charles owned 100% of the Charco stock throughout 1997. Assume also that Charco was profitable in 1997 and reported $175,000 of ordinary income and no separately reported or tax exempt items. The 1996 and 1997 tax situations would be:

	Ordering Rule	
	General	*Special*
1996		
Beginning basis	$ 30,000	$ 30,000
Reduce for		
Ordinary loss deduction	(0)	(20,000)
Charitable deduction	(30,000)	(10,000)
Basis at end of 1996	$ 0	$ 0
Carryforwards at end of 1995		
Ordinary loss	$ 20,000	$ 0
Charitable contribution	$ 0	$140,000
Total 1996 deduction to Charles	$150,000	$170,000
1997		
Beginning basis	$ 0	$ 0
Increase for 1997 ordinary income	175,000	175,000
Reduce for suspended 1995 loss	(20,000)	(140,000)
Basis at end of 1996	$155,000	$ 35,000
Total 1997 income to Charles	$155,000	$175,000

Thus, under most circumstances Charles would be well served to use the general ordering rule and forgo the ordinary deduction in 1996. The principal reason is the reduced basis caused by the elective ordering rule.

10

Under some circumstances, the elective ordering rule would be preferred. If a shareholder had disposed of all of his or her stock during or after the year of the charitable contribution, he or she would receive no future tax benefit from stock basis and would thus be better off claiming all possible deductions in that year. Similarly, if the shareholder had died, and the executor wanted to claim the greatest possible deductions on the shareholder's final return, the elective ordering rule would be beneficial.

OBSERVATION: The elective ordering rule is irrevocable and is binding on the shareholder for all future years. Thus, it should be chosen only when the shareholder is reasonably certain that the required basis reduction will have little or no future adverse effects. The elective ordering rule can be made on an amended return for the year in which the deductible and nondeductible items occur. Again, a shareholder would probably be best served to wait to make this election until he or she is certain that the elective ordering rule will not have any adverse effects.

In other circumstances, an S corporation might report positive income, exclusive of the charitable contribution, and make a contribution that exceeds the shareholder's basis, after adjustment for the year's income. In this situation, there is no combination of deductible and nondeductible losses. Therefore, there is no ordering rule.

EXAMPLE 10 - 43: Assume the same facts as in Example 10 - 42, except that Charco has ordinary income of $5,000 in 1996. Charles's basis before the charitable contribution would be $35,000 ($5,000 + $30,000). He would reduce his basis to zero for the charitable contribution and claim a deduction of $150,000 on his 1996 return. Thus his charitable deduction would exceed his basis by $115,000. There is no provision that would require him to carry that amount forward as a future reduction of basis.

1045. State and local income taxes.

States that recognize the federal S election (or a state equivalent) impose their own taxes on the shareholders. These taxes may be paid by the shareholders from their personal funds, or the corporation may make state tax deposits on its shareholders' behalf. In the latter case, the corporation should treat the tax deposits as distributions to the shareholders[11] and make tax deposits in proportion to shareholdings, in order to avoid any possible complications with class-of-stock rules.

A shareholder is able to claim state and local taxes as an itemized deduction on his or her federal income tax return. If the shareholder pays the state taxing authority from his or her personal funds, the deduction would not be subject to any basis, at-risk, or passive activity loss limits. It may be subject to two important limitations on the shareholder's return:

- As an itemized deduction, it is subject to the phaseout of 3% of the adjusted gross income in excess of a certain threshold. The threshold, which is indexed annually for inflation, is $114,700 for 1995 ($57,350 if the taxpayer is married and files a separate return), but is limited to 80% of the total itemized deductions. [§68]
- The deduction for taxes is an addition to taxable income in arriving at alternative minimum taxable income. [§56(b)(1)(A)(ii)]

EXAMPLE 10 - 44: Tom and Ellen are equal shareholders in Eltoco, an S corporation. In the current year, Eltoco reports $2,000,000 of taxable income. Tom and Ellen, therefore, each report $1,000,000 of income from Eltoco. They live in a state that imposes a personal income tax at the rate of 5%. Each would claim a deduction for $50,000 for the state taxes they must pay on Eltoco's taxable income. The phaseout of itemized deductions would approximate $30,000 for each shareholder (3% of $1,000,000), leaving each shareholder with a deduction of $20,000. In addition, each shareholder would have an additive adjustment of $20,000 (the deductible portion of the tax) in arriving at alternative minimum taxable income.

10

If the corporation pays the tax on the shareholders' behalf, the payment will be treated as a distribution and will be subject to the distribution rules discussed in Chapter 7. Usually, an S corporation will pay its shareholders' income taxes only in a year in which it anticipates taxable income. Accordingly, the distribution would usually be a reduction of basis and would reduce the S corporation's Accumulated Adjustments Account. In some cases, however, the distribution could be a dividend, as suggested below.

If the corporation makes a state tax deposit for its shareholders early in the year in anticipation of reporting taxable income, and later events cause the corporation to show a loss for the year, the corporation may not have an Accumulated Adjustments Account sufficient to absorb the distribution. Similarly, if the corporation elects to distribute accumulated earnings and profits before the Accumulated Adjustments Account, under §1368(e)(3), the distributions, including the tax deposits, would be treated as dividends to the shareholders. In either instance, the shareholders would report dividend income to the extent of the distribution or the corporation's accumulated earnings and profits, whichever is less.

1050. Miscellaneous expenses.

Certain expenses characterized as itemized deductions might also flow through from an S corporation to its shareholders. As was discussed in Chapter 6, at 630.6., these expenses will

[11] See PLR 9142029, which specifically treated tax deposits as distributions. This ruling also has important implications for Qualified Subchapter S Trusts.

be treated as reductions of basis to the shareholders. These itemized deductions will still be subject to the at-risk and passive activity loss limits on deductibility, even after the shareholder has met the basis test to claim them.

> **OBSERVATION:** Expenses that are not deductible at the corporate level, such as charitable contributions, meal and entertainment expenses, etc., should probably reduce a shareholder's amount at risk with respect to the S corporation in the same manner as they affect a shareholder's basis. See discussion at 1020.4. Such expenses, however, should have no effect on any shareholder's passive activity income, since the passive loss rules apply only when the *deductions* from an activity exceed the gross income from passive activities.

1055. Summary of loss limits.

Tables 10 - 2 and 10 - 3 provide a reference for the multiple loss limits and carryforwards.

1060. Practice aids.

Checklist 10-1 and Worksheets 10-1 and 10-2 are similar to the basis practice aids at the end of Chapter 9. They are adapted slightly to be used in computing the amount at risk for each block of stock or debt instrument. Worksheets 10-1 and 10-2 should be useful after the year

10

TABLE 10 - 2: Summary of Loss Limits for Trade or Business

Priority	*Limitation*	*Treatment of Excess*	*Treatment on Disposition*
1.	Stock basis	Carry forward until basis is restored	No benefit
2.	Debt basis	Carry forward until basis is restored	No benefit
3.	Amount at risk	Carry forward until amount is increased	No benefit (except that gain adds at-risk)
4.	Passive limit	Carry forward until subsequent passive income	All suspended losses are deductible
5.	Capital loss	Carry forward until subsequent capital gain	No benefit (except that gain may be capital)

TABLE 10 - 3: Summary of Loss Limits for Investment Interest

Priority	*Limitation*	*Treatment of Excess*	*Treatment on Disposition*
1.	Stock basis	Carry forward until basis is restored	No benefit (except that gain may be investment income)
2.	Debt basis	Carry forward until basis is restored	No benefit (except that gain may be investment income)
3.	Investment interest	Carry forward to investment income	No benefit (except that gain may be investment income)
4.	Amount at risk	Carry forward until amount is increased	No benefit (except that gain adds at-risk)

end to determine a shareholder's stock and debt amount at risk after the year end. As Worksheet 10-1 indicates, a shareholder who owns more than one block of stock should keep a worksheet for each block. Similarly, a shareholder who has made more than one loan to the corporation should keep a separate worksheet for each loan.

Note that there is an inconsistency between the amount at risk for stock basis and the amount at risk for debt basis. Certain nonrecourse financing does not give an amount at risk for stock, whereas the same financing will give an amount at risk for shareholder debt. Thus, there are slight differences in the basis worksheet and the amount-at-risk worksheet for stock, but virtually no differences for debt.

Each shareholder should also keep separate schedules for the alternative minimum tax amount at risk of each block of stock and for each debt instrument. The same worksheets can be used for this purpose, except that the beginning amount at risk, income, and losses should be calculated separately by the alternative minimum tax rules.

Finally, Worksheet 10-3 provides a handy place to keep track of the multiple loss limitations that might apply to any loss or deduction that has been passed through from the corporation to each shareholder. By completing this worksheet at the beginning and end of each year, the tax preparer will remember to look for items that might have been carried forward from the prior year. Further, this worksheet will help the taxpayer recognize valuable tax benefits that might otherwise be lost. Filling out the final column for the end of the year will provide a good head start on next year's tax return.

Checklist 10 - 1: Year-end amount-at-risk planning

	Applicable (Yes/No)	*Completed (Date)*
1. Shareholder considerations (complete for each shareholder)		
a. Amount at risk for potential losses	______	______
i. If insufficient, consider increasing amount at risk by:	______	______
(1) Contributing to capital	______	______
(2) Making loan to corporation	______	______
(3) Substituting on bank loan	______	______
(4) Postponing payment of salary, rent, or interest—be wary of insufficient salary, effects on pension funding, or debt reclassification problems.	______	______
(5) Repaying any nonrecourse debt used to finance stock with recourse debt	______	______
ii. Examine any refinancing with nonrecourse debt, and possible recapture of prior year losses	______	______
iii. If amount at risk is sufficient, consider reducing amount at risk to suspend loss.	______	______
(1) Anticipated losses might overshoot personal exemptions and itemized or standard deduction.	______	______
(2) Losses may yield better tax result next year.	______	______

Copyright © 2000 by Harcourt, Inc. All rights reserved.

b. Amount at risk for distributions
If amount at risk after losses is insufficient to absorb distributions, consider increasing amount at risk. ______
   i. Loan to corporation will not help. ______ ______
   ii. If unable to increase amount at risk, consider AAA bypass election. ______
c. Possible benefits of corporate actions ______
   i. Charitable contributions ______
   ii. Recognized corporate-level capital losses ______ ______
   iii. Other items ______ ______

Worksheet 10 - 1: Stock amount at risk

Keep a separate worksheet for each block of stock.

If the corporation has terminated a year under §1.377(a)(2) or Regulations §1.1368-1(g), complete a separate worksheet for each portion of the year.)

10

1. Amount at risk at beginning of year, or at acquisition date if acquired during year. $ ______

2. Additions to amount at risk
(CAUTION: Make sure that any debt amount at risk has been restored to extent of prior reductions.) ______
   a. Add all taxable items from shareholder's K- 1
   (to the extent allocated to this block) $ ______
   b. Add all tax-exempt income
   (CAUTION: If including corporate cancellation of debt income, review current IRS position and consider disclosure.)
   See discussion at 610.9. $ ______
   c. Add any deemed dividend allocated to this block
   (See Chapter 7, at 740.5.) $ ______
   d. Any nonrecourse financing that has been reduced by cash payment or refinancing with recourse debt. $ ______

3. Subtotal (1 + 2a + 2b + 2c + 2d) $ ______

4. Reductions of amount at risk
(CAUTION: Determine if prior or current election to reduce for deductible expenses under Regulations §1.1367-l(f) is in effect.
If such election is in effect, skip line 4a and go directly to line 4c.) ______
   a. Nondeductible expenses, not capitalized
   (Include any spillovers from other blocks of stock.)
   (Do not reduce amount at risk below zero.)

Copyright © 2000 by Harcourt, Inc. All rights reserved.

(Check to see if other block of stock has sufficient amount at risk to absorb excess.)
(Check to see if shareholder debt has sufficient amount at risk to absorb excess.)
(Do not carry forward any excess expense to next year.) $ ________

b. Subtotal (3a – 4a) $ ________

c. Deductible expenses and losses
(Include any spillovers from other blocks of stock.)
(Include any amounts carried forward from last year.)
(Do not reduce amount at risk below zero.)
(Check to see if other block of stock has sufficient amount at risk to absorb excess.)
(Check to see if shareholder debt has sufficient amount at risk to absorb excess.)
(Carry forward any excess expense to next year.) $ ________

d. Subtotal (4b – 4c)
(CAUTION: If prior or current election to reduce for deductible expenses under Regulations §1.1367-1(f) is not in effect, skip line 4e and go directly to line 4f.) $ ________

e. Nondeductible expenses, not capitalized
(Include any spillovers from other blocks of stock.)
(Include any amounts carried forward from last year.)
(Do not reduce amount at risk below zero.)
(Check to see if other block of stock has sufficient amount at risk to absorb excess.)
(Check to see if shareholder debt has sufficient amount at risk to absorb excess.)
(Carry forward any excess expense to next year.) $ ________

f. Subtotal (4d – 4e)
Distributions received by shareholder during year
(Do not include any dividend from earnings and profits or deemed dividend.)
(Do not reduce amount at risk below zero: If distributions exceed amount at risk, check to see if other block of stock has sufficient amount at risk to absorb excess.) $ ________

g. Refinancing of amount at risk by nonrecourse debt $ ________

5. Ending amount at risk (4f – 4g – 4h) $ ________

10

Worksheet 10 - 2: Debt amount at risk

Keep a separate worksheet for each note.

If the corporation has terminated a year under §1377(a)(2) or Regulations §1.1368-1(g), complete separate worksheet for each portion of the year.

Copyright © 2000 by Harcourt, Inc. All rights reserved.

1. Amount at risk at beginning of year, or at loan date if loaned during year $ ________
2. Additions to amount at risk
(CAUTION: Limit to extent of prior reductions.) (If debt amount at risk has never been reduced, skip to line 3.) ________
   a. Add all taxable items from shareholder's K-1
   (to the extent allocated to this block) $ ________
   b. Add all tax-exempt income
   (CAUTION: If including corporate cancellation of debt income, review current IRS position and consider disclosure.)
   See discussion at 610.68. $ ________
   c. Less distributions received by shareholder during year
   (Do not include any dividend from earnings and profits or deemed dividend.), limit to 2a + 2b $ ________
3. Subtotal (1 + 2a + 2b – 2c) $ ________
4. Reductions of amount at risk
(CAUTION: Determine if prior or current election to reduce for deductible expenses under Regulations §1.1367-1(f) is in effect. If such election is in effect, skip line 4a and go directly to line 4c.) ________
   a. Nondeductible expenses, not capitalized
   (to extent expenses exceed amount at risk of stock)
   (Do not reduce amount at risk below zero.)
   (Do not carry forward any excess expense to next year.) $ ________
   b. Subtotal (3 – 4a) $ ________
   c. Deductible expenses and losses
   (to extent expenses exceed amount at risk of stock)
   (Include any amounts carried forward from last year.)
   (Do not reduce amount at risk below zero.)
   (Carry forward any excess expense to next year.) $ ________
   d. Subtotal (4b – 4c)
   (CAUTION: If prior or current election to reduce for deductible expenses under Regulations §1.1367-1(f) is not in effect, skip line 4e and go directly to line 4f.) $ ________
   e. Nondeductible expenses, not capitalized
   (to extent expenses exceed amount at risk of stock)
   (Include any amounts carried forward from last year.)
   (Do not reduce amount at risk below zero.)
   (Carry forward any excess expense to next year.) $ ________
   f. Subtotal (4d – 4e) $ ________
   g. Partial repayments received by shareholder during year $ ________
5. Ending amount at risk (4f – 4g) $ ________

10

Copyright © 2000 by Harcourt, Inc. All rights reserved.

Worksheet 10 - 3: Loss limits and carryovers

Description	*Beginning of year*	*End of year*
Casualty loss on rental or business property		
Basis limit carryforward	________	________
At-risk limit carryforward	________	________
Other shareholder limits (list)	________	________
Capital loss on rental or business property		
Basis limit carryforward	________	________
At-risk limit carryforward	________	________
Passive activity loss limit carryforward	________	________
Other shareholder limits (list)	________	________
§1231 loss on rental or business property		
Basis limit carryforward	________	________
At-risk limit carryforward	________	________
Passive activity loss limit carryforward	________	________
Other shareholder limits (list)	________	________
Investment interest		
Basis limit carryforward	________	________
At-risk limit carryforward	________	________
Investment income carryforward	________	________
Other itemized deductions		
Basis limit carryforward	________	________
At-risk limit carryforward	________	________
Passive activity loss limit carryforward	________	________
Other shareholder limits (list)	________	________
______________________________		
______________________________		
______________________________		
Charitable contributions		
AGI limit carryforward	________	________

10

Copyright © 2000 by Harcourt, Inc. All rights reserved.

Part III

Corporate-Level Taxes and Termination

TAXES ON PROPERTY DISPOSITIONS

Contents

11

1100. Overview.

An S corporation is generally exempt from any form of the income tax. This rule is stated in §1363(a). However, there is a caveat that Subchapter S may provide exceptions. The most important of these exceptions is the built-in gains tax.

SUMMARY OF AUTHORITY: CODE SECTION 1363(a)

- The term *this chapter* means Chapter 1 of Subtitle A of the Internal Revenue Code of 1986.
- Chapter 1 contains Sections 1 through 1399.
- Chapter 1 imposes the regular corporate income tax, the alternative minimum tax, the environmental income tax, the personal holding company tax, and the accumulated earnings tax.
- The phrase "except as otherwise provided in this subchapter" gives exclusive authority to Subchapter S to impose corporate-level taxes on S corporations.
- The term *this subchapter* means Subchapter S, which contains only Sections 1361 through 1379.

The taxes avoided by the S election include the regular corporate income tax of §11, the corporate alternative minimum tax, the taxes on personal holding companies, and the accumulated earnings tax.

A corporation that made an S election at its inception is exempt from these taxes under most circumstances. S corporations that were former C corporations may be subject to certain other taxes, intended to lock in at least some of the double tax that the corporation would have paid if it had remained a C corporation. There are five forms of tax listed directly in Subchapter S. These taxes meet the exception provided for in §1363(a).

1. The *built-in gains tax* [§1374], enacted by the Tax Reform Act of 1986, is particularly troublesome, because it may affect an S corporation for at least 10 years after its S election takes effect. The built-in gains tax is the most complicated tax imposed on S corporations. Part of its complexity, however, consists of legitimate opportunities to minimize its impact. This tax is the principal topic of this chapter.
2. The *LIFO recapture tax* is imposed on the corporation in its last year as a C corporation, although it is payable during the period of the S election. [§1363(d)] See Chapter 3, at 320., for a discussion of the LIFO recapture tax.
3. The *passive investment income tax* is an extremely important issue, but probably affects very few S corporations. [§1375] Chapter 12 discusses passive investment income and its related problems.
4. The *capital gains tax* [§1374, as in effect before the Tax Reform Act of 1986, with limited transitional effect for years after 1986] is gradually disappearing from the law, but it manages to stay alive through some transitional rules. It is discussed briefly in this chapter under transitional rules.
5. An S corporation is usually exempt from the *investment tax credit recapture tax*, although some S corporations may have some recapture tax liability. [§1371(d)] The investment tax credit recapture tax is rapidly diminishing in importance. It is discussed briefly in this chapter under transitional rules.

1110. Background.

One of the major thrusts of the Tax Reform Act of 1986 was the repeal of the "General Utilities" rule. [From *General Utilities & Operating Co. v. Helvering*, 36-1 USTC 9012] Under the General Utilities doctrine, a corporation recognized no gain or loss on the distribution of property to its shareholders. By the mid-1980s the doctrine had eroded significantly, so that it no longer applied to most distributions, except in the case of a complete liquidation.[1] [§§336 and 337, as in effect before the Tax Reform Act of 1986] The major thrust of the rule was to exempt capital gains, §1231 gains, and gains on inventory[2] from recognition at the corporate level. A shareholder receiving property in liquidation would treat the transfer of property as a fully taxable sale of his or her stock. The shareholder's basis in the distributed property was its fair market value at the time of receipt.[3] [§331, §334(a)] The principal impact of the General Utilities rule was the avoidance of the corporate double tax on a liquidating distribution.

The corporate liquidation rules, which apply to both C corporations and S corporations, receive detailed discussion in Chapter 15, at 1525. The examples in this chapter are extremely simplified and are used only to illustrate the purpose of the built-in gains tax.

> **EXAMPLE 11 - 1:** Darco was a C corporation that was liquidated in 1986. The fair market value of Darco's assets at the date of liquidation was $10,000,000, and its adjusted basis in those assets was $4,000,000. None of the difference between the fair market value and the adjusted basis was due to depreciation recapture, LIFO inventories, or other types of gain that it would be required to report under the rules then in effect. Darco had one shareholder, Darrell, who had a basis of $3,500,000 in his stock. On liquidation, Darco would report no taxable gain or loss. Darrell would report $6,500,000 of capital gain and take a basis of $10,000,000 in the assets received from Darco.

The Tax Reform Act of 1986 extended the double taxation of C corporations to liquidating sales and distributions. Under the new law, a corporation recognizes gains and losses on distributions of property in complete liquidation. [§336(a)]

> **EXAMPLE 11 - 2:** Assume the same facts as in Example 11 - 1, except that Darco was liquidated in 1987. Under post-1986 law, Darco would recognize $6,000,000 of gain, resulting in a corporate-level tax. Darrell's recognized gain would be reduced by the tax on Darco.

11

If Congress had not added the built-in gains tax to the law, many corporations could have avoided the double tax on liquidation by making an S election. There was already a capital gains tax imposed on S corporations, but it was limited in scope.

> **EXAMPLE 11 - 3:** Refer to Examples 11 - 1 and 11 - 2. Assume that all of the difference between Darco's basis in its property and the fair market value was due to appreciation in inventory and that Darco did not use LIFO. Assume that Congress had not enacted the built-in gains tax for S corporations. If Darco was not liquidated in 1986, filed an S election that took effect in 1987, and then liquidated when the S election was in effect, all of Darco's gain would have passed through to Darrell. Darrell would be liable for income tax on Darco's gain, under the general rules of Subchapter S. The gain flowing through from Darco, however, would allow Darrell to increase the basis in his stock and would reduce the capital gain Darrell would report on the liquidating distribution.

Congress anticipated the planning strategy illustrated in Example 11 - 3. Accordingly, it replaced the old capital gains tax with a tax on built-in gains. In general, this tax is intended to approximate the double tax that would be imposed on a corporation that distributes its property in liquidation.

> **EXAMPLE 11 - 4:** Refer to Example 11 - 3. Darco's gain realized on the distribution of all its property in complete liquidation would be subject to the built-in gains tax. This tax, which

---

[1] Depreciation recapture, installment gains, and some other items produced taxable gains before the 1986 repeal.

[2] After 1980, liquidating corporations were required to recapture LIFO reserves. There was no income to the corporation from a distribution in complete liquidation of any inventory for which the corporation did not use LIFO.

[3] Generally, the tax treatment of a shareholder receiving property in a corporate liquidation was not amended by the Tax Reform Act of 1986. There was a provision whereby shareholders could limit gain recognition in a one-month liquidation under §333. This provision was repealed by the Tax Reform Act of 1986.

is imposed directly on the S corporation, would give both Darco and Darrell approximately the same tax treatment as if Darco had never become an S corporation. The results would be the same as those illustrated in Example 11 - 2.

Although the built-in gains tax was enacted as part of the revised liquidation rules, it applies to many more situations than corporate liquidations. It applies to sales and other transactions in the ordinary course of an S corporation's business, as well as distributions of property to shareholders in nonliquidating transactions.

The IRS has considerable power to issue Regulations interpreting the built-in gains tax. Legislative Regulations are authorized in §1374(c)(1), §1374(d)(8)(A), and §1374(e). There is also a broad grant of regulatory authority in §337(d), which states that the IRS shall have the power to issue Regulations interpreting Subtitle D of Title IV of the Tax Reform Act of 1986. That subtitle contains the new corporate liquidation rules and the built-in gains tax for S corporations. Therefore, if there are any challenges to Regulations, those Regulations should have extremely strong legislative support.

SUMMARY OF AUTHORITY: CODE SECTION 1374(e)

- The IRS has broad regulatory authority in enforcement of the built-in gains tax.

1110.1. Impact of the built-in gains tax. The built-in gains tax forces immediate recognition of the double tax on certain items of an S corporation's income. The tax on built-in gains is imposed at the highest rate specified for corporations (currently 35%). [§1374(b)(1)]

Each S corporation must properly compute its built-in gains tax, then recalculate its taxable income for allocation to the shareholders. In addition, each S corporation that is subject to the built-in gains tax must recalculate its net unrealized built-in gain at the end of each year. The overall structure is shown in Figure 11 - 1.

The built-in gains tax applies primarily to former C corporations. In limited instances, this tax can be imposed on S corporations that have never been C corporations but have acquired the property of a C corporation in a tax-free reorganization. See the discussion of this rule at 1140.2., below.

11

In some cases, the built-in gains tax can make electing S status more costly than remaining a C corporation. Example 11 - 5 presents an extremely simplified set of facts to illustrate the economic impact of this tax.

EXAMPLE 11 - 5: In 1999, the highest marginal rate of tax imposed on individuals is 39.6%, and the highest rate on corporations is 35%. No changes in the marginal rates are expected. GHI Corporation is a C corporation that is eligible to make an S election. GHI anticipates taxable income of $500,000 per year. As this chapter will demonstrate, there is a presumption that all income recognized within the first 10 years of an S election is taxable as a recognized built-in gain. This presumption may be rebutted in most circumstances, but assume that GHI is not able to rebut the presumption. The corporation does not believe it could safely avoid the corporate income tax by making compensation or other deductible payments to its shareholders. If it were to make an S election, all of its first 10 years of taxable income would be subject to the built-in gains tax. Its shareholders are all individuals in the 39.6% tax bracket. As an S corporation, GHI could anticipate, for each of the next 10 years, tax liability of:

	Income	*Tax*
Corporation's income	$500,000	
Corporation's tax at 35%		$175,000
Deduction at corporate level	(175,000)	
Income passing through to shareholders	$325,000	
Shareholders' tax at 39.6%		128,700
Total corporation and shareholder tax		$303,700

11

Figure 11 - 1: Overview of the built-in gains tax structure.

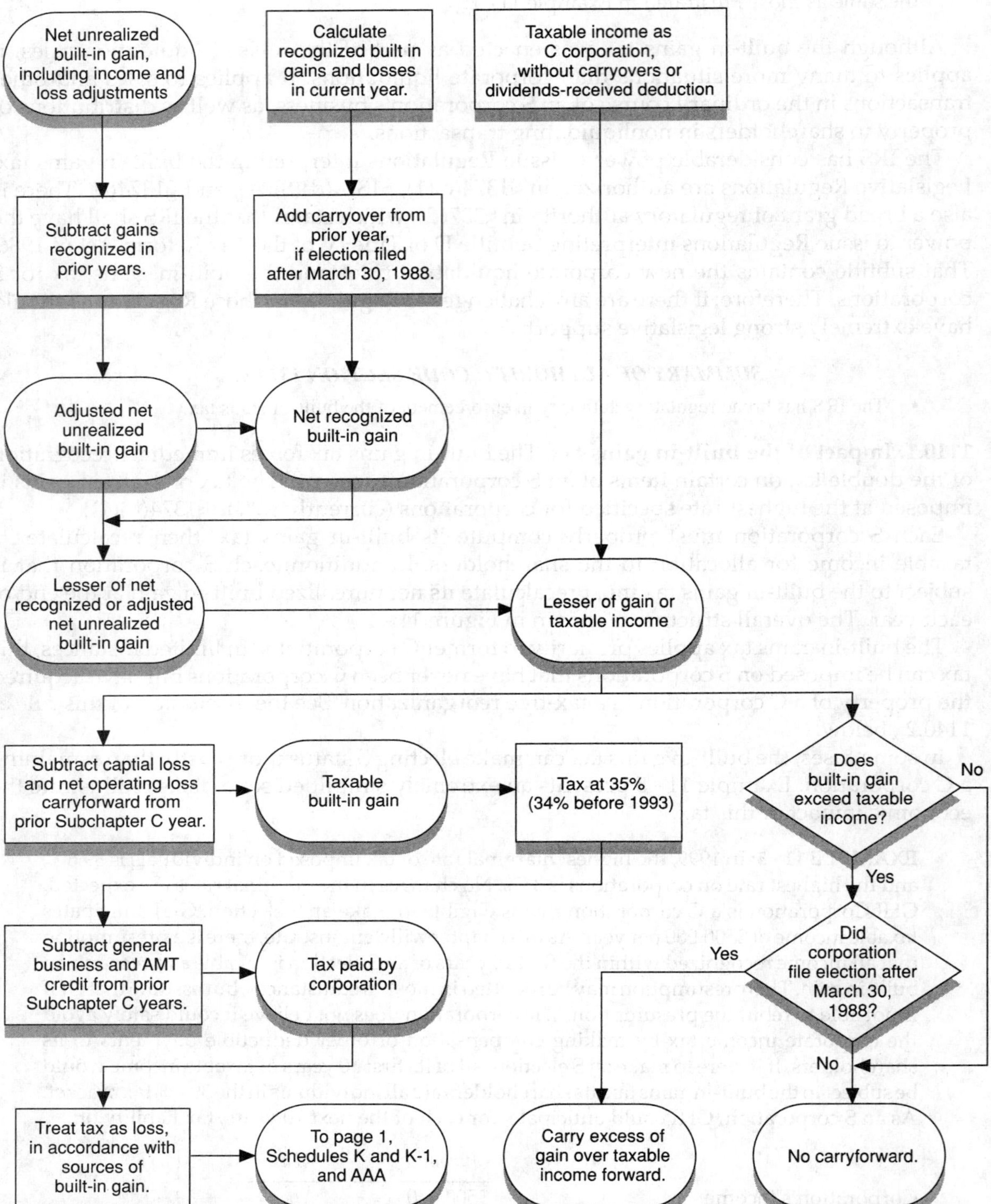

If GHI were to remain a C corporation, the annual income tax would be only $170,000 using the rate schedule of §11. Accordingly, it appears that GHI would be ill-advised to make an S election. Additional considerations, however, might mitigate in favor of an S election:

- The corporation may be facing imposition of the accumulated earnings tax or the personal holding company tax, in which case it would be subject to double taxation as a C corporation. Either of these taxes, imposed at a 39.6% rate, would make remaining a C corporation as expensive as becoming an S corporation and paying the built-in gains tax.
- The shareholders might intend to withdraw a significant portion of the corporation's income. If the corporation remained a C corporation, these distributions would be taxable as dividends, with no corresponding deduction to the corporation. The double tax on dividends from a C corporation would approximate the results shown above.
- The corporation might be subject to the alternative minimum tax, due to significant adjusted current earnings. An S election would eliminate this tax at the corporate level and would not impose a similar tax on the shareholders.
- The corporation may be anticipating profitable operations in the future, which would be subject to built-in gains tax only on gains that had economically accrued at the time the S election took effect. Activities that commenced after the S election took effect would be exempt from the built-in gains tax; if the corporation remained a C corporation it would still be subject to the double tax.

1110.2. General applicability limited to former C corporations. It is important at this point to understand that the tax applies only to S corporations that recognize certain gains after the S election takes effect. As was discussed in Chapter 3, the LIFO recapture tax becomes a liability at the time the corporation makes its S election. The built-in gains tax, by contrast, is not an immediate liability. It is only a potential liability at the time the S election takes effect.

SUMMARY OF AUTHORITY: CODE SECTION 1374(c)(1)

- The built-in gains tax does not apply to a corporation if it has always been an S corporation.
- The tax history of certain predecessor corporations must be taken into account.

11

A predecessor corporation may include a corporation that has been absorbed in a tax-free reorganization or liquidation. (See discussion at 1140.2., below.) Generally, however, a corporation that has always had an S election in effect is completely exempt from the built-in gains tax.

1110.3. Effective dates. The tax on built-in gains is applicable to a corporation that filed its S election after 1986. [§1374] Some special transitional rules apply to other corporations. There are limited exceptions for corporations that filed elections between January 1, 1987, and December 31, 1988. See discussion at 1160.2., below, for discussion of the transitional rules. It is the filing date, rather than the effective date, of the S election that governs the applicability of the built-in gains tax. The tax applies only to corporate years beginning after 1986.

EXAMPLE 11 - 6: XYZ Corporation filed Form 2553 on January 2, 1987. The election took effect for the corporation's fiscal year beginning November 1, 1986. The corporation retained its October year-end. XYZ is exempt from the built-in gains tax for its first fiscal year as an S corporation, since that year began before 1987. It is subject to the built-in gains tax for its next nine years, since it filed its S election after 1986.

EXAMPLE 11 - 7: ABC Corporation filed Form 2553 on December 30, 1986. The election took effect in the corporation's taxable year beginning December 1, 1987. ABC is exempt from the built-in gains tax, since it filed its S election before 1987.

In December 1992, the IRS issued Proposed Regulations that interpret some of the problems of the built-in gains tax. These Proposed Regulations were issued as Final Regulations, with

TABLE 11 - 1: Effective Dates of Built-In Gains Tax Rules

Date of election or transaction	*Rules*
Filed election before 1987	Not subject to tax, unless party to reorganization or other tax-free acquisition.
Filed election after 1986, before 1989	Not subject to tax on capital gains or §1231 gains, if qualified for transitional relief, unless party to reorganization or other tax-free acquisition. If not subject to transitional relief, then subject to the general rules of §1374 and legislative history thereof, but not to most provisions of the §1374 Regulations. Not subject to the built-in gain carryover.
Filed election before March 31, 1988	Not subject to built-in gain carryforward.
Filed election after 1988, before 12/28/94	Subject to the general rules of §1374 and legislative history thereof, but not to most provisions of the §1374 Regulations.
Installment sale before 3/26/90	Not subject to extended recognition period on installment gain.
Filed election after 12/27/94	Subject to all rules of new Regulations.
Acquired property in tax-free reorganization or liquidation after 12/27/94,	Subject to rules of new Regulations, but only on property acquired in liquidation or reorganization.

some revisions, on December 27, 1994. They are cited in the text and examples in this chapter. The Regulations cover limited aspects of the law. Their general effective date is for years beginning after December 27, 1994, but only when the corporation filed its S election after December 27, 1994. [Regs. §1.1374-10(a)] The rules contained in the Final Regulations also apply to property received in a tax-free reorganization or liquidation when the transaction occurs after December 27, 1994. See discussion of these transactions at 1140.2. Table 11 - 1 illustrates the general effective dates of the code, legislative history, and regulations.

TABLE 11 - 2: Effective Dates of Special Rules in the Built-In Gains Tax Regulations

Date	*Transaction*
Election after 12/27/94	All rules
Assets acquired in carryover basis transaction from C corporation after 12/27/94	All rules applicable to assets acquired in transaction.
1/1/87	Property transferred by the corporation to a partnership with the intent to avoid the built-in gains tax on the disposition of the asset is disregarded. [Regs. §1.1374-10(b)(1)]
1/1/87	The amount of built-in gain on disposition of inventory is determined by reference to the inventory method used by the corporation. [Regs. §1.1374-10(b)(2)]
1/1/87	The IRS can disregard the effect of any asset that was contributed to the corporation in order to reduce net unrealized built-in gain. [Regs. §1.1374-10(b)(3)]
After March 26, 1990	Any built-in gain recognized on an installment sale is subject to the built-in gains tax, regardless of the recognition period. [Regs. §1.1374-10(b)(4)]

Although the Regulations are incomplete and will not affect most corporations that currently have S elections in effect, it is important to understand the legislative history of this tax. Such understanding will allow the tax professional to take positions on tax returns that produce the least possible tax liability, without running afoul of any authoritative pronouncement, in areas that are not covered by the Regulations. There *are* exceptions to the general effective date, which are discussed in context at various places in this chapter. [Regs. §1.1374-10(b)] Table 11 - 2 illustrates the significant effective dates in the Regulations.

1110.4. Key terms. There are several terms relating to the built-in gains tax for which it is necessary to understand the precise meaning. For some of these, the statute is reasonably clear; others need considerable discussion. Table 11 - 3 provides a brief overview of the terms. Although the Final Regulations generally do not apply to most S corporations, they give some useful terminology; accordingly, Table 11 - 3 includes terminology from these Regulations.

1115. Recognition period.

The *recognition period* is the time span for which the built-in gains tax applies to an S corporation. In general, the recognition period consists of the first 10 years that the corporation has an S election in effect.

TABLE 11 - 3: Key Terms Used in the Built-In Gains Tax

Term	*Definition*	*Cite*
Recognition period	Ten years including the date the S election takes effect	§1374(d)(7)
Recognized built-in gain	Presumed, all income items in recognition period. All gains and income attributable to time before S election took effect	§1374(d)(3), §1374(d)(5)(A)
Recognized built-in loss	Presumed, no losses or deductions. Losses and deductions attributable to time before S election took effect	§1374(d)(4), §1374(d)(5)(B)
Net unrealized built-in gain	Net gain that corporation would have recognized if it disposed of all property and liquidated on date S election took effect	§1374(d)(1), §1374(d)(5)(C)
Net recognized built-in gain	Recognized built-in gains less recognized built-in losses in a taxable year in the recognition period	§1374(d)(2)
Net recognized built-in gain must be calculated in three ways, defined in the Regulations as follows:		
Pre-limitation amount	Taxable income of the corporation, including only recognized built-in gains and losses	Regulations §1.1374-2(a)(1)
Taxable income limitation	Taxable income of the corporation, including all income and deductions	Regulations §1.1374-2(a)(2)
Net unrealized built-in gain limitation	Net unrealized built-in gain of the corporation, reduced by net recognized built-in gain in all prior years	Regulations §1.1374-2(a)(3)

SUMMARY OF AUTHORITY: CODE SECTION 1374(d)(7)

- The recognition period begins on the day the S election takes effect.
- The recognition period is exactly 10 years.

1115.1. Ten-year horizon. The definition uses the term *10-year period* and does not state 10 specific taxable years. Therefore, the recognition period cannot be reduced by using short years.

EXAMPLE 11 - 8: A C corporation that has been using a June 30 fiscal year makes an S election for its taxable year beginning July 1, 1991. For its first year as an S corporation, it makes a §444 election to use a September 30 year. (See Chapter 4.) Immediately after calendar year 1992, it terminates its §444 election and files a short-year return for October through December 1992. These two short years have no impact on the corporation's recognition period, which would be as follows:

1. Short year ended September 30, 1991
2. Full year ended September 30, 1992
3. Short year ended December 31, 1992
4. Full year ended December 31, 1993
5. Full year ended December 31, 1994
6. Full year ended December 31, 1995
7. Full year ended December 31, 1996
8. Full year ended December 31, 1997
9. Full year ended December 31, 1998
10. Full year ended December 31, 1999
11. Full year ended December 31, 2000
12. First six months of year ended December 31, 2001

11 When the final year of the recognition period does not correspond with the end of the corporation's taxable year, the corporation must have an interim closing. Items occurring on or before the closing date will be subject to the built-in gains tax, whereas those following the closing will not. [Regs. §1.1374-1(d)]

EXAMPLE 11 - 9: Cajco was a C corporation that used a June 30 fiscal year. It became an S corporation for its taxable year beginning July 1, 1992, and changed to the calendar year immediately. Thus, its first taxable year as an S corporation began on July 1, 1992, and ended on December 31, 1992. Cajco's recognition period will end on June 30, 2002. It must divide its 2002 taxable year into two portions. The first portion, ending June 30, 2002, will be subject to the built-in gains tax, and Cajco must compute its net recognized built-in gain for that period. Nothing that occurs after June 30, 2002, will be subject to the built-in gains tax.

1115.11. New S elections. The recognition period runs through a continuous S election. If a corporation makes an S election, revokes an S election, and makes another S election, it will have a new recognition period.

SUMMARY OF AUTHORITY: CODE SECTION 1374(d)(9)

- The most important reference to the first taxable year for which a corporation was an S corporation is the determination of the recognition period.
- An S corporation that has made and terminated one or more S elections in the past determines its recognition period from the effective date of its most recent S election.

EXAMPLE 11 - 10: A corporation makes an S election that takes effect on January 1, 1993. It terminates its S election in 1995. In 1996, new shareholders purchase all of the corporation's stock, and they request permission to make a new S election for the 1996 taxable year. The IRS grants permission for the new election, which takes effect on January 1, 1996.[4] The corporation's recognition period would begin on January 1, 1996, and end on December 31, 2005.

1115.12. Effect of inadvertent termination. If an S corporation inadvertently terminates its S election, it may apply for relief under §1362(f). The IRS generally grants these requests and treats the corporation as if its S election had been continuously in effect. (See Chapter 13, at 1350., for discussion of the inadvertent termination relief rules and procedures.) When an S corporation is granted inadvertent termination relief, there is no new recognition period. The general applicability of the built-in gains tax should be governed by the date the corporation filed its S election, rather than the date that it was approved for inadvertent termination relief.

> **EXAMPLE 11 - 11:** A former C corporation inadvertently terminated its S election by issuing shares to an ineligible trust on April 17, 1995. Upon discovery of the error, it redeemed the shares and applied for inadvertent termination relief. The IRS granted relief on May 7, 1996. The IRS treats the corporation as if it had been an S corporation from April 17, 1995, through May 7, 1996.
>
> If the corporation had filed its S election before 1987, it would be exempt from the built-in gains tax. If it had filed its S election after 1986, it would be subject to the built-in gains tax (possibly subject to the transitional rules discussed below), but only from the date that its S election first took effect, not from April 17, 1995, or May 7, 1996.

1115.2. Effect of liquidation, reorganization, or QSub conversion. If a corporation with an S election in place acquires assets from a C corporation in a tax-free reorganization or liquidation, the date of the reorganization starts a new recognition period for the assets acquired in the transaction. See at 1140.2. for further discussion. Under general tax rules, the conversion of an existing C corporation to a QSub will constitute a tax-free liquidation. See Chapter 14, at 1435.42, for discussion of this problem.

1115.21. Separate recognition periods. When an S corporation acquires another S corporation in a tax-free reorganization or liquidation, the recognition period may become quite complicated. For example, in one ruling, an S corporation acquired two other S corporations and two C corporations in simultaneous mergers. The surviving corporation had filed its election before 1987 and was not subject to the built-in gains tax on any of its assets. The two extinguished S corporations had filed S elections in 1987, but were not entitled to transitional relief, discussed at 1160.2., below.[5] The ruling held that the surviving corporation was subject to the built-in gains tax on the assets that the extinguished S corporations possessed on the dates the S elections took effect, for the 10-year periods following the merged corporations' S elections.

In some complicated transactions, the corporation surviving a reorganization can end up with several different recognition periods. Letter Ruling 9117055 provides the most inclusive example to date of the applicability of §1374 to merged corporations. In that ruling an S corporation acquired two other S corporations and two C corporations in simultaneous mergers. The extinguished S corporations had filed their S elections after 1986 and were subject to the built-in gains tax. The surviving corporation had filed its election before 1987 and was not subject to the built-in gains tax on any of its assets. The ruling held that the built-in gains tax would apply as follows:

---

[4] The IRS generally grants permission to make a new S election before the five-year statutory waiting period specified in §1362(g) if there has been a change in ownership of more than 50% of the shares since the corporation terminated its prior election. See Chapter 5 for more complete discussion.

[5] The letter ruling does not state why the corporations were not entitled to transitional relief. As is discussed at 1160.23., below, there was a net worth test and an ownership test. The merged corporations might have failed to meet these criteria.

11

Assets Covered	*Extent Subject to Tax*
Owned by surviving corporation prior to reorganization	Not subject to tax
Owned by either C corporation	Subject to tax for 10 years following reorganization, to the extent of each C corporation's net unrealized built-in gain
Owned by extinguished S corporations on date old S elections took effect	Subject to tax, for 10 years following extinguished corporation's S election, limited to each extinguished S corporation's net unrealized built-in gain
Acquired by extinguished S corporations after S elections took effect	Not subject to tax

1115.22. Divisive reorganizations. The IRS has also ruled that an S corporation that emerges from a divisive reorganization retains the same recognition period of the corporation that existed prior to the reorganization. See Chapter 17, at 1735.25. for further discussion and citations.

1115.23. Type F reorganizations. In some cases, such as a Type F reorganization, the new corporation and the old corporation are treated as one tax entity. The IRS has ruled that the recognition period of the new corporation includes the recognition period of the old corporation. [PLR 9309031]

> **EXAMPLE 11 - 12:** Cayco, a California corporation, was a C corporation. Cayco elected S status for its taxable year beginning January 1, 1993. On July 29, 1995, Cayco reorganized as a Nevada corporation in a Type F reorganization. The recognition period of the new Cayco would continue through December 31, 2002.

1115.3. Special rules for installment sales. If a corporation sells built-in gain property within the recognition period (or had sold the property before it became an S corporation) and uses the installment method, there is no expiration of the recognition period for any built-in gain on that sale. To comply with these rules, the corporation must calculate the gain that would have been subject to the built-in gains tax if the corporation had elected out of the installment method. The tax will continue to be imposed on the installment receipts, even though they occur after the recognition period normally would end. [Regs. §1.1374-4(h)]

Long before the issuance of Regulations in this area, the IRS announced that it would treat installment gains resulting from the sale of built-in gain property as recognized built-in gains, even if the installments were collected beyond the normal end of the recognition period. [Notice 90-27, 1990-1 CB 336] This rule applied to all installment gains from sales completed after March 26, 1990. The Final Regulations issued in 1994 retained this effective date. [Regs. §1.1374-10(b)(4)] This is one of the few effective dates in the new Regulations before December 27, 1994.] See further discussion at 1140.3.

1115.4. Final year of the recognition period. In general, as discussed above, a corporation's recognition period ends 10 years from the day on which the S election first takes effect. As long as the corporation maintains the same taxable year throughout the recognition period, there will be no special problems during its final year. It will simply begin its eleventh year as an S corporation free from the built-in gains tax.

1115.41. Effect of short taxable years in recognition period. Some potential interpretive problems deserve further discussion. One problem that will begin to surface in the late 1990s occurs when a single taxable year is partly within, and partly outside of, the recognition period.

EXAMPLE 11 - 13: Perco was a C corporation that used a June 30 year-end. On August 1, 1987, Perco filed an S election, which took effect on July 1, 1987. Perco's recognition period ends on June 30, 1997.

When Perco filed its S election, it changed to the calendar year. Its taxable year ending December 31, 1997, is partly within and partly beyond its recognition period.

In a year that bridges the end of a corporation's recognition period, the corporation must take care to segregate any recognized built-in gains that occur before the end of the recognition period from those that occur thereafter. The Regulations provide that the corporation must close its books at the end of any recognition period that does not coincide with the end of the corporation's taxable year. [Regs. §1.1374-1(d)]

The recognition period may also be affected by receipt of property in a tax-free reorganization. For assets received in such a transaction, the recognition period begins on the date of the reorganization. This situation will require the maintenance of separate asset ledgers.

EXAMPLE 11 - 14: Surco was a C corporation through 1989. Its S election took effect for its taxable year beginning January 1, 1991. On July 1, 1993, Surco acquired all of the assets of Exco, a C corporation, in a tax-free reorganization. Surco will have two recognition periods, as follows:

Assets Covered	*Recognition Period Expires*
Owned on January 1, 1991	December 31, 2000
Acquired from Exco	June 30, 2003

1115.42. S termination year problems. An S corporation that terminates its S election within the recognition period will simultaneously terminate its recognition period. See Chapter 13, at 1335., for discussion of the accounting rules applicable to the S termination year. The IRS has issued a Field Service Advice (FSA) in which it instructed its agents to pay special attention to income that should be taxable as built-in gains in the S termination year. [FSA 1999-685]

11

1120. Net unrealized built-in gain.

Net unrealized built-in gain may be an important limitation on the built-in gains tax. If an S corporation can conclusively demonstrate its calculation of net unrealized built-in gain, this amount will serve as the cap on all taxable built-in gains during the recognition period. If a corporation can conclusively demonstrate that its net unrealized built-in gain is zero, or negative, at the time of conversion to S status, it will completely avoid any built-in gains tax.

1120.1. Significance of unrealized built-in gain. The principal importance of net unrealized built-in gain is that it acts as a limit on the total amount of built-in gains that will be subject to tax in the recognition period. As explained at 1135.2., the net unrealized built-in gain limitation is adjusted annually to reflect the corporation's net recognized built-in gain. The following brief example illustrates the importance of net unrealized built-in gain.

EXAMPLE 11 - 15: A corporation filed its S election in 1997. As of the first day of its 1997 taxable year, it had net unrealized built-in gains of $250,000. During its 1997 taxable year, it had net recognized built-in gains of $45,000. In 1997, the corporation's net unrealized built-in gain exceeded its recognized built-in gain. Therefore, its net recognized built-in gain would be $45,000. At the beginning of 1998, the corporation's adjusted net unrealized built-in gain would be:

Net unrealized built-in gain on 1/1/97	$250,000
Less gain recognized in 1997	(45,000)
Net unrealized built-in gain on 1/1/98	$205,000

In 1998, the corporation had net recognized built-in gains of $250,000. It would limit its net recognized built-in gain to its net unrealized built-in gain of $205,000. The corporation would be exempt from the built-in gains tax in all future years.

In many cases, S corporations will be able to control the level of built-in gains tax imposed in the recognition period without relying on net unrealized built-in gain. This situation could arise when a corporation believes that its net unrealized built-in gain is considerably higher than all of the built-in gains it will recognize during its recognition period.

EXAMPLE 11 - 16: Mapco was a C corporation through 1995 and elected S status for its taxable year beginning January 1, 1996. It owns some highly appreciated real estate, has developed some successful patents, and has considerable goodwill. The shareholders believe they could sell the corporation for $50,000,000, plus the assumption of all of the corporation's debts. The adjusted basis of the corporation's assets is only $5,000,000, so Mapco's net unrealized built-in gain is $45,000,000. The only property on-hand that Mapco actually plans to sell, however, is one asset that has a fair market value of $6,000,000 and adjusted basis of $3,500,000. Mapco sells that asset in 1996 and has a net recognized built-in gain of $2,500,000 for that year.

Mapco's net unrealized built-in gain far exceeds its recognized built-in gain for 1996, and it offers no possibility for reducing the built-in gains tax. For the remainder of its recognition period, however, Mapco is able to demonstrate conclusively that all its recognized gains and other income items are attributable to activities that began after the S election took effect. Therefore, Mapco will be able to rebut the presumption of built-in gains on all of its future income, and it will pay no more built-in gains tax.

11 Throughout the remainder of Mapco's recognition period, its net unrealized built-in gain will remain at $42,500,000 (the original $45,000,000 less the $2,500,000 of built-in gains recognized in 1996). This high net unrealized built-in gain value will have absolutely no adverse effect on Mapco, unless it sells some of the property it actually held on January 1, 1996, during the recognition period.

OBSERVATION: A corporation that believes its net unrealized built-in gain is less than the built-in gains it expects to recognize should be extremely careful to obtain credible valuation of its assets. The corporation should also account for other items that might reduce its net unrealized built-in gain, such as unfunded deferred compensation liabilities that exist at the time its S election takes effect. When a substantial portion of the corporation's assets is subject to depressed prices, net unrealized built-in gain might be low.

Unless the net unrealized built-in gain is established by thorough documentation, including appraisals, it will be useless. The presumption that all gains are built-in gains requires effective documentation for rebuttal.

A corporation's net unrealized built-in gain is useful only if it will reduce the built-in gains tax. Therefore, a corporation with substantial appreciation in assets that it does not intend to sell may benefit very little from an accurate calculation of net unrealized built-in gain. For instance, during its recognition period, a corporation may sell only a minor portion of the total assets it had on hand when its S election took effect. Effective rebuttal of the presumption of recognized built-in gain on recognized transactions will be more effective than reliance on net unrealized built-in gain.

EXAMPLE 11 - 17: Century Corporation filed an S election on February 2, 1987, effective for its tax year beginning January 1, 1987. Since the election was filed after December 31, 1986,

Century is subject to the built-in gains tax. It will be subject to the tax on any property sold through its tax year ending December 31, 1996.

On January 1, 1987, the fair market value of its assets was $600,000. Total adjusted basis was $350,000, so Century's net unrealized built-in gain is $250,000.

Century Corporation owns some land that had a basis of $80,000 and fair market value of $125,000 on January 1, 1987. On July 1, 1987, a major corporation announces that it will build a new distribution center near the site of Century's land. On September 30, 1987, Century sells the land for $200,000, resulting in a gain of $120,000. The entire gain will be presumed to be a built-in gain, unless Century has other evidence of its January 1, 1987, value in its records.

1120.2. Definition of unrealized built-in gain. As is the case with many tax terms, the definition of *net unrealized built-in gain* requires some explanation. The general rule is given in §1374(d)(1).

SUMMARY OF AUTHORITY: CODE SECTION 1374(d)(1)

- Net unrealized built-in gain is calculated on the first day of the corporation's first year as an S corporation.
- Net unrealized built-in gain is calculated by subtracting the corporation's adjusted basis in all of its assets from their aggregate fair market value.

The term *assets* includes intangible property, such as goodwill. The valuation of a corporation's entire asset base, which is necessary for the determination of net unrealized built-in gain, may be a difficult process. An S corporation's net unrealized built-in gain approximates the net gain that it would have recognized if it had liquidated on that date.

The above definition includes only those assets that were in existence at the time the S election took effect. It does not take into account any items that would not be shown on the asset side of the balance sheet, such as unrealized payables. If the definition given in §1374(d)(1) were inclusive, it could work some hardships, especially for cash-basis taxpayers. 11

EXAMPLE 11 - 18: Merco, a cash-basis personal service corporation, was a C corporation through 1995. Its S election took effect for its taxable year beginning January 1, 1996. On January 1, 1996, its balance sheet showed the following:

	Adjusted Basis	*Fair Market Value*
Accounts receivable	$ 0	$ 80,000
Fixed assets	120,000	120,000
Total assets	$120,000	$200,000
Accounts payable	$ 0	$ 65,000

According to the definition given in §1374(d)(1), Merco would appear to have $80,000 net unrealized built-in gain, since the fair market value of its assets exceeds the adjusted basis of its assets by that amount.

1120.21. Cash-method accounting items. The Technical and Miscellaneous Revenue Act of 1988 addressed this ambiguity by adding §1374(d)(5)(C), which broadens the definition of *net unrealized built-in gain.*

SUMMARY OF AUTHORITY: CODE SECTION 1374(d)(5)(C)

- Net unrealized built-in gain is adjusted for income and deduction items not included in the measurement of the difference between fair market value and adjusted basis of assets on the date the S election takes effect.

- Net unrealized built-in gain must be increased for any item that is a potential recognized built-in gain at the date the S election takes effect.
- Net unrealized built-in gain must be decreased for any item that is a potential recognized built-in loss at the date the S election takes effect.
- If an S corporation has an unrealized loss at the time the S election takes effect, the loss need not actually be recognized during the recognition period.

EXAMPLE 11 - 19: Refer to Example 11 - 18. If and when Merco pays its accounts payable, they will be deductible and treated as recognized built-in losses. Therefore, the modification to net unrealized built-in gain pursuant to §1374(d)(5)(C) treats Merco's accounts payable as a reduction in net unrealized built-in gain. Merco's net unrealized built-in gain is $15,000, the excess of the accounts receivable over the accounts payable on January 1, 1996.

1120.22. Regulations Definition. The Regulations under §1374 give a straightforward definition of *net* unrealized built-in gain. In short, the definition is:

- The amount that would be realized if the corporation sold all of its assets at fair market value
- Less the corporation's liabilities, if they would result in a deduction when paid
- Less the adjusted basis of the corporation's assets
- Plus or minus the deferred income and deductions from changes in accounting methods under §481 [Regs. §1.1374-3(a)] (See the discussion of §481 adjustments at 1145.6.)

All of these items are to be measured as of the first day of the first S corporation year. This date is often termed the *conversion date*, or the date that a C corporation converts to S status.

11

1120.3. Initial calculation of net unrealized built-in gain. When a C corporation intends to make an S election, it should first estimate its net unrealized built-in gain. An extremely low total might save the corporation a considerable amount of taxes.

EXAMPLE 11 - 20: Virco is a corporation located in metropolitan Washington, DC. At the end of 1989, it was considering making an S election. At the time, real estate prices were substantially depressed in the area. Virco's balance sheet showed the following:

	Adjusted Basis	*Fair Market Value*
Current assets	$100,000	$180,000
Real estate	220,000	120,000
Total assets	$320,000	$300,000

Since the total fair market value of Virco's assets was less than Virco's adjusted basis in those assets, Virco had no net unrealized built-in gain.

Assume that Virco made an S election that took effect for its taxable year beginning January 1, 1992. Also assume that Virco converted its current assets in 1992, and therefore had a net recognized built-in gain of $80,000. Since Virco has no net unrealized built-in gain, however, it paid no built-in gains tax in 1992 or in any other year in its recognition period. The economic condition at the end of 1991 created ideal timing for Virco to make an S election.

CAUTION: Since the net unrealized built-in gain is calculated by reference to recognized built-in gains and losses, there is an indirect presumption that net unrealized built-in gain is practically limitless. One particular hazard that might arise in the calculation of net unrealized built-in gain is the existence of unrecorded assets. Goodwill is a special problem, since its valuation is largely subjective.

EXAMPLE 11 - 21: Refer to Example 11 - 20. An IRS audit for 1992 determined that the value of Virco's goodwill was $100,000. Accordingly, it adjusted net unrealized built-in gain as of January 1, 1992, to $80,000. The IRS assessed a built-in gains tax on Virco for the $80,000 net recognized built-in gain in 1992.

1120.31. Property subject to liabilities. Since net unrealized built-in gain must be computed in the absence of any arm's-length transaction, there are inevitable valuation problems. There is no guidance on the valuation of property subject to liabilities for determination of net unrealized built-in gain. Code §7701(g) provides that fair market value of any asset shall not be less than any nonrecourse liability to which property is subject. These rules apply to any exchange or "deemed exchange" in Subtitle A (Income Taxes, §§1–1563). It is not clear whether an S election constitutes a deemed exchange. If it does, the net unrealized built-in gain on depreciated property, such as real estate, could be measured by the liabilities, rather than the fair market value.

EXAMPLE 11 - 22: Resco Corporation makes an S election, effective January 1, 1996. On that date, Resco held real estate with a market value of $500,000 and adjusted basis of $750,000 that is subject to nonrecourse liabilities of $800,000. The actual value of the property would indicate that Resco has an unrealized built-in loss of $250,000, although the difference between the nonrecourse liability and the adjusted basis results in an unrealized built-in gain of $50,000. If the election constitutes a deemed exchange, the fair market value of the real estate is $800,000. However, since there is no express treatment of an S election as a deemed exchange, the corporation would be justified in treating the fair market value of the property as $500,000.

OBSERVATION: The election of S status by a C corporation is not treated as a taxable exchange. The Final Regulations under §1374, as well as the legislative history, make no reference to §7701(g). Therefore, at least until Regulations provide otherwise, there is no requirement that net unrealized built-in gain be measured by any amount other than a market price of property. In areas where real estate values are depressed, market values of some properties may be less than the amount of liabilities to which the properties are subject. Use of the true market value, rather than the liabilities, may help to reduce net unrealized built-in gain.

If an S corporation actually sells property subject to liabilities, and the liabilities exceed the fair market value of the property at the time of disposition, there is an actual exchange to which §7701(g) would apply. Under the general presumption, all of the gain would be treated as a built-in gain. The actual wording of the statute allows a taxpayer to rebut the built-in gain characteristic by demonstrating that a recognized gain exceeds the fair market value minus the adjusted basis of the property on the date the S election took effect. [§1374(d)(3)(B)] See at 1125.11.

EXAMPLE 11 - 23: Refer to Example 11 - 22. In 1993, Resco sells the property. The buyer assumes the liabilities and gives Resco no other consideration. At the time of sale, the liabilities are $780,000 and the property's basis is $720,000. The gain recognized on the sale is $60,000.

Resco should attempt to treat the gain as other than a built-in gain. By following the language of the statute, it should be able to demonstrate that the property's fair market value was less than its adjusted basis on the date the S election took effect.

If the IRS (possibly pursuant to Regulations not issued at the time of this writing) should assert that §7701(g) was the proper measure of fair market value at the date of the S election, Resco has a secondary argument. If the property had been sold on January 1, 1996, the gain would have been $50,000. That amount is the maximum gain that could be a built-in gain on that particular property. The Regulations under §1374 are silent on this problem.

1120.32. Capital and other assets. In measuring net *unrealized* built-in gain, there is no requirement to separate capital assets from ordinary assets. Therefore, a capital loss may offset ordinary gains, even though there would be no offset on an actual sale of those properties.

EXAMPLE 11 - 24: JTCO, a former C corporation, has the following assets on the date its S election becomes effective:

	Adjusted Basis	*Fair Market Value*
Ordinary assets	$450,000	$600,000
Capital assets	375,000	210,000
Total	$825,000	$810,000

Since the corporation's basis exceeds the fair market value of all of its assets, the corporation has no net unrealized built-in gain, even though the corporation would not be able to offset the ordinary income from the sale of its ordinary assets with the loss on its capital assets.

In its first year as an S corporation, JTCO sells all of the ordinary assets it owned when its S election took effect. Its recognized built-in gain is $150,000. However, its net recognized built-in gain is limited to its net unrealized built-in gain of zero. JTCO would pay no built-in gains tax in this year, or in any other year during the recognition period.

11

1120.33. Accruals to related parties. According to the Regulations, certain accruals to related parties, as well as payments under nonqualified deferred compensation arrangements, may not be treated as recognized built-in losses unless they are paid within 2 months and 15 days after the beginning of the first S year. [Regs. §1.1374-4(c)(1)] See at 1125.19. for comprehensive discussion of this topic as it relates to net *recognized* built-in gains. However, there is no express treatment of these items for *unrealized* built-in gain. Therefore, the corporation should be able to use the general rule that includes all potential deductions as reductions of unrealized built-in gain if they would be recognized during the recognition period. [§1374(d)(5)(C)]

1120.34. State and local taxes. For a cash-method corporation, state and local income taxes that would be imposed on any recognized built-in gains should be allowed as deductions in arriving at net unrealized built-in gain. As is discussed at 1120.2., this computation begins with the comparison of asset values and basis on the conversion date. It is also adjusted for any income or losses that are treated as recognized built-in gains and losses under §1374(d)(5). [§1374(d)(5)(C)]

Undoubtedly, many corporations that qualify for S status do not have audited financial statements. Consequently, they may overlook some financial accounting rules, especially if all parties that receive the reports are satisfied with cash-basis financial statements. All corporations contemplating an S election should review the rules of Financial Accounting Standards Board Statement No. (FAS)-109, which gives rules for the financial statement treatment of federal and state income taxes. Under its general matching concept, a tax liability would be associated with each income item that has not yet been reported for tax purposes. A corporation that uses the cash method of accounting for tax purposes would be required to accrue a deferred tax liability on its unbooked accounts payable, if it were to prepare an accrual-method financial statement. Therefore, it should consider any such liability in measuring its unrealized built-in gain.

> **EXAMPLE 11 - 25:** Cashco, a C corporation, uses the cash method of accounting. Its operations are conducted in a state that imposes a 6% income tax on corporations. Cashco's S election takes effect on January 1, 2000, at which time it has $40,000 accounts payable. Under the rules of FAS-109, Cashco would book $2,400 as a deferred state income tax liability on that date. Therefore, it may be able to reduce its unrealized built-in gain by that amount.

However, FAS-109 requires corporations to eliminate their deferred tax liabilities if they convert to tax-exempt status. Potential shareholder-level taxes are not measured for FAS-109 purposes. Therefore, conversion to S status may have the effect of eliminating such tax liabilities. However, a corporation converting to S status must leave a sufficient balance in its deferred tax liability to cover anticipated built-in gains tax. Therefore, if a state imposes a tax on S corporations' recognized built-in gains, the reserve must continue to appear, at the state built-in gain tax rate. If the state taxes an S corporation's income at the corporate level, the reserve must continue to reflect such anticipated liability.

> **EXAMPLE 11 - 26:** Refer to Example 11 - 25. The state imposes a 2.5% tax on all income of S corporations. Cashco should adjust its deferred state income tax liability attributable to the accounts receivable to $1,000 (2.5% of $40,000). This amount should be treated as a reduction of Cashco's unrealized built-in gain.

1125. Net recognized built-in gain.

Net recognized built-in gain is the taxable amount of gain, subject to some relief provisions. One important aspect of this term is that an S corporation must have a net recognized built-in gain in order to be subject to the built-in gains tax.

SUMMARY OF AUTHORITY: CODE SECTION 1374(a)

- Section 1374 imposes a tax on an S corporation that has a net recognized built-in gain in a taxable year in its recognition period.
- The tax is imposed on the income of the S corporation.

11

This subsection uses several terms that must be read carefully. The statute is, at times, awkwardly constructed. Accordingly, these terms, as well as several others, receive detailed discussion throughout this chapter. The phrase "income from the S corporation" has no definition, per se. Therefore, it is necessary to look to §1374(b)(1) for more useful terminology:

SUMMARY OF AUTHORITY: CODE SECTION 1374(b)(1)

- The tax rate is the highest stated rate imposed on C corporations for the taxable year.
- The base for the tax is the S corporation's net recognized built-in gain.

The term *net recognized built-in gain* is a rather complicated provision that can be understood only after exploring some other terms, such as *recognized built-in gain*, *recognized built-in loss*, *net unrealized built-in gain*, and *taxable income*, each of which has special rules applicable only to this tax. Depending on the corporation's circumstances in any given taxable year, *net recognized built-in gain* has three possible definitions:

- The pre-limitation amount, which includes only the corporation's recognized built-in gains and recognized built-in losses for the year.
- The taxable income limitation, which includes all of the corporation's gross income and deductions for the taxable year.
- The net unrealized built-in gain limitation, adjusted for all recognized built-in gains and losses to date

1125.1. Pre-limitation amount. The first calculation of net recognized built-in gain is the pre-limitation amount. In determining this figure, the corporation ignores all activities except for its recognized built-in gains and recognized built-in losses.

SUMMARY OF AUTHORITY: CODE SECTION 1374(d)(2)(A)(i)

- The first calculation of net recognized built-in gain is the difference between recognized built-in gains in a taxable year and recognized built-in losses in the same year.

1125.11. Recognized built-in gain, in general. *Recognized built-in gain* is an extremely important term upon which the entire tax is based. The definition is actually found in two parts of the statute. The general definition appears in §1374(d)(3). A careful reading reveals a presumption that all gains recognized by the corporation in its recognition period are built-in gains.

SUMMARY OF AUTHORITY: CODE SECTION 1374(d)(3)

- All gains on the disposition of property during the 10-year period are recognized built-in gains, according to the presumption built-into the law.
- The burden is always on the S corporation to establish that a gain is not built-in and therefore is exempt from the tax on built-in gains.
- A gain is not a built-in gain if it is recognized on property that was not held by the corporation on the first day of its first taxable year as an S corporation.
- A gain recognized on the disposition of property held by the corporation when the S election took effect may not be a built-in gain, to the extent that the gain accrued economically after the corporation's S election took effect.

11

A complete inventory and appraisal of assets on the first day of the first S year will serve the corporation well if it needs to effectively rebut the presumption later on a sale of property.

EXAMPLE 11 - 27: Marianna Corporation is a newly established accounting corporation in 1988. It makes an S election for 1989. At the time of its S election, its fair market value is approximately $100,000. In 1997, the sole shareholder sells all of the practice to a national accounting firm at a gain of $1,000,000. Most of the gain represents goodwill. Since the corporation was a C corporation and recognized the gain within 10 years of its S election, the entire gain is presumed to be a built-in gain.

Unless the corporation had its assets, including goodwill, appraised as of January 1, 1989, it will be difficult to rebut the presumption.

OBSERVATION: When a former C corporation's S election takes effect, it is advisable to have a view to the tax consequences of the sale of all of the corporation's assets within 10 years. Since goodwill is now amortizable under §197, a purchaser may want to structure an asset acquisition so that a significant portion of the price is allocated to goodwill. Accordingly, S corporations should attempt to make a reasonable, albeit low, valuation of goodwill when the S election takes effect. Without any appraisal of this now highly marketable asset, any goodwill sold within the recognition period will be assumed to have existed on the first day of the corporation's S election. See Chapter 16, at 1620.3., for discussion of goodwill.

1125.12. Cash-method income items. For approximately two years, §1374(d)(3) contained the exclusive definition of *recognized built-in gain*. The terminology created some confusion. For instance, the phrases *gain recognized* and *disposition of any asset* might appear inapplicable to certain other income items. A person could challenge whether the term was applicable to collection of an account receivable by a cash-basis taxpayer. This transaction would generate ordinary income, which may not be the same as a gain, per se. In order to resolve such doubts, in 1988 Congress expanded the definition as phrased in §1374(d)(5)(A).

SUMMARY OF AUTHORITY: CODE SECTION 1374(d)(5)(A)

- Income that is not considered a gain, per se, must be treated as a recognized built-in gain.
- To be treated as a recognized built-in gain, an item of income must have economically accrued before the S election took effect and must be recognized as income during the corporation's recognition period.

The addition of §1374(d)(5)(A) to the Code has specifically broadened the definition of *built-in gains.* As discussed below, it does not resolve all potential controversy. It will, however, make excluding income items from classification as built-in gains very difficult, unless the corporation can establish that no part of the income was attributable to years before the S election took effect.

EXAMPLE 11 - 28: ABC Corporation is a C corporation that uses the cash method of accounting. It made an S election that took effect for its year beginning January 1, 1992. Under the presumption in the law, all of its collections on accounts receivable through December 31, 2001, are built-in gains. Assume, however, that ABC has records demonstrating that $100,000 was actually outstanding on January 1, 1992. By keeping a careful record of which balances ABC actually collects, ABC can limit built-in gains treatment to those receivables that were outstanding on January 1, 1992. The remainder of its collections will be exempt from taxation as built-in gains.

1125.13. Recognition. A recognition event occurs according to the normal accounting rules. A sale of property, collection of a cash-basis receivable, or receipt of payment on an installment receivable are all instances of recognized gain. A like-kind exchange, involuntary conversion, or tax-free contribution to a partnership or other corporation would not cause a recognized gain and therefore would be exempt from tax as a built-in gain. 11

EXAMPLE 11 - 29: XYZ Corporation is a former C corporation whose S election took effect for its year beginning January 1, 1996. In 1996, it sold some land at a gain of $50,000. The corporation's basis in the land was $100,000 and the sale price was $150,000. It also traded in some old machinery on some new machinery. The book value of the old machinery was zero, and it was given a realistic trade-in allowance of $10,000. The presumed recognized built-in gain for 1996 is the $50,000 gain on the sale of the land. The gain on the equipment exchanged is not recognized under §1031 and therefore is not taxable as a built-in gain. (There is a problem with the replacement equipment, discussed below at 1140.1.) XYZ's built-in gain on the sale of the land could be less than the $50,000 reported gain, if XYZ can establish that the value as of January 1, 1996, was less than the $150,000 ultimate selling price.

There was one challenge in the Tax Court concerning the retroactive effective date of §1374(d)(5)(A). A cash-basis taxpayer claimed that it was not required to treat collections of accounts receivable as recognized built-in gains. The Tax Court, however, upheld the IRS and declared that such income was a recognized built-in gain, even if it occurred before 1988. [*Leou*, TC Memo 1994-393]

In some cases, a recognized gain may be only partly a built-in gain. An S corporation can reduce the portion of any gain treated as a built-in gain by demonstrating that some of the gain is attributable to years after the S election took effect.

EXAMPLE 11 - 30: Davco is a former C corporation whose S election took effect for its taxable year beginning January 1, 1992. In 1995, it sold some property that had an adjusted basis of

$140,000. The sale price was $230,000. Davco recognized a gain of $90,000 on the sale. Under the general presumption, the entire $90,000 is a built-in gain. However, Davco has strong evidence that the value on January 1, 1992, was only $210,000. Had Davco sold the property on January 1, 1992, its recognized built-in gain would have been $70,000. Therefore, Davco's recognized gain of $90,000 is treated as a built-in gain only to the extent of $70,000.

1125.14. Accrual accounting. The Regulations under §1374 treat any item of income as a recognized built-in gain if it would have been included in the corporation's income before the S election took effect, under the accrual method of accounting. [Regs. §1.1374-4(b)(1)] The accrual method of accounting may, however, need to be adapted to the actual transaction in which the corporation recognizes the income.

EXAMPLE 11 - 31 [adapted from Regs. §1.1374-4(b)(3), Example 1]: X Corporation uses the cash method of accounting and was a C corporation through 1994. X files an S election that takes effect for its taxable year beginning January 1, 1995. On that date, it has accounts receivable with a face amount of $50,000 and a fair market value of $40,000 to reflect uncollectible accounts. If the corporation collects the entire $50,000 within its recognition period, the $50,000 will be a recognized built-in gain. If the corporation sells its accounts receivable for $40,000 or more during its recognition period, its recognized built-in gain will only be $40,000, since that is the amount of income it would have recognized under the accrual method of accounting if it had sold the accounts in bulk on January 1, 1995.

OBSERVATION: In some cases, the accrual method of accounting may exclude certain items, even though they may be attributable, to some extent, to years before the S election took effect. Thus, a recovery of a bad debt that had been written off before the S election took effect might not be a recognized built-in gain. If accrual accounting would not have shown the account as an asset at the time the S election took effect, the corporation would certainly have grounds to claim that a recovery was not a built-in gain. Similarly, a refund from a payment that occurred before the S election took effect may or may not be a recognized built-in gain. If the refund were expected and were properly classified as an asset when the S election took effect, the refund would be a recognized built-in gain if the corporation used the cash method of accounting. By contrast, a contingent claim that existed at the time of conversion to S status would not be properly shown as an asset on an accrual method balance sheet. Therefore, the realization of this item after the S election took effect should not cause the resultant income to be a recognized built-in gain.

11

A taxpayer who receives prepaid service income may elect to defer the income until the period in which the services are performed. [Rev. Proc. 71-21, 1971-2 CB 549] When a C corporation has made this election, any income that was deferred on the conversion date is not treated as a recognized built-in gain when it is reported. [Regs. §1.1374-4(b)(3), Example 4]

The Regulations also address corporations that use the completed-contract method of accounting. Any income deferred under that method is a built-in gain, to the extent that it would have been reported as income under the percentage-of-completion method before the S election took effect. [Regs. §1.1374-4(g)]

1125.15. Inclusion of built-in gain carryforward. An S corporation is required to make a calculation of gain carryforward if the taxable income limitation is the final net recognized built-in gain. See discussion below at 1135.1. This amount must be treated as a recognized built-in gain in the next taxable year. If there is a gain carryforward from the final year of the recognition period, it disappears with no further tax consequences.

1125.16. Recognized built-in loss, in general. An S corporation is allowed to offset its recognized built-in gains with built-in losses sustained in the same taxable year. Code §1374(d)(4) defines *recognized built-in loss.*

SUMMARY OF AUTHORITY: CODE SECTION 1374(d)(4)

- The presumption is that there are no recognized built-in losses.
- The corporation may rebut the presumption by establishing that fair market value was less than basis on the first day of the first S year, or that unrealized payables existed at that date.
- As is the case with net unrealized built-in gain, the burden is on the corporation to keep careful records. The only benefit of cash-method liabilities will be treatment as a built-in loss.
- There is apparently no benefit from recognized built-in losses to the extent they exceed recognized built-in gains in the same year. They should, however, limit net unrealized built-in gain.

EXAMPLE 11 - 32: Hico, Inc., is a cash-basis corporation. Through December 31, 1995, it was a C corporation. Its S election took effect for its taxable year beginning January 1, 1996. In 1996, it sold some land, for which its basis was $250,000. Hico received $180,000 on the sale. In order to treat the $70,000 loss as a recognized built-in loss, Hico must demonstrate two facts:

- Hico owned the property on January 1, 1996.
- The fair market value of the property on that date was no greater than $180,000.

1125.17. Cash-method deduction items. As was the case with *recognized built-in gains*, there are some weaknesses in the definition of *recognized built-in losses*. Specifically, it is not clear whether losses include any transaction other than a sale of property. Fortunately, §1374(d)(5)(B) expands the definition to include other items.

SUMMARY OF AUTHORITY: CODE SECTION 1374(d)(5)(B)

- Recognized built-in losses include any deductions allowed during the recognition period that are attributable to tax years of the corporation before the S election took effect.

An S corporation is allowed to treat any deduction as a recognized built-in loss, provided it can sustain the burden of proof that the deduction is attributable to a year before the S election took effect. This rule has important implications for cash-basis corporations.

11

EXAMPLE 11 - 33: Teeco is a cash-basis corporation that was a C corporation through 1990. Its S election took effect for its taxable year beginning January 1, 1995. In 1995, Teeco paid $150,000 deductible expenses. Teeco can demonstrate that $30,000 of these expenses had actually arisen before 1995, but were not yet taken into account under the cash method. These $30,000 of expenses are treated as recognized built-in losses. Teeco has the burden of proving that these expenses were actually accrued economically before its S election took effect.

The Regulations provide that a recognized built-in loss includes any item that would have been allowed as a deduction to an accrual-method taxpayer. To be deductible, an accrued expense must meet three tests of deductibility. The first two tests are found in Regulations §1.451-1(a):

- All events must occur to fix the taxpayer's right to receive the income.
- The amount of income must be determinable with reasonable accuracy.

In addition, an accrued expense must meet the *economic performance* test to be allowed as a deduction. [§461(h)] In general, economic performance occurs when the services, delivery of property, or use of property for which the payment is made occurs. [§461(h)(2)(A)]

EXAMPLE 11 - 34: Tenco, a C corporation through 1995, converted to S status for its taxable year beginning January 1, 1996. In December 1995, Tenco obligated itself on a lease on some property for a five-year period beginning January 1, 1996. The payments it makes under the lease will be deductible over the period of the lease. Therefore, none of the payments may be treated as a recognized built-in loss.

In computing a deduction under the accrual method, a taxpayer may be subject to §461(h)(2)(C), which does not allow a deduction for the payment of tort liabilities and workers' compensation until the payment is actually made. The Regulations under §1374 allow an accrued tort or workers' compensation liability to be treated as a built-in loss if the amount and obligation were fixed at the time the S election took effect, even though the payment had not yet been made.

1125.18. Passive activity loss limits. The Proposed Regulations also allowed a built-in loss for an expense or loss that would have been deductible if not for the passive activity loss limit of §469. [Proposed Regs. §1.1374-4(b)(2)] The Final Regulations, however, do not allow a corporation to utilize any deduction suspended under §469. [TD 8579, Sec. C3]

EXAMPLE 11 - 35: Close Corporation was a C corporation through 1995. Its S election took effect for its taxable year beginning January 1, 1996. At the end of 1995, Close had $50,000 of rental deductions that had been suspended under §469. Under the Final Regulations, these deductions would never be allowed to Close as long as its S election is in effect. Thus, the $50,000 would not be treated as a built-in loss.

OBSERVATION: The rationale for disallowing any suspended loss from §469 from being treated as a recognized built-in loss is found in TD 8579, the preamble to the Final Regulations. The IRS position is that §1371(b)(1) bars an S corporation from using any carryover from a C corporation year in any S corporation year. (See discussion in Chapter 6, at 610.3.) By inference, an S corporation cannot claim any item suspended under §465, or any other provision, as a deduction while the S election is in effect.

This position appears harsh, and arbitrary, especially with respect to recognized built-in losses. The loss disallowance rules, such as §465 and §469, offer clear rules whereby a taxpayer may deduct suspended items in future years. There is nothing in the legislative history of either of these provisions to indicate that Congress intended for these deductions to be suspended permanently if the deductions were disallowed to a C corporation and the corporation then made an S election. However, the IRS has the power to write legislative regulations in the built-in gain area, and this rule must not be taken lightly.

11

1125.19. Related party accruals. The Final Regulations under §1374 state that a deduction is treated as a built-in loss if it would have been deductible under the accrual method, together with all of the restrictions on the accrual method for tax purposes. Thus, a cash-method corporation could not treat an amount accrued to a controlling shareholder as a deduction unless the amount were paid during the final C year. [§267(a)(2)] See discussion in Chapter 8, at 815.

The Regulations allow certain expenses that would be disallowed under §267(a)(2) to be treated as built-in losses. For the corporation to claim this treatment, the accrued expenses must be paid within 2 months and 15 days of the beginning of the recognition period. [Regs. §1.1374-4(c)(1)] The same rule applies if the corporation uses the accrual method of accounting.

EXAMPLE 11 - 36: Relco was a C corporation that used the accrual method of accounting. Its S election took effect on January 1, 1995. On March 14, 1995, Relco paid $50,000 as a bonus to its controlling shareholder, Reggie. On April 15, 1995, the corporation paid $75,000 to Reggie. If these amounts had been accrued on December 31, 1994, they would not have been deductible until paid, pursuant to §267(a)(2).

Relco intends to take the position that both of these amounts are attributable to services the shareholder performed before 1995. If that position were sustained, each of the payments would qualify as a recognized built-in loss. Under the Regulations, the first payment could be treated as a recognized built-in loss, since it was paid within 2 months and 15 days of the beginning of the first S corporation year. The second payment could not be treated as a recognized built-in loss under the Regulations, because it was paid more than $2^1/_2$ months after the beginning of the first S year.

Regulations §1.1374-4(c)(1) appears to apply equally to cash-method and accrual-method corporations. In the immediately preceding example, therefore, it would make no difference if the corporation used the cash method rather than the accrual method. The amounts paid within 2 months and 15 days of the beginning of the first S year would be deductible as built-in losses, and the amounts paid later would not.

OBSERVATION: The position of the Regulations with respect to amounts accrued to controlling shareholders has no specific support in the statute or in legislative history. Thus, a corporation that filed its Form 2553 before December 27, 1994, would not be bound by this position, per se. Such a corporation arguably could take a position that any payment to a controlling shareholder within the ten-year recognition period is a built-in loss, if the corporation were able to sustain the burden of proof that the amount was attributable to events that occurred before the S election took effect.

Similarly, the IRS would not be bound to follow the position of the Regulations with respect to a corporation that filed Form 2553 before December 27, 1994. The IRS could refuse to allow any payment to a shareholder to be treated as a recognized built-in loss, even if it were paid by the corporation within 2 months and 15 days of the beginning of the first S year.

The Regulations are more lenient with respect to amounts accrued to persons who own less than 5% of the voting power and value of the corporation's stock, using the constructive ownership rules of §267. The shareholder in question must own less than 5% of the voting power, both at the time the election takes effect, and the time the corporation actually pays the amount. [Regs. §1.1374-4(c)(1)(ii)(B)] These amounts need not be paid within the first two months and 15 days of the first S year in order to be treated as recognized built-in losses. [Regs. §1.1374-4(c)(1)(ii)(B)]

11

OBSERVATION: This provision could be of benefit only if a corporation was a personal service corporation before its S election took effect. All shareholders in a personal service corporation are covered by the accrual disallowance of §267(a), even if they own 50% or less of the corporation's stock. [§267(e)] In any other corporation, a person who owns less than 5% of the stock would not be subject to the limits of §267.

EXAMPLE 11 - 37: Profco was a personal service corporation that did not make an S election until January 1, 1996. Profco had 30 equal shareholders, none of whom were related to each other within the meaning of §267(b). In 1996 and 1997, Profco made several payments to each of its shareholders. Profco could take the position that these payments were attributable to activities before the S election took effect and thus could treat the payments as recognized built-in losses on its 1996 and 1997 tax returns. Profco would not need to disclose the position as being contrary to any Regulations. The IRS could adjust these built-in losses if Profco's returns were audited.

1125.110. Deferred compensation. The Regulations also provide some special rules for deferred compensation. Deferred compensation payments within the recognition period may not be treated as recognized built-in losses if they are made to related persons, within the meaning of §267. [Regs. §1.1374-4(c)(2)] In addition, the amount of the liability must be fixed at the conversion date.

1125.111. Limitations and offsets. The Regulations state that the corporation must follow the rules applicable to C corporations for computation of taxable income, if the only income, deductions, and losses for the year were built-in gains and losses. This rule implies that the corporation must follow all limitations, such as those imposed on capital losses, passive activity losses, and the like.

The Regulations under §1374 state that the corporation must compute its pre-limitation amount of net recognized built-in gain using the rules that apply to C corporations—but only including recognized built-in gains (including any gain carryover) and recognized built-in losses. The rules applicable to a C corporation forbid the deduction of a corporation's capital losses against ordinary income.

EXAMPLE 11 - 38: Ordco recognizes $50,000 of ordinary gains, which are built-in gains, in a taxable year within its recognition period. In the same year, it recognizes $20,000 of capital losses, which are also built-in losses. Its pre-limitation amount of net recognized built-in gain is $50,000, which is its ordinary gains, not reduced by its capital losses.

EXAMPLE 11 - 39: Quay Corporation is a cash-method corporation. It was a C corporation until it filed an S election in 1995, effective for calendar year 1996. As of January 1, 1996, it had $50,000 in unrealized accounts receivable and $31,000 in unrealized accounts payable. In 1991 and all later years in the recognition period, Quay must separate its recognized built-in gains and losses from its other income and loss items for the year.

In 1996, Quay recognizes $300,000 of income and $285,000 of deductions. The income included collection of $43,000 of the receivables that existed on January 1, 1996. The deductions included payment of $22,000 of the accounts payable that existed on that date. Quay's pre-limitation amount disregards everything except the recognized built-in gains and losses. The calculation is:

Gross income	$43,000
Deductions	(22,000)
Pre-limitation amount	$21,000

Because of the difference between the individual and the C corporation taxable income rules, the taxable income computed for the built-in gains tax may be considerably different from that which flows through to the shareholders.

EXAMPLE 11 - 40: Martco has the following items to report on its 1992 Form 1120S:

Ordinary loss	$(140,000)
Income from rental activity	60,000
Interest income	35,000
Long-term capital gain	80,000
Short-term capital loss	(7,500)
§1231 loss	(5,000)
Charitable contributions	(2,000)

On Schedules K and K-1, each of the above items would be reported separately, with page 1 showing only the ordinary loss of $140,000. For the dummy Form 1120, on which the corporation must calculate its taxable income for the built-in gains tax, all of the above items would be combined and would result in taxable income of $20,500.

1125.112. Tax character of net recognized built-in gain. Since an S corporation uses the corporate rules, it must keep track of the character (ordinary, capital, or §1231) of the gains and losses. The Regulations provide that the built-in gain is to be treated as coming proportionately from each class of income, after losses and deductions are matched up. [Regs. §1.1374-2(b)] Worksheet 11 - 1 provides a useful way to separate and classify the various items of recognized built-in gain and recognized built-in loss. This worksheet uses all of the categories necessary for individuals, since the tax must be apportioned among the categories of built-in gain. See discussion below at 1136.3.

Worksheet 11 - 2 then apportions the net overall gain of each category to each category. In using this worksheet, the corporation should apply all of the usual corporate rules. In other words, a capital loss of one type may offset a capital gain of another type, but a net capital loss may not offset ordinary income.

1125.2. Taxable income limitation. The second measure of net recognized built-in gain is the corporation's taxable income, including all income, losses, and deductions in addition to recognized built-in gains and recognized built-in losses. The statutory authority is somewhat tangled, and it calls upon two different Code sections.

SUMMARY OF AUTHORITY: CODE SECTION 1374(d)(2)(A)(ii)

- The second calculation of net recognized built-in gain is the corporation's taxable income for the same year (with special rules discussed in this portion of the chapter).

1125.21. General rules. To arrive at the second calculation of net recognized built-in gain, it is necessary to examine §1375(b)(1)(B). That provision defines *taxable income,* for purposes of the passive investment income tax discussed in Chapter 12.

SUMMARY OF AUTHORITY: CODE SECTION 1375(b)(1)(B)

- For built-in gains tax purposes, an S corporation must compute its taxable income in the same manner as a C corporation.
- The corporation follows all of the corporate rules for allowances of deductions, offsets of gains and losses, and any other special rules applicable to C corporations.
- For this determination, an S corporation is not entitled to the dividends-received deduction.
- At this point in the calculations, the corporation is not allowed to use any net operating loss deduction (this rule is relaxed later).

11

In general, an S corporation follows the individual, rather than the corporate, rules in determining its taxable income. [§1363(b)] See Chapter 6, at 610., for discussion of the requirement for separate computation and statement of certain items. When an S corporation computes its C taxable income, however, it must offset all items of income and deduction as if it were a taxpayer rather than a conduit. The corporation follows all of the income tax rules of §63(a) except for the dividends-received deduction and the net operating loss carryforward allowed by §172. [§1375(b)(1)(B)]

The cross-reference to §1375(b)(1)(B) that allows the corporation to compute its taxable income under §63(a) deserves some explanation. When the statute was written, §63(a) applied only to corporations. Therefore, the two Code provisions, when read in conjunction, allowed the S corporation to use all of the C corporation rules in calculating its taxable income. The IRS instructions have consistently required that an S corporation that is subject to the built-in gains tax (or the passive investment income or prior capital gains tax) fill out a dummy Form 1120 and observe all of the C corporation rules and limitations. Regulations under §1374 specifically require S corporations to use the C corporation rules in both the calculation of the pre-limitation amount of net recognized built-in gain and the taxable income limitation thereof. [Regs. §1.1374-2(a)(1) & (2)] The Regulations term this second calculation the *taxable income limitation* [Regs. §1.1374-2(a)(2)] and specifically require that the corporation compute its taxable income as if it were a C corporation.

EXAMPLE 11 - 41: Refer to Example 11 - 40. Quay's calculation of its taxable income limitation includes all of its gross income and deductions for 1990:

Gross income	$300,000
Deductions	(285,000)
Taxable income limitation	$ 15,000

1125.22. Tax character of net recognized built-in gain. If the corporation's taxable income limitation applies to limit the net recognized built-in gain, the corporation must apportion the various components by character. [Regs. §1.1374-2(b)] Worksheet 11 - 2, which is designed for this purpose, takes data from Worksheet 11 - 1 and allocates the taxable income limitation in the same ratio as the built-in gains and losses were to the pre-limitation amount.

1125.3. Net unrealized built-in gain limitation. The third calculation of net recognized built-in gain is somewhat more obscure. Code §1374(c)(2) limits a corporation's net recognized built-in gain to its net unrealized built-in gain, as adjusted for net recognized built-in gains of prior years within the recognition period. The Regulations refer to this calculation as the *net unrealized built-in gain limitation.* [Regs. §1.1374-2(a)(3)]

SUMMARY OF AUTHORITY: CODE SECTION 1374(c)(2)

- When net unrealized built-in gain is less than net recognized built-in gain, the corporation's taxable built-in gain is limited to net unrealized built-in gain.
- An S corporation's net unrealized built-in gain is adjusted each year by removing the recognized built-in gain for that year.

1125.31. First year of the recognition period. In the first year of the recognition period, the net unrealized built-in gain limitation is the net unrealized built-in gain calculated as of conversion date. See 1120. above.

11

EXAMPLE 11 - 42: Refer to Examples 11 - 40 and 11 - 41. Assume that Quay had no other assets, liabilities, or other items that would have affected its net unrealized built-in gain as of January 1, 1990. Its net unrealized built-in gain would be $19,000—the difference between its unrealized receivables and its unrealized payables. Therefore, its net unrealized built-in gain limitation (of its net recognized built-in gain) for 1990 is $19,000. Quay's taxable built-in gain for the year is $15,000, since the taxable income limitation is the lowest measure of net recognized built-in gain.

1125.32. Subsequent years. Each year the S corporation must adjust its unrealized built-in gain limit to reflect the current year's activity. The corporation reduces its net unrealized built-in gain limitation by the amount, if any, of its net recognized built-in gain of the current year. These rules are discussed below, at 1135.2.

1125.33. Tax character of net recognized built-in gain. If the corporation's net unrealized built-in gain limitation applies to limit the net recognized built-in gain, the corporation must apportion the various components by character. [Regs. §1.1374-2(b)] Worksheet 11 - 2, which was used to apportion the taxable income limitation, is designed for this purpose.

1130. Computation of tax.

To calculate its built-in gains tax properly, the corporation must determine its net recognized built-in gain, compare that total with net unrealized built-in gain and taxable income, and then calculate the tax on the least amount of the three figures. Worksheet 11 - 5, at 1170., provides a useful way to order the computations.

EXAMPLE 11 - 43: JLCO, Inc., was a C corporation through 1995. It makes an S election for its taxable year beginning January 1, 1996. On January 1, 1996, its net unrealized built-in gain is $350,000. In 1996, it reports the following:

Recognized built-in gains	$ 85,000
Recognized built-in losses	$ (15,000)
Taxable income (modified C corporation rules)	$ 75,000

JLCO enters the information on its worksheet as follows:

JLCO, Inc., Net Recognized Built-In Gain Worksheet

1a. Determine recognized built-in gains (Including income items attributable to prior C years)	$ 85,000
1b. Subtract recognized built-in losses (Including deductions attributable to prior C years)	(15,000)
1c. Add carryforward of built-in gain from last year (If election filed after 3/30/88)	0
1d. Pre-limitation amount	$ 70,000
2. Net unrealized built-in gain limitation	$350,000
3. Lesser of 1d or 2	$ 70,000
4. Taxable income limitation	$ 75,000
5. Taxable recognized built-in gain (lesser of 3 or 4)	$ 70,000
6. Subtract net operating loss and capital loss carryforwards from C years	(0)
7. Taxable recognized built-in gain (after carryforwards)	$ 70,000
8. Tax on 7 at highest corporate rate (currently .34)	23,800
9. Subtract general business credit and alternative minimum tax carryforwards from C years	(0)
10. Tax payable in current year (subject to estimated tax requirements)	$ 23,800
11. If election filed after 3/30/88 and 3 exceeds 4, carry excess forward to next year; otherwise, zero	0

11

1130.1. Tax rate. The tax rate is specified by reference to the highest corporate tax rate. From 1988 through 1992, the rate was 34%. For taxable years beginning after 1993, Congress raised the maximum specified rate to 35%. This rate applies to C corporations with taxable income in excess of $110,000,000. It also applies to personal service corporations [§11(b)(2)] and, by inference, to S corporations subject to the built-in gains tax.[6] [§1374(b)(1)] For corporations with fiscal years beginning in 1992 and ending in 1993, the two tax rates must be blended, based on the number of days of the corporation's taxable year that fall within each of the two calendar years. [§15] Practitioners can expect a similar rule in the future, if Congress changes the top corporate tax rate.

[6] In some instances, a C corporation is subject to a surtax. This can occur between $100,000 and $335,000 of taxable income or between $15,000,000 and $18,333,333 of taxable income. These surtaxes are not incorporated into the stated tax rates of corporations, per se. Therefore, they do not apply to the built-in gains tax, or the passive investment income tax, imposed on S corporations.

1130.2. Loss carryforwards from C years. A C corporation may have incurred net operating losses when its allowable deductions in one taxable year exceed its gross income for the same taxable year. In general, a C corporation is allowed to carry a net operating loss back 3 years and forward 15 years. [§172] If a corporation has an unused loss carryforward at the time its S election takes effect, it generally cannot deduct the loss in any year, unless it revokes its S election and again becomes a C corporation. [§1371(b)(2)] See Chapter 6, at 610.3., for discussion. There is, however, a relief provision that allows a former C corporation to use net operating loss (NOL) carryforwards from prior years to offset its taxable built-in gain.

SUMMARY OF AUTHORITY: CODE SECTION 1374(b)(2)

- An S corporation is allowed to offset its taxable built-in gain (preliminary) with a net operating loss carryforward from a prior C corporation year.
- The corporation's net recognized built-in gain absorbs the portion of the loss carryforward allowed as a deduction.
- Similar rules shall apply to a capital loss carryforward from a prior C year.

The loss is applied to reduce the corporation's net recognized built-in gain. Recall that this term has three different meanings. To be consistent with the terminology adopted at 1110.4, the loss is applied to the corporation's taxable built-in gain (preliminary).

EXAMPLE 11 - 44: R Corporation has a recognized built-in gain of $35,000 in 1997. R's taxable income limitation is $30,000 in 1997. It had a NOL carryforward of $12,000 from 1995. It would compute its built-in gains tax in the following manner:

Built-in gains	$35,000
Limited to taxable income (before NOL)	30,000
Lesser of two figures	$30,000
Less NOL	(12,000)
Final taxable amount	$18,000
Tax at 35%	$ 6,300

11

The years will continue to run on the carryovers. The loss carryover will be absorbed by the corporation's taxable built-in gain (preliminary).

EXAMPLE 11 - 45: Barco is a former C corporation whose S election took effect in its taxable year beginning January 1, 1994. As of that date, Barco's net unrealized built-in gain was $150,000, and it had a net operating loss carryforward of $80,000 from 1993. Its taxable built-in gain (preliminary) for the next three years was:

1994	$40,000
1995	20,000
1996	30,000

Barco would utilize its net operating loss carryforward as follows:

1994	$40,000
1995	20,000
1996	20,000
Total	$80,000

Barco would have no taxable built-in gain (final) in either 1994 or 1995. Barco's taxable built-in gain (final) for 1996 is $10,000. Barco's net operating loss carryforward from its C years is exhausted at the end of 1996 and could not be utilized against any future taxable income.

The statute states that similar rules shall apply for capital losses carried forward from C years. Exactly what such similar rules will be is speculative at the time of this writing. Most likely, such capital loss carryforwards will be limited to capital gains incurred within the recognition period. However, the capital loss carryforward period is only five years. Therefore, it would appear that the corporation must utilize such losses before the carryforward period expires, and that such loss carryforwards could be used against any built-in capital gains.

> **OBSERVATION:** The Code is not clear on the treatment of net capital losses carried forward from C corporation years or on their effect on taxable built-in gains. The Regulations seem to ignore the existence of these carryforwards and provide no operating rules for their use. However, Regulations §1.1374-5(a) limits loss carryforwards "to the extent their use is allowed under the rules applying to C corporations."

1130.3. Distinctions between carryover and recognized built-in loss. In many cases, using a net operating loss carryover against built-in gains may have the same effect as recognizing a built-in loss. There are three primary and important distinctions, however, between a loss carryforward from a C year and a built-in loss that is recognized during the recognition period:

1. The existence and utilization of a loss carryforward have no effect on the corporation's net unrealized built-in gain. By contrast, a recognized built-in loss, or potential recognized built-in loss, reduces the corporation's net unrealized built-in gain.

> **EXAMPLE 11 - 46:** Magco, Inc., was a C corporation through 1995. Its S election took effect for its taxable year beginning January 1, 1996. On that date, Magco's assets had fair market value of $1,000,000 and adjusted basis of $650,000. Magco also had a net operating loss carryforward of $200,000. Magco's net unrealized built-in gain was $350,000 and was not affected by the net operating loss carryforward.
>
> If Magco recognizes all of its built-in gains before the net operating loss carryforward expires, it will have a taxable built-in gain (final) of only $150,000. If, however, it has actual recognition of built-in gains after the net operating loss carryforward expires, its taxable built-in gain (final) could reach $350,000.

11

2. A loss carryforward may expire before the end of the corporation's recognition period, whereas a built-in loss can yield a tax benefit any time during the recognition period. An S corporation must be aware of the period in which a net operating loss carryforward may be allowed. In general, a net operating loss can be carried forward for no more than 15 years, including short years. A built-in loss, by contrast, may offset recognized built-in gains at any time during the corporation's recognition period.

> **EXAMPLE 11 - 47:** Corporation 1 and Corporation 2 are both former C corporations. In their sixth year as S corporations, they each recognize $100,000 of built-in gains. Both corporations' net unrealized built-in gain and taxable income are considerably in excess of $100,000, and they provide no relief in the calculation of net recognized built-in gain. Corporation 1 recognizes a built-in loss of $100,000 in its sixth year as an S corporation. Corporation 2 has no recognized built-in loss in its sixth year as an S corporation, but it has a net operating loss carryforward of $150,000 from a C year. The carryforward is 10 years old at the time the S election takes effect. By the sixth year, the carryforward has expired. Corporation 1 would have no net recognized built-in gain, but Corporation 2 would have a net recognized built-in gain of $100,000.

3. A corporation may receive no benefit if its recognized built-in losses exceed its recognized built-in gains in a single tax year, whereas a loss carryforward can provide benefits until it expires. An S corporation's net recognized built-in gain can only be positive (or zero). There is no prescribed tax treatment for an S corporation whose

recognized built-in losses exceed its recognized built-in gains in the same taxable year. A loss carryforward, by contrast, is carried forward to the next taxable year to the extent that it exceeds the taxable built-in gain (preliminary).

EXAMPLE 11 - 48: Corporation A and Corporation B are both former C corporations. In their first year as S corporations, they each recognize $100,000 of built-in gains. Both corporations' net unrealized built-in gain and taxable income are considerably in excess of $100,000, and they provide no relief in the calculation of net recognized built-in gain. Corporation A recognizes a built-in loss of $150,000 in its first year as an S corporation. Corporation B has no recognized built-in loss in its first year as an S corporation, but has a net operating loss carryforward of $150,000 from a C year. In the second year, each corporation recognizes built-in gains of $40,000, and neither corporation recognized any built-in losses. The results would be:

	Corporation A	*Corporation B*
First year:		
Recognized built-in gains	$100,000	$100,000
Recognized built-in losses	(150,000)	(0)
Loss carryforward allowed	(0)	(100,000)
Taxable built-in gain (final)	$ 0	$ 0
Second year:		
Recognized built-in gains	$ 40,000	$ 40,000
Recognized built-in losses	(0)	(0)
Loss carryforward allowed	(0)	(40,000)
Taxable built-in gain (final)	$ 40,000	$ 0

11

The Code omits reference to any carryforwards other than the net operating loss or capital loss carryforward. The Regulations state that an S corporation cannot offset its taxable built-in gain with any other carryforward, such as a charitable contribution carryforward. [Regs. §1.1374-5(a)]

OBSERVATION: If a cash-method C corporation incurs some expenses in the year before its S election is to take effect, it should consider borrowing the money and paying the expenses out, rather than waiting to pay them in the ordinary course of business. By doing so, the corporation could use these deductions to offset income from the final C corporation year or to create a loss for that year. If a loss for the final C corporation year will result in a carryforward of the loss to a profitable C corporation year, the corporation would receive an immediate refund of its income tax. This strategy would produce better results than using these accrued deductions as recognized built-in losses in subsequent years. If the corporation's marginal tax rate has been considerably lower than 35% in its final three C years, however, the corporation might be better off not paying these expenses, and instead treating them as recognized built-in losses in the future.

If some of these unpaid expenses would exceed the corporation's recognized built-in gain in any year, it might be better to create a net operating loss in the final C corporation year and carry the loss forward for use as an offset to taxable built-in gains. Under current law, a loss carryforward may be used up to 15 years following the loss year and thus would be available at any time throughout the corporation's recognition period.

1130.4. Credit carryforwards. The S corporation computes its built-in gains tax by multiplying its taxable built-in gain (final) by the highest corporate rate in effect for the year. At that point, there is a limited ability to use credits to offset the tax. [§1374(b)(3)]

SUMMARY OF AUTHORITY: CODE SECTION 1374(b)(3)

- Generally, an S corporation may not offset any of its built-in gains tax liability with any credits, since credits must usually pass through to the S corporation's shareholders.
- An S corporation may offset its tax liability with the fuels credit of §34, since this credit is fully refundable.
- If an S corporation was unable to utilize all of its general business credit when it was a C corporation, it may utilize the general business credit carryforward against its built-in gains tax.
- An S corporation that paid the corporate alternative minimum tax when it was a C corporation may use the alternative minimum tax credit to offset its built-in gains tax.

The use of a credit carryover will reduce the amount available for future years. The general business credit is limited to the same proportion of built-in gains tax liability as it would be to the regular income tax liability of a C corporation. [Regs. §1.1374-6(b)] In the case of the general business credit, the limit in any one year is a complete offset of the first $25,000 tax liability plus 25% of the excess of the tax liability over $25,000. [§38(c)]

EXAMPLE 11 - 49: Venda, Inc., is a former C corporation. When its S election took effect, it had an unused general business credit of $80,000. In its first year as an S corporation, Venda reports net recognized built-in gain of $100,000. Venda's built-in gains tax, before credits, is $35,000. Its general business credit would be:

	Credit Allowed
First $25,000 of built-in gains tax	$25,000
25% excess (.25 x $10,000)	2,500
Credit allowed	$27,500
Credit carried forward to next year	52,500
Total	$80,000

Venda's built-in gains tax liability, after the general business credit, would be $7,500 ($35,000 – $27,500). Note that Venda is able to utilize only the credit carried forward from its years as a C corporation against its built-in gains. If Venda qualified for a general business credit in one of its years as an S corporation, the credit would be reported to the shareholders, who could use it to offset their personal tax liabilities.

An S corporation that uses the alternative minimum tax credit against its built-in gains tax liability is subject to limitations similar to those of a C corporation. In general, the alternative minimum tax credit reduces a taxpayer's regular tax liability in a year when its alternative minimum tax is less than its regular tax. [§53(c)] Presumably, an S corporation must compute its tentative alternative minimum tax by the regular corporate rules and compare that total to its built-in gains tax in order to determine its credit limitation. [Regs. §1.1374-6(b)]

EXAMPLE 11 - 50: Recco was a C corporation through 1996. Its total alternative minimum tax liability from 1987 through 1996 was $39,000. Recco became an S corporation in its taxable year beginning January 1, 1997. In 1997, its recognized built-in gains were $135,000 and its taxable income (by the modified C corporation rules) was $100,000. Its built-in gains tax liability, before the alternative minimum tax credit, was $35,000. Recco had tax preferences of $15,000. Its computation of adjusted current earnings (ACE)[7] is $155,000. It would make a dummy calculation of its alternative minimum tax as follows:

[7] A C corporation must compute adjusted current earnings (ACE) to determine its alternative minimum tax adjustments. The rules are contained in §56(d), and they receive brief discussion in Chapter 1.

11

Taxable income	$100,000
Tax preferences	15,000
Alternative minimum taxable income before ACE	115,000
ACE [.75 x ($155,000 – $115,000)]	30,000
Exemption	(40,000)
Alternative minimum taxable income	$105,000
Tax rate	.2
Tentative alternative minimum tax	$ 21,000

Recco would use its alternative minimum tax credit as follows:

Regular tax liability	$ 35,000
Less tentative alternative minimum tax	(21,000)
Limitation on alternative minimum tax credit	$ 14,000

Recco would pay a built-in gains tax of $21,000 and carry forward $25,000 of its alternative minimum tax credit to future years ($39,000 – $14,000).

- The corporation offsets the tax with any business credit carryforward and alternative minimum tax credit from a C corporation year.
- The corporation cannot utilize any other credit (except for the fuel credit) from an S year. These credits pass through to the shareholders.

1130.5. Estimated tax payments. Until 1990, S corporations were not required to make estimated tax payments on the corporate-level taxes. The Revenue Reconciliation Act of 1989, however, subjected S corporations to some strange payment rules.

1130.51. General requirement for S corporations. For taxable years beginning after 1989, S corporations are required to estimate tax payments to cover built-in gains, excess net passive income, capital gains, and investment tax credit recapture taxes. [§6655(g)(4); Revenue Reconciliation Act of 1989, §7209(a)] The requirements vary, depending upon the particular tax imposed.

To avoid a penalty for underpayment, the S corporation should make the following estimated tax payments:

- For its passive investment income tax liability
  - — The lesser of
    - (i) 100% of the current year's liability, or
    - (ii) 100% of the immediate prior year's liability [§6655(g)(4)(C)(II)(ii)]
- For its built-in gains tax liability
  - — At least 100% of the current year's liability [§6655(g)(4)(C)(II)(i)]
- For its capital gains liability
  - — At least 100% of the current year's liability [§6655(g)(4)(C)(II)(i)]
- For its investment tax credit recapture tax liability
  - — At least 100% of the current year's liability [§6655(g)(4)(C)(II)(i)]

OBSERVATION: There is no apparent policy reason for the liberal treatment of the passive investment income tax compared to the other taxes. To comply with the requirement for estimated payments on the built-in gains tax, the corporation will need to determine its taxable built-in gain (final) for each portion of the year.

The general rule for estimated tax payments is that they must be made quarterly, in even installments. There are some annualization rules, however, that allow S corporations to base each quarter's payment on the activity to date. [§6655(e)]

1130.52. Effect of underpayment penalty on shareholders. An S corporation's penalty for underpayment of its estimated taxes is a nondeductible expense. [Ann. 93-42, 1993-11 IRB 55] The corporation should allocate to each shareholder his or her portion of the penalty, as it would any other income or expense item for the appropriate taxable year. The penalty is not deductible at the shareholder level, but it does reduce each shareholder's basis. [Regs. §1.1367-1(c)(2)] Since the penalty is not connected with the production of tax-exempt income, it does not flow to the Other Adjustments Account (OAA). Instead, it is a reduction of the corporation's Accumulated Adjustments Account (AAA), in the same manner as any other corporate-level tax paid by an S corporation.

1135. Other computations.

Each year during the recognition period an S corporation must make some computations in addition to its built-in gain tax liability. It must determine the effects of the current year's gains on future built-in gains, and it must incorporate the current year's built-in gain tax into the shareholder basis adjustments and the corporation's AAA.

1135.1. Gain carryforward. If the corporation's taxable income is less than the gain that is otherwise taxable, there may be a gain carryover. The carryover is a Technical and Miscellaneous Revenue Act of 1988 amendment that closed a loophole in the 1986 legislation. Corporations that filed S elections before March 31, 1988, are exempt from the carryover.

SUMMARY OF AUTHORITY: CODE SECTION 1374(d)(2)(B)

- When the corporation's net recognized built-in gain in any year exceeds its taxable income (by the modified C corporation rules), the excess is carried forward and treated as a recognized built-in gain in the next year if the corporation filed its S election after March 30, 1988.
- The carryover means that the built-in gains that escape taxation in a given year due to the taxable income limitation will roll forward into future years.

Corporations that filed their S elections prior to March 31, 1988, were able to use a planning strategy to reduce their built-in gains tax. By eliminating or substantially reducing taxable income in a year in which a corporation had significant recognized built-in gains, such corporations were able to eliminate the tax completely on the gains recognized in that year.

EXAMPLE 11 - 51: XYZ Corporation filed its S election in 1988, effective January 1, 1989. As of January 1, 1989, it had net unrealized built-in gains of $105,000. In 1989, it had net recognized built-in gains, pre-limitation amount, of $90,000 and taxable income of $10,000. Since the taxable built-in gains are limited to the taxable income, XYZ's tax is $3,400.

In 1990, the corporation recognized no built-in gains. Its taxable income was $200,000. If XYZ filed its S election before March 31, 1988, its recognized built-in gains for 1990 would be zero. Its net unrealized built-in gain would be reduced by $10,000, reflecting its final calculation of net recognized built-in gain in 1989. If XYZ could rebut the built-in gains presumption on all of its future gains, it would pay no further built-in gains tax. Note that it would recognize $90,000 of built-in gains in its recognition period, but it would pay a total tax of only $3,400.

In the Technical and Miscellaneous Revenue Act of 1988, Congress made this planning technique much more difficult to utilize. The taxable income limit on the taxable built-in gains may defer the tax, but the corporation will face the potential tax liability for all gains recognized, even though they may be shielded by low taxable income.

EXAMPLE 11 - 52: Refer to Example 11 - 51. Assume that XYZ filed its S election after March 31, 1988. In 1989, the S corporation would pay only $3,400 tax, due to its low taxable income. It would, however, need to measure the difference between its net recognized built-in gain and its taxable income. In 1989, that amount would be $80,000. XYZ would treat the $80,000 as a recognized built-in gain in 1990 and pay a tax of $27,200 ($80,000 x .34).

As is the case for other transitional rules, it is the filing date of Form 2553, rather than the effective date of the S election, that governs the carryover. A corporation that filed its election on or before March 30, 1988, is exempt from the carryover rule.

EXAMPLE 11 - 53: Oneco was a C corporation that used a February year-end. On March 15, 1988, Oneco filed Form 2553. On March 1, 1988, some of Oneco's stock had been owned by a nonresident alien. The shares were purchased by qualified shareholders on March 10, 1988. Oneco's S election cannot take effect until its taxable year beginning March 1, 1989. Since it filed its S election before March 31, 1988, it is exempt from the gain carryover rule.

The gain carryover is created only when the pre-limitation amount (taxable income including only recognized built-in gains and losses) is greater than the taxable income limit. [Regs. §1.1374-2(c)] The excess of a pre-limitation amount over a net unrealized built-in gain limit does not create a gain carryforward.

EXAMPLE 11 - 54: Duco is a former C corporation that filed its S election in January 1995 for its taxable year beginning January 1, 1995. As of January 1, 1995, its net unrealized built-in gain was $25,000. Duco's net unrealized built-in gain consisted of $250,000 unrealized built-in gain and $225,000 unrealized built-in losses. In 1995, it sold property on which it recognized built-in gains of $180,000. Its taxable income was $40,000. Duco's taxable built-in gain is limited to its net unrealized built-in gain of $25,000. The excess of built-in gains recognized over net unrealized built-in gain—$155,000—is not carried forward. Duco will not be subject to any built-in gains tax for the remainder of its recognition period, since it has exhausted its net unrealized built-in gain.

Similarly, utilization of a loss carryover from a C corporation year does not create a gain carryover. As discussed above, the S corporation applies its carryover to the lesser of the net recognized built-in gain or taxable income.

EXAMPLE 11 - 55: JYB Corporation is an S corporation that is subject to the built-in gains tax. In the current year, its taxable income is $80,000 and its net recognized built-in gain is $50,000. It has a net operating loss carryforward of $35,000 from its last year as a C corporation. It applies the loss carryforward to its net recognized built-in gain. Its final taxable built-in gain is $15,000. Since its taxable built-in gain for the current year was not limited by its taxable income, the corporation does not carry any of its current year gains into the next taxable year.

OBSERVATION: A corporation that filed its S election before March 31, 1988, may effectively eliminate its built-in gains tax exposure by reporting little or no taxable income in a year in which it recognizes substantial built-in gains. A corporation that filed its S election on or after March 31, 1988, will need to be aware of the carryover. To use the taxable income limit effectively, such a corporation must eliminate its taxable income in the year in which it recognizes substantial built-in gains and must continue to eliminate its taxable income for each year remaining in the recognition period.

1135.2. Annual adjustment to net unrealized built-in gain. As discussed above, a corporation's net unrealized built-in gain may be a limitation on net recognized built-in gain. [§1374(c)(2)] The amount of net unrealized built-in gain taken into account each year is the corporation's initial net unrealized built-in gain less the net recognized built-in gain of all prior years during the recognition period.

Worksheet 11 - 6, at 1170., illustrates the calculation of a corporation's net unrealized built-in gain. Part 1 shows the computations necessary for the beginning of the corporation's first year as an S corporation. Parts 2 and 3 deal with the adjustments required each year during the recognition period. Example 11 - 56 illustrates the use of the worksheet over several years.

EXAMPLE 11 - 56: MNO Corporation files its S election in 1993, effective January 1, 1993. The following accounts affect its net unrealized built-in gain:

	Adjusted Basis	*Fair Market Value*
Accounts receivable	$ 0	$ 80,000
Investments	50,000	40,000
Fixed assets	80,000	120,000
Total assets	$130,000	$240,000
Accounts payable	$ 0	$ 45,000

MNO Corporation
Net Unrealized Built-In Gain Worksheet

1. **Date S election takes effect**	1/1/93
Value of assets	$240,000
Subtract basis of assets	(130,000)
Subtract cash-basis liabilities	(45,000)
Add potential income items not on balance sheet	
Subtract potential deduction items not on balance sheet	( )
Result: Net unrealized built-in gain limitation at beginning of first S year	$ 65,000

In 1993, MNO collects the receivables, pays the payables, and sells the investments. Its taxable income, by C corporation rules, is $40,000. Using the recognized built-in gain worksheet, as shown above, it calculates its net recognized built-in gain for 1993.

MNO Corporation
Net Recognized Built-In Gain Worksheet, 1993

1a.	Determine recognized built-in gains (Including income items attributable to prior C years)	$80,000
1b.	Subtract recognized built-in losses (Including deductions attributable to prior C years)	(55,000)
1c.	Add carryforward of built-in gain from last year (If election was filed after 3/30/88)	0
1d.	Pre-limitation amount	$25,000
2.	Net unrealized built-in gain limitation	$65,000
3.	Lesser of 1d or 2	25,000

4.	Taxable income limitation	$40,000
5.	Taxable recognized built-in gain (lesser of 3 or 4)	$25,000
6.	Subtract net operating loss and capital loss carryforwards from C years	(0)
7.	Taxable recognized built-in gain (after carryforwards)	$25,000
8.	Tax on 7 at highest corporate rate	8,750
9.	Subtract general business credit and alternative minimum tax carryforwards from C years	(0)
10.	Tax payable in current year (subject to estimated tax requirements)	8,750
11.	If election filed after 3/30/88 and 3 exceeds 4, carry excess forward to next year; otherwise, zero	0

MNO adjusts its net unrealized built-in gain to reflect 1989 activity, using the second part of Worksheet 11 - 6.

2.	**End of first S year**	
	Net unrealized built-in gain from line 1	65,000
	Less net recognized built-in gain this year	(25,000)
	Result: Net unrealized built-in gain limitation at beginning of next S year	$40,000

11

In 1994, MNO sells some fixed assets and recognizes a built-in gain of $15,000. Its taxable income for that year, by C corporation rules, is $5,000. It calculates its net recognized built-in gain as follows:

MNO Corporation
Net Recognized Built-In Gain Worksheet, 1994

1a.	Determine recognized built-in gains (Including income items attributable to prior C years)	$15,000
1b.	Subtract recognized built-in losses (Including deductions attributable to prior C years)	(0)
1c.	Add carryforward of built-in gain from last year (If election was filed after 3/30/88)	0
1d.	Pre-limitation amount	$15,000
2.	Net unrealized built-in gain limitation	$40,000
3.	Lesser of 1d or 2	15,000
4.	Taxable income limitation	$ 5,000
5.	Taxable recognized built-in gain (lesser of 3 or 4)	$ 5,000
6.	Subtract net operating loss and capital loss carryforwards from C years	(0)
7.	Taxable recognized built-in gain (after carryforwards)	$ 5,000

8.	Tax on 7 at highest corporate rate	1,750
9.	Subtract general business credit and alternative minimum tax carryforwards from C years	(0)
10.	Tax payable in current year (subject to estimated tax requirements)	1,750
11.	If election filed after 3/30/88 and 3 exceeds 4, carry excess forward to next year; otherwise, zero	10,000

MNO's adjustment to net unrealized built-in gain at the end of 1990 is:

3.	**Subsequent S years**	
	Net unrealized built-in gain at end of last year	$40,000
	Less net recognized built-in gain this year	(5,000)
	Result: Net unrealized built-in gain limitation at beginning of next S year	$35,000

1135.3. Pass-through to shareholders. The corporation reduces the gain for the amount attributable to the tax in determining pass-through to shareholders. Consequently, the shareholders take the gain, net of tax, into income.

SUMMARY OF AUTHORITY: CODE SECTION 1366(f)(2)

- The S corporation treats the built-in gains tax as a loss that corresponds to the gain (or gains) that created the tax.
- The corporation must allocate tax carefully among the separately reported and bottom-line gains.

11

1135.31. Apportionment of tax by character. When there are recognized built-in gains of different character, such as ordinary income and capital gains, in one year, the corporation must allocate any built-in gains tax between the multiple types of gains. The allocation is made in accordance with the contribution of each type of gain to the total built-in gains of the corporation for the year. [Regs. §1.1374-2(b)] The tax apportioned to each type of gain is treated as a loss of the same character, in determining the effects of the corporate tax on the flow-through to shareholders. [§1366(f)(2)] Worksheet 11 - 3 may be used for this purpose.

This apportionment must be used regardless of the final measure of net recognized built-in gain for the taxable year. Worksheet 11 - 4 may be used to apportion the tax, other deductions, and all income items to the shareholders.

EXAMPLE 11 - 57: Dapco is a calendar-year S corporation that has net unrealized built-in gain of $50,000. In the first year of its recognition period, Dapco recognizes built-in gains of $20,000, of which $15,000 is ordinary income and $5,000 is a long-term capital gain. Dapco's taxable income limitation is $12,000, and Dapco's built-in gains tax is $4,200 (.35 x $12,000). Dapco must apportion the gain, and tax, as follows:

	Capital Gain	*Ordinary Income*	*Total*
Pre-limitation amount	$5,000	$15,000	$20,000
Percentage	25%	75%	100%
Tax	$1,050	$ 3,150	$ 4,200

Dapco's income that passes through to the shareholders consists of the $5,000 capital gain and ordinary income of $7,000, before reduction for the built-in gains tax. Dapco's final measurement of allocation to the shareholders is:

	Capital Gain	*Ordinary Income*	*Total*
Income, before built-in gains tax	$5,000	$7,000	$12,000
Less built-in gains tax	(1,050)	(3,150)	(4,200)
Pass-through to shareholders	$3,950	$3,850	$ 7,800

1135.32. Effect of gain carryforward from prior years. If the tax is payable by the corporation in the same year the gain is recognized, the application of this rule will reduce the gain passing through to the shareholders. If the tax is payable in a different year, due to the operation of the gain carryover, it may create some timing problems.

EXAMPLE 11 - 58: MLC Corporation filed its S election in 1993, effective for calendar year 1993. In 1993, its only recognized built-in gain was a long-term capital gain of $100,000, it had an ordinary loss of $90,000, its taxable income was $10,000, and its tax was $3,500.

In 1994, its taxable income is $250,000, all ordinary. It has no recognized built-in gain in that year, except for the carryforward of $90,000 from 1993. The corporation paid a built-in gains tax of $31,500 in 1994, which was treated as a long-term capital loss. The pass-through to the shareholders is as follows:

	1993	*1994*
Ordinary income (loss)	$(90,000)	$250,000
Long-term capital gain (loss)	96,500	(31,500)

The timing problem from the loss characterization is that the shareholders reported the capital gain in 1993. The capital loss resulting from the payment of the built-in gains tax was only $3,500 in 1993 and $31,500 in 1994. Unless a shareholder had capital gains from other sources in 1994, he or she would be subject to the $3,000 deduction limit for 1994, even though the gain was reported in full in 1993.

11

In this example, the shareholders might be better served if the corporation had not been able to limit its net recognized built-in gain to its taxable income in 1993. The capital loss resulting from the built-in gains tax on the capital gain would have been allowed as an offset to the capital gain in the year in which it was incurred.

As of this writing, there is no guidance on the allocation of built-in gains to the shareholders. Normally, such gains should be allocated in accordance with the per-day, per-share rule discussed in Chapter 6, at 630. When a shareholder terminate his or her entire interest, and the corporation elects to split years, the gains actually recognized in each portion of the year should be specified. When there is a gain carryforward, presumably it should be allocated to the first day of the first short period.

OBSERVATION: While the statute requires that a built-in gains tax be treated as a loss of the same character as the gain that resulted in the tax, it offers no further explanation. Thus, the loss should be subject to the dual classification problems, such as ordinary vs. capital, active vs. passive vs. portfolio, etc. See Chapter 6, at 615.1., for the dual classification problems of income and losses from S corporations.

EXAMPLE 11 - 59: Carico was a C corporation that used the calendar year. It became an S corporation for its taxable year beginning January 1, 1996. On that date, Carico's net unrealized built-in gain was $650,000. In 1996, Carico's pre-limitation amount of net recognized built-in gain was $80,000, and its taxable income limitation was $50,000. All of the 1996 recognized built-in gains were ordinary income. Pursuant to §1374(d)(2)(B), Carico carried $30,000 of its 1996 recognized built-in gain to 1997. On July 30, 1997, Carico's sole shareholder, Caroline, sold all of her stock to Richard. The corporation properly elected to split its 1997 taxable year into two portions under §1377(a)(2). Its recognized built-in gains for the year were:

	1/1 to 7/30	7/31 to 12/31	Total
Pre-limitation amount (excluding carryforward from 1996)	$ 0	$20,000	$ 20,000
Gain carried from 1992	30,000	0	30,000
Total pre-limitation amount	30,000	20,000	50,000
Taxable income limitation	40,000	60,000	100,000

For 1997, the pre-limitation amount is the final measure of net recognized built-in gain. The corporation should probably allocate 60% of the tax to the first portion of the year and 40% to the second portion, although there is no guidance on this matter.

1140. Extensions of the rules.

There are two extensions of the built-in gains tax to property that the corporation did not own at the time the S election took effect. Both deal with situations where careful planning could easily circumvent the built-in gains tax. There is also an extension of the rule to certain installment receivables from sales that occur before the end of the recognition period. Another extension relates to certain property held by a partnership in which the S corporation is a partner.

1140.1. Substituted basis property. When a taxpayer exchanges property in a transaction that qualifies as a like-kind exchange, no gain is recognized on the transfer. Accordingly, there could be no recognized built-in gain if property held at the time the S election took effect is exchanged for new property within the recognition period. If the replacement property were sold at a later time, but still within the recognition period, the S corporation would be able to establish conclusively that it did not own the property when the S election took effect. Such an exchange would provide a marvelous planning opportunity to circumvent the built-in gains tax. Example 11 - 60 illustrates the planning strategy that could be useful in the absence of a specific provision to the contrary.

EXAMPLE 11 - 60: Exco was a C corporation through December 31, 1995. Its S election took effect on January 1, 1996. On January 1, 1996, Exco owned a building with an adjusted basis of $100,000 and fair market value of $250,000. In 1996, it intended to sell the building. Instead of selling the building for cash, Exco exchanged the building for some unimproved real estate. The exchange met all of the rules for a like-kind exchange. The unimproved real estate had a fair market value of $250,000, and neither property was subject to a mortgage. There would be no tax on the disposition of the building. Exco's basis in the unimproved real estate would be $100,000.

In 1997, Exco sold the unimproved real estate. Exco's records could prove conclusively that it did not own the unimproved real estate on January 1, 1996. Therefore, it would be able to rebut the presumption that the gain on the sale was a built-in gain. [§1374(d)(3)(A)] (See discussion at 1125.11.)

When Congress became aware of such planning opportunities, it enacted corrective legislation in the Technical and Miscellaneous Revenue Act of 1988, as follows.

SUMMARY OF AUTHORITY: CODE SECTION 1374(d)(6)

- When property with built-in gains accrued is exchanged for like-kind property, or is replaced with qualified property in an involuntary conversion, there is no recognition of a gain.
- When such an exchange occurs, the built-in gains potential from the surrendered property will attach to the replacement property.
- The extension of the built-in gain to the replacement property does not start a new 10-year recognition period.

EXAMPLE 11 - 61: Refer to Example 11 - 60. The gain on the sale of the unimproved real estate would be subject to treatment as a built-in gain. The recognized built-in gain would, however, be limited to the gain that Exco would have recognized if it had sold the building on January 1, 1996.

The built-in gain is limited to the gain accrued at he time of the S election. Under the general presumption, however, the corporation must establish this limitation.

EXAMPLE 11 - 62: CAI Corporation files its S election on January 1, 1989, effective for calendar 1989. On that date, it has a warehouse with adjusted basis of $300,000 and fair market value of $500,000. In 1993, the warehouse is completely destroyed by fire. At that time, CAI's adjusted basis in the warehouse is $260,000. CAI collects insurance proceeds of $600,000. CAI invests $750,000 in a new warehouse and elects under §1033 to defer the gain of $340,000. The basis of the new warehouse is $410,000. In 1997, when the basis of the warehouse is $340,000, CAI sells it for $850,000, resulting in a gain of $510,000. Since the gain is recognized within the first 10 years of the S election, it is presumed to be a built-in gain.

If the corporation had the old warehouse appraised as of January 1, 1989, it could establish that the built-in gain is $200,000. If it cannot do so, it may have some other options. First, its records should show that depreciation of $40,000 on the old warehouse had occurred after the S election. Second, it should have records to show that the gain deferred on the old warehouse was $340,000. The combination of those records should be adequate to establish that the built-in gain was no more than $300,000.

1140.2. Property received in a tax-free reorganization or liquidation. As Chapter 17 demonstrates, S corporations are allowed to engage in certain tax-free reorganizations. One popular form of reorganization is the merger of one corporation (the extinguished corporation) into another corporation (the surviving corporation). As a general rule, neither corporation nor any of the shareholders of either corporation recognizes gain or loss. This nonrecognition extends to any built-in gains that have not yet been recognized. The merger itself does not accelerate the recognition of a built-in gain. [PLR 9801056]

11

The shareholders who surrender stock in the extinguished corporation substitute the basis of the surrendered stock as basis for the new stock. The surviving corporation takes a carryover basis from the extinguished corporation in each of the assets received.[8]

The general authority for applying the Subchapter C reorganization rules to S corporations is found in §1371(b), which applies all rules of Subchapter C to S corporations, to the extent that those rules do not conflict with the purposes of Subchapter S. The IRS ruling policy on reorganizations of S corporations, however, predates the Subchapter S Revision Act of 1982. As discussed in Chapter 17, at 1715., S corporations often merge with C corporations. Either the S corporation or the C corporation may survive the reorganization. When an S corporation emerges as a surviving corporation, the reorganization, per se, does not terminate the corporation's S election.[9] At first glance, the ability to use a tax-free reorganization might appear to provide an escape from the built-in gains tax.

EXAMPLE 11 - 63: Charlie Corporation is a C corporation that could benefit from an S election. If Charlie made an S election, it would have substantial net recognized built-in gains for several years. It could not effectively eliminate its taxable income without considerable audit risk.

Delta Corporation is an S corporation, and it has had an S election in effect from its inception. Charlie's shareholders purchase all of Delta's stock and merge Charlie into Delta. Looking only at the general exemption from the built-in gains tax for corporations that have always been S corporations, it might appear that the shareholders have accomplished the following:

---

[8] Each of these rules has a specific statutory source. Citations for the general reorganization rules are given in Chapter 17.

[9] This result is stated frequently in letter rulings, many of which are cited in Chapter 17, at 1730.34.

- Neither the shareholders nor Charlie corporation would report any taxable gain as a result of the reorganization.
- Delta would be exempt from the built-in gains tax.

Congress foresaw this possible loophole. In 1988, an amendment to the built-in gains tax formally stated the rule.

SUMMARY OF AUTHORITY: CODE SECTION 1374(d)(8)

- When an S corporation acquires property in a carryover basis transaction from a C corporation, the property so acquired is subject to the built-in gains tax.
- The corporation begins a new 10-year recognition period for the assets acquired in the transaction.
- The general exemption under §1374(c)(1) (which exempts corporations that have always had an S election in effect) does not apply to the corporation.

The two transactions in which an S corporation can receive property from a C corporation and determine basis in the property received by reference to the C corporation's basis are a tax-free reorganization and a tax-free liquidation. [§362(b), §334(b)] Both of these transactions require an extensive knowledge of Subchapter C. They receive brief explanation in Chapter 15, at 1525.7., and Chapter 17, at 1730.3.

OBSERVATION: Until recently, the IRS had taken the ruling position that an S corporation could not use the tax-free liquidation rules, since this transaction involves the liquidation of a subsidiary into a parent corporation that owned at least 80% of the subsidiary's stock. [§332] See Chapter 15, at 1525.8., for discussion. Although the IRS has long been willing to waive momentary ownership of 80% or more of a corporation's stock by an S corporation, it held that an S corporation must be treated as an individual, rather than as a parent corporation, when it liquidates a subsidiary. [PLR 8818049] Recently, the IRS has admitted that this position was in error [PLR 9323024], and has held that an S corporation that liquidates a subsidiary will be treated as a parent corporation, so that the liquidation is tax-free to the subsidiary. [TAM 9245004][10]

The IRS has ruled that property acquired by an S corporation from a C corporation in a tax-free reorganization is subject to the built-in gains tax for 10 years following the reorganization. When an S corporation acquires another S corporation in a tax-free reorganization, the IRS has ruled that the assets acquired in the reorganization are subject to the built-in gains tax, to the same extent and for the same period, that they would have been if the extinguished S corporation had continued in existence. [PLRs 8806031, 8826015, 8922004, 9002051, 9115029, 9115059, 9117055, 9117062, 9118029, 9123049, 9139012, 9140054]

EXAMPLE 11 - 64: Refer to Example 11 - 63. Delta would be subject to the built-in gains tax on all property received from Charlie in the reorganization. Delta's recognition period for that property would be 10 years from the date of the reorganization. However, Delta would be exempt from the built-in gains tax on any other property it owned. The result would be the same if Delta had secured waiver of momentary ownership, purchased all of the stock of Charlie, and liquidated Charlie in a transaction in which §334(b) governed the basis of the assets acquired from Charlie.

---

[10] This Memorandum specifically held that the assets acquired in the tax-free liquidation would be subject to the built-in gains tax for ten years following the liquidation.

CAUTION: The Regulations issued in December 1994 apply to reorganizations and liquidations after December 27, 1994. [Regs. §1.1374-10(a)]

EXAMPLE 11 - 65: Refer to Examples 11 - 63 and 11 - 64. Assume that Charlie had filed Form 2553 before December 27, 1994, but that the reorganization took place in 1995. All the assets acquired from Delta would be subject to the rules of Final Regulations §§1.1374-0 through 1.1374-10.

1140.3. Installment sales. One potential escape from the built-in gains tax would be to sell property using the installment method and schedule receipts to occur beyond the end of the recognition period.

If a corporation sells built-in gain property within the recognition period and uses the installment method, it must calculate the gain that would have been subject to the built-in gains tax if it had elected out of the installment method. The tax will continue to be imposed on the installment receipts, even though they occur after the recognition period normally would end. [Regs. §1.1374-4(h)]

EXAMPLE 11 - 66: Insco was a C corporation through 1988; its S election took effect for its taxable year beginning January 1, 1989. In 1996, Insco sells property using the installment method. The sale price is $150,000, and the adjusted basis is $50,000. All of the gain is a built-in gain. The payment is to be made in 10 equal annual installments (plus interest at the *applicable federal rate* for the date of sale). The principal of each installment is $15,000, and the gain to be reported on each installment is $10,000. For 1996 through 2005, the installment method will result in recognition of $10,000 per year. The entire gain, even that recognized after the year 1998, may be a recognized built-in gain.

11 There may, however, still be some opportunities to reduce the taxable gain. The taxable built-in gain is limited to the taxable gain that would have resulted if the corporation had elected out of the installment method in the year of sale. Accordingly, the S corporation must be careful to calculate any limits from net unrealized built-in gain, C corporation taxable income, or both. To determine the amount taxable, a corporation must calculate the taxable built-in gain (final) as if the corporation had elected out of the installment method.

EXAMPLE 11 - 67: Refer to Example 11 - 66. Assume that Insco's net unrealized built-in gain at the beginning of 1996 was $60,000. If Insco had elected out of the installment method, its taxable built-in gain (final) for 1996 would have been $60,000. Therefore, only the first six installments of $10,000 should be taxable as built-in gains.

In determining the amount that would have been taxable if the corporation had elected out of the installment method in the year of sale, the corporation must observe the effects of any gain carryover. If the corporation filed its S election before March 31, 1988, it may limit the total gain recognition to its taxable income for the year of sale. By contrast, if the corporation filed its S election on or after March 31, 1988, it could not limit the total gain recognition to its taxable income for the year of sale.

EXAMPLE 11 - 68: Refer to Example 11 - 67. Assume that Insco filed its S election *before* March 31, 1988. Assume also that its net unrealized built-in gain at the beginning of 1996 was $60,000, but that its taxable income for the year would have been only $20,000 if it had elected out of the installment method. The taxable built-in gains for that year would have been limited to $20,000. Therefore, only Insco's first two installments received should be taxable as built-in gains.

EXAMPLE 11 - 69: Assume the same facts as in Example 11 - 68, except that Insco filed its S election *after* March 30, 1988. Its taxable built-in gains for 1996 would have been only $20,000.

The difference between its net unrealized built-in gain and its taxable income—$40,000—would carry forward to 1999 and be recognized as built-in gains in that year. Therefore, the entire $60,000 of the corporation's net unrealized built-in gain would have been taxed if the corporation had elected out of the installment method, and the results apparently would be the same as those in Example 11 - 66.

If a corporation that filed its S election after March 30, 1988, makes an installment sale after March 26, 1990, it may still be able to avoid tax on the installments received after the recognition period expires. To do so, it must eliminate its taxable income for the year of the sale and for every remaining year in the recognition period.

EXAMPLE 11 - 70: Refer to Example 11 - 69. Assume the same facts except that Insco has a loss of $100,000 (excluding any gain on the installment sale) in 1996. In 1997 and 1998, the only years remaining in the recognition period, the corporation's taxable income, including $10,000 per year from the installment sale, is zero. If the corporation had elected out of the installment method in 1996, its taxable built-in gain (final) for that year would have been zero. Since its taxable income would not have exceeded zero for the remainder of its recognition period, it would not have paid any built-in gains tax on the installment receivable, if it had elected out of the installment method. Therefore, it should not be subject to the built-in gains tax on the installment gain after its recognition period expires.

The Final Regulations offer some additional relief for a corporation that makes an installment sale before the end of the recognition period. The taxable income limitation for the installment gain is based on the amount of taxable income the corporation would have reported in the year of sale and in all succeeding years within the recognition period if the corporation had elected out of the installment method in the year of sale. [Regs. §1.1374-4(h)(2)] Thus, any built-in losses recognized in subsequent years within the recognition period, as well as any loss carryforwards allowed during the same period, may reduce the taxable built-in gain. [Regs. §1.1374-4(h)(4)]

According to the Regulations under §1374, an installment sale that occurs before the corporation's S election took effect is treated as if it were made during the first year of the recognition period. [Regs. §1.1374-4(h)(1)] Any gain that remains to be taken into account when the S election takes effect is treated as a recognized built-in gain, regardless of when the corporation takes the gain into income.

EXAMPLE 11 - 71: Slowco was a calendar year C corporation through 1996. In 1995, Slowco sold some property on the installment method. The contract price is $150,000. The contract requires payment of interest, plus $10,000 on the principal, each year from 1995 through 2008. The gross profit ratio is 90%, so Slowco would recognize $9,000 of gain on the receipt of each payment. The buyer made timely payments in 1995 and 1996. On January 1, 1997, Slowco's deferred gain was $117,000 (13 payments x $10,000 x 90%). Assuming Slowco's net unrealized built-in gain is at least $117,000, all of the gains recognized on this sale, including those recognized after the recognition period, will be taxable as built-in gains.

OBSERVATION: Although the rules of Regulations under §1374, as issued in December 1994, generally affect only those corporations that file Form 2553 after December 27, 1994, the installment sale rules are in effect for any installment sales made after March 26, 1990. [Regs. §1.1374-10(b)(4)]

1140.4. Income and deductions from partnerships. The Regulations under §1374 establish some rules for determining an S corporation's recognized built-in gain or recognized built-in loss from its distributive share of items from partnerships. Chapter 14 contains a brief discussion of partnership taxation, at 1435.11. In brief, a partnership allocates its income, losses, and deductions much like an S corporation does. Each line item of income, loss, or deduction must be separately stated to each partner, in the same manner as the separately stated items of an S corporation.[11] [§702, §703] For purposes of the built-in gains rules, every item of partnership income that is allocated to a partner that is an S corporation is treated as a recognized built-in gain unless the corporation can rebut the presumption of built-in gains.

If a partnership had an S corporation as a partner when the corporation's S election took effect, the property held by the partnership when the S election took effect is subject to the built-in gains tax. In other words, the Proposed Regulations look through the existence of the partnership, and treat each asset held by the partnership as if it were held by the corporate partner on the day its S election took effect.

> **EXAMPLE 11 - 72:** Parco was a C corporation through 1994. Parco became an S corporation for its taxable year beginning January 1, 1995. On that date, Parco held a 50% interest in PG Partnership. On that date, PG held property with an adjusted basis of $50,000 and fair market value of $80,000. During Parco's recognition period, PG sold the above-mentioned property for $110,000 and reported a gain of $60,000, of which $30,000 was allocated to Parco. Tentatively, Parco must treat its $30,000 gain from GP as a recognized built-in gain. However, if Parco can establish that the value of the property on January 1, 1995, was $80,000, only $15,000 (its proportionate share of the unrealized gain on January 1, 1995) would be treated as a recognized built-in gain.

The steps under the Regulations for calculating an S corporation's recognized built-in gain or recognized built-in loss from its distributive share of items from partnerships are rather complicated. Conceptually, the steps required are as follows:

11

1. Determine if the corporation contributed property to the partnership to avoid the built-in gains tax. If so, the corporation must ignore the remaining partnership rules and treat each income item from the partnership as a recognized built-in gain (RBIG), unless the corporation can rebut the built-in gain presumption under the general rules, discussed at 1125.11. Any loss or deduction is not treated as a recognized built-in loss (RBIL) unless the corporation can satisfy the burden of proof that the loss or deduction is a built-in loss. [Regs. §1.1374-10(b)(1)] This rule applies as of January 1, 1987. See at 1125.16. for further discussion.
2. Determine the S corporation's percentage interest in the partnership, and value thereof, for each year in the recognition period. If the S corporation owns less than 10% of partnership capital and profits, and the fair market value of the S corporation's interest on and before the conversion date is less than $100,000, the S corporation ignores the income or loss from the partnership in computing its RBIG. [Regs. §1.1374-4(i)(5)(i)] This rule does not apply if the partnership was formed or availed of with a principal purpose of avoiding the built-in gains tax. [Regs. §1.1374-4(i)(5)(ii)] The corporation must still include partnership income or loss in computing its taxable income limitation to net RBIG.
3. If the partnership was not formed or availed of to avoid the built-in gains tax, the S corporation must calculate a hypothetical gain or loss. This is what the corporation would have recognized on the first day of the recognition period if the corporation had sold its partnership interest at fair market value. [Regs. §1.1374-4(i)(4)(i)] This hypothetical gain or loss is adjusted for the S corporation's distributive share of the partnership's pending §481(a) adjustments due to changes in accounting methods.[12] [Regs. §1.1374-4(i)(4)(i)]

---

[11] The apportionment of income and other items among the partners is considerably different from the rules used by S corporations and is beyond the scope of this book. The separately stated and nonseparately stated items, however, are nearly identical.

[12] There is no requirement that the corporation must calculate its ordinary income under §751(a) separately from its capital gain or loss under §741. These amounts are combined and treated as one gain or one loss for measurement of the results of the hypothetical sale.

a. If the hypothetical sale of the partnership interest on the first day of the recognition period would result in a gain, the corporation treats this gain as its *partnership RBIG limitation* and computes a *partnership RBIL limitation* of zero. [Regs. §1.1374-4(i)(4)(ii)]

b. If the hypothetical sale of the partnership interest on the first day of the recognition period would result in a loss, the corporation treats this gain as its *partnership RBIL limitation* and computes a *partnership RBIG limitation* of zero. [Regs. §1.1374-4(i)(4)(ii)]

4. Each year in the recognition period, the S corporation treats its distributive share of partnership income, loss, and deduction items as if they were RBIGs or RBILs, subject to the general presumptions. [Regs. §1.1374-4(i)(1)(i)] The corporation must then make several dummy computations of its RBIG.

   a. The corporation computes its net RBIG without including any items from the partnership. [Regs. §1.1374-4(i)(1)(ii)] Although the Regulations are not specific on the details of the computations, presumably the corporation must calculate its pre-limitation amount, its taxable income limitation, and its net unrealized built-in gain limitation in this step.

   b. The corporation computes its net RBIG including all items from the partnership. [Regs. §1.1374-4(i)(1)(iii)] Presumably, the corporation must calculate its pre-limitation amount, its taxable income limitation, and its net unrealized built-in gain limitation in this step.

   c. The corporation finds the difference in its net RBIG with the partnership items from its net RBIG without the partnership items. [Regs. §1.1374-4(i)(1)(iv)] If the difference is positive, the difference is termed the corporation's *partnership RBIG.* If the difference is negative, the difference is termed the corporation's *partnership RBIL.*

5. If the corporation has a partnership RBIG, it must compare this amount with its partnership RBIG limitation, which it computed in step 3, above. It adds the lesser of these two amounts to its net RBIG, which it computed without including any partnership items. The result is the corporation's final measure of RBIG for the year. [Regs. §1.1374-4(i)(1)(iv)] The corporation must then reduce its partnership RBIG limitation for the partnership RBIG included in its net recognized built-in gain for the year, to determine its remaining partnership RBIG limitation for the next year. [Regs. §1.1374-4(i)(2)(i)]

6. If the corporation has a partnership RBIL, it must compare this amount with its partnership RBIL limitation, which it computed in step 3, above. [Regs. §1.1374-4(i)(1)(iv)] It subtracts the lesser of these two amounts from its net RBIG, which it computed without including any partnership items. The result is the corporation's final measure of net RBIG for the year. The corporation must then reduce its partnership RBIL limitation for the next year by its allowed partnership RBIL. [Regs. §1.1374-4(i)(2)(ii)]

Examples 11 - 73, 11 - 74, and 11 - 75 illustrate the steps for an S corporation that has a positive partnership RBIG limitation.

EXAMPLE 11 - 73: Winco, a C corporation through 1994, became an S corporation in its taxable year beginning January 1, 1995. On that date, Winco owned a 50% interest in BG, a partnership. The fair market value of Winco's interest in BG was $300,000, and the adjusted basis was $120,000 on that date. The value of Winco's other assets on January 1, 1995, was $500,000, and its adjusted basis in the other assets was $200,000. Winco had no other items that would affect its built-in gains on January 1, 1995. As of January 1, 1995, Winco should make the following calculations:

11

Fair market value of interest in BG	$300,000
Adjusted basis of interest in BG	(120,000)
RBIG limitation of BG	$180,000
RBIL limitation of BG	$ 0
Fair market value all property	$800,000
Adjusted basis all property	(320,000)
Net unrealized built-in gain	$480,000
Fair market value all property, excluding BG	$500,000
Adjusted basis all property, excluding BG	(200,000)
Net unrealized built-in gain, excluding BG	$300,000

EXAMPLE 11 - 74: Refer to Example 11 - 73. In 1995, Winco has net RBIG of $125,000 (pre-limitation amount) exclusive of its distributive share of BG's items for the year. Its distributive share of BG's items resulted in RBIG of $100,000 and no RBIL. Winco's taxable income, exclusive of its distributive share of income and deductions from BG was $100,000. Its taxable income, including a net loss from BG, was $80,000. Winco makes the following calculations for 1995:

Net RBIG	*Without BG items*	*With BG items*
Pre-limitation amount	$125,000	$225,000
Taxable income limit	100,000	80,000
Net unrealized built-in gain limit	300,000	480,000
Net RBIG (least of above)	100,000	80,000

At this stage, the inclusion of BG items appears to result in a reduction of Winco's net recognized built-in gain. However, since Winco's partnership RBIL limitation with respect to BG is zero, Winco's net recognized built-in gain for 1995 is $100,000. Winco must report $100,000 as a taxable built-in gain and reduce its net unrealized built-in gain to $380,000 for 1996. It does not adjust its RBIG or RBIL limitation from Winco. At the beginning of 1997, Winco's unused net unrealized built-in gain and unused partnership RBIG limitation are:

RBIG limitation of BG	
Beginning of year	$180,000
Adjustment for year	(0)
End of year	$180,000
Net unrealized built-in gain	
Beginning of year	$480,000
Adjustment for year	(100,000)
End of year	$380,000
Net unrealized built-in gain, excluding BG	
Beginning of year	$300,000
Adjustment for year	(100,000)
End of year	$200,000

EXAMPLE 11 - 75: Refer to Examples 11 - 73 and 11 - 74. In 1996, Winco has net RBIG of $150,000 (pre-limitation amount) exclusive of its distributive share of BG's items for the year. Its distributive share of BG's items resulted in recognized built-in gains of $120,000 and no recognized built-in losses. Winco's taxable income, exclusive of its distributive share of income and deductions from BG, was $130,000. Its taxable income, including net income from BG, was $180,000. Winco makes the following calculations for 1996:

Net RBIG	*Without BG items*	*With BG items*
Pre-limitation amount	$150,000	$270,000
Taxable income limit	130,000	180,000
Net unrealized built-in gain limit	200,000	380,000
Net RBIG (least of above)	130,000	180,000

In 1996, Winco's taxable built-in gain is $180,000. Winco's partnership RBIG from BG is $50,000, which represents BG's contribution to Winco's taxable built-in gains. Winco should then reduce its overall net unrealized built-in gain by its recognized built-in gain of $180,000. It will reduce its partnership RBIG limitation by $50,000. At the beginning of 1997, Winco's unused net unrealized built-in gain and unused partnership RBIG limitation are:

RBIG limitation of BG	
Beginning of year	$180,000
Adjustment for year	(50,000)
End of year	$130,000
Net unrealized built-in gain	
Beginning of year	$380,000
Adjustment for year	(180,000)
End of year	$200,000
Net unrealized built-in gain, excluding BG	
Beginning of year	$200,000
Adjustment for year	(130,000)
End of year	$ 70,000

Note that the taxable income limitation of $180,000 reduced the corporation's taxable built-in gain from $270,000. Thus, Winco would have a recognized built-in gain carryover of $90,000 to 1997.

> **OBSERVATION:** Unless the steps laid out in the Regulations are followed precisely, the rules for calculating RBIG and RBIL from partnerships may not make any sense. In the above examples, the partnership has passed through a total of $220,000 of RBIG ($100,000 in 1995 and $120,000 in 1996), even though its RBIG limitation was only $180,000 at the beginning of the S corporation's recognition period. This situation is not unrealistic, since the partnership may have had some economically depreciated property at the beginning of the S corporation's recognition period that has not yet been sold. Although the partnership RBIG limitation began at $180,000 and the partnership has passed through $220,000 of RBIGs, the partnership RBIG limitation remains at $130,000.

An S corporation may dispose of a partnership interest during the recognition period. The disposition of the interest may be taxable as a built-in gain or deductible as a built-in loss. If the disposition results in a gain, the gain is a built-in gain, to the extent that the original partnership RBIG limitation exceeds the partnership RBIGs that have already passed through from the partnership. [Regs. §1.1374-4(i)(3)]

EXAMPLE 11-76: Refer to Examples 11-73, 11-74, and 11-75. At the beginning of 1997, Winco sells its entire interest in BG and recognizes a gain of $250,000. The amount of gain that is treated as a RBIG is $130,000, which is the unused partnership RBIG limitation at the end of 1996.

11

The Regulations under §1374 provide parallel rules for losses that pass through from partnerships. If the S corporation disposes of its partnership interest at a loss during the recognition period, the loss is treated as a RBIL, but only to the extent the partnership RBIL limitation has not been reduced by the pass-through of RBILs during the recognition period. [Regs. §1.1374-4(i)(3)]

The Regulations also provide special treatment for the disposition of an asset that had been held by a partnership and distributed to the S corporation. In general, a distribution of property from a partnership does not result in a taxable gain or deductible loss to either the partnership or the partner who receives the property. [§731] The basis of the property to the partnership, prior to distribution, becomes the basis of the property to the receiving partner. [§732]

Therefore, there is no RBIG or RBIL when a partnership distributes property to an S corporation. If a partnership owns property at the beginning of an S corporation partner's recognition period and distributes the property to the S corporation during the recognition period, the potential RBIG or RBIL remains with the property. The S corporation is treated as if it had owned the property on the first day of the recognition period. [Regs. §1.1374-4(i)(7)] If it sells the property during the recognition period, any gain is presumed to be a built-in gain, and any loss is presumed not to be a built-in loss, under the general rules regarding built-in gains and losses. The corporation may rebut either presumption by conclusively establishing the fair market value and basis of the property on the first day of the recognition period.

EXAMPLE 11 - 77: Cateco was a C corporation through 1994. Its S election took effect for its taxable year beginning January 1, 1995. On that date, Cateco owned a 50% interest in DAP, a partnership. DAP owned some nondepreciable real estate on January 1, 1995, with an adjusted basis of $50,000 and fair market value of $120,000. In 1997, DAP distributed the real estate to Cateco. Cateco's basis in the distributed property was $50,000, according to §732. The distribution of the property from DAP to Cateco was not a taxable event, and there was no recognition of a built-in gain in 1997. In 1999, Cateco sold the real estate for $150,000, reporting a gain of $100,000. Cateco had documentation to prove that the fair market value of the property on January 1, 1995, was $120,000. Therefore, $70,000 of the gain was a recognized built-in gain in 1998. This is the same treatment as would be used if Cateco had owned the property on January 1, 1995.

11

When a partner contributes property to a partnership in exchange for an interest therein, no gain or loss is recognized on the transfer. [§721] The gain or loss that is avoided on the transfer is often termed the *pre-contribution* gain or loss. The partnership must allocate all pre-contribution gain or loss to the contributing partner. [§704(c)] Pre-contribution gain or loss may be eroded by allocation of depreciation for periods after the contribution. [Regs. §1.704-1(c)(2), Example 1] The Regulations under §1374 provide that there is no adjustment to an S corporation's pre-contribution gain or loss for measurement of the built-in gain that results from the ultimate disposition of the property by the partnership.

EXAMPLE 11 - 78 [adapted from Regs. §1.1374-4(i)(8), Example 8]: Dateco was a C corporation through 1994. Its S election took effect for its taxable year beginning January 1, 1995. On that date, Dateco contributed property to a partnership in exchange for a 50% interest in the partnership. The property had an adjusted basis of zero and fair market value of $40,000 on the contribution date. In 1995, the partnership claimed $8,000 depreciation on the property for accounting purposes (none for tax purposes), and none of the book depreciation was allocated to Dateco. In early 1996, the partnership sold the property for $40,000. Pursuant to §704(c), Dateco was allocated $32,000 of the gain, and the other partner was allocated the remaining $8,000 of gain. Dateco, however, was required to treat all $40,000 as a recognized built-in gain.

The Regulations under §1374 do not cover all potential problems of built-in gains when an S corporation is a partner in a partnership. For instance, there is no direct statement about, and no example of, an S corporation that is a partner in two or more partnerships on its date of conversion to S status. Presumably, the corporation would need to make separate calculations of net RBIG, with and without the pass-through, for each partnership in which it owns an interest.

Similarly, the Regulations do not explicitly coordinate the partnership rules with the tax-free reorganization rules. Presumably, a C corporation with an interest in a partnership, which is then acquired by an S corporation in a tax-free reorganization, would need to measure its partnership RBIG or RBIL limit on the date of acquisition. The surviving S corporation would then need to follow the same rules as if it had owned the partnership directly.

OBSERVATION: The partnership provisions of the built-in gains Regulations do not take effect for any corporation unless it filed its S election after December 27, 1994. (There is a significant exception if the contribution of property to a partnership has a principal purpose of avoiding the built-in gains tax; see at 1140.4, below.) Therefore, there is no guidance on the treatment of partnership items for existing S corporations. The Regulations may provide some approximation of guidance for S corporations that face the problems discussed in this portion of the chapter.

The accounting rules for built-in gains will undoubtedly become more complex for any S corporation that owns interests in two or more partnerships. The Regulations do not even attempt to give an example of this situation. It is a problem that many S corporations may need to deal with, and this discussion may provide some defensible positions.

EXAMPLE 11 - 79: Twoco was a C corporation that used the calendar year. It became an S corporation for its taxable year beginning January 1, 1993. On that date, Twoco owned interests in two partnerships, Onepar and Twopar. It had not transferred any assets to either of the partnerships in anticipation of the S election, and Twoco owned more than 10% of the capital and profits interests in each partnership. Twoco computes its net unrealized built-in gain as follows, on January 1, 1993:

	Fair Market Value	*Adjusted Basis*
Interest in Onepar	$150,000	$ 95,000
Interest in Twopar	220,000	235,000
All other assets	450,000	350,000
Total	$820,000	$680,000
Overall net unrealized built-in gain		$140,000

Twoco must compute its RBIG and RBIL limitations for the interest in each partnership. The computations would be as follows:

1. RBIG and RBIL limitations with respect to Onepar.

Net Unrealized Built-In Gain without Onepar	*Fair Market Value*	*Adjusted Basis*	*Net Unrealized Built-In Gain*
Interest in Twopar	$220,000	$235,000	
All other assets	450,000	350,000	
Total	$670,000	$585,000	$85,000

11

Overall net unrealized built-in gain with Onepar	$140,000
Overall net unrealized built-in gain without Onepar	(85,000)

The comparison of these figures reveals that Twoco's net unrealized built-in gain would be $55,000 less without its interest in Onepar than it is with that interest. Therefore, its RBIG and RBIL limitations with respect to Onepar are:

RBIG limitation with respect to Onepar	0
RBIL limitation with respect to Onepar	55,000

2. RBIG and RBIL limitations with respect to Twopar.

Overall net unrealized built-in gain	$ 140,000

Net Unrealized Built-In Gain without Twopar	*Fair Market Value*	*Adjusted Basis*	*Net Unrealized Built-In Gain*
Interest in Onepar	$150,000	$ 95,000	
All other assets	450,000	350,000	
Total	$600,000	$445,000	$155,000

The comparison of these figures reveals that Twoco's net unrealized built-in gain would be $15,000 less without its interest in Twopar than it is with that interest. Therefore, its RBIG and RBIL limitations with respect to Twopar are:

RBIG limitation with respect to Twopar	$15,000
RBIL limitation with respect to Twopar	0

11

The implications of these calculations are as follows:

1. In any year in which Onepar reports income that would otherwise be treated as a recognized built-in gain, the gain is ignored in Twoco's calculations of net recognized built-in gain. The gain passed through from Onepar does not adjust Twoco's net unrealized built-in gain, nor does it affect Twoco's RBIG or RBIL limit with respect to Onepar.
2. In any year in which a loss passes through from Onepar and the loss is substantiated as a built-in loss, such loss may offset any other built-in gains recognized by Twoco. By reducing Twoco's net recognized built-in gain, the loss will indirectly reduce Twoco's net unrealized built-in gain limitation for all succeeding years. Such loss will also reduce Twoco's partnership RBIL limitation for future years.
3. If Twoco disposes of its interest in Onepar during its recognition period, any gain on the disposition will not be treated as a recognized built-in gain. A loss on the disposition would be treated as a recognized built-in loss, but only to the extent of $55,000, reduced by any recognized built-in loss from Onepar in preceding years.
4. In any year in which Twopar reports income that would otherwise be treated as a recognized built-in gain, the gain is included in Twoco's net recognized built-in gain for the year. Such gain will reduce Twoco's net unrealized built-in gain, and it reduces Twoco's RBIG limit with respect to Twopar. Such gain has no effect on Twoco's RBIL limitation with respect to Twopar.
5. In any year in which a loss passes through from Twopar and the loss is substantiated as a built-in loss, such loss will not affect Twoco's net recognized built-in gain. The loss passed through from Twopar does not adjust Twoco's net unrealized built-in gain, nor does it affect Twoco's RBIG or RBIL limit with respect to Twopar.

6. If Twoco disposes of its interest in Twopar during its recognition period, any loss on the disposition will not be treated as a recognized built-in loss. A gain on the disposition would be treated as a recognized built-in gain, but only to the extent of $15,000, reduced by any recognized built-in gain from Twopar in preceding years.

The possible combinations of gains and losses from interests in more than one partnership are practically infinite. However, if an S corporation runs several dummy calculations of its net recognized built-in gain and excludes only one partnership's items from each calculation, the results should be defensible.

1145. Problem areas.

Application of the built-in gains rules to specific situations presents numerous problems. Some of the topics covered here receive little or no guidance from any source. Others are addressed in the Regulations, but often the explanations and examples cover only simple situations. This portion of the chapter clarifies some existing positions and attempts to develop defensible approaches to situations where guidance is lacking.

1145.1. Non negativity of built-in gain. One final aspect of net recognized built-in gain deserves mention: The amount can only be positive or zero. There is no mention of *net unrealized built-in loss* in §1374. In fact, there is no definition of this term in Subchapter S, or in the Regulations under §1374.

EXAMPLE 11 - 80: R Corporation makes an S election on March 1, 1994, effective for calendar year 1994. On January 1, 1994, it had the following properties:

	Adjusted Basis	*Fair Market Value*
Inventory	$ 40,000	$ 75,000
Land	20,000	80,000
Securities	80,000	35,000
Total	$140,000	$190,000

Its net unrealized built-in gain is $50,000, according to the above information.

In 1994, R sells the inventory and securities. Its recognized built-in gain is $35,000. Its recognized built-in loss is $45,000. Its taxable built-in gain (preliminary) is zero. There is no provision for the net loss of $10,000 from the sales of built-in gain property.

Each year, an S corporation's net unrealized built-in gain is reduced by the amount of net recognized built-in gain [*taxable built-in gain (preliminary)*, as used in this book]. Since R's taxable built-in gain (preliminary) for 1994 is zero, R does not adjust its net unrealized built-in gain for any 1994 transactions.

In 1995, R sells the land and recognizes a gain of $60,000. There is no provision in the Code that allows it to utilize any of the 1994 built-in loss against the 1995 built-in gains, since that loss was not recognized in 1995. Therefore, its net recognized built-in gain is $60,000.

If R can establish that its net unrealized built-in gain was $50,000, the taxable built-in gain (preliminary) would be limited to that amount. However, if the IRS asserted that the corporation had at least $10,000 fair market value of unrecorded assets, such as goodwill, when the S election took effect, R's taxable built-in gain (preliminary) for 1995 would be $60,000.

OBSERVATION: In Example 11 - 80, the corporation may have wasted built-in losses by recognizing them in the wrong year. Although tax consequences cannot always dictate business decisions, such as the disposition of property, the corporation

11

should be aware of the tax consequences and, whenever possible, plan the timing of its transactions to achieve the best tax results. In the above example, if the corporation could have waited until the second year to recognize $10,000 of its losses, it could have reduced its risk of paying built-in gains tax.

1145.2. Coordination of built-in gains tax and §382. In 1986, Congress was concerned with deduction of corporate loss carryovers following a change in ownership. The major concern was that a buyer might acquire a corporation with little motivation except to deduct the corporation's loss carryforwards. The purchaser might be able to infuse new operating assets into a corporation that had sustained losses, and use the old losses to offset new income. In response, the Tax Reform Act of 1986 enacted §382, which limits a corporation's ability to use old losses following a change in ownership. The operating rules of §382 are discussed briefly in Chapter 16, at 1630.1.

On the surface, §382 has limited applicability to S corporations, since §382 limits deductions available to corporations [§382(a)] and an S corporation must compute its taxable income in the same manner as an individual. [§1363(b)] When an S corporation must use the C corporation rules to compute its taxable income, however, the IRS has justification to impose the §382 limitations on S corporations. An S corporation must use the C corporation rules to compute its taxable income (both the pre-limitation amount and the taxable income limitation) for the built-in gains tax calculations. [Regs. §1.1374-2(a)(1); Regs. §1.1374-2(a)(2)] The Regulations under §1374 require that an S corporation be subject to the limits of §382, in the same manner as a C corporation, when it uses the C corporation rules to compute its taxable income. [Regs. §1.1374-1(b)] Probably the most frequent application of §382 to the calculation of taxable built-in gain is the limitation on the use of net operating loss carryforwards when there has been a change in ownership in an S corporation, the S corporation has a net operating loss carryforward which occurred before the ownership change, and the S corporation has net recognized built-in gain in a year after the ownership change.

11

In general, the limitation imposed by §382 is that the corporation may use only a portion of loss carryforwards that are being carried forward from years prior to the ownership change. The portion is the value of the corporation on the date the ownership changed, multiplied by the long-term tax-exempt interest rate, which is published monthly by the Internal Revenue Service. [§382(b)(1)]

EXAMPLE 11 - 81 [adapted from Regs. §1.1374-5(b)]: Ownco was a C corporation through 1994. On January 1, 1995, Owen, who had not previously been a shareholder in Ownco, bought all of Ownco's stock for $500,000. At the end of 1994, Ownco had a net operating loss carryforward of $400,000. On that date, the long-term tax-exempt interest rate was 8%. Ownco's annual §382 limit is $40,000 ($500,000 x 8%). Ownco remained a C corporation until January 1, 1997, when its S election took effect. It had not used any of its net operating loss carryforward in 1995 or 1996.

Ownco used the cash method of accounting. On January 1, 1997, its accounts receivable were $100,000. It collected all of these accounts in 1997. Its taxable built-in gain, before the net operating loss deduction, was $100,000. Ownco can use only $40,000 of the pre-1995 net operating loss carryforward to reduce its taxable built-in gain in 1997, due to the §382 limit.

Section 382 uses some of the same terms as does §1374. In particular, both Code provisions contain the following terms:

- Recognized built-in gain
- Recognized built-in loss
- Net unrealized built-in gain

There are some different terms in the two provisions. Code §382 uses the term *recognition period* but defines the term as a five-year period following an ownership change. Section 382

TABLE 11 - 4: Desired Treatment Under §382 and §1374

	§382		*§1374*	
Type of transaction:	Gain	Loss	Gain	Loss
Taxpayer prefers:	Built-in	Not built-in	Not built-in	Built-in
IRS prefers:	Not built-in	Built-in	Built-in	Not built-in

also uses the term *net unrealized built-in loss*, which does not appear in §1374. Section 382 does not use the term *net recognized built-in gain*.

Although §1374 and §382 contain similar terminology and were enacted in the same legislative package, they must be approached from opposite points of view. In general, §382 limits the ability of a corporation to deduct a recognized built-in loss and relaxes the limit for the corporation's recognized built-in gains. A corporation facing §382 problems is penalized on its built-in losses and rewarded for finding built-in gains. Therefore, the position favorable to a taxpayer with §382 problems is the opposite of the position favorable to a taxpayer with §1374 problems. Table 11 - 4 shows the preferred treatment of gains and losses for both the taxpayer and the IRS and highlights the contrasts between §382 and §1374.

The IRS is attempting to develop some consistency in the definitions of *built-in gains* and *built-in losses* for both §382 and §1374.[13] Although there have been several letter rulings under §1374, most of them to-date relate to effective dates and tax-free reorganizations. Few letter rulings have dealt with the definitions of *built-in gains* and *built-in losses*. Some, but not very many, rulings have been issued under §382 that define *built-in gains* and *built-in losses*. When rulings issued under §382 are cited in this chapter, they are clearly labeled as rulings under §382. In interpreting these rulings in relation to §1374, the reader should be aware that the taxpayer requesting a ruling under §382 has sought assurance that gains are built-in gains. A taxpayer who requests a ruling under §1374 would be attempting to establish the opposite position.

11

As explained in Chapter 1, a letter ruling is not valid precedent and cannot be relied on by any person other than the taxpayer to whom it was issued. Usually, however, letter rulings are a useful indicator of the IRS position on the tax problem for which the ruling was issued. A position held by the IRS in a letter ruling issued under §382 may be of only limited use for a taxpayer with §1374 problems. At a minimum, however, a taxpayer requesting a ruling under §1374 can indicate to the IRS its own position by citing a ruling issued under §382.

Another Code section that uses the same terminology is §384. That provision is designed to curb what was commonly known as a "mirror" transaction to avoid the application of §382. In brief, §384 provides that a corporation that is subject to the loss limitations of §382 cannot acquire a corporation with substantial built-in gains and offset the built-in losses of the parent corporation with the built-in gains of the newly acquired corporation. A taxpayer faced with §384 problems will want to minimize the built-in gains of the acquired corporation. Accordingly, planning strategies under §384 will follow principles that are the opposite from those employed under §382 and will be similar to those used by an S corporation that is having built-in gains problems.

The Regulations under §1374 apply the principles of §384 to S corporations when there has been a change in ownership, usually a merger, and an S corporation has recognized built-in gains from one pre-merger corporation and losses from another corporation. [Regs. §1.1374-1(b)] In addition, the Regulations forbid a corporation with built-in losses or loss carryforwards to offset those losses against income that results from the operations of an acquired business.

[13] See, for example, Notice 90-27, 1990-1 CB 336 (discussed above), which governs treatment of installment sales of built-in gain property during the recognition period. That Notice applies to both §1374 and §382.

EXAMPLE 11 - 82: Lossco was a C corporation through 1993. It became an S corporation for its taxable year beginning January 1, 1994. In 1995, Lossco acquired all of the assets of Gainco, a C corporation, in a tax-free reorganization. In 1996, Lossco recognizes a built-in loss of $50,000 from the sale of an asset that it had owned on January 1, 1994. Lossco can demonstrate conclusively that the loss is a built-in loss. In 1996, Lossco also sells one of the assets it acquired from Gainco and reports a gain of $75,000. The Regulations do not permit the offset of the gain and the loss.

When an S corporation is subject to the built-in gains tax from more than one asset acquisition, and is subject to the taxable income limitation, the Regulation under §1374 allocate the taxable income limit proportionately. The pre-limitation amount of assets sold from each asset acquisition is apportioned to the corporation's taxable income.

EXAMPLE 11 - 83: Getco was a C corporation through 1994, and it converted to S status for its taxable year beginning January 1, 1995. On January 1, 1995, Getco's net unrealized built-in gain was $50,000. Getco had a net operating loss carryforward of $30,000 on January 1, 1995. In 1995, Getco sold some assets for a net recognized built-in gain of $40,000 (pre-limitation amount).

Also in 1995, Getco acquired all of Hadco's assets in a tax-free reorganization. Hadco was a C corporation until it was acquired by Getco. The calculation of net unrealized built-in gain with respect to Hadco's assets was $100,000. Getco recognized built-in gains of $20,000 on the sale of assets it acquired from Hadco in 1995. Getco's taxable income limitation for 1995 was $30,000. Getco must apportion its taxable income limitation as follows:

	Assets Owned on 1/1/95	*Acquired from Hadco*	*Total*
Pre-limitation amount	$40,000	$20,000	$60,000
Percentage	66.7%	33.3%	100%
Taxable income limitation	$20,000	$10,000	$30,000

Pursuant to the Regulations, Getco could use only $20,000 of its net operating loss carryforward to offset its taxable built-in gains for 1995. Therefore, Getco's taxable built-in gain for 1995 is $10,000.

The separation of losses resulting from predecessor corporations is not limited to situations in which §382 or §384 applies. These sections are effective only when there is a change in ownership.

EXAMPLE 11 - 84: Refer to Example 11 - 83. Assume that Getco and Hadco were brother–sister corporations with identical ownership for at least three years before the reorganization. There would be no limitation from §382 or §384 on the ability of the surviving corporation to offset pre-reorganization gains and losses. The results would be the same as those in Example 11 - 62.

1145.3. Valuation of inventories. Valuation of inventory may vary considerably depending upon the valuation assumptions. Replacement cost, comparative sales value, and net realizable value (adjusted for completion costs) are all legitimate methods, according to Revenue Procedure 77-12. [Rev. Proc. 77-12, 1977-1 CB 569] That Revenue Procedure was issued under prior corporate liquidation rules, in which a purchasing corporation could liquidate a recently purchased subsidiary and allocate its cost of the subsidiary's stock to basis in the assets received in liquidation. [(§334(b)(2), before its repeal by the Tax Equity and Fiscal Responsibility Act of 1982. Similar rules apply under current §338.] The rules of the Revenue Procedure state that replacement cost is an appropriate measure of value for a retail or wholesale concern but may need to be adjusted. For example, a well-balanced inventory might have a greater value than replacement cost, whereas the presence of obsolete goods may lower the value. A retail corporation making an S election may want to consider using the replacement cost method.

> **EXAMPLE 11 - 85:** JY Corporation is a C corporation that makes an S election for its taxable year beginning January 1, 1996. JY uses the FIFO cost method of valuing its inventory for tax purposes. As of January 1, 1996, its FIFO cost of inventory is $700,000. The replacement cost of its inventory is also $700,000. According to Revenue Procedure 77-12, JY has a position for valuing its inventory at $700,000. Since the position is not in contrast to any authority, it should be justifiable on a tax return.

A manufacturer's inventory may involve valuation problems different from those of a retailer or wholesaler. Revenue Procedure 77-12 advises the use of the comparative sales method or the income method. The comparative sales method uses the actual selling price to customers as its starting point. This value is then reduced for an amount that considers the time to dispose, the costs to dispose, and a reasonable amount of profit commensurate with the degree of risk. The income method, not described comprehensively in the Revenue Procedure, applies when the inventory is the only asset that is expected to provide revenue as of the valuation date. Therefore, the value must be reduced for any necessary costs, and for a reasonable return on investment, during the period of disposition.

When inventories are normal in quantity for the owner's usual level of sales, the comparative sales method is probably the best measure. If they are abnormally large, the income method may be a better valuation. The Revenue Procedure states that work in process is to be valued using the same method as that used for finished goods. Replacement cost is appropriate for raw materials. The requirement that manufacturers' finished goods and work in process be valued by subtracting anticipated profits, as well as disposition costs, should enable S corporations to state a relatively low market value for their inventories.

A final consideration in comparing value with basis is the requirement to apply uniform capitalization rules to the basis of inventory. These rules may require that considerably more costs be added to the tax basis of inventory than are included on the financial statement book value. By following the rules in Revenue Procedure 77-12, a retailer, wholesaler, or manufacturer should be able to place a value somewhere near tax basis on its inventory for measurement of net unrealized built-in gain.

11

> **OBSERVATION:** The Regulations under §1374 instruct corporations to value inventories on the conversion date as if they were sold from a willing buyer to a willing seller in one transaction. [Regs. §1.1374-7(a)] This position is not a radical departure from Revenue Procedure 77-12. In most circumstances, the value of inventory in a bulk sale is considerably less that the amount that would be received from orderly sales in the ordinary course of business. The guidance from Revenue Procedure 77-12 should help to justify relatively low inventory values for measurement of net unrealized built-in gain.
>
> The IRS indicated in the preamble to the Proposed Regulations under §1374 that it was reconsidering the applicability of the principles of Revenue Procedure 77-12 to the built-in gains problem. [Preamble to Proposed Regs. §1.1374-1-10, CO-80-87, December 4, 1992] If the IRS should take further action, it may apply a profit percentage to the ultimate disposition value. This technique has been used by the courts in valuing inventories in bulk purchases. [See *Knapp King-Size Corp. v. U.S.*, 75-1 USTC 9461 (Ct. Cls.), and *Zeropack Company*, TC Memo 1983-652.] The Final Regulations did not adopt any safe harbor for inventory valuation. Thus, the final word on inventory valuation, as of this writing, is Revenue Procedure 77-12, discussed above.

In the normal course of business, physical inventory turnover occurs quickly. Under the FIFO cost flow assumption, the gross profit on the first sales in the first S year might be considered a recognized built-in gain. Under the rationale of Revenue Procedure 77-12, however, the gross profit may be attributable to events that occur after the S election takes effect.

> **EXAMPLE 11 - 86:** Refer to Example 11 - 85. JY generally realizes a 30% gross profit on the sale of its goods. In 1996, JY sells its beginning inventory for $1,000,000. Using reproduction, or replacement, cost of its inventories, it determines that the value of its inventory on January 1, 1996, was only $700,000. Therefore, the $300,000 gain recognized on the sale of inventory is attributable to activities after the S election took effect, and it does not result in a recognized built-in gain. Consistent with this position, JY reports net unrealized built-in gain of zero with respect to its inventory.

The preamble to the Proposed Regulations adopted a safe-harbor rule for determining the recognized built-in gain from the sale of inventory. The safe-harbor formula was based on the gross profit from the beginning inventory, less direct selling expenses. Although the Final Regulations did not adopt any safe harbor, this book continues to demonstrate the formula that the IRS considered in 1992. Although it cannot be relied on as authority, the formula is reasonably objective and could provide at least an arguable position.

To compute the gross profit, an S corporation would apply the following formula:

1. Compute the gross profit for the year as follows:

   Gross receipts from sales
   Less cost of goods sold
   Less direct selling expenses
   ___
   Equals gross profit

2. Compute percentage of gross profit to reflect any costs that add to value but were not taken into account in determining gross profit. (The preamble provides no guidance on this computation.)

   $$\frac{\text{Gross profit, adjusted}}{\text{Gross receipts from sales}}$$

3. Compute the turnover rate of the beginning inventory (inventory turns) for the first year of the recognition period, as follows:

   $$\frac{\text{Cost of goods sold in year}}{\text{Beginning FIFO value}}$$

4. Compute the gross profit of one turn of inventory for the year. The result is assumed to be the gross profit attributable to the opening inventory, and it is treated as a recognized built-in gain.

> **EXAMPLE 11 - 87:** Zerosize Corporation was a C corporation through calendar year 1994. It converted to S status for its taxable year beginning January 1, 1995. Zerosize used the FIFO inventory method. Zerosize's sales and inventory data for 1995 follow:

Beginning inventory	$ 650,000
Sales for 1995	$7,350,000
Cost of goods sold	$4,950,000
Direct selling expenses	$ 785,000

Zerosize includes all costs that add value to inventory in its cost of goods sold. Thus, there is no adjustment to the gross profit percentage. To compute the safe-harbor built-in gain from the sale of inventory for 1995, Zerosize makes the following computations:

Gross receipts from sales	$7,350,000
Less cost of goods sold	(4,950,000)
Less direct selling expenses	(785,000)
Equals gross profit	$1,615,000
Inventory turns	
Cost of goods sold	$4,950,000
Divide by beginning inventory	650,000
Number of turns	7.62
Gross profit	$1,615,000
Divide by number of turns	7.62
Gross profit from one turn	$ 211,942

Thus, Zerosize would treat $211,942 as a recognized built-in gain from the sale of its opening inventory.

The Regulations also provide that gains on the sale of inventory are determined according to the corporation's inventory method. If a corporation adopts LIFO when it becomes an S corporation, in order to avoid the built-in gains tax, the corporation must use FIFO to measure its built-in gains. [Regs. §1.1374-7(b)]

1145.4. Income from property. Income from property, such as rents, royalties, interest, and dividends, will generally not result in built-in gains, even when the property producing the income was held by the S corporation at conversion date. These types of income would be treated as recognized built-in gains only if they could be included, by the accrual method of accounting, at conversion date. Therefore, corporations that used the accrual method of accounting before the conversion date would have already included these items in taxable income for the final C year, and they would not be included again in the first S year. A cash-method taxpayer would include these items as recognized built-in gains only if the right to receive such income was fixed, and determinable with reasonable accuracy, under the general accrual tests. (See Regulations §1.1374-4(a), Examples 1 and 2, for an application of this principle to mineral interests. Also see PLR 9825008, specifically ruling that a coal royalty is not a recognized built-in gain.) A recognized gain or loss from the disposition of the property, however, is treated as a recognized built-in gain or recognized built-in loss.

In some previous rulings, regarding timber companies that intended to become S corporations, the IRS held that any increase in value in unharvested timber, as of the conversion date, would not be treated as a recognized built-in gain when the timber was sold. Any logs harvested at the conversion date, however, would produce recognized built-in gains when they were sold. [PLRs 9430026, 9712027, 9712028, 9719032, 9732030, 9739046, 9732030, 9802005, 9826017, 9826016, 9825018, 9827020]

In 1998, the IRS changed its ruling policy on this issue, stating in Revenue Procedure 98-56 that it would no longer issue rulings on whether timber that was uncut on conversion date and is cut and sold after conversion will be subject to the built-in gains tax. [Rev. Proc. 98-56, 1998-46 IRB] This Revenue Procedure also applies to coal and other mineral income. As a result, S corporations engaged in timber and mineral extraction will not be able to obtain rulings under the current IRS policy.

11

1145.5. Contingencies. In general, an asset cannot be accrued for income tax purposes until it meets two tests [Regs. §1.451-1(a)]:

- All events must occur to fix the taxpayer's right to receive the income.
- The amount of income must be determinable with reasonable accuracy.

Any potential claim that does not meet these two tests is a contingent asset. The Regulations under §1374 use the accrual method to value contingencies in measuring net unrealized built-in gain. Therefore, if any income item could not be reported on the corporation's accrual-method tax return, it will not result in a recognized built-in gain when it is taken into account.

> **EXAMPLE 11 - 88:** Suemco, Inc., was a C corporation through 1995. Its S election took effect on January 1, 1996. On that date, it was a plaintiff in a lawsuit in which it was seeking $1,000,000 damages. In 1996, Suemco received a settlement of $400,000. Under general rules for the accrual method of accounting, Suemco would not take any of the damages into income in 1995, since neither the unconditional right nor the final amount was fixed at that time. Therefore, Suemco would not report a recognized built-in gain when it receives the award. Suemco would not include any portion of the damages in its net unrealized built-in gain as of January 1, 1996.

Similarly, any contingent liability will not be allowed as a built-in loss, since it would not be deductible under the accrual method of accounting. [See Regs. §1.1374-4(b)(3), Example 3] A tort liability or worker's compensation payment that is fixed at the date of conversion to S status is deductible as a built-in loss when paid. [Regs. §1.1374-4(b)(2)]

11

1145.6. Accounting changes. An application of considerable importance for a few years following the Tax Reform Act of 1986 is §481 adjustments. Many corporations, for example, changed from the reserve method to the direct write-off method for bad debts. A voluntary accounting change is followed by a §481 adjustment, in which the taxpayer reports the income or loss form the cumulative effect of the change over four years, beginning with the year of change. [Rev. Proc. 97-27 1997-21 IRB, §3.06]

Any such corporation that had created its bad debt reserve while it was a C corporation would have a concern about the treatment of the remaining adjustment as a built-in gain or loss. The current IRS position is that the remaining §481 adjustment is not accelerated when a C corporation becomes an S corporation or when an S corporation terminates its election. [Rev. Proc. 98-60, 1998-51 IRB]

The Tax Court has held that income from a §481 adjustment was a recognized built-in gain, in a year unaffected by the Final Regulations. [*Argo Sales Company, Inc.*, 105 TC No. 7 (1995)] Similarly, the IRS has ruled that §481 adjustments resulting from a bank's change in bad debt accounting method was a recognized built-in gain. [Rev. Proc. 97-37, 1997-33 IRB 18]

The Regulations issued in December 1994 treat all §481 adjustments as built-in gains or losses when they are taken into account, if the accounting change occurred before the conversion date. [Regs. §1.1374-4(d)] In addition, the Regulations treat income or deductions from accounting changes made in the first S corporation year as net unrealized built-in gains or losses. [Regs. §1.1374-3(a)(4)]

The IRS has ruled that a former C corporation was a farming corporation that had been required to change to the accrual method and took the extra income for the year of change into account under §447(i).[14] The ruling held that the reorganization did not accelerate the §447 adjustment, but the remaining adjustment would be treated as a built-in gain, taxable to the surviving corporation under §1374. [PLR 9117055]

1145.7. Cancellation of debt income. A solvent taxpayer who is not involved in a bankruptcy proceeding must report any reduction of indebtedness as gross income. [§61(a)(12)] The IRS has ruled that income from discharge of indebtedness is a built-in gain under §382. [PLR 8932049] The circumstances of that ruling, however, clearly indicate that the reduction of indebtedness had been negotiated at the time of the ownership change. It would stand to reason that if a reduction of debt were in process at the time the S election took effect, any income resulting therefrom should be a recognized built-in gain. The Proposed Regulations under §1374 took a reasonably objective position on this problem. Income from cancellation of debt would have been treated as a recognized built-in gain if the debt existed when the S election took effect and the reduction occurred in the first year of the recognition period. [Proposed Regs. §1.1374-4(e)] The Final Regulations merely state that such income is a recognized built-in gain if the debt was outstanding at the beginning of the recognition period. [Regs. §1.1374-4(f)]

> **OBSERVATION:** S corporations that already had filed elections before December 28, 1994, are not subject to this arbitrary rule, and they may be able to argue that the debt forgiveness is the triggering event. The IRS, similarly, will not be bound by the new Regulations in matters concerning any S corporation that filed its election before December 28, 1994.

The Regulations do not treat any reduction of indebtedness as a built-in gain if the corporation is able to exclude the reduction from income under §108, due to bankruptcy or insolvency. Under the general rules of §108, a taxpayer in either of these circumstances does not report the reduction of debt as gross income. Therefore, the reduction would not be included in the calculation of either the pre-limitation amount of net recognized built-in gain or the taxable income limitation thereof. See Chapter 6, at 610.6., for a discussion of these rules.

An unusual problem may arise when an S corporation's debt is reduced and the reduction meets the tests for qualified real property business indebtedness. If the debt reduction occurs in the first year of the S election, and the corporation elects to reduce basis of its real property, there will be no gross income (within the limits of §108(d)) for reporting its income to its shareholders. This same reduction, however, would be taxable as a recognized built-in gain for measurement of the corporation's pre-limitation amount and taxable income limitation. As discussed at 1125.111. and 1125.21, an S corporation calculates these figures using the rules applicable to C corporations. A C corporation may not exclude cancellation of debt under the qualified real property business indebtedness rules.

11

> **EXAMPLE 11 - 89:** Qualco was a C corporation through 1996. Its S election took effect for its taxable year beginning January 1, 1997. In 1997, Qualco arranges a reduction of qualified real property business indebtedness of $50,000. Qualco reduces the basis of real property and reports no gross income to its shareholders. In computing its pre-limitation amount and taxable income limitation of net recognized built-in gain, however, Qualco must include the $50,000 reduction of debt as gross income. If the reduction occurred in 1994, Qualco would not treat the reduction as a recognized built-in gain. It would, however, include the reduction in its taxable income limitation.

1145.8. Bad debt deductions. The Regulations' treatment of bad debt deductions mirrors the treatment of cancellation of debt income. If an S corporation was owed a debt on the date of conversion to S status, and the debt becomes uncollectible in the recognition period, the deduction is treated as a recognized built-in loss. [Regs. §1.1374-4(f)]

> **EXAMPLE 11 - 90:** Credco was a C corporation through 1996. Its S election took effect for its taxable year beginning January 1, 1997. In 1997, one of its customers becomes bankrupt, and Credco writes off the account receivable. The bad debt is treated as a recognized built-in loss

under the Regulations. It would not be necessary to prove that the account had been in existence on January 1, 1997.

1145.9. Effects of state and local income taxes. The statute, legislative history, and Regulations are all silent on any specific treatment of state and local income taxes attributable to built-in gains. The S corporation that is subject to such a tax should not neglect its effects on net recognized built-in gain and net unrealized built-in gain.

When computing the pre-limitation amount, as is discussed above at 1125.1, the corporation must include only recognized built-in gains and losses. If the net effect is a net gain, the corporation should compute the state and local income taxes that would be imposed on that level of income. The language of §1374(d)(5)(B), discussed at 1125.16, treats all expenses attributable to events that occurred prior to the S election as recognized built-in losses. Therefore, any state or local tax attributable to pre-conversion appreciation should meet this definition.

The effect of state and local taxes on the taxable income limitation is perhaps more straightforward. This computation includes all income and deductions of the current year, as if the corporation had no S election in effect. Thus, any state or local taxes would be allowed as deductions in computing this limitation.

In jurisdictions that impose lower rates of tax on S corporations than they do on C corporations, it would appear that the taxes actually imposed should be deducted. There is no authority for deducting an imputed state tax at the C corporation rate.

> **EXAMPLE 11 - 91:** Anberco is an S corporation that has taxable built-in gains. Anberco is subject to State X income taxes. State X imposes tax on net income of S corporations at the rate of 1.5%. Its rate on C corporations is 4%. When computing its net recognized built-in gain, Anberco should deduct the tax actually imposed at the 1.5% rate.

11

1145.10. Miscellaneous loss problems. An S corporation may face other problems in determining that losses are usable against built-in gains. One problem that is likely to arise in the 1990s is the treatment of tax depreciation on economically depressed property, such as real estate. If an S corporation owns depreciated property when the election takes effect, the unbooked loss will enter into the calculation of net unrealized built-in gain, whether or not the corporation actually recognizes the loss on a sale of the property during the recognition period. [§1374(d)(5)(C)] See discussion at 1120.

An S corporation that does not recognize the loss by an actual sale during the recognition period might be able to claim a recognized built-in loss for the depreciation allowed on the excess of the property's basis over its fair market value.

> **EXAMPLE 11 - 92:** Depco was a C corporation through 1991. At the beginning of 1992, when Depco's S election took effect, it owned a building with an unadjusted basis of $315,000. The building was MACRS property, and Depco used straight-line depreciation over a life of 31.5 years. At the beginning of 1992, the property's adjusted basis was $275,000. Its fair market value was $220,000, or 80% of its adjusted basis. Two aspects of the building's economic depreciation are clear:
>
> 1. The unrealized loss of $55,000 at the beginning of 1992 will reduce Depco's net unrealized built-in gain.
> 2. If Depco sells the building any time before 2002, up to $55,000 of loss on the sale would be a recognized built-in loss.
>
> What is not clear is the treatment of Depco's depreciation deduction during its recognition period. Under MACRS, the corporation will deduct $10,000 per year. Since the building's value is only 80% of its basis, it would appear that 20% of the depreciation deduction may be treated as a recognized built-in loss each year.

When an asset's basis exceeds its fair market value, the depreciation on the excess of basis over value is a built-in loss within the meaning of §382. [§382(h)(2)] There is no comparable statement in §1374, nor is there any prohibition against such treatment in either the statutory language or the legislative history of §1374. The Regulations under §1374, issued in December 1994, are silent on this matter.

> **OBSERVATION:** Treatment of depreciation as a recognized built-in loss, to the extent the depreciation is claimed on basis in excess of fair market value at conversion date, is a questionable position. The argument for such treatment has some support in the language of §1374(d)(5)(B), which treats a deduction as a recognized built-in loss if it is attributable to periods before the S election took effect. The treatment of such depreciation as a built-in loss under §382 is ambiguous with respect to §1374. The express statutory authority for such treatment within §382 may be viewed as indirect authority for similar treatment under §1374. On the other hand, the express inclusion of the rule in §382 and the exclusion of the same rule within §1374 may indicate that Congress intended to limit this treatment to §382.

1150. Interaction of multiple taxes on an S corporation.

An S corporation may be subject to more than one tax in the same year. This portion of the chapter deals with the treatment of the built-in gains tax, LIFO recapture tax, and the tax on passive investment income.

1150.1. Interaction of the built-in gains and the passive investment income tax. In some cases, the sale of an asset might result in a recognized built-in gain and excessive passive investment income. In such a case, the built-in gains classification dominates the passive investment income character. Chapter 12 contains discussion and an example, at 1220.1.

1150.2. Interaction of the built-in gains tax and the LIFO recapture tax. The integrative effects of the built-in gains tax and the LIFO recapture tax can lead to some complications in calculating net unrealized built-in gain. As discussed in Chapter 3, the LIFO recapture occurs on the last day of the corporation's final year as a C corporation. [§704(c)] The basis adjustment to the inventory would also occur on that date. [§1363(d)(1)(B)] Therefore, the basis of the inventory would be stepped up to FIFO cost (or market, if lower) as of the date on which the corporation measures its net unrealized built-in gain.

A corporation that uses LIFO does not change its inventory method when it becomes an S corporation. The actual recognition of gain on inventory is determined by the corporation's inventory method. [Ann. 86-128, 1986-51 IRB 22; Regs. §1.1374-7(b); Regs. §1.1374-10(b)(2)] Therefore, an S corporation that uses LIFO will not be subject to any built-in gains tax unless it liquidates a layer during its recognition period.

1155. Planning techniques.

Some corporations will find it profitable to remain C corporations, even if they want to distribute income to shareholders. The built-in gains tax is a substitute for the corporate income tax. It may be more than, less than, or approximately the same amount as the tax paid if the corporation did not make the S election. It is possible to find the break-even point for the S election by comparing the taxes paid as an S corporation with those paid as a C corporation. A corporation that appears to be facing a significant built-in gains tax should anticipate that future activities will be exempt from the tax, if they are undertaken after the S election takes effect.

1155.1. Making S election for new corporation at inception. As discussed in Chapter 5, a newly formed corporation must make its S election within 2 months and 15 days of the beginning of its first taxable year or it will be a C corporation. Chapter 5, at 520.2., discusses a planning strategy of creating a short fiscal year as a C corporation if the corporation misses the deadline for filing the S election. Some examples from that chapter are worth repeating at this point, to illustrate some of the problems involved.

EXAMPLE 11 - 93: AGM Corporation begins business on June 23, 1996. Its deadline for filing an S election for its first year is September 7, 1989. On September 14, 1996, it realizes that it should have made an S election. It can file a return on September 15 for its year ended June 30. It can file Form 2553 on September 15, which will cause the election to take effect for the taxable year beginning July 1, 1996.

When a corporation has been a C corporation for any amount of time, it will face problems such as corporate-level taxes. The LIFO recapture tax and passive income tax will probably not be serious if, as in Example 11 - 93, the corporation has had little time to accumulate earnings and profits or build up a LIFO reserve. The built-in gains tax, however, may be significant. When a corporation has spent any amount of time, even one day, as a C corporation, it will be subject to the built-in gains tax. The corporation's net unrealized built-in gain is the fair market value of its assets, less the aggregate adjusted basis of its assets. When the corporation has received appreciated property from one or more shareholders in a §351 transfer, the corporation's basis will be the same as the shareholder's basis. [§362] See discussion in Chapter 14.

EXAMPLE 11 - 94: AGM, in Example 11 - 93, was capitalized by one shareholder, Hubert. He transferred in property with a basis of $100,000 and fair market value of $1,000,000. The transfer was covered by §351 and no gain was recognized. If AGM had filed its S election in time for it to take effect on June 23, AGM would not be subject to the built-in gains tax.

11

If AGM files its first return as a C corporation, with an eight-day taxable year, it is subject to the built-in gains tax in later years when it is an S corporation. The corporation's net unrealized built-in gain is $900,000.

OBSERVATION: Although the built-in gains tax is intended to subject corporations to the double tax on appreciation realized in Subchapter C years, it is not limited to appreciation in value during those years. A gain realized by an individual shareholder that was not recognized in a §351 transfer, or any other tax-free exchange, is not exempt from the built-in gains tax if the corporation is ever a C corporation. A gain realized by an individual shareholder on property transferred to the corporation will be exempt from the built-in gains tax only if the corporation files an effective S election for its first taxable year.

1155.2. Minimizing taxable income. An S corporation that faces the built-in gains tax would generally employ the same planning strategies as a C corporation. It should seek to reduce its taxable income using compensation, interest, rents, and other deductible payments to its shareholders. As the IRS begins to audit more S corporations on this issue, tax professionals can expect to find the same types of adjustments that the IRS imposes on C corporations.

If the corporation filed its S election after March 30, 1988, any recognized built-in gains that are not taxed due to the taxable income limit are carried forward. (See discussion at 1135.1.) Therefore, minimizing taxable income when the recognized gains are high will only provide deferral. If the corporation is able to keep its taxable income at zero for the entire recognition period, it should be able to eliminate its built-in gains tax completely.

EXAMPLE 11 - 95: Minco is a former C corporation whose S election took effect for its taxable year beginning January 1, 1989. In 1989, it recognizes built-in gains of $500,000. Its net unrealized built-in gain was also $500,000. In 1989 its taxable income is zero. It pays no tax for 1989, since its taxable built-in gain (final) is zero.

If Minco filed its S election before March 31, 1988, it should have no further built-in gains problems. It will have to rebut the presumption of built-in gains on further sales, and its net unrealized built-in gain remains at $500,000.

If Minco filed its S election after March 30, 1988, its recognized built-in gain of $500,000 will carry forward as a recognized built-in gain in 1990. Minco may avoid tax in 1990 by showing zero taxable income, but the gain will carry forward to 1991. If Minco cannot reduce its taxable income to zero for every year in the recognition period, which ends on December 31, 1999, it will eventually pay some built-in gains tax. However, it will manage to defer the tax liability from 1989 to some future year. If Minco does bring its taxable income to zero every year through 1999, it will never pay any built-in gains tax (except possibly for gains on installment sales, for which the recognition period never expires).

1155.3. Minimizing net unrealized built-in gain. Since an S corporation's net recognized built-in gain is limited to its net unrealized built-in gain, it should take careful steps to give as low a measure of net unrealized built-in gain as it can justify.

The corporation may, for example, accrue compensation to shareholder-employees as of the end of the last Subchapter C year. This action would create an unrealized built-in loss. There are several cautions to be observed:

- In Announcement 87-3, the IRS stated that it would carefully scrutinize deferred compensation agreements of controlled entities. [Ann. 87-3, 1987-2 CB 40] If appropriate, it will assert constructive receipt for the year of accrual. The intent of this Announcement was to prevent shifting of income from 1986 or 1987 to later years, but it is still viable.
- The IRS could challenge the deferred compensation as excessive compensation and disallow the deduction entirely.

If the deferred compensation agreement withstands IRS scrutiny, it should reduce net unrealized built-in gain. When the corporation actually pays the compensation in a year in which it realizes built-in gains, it will create a recognized built-in loss. This strategy can produce tax savings that may be substantial.

EXAMPLE 11 - 96: At the end of 1996, P Corporation has decided to be an S corporation. Its election will take effect on January 1, 1997. It uses the cash method of accounting. At the end of 1996, its receivables are $150,000 and its payables are $60,000. With no further action, its net unrealized built-in gain will be $90,000. If it collects its receivables and pays its payables in 1997, it will have a net recognized built-in gain of $90,000. It anticipates taxable income of approximately $200,000 per year, so it will get no relief from the taxable income limitation. It is considering accruing $90,000 as deferred compensation to its sole shareholder, who is married and files a joint return. The total tax liability on the corporation's income for 1997 without the accrued bonus—and with it—will be:

	Without Bonus	*With Bonus*
Corporate liability:		
Built-in gains tax (.35 x $90,000)	$ 31,500	$ 0
Shareholder taxable income:		
Accrued bonus	$ 0	$ 90,000
Corporation's taxable income:		
	($200,000 – $31,500)	168,500
	($200,000 – $90,000)	110,000
Taxable income	$168,500	$200,000
Shareholder tax	$ 66,726	$ 79,200
Built-in gains tax	31,500	0
Total	$ 98,226	$ 79,200
Savings from accrual of bonus		$ 19,026

CAUTION: If an S corporation is subject to the Regulations under §1374, it must be very careful when paying bonuses, salary, interest, rents, or any other deductible payment to a controlling shareholder. The Regulations take the position that such a payment can be a recognized built-in loss only if it is paid within 2 months and 15 days of the beginning of the first S year. [Regs. §1.1374-4(c)(1)] See discussion above at 1125.19.

An S corporation may make a mistake by focusing entirely on the built-in gains tax. It may be advantageous to deduct payments in the last C year. Doing so might create a loss, which could be carried back to a C corporation year. The corporation might also prefer to use a large expense to offset LIFO recapture.

As noted above, installment sales may be of only limited usefulness for avoiding the built-in gains tax, although they still may provide valuable deferral of tax liability. Alternatives to sales of property that may enable the corporation to avoid the built-in gains tax include the following.

1155.4. Leases and like-kind exchanges. As noted above, installment sales may be of only limited usefulness in avoiding the built-in gains tax, although they still may provide valuable deferral of tax liability. Alternatives to sales of property that may enable the corporation to avoid the built-in gains tax include the following:

- An S corporation might use options or leases, where the property will not be sold before the end of the recognition period. The transactions should be structured so that they will not be reclassified as sales.
- An S corporation that intends to dispose of real or personal property held for business or investment might exchange the property in a transaction that qualifies as a like-kind exchange. Although the built-in gain taint would attach to the replacement property, the corporation could hold the replacement property until the recognition period has expired, with results as found in Example 11 - 97.

EXAMPLE 11 - 97: Gavco is in the seventh year of its recognition period. A prospective purchaser has made an offer on some land and a building. An outright sale would be taxable as a built-in gain. If the deal could be structured so that Gavco could receive some investment land, or a rental property with a value equal to that of the land and building, instead of cash, the exchange would not be taxable. The property received could be held or rented for approximately three years, until the recognition period has expired. At that time, Gavco could sell the new property, and the sale would not be taxable as a built-in gain.

1155.5. Contributing built-in loss property to corporation by shareholder. A shareholder (or shareholders) might attempt to reduce a corporation's net unrealized built-in gain by contributing loss property to the corporation shortly before the S election takes effect. Congress anticipated that taxpayers might attempt this technique. The legislative history to the Technical and Miscellaneous Revenue Act of 1988 authorized the IRS to prevent corporations from using this technique to avoid the built-in gains tax.[15] [Senate Finance Committee Report to Technical Corrections Bill of 1988 (8/3/88), page 79]

EXAMPLE 11 - 98: Jayco, which is a C corporation at the end of 1995, files an S election for its taxable year beginning January 1, 1996. It estimates that its net unrealized built-in gain will be $250,000. Its sole shareholder, Jay, owns some real estate that has an adjusted basis of $1,500,000 and fair market value of $1,250,000. Jay could contribute the property to the

---

[15] The House Ways and Means Committee Report to the Miscellaneous Revenue Bill of 1988 (7/26/88) contains the same language at page 65.

corporation as a tax-free transfer under §351 or as a contribution to capital. (See Chapter 14 for discussion of the tax rules involved.) In either case, Jay's basis of $1,500,000 would become the corporation's basis in the property received. Jayco's net unrealized built-in gain would now apparently be zero. The IRS has authority to prevent the avoidance of the built-in gains tax through this contribution.

The IRS has exercised its authority in Regulations §1.1374-9, appropriately titled *anti-stuffing rules*. The rule provides, briefly, that any acquisition of property during or before the recognition period, with a principal purpose of avoiding the built-in gains tax, is a stuffing transaction. Any loss sustained on such property is disregarded in determining the corporation's taxable built-in gain. Similarly, any net operating loss or credit carryforward is disregarded in determining the corporation's built-in gains tax.

OBSERVATION: The anti-stuffing rules require that the contribution of property have avoidance of the built-in gains tax as a *principal purpose*, but this need not be the only purpose of contributing the property. Therefore, even if a contribution of property has other valid business purposes, the IRS could disallow any loss or credit that resulted from property that was contributed before or during the corporation's recognition period. There is no specified time limit on the anti-stuffing rule. Therefore, property contributed several years before the S election took effect could be tainted by this limitation, if the corporation contemplated an S election when it received the property.

1155.6. Contributing built-in gain property to another entity. A corporation that wants to avoid the built-in gains tax might contribute property to a corporation or a partnership in a nonrecognition transaction. Two nonrecognition transactions that the corporation might consider are contribution of property to a controlled corporation and contribution of property to a partnership. See Chapter 14, at 1415. and 1435.11., respectively, for considerable discussion of the former and limited discussion of the latter.

Contributing property to another corporation in a §351 transfer will likely have little potential for avoidance of double tax. An S corporation may be a shareholder in another corporation, as long as it does not directly own at least 80% of the stock. If the S corporation continues to be a shareholder, the subsidiary corporation must remain a C corporation. Its assets will be subject to double tax.

Contributing property to a partnership might appear to have more appeal. A transfer in exchange for a partnership interest is a tax-free event. The partnership would be exempt from double taxation on income and distributions.

In the Regulations under §1374, the IRS announced it would ignore contributions of property to partnerships if the property is transferred in contemplation of an S election, or at any time during the recognition period. [Regs. §1.1374-10(b)(3)] Therefore, if the partnership disposed of property transferred to it by the S corporation at any time during the recognition period, the corporation is treated as if it had sold the property directly.

EXAMPLE 11 - 99: JMC Corporation is a C corporation with two shareholders, Jane and Mike. Near the end of 1995, the corporation owns several unsold homes on which it would recognize built-in gains if they were sold. JMC is anticipating an S election for its taxable year beginning January 1, 1996. JMC forms the JMP Partnership with Jane and Mike and contributes the unsold homes to JMP. At the time of the contribution, the homes have an aggregate fair market value of $1,000,000 and adjusted basis to JMC of $800,000.

In 1996, JMP sells all of the homes for $1,000,000. Under the partnership rules, JMP must allocate all of the gain to JMC, since JMC contributed the property to the partnership. [§704(c)] When JMP sells the homes received from JMC, JMC must report the gains as if JMC had sold the homes directly. Therefore, all gains on sales of property by JMP are treated as built-in gains to JMC, unless JMC can rebut the presumption.

11

OBSERVATION: The Regulations provision covering transfers to partnerships applies as of the effective date of §1374.[16] Therefore, this rule applies to any sale of property by a partnership that received property from a corporation that is subject to the built-in gains tax. In most cases, this rule applies if the former C corporation filed its S election after December 31, 1986. The retroactive date of this portion of the Proposed Regulations may seem harsh and arbitrary. It is, however, specifically authorized by the legislative history of the Technical and Miscellaneous Revenue Act of 1988. [Senate Finance Committee Report to Technical Corrections Bill of 1988 (8/3/88), page 80]

1160. Transitional rules.

A tax on capital gains was the predecessor to the built-in gains tax. [§1374 tax imposed on certain capital gains, repealed by Tax Reform Act of 1986] Its purpose was to impose a tax cost on corporations that made one-shot S elections when they anticipated abnormally large gains and wanted to distribute excess liquidity.

The transition between the capital gains tax and the built-in gains tax was phased in between 1986 and 1989. Because of these phase-in rules, tax professionals will need to keep careful records concerning the dates of S elections, financial status and ownership of corporations, and other activities of corporations that became S corporations during these years.

1160.1. Capital gains tax. A tax on capital gains was the predecessor to the built-in gains tax. [§1374 tax imposed on certain capital gains, repealed by Tax Reform Act of 1986] Its purpose was to impose a tax cost on corporations that made one-shot S elections when they anticipated abnormally large gains and wanted to distribute excess liquidity. Although its was repealed by the Tax Reform Act of 1986, its effects will remain for several more years.

11

As of this writing, the capital gains tax has almost completely disappeared. The details of the tax are retained in this edition to assist tax professionals in preparing amended returns or handling audits. The most important aspects of this tax, which must be kept in mind for many years to come, are its effective dates and the period of its applicability.

1160.11. General applicability limited to former C corporations. Like the built-in gains tax, the capital gains tax is imposed generally on former C corporations. Corporations whose S elections were in effect from inception are exempt from this tax, with some exceptions. For example, an S corporation that receives property from a C corporation in a tax-free reorganization is subject to the capital gains tax, but only on the assets received in the reorganization.

1160.12. Effective dates. The tax on capital gains is limited to corporations whose elections were filed before 1987. It is not applicable, generally, if the election was filed after December 31, 1986. See a limited exception below. Corporations that filed S elections after 1986 are now subject to the built-in gains tax.

If the corporation filed an early election for its tax year beginning in 1987, the capital gain tax applied. The filing date of election, rather than the effective date, was the governing factor. [Tax Reform Act of 1986, §633(b); Rev. Rul. 86-141, 1986-2 CB 151]

EXAMPLE 11 - 100: Z Corporation has used a September 30 year-end. On October 1, 1986, it filed an S election to be effective for its tax year beginning October 1, 1987. Z Corporation was subject to the capital gains tax. If it had filed on or after January 1, 1987, it would be subject not to the capital gains tax, but to the built-in gains tax.

---

[16] The House Ways and Means Committee Report to the Miscellaneous Revenue Bill of 1988 (7/26/88) contains the same language at page 65.

OBSERVATION: Many corporations filed S elections between October 22, 1986 (the date that the Tax Reform Act of 1986 became law), and December 31, 1986. One of the primary motivations for filing S elections in late 1986 was to escape the built-in gains tax.

1160.13. Period of applicability. A former C corporation was subject to the capital gains tax for its first three taxable years as an S corporation. Unlike the built-in gains recognition period, the capital gains recognition period counted a short year as a full taxable year. [PLRs 8651019, 8743046, 8829046, 8836019, 8911049, and 8924043]

As discussed above, an installment sale may lengthen the recognition period for the built-in gains tax. This was not the case with the capital gains tax. Installments received after the corporation's first three taxable years as an S corporation were exempt from the tax.

1160.14. Taxable gain computed. Measurement of the taxable gain had its own special rules. The corporation used the same process as a C corporation in netting out:

- §1231 casualty and theft gains and losses
- Gains and losses from sales of §1231 property
- Long-term capital gains and losses
- Short-term capital gains and losses[17]

If the process yielded a net (long-term) capital gain of less than $25,000, there was no tax. If the net capital gain exceeded $25,000, the corporation computed its taxable income. The taxable income for the capital gains tax was measured in the same manner as it now is for the built-in gains tax and the passive investment income tax. The corporation was not allowed to use any carryovers from C corporation years to offset the taxable capital gain.

At this point, the corporation compared the net capital gain with the taxable income. In order to be liable for tax, the corporation's net capital gain must have exceeded 50% of its taxable income, and its taxable income must have exceeded $25,000. The corporation then computed its potential tax in one of two ways:

11

- It used a flat rate of 34% on the net capital gain in excess of $25,000. [Technical and Miscellaneous Revenue Act of 1988, §1006(g)(2)] Presumably, if any corporation is still subject to this tax for a year beginning after 1992, the rate would be 35%.
- The corporation used the graduated §11 rate schedule on its entire taxable income (as computed above).

EXAMPLE 11 - 101: V Corporation was an S corporation since its inception in 1984. In 1987, it merged with W Corporation in a Type A reorganization. (See Chapter 17.) V survived and kept its S election. It received §1231 assets from W. The assets had a basis of $150,000. Pursuant to §361, W's basis carried over to V.

In 1988, V sells the §1231 assets for $575,000, resulting in a capital gain of $425,000. In 1988, V's other operations resulted in a loss of $350,000.

V made the following computations:

	Gain	*Tax*
Net capital gain	$425,000	
Less excluded amount	(25,000)	
Taxable capital gain	$400,000	
Tax at 34%		$136,000

[17] Gains realized by commodities and options dealers, including mark-to-market gains of §1256, were excluded from taxable capital gains. [prior §1374(c)(4)]

V's tax was limited to the tax on corporate taxable income:

	Income	Tax
Capital gain	$425,000	
Ordinary loss	(350,000)	
Taxable income	$ 75,000	
Corporate income tax		$ 13,750

V's income tax was $13,750, the lower of the two figures.

1160.15. Effect of the tax on the shareholders. The tax reduced the flow-through of gains to the shareholders. The tax was first applied to pure long-term capital gains. If the tax was greater than the pure capital gains, it reduced the §1231 gain.

EXAMPLE 11 - 102: Refer to Example 11 - 101. V's shareholders would report ordinary loss of $350,000 and net capital gains of $411,250 ($425,000 – $13,750).

1160.2. Certain elections before 1989. The transition between the capital gains tax and the built-in gains tax was phased in between 1986 and 1989. Because of these phase-in rules, tax professionals will need to keep careful records concerning the dates of S elections, financial status and ownership of corporations, and other activities of corporations that became S corporations during these years.

1160.21. Background. The Tax Reform Act of 1986 changed the treatment of corporations undergoing complete liquidation. Under prior law, gains and losses were generally not recognized on the distribution or sale of property during the liquidation period. Under the new law, most of such sales and distributions are taxable events. The 1986 Act provided some transitional relief for corporations that were completely liquidated before 1989. The built-in gains tax was enacted as a companion measure to the new corporate liquidation rules. Although it has a broader reach than liquidations, it prevents corporations from making an S election to avoid the new liquidation rules. As a companion to the transitional liquidation relief, the new law provides some transitional exceptions to the built-in gains tax for certain corporations that filed S elections before 1989.

11

1160.22. General effects of transitional rules. Certain "qualified corporations" (the term is defined in the Tax Reform Act of 1986, §633(d)(5)) that met the criteria discussed below were subject to one of two transitional rules. Understanding the liquidation relief rule is important to interpreting the rationale of the built-in gains relief rule, which will continue to have its effects throughout most of the 1990s.

Liquidation relief. If a qualified corporation (whether or not it was an S corporation) was completely liquidated in 1987 or 1988, its long-term capital gains (including §1231 and §1239 gains) were exempt from recognition. [Tax Reform Act of 1986, §633(d)(1)] Qualified corporations were also prohibited from deducting losses on capital or §1231 assets sold or distributed in the liquidation during this period. Ordinary gains and losses (excluding §1239 gains) realized on a liquidating sale or distribution, however, were included (or deducted) by the liquidating corporation.[18] The exclusion and inclusion rules applied to all qualified corporations, including S corporations. Therefore, gains that were not recognized on a liquidating sale or distribution were exempt from the capital gains tax and the built-in gains tax. These

[18] Tax Reform Act of 1986, §633, contains several other transitional rules that are no longer relevant.

gains did not flow through as taxable income to the shareholders. This rule was extremely important through 1988, but it has now ceased to exist, with the possible exception of some open returns that are still undergoing examination. Accordingly, it receives no further discussion in this text.

Built-in gains relief. A qualified corporation that filed its S election before January 1, 1989, is exempt from the built-in gains tax on capital and §1231 assets. [Tax Reform Act of 1986, §633(d)(8), as amended by the Revenue Act of 1987 and the Technical and Miscellaneous Revenue Act of 1988] However, the assets exempt from the built-in gains tax were subject to the capital gains tax. [Tax Reform Act of 1986, §633(b)(2)] Since the capital gains tax could affect a corporation only for its first three taxable years as an S corporation, most, if not all, of those properties are completely exempt from tax on their disposition by the time of this writing.

> **EXAMPLE 11 - 103:** Transco was a C corporation that used a November 30 taxable year. On December 31, 1988, Transco filed an S election that took effect for its taxable year beginning December 1, 1989. It made a §444 election to retain its November year. Its first three taxable years as an S corporation are its years ended November 30, 1990, 1991, and 1992. Any later year would be beyond the capital gains tax recognition period.

A corporation cannot make a valid S election for a year beyond its next taxable year. December 31, 1988, was the last day a corporation could make an election and qualify for the built-in gains relief. Therefore, the situation presented in Example 11 - 103 demonstrates the last possible taxable year for the capital gains tax.

1160.23. Qualified corporation defined. A corporation must have met two criteria for liquidation relief, or built-in gains relief, based on net worth and stock ownership:

11

- Stock ownership
  - More than 50% of the stock must have been held by or for 10 or fewer individuals, estates, or trusts ("Qualified Group") on August 1, 1986, and at all times thereafter, until the corporation liquidated or filed Form 2553.
  - The attribution rules of §318 treat stock owned by corporations, partnerships, or trusts as being held proportionately by owners or beneficiaries. Family attribution rules of §318(a)(1) are also used. In this case, the constructive ownership rules make it easier to meet the maximum shareholder count. Transfers among family members during the test period will have no effect.
  - The corporation qualified (for liquidation relief) only if a qualified group of shareholders owned stock at all times during the five years preceding adoption of the liquidation plan—or the period of the corporation's existence, if shorter. [Technical Corrections Act of 1987, §1206(g)(3)] For built-in gains relief, a corporation would meet this criterion if more than 50% of its stock were owned directly or indirectly by 10 or fewer individuals for five years on the date the S election was filed. [Rev. Rul. 86-141, 1986-2 CB 151]
- Net worth
  - For complete relief, the fair market value of the corporation's stock must not have exceeded $5,000,000 on either August 1, 1986, or the date of filing the S election.
  - Reduced relief was available if the fair market value of the corporation's stock exceeded $5,000,000 but did not exceed $10,000,000 on either of those dates.

EXAMPLE 11 - 104: Qualco filed an S election on December 31, 1988. If more than 50% of its stock had changed hands since December 31, 1983, Qualco could not qualify for transitional built-in gains relief. If the transfer had been among family members, or among entities controlled by the persons who own more than 50% of the stock on December 31, 1988, however, the corporation could qualify.

EXAMPLE 11 - 105: In 1988, a calendar-year C corporation filed an S election, which took effect on January 1, 1989. The corporation's stock was held by three individuals. The fair market value of its stock is $3 million. In 1992, the corporation recognized a long-term capital gain of $250,000. Since the corporation had been an S corporation for more than three taxable years in 1992, it was not subject to the capital gains tax of old §1374.

EXAMPLE 11 - 106: Assume the same facts as in Example 11 - 105, except that the fair market value of the corporation's stock on the date the gain was realized was $8 million. The percentage of the gain not qualifying for relief would be:

$$\frac{\text{Excess of value over \$5 million x Gain}}{\text{\$5 million}}$$

$$\frac{\$3{,}000{,}000}{\$5{,}000{,}000}$$

Of the gain, $100,000 would be completely exempt from tax at the corporate level. The remaining $150,000 is subject to the built-in gains tax.

11

1160.24. Major benefits of the transitional exclusion. The principal benefit of the transitional rule was the exemption of capital, §1231, and §1239 gains from the built-in gains tax. The exemption of these gains from the built-in gains tax was not a completely unmixed blessing, since these same gains were subject to the old capital gains tax, which was imposed at the same 34% rate as the built-in gains tax. The main benefit was that the capital gains tax was imposed in only the first three S corporation taxable years. After that period, those gains became completely exempt from any corporate-level tax. A net unrealized built-in gain, by contrast, presents a potential tax liability for 10 years following the effective date of the S election.

During the years in which a corporation was still subject to the old capital gains tax, there was a secondary benefit, in that the first $25,000 of capital gains in any taxable year were exempt from tax. There is no comparable exemption from the built-in gains tax.

There were, however, some hazards to the old capital gains tax that are not present with the built-in gains tax. First, a capital gain was subject to tax, even though it was not attributable to years before the S election took effect. Second, there was no provision equivalent to the net unrealized built-in gain limit. A corporation was subject to the tax on any recognized capital gain, even if it had no net unrealized built-in gain at the time its S election took effect. Finally, a taxable capital gain could not be offset by an ordinary loss, even if the loss was incurred on the disposition of an asset that had declined in value before the S election took effect. By the time of this writing, most of the hazards of the old capital gains tax have disappeared, since there are few corporations still subject to the tax.

1160.25. Summary of transitional rule. Two important aspects of the built-in gains tax are (1) the effects of the transitional rules on property subject to the tax and (2) the set of calculations required. The effects of different election dates and the types of taxable gain are summarized in Table 11 - 5.

TABLE 11 - 5: Transitional Rules and Gain Taxability

Date Election Filed	*Long-Term Capital §1231 Gains*	*Other Gains*
Before 1/1/87	Taxable for 3 years	Not taxable
Between 1/1/87 and 12/31/88	Taxable for 3 years (if corporation qualifies, 10 if it does not)	Taxable for 10 years
After 12/31/88	Taxable for 10 years	Taxable for 10 years

1160.26. Problems in interpreting transitional rules. The transition from the capital gain tax to the built-in gains tax is not entirely smooth. The exact language of the statute bears careful examination. The transitional rule for S corporations is contained in Tax Reform Act of 1986 §633(b)(1).

SUMMARY OF AUTHORITY: TAX REFORM ACT OF 1986, SECTION 633(b)(1)

- Section 632 of the Tax Reform Act of 1986 was the provision that changed the corporate liquidation rules and contained the new version of §1374 that imposes the built-in gains tax.
- Subsection (b) of §632 was the provision that exempted corporations from recognition of gain or loss on certain distributions in tax-free reorganizations. See Chapter 17.
- None of the rules of §1374 can apply to an S corporation if it filed its S election before January 1, 1987.

This portion of the chapter discusses some of the problems that result from incomplete Congressional guidance. The reader should be alert for new Regulations or other pronouncements that might affect these problem areas.

OBSERVATION: The positions taken in this portion of the book are based on the law as it exists at the time of this writing. There are no authoritative pronouncements that contradict any of the positions. When dealing in areas of uncertainty regarding the built-in gains tax, the reader should always be aware that Congress has delegated authority to the IRS to write legislative Regulations to prevent abuse of the revised corporate rules, which include the built-in gains tax. [§337(d)] Accordingly, the reader should always check for the most recent pronouncements that might affect the problems covered in this discussion.

11

Fiscal years beginning in 1986. In a few cases, corporations filed S elections after December 31, 1986, for fiscal years beginning in 1986. For instance, a corporation could have filed an election on or before February 15, 1987, for its year beginning December 1, 1986. The corporation would be exempt from the built-in gains tax for its year beginning in 1986 but subject to the tax in later years. A corporation in this situation could face several problems not explained in the statute:

- The corporation's recognition period would probably begin in 1986.
- The corporation would probably need to measure its net unrealized built-in gain on the date its S election took effect in 1986.
- The corporation's net recognized built-in gain for the year beginning in 1986 would probably reduce its net unrealized built-in gain.

It is likely that there are only a few corporations in this situation, since many corporations filed their S elections in 1986 to avoid the tax in its entirety. The major concerns by the time of this writing are the extent of the recognition period and the effect of the first year's transactions on net unrealized built-in gain.

Relationship of transitional exemption to measurement of net unrealized built-in gain. The statute and legislative history do not mention the inclusion or exclusion of exempt transitional assets in net unrealized built-in gain. Since the transitional exception applies to all capital and §1231 assets, they should be removed from the asset base on the first day of the first S year so that the net unrealized built-in gains can be measured.

EXAMPLE 11 - 107: Z Corporation files an S election that takes effect on January 1, 1988. On that date its assets consist of:

	Fair Market Value	*Adjusted Basis*
Capital	$ 800,000	$ 600,000
Other	1,500,000	1,200,000
Total	$2,300,000	$1,800,000

Since the capital assets are exempt from the built-in gains tax, they should not be used to determine net unrealized built-in gains. The difference between the fair market value and the adjusted basis of the other assets—$300,000—is the valid measure of net unrealized built-in gains.

There could also be a holding period problem. Since the exemption from the built-in gains tax applies only to long-term capital and §1231 gains (§1231(b)(1) states that the §1231 property includes only those assets held at least one year), any capital or §1231 asset that has not been held for more than one year on the first day of the S year remains subject to question.

- If a capital asset is sold at a gain before it qualifies for long-term capital gain treatment, it should be exempt from the capital gains tax but subject to the built-in gains tax.
- If the asset is sold at a gain after it qualifies for long-term capital gain treatment, the gain should be exempt from the built-in gains tax but subject to the capital gain tax.
- Including a capital asset in the asset base for measurement of net unrealized built-in gains will depend upon its being sold while it still represents a short-term gain.

Transitional rules and reorganizations. As stated above, an S corporation that filed its S election before January 1, 1987, is exempt from all provisions of Tax Reform Act of 1986 §632, except for §632(b). Code §632(b) holds that gains and losses are not recognized on the transfer of property in a tax-free reorganization. See Chapter 17. Therefore, the statute seems to say that an S corporation that filed its election before 1987 is exempt from all provisions of the built-in gains tax.

A literal reading of the statute exempts a corporation from the built-in gains tax following a reorganization, if the surviving S corporation filed its S election before 1987. However, it would be subject to the capital gains tax. [Tax Reform Act of 1986, §633(b)(1)]

PLANNING TIP: An S corporation that filed its S election before 1987 might be an ideal survivor in a tax-free reorganization. Former §1374 would apply to any capital gain recognized for three years following the reorganization. Any reorganization must withstand the tests of business purpose, substance over form, continuity of business enterprise, and continuity of proprietary interest. See Chapter 17. The reorganization should be well structured and protected from attack as a step transaction.

OBSERVATION: The IRS subjected an old (pre-1987) S corporation to the built-in gains tax after a tax-free reorganization, in direct contradiction to the language of the statute. [PLR 9005021] However, the IRS does have authority to write legislative Regulations in this area [§337(d)], so the outcome of a contest on a similar situation is uncertain.

1160.3. Investment tax credit recapture. The investment tax credit was available to taxpayers who purchased qualifying property through December 31, 1985. The Tax Reform Act of 1986 repealed this credit, although there were several transitional rules. Most of the transitional rules have expired as of this writing. The one that still may be applicable in a few cases is the recapture of investment tax credit.

When a taxpayer disposes of investment tax credit property before a certain period of ownership (generally, five years), the taxpayer is required to pay a portion of the credit claimed as an additional tax. The credit has largely, if not completely, disappeared from the tax law. The recapture of the credit has also nearly completely vanished. However, to provide a limited reference for tax professionals who may be concerned about open years, this book contains a brief discussion of the credit and recapture as they related to S corporations and their shareholders.

This tax may be imposed when an S corporation disposes of property on which it claimed the credit. Note that dispositions after December 1990 will be exempt from recapture, unless the property qualified for the credit under one of the numerous transitional rules of the Tax Reform Act of 1986.[19] Preparers of an S corporation's tax returns through fiscal years ending in 1991 will need to study carefully the acquisition date of property disposed of in the tax year of the return being prepared. Returns for years after 1991 will be affected by this rule only if the corporation had property that qualified for the transitional relief.

1160.31. General exemption. Under most circumstances, an S corporation is exempt from the investment tax credit recapture. Thus, a newly formed corporation that was an S corporation from its inception could not be subject to the tax. If property was contributed by a shareholder and the shareholder did not recapture at contribution, the shareholder was required to recapture the credit if either one of two conditions existed:

- The corporation disposed of the property. [Regs. §1.47-3(f)(1)]
- The shareholder disposed of his or her stock. See Chapter 15.

If an S election was in effect when the corporation acquired the property, the credit passed through to shareholders. [§1366(a)(1)(A)] The shareholder recaptured the credit when the corporation disposed of the property or when the shareholder disposed of his or her stock.

The S election itself was a recapture event under prior Subchapter S. Shareholders could agree to assume the liability and relieve the corporation of the recapture. As of this writing, this problem has been completely phased out of the law. It receives no further discussion in this book.

1160.32. Rule for former C corporations. After the Subchapter S Revision Act of 1982, an S election by an existing corporation does not trigger investment tax credit recapture. The corporation continues to be liable for recapture upon premature disposition of the §38 property.

SUMMARY OF AUTHORITY: CODE SECTION 1371(d)

- Making an S election does not make the corporation or its shareholders liable for investment tax credit recapture.
- The corporation continues to be liable for investment tax credit recapture if the property is disposed of prematurely.

---

[19] Many transitional rules were custom-made for important constituents. In order to determine if an S corporation received any of the transitional benefits, it will be necessary to examine the corporation's tax returns for years after 1985.

11

EXAMPLE 11 - 108: On October 1, 1985, XYZ Corporation was a C corporation. It placed in service qualified §38 property at a cost of $100,000. It claimed $10,000 investment tax credit and reduced the property's basis to $95,000. In 1986, XYZ made an S election. On February 29, 1988, it sold the property. Since more than three but fewer than four years had elapsed, it recaptures 40% of the credit, or $4,000. XYZ increases the gain or loss basis of the property by $2,000.

The shareholders are not liable for the credit, but they get the benefit of the reduced gain (or increased loss) on the sale of the property. If XYZ has any accumulated earnings and profits as of February 1, 1988, they are reduced by the $2,000 recapture.

The corporation computes the recapture tax on Form 4255. It shows the tax as a write-in entry on Form 1120S, line 22c.

1165. Summary.

The built-in gains tax is the most complicated aspect of the S corporation. This tax alone is a major reason for new corporations to become S corporations from their inception. This tax forces immediate double taxation on the corporation and its shareholders on the recognized gains from prior C corporation years. To understand this tax, the practitioner must merge the concepts of Subchapter S and Subchapter C. General tax rules such as accounting method and gain and loss characterization are also crucial to proper application of these tax rules.

1170. Practice aids.

Certain examples in this chapter used worksheets developed as part of this treatise. They are reproduced in this portion of the chapter so that they can be easily copied and adapted to the needs of specific clients. In addition, Checklist 11 - 1 is designed to help a C corporation that is contemplating an S election analyze the impact of the built-in gains tax. Checklist 11 - 2 provides some additional aids to assist a tax preparer who might be unfamiliar with the S corporation's history to look for certain key events, such as the date the election was filed, and any asset acquisitions that might subject some of the corporation's activities to a special recognition period. Worksheet 11 - 3 would be useful for a corporation that has acquired assets in one or more tax-free reorganizations or liquidations.

Worksheet 11 - 1: Tax classification of recognized built-in gains and losses

Tax character	(a) Description	(b) Amount realized	(c) Adjusted basis	(d) Gain or loss	(e) Less post-conversion gain or loss	(f) Recognized built-in gain or loss (d)–(e)
(1) Ordinary						
(2) Short-term capital						
(3) Long-term capital (20%)						
(4) Long-term capital (28%)						
(5) Sec. 1231 (20%)						
(6) Sec. 1231 (25%)						
(7) Sec. 1231 (28%)						

Copyright © 2000 by Harcourt, Inc. All rights reserved.

Worksheet 11 - 2: Apportionment of classification of recognized built-in gains to pre-limitation amount, taxable income limitation, or net unrealized built-in gain limitation

Tax character	(a) Recognized built-in gain and loss, from Worksheet 11 - 1	(b) Net built-in gain for each category (enter 0 if loss, not usable against other gain)	(c) Percent of total (line 8)	(d) Apply percentage to pre-limitation amount, taxable income limitation, or net unrealized built-in gain limitation
(1) Ordinary				
(2) Short-term capital				
(3) Long-term capital (20%)				
(4) Long-term capital (28%)				
(5) Sec. 1231 (20%)				
(6) Sec. 1231 (25%)				
(7) Sec. 1231 (28%)				
(8) Total			100.00	

11

Worksheet 11 - 3: Apportionment of built-in gains tax to gains of differing characters

Tax character	(a) Net gain from Worksheet 11 - 2, column (d)	(b) Percent of total (line 8)	(c) Apply percentage to final built-in gains tax for year
(1) Ordinary			
(2) Short-term capital			
(3) Long-term capital (20%)			
(4) Long-term capital (28%)			
(5) Sec. 1231 (20%)			
(6) Sec. 1231 (25%)			
(7) Sec. 1231 (28%)			
(8) Total		100.00	

Copyright © 2000 by Harcourt, Inc. All rights reserved.

Worksheet 11 - 4: Apportionment of income, deductions, and built-in gain tax to shareholder pass-through and to corporation's AAA

Tax character	(a) Recognized gain and loss, from Worksheet 11 - 1, column (d)	(b) Net gain or loss for each category	(c) Less any other deductions attributable to income type	(d) Less tax, allocated from Worksheet 11 - 3	(e) Net to Schedule K, Form 1120S, allocate to shareholders on Schedule K-1.
(1) Ordinary					
(2) Short-term capital					
(3) Long-term capital (20%)					
(4) Long-term capital (28%)					
(5) Sec. 1231 (20%)					
(6) Sec. 1231 (25%)					
(7) Sec. 1231 (28%)					
(8) Other					
(9) Total					
(10) To AAA					

11

Worksheet 11 - 5: Net recognized built-in gain

1. a. Determine recognized built-in gains (including income items attributable to prior C years)	$
b. Subtract recognized built-in losses (including deductions attributable to prior C years)	( )
c. Add carryforward of built-in gain from last year (if election was filed after 3/30/88)	$
d. Pre-limitation amount	$
2. Net unrealized built-in gain limitation	$
3. Lesser of 1.d or 2	$
4. Taxable income limitation	$
5. Taxable recognized built-in gain (lesser of 3 or 4)	$
6. Subtract net operating loss and capital loss carryforwards from C years	( )
7. Taxable recognized built-in gain (after carryforwards)	$
8. Tax on 7 at highest corporate rate	$
9. Subtract general business credit and alternative minimum tax carryforwards from C years	( )
10. Tax payable in current year (subject to estimated tax requirements	$
11. If election filed after 3/30/88 and if 3 exceeds 4, carry excess forward to next year; otherwise, zero.	$

Copyright © 2000 by Harcourt, Inc. All rights reserved.

Worksheet 11 - 6: Net unrealized built-in gain

1. Date S election takes effect	
Value of assets	$
Less basis of assets	( )
Less cash-basis liabilities	( )
Plus potential income items not on balance sheet	$
Less potential deduction items not on balance sheet	( )
Result: Net unrealized built-in gain at beginning of first S year	$
2. End of first S year	
Net unrealized built-in gain from line 1	$
Less net recognized built-in gain this year	( )
Result: Net unrealized built-in gain at beginning of next S year	$
3. Subsequent S years	
Net unrealized built-in gain at end of last year	$
Less net recognized built-in gain this year	( )
Result: Net unrealized built-in gain at beginning of next S year	$

11

Checklist 11 - 1: Impact of built-in gains tax

Complete before S election takes effect.

	Applicable (Yes/No)	*Completed (Date)*
1. Value all assets at market		
2. Reduce for any potentially deductible liabilities		
3. Consider any §481 adjustment		
4. Evaluate offset for any NOL carryforwards		
5. Evaluate offset for any NOL carryforwards		
6. Consider trade-off of taking loss in last C year or postponing to S year		
a. Accrual or payment of bonus to shareholders		
b. Other items that corporation can control depreciation elections		
Asset expensing		
Other (list)		

Copyright © 2000 by Harcourt, Inc. All rights reserved.

Checklist 11 - 2: History of important events

Complete each year of recognition period.

	Applicable (Yes/No)	Completed (Date)
1. Date S election filed (If filed before 1987, no built-in gains tax applies)		
2. If filed in 1987 or 1988, check for transitional exemption of capital and §1231 assets.		
3. If corporation has survived a reorganization or liquidated a subsidiary tax- free, complete Checklist 11 - 3 for each asset acquisition.		

Checklist 11 - 3: Assets acquired in tax-free reorganizations or liquidations

Complete for each asset acquisition.

	Applicable (Yes/No)	Completed (Date)
Date recognition period began		
Net unrealized built-in gain on acquisition less prior years' adjustments		
Pre-limitation amount		
Recognized built-in gains		
Check for post-acquisition appreciation		
Consider §384 limitation		
Recognized built-in losses		
Check for post-acquisition depreciation		
Consider §382 limitation		
Taxable income limitation		
Consider §382 limitation		

11

Copyright © 2000 by Harcourt, Inc. All rights reserved.

PASSIVE INVESTMENT INCOME

Contents

12

1200. Overview.

The original version of Subchapter S adopted the phrase "small business corporation" as the designation of a corporation eligible to elect S status. The emphasis on the term *business* was intended to restrict the S election to operating, rather than investment, corporations. As a means of enforcement, the original law provided that no more than 20% of an S corporation's gross receipts could come from sources classified as personal holding company income (other than personal service income).

The terms *passive income* and *investment income* have major significance for individuals. Since the Tax Reform Act of 1969 added the investment interest limits, and the Tax Reform Act of 1986 enacted the passive activity loss restrictions, taxpayers must go to considerable pains to distinguish between the two income types. An S corporation must comply with all of the individual classification rules in order to report the character of income and deductions properly to its shareholders. An S corporation has entirely different concerns in the measurement of passive investment income.

The phrase "passive investment income," as used within Subchapter S, is a mix between the two classifications used by individuals. It contains some items that will be classified as "portfolio" or "investment" income to shareholders. It contains some items that will be classified as "passive" at the shareholder level. It also excludes some of the items that receive one of these two classifications for an individual.

The definitions of *passive investment income* within Subchapter S are not the same as those of *passive income* as used in §469, discussed extensively in Chapters 6 and 10. In recent rulings, the IRS has held that income which is not passive (within the meaning of Subchapter S) was nevertheless passive income according to §469. [PLRs 9510064, 9514005, 9543032, 9548012]

Under old Subchapter S, a corporation would lose its election if it obtained more than 20% of its gross receipts from passive sources. [§1372(e)(5), prior law] (There was a *de minimis* exception for new corporations with small dollar amounts of interest.) The loss of the S election was retroactive to the beginning of the taxable year in which the disqualifying event occurred, and there was no relief provision. A combination of factors—such as a strike or casualty (which might reduce the usual source of gross receipts) and a rise in market interest rates (which could raise the amount of passive income)—could result in an unpleasant surprise. The S corporation would find that it had lost its election, even though the causes of the loss were beyond its control.

One of the objectives of the Subchapter S Revision Act of 1982 was to remove "traps for the unwary" (the phrase is used frequently in the Congressional committee reports). Another objective was to broaden the applicability of Subchapter S. Congress saw no reason to continue the policy of restricting the election to operating companies, since it was now denying S corporations the tax deductions for fringe benefits and limiting the fiscal years. It was concerned, however, that corporations with accumulated earnings problems, as well as personal holding companies, could abuse the tax law through an S election. These corporations would already have used the corporate tax structure to shield earnings. Congress felt that the S election should be available only to corporations with substantial business operations, rather than significant investment income. Accordingly, the Subchapter S Revision Act of 1982 adopted three compromises:

1. To permit a corporation with no accumulated earnings and profits to have unlimited passive investment income. (The Small Business Job Protection Act of 1996 eliminated pre-1983 earnings and profits accumulated while a corporation was an S corporation. See discussion at 1230.22. for rules related to tax years beginning before 1/1/97, when an S corporation could have accumulated earnings and profits for S corporation years.)

2. To prevent sudden and unexpected increases in the relative percentage of passive income from causing a surprise termination. The Subchapter S Revision Act of 1982 raised the limit to 25% from its former level of 20%. It also provided that a corporation could temporarily violate the limit and keep its S election. An S election is terminated by excessive passive income only if the corporation's passive investment income exceeds the 25% ceiling for three consecutive years.
3. To enact a corporate-level tax on corporations with excessive passive income. Like the termination rule, this rule applies only to corporations with accumulated earnings and profits.

The classification problems of individuals' investment and passive income may be viewed as inconsistent. There are no Regulations defining *investment income*, although the investment interest limits have been in effect since 1970. By contrast, the passive income rules, which have existed since 1986, have been the subject of massive Regulations that develop mechanical tests for nearly every conceivable situation. Also, passive investment income of S corporations has a lengthy history of cases and rulings.

In addition, the IRS has issued Final Regulations under new Subchapter S that give some reasonably straightforward operating rules. Final Regulations §1.1375-1, issued in 1986 and modified (slightly) in 1992,[1] is concerned with the passive investment income tax.

In November 1992, the IRS issued Final Regulations §1.1362-2. This Regulation deals, in part, with the definitions of *passive investment income*. The Final Regulations provide more liberal treatment of gross receipts from stock or securities, royalty income, and disposition of partnership interests than had been available under prior guidelines. The Final Regulations are generally applicable to all S corporation tax years beginning after December 31, 1992. [Regs. §1.1362-7(a)]

In one situation, an S corporation was a securities broker. According to the Proposed Regulations in effect during the corporation's fiscal year ended March 31, 1988, the interest it received on margin accounts was passive investment income. Accordingly, the corporation elected to distribute its earnings and profits under §1368(e)(3). The corporation did not have sufficient cash to make the entire distribution. There was no deemed dividend election available at the time.[2] The corporation made cash distributions to its shareholders, who immediately transferred much of the cash back to the corporation as a contribution to capital. According to the 1992 Final Regulations, interest received by a broker-dealer on a margin account is not passive investment income. [Regs. §1.1362-2(c)(5)(iii)(B)] After the 1992 Final Regulations were issued, the corporation requested permission to revoke its election to bypass earnings and profits. The year was not closed under the statute of limitations. The IRS allowed the corporation and its shareholders to amend their returns. The distribution was recharacterized under the normal ordering rules and was reduced by the amount that the shareholders contributed back to the corporation. [PLR 9312027] (See similar rulings with respect to revocation of the bypass election, but not rescission of the distribution, in PLRs 9341010, 9342018.)

The Subchapter S Revision Act of 1982 made few changes to the definitions of *passive investment income*. Accordingly, many of the cases and rulings under prior law remain valid precedent. Figure 12 - 1 gives an overview of the passive investment income problems of S corporations.

---

[1] Until May 28, 1992, this Regulation was designated as Regulations §1.1375-1A. The change in designation was the most significant modification in 1992.

[2] See Chapter 7, at 740.7, for a discussion of the elections to bypass AAA and the deemed dividend election.

Figure 12 - 1: Overview of the passive investment income rules.

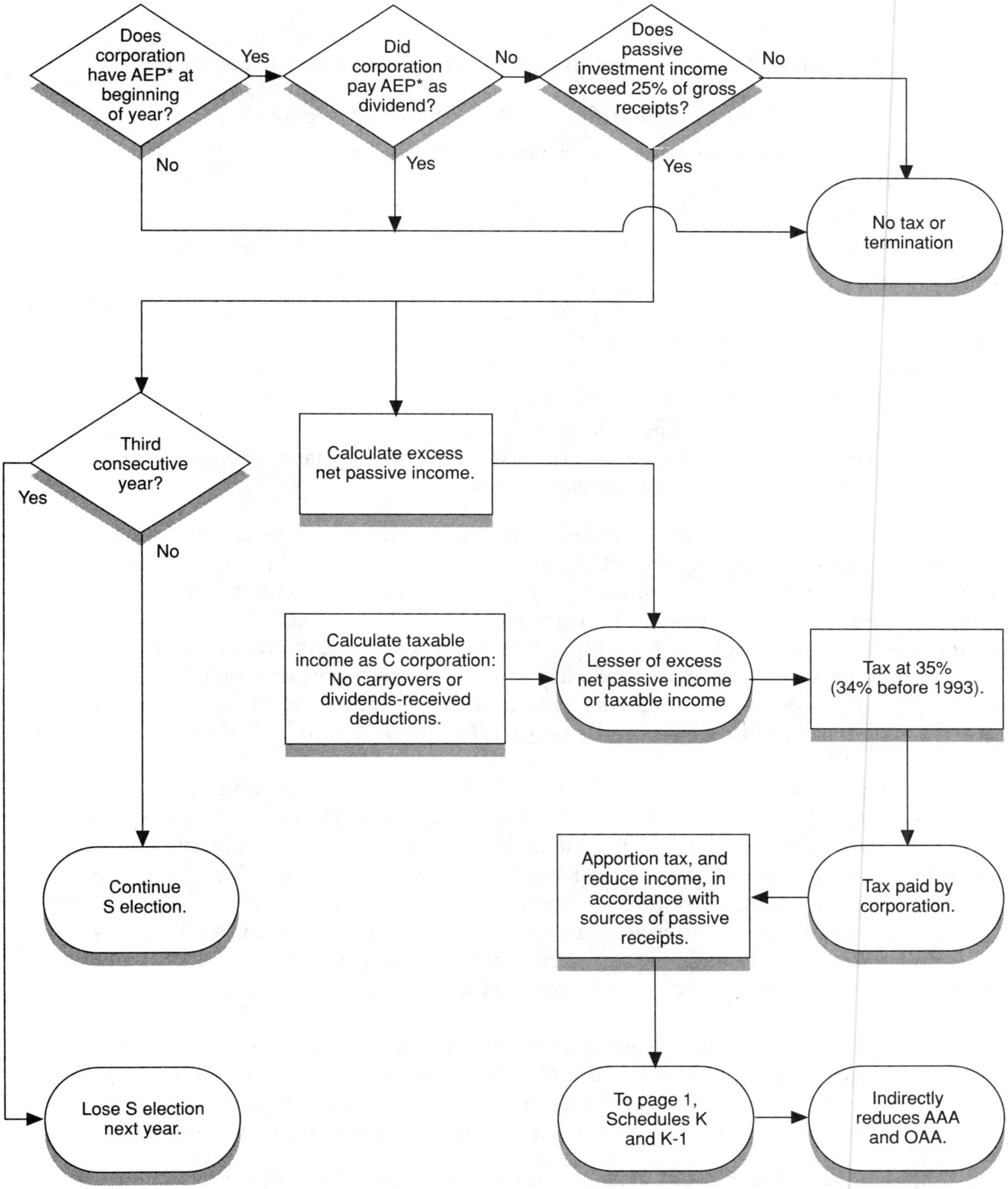

*Disregard EP accumulated while S corporation from 1958 through 1982.

*For years beginning after 12/31/96, EP accumulated while S corporation is eliminated. For years beginning before 1/1/97, disregard EP accumulated while S corporation from 1958 through 1982.

12

1210. Definitions of passive investment income.

The term *passive investment income*, as used in Subchapter S, has its own definitions. It bears only superficial resemblance to the terms *passive income* and *investment income* as used by individuals.

1210.1. Statutory rules. The Code provides some definitions of *passive income* in §1362(d)(3).

SUMMARY OF AUTHORITY: CODE SECTION 1362(d)(3)(C)

- Briefly, the sources of passive investment income are:
  — Interest
  — Dividends
  — Annuities
  — Rents
  — Royalties
  — Gains from sale of stock or securities
- By definition, the statute excludes:
  — Interest on notes from sale of inventory
  — Interest derived by a lending or finance company
  — Gains from exchange of stock in complete liquidation of a subsidiary when the corporation owned more than 50% of the subsidiary's stock

A separate provision excludes gains realized by dealers from the sale of passive investment income options and commodities, including "mark-to-market" gains under §1256. [§1362(d)(3)(E)] Therefore, it is possible for options and commodities dealers to make S elections without fear of the passive investment income problems. With little discussion, the Regulations under §1362 allow an exemption from passive investment income of gains from sales of stock or securities in the ordinary course of the S corporation's business. [Regs. §1.1362-2(c)(5)(iii)(B)(1)] There are also some new rules that provide relief for certain gains from sales of partnership interests. [Regs. §1.1362-2(c)(4)(ii)(B)(4)(i)] These rules are discussed below at 1210.5.

The Small Business Job Protection Act of 1996 added another exception to the general rule of §1362(d)(3)(c). For tax years beginning after December 31, 1996, an S corporation is allowed to own 80% or more of the stock of a C corporation. (Under prior law, such ownership was limited to <80%.) Accordingly, Congress added §1362(d)(3)(E), which excludes dividends from a C corporation from the definition of *passive investment income* if the S corporation receiving the dividends owns at least 80% of the C corporation. Such dividends are excluded to the extent they are "attributable to the earnings and profits of such C corporation derived from the active conduct of a trade or business." See discussion at 1210.7., below.

Since these definitions have been modified only slightly since the enactment of the original Subchapter S in 1958, many interpretations are currently applicable. Regulations, cases, Revenue Rulings, and private letter rulings have developed guidelines, under both prior and current Subchapter S. Unfortunately, there is not always a "bright line" test.

1210.2. Special rules for interest. There are some special problems with interest income. For instance, a taxpayer who receives leveraged interest, such as interest on a wraparound contract, must use the gross, rather than the net, interest received in measuring passive gross receipts. [*Llewellyn*, 70 TC 370 (1978)]

Under Regulations issued in 1986, tax-exempt interest is passive income. [Regs. §1.1375-1(f) (Example 2)] The Regulation includes tax-exempt income for both the calculation of passive gross receipts and the calculation of the tax.

OBSERVATION: The treatment of tax-exempt interest as taxable income for this particular tax is a curious reach of regulatory authority. As of this writing, the validity of the Regulation has not been challenged.

In some situations, interest derived in the ordinary course of the corporation's trade or business is not treated as passive investment income. The statute specifically excludes interest from sales of the taxpayer's inventory from categorization as passive. [§1362(d)(3)(C)(ii)] Similarly, interest derived in the course of business by a lending or finance institution is not passive investment income. [§1362(d)(3)(C)(iii)] The Regulations have expanded this exclusion so that interest derived in the trade or business of dealing in property is not passive investment income. [Regs. §1.1362-2(c)(5)(iii)(B)] Accordingly, interest received by brokers on margin accounts is no longer passive investment income.

OBSERVATION: The exclusion of interest on the sale of inventory incorporates a reference to §1221(1). That provision includes all property held for sale in the ordinary course of business. Thus, the interest not treated as passive should extend to interest received on land held for resale by a real estate dealer, even though such property is not normally called "inventory." Similarly, if an S corporation sells all of its business activity on an installment sale, the interest attributable to the value of the inventory should not be treated as passive investment income.

CAUTION: As banks start to consider the S election, they should pay special attention to the rules regarding interest income. Banks typically have two sources of interest income. The interest derived from loans made in the course of the banking business will not be passive investment income. The interest on portfolio investments, including any tax-exempt interest income, will be treated as passive investment income. [Regs. §1.1362-2(c)(5)(iii)(B)(2)]

1210.3. Income from "rents." Although the statute makes a blanket statement that rents are passive investment income, there has been considerable ruling activity, and a few cases, in this area. Two major questions arise in the classification of rents:

12

- Are certain types of income considered to be rent?
- Are certain types of rent not considered to be passive income?

There are no detailed mechanical tests contained in any Regulations, either under the current or under the former version of Subchapter S. There are, however, many cases and rulings in the approximately 30-year history of the provision. Contrast this situation with the definition of *rents* under §469, described in Chapter 6. The tests employed in determining passive investment income under the S corporation rules are different from those that define *rent* under §469. Thus it is possible for a payment to be classified as rent under §469, even though it is not classified as passive investment income under §1362. [PLR 9423023]

The history of cases and rulings must be evaluated in terms of Regulations §1.1362-2, which was issued in November 1992. As is discussed at 1210.35., below, this Regulation adopted a new criterion for determining whether rent is passive or active income: Rent is not passive if it is received in the conduct of an active trade or business of renting property. The new standard, however, is not completely divorced from the rulings and cases that occurred before the Regulation was issued. Thus the rulings issued before 1993 could still provide valuable guidance.

1210.31. Items not considered rent. The statute gives no clear definition of *rent*, though some cases and rulings have dealt with the term. For example:

- An oil and gas lease bonus is not rent. [*Swank & Son v. U.S.*, 73-2 USTC 9677 (DC Mont.)]
- Broadcast right payments do not constitute rent, and are not passive investment income. [PLR 8924094]
- Revenues from crop sharing are not passive investment income.[3] [Rev. Rul. 61-112, 1961-1 CB 399; PLRs 8927039, 9003056, 9514005]
- Software license income is not passive investment income. [PLR 8952072]
- An auto dealer's open-ended contract is a conditional sale, and not a lease. [PLR 8926044] Since a sale of property other than stock and securities does not create passive investment income, the characterization is important. If a transaction is a sale, rather than a lease, the amount of services provided by the seller is immaterial. If the transaction is characterized as a lease, the amount of services provided by the lessor becomes extremely important.
- Warehouse storage charges are not rents. [Rev. Rul. 65-91, 1965-1 CB 431]

Pre-1993 cases, rulings, and Proposed Regulations made a distinction between personal and real property. [Proposed Regs. §1.1362-3(d)(5)(ii)(B)] The Final Regulations do not make an overt distinction between real and personal property. Therefore, as new rulings and cases occur, the distinction, which had been critical, may be relatively unimportant.

1210.32. Personal property rents, before the Final Regulations. For personal property, any amount of services provided by the lessor appeared to be "significant." Equipment leasing was an important, diverse ruling area, perhaps because the level of services provided can vary almost infinitely on different equipment rental arrangements.

In one instance, the lessor of equipment provided its own operators. The level of service was significant, and the income was not treated as passive. [*Lausman*, 37 TCM 1740 (1978)]

Another ruling illustrates that transactions that appear to produce similar types of revenue can have considerably different outcomes. Revenue Ruling 81-197 addresses income from airplanes. In one situation, the lessor chartered flights, providing all maintenance as well as the flight crew. Such services are significant and the income thus was not rent. The second situation involved a dry lease, where the lessee was responsible for all maintenance and operation of the plane. The income received by the lessor in this instance was passive. [Rev. Rul. 81-197, 1981-2 CB 166]

12

In several other instances, the IRS has ruled that certain types of payments are not passive investment income. Table 12 - 1 provides an overview of rulings to date.

In PLR 9148013, the S corporation leased portable office trailers, used in construction sites. The S corporation provided installation, refurbishing, mechanical maintenance, and certain other services. The IRS held that the services were significant. Per Revenue Ruling 65-83, the gross income would not be treated as passive. [Rev. Rul. 65-83, 1965-1 CB 430]

Perhaps the most illustrative ruling involved an S corporation that leased automobiles on a long-term basis. The leases customarily exceeded one year. The lessor provided ordinary services, such as installing any special equipment and delivering the vehicle. The lessor maintained a repair shop for its leased vehicles, but also gave each lessee a credit card on which the lessee could charge maintenance and repair work done elsewhere. The IRS held that the services were significant and the income was not passive. [Rev. Rul. 76-469, 1976-2 CB 252]

1210.33. Real property rents, before the Final Regulations. Prior to the Final Regulations issued in 1992, cases and rulings held that services provided in connection with real property

---

[3]However, see *Gladys M. Kennedy*, 33 TCM 655, TC Memo 1974-149, where the shareholder performed no services.

TABLE 12 - 1: Items Held Not to Constitute Rent

Source of Income	*Cite*
Full-service yacht charter	PLR 7718003
Short-term car rental	Rev. Rul. 65-40, 1965-1 CB 429
Dress clothing and cranes	Rev. Rul. 65-83, 1965-1 CB 430
Equipment lease, where lessor provided parts, training, repair, and maintenance	PLR 8321060
Equipment lease, where S corporation spent 39% of its staff-hours on maintenance of leased equipment	PLR 8950020
Tractor leasing company provided screening and training for drivers	PLR 8825050 [See also Rev. Rul. 76-469, 1976-2 CB 252.]
Rental of office furniture	PLR 8926039
Leasing of railroad cars	PLR 9314018

had to exceed services customarily provided by a landlord in order for the income not to be classified as rent. The cases and rulings in this area followed the same line of reasoning as those in the self-employment tax area. For either purpose, the level of services provided by the owner determines the characterization of the income. One of the most often cited cases in the IRS rulings is *Bobo*, which dealt with the self-employment tax issue. [*Bobo*, 70 TC 706 (1978), acq. 1983-2 CB 1] In that case, the lack of services provided by the landlord caused the rent not to be treated as trade or business income. Therefore the rent was not subject to self-employment tax. Although *Bobo* did not involve an S corporation, the principles from that case were adapted to S corporations. If the services were sufficient to subject the income to self-employment tax, they were sufficient to avoid classification as passive investment income.

When the property being rented was residential real property, apparently no amount of services was sufficient to prevent the income from being classified as passive. In one leading case, the maintenance of pool, laundry, and other facilities in connection with luxury apartments did not constitute significant services. [*Crouch v. U.S.*, 82-2 USTC 9651 (10th Cir.)] Similarly, advertising, cleaning, and lease management of residential realty did not constitute significant services. [*Lillis*, 45 TCM 1000 (1983)] Similar facts and circumstances with the same conclusion can be found in *Bramlette*, 52 TC 200 (1969), and *City Markets*, 28 TCM 1055 (1969).]

12

Owners of mobile home parks had mixed success in avoiding classification of the rental income as passive investment income. In one case, the maintenance of utility hookups in a mobile home park did not constitute significant services. Since the landlord did not perform any other significant services, the income was deemed to be passive. [*Stover, A.M.*, 86-1 USTC 9149 (8th Cir., 1986)]

The IRS ruling policy, however, appeared to become more lenient in recent years as far as mobile home parks are concerned. In one letter ruling, the operation by the landlord of recreational facilities in a mobile home park did constitute significant services, and the income was not passive. [PLR 7718007] In another letter ruling, an S corporation owned a mobile home park. The corporation provided sewage and garbage removal, exterior lighting, grounds maintenance, shelter with kitchen, recreational facilities, and assistance to tenants selling their units. The rental income was not considered passive. [PLR 9003039. There were similar facts, and the same conclusion, in PLR 9018050 and PLR 9710014.]

Owners of shopping centers were also reasonably successful in securing favorable rulings when they sought to avoid passive classification for their income. For instance, advertising and promotional activities conducted by an S corporation that owned a shopping center were significant services. The corporation's income was not passive. [PLR 8906035] Likewise, maintenance, advertising, and miscellaneous services constituted significant services by the owner of the shopping center, and the income was not passive. [PLRs 8946043, 9311011, 9643017, 9702007]

Similarly, an S corporation that owned a light manufacturing facility was deemed to provide significant services. The owner provided maintenance, cafeteria, recreation facilities on site, and a day care center. The IRS held that the services were significant and that the income was not passive. [PLR 9345048]

1210.34. Means of providing services. The current Regulations, as well as prior Regulations and rulings, do not specify any means by which the S corporation must provide the significant services. It appears, at least in the case of personal property, that the corporation must be financially responsible for the services but need not actively provide the services.

The question of who must actually perform the services often arises when an S corporation owns an interest in the business or rental activity through a partnership. The issues that arise in this context, including the provision of services for rented property, are discussed at 1210.34.

A 1990 case explored the problem of provision of services for activities that the S corporation owns outright. [*Nigh*, 60 TCM 91, TC Memo 1990-349] (This case also contains basis issues, discussed in Chapter 9.) In *Nigh*, an S corporation owned some barges. It used an agent, who was not an employee of the corporation, to manage the barges. The agent was responsible for the rental and maintenance of the barges and was compensated by the corporation. The S corporation and its shareholders had no day-to-day involvement with the barge operations. The IRS claimed that the income from the barge rental should be passive investment income, since the corporation, per se, provided no services. The Tax Court, however, held that the income was not passive: The corporation bore the financial burden of providing the services, and that burden was sufficient to avoid classification of the income as passive.

Another recent case involved an owner of a ferry service. The corporation that owned the ferry had contracted with another organization that was controlled by one of the shareholders of the owner. The operating corporation provided most of the day-to-day services involved in the ferry's operation. The controlling shareholder of the operating corporation, who was also a shareholder in the owner, spent substantial time, on behalf of the owning corporation, supervising maintenance and solving other problems. The owning corporation continued to bear certain risks of loss for any days in which the ferry could not operate. The Tax Court found that the operating agreement was not a lease, and thus the receipts from the operator did not constitute rent. [*White Ferry, Inc.*, TC Memo 1993-639, 66 TCM 1855]

1210.35. Rules adopted in Final Regulations. The Final Regulations adopted in November 1992 departed from the piecemeal approach of earlier years. The new Regulations provide some general tests for determining whether rent is passive or active.

SUMMARY OF AUTHORITY: REGULATIONS SECTION 1.1362-2(c)(5)(ii)(B)

- Rents generally include amounts received for the use of property.
- Rents exclude receipts from the use of property under any of the following circumstances:
  - The amount is received in connection with the active trade or business of renting property.
  - The amount is received for the use of a produced film.
  - The owner has produced the property.
  - There is no overt difference in the treatment of real and personal property.

The Final Regulations specifically state that the incurrence of substantial costs, other than depreciation, is an indicator that the corporation is in the active trade or business of renting property. Thus they appear to incorporate the rationale of the *Nigh* case, discussed above.

> **OBSERVATION:** The November 1992 Final Regulations appear to take a more liberal stance on treatment of rents as active, rather than passive, income. Thus the favorable rulings cited above should still be reasonably good precedent, and the letter rulings cited above should continue to be valid indicators of the IRS position. As discussed below, the private letter rulings issued after the Final Regulations may signal subtle, but important, tendencies of the IRS to rule that more types of rent are active.

1210.36. Rulings after the Final Regulations. By 1994, the IRS was beginning to issue rulings on rental income with reference to the active trade or business test included in the Regulations. The rulings issued in early 1994 indicate that the IRS is at least as liberal in classifying rent as active as it had been before the new Regulations. The early private letter rulings held that the items in Table 12 - 2 are not rental income.

TABLE 12 - 2: Rulings Holding That Rent Was Active Trade or Business Income

Type of Property	*Services Performed*	*PLR Reference*
Office building	Maintenance, garbage, collection of checks, major repairs, capital improvements	9404010
Warehouse	Maintenance, garbage, collection of checks, major repairs, capital improvements	9404010
Equipment, not self-manufactured	Solicitation of customers, credit approval, delivery	9404016
Mobile home park	Roadways, water, sewer, backup electricity, maintenance, auto repair areas, yard sales, recreation hall, storage facility, park area, basketball court, security guards	9404019
Automobile, long-term	Orders for autos, delivery, maintenance and repair assistance, loaners, warranty negotiation, disposition at end of term	9404026
Apartment management	Lease negotiations, credit checks, maintenance and repair	9411006
Self-owned office building	Lease negotiation, credit checks, janitorial, trash removal, maintenance of offices and common areas	9411006
General partner in apartment rental	Supervision of employees of partnerships, who provide snow removal and perform maintenance for swimming pools, clubhouses,	9411006

12

Type of Property	*Services Performed*	*PLR Reference*
	vending machines, laundry, basketball courts, playgrounds, tennis courts, other recreational facilities, newsletters, satellite television	
Office building	Budgets, lease negotiation, planning layouts, assistance with tenant improvements, supervision of maintenance and repair, payment of utilities	9411015
Partnership interest in recreational vehicle park	Partnership provides insurance, taxes, building and ground maintenance, hook-ups, message service, reservations, laundry facilities, recreation hall, pool, coffee, vending machines, company-owned store on premises	9411034; see also Rev. Rul. 71-455, 1971-2 CB 318.
Full-service storage facility	Security, air conditioning, routine maintenance, messages, rental negotiations	9419029
Shopping center	Lease negotiation, collections, maintenance, security. Some services are provided by independent contractors.	9420014
Commercial, industrial property and parking lot	Regular inspections, landscape maintenance, minimal storage space, odd-job maintenance on individual properties, maintenance of common areas, interpretation of zoning ordinances, troubleshooting, lease and sublease assistance, repair of vacant units	9421007
Office complex	Lease negotiations, layout design, grounds maintenance, snow removal, forklift, service center for copies and faxes	9421023
Mobile home park	Security, emergency service, trash pickup, lawn care in common areas and at homesites, maintenance of roads, sidewalks, water, sewer and other utilities, monitoring compliance with local ordinances, marketing and financing assistance upon sale of a unit	9421045
Shopping center, office, light industrial, car wash	Two full-time employees provided general maintenance, trash pickup, pest control; had active roles in site development, promotion; advised on construction and zoning. Owner	9417021

	carries insurance, environmental cleanup.	
Shopping center	Maintenance of common areas, repairs on leased space, advertising, marketing research	9422049

In another recent ruling, a corporation's S election had terminated due to excessive passive investment income, under the interpretation of the law as it existed before Final Regulations §1.1362-2. The corporation operated a commercial office building, a warehouse, and storage space. The owner provided some, but not all, of the utilities. The owner negotiated all leases, although some space was leased to related corporations. The owner reviewed property tax assessments, although the tenants paid the property tax. The owner maintained common areas and provided limited maintenance on leased space. The IRS held that the corporation could apply the new tests to its open years, and thus its S election was retroactively reinstated. The IRS required that all of the persons who owned shares in all open years file returns consistent with the S election being in effect. [PLR 9423023]

> **OBSERVATION:** The rulings issued in 1994 and 1995 have allowed several S corporations with long-term tenants to treat the rent income as not passive. In each of the rulings, the corporation provided services beyond those customarily found in a net leasing agreement. The corporations had employees who were actively involved in the management of the rental properties, although some of the services were contracted out. These rulings appear to indicate a relaxation of the standards that had been applied to real property rents, discussed at 1210.33., above.
>
> The new rulings may be of special interest to S corporations that own and operate apartment houses. PLR 9411006 allowed an S corporation that was a general partner in a partnership that owned an apartment house to claim that the rent income was not passive, due to the nature of the services provided. In contrast, the case of *Crouch v. U.S.* [82-2 USTC 9651 (10th Cir.)], held that rental income was passive even though the services performed were essentially the same. Thus the change in IRS policy from the years in the *Crouch* case to the present should allow many more S corporations to avoid the passive investment income problems. Some corporations that own rental real estate and have avoided elections due to the nature of their income may want to reconsider.

12

Through late 1996 to date, the IRS has continued to issue rulings treating rent as nonpassive when it was connected with the active trade or business of renting property. [PLRs 9602020, 9644060, 9645008, 9647018, 9649028, 9650026, 9731017, 9736017, 9801022, 9808009, 9811010, 9811015, 9812019, 9812026, 9813011, 9823019, 9824018, 9824019, 9824023, 9824031, 9824032, 9828023, 9828024, 9828028, 9839006, 9844007, 199908008, 199909028, 199917017, 199917019, 199917029, 199917055, 199921014, 199921017, 199921018, 199921021, 199921049, 199923008] In contrast to the treatment under prior law, discussed above, several rulings have indicated that rents received by residential property are not passive investment income. [PLRs 9540049, 9543028, 9624015, 9752045, 9815002, 9848021, 9811011, 9823011, 199919010, 199919011, 199919012, 199919013, 199919014, 199919015] The IRS has also ruled that real property rent was not passive investment income when the corporation developed and constructed the property. [PLRs 9430016, 9430017, 9430018, 9540068, 9734051, 9734052, 9808008, 9825014, 9828019, 9850004, 199904028, 199912036]

Although most of the rulings issued by the IRS deal with real property rents, the IRS has also ruled that personal property rents are not passive investment income. In PLR 9548012, the S corporation leased computer equipment and provided services such as installation, repossession, accounting, lease negotiation, refinishing, and sale of used equipment. The income from the leases was not considered passive investment income. The IRS has also ruled that rental payments for floating boat houses are not passive investment income, where the S corporation provided services such as security, repairs, cleaning, billing, and other administrative functions. [PLR 9625034] See also PLR 9630007, in which the S corporation provided similar services related to leasing heavy construction equipment and a radio tower. For additional rulings on personal property rents not classified as passive income, see PLRs 9853030 and 9851041.

1210.4. Royalty income. Generally, royalties are payments for the use of property, including oil, gas, and minerals, as well as patents, copyrights, secret processes and formulas, goodwill, trademarks, tradebrands, and franchises. The general rule is contained in Regulations §1.1362-2(c)(5)(ii)(A), summarized here:

SUMMARY OF AUTHORITY: REGULATIONS SECTION 1.1362-2(c)(5)(ii)(A)(1)

- Royalty income includes amounts received for:
  — Minerals, including oil and gas
  — Patents
  — Copyrights
  — Secret processes and formulas
  — Goodwill, trademarks, and tradebrands
  — Franchises
  — "Other like property," not specified in the Regulations
- The gross income from royalties is not reduced by any deductions, when testing for the percentage of gross receipts.

12

For many of the items listed above, there is no relief from classification as passive investment income. There are some relief provisions, however, for copyright, software, and oil, gas, and mineral royalties. The special rules are derived from the personal holding company provisions, which were the origin of the passive investment income rules. In addition, the 1992 Regulations treat certain royalties derived in the ordinary course of a trade or business as not being passive income.

1210.41. Royalties derived in the ordinary course of business. Perhaps the most significant development in the IRS treatment of royalties was the modification of Proposed Regulations §1.1362-2 in 1992. Before this modification, there were only narrowly defined exceptions to the treatment of royalties as passive investment income. The liberalized language of the Proposed Regulation, as modified in April 1992, was adopted in the Final Regulations in November 1992.

SUMMARY OF AUTHORITY: REGULATIONS SECTION 1.1362-2(c)(5)(ii)(A)(2)

- Certain royalties are not passive investment income.
- To qualify, the royalties must be received in the active conduct of the S corporation's trade or business.
- The S corporation must have created the royalties or must perform significant services with respect to the property.

This treatment will probably apply to many franchisors, as well as to holders of other licensed property. An example adapted from the Regulations illustrates the treatment of royalties under this exception.

EXAMPLE 12 - 1 [adapted from Regs. §1.1362-2(c)(6), Example 5]: In 1997, Sierra Corporation, an S corporation with accumulated earnings and profits, has the following gross receipts:

Trademark A royalties	$ 5,000
Trademark B royalties	8,000
Other trade or business receipts	62,000
Total	$75,000

Sierra created Trademark A, but it did not create Trademark B or perform significant services or incur substantial costs with respect to the development or marketing of Trademark B.

Because Sierra created Trademark A, the royalty payments with respect to Trademark A are derived in the ordinary course of Sierra's business and are not included in the term *royalties* for purposes of determining Sierra's passive investment income. However, the royalty payments with respect to Trademark B are passive investment income. Sierra's passive investment income for the year is $8,000, and its passive investment income percentage for the taxable year is 10.67% ($8,000/$75,000). This does not exceed 25% of gross receipts, and consequently the three-year period for termination of the S election does not begin to run. Nor would Sierra be subject to the passive investment income tax for 1997.

Certain other royalties may be excluded from treatment as passive investment income. These royalties have special provisions in the personal holding company area if they meet certain conditions. The Regulations under Subchapter S adopt the same tests. As a general rule, copyright, software, and oil, gas, and mineral, timber, coal, and domestic iron ore royalties are not passive income if the corporation's principal business is producing those royalties. [Regs. §1.1362-2(c)(5)(iii)] The specific rules related to the personal holding company rules are detailed below, under each type of royalty. The authority for the treatment of these royalties is found in Regulations §1.1362-2(c)(5)(ii)(A)(3).

SUMMARY OF AUTHORITY: REGULATIONS SECTION 1.1362-2(c)(5)(ii)(A)(3)

12

- Copyright royalties are not passive investment income if they would not be treated as personal holding company income.
- Oil, gas, and mineral royalties are not passive investment income if they would not be treated as personal holding company income.
- Active business computer software royalties are not passive investment income if they would not be treated as personal holding company income.
- Disposition of timber with a retained economic interest is not passive investment income.
- Disposition of coal or domestic iron ore with a retained economic interest is not passive investment income.

The copyright, oil, gas, mineral, and active business computer software royalties are discussed below. The exceptions relating to timber, coal, and domestic iron ore are so narrowly crafted that they receive no discussion in this book.

1210.42. Oil, gas, and mineral royalties. Oil, gas, and mineral royalties are not personal holding company income if:

- They constitute 50% or more of the corporation's adjusted ordinary gross income.
- The corporation's other personal holding company income is not more than 10% of the ordinary gross income.

- The corporation's trade or business deductions (other than compensation to shareholders, interest, taxes, losses, and depreciation) exceed 15% of adjusted ordinary gross income. [§543(a)(3); Regs. §1.543-1(b)(11)]

The Regulations under Subchapter S treat oil, gas, and mineral royalties as other than passive investment income if they meet these same tests. [Regs. §1.1362-2(c)(5)(ii)(A)(3)] Accordingly, an S corporation will not have passive investment income from its oil, gas, and mineral royalties in any year in which it meets all of these criteria. See PLR 9825008, specifically ruling that a coal royalty is not passive investment income. If, however, the corporation should fail to meet any one of the above tests in a taxable year, such royalty income would be considered passive investment income for that year.

1210.43. Copyright royalties. Copyright royalties are not personal holding company income if they are from artistic or literary creations by any shareholder. Other copyright royalties are not passive if:

- The royalties are at least 50% of the corporation's adjusted ordinary gross income.
- The corporation's other personal holding company income (excluding copyright royalties, but including copyright royalties from property created by any 10% shareholder, and excluding any dividend received from corporations in which the corporation owns at least 50% of the stock) is not more than 10% of the ordinary gross income.
- The corporation's trade or business deductions (other than compensation to shareholders, interest, taxes, losses, and depreciation) exceed 25% of adjusted ordinary gross income, less compensation to shareholders and royalties paid. [§543(a)(4); Regs. §1.543-1(b)(12)(iv)]

The Regulations under Subchapter S provide similar treatment for excluding copyright royalties from passive investment income. Therefore, an S corporation that meets all of these tests for any given taxable year will not have passive investment income from its copyright royalties. [§543(d)]

1210.44. Active business computer software royalties. Active business computer software royalties are also excluded from passive investment income if they would be excluded from personal holding company income. To meet these tests, the corporation must be in the active business of manufacturing, developing, or producing software. The additional tests are as follows:

- The royalties are at least 50% of the corporation's adjusted ordinary gross income.
- The corporation's trade or business deductions (other than compensation to the five largest shareholders, interest, taxes, losses, and depreciation, but including research and development costs and business start-up amortization) exceed 25% of adjusted ordinary gross income, for the five most recent years (or the corporation's entire existence, if less than five years). [Regs. §1.1362-2(c)(5)(ii)(A)(3)]

Regulations under Subchapter S provide a similar exclusion from passive investment income. Accordingly, an S corporation whose principal activity is the development and licensing of software will not have passive investment income from its software royalties. [Regs. §1.1362-2(c)(5)(ii)(A)(3)]

> **OBSERVATION:** The regulatory exclusions from passive investment income for oil, gas, mineral, copyright, and computer software royalties require that a corporation

engaged in one of these activities meet certain rigid mechanical tests. Note that each type of royalty stands alone and cannot be aggregated with royalties from other types of property. Accordingly, the owners of an S corporation that engages in one of these activities should not combine other business or investment operations within the same corporation.

As a practical matter, most S corporations that meet the personal holding company exclusion will probably also qualify for the active business exclusion, discussed above. As a consequence, the specific exclusions for oil, gas, copyright, and active business software royalties will probably generate little, if any, relief.

1210.5. Gains from property sales. Most gains from the sale of property do not produce passive investment income. Gains from sales of stock and securities, however, are passive. For measuring an S corporation's passive investment income, the gains from individual sales are not offset by losses from sales of other shares or securities.

SUMMARY OF AUTHORITY: CODE SECTION 1362(d)(3)(C)(i)

- For purposes of the passive investment income test, the gross receipts from sales of stocks and securities are limited to the gains from such sales.
- The gains are not offset by losses.

Until the IRS issued Final Regulations §1.1362-2 in November 1992, there was no distinction between sales of stocks and securities by purely passive investors from sales by traders or dealers. Such gains were treated as passive, without regard to their characterization as capital or ordinary. Therefore, this provision could apply to an S corporation that is a securities dealer. The Final Regulations, however, provide that gains from the sale of stock and securities in the ordinary course of an active trade or business are not passive investment income. [Regs. §1.1362-2(c)(5)(iii)(B)(1)]

OBSERVATION: Any S corporation dealing in securities can file amended returns for all open years to treat gains as not being passive investment income. See discussion of these procedures at 1200., above.

12

Before the issuance of the Final Regulations under §1362, an interest in a partnership was considered a security. Therefore, a gain from the sale of a partnership interest resulted in passive investment income. [PLR 7922083] The Proposed Regulations under Subchapter S treated all sales of partnership interests as sales of securities. [Proposed Regs. §1.1362-3(d)(4)(ii)(B)]

The Final Regulations under Subchapter S provide different treatment for sales of partnership interests. If an S corporation sells a limited partnership interest, the gain (or loss) on the sale is treated as a gain or loss recognized on the sale of a security. [Regs. §1.1362-2(c)(4)(ii)(B)(3)] The sale of a general partnership interest, however, is somewhat more complicated.

The Regulations treat the sale of a general partnership interest by an S corporation as if it were a sale of the partner's share of each partnership asset. Therefore, passive investment income is limited to the gain that would have been allocated to the S corporation if the partnership had sold all of its stock and securities. [Regs. §1.1362-2(c)(4)(ii)(B)(4)(i)]

EXAMPLE 12 - 2: GPR Corporation is an S corporation. On December 22, 1992, GPR sold a 10% general partnership interest in the MAJ partnership. On that date, MAJ held some XYZ stock that had a basis of $500,000 and fair market value of $750,000. MAJ had no other stocks or securities. Under the general rule from the Regulations, GPR would treat $25,000 as passive investment income from a sale of stock or securities on December 22, 1992.

The Regulations allow an S corporation to treat the sale of a general partnership interest as if it were a sale of a limited partnership interest. [Regs. §1.1362-2(c)(4)(ii)(B)(4)(ii)] This election will most likely be useful when the corporation's gain on the sale of the limited partnership interest is less than the amount that would have been allocated to the S corporation if the partnership had sold its stock and securities.

EXAMPLE 12 - 3: Refer to Example 12 - 2. GPR's gain on the sale of its interest in MAJ was only $3,000. By electing to treat its MAJ interest as an interest in a limited partnership, GPR has passive investment income of only $3,000 from the sale.

OBSERVATION: An investment in a limited liability company may be viewed as a general partnership interest or as a limited partnership interest. The distinction is not entirely clear. At first it might appear that all members of a limited liability company are limited partners, due to the limited liability of all members. However, in Revenue Procedure 89-12, 1989-1 CB 798, a partner who actively participates in management of a partnership is not considered to be a limited partner. See PLRs 9350013 and 9407030 for holdings that members of limited liability companies are not necessarily limited partners. Thus, classification of an interest in a limited liability company as a general partnership or limited partnership interest may depend on the S corporation's management role.

When an S corporation has several blocks of the same security, it must be careful to identify the securities sold, if it can avoid significant gains by doing so. Unless securities are identified, the IRS uses the FIFO rule. [*Gann*, 43 TCM 682 (1982)]

Although gains from the sale of property other than stock or securities are not treated as passive, it is important to determine the gross receipts from such sales. If these sales, as well as other gross receipts, exceed 75% of the corporation's total, the corporation will not be subject to the passive investment income problems. Gross receipts from other capital assets are limited to capital gain net income. [§1362(d)(3)(B)]

EXAMPLE 12 - 4: Q Corporation sells the following assets in 1988:

	Amount Realized	*Adjusted Basis*	*Gain (Loss)*
Stocks	$75,000	$40,000	$35,000
Bonds	80,000	90,000	(10,000)
Land parcel 1	90,000	20,000	70,000
Land parcel 2	50,000	95,000	(45,000)
Inventory	60,000	15,000	45,000

According to the passive investment income rules, Q's total gross receipts are:

Stocks	$ 35,000	(gains only)
Bonds	0	(losses are not counted)
Land parcels	25,000	(gains less losses)
Inventory	60,000	(amount received)
	$120,000	

Since its passive gross receipts ($35,000) exceed 25% of its total gross receipts ($30,000), the corporation has excessive passive investment income. If the corporation has accumulated Subchapter C earnings and profits, it may be subject to the tax on excess net passive income. If the situation continues for three consecutive years, the corporation could lose its S election.

Certain other types of property may be considered securities. Case law under old Subchapter S held that commodities futures traded in the active conduct of a trade or business were not passive investment income. [*New Mexico Timber Co.*, 84 TC 1290 (1985)] By contrast, mortgage notes sold by a mortgage lender were treated as securities, and they created passive investment income. [*Buhler Mortgage Co.*, 51 TC 971, 1969] The latter case is of dubious precedential value, after the issuance of Regulations §1.1362-2(c)(5)(iii)(B)(1). It would now appear that the sale of mortgages could qualify as active income if such sales were a part of the corporation's ordinary trade or business activities.

1210.6. Character of income from partnerships. If the S corporation is a partner in a partnership, certain attributes of income from the partnership will pass through to the S corporation. For instance, the nature of the gross receipts as passive or otherwise will be determined at the partnership level. [Regs. §1.702-1(a)(8)(ii)] In this case, an S corporation's share of partnership gross receipts is used in the test for 25% passive investment income. [Rev. Rul. 71-455, 1971-2 CB 318; PLRs 8804015, 8917043, 8950053, 9321041, 9435010, 199923007, 199923030]

EXAMPLE 12-5: Pico, an S corporation, is a 30% partner in partnership PYZ. For the current year, PYZ's gross income is $500,000 and its taxable income is $50,000.

Pico has gross receipts of $250,000 from sources other than its interest in PYZ. In determining its gross receipts for the passive investment income test, Pico's total is:

Share of gross receipts from PYZ (30%)	$150,000
Gross receipts from other sources	250,000
Total	$400,000

Therefore, up to $100,000 of Pico's gross receipts may be passive investment income, and Pico's passive investment income will not exceed the allowable limit. Any of Pico's share of passive investment income from PYZ would retain its character to Pico. It would be combined with any of Pico's passive investment income from other sources to test for the 25% limit.

To comply with an S corporation's need for information, a partnership that sells some stock and securities should report the gains separately from the losses incurred on such sales. If the partnership receives rental income, it should determine the significance of the services it performs in connection with such rents.

An S corporation's share of income from a partnership is passive investment income, to the extent of its rents, royalties, interest, dividends, and annuities. [PLR 8852021] Especially where rents are concerned, the services provided by the partnership may be sufficient for the income not to be classified as passive to the S corporation partner. For example, an S corporation's share of rental income from a partnership that operated a parking lot was not passive investment income. Services provided at the partnership level were significant, so the income was not passive rent within the meaning of Subchapter S. [PLR 8931007]

In a similar ruling, charter boats rented by a limited partnership were not passive investment income to an S corporation that was a limited partner. [PLR 8916057] Another ruling involved an S corporation that was a limited partner in a partnership that owned a natural gas pipeline. [PLR 9144024] The partnership provided significant services, and the income was not classified as rent. The S corporation was required to take into account its distributive share of the gross income from the partnership in testing for excessive passive investment income. This requirement would appear to work to the S corporation's advantage, because the IRS also held that the income from the partnership would not be passive.

OBSERVATION: The information an S corporation needs for classification of passive investment income may differ from that which a partnership normally reports to its partners. When an S corporation with passive income concerns is a partner, the corporation should inform the partnership of the information it needs.

EXAMPLE 12 - 6: An S corporation is a limited partner in a partnership. The partnership owns and operates a motel. Since the partnership provides significant services, the S corporation's share of the partnership's gross receipts will not be passive investment income. The net income or loss that passes through from the partnership to the S corporation must be again passed through to the S corporation's shareholders. Unless one or more of the shareholders can meet a material participation test (which is extremely unlikely for a limited partner), the net income or loss will most likely be passive to the shareholders. (See Chapter 10 for discussion of the material participation tests.)

OBSERVATION: For many years, Revenue Ruling 77-220, 1977-1 CB 263, raised the possibility that being a member of a partnership could endanger a corporation's S status. The change in IRS policy in 1994, as expressed in Revenue Ruling 94-43, 1994-27 IRB 8, however, signals a new tolerance for such arrangements. See discussion in Chapter 2, at 235.2., and in Chapter 14, at 1435.21. Thus the planning potential for using an interest in a partnership that has active income to avoid the 25% test on passive gross receipts should be even more viable in the future.

As is discussed in Chapter 14, at 1435.21., most states now permit limited liability companies. If one of these companies is classified as a partnership for federal tax purposes, it might make an ideal investment opportunity for an S corporation that wants to avoid the passive investment income test. If the services provided by a partnership or a limited liability company are similar to those that an S corporation provided in the rulings listed in Table 12 - 2, at 1210.36., it should be easier now than ever before for an S corporation to invest in vehicles that provide active gross receipts.

If an S corporation invests as a limited partner, it should plan carefully for the year of sale of its interest therein. As was discussed above, at 1210.5., any gain from the sale of a limited partnership interest is passive investment income. Thus there is no distinction between a general partnership interest and a limited partnership interest as to the nature of gross receipts while the S corporation owns the interest. There is an important difference in the year of sale.

12

CAUTION: An S corporation that is considering investment in a partnership (including a limited liability company) in order to use the partnership's gross receipts to avoid the passive investment income test should be careful not to confuse gross receipts with gross income. For instance, if an S corporation has gross receipts of $100,000 and has cost of goods sold of $90,000, its gross receipts are $100,000 and its gross income is only $10,000.

1210.7. Character of dividends from subsidiaries. As discussed above, dividend income is normally passive investment income, per se. However, the Small Business Job Protection Act of 1996 amended the law to provide special rules for subsidiary corporations in which the S corporation owns 80% or more of the stock. The Code states that dividends are not passive investment income to the extent that they are "attributable to the earnings and profits of such C corporation derived from the active conduct of a trade or business." In 1998, the IRS issued Proposed Regulations to interpret this phrase. [Proposed Regs. §1.1362-8] In essence, the Proposed Regulations require a two-step process:

1. Determine the mix of the subsidiary corporation's earnings and profits.
2. Apply the mix of the earnings and profits to the actual dividend received by the S corporation.

In general, the subsidiary corporation can use any "reasonable method" to allocate its earnings and profits between passive and nonpassive. [Proposed Regs. §1.1362-8(b)(1)] The Regulations suggest, but do not require, a safe harbor method. The corporation calculates the percent of gross receipts from passive and nonpassive and applies these percentages to its earnings and profits for the taxable year. [Proposed Regs. §1.1362-8(b)(5)] A *de minimis* rule provides that if less than 10% of the corporation's gross receipts in any year are from passive sources, then none of the earnings and profits for that year are considered passive. [Proposed Regs. §1.1362-8(b)(3)]

> **EXAMPLE 12 - 7:** Jenco, an S corporation., owns 90% of the stock of Filco. In 1998 Filco had active gross receipts of $85,000 and passive gross receipts of $15,000. Thus 15% of Filco's current earnings and profits are treated as passive investment income under the safe harbor rule. Filco could use another "reasonable method" to make this allocation.

If the C corporation's distributions in a taxable year do not exceed its current earnings and profits, the dividend to the S corporation will be allocated to passive and nonpassive income in the same percentage in which the current earnings and profits were determined. If a corporation uses the gross receipts safe harbor, the gross receipts percentages will apply to the distribution.

> **EXAMPLE 12 - 8:** Refer to Example 12 - 7. Filco's current earnings and profits for 1998 were $70,000. If Filco did not distribute more than $70,000, 15% of its distribution to Jenco would be treated as passive investment income to Jenco.

If a distribution exceeds the subsidiary's current earnings and profits, the Regulations provide a reasonable allocation mechanism for the subsidiary's accumulated earnings and profits. Distributions from accumulated earnings and profits are treated as passive investment income based on the percentage of the immediate prior year's current earnings and profits, as calculated above.

> **EXAMPLE 12 - 9:** Assume the same facts as in Example 12 - 8, except that Filco distributed $100,000 of dividends in 1998 ($90,000 to Jenco, the 90% shareholder). Thus $70,000 ($63,000 to Jenco) of the 1998 distribution would be from 1998 earnings and profits and $30,000 would be from accumulated earnings and profits as of January 1, 1998. Further assume that 40% of Filco's 1997 earnings and profits was passive investment income. The 1998 distribution to Jenco would be treated as follows:

	Passive	*Nonpassive*
Dividend from current earnings and profits		
($63,000 x .15)	$ 9,450	
($63,000 x .85)		$53,550
Dividend from current earnings and profits		
($27,000 x .4)	10,800	
($27,000 x.6)		16,200
Total	$20,250	$69,750

12

There are also special rules for C corporation subsidiaries that in turn have other subsidiaries. [See Proposed Regs. §1.1362-8(b)(2) for treatment of lower-tier subsidiaries that do not file consolidated returns, and see Proposed Regs. §1.1362-8(c) for lower-tier subsidiaries that do file consolidated returns.] Finally, there are some special rules for aggregating any of the subsidiary's accumulated earnings and profits for years before the S corporation was the 80% shareholder. The subsidiary computes its average passive gross receipts for the three most recent pre-affiliation years and applies that percentage to all of its pre-affiliation accumulated earnings and profits. [Proposed Regs. §1.1362-8(b)(4)]

1210.8. Other gross receipts problems. When a taxpayer receives amounts that are subject to commissions, there may be a question about whether the gross receipts are measured before or after the commission. In one ruling, an insurance agency collected gross commissions and then remitted a portion to the insurer. The agency owned the net premium to the insurer regardless of whether it collected anything from the insured. The IRS held that the gross receipts were the full amounts received by the agency before the insurer was paid the commissions. [Rev. Rul. 69-192, 1969-1 CB 206]

Recently, the IRS has ruled similarly when an S corporation resells goods (the type of goods is not specified in the ruling) and pays the supplier based on the amount of goods sold. This situation might be similar to that of a dealer who receives credit terms from a manufacturer. The IRS ruled that the reseller's gross receipts are the amounts that it receives from its customers, and the gross receipts are not reduced by any amount owed to the S corporation's supplier. [PLR 9853031]

1210.9. Summary of income classification. As discussed above, the various categories of income have special rules for classification. The different types of potentially passive income may be subject to some unique rules, which tend not to follow any logical consistency. Figure 12 - 2 summarizes the rules.

1215. Passive income tax.

If, at the end of a taxable year, an S corporation has accumulated earnings and profits, and its passive investment income exceeds 25% of the gross receipts for the same year, the corporation is subject to the passive investment income tax.

SUMMARY OF AUTHORITY: CODE SECTION 1375(a)

- When an S corporation has accumulated earnings and profits at the close of the year, and its passive investment income exceeds 25% of its gross receipts, the corporation is subject to a corporate-level tax.
- The tax is imposed on the S corporation's excess net passive income.
- The corporation must use the highest corporate tax rate.

Like the built-in gains tax, the passive investment income tax is imposed at the highest corporate rate. From 1988 through 1992, this rate was 34%. For taxable years beginning after 1992, the rate is 35%. See Chapter 11, at 1130.1., for the rules regarding fiscal years that begin in 1992 and end in 1993.

1215.1. Excess net passive income defined. The preceding discussion covered the rules on defining *passive investment income*. The focus was on definition and measurement of gross receipts and on classification of gross receipts as passive or otherwise. Once a corporation has exceeded the allowable limit, it must compute its tax liability. The tax is imposed not on the passive gross receipts, per se, but on the corporation's "excess net passive income."

Net passive income is the first quantity that must be identified. The Code provides a straightforward definition.

SUMMARY OF AUTHORITY: CODE SECTION 1375(b)(2)

- Net passive income is the difference between the gross receipts from passive sources and the deductions directly connected with the passive gross receipts.
- Passive gross receipts cannot be reduced by any net operating loss deductions.
- Passive gross receipts cannot be reduced by any dividends-received deductions or amortization of the corporation's organizational expense (part VIII of Subchapter B).

Figure 12 - 2: *Classification of passive investment income by category.*

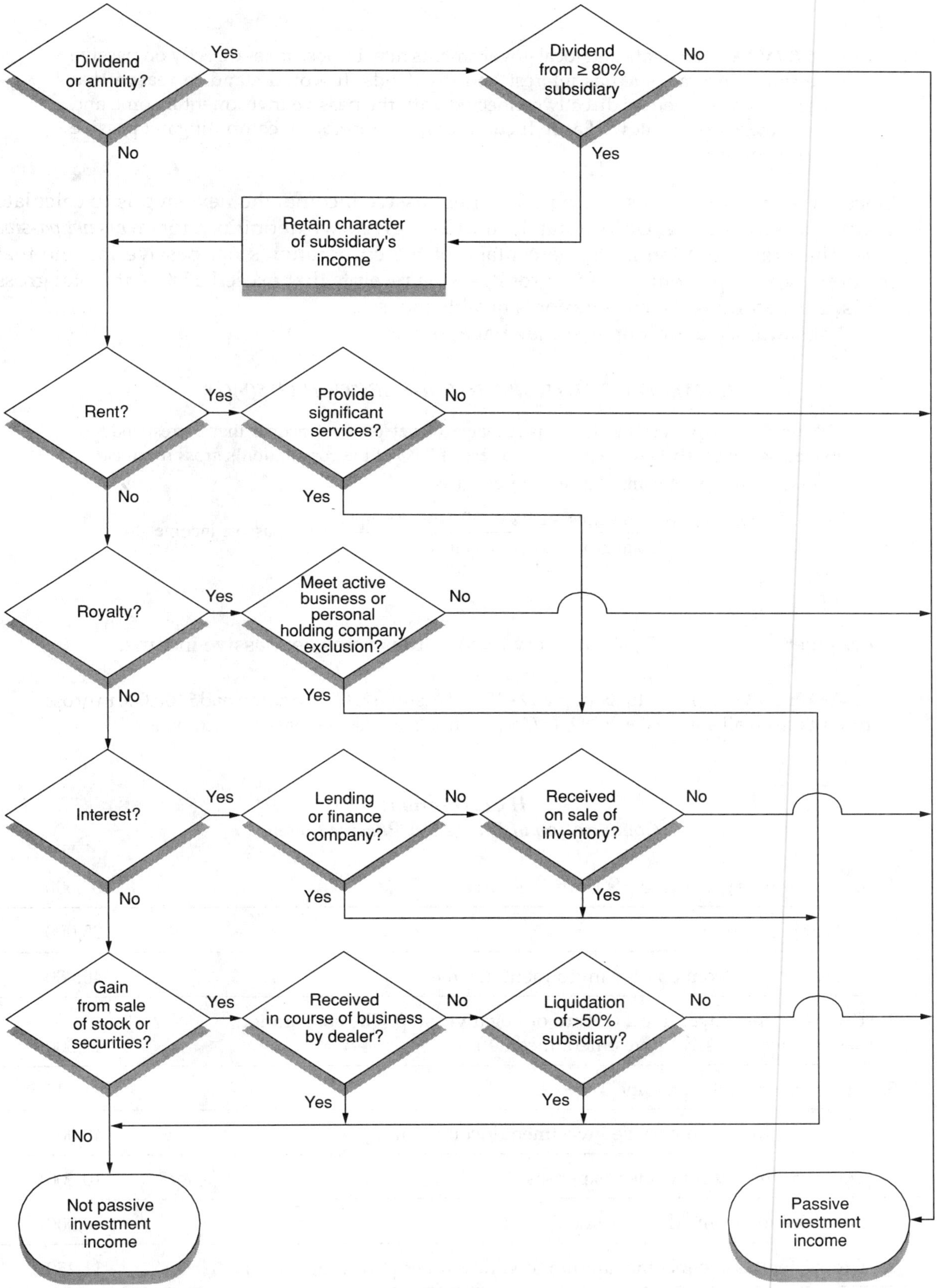

EXAMPLE 12 - 10: In 1989, H Corporation has $40,000 of passive gross receipts. It has $10,000 expenses directly connected with the passive income. Its net passive income is $30,000.

OBSERVATION: State and local governments may impose taxes directly on passive investment income, such as interest and dividends. It would stand to reason that these taxes are expenses directly connected with the passive investment income and should therefore be allowed as reductions of gross receipts in computing net passive investment income.

Once an S corporation has computed its net passive income, the next step is to calculate excess net passive income. Unfortunately, the Code gives two definitions for *excess net passive income.* The first definition is the percentage of the corporation's net passive income that corresponds to the percentage of its gross passive receipts that exceed 25% of its total gross receipts. The second is the corporation's taxable income.

The first statutory definition is somewhat awkward.

SUMMARY OF AUTHORITY: CODE SECTION 1375(b)(1)

- Excess net passive income is the percentage of net passive income that corresponds to the percentage of passive gross income in excess of 25% of the corporation's gross receipts.
- Excess net passive income can be represented as:

$$\frac{\text{(Gross passive receipts} - 25\% \text{ of all gross receipts)}}{\text{Total gross passive receipts}} \times \text{net passive income}$$

Worksheet 12 - 1, at 1235., shows how to compute excess net passive income.

12

EXAMPLE 12 - 11: Refer to Example 12 - 10 and assume H Corporation had $100,000 in gross receipts from all sources. In 1989, H Corporation's excess net passive income is:

H Corporation
Computation of Excess Net Passive Income

1. Corporation's gross receipts from all sources	100,000
2. 25% of gross receipts	25,000
3. Gross receipts from passive investment income	40,000
4. Excess of line 3 over line 2 (If zero or negative, stop. The corporation has no excess passive investment income.)	15,000
5. Line 4 as percentage of line 3	37.5%
6. Gross receipts from passive investment income (line 3)	40,000
7. Subtract directly connected expenses	(10,000)
8. Net passive income (line 6 – line 7)	30,000
9. Excess net passive income (amount on line 8 times percentage on line 5)	11,250

OBSERVATION: As discussed above, passive income includes tax-exempt interest. Therefore, according to the Regulations, the tax results shown in Example 12 - 8 would be the same if the corporation's passive investment income consisted of taxable receipts, tax-exempt interest, or a combination thereof. [Regs. §1.1375-1(f), Example 2]

1215.2. Limitation on excess net passive income. As was the case with the built-in gains tax, discussed in Chapter 11, an S corporation with passive investment income tax exposure can limit its taxable passive income to its taxable income. The literal language of the Code provides that this amount is the second definition of *excess net passive income.*

SUMMARY OF AUTHORITY: CODE SECTION 1375(b)(1)(B)

- An S corporation's taxable passive income cannot exceed its taxable income for any year.
- The corporation's taxable income is computed in the same general manner as if it were a C corporation *except that* the corporation is not allowed to claim a net operating loss deduction or a dividends-received deduction

The rules for computing the corporation's taxable income for the passive investment income limit are exactly the same as those discussed in Chapter 11, at 1125.2. In fact, the computation for the built-in gains tax is defined only by reference to the passive investment income tax. Therefore, the same rules apply for both taxes—but only up to a limit. As discussed in Chapter 11, an S corporation can offset its net recognized built-in gain [this book uses the phrase "taxable built-in gain (preliminary)"] with net operating loss and net capital loss carryforwards from C years. There is no provision, however, allowing a corporation to utilize these carryforwards to reduce taxable passive investment income.

Similarly, an S corporation with a built-in gains tax liability may offset that tax with general business credit and alternative minimum tax credit carryovers from C years. The passive investment income tax may not be offset by any credit, except for the off-the-road fuel tax credit allowed by §34.

As of this writing, the Regulations under §1375 give no additional information on the computation of taxable income. The only regulatory guidance is in Regulations §1.1374-1(d), which was issued under the now-repealed capital gains tax on S corporations. That Regulation merely restates the rules of the Code, which were stated above, and requires that the corporation attach a properly completed Form 1120 to its Form 1120S for the year.

The Regulations interpreting the built-in gains tax are discussed in Chapter 11. In particular, the taxable income limitation, discussed at 1110.55.2., interprets the definition of *taxable income* used for the passive investment income tax, as well as the built-in gains tax. As also discussed in Chapter 11, the corporation must observe all deduction limitations and other corporate rules when computing its taxable income.

OBSERVATION: In computing its taxable income, a corporation must begin with gross income and subtract all allowable deductions. [§63(a)] In this case, it appears that tax-exempt interest would not be included in the tax base, since such interest is specifically excluded from gross income. [§103(a)] Example 12 - 12 illustrates the divergent treatment of tax-exempt income in the two computations of excess net passive income.

EXAMPLE 12 - 12: RS Corporation is an S corporation in 1988. It has the following gross income and deductions:

12

Gross income:	
Equipment rentals	$100,000
Real estate rental	200,000
Service income	450,000
Total	$750,000

Expenses:	
Directly connected with equipment	$135,000
Directly connected with real estate	180,000
Other expenses	440,000
Total	$755,000

Note that the majority of the corporation's income is from services. If the corporation were a C corporation, it would be classified as a personal service corporation and would be subject to the passive activity loss limits of §469 in the same manner as an individual.

RS Corporation also has tax-exempt interest of $50,000. The equipment rents are not passive income, due to the services the corporation provides. The real estate rents are passive. The computations would be:

1. First computation of excess net passive income:

Gross receipts:	
Total	$800,000
Passive	$250,000
25% of total	(200,000)
Excess passive income	$ 50,000

Net passive income:	
Gross passive income	$250,000
Directly connected expenses	(180,000)
Net passive income	$ 70,000
Excess net passive income (50,000/250,000) x 70,000	$ 14,000

Tax on excess net passive income:	
Tax on $14,000 at 34%	$ 4,760

Assume that the equipment rental is a "significant participation activity" and that the loss is treated as passive for §469, even though it is not passive for §1375.

2. Second computation of excess net passive income:

Income from passive activity:	
Rent of real estate	$200,000
Less rental expenses	(180,000)
	$ 20,000

Loss from passive activity:	
Rent of equipment	$100,000
Less rental expenses	(135,000)

Loss	(35,000)
Limit	(20,000)
Other income	450,000
Other deductions	(440,000)
Taxable income	$ 10,000
Income tax	$ 3,400

The tax imposed on the corporation for 1988 would be $3,400, since the corporation's taxable income is less than the first computation of excess net passive income.

OBSERVATION: Example 12 - 12 includes tax-exempt income in the first computation of excess net passive income, in accordance with Regulations §1.1375-1(f) (Example 2). The example excludes such interest from the second calculation of excess net passive income—the corporation's taxable income as if it were a C corporation—because such interest is not included in gross income.

PLANNING TIP: An S corporation which faces the passive investment income tax for any year should use the same planning techniques a s a corporation to avoid the double tax. Thus, salaries and bonuses to shareholder-employees, immediate expensing of asset acquisitions, deferred billings, etc., could all provide ways to reduce the corporation's taxable income for the year, and thus reduce or eliminate its passive investment income tax. These techniques will not work to save the corporation from losing its S election if it has excessive passive gross receipts for three consecutive years.

When a corporation calculates its taxable income under these rules, it should not neglect to claim deductions for any state or local taxes. In jurisdictions that impose lower rates of tax on S corporations than they do on C corporations, it would appear that the taxes actually imposed should be deducted. There is no authority for deducting an imputed state tax at the C corporation rate. 12

EXAMPLE 12 - 13: Anberco is an S corporation with excessive passive investment income. Anberco is subject to State X income taxes. State X imposes tax on net income of S corporations at the rate of 1.5%. Its rate on C corporations is 4%. When computing its C corporation taxable income, Anberco should deduct the tax actually imposed at the 1.5% rate.

1215.3. Tax computation and payment. An S corporation's passive investment income tax may not be reduced by any credits, except for the fuel credit allowed by §34. Code §1375(c) provides the rule.

SUMMARY OF AUTHORITY: CODE SECTION 1375(c)

- No credit, other than the fuel credit, is allowed to offset the passive investment income tax.
- No credit carryforward from Subchapter C years may offset the passive investment income tax.

The passive investment income tax is subject to estimated tax rules that allow estimates based on the prior year's tax liability.

In summary, the tax payment rules for the built-in gains tax are more lenient than those for the passive investment income tax, in that credit carryovers may reduce the former, but not the latter. The estimated tax rules, however, are more stringent for the built-in gains tax than for the passive investment income tax. There is no clear legislative history to distinguish the estimate and credit rules of the two taxes. See Chapter 11, at 1130.5., for the estimated tax rules.

1215.4. Effect of the tax on income to shareholders. The passive investment income tax is treated as a reduction of the income passed through to the shareholders. Code §1366(f)(3) provides the rule.

SUMMARY OF AUTHORITY: CODE SECTION 1366(f)(3)

- The corporation's passive investment income tax reduces the pass-through of income from the corporation to its shareholders.
- The tax is allocated to each source of passive investment income in proportion to that source's contribution to gross passive investment income.

Apparently, the apportionment formula does not depend on the measure of excess net passive income that the corporation actually uses. The allocation is made in proportion to the gross receipts, even if the corporation's taxable income is the final measure of excess net passive income.

EXAMPLE 12 - 14: RS Corporation, in Example 12 - 12, would apportion its passive income tax as follows:

	Passive Income		*Tax*
	Percent	*Amount*	*Allocation*
Exempt interest	20	$ 50,000	$ 680
Rental income	80	200,000	2,720
	100	$250,000	$3,400

12

The final allocations of income to the shareholders would be:

	Income	*Tax*	*Expenses*	*Net*
Exempt interest	$ 50,000	$ 680	$ 0	$ 49,320
Real estate rent	200,000	2,720	180,000	17,280
Equipment rent	100,000	0	135,000	(35,000)
Ordinary	450,000	0	440,000	10,000

OBSERVATION: The criteria used to define *passive investment income* by the Subchapter S rules are completely different from those used to define *passive income* or *investment income* by the individual rules. Therefore, an item that is considered as other than passive for the passive investment income tests may still pass through to the shareholders as passive income, passive loss, or portfolio income.

1215.5. Waiver of passive investment income tax. The IRS may waive the tax on an S corporation's passive investment income for an S corporation that has miscalculated its earnings and profits. The rule is found in §1375(d).

SUMMARY OF AUTHORITY: CODE SECTION 1375(d)

- To qualify for a waiver of the passive investment income tax, an S corporation must meet two conditions:

— The corporation must have made a good-faith determination that it had no accumulated earnings and profits at the end of the year.
— Within a reasonable time after discovery of the earnings and profits, it must distribute all accumulated earnings and profits.

The statute provides no guidance on the mechanism for applying for relief from the tax. The Regulations, however, provide specific instructions.

SUMMARY OF AUTHORITY: REGULATIONS SECTION 1.1375-1(d)(2)

- An S corporation may request that the District Director of the IRS in the appropriate jurisdiction waive the passive investment income tax.
- The request must explain the erroneous calculation of the corporation's earnings and profits.
- The corporation must specify the actual or planned disposition of its earnings and profits.

In contrast to several other relief provisions (such as inadvertent terminations, discussed in Chapter 13), the passive investment income tax waiver is submitted to the District Director. Most requests are submitted to the National Office of the IRS. The National Office issues rulings (usually in the form of private letter rulings) that are publicly available; District Directors do not issue rulings. It is difficult, therefore, to assess the policy of the IRS.

EXAMPLE 12 - 15: Robco was a C corporation through 1986, and its S election took effect for its taxable year beginning January 1, 1987. The corporation's retained earnings at December 31, 1986, showed a deficit of $50,000. The corporation's officers assumed that it had no earnings and profits. From 1987 through 1992, the corporation's passive investment income exceeded 25% of its gross receipts consistently.

In 1993, the corporation engaged a new tax professional, Zeke. In reviewing past returns, Zeke discovered that the corporation had claimed $10,000 depreciation in excess of straight-line on its tax returns. Also, upon the death of a key employee in 1984, it had received $50,000 in life insurance, which the accountant who was employed at that time had treated as an extraordinary item. The corporation had used the $50,000 to redeem the stock of the deceased employee's estate, and had never properly accounted for the receipt or the redemption. According to Zeke's calculations, the corporation's earnings and profits should have been a positive $6,000 balance, rather than a $50,000 deficit.

Zeke advises the corporation and its shareholders to distribute the $6,000 as soon as possible. Zeke then writes a letter, which is signed by the corporation's president, to the District Director to request waiver of the passive investment income tax, which should have been paid for the years 1987 through 1989. Zeke also prepares a ruling request for inadvertent termination relief (discussed in Chapter 13).

The District Director will probably grant relief from the passive investment income tax, and the National Office will most likely grant inadvertent termination relief.

OBSERVATION: The only reason for which the IRS may grant a waiver of the passive investment income tax is the unintentional miscalculation of the corporation's earnings and profits. Other errors, such as failure to properly classify passive investment income or miscalculation of the percentage for gross receipts from passive sources, do not qualify the corporation for waiver of the tax. Even if a corporation cannot qualify for the waiver of the tax, however, it may successfully gain relief from termination of its S election. See discussion in Chapter 13, at 1350.

PLANNING OPPORTUNITY: As is discussed in Chapter 13, at 1350., there have been numerous ruling requests in which the IRS has granted inadvertent termination relief when a corporation has miscalculated its accumulated earnings and profits and run afoul of the 25% passive investment income ceiling for three consecutive years. In some cases, this relief may be unnecessary, if the third consecutive year is still open at the time of discovery. The corporation, with the consent of the shareholders, may be able to elect to bypass AAA on an amended return, and thus avert the termination entirely.

EXAMPLE 12 - 16: Kaji Corporation was an S corporation that used the calendar year. Its S election took effect on January 1, 1990, after Kaji had been a C corporation for many years. Kaji's independent accountant determined that there were no AEP as of January 1, 1990. Kaji's principal source of income for all years was from net leases on real estate, and Kaji could not meet any of the active income definitions.

In 1995, a new independent accountant determined that Kaji had $25,000 of AEP as of January 1, 1990. Kaji had filed S corporation returns for 1990 through 1993 and had not distributed its AEP in those years. Thus it would appear that Kaji's S election had terminated after 1992, the third consecutive year in which its passive investment income exceeded 25% of its gross receipts.

As is discussed in Chapter 13, at 1350., the IRS would likely grant inadvertent termination relief. The probable cost would be that Kaji's shareholders would need to take a dividend distribution in 1995.

There might be a much better alternative. Kaji and its shareholders could amend their returns for 1992, which has not yet closed under the statute of limitations as of the discovery of the AEP. If Kaji had distributed at least $25,000 in that year, and the parties made a proper election to bypass AAA, the corporation would not have any AEP as of the close of 1992. Thus it would not have terminated its S election, and inadvertent termination relief would be unnecessary.

When the corporation and the shareholders acknowledge the problem of the AEP, they would still be faced with the corporation's passive investment income tax for 1991 and 1992. They would need to either pay that tax or apply for waiver of the tax under §1375(d).

When an S corporation in these circumstances is faced with the choice of the tax or the waiver, the first course of action should be to apply for the waiver. All that is required on the waiver request is that there must have been an erroneous, but good-faith, determination that there were no AEP. It would seem unlikely that the IRS would penalize a corporation that had relied in good faith on the erroneous work of a prior tax advisor. The IRS should be willing to grant the waiver, even if the former tax advisor's determination was negligent.

1220. Interaction of passive investment income tax with other taxes.

The taxes imposed on an S corporation's income can include:

- LIFO recapture tax
- Built-in gains tax
- Passive investment income tax

In addition, some S corporations might still be subject to the investment credit recapture tax and the capital gains tax. An item of passive income cannot also be treated as LIFO recapture and may not result in investment tax credit recapture. It is possible, however, for one item of gain to be subject to two taxes (or even three, for certain corporations). This portion of the chapter illustrates the overlapping classifications and the prevention of double jeopardy for one item of gain.

It is possible for one gain on a sale of securities to be both passive investment income and either a taxable capital gain or a recognized built-in gain. There are some protections against overlapping classifications. To be consistent with the approach used in Chapter 11, the capital gain and passive investment income overlap is described below, although there are few returns remaining that are subject to the capital gain tax.

1220.1. Passive income and built-in gains. A single gain may literally meet the definitions of *passive investment income* and *built-in gain,* as Example 12 - 17 illustrates.

EXAMPLE 12 - 17: MAB Corporation was a C corporation through 1988. It filed its S election effective January 1, 1989. It had accumulated earnings and profits at the time. It had some securities with adjusted basis of $400,000 and fair market value of $700,000. In 1992, when the value of the securities reaches $900,000, it sells. The resultant gain is $500,000. Under the general rule of §1374 (discussed in Chapter 11), the entire gain is presumed to be a built-in gain. Because the gain is from the sale of securities, it also meets the definition of passive investment income.

Since the addition of the built-in gains tax in 1986, the Code has provided that no single item of gain shall be subject to both taxes. Originally, the classification as passive investment income dominated. A 1988 amendment gave the built-in gain classification priority over the passive investment income status.

SUMMARY OF AUTHORITY: CODE SECTION 1375(b)(4)

- A gain that is treated as a recognized built-in gain shall not also be treated as passive investment income, *but*
- Any gain that is not a recognized built-in gain may be treated as passive investment income if it results from the sale of stock or securities.

EXAMPLE 12 - 18: MAB, from Example 12 - 17, has adequate records to demonstrate that its built-in gain on the sale of securities is $300,000 (the excess of the fair market value over the adjusted basis of the securities on the date that its S election took effect). Therefore, MAB treats $300,000 of the gain on the sale of the securities as a recognized built-in gain. Since the remainder of the gain is from the sale of securities but is not a built-in gain, it is passive investment income. Therefore, the classification of the $500,000 gain on the securities is:

Recognized built-in gain	$300,000
Passive investment income	200,000
Total	$500,000

12

Since the passive income tax and the built-in gain tax are imposed at the same rate, it may make little difference how one gain that meets both definitions is classified. Depending on the situation, however, taxpayers may prefer the built-in gains classification over the passive income category, or vice versa.

1220.11. Preference for built-in gain treatment. If classification as a built-in gain keeps passive income below 25% of the gross receipts, the corporation's S election will not be endangered. In such a case, an S corporation may benefit from failing to rebut the presumption of built-in gain. This consideration may be especially important if there is a danger that passive income will exceed 25% of gross receipts for three consecutive years. If that is the case, the corporation will lose its S election unless it pays out all of its accumulated earnings and profits as dividends.

EXAMPLE 12 - 19: MAB, from Examples 12 - 17 and 12 - 18, can establish that the built-in gain on security sales was $300,000. It has no other passive income in 1992, but its gross receipts (including the gain of $500,000 on the securities) are $600,000. MAB's passive investment income exceeded 25% of its gross receipts in 1990 and 1992. If its passive investment income exceeds 25% of its gross receipts in 1992, it may lose its S election.

Only $200,000 of the 1992 gain is passive income, but it exceeds 25% of the total. As a consequence, the corporation may be subject to both taxes, and it will lose its S election unless it pays out all of its earnings and profits by the end of 1992.

MAB may benefit from the presumption that its entire $500,000 gain is a recognized built-in gain. If it fails to rebut the presumption, its built-in gain will be $500,000, it will have no passive gross receipts, and its S election will be safe for at least two more years. (See discussion of terminations at 1225.)

A corporation may also prefer to classify a gain that meets both definitions as a built-in gain, rather than as passive investment income, if it has certain favorable tax attributes. Recognized built-in losses in the same year, or net operating loss or capital loss carryforwards from C corporation years, may reduce taxable built-in gains but not excess net passive income. A corporation may prefer the treatment as built-in gain over passive investment income if it has general business credit or alternative minimum tax carryforward from C corporation years. These credits may reduce the tax imposed on built-in gains, but not the tax imposed on excess net passive income.

Finally, a corporation would prefer built-in gain treatment over passive investment income if its net unrealized built-in gain, adjusted for net recognized built-in gain of prior S years, was less than the gain that would be taxable as passive investment income. As discussed in Chapter 11, an S corporation's total taxable built-in gains cannot exceed its net unrealized built-in gain. There is no similar limitation for passive investment income.

OBSERVATION: There is no elective treatment of any single item of gain as a built-in gain or as passive investment income. The structure of the built-in gains tax rules, however, requires that an S corporation treat all gains within the recognition period as built-in gains unless the corporation demonstrates that the gain is not a built-in gain. [§1374(d)(3)] See discussion in Chapter 11. Therefore, failure to rebut the presumption should give an S corporation sufficient authority to treat any item of gain as a built-in gain. When it is profitable to avoid passive investment income treatment, this strategy may be beneficial.

1220.12. Preference for passive investment income. There are also instances where the S corporation would prefer to have a gain treated as passive investment income, rather than as a recognized built-in gain. This is perhaps most obvious when the corporation's gross receipts *from passive sources*, including the gain in question, do not exceed 25% of the total gross receipts. In such a case, passive investment income is not subject to any corporate-level tax. Even if the gain exceeds 25% of the gross receipts, the exclusion of 25% of the gross receipts from taxation may make the treatment as passive investment income preferable.

EXAMPLE 12 - 20: Pearl Corporation is a former C corporation whose S election took effect for its taxable year beginning January 1, 1992. At the end of 1991, Pearl's accumulated earnings and profits had a balance of $25,000.

In 1993, Pearl sold, for $80,000, some securities that had a basis of $50,000. Pearl's gross receipts from other sources were $70,000, and Pearl had no other item of passive investment income and no other recognized built-in gain in 1993. Pearl has no expenses directly connected with the sale of the securities, and thus its net passive income is $30,000. Pearl's taxable income, including the gain from the securities, is $38,000. Pearl's total gross receipts are $100,000.

The entire gain of $30,000 is presumed to be a built-in gain. Pearl could limit the built-in gains treatment by establishing conclusively that the fair market value of the securities was less than $80,000 on January 1, 1992. If, for example, Pearl could establish that the fair market value on that date was only $50,000, none of the gain would be a recognized built-in gain in 1993. Instead, the entire $30,000 gain would be passive investment income. Because of Pearl's gross receipts of $100,000, $25,000 of the passive income would not be subject to this tax. Pearl's taxable passive investment income would be $5,000, and Pearl would pay a tax of $1,700.

If Pearl cannot rebut the presumption that any of the gain is not a built-in gain, the taxable gain would be $30,000, and Pearl would pay a tax of $10,200. Pearl could save $8,500 by rebutting the presumption of built-in gain on the sale of the securities.

A corporation could also benefit by treating a gain as passive investment income, rather than a built-in gain, when the corporation's taxable gain is limited to its taxable income by the modified C corporation rules. As discussed in Chapter 11, for a corporation that filed its S election after March 30, 1988, any recognized built-in gains that are limited by taxable income must be treated as gains recognized in the next taxable year. There is no corresponding carryover for passive investment income.

EXAMPLE 12 - 21: Refer to Example 12 - 20. Assume that Pearl's taxable income is only $1,000. The tax would be $340, whether the gain is passive investment income or a recognized built-in gain, since both taxes are imposed at the same rate.

If the entire gain is classified as a built-in gain, Pearl would carry the untaxed $29,000 of the gain forward to 1994 and treat that amount as a recognized built-in gain in 1994. However, if the gain is not a built-in gain but passive investment income, Pearl would not carry forward any of the gain.

An S corporation would also prefer passive investment income over a built-in gain if the corporation has made an installment sale. As discussed in Chapter 11, an installment sale of built-in gain property may result in an extension of the recognition period with respect to the gain. If the installment receipts treated as gain were likely to be less than 25% of its gross receipts in each of the years of collection, the corporation could most likely avoid tax on the gain if it were passive investment income. It would, however, be required to treat the gain component of each of the installments as a recognized built-in gain in the years of collection.

Finally, an S corporation would prefer to have a gain treated as passive investment income if its earnings and profits were relatively low. If the corporation could distribute its earnings and profits before the year end, it would not be subject to any passive investment income tax. An S corporation's accumulated earnings and profits, or lack thereof, have no effect, however, on the built-in gains tax.

12

1220.2. No relief from multiple taxes. Although no item of gain can be a recognized built-in gain and passive investment income simultaneously, a corporation may be subject to both taxes in a single year. In some cases, the taxes imposed on the corporation could approach or equal 68% of taxable income.

EXAMPLE 12 - 22: Casco is an S corporation. It filed its S election after 1986, and has accumulated earnings and profits. In 1994, it has recognized built-in gains of $55,000 and no recognized built-in losses. It also has excess net passive income of $60,000. Its taxable income, by the modified C corporation rules, is $50,000. It calculates its built-in gains tax and passive investment income tax as follows:

Built-in gains tax:		
Recognized built-in gains, net of losses	$55,000	
C corporation taxable income	50,000	
Tax on lesser of two amounts at 35%		$17,500
Passive investment income tax:		
Excess net passive income	60,000	
C corporation taxable income	50,000	
Tax on lesser of two amounts at 35%		17,500
Total built-in gains and passive investment income tax		$35,000

Assuming that the shareholders are all in the top marginal bracket of 39.6% and that all of the corporation's income was ordinary, the shareholder tax would be as follows:

Income from corporation, before built-in gains and passive investment income taxes	$50,000
Less:	
Built-in gains tax	(17,500)
Passive investment income tax	(17,500)
Net to shareholders	$15,000
Less tax to shareholders	(5,940)
Net after tax income	$ 9,060

The combined tax rate on the corporation's taxable income is 81.88%.

OBSERVATION: Although taxable passive income and taxable built-in gains are each limited to taxable income, there is no overall limit on both. In the absence of corrective legislation or Regulations, the tax law could force payment of tax on up to twice the taxable income.

1220.3. Comparison of passive investment income tax and built-in gains tax. The passive investment income tax and built-in gains tax are certainly the most important corporate-level taxes, especially as the transitional years from the Tax Reform Act of 1986 come to an end. The two taxes have some aspects in common, but also have significant differences. Table 12 - 3 compares the tax on excess net passive income with the tax on built-in gains.

1220.4. Passive income and capital gain. A gain could be subject to both the passive investment income tax and the capital gains tax. When a gain meets both definitions, the classification as passive investment income predominates. ([§1375(c), prior to amendment by the Technical and Miscellaneous Revenue Act of 1988. Current law is silent on the issue, but the Regulations issued before the Tax Reform Act of 1986 have not been amended.) The allocation formula is given in Regulations §1.1375-1(c)(2).

12

SUMMARY OF AUTHORITY: REGULATIONS SECTION 1.1375-1(c)(2)

The allocation formula may be restated as follows:

- The portion of net capital gain that is subject to passive income tax is:

$$\frac{\text{Net capital gain} - \text{Related expenses}}{\text{Net passive income}}$$

- The remaining gain is potentially taxable as a capital gain.

Refer to the 1994 edition of the *S Corporation Tax Guide* for discussion and examples.

1220.5. Transitional corporations. A corporation that filed its S election in 1987 or 1988 may be partially subject to the built-in gains tax and partially subject to the old capital gains tax. Any former C corporation could be subject to the passive investment income tax. Therefore, a transitional corporation may have all three types of taxable gains in one year.

By the time of this writing, few, if any, corporations could be subject to all three taxes. Refer to the 1994 edition of the *S Corporation Tax Guide* for discussion and examples.

1225. Termination of S election due to excess passive income.

An S corporation may lose its S election if it violates the passive income ceiling for three consecutive years. If a corporation has accumulated earnings and profits and has passive

TABLE 12 - 3: Relative Features of the Passive Investment Income, Built-in Gains, and Capital Gains Taxes on S Corporations

Feature	*Passive Income*	*Type of Tax Built-in Gain*	*Capital Gain*
Applicable to "always S" corporations	No*	No**	No**
Applicable to former C corporations	Only if the corporation has accumulated earnings and profits	Yes	Yes
Minimum threshold	25% of gross receipts	None	$25,000
Expires years after S election in effect	No expiration	10	3
Gains covered by tax	Only stock and securities	Any property	Capital and §1231 only
Other receipts covered	Any passive income	Income accrued before S election	None
Limit on taxability	Taxable income or net unrealized built-in gain	Taxable income	Taxable income
Limited to pre-election accrued gain	No	Yes	No
Generally applicable to elections filed	After 1957	After 1986	Before 1987
Special rule for transitional corporations	None	Ordinary and portion of capital and §1231 gain attributable to net worth $5,000,000	Portion of capital and §1231 gain attributable to net worth not over over $5,000,000

* An S corporation may acquire accumulated earnings and profits if it survives a tax-free reorganization.

**An S corporation may acquire built-in gain property if it survives a tax-free reorganization.

12

income in excess of 25% of its gross receipts in three consecutive tax years, the S election is terminated on the first day of the following year. Code §1362(d)(3)(A) provides the rule:

SUMMARY OF AUTHORITY: CODE SECTION 1362(d)(3)

- An S corporation with accumulated earnings and profits could lose its S status due to excessive passive investment income.
- For the election to be lost, passive investment income must exceed 25% of the corporation's gross receipts in three consecutive years and the corporation must have accumulated earnings and profits at the end of each of those years.

EXAMPLE 12 - 23: O Corporation is an S corporation with accumulated Subchapter C earnings and profits. In 1991, 1992, and 1993 it had passive income in excess of 25% of its total gross receipts. Its S election is terminated on January 1, 1994.

An S corporation may have accumulated earnings and profits and excessive passive investment income and not be subject to the passive investment income tax, due to a lack of taxable income. The three-year period for termination, however, is not related to the corporation's tax liability. A corporation can even sustain a *loss* in one or more of the three consecutive years and still lose its election.

EXAMPLE 12 - 24: Refer to Example 12 - 23. The corporation had losses in 1991, 1992, and 1993. Therefore, it paid no passive investment income tax in any of those years. It will, nevertheless, lose its S election on January 1, 1994.

Once an S corporation loses its S election, it generally may not make a new election within five years. [§1362(g), discussed in Chapter 5] Generally, the IRS does not grant a corporation permission to make a new election before that period expires unless there is new ownership of more than 50% of the shares. See discussion in Chapter 5. Therefore, the failure of an S corporation to monitor its passive income properly, or to compute its earnings and profits accurately, can have drastic consequences.

A corporation that innocently violates any of these rules can apply for inadvertent termination relief under §1362(e). As discussed in Chapter 13 at 1350., the IRS frequently grants such relief. Usually, the main cost to the corporation and its shareholders is the payment of all the corporation's accumulated earnings and profits as a dividend.

As discussed below, at 1230., an S corporation may seek to alter its source of gross income, within certain limitations. It may also pay out all of its earnings and profits as a dividend at any time in one of the three consecutive years.

OBSERVATION: Most passive investment income also meets the definition of *personal holding company income.*[4] When a C corporation is closely held (within the meaning of §542(a)[5] and has more than 50% of its income from personal holding company sources (subject to some adjustments), it will be classified as a personal holding company. As such, it will be subject to a tax of 39.6% on certain undistributed income, as well as the regular income tax and alternative minimum tax. In many, but not all, cases where the corporation loses its S election due to passive sources, it may become a personal holding company. As such, it will be subject to a full round of double taxation each year. Therefore, an S corporation that might be a personal holding company should take special precautions to avoid losing its S election.

1230. Planning strategies.

An S corporation that has accumulated earnings and profits and anticipates significant passive investment income should consider ways to avoid the passive investment income tax and termination worries. The course of action taken will depend largely on business, rather than tax, considerations. The options to be considered are:

- Becoming a C corporation and finding other means to avoid double taxation (See Chapter 3, at 335.)

---

[4] Code §543(a) defines *personal holding company income* as interest, dividends, annuities, royalties (exceptions to treatment of royalty income as personal holding company income were discussed above), and rents. There are some complicated exceptions to classification of rents as personal holding company income.

[5] Most S corporations meet the personal holding company ownership rules.

- Distributing all of the accumulated earnings and profits (See Chapter 7, at 720.2. and 740.)
- Distributing investment property to the shareholders (See Chapter 7, at 730.)
- Investing in ventures that will produce income that is not passive (See at 1210.6.)
- Liquidating the corporation and operating as a proprietorship or partnership (See Chapter 15.)

Of course, not all S corporations with temporary excess passive investment income need to consider any of these alternatives. For instance, a corporation that has excessive passive investment income in one year and does not anticipate continuing this situation might be best served by merely paying the tax in that year and then continuing business as usual.

> **EXAMPLE 12 - 25:** Selco, an S corporation, has sold the retail clothing store that accounted for all of its business operations. It is in the process of acquiring a franchise to own and operate an auto parts store. Between the sale of the clothing store and the commencement of business in auto parts, its sole source of income is interest on municipal bonds. The corporation has considerable accumulated earnings and profits. Therefore, distributing all earnings and profits would result in an extremely large tax liability to the shareholders.
>
> In the current year, the bond interest will be approximately 90% of the corporation's gross receipts. Apparently, such bonds are subject to the passive investment income tax, pursuant to Regulations §1.1375-1(f) (Example 2). (See at 1210.2.) The bond interest will, however, pass through to the shareholders (net of the corporation's passive investment income tax) as exempt income. The tax will not be unduly onerous for a single year. Once the corporation commences active business selling auto parts, it will no longer have any passive investment income worries. Therefore, Selco decides to pay the passive investment income tax, since this option is the least expensive.

1230.1. Terminating S status. As discussed in Chapter 13, terminating an S election is an extremely simple process. The corporation merely sends a letter to the IRS Service Center informing the government that it is no longer an S corporation. The letter requires the signature of a corporate officer and consent of the holders of a majority of the shares. 12

As is mentioned often in this text, an S election is not the only way to eliminate the double tax. If a corporation could accomplish this objective by paying reasonable compensation to its shareholder-employees, renting property from shareholders, paying interest to shareholders, and covering its shareholder-employees with deductible fringe benefits and tax-deferred retirement plans, it may find C corporation status more advantageous than S status.

However, if the corporation might benefit from S corporation status at some time in the future, terminating an S election would have its drawbacks:

- The corporation would not be able to make a new election within five years, unless the majority of stock was sold to new owners.
- The corporation would be a former C corporation when the new election took effect. As such, it could be subject to LIFO recapture, the built-in gains tax (with a new recognition period), the passive investment income tax, or more than one of these taxes.

1230.2. Eliminating earnings and profits. An S corporation with passive investment income tax may eliminate its accumulated earnings and profits by distributing the entire balance to the shareholders as a dividend, in one of three ways:

1. It may distribute its entire Accumulated Adjustments Account and make an additional distribution sufficient to exhaust its accumulated earnings and profits.

2. It may elect to treat its accumulated earnings and profits as the first source of distributions during the tax year.
3. It could make a deemed dividend election, as discussed in Chapter 7, at 740.5. [Regs. §1.1368-1(f)(3)]

The first option will normally require a greater amount of distribution than the second. This option may also pose some risk, in that the corporation will need to anticipate its year-end Accumulated Adjustments Account (after adjustment for the current year's taxable income and deduction items). It must be certain that it distributes this total, plus all of its accumulated earnings and profits, before year end.

The election to distribute earnings and profits first, known as the *bypass election*, is permitted by §1368(e)(3). (This election and the mechanics of it are discussed in Chapter 7, at 740.) This procedure will require the consent of all shareholders who receive distributions, but it will avoid the need to estimate the year-end balance in Accumulated Adjustments Account. If a corporation has insufficient cash to give its shareholders, it may use other property, including notes, to fund the distribution. [PLR 9003042]

EXAMPLE 12 - 26: FR Corporation is an S corporation with $200,000 accumulated earnings and profits. FR purchased a patent several years ago. It used the patent briefly in a manufacturing process, but discontinued its active business. Its principal source of income is now the patent royalty. It is still an active business, engaged in the development of other products, but it has significant revenues from the patent. The corporation provides no services with respect to the patent, and the patent cannot meet one of the exceptions from classification as passive investment income.

Its patent has become extremely profitable, and the royalties exceed $500,000 for 1995. Its taxable income for 1995 is $500,000. It has little need for retention of earnings, so the S election will avoid either the double tax on distributions or the personal holding company tax. Its sole shareholder is in the 39.6% federal income tax bracket.

Compare the consequences of paying the passive income tax and distributing all of the earnings and profits as a dividend in 1995:

	Without Dividend	*With Dividend*
Corporate taxable income	$500,000	$500,000
Corporate passive income tax	(175,000)	(0)
Pass-through income to shareholder	325,000	500,000
Dividend income to shareholder	0	200,000
Shareholder's taxable income from corporation	$325,000	$700,000
Shareholder's income tax	$128,700	$277,200
Corporation's tax	175,000	0
Total income tax	$303,700	$277,200

Although payment of an unnecessary dividend may seem counterintuitive, it pays off in this case. It has two additional benefits:

- It will prevent termination of the S election due to excessive passive income.
- It will result in even greater savings in the next two years.

For 1996, assuming all the facts are the same, the comparison is:

	Without 1995 Dividend	*With 1995 Dividend*
Corporate taxable income	$500,000	$500,000
Corporate passive income tax	(175,000	(0)
Income to shareholder	325,000	500,000
Shareholder's income tax	$128,700	$198,000
Corporation's tax	175,000	0
Total income tax	$303,700	$198,000

1230.21. Effects of previously taxed income. If an S corporation has shareholder previously taxed income (PTI) accounts from before 1983, the election to bypass the Accumulated Adjustments Account (AAA) will leave PTI as the first source of distributions. A corporation in this situation may wish to distribute all of its PTI, in addition to its accumulated earnings and profits. The distribution should be sufficient to exhaust both accounts. On the other hand, if the corporation intends to leave PTI unchanged and distribute only its accumulated earnings and profits, it should make a second election to bypass place both AAA *and* PTI. See Chapter 7 at 740.2. for a discussion of the election to bypass PTI.

1230.22. Effects of old Subchapter S earnings and profits (for taxable years beginning before 1/1/97). Since the Subchapter S Revision Act of 1982 took effect, for taxable years beginning after December 31, 1982, a corporation with an S election in effect generates no current earnings and profits. Since an S corporation has no current earnings and profits, it normally cannot add to its accumulated earnings and profits. Further, the Small Business Job Protection Act of 1996 eliminated pre-1983 earnings and profits attributable to S corporation years, for taxable years beginning after 12/31/96.

See the 1997 *S Corporation Taxation Guide,* at 1230.22., for further discussion.

1230.3. Distributing investment property. An S corporation with both business and investment activities may distribute to its shareholders the property that produces passive investment income. To use this alternative, an S corporation must be free from certain hazards.

1. The property should not be substantially appreciated in value. If it is, the corporation must recognize gains on the distribution. The distribution may also result in a built-in gains tax, passive investment income tax, or both, to the corporation.
2. The property should not have depreciated in value. If it has, the shareholder will take the low fair market value as a basis, and the corporation will not be able to recognize any loss.
3. If the value of the property exceeds the balance in the corporation's Accumulated Adjustments Account, a portion of the distribution will be treated as a dividend.

The existence of one or more of these obstacles will rarely cause distribution of investment property to be a better strategy than making the bypass election.

1230.4. Alternative investment strategies. An S corporation that anticipates a continuing passive investment income problem should consider finding other investments to replace its holdings that produce passive investment income. The corporation should evaluate the business consequences, as well as the tax consequences, of divesting itself of its current sources of income. For example, if a corporation has a substantial portion of its assets leased out and does not provide significant services, it might need to change its entire business. This would hardly be a sound business decision if the sole motivation were to avoid the passive investment income tax.

On the other hand, if the primary sources of passive investment income were bonds that had no relation to the corporation's major business activities, changing investments could make sense. There may be several forms of investment that require little effort or expertise from the corporation or its shareholders, but do not produce passive investment income.

> **PLANNING TIP:** An S corporation with funds to invest may consider investing in a partnership, as opposed to a portfolio of stocks, taxable bonds, or tax-exempt bonds. If the partnership is involved in a nonrental business activity, the S corporation's share of the partnership's gross income will be treated as other than passive. That treatment may make it possible for the S corporation to avoid passive investment income problems.

The principal drawback to alternative investments is the lack of liquidity. It may not be as easy to divest of an interest in a partnership or other investment vehicle as it is to simply sell a stock or bond portfolio.

1230.5. Using a QSub. Because a QSub is treated as a nonentity for federal income tax purposes, it stands to reason that the gross receipts of a QSub would be combined with those of the parent S corporation. The IRS has agreed with this reasoning. [PLR 199923030] Accordingly, if the total passive investment income of the corporations, in combination, would not exceed 25% of the total gross receipts of the group, it should be possible to avoid the passive investment income problems when one corporation has excessive passive gross receipts and another corporation has active income. Thus, a combination of two or more S corporations could avert passive investment income problems. See Chapter 17 for descriptions of various tax-free reorganizations that might help accomplish this goal.

1230.6. Liquidating the corporation. A final, and drastic, alternative, to avoid passive investment income problems is to liquidate the corporation. Although the tax rules governing liquidations are discussed in Chapter 15, it is appropriate to describe a few of these rules briefly here.

12

In general, a corporate liquidation is a fully taxable event to all parties concerned. The corporation recognizes gains and losses on the distribution of property, as if it had sold all of its assets for their fair market value on the date of the liquidating distribution. The gains and losses will pass through to the shareholders, but they may also be subject to the built-in gains tax, the passive investment income tax, or both, at the corporate level.

Each shareholder will adjust his or her basis to reflect the gains and losses passed through from the corporation on the liquidating distribution. The gains and losses passed through from the corporation will retain their character. See Chapter 8 for a discussion of gains and losses on sales or distributions of property to shareholders.

Each shareholder will then be treated as having sold his or her stock back to the corporation for the fair market value of the property received. The selling price of the stock is reduced for any liabilities assumed or otherwise taken by the shareholder as part of the transaction.

The obvious tax disadvantage to liquidating a corporation is the complete incidence of double taxation. However, if a corporation has some depreciated property, the incidence of taxation may be reduced or even eliminated. As discussed in Chapter 15, a liquidating distribution is the only instance in which a corporation can recognize losses on the distribution of property to a shareholder.

> **OBSERVATION:** If the shareholders liquidate a corporation and then immediately transfer property to another corporation, the IRS may treat the entire series of

transactions as a corporate reorganization. In that case, all of the old corporation's attributes, including its earnings and profits, would carry over to the surviving corporation. See Chapter 16 for further discussion.

Another advantage to liquidating the corporation is the elimination of any passive investment income tax for the year of liquidation. The taxable year of the corporation closes immediately after the distribution of all property in complete liquidation. The IRS has ruled that, for purposes of §1375, a liquidating distribution will rid the corporation of all accumulated earnings and profits. [PLRs 9747035, 9752038] Thus, for its last hypothetical moment of existence the corporation has no accumulated earnings and profits and is not subject to the passive investment income tax for its final year, even if its passive gross receipts exceeded 25% of its total and it had AEP at the beginning of its final year.

1235. Practice aids.

The practice aids in this chapter consist of a worksheet for evaluating the sources of an S corporation's income and a checklist for spotting passive investment income problems and possible remedies. There is a brief worksheet provided in the instructions to Form 1120S, but that worksheet does not provide for an analysis of income by source. It is probably a good idea for any S corporation that has accumulated earnings and profits to complete Checklist 12 - 1 before the deadline for filing Form 1120S, so that tax advisors can determine if any corrective action is necessary.

> **CAUTION:** Checklist 12 - 1 advises consideration of the deemed dividend election, discussed in Chapter 7. This election is available only for taxable years beginning after 1993, unless the corporation secures permission from the IRS.

Sample Letters 12 - 1 and 12 - 2 are models for requesting relief from the passive investment income tax under §1375(d). This relief request is sent to the Director of the IRS district in which the corporation is located. Mechanically, these letters are extremely simple. There is no requirement in the Code or Regulations that these requests must be signed by a corporate officer, no required statement under penalties of perjury, and no required shareholder consents.

Sample Paragraphs 12 - 1 and 12 - 2 can be used in either of the sample letters to help explain the specifics of the miscalculation of earnings and profits. Sample Paragraph 12 - 1 is useful when there is a specific error in determining earnings and profits, such as a miscalculation of one or more of the provisions discussed in Chapter 3, at 325. Sample Paragraph 12 - 2 is useful when a tax advisor has neglected to advise the corporation on the earnings and profits problems.

Sample Paragraph 12 - 3 should be included as part of the request for relief from the passive investment income tax when the corporation is also applying for inadvertent termination relief. The Code and Regulations contain no formal requirement for this statement, but it is probably best to let the District Director know that the corporation has applied for this relief. Incidentally, it also is probably a good idea to inform the National Office of the application for waiver of the tax, as part of the ruling request for inadvertent termination relief.

Sample Statement 12 - 1 specifies that an S corporation will treat a disposition of a general partnership interest as if it were a limited partnership interest under Regulations §1.1362-2(c)(4)(ii)(B)(4)(ii). While there is no requirement that this treatment be formalized in an election statement, it is probably a good idea to include this statement in the tax file for the year, in case the IRS challenges the treatment on audit.

Worksheet 12 - 1: Passive investment income, by source

Complete only if corporation has accumulated earnings and profits.
Include flow-through from any partnership interest.

1	2	3	4
Type of income	passive	nonpassive	total
Interest			
Lending activities			
Sale of inventory			
All other			
Excluded dividends from a >80% owned C corporation (apportion)			
Other dividends			
Annuities			
Rents			
Significant services provided			
Significant costs incurred			
Trade or business of rental			
Other			
Royalties			
Trade or business, self-developed			
Trade or business, significant cost			
Oil gas (phc exempt)			
Copyright (phc exempt)			
Software (phc exempt)			
Other			
Sales of stock and securities			
Ordinary business			
Other			
Stock			
General partnership			
Limited partnership			
All other gross receipts			
Capital gain net income			
Ordinary gross receipts			
Total columns			
Passive % (Col 2/Col 4)			

Copyright © 2000 by Harcourt, Inc. All rights reserved.

Checklist 12 - 1: Passive income hazards

Complete only if passive gross receipts >25% total.

	Applicable (Yes/No)	*Completed (Date)*
1. Does corporation have any earnings and profits?	______	______
If not, no passive investment income problems. (Be sure to check tax history if corporation ever survived a reorganization or liquidated a subsidiary.)	______	______
FOR TAX YEARS BEGINNING BEFORE 1/1/97 ONLY:	______	______
2. Was corporation an S corporation before 1983?	______	______
If no, all earnings and profits are from Subchapter C years.	______	______
If yes, separate Subchapter C EP from old Subchapter S EP.	______	______
3. Is this the third consecutive year of excess passive investment income?	______	______
If yes, must distribute all Subchapter C EP or lose S election.	______	______
If no, may be subject to passive investment income tax.	______	______
4. To avoid tax:	______	______
a. Reduce taxable income to zero.	______	______
b. Invest in assets producing active income for future.	______	______
c. Consider bypass election. (CAUTION: Bypass PTI if any exists.)	______	______
d. Consider deemed dividend election.	______	______

12

Sample Letter 12 - 1: Request for waiver of passive investment income tax under §1375(d), after distribution of AEP

(Without simultaneous application for inadvertent termination relief)

[Company]
[Address]
[City, State ZIP Code]
[FEIN]

[Date]

District Director
Internal Revenue Service
[City, State ZIP Code]

[Company] requests a waiver of the tax on excess net passive income for the years [beginning] [ending] and [beginning] [ending]. [Company] requests this waiver under §1375(d) of the Internal Revenue Code and Regulations §1.1375-1(d)(2).

Copyright © 2000 by Harcourt, Inc. All rights reserved.

Code §1375(d)(1) requires that the corporation must have determined in good faith that there were no earnings and profits as of the close of a taxable year. [Company] believes that it satisfies this test for the following reasons:

[Insert Sample Paragraph 12 - 1 or 12 - 2 here.]

[Company] has distributed out all of its earnings and profits on [dates], and shareholders have reported the distribution on their tax returns for [years].

[Insert Sample Paragraph 12 - 3 here, if appropriate.]

Sample Letter 12 - 2: Request for waiver of passive investment income tax under §1375(d), before distribution of AEP

(Without simultaneous application for inadvertent termination relief)

[Company]
[Address]
[City, State ZIP Code]
[FEIN]

[Date]

District Director
Internal Revenue Service
[City, State ZIP Code]

[Company] requests a waiver of the tax on excess net passive income for the years [beginning] [ending] and [beginning] [ending]. [Company] requests this waiver under §1375(d) of the Internal Revenue Code and Regulations §1.1375-1(d)(2).

12

[Insert Sample Paragraph 12 - 1 or 12 - 2 here.]

[Company] will distribute out all of its earnings and profits on [dates], and shareholders will report the distribution on their tax returns for [years]. [Company] believes that this schedule is reasonable in that it allows sufficient time to prepare directors' resolutions and secure permission from creditors in order to default on loan provisions.

[Insert Sample Paragraph 12 - 3 here, if appropriate.]

Sample Paragraphs

Sample Paragraph 12 - 1: Explanation of erroneous calculation of earnings and profits

On [date], when [Company's accountant] was advising on [Company's] S election, [accountant] determined that [Company's] accumulated earnings and profits were [$]. In making this calculation, [accountant] did not properly consider the effects of the following transactions:

[e.g., depreciation, installment sales, tax-exempt income]

which occurred in

[years]

Copyright © 2000 by Harcourt, Inc. All rights reserved.

After recalculation of the earnings and profits, including the effects of [transactions], [Company's] accumulated earnings and profits balance as of [conversion date] should be [$].

Sample Paragraph 12 - 2: Regarding reliance on tax advisor in belief that there were no earnings and profits

When [Company] filed its S election on [date], [company's] tax advisor assured management that there would be no adverse effects to making an S election. [Company] relied on this advice and was unaware that it had accumulated earnings and profits as of the end of its last year as a C corporation. If [Company] had known that it had accumulated earnings and profits and was facing a problem with the passive investment income tax, it would have cured the problem in the first taxable year of its existence by distributing all of its accumulated earnings and profits to the shareholders in the form of a dividend. A subsequent tax advisor has informed [Company] that the earnings and profits as of date were [$].

Sample Paragraph 12 - 3: To inform District Director that the corporation has also applied for inadvertent termination relief

[Company] violated the passive investment income limits for three consecutive years, ending [date], [date], and [date]. Accordingly, [Company's] S election was terminated on [date]. [Company] has applied to the National Office of the Internal Revenue Service for inadvertent termination relief under Code §1362(f).

Sample Statement 12 - 1

[Company] elects to treat the disposition of the general partnership [name of partnership] on [date] as if it were an interest in a limited partnership, pursuant to Regulations §1.1362-2(c)(4)(ii)(B)(4)(ii). Thus all gain from the disposition of this interest is treated as passive investment income.

Copyright © 2000 by Harcourt, Inc. All rights reserved.

TERMINATION OF THE S ELECTION

CONTENTS

1300. Overview.

Once a corporation elects S status, the election remains in effect for all future years—unless it is revoked or terminated, which may be done at any time. *Revocation* requires shareholder consent, and the corporation needs to observe certain filing and effective dates. *Termination* can happen in one of two ways:

- The corporation might have accumulated earnings and profits years and exceed the 25% passive investment income limit for three consecutive years.
- The corporation could cease to meet the definition of "small business corporation," if, for example, there is an ineligible shareholder, there are too many shareholders, or there is a second class of stock.

An S election may take effect only at the beginning of a taxable year. By contrast, a termination or revocation may occur at any time during a taxable year, in which case the corporation must file two tax returns for one year. This situation presents some compliance problems—and some planning opportunities.

The Subchapter S Revision Act of 1982 adopted a relief provision for inadvertent terminations. The IRS can allow the corporation's S election to continue uninterrupted, even though the corporation has violated one or more of the qualifications. The IRS has the power to require certain adjustments at the corporate and shareholder levels. Inadvertent terminations have been the source of numerous private letter rulings. One of the most frequent violations is that of an ineligible trust owning shares. Trusts have often lacked one or more of the requirements of a QSST or failed to file the QSST election. To date, the IRS appears to have interpreted the inadvertent termination rules liberally and fairly.

Election after termination is permitted after a five-year waiting period. The IRS may reduce the period to one year. Chapter 5 contains a complete discussion of this topic, as well as the special reelection provisions of the Small Business Job Protection Act of 1996.

1310. Voluntary terminations.

This book devotes considerable effort to discussion of the advantages of the S corporation compared to the C corporation. However, there are certain corporations for which the S election is no longer feasible or advantageous. Some of the circumstances that may lead to consideration of termination of an S election are:

- The corporation intends to go public or to have ineligible investors in the near future. The current shareholders want to control the income or loss during the last days that the S election is in effect.
- The corporation may be able to provide valuable tax-free fringe benefits to its shareholders, such as health insurance or meals and lodging for the convenience of the employer. See Chapter 8, at 825., for discussion of these and other benefits.
- The shareholders might be in the top tax brackets, thus forcing the corporation to make distributions to pay taxes at individual rates. The corporation might be able to reduce current cash outflow by becoming a C corporation and paying its taxes directly at the corporate rates.

> **CAUTION:** A corporation that intends to revoke its S election for the sole purpose of reducing its current cash outflow should weigh other costs that might be associated with becoming a C corporation. For example:

- The savings in the federal taxes may be offset by increased state and local income tax imposed on C corporations.
- The corporation will probably not be able to make another S election for five years.
- At the time of a new S election, the corporation would be subject to the built-in gains tax for a new 10-year recognition period.
- If the corporation were to sell substantially all of its assets in the future, the sale would be subject to double tax.
- The shareholders would lose their ability to participate in a §338(h)(10) election on the sale of stock. See Chapter 15, at 1525.84., for a discussion of this stock sale technique.

After the corporation and its tax advisors have evaluated the consequences, they may decide that the time has come for the corporation to revoke its S election. At that point, the revocation procedures become important.

Voluntary terminations are termed *revocations*. Any S election may be terminated by revocation. The termination is not generally a taxable event.[1] Upon termination, the corporation becomes a C corporation. The general rules are laid out in §1362(d)(1).

SUMMARY OF AUTHORITY: CODE SECTION 1362(d)(1)

- An S corporation may revoke its S election and become a C corporation.
- Revocation requires consent of the holders of a majority of the corporation's stock.
- For the revocation to be effective on the first day of the corporation's taxable year, the corporation must revoke its election by the 15th day of the third month of that year.
- A revocation made after that date takes effect at the beginning of the corporation's next taxable year.
- A corporation may specify a prospective effective date for revocation of its election.

The Code specifies the general rules for revocation, but it is not overly concerned with the details. Almost immediately after the Subchapter S Revision Act of 1982 took effect, the IRS specified the procedures in Temporary Regulations §18.1362-3. In late 1988, the IRS issued Proposed Regulations §1.1362-3, which provided identical procedural rules. Final Regulations, issued in late 1992, adopt consistent positions on all material aspects of the Temporary and Proposed Regulations. The Final Regulations apply to years beginning after December 31, 1992. The Temporary and Proposed Regulations are authority for years beginning prior to that date. [Notice 92-56, 1992-49 I]

13

1310.1. General rules. There is no printed form prescribed for revocation of the S election. The corporation files a statement with the IRS Service Center where the S election was filed indicating the effective date of the revocation. The statement must be signed by any person authorized to sign the corporation's income tax returns. [Regs. §1.1362-6(a)(3)(i)] The revocation requires no consent of the IRS to be effective. In PLR 9750036, the IRS ruled that an S corporation successfully terminated its election by writing "Final Return as S Corporation. Corporation elects to file as 1120 Corporation," across the top of Form 1120S.

Attached to the revocation statement there must be a statement of consent, signed by the holders of more than 50% of the number of shares of stock, *including nonvoting stock*, on the date that the revocation is filed. The corporation must be careful to account for all of its shares when filing its revocation.

---

[1] One of the few exceptions to this rule is foreign loss recapture, discussed in Chapter 3. Foreign loss recapture is required when a C corporation makes an S election or when an S corporation becomes a C corporation.

In one instance, a corporation had equal numbers of voting and nonvoting shares. The holder of the voting stock, representing exactly 50% of the total outstanding stock, was the only person who consented to the revocation. The revocation statement was invalid and the S election continued. [PLR 9028039]

EXAMPLE 13 - 1: XYZ Corporation is an S corporation that uses the calendar year. Xaviera holds 40 voting shares. Yancey and Zenon each hold 30 nonvoting shares. On March 5, 1992, XYZ files a revocation statement with the IRS Service Center where it files all tax returns. The revocation statement does not disclose that Yancey and Zenon are shareholders. Xaviera signs her consent, as the holder of all voting shares. The revocation is invalid and XYZ remains an S corporation.

EXAMPLE 13 - 2: On March 1, 1992, Vasant purchases 40% of the stock in Vijay Corporation, an S corporation. On March 6, 1992, Vasant sends a letter to the IRS Service Center where the corporation files its returns, stating that he does not consent to the continuation of the S election. The statement is not signed by a corporate officer, and no other shareholder consents to the statement. The statement has absolutely no impact on Vijay's status as an S corporation. The S election remains in effect until it is properly revoked or is terminated by operation of law.

CAUTION: Shareholders with effective voting control of an S corporation must be aware that revocation requires the consent of the holders of a majority of all shares. Thus, when a substantial number of nonvoting shares are outstanding, the persons in control will need to consider all of these shareholders when planning to revoke the S election. It may be possible to issue nonvoting shares to voting trusts, or for a controlling shareholder to obtain proxy or power of attorney to effectively control the consent of holders of nonvoting stock. Any controlling shareholder who wishes to maintain this level of control should check with competent local counsel to be sure that the terms are enforceable.

1310.2. Default dates. In general, a revocation filed within the first 2 months and 15 days of the corporation's taxable year takes effect on the first day of that year. [§1362(d)(1)(C)(i)] A revocation statement filed after that date becomes effective on the first day of the corporation's next taxable year. [§1362(d)(1)(C)(ii)] A corporation may be able to choose another date, but it must be careful to specify the date in the revocation statement.

13

1310.3. Retroactive revocation. If a revocation statement, and the required consent, are filed within 2 months and 15 days of the beginning of the corporation's tax year, the revocation may be effective as of the first day of that tax year. [§1362(d)(1)] If the corporation either specifies that the revocation is to be effective on the first day of the current year or does not specify a date, the revocation will be retroactive to the beginning of the year. A revocation is effective on the first day of the taxable year for which it is filed, under any of three circumstances:

- The revocation is filed within the 2-month, 15-day period and does not specify an effective date.
- The revocation is filed within the 2-month, 15-day period and specifies that it is to be effective on the first day of the year.
- The revocation is filed within the 2-month, 15-day period and specifies an invalid effective date.

EXAMPLE 13 - 3: The F Corporation uses the calendar year. On March 2, 1987, it files a revocation statement, with the proper consent, but does not specify the effective date. The corporation's S election is revoked as of January 1, 1987. The corporation has no opportunity to restore its S election.

A corporation may file a revocation statement within 2 months and 15 days of the beginning of the tax year and specify a later date for the revocation to take effect. If it follows the rules discussed below, the revocation will be effective on the date stated.

OBSERVATION: The only retroactive revocation permitted is for the first day of the tax year in which the corporation files the proper statement with the IRS. To qualify for this treatment, the corporation must file the proper statement, together with the required consents, on or before the 15th day of the third month of the year in which it is to take effect.

EXAMPLE 13 - 4: Leading Corporation is an S corporation that uses the calendar year. On March 10, 1992, the corporation prepares a revocation statement, and the holders of more than 50% of the shares attach their consents. The corporation specifies that the revocation is to occur on January 1, 1992. The corporation's accountant does not mail the statement until March 16, 1992. Since the corporation failed to meet the deadline for retroactive termination, the revocation cannot be effective until January 1, 1993. (See discussion below.)

OBSERVATION: When a corporation files a retroactive revocation of its election, it will have no opportunity to change its mind. The revocation will have already taken effect. There will be no opportunity to receive inadvertent termination relief or to rescind the revocation.

In some instances, a corporation's S election may terminate within the first 2 months and 15 days of a taxable year. At that time, the shareholders may decide that they would rather not have any portion of the year as an S corporation. There is no prohibition against retroactive termination by a corporation that has already become ineligible.[2]

EXAMPLE 13 - 5: Termco, Inc., was a calendar-year S corporation until February 25, 1992. On that date, it issued some shares to a C corporation and thus terminated its S election. There is no prohibition against Termco filing a revocation statement on or before March 15, 1992, which would terminate the S election as of January 1, 1992.

OBSERVATION: Recent bankruptcy cases involving S corporations and their shareholders have treated S elections as valuable assets and have sought to protect them on behalf of creditors. In one recent case, a federal bankruptcy court estopped a debtor shareholder from revoking an S election. [River City Hotel Corp., 75 AFTR 2759 (Bankr E.D. Tenn., 1995)] In another case, a creditor sued shareholders and the U.S. government in an attempt to keep an S election from being terminated. [In re Urban Broadcasting of Cincinnati, 180 BR 153 (Bankr E.D. LA, 1995)] In a third case, a bankruptcy court determined that an S election was a valuable asset and could be protected by preventing distribution of shares to ineligible persons. [In re Cumberland Farms, Inc., 162 BR 62 (Bankr D. Mass., 1993)]

13

1310.4. Prospective revocation. A corporation may file a revocation statement that specifies a prospective date. The prospective date may be any date on or after the filing of the statement. [Regs. §1.1362-2(a)(2)(ii)]

A prospective revocation statement must state the date on which the revocation occurs. It must not be given in terms of some event. [Regs. §1.1362-2(a)(2)(ii)] For instance, the corporation cannot state that a revocation will be effective at the time a new shareholder buys into the corporation, a major contract is completed, or any other such prospective event. If the revocation is filed after the 2-month, 15-day period and does not specify an effective date, the S election will be in effect until the first day of the corporation's next taxable year.

---

[2] Neither the Code nor the Regulations contain any requirement that the corporation be an S corporation at the time of the revocation statement.

In one instance, an S Corporation revoked its election, stating October 27, 1988, as the effective date. The corporation did not actually mail the statement until November 3, 1988. The date was not prospective, so the revocation took effect on January 1, 1989. [PLR 8938008]

EXAMPLE 13 - 6: The F Corporation uses the calendar year. On April 2, 1987, it files a revocation statement, with the proper consent, but it does not specify the effective date. If the revocation is not accompanied by a consent statement signed by the holders of more than 50% of its shares (on April 2), the S election continues to be in effect. If the revocation *is* accompanied by the proper consent, the corporation faces the following possibilities:

- If the revocation does not specify a date, the election is revoked as of January 1, 1988.
- If the revocation specifies an effective date of January 1, 1988, it is effective as of the specified date.
- If the revocation specifies any date between January 2 and April 1, 1987, the revocation is effective as of January 1, 1988.
- If the revocation specifies any date after April 1, 1987, the corporation's S election is terminated on the date stated in the letter.

The filing date should be evident from a certified mail receipt or a stamped duplicate copy from the IRS. If the prospective date is any day other than the first day of the next taxable year, the corporation will have an *S termination year*, which requires some special accounting rules, discussed later in this chapter. In an S termination year, the corporation will be treated as having a short S year from the first day of the tax year to the day before the revocation is effective. The period beginning on the revocation date and ending on the last day of the corporation's tax year will be treated as a short C corporation year.

EXAMPLE 13 - 7: L Corporation is an S corporation using the calendar year. On May 27, 1987, it files a revocation with the proper consent statement attached. The statement specifies that May 27, 1987, is the day on which the S election is no longer effective. The period from January 1 through May 26, 1987, is treated as a short S year. The remainder of the year is treated as a short C year.

1310.5. Revocation before election takes effect. As mentioned above, a corporation is not required to actually have an election in effect before it terminates an election. The IRS has indicated, both in Regulations and in its ruling policy, that an S election that terminates before it ever takes effect is, in essence, a nullity. [Regs. §1.1362-5(c)] The corporation may make a new S election without being subject to the five-year waiting period required by §1362(g). (See discussion in Chapter 5.) The Regulations further state that an election that never takes effect has no impact on the corporation's taxable year. [Regs. §1.1362-2(a)(3)]

13

EXAMPLE 13 - 8: Mario Corporation is a C corporation that has been using a June 30 taxable year. On June 17, 1992, it files an S election for its taxable year beginning July 1, 1992. On Form 2553 it indicates that it is changing to the calendar year. On September 14, 1992, Mario revokes its S election, effective July 1, 1992. According to the IRS, Mario is still a C corporation with a June 30 year end.

A corporation that has been too hasty in filing an S election may eliminate any disadvantage of being an S corporation by filing a revocation that completely nullifies its S election. By doing so, it may be able to avoid certain adverse consequences such as LIFO recapture or foreign loss recapture. See Chapter 3 for a discussion of these problems.

OBSERVATION: A corporation that is considering an S election might also anticipate an adverse change in the tax law. For instance, in 1990 there was a possibility that a C corporation would be treated as constructively liquidated when an S election took effect. (See discussion of 1990 legislative proposals in Chapter 1.) A C corporation might have pursued the strategy that is illustrated in Example 13 - 9.

EXAMPLE 13 - 9: Avoco was a calendar-year C corporation in 1990 and was weighing the benefits and drawbacks of an S election. In April 1990, the corporation's tax advisor learned that Congress might introduce legislation to make the S election by a C corporation a constructive liquidation. The corporation filed Form 2553 immediately, since the effective date of new legislation is not usually before the introduction of a bill in Congress. By the end of 1990, the corporation had decided that an S election would not be worthwhile. Therefore, it revoked its S election before it took effect. Avoco has never been an S corporation, and it is not prevented from making an S election in the future.

1310.6. Rescission of revocation. An S corporation that has revoked its S election and then changes its mind may rescind the revocation. (All rules discussed in this portion of the chapter are found in Regulations §1.1362-2(a)(4).) The mechanics of a rescission are relatively straightforward. The corporation files a statement with its regional IRS Service Center to the effect that it is rescinding the revocation of its S election. The rescission must have the consent of all persons who consented to the revocation and of each person who has become a shareholder since the corporation filed its revocation.

EXAMPLE 13 - 10: Changeco, Inc., is an S corporation that uses the calendar year for tax purposes. On December 1, 1991, Changeco's shares were held in equal portions by John, Kathy, and Hannah, each of whom owned 30 shares. On that date, Changeco revoked its S election. John and Kathy consented to the revocation. On December 10, 1991, the corporation issued 10 new shares to Miguel. At that time, the shareholders began to have doubts about the wisdom of revoking the S election. In order to rescind the revocation, the corporation must file a statement properly describing its rescission to the IRS. John, Kathy, and Miguel must consent to the rescission.

It is important to note that the corporation must file the rescission before the revocation is to take effect. Unlike the rules for electing or terminating S status, there is no grace period for revocation. A retroactive revocation, by definition, is filed after the revocation is to be effective. Therefore, there is no opportunity to rescind a retroactive revocation.

EXAMPLE 13 - 11: Refer to Example 13 - 10. If Changeco decides to rescind the revocation and retain its status as an S corporation, it must file the rescission before January 1, 1992. If it waits until January 1, 1992, its S election will be terminated.

1310.7. Summary of revocation rules. The revocation rules are not inherently complicated. The shareholders, however, must pay careful attention to the dates. Figure 13 - 1 illustrates the steps involved.

1315. Termination by operation of law.

If an S corporation violates one or more of the requirements of a small business corporation, it ceases, at that time, to be an S corporation.

SUMMARY OF AUTHORITY: CODE SECTION 1362(d)(2)

- If a corporation has an S election in effect and fails at any time to meet one of the eligibility requirements, the S election is terminated. Likely causes of termination include:
  - — More than 75 shareholders
  - — One or more ineligible shareholders
  - — More than one class of stock
- The termination is effective on the date the corporation ceases to meet any eligibility requirement.

Figure 13 - 1: *Termination of an S election.*

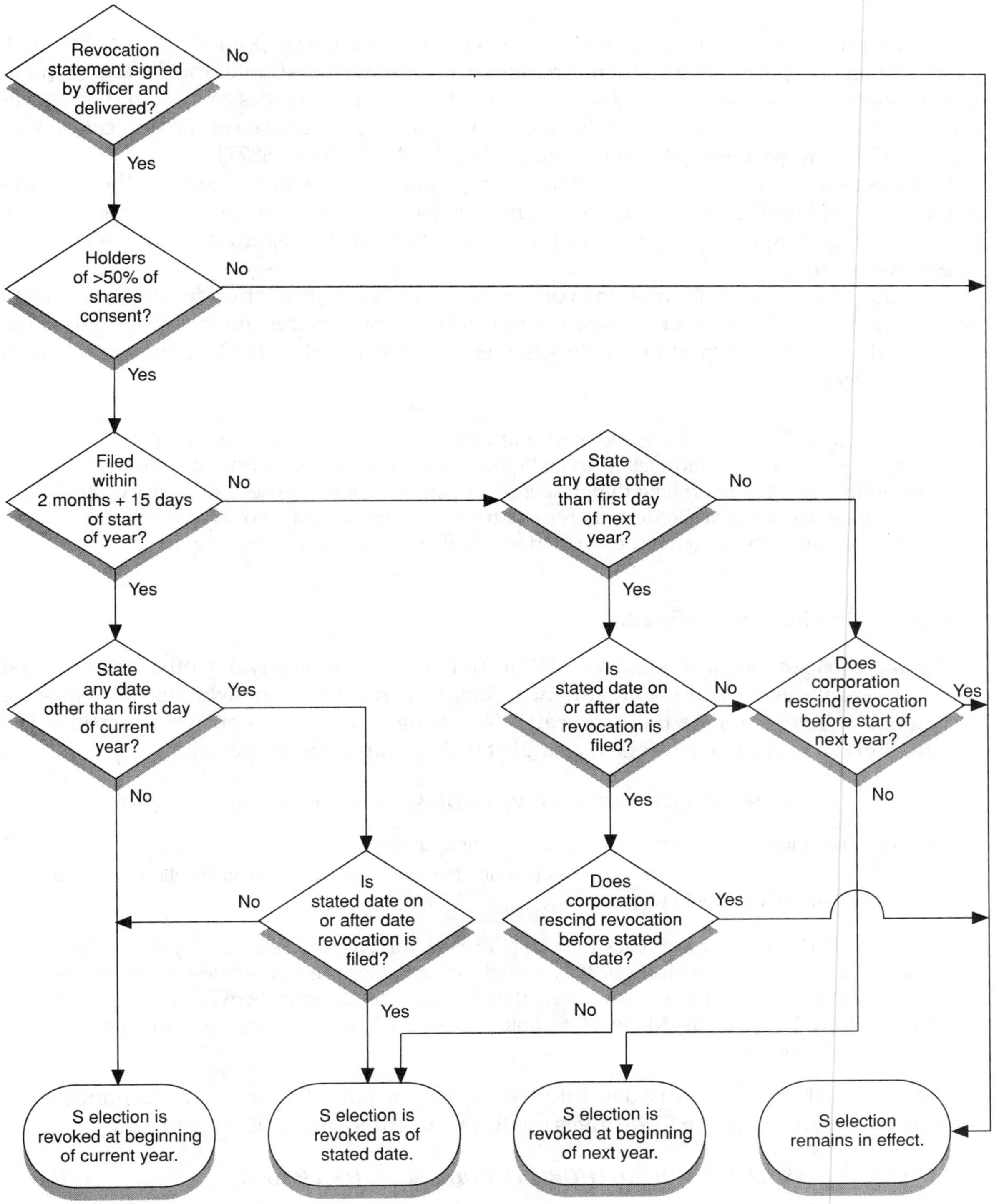

EXAMPLE 13 - 12: Calco was an S corporation through June 23, 1992. On that date, one of its shareholders sold her stock to Kim, a Korean citizen who was not a U.S. resident. On June 23, 1992, the corporation became a C corporation.

Note that the filing of a bankruptcy petition does not cause a corporation to cease being a small business corporation, and therefore does not cause termination of the S election. [*In re Stadler Associates, Inc., et al.*, 76 AFTR 2d 95-5146] Bankruptcy trustees can avoid the revocation of an S election made prior to filing for bankruptcy if the purpose of the revocation was to manipulate the tax laws. [*Parker v. Sanders et al.*, 82 AFTR 2d 98-6877]

An S election can also be terminated in the year following the third year that the corporation has accumulated earnings and profits and passive investment income in excess of 25% of its gross receipts. Refer to Chapter 12 for a description of the operating rules relating to excess passive income.

If the termination is accidental, the corporation may request relief under the inadvertent termination rules, discussed below at 1350. Since the inadvertent termination relief provision was added to the law as part of the Subchapter S Revision Act of 1982, rulings in this area have been frequent.

OBSERVATION: A shareholder who attempted to terminate a corporation's election by transferring his stock to an ineligible person was estopped from doing so in a non-tax case. The court held that the consent to an S election imposes a fiduciary duty to one's fellow shareholders to refrain from any action that would devalue the corporation. [*Chesterton, Inc. v. Chesterton*, 951 F. Supp. 291 (D. Mass., 1997)]

1320. S termination year defined.

An *S termination year* occurs whenever an S election terminates on any day other than the first day of a taxable year. The tax treatment is identical regardless of whether the cause of termination is revocation or the corporation's ceasing to qualify as an S corporation. The definition given in the Code refers to a single taxable year of the corporation.

SUMMARY OF AUTHORITY: CODE SECTION 1362(e)(4)

13

- The Code refers to an S termination year as a single taxable year.
- An S termination year occurs when a corporation terminates its S election on any day other than the first day of its taxable year.

EXAMPLE 13 - 13: Manoco uses the calendar year for tax purposes. On April 17, 1992, Manoco terminates its S election. It is immaterial whether the termination is caused by revocation or disqualification. Assuming that no other events occur between April 17 and December 31, 1992, to cause Manoco's taxable year to end, Manoco's S termination year is the calendar year of 1992.

An S termination year is divided into two short portions. The statutory terminology is perhaps confusing, since the Code gives the term *year* three different meanings.

SUMMARY OF AUTHORITY: CODE SECTION 1362(e)(1)

- An S termination year consists of the entire taxable year of the corporation.
- The first portion of the year is the S short year.
- The second portion of the year is the C short year.

The phrase "for purposes of this title" is especially bothersome. As of this writing, there is some uncertainty as to what attributes of a taxable year attach to the termination year in its entirety and what attributes attach to each portion thereof. It is probably best to think of the termination year as one tax year and each of the short years as an accounting period, for limited purposes.

> **EXAMPLE 13 - 14:** Refer to Example 13 - 13. Manoco's S short year starts January 1, 1992, and ends April 16, 1992. The C short year starts April 17, 1992, and ends December 31, 1992.

The termination of an S election does not, per se, cause the corporation's taxable year to end prematurely. Accordingly, the S termination year is generally the 12-month period that has served as the corporation's taxable year for all purposes. However, other events could cause the corporation's year to end. For example, the corporation may be acquired by another corporation that files consolidated returns. In that event, the former S corporation would close its taxable year on the date of acquisition and join in the taxable year of its new parent corporation. [Regs. §1.1502-76(b)(2)] See Chapter 16, at 1630.33 for further discussions.

In other instances, a corporation might be merged into another corporation, or might liquidate, before the normal year end. In either of these cases, the corporation will cease to exist at that date, and the S termination year will end as of the date of merger or liquidation. Finally, if the corporation has been using a fiscal year-end under §444 and becomes a personal service corporation when it terminates its S election, the corporation may revoke its §444 election and change to the calendar year.

> **EXAMPLE 13 - 15:** Darco, PC, is a public accounting firm that was incorporated in 1985. It has used a September 30 taxable year since its first year of business. When the §444 year became available, it elected to keep its fiscal year. The corporation has had an S election in effect since 1986. The shareholders have decided to avail themselves of the fringe benefits that are available only to shareholders in a C corporation. The shareholders are wary of the hazards of using a fiscal year under §444 for a personal service corporation.[3]
>
> On December 12, 1992, the corporation revokes its S election. On January 10, 1993, Darco revokes its §444 election, effective January 1, 1993. Although the termination of the S election had no effect on the corporation's taxable year, the termination of the §444 election causes the S termination year to end on December 31, 1992. Therefore, the corporation's S termination year is the period from October 1, 1992, through December 31, 1992.
>
> The S short year runs from October 1, 1992, through December 12, 1992. The shareholders must report their S corporation items for that period—as well as the S corporation items for the year ended September 30, 1992—on their 1992 tax returns. Darco's C short year is December 13, 1992, through December 31, 1992.

1325. Corporate treatment of the S termination year.

In certain respects, the corporation treats the S termination year as a single taxable year. Among the more important aspects of this rule are the requirements for filing tax returns and the expiration of C corporation carryovers. In other respects, however, the corporation treats the S termination year as two taxable years. The specific accounting rules are discussed below at 1335. The rules discussed here are applicable to any S termination year, regardless of the method of accounting used by the corporation.

1325.1. Returns and carryovers. The corporation's S termination year is a single year for filing both the S corporation and C corporation returns. The authority is found in §1362(e)(6)(A).

---

[3] Code §280H(e) prohibits the carryback of a personal service corporation's net operating loss either to or from a §444 year. There is no equivalent prohibition for a personal service corporation using the calendar year.

SUMMARY OF AUTHORITY: CODE SECTION 1362(e)(6)(A)

- The S termination year is treated as a single year for C corporation carryover purposes.
- The corporation's tax return for the S corporation portion of the S termination year is due on the same date as the return for the C corporation portion of that year.
- Both returns are subject to the usual corporate extension rules.

In general, a corporation must file its return by 2 months and 15 days following the close of its taxable year.[4] Any corporation may receive an automatic 6-month extension by filing Form 7004 on or before the due date for its return.[5] Therefore, the due date for both the S corporation return and the C corporation return for the S termination year is 2 months and 15 days following the end of the S termination year and may be extended for six additional months.

EXAMPLE 13 - 16: Acme Corporation is a calendar-year taxpayer that terminates its S election in 1989, splitting its tax year into an S short year and a C short year. It had been a C corporation through 1986 and had sustained a net operating loss in 1985. It had insufficient taxable income in 1986 to utilize the net operating loss deduction. It was unable to use any of the loss in 1987 and 1988, because it was an S corporation.

When it becomes a C corporation in 1989, Acme will be able to use the carryforward from 1985 against its taxable income during the C short year. If it cannot deduct the loss in full in 1989, it will carry it forward to 1990. As of 1990, four years of loss eligibility will have expired:

1986:	C corporation year
1987:	S corporation year
1988:	S corporation year
1989:	S corporation short year and C corporation short year are treated as one year

Acme must file Form 1120S for the S short year and Form 1120 for the C short year. The due date for both returns is March 15, 1990. The date can be extended to September 15 for either or both of the returns.

When the S termination year ends prematurely, the due date for the corporation's tax return is also affected. If the S termination year ends because the corporation has been purchased by another corporation, the acquired corporation's year may end on the date of the purchase. This would be the case if the purchasing corporation files consolidated returns, liquidates or merges the acquired corporation, or makes a §338 election. These transactions are discussed in Chapter 15.

If the S termination year ends because the new parent corporation files consolidated returns, the returns for the S termination year are due on the date that the parent corporation's consolidated return is due. [Regs. §1.1502-76(c)(1)] If the acquired corporation is dissolved due to liquidation, merger, or a deemed liquidation under §338, the returns for the S termination year are due 2 months and 15 days after the end of the month in which the corporation's dissolution occurs. [Rev. Rul. 71-129, 1971-1 CB 397]

1325.2. Return for the S short year. The tax on all items of income for the S short year is subject to the usual Subchapter S rules. The shareholders must include their portions of all of the Subchapter S items on their personal tax returns. The corporation may be subject to one or more corporate-level taxes, such as the built-in gains tax, the passive investment income tax, or both.

---

[4] Code §6071(a) states a due date of March 15 for calendar-year corporations. Regulations §1.6072-2(a) states the general rule of the 15th day of the third month following the end of the taxable year for fiscal year corporations.

[5] Code §6081(a) generally limits extensions to six months. Regulations §1.6081-3(a) states that any extension granted to a corporation is for six months.

Since the built-in gains and passive investment income taxes are both imposed at a flat rate, there is no need to annualize the corporation's income. Similarly, there is no need to annualize the income reported to the shareholders.

1325.3. Return for the C short year. The corporation will be liable for a tax on its own income for the C short year. To compute this tax properly, the corporation must annualize its taxable income on a daily basis and apply the corresponding adjustment to the computed tax.

SUMMARY OF AUTHORITY: CODE SECTION 1362(e)(5)

- The corporation multiplies its taxable income by the number of days in the S termination year and divides the result by the number of days in the C short year.
- After computing the tax on the above figure, the corporation multiplies the tax by the number of days in the C short year and divides the result by the number of days in the S termination year.
- The corporation annualizes its alternative minimum tax for the C short year on a monthly basis.

The annualization rule for the income tax for the C short year is different from the general rules provided for other corporate short years. In most other instances, when a corporation has a short year it annualizes on a monthly basis. [§443(b)] As long as the entire S termination year is a period of 12 months, the corporation will use the daily annualization method.

EXAMPLE 13 - 17: Linco is a corporation that uses the calendar year. It terminated its S election on June 29, 1992 (a leap year). Its S short year is the 180-day period from January 1 through June 28, 1992. Its C short year is the 186-day period from June 29 through December 31, 1992. The corporation does not terminate its taxable year during the C short year. Linco reports $55,000 taxable income in its C short year. Its tax calculation is as follows:

Taxable income of C short year	$ 55,000
Annualized (366/186)	108,226
Tax on $108,226*	25,458
Annualized tax (186/366)	$ 12,938

*At C corporation rates in §11.

The annualization rules compound when the S termination year, in and of itself, is a taxable year of less than 12 months. In that case, the corporation will be subject to both the special annualization rule of Subchapter S and the general annualization rule of §443(b). The corporation will need to use a two-step annualization process. Since the only mathematics involved are multiplication and division, the ordering is not terribly important. The next example suggests a reasonable ordering of the steps. 13

EXAMPLE 13 - 18: Gorco had used the calendar year for tax reporting. On April 17, 1993, the shareholders revoked the S election. On August 31 of the same year, Gorco was merged into Bayco. Since Gorco's existence was terminated on August 31, its S termination year terminated on the same day. For the C short year (April 17 through August 31), Gorco's taxable income was $30,000. The steps required are:

Taxable income of C short year	$30,000
Annualized by days (243/136)	53,603
Annualized by months (12/8)	$80,404
Tax on $80,404*	$16,938
Annualized tax by months (8/12)	11,292
Annualized tax (136/243)	$ 6,320

*At C corporation rates in §11.

OBSERVATION: The calculation of a corporation's alternative minimum tax is beyond the scope of this book. The corporation will need to observe any special rules for adjusted current earnings and other tax preferences and adjustments. It will also need to compute an annualized alternative minimum tax exemption.

The corporation will be subject to all estimated tax requirements for the C short year. In general, if the short year is less than four months long, the corporation is not required to make estimated tax payments. [Proposed Regs. §1.6655-5(b)] Short years that are at least four months long, however, are subject to estimated tax payments.

1330. Shareholder treatment of the S termination year.

Each shareholder will include his or her portion of the S corporation's items for the S short year on his or her personal tax return in the same manner as in any other year. The basis and distribution rules for the S short year will also be subject to the usual rules of Subchapter S. (There are some special distribution rules for a period after the end of the S short year, discussed below.)

1330.1. Timing of pass-through. In spite of the statement that the S short year and the C short year are each treated as separate taxable years, the termination of an S election does not accelerate the reporting to the shareholders. Each shareholder takes his or her portion of the corporation's income, losses, deductions, and other items into account at the end of the S termination year.

SUMMARY OF AUTHORITY: REGULATIONS SECTION 1.1362-3(c)(6)

- Each shareholder reports his or her share of the S corporation's items for an S termination year on the personal tax return that includes the last day of the S termination year.
- The date on which the items pass through is the final day of the C short year.

EXAMPLE 13 - 19: Yanco uses a September 30 fiscal year. All of Yanco's shareholders use the calendar year. On December 1, 1992, Yanco terminates its S election. The items of income, loss, and deduction from October 1 through November 30, 1992, must be reported to the shareholders on Form 1120S, Schedule K-1. The date for inclusion by each of the shareholders would be September 30, 1993.

13

There are, however, instances in which a shareholder must report his or her portion of the S corporation items before the year normally would end. For instance, as discussed in Chapter 6, a shareholder who dies within an S corporation's taxable year must report all of the S corporation items on his or her final return. [§1366(a)] The shareholders must also be alert for any instance that accelerates the closing of the corporation's taxable year.

EXAMPLE 13 - 20: Refer to Example 13 - 19. Assume that the corporation is liquidated on December 22, 1992. The S termination year that began on October 1, 1992, would end on December 22, 1992. Accordingly, all of the shareholders must report their portions of the S corporation items on their 1992 tax returns.

1330.2. Interaction of election termination and passive activity loss rules. As a general rule, a taxpayer's interest in a passive activity does not include an interest held through a C corporation.[6] When a taxpayer has held an interest in an S corporation, however, and the corporation terminates its S election, there are some special rules:

---

[6] Temporary Regulations §1.469-4T(b)(2)(ii)(B) provided this rule for the years in which that Temporary Regulation was in effect. Proposed Regulations §1.469-4 is not as specific on the subject, but provides only for aggregation of a taxpayer's interest in pass-through entities.

1. Under the general rules applicable to C corporations, the income or loss from the activity held by the C corporation will no longer pass through to the shareholders.
2. Income realized by the shareholder from the corporation will be active in the case of compensation, or portfolio in the case of interest. There may be some opportunity for the shareholder to create passive income by renting property to the corporation.

The suspended losses from the activity during the years the S election was in effect continue to be treated as passive activity losses. [Temporary Regs. §1.469-1T(f)(4)(ii)] Apparently, termination of an S election would not be treated as a complete disposition of the shareholder's interest in an activity and the Regulations provide that the shareholder is treated as continuing to own the interest in the activity. This activity, however, cannot generate any future passive income to the shareholder. Accordingly, any suspended losses from S years remain as passive activity losses from the same activity that can no longer generate any passive income. They are deductible only to the extent of the shareholder's passive income from other sources. They should be allowed in full if the corporation disposes of its entire interest in the activity or if the shareholder disposes of his or her entire interest in the corporation, as long as the shareholder has no other ownership interest in the activity.

EXAMPLE 13 - 21: SF Corporation is an S corporation through 1991. It has one shareholder, Sally. Through 1991, it generates $50,000 in losses from a rental activity. Sally has not been able to use any of those losses at the end of 1991. In 1992, SF revokes its S election. In 1992 and future years, any net rental income would not generate any passive income to Sally, but would be treated as passive income within the corporation. Sally's $50,000 suspended losses would continue to be identified with her interest in SF Corporation and the activity it continues to conduct. Assume that SF Corporation realizes $20,000 net income from the rental activity in 1992. The losses from earlier years would not be deductible by the corporation, since they were suspended at the shareholder level. The net rental income does not pass through to Sally, since the S election is no longer in effect.

1335. Accounting for the S termination year.

An S corporation may use one of two methods for accounting for its income and deductions in an S termination year. In some instances, S corporations may prorate all income and deduction items for the entire termination year on a daily basis and assign the appropriate amounts to each of the short periods. In other cases, the corporation will close its books on that last day of the S short year and begin a new accounting period for the C short year. 13

1335.1. Interpretive problems. Both the Code and the Regulations state that the S short year and the C short year are treated as separate taxable years for all tax purposes. [§1362(e)(1); Regs. §1.1362-3(c)(3)] Specific exceptions are the treatment as one year for expiration of carryovers and the due date for filing the return of the S short year. If the language applies literally, some of the implications are as follows:

- The corporation must use short-year depreciation in both the S portion and the C portion of the year.
- The corporation may make a §179 expensing election for property placed in service in either or both of the two short years.
- The corporation must make any LIFO and uniform capitalization adjustments to its inventory for each portion of the termination year.
- The corporation must make all other year-end adjusting entries on its books.

For a corporation that uses the pro rata allocation method to allocate its income in its S termination year, the rules would be nearly impossible to apply. Fortunately, the Regulations provide that the corporation does not close its books on the termination date if the corporation uses the pro rata allocation method. [Regs. §1.1362-3(a)] When the corporation uses this method, it will not need to make any special adjustments at the end of the S short year.

> **OBSERVATION:** It would be helpful to tax practitioners if Congress or the IRS would clarify the extent of the treatment of an S termination year as two separate taxable years. There should be a list of what calculations must be made at the end of the S short year and what items may be computed for the entire S termination year. The ambiguity of the treatment of the S termination year leads to some problems in filling out tax returns.

1335.2. Pro rata allocation generally required. The general accounting rule for an S termination year is that the corporation must prorate its income and deductions throughout the entire S termination year.

SUMMARY OF AUTHORITY: CODE SECTION 1362(e)

- The general accounting rule for the termination year requires pro rata allocation.
- The corporation must divide each line item for which separate reporting to a shareholder is required in an S corporation by the number of days in the S termination year.
- The corporation must then assign each line item to the S short year and the C short year based on the number of days in each.

EXAMPLE 13-22: Albuco uses a September 30 year end. On February 13, 1993, the corporation revokes its S election, effective February 14, 1993. The corporation does not elect, and is not required, to close its books as of February 13, 1993. For the corporation's S termination year (October 1, 1992, through September 30, 1993), Albuco reports the following:

13

Long-term capital gain	$50,000
Short-term capital loss	(60,000)
Section 1231 losses	(30,000)
Charitable contributions	(45,000)
Investment interest	(15,000)
Rental loss	(18,000)
Accident and health insurance paid on behalf of shareholder-employees	(24,000)
Ordinary income*	150,000

*After deduction of health insurance. See Chapter 8.

Albuco's S termination year consists of 365 days, of which 146 are in the S short year and 219 are in the C short year. Accordingly, 40% (146/365) of each item is allocated to the S short year and the remaining 60% is assigned to the C short year. Albuco's accounting would be:

	Total	*40% to S Short Year*	*60% to C Short Year*
Long-term capital gain	$50,000	$20,000	$30,000
Short-term capital loss	(60,000)	(24,000)	(36,000)
Section 1231 losses	(30,000)	(12,000)	(18,000)
Charitable contributions	(45,000)	(18,000)	(27,000)
Investment interest	(15,000)	(6,000)	(9,000)
Rental loss	(18,000)	(7,200)	(10,800)
Accident and health insurance	(24,000)	(9,600)	(14,400)
Ordinary income	150,000	60,000	90,000

Albuco would report the following to its shareholders on Form 1120S, Schedule K-1, for its year ended September 30, 1993:

Long-term capital gain	$20,000
Short-term capital loss	(24,000)
Section 1231 losses	(12,000)
Charitable contributions	(18,000)
Investment interest	(6,000)
Rental loss	(7,200)
Ordinary income	60,000

The accident and health insurance of $9,600 would be reported to the shareholder-employees on Form W-2. This item would require a further breakdown, since some of the amount was paid in calendar year 1992 and some was paid in calendar year 1993. The shareholders would probably not need to report any of the $14,400 accident and health insurance premiums allocated to the C short year on their personal income tax returns, since this fringe benefit is excludable from the gross income of a shareholder-employee in a C corporation.

A corporation in an S termination year must then calculate its taxable income and income tax for the C short year using the offsets and limitations prescribed for C corporations. A corporation in this situation should be aware of any special rules governing its taxable income and tax computations; for example:

- The corporation may be required to switch to the accrual method.
- The corporation may be a closely held corporation, subject to the at-risk and passive activity loss rules.
- The corporation may be a personal service corporation, subject to several special requirements.[7]

EXAMPLE 13 - 23: Refer to Example 13 - 22. Albuco is not a personal service corporation. Its shares are owned in equal portions by 15 shareholders, so the corporation is not subject to the passive activity loss rules. It is, however, subject to all of the usual C corporation limits. Albuco would compute its income for the C short year as follows:

	Capital Gain and Loss	*Taxable Income*
Ordinary income		$ 90,000
Long-term capital gain	$30,000	
Short-term capital loss, limited to capital gains	$30,000*	
Section 1231 losses		(18,000)
Investment interest		(9,000)
Rental loss		(10,800)
Taxable income before charitable deduction		52,200
Charitable deduction (limited to 10% taxable income)**		(5,220)
Taxable income		$46,980

* The corporation may carry $6,000 back three years (if its S election was not in effect for any of those years) or forward five years. It is treated as a short-term capital loss and may be used to offset capital gains in any of those years.

** The corporation's contributions allocated to the C short year were $27,000, but the deduction was limited to $5,220. The corporation could carry the nondeductible $21,780 forward five years.

13

[7] A personal service corporation is subject to the passive loss limitations and to nondeductibility of accruals to shareholders, for example. See Chapter 1 for a brief discussion of the tax problems of personal service corporations.

1335.3. Election to use separate accounting periods. Any S corporation may make an election to split its S termination year into two separate accounting periods. When it does so, the corporation closes its books on the last day of the S short year.

SUMMARY OF AUTHORITY: CODE SECTION 1362(e)(3)

- A corporation may elect to split its S termination year into two separate accounting periods.
- This election requires the consent of:
  — All persons who were shareholders at any time during the S short year
  — All shareholders on the first day of the C short year

The election to use separate accounting periods will add some complexity to the S termination year. If the corporation elects to close its books on the final day of the S short year, it will need to make all of the year-end adjustments twice during the S termination year. The decision to use the general pro rata rule or the separate accounting rule should be made on a case-by-case basis. Examples comparing the impact of the two methods are presented at 1345.

The formalities of the election are simple. The corporation attaches a statement to its return for the C short year. The statement must describe the cause and the date of the termination of the S election. The statement must be signed, separately from the return itself, by a corporate officer. The required shareholder consents may be on the same page or on attached letters. [Regs. §1.1362-3(b)]

1335.4. Requirement to use separate accounting periods. In some instances, an S corporation is required to use separate accounting periods for the S short year and the C short year. In these instances, the corporation must close its books on the final day of the S short year.

SUMMARY OF AUTHORITY: CODE SECTION 1362(e)(6)(C) AND (D)

- A corporation must account for its S short year and its C short year separately if the purchaser of the corporation's stock or assets makes a §338 election.
- A corporation must account for its S short year and its C short year separately if there is a sale or an exchange of 50% or more of its stock in the S termination year.

The §338 election is relatively rare under current law. Therefore, the discussion begins
13 with the sale or exchange of 50% or more of the shares.

1335.41. Sale or exchange of 50% of shares. If there is a sale or an exchange of 50% or more of the corporation's stock in the S termination year, the corporation is required to close its books on the last day of the S short year. The phrase "sale or exchange" is not defined in the Code, but the Regulations provide some guidance.

The Regulations base the 50% test on newly owned stock, which is determined as follows:

- Measure each shareholder's percentage of ownership at the end of the S termination year.
- Compare that percentage with each shareholder's percentage of ownership at the end of the immediate prior year.

The difference is the total percentage of newly owned stock. If the total is at least 50%, the corporation must close its books on the last day of the S termination year. [Regs. §1.1362-3(b)(3)] This rule includes certain shares transferred by means other than a sale or an exchange between shareholders, such as issuance of new stock and redemption by the corporation of some of its shares.

EXAMPLE 13 - 24: At the end of 1991, the stock of BMJ Corporation, an S corporation that uses the calendar year, is owned as follows:

	Shares	*% of Total*
Bob	20	20%
John	40	40%
Maggie	40	40%

In 1992, the corporation issues 100 new shares to Bob. In addition, Clyde buys 24 shares from Maggie and 16 shares from John. The corporation terminates its S election in 1992. The calculation of newly owned stock is as follows:

	End of 1992		*End of 1991*	
	Shares	*% of Total*	*% of Total*	*Increase*
Bob	120	60%	20%	40%
John	24	12%	40%	n/a
Maggie	16	8%	40%	n/a
Clyde	40	20%	0%	20%
Total percentage newly owned at the end of 1992				60%

Since the newly owned shares exceed 50% of the total at the end of the S termination year, the corporation must close its books on the final day of the S short year.

Certain transfers are completely disregarded in determining newly owned shares. Such transfers include gifts and transfers at death, if the transferor held the stock on the last day of the immediate preceding taxable year. [Regs. §1.1362-3(d), Example 4]

EXAMPLE 13 - 25: Derco was an S corporation that used the calendar year. At the end of 1991, 40% of its shares were owned by Dean and 60% were owned by Sue. In 1992, Sue died and her shares were transferred to her estate. In 1992, Derco terminated its S election. At the end of the year, 40% of the shares are owned by Dean and the remaining 60% are still owned by Sue's estate. According to the Regulations, there are no newly owned shares at the end of 1992. Therefore, unless Derco, with the consent of its shareholders, elects to close its books at the end of the S short year, the corporation must prorate all of its Subchapter S items between the S short year and the C short year on a daily basis.

There may be multiple transfers by gift or at death during a single taxable year without creating newly owned shares. Examples would include transfers into or out of trusts. 13

EXAMPLE 13 - 26: Refer to Example 13 - 25. In 1992, Sue's estate transferred all of Sue's shares to a trust. Later in 1992, the trust terminated, and it distributed all of the shares to Ellen. Since none of Ellen's shares was transferred by sale or exchange, none is treated as newly owned at the end of 1992.

There are no attribution rules for ownership of stock for the calculation of newly owned shares. Any sale will require calculation of the newly owned percentage.

EXAMPLE 13 - 27: Majco is a corporation that uses the calendar year. At the end of 1991, Mary Jane owned all of the stock. In early 1992, Mary Jane sold all of the shares to her daughter, Kelly. In late 1992, Majco terminated its S election. All of Kelly's shares are treated as newly owned, so the corporation must close its books on the final day of the S short year.

The sale or exchange of stock in the S termination year need not be connected to the terminating event in order to require closing of the books. For the sale and the termination to occur in the same year is sufficient to require the use of separate accounting periods.

EXAMPLE 13 - 28: Refer to Example 13 - 27. Kelly bought the shares from Mary Jane on March 2, 1992. Kelly caused the corporation to revoke its S election on November 13, 1992. The corporation must close its books as of November 12, 1992. In addition, Mary Jane and Kelly could elect to have another interim closing on March 1, 1992, since Mary Jane has terminated her entire interest in the S corporation at that time. [§1377(a)(2)] (See discussion in Chapter 6.)

1335.42. Effect of §338 election. An S corporation that acquires a controlling interest in another corporation may make a §338 election to treat the stock purchase as an asset purchase. The effect of the election is that the purchased corporation may make a §338 election to treat the stock purchase as an asset purchase. This election is advisable in few situations, since the Tax Reform Act of 1986 has made liquidation of a corporation a fully taxable event. The mechanics of this election are discussed briefly in Chapter 15, at 1525.8.

To qualify for a §338 election, the purchasing corporation must acquire at least 80% of the target corporation's shares within a 12-month period. [§338(h)(1)] The constructive liquidation occurs on the date of the first purchase of shares. [§338(h)(2)]

In many cases, such a purchase will require the corporation to use separate accounting periods. (Proposed Regulations §1.1362-4(c)(3)(ii) provided an exception for certain transactions occurring before July 18, 1984.) In some cases, however, there might be a staggered purchase of stock that bridges two taxable years of the S corporation. In this instance, the corporation must close its books at the end of the S short year, even though there is not a sale or an exchange of at least 50% of the stock in the S termination year.

OBSERVATION: The provision requiring separate accounting periods for the S termination year when the purchaser makes a §338 election protects the selling shareholders from the tax burden of the constructive liquidation. If the selling shareholders want the tax burden, allowing them to step up their basis in their shares at the date of sale, they can structure the transaction as an asset sale. See Chapter 16 for a discussion of stock and asset sales.

Another effect of the §338 election is that it terminates the year of the acquired corporation. [§338(a)(2)] If the acquired corporation is an S corporation that has been using a fiscal year, the purchaser's §338 election may accelerate the reporting of the S short year's items to the shareholders of the acquired corporation.

13

1335.43. Effect of §338(h)(10) election. When a C corporation acquires at least 80% of the stock in an S corporation on one day, the acquiring corporation and the selling shareholders may elect to treat the transaction as an asset sale under §338(h)(10). The mechanics of this election are discussed briefly in Chapter 15, at 1525.84. In this situation, there is no S termination year. The selling shareholders report the deemed asset sale on their own returns as if such sale had occurred on the acquisition date. [Regs. §1.338(h)(10)-1(e)(2)(ii)]

EXAMPLE 13 - 29: Johnco was an S corporation that used a September 30 fiscal year. John, the sole shareholder, used the calendar year. On December 5, 1994, he sold all of his stock in Johnco to Brooke Corporation, a C corporation. John and Brooke made a joint election under §338(h)(10) to treat the stock sale as an asset sale. For all tax purposes, Johnco's year ends on December 5, 1994. Johnco is considered an S corporation through that date, on which it is treated as if it sold all of its assets at fair market value. Thus John must report all of the gains and losses from the deemed asset sale on his 1994 tax return. If Brooke does not liquidate Johnco, Johnco will be treated as a new corporation with a year that begins on December 6, 1994.

1335.5. Special accounting problems. Treating the S termination year as a single taxable year for some purposes but as two taxable years for others raises some questions about certain computations. In particular, depreciation and the reporting of income and deductions from partnerships may cause some concern.

1335.51. Depreciation in the S termination year. The calculation of the corporation's depreciation in the S termination year has not been addressed in any Regulation. The treatment of the S short year and the C short year could require short-year depreciation computations for each portion of the year. It is probably safe to assume, however, that the corporation merely calculates its depreciation for its entire S termination year and allocates the deduction on a daily basis between the S short year and the C short year.

This method is consistent with that used when depreciable property is transferred in a nontaxable transaction. (See Proposed Regulations §1.168-5(b)(2) for a description of nontaxable transfers and depreciation calculations under original ACRS. Also see the Example in Proposed Regulations §1.168-5(b)(4)(iii).) See Chapter 14 for a discussion of transfers under §351 and the resulting depreciation calculations. Termination of the S election is not a nontaxable transfer, per se, since there is no actual transfer of the asset. However, a nontaxable transfer is analogous to termination of an S election. Since there are no rules directly on this point, the rules for nontaxable transfers should be equally applicable. The calculations should be the same if the corporation uses pro rata allocation or separate accounting periods for the S short year and the C short year.

> **EXAMPLE 13-30:** Depco, which uses the calendar year, terminates its S election on June 30, 1992 (181 days have elapsed). Depco owns a building that it placed in service in 1989. The building cost was $315,000, and the full year's depreciation deduction for 1992 would be $10,000. Allocating the depreciation on a daily basis would assign $4,945 [$10,000 x (181/366)] to the S short year. The C short year would be assigned $5,055 [$10,000 x (186/366)]. The result should not be affected by pro rata accounting or separate-period accounting for Depco's S termination year.

1335.52. Income or loss from a partnership interest. If the S corporation is a partner in a partnership, it must account for its pro rata share of partnership income through the day before termination. Although this rule would automatically be implemented if the corporation used the pro rata allocation method, the Regulations apply the rule to a corporation that uses separate accounting periods.

SUMMARY OF AUTHORITY: REGULATIONS SECTION 1.1362-3(c)(1)

- When a corporation is a partner in a partnership and terminates its S election, the termination is treated as a sale or an exchange of the corporation's entire interest in the partnership.
- However, the termination is only for §706(c), which relates to the reporting of income by a selling partner.

13

The Regulations state this rule awkwardly. They state that a termination of an S election is a sale or an exchange of the corporation's interest in the partnership *for purposes of §706(c)*. There are numerous consequences, at the partnership level, to the sale or exchange of a partnership interest. For example, a sale or exchange of 50% or more of the interests may result in termination of the partnership under §708. Also, admission of a new partner may trigger basis adjustments to partnership property under §754.

Code §706(c), however, states only that the partner's year shall close with respect to the partnership, so that the partner must report his, her, or its share of partnership income, loss, etc., on the date of the sale or exchange. Therefore, the only function of Regulations §1.1362-3(c)(1) is to require that the corporation apportion partnership income between the S short year and the C short year, even if the corporation elects to use separate accounting periods. The Regulation imposes no consequences at the partnership level. The partnership may, however, be able to have an interim closing as of the S corporation's termination date, in allocating the income to the corporation. There is no corresponding portion of the extraordinary personal services Regulations dealing with this issue. As a result, there is no express requirement for the partnership to issue Schedule K-1 to the S corporation as of the date of termination.

EXAMPLE 13 - 31: GV Corporation is a corporation that terminates its S election on May 27, 1989. It is a partner in the MG Partnership. Both GV and MG use the calendar year. For the entire 1989 calendar year, GV's share of MG's taxable income is $100,000. Under the Regulations, GV will have "sold" its interest in GV on May 26, 1989. If the partnership agreement does not require an interim closing, GV's share of partnership income would be allocated as follows:

January 1–May 26 [(146/365) x 100,000]	$ 40,000
May 27–December 31 [(219/365) x 100,000]	60,000
	$100,000

The Regulation apparently does not apply when the termination year, in and of itself, is a short year. (As stated above, Regulations §1.1362-3(c)(1) applies this rule only when the partnership year ends in the C short year.) A S termination year may be a short year if the purchaser makes a §338 election, if the former S corporation joins an affiliated group filing consolidated returns, or if the former S corporation is merged or liquidated.

EXAMPLE 13 - 32: Refer to Example 13 - 31. Assume that GV was purchased by another corporation that filed a consolidated return for 1989. GV's S termination year would end on May 27, 1989. The remainder of GV's taxable year would be that of the affiliated group of corporations of which it is now a member. Therefore, there would be no C short year. The partnership's taxable year would not end in a C short year, and the Regulations would not require allocation of any portion of the income from the partnership to the S short year.

1335.6. Effect of accounting method on pass-through to shareholders. As the examples below at 1345. indicate, the use of pro rata or separate-period accounting may have a significant impact on the number of different Subchapter S items that pass through to the shareholders in the S termination year. The accounting method, however, has no effect on the timing of the pass-through to the shareholders.

EXAMPLE 13 - 33: Zeeco has been an S corporation that uses a September 30 taxable year. On December 15, 1992, the corporation terminates its S election. It closes its books and reports $125,000 ordinary income from October 1 through December 14, 1992. There is no event before January 1, 1993, that causes the S termination year to end prematurely. The shareholders will report the $125,000 taxable income in 1993, since the S termination year ends in that year.

As discussed below, there are some special rules for distributions and basis in the post-termination transition period that follows the termination of a corporation's S election. The use of pro rata or separate-period accounting does not affect the length of this period.

1335.7. Summary of accounting rules for the S termination year. The required and elective accounting rules for the S termination year may have a significant impact on the tax liabilities of the corporation and its shareholders. The rules are summarized in Figure 13 - 2.

1340. Post-termination transition period.

A corporation that has terminated its S election is subject to some special rules during its post-termination transition period. The two principal aspects of the post-termination transition period are:

- The ability to withdraw the former S corporation's Accumulated Adjustments Account
- The ability of the shareholders to restore basis and deduct losses from the S corporation years

Figure 13 - 2: S corporation termination year.

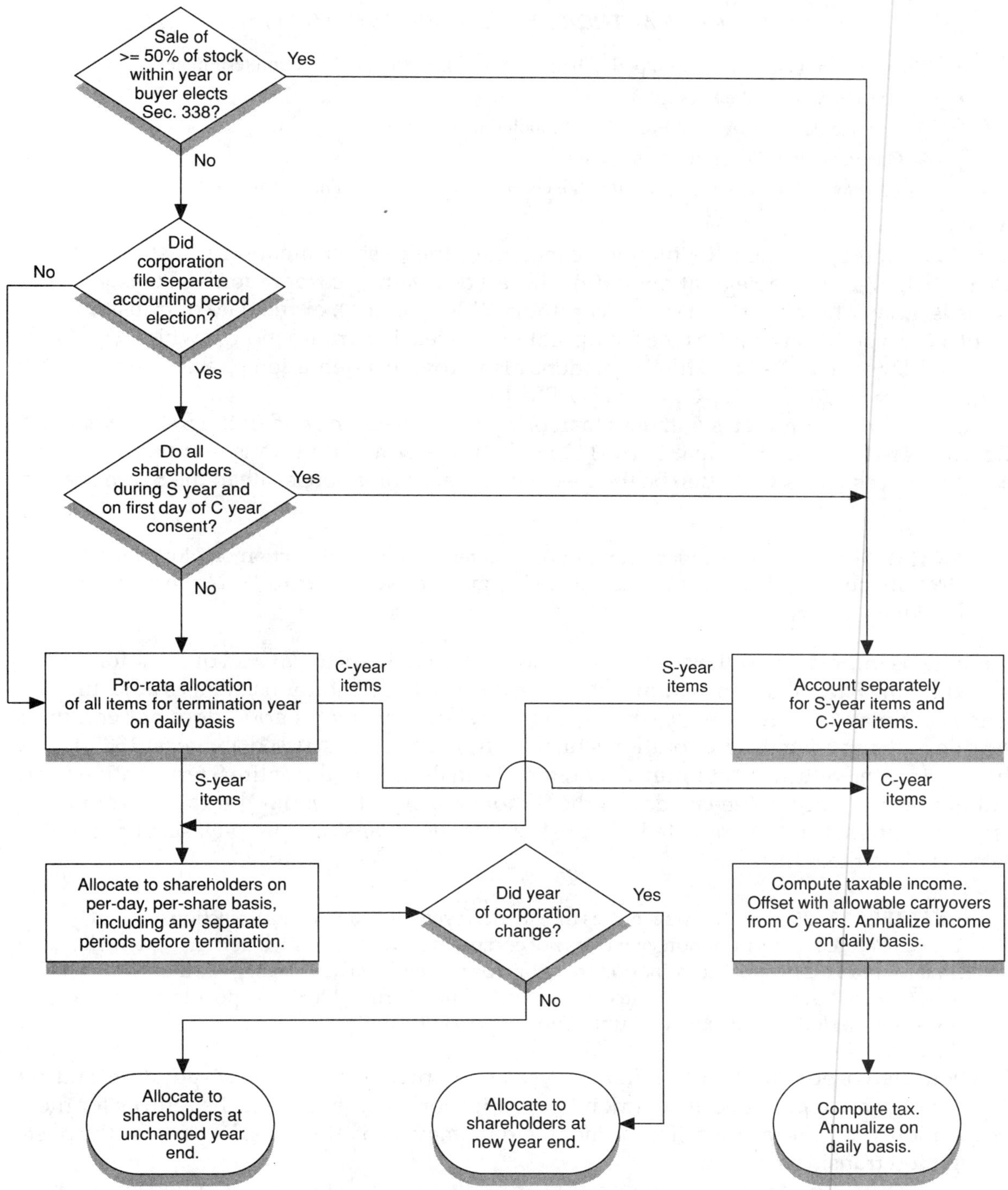

1340.1. Post-termination transition period defined. The post-termination transition period begins on the day the S election is no longer effective. It ends one year after the day on which the S election terminates or on the due date for the corporation's final S corporation tax return.

SUMMARY OF AUTHORITY: CODE SECTION 1377(b)

- The post-termination transition period begins on the day after an S election terminates.
- The period ends on the latest of:
  — The due date for the final Form 1120S, including extensions
  — One year after the termination occurs
  — 120 days after a determination that the corporation's S election has terminated

In 1996, the IRS issued Regulations concerning the post-termination transition period. [Regs. §1.1377-2] These Regulations define the last day of the S corporation's last taxable year as the last day of the short S taxable year under §1362(e)(1)(A), or the date of transfer in the event a C corporation acquires the S corporation's assets in a transaction to which §381(a)(2) applies. [Regs. §1.1377-2(c)] The Regulations also provide a definition of a *determination* for purposes of §1377(b)(1)(B). [Regs. §1.1377-2(d)]

If an S election terminates with less than one year between the end of the S short year and the due date for filing the final Form 1120S, the post-termination transition period will be exactly one year. This will often be the case when the termination is late in the S termination year.

EXAMPLE 13 - 34: A calendar-year corporation terminates its S election on November 5, 1992. Its post-termination transition period begins on November 6, 1992, and ends on November 5, 1993.

It may be important for the corporation and its shareholders to have all of the information regarding the S termination year in order to make timely distributions or basis adjustments, as the case may be. Accordingly, the post-termination transition period does not end until the due date for filing the corporation's final Form 1120S. As discussed above, at 1325.1., the due date for the return is determined by reference to the end of the entire S termination year, and not by reference to the last day of the S short year. [§1362(e)(6)(A)] If the S termination year is not prematurely terminated, the post-termination transition period lasts until the due date for filing the return.

13

EXAMPLE 13 - 35: Paintco, which uses the calendar year, terminated its S election on March 1, 1992. Paintco's S termination year does not end prematurely. If Paintco does not extend its final Form 1120S, its post-termination transition period ends on March 15, 1993, the due date for its final Form 1120S. If Paintco extends its final Form 1120S, the post-termination transition period is also extended until September 15, 1993.

When the corporation's S termination year ends prematurely, the corporation and its shareholders must pay special attention to the appropriate due date for the returns for the S termination year. The acceleration of the due date may also affect the duration of the post-termination transition period.

If a corporation discovers, in the process of an audit, that its S election has ended in an earlier year, the post-termination transition period ends 120 days after the final determination that the S election has terminated. The *final determination* date is the date on which the corporation agrees to the adjustment for the year in question. If the corporation does not agree with the IRS, but appeals the issue in court, the post-termination transition period is extended until the court decides that the S election has terminated. The extension of the post-termination transition period, however, has absolutely no effect on the date of termination of the S election.

EXAMPLE 13 - 36: On March 3, 1988, Barbco, an S corporation that used the calendar year, formed an operating subsidiary. Barbco and its shareholders did not realize that this action caused the termination of the S election. In 1991, Barbco's 1988 return was audited by the IRS. The agent discovered the formation of the subsidiary and terminated Barbco's S election as of March 2, 1988. Barbco and its shareholders did not request inadvertent termination relief and did not contest the termination. On July 24, 1991, Barbco agreed to the results of the audit.

Barbco's S termination year was the calendar year 1988, since its S election terminated in that year. Barbco's post-termination transition period began on March 3, 1988, but does not end until November 21, 1991, 120 days after the closing agreement.

OBSERVATION: As of this writing, there have been no cases or rulings involving the duration of the post-termination transition period following a determination that a corporation's S election had terminated in an earlier year. The availability of inadvertent termination relief, discussed at 1350., has allowed many S corporations to avoid the loss of S elections. If the corporation does not qualify for inadvertent termination relief, however, the extension of the post-termination transition period may be useful.

1340.2. Impact of post-termination period. The post-termination transition period is important to the shareholders because of its effect on:

- Losses incurred by the corporation before the S election terminated
- Distributions made by the S corporation after the termination of the S election but before the end of the post-termination transition period

1340.21. Impact on pre-termination losses. The S corporation may have incurred losses while its S election was in effect, and the shareholders may not have had sufficient basis to deduct those losses. The amount of the suspended losses may not be known until the S corporation closes its books for the period before termination. If there were no post-termination transition period rule, a shareholder would be permanently barred from claiming losses for the final year of the S election.

EXAMPLE 13 - 37: Losco was an S corporation that used the calendar year. It terminated its S election on May 2, 1992. The corporation's S termination year did not end prematurely, and the corporation extended the due date for its 1992 returns until September 15, 1993.

Losco has one shareholder, Leona. Her basis in her Losco stock on January 1, 1992, was $3,000. For its S short year ended May 1, 1992, Losco reported $12,000 loss. Leona was unaware of the magnitude of the loss until June 1993, when the accountant was preparing Losco's 1992 returns. In the absence of the post-termination transition period rules, Leona's loss deductions would be limited to $3,000, her basis in the Losco stock.

13

Within the post-termination transition period, a shareholder may restore basis and may claim the otherwise suspended losses. This aspect of the post-termination transition period may provide considerable relief.

SUMMARY OF AUTHORITY: CODE SECTION 1366(d)(3)

- If a former S corporation's losses allocated to a shareholder exceeded that shareholder's basis, as of the end of the S short year in the S termination year the shareholder may be able to deduct those losses in the post-termination transition period.
- Any increase in a shareholder's stock basis during the post-termination transition period will allow the shareholder to deduct pre-termination losses.
- Any deduction of pre-termination losses will result in a reduction of stock basis.
- Any losses that are suspended under the at-risk rules of §465 are called forward to the post-termination transition period.

It is important to note that the basis of indebtedness resulting from loans to the corporation by the shareholder will not allow the deductibility of losses after the S election terminates. Accordingly, a shareholder who wishes to take advantage of this rule must either purchase additional shares in the corporation or make a contribution to capital. The resultant increase in basis will allow the shareholder to claim the loss in the year of contribution.

EXAMPLE 13 - 38: Refer to Example 13 - 37. Leona's loss deduction for 1992 is limited to her basis of $3,000, and the remaining $9,000 loss is carried into 1993. The corporation was not an S corporation at any time during 1993, but the post-termination transition period does not expire until September 15, 1993.

In June 1993, when Leona discovers that she needs $9,000 additional basis, she contributes $9,000 to the corporation's capital. This contribution increases her basis to $9,000 and allows her to deduct the suspended $9,000 loss in 1993. The loss deduction reduces her stock basis back to zero.

Since a corporation is no longer an S corporation in its post-termination transition period, the shareholder who wants to establish basis may purchase preferred stock from the corporation. This strategy may work well if there has been a change in ownership since the corporation terminated its S election.

OBSERVATION: A corporation that has sustained substantial losses may be a risky financial proposition. Accordingly, the shareholders may want to ensure themselves of §1244 ordinary loss treatment (discussed in Chapter 14). A contribution to the corporation's capital would not result in §1244 loss on the sale or worthlessness of stock, whereas the purchase of additional shares could achieve that result. If the shareholders contribute only enough cash or property to establish sufficient basis to claim the losses suspended from prior S years, the increase in basis will be eliminated instantaneously by the losses that pass through. In this instance, §1244 treatment is not important.

A shareholder who wants to establish basis during the post-termination transition period should be wary of the financial risks involved. Additional basis will require an outlay of cash, which may not be a sound investment. In some cases, the shareholder would be well advised to forego the loss deduction, rather than make the additional investment. However, if the shareholder is committed to the enterprise or has guaranteed loans that he or she will probably need to pay, it would be wise to make the contribution to capital or purchase additional shares during the post-termination transition period. By doing so, the shareholder could claim a tax deduction on money that he or she would likely be required to pay in any circumstance.

CAUTION: If a shareholder wants to obtain additional basis by making loans or contributions of noncash property to the corporation, these transactions must be completed while the S election is still in effect. Similarly, a shareholder who wants to increase basis by purchasing new stock should complete the purchase before the S election terminates. During the post-termination transition period, the only basis increments that will allow a shareholder to deduct suspended losses will be through direct contributions of cash to the corporation by the shareholder.

1340.22. Distributions during the post-termination transition period. If an S corporation was profitable before it terminated its S election, the shareholders would have been subject to tax on all of its income, and the corporation may have generated a balance in the Accumulated Adjustments Account. The corporation is now a C corporation, however, and its distributions are dividends to the extent of the corporation's current and accumulated earnings and profits. Absent any special rules, the shareholders cannot receive any distributions without being subject to a second round of taxation.

EXAMPLE 13 - 39: Profco terminated its S election on July 2, 1992. Profco used the calendar year, and there was no event that terminated Profco's S termination year before December 31, 1992. For 1992, Profco's taxable income was $366,000, all of which was ordinary. Profco used the pro rata allocation method of accounting for its S termination year of 1992. Therefore, Profco's taxable income is $183,000 for its S short year and also $183,000 for its C short year. Profco's income tax for its C short year is $50,470. Assuming Profco had no adjustments to its earnings and profits other than its income tax, its current earnings and profits for its C short year would be $132,530 ($183,000 – $50,470). (See Chapter 3 for the rules governing the calculation of a C corporation's current earnings and profits.)

Profco had no balance in its Accumulated Adjustments Account or its accumulated earnings and profits at the beginning of 1992. The corporation made no distributions before July 2, 1992. Therefore, its AAA as of that date would be $183,000, its taxable income for its S short year. Any distribution up to $132,530 (current earnings and profits) made by the corporation between July 2, 1992, and December 31, 1992, would be a dividend to the shareholders, under the general rules of Subchapter C. Therefore, under those rules, a shareholder could not even receive a distribution to pay income tax on the income for the S short year without being subject to double taxation. According to the post-termination transition period rules, however, distributions up to $183,000 would be from the AAA.

Fortunately, a former S corporation is allowed to distribute its AAA during its post-termination transition period. This rule allows the corporation adequate time to determine its final AAA balance and to distribute any or all of that amount to the shareholders without its being treated as a dividend.

SUMMARY OF AUTHORITY: CODE SECTION 1371(e)

- A distribution during the post-termination transition period is treated as a distribution of the corporation's AAA, to the extent thereof.
- To qualify for this treatment, the distribution must be in the form of cash.
- A corporation may make a bypass election to distribute its earnings and profits in the post-termination transition period.

The election to bypass the Accumulated Adjustments Account during the post-termination transition period is of limited use. A corporation may want to do so if it faces the accumulated earnings tax or personal holding company tax. In most other cases, however, a former S corporation will probably choose to distribute its Accumulated Adjustments Account during this period.

13

The balance that can still be distributed under the Subchapter S rules is limited to the corporation's AAA, as adjusted through the final day as an S corporation. Previously taxed income (PTI) and the Other Adjustments Account (OAA) are not available, and they should be closed to paid-in capital. No property other than cash will qualify as a distribution of AAA in the post-termination transition period.

As discussed in Chapter 7, before the issuance of Proposed Regulations §1.1368-1 the IRS instructed corporations to include all tax-exempt income and related expenses in the AAA. For corporations with no earnings and profits, and whose expenses relating to tax-exempt income exceeded tax-exempt income, this instruction could have caused a corporation to compute a balance in the AAA that was less than that authorized by law.

EXAMPLE 13 - 40: Alpha Corporation and Bravo Corporation are both S corporations. Each corporation has $50,000 taxable income and $3,000 premiums paid on employee life insurance. Alpha has no accumulated earnings and profits, and Bravo has $1 accumulated earnings and profits. Per the IRS instructions, Alpha's AAA would be $50,000 and Bravo's would be $47,000. If the corporations terminated their S elections, Alpha could still distribute $50,000 tax-free during the post-termination transition period. Bravo could distribute only $47,000. This divergent treatment seems unwarranted. Bravo should recalculate its AAA, by posting the $3,000 of life insurance premiums to its OAA, bringing the balance in its AAA up to $50,000.

OBSERVATION: The rules relating to distributions of the AAA during the post-termination transition period are not limited to apply to only the shareholders who owned their stock during the period in which the S election was in effect. Therefore, it appears that new shareholders, including ineligible shareholders, such as partnerships and corporations, could also receive distributions as basis reductions, rather that dividends, during the post-termination transition period. If a new shareholder actually prefers dividend treatment, the corporation can make a bypass election during the post-termination transition period to attain this result. [§1371(e)(2)]

1340.3. Special rules governing post-termination distributions. At the time of this writing, there are no Regulations or rulings concerning distributions during the post-termination transition period. There is a limited analogy, however, in prior law.

1340.31. Rules of prior law. Before the Subchapter S Revision Act of 1982, a corporation that had terminated its S election was allowed to distribute its undistributed taxable income (UTI) within 2 months and 15 days after the end of its last year as a Subchapter S corporation. The effect of a distribution of UTI was the same as the effect of a distribution of AAA under current law. It reduced the shareholder's basis and was not included in gross income. An effective distribution of UTI could only be a cash distribution. A distribution of property, including a corporate obligation, was considered to be a dividend.

In one case a corporation wrote checks within the 2-month, 15-day period following its last year as an S corporation. It did not have the funds on hand to cover the checks. It did, however, have sufficient credit that it could have borrowed the funds to cover its checks. The shareholders loaned money back to the corporation, on the same day, in the same amount of the distribution, and took back notes from the corporation. The court held that the distribution was a valid distribution of cash. [*Hauer*, 85-2 USTC 9447 (DC N.D.)]

Another case involved a triangular distribution scheme. The S corporation terminated its election and distributed its UTI to its shareholders within the 2-month, 15-day period. The shareholders then made a loan to a second corporation, and the second corporation made a loan to the former S corporation to cover the distribution. The court held that this distribution was a valid distribution of cash. [*Oswald*, 54 TCM 436 (1987), appealed in 1989]

13

In a case where the bookkeeping was unreliable, a corporation tried to extend this period several months by treating a distribution as a payment of a debt. The directors had authorized payment of a dividend that qualified as a distribution of UTI. The actual distribution made within the 2-month, 15-day period, however, was $100,000 less than that authorized by the board of directors. The corporation later paid the $100,000 and treated it as a payment of a note. The corporation claimed that it had in fact distributed the debt while its S election was still in effect. The court found that the shortfall of the distribution during the allowable period had not created a bona fide liability. The shareholders were deemed to have received dividend income for the later payment of $100,000. [*Segel*, 89 TC 816 (1987)]

1340.32. Rules of current law. While a corporation's S election is in effect, it can make a distribution of cash or other property from its AAA. During the post-termination transition period, however, cash is the only property that may be distributed from the AAA. Any other property distributed is from the corporation's current earnings and profits. The corporation also must be careful to observe the time limits on the post-termination transition period.

EXAMPLE 13 - 41: G Corporation plans to terminate its S election at the end of 1991. In late 1991, it estimates that its AAA balance will be $100,000. It does not anticipate sufficient cash flow to pay out $100,000 in cash within 1992. It actually pays $100,000 to its shareholders in 1993, after its post-termination transition period had expired.

G Corporation's shareholders would treat the distribution as a dividend, to the extent of the corporation's current and accumulated earnings and profits.

A corporation that has a significant AAA, but lacks cash to make the distribution before the expiration of the post-termination transition period, should plan its actions carefully. Under current law, only cash paid out within the post-termination transition period is treated as a distribution from the AAA. Distribution of a note does not qualify.

EXAMPLE 13 - 42: Refer to Example 13 - 41. G Corporation could borrow an amount of cash equal to its AAA at any time during the post-termination transition period and distribute the cash to its shareholders. The shareholders should be able to loan the cash back to the corporation, which could then pay off its debt. At any time in the future, the corporation would be able to repay the loan from the shareholders. The corporation and shareholders would need to observe the formalities of a debtor–creditor relationship, in order to avoid possible reclassification of the debt as equity by the IRS.

A corporation may distribute notes to its shareholders before the S election terminates. Corporations that anticipate terminating the S election and want to distribute all AAA balances but are short of cash must plan carefully to observe all of the formalities of creating valid debt before the election terminates.

EXAMPLE 13 - 43: Refer to Example 13 - 42. G Corporation distributes notes in the total amount of $100,000 before the S election terminates. The corporation then redeems the notes in 1993, when it has sufficient cash to do so.

If G can establish that the $100,000 was a bona fide debt at the end of 1991, the shareholders can avoid dividend treatment, since they would have received the distribution while the S election was still in effect. If G cannot establish that the debt existed before 1992, the shareholders will have dividend income, to the extent of G's current (1993) and accumulated (in 1992 and in any years prior to G's S election) earnings and profits.

OBSERVATION: There is no policy reason to limit distributions of AAA during the post-termination transition period to cash only. It is a statutory rule, however, and must be observed by any corporation that intends to take advantage of the post-termination transition period distribution rules.

The post-termination transition period distribution rules apply to any shareholder, including a person or an entity that was not a shareholder when the S election was in effect. Therefore, the AAA may be allocated, at least in part, to shareholders who have no liability for tax for the income from the S short year.

EXAMPLE 13 - 44: Virgil owned 100 shares—all of the outstanding stock—in Virco, an S corporation that used the calendar year. On July 1, 1992, Virco issued 100 new shares to Holco, a domestic C corporation, thereby terminating Virco's S election on that date. Virco was not liquidated or merged in 1992, and its S termination year ended on December 31, 1992. Virco's AAA as of June 30, 1992, was $200,000.

Virco extended its 1992 tax returns so its post-termination transition period ended on September 15, 1993. Virco intends to distribute $200,000 to Virgil, who would treat the amount as a reduction of his basis. However, if Virco made any distributions to Holco during the post-termination transition period, those distributions would receive their proportionate allocations of the AAA.

Holco could benefit from a distribution of AAA, since it would be tax free, at least to the extent of Holco's basis. If the distribution to Holco were treated as a dividend, however, Holco would receive a dividends-received deduction of 80%. [§243(c)(1)] Therefore, Holco would not have a strong preference for a distribution of AAA, as opposed to a dividend. Virco and its shareholders could consider the following:

1. Virco could make distributions to Virgil before the post-termination transition period ended, but postpone any distribution to Holco until after that date.
2. Virco could make cash distributions to Virgil, but property distributions to Holco, during the post-termination transition period.

Either of these approaches would assure that Virgil would be the only shareholder to receive a distribution of AAA during the post-termination transition period. These transactions should be carefully planned and agreed to by both of the shareholders.

1345. Planning strategies for an S termination year.

A corporation that terminates its S election and is not required to use separate accounting periods for its S short year and C short year should calculate the tax effects of either allowable method before it files its tax returns for the S termination year. Depending on the timing of transactions during the post-termination transition period, the two methods may yield significantly different tax results. Examples 13 - 44 and 13 - 45 illustrate a situation in which the allocations are affected by the choice of accounting method.

EXAMPLE 13 - 45: Z Corporation is a calendar-year corporation that terminates its S election on October 19, 1989 (at 80% of the year). It has the following items of income and deduction:

Dividend income	$10,000
Payments to fringe benefit plans*	12,000
Capital gains on stock sales	30,000
Ordinary taxable income	20,000

*For benefit of shareholder-employees

Under the pro rata allocation rule, 80% of each of these items would be apportioned to the S portion of the year. The portions and possible ramifications for the S short year are:

- Dividend income of $8,000 would be passive income to the S corporation, with the possible imposition of the tax on excess net passive income. It would flow through to the shareholders as portfolio income. It would add to the shareholders' AAA.
- Fringe benefit payments of $9,600 would be deductible by the corporation, but they would be treated as taxable compensation to the shareholders.
- The capital gains of $24,000 on stock sales would be passive income to the S corporation. Along with the dividend income, these gains might result in the imposition of the tax on excess net passive income at the corporate level. They may be subject to the tax on built-in gains, and they would probably be treated as portfolio income to the shareholders, adding to the shareholders' AAA.
- The ordinary income of $16,000 may have elements of built-in gains, subject to the corporate-level tax. It would flow through to the shareholders as ordinary income. It would be active or passive to each shareholder (for §469) depending on the degree of each shareholder's participation in the corporation's business activity. It would also add to the AAA.

The portion of each income or expense item for the C short year and its ramifications to the corporation are:

- Dividend income of $2,000 would be subject to the dividends-received deduction of 70% or 80%, depending on the amount of stock Z Corporation owns in the paying corporations.

- Fringe benefit payments of $2,400 would be deductible to the corporation, subject to the anti-discrimination requirements in effect. This amount would not be included in the shareholders' gross income.
- The capital gains of $6,000 would be taxed at the same rate as ordinary income to the corporation. They could, however, be reduced for capital losses carried forward or back from another taxable year.
- The ordinary income of $4,000 would have no special characteristic. Combining it with the other items, however, apparently would put the corporation in the 15% income tax rate bracket.

EXAMPLE 13 - 46: Refer to Example 13 - 45. Z Corporation terminated its election so that it could take advantage of the tax benefits available to C corporations. It had earned all of its ordinary taxable income between January 1 and October 18. On October 19, it sold its stock portfolio and reinvested its proceeds in high-yield common stocks. It adopted the fringe benefit package at that time. All of its dividend income, fringe benefit payments, and capital gains occurred between October 19 and December 31. By using separate accounting periods, it could achieve the following:

- Dividend income would not be passive income to the S corporation, since it was received in the C short year. It would all be subject to the dividends-received deduction for the C corporation.
- Fringe benefit payments of $12,000 would be deductible items for the C short year and not included in the shareholders' gross income.
- The capital gains on stock sales would not be passive income to the corporation. They would not be subject to the tax on built-in gains.
- The ordinary income would pass through to the shareholders, since it occurred in the S short year. It would give the shareholders an AAA of $20,000, which they could withdraw at any time during the post-termination transition period.

Example 13 - 47 illustrates another situation in which a corporation may use separate accounting periods. It compares the total tax liabilities, and raises some other issues for consideration.

EXAMPLE 13 - 47: N Corporation commenced operations in January 1993 and filed an S election at that time. It was engaged to develop computer software and had a net loss of $20,000 through May 26, 1993. On that date it succeeded in obtaining a commitment from an important customer. It immediately filed a proper statement revoking its S election, effective May 27, 1993. From May 27 through December 31, 1993, its taxable income was $100,000. The taxable income for the entire year is $80,000.

N's sole shareholder, Norman, is in the 31% tax bracket.

If the corporation computes its income by the general rule (pro rata throughout the year), it will be allocated as follows:

To the S year [(146/365) x $80,000]	$32,000
To the C year [(219/365) x $80,000]	$48,000

The shareholder's tax resulting from the S short year is $9,920 (31% of $32,000). The corporation's liability is:

Taxable income of C year	$48,000
Annualized (365/219)	80,000
Tax on $80,000*	15,450
Annualized (219/365)	$ 9,270

*At C corporation rates in §11.

If the corporation elects to use separate accounting periods, Norman would include the $20,000 loss from the S period in his taxable income for 1993, resulting in a tax savings of $6,200. The corporation's liability would be as follows:

Taxable income of C year	$100,000
Annualized (365/219)	166,667
Tax on $166,667*	48,250
Annualized (219/365)	$ 28,950

*At C corporation rates in §11.

Comparison of the two tax liabilities:

	Using Pro Rata	*Separate Periods*	*Tax Cost (Savings)*
Tax on corporation	$ 9,270	$28,950	$19,680
Tax on shareholder	9,920	(6,200)	(16,120)
Total	$19,190	$22,750	$ 3,560

Note that the total tax difference is not significant. The shareholder would save $16,120 by using separate periods, but the corporation would save $19,680 by using pro rata allocation. Although the pro rata allocation would cost the shareholder taxes, it would also create an AAA balance of $32,000. The shareholder could withdraw this amount during the post-termination period and have approximately $16,000 cash after paying the extra tax. In an actual situation, the indirect effects on shareholder taxable income, such as the deductibility of medical expenses, casualty losses, miscellaneous itemized deductions, rental losses, and individual retirement accounts, would be important factors. Another important consideration would be the limitation on losses. If, in this example, the shareholder had a basis of less than $20,000 at the start of the year, he would not realize the full tax benefit of the pre-termination loss.

PLANNING TIP: The following points may be useful considerations when the choice of accounting methods brings about a shift of income between the S short year and the C short year:

- It is desirable to shift income into the S short year when:
  - —The effective rate of tax is lower at the shareholder level and the corporation is able and willing to distribute income to the shareholders
  - —The corporation will be able to distribute the AAA, and the shareholders want to withdraw cash
  - —There are no adverse effects to increasing adjusted gross income at the shareholder level
  - —There are corporate-level capital gains that would result in favorable treatment for an individual, but not for a corporation
  - —The corporation has passive investment income, and shifting other gross receipts to the corporation would cause its passive income to be less than 25% of gross receipts
- It is desirable to shift income into the C short year when:
  - —The effective rate is lower at the corporate level, and the corporation wants to distribute as little as possible
  - —The increased adjusted gross income at the shareholder level would have secondary ill effects, such as increased phaseouts of personal exemptions and itemized deductions
  - —There are items of income and deduction for which a C corporation would receive beneficial treatment, but not an S corporation

— There is a substantial amount of passive investment income that, if shifted to the C short year, could reduce or eliminate the S corporation tax on excess net passive income

— There are substantial built-in gains, and the shift of either the gains or taxable income to the C short year would eliminate or reduce the S short year's built-in gains tax

1350. Inadvertent termination relief.

When Congress was drafting the Subchapter S Revision Act of 1982, the writers realized that many closely held businesses do not pay close attention to tax matters. Under old Subchapter S, there was no inadvertent termination relief provision. The courts were full of cases in which it appeared to be inequitable that S elections were terminated, but the law was so rigid that the IRS and the courts had no choice in the matter. Accordingly, the Subchapter S Revision Act of 1982 added a rule allowing the IRS to waive certain inadvertent terminations of S elections. Congress instructed the IRS to be reasonable in granting such waivers. [Senate Report No. 97-640, 97th Cong., 2d Sess., H.R. 6055, pages 12, 13] As of this writing, the IRS has granted literally hundreds of requests for such relief. Thus, the inadvertent termination relief rules allow tax professionals to protect their clients' S elections.

1350.1. General rule. The statute gives most of the necessary rules for the definition of an *inadvertent termination*. It also gives the IRS the authority to waive such terminations.

SUMMARY OF AUTHORITY: CODE SECTION 1362(f) AS AMENDED BY THE SMALL BUSINESS JOB PROTECTION ACT OF 1996

- If an S corporation loses its S election because it fails to meet one or more of the requirements to be an S corporation, it may, with the consent of the IRS, treat its S election as continuing in force.
- The reason for termination must be a violation of one of the eligibility standards, and not a revocation.
- The corporation must have been unaware that the disqualifying event would cause it to lose its S election.
- Upon discovery of the terminating event, the corporation must take the necessary steps to restore its eligibility.
- All persons who have been shareholders from the date of the terminating event to the date the corporation requests inadvertent termination relief must agree to the request.
- The corporation must file a formal request for relief under this rule.

13

Typically, a corporation that has inadvertently terminated its S election makes a request to treat the S election as if it had never terminated. Regulations §1.1362-4(f) offers a corporation two options for inadvertent termination relief.

SUMMARY OF AUTHORITY: REGULATIONS SECTION 1.1362-4(f)

- An S corporation that is granted inadvertent termination relief may be treated as if its S election had never terminated.
- An S corporation that is granted inadvertent termination relief may be treated as if it was a C corporation from the date of the terminating event until the date on which it again became eligible for S status.

The first option is the one chosen in most, if not all, requests. Accordingly, the second option receives no further discussion in this book.

A representative sample of situations in which the IRS has granted inadvertent termination relief is discussed below. A significant percentage of the rulings granting such relief involve an S corporation transferring stock to a trust, but the trust failing to make the proper election to be a Qualified Subchapter S Trust. The Small Business Job Protection Act of 1996 relaxed the rules regarding trusts as S corporation shareholders, so there should be fewer requests for inadvertent termination relief in this area in the future. (See Chapter 2 for a description of trusts that qualify as shareholders in S corporations.)

EXAMPLE 13 - 48: Truco made a valid S election in 1986. In 1991, one of Truco's shareholders died. As requested in his will, his shares were transferred to a trust. The trust met all of the requirements to be a Qualified Subchapter S Trust, but the beneficiary failed to make a timely election to treat the trust as a Qualified Subchapter S Trust. Truco's S election was terminated when the grace period passed for the beneficiary to make the election. Truco and its shareholders did not understand that the corporation would lose its S election as a result of the trust's ownership of stock. Truco's accountant (who was not the tax advisor for the deceased shareholder or his family) discovered, while preparing Truco's 1991 tax return, that the trust had acquired the shares.

The failure of a trust beneficiary to make a timely QSST election under §1362(d) has been a frequent cause of ruling requests. More recently, S corporations have also terminated eligibility when a fiduciary of a purported ESBT failed to make a timely election on behalf of the trust.

In 1998, the IRS revised a simplified procedure for inadvertent termination relief when the sole cause of the termination is the failure to make a timely QSST election. This rule now applies to a late ESBT election. This simplified method does not apply to any other cause of inadvertent termination. See 1350.22 and 1350.23, below, for discussion of the simplified procedures.

1350.2. Procedures. The statute requires the consent of the IRS to inadvertent termination relief, but does not state the procedures necessary to request such action. The statute clearly gives the IRS the authority to issue its own procedural rules.

1350.21. General procedures. The general procedures have been in effect since 1983. They were formalized in Final Regulations in 1992. As of 1999, they still apply to all inadvertent terminations except for failure to make a timely QSST or ESBT election. The general rules are stated in Regulations §1.1362-4(c).

SUMMARY OF AUTHORITY: REGULATIONS SECTION 1.1362-4(c)

- The corporation must submit a request for a private letter ruling to the National Office of the IRS.
- The ruling request must be prepared in the form acceptable to the IRS.

The IRS usually issues a Revenue Procedure each January that gives detailed instructions on preparation of a ruling request. At the time of this writing, the processing fee that must accompany the request is $5,000. [Rev. Proc. 99-1, 1999-1 IRB 6, Appendix A, (3)(c)] When the IRS issues the ruling, it is in the form of a private letter ruling. The ruling repeats all of the information sent in the request, except for names and other information for which the taxpayer may request confidentiality. Any of the rulings cited in this book will be useful guidelines for the information the IRS needs to process the request.

At a minimum, the ruling request must contain the following:

- A statement acknowledging the corporation's ineligibility because of a terminating event
- The description and date of the terminating event

- A representation that there was no tax avoidance motive to the termination
- The description and date of the actions taken to restore the corporation's eligibility
- A statement signed by all of the shareholders during the time of the inadvertent termination, indicating that they agree to any adjustments required by the IRS to restore the corporation's S election [Regs. §1.1362-4(a)(4)]

EXAMPLE 13 - 49: Refer to Example 13 - 48. Truco's accountant discovers the terminating event on March 1, 1992. On March 2, 1992, the beneficiary of the trust files a QSST election, even though the election is long past the statutory grace period. Shortly thereafter, the accountant prepares a ruling request. A corporate officer signs the request, and all shareholders agree to the adjustments necessary for the IRS to grant the request. The corporation's accountant mails the request, along with the $5,000 filing fee, to the National Office of the IRS. It is extremely likely that the IRS will grant the request.

The requirement that all shareholders must agree to any adjustments necessary to keep the S election in force may seem to pose a formidable risk. Actually, the adjustments, which are specified in the Regulations, are quite reasonable. Since the corporation is attempting to be treated as an S corporation throughout the period of its ineligibility, the shareholders must all agree to be treated as S corporation shareholders during that period. [Regs. §1.1362-4(d)] In some rulings, an ineligible shareholder has agreed to be treated as an eligible shareholder and include all items of the corporation's income and losses on its own tax returns. [PLRs 8825042, 8830020] In other rulings, a person other than the actual shareholder has agreed to include all items that were allocated to the ineligible person. [PLR 8838046]

EXAMPLE 13 - 50: Refer to Example 13 - 48. The beneficiary of the trust in question agrees to include all of her portion of the Subchapter S items on her own return, as if the trust had been a grantor trust. All other shareholders agree to report their allocable portions of the Subchapter S items on their returns, as if the S election had never terminated. Since the shareholders have agreed to the necessary adjustments, the IRS is almost certain to grant the ruling request, and the corporation will be treated as if its S election had continued uninterrupted.

OBSERVATION: The parties who must agree to the inadvertent termination relief provisions include all persons who were shareholders during the time of technical disqualification. Therefore, any person who held shares at any time during the period of disqualification can block the request.

13

EXAMPLE 13 - 51: Refer to Example 13 - 48. A person who holds 1% of the shares feels that he has been unfairly excluded from important corporate decisions. He has the right to be treated as a shareholder in a C corporation, since the corporation has terminated its S election. By refusing to sign the ruling request, he may unilaterally veto the request for inadvertent termination relief. The corporation would be a C corporation from the date the trust was disqualified. Obviously, the dissident shareholder could command an exorbitant price for consent.

1350.22. Lack of timely QSST or ESBT election. As discussed below, under actions of the IRS, the lack of a timely QSST election was one of the most frequent cause of inadvertent termination of an S election. Therefore, the IRS issued a simplified procedure to deal with this cause of termination. [Rev. Proc. 94-23, 1994-1 IRB, made obsolete by Rev. Proc 98-55] This procedure was broadened to include the ESBT in Revenue Procedure 98-55, 1998-46 IRB-1. Instead of filing a ruling request, the corporation may file a statement and receive automatic relief. To qualify for this expedited relief, the corporation must show that the sole cause of the termination was the failure to file a timely QSST election.

- The QSST election must contain all of the information required for a timely filing, including the identification of the trust, the name, the address, and the identification number of the beneficiary.
- This election must be filed with the IRS within two years of the original due date for the QSST election.
- The beneficiary must file the QSST election, complete with trust documentation, which demonstrates that the trust meets all requirements of a QSST. See Chapter 2, at 215.34., for a description of these requirements.
- The election must also be accompanied by trust documentation, or an affidavit from the trustee, that the trust meets the requirement to distribute all trust accounting income annually and will continue to meet this requirement.
- This filing should be labeled at the top, "FILED PURSUANT TO REV. PROC. 98-55."
- The election must be accompanied by affidavits from the corporation and all persons who have been shareholders during the period of the termination. These parties must state that they have filed all relevant tax returns for the termination period as if the S election had been in effect.
- The current income beneficiary must state, "Under penalties of perjury, I declare that, to the best of my knowledge and belief, the facts presented in support of this election are true, correct, and complete." [Rev. Proc. 98-55, 1998-46 IRB 1, §6]

When a corporation qualifies for expeditious relief under Revenue Procedure 98-55, it does not need to file a request for a letter ruling. There is no user fee required for relief under this Revenue Procedure. However, if there is any other cause of termination, or if more than two years have elapsed since the original due date for the QSST election, the corporation must request a ruling, as discussed above at 1350.21.

1350.23. Lack of timely ESBT election. Even though the ESBT election is a relatively new phenomenon, it is becoming a compliance problem. Accordingly, the IRS has extended the simplified and expedited relief rules of Revenue Procedure 98-55 to cover inadvertent termination caused by a late ESBT election. The procedures are almost identical to those discussed above for the QSST election. They differ only in that the ESBT is a different entity than the QSST. The procedures are as follows:

- The ESBT election must contain all of the information required for a timely filing, including the name, address, and identification number of the trust.
- This election must be filed with the IRS within two years of the original due date for the ESBT election.
- The trustee must file the ESBT election, complete with trust documentation that demonstrates that the trust meets all requirements of an ESBT. See Chapter 2, at 215.36, for a description of these requirements.
- The election must also be accompanied by an affidavit from the trustee stating that the trust meets all requirements to be an ESBT (except for a timely election) and that all potential current beneficiaries meet the shareholder requirements of the ESBT.
- This filing should be labeled at the top, "FILED PURSUANT TO REV. PROC. 98-55."
- The election must be accompanied by affidavits from the corporation and all persons who have been shareholders during the period of the termination. These parties

must state that they have filed all relevant tax returns for the termination period as if the S election had been in effect.

- The trustee must state, "Under penalties of perjury, I declare that, to the best of my knowledge and belief, the facts presented in support of this election are true, correct, and complete." [Rev. Proc. 98-55, 1998-46 IRB 1, §6]

As is the case with a QSST filed under this procedure, there is no need for a ruling request or a user fee.

1350.3. Actions of the IRS. As of this writing, the IRS has evidently complied with the spirit and the letter of its directive to be reasonable in granting inadvertent termination relief. Most rulings it issues in this area (usually about 10 per month) are private letter rulings and are of no precedential value. Therefore, this book cites only a few of those rulings. Table 13 - 1 cites some of the rulings that have been issued to date involving late QSST elections. These rulings can be expected to diminish in the future, as more of these terminations are covered by the expeditious rule of Revenue Procedure 98-55.

> **OBSERVATION:** Inadvertent termination relief has saved many clients from permanent loss of an S election. Undoubtedly, it has saved many tax practitioners from extensive malpractice exposure. The remedy, however, is not entirely painless. Although the IRS usually grants relief, such relief has its costs. At a minimum, the tax advisor may find an extremely irritated client. The cost of preparing the ruling request, and paying the user fee, could be avoided by meticulously observing all of the criteria of a small business corporation. Tax advisors should periodically remind their clients of these requirements. The time between submission of the request and issuance of the ruling is four to six months in many of the rulings cited above. During that period, the corporation has an uncertain status, which raises its share of compliance and planning problems. Finally, the disqualification of the corporation's S election gives every shareholder the right to block the inadvertent termination relief request by failing to agree to the adjustments. Especially when there is hostility among shareholders, an inadvertent termination may result in the permanent loss of the S election.

TABLE 13 - 1: Inadvertent Termination Relief Granted in Situations Involving Late QSST Elections

The following private letter rulings involve inadvertent termination that resulted from failure to make a timely QSST election, when trusts met all other QSST requirements.

PLRs 9401007, 9402009, 9404014, 9406014, 9406023, 9406036, 9406037, 9409012, 9412028, 9413036, 9417022, 9417023, 9417025, 9419017, 9420005, 9424044, 9425039, 9426022, 9428016, 9432007, 9441019, 9447037, 9507034, 9508024, 9511024, 9513016, 9515015, 9515022, 9518016, 9528024, 9527018, 9542010, 9543027, 9546023, 9547012, 9547021, 9549024, 9603028, 9629003, 9642030, 9642042, 9644036, 9645012, 9701017, 9701019, 9701033, 9714024, 9716015, 9718008, 9730017, 9739030, 9742033, 9749008, 9815041, 9821031, 9821032, 9822017, 9824015, 9825012, 9827030, 9827033, 9827036, 9832016, 9832030, 9838025, 199901017, 199903018, 199903023, 199906010, 199907012, 199912037, 199913025, 199920015

Table 13 - 2 cites some of the rulings that have been issued to corporations whose inadvertent termination was caused by transfer of stock to a trust and that included some problem other than a late QSST election.

TABLE 13 - 2: Inadvertent Termination Relief Granted in Situations Involving Trusts

Situation	Authority
Inadvertent termination waived when stock transferable to ineligible trust. Within reasonable time, situation was corrected.	Rev. Rul. 86-110, 1986-2 CB 150; PLRs 8523097, 8537034, 8540031, 8541059, 8546033, 9321064, 9334008, 9336019, 9340045, 9342049, 9403020, 9407011, 9422017, 9422018, 9422019, 9422020, 9422021, 9422022, 9422023, 9424014, 9426036, 9436033, 9443008, 9508017, 9510017, 9511015, 9527016, 9552031, 9625008, 9642011, 9648040, 9807003, 9812008, 9852016, 199908046
Transfer to testamentary trust was inadvertent termination.	PLRs 8839025, 8834033, 9321033
Transfer to exempt retirement trust was inadvertent termination.	PLRs 8850034, 8834033, 9332016
Inadvertent termination was recognized by corporation, which filed as C corporation for two years. Cause was transfer to testamentary trust. Corporation was allowed to file amended returns and remain an S corporation.	PLR 8833041
A grantor trust held stock for more than two years after the grantor's death	PLRs 9231023, 9305020, 9426035, 9623008, 9642003, 9801029, 9804008
Several trusts that had qualified as QSSTs failed to distribute all trust accounting income currently. Upon discovery, the trusts made the proper distributions.	PLRs 9302025, 9509007, 9603007 9649038, 199906027
A testamentary trust with multiple beneficiaries was allowed to be a QSST when all beneficiaries except for the surviving spouse disclaimed their interests.	PLR 9324032
A testamentary trust with two beneficiaries transferred its shares to two newly created trusts that qualified as QSSTs.	PLR 9324032
Testamentary trust held stock for more than 60 days.	PLRs 9401028, 9413037, 9432014, 9733013, 9853008
QSST elections were executed by trustee rather than by income beneficiaries. Upon discovery, income beneficiaries filed QSST elections.	PLRs 9430009, 9749008
ESBT and QSub elections filed late. Termination was inadvertent.	PLRs 9828005, 9829019, 9833023 9846010, 9848019, 199911021, 199916016, 199921009

Transfer of S corporation stock to a qualified ESBT was done prior to first taxable year after 12/31/96.	PLR 9842043
Trust failed to file QSST election, had accumulated earnings and profits and excess passive investment income.	PLR 9847007
Grantor trust held stock for more than two years after the grantor's death. IRS taxed the trust as an ESBT.	PLRs 199907009, 199916047
Beneficiaries failed to file timely QSST elections, then trust failed to distribute all income currently. Both events were considered inadvertent termination.	PLRs 9551016, 9842021, 9846007

Although transfer of stock to a trust has been the most frequent cause of inadvertent termination relief, there have been numerous rulings for other causes of termination. Tables 13 - 3 through 13 - 6 cite some of the rulings that have been issued to corporations whose inadvertent termination was caused by ownership of stock by an ineligible shareholder other than a trust.

TABLE 13 - 3: Inadvertent Termination Relief Involving Ineligible Shareholders

Donation of stock to charitable organization was inadvertent termination. Individual donor was treated as shareholder throughout charity's ownership.	PLRs 8907044, 9702020, 9750041 9846013
Transfer of shares to an ineligible charitable corporation was inadvertent termination. The corporation was deemed not to have held the stock until after 12/31/97 when it became an eligible shareholder.	PLR 9834031
C corporation had maintained ESOP, but distributed all stock. Employees rolled stock into IRA after corporation had made S election.	PLR 8821020
Issue of stock to ineligible stock plan. Plan sold its shares to the shareholder.	PLR 199904005
Issue of stock to IRA was inadvertent termination.	PLRs 8914005, 9426036, 9434026, 9528008, 9539004, 9540055, 9542038, 9551004, 9627006, 9644030, 19990926
Mistaken issue of stock to corporation did not terminate S election. Corporation that temporarily owned stock was required to include its share of S corporation's income on its corporate return.	PLRs 8825042, 8830020, 9317036 9651011, 9714021, 9831027, 9834001, 199915020
Mistaken transfer of shares to ineligible shareholder was inadvertent termination.	PLRs 8830032, 8852020, 8938023, 9342032, 9444014, 9506014, 9524006, 9603014, 9628005, 9715007, 9716022, 9710017, 9818062 9821013, 199913033

13

Mistaken transfer of shares to other corporation was inadvertent termination when corporation held shares for nearly two years. Corporate shareholder was required to include share of S corporation's taxable income.	PLR 8839034
Mistaken transfer of one share to Canadian citizen was inadvertent termination. U.S. shareholder was required to include all income.	PLR 8838046
Surrender of Green Card by resident alien shareholder was inadvertent termination; change of status to non-resident alien.	PLRs 8923030, 9808018
Resident alien shareholder returned to his home and became ineligible. Upon discovery of ineligibility, the shareholder gave all of his stock to his wife, a U.S. citizen. The IRS held the termination inadvertent.	PLR 9015020
Issuance of stock to a partnership caused inadvertent termination. Upon discovery, transaction was rescinded and stock was transferred to individuals.	PLRs 9348005, 19990923
Gift of shares to nonresident alien was inadvertent termination. Upon discovery, donor reacquired shares. Nonresident alien was required to report his share of income and deductions for the time he held the shares.	PLR 9431009
Transfer of shares to a bank under a transfer, and settlement agreement was inadvertent termination.	PLR 9431011
Transfer of shares to a partnership by a shareholder was an inadvertent termination. Corporation redeemed stock, and transferring shareholder agreed to pay adjustments required by IRS.	PLR 9527017

TABLE 13 - 4: Inadvertent Termination Relief Involving Affiliated Groups*

Purchase of 100% stock of other corporation, when both attorney and accountant assumed the other party was responsible for tax matters, was inadvertent termination. After discovery of ineligibility, S corporation divested.	PLR 8842022
Formation of operating subsidiary was inadvertent termination. Shortly after discovery, S corporation merged with subsidiary.	PLRs 8842023, 9130018
Incorporation of two active subsidiaries was inadvertent termination. S corporation could not reflect income and loss of subsidiaries on its own return.	PLR 8914033
Mistaken purchase of subsidiary, when accountants thought it was asset purchase, was inadvertent termination.	PLR 8917038
Inadvertent termination was waived for an S corporation that temporarily held a subsidiary as nominee.	PLR 8550033

* These rulings were issued prior to the Small Business Job Protection Act of 1996, which removed the prohibition against membership in affiliated groups.

Failure to file merger document resulted in inadvertent termination.	PLR 8946063
S corporation bought 95% of the stock of another corporation. It disregarded the second corporation's existence and operated it as a division, but did not liquidate or dissolve it. When filing the S corporation's tax return, the accountant discovered the second corporation. It was immediately dissolved. The IRS held that the termination of the S election was inadvertent.	PLR 8949080
Acquisition of shell corporation along with significant other property caused membership in affiliated group. When S corporation discovered existence, it sold all stock in the purchased corporation to its sole shareholder. The IRS held the termination inadvertent.	PLR 9001050
Acquisition of subsidiary, with no tax advice, caused termination. The acquired subsidiary was merged into the parent corporation and inadvertent termination relief was granted.	PLR 932200
Stock of a foreign subsidiary held through a trust, which was treated as a grantor trust created by the S corporation, caused an affiliated group. Trust was modified and inadvertent termination relief was granted.	PLR 9322030
Subsidiary corporation issued new shares to parent corporation that created affiliated group. Upon discovery, parent corporation divested.	PLR 9406022
Chinese counsel created subsidiary corporation, rather than limited liability company. Upon discovery, one of the parent corporation shareholders purchased all of subsidiary's stock.	PLR 9331049
Subsidiary redeemed some of minority shareholders' stock, which caused parent corporation's ownership to exceed 80%. Upon discovery, one of parent corporation's shareholders purchased enough stock from parent to reduce parent's ownership to 71.81%.	PLR 9331008
Partnership in which S corporation owned 80% interest was incorporated, and S corporation became 80% shareholder. Upon discovery, subsidiary corporation issued additional shares to other shareholder, which reduced parent corporation's ownership to less than 80%.	PLR 9336039
Newly formed subsidiary issued more than 80% of its common and preferred stock to S corporation. Subsidiary then acquired operating assets. Upon discovery, subsidiary was liquidated.	PLRs 9422040, 9648038
Temporary ownership of more than 80% of stock in investment companies, pending sale of stock in each company to public, caused inadvertent termination of parent corporation's S election. Upon discovery, parent corporation divested to less than 80% ownership.	PLR 9421004

13

S corporation formed a wholly owned holding company to hold stock in a foreign corporation. Upon discovery, holding company and foreign corporation were liquidated.	PLR 9427004
Corporation's redemption of shareholders' stock, resulting in S corporation shareholder holding more than 80% of outstanding stock, was inadvertent termination.	PLRs 9434021, 9626025
Purchase or transfer of remaining stock of a C corporation of which an S corporation had previously owned less than 80% was inadvertent termination. Upon discovery, S corporation sold enough stock to reduce its ownership of C corporation to less than 80%.	PLRs 9440013, 950931, 9750042
S corporation entered into a plan for a Type A merger with another corporation. Filings with the state erroneously indicating a Type B share exchange rather than a Type A merger resulted in an inadvertent termination.	PLR 9435028
Ownership by an S corporation of 80% of an LLC that was taxable as a corporation resulted in an inadvertent termination.	PLR 9433008
Purchase of 100% stock of other corporation when attorney was not aware of adverse consequences and accountant was not advised of transaction was inadvertent termination.	PLRs 9547006, 9648036, 9643010, 9643019, 9642031
Formation of a new subsidiary based on poor tax advice was inadvertent termination.	PLRs 9551012, 9625041, 9627021 9648031, 9730005, 9750022
Purchase of stock by an LLC that subsequently distributed the stock to the LLC partners.	PLRs 9750004, 9750005, 9750006 9750007, 9750008

The following are rulings that have been issued since the Small Business Job protection act of 1996, which removed the prohibition against membership in affiliated groups.

QSub election filed late was an inadvertent termination.	PLR 199911021
S corporation acquired less than 100% of another S corporation. Remainder of stock was acquired and timely QSub election was filed.	PLR 199919017
S corporation's ownership of a foreign entity was an inadvertent termination. The corporation sold its holdings.	PLR 199921024
S corporation inadvertently became sole owner of a joint venture. The joint venture was liquidated.	PLR 9841031

TABLE 13 - 5: Inadvertent Termination Relief Involving Passive Investment Income

An S corporation's new accountant discovered accumulated earnings and profits. Corporation had excessive passive investment income for three years. Corporation immediately paid dividend with §1368(e)(3) election. IRS held inadvertent termination.	PLR 8952033

Late discovery of accumulated earnings and profits, with more than 25% gross receipts from passive sources, was inadvertent termination.	PLRs 8848065, 8937006, 9342020, 9602008
A corporation made an ineffective election to distribute its accumulated earnings and profits. It had excess passive investment income. The IRS held the termination inadvertent.	PLR 895204
Mistaken classification of passive gross receipts resulted in inadvertent termination.	PLRs 9253015, 9309014, 9752058
Mistaken projection resulted in passive gross receipts. No evidence of a dividend payout, but IRS granted inadvertent termination relief.	PLR 199910022
S corporation's accounting firm was unaware of corporation's passive investment income.	PLRs 9301016, 9318006, 9335052, 9642015, 9642016, 9817008
S corporation's accounting firm was unaware of rules regarding termination for excessive passive investment income.	PLRs 9322018, 9333034, 9411029
S corporation's accounting firm was aware of passive investment income rules, but did not seek inadvertent termination relief. Corporation filed as a C corporation for three years. Attorney became aware of problem and filed for inadvertent termination relief. IRS allowed corporation to file as S corporation for all years during termination.	PLR 9321038
As a condition of inadvertent termination relief, an S corporation was required to file amended returns with elections to distribute AEP under §1368(e)(3). (See Chapter 7, at 740., for discussion.) In addition, the corporation was required to distribute the remainder of its AEP within 30 days of receipt of a favorable ruling.	PLR 9349017, 199901035 199917070
In several recent rulings, the IRS has permitted inadvertent termination relief for excessive passive investment income, if the corporation and its shareholders would make a deemed dividend election. Thus, in these situations the IRS has permitted deemed dividend elections for years beginning before 1994, in contrast to the general effective date of the deemed dividend election.**	PLRs 9342034, 9342035, 9342036, 9342040* 199906002
Corporation's owners and accountant were unaware that original S election prepared by attorney was not effective, so corporation had been a C corporation for a period of time and thus had accumulated earnings and profits. Three consecutive years of passive investment income resulted in termination of the S election. IRS ruled the termination was inadvertent.	PLR 9545005

---

*These rulings were issued prior to the issuance of Final Regulations that permit the deemed dividend election.

** See Chapter 7, at 740.5., for discussion of the deemed dividend election, which generally applies to years beginning after 1993.

TABLE 13 - 6: Inadvertent Termination Relief Involving Classes of Stock

S corporation had second class of stock unissued. It issued some of this class as a stock dividend, then amended rights of class to eliminate differences.	PLR 9003015
Agreement between shareholders created second class of stock. Agreement was rescinded.	PLR 9322020
Preferred stock was replaced by common stock and notes.	PLR 9432032
At incorporation, second class of stock was issued but no distributions or liquidation rights were ever exercised. Termination was inadvertent.	PLR 9843026
Amendment of articles of incorporation to create a second class of stock was inadvertent termination.	PLRs 9608012, 9731027

As Tables 13 - 1 through 13 - 6 indicate, S corporations have been granted relief for nearly every conceivable violation of the Subchapter S eligibility rules. The sheer volume of rulings issued, of which only a small number are cited in this book, indicates that inadvertent termination relief has been a valuable provision for corporations that have innocently violated the complex and confusing requirements of Subchapter S.

> **OBSERVATION:** Ruling requests for inadvertent termination relief must disclose the reason for the termination. In many cases, the corporation represents in the request that it had relied on its tax advisor and believed that the corporation's S election would not be endangered. When an S corporation's inadvertent termination is the result of acting on the advice of the corporation's tax accountant or attorney, the tax professional will need to admit his or her error in the ruling request. The tax professional should not undertake such action without the advice of legal counsel.

13

1350.4. Denial of inadvertent termination relief. Although inadvertent termination relief has been granted for many violations of the Subchapter S eligibility requirements, there are certain situations in which the IRS cannot grant such relief, principally:

- The terminating event occurred before 1983.
- The corporation did not have a valid S election in effect.
- The corporation revoked its S election.

The inadvertent termination rule was added by the Subchapter S Revision Act of 1982. As was the case with most provisions in that legislation, the effective date was for taxable years beginning after 1982. Since prior Subchapter S had no equivalent provision, the IRS has no authority to grant relief where the termination occurred in any year beginning before 1983. [Proposed Regs. §1.1362-5(a). Also see PLR 8832055.]

For the IRS to consider a request for inadvertent termination relief pursuant to a ruling request before August 20, 1996, the corporation must have had a valid S election in effect before the terminating event. As stated in §1362(f)(1), the inadvertent termination provision applies if "*an election under subsection (a)* by any corporation was terminated . . ." [emphasis added]. As was discussed in Chapter 5, a corporation must comply with all eligibility requirements, and must observe the filing dates and consent conditions, before its S election may take effect. The Regulations, which are perhaps more clearly worded, state that the corporation must have had a *valid* S election in effect before the termination. [Regs. §1.1362-4(a)(1)]

OBSERVATION: The Small Business Job Protection Act of 1996 added language to §1362 that allows the IRS to waive defective or late S elections for good cause. The standards are similar to those established for inadvertent termination relief. As with inadvertent termination relief, the provisions apply to taxable years beginning after 12/31/82.

A request for inadvertent termination relief can be considered only when a corporation has lost its eligibility by failing to meet one of the requirements. Again, the wording of the statute is specific, although it may take some careful reading. As stated in §1362(f)(1), the inadvertent termination provision applies if "an election . . . was terminated *under paragraph (2) or (3) of subsection (d)*" [emphasis added]. As discussed earlier in this chapter, there are several ways to terminate an S election. By limiting application of inadvertent termination to terminations under §1362(d)(2) (cessation as a small business corporation) and §1362(d)(3) (excess passive investment income for three consecutive years if the corporation has accumulated earnings and profits), the statute provides no possibility of such relief if the corporation has revoked its S election.

A revocation that occurs under §1362(d)(1) is not a cause for granting inadvertent termination relief. Therefore, an S corporation that has revoked its election, and secured the requisite consents from the holders of a majority of its shares, cannot request inadvertent termination relief, even if the shareholders were completely ignorant of the consequences of their actions.

EXAMPLE 13 - 52: Dumco was an S corporation through May 31, 1992, when it filed a statement that revoked its S election immediately. The corporation acted on incompetent tax advice. When the corporation changed accountants, the new tax advisor determined that Dumco would have benefited substantially from keeping its S election. Dumco cannot apply for inadvertent termination relief. In addition, it is unlikely that the IRS would grant Dumco permission to make a new S election before five taxable years have expired. [§1362(g)] See discussion in Chapter 5. It would require a substantial restructuring of the corporation's business, or a change in the ownership of a majority of its shares, for a quick re-election to be likely. Dumco may have a cause of action against its former tax advisor, but it will not be entitled to any special consideration by the IRS.

There have been few rulings in which the IRS has declined to grant inadvertent termination relief, but they occasionally occur. For instance, an S corporation that waited approximately $2^1/_2$ years after the discovery of a terminating event was denied inadvertent termination relief. The IRS based the denial, in part, on the fact that the corporation had agreed to an audit that terminated the S election and did not take timely action to request relief. [PLR 9309052] In another situation, the corporation was aware of the passive investment income rules It was also aware that it had Subchapter C AEP, and it continued to violate the passive investment income limits for three consecutive years. The IRS declined to grant inadvertent termination relief. [PLR 9403007] The IRS also refused to grant inadvertent termination relief to a corporation that acquired 100% of a subsidiary. The IRS contended that the terminating event was not acquisition of the subsidiary, but the filing of Form 1120, rather than Form 1120S, by the corporation for 8 years. [PLR 9523004]

Finally, since inadvertent termination rulings cover only those situations in which the corporation could properly request a ruling, there is no public record of situations in which a corporation could not properly file a ruling request. For example, there is no record of income tax relief that might have been granted if one or more shareholders had not refused to consent to the necessary adjustments.

1350.5. Summary of inadvertent termination relief. Inadvertent termination relief has become a valuable remedy for S corporations. The relief is not free—recall the $3,000 processing fee due with the submission of a ruling request. It may take from two to six months for the IRS to process a ruling, during which time the corporation and its shareholders are not completely certain of their tax status. It is, however, one of the important tax planning opportunities in all of Subchapter S. The rules are summarized in Figure 13 - 3.

1355. Termination of a QSub (QSSS).

A corporation that terminates its status as a QSub is treated as a new corporation that received all of its assets and liabilities immediately before its termination. [Proposed Regs. §1.1361-5(b)(1)]

1355.1. In General. A termination is most likely to result from one of three causes:

1. The parent corporation terminates its S election.
2. The parent corporation retains its S election but sells or distributes some or all of the QSub stock to other persons.
3. The parent corporation retains its S election but revokes the QSub election of the subsidiary.

There is no need for a split year, as is the case with an S termination year, since the former QSub does not even come into existence for tax purposes until the terminating event. Therefore the new corporation will select its taxable year by the usual rules for C corporations or for S corporations, depending on its status after the termination. See Chapter 5, at 525., for discussion of the reelection and waiting period rules. Also see Chapter 14, at 1435.45., for problems regarding the disposition of a QSub. The topic in connection with a §338 election is covered in Chapter 16, at 1630.38.

The revocation of the election is covered in the Proposed Regulations. In general, the parent S corporation files a statement with the IRS service center where it normally files its returns. [Proposed Regs. §1.1361-3(b)(1)] The revocation identifies both the parent and the QSub and is signed by a corporate officer (of the parent S corporation). The revocation must be made within 2 months and 15 days after the date for which it is to be effective. The corporation may specify a prospective date, not more than 12 months after the date of the filing of the revocation statement. [Proposed Regs. §1.1361-3(b)(2)] An S corporation may not file a retroactive revocation for the QSub after the occurrence of an event that has already invalidated the Qualified Subchapter S Subsidiary status. [Proposed Regs. §1.1361-3(b)(2)]

13

The Proposed Regulations also direct the IRS to allow inadvertent termination relief for QSSS corporations. [Proposed Regs. §1.1361-5(c)] The Proposed Regulations do not contain any statement that would allow relief from an inadvertently defective QSub election or a late election, even if there is reasonable cause.

1360. Practice aids.

The practice aids in this chapter deal with the elections necessary to terminate an election and the simplified procedure for obtaining inadvertent termination relief.

1360.1. Planning for a revocation. As business conditions change, tax professional should always consider the advantages of maintaining, or revoking, an S election. Checklist 13 - 1 provides a list of factors to consider before revoking an election.

1360.2. Revocation statement and consents. Checklist 13 - 2 contains factors that should be considered in a year in which a corporation terminates an S election, either by revocation or by operation of law. The revocation statement must be signed by a corporate officer. It must

Figure 13 - 3: *Inadvertent termination relief.*

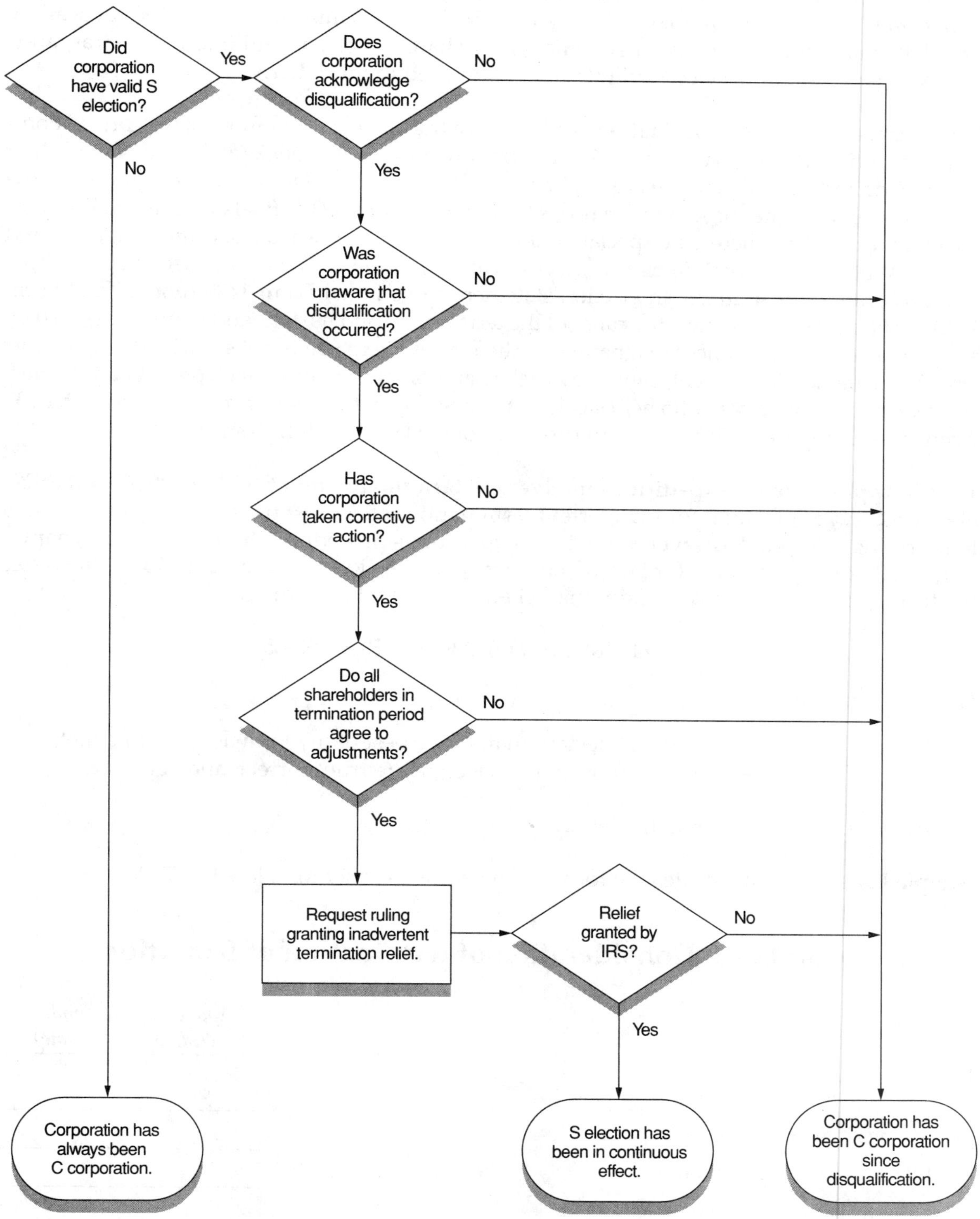

13

state the number of shares issued and outstanding on the date that the statement is filed, including both voting and nonvoting stock. Sample Letter 13 - 1 shows a sample letter revoking an S election. The revocation statement should list all shares, both voting and nonvoting, of which the holders of more than 50% in total must consent to the revocation. This letter also contains consent statements for shareholder use, although the paragraphs indicating consent may be on separate pages, attached to this letter.

1360.3. Election to split S termination year. When a transfer of 50% or more of the corporation's stock occurs in an S termination year, the corporation must close its books at the end of the S short year (a required closing). If there is not a transfer of 50% or more of the corporation's stock in the S termination year, the corporation may elect to close its books on the final day of the S short year (an elective closing). There is no special disclosure necessary for pro rata allocation or a required closing. When the corporation uses an elective closing, however, there is an election procedure. The corporation must attach an election statement to its initial Form 1120 (not its final Form 1120S). The statement contains the cause of the termination and its date, and it must be signed by a corporate officer (the officer's signature on the face of the return is not sufficient). There must also be a statement of consent, signed by each shareholder who held stock on any day of the S short year and any person who held stock on the first day of the C short year. Sample Letter 13 - 2 contains a sample election to close the books as of the last day of the S short year.

1360.4. Application for expeditious inadvertent termination relief for late QSST and ESBT elections. An application for inadvertent termination relief must usually be in the form of a letter ruling request. However, there is an expeditious procedure, discussed in this chapter at 1350.22., to request relief for lack of a timely QSST election. Sample Letter 13 - 3 illustrates the form that must be used to claim this relief. Note that the heading:

FILED PURSUANT TO REV. PROC. 98-55

and the statement:

> Under penalties of perjury, I declare that, to the best of my knowledge and belief, the facts presented in support of this election are true, correct, and complete

should be copied verbatim in the letter.

Sample Letter 13 - 4 illustrates the form for expeditious relief for a late ESBT election.

Checklist 13 - 1: Consideration of termination of S election

	Applicable (Yes/No)	*Completed (Date)*
1. Viability of revocation	______	______
Savings in federal taxes	______	______
Effect of state and local taxes	______	______
Long-term exposure to double tax	______	______
2. Timing of revocation (See Checklist 13 - 2.)	______	______
3. Basis adjustments to absorb		

Copyright © 2000 by Harcourt, Inc. All rights reserved.

	Applicable Completed	
	(Yes/No)	(Date)
S corporation losses		
If loan, must complete before termination.		
If noncash property contribution, must complete before termination.		
4. Disposition of corporate assets		
a. Any unwanted assets?		
Consider distribution or sale to shareholders before double taxation takes effect. (All property distributions will be taxed as dividends after termination.)		
b. Distributions to shareholders		
Only cash may be from AAA in post-termination transition period. Therefore, any notes or other property must be distributed while election is still in effect.		
c. Elections with respect to split year (See Sample Letter 13 - 2.)		

Checklist 13 - 2: Termination of S election

	Applicable (Yes/No)	Completed (Date)
1. Revocation of election		
a. For retroactive:		
i. File within 2 months and 15 days of beginning of taxable year.		
ii. List all shares, voting and nonvoting, and all shareholders.		
iii. Obtain consent statements from holders of more than 50% of stock.		
b. For prospective:		
i. File on or before stated date.		
ii. List all shares, voting and nonvoting, and all shareholders.		
iii. Obtain consent statements from holders of more than 50% of stock.		
2. Termination by disqualification		
a. If inadvertent termination:		
i. Determine if inadvertent termination relief is desired.		
ii. Take or resolve to take corrective action.		
iii. Begin preparing ruling request for inadvertent termination relief.		
iv. Get shareholder agreements on file.		

13

Copyright © 2000 by Harcourt, Inc. All rights reserved.

	Applicable (Yes/No)	*Completed (Date)*
b. If inadvertent termination impossible or not wanted:		
i. If more than 50% stock sold in year, must close books at end of S short year.		
ii. If not more than 50% of stock sold, determine whether pro rata or interim closing is desired.		
(1) If pro rata accounting is desired, no election is necessary.		
(2) If interim closing is desired:		
• Prepare election for signature of officer.		
• Prepare consent for each shareholder during S short year and all shareholders on first day of C short year.		
• File election and consents with final Form 1120S.		

Sample Letter 13 - 1: Revocation of corporation's S election

Revocation of S election under Internal Revenue Code §1362(d)(1)

[Date]

[Company]
[Address]
[City, State ZIP Code]
[FEIN]

[Company] revokes its election under §1362(a) to be an S corporation. Such revocation is to be effective as of [date]. On [date], [Company] had issued and outstanding [number] shares of voting stock and [number] shares of nonvoting stock.

13

____
[Name]
President, [Company]

I am the holder of [number] shares of voting stock in [Company] on [date]. I consent to the revocation of [Company]'s election to be an S corporation under Internal Revenue Code §1362(a) as of [date].

____
[Name]
Shareholder, [Company]

I am the holder of [number] shares of nonvoting stock in [Company] on [date]. I consent to the revocation of [Company]'s election to be an S corporation under Internal Revenue Code §1362(a) as of [date].

____
[Name]
Shareholder, [Company]

Copyright © 2000 by Harcourt, Inc. All rights reserved.

Sample Letter 13 - 2: Election to terminate taxable year

Election to terminate taxable year under Internal Revenue Code §1362(e)(3)

[Date]

[Company]
[Address]
[City, State ZIP Code]
[FEIN]

[Company] elects to treat its taxable year beginning [date] and ending [date] as two taxable years under Internal Revenue Code §1362(e)(3). The first taxable year, within the meaning of §1362(e)(3), begins on [date] and ends on [date]. On that date, [Company] revoked its election under §1362(a) by filing a statement under Internal Revenue Code §1362(d)(1).

The second taxable year, within the meaning of §1362(e)(3), begins on [date] and ends on [date].

____
[Name]
President, [Company]

As a shareholder in [Company] during the corporation's taxable year beginning [date] and ending [date], I consent to the corporation's election under Internal Revenue Code §1362(e)(3) to treat that year as two taxable years.

____
[Name]
Shareholder, [Company]

As a shareholder in [Company] during the corporation's taxable year beginning [date] and ending [date], I consent to the corporation's election under Internal Revenue Code §1362(e)(3) to treat that year as two taxable years.

____
[Name]
Shareholder, [Company]

As a shareholder in [Company] during the corporation's taxable year beginning [date] and ending [date], I consent to the corporation's election under Internal Revenue Code §1362(e)(3) to treat that year as two taxable years.

____
[Name]
Shareholder, [Company]

Copyright © 2000 by Harcourt, Inc. All rights reserved.

Sample Letter 13 - 3: Inadvertent termination relief for failure to file timely QSST election

FILED PURSUANT TO REV. PROC. 98-55

Income beneficiary
[Name]
[Address]
[Tax ID number]

Trust
[Name]
[Address]
[Tax ID number]

Corporation
[Name]
[Address]
[FEIN]

Election to be a qualified Subchapter S trust under §1361(d)(2)

Date stock was transferred to trust [date]______________________

Enclosed are copies of all relevant pages of the trust to demonstrate that the trust satisfies all requirements of §1361(d)(3)(A)(i) through (iv).

Affidavit from trustee stating that all trust income has been distributed no less than annually to the current income beneficiary, if not required to be distributed under terms of the trust:

I, [Name], am trustee of the [name of trust] trust. I affirm that the trust distributes all of its trust accounting income no less than annually to [Name], the current income beneficiary, and that the trust will continue to make such distributions to such beneficiary no less than annually.

____

Signature of trustee

13

I, [Name], am the current income beneficiary of the [name of trust] trust, which received stock in [Company] Corporation on [date]. I affirm that the failure to file an election under §1361(d)(2) within 2 months and 15 days of receipt of the stock was inadvertent.

Upon discovery I acted diligently to file this election.

____

Signature of current income beneficiary [or parent or legal guardian]

I, [Name], am (officer) of the [Company] Corporation. To the best of my knowledge all shareholders whose tax liability would have been affected by the required election under §1361(d)(2) have filed their personal tax returns as if the S election had been in effect for all taxable years including and subsequent to the transfer of stock to the [name of trust] trust.

____

Signature

____

Title

Copyright © 2000 by Harcourt, Inc. All rights reserved.

We, the shareholders of [Company] from [date stock transferred to trust] to [date of this letter], affirm that we have filed our personal tax returns as if the S election had been in effect for all taxable years including and subsequent to the transfer of stock to the [name of trust] trust.

____

Shareholder Signature

____

Shareholder Signature

____

Shareholder Signature

____

Shareholder Signature

____

Shareholder Signature

____

Shareholder Signature

____

Shareholder Signature

Under penalties of perjury, I declare that, to the best of my knowledge and belief, the facts presented in support of this election are true, correct, and complete.

____

Signature of current income beneficiary

____

Date

Encl: pp. [range of pages] of [name of trust] trust.

13

Copyright © 2000 by Harcourt, Inc. All rights reserved.

Sample Letter 13 - 4: Inadvertent termination relief for failure to file timely ESBT election

FILED PURSUANT TO REV. PROC. 98-55

Trust

[Name]
[Address]
[Tax ID number]

Corporation

[Name]
[Address]
[FEIN]

Election to Be an Electing Small Business Trust under §1361(e)

Date stock was transferred to trust [date] ____________________

Enclosed are copies of all relevant pages of the trust to demonstrate that the trust satisfies all requirements of §1361(e).

I affirm that the failure to file an election under §1361(e) within 2 months and 15 days of receipt of the stock was inadvertent.

Upon discovery I acted diligently to file this election.

____

[Signature of trustee]

13

I, [Name], am (officer) of the [Company] Corporation. To the best of my knowledge, all shareholders whose tax liability would have been affected by the required election under §1361(d)(2) have filed their personal tax returns as if the S election had been in effect for all taxable years including and subsequent to the transfer of stock to the [name of trust] trust.

____

[Signature]

____

[Title]

We, the shareholders of [Company] from [date stock transferred to trust] to [date of this letter], affirm that we have filed our personal tax returns as if the S election had been in effect for all taxable years including and subsequent to the transfer of stock to the [name of trust] trust.

____

[Shareholder Signature]

Copyright © 2000 by Harcourt, Inc. All rights reserved.

____
[Shareholder Signature]

____
[Shareholder Signature]

____
[Shareholder Signature]

____
[Shareholder Signature]

____
[Shareholder Signature]

____
[Shareholder Signature]

Under penalties of perjury, I declare that, to the best of my knowledge and belief, the facts presented in support of this election are true, correct, and complete.

____
[Signature of current income beneficiary]

____
[Date]

Encl: pp. [range of pages] of [name of trust] trust.

Copyright © 2000 by Harcourt, Inc. All rights reserved.

Part IV

Relationship to Other Tax and Accounting Rules

CAPITAL STRUCTURE OF THE S CORPORATION

CONTENTS

1400. Overview.

Subchapter S is primarily concerned with the treatment of income, deductions, and distributions while the S election is in effect. Much of the Code in Subchapter S is concerned with qualifications, elections, and termination procedures. It also devotes considerable attention to the corporate-level taxes unique to the S corporation.

Many transactions, however, are not covered directly within Subchapter S, including corporate formations (at 1415.), stock redemptions (Chapter 15, at 1510.), liquidations (Chapter 15, at 1525.), and reorganizations (Chapter 17, at 1735. and 1710.). As a general rule, Subchapter C governs these transactions for all corporations, even those which have an S election in effect. In some cases, Subchapter S is silent; in others, it offers some slight modifications.

Chapter 14 is concerned with the capital structure of an S corporation, as well as the use of S corporations within a larger group of closely held businesses. Principal areas of discussion include establishment and maintenance (at 1415.7.) of the corporation's eligibility for S corporation status.

This chapter begins with a discussion of the transfer of property into a corporation—usually the first event in a corporation's existence.

1410. General applicability of Subchapter C.

Subchapter S has no specific rules governing most of the important transactions discussed in this chapter. There are, however, some specific rules of Subchapter C, dealing with a corporation's capital structure, which are applied instead. With somewhat cryptic language, Subchapter S applies many of the Subchapter C rules to S corporations.

SUMMARY OF AUTHORITY: CODE SECTION 1371(a)

- The rules of Subchapter C generally apply to S corporations.

As of this writing, there have been no Regulations, cases, Revenue Procedures, or published Revenue Rulings interpreting the above statement. The legislative history of the Subchapter S Revision Act of 1982 is silent on the meaning of the phrase "inconsistent with this Subchapter." There have, however, been numerous letter rulings that tend to treat S corporations much like C corporations when Subchapter S is silent.

1415. Contributions of property to the corporation.

When a person transfers property to a corporation in exchange for stock, there is an exchange of one item of property for another. Under general rules of taxation, the fair market value of the property received (stock in the corporation) less the adjusted basis of the property relinquished creates a gain or loss realized by the person contributing the property. [§1001(b)] If there were no exceptions to this rule, it would be impossible to alter the form of a business without the immediate imposition of tax.

There are two areas of general exception to taxability:

- Taxation related to the transfer of property to a partnership in exchange for an interest therein
- Taxation related to a transfer of property to a corporation in exchange for stock

Although full exploration of either subject is beyond the scope of this book, a brief exposure to each is necessary.

Transfers of property to a partnership are relevant later in this chapter, at 1435., where the main concern is the existence of an S corporation within a larger business setting. The transfer of property to a corporation, by contrast, is a matter requiring immediate attention. The taxation of such transfers is of extreme importance in two situations:

- The establishment of a new corporation
- The restructuring of the ownership of an existing corporation

In both instances, the tax professional must be aware that C corporation rules discussed in 1415.1. govern transfers to S corporations. The taxability of such transfers must be examined from two vantage points—that of the corporation and that of the shareholders.

1415.1. Tax-free transfers. It is possible to structure a transfer of property from a shareholder to a corporation as a tax-free event. From the corporation's point of view, nearly any transfer of its own stock in exchange for property is tax-free. A corporation does not recognize gain or loss in dealings involving its own stock. [§1032] This treatment does not depend on the tax consequences to the shareholder. The corporation, however, will need to know the taxability of the shareholder in order to determine its own basis in the property received.

A shareholder who transfers property to a corporation in exchange for stock is not subject to tax on the transfer, if the transfer meets the requirements of §351. It is the only provision that allows shareholders to receive stock in a corporation in exchange for property without recognition of gain or loss.

SUMMARY OF AUTHORITY: CODE SECTION 351(a)

- A shareholder recognizes no gain or loss on certain transfers to a corporation if:
  — The shareholder transfers property
  — The shareholder receives stock in the corporation
  — The shareholder (when his or her shares are combined with the shares owned by other persons who transfer property in the same exchange) is in control of the corporation immediately after the exchange
- The rules of §351 are mandatory, rather than elective.

The rules of §351 apply equally to C corporations and S corporations. This particular Code section does not define the critical terms *property, stock,* or *control. Property* includes real or personal property, tangible or intangible property, and money. *Stock* issued for services is not considered as issued for property. [§351(d)(1)] Nor does it include indebtedness of the corporation (unless evidenced by a security) [§351(d)(2)] or accrued interest from the corporation. [§351(d)(3)] *Control* is defined as ownership of 80% of the total combined voting power of all classes of stock entitled to vote and 80% of total number of shares of all other classes of stock. [§368(c)] When there are two or more transferors (shareholders), the group must collectively be in control of the corporation. [Regs. §1.351-1(a)(1)] A prearranged commitment to divest of the requisite control will invalidate the tax-free exchange. [Rev. Rul. 79-70, 1979-1 CB 144]

> **EXAMPLE 14 - 1:** Fran and George are forming a corporation. Fran contributes property worth $50,000 which had a basis of $30,000. George transfers property worth $50,000 that had a basis of $60,000. Each of the shareholders receives 50% of the stock in the corporation. Since the two persons, in combination, own at least 80% of the stock, the transfer qualifies as a §351 exchange. Fran does not recognize a gain, and George does not recognize a loss. The corporation does not recognize any gain or loss.

OBSERVATION: The rules of §351 are mandatory. Thus gains and losses on contributions generally are unrecognized at the time of the transfer. When a shareholder desires recognition of a loss, the transfer must be carefully planned so that it does not fall within §351. The IRS has considerable latitude in grouping transactions together (known as the "step-transaction" approach), so there must be some real economic divergence from the typical contribution pattern. In some cases, it may be better for a shareholder with high basis property to lease it to the corporation. Beware of selling property to a controlled corporation at a loss. As is discussed in Chapter 8, at 835.1., a loss on the sale of property to a related party cannot be recognized.

There are no attribution rules governing §351, so ownership by parties related to the transferor is not taken into account. The transfer must be "solely" in exchange for stock of the corporation. [§351(a)]

OBSERVATION: For transfers prior to October 2, 1989, transferors could receive securities as nonrecognition property. The Revenue Reconciliation Act of 1989 removed securities from the definition of nonrecognition property. Securities are debt obligations of corporations with maturity of at least ten years. Securities received in the exchange (after October 2, 1989) apparently qualify the transferor for installment recognition.

OBSERVATION: Recent changes to §351 treat certain preferred stock as boot, or recognition property if received in exchange for property. Since S corporations can have only one class of stock, these new rules have no relevance to this book and are not discussed herein.

1415.2. Effects of receipt of other property. In many tax-free or partially tax-free transactions, one or more parties may receive some property that does not qualify for tax-free treatment. In a §351 transfer, the disqualifying property is anything other than stock of the corporation involved. The common term for nonqualifying property is *boot*.

If boot, including corporate debt obligations, is received by any transferor in a transfer of property in a §351 exchange, that person may have to recognize gain on the transfer. The gain recognized by that person is the lesser of gain realized on the exchange or boot received. [§351(b)] Boot (and resulting gain) is apportioned among assets transferred. [Rev. Rul. 68-55, 1968-1 CB 140] No loss is recognized on any exchange covered by §351. [§351(b)(2)]

EXAMPLE 14 - 2: Ferdinand and Imelda are forming the FI Corporation, which will sell shoes. The two persons intend to be equal shareholders. The properties to be transferred by each person are as follows:

Ferdinand:	
Basis	$ 40,000
Fair market value	100,000
Imelda:	
Basis	$ 60,000
Fair market value	110,000

To equalize the two persons' interests, the corporation will issue each shareholder $100,000 worth of stock. The corporation will also issue Imelda a note with a value of $10,000.

Since both persons transferred property, the exchange qualifies under §351. Ferdinand will recognize no gain, since he received nothing but stock. Imelda, however, must recognize $10,000 gain, equal to her boot.

14

When a shareholder receives an obligation of the corporation in addition to stock, the shareholder may be able to defer gain through the use of the installment method. Installment reporting is not available, however, to the extent that any gain recognized on the transfer is depreciation recapture. [§453(i)] Installment gain is accelerated to the shareholder if that shareholder owns more than 50% of stock of the corporation and the corporation sells the property within two years (anytime for marketable securities). [§453(e)]

1415.3. Assumption of liabilities. As a general rule, assumption of liabilities by the corporation is not treated as boot. [§357(a)] Without this rule, it would not be possible to incorporate a business unless it were free of debt.

EXAMPLE 14 - 3: Jules is incorporating his proprietorship. He transfers property with a fair market value of $300,000 and adjusted basis of $200,000. The property is subject to liabilities of $150,000, which the corporation assumes. The liabilities were incurred in the ordinary course of business, and there was no tax-avoidance motive in transferring them to the corporation. Jules receives no property other than stock in the corporation. Jules recognizes no gain on the transfer. The liabilities assumed by the corporation will, however, reduce his basis in the shares received. (See discussion at 1415.4.)

There are two instances in which the assumption of (or taking of property subject to) liabilities does create boot and gain recognition for the shareholder. If the transfer of liabilities lacks a business purpose or has a tax-avoidance motive, §357(b) treats all liabilities transferred from that particular shareholder as boot. This rule does not affect the tax treatment of any other shareholder who is a party to the exchange.

EXAMPLE 14 - 4: Jennifer and Karl are forming the JK Corporation. The properties to be transferred by each person are as follows:

Jennifer:	
Basis	$ 40,000
Fair market value	130,000
Liabilities assumed	30,000
Karl:	
Basis	$ 60,000
Fair market value	140,000
Liabilities assumed	40,000

14

Each shareholder receives $100,000 worth of stock, and the corporation assumes the liabilities of each. All of Jennifer's liabilities were incurred in the ordinary course of her business. Karl, however, had recently refinanced a mortgage and kept $1,000 for his personal use. Since $1,000 of Karl's liabilities were assumed with a tax-avoidance motive, all of the liabilities assumed from Karl are treated as boot. Therefore, Karl recognizes $40,000 gain on the transfer.

CAUTION: When a tax advisor is reviewing a planned transfer of property to a controlled corporation, he or she should be certain that the client has not included any personal liabilities in with the business debt to be transferred. Any personal expenses that will be paid by the corporation will be a transfer of liabilities without a valid business purpose and will thus taint all liabilities transferred by the shareholder.

If there is no tax-avoidance motive for the transfer of liabilities in connection with a §351 exchange but the liabilities assumed from a shareholder exceed that person's basis in all property transferred, there is partial gain recognition. That shareholder treats the excess of liabilities assumed over basis of property as boot and recognizes gain accordingly. [§357(c)] For §357(c) to apply to liabilities in excess of basis, it is not necessary that a corporation formally assume the debt from the shareholders. If the corporation takes property subject to the liabilities, the boot rule of §357(c) applies. [*Doe*, TC Memo 1993-543, 66 TCM 1376] However, if the transfer of liabilities from the shareholder to the corporation is ineffective under state law, there is no boot within the meaning of §357(c). [*Doe v. Comm'r*, 80 AFTR 2d 97-5535 (10th Cir.)]

EXAMPLE 14 - 5: Leann transfers property to a new corporation in exchange for all of the corporation's stock. The details of the transfer are:

Basis	$ 70,000
Fair market value	100,000
Liabilities assumed	80,000

All of Leann's liabilities were incurred in the ordinary course of her business. Since the liabilities assumed by the corporation exceed Leann's basis in the transferred property by $10,000, she must recognize $10,000 of gain on the transfer.

A shareholder who uses the cash method of accounting may transfer unrealized assets and unrealized liabilities to a corporation. In some instances, the amount of liabilities may exceed the shareholder's basis in assets transferred. In this case, the liabilities are not treated as boot. The corporation is allowed to deduct those liabilities when they are paid. [§357(c)(3)]

1415.4. Basis considerations. The deferral of recognition on the exchange causes two basis calculations to reflect the gain not recognized:

1. The corporation acquires a carryover basis in the assets received in the transfer, increased by any gain recognized by the transferor. [§362(a)]

EXAMPLE 14 - 6: Refer to Example 14 - 5. The corporation's basis in the assets transferred from Leann is $80,000, which equals Leann's basis before the transfer plus the gain Leann recognized on the transfer.

2. The basis of the shares received by shareholders is the same as the basis of property they transferred to the corporation, increased by any gain recognized, less shareholder liabilities taken over by the corporation. [§358(a)]

EXAMPLE 14 - 7: Refer to Example 14 - 5. Leann's basis in the new corporation stock is:

Basis of property transferred	$ 70,000
Add gain recognized	10,000
Less liabilities assumed	(80,000)
Basis in shares received	$ 0

EXAMPLE 14 - 8: Marvin transferred property to a corporation in exchange for stock. Marvin's basis in the property was $100,000. He received $150,000 in stock and $10,000 of a corporate debt, and he was relieved of $40,000 of liabilities. Marvin's basis in his shares is:

Basis of property transferred	$100,000
Add gain recognized	10,000
Less boot received	(10,000)
Less liabilities assumed	(40,000)
Basis in shares received	$ 60,000

14

When a shareholder contributes intangible property to a corporation, the basis of the property must be reduced by prior amortization allowed or allowable. Thus the amortization will reduce the shareholder's basis in the stock and the corporation's basis in the intangible asset. [*Spencer*, 110 TC 62 (1998)]

According to the IRS, contribution of a shareholder's personal note to the corporation does not give the shareholder basis. [Rev. Rul. 81-187, 1982-2 CB 167] However, the Ninth Circuit recently held that a shareholder may contribute a personal note in order to avoid gain recognition under §357(c). [*Peracchi v. Comm'r*, 81 AFTR 2d 98-1754 (9th. Cir., 1998), rev'g *Peracchi*, TC Memo 1996-161]

A shareholder may borrow money and contribute it to a corporation in exchange for stock. The shareholder's basis is usually the amount of money paid for the stock. If the shareholder borrows the money on a nonrecourse note, however, pledging the stock as collateral, the shareholder will have no basis in the stock. [Rev. Rul. 80-236, 1980-2 CB 240]

1415.5. Summary of §351. Figure 14 - 1 summarizes the gain, loss, and basis rules of §351 and its related provisions.

1415.6. Collateral issues. Some important issues follow the transfer of property to a corporation. Foremost in the minds of tax advisors should be the corporation's ability to elect S status immediately, as discussed at 1415.7. There are also rules governing accounting methods, especially depreciation, which may be related to a §351 transfer, as follows.

1415.61. Depreciation rules relating to transfers of property. Depreciation rules relating to formations of corporations depend on the taxability of the exchange and on the relative interest held by the shareholder in the corporation. In the years following the Tax Reform Act of 1986, shareholders may be contributing property that was placed in service under the prior ACRS rules.

If the transfer is tax-free, as under §351, the corporation will use the same life and method that the shareholder had used. [§168(i)(7)] If the transfer is taxable, the corporation will most likely be subject to the modified ACRS (MACRS) rules. [§168(f)(5)]

> **OBSERVATION:** Regulations regarding depreciation related to transfers of property have never been issued under either old or new ACRS. Certain Temporary Regulations have been issued to deal with leasing. Regulations for general operation of ACRS were proposed in February 1984, but have never been adopted.

14

1415.62 Other tax attributes. There is no provision requiring or allowing the survival of tax attributes other than depreciation following a transfer of property to a corporation. Therefore, a new corporation must make all of the appropriate elections, such as its accounting method. Chapter 6 discusses several of these elections, including those made directly by shareholders in an S corporation.

In one letter ruling, a sole proprietorship had been using the LIFO inventory method. When the proprietorship incorporated, it made an S election immediately. The proprietor was not required to recapture the LIFO reserve upon the transfer of the inventory to the new corporation. The IRS also held that the corporation would be exempt from the built-in gains tax on the transferred property. [PLR 9039005]

1415.7. Planning for immediate S status. A newly formed corporation that may be eligible for an S election and may benefit from treatment as an S corporation should take steps to be certain that it makes the S election for its first taxable year. It should be certain that it is eligible from the first day of its existence, and it must observe the 2-month, 15-day period for which an S election may be made retroactively.

Figure 14 - 1: *Rules of Section 351.*

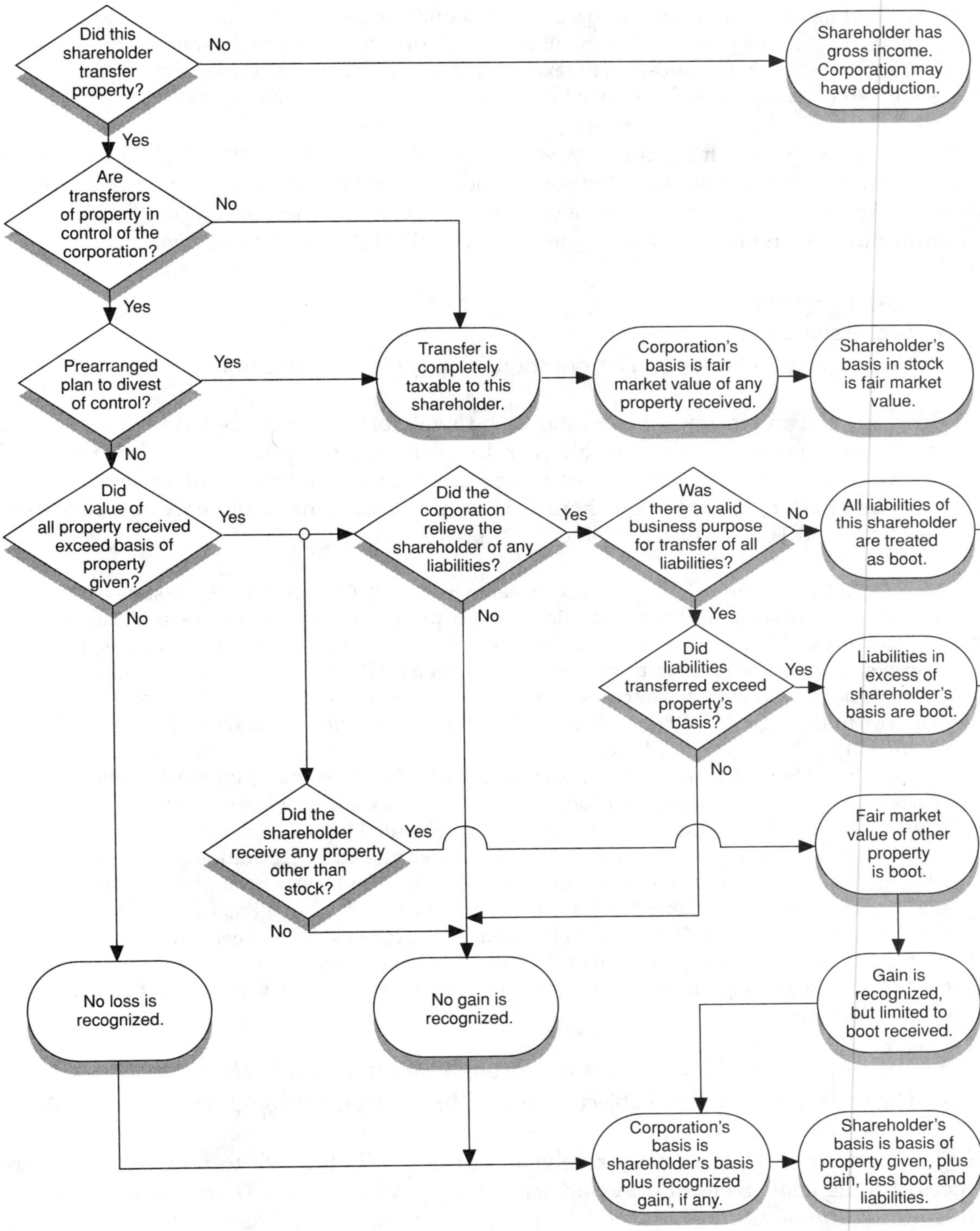

OBSERVATION: If a new corporation is uncertain whether to be an S corporation or a C corporation, it should make an immediate S election. If the corporation later decides it would be better off as a C corporation, it can easily revoke its S election. There are virtually no adverse effects to converting a corporation from S status to C status (except for foreign loss recapture, which is a consideration for few corporations). There are, however, significant drawbacks to postponing an S election beyond the first taxable year. If the corporation does not make an S election that takes effect for its first taxable year, it will begin its life as a C corporation. If it makes an S election that takes effect in any subsequent taxable year, it will be a former C corporation and will be subject to the built-in gains tax for its first 10 years as an S corporation.

1415.71. Timely election for the first year. To make an S election that will take effect for the corporation's first taxable year, the corporation and its tax advisors must be aware of the date on which the corporation's taxable year begins. As mentioned in Chapter 5, at 515., the new corporation's first taxable year begins on the earliest date that the corporation:

- Acquires assets
- Issues shares
- Commences business as a corporation [Regs. §1.1362-6(a)(2)(ii)(C)]

The corporation and its tax advisors should be aware of local statutes that might affect the opening of the corporation's first taxable year. In one case, the applicable state law provided that a corporation was deemed to have issued stock on the date that the state issued the corporation's charter, even though there was no physical transfer of shares on that date. [*William C. Lyle*, 30 TCM 1412, TC Memo 1971-324]

EXAMPLE 14 - 9: Corporation A is incorporated in State X. On July 7, 1992, the state issues the corporation its charter. The corporation does not physically issue any shares until August 31, 1992, on which date the sole shareholder transfers property to the corporation. The shareholder's adjusted basis in the property transferred is $200,000, and the fair market value of the property is $1,500,000. The corporation's tax advisor was not aware of the corporation's existence until August 31, 1992, and believed that the corporation could file an S election on any date up to November 15, 1992.

The laws of State X provide that a corporation legally issues shares on the date that its charter is granted. Accordingly, Corporation A's initial taxable year begins on July 7, 1992. If an S election is to take effect for that year, it must be filed before September 22, 1992.

14

Assume that the corporation files its election to become an S corporation on October 5, 1992, and states that the election is to take effect for its taxable year beginning August 31, 1992, and ending December 31, 1992. The corporation met all qualifications to be an S corporation on October 5, 1992, so the election is valid. However, the election is not timely for the taxable year ending December 31, 1992, and will take effect for the corporation's taxable year beginning January 1, 1993. Among the more significant results of filing the election late are:

- The corporation is a C corporation through December 31, 1992.
- The corporation will be subject to the built-in gains tax through December 31, 2002.

Once a corporation has actually received property, it is too late to remedy the consequences of filing a late S election. A transfer of property back to the shareholders generally results in full double tax, even if the transfer is in complete liquidation of the corporation. [§336] See discussion in Chapter 15, at 1525. A transfer by merger into another corporation will subject the assets transferred to the built-in gains tax for a period of 10 years following the merger. [§1374(d)(8)] (This rule is discussed in Chapter 11. Also see the discussion of tax-free reorganizations in Chapter 17.) There appears to be no remedy for failure to observe the proper beginning of the new corporation's first taxable year.

If a corporation has not received any property by the time the deadline for filing the S election has passed, there may be a simple remedy. The shareholders may apply for a new corporate charter, and transfer the property to the new corporation. The other charter could be revoked, or used for other purposes, as long as an S election was unimportant. Alternatively, the corporation might defer the transfer of any assets with built-in gain potential until the beginning of the next taxable year, for which the S election could be effective. The corporation, which is already a C corporation, could end its taxable year before any property is transferred. The property transfer would then take place after the S election took effect. Either of these techniques would circumvent the corporation's exposure to the built-in gains tax.

EXAMPLE 14 - 10: The laws of State Z provide that a corporation issues stock on the day the corporation's charter is granted. On April 17, 1992, Corporation M is granted a charter by State Z. According to Regulations §1.1362-6(a)(2)(ii)(C), M's taxable year began on that date. Therefore, the corporation must file an S election by July 1, 1992, for the election to be in effect for M's first taxable year.

As of July 15, the shareholders have transferred no property into the corporation. They consult with their tax advisor, who checks on the date of incorporation. The advisor informs the shareholders that the corporation has missed its opportunity to become an S corporation for its first taxable year. The advisor suggests two plans:

- The corporation could prepare complete books and records for its taxable year beginning April 17, 1992. It could terminate the year on the last day of any month. If it selected a June 30 year end, for example, the corporation could begin a new year on July 1, 1992, file a timely S election for that year, and transfer property from the shareholders in that year.
- The shareholders could apply for another charter. When that charter is received, they could transfer property to the new corporation and file a timely S election.

When a corporation issues shares by operation of law, the corporation should be careful to ascertain the identity of all shareholders. It must obtain the consent of each shareholder who is treated as owning shares under state law. If the standing of any shareholder is in doubt, that person should consent to the S election. If it was ultimately determined that the questionable party was not a shareholder, the consent would be superfluous but would not endanger the S election. If that person were ultimately determined to be a shareholder, but his or her shares were not listed on Form 2553, the election would be invalid.

1415.72. Immediate eligibility for S status. The corporation and its tax advisors should be certain that the corporation is eligible for an S election from the beginning of its initial taxable year. It should not only ascertain the identity of the shareholders, but also make sure that each is eligible to hold stock in an S corporation.

EXAMPLE 14 - 11: Sally Talbot owns all of the shares in Salco, a C corporation. She intends to transfer some of Salco's assets, along with some other business property, into Talco, a corporation yet to be formed. Sally has no intention of making an S election for Salco. She does intend to make an immediate S election for Talco.

The property that she wants to transfer from Talco has basis of $50,000 and fair market value of $75,000. Sally realizes that this property cannot be transferred from one corporation to another without recognition of gain. She has two possible courses of action with respect to the property to be transferred from Salco to Talco. Salco could transfer the property directly to Talco, in exchange for Talco stock, then distribute the Talco stock to Sally. Alternatively, Salco could distribute the property to Sally, who would then contribute the property to Talco in exchange for stock.

The first course of action would not invalidate the §351 incorporation, but it would have two serious drawbacks. First, Talco would take Salco's basis of $50,000, rather than the fair market value of $75,000. Upon receipt of the stock as a distribution from Salco, Sally would take a fair market value basis of $75,000 in the stock she received. The second problem is more onerous. Since Salco, a corporation, would be a shareholder in Talco at some time during Talco's first taxable year, Talco could not make an S election for that year. Talco would be subject to the built-in gains tax on the property received from Salco.

The second plan would allow Sally and Talco to avoid both problems. When Salco transfers the property to Sally, Talco would recognize gain on the transfer, but the gain would be no greater than Talco would have recognized on the transfer under the first plan. Sally would have dividend income in the same amount as under the first plan. She would then contribute the property to Talco, and Talco would receive a fair market value basis in the property. Sally would also receive fair market value as her stock basis. Salco would never own any of Talco's stock. Therefore, Talco would be eligible to be an S corporation from the first day of its existence.

Another potential trap with a §351 transfer relates to the classes of stock issued by the corporation. In one case, a corporation that had received cash from some shareholders and property from others was found to have a second class of stock, even though the shareholders all intended for there to be a single class of stock. The applicable state law required that all shareholders who had contributed cash were entitled to a preference in liquidation over those shareholders who had contributed other property. [*Paige v. U.S.*, 78-2 USTC 9702 (9th Cir.)]

EXAMPLE 14 - 12: Norma, Oliver, and Pauline are intending to incorporate a business. Norma will contribute property, whereas Oliver and Pauline will contribute only cash. The shareholders have no intention of issuing any shares with different rights, and they want the corporation to be an S corporation. Their home state requires that, upon liquidation of the corporation, any shareholder who contributes cash must be able to recoup his or her investment before any shareholder who contributes property other than cash.

They cannot incorporate in their home state and be eligible for the S election. Therefore, they should select another state for incorporation.

1415.8. Structuring a transfer for basis step-up. Usually, a corporation and its shareholders will structure a transaction so that it qualifies under §351, to avoid immediate gain recognition. On some occasions, however, especially when the corporation is an S corporation, the basis considerations may dominate the taxation of the initial transfer. Consider the following examples.

14

EXAMPLE 14 - 13: Allen and Beulah are forming AB Corporation. AB will make an immediate S election. The contributions are:

	Property	*Basis*	*FMV*
Allen	Cash	$10,000	$10,000
Beulah	Land	$10,000	$50,000

The property received by Allen and Beulah is:

	Property	*Basis*	*FMV*
Allen	Stock	$10,000	$10,000
Beulah	Stock	$ 2,000	$10,000
	Securities	$ 8,000	$40,000

If the transfer were made prior to October 2, 1989, or if Beulah had received additional stock instead of the securities, no gain would be recognized to any party at time of formation.

The basis of land to the corporation would be $10,000. Under current law, the securities constitute boot to Beulah and would cause recognition of $40,000 gain.

The only way to accomplish the transfer without recognition of gain would be to give Beulah $50,000 worth of stock. That would give Beulah considerably more stock than Allen, which might not be what the parties desire. The corporation could issue an equal number of voting shares to each party and issue nonvoting shares to Beulah to compensate her for her greater contribution of property.

AB Corporation is a real estate dealer. Assume that the corporation sells the land. Gain recognized to the corporation is $40,000 and will be ordinary income. The income will be allocated to each shareholder in accordance with his or her percentage ownership in the corporation.

The parties in this case may benefit from the gain recognition. Accordingly, the corporation might want to issue debt to Beulah, in accordance with the initial plan. The debt received by Beulah would be an installment obligation and would allow her to defer her gain on the transfer.

Beulah will also recognize $32,000 of capital gain when the securities she received from the corporation are redeemed. The effects of the transaction under this scenario are as follows:

	Property	*Basis*	*FMV*
Allen	Cash	$10,000	$10,000
Beulah	Land	$10,000	$50,000

The property received is:

	Property	*Basis*	*FMV*
Allen	Stock	$10,000	$10,000
Beulah	Stock	$10,000	$10,000
	Notes	$40,000	$40,000

The basis of land to the corporation is $50,000.

Beulah recognizes $40,000 gain upon the transfer of the property to the corporation. Under the installment method, Beulah recognizes the gain when the corporation pays off the notes. If Allen and Beulah are not related, gain to Beulah will not be accelerated upon sale of the land by the corporation.

There are some cautions to be observed:

- If Allen and Beulah are related, Beulah would own (actually and constructively) a majority of the stock of the corporation. [§267(b)] See discussion in Chapter 8. In this case, if the corporation sold the land within two years of receipt from Beulah, she could not treat the initial transfer as an installment sale. [§453(e)]
- Installment treatment would not be available to the extent of any depreciation recapture on the property transferred by Beulah. [§453(i)]

1415.9. Incorporation of a partnership. A partnership that plans to incorporate must observe all eligibility requirements if it intends to be an S corporation for its first taxable year as a corporation. Revenue Ruling 84-111 respects three different forms of incorporation [Rev. Rul. 84-111, 1984-2 CB 88]:

- Distribution followed by contribution. The order of the transactions is:
  - — The partnership distributes all assets to its partners.
  - — The partners contribute the distributed property to the corporation in exchange for stock.

  Assuming all of the partners are eligible to hold shares in an S corporation, the corporation could file an immediate S election.

- Transfer directly from shareholders to the corporation. The order of the transactions is:
  — All of the partners transfer their partnership interests to the corporation in exchange for its stock.
  — The partnership is dissolved by operation of law since there is only one owner.
  Assuming all of the partners are eligible to hold shares in an S corporation, the corporation could file an immediate S election.
- Transfer directly from partnership to corporation. The order of the transactions is:
  — The partnership transfers all of its assets in exchange for stock.
  — The partnership then distributes the stock to partners in the liquidation of partnership interest.

The third situation described above puts the partnership in control of the corporation at time of transfer. The IRS holds, in Revenue Ruling 84-111, that the immediate liquidation of the partnership does not violate the control requirement of §351. Note, however, that the partnership is a shareholder in the corporation. The ability of the new corporation to make an S election is in question. In a similar situation, the IRS disregarded momentary ownership by a partnership and allowed an S election. [PLRs 8926016, 9421022]

In any of these transactions, the partners may have negative capital accounts. Upon incorporation, the transfer of liabilities to the corporation may result in the receipt of boot and recognition of gain under §357(c). Although the gain recognized may not differ among these three incorporation methods, the basis of property to the new corporation may be affected by the form of the transfer. Revenue Ruling 84-111 respects the form, as well as the substance, of the transaction.

If the new corporation is never a C corporation, it will not be subject to the built-in gains tax, LIFO recapture, or the passive investment income tax if it makes an S election immediately. If it is a C corporation for any period of time, however, it may be subject to any or all of these taxes.

1420. Contributions to the corporation's capital.

A corporation may receive a contribution to its capital without issuing new shares. Usually, a contribution is made by shareholders who need to shore up the corporation's financial situation. Occasionally, a corporation receives a contribution of property from someone who is not a shareholder. For this second type of transaction, it may be difficult to distinguish a capital contribution from a receipt of income. When a closely held corporation receives a contribution from a person who owns no stock, the economic realities of the transaction may require that it be recognized as a gift.

If property is contributed to the corporation's capital, the corporation recognizes no income. There are special basis rules for property received as a contribution to capital, depending upon the relationship of the transferor to the corporation. This portion of the chapter explores these rules briefly, with a view to the special problems of S corporations.

1420.1. Tax consequences of a contribution to capital. Under general tax rules, a corporation that receives a contribution to capital does not include the contribution in its gross income. [§118] There is one exception, relating to a contribution of the corporation's indebtedness, that is extremely important for S corporations. This rule is discussed below. This portion of the discussion deals with the rules for contribution of other property.

1420.11. Contribution by shareholders. The tax consequences to both the receiving corporation and the contributing shareholder closely resemble the consequences of a transfer in exchange for stock under §351. Neither the corporation nor the shareholder recognizes gain.

The shareholder increases his or her stock basis to reflect the additional contribution. The basis increase corresponds to the amount of money (or the basis in property other than money) contributed. [Regs. §1.118-1. See also *Frantz*, 83 TC 162 (1984).] The corporation's basis in the property received is the same as the shareholder's basis in the contributed property. [§362(a)]

1420.12. Contribution by other entities. An entity other than a shareholder may contribute property to a corporation. Often, a contribution of this nature occurs when a governmental unit seeks to induce an employer to relocate.

> **EXAMPLE 14 - 14:** The citizens of the village of Hoover suffered a serious financial decline when Herbco, a major local employer, closed down. Hoover claimed title to Herbco's property and plant, due to Herbco's failure to pay property taxes. The city council wants to induce Franklin Corporation to locate its manufacturing operations in Hoover. Therefore, Hoover offers Franklin clear title to the property vacated by Herbco.

When a corporation receives property in this manner, the corporation has no gross income, under the general rule. The corporation takes a zero basis in the property received. [§362(c)(1)] If the contributor provides cash to the corporation, the recipient must reduce the basis of any property purchased within the next 12 months, up to the amount of cash received. [§362(c)(2)]

> **EXAMPLE 14 - 15:** Refer to Example 14 - 14. Hoover offers Franklin $100,000 cash to help it remodel the facilities. Franklin accepts the offer. Franklin's basis in the plant is zero. Franklin then purchases $400,000 worth of new equipment. Franklin's basis in the equipment is $300,000.

1420.13. Special problems of S corporations. The treatment of a contribution to capital of an S corporation is not stated directly in the Code. A literal reading of the provisions applicable to contributions to capital leads to a paradox.

As discussed above, the rules of Subchapter C generally apply to S corporations. Accordingly, the basis rules for contributions to capital, which are found at §362, should apply to S corporations as well as C corporations. The general rule for exclusion of income, however, is §118, in Subchapter B. By its literal wording, §118 applies only to *corporations*. Yet, as discussed in Chapter 6, an S corporation computes its taxable income like an individual, not a corporation. Therefore there is no direct link from §118 to S corporations.

The only sensible rule is to allow an S corporation to exclude a contribution to capital from its gross income. This is actually the rule in two situations:

- If the corporation is subject to the built-in gains tax or the passive investment income tax, it must compute its taxable income like a C corporation. (See Chapters 11 and 12 for discussion.)
- The separate rule for contribution of a corporation's indebtedness does apply to S corporations. (See discussion below.)

14

In several cases, the courts have treated debt from a corporation to a shareholder like a contribution to capital. [*W. C. Gamman*, 46 TC 1 (1966); *August F. Nielsen Co., Inc.*, 27 TCM 44, TC Memo 1968-11; *Amory Cotton Oil v. U.S.*, 72-2 USTC 9714 (5th Cir.)] These cases were decided before the Subchapter S Revision Act of 1982, however, and have no direct bearing on the problem. One major aspect of the Subchapter S Revision Act of 1982 was to require S corporations to calculate taxable income like partnerships do. There is no express rule in partnership tax law that deals with contributions to capital, for which the contributor receives no interest in the partnership. The IRS, however, has privately ruled that a partnership may exclude a contribution to capital from its gross income just as a corporation does. [PLR 8038037] The IRS has followed this sensible policy with respect to S corporations. [PLR 8303018]

> **OBSERVATION:** Exclusion of a contribution to capital from the gross income of an S corporation is a logical and sensible policy. Unfortunately, the Code and Regs. under Subchapter S, as well as §118 and its sole Regulation, are completely silent on this issue. An S corporation cannot be certain of obtaining this tax treatment without obtaining a ruling.

1420.2. Contribution distinguished from other transactions. A contribution to capital must be voluntary and must not involve the issuance of new shares. [Regs. §1.118-1] The determination of a contribution, as opposed to another type of transaction, is a question of fact, rather than law, and cases with similar facts may have different outcomes. Typically, a payment from a customer is gross income, even if it is not the result of a direct sale of products or services. For example, discount stores that require membership fees are required to include those fees in gross income. [*Affiliated Government Employees' Distributing Co. v. U.S.*, 63-2 USTC 9707 (9th Cir.); *Federal Employees' Distributing Co. v. U.S.*, 63-2 USTC 9712 (9th Cir.)]

In some cases, a contribution is in the nature of a gift. This situation arises most often in a family-owned business. When a person makes a gift directly to a corporation, it is usually for the benefit of the shareholders. The federal gift tax Regulations treat such a contribution as a gift to the shareholders in proportion to their ownership of the corporation. [Regs. §25.2511-1(h)(1)]

> **EXAMPLE 14 - 16:** Moses, Jerome, and Sherman are three brothers who own equal numbers of shares in Threeco. There are no other shareholders. Their mother contributes $120,000 directly to Threeco in order to help her sons' business. Given the relationship of the parties, the mother has made a gift of $40,000 to each of her sons.

1420.3. Corporate debt contributed to capital. Contributions of a corporation's debt to capital are not covered by the general rule discussed above. Under general tax rules, any taxpayer who settles a debt for an amount less than its face value realizes income from discharge of indebtedness. [Regs. §1.61-12(a)] Therefore, a contribution of indebtedness to capital could result in income to the corporation. In one sense, the corporation has satisfied debt for no consideration, when a shareholder-creditor gives the corporation's obligation back and receives no property in exchange.

From a shareholder's perspective, however, it would be inequitable to treat the corporation as having been gratuitously forgiven its debt. The shareholder would not be entitled to a deduction for a contribution of debt to the corporation, but instead would increase his or her stock basis in the amount of the property (debt) contributed to the corporation.

There is another alternative to treating debt from a shareholder-creditor as a contribution to capital. A corporation could exchange new shares for the debt. As long as the shares had a fair market value equal to the face amount of the debt, the corporation would not have any forgiveness-of-debt income [§108(e)(10)(A)], and it would make little sense to treat a corporation as having recognized income from the contribution of debt to capital. Accordingly, §108(e)(6) states that when a corporation receives debt owed to a shareholder as a contribution to capital, the corporation is treated as having satisfied the debt with an amount equal to the shareholder's basis in the debt.

> **EXAMPLE 14 - 17:** Bill and Al are equal shareholders in Campaign Corporation, an S corporation. Campaign has no other shareholders. In the past, each of the two shareholders had loaned the corporation $10,000. The debt basis of each shareholder-creditor had been

reduced to zero, due to the corporation's losses in earlier years, but subsequent profits have increased each shareholder's basis back to $10,000.

Both shareholders live in a state that imposes an income tax on certain investment income, such as interest, but does not impose a tax on the income that flows through from S corporations. The two shareholders have agreed to give the corporation back the two debts, so that they no longer have any interest income.

They could choose one of two structures for the transaction. They could have the corporation issue stock with a fair market value of $10,000 to each shareholder, or they could take no new stock and contribute the debt back to capital. Since Bill and Al are the only shareholders, there is no essential economic difference between the two methods of extinguishing the debt.

Under either alternative, each shareholder would increase his basis in Campaign stock by $10,000. In either case, the corporation would not have income from discharge of indebtedness.

This rule does not apply to debt contributed by nonshareholders. Thus, unless the corporation is bankrupt or insolvent, it will have gross income from the cancellation of such debt. (The rules of §108, to the extent that they have special applicability to S corporations, are discussed in Chapter 6.) The person who forgives the debt, however, is likely to be entitled to claim a bad debt deduction.

When a corporation receives its own debt as a contribution to capital, it must be aware of the shareholder's basis in the debt, since such basis is treated as the amount paid by the corporation to discharge the debt. In many cases, the shareholder's basis will be the same as the face value of the debt. In some instances, however, the shareholder's basis will be less than the face value. There are three general causes of such a differential:

- The debt could be the result of an installment sale of property from the shareholder to the corporation, where the shareholder has deferred recognition under the installment sale provisions of §453.
- The debt could be a security issued in a §351 exchange before October 2, 1989, at which time securities were nonrecognition property and received a substituted basis.
- The shareholder could have reduced debt basis due to the pass-through of losses, if the borrower is an S corporation.

If the shareholder's basis in the debt is less than its face amount, due to either of the first two causes, the corporation will have income from discharge of debt. The income to the corporation will be the face amount of the debt, less the shareholder's adjusted basis in the debt.

EXAMPLE 14 - 18: Ross owns all of the stock in Peroco, an S corporation. In 1990, he sold the corporation property with a basis of $350,000,000 and received a note of $1,000,000,000 in exchange. The note bore interest at a reasonable rate. The corporation was to pay the principal in full in the year 2000. The sale qualified for installment sale treatment. Therefore, Ross' basis in the note is $350,000,000. In 1993, Ross decides that he really doesn't need the money and the corporation has better uses for the interest it is paying annually, so he contributes the note to the corporation. The corporation is treated as having satisfied a debt of $1,000,000,000 in the amount of $350,000,000, and it recognizes income of $650,000,000. This income passes through to Ross, the sole shareholder, who adjusts his basis in his Peroco stock.

If the shareholder's adjusted basis in the debt is less than its face amount, due to the pass-through of losses from an S corporation, those particular basis adjustments are ignored. [§108(d)(7)(C)] Therefore, the corporation recognizes no income when a shareholder contributes debt to the corporation's capital if the only basis reduction is due to losses in prior S corporation years.

EXAMPLE 14 - 19: Hillary is the sole shareholder in Tipco, an S corporation. In 1990, the corporation was sustaining substantial losses, so Hillary loaned the corporation $50,000. The losses in that year reduced her debt basis to $15,000. In 1991, the corporation continues to be in a cash-flow crunch, and Hillary wants to remove the $50,000 debt from the corporation's balance sheet as well as relieve the corporation of its obligation to make interest payments. To achieve this, in 1991 Hillary contributes the note to Tipco and receives no additional stock. Hillary will report no income or loss from the contribution and will increase her stock basis by $15,000. Tipco will be treated as having satisfied its debt for $50,000, which is the same as Hillary's basis in the debt except for the adjustments for the 1990 losses.

OBSERVATION: The tax rules regarding the contribution of debt to an S corporation's capital by a shareholder are well structured and sensible. A shareholder-creditor who has reduced his or her basis in the debt due to the S corporation's losses is able to contribute the debt to the corporation's capital without any recognition of gain and will increase stock basis for his or her basis in the debt. The corporation's tax treatment mirrors that of the shareholder's: It reports no income, and it increases its paid-in capital by the shareholder's basis in the debt of which it is relieved.

CAUTION: A contribution to capital, including a contribution of debt, to the corporation will give the shareholder additional basis to protect the deduction of losses, or the classification of distributions as tax-free. See Chapter 9, at 935.4. As is discussed below, at 1430.41., a contribution of capital will not give the shareholder additional basis for §1244 loss purposes.

1425. Debt and equity classification problems.

Most corporations have both debt and equity in their capital structures. As long as the shareholders and the creditors are not the same persons, there is usually no problem in distinguishing the two forms of financing. It has been a common practice of many closely held corporations to issue some debt to the shareholders, in addition to their equity interests. Reasons for issuing debt to shareholders include the following:

- Payment of interest to a shareholder-creditor is deductible to the corporation, whereas a payment in respect of stock is a nondeductible dividend.
- Redemption of principal of a debt is usually a tax-free exchange, whereas a redemption of stock may be taxable as a dividend.
- If the corporation becomes worthless, a creditor may have a bad-debt deduction, whereas a shareholder will typically have a capital loss.

The issuance of debt by a new corporation was probably more common before October 2, 1989, than it is today. Until that date, a corporation could issue securities in a §351 transfer, and the shareholder did not treat the securities as boot. The 1989 change to §351 was probably motivated by a desire on the part of Congress to discourage the use of excessive debt.[1]

There are two ways to mitigate the adverse consequences of an equity investment. The first is an S election, which will allow the shareholder to avoid dividend treatment on amounts received from the corporation. The second is qualification of stock under §1244, which will allow a shareholder an ordinary loss deduction if the corporation becomes worthless.

1425.1. General considerations for S corporations. The shareholders of an S corporation can deduct losses as they are incurred by the corporation. Therefore, the debt and equity considerations may not be as important for an S corporation as they are for a C corporation. There are certain situations, however, in which an S corporation uses the same planning techniques as a C corporation:

---

[1]There is no legislative history to the 1989 change.

- The S corporation may be subject to the built-in gains tax or the passive investment income tax, and it may save corporate-level taxes by paying interest rather than by making distributions. (See Chapter 11 for discussion of the built-in gains tax and Chapter 12 for discussion of the passive investment income tax.)
- The corporation may be subject to state or local taxes on its own income. Such taxes can be reduced by paying interest, but not by making distributions of income.
- A shareholder may be subject to a state or local tax on distributions from S corporations, but not subject to tax on the repayment of a debt.
- One shareholder may be willing to risk investment in a corporation only if he or she has a preference in distribution and liquidation rights. Since this cannot be accomplished by issuing preferred stock, a corporation may issue debt to a shareholder to attain this result.

In some jurisdictions, shareholders may be subject to tax on interest income, but not other forms of income. In these situations, the shareholders improve their state tax consequences by structuring the corporation's capital with all equity and no debt.

As a general proposition, taxpayers prefer to load a corporation's capital structure with debt. The IRS, by contrast, often seeks to reclassify debt as equity. If the corporation under examination is a C corporation, the IRS usually hopes to disallow a corporate-level interest deduction. When the corporation involved is an S corporation, the IRS has sought to find that the corporation has a second class of stock. There are other potential risks. For instance, the holder of a debt instrument may be ineligible to hold shares in an S corporation. Reclassification of the debt as equity may cause the corporation to lose its S election by virtue of having an ineligible shareholder.

EXAMPLE 14 - 20: Lenco, a corporation, lends $100,000 to Borco, an S corporation. Borco is highly leveraged and has no equity. Lenco's terms are much more generous than loans that are available in the market. If the IRS were to recharacterize the loan as equity, it could treat Lenco as a shareholder, rather than as a creditor. Since Lenco is ineligible to be a shareholder in an S corporation, Borco would lose its S election.

There may be advantages to structuring financing as stock, rather than debt, when the corporation is an S corporation. As is discussed in Chapter 8, at 845.3, loans must bear interest not less than the applicable federal rate. If the corporation does not pay interest, it may be imputed under §7872. This provision is a bookkeeping nuisance, to say the least. By contrast, an equity investment does not necessitate any regular payments.

In other circumstances, the corporation may want to present a healthy balance sheet to potential investors or independent lenders. The corporation is more likely to obtain favorable terms when it can present a strong equity position to these parties.

1425.11. Treatment of debt as second class of stock. There is always a possibility that reclassification of a debt instrument as equity will create a second class of stock. Cases on this issue were discussed extensively in Chapter 2, at 225.7. The IRS met with some early successes in these cases, but with unmixed failure thereafter. The Subchapter S Revision Act of 1982 contained the safe harbor for straight-debt instruments, in part to protect taxpayers from a renewed effort by the IRS to litigate this issue. [§1361(c)(5)] In May 1992, the IRS issued Final Regulations §1.1361-1, which provides for other safe harbors under which debt will not create a second class of stock. The class-of-stock issue was discussed extensively in Chapter 2 and is not repeated in this chapter. It is also mentioned in Chapter 16 as it relates to financing a purchase of an S corporation.

1425.12. Bad debt deduction to shareholder-creditors. The IRS has also been successful in reclassifying debt as equity in order to deny a shareholder a bad-debt deduction. Occasionally, the IRS has prevailed on this issue when the lender was a shareholder and the borrower was an S corporation. [Cf. *Miles Production Co. v. Commissioner*, 72-1 USTC 9331 (5th Cir.)] This risk of reclassification is discussed in Chapter 8. As a practical matter, few S corporation shareholders should be troubled by this particular risk, since this problem usually arises when a corporation is in serious financial trouble and incurs losses that pass through to the shareholder-creditor. The shareholder-creditor's basis in all stock and debt has often been reduced to zero for the corporation's losses, which makes the deduction of a loss on disposition a moot point.

A recent case illustrates several of the factors the IRS uses to distinguish debt from equity. In *Sutherland,* several shareholders had loaned money to an ailing S corporation. [*Sutherland,* 58 TCM 1117, TC Memo 1991-619] The shareholder-creditors had claimed a bad-debt deduction when the corporation failed. The Tax Court held that the purported debts were really contributions to capital, rather than valid debts. Therefore, the shareholders were limited to a capital loss on the worthlessness of stock, rather than an ordinary deduction for a bad debt. The court based its conclusion on the following factors:

1. The loans provided the corporation with essential working capital.
2. Repayment was expected to come from business profits.
3. The terms of the debts were ignored, and the corporation had not met the schedule of principal and interest payments.
4. The shareholder-creditors had made no attempt to enforce the terms.
5. The corporation had a high debt/equity ratio.
6. The notes were unsecured and subordinated.
7. The corporation could not obtain funds from outside lenders.

In rare cases, the IRS has treated a loan to a corporation from a lender who is not a shareholder as a loan made to the shareholder, followed by a contribution to the corporation's capital by the shareholder. [*Plantation Patterns, Inc., v. Commissioner*, 72-2 USTC 9494 (5th Cir.), cert. denied] In one recent case, the IRS prevailed in reclassifying debt as equity when the borrower was an S corporation and the lender was a C corporation that was under substantial control of the shareholders of the S corporation. [*Georgia Cold Storage Company v. U.S.*, 90-2 USTC 50,450 (M.D. Ga.)] In that case, the court disallowed the interest deduction to the S corporation. The case did not address the possibility of disallowing the S election, even though the equity holder was a corporation. In most cases, however, the IRS has limited reclassification to loans made directly by a shareholder to a corporation.

If a shareholder is successful in claiming a bad debt for a loan to a worthless S corporation, the deduction may be an ordinary loss or a capital loss. If it is a business bad debt, it is an ordinary deduction. If it is a nonbusiness bad debt, it is treated as a short-term capital loss. See Chapter 6, at 610.54., for a brief discussion of the distinction between the two types of bad debts. An individual shareholder (including an estate or trust) is subject to the same rules as is an S corporation in making this determination.

Recently, the Tax Court ruled that bad debts from S corporations to their controlling shareholders entitled the shareholders to bad debt deductions. The Court also held, however, that the deduction was a nonbusiness bad debt. [*Boatner*, TC Memo 1997-379; *Kaiser*, TC Memo 1998-264]

1425.2. Statutory classification rules. In 1969, Congress decided to address the debt and equity problem by statute. The Tax Reform Act of 1969 added Code §385, which was intended to give the IRS authority to give definitive rules on the subject.

SUMMARY OF AUTHORITY: CODE SECTION 385

- Section 385 authorizes the IRS to prescribe Regulations that distinguish debt from equity.
- Section 385 lists five factors that the IRS may consider in writing those Regulations.
- Section 385 does not attempt to define *debt* and *equity* in the absence of Regulations.

In the early 1980s the IRS made several attempts to issue Regulations under §385. Each draft of the Regulations was met with substantial criticism. On August 5, 1983, the IRS withdrew the §385 Regulations. [T.D. 7920, 1983-2 CB 69] As of this writing, there has been no attempt to introduce any subsequent Regulations on the topic.

1425.3. Areas of litigation. There is an extensive history of cases that distinguish debt and equity. Various courts have set forth factors to be considered in making the distinction. Among the most important are:

- The designation of the certificates evidencing the indebtedness
- The presence or absence of a maturity date
- The source of the payments
- The right to enforce the payment of principal and interest
- The creditor's participation in management
- The creditor's status being equal to or inferior to that of regular corporate creditors
- The intent of the parties
- "Thin" vs. adequate capitalization
- Creditor and stockholder are the same, or different, persons
- Source of interest payments
- The ability of the corporation to obtain loans from outside lending institutions
- The extent to which the advance was used to acquire capital assets
- The failure of the debtor to repay on the due date or to seek a postponement [Cf. *Texas Farm Bureau v. U.S.*, 84-1 USTC 9247 (5th Cir.).]

As stated quite sensibly by the Supreme Court in the landmark case *John Kelley Co. v. U.S.*, there is no one factor that distinguishes debt from equity. [*John Kelley Co. v. U.S.*, 46-1 USTC 9133 (S. Ct.)] It is perhaps most important to be aware of situations in which taxpayers have prevailed or lost on each of these issues.

1425.31. Thin capitalization. The absence of any risk capital may lend credence to the reclassification of debt as equity. In some cases, the lack of other equity capital appeared to influence a court's decision that purported debt was in fact equity. [*Henderson v. U.S.*, 65-2 USTC 9598 (Mid. D. Ala.); *W.C. Gamman*, 46 TC 1 (1966)] In other instances, courts have respected the form of debt, even though the corporation was thinly capitalized. [*Byerlite Corp. v. Williams*, 61-1 USTC 9138 (6th Cir.); *Austin Village v. U.S.*, 70-2 USTC 9620 (6th Cir.); *Piedmont Corp.*, 68-1 USTC 9189 (4th Cir.); *Mills v. IRS*, 88-1 USTC 9180 (4th Cir.)] 14

1425.32. Loans in proportion to stock. Loans held in proportion to shareholdings are more likely to be subject to equity classification than loans held in part by shareholders and in part by others. Indeed, if any portion of a debt is held by persons who are not shareholders, the corporation may be able to use this fact in its defense. [*Mills v. IRS*, 88-1 USTC 9180 (4th Cir.); *Baker Commodities*, 69-2 USTC 9589 (9th Cir.); *Jaeger Auto Finance Co. v. Nelson*, 61-1 USTC 9465 (DC Wis.)] In some cases, however, loans in proportion to shareholdings have successfully resisted reclassification as equity. [*Milton T. Raynor*, 50 TC 762 (1968)]

For the proportionality test, a court may consider a loan by a related party to a shareholder as a loan made by the shareholder. Courts do not always agree to this treatment, however. Especially when the parties are independent adults, the courts tend to not force attribution of ownership. [*Proctor Shop, Inc.*, 36-1 USTC 9203 (9th Cir.); *McDermott*, 13 TC 468 (1949); *Curry*, 43 TC 667 (1965); *Hofert Co. v. U.S.*, 69-1 USTC 9220 (CD Cal.)]

1425.33. Lender's business purpose. If the loan is related to the lender's business, rather than being merely an investment in the borrowing corporation, the courts tend to respect the form of the debt. This argument has proved useful in several cases. [*Lots, Inc.*, 49 TC 541 (1968); *Piedmont Corp.*, 68-1 USTC 9189 (4th Cir.); *Baker Commodities*, 69-2 USTC 9589 (9th Cir.)]

1425.34. Consistent treatment by parties. If the parties want a financing instrument treated as debt, *both* the borrower and the lender should treat the instrument as debt, rather than equity, on *both* their financial statements and their tax returns. [*Bauer v. IRS*, 84-2 USTC 9996 (9th Cir.)] There is a general policy that a taxpayer is bound by the tax consequences of the form chosen for the transaction. [*Danielson*, 50 TC 782 (1968)] The position taken on a tax return is more important than that taken on a financial statement and may prove to be decisive. [*Comdisco, Inc., v. U.S.*, 85-1 USTC 9245 (7th Cir.); *Weinert's Estate v. Commissioner*, 61-2 USTC 9644 (5th Cir.)] When a taxpayer takes a position on its tax return that is inconsistent with the desired tax treatment, the courts are likely to force the taxpayer to abide by the tax consequences of the tax return. [*Illinois Power*, 87 TC 1417 (1986)]

1425.35. Enforcement of terms. Enforcement of the terms of a debt, such as timely payments of principal and interest, may have an important effect on an instrument's classification. Failure of the debtor to make these payments has caused courts to uphold the reclassification of debt as equity. [*Henderson v. U.S.*, 65-2 USTC 9598 (Mid. D. Ala.)] There may, however, be valid reasons for having no fixed payment schedule.

> **CAUTION:** Whenever a client is claiming that debt from the corporation to the shareholder in fact exists, the tax advisor should be certain that the documentation is in place. See Chapter 9, at 920.32., for discussion of cases where a loss deduction was denied on the basis of failure to substantiate the existence of debt. Also see Chapter 8, at 845., for the rules regarding interest on loans between corporations and shareholders. Contemporaneous documentation of properly drawn debt instruments will serve as better evidence on audit than a few self-serving statements.

1425.36. Repayment subject to sale of property. Repayment of a loan may depend upon the sale of property, especially if the loan was a purchase money financing arrangement. If the property is not readily salable, the entire transaction might appear to be an equity investment in the borrowing corporation by the lender. [*Aqualane Shores, Inc., v. IRS*, 59-2 USTC 9632 (5th Cir.)] On the other hand, if the connection between the sale of property and the repayment of the loan is a reasonable business arrangement, the courts have held that the purchase money loan is valid debt. [*Bauer v. IRS*, 84-2 USTC 9996 (9th Cir.); *Hardman v. IRS*, 87-2 USTC 9523 (9th Cir.)] In these circumstances, the taxpayer's case is strengthened if the property is readily salable. [*Sun Properties*, 55-1 USTC 9261 (5th Cir.); *Piedmont Corp.*, 68-1 USTC 9189 (4th Cir.)]

> **OBSERVATION:** This portion of the chapter has provided a brief overview of the issues marking the distinction between debt and equity. It has also discussed some of the risks of reclassification, which are unique to S corporations. Reclassification has been the subject of many court cases, and the courts decide facts, not law, by the very nature of the problem. A tax professional who intends to use substantial amounts of debt in the corporation's capital structure, especially when the debt is issued to persons who are also shareholders, should consult these, and perhaps other, cases, in order to ensure that the corporation's and shareholders' risk of IRS reclassification will be minimized.

1425.37. Loss deduction on guarantee of debt by shareholder. As Chapter 9 discusses extensively, at 920.2., many shareholders have attempted to use their guarantee of an S corporation's debt to establish basis in order to deduct losses passing through from an S corporation. This argument has met with little success. When a shareholder is required to perform on the guarantee and actually pays the corporation's debt, however, the basis is clearly established. [Rev. Rul 70-50, 1970-1 CB 178] The question that may arise when a shareholder pays on the guarantee and then loses his or her investment in the corporation is the character of the loss deduction.

A taxpayer is allowed a deduction for the adjusted basis of any debt that becomes worthless. [§165(b)] If the holder of the debt is not a corporation, the character of the deduction depends on the debt's categorization as a business bad debt or a nonbusiness bad debt. A loss on the worthlessness of a business bad debt is an ordinary deduction in the year of the worthlessness. [§165(a)] A loss on a nonbusiness bad debt, however, is treated as a short-term capital loss. [§165(d)(1)(B)] The Supreme Court has allowed taxpayers to deduct payments of debts on behalf of defunct corporations. [*F. D. Arrowsmith*, 52-2 USTC 9527 (S.Ct.)]

The question most often comes up when a shareholder-creditor is also relying on the corporation for his or her livelihood. If the nature of the guarantee is one that protects the taxpayer's investment, the debt will be treated as a nonbusiness bad debt. If the taxpayer has made the guarantee in order to protect his or her employment, the debt is a business bad debt, and the deduction is allowed in full. On occasion, taxpayers have been allowed ordinary deductions for debts that were paid on behalf of one business in order to protect the debtor's reputation in another business.[2]

The Supreme Court has established the standard that the taxpayer must prove that protecting his or her livelihood was the dominant motive for making the guarantee. [*U.S. v. Generes*, 72-1 USTC 9259 (S.Ct.)] A recent case holds that the burden of proof is on the taxpayer to establish that protection of livelihood, rather than investment, was the dominant motive at the time the guarantee was entered into. [*Garner v. Commissioner*, 93-1 USTC 50,167 (5th Cir.)] Another recent case points out that the classification of the bad debt as a *debt*, rather than an equity investment, may be critical to the determination of a business bad debt deduction. [*Cerbone*, 65 TCM 2425, TC Memo 1993-167]

1425.4. Planning considerations for S corporations. Issuing debt to shareholder-creditors in a C corporation can be an important way to minimize the double taxation of corporate distributions. An S corporation may have less use for this planning technique than a C corporation, but still may face some double taxation. For instance, an interest deduction on debt to a shareholder-creditor may reduce the S corporation's built-in gains tax, passive investment income tax, or state or local income tax liability. However, there are other uses of debt by an S corporation, which can allow it to have some flexibility in financing its operations.

> **CAUTION:** The major caution to be observed by an S corporation that intends to use significant debt financing is to avoid classification of any of its obligations as a second class of stock, which would thereby terminate its S election. An S corporation will eliminate this risk by assuring that debt instruments meet the statutory definition of *straight-debt safe harbor*. As discussed in Chapter 2, at 225.72., such debt must be written, must have interest rates and payment dates that are not within the corporation's discretion, must not be convertible into stock, and must be held by a person eligible to be a shareholder in an S corporation. [PLR 9308006] An S corporation will find debt a useful way to provide certain persons with priorities to current and liquidating distributions.

---

[2]The most amusing case in point is *Harold L. Jenkins*, 47 TCM 238, TC Memo 1983-667. Mr. Jenkins, also known as Conway Twitty, satisfied some debts relating to a defunct restaurant business, in order to protect his reputation in the country music business.

EXAMPLE 14 - 21: Regina and Sam are forming the RS Corporation, which will be an S corporation. The two individuals intend to be equal shareholders with respect to profits, losses, and voting power. Sam has only $10,000 to invest, whereas Regina will contribute $110,000 to the corporation. Both shareholders believe that Regina should be able to withdraw an annual return on her investment before the corporation splits the profits between the two shareholders. Regina also wants to receive the first $100,000 of assets, in the event that the corporation liquidates or sells all of its business.

If the corporation were not concerned with an S election, it could accomplish these objectives by issuing $100,000 of preferred stock to Regina and $10,000 of common stock to each of the two shareholders. Since an S corporation cannot issue any preferred stock, it could issue debt to Regina.

Regina is now entitled to an annual payment of interest and will have priority in liquidation, since she is a creditor of the corporation. RS Corporation should write the debt instrument so that it will be within the straight-debt safe-harbor.

It is not always possible to issue debt that falls within the safe harbor. The most obvious case of the safe harbor not providing protection is when the financing comes from a person not eligible to be a shareholder. The position of the IRS is stated in Regulations §1.1361-1(l)(4)(ii)(A).

SUMMARY OF AUTHORITY: REGULATIONS SECTION 1.1361-1(l)(4)(ii)(A)

- Debt (or any other financing arrangement) that does not meet the safe harbor of §1361(c)(5) must meet two criteria to be treated as a second class of stock:
  - — The arrangement must be treated as equity under general principles of federal tax law.
  - — A principal purpose of the arrangement must be to circumvent the limitations of a single class of stock.

An S corporation may also issue debt to persons or organizations that could not own stock in an S corporation. In this manner, an S corporation may be able to obtain long-term funding from ineligible persons or more than 75 investors. If the financing instrument cannot comply with the straight-debt safe harbor, as in the case of financing by ineligible investors, the corporation should observe the necessary formalities to minimize the risk of reclassification. The corporation should be aware of the factors discussed above, at 1425.3. It should take all possible steps to minimize the risk of reclassification of debt. It should also document the business purpose for any such financing, in a manner that demonstrates that the corporation and its shareholders were not trying to circumvent the single-class-of-stock rule.

OBSERVATION: Unless a debt instrument is extremely ill-structured or is an obvious masquerade of a second class of stock, an S corporation should be relatively safe in issuing debt. It appears that the IRS will need to demonstrate the reclassification as equity, as well as the principal purpose of circumvention of the class-of-stock limit. For several years, there were no rulings on the status of S corporations' debt as a second class of stock. Subsequent to the issuance of Final Regulations §1.1361-1, however, the IRS has ruled that certain debts to eligible shareholders are within the safe harbor, although the statute seems to be worded well enough to avoid confusion in this area. [PLR 9308006] It is perhaps more significant that the IRS has ruled that debt to an ineligible shareholder that cannot meet the safe harbor is not a second class of stock. [PLR 9308006] See Chapter 2, at 225.75., for discussion of these rules.

In some cases, a creditor may want a potential equity interest in return for a long-term commitment of funds. To accommodate such investors, or to obtain reduced interest rates from commercial lenders, an S corporation may issue stock options. Options can also be used to give potential equity interests to employees. Under general principles of tax law, options generally are not equity and therefore cannot be a class of stock. However, an option may be a second class of stock, if it is "substantially certain to be exercised." [Regs. §1.1361-1(l)(4)(iii)(A)] There is no definition of the phrase "substantially certain to be exercised." The Regulations do provide that this probability is to be determined in light of all facts and circumstances. In addition, the "strike" (exercise) price of the option must be substantially below the fair market value of the stock. Example 14 - 22 illustrates an option arrangement that may be similar to a second class of stock.

EXAMPLE 14 - 22: Shadyco has one shareholder, Sherman. His cousin, Vinnie, is willing to provide substantial funding to Shadyco but does not want to be taxed on any of the corporation's income. He wants to take a 50% equity interest in the corporation if its assets should materially appreciate. At the present time, the value of Sherman's equity interest is $250,000, represented by 250 shares. Sherman and Vinnie come to the following agreement:

- Vinnie will loan Shadyco $249,000.
- Shadyco will give Vinnie an option to purchase 250 shares for a total exercise price of $1,000.

Vinnie will receive a reasonable interest rate on the loan. The debt may well be within the safe harbor, but the treatment of the option is questionable. The option could entitle Vinnie to own one-half of the corporation, and it would cost him only $1,000 cash to exercise. At the current time, the value of the option would be approximately $125,000, less the cost of $1,000 to exercise. It is highly unlikely that Vinnie would not exercise the option. The only question would be the timing of the exercise.

The substantial certainty of exercise must be determined on the date the option is issued, materially modified, or transferred from an eligible shareholder to an ineligible shareholder. The Regulations, although they do not define *substantial certainty*, do provide some conditions under which an option will not be classified as a second class of stock:

- The option cannot be exercised at a price less than the fair market value of the stock on the date of exercise. [Regs. §1.1361-1(l)(4)(iii)(A)]
- The option is issued to a lender in connection with a loan, as long as the loan is made in the course of the lender's trade or business and the loan's terms are commercially reasonable. [Regs. §1.1361-1(l)(4)(iii)(B)(1)]
- The option is issued to an employee (or independent contractor) in connection with services performed for the corporation. In this situation, the option must be non-transferable and have no readily ascertainable fair market value. [Regs. §1.1361-1(l)(4)(iii)(B)(2)]

1430. Section 1244 stock.

It may be important for a corporation to protect its shareholders from the downside risk if the investment is unprofitable. An S election is one of the most important considerations at this juncture, since an S corporation can pass through losses to its shareholders. Another important consideration is the issuance of §1244 stock, which may allow certain shareholders to claim an ordinary loss deduction on the disposition of stock.

Under general tax rules, the disposition of stock results in a capital gain or capital loss. Capital losses are subject to severe limitations on deductibility for both individuals and corporations. In 1958, Congress was concerned with the idea of tax neutrality between the different forms of business organizations. A portion of the Technical Amendments Act of 1958 contained in §1244, which allowed certain shareholders a limited ordinary loss deduction on the disposition of stock in a *small business corporation*. [PL 85-866, §202]

SUMMARY OF AUTHORITY: CODE SECTION 1244(a)

- An individual may claim an ordinary loss deduction on the disposition of §1244 stock.
- Section 1244 does not affect the character of any gain on the disposition of stock.

Since its initial appearance in 1958, §1244 has been substantially amended. The most important change occurred in 1978, when the Revenue Act of 1978 simplified the procedures for issuing §1244 stock. Stock issued before the 1978 changes was subject to rigorous procedural rules. Those rules are still in effect for stock that was issued on or before November 6, 1978, regardless of the year in which a shareholder sustains the loss. (Regulations §1.1244(c)-1(f) contains the rules regarding substantiation of losses on the disposition of stock that was issued before November 7, 1978.) The Deficit Reduction Act of 1984 further liberalized the rules by allowing ordinary loss treatment for both preferred and common stock (which is, of course, irrelevant to shareholders in S corporations). The discussion in this chapter is concerned with the rules as they apply to stock issued after November 6, 1978.

Code §1244 is limited in its application. It characterizes certain losses as ordinary, whether they are incurred when stock is sold or when the stock becomes worthless. Section 1244 has no effect on any gains on the disposition of stock. Although the 1978 amendments simplified the procedures for issuing §1244 stock, the form of issuance is still extremely important. Therefore, taxpayers need to be careful to qualify an issue of stock for eventual §1244 treatment.

The shareholder must be allowed, under general tax rules, to claim a deduction for the loss. Usually, the loss is incurred on the date of sale. If stock becomes worthless, however, the holder is treated as if he or she had sold the stock on the last day of the taxable year in which the stock becomes worthless.[3] [§165(g)]

> **EXAMPLE 14 - 23:** Pete, a single taxpayer, owned shares in Lessco. In 1992, Lessco filed for bankruptcy. The trustee in bankruptcy distributed all of Lessco's assets in payment of its debts. The shareholders received nothing. Even though Pete did not actually dispose of his Lessco stock, he is allowed to treat his investment in this corporation as if he had sold it on December 31, 1992. His basis in Lessco had been $7,000, so he is allowed to report a loss of $7,000 on his Lessco stock.

When a shareholder claims a §1244 deduction for the worthlessness of stock, rather than a sale, the taxpayer must bear the burden of proof that the stock became worthless in the year in which the deduction is claimed. Failure to meet this burden can be fatal to the §1244 loss deduction. [*Cerbone*, 65 TCM 2425, TC Memo 1993-167]

> **CAUTION:** A taxpayer who wants to claim a deduction for worthless securities must carefully document that the debt has become worthless. Failure to do so may endanger the bad-debt deduction entirely. For instance, a taxpayer may claim worthlessness of a security in a later year than the one in which the security actually became worthless. Upon audit, the IRS might disallow the deduction for the year in which it was claimed. If the year in which the worthlessness occurred is allowed by the statute of limitations, the taxpayer might lose the deduction.

1430.1. Qualified shareholders. The ordinary loss deduction of §1244 is allowable only to individual shareholders in S corporations. (Section 1244 also permits the deductions to individual partners in partnerships that hold the stock, but a partnership is not eligible to hold S corporation stock.) The term *individual* does not include any estate or trust, regardless of how the entity acquired the stock. [Regs. §1.1244(a)-1(b)(2)] Therefore, an estate of a deceased or bankrupt shareholder could not claim an ordinary loss on the disposition of stock under §1244.

---

[3]There are also rules that allow a loss deduction for partially worthless securities, including stock. [§166(a)(2)]

There are no rules permitting a beneficiary of a grantor trust or Qualified Subchapter S Trust to claim a deduction for a loss sustained on disposition of stock owned by the trust. A deemed owner of a grantor trust, however, treats all of his or her income and deductions as if they were received directly from the source, as if the trust did not exist. [Regs. §1.671-1(c)] Therefore, it would not be unreasonable for a beneficiary of a grantor trust to claim a §1244 loss deduction if the trust incurred a loss on the sale of stock, provided the deemed owner was the original holder of the stock. The same principal should hold for stock held by a QSST. However, if a person other than the deemed owner had acquired the stock from the corporation and placed the stock in trust for the beneficiary, there would be no opportunity to claim a §1244 loss on disposition.

The only person entitled to claim an ordinary loss deduction under §1244 is the original holder of the stock. [Regs. §1.1244-(a)(1)(b)(2). Also see *Harwell*, 33 TCM 669, TC Memo 1974-153.] Therefore, it would appear that any transfer, even a gift between husband and wife, would cause the stock to lose its §1244 character.[4]

The holder claiming a §1244 loss must have purchased the shares directly from the corporation, not from another shareholder. The Tax Court has disallowed §1244 loss when a corporation redeemed shares from one shareholder and issued shares to another person. [*M.R. Adams, Jr.*, 74 TC 4 (1980)] In that case, the court stated that the purpose of §1244 was to protect investors who had created an infusion, rather than a substitution, of capital to the corporation.

EXAMPLE 14 - 24: Harry owned 500 shares of Harco, a small business corporation within the meaning of §1244. In May 1992, Harco redeemed Harry's shares for $50,000. In July 1992, Harco issued new shares to Larry, in exchange for $50,000 cash. If Harry's redemption and Larry's purchase are connected, Larry will not be allowed §1244 treatment on the disposition of his shares.

The burden of proof is on the shareholder claiming the loss to prove that he or she purchased the shares directly from the corporation. In one case, a shareholder claimed a §1244 loss on shares that had been issued in another person's name. The shareholder was not allowed a §1244 loss deduction on the worthlessness of the stock. [*Rookard v. U.S.*, 71-1 USTC 9457 (DC Ore.)] In another recent case, the taxpayer failed to substantiate that the provisions of §1244 were applicable. The §1244 loss was not allowed. [*Zand*, TC Memo 1996-19, 71 TCM (CCH) 1758]

In 1991, the question arose as to whether an S corporation that held shares in a C corporation could claim §1244 ordinary loss treatment on the disposition of stock. In principle, the argument appears to be reasonable. The benefits of §1244 loss are allowed only to individuals, the S corporation's shareholders were individuals, and the S corporation was a pass-through entity. Therefore, treating the S corporation as a qualified holder of §1244 stock did not appear to frustrate any policy objective in either Subchapter S or §1244. 14

The argument was in part strengthened, and in part weakened, by the language of §1371(a)(2), which treats an S corporation, in its capacity as a shareholder in another corporation, as an individual. That provision, however, limits the treatment as an individual to the rules of Subchapter C (§§301–385). The IRS has limited this treatment to Subchapter C rules, and has not extended it to §1244. Therefore, an S corporation that sustains losses on the disposition of stock in a small business corporation (§1244 definition) is not entitled to an ordinary loss deduction and must pass the loss through to its shareholders as a capital loss.[5] [9130003 (TAM). The Tax Court recently disallowed a §1244 loss deduction to an S corporation that held stock in

---

[4] See *Prizant*, 30 TCM 817, TC Memo 1971-176, where a partnership that had held §1244 stock had transferred its shares to a partner before the stock was disposed. The partner could not claim §1244 loss treatment.

[5] This Technical Advice Memorandum points out that Congress did not add S corporations as qualified §1244 shareholders when it enacted the Subchapter S Revision Act of 1982.

another corporation. [*Rath*, 101 TC No. 13 (1993)] The court pointed out that it would have been reasonable for Congress to have expanded §1244 to include S corporations as qualified shareholders, but the statutory language of §1244 forbade this treatment. The taxpayer had also tried to use Revenue Ruling 93-36, which held that S corporations are subject to individual rules on bad debt deductions, to impute §1244 treatment to an S corporation. [Rev. Rul. 93-36, 1993-1 CB 187] (See Chapter 6, at 610.54., for discussion of bad debts incurred by S corporations.)

As is the case with many business deductions, the shareholder must have acquired the stock with a profit motive. A sham transaction, lacking any economic substance, can be disregarded by the IRS and will not allow a §1244 loss deduction. [*Perrett*, 74 TC 111; *Webb v. U.S.*, 83-1 USTC 9114 (DC E. Miss.)]

A shareholder who received stock in a tax-free reorganization is generally not allowed to claim §1244 treatment on the sale or worthlessness of such stock. Chapter 16 contains a discussion of these transactions and the extremely narrow exceptions.

1430.2. Limitation on §1244 loss deduction. The principal benefit of §1244 is that it allows an investor to claim a loss deduction in excess of that normally allowed for capital losses. The benefit of this characterization, however, has its own limits.

SUMMARY OF AUTHORITY: CODE SECTION 1244(b)

- An investor is limited to $50,000 ordinary loss deduction from §1244 in any taxable year.
- The limit is doubled to $100,000 if the shareholder files a joint return.

The $100,000 limit for joint filers does not depend on the actual losses sustained by each of the spouses. If one of the spouses disposes of §1244 stock, and the stock is separate property, that person may claim the entire $100,000 limit on a joint return.

The loss limit is applied at the shareholder level and applies to all §1244 losses sustained in a single taxable year. The investor must aggregate the losses sustained on all dispositions of §1244 stock, if the shareholder has losses on two or more corporations in the same year.

> **EXAMPLE 14 - 25:** In 1992, Barb, a married taxpayer, sells stock in Barco, which she had purchased in 1989. She had a basis of $125,000 in her Barco stock and realized $45,000 on the sale. In 1992, she purchased stock in Berico, which was a highly risky enterprise. She invested $70,000 in Berico, but the corporation became worthless in September of that year. At the end of the year, she still held her Berico certificates, which were now completely worthless. The stock in both corporations met all of the criteria for §1244. Barb's husband sold no stock in 1992. Her combined losses are $150,000 on her dispositions of §1244 stock. Of this amount, $100,000 would be treated as an ordinary loss incurred in 1992. The remaining $50,000 would be treated as a capital loss sustained in 1992.

Section 1244 has no effect on the timing of the loss recognition. A shareholder may not treat losses on §1244 stock that exceed the limit as §1244 losses incurred in any other taxable year. The excess of losses sustained on §1244 stock over the $50,000 or $100,000 limit is treated as a capital loss in the year of disposition. [Regs. §1.1244(d)-2(b)]

If an allowed ordinary loss under §1244 exceeds a shareholder's taxable income, it may create a net operating loss to that shareholder. [§1244(d)(3)] Under general tax principles [§172], the shareholder could carry his or her personal net operating loss back 3 years or forward 15 years. If a shareholder has a net operating loss resulting in whole or in part from §1244 losses and carries the loss into another year in which he or she had §1244 losses, the actual tax benefit of §1244 losses may exceed the $50,000 or $100,000 limit in the year in which the deduction is ultimately allowed. [Regs. §1.1244(d)-4(b)]

> **EXAMPLE 14 - 26:** Maggie, a single taxpayer, deducted a §1244 loss of $50,000 in 1989, after which her taxable income was $80,000. In 1992, she sustains another §1244 loss of $50,000. In

1992, her allowable deductions from all sources exceed her gross income, and she has a net operating loss of $35,000. Under general tax principles, she carries the loss back three years to 1989. She is allowed to claim the $35,000 loss deduction in 1989, and reduces her taxable income to $45,000. Her final determination of her 1989 taxable income has been affected by $85,000 of §1244 losses, the $50,000 incurred and deducted in 1989, and the $35,000 incurred in 1992. The Regulations under §1244, however, expressly permit her to use her 1992 net operating loss deduction in 1989.

The $50,000 (or $100,000) limits are imposed on the shareholder, not on the stock of any particular corporation. Therefore, an investor may actually recognize more than the $50,000 or $100,000 limit on §1244 stock, if the shareholder sells portions of his or her holdings in two separate taxable years.

EXAMPLE 14 - 27: Hope, a single taxpayer, purchased $300,000 of stock in Bluskyco in 1989. The corporation was not as profitable as expected, but it never became worthless. In December 1992, Hope agreed to sell all of her Bluskyco stock to Gouger for $200,000. If she sells all of her stock in either 1992 or 1993, her loss of $100,000 will be half ordinary and half capital. If she sells half of her shares to Gouger in 1992 and the other half in 1993, she can claim $50,000 of ordinary loss on each sale.

OBSERVATION: A shareholder who sells two blocks of stock in two separate years should make sure that the sale is not aggregated into one transaction. If the shareholder delivered all of the shares to an escrow agent in one transaction, the IRS would probably succeed in treating the sale as occurring in one transaction, when the seller transferred the stock into escrow. [Pacific Coast Music Jobbers, Inc., 55 TC 866 (1971), aff'd 72-1 USTC 9317 (5th Cir.)]

If a taxpayer realizes a loss on the sale of §1244 stock in a C corporation, the loss would not be subject to the passive loss limits of §469, since a taxpayer's interest in an activity subject to the passive activity loss limits does not include stock in a C corporation. (See discussions in Chapters 8 and 10.) However, if a shareholder sustains a §1244 loss on shares in an S corporation, the ability to claim an ordinary loss deduction may be affected by the passive activity loss limits. If the sale is a complete disposition of the shareholder's interest in the activity, the loss is not subject to the passive activity loss limits. That loss, together with any losses from that activity suspended from earlier years, would be deductible in the loss year. [§469(g)] A disposition of less than the taxpayer's entire interest, however, would subject the loss to the §469 limits.

EXAMPLE 14 - 28: Refer to Example 14 - 27. Hope owned no interest, directly or indirectly, in Bluskyco's activities, other than her shares. She never participated in Bluskyco's business activities. Her 1992 sale would be subject to the passive activity loss limits. Her 1993 sale, however, would be a complete disposition, assuming that Gouger was not related to Hope.

Hope had no income from passive activities in either year. Therefore, she would suspend the 1992 loss as a passive activity deduction. She could claim that loss, together with the 1993 loss, in 1993.

1430.3. Section 1244 stock defined. Section 1244 stock has three essential requirements, as articulated in §1244(c).

SUMMARY OF AUTHORITY: CODE SECTION 1244(c)

- The issuing corporation must have been a small business corporation at the time the stock was issued.
- The stock must have been issued directly to a holder in exchange for property.

- The corporation's gross receipts from certain passive sources must not have exceeded 50% of its total receipts for a five-year period ending with the corporation's taxable year immediately preceding the shareholder's loss.

Each of these requirements deserves further discussion. The terms *small* and *business* relate to different times in the corporation's history. In short, the corporation must have been small on the date the stock was issued and involved in business for five years preceding the loss.

1430.31. Qualification at time of issue. At the time the stock is issued, the corporation must have received no more than $1,000,000 of property in exchange for stock or as a contribution to capital. [§1244(c)(3)(A)] The test is made with respect to the adjusted basis of the property to the corporation. Thus, if property were received in a §351 exchange, the corporation would use the shareholder's basis plus any gain the shareholder recognized. If the property were received in an exchange that did not qualify under §351, the corporation's basis would be the fair market value of the property. The basis for this test is also reduced by liabilities the corporation has assumed (or transferred in connection with the property transfer). [§1244(c)(3)(B)]

EXAMPLE 14 - 29: Lisa contributes property to her newly formed corporation, Lico, in 1991. The property had an adjusted basis to Lisa of $900,000 and a fair market value of $3,000,000. The property was taken subject to liabilities of $850,000. Lisa received no consideration other than stock in Lico, and she receives all of the outstanding shares in Lico. Therefore, the exchange qualifies under §351. Neither Lisa nor Lico recognizes any gain on the transfer. Lico's basis is $900,000. Lisa's basis in her stock is $50,000 ($900,000 basis of property contributed less $850,000 liability relief). Lico's basis for §1244 rules is $50,000.

The $1,000,000 capitalization test is made as of the end of the year in which the stock in question is issued. [Regs. §1.1244(c)-2(b)] In performing the test, the corporation must consider the aggregate amount of property received as of the end of a year, rather than just the property received within that year.

EXAMPLE 14 - 30: In 1990, 10 individuals contributed property to a corporation in exchange for stock. Each individual's basis in the property contributed was $100,000, and the total basis to the corporation was $1,000,000.

Most of the property was depreciable, with a relatively short depreciation period. By the beginning of 1993, the property had a basis of $350,000. In 1993, the corporation issued stock to five other individuals for a total of $500,000 cash. The stock issued in 1990 qualifies for §1244 treatment. The stock issued in 1993 does not qualify, since the corporation had already received its $1,000,000 limit.

A distribution of property from the corporation will not reduce the aggregate amount of basis, whether or not the distribution is treated as a return of capital. This rule is important for an S corporation, since most distributions are treated as return of capital to the shareholder.

Property received by the corporation that is not the result of a sale of stock or capital contribution does not exhaust the $1,000,000 limit. The most likely source of such property is the retention of corporate earnings.

EXAMPLE 14 - 31: In 1992, five individuals each invest $100,000 in stock of Fiveco, a newly formed corporation. In 1992 and 1993, Fiveco is profitable and retains $600,000 of income. At the end of 1993, the corporation's total assets are $1,100,000. In 1994, another individual invests $100,000 to purchase stock in Fiveco. Assuming the corporation and the newest shareholder meet all other qualifications, the stock issued in 1994 is §1244 stock, since the corporation has received only $600,000 from the sale of stock by the end of 1994.

The property tested for the $1,000,000 limit includes all property received from any shareholder. Therefore, contributions by a nonqualifying shareholder can exhaust the corporation's ability to issue §1244 stock.

EXAMPLE 14 - 32: In 1992, eight individuals and an estate have decided to form a corporation. In that year, individuals Allen, Brenda, and Clyde each contribute $100,000 in exchange for stock, and the estate contributes $700,000. In 1993, individuals Debbie, Earl, Fiona, Gary, and Helen each contribute $100,000 and receive shares in the corporation. The stock issued to Allen, Brenda, and Clyde qualifies as §1244 stock, since the corporation had not exceeded its $1,000,000 limit by the end of 1992. The stock received by the estate does not qualify, since an estate cannot hold §1244 stock. The stock received by Debbie, Earl, Fiona, Gary, and Helen does not qualify as §1244 stock, since the corporation had reached its $1,000,000 limit before the year in which they purchased their stock.

OBSERVATION: If a corporation has some flexibility in the order in which it issues shares, it should determine which, if any, shareholders will be eligible to benefit from §1244 treatment. The corporation should then issue shares to those persons first and to the disqualified shareholders later. If the ordering of the contribution of property to the corporation demands that ineligible persons contribute money or property before eligible persons will be able to do so, the corporation might want to issue debt securities and stock options to the ineligible persons.

EXAMPLE 14-33: Assume the same facts as in Example 14-32, except the corporation issues no stock and a $700,000 note to the estate in 1992. The property received from the estate will not absorb any of the $1,000,000 limit, since that property was not received by the corporation in exchange for stock.

The corporation also issues the estate an option to purchase the shares that would have been issued under the original plan, at the fair market value of that number of shares in 1992. This option's exercise price is within the safe harbor limits of Regulations §1.1361-1 and would not be treated as a second class of stock. The estate does not exercise the option until 1994. Therefore, the corporation has not exceeded its $1,000,000 by the end of 1993, and all of the individuals' shares qualify as §1244 stock. The estate is not concerned with §1244 treatment, since it is not an eligible shareholder for §1244 purposes.

There may be a year in which the corporation is eligible to issue §1244 stock but receives enough cash or property during that year to cause it to exceed the $1,000,000 limit. The Regulations refer to such a year as a *transitional year* and provide two alternative rules:

14

1. The corporation may designate which of the shares it issues are §1244 and which are not. [Regs. §1.1244(c)-2(b)(2)] This rule allows a corporation to issue §1244 stock to persons who may benefit from ordinary loss treatment and to designate shares issued to other persons as not being §1244 stock. This designation must be made by $2^1/_2$ months following the close of the transitional year.
2. If the corporation fails to designate the §1244 shares in the transitional year, the corporation must make an allocation based on the value of shares issued in the transitional year. [Regs. §1.1244(c)-2(b)(3)] The allocation is made according to the following formula:

$$\frac{\text{Unused limit at the beginning of transitional year}}{\text{Stock issued for property during transitional year*}} = \text{Percentage of stock treated as §1244}$$

*Includes any contributions to capital or paid-in surplus received in transitional year.

EXAMPLE 14 - 34: A corporation had issued stock in exchange for $900,000 (adjusted basis) of property as of the end of 1992. In 1993, it issued stock in exchange for $300,000 cash. It did not designate which shares were §1244 stock and which shares were not. Accordingly, one-third of the stock issued in 1993 is §1244 stock.

This allocation can be calculated at any time. In practice, it probably is not done until the stock has become worthless.

1430.32. Qualification at time shareholder sustains loss. The corporation must meet an entirely different criterion as a small business corporation at the time the shareholder sustains a loss on the disposition of stock. At that time, the corporation must look to its gross receipts for the five taxable years preceding the loss. If the corporation has been in existence less than five years, the corporation tests for the entire period of its existence.

Within that period of time, the corporation must have derived no more than 50% of its gross receipts from royalties, rents, dividends, interest, annuities, and sales or exchanges of stocks or securities. [§1244(c)(1)(C)] These receipts are from sources similar to those for *passive investment income*, as used in Subchapter S. [§1362(d)(3)(D)] These rules are discussed extensively in Chapter 12. There are some differences, however:

1. There is no exception for interest received by a lending company or on the sale of inventory. Therefore, stock in a loan company that derives more than 50% of its gross receipts from interest, even though the interest is received in the active conduct of the corporation's business, cannot be §1244 stock. [Rev. Rul. 75-431, 1975- 2 CB 346]
2. There is no relief provision for any royalty income.
3. There is an exception for rent, if the corporation provides significant services. [Regs. §1.1244(c)-1(b)(iii)] The test for these receipts is made for the aggregate period, not on a year-by-year basis. However, the corporation eliminates from the testing period any year in which it sustains a net operating loss. [§1244(c)(2)(C)]

OBSERVATION: When a shareholder disposes of stock for which he or she can claim a potential ordinary loss deduction pursuant to §1244, it is quite likely that the corporation has sustained operating losses in its recent history. Therefore, the passive income limit probably applies in few cases.

If a corporation has few or no gross receipts during the testing period, the corporation's principal activities may be the determining factor. In one case, a corporation that had no receipts, but provided management services to related corporations, failed to meet the requisite active business criterion, and the shareholders were denied §1244 loss treatment. [*A. O. Bates v. U.S.*, 78-2 USTC 9592 (6th Cir.)]

1430.33. Summary of definitions. Although the term *small business corporation* appears in both §1244 and §1361, the definitions are not identical, as illustrated in Table 14 - 1.

1430.4. Shareholder's basis for §1244 loss. A shareholder must have acquired §1244 stock directly from the corporation in exchange for property contributed to the corporation. As discussed above, the shareholder must not have acquired the stock directly or indirectly from any other shareholder. The basis at the time of the loss must be due to the original contribution of property, not due to any other basis increase. There are limitations to the definition of *property* and special rules dealing with stock whose basis is partly due to the initial contribution and partly caused by other transactions.

1430.41. Property qualifying for §1244 basis. The property contributed to the corporation must not have been stock or securities. [§1244(c)(1)(B)] A shareholder may be able to claim

TABLE 14 - 1: Small Business Corporation Definitions Compared

Criterion	*Subchapter S*	*Section 1244*
Types of shareholders	Individuals, estates, certain trusts	Unlimited, but only certain shareholders can claim §1244 treatment
Number of shareholders	35 maximum (75 after 1996)	Unlimited, but only individuals and partnerships can claim §1244 treatment
Classes of stock	Common only	Common or preferred
Eligible corporation	No insurance company, bank (before 1997), etc., or foreign corporation	Domestic corporation, no other restrictions
Passive income limit	25% if corporation has accumulated earnings and profits, no limit for other corporations	50%, except in loss year
Limit on equity	Unlimited	$1,000,000

§1244 treatment on stock issued in exchange for debt from the corporation, as long as the debt is not evidenced by a security. [Regs. §1.1244(c)-1(d)] However, the shareholder has the burden of proof that he or she actually received §1244 stock in exchange for the cancellation of debt. [*Shapiro*, 25 TCM 654, TC Memo 1966-128]

The basis for §1244 is, generally, the shareholder's basis in the stock. If the stock is received in a §351 transfer, the shareholder's basis in the stock is the same as that person's basis in the property transferred (plus any gain recognized and less any boot received; see the discussion above). Sometimes, the fair market value of the property is less than the shareholder's basis, in which case the shareholder keeps the relatively high basis from the property as basis in his or her stock. For §1244, however, the shareholder's stock basis is limited to the fair market value of the property at the date of contribution. [§1244(d)(1)]

If the contribution of property, including cancellation of debt, is structured as a contribution to capital, the shareholder making the contribution will increase his or her basis in the stock. [Regs. §1.118-1] The additional basis received, however, would not allow an increase in the allowable §1244 loss deduction. [Regs. §1.1244(d)-2(b)]

14

Any stock issued in exchange for services is not §1244 stock, since services are not considered property. [Regs. §1.1244(c)-1(d)] When a shareholder receives stock in exchange for guarantee of a corporate loan, the stock is received in exchange for services and not property. [*Schneiderman*, 54 TCM 1006, TC Memo 1987-551] A shareholder may, however, contribute cash to a corporation in exchange for stock if the corporation uses the contribution to pay off debts. [*Smyers*, 57 TC 189 (1971)]

1430.42. Basis adjustments to stock in S corporations. If a corporation's losses have reduced a shareholder's basis, such adjustments must be taken into account before determining the loss on disposition of stock. [§1367(b)(3)] Therefore, any loss that passes through to a shareholder will reduce the ability of that person to claim §1244 (or even capital) loss on the disposition.

EXAMPLE 14 - 35: In 1992, Oliver invested $100,000 in Olco, an S corporation. He received 50% of Olco's stock, which qualified as §1244 stock. In 1992, Oliver's share of Olco's loss was

$80,000, which reduced Oliver's basis to $20,000. On May 26, 1993, Oliver sold his shares for $5,000. In 1993, Olco sustained a capital loss of $80,000, of which $16,000 was allocated to Oliver under the pro rata allocation method of §1377(a)(1). (See Chapter 6 for discussion.) Oliver must take his allocable loss from Olco into account before determining his basis for the disposition. Such allocation would reduce Oliver's basis to $4,000 at the time of disposition, and he would report a gain of $1,000 on the sale of his Olco stock.

By contrast, an increase in a shareholder's basis through the operation of Subchapter S will not increase a shareholder's §1244 loss potential. [Regs. §1.1244(d)-2(a). This Regulation has not been updated to reflect the Subchapter S Revision Act of 1982.] When a shareholder sustains a loss after a basis increase, he or she must apportion the loss between the §1244 basis and the other basis.

EXAMPLE 14 - 36: In 1992, Lucy contributed $40,000 to Lucia, a newly formed corporation, in exchange for all of its stock. Lucia immediately made an S election, which was effective from the corporation's inception. In 1992, Lucia was slightly profitable and reported $5,000 of taxable income to Lucy. Lucia did not make any distribution to Lucy, so Lucia's basis was $45,000 at the end of 1992. In early 1993, Lucy faced serious health problems, and she sold her shares to Ricky (an unrelated person) for $30,000. Lucia's loss is $15,000. She apportions the loss between her §1244 basis and her other basis, as follows:

§1244 loss [$15,000 x ($40,000/$45,000)	$13,333
Capital loss [$15,000 x ($5,000/$45,000)]	1,667
Total	$15,000

When a shareholder in an S corporation is concerned with preserving the §1244 character of his or her stock investment, there are means of preserving the basis. If the shareholder takes all positive adjustments to basis out of the corporation as distributions, then uses the distributions to purchase additional stock, the new shares could be §1244 stock. The corporation would need to be under the $1,000,000 capitalization limit in the year in which the shareholder purchased the new stock.

EXAMPLE 14 - 37: Refer to Example 14 - 36. If, before the sale to Ricky, Lucy had taken $5,000 as a distribution from the corporation and had used the $5,000 to purchase new shares, she would have been entitled to §1244 treatment on the entire loss.

1430.5. Compatibility of §1244 with S corporations. A corporation may meet both of the definitions of *small business corporation*, as used in Subchapter S and §1244. As a practical matter, §1244 may be of little use to the holder of S corporation stock. The holder may already have exhausted his or her stock basis by the time of the sale or other disposition of the stock. Therefore, there will be no remaining loss to use for tax purposes, and the treatment of the loss as ordinary or capital will be insignificant. However, if a shareholder sells the stock before the corporation recognizes losses for tax purposes, the §1244 treatment may prove useful.

EXAMPLE 14 - 38: On February 23, 1991, individuals Karen, Mike, and Leon form the KML Corporation. The corporation immediately files an S election. Karen contributes property worth $20,000, basis $45,000. Mike contributes property worth $40,000, basis $60,000. Leon contributes services worth $15,000. The transaction qualifies under §351.

In 1991, the corporation operates at break-even. On January 1, 1992, Mike sells his stock to Diane for $30,000. Mike recognizes $20,000 of capital loss and $10,000 of §1244 loss. In 1992, the corporation again operates at break-even, but becomes the target of a large lawsuit. On January 1, 1993, all of the shareholders sell their stock at a loss. The losses are characterized as follows:

Karen—ordinary. She was an original holder of stock issued for property. Her §1244 loss, however, is limited to the fair market value of the property at the time of contribution, which was $20,000. The remainder of her loss will be capital.

Leon—capital. He received his stock for services.

Diane—capital. She was not an original shareholder.

1430.6. Interpretive problems for S corporation shareholders. The Regulations under §1244 have not been amended to reflect the Subchapter S Revision Act of 1982. As of this writing, there have been no cases or ruling dealings with a shareholder who has had both upward and downward adjustments to his or her stock under either version of Subchapter S. Until the §1244 Regulations are updated to deal with post-1982 basis adjustments to S corporation stock, tax professionals are forced to extrapolate from the old rules in order to determine the equivalent treatment under the new version of Subchapter S.

1430.61. Relation of §1244 to basis adjustments under old Subchapter S. The Regulations under §1244 prohibit a shareholder from claiming §1244 loss due to an increase in stock basis "under §1376(a)." [Regs. §1.1244(d)-2(a)] The cited Code section, §1376(a), was repealed by the Subchapter S Revision Act of 1982. When it was in effect, §1376(a) required a shareholder to increase his or her stock basis for the allocable portion of "Undistributed Taxable Income." (See Chapter 7 for discussion of undistributed taxable income.) Unfortunately, the existing Regulations under §1244 do not address the basis adjustments under old Subchapter S comprehensively.

There are no references within the §1244 Regulations to any other provision of Subchapter S. There were, however, two other basis adjustments required under old Subchapter S:

- The Code required a shareholder to reduce stock and debt basis for losses. [§1376(b)]
- The Regulations required a shareholder to reduce basis for a distribution of undistributed taxable income or previously taxed income. [Regs. §1.1375-4(a) (prior law)]

Each of these basis adjustment rules has a parallel provision in the current version of Subchapter S. It is a relatively simple matter to compare the adjustment required under §1376(a), which is explicitly addressed in the §1244 Regulations, to the current rules, as long as all adjustments take place in the same taxable year.

1430.62. Increases and decreases in the same taxable year. The only provision under old Subchapter S that permitted a shareholder to increase his or her stock basis was §1376(a), cited in the §1244 Regulations. Although a detailed description of this rule serves little purpose, more than 10 years after its repeal, a brief restatement of the rule will help to interpret the application to §1244 stock.

Between 1958 and 1982, an S corporation computed its taxable income in a manner similar to that of a C corporation.[6] Thus income and deductions of dissimilar character (such as capital and ordinary) were combined at the corporate level. Distributions from an S corporation generally were treated as dividends, unless they were from undistributed taxable income (UTI) or previously taxed income (PTI). These concepts are discussed briefly in Chapter 7. Like dividends from a C corporation, dividends from an S corporation had no effect on a shareholder's basis, but were treated as ordinary income at the time of receipt. If an S corporation's dividend distributions were equal to or greater than its taxable income, there was no creation of UTI. If the corporation distributed less than its taxable income, the difference was UTI, which was treated as a dividend to the shareholders on the final day of the corporation's taxable year. The

[6]The terms *S corporation* and *C corporation* did not actually appear in the law until the Subchapter S Revision Act of 1982.

shareholders would increase basis for their portions of UTI. Therefore, an increase in basis was each shareholder's portion—in a single taxable year—of:

- The corporation's gross income
- Less the corporation's allowable deductions
- Less the distributions made by the corporation

To analyze the impact of the §1244 Regulations on a shareholder's basis, it is perhaps best to use a simple example that compares the basis adjustments under both old and new law.

EXAMPLE 14 - 39: Fay contributes $45,000 to Vincent Corporation, a newly formed corporation, in exchange for all of Vincent's stock. The stock meets all of the §1244 requirements. Vincent makes a valid S election for its first year of operations. In that year, Vincent's income, losses, and distributions are as follows:

Ordinary income	$25,000
§1231 loss	(8,000)
Distributions to Fay	12,000

If the year in question began before 1983, the corporation would combine its ordinary income and its §1231 loss to report taxable income of $17,000. Fay would treat the distribution of $12,000 as a dividend. The corporation would have distributed $5,000 less than its taxable income. It would have reported this $5,000 as a deemed dividend to Fay on the last day of its taxable year. Fay's basis adjustment under §1376(a) would be $5,000. Fay's basis would be $50,000. If Fay sold his stock for $40,000, he would recognize a loss of $10,000. He would apportion the loss between the §1244 basis and the other basis, as follows:

§1244 loss [$10,000 x ($45,000/$50,000)]	$ 9,000
Capital loss [$10,000 x ($5,000/$50,000)]	1,000
Total	$10,000

If the corporation's year began after 1982, the tax treatment would be different. Fay's basis adjustments would be:

	Amount	*Statutory Reference*
Ordinary income	$ 25,000	§1367(a)(1)(B)
§1231 loss	(8,000)	§1367(a)(2)(B)
Distributions to Fay	(12,000)	§1367(a)(2)(A)

His net basis adjustment for the year would be $5,000, and his basis at year-end would be $50,000. In this example, there is no difference between the basis adjustment required under old Subchapter S and the net adjustment required by new law.

1430.63. Decreases in a year following increases. Under either old or new Subchapter S, it is possible for a decrease in basis to occur after an increase. The statute and Regulations under §1244, as well as those under Subchapter S, are unclear as to the treatment of downward adjustments following upward adjustments. Example 14 - 40 illustrates the problem.

EXAMPLE 14 - 40: In 1992, Quincy purchases qualified §1244 stock from Quinco, an S corporation. Quincy's basis at the time of purchase is $75,000. In 1992, Quinco is profitable. Quincy's share of the corporation's income is $40,000. Quincy takes no distributions in 1992 and adjusts his basis to $115,000. In 1993, Quincy receives a distribution of $20,000 from the corporation's AAA. In 1993, the corporation sustains a loss, of which Quincy's share is $25,000. Therefore, at the end of 1993, Quincy's basis is $70,000. In 1994, the corporation reports no income or loss. Quincy sells all of his Quinco stock for $40,000, and sustains a loss of $30,000 on the sale. The treatment of this loss as ordinary, or partly ordinary and partly capital, is uncertain.

If the Regulations under either Subchapter S or §1244 stated that an adjustment for losses and distributions would reduce the basis acquired through the initial contribution of capital, Quincy's §1244 basis would be:

Initial investment	$75,000
Less 1993 loss	(25,000)
Less 1993 distribution	(20,000)
Basis remaining from original investment	$30,000

If the Regulations under either statute stated that an adjustment for a loss or distribution would cancel out previous adjustments for income, Quincy's §1244 basis would be:

Initial investment	$75,000
Adjustments	
Add 1992 income	$40,000
Less 1993 loss	(25,000)
Less 1993 distribution	(20,000)
Net adjustments under Subchapter S	(5,000)
Basis remaining from original investment	$70,000

The Regulations under §1244 do not expressly permit an offset of basis increases with basis reductions. Nor do they explicitly (or implicitly) prohibit such an offset. Therefore, they provide no solution to the problem illustrated in Example 14 - 40.

The Regulations under §1244 are completely silent as to the tax treatment of a shareholder who has had both upward and downward adjustments to basis under either version of Subchapter S. A distribution of UTI would reduce basis, but only to the extent that the creation of UTI had caused an increase in basis. Therefore, it would appear to serve no purpose for the IRS to allow a shareholder to reduce additional basis created by the operation of Subchapter S. Accordingly, a shareholder should be able to claim §1244 basis for any basis remaining at the time of disposition of the stock, to the extent there has not been a net increase in any taxable year for income from the S corporation.

EXAMPLE 14 - 41: Refer to Example 14 - 40. By extrapolating from the old Subchapter S rules, Quincy should be allowed to offset his basis increase from the corporation's 1992 income with his 1993 distribution, as well as his share of the corporation's 1993 loss. Therefore, his remaining basis at the date of sale should be entirely attributable to his initial invested capital, and his entire loss on the sale should be treated as an ordinary loss under §1244.

OBSERVATION: The solution in Example 14 - 41 has never been approved in any Regulation or other pronouncement. Nor has it ever been disallowed. It is based on a sound analysis of the operative provisions of old Subchapter S adapted to current law. Such an analysis is necessary to fit the obsolete reference to S corporations in the §1244 Regulations to current tax problems. It should not be viewed as a frivolous position, and it is not contrary to any authority. Therefore, a taxpayer should be able to take this position on a tax return without fear of a negligence penalty. If a tax preparer uses this position on a return, however, he or she should check carefully for any new rules that may have been published since this writing.

1430.64. Increases in a year following decreases. A shareholder may have reduced basis for losses in one year, increased basis for income in a later year, and then sold his or her stock. Literal reading of Regulations §1.1244(d)-2(a) leads to the unfortunate conclusion that any upward adjustment to a holder's S corporation shares does not qualify for §1244 treatment, even if an upward adjustment cancels out a previous downward adjustment.

EXAMPLE 14 - 42: In 1992, Pamela purchases §1244 stock in Pamco, an S corporation. Pamela's initial basis is $80,000. In 1992, her share of Pamco's loss is $75,000, and she reduces her basis to $5,000. In 1993, the corporation has taxable income, of which Pamela's share is $30,000. Pamela receives no distributions in 1993 and adjusts her basis to $35,000. In 1994, the corporation reports no income or loss, and Pamela sells her shares for $10,000. Her loss on the sale was $25,000. The stock was originally §1244 stock, so it might appear that she should be entitled to claim §1244 ordinary loss on the sale. Unfortunately, most of her basis is due to adjustments subsequent to her acquisition of the shares. She probably must allocate her loss between §1244 and capital, in the same manner as shown in Example 14 - 36.

1430.65. Tracking basis adjustments to individual shares. When a shareholder has acquired different blocks of stock at different times, the IRS requires that the basis adjustments for income, losses, and distributions be apportioned to individual shares. [Regs. §1.1367-1(c)(3)] This rule is especially important when a shareholder has some stock that qualifies for §1244 treatment and some that does not.

EXAMPLE 14 - 43: In December 1992, David paid $100,000 cash directly to Boyco, a calendar-year S corporation, in exchange for 100 shares of stock. David's 100 shares qualified as §1244 stock and constituted half of the corporation's outstanding shares.

The corporation had no activity in 1992, so David had no adjustment to his basis in that year. On May 26, 1993 (exactly 40% of the corporation's year had expired), David purchased all of the other shares from Ted. David paid Ted $80,000 for his stock. This stock does not qualify as §1244 stock to David, since he is not the original holder. In 1993, the corporation sustains a loss of $120,000. The corporation does not elect to close its books as of May 26, 1993. David would apportion the loss between his two blocks of shares as follows:

	Date Block Acquired	
	12/92	*5/26/93*
Percent of outstanding shares	50%	50%
Percent of 1993 held by David	100%	60%
Percent of loss allocated to each block	50%	30%
Corporation's 1993 loss	$120,000	$120,000
Loss to each block	$ 60,000	$ 36,000

The basis for each block would be determined as follows:

	Date Block Acquired	
	12/92	*5/26/93*
Basis before 1993 loss	$100,000	$ 80,000
Loss allocated for 1993	(60,000)	(36,000)
Basis at end of 1993	$ 40,000	$ 44,000

In early 1994, David sells all of his Boyco stock for $70,000. The treatment of the loss will be:

	Date Block Acquired	
	12/92	*5/26/93*
Amount realized on sale	$35,000	$35,000
Basis at end of 1993	(40,000)	(44,000)
Loss on each block	$ 5,000	$ 9,000
Character of loss	Ordinary	Capital

14

1435. S corporation within a general business structure.

If an S corporation is mindful of the ownership and affiliation restrictions, it can be one entity in a larger group of businesses under common control of a few shareholders (or even one shareholder). The constraints of real importance to the S corporation are its eligibility rules. No taxpayer other than a U.S. citizen or resident (or estate or permitted trust) can own any of the S corporation's shares at any time. The S corporation, under current law, cannot be the parent corporation in an affiliated group before January 1, 1997, or before the taxable year beginning in 1997. After 1996, however, an S corporation may be a member of an affiliated group of corporations. Undoubtedly this change in the law will result in numerous new business combinations involving S corporations.

The strategies employed in past years to circumvent the affiliated group problems will still serve their purposes. S corporations will often find it beneficial to join with other businesses and investors, domestic and foreign, in joint ventures. A joint venture is a partnership for tax purposes, and the S corporations that participate in these investments will need to be mindful of the partnership tax rules.

1435.1. S corporations as members of partnerships. Occasionally, it makes good sense to structure a business as a partnership and have one or more of the partners be S corporations. The principal purpose of the structure, at least as far as federal taxes are concerned, is to avoid the double taxation of income while adding some flexibility to the ownership of the business. Before 1994, the IRS was suspicious of partnerships with S corporations as partners. [See Rev. Rul. 77-220, 1977-1 CB 263.] In 1994, however, it reversed its position and ruled that membership in a partnership would no longer endanger a corporation's S status. [Rev. Rul. 94-43, 1994-27 IRB 8] The cases and rulings that preceded 1994 may be of little relevance as precedent, in today's liberalized climate. They do, however, point out some interesting uses of this structure, some of which will have continuing relevance for the foreseeable future.

In many cases and rulings, the IRS has either explicitly or tacitly approved such structures. For example, the Milwaukee Brewers baseball franchise was established as a limited partnership, with its general partner being an S corporation.[7] [See *Selig v. U.S.*, 83-2 USTC 9442 (E.D. Wis.), and *Selig v. U.S.*, 84-2 USTC 9696 (7th Cir.).]

Revenue Ruling 71-455 dealt with a situation where an S corporation was a member of a partnership. [Rev. Rul. 71-455, 1971-2 CB 318] That ruling did not address the eligibility of the corporation for an S election, per se, but implied that an S corporation could be a partner in a partnership and retain its S status. The IRS continues to acknowledge the existence of these structures. [See PLRs 9341018, 9409021, 9409027, 9411012.] In a 1995 private letter ruling, the IRS allowed two S corporations to form a limited liability company that would be a partnership for federal tax purposes. Again, the retention of the two corporations' S status was implied but not commented on. [PLR 9529015]

1435.11. Overview of partnership taxation. A comprehensive discussion of partnerships is far beyond the scope of this book. It is important, however, to understand the basic nature of the operation of this type of entity. A partnership is exempt from the federal income tax at its own level. [§701] The income of a partnership is taxed to the partners, and losses are deductible by partners. [§702] These rules resemble those applicable to S corporations and their shareholders, but there are some exceptions:

- Although an S corporation may be subject to corporate-level taxes, such as the built-in gains tax or passive investment income tax, no equivalent taxes are imposed on partnerships.

---

[7] See also PLR 8711020, in which a C corporation and an S corporation were allowed to be equal partners in a partnership.

- Although partners are subject to tax on their portions of income, the rules for allocating income from partnerships to partners may be quite different from the S corporation rules. [§704]

Aside from the income and loss pass-through rules, the partnership provisions differ markedly from those applicable to S corporations. For instance, transfers to a partnership in exchange for a partnership interest are tax-free to both the partner and the partnership. [§721] Unlike the rules of §351, discussed earlier in this chapter, there is no requirement that the transferring partners be in control of the partnership. A partner's basis in his or her partnership interest includes that partner's portion of partnership debts, whether or not the partner has personally guaranteed the debts.[8] [§752] A distribution of property from a partnership to a partner is generally tax-free to both the partnership and the recipient partner. [§731] Property received in a distribution generally retains its basis and is not adjusted to fair market value. [§752] A partnership may adjust the basis of its assets to reflect changes in the basis of the partners when there is a sale or an exchange of a partnership interest or when there is a distribution of property. [§§754, 743(b), 734(b), 755]

The principal use of the S election is to avoid the double taxation of business income. A partnership can accomplish the same objective, but it has some disadvantages and some advantages. The primary disadvantage is that there must be at least one general partner, who has unlimited personal liability for all debts of the business. (In some cases, a partnership or other entity may obtain nonrecourse financing, whereby the lender seeks only an interest in specified property as security for repayment. Since the demise of the savings and loan associations in the early 1990s, this form of financing generally is not available in a commercial environment.) An S corporation absolves the owners of the business from personal liability for any corporate debts, except those that the shareholders specifically underwrite.

Partnerships often cope with the problem of personal liability by adopting the limited partnership structure. A limited partner has no personal liability for debts of the partnership and has an economic relation to the partnership that is similar to that of a shareholder in a corporation. In order for there to be a valid partnership, however, there must be at least one general partner. The general partner may be a corporation, but if the corporation does not have substantial assets the IRS may disregard its existence. The IRS retains the power to reclassify unincorporated entities as associations, which are treated as C corporations for federal income tax purposes. (See Regulations §301.7701-2 and Rev. Proc. 89-12, 1989-1 CB 798, for descriptions of the factors that the IRS uses to distinguish partnerships from associations.)

OBSERVATION: At the time of this writing, all states have adopted the business form of the "limited liability company," which resembles a partnership except that there are no general partners. An entity of this nature may provide a viable substitute for the S corporation. The limited liability company has three primary advantages over the S corporation. First, a limited liability company need not meet the eligibility requirements imposed on S corporations. Second, the limited liability company may, in many circumstances, distribute its noncash property without recognition of gain or loss. [§731] This aspect of partnership taxation facilitates business contractions and liquidations. Third, if a new owner acquired an interest (either through purchase or inheritance) in a limited liability company with appreciated assets, the limited liability company may adjust the basis of its assets to match the new owner's basis. [§743(b)] (The limited liability company must have a §754 election in effect to achieve this result.) Each of these advantages requires that the limited liability company receive *partnership* tax status. The IRS has issued Regulations that allow an unincor-

[8]There are special rules that distinguish recourse debts from nonrecourse debts and general partners from limited partners.

porated organization to choose its business form by election. [Regs. §301.7701-3] In general, a domestic unincorporated organization with two or more members would be treated as a partnership if it did not elect to be an association (corporation). There are other rules for single owner organizations and for foreign companies.

It is extremely unlikely that the limited liability company would replace the S corporation, however, for three reasons.

First, an existing corporation cannot become a partnership without liquidating. As discussed in Chapter 15, at 1525., a liquidation is a taxable event. Therefore, the cost of transition from corporate form to limited liability company form may be prohibitive.

Second, the business may have only one owner. Some states require that the limited liability company must have at least two owners. An S corporation, by contrast, may have a sole shareholder without risk of losing its tax status. However, enough states now permit single-owner limited liability companies that this particular problem should be easily remedied, merely by chartering the limited liability company in a state that permits a single-member limited liability company.

Third, in some jurisdictions the body of common law may be incomplete with respect to limited liability companies, whereas the rules are well established for corporations and their shareholders. For this reason, competent attorneys may steer clients away from limited liability companies if they are likely to encounter a problem for which the legal situation of the limited liability company and its members has not been resolved.

1435.12. Uses of the organizational structure. The restrictions on eligibility of S corporations make the simple S corporation form of entity unavailable to many businesses. When a business intends to have more than 75 shareholders, to have owners who are not U.S. citizens, not individuals, or to divide current profits in any manner different from future profits or liquidation rights, the business must turn to another form. The two alternatives become the partnership and the C corporation. If the business is not able to avoid double taxation, the partnership becomes the only suitable form.

The federal taxing statutes offer no restrictions on the types of entities that can be partners in a partnership. Individuals, trusts of any type, C corporations, estates, nonresidents, foreign trusts and corporations, and even tax-exempt organizations are all partners in many partnerships. S corporations can also be partners and may find several benefits from this form of doing business.

First, if the partnership interest is held merely as an investment, rather than as a substantial part of the S corporation's business, the S corporation may be able to avoid classification of some of its income as passive investment income. (See Chapter 12 for discussion.) Second, if the S corporation conducts substantial business through the partnership entity, the S corporation may be able to serve as a general partner. By doing so, the S corporation may be able to shield its owners from potential unlimited liability for corporate debts yet not cause any component of the organization to be subject to the double tax. This aspect of limited liability for a flow-through entity may have been the rationale behind the organization of the Milwaukee Brewers baseball franchise, described above.[9] If the structure becomes inconvenient, however, a shareholder in an S corporation cannot treat the S corporation as nonexistent and treat himself or herself as the direct owner of the partnership interest. Accordingly, it may not be possible to get assets from a partnership in which an S corporation is a partner into the hands of the S corporation's shareholders without taxation. [*Patterson*, 47 TCM 1029, TC Memo 1984-58. In this case the corporation had no assets except for its interest in the partnership and conducted no business activity in its own right.]

14

[9] The reason for adoption of the S corporation and limited partnership structure was not an issue in either case, and was not discussed.

EXAMPLE 14 - 44: Woodley Corporation is an S corporation with one shareholder, Ms. Woods. Woodley has no assets, except for its interest in Zooco, a partnership. Zooco distributes some appreciated property to its partners. Woodley receives property that had a basis of $10,000 to the partnership and fair market value of $100,000 at the time of the distribution. The distribution of appreciated property by a partnership does not cause the recognition of gain to either the partnership or the partner. [§731(a)] The partner takes a basis in the property that is the same as the partnership's basis before the distribution.[10] [§732]

Ms. Woods would like to own the property in her own name. Unfortunately, she will not be able to do so without having Woodley distribute the property to her. Such distribution will cause Woodley to recognize gain on the distribution, and Ms. Woods would receive a basis equal to the fair market value of the property. If Ms. Woods were to conveniently forget about the existence of Woodley, she could face serious audit problems.

This structure of S corporations as partners in partnerships may diminish in importance, as more states permit the formation and operation of limited liability companies, discussed above. Until these companies are available in most jurisdictions, however, making an S corporation a partner in a partnership is likely to be a useful method for structuring certain businesses.

1435.13. Classification problems. Between 1977 and 1994 there was a danger of an S corporation being a partner in a partnership. In Revenue Ruling 77-220, there were three supposed S corporations, each with 10 shareholders. (In 1977, an S corporation could have no more than 10 shareholders.) The three corporations conducted all business operations through a single partnership. The IRS combined all three of the corporations and disregarded the existence of the partnership, determining that there was only one association. The IRS's principal justification for its approach was that the entire structure lacked any business purpose and had been undertaken solely to circumvent the limitation on the number of shareholders. Since the combined association had 30 shareholders, it could not be an S corporation.

In 1994, the IRS revoked the earlier ruling. [Rev. Rul. 94-43, 1994-27 IRB 8] (See discussion in Chapter 2, at 220.2.) Thus, it now appears that membership in a partnership will not endanger an S corporation's status. Before 1994, many S corporations that intended to enter into partnerships received letter rulings. The purpose of obtaining such a ruling was to ensure that the IRS would not reconstruct the partnership arrangement in a manner similar to that in Revenue Ruling 77-220. There are at least three potential risks of reclassifying the entire structure as one association, as far as the S corporation eligibility requirements are concerned:

14

- There could be too many shareholders, as in Revenue Ruling 77-220.
- There could be an ineligible shareholder or shareholders.
- The division of partnership profits may be tantamount to a second class of stock.

The 1994 edition of the *S Corporation Tax Guide*, in Chapter 14 at 1435.13., contained discussion and examples of this problem. They now appear to be obsolete, in light of the new IRS policy.

OBSERVATION: The shift in IRS policy is based on valid grounds. In Revenue Ruling 94-43 [1994-27 IRB 8], the IRS stated that the sole purpose of the shareholder limit was to simplify tax matters with respect to the S corporation and acknowledged that the classification problem in Revenue Ruling 77-220 was beyond the scope of the reasons for the shareholder limits.

---

[10] In some cases, the basis to the partner may be the same as the partner's basis in the partnership interest. Further discussion of this issue is beyond the scope of this book.

> **EXAMPLE 14 - 45:** The CPA firm of Young and Olds has 300 partners. The firm is currently a general partnership with offices in several states. The firm is mindful of the risk of conducting business as a general partnership. On the advice of counsel, the partners have decided that each person will form his or her own corporation, which will be in compliance with the personal service corporation statutes for the state. Each partner will then transfer the interest in Young and Olds to his or her own corporation. After the transfers take place, Young and Olds will be a general partnership with 300 different personal service corporations as its partners. Counsel has advised the parties that each individual will be insulated from potential malpractice liability caused by the actions of other members of the firm.

The situation illustrated in Example 14 - 45 was the subject of several ruling requests. The IRS has held that the division of malpractice liability was a sufficient business purpose for the structure. Each corporation was allowed to be an S corporation, even though there were more than 35 members of the partnership. [PLRs 8823023, 8823027, 8950066]

S corporations requested and received favorable rulings on other issues as well. In one situation the IRS ruled that having S corporations as partners would not violate the 35-shareholder requirement, even though there were more than 35 partners; but it did not rule on any other issue. [PLR 9026044]

Taxpayers were concerned about extension of the IRS rationale to other issues. For instance, a partnership does not need to allocate its income in proportion to the various partner's interests.[11] Therefore, a partnership of two or more S corporations could resemble a corporation that has more than one class of stock.

> **EXAMPLE 14 - 46:** Marco and Anco, two S corporations, form a partnership and receive equal capital accounts. The partnership agreement provides for Marco to receive 70% of the partnership income for three years, after which the two partners will receive equal divisions of profits. The partnership agreement has substantial economic effect. If the IRS were to treat the two S corporations and the partnership as a single tax entity, the uneven allocation of profits would be equivalent to two classes of stock.

In some instances, taxpayers have asked the IRS to rule that such an allocation scheme does not create a second class of stock. In one ruling the taxpayer represented that the allocation of partnership income would not be in accordance with ownership percentages. The IRS did not address the class-of-stock problem directly, but stated that the partners could be S corporations. In another ruling, the IRS held that the division of partnership profits did not create a second class of stock. The partnership was allowed to allocate its income and losses among the partners under the normal partnership allocation rules, which are much more flexible than the S corporation rules.

When an S corporation is a partner in one or more partnerships, the recordkeeping requirements for the corporate-level taxes may be onerous. As discussed in Chapter 11, at 1140.4., the flow-through of built-in gains from a partnership to an S corporation can be quite complex. See Chapter 12, at 1210.5. and 1210.6., for the treatment of partnership income and gains from sales of partnership interests with respect to the S corporation's passive investment income.

1435.2. S corporations as members of limited liability companies. The role of an S corporation as a member of a limited liability company is similar to that of a member of a partnership. From a tax point of view, there are few differences between the partnership and the limited liability company.

---

[11] Such allocation must have substantial economic effect, pursuant to §704(b). The rules defining substantial economic effect are extensive, and are beyond the scope of this book.

1435.21. Classification problems. If an S corporation is a member of a limited liability company, there may be some additional complications if the limited liability company is treated as an association.

In one ruling, the S corporation involved owned 80% of the interest in a limited liability company, and the sole shareholder of the S corporation owned the other 20%. The IRS held that the limited liability company was an association taxable as a corporation. Therefore, the S corporation lost its S election as a result of the affiliation. [PLR 9433008] The S corporation was granted inadvertent termination relief, as discussed in Chapter 13, at 1350.

> **OBSERVATION:** After 1996, an S corporation may own more than 80% of the stock of another corporation. Thus, the affiliation problem from PLR 9433008 has disappeared. From another point of view Regulations §301.7701-3 (dealing with elective classification of limited liability companies) has solved the classification issue of limited liability companies. In this case, an S corporation with a less-than-100% interest in a limited liability company would always be treated as a partner in a partnership, unless the limited liability company elected to be taxed as a corporation. An S corporation with 100% ownership of an limited liability company (in a jurisdiction that allows single-member limited liability companies) is treated as the owner of the assets and liabilities of the limited liability company. The single-member limited liability company owned by an S corporation would be remarkably similar to the new qualified Subchapter S subsidiary permitted after 1996.

In a different situation, two S corporations were the sole members of a limited liability company. The IRS ruled that the limited liability company was a valid partnership. There was no ruling on the status of the S corporations, although the ruling implicitly permitted the arrangement. [PLR 9529015]

1435.22. Uses of the organizational structure. As is discussed in Chapter 15, liquidation of an S corporation is treated as a fully taxable event. Conversion of an S corporation into a limited liability company is treated as a taxable liquidation, unless the limited liability company is treated as a corporation. This is an unusual situation after the "check the box" Regulation. [§301.7701-3] Also, conversion of an existing S corporation into a limited liability company classified as an association accomplishes absolutely nothing for federal income tax purposes. See Chapter 17, at 1730.36., for discussion.

There may be many instances in which an S corporation would rather be a limited liability company, but cannot afford the tax cost of the liquidation. Having an existing corporation contribute its assets to a limited liability company can accomplish part of this objective. The S corporation can transfer some or all of its assets to the limited liability company in exchange for an interest therein. The transfer of property into the limited liability company is tax free. [§721] See at 1435.11. for discussion.

There is no opportunity to use a partnership or a limited liability company to shift any unrealized appreciation to other parties. [§704(c)(1)(A)] There are flexible, but extremely complicated, rules regarding the allocation of income and other items among the members of a partnership or a limited liability company. [§704(b)] Thus the transfer of assets from an S corporation to a limited liability company in which it is a member offers no immediate tax-saving strategies.

One possible tax-saving strategy relates to the portion of Social Security taxes covering Medicare. There is no ceiling amount for this tax, which is 1.45% employer tax plus an equal amount of withholding. A similar tax is imposed on self-employment income. [§1401] A partnership passes self-employment income through to general partners and to limited partners who receive guaranteed payments for services. [§1402] An individual who is a member of a limited liability company has a strong likelihood of being treated as a general partner. An S corporation, however, does not pass self-employment income through to its shareholders. See Chapter 8, at 820.1. Therefore, interposing an S corporation between a partnership (including a limited liability company) and individual members may prevent income from the Medicare portion of the FICA or self-employment tax. See Chapter 8, at 820.3., for a discussion of the rules regarding compensation.

1435.23. Multiple-owner companies. A multiple-owner limited liability company is identical to a partnership for tax purposes. Therefore, the structure of one or more S corporations as members in a limited liability company allows the flexibility of partnerships, without double taxation. It might also be useful when an S corporation wants to disperse ownership in one or more, but not all, of its business enterprises. Several of the split-off rulings, discussed in Chapter 17, have dealt with similar situations.

1435.24. Single-owner companies. An S corporation may want to own property through a single-member limited liability company for the liability shield, although parties desiring this protection should seek competent local legal counsel to ascertain the degree of protection afforded.

The tax classification of a single-owner limited liability company under the "check the box" regulations is that of a nonentity. [Regs. §301.7701-3(b)(1)(ii)] If an S corporation transfers assets to a single-member limited liability company or acquires all of the interest in a limited liability company, the company itself would be disregarded for tax purposes. The tax treatment would be identical to that of a parent S corporation and a QSSS (QSub), with one important distinction. If a parent S corporation wanted to dispose of a part interest in a QSub, the QSub would become a C corporation, unable to elect S status for five years. A disposition of a part interest in a single-member limited liability company would create a partnership, which would continue to be a pass-through entity for tax purposes.

> **OBSERVATION:** Proposed Regulations issued in 1998 allow a single-member limited liability company to be treated as a QSub. [Proposed Regs. §1.1361-2(c), Example (2)] It is difficult to see where this classification would have any advantage over the default classification of a single-member limited liability company, which is disregarded for tax purposes without a QSub election.

1435.25. Disposition of interest. When a partner disposes of an interest in a partnership, there are several complex rules. Among these is §751(a), which treats the disposition of the interest as a disposition of a partner's pro-rata share of unrealized receivables and inventory items. This deemed disposition can cause the partner to recognize ordinary income on part of the disposition and the remainder as capital gain or loss. The same rules apply to dispositions of interest in a limited liability company, assuming that the limited liability company is treated as a partnership for tax purposes.

1435.3. S corporations in controlled group of corporations. There are *controlled* groups of corporations, defined in §1563, in which two or more corporations are controlled by common owners, for example, in a parent–subsidiary or brother–sister controlled group structure. The principal nontax reasons for controlled groups of corporations are the insulation of business assets from certain claims and the dispersion of ownership of different areas of the business. An S corporation *may* be a member of a controlled group of corporations, whether the controlled group is a parent–subsidiary or a brother–sister arrangement. However, an S corporation cannot be a subsidiary member of a parent–subsidiary group. A brother–sister group may include several S corporations, as long as each meets all of the eligibility requirements.

EXAMPLE 14-47: Allen, Brenda, and Clyde are equal shareholders in the ABC Corporation, an S corporation. ABC has substantial business assets and is considering purchasing some property for expansion of its business. The property under consideration was once the site of an automobile service station. Allen, Brenda, and Clyde are concerned about the potential liability for environmental cleanup costs if they purchase the new building. Their attorney has advised them to keep the property in a corporation that is completely separate from any other assets. Therefore, they establish BCA Corporation, of which Allen, Brenda, and Clyde become equal shareholders. BCA's only asset is the new property. ABC and BCA are not members of an affiliated group of corporations, since neither corporation directly owns any stock in the other. ABC does not endanger its S election. BCA is also eligible to become an S corporation, if the shareholders desire.

1435.31. Tax advantages of controlled group. From a tax point of view, this type of structure could allow ineligible persons to own portions of the business and provide certain fringe benefits to shareholders. The availability of fringe benefits to shareholder-employees of a C corporation may make a controlled group of corporations an ideal blend between the benefits of C corporations and those of S corporations.

EXAMPLE 14-48: Vicki owns all of the stock of Vico, an interior design consulting firm. She has also agreed to a distributorship arrangement with a Mexican producer of furnishings and decorative items. The consulting business derives most of its income from Vicki's activities. Vicki and her tax advisors do not believe that there is any substantial risk that this business would ever generate extremely high income. Therefore Vicki's salary would be able to exhaust the corporation's taxable income without being reclassified as excessive compensation. In addition, Vicki wants the tax advantage of having the corporation provide her with accident and health insurance coverage. Therefore, she has conducted the design consulting business as a C corporation and intends to do so in the future.

The distributorship arrangement is likely to be a much more volatile business. It is likely to suffer a loss in its first year or two, and then it could be extremely profitable. If it becomes as profitable as she expects, the corporation's income would exceed any allowance for reasonable compensation. This operation could place the corporation in serious danger of double taxation. Therefore, it makes sense to place the distributorship arrangement in a separate corporation and make an S election for that corporation. The end result will be that Vicki receives tax-free accident and health insurance, but does not need to worry about unreasonable compensation problems.

When a C corporation is a member of a controlled group with other C corporations, certain tax attributes must be split among the component members. For instance, the graduated rate schedule, the alternative minimum tax exemption, and the §179 asset expensing election (discussed in Chapter 6, at 610.53.) must be divided so that the entire group is allowed no more of these tax benefits than a single corporation. An S corporation is not a component member of a controlled group of corporations. Therefore the S corporation will be able to expense property under §179 without causing a reduction of the limit for the C corporations that are also under common control. Similarly, the C corporations that are members of the group will not need to allocate any of their other favorable tax attributes to the S corporation.

1435.32. C corporation subsidiary. An S corporation may find several uses for holding a C corporation as a subsidiary. Among these could be the avoidance of LIFO recapture tax.

EXAMPLE 14-49: Licor is a C corporation that uses the LIFO inventory method. It has decided to convert as much of its operations as possible to S corporation status. One of its lines of business, however, uses the LIFO inventory method. The LIFO recapture tax on conversion of this part of the operation would be extremely expensive. Therefore, the corporation decides to contribute the line of business with the LIFO inventory to a brand new subsidiary. The subsidiary will be a C corporation, and Licor will elect S status for its next taxable year.

CAUTION: There must be some valid nontax purpose for the division of a business. If a corporation merely contributes its LIFO inventory to a subsidiary, and the subsidiary has no other assets and no independent businesses, the IRS could invoke the doctrine of substance over form and treat the parent corporation and the subsidiary as one corporation. The IRS could then collect the LIFO recapture tax.

1435.33. Disposition of interest. A disposition of interest in a C corporation subsidiary would receive no special tax treatment. The S corporation would generally report capital gain or loss on the disposition of its stock in the subsidiary, as discussed in Chapter 16. It would appear that the transaction could not be the subject of a §338(h)(10) election, since the S corporation and the subsidiary would not be members of an affiliated group of corporations. [§1504(b)(8); Regs. §1.338(h)(10)-1(a)]

1435.4. Qualified Subchapter S Subsidiary. A QSub may have many uses. Among the most important is the liability shield under local law. For example, if an S corporation acquires a corporation that has some potential liabilities, the S corporation need not liquidate the target corporation and expose itself (the parent corporation) to the liabilities of the target.

1435.41. Definition and tax treatment. As discussed in Chapter 2, at 230., an S corporation may elect to treat a 100% owned domestic corporation as a QSub. In general, the subsidiary is treated as a nonentity (in the same manner as a single-owner limited liability company) for federal income tax purposes. [§1361(b)(3)] Thus this method can be effective for consolidating operations of various corporations.

EXAMPLE 14 - 50: Reno, Inc., is an S corporation with 100% active gross receipts (within the meaning of §1362(d)(3)(C)). It expects its active gross receipts to be in the range of $1,000,000 per year. Rentco, Inc., is another S corporation, owned by Reno's shareholders. Reno's gross receipts are expected to be around $300,000 per year. Most of Rentco's gross receipts will be passive investment income. Rentco has substantial accumulated earnings and profits. As an S corporation, Rentco will be subject to the passive investment income tax, and it will likely lose its S election unless it pays out its accumulated earnings and profits as dividends. The shareholders do not want to claim the dividend income that would result from a distribution or distribution election. The shareholders intend to continue to treat Rentco and Reno as separate corporations for local law purposes.

The shareholders could contribute their Rentco stock to Reno (or vice versa). They could use a transaction such as a Type B reorganization (see Chapter 17) to make the contribution tax-free. By having the acquiror treat the acquired subsidiary as a loss, the gross receipts from both corporations would be combined for purposes of the passive investment income tests. Thus the combined entities would not be in any danger of the passive investment income tax or loss of an S election.

14

1435.42. Acquisition of a QSub. There are no rules regarding the acquisition of a QSub. Therefore, the acquisition could be done in any manner, such as a §351 incorporation, discussed in this chapter; a purchase of a going-concern corporation, as discussed in Chapter 16; or by means of one of the tax-free reorganization provisions discussed in Chapter 17. Within 2 months and 15 days after acquisition, the parent corporation must file the appropriate election for the QSST status to begin at the time of acquisition. See discussion in Chapter 5, at 545, for a discussion of the QSub election in general. Also see Chapter 16, at 1630.38., for discussion of the effects of a §338 election and QSub election.

The 1998 Proposed Regulations generally provide that a QSub election for an existing corporation is to be treated as a liquidation of the subsidiary under general tax principles. As is discussed in Chapter 15, liquidation of a wholly owned subsidiary is generally tax-free under §§332 and 337. To qualify for this tax-free treatment, the parent corporation must own at least 80% of the stock of the subsidiary at the time of the adoption of the plan to liquidate and at all times thereafter. [§332(b)(1)] Furthermore, the subsidiary must not be insolvent (i.e., liabilities exceed fair market value of all assets).

1435.43. Step-transaction problems. The QSub election could be violated if the parent did not own the requisite 80% of the stock of the subsidiary at the time the plan to liquidate was adopted. Application of the step-transaction doctrine could have a drastic effect on the tax consequences of acquiring a corporation and converting it to QSub status.

> **EXAMPLE 14 - 51:** John owns 100% of the stock of Johnco. Johnco owns 79% of the stock of Subco and John owns the other 21% of Subco's stock. John contributes his Subco stock to Johnco in exchange for additional Johnco stock (as a §351 transfer or as a contribution to Johnco's capital). This contribution would be tax-free under either §351 or §118. If Johnco now liquidates Subco, the liquidation could also be tax-free under §332. If, however, the facts indicated that Johnco did not own the requisite 80% of Subco at the time the plan to liquidate Subco was adopted, the liquidation of Subco would be taxable.

The Proposed Regulations do not provide a permanent protection from imposition of the step-transaction doctrine, but they do provide that the doctrine will not be invoked with respect to any QSub election that occurs before 60 days after the Final Regulations are adopted. [Proposed Regs. §1.1361-4(a)(5)] Accordingly, the Regulations provide that filing the QSub election constitutes the adoption of the plan to liquidate. This rule could be very useful if S corporations are acquiring the minority interests of subsidiaries that were necessary to avoid the pre-1997 affiliated group rules.

> **EXAMPLE 14 - 52:** Refer to Example 14 - 51, above. If John contributes the Subco stock to Johnco and Johnco makes the QSub election within 60 days after adoption of the Final Regulations, the step-transaction doctrine would not be invoked and the deemed liquidation of Subco would be tax-free under §332.

1435.44. Tiers of QSub corporations. A QSub is treated as nonexistent for all federal tax purposes. Accordingly, there can be limitless levels, and arrangements of ownership, as long as all parties concerned are the parent S corporation and the QSub corporations.

> **EXAMPLE 14 - 53:** Margco, an S corporation, owns all of the stock of Sub1, a QSub. Margco and Sub1 each own 50% of the stock of Sub2. Margco is treated as the sole owner of the Sub2 stock, since Sub1 is disregarded for all federal tax purposes. Accordingly, Sub2 can also be a QSub.

1435.45. Disposition of a QSub. Since the existence of the QSub is ignored for tax purposes, the disposition of stock should be treated as a disposition of the assets within the QSub. If these assets consist of a separate business, an allocation under §1060 may be needed. See Chapter 16, at 1620. If the assets do not constitute a going concern, or if they are not sufficient for any going-concern value to be attached, there are no special rules on the allocation of the consideration.

The Proposed Regulations issued in 1998 provide some guidance on the disposition of a QSub; they merely restate the Code that when a QSub loses its status as such, it is treated as a newly formed corporation. The tax fiction is that the parent S corporation transfers assets and liabilities (those actually held inside the QSub for nontax purposes) to a new corporation. The Proposed Regulations treat this as a hypothetical formation of a new corporation. [Proposed Regs. §1.1361-5(b)(1)] Accordingly, if the parent corporation retains at least 80% control, the formation of the "new" corporation will be covered by §351. The control rule would not be violated if the parent S corporation distributed the stock of the subsidiary to shareholders of the parent corporation. [§351(c)]

However, the sale of a QSub to other persons would disqualify the formation of the "new" corporation from §351, since there would be a prearranged plan to divest control. The parent corporation's transfer of assets and liabilities to the "new" corporation would be a taxable event. In addition, the sale of the QSub's stock would be treated as occurring on the first day of its holding period by the parent corporation; it could not be considered long-term capital gain, even if the parent corporation had actually held the stock for an extended period of time.

1435.46. Special rules for banks. The Small Business Job Protection Act of 1996 allows banks to be S corporations. Similarly, bank holding companies can now be S corporations, and a bank can be a QSub. Some special rules limit certain deductions of banks and do not permit the bank's income to be combined with that of any other corporation. For this purpose, each bank is treated as a corporation separate from its parent or its non-bank QSub. [See Proposed Regs. §1.1361-4(a)(3).]

1435.5. Ownership of real estate. Due to its volatile nature, real estate is often kept out of the corporation entirely. This separate ownership has several distinct advantages. See the discussion in Chapter 8, at 840.2., for some of the tax ramifications. In some instances, the real estate is held by a partnership or a limited liability company that is owned by the owners of the S corporation. In other situations, the real estate partnership or limited liability company is owned by different persons, such as members of the controlling shareholder's family.

Among the advantages to be considered are the following:

- The rent that the S corporation pays to the partnership will distribute some of the earnings of the S corporation to owners in the form of payments that are not subject to FICA tax.
- The real estate, which potential buyers of the corporation may not want, may be kept out of the assets measured in a disposition of stock in a tax-free reorganization. See Chapter 17.
- If a shareholder in a family corporation is to be redeemed out of the S corporation in a transaction that qualifies under §302(b)(3), the corporation may still rent property from the shareholder without jeopardizing the redemption's tax treatment. [PLR 9837022] See Chapter 15, at 1510.4.
- The real estate may be distributed to partners or members of an limited liability company without recognition of gain or loss. In addition, basis of the real estate often carries over to the partners or members after a distribution. [§731, §733] This tax treatment is not available to S corporations and their shareholders.

1435.6. Hazard of income reallocation. When two or more businesses are under common control, the IRS can reallocate income to reflect arm's-length transfer pricing. [§482] This rule usually is applied in the area of international trade, but the IRS could apply the rule to an S corporation and a C corporation combined. Unlike other areas of the tax law, §482 has no specified definition of *common control*. This area of the tax law is extremely complex and is beyond the scope of this book.

1435.7. Treatment of common paymasters. When one person is an employee of two or more corporations, there could be a duplication of employer FICA and unemployment taxes. The burden of these taxes on the employers can be substantially reduced if the employers qualify to select a common paymaster. If they do so qualify, they are treated as one employer for FICA tax [§3121(s)] and for federal unemployment tax. [§3306(p)] In order for a group of corporations to qualify to use a common paymaster, they must meet one of the following tests [Regs. §31.3121(s)-1(b)]:

- They must be members of a controlled group of corporations (with a 50%, rather than an 80%, minimum ownership test), or
- Both corporations must have common holders of at least 50% voting power, or
- At least 50% of one corporation's officers must also be officers of the other corporation, or
- At least 30% of one corporation's employees must be concurrently employed by the other corporation.

Note that the requisite relationships are diverse enough for most brother–sister controlled groups to qualify.

When a qualifying group of corporations designates a common paymaster, that corporation issues the payroll checks and performs all withholding and tax payment functions. [Regs. §31.3121(s)-1(a)] If the separate corporations issue checks directly to employees and bypass the common paymaster, they are treated as separate employers and they lose the benefits of common paymaster status. [Rev. Rul. 81-21, 1981-1 CB 482]

> **EXAMPLE 14 - 54:** Refer to Example 14 - 48. Vicki establishes a new corporation, Kico, to conduct the distributing business. Vico remains a C corporation and Kico makes an immediate S election. Vico becomes the common paymaster for both corporations.
>
> On a given payday, Kico owes $3,000 to an employee. Vico's obligation to that same person is $2,000. The employer's portion of payroll taxes on $5,000 is $400. Vico writes a check for $5,000 (less withholding to the employee) and also pays the payroll taxes of $400. Vico then determines that Kico's total payroll obligation is $3,000 plus $240 [(3,000/5,000) x 400] for the payroll tax. Kico then reimburses Vico $3,240.

The common paymaster is treated as a sole employer for FICA and other payroll tax purposes. Therefore the employers can combine all of their payments to one employee for purposes of the wage ceilings.

> **EXAMPLE 14 - 55:** Refer to Example 14 - 54. Assume, for the current year, that the FICA old age tax ceiling is $60,000. By mid-year, Vicki has received $40,000 salary from Vico and $20,000 from Kico. The remainder of her compensation from either or both corporations during the current year will be exempt from FICA.

No formal election is filed with the IRS to secure common paymaster status. The board of directors of each corporation participating in the arrangement must adopt a resolution that designates one of the corporations as the common paymaster. [PLR 8352049]

14

The statute states literally that each employer must be a *corporation*. Thus any corporation, including an S corporation, should be allowed to participate in a common paymaster arrangement. Where the compensation involves an officer of the S corporation, it is prudent to show the amount as compensation of officers on the S corporation's Form 1120S. Failure to classify the payments in this manner can result in an audit for unreasonably low compensation, as discussed in Chapter 8, at 820.3.

The IRS has ruled that partnerships [PLRs 8510026, 9315007] and even a university [PLR 9224013] can act as common paymasters, even though they are not corporations. If a group of employers contains one or more unincorporated enterprises, it is probably prudent to request a letter ruling, since the statute does not literally allow this treatment.

> **OBSERVATION:** The lack of formal procedures to elect common paymaster status has its benefits and its drawbacks. The major benefit is that this status will not be disallowed because of failure to file some specific form. The major drawback is that some IRS offices might request lengthy and repeated explanations of the failure of employers other than the common paymaster to file payroll tax returns.

1440. Practice aids.

The following practice aids are checklists to help the user keep track of the different tax problems discussed in this chapter. The principal focus of each checklist is to serve as a reminder of some of the most important S corporation planning opportunities and pitfalls.

Checklist 14 - 1 provides a convenient review of factors to consider before incorporating a business.

Checklist 14 - 2 is useful for evaluating the potential tax treatment of a purported loan, and it can help drafters of a loan recall the important criteria for distinguishing debt from equity. The user is also reminded to document each of the factors that could be useful in defending the tax classification of a debt. There is also a checklist in Chapter 2 for the straight-debt safe harbor.

Checklist 14 - 3 summarizes the requirements of §1244. It should be prepared at the time stock is issued, and again when a holder disposes of stock.

Checklist 14 - 4 provides a list of factors to consider when an S corporation owns interests in one or more other entities, including corporations, partnerships, and limited liability companies.

Checklist 14 - 1: Pre-incorporation

Corporate considerations	*Yes*	*No*
Nonrecognition treatment desired under §351?	______	______
Identity of all transferors in an integrated exchange	______	______
Review the following in assuring 80% control:	______	______
All shares voting stock	______	______
Each class nonvoting	______	______

Corporate considerations	*Yes*	*No*
Transferors of property in control?	______	______
Any existing shareholders?	______	______
If yes, is new property contribution sufficient?	______	______
Any receiving stock for services?	______	______
If yes, is new property contribution sufficient?	______	______
Determine any shareholder's recognized gain.	______	______
Allocate gain to assets contributed.	______	______
Eligibility for S status	______	______
Review Chapter 2 checklists.	______	______
State law governing issuance of shares	______	______
File election to be in effect first year.	______	______
Shareholder considerations (Complete for each)	______	______
Identity of property to be transferred	______	______
Any timing delays?	______	______
If yes, be sure to include in shareholder agreement.	______	______
Any liabilities to be transferred?	______	______
Any liabilities without business purpose or with tax avoidance motive?	______	______

14

Consider keeping liabilities out of corporation.	___	___
Liabilities exceed basis?	___	___
Consider keeping liabilities out of corporation.	___	___
Consider transferring other property.	___	___
Consider lease, rather than contribution.	___	___
Any other boot?	___	___
If currently a partnership, consider three options:	___	___
Contributing partnership property to corporation, then liquidating distribution of stock	___	___
Contributing partnership interests to corporation	___	___
Liquidating distribution of all partnership property, then contributing of property to corporation	___	___

Checklist 14 - 2: Debt and equity

(Also see Checklist 2-4, for straight-debt safe harbor.)

Characteristics of debt	*Yes*	*No*
Written instrument	___	___
Maturity date or demand	___	___
Enforcement of terms	___	___
Consistent treatment by lender and debtor	___	___

Characteristics of debt	*Yes*	*No*
Lender's business purpose	___	___
Thin capitalization	___	___
Proportion to stock ownership	___	___
Repayment subject to sale of property	___	___
Use of funds for essential assets	___	___
Adequate interest? See Chapter 8.	___	___

14

Checklist 14 - 3: Section 1244

	Yes	*No*
At issue:		
Stock received for cash or property?	___	___
Under $1,000,000 capitalization	___	___
If pre-11/7/78, check for plan	___	___
At disposition:	___	___
Original holder?	___	___
Determine §1244 basis, without adjustments	___	___

Copyright © 2000 by Harcourt, Inc. All rights reserved.

Determine loss limit	______	______
Evaluate other §1244 stock sales in year	______	______
Determine any apportionment and treatment of excess	______	______
Active trade or business	______	______

Checklist 14 - 4: Affiliations

	Applicable (Yes/No)	*Completed (Date)*
All subsidiary corporations – 100% stock?	______	______
If yes, consider QSub election	______	______
Check for changed ownership percentage	______	______
Stock redemption of minority	______	______
Issue new stock to parent	______	______
Check for incorporation of any partnership in which corporation owns interest	______	______
Check for all employers under common influence or control	______	______
Common paymaster agreements	______	______
Consistent federal state and local payroll tax return	______	______

14

Copyright © 2000 by Harcourt, Inc. All rights reserved.

CONTRACTION OF THE S CORPORATION

CONTENTS

15

1500. Overview.

S corporations occasionally want to contract their operations for any number of reasons. For instance:

- The corporation may have excessive assets for the level of business it intends to conduct.
- The shareholders may have decided to split up the business and go their separate ways.
- The shareholders have decided to split up the business into smaller entities, but retain proportionate ownership in each.
- One or more of the shareholders have decided to terminate their business interest entirely.

The simplest way to accomplish this objective is to distribute the unwanted property to the shareholders. There are, however, some potential tax problems:

- If the property has appreciated in value, the corporation will recognize gain on the distribution. See Chapter 7, at 730.4.
- If the property has declined in value, the corporation will not be allowed to recognize any loss, but the shareholders receiving the property will adjust their basis to the property's fair market value. See Chapter 7, at 730.5.
- If the corporation has a relatively low Accumulated Adjustments Account (AAA) and significant accumulated earnings and profits, the shareholders receiving the property will have dividend income. See Chapter 7, at 720.
- If the distribution is not proportionate to all shares, the corporation may have a second class of stock. See Chapter 2, at 225.3.

Besides a straightforward distribution of property, there are two other techniques by which a corporation may contract its operations:

- A stock redemption
- A corporate division

A stock redemption may mitigate the taxability of certain distributions. The shareholder who receives the proceeds will be able to recover basis in his or her stock and report a capital gain or loss on the transaction. From the corporation's point of view, however, a stock redemption is similar to any other distribution. The corporation must recognize any gain, but it cannot recognize a loss on the distribution of property.

A divisive reorganization may allow a corporation to divest itself of some of its properties in a completely tax-free transaction. The property so distributed must be sufficient to constitute an entire trade or business, and it must be distributed in the form of stock. Neither the shareholders who receive stock nor the corporation making the distribution recognizes any gain or loss on the transfer. The tax benefits of this transaction are so great that the rules are extremely rigid.

The rules governing both types of transactions are contained in Subchapter C, but are applicable to S corporations. The unique aspects of S corporations require that a corporation contemplating such a transaction follow some special rules. This chapter provides a basic discussion of these rules. It is not intended to be a comprehensive discussion of the Subchapter C problems. It addresses the most commonly encountered problems and suggests planning strategies to S corporations and their shareholders.

1510. Stock redemptions.

A stock redemption occurs when an issuing corporation buys its own stock. [§317(b)] The term *stock redemption* does not indicate the tax treatment. In some cases, a stock redemption is equivalent to any other sale or exchange. In others, the redemption is not significantly different from a distribution. The next two examples illustrate two fundamentally different transactions.

> **EXAMPLE 15 - 1:** Steve owns 100 shares of stock in Public, Inc., a publicly traded corporation with 150,000,000 shares outstanding. Steve places a sale order with his broker, who sells the shares on the same day. On that day, Public, Inc., was buying back some of its own shares and happened to buy Steve's block. Although neither Steve nor his broker is aware of the purchaser's identity, the transaction is a stock redemption.

> **EXAMPLE 15 - 2:** Bob owns all of the stock in Bobco, a C corporation with substantial earnings and profits. Bobco has $1,000,000 in liquid assets and is facing the possibility of the accumulated earnings tax. Bob's basis in his Bobco stock is $1,500,000. Bob sells two-thirds of his Bobco stock back to Bobco. The transaction is a stock redemption.

Each of the two preceding examples illustrates a stock redemption. Although the transactions are similar in form, they are completely different in substance. The first instance is no different from any other sale of securities. The second, however, is no different from a dividend. The shareholder has surrendered nothing of substance and has attempted to convert a fully taxable distribution into an exchange.

Not all transactions are as easy to categorize as the two examples above, so Subchapter C contains several tests for redemption transactions, described below at 1510.1. If a transaction meets one of these tests, it is treated as a sale or an exchange, from the shareholder's point of view.

An S corporation may redeem stock of a shareholder. The redemption may be treated as a sale or a distribution of income. The stock redemption rules are found in Subchapter C, with only one slight modification in Subchapter S. As a general rule, shareholders of C corporations prefer to have a redemption treated as a sale or an exchange. In the C corporation context, a sale or exchange allows the shareholder to recover basis in the redeemed shares and report capital gain for the remainder of the proceeds. If it does not qualify as a sale or an exchange, it usually is treated as a dividend. The dividend is ordinary income, to the extent of the entire redemption proceeds or the corporation's current and accumulated earnings and profits (AEP), whichever is less.

When an S corporation redeems its own stock, the treatment as an exchange or a distribution may be immaterial. If the corporation has no AEP, a distribution is recovery of basis, then gain—exactly the same treatment as a distribution. If an S corporation does have AEP, the shareholder may desire exchange treatment. The other shareholders might also have a vested interest in treating the redemption as an exchange, since a distribution of the corporation's Accumulated Adjustments Account to one shareholder may make distributions to other shareholders taxable as dividends.

In a recent case, a split-off that failed to meet the tests of §355 (see Chapter 17, at 1735) was held to be a redemption. Accordingly the corporation and the shareholder who received the distribution were required to recognize gain. [*Martin Ice Cream Co.*, 110 T.C. No. 18(1998)]

1510.1. Sale or exchange tests, in general. A *stock redemption* is defined as a transaction whereby a corporation buys its own stock from a shareholder. [§317(b)] That term *redemption*, however, does not distinguish between an exchange and a distribution. Section 302(b) gives four tests for determining whether the transfer will qualify for exchange treatment. Three of the tests are made by measuring the effects at the shareholder level:

- "Not essentially equivalent to a dividend"—§302(b)(1)
- "Substantially disproportionate"—§302(b)(2)
- "Complete termination"—§302(b)(3)

The fourth test is made at the corporate level:

- "Partial liquidation"—§302(b)(4)

Another transaction that may be treated as an exchange is the redemption of stock that had been held by a deceased shareholder. Section 303 allows the surviving shareholder to use corporate assets to redeem stock in order to pay certain estate and inheritance taxes.

In all other cases, if the redemption passes any of the four tests, it is a sale or an exchange. If the transaction is a sale or an exchange, the shareholder recovers basis and reports gain or loss realized. [§302(a)] If the transaction is not treated as a sale or an exchange, the shareholder treats it as a corporate distribution with respect to stock. [§302(d)] If the corporation is not an S corporation, the shareholder will treat the redemption proceeds as a dividend to the extent of the corporation's AEP.

As stated in earlier chapters, there is a general rule that Subchapter C provisions apply to S corporations. Subchapter S contains no rules that modify any of the Subchapter C redemption tests. The IRS has ruled that C corporation redemption tests apply to S corporations. [PLRs 8739007, 8748034] Therefore, the rules of Subchapter C and Subchapter S have some interesting interactions.

1510.11. Significance of redemption rules for S corporations. If a redemption of stock is treated as a sale or an exchange, there is almost no difference between the treatment of S corporation stock and the treatment of C corporation stock. The proceeds are treated as the amount realized on the sale of stock. The shareholder whose stock is redeemed reports a taxable gain or loss for the difference between the proceeds and the adjusted basis of the stock surrendered.

Although the rules for testing redemptions are identical for C corporations and S corporations, the consequences of a distribution may be considerably different for shareholders in the two types of entities when the distribution is not treated as a sale or exchange. Whereas the shareholder in a C corporation nearly always reports dividend income, the treatment is different for S corporation shareholders when a redemption is treated as a dividend.

The reason for this difference is that §302(a) treats any redemption that fails to meet one of the exchange tests as a *distribution subject to §301*. Subchapter S, however, preempts any distribution that would be subject to §301. Therefore, a distribution, whether or not in redemption of stock, will be subject to the normal ordering rules of §1368: 15

- AAA
- PTI (if it exists)
- AEP
- Recovery of basis
- Gain

Therefore, the shareholder will not have dividend income except to the extent that the distribution is treated as coming from the corporation's AEP.

If the S corporation has no AEP or has sufficient AAA to cover the entire redemption distribution, treatment as a sale or an exchange, as opposed to a corporate distribution, has no significant effect on a shareholder whose stock is redeemed.

EXAMPLE 15 - 3: Aqua Corporation is an S corporation with no AEP. Shareholder Alvin's stock is redeemed for $150,000. His basis in the stock is $15,000. He will recognize a gain of $135,000, regardless of whether the redemption passes one of the tests in §302(b), since the corporation has no AEP.

If the S corporation has AEP and insufficient AAA to cover the distribution, the treatment as a sale or an exchange can have important tax consequences.

EXAMPLE 15 - 4: Assume that Aqua, from Example 15 - 3, has $55,000 AAA and $120,000 AEP on the date that the shares are redeemed. If Alvin's redemption is viewed as a distribution, he will treat it as follows:

From AAA	
Reduction of basis	$ 15,000
Gain	40,000
From AEP	
Dividend	95,000
Total	$150,000

If Aqua made other distributions in the same year, the AAA would be apportioned among them. All of the shareholders who received distributions during the year might be affected.

1510.12. Situations where distribution is preferable to exchange. If a C corporation redeems its shares, shareholders usually prefer to have the transaction treated as an exchange rather than a distribution. In an exchange, the shareholder is allowed to recover his or her basis, and only the excess of the redemption proceeds over the basis is taxable as a gain. In addition, a gain on a redemption is typically a capital gain, whereas a distribution from a C corporation is usually ordinary income.

When the corporation is an S corporation, however, the shareholder may actually prefer to have ordinary distribution treatment rather than classification as an exchange. In an ordinary distribution, the shareholder is allowed to recover all of his or her stock basis, including basis in shares that are not redeemed. By contrast, in an exchange transaction the shareholder would be able to recover only the allocable portion of basis of the shares actually redeemed.

15

EXAMPLE 15 - 5: Kevin owns 50 shares in Walco, an S corporation. Teresa owns the other 50 shares. All 100 outstanding shares are voting stock. Kevin and Teresa are not related. In the current year, the corporation plans to redeem 20 of Kevin's shares at $1,000 per share, or $20,000 in total. Kevin's basis in those shares, after reflecting all of the current year's income and deductions, is $600 per share, or $12,000 in total. His basis in the 30 shares he retains is also $600 per share.

The transaction appears to meet the definition of a *substantially disproportionate redemption* under §302(b)(2). After the redemption, Kevin only holds 37.5% (30 of 80 outstanding shares). This reduction from his former position is sufficient to meet the required tests. Therefore, Kevin's tax treatment is:

Amount realized on the redemption	$20,000
Adjusted basis	(12,000)
Gain on redemption	$ 8,000

If the redemption did not pass the exchange test, the entire $20,000 would be treated as an ordinary distribution. In that case, however, Kevin could actually benefit from the characterization as an ordinary distribution. Assuming that the corporation had no AEP, or, alternatively, that it had at least $20,000 in its AAA, Kevin would recognize no gain on an ordinary distribution. He would merely reduce his basis in all of his shares by the $20,000 realized in the redemption.

A shareholder who wants to avoid exchange treatment on a redemption might select one of several alternative structuring arrangements. If, for example, the corporation has both voting and nonvoting stock, the shareholder might retain substantially all of his or her voting stock and have the corporation redeem the nonvoting stock. Since the tests in §302(b)(2) are based on both the shareholder's voting percentage and the number of shares, it may be relatively simple to arrange the redeemed shares so that the shareholder retains enough voting stock to treat the redemption as a distribution.

A complete termination of a shareholder's interest can be avoided in any one of several simple arrangements. For instance, the redeemed shareholder may retain status as an employee or as a director.

Perhaps the simplest way to ensure that a redemption fails to meet the exchange test is to give the redeemed shareholder options to purchase stock. Under §318(a)(4), an option 1 holder is treated as the owner of all shares subject to the option. The option need not be immediately exercisable and may have an exercise price that is high enough that it is unlikely to be exercised.

OBSERVATION: The nature of distributions by S corporations, when viewed in the context of the Subchapter C redemption rules, gives S corporations some strange considerations. Before a corporation and its shareholders arrange a redemption plan, however, they should be sure of the side effects. If the corporation has significant AEP and minimal AAA, treatment of a redemption as a distribution will likely cause the shareholder to report dividend income. The corporation should also consider the side effects of the AAA that will be allocated to the redemption. A large reduction of AAA by the shareholder whose stock is redeemed may leave the remaining shareholders little protection from dividend treatment.

1510.13. Situations where exchange is preferable to distribution. An S corporation with little AAA and substantial AEP should employ similar tax planning strategies as a C corporation. In the case of a redemption, the redeemed shareholder would report dividend income if the redemption proceeds exceed the AAA, the corporation has AEP and the redemption is treated as a distribution.

EXAMPLE 15 - 5a: Refer to Example 15-5. Assume that the corporation had only $1,000 of AAA and over $19,000 of AEP. Kevin would reduce basis by $1,000 and report $19,000 of dividend income if the redemption were classified as a distribution. If the redemption were classified as an exchange, he would have only reported $8,000 gain.

The classification of a redemption as an exchange or a distribution is important to the continuing shareholders, as well as the person whose stock is redeemed. As is discussed below, at 1515.3., a redemption treated as a distribution reduces AAA first, to the lesser extent of the AAA or the redemption proceeds. In contrast, a redemption tread as an exchange reduces AAA proportionate to the number of shares redeemed.

There is another issue when the redemption proceeds are not all to be received in the same year. The installment sale rules will generally apply to sales of stock, and may allow the redeemed shareholder to report his or her gain ratably over the period in which the installment note is satisfied. [§453] In order to qualify for installment sale treatment, there must be disposition of property. [§453(b)(1)] It would be risky to claim that a redemption that was treated as a distribution for tax purposes would be a disposition of property.

EXAMPLE 15 - 5b: Roger owned 100 shares in Roco, an S corporation. His basis was $100,000 and the redemption price was $500,000, payable in equal installments, plus interest at the applicable federal rate, over ten years. If the redemption is an exchange, he could report $40,000 gain per year. If the redemption were treated as a distribution he would be treated as receiving a $500,000 property distribution immediately, and would report all gain in the year of the agreement.

1510.14. Recognition of loss on redemption. If a redemption is treated as an ordinary distribution, the proceeds are subject to the usual distribution treatment at the shareholder level. Therefore, it is impossible to recognize a loss, even if the proceeds of the redemption are less than the shareholder's basis. When a shareholder's stock has been redeemed for less than the shareholder's basis, the shareholder merely adds the remaining basis to his or her other shares. [Regs. §1.302-2(c)] If the shareholder retains no direct interest in the corporation, but the redemption is treated as an ordinary distribution due to continued constructive ownership, the basis of the redeemed shares attaches to the basis of the actual owner of the shares. See discussion of constructive ownership, at 1510.2.

EXAMPLE 15 - 6: Brenda was a 50% shareholder in BB Corporation until BB redeemed all of her stock. After the redemption, Brenda's husband, Bruce, owned all of the outstanding stock. Brenda's basis in her shares was $100,000, and the amount realized on the redemption was $75,000. Assuming that the redemption did not qualify as an exchange (see 1510.3. and 1510.4., below), Brenda would be treated as having received a distribution of $75,000. Any remaining basis in her shares, after the application of the usual basis reduction rules, would be transferred to Bruce.

If a redemption does qualify as an exchange, the shareholder generally recognizes gain or loss. If, however, the shareholder is considered a constructive owner of more than 50% of the stock under the attribution rules of §267, the shareholder cannot recognize a loss. [PLR 9412032] See Chapter 8, at 835.1., for discussion of the related-party loss disallowance rules.

EXAMPLE 15 - 7: Assume the same facts as in Example 15 - 6, except that the redemption qualified as a complete termination of Brenda's interest in BB Corporation. (See 1510.4., below.) Brenda would not be allowed to recognize the $25,000 loss on the stock redemption. Furthermore, the disallowed loss would not benefit any other taxpayer in the future, since the owner of the stock is now BB Corporation. A corporation can never recognize a gain or loss on a transaction involving its own stock. [§1032(a)]

OBSERVATION: The constructive ownership loss disallowance rules are not the same constructive ownership rules used for determining whether a redemption constitutes an exchange. The loss disallowance rules are contained in §267, which is discussed in Chapter 8, at 835.1. The constructive ownership rules for testing redemptions are found in §318 and are discussed at 1510.4. below. By contrast, the constructive ownership rules of §267(a) are never waived. The only loss allowed on a disposition of stock to the issuing corporation by a greater-than-50% shareholder occurs when the corporation is completely liquidated. See at 1525.4.

1510.15. Constructive distribution problems. A redemption may be used as part of the consideration for the sale of an entire corporation. In some cases, it may be possible to transfer some liquid or unwanted assets directly from the corporation to the selling shareholder and have the buying shareholder purchase the remainder of the stock. This technique, often called a "bootstrap acquisition," must be carefully worked out in advance. (If the corporation issues its own obligations to the seller, the transaction is termed a "leveraged buyout.") The rationale is that the selling shareholder would report gain or loss on the sale, or on a redemption. Thus the seller has no preference for a sale to the buyer or redemption from the corporation. The buyer might prefer to use some of the corporation's own assets to acquire some of the stock from the seller. If the buyer were to receive a distribution after the sale, to cover part of the purchase price, the distribution would be treated as an ordinary distribution.

> **CAUTION:** In *Waterman S.S. Corp. v. CIR* [430 F2d 1185, 26 AFTR 2d 70-5185, 70-2 USTC ¶9514 (5th. Cir.)], a target corporation distributed notes to the selling shareholder immediately before a sale of the entire corporation. The purchaser then advanced funds to the target corporation to enable it to pay the pre-sale dividend. In this case, the seller was able to take advantage of the dividends-received deduction, which yielded better results than a gain from the sale of stock. The IRS could apply this doctrine to the sale of an S corporation's stock, if the arrangement between the purchaser and the seller appeared to present some sort of tax avoidance scheme. As of this date, **there is no record of this doctrine having been applied to the sale of an S corporation's stock.**

When a person has agreed to purchase stock from a shareholder, and the corporation redeems some stock from the seller, the corporation may have relieved the buyer of an obligation. If the corporation of concern is a C corporation, the redemption will be treated as a dividend to the extent of the corporation's current and accumulated earnings and profits. [*Wall v. U.S.*, 164 F2d 462 (4th. Cir., 1947); *Sullivan v. U.S.*, 363 F2d 724 (8th. Cir., 1966); *Schroeder v. CIR*, 831 F2d 856 (9th. Cir., 1987)] The IRS has ruled that a stock redemption is a constructive distribution if it relieves a person of a primary and unconditional obligation to purchase the stock. [Rev. Rul. 69-608, 1969-2 CB 42] In the same ruling, however, the IRS held that a redemption is not a constructive distribution to the buying shareholder if the obligation is conditional or secondary.

> **EXAMPLE 15 - 8:** Michelle has agreed to purchase all of the outstanding stock in Elco from Ellen for $250,000. The transaction is accomplished by having Elco redeem 60% of Ellen's stock for $150,000. Michelle then pays Ellen $100,000 for the remaining 40% of her stock.
>
> If Michelle had a primary and unconditional obligation to purchase all of Ellen's stock, the redemption to Ellen would be treated as a constructive distribution from Elco to Michelle. By contrast, if the parties had agreed that Elco was to redeem all of Ellen's stock and Michelle would guarantee that obligation, there would be no constructive distribution to Michelle as a result of the redemption.

When an S corporation engages in a bootstrap acquisition, the constructive distribution may not be a serious problem. If the corporation has sufficient AAA to cover the redemption, or if the corporation has no AEP, the buying shareholder would treat the distribution as a reduction of basis. Since the buyer would be treated as having constructively purchased the shares, he or she would always have sufficient basis so that none of the constructive distribution would be treated as a gain. If, however, the corporation had little AAA and substantial AEP, the buyer could be treated as receiving a constructive dividend.

15

> **EXAMPLE 15 - 9:** Refer to Example 15 - 8. Assume that Elco was an S corporation. Also assume that Michelle's obligation was primary and unconditional. She would have $250,000 basis from the actual and constructive purchase of all of Ellen's stock, followed by a constructive distribution of $150,000.
>
> If the corporation had at least $150,000 of AAA or had no AEP, the constructive distribution to Michelle would reduce her basis to $100,000. Alternatively, assume that the corporation has only $10,000 of AAA and $200,000 of AEP. The constructive distribution

would reduce Michelle's basis by $10,000. The remaining $140,000 of constructive distribution would be a dividend.

Several recent cases have concerned divorce settlements and stock redemptions [*Joann C. Arnes v. U.S.*, 91-1 USTC 50,207 (WD Wash.), aff'd in *Joann C. Arnes v. U.S.*, 981 F2d 456, 93-1 USTC 50,016, 71 AFTR 2d 93-369 (9th. Cir.); *Pozzi v. U.S.* (D. Ore., 1993); *Hayes*, 101 TC No. 40 (1993); *Blatt*, 102 TC No. 5 (1994); *John A. Arnes*, 102 TC No. 20 (1994)], including corporations held jointly by a husband and wife. At the time of the divorce, the corporation has redeemed the wife's shares, leaving the husband as the sole shareholder. In other cases, the wife whose shares were redeemed claimed that the amounts received in exchange for the stock were marital property settlements, and not taxable sales. [§1041] To arrive at this conclusion, the wife has reasoned that the stock was constructively redeemed from the husband and the cash received in the redemption was then transferred from the husband to the wife. To follow through on the wife's reasoning, the husband would report gain from the redemption.

The husband has reasoned that the corporation redeemed the stock directly from the wife. Therefore, any gain from the redemption should be reported by the wife, in accordance with the literal form of the transaction. The decisions have been conflicting. In the case of *Joann C. Arnes*, the courts held that the cash received by Mrs. Arnes was in satisfaction of her husband's marital obligation, and thus she should not report gain from the redemption. [*Joann C. Arnes v. U.S.*, 91-1 USTC 50,207 (WD Wash.), aff'd in *Joann C. Arnes v. U.S.*, 981 F2d 456, 93-1 USTC 50,016, 71 AFTR 2d 93-369 (9th Cir.)] Note that this case involved only Mrs. Arnes' tax treatment. Her husband took his case to the Tax Court. The Tax Court found that Mr. Arnes did not have a primary and unconditional obligation to redeem his wife's shares. Therefore, the redemption did not relieve him of such obligation, and there was no constructive dividend. [*John A. Arnes*, 102 TC No. 20 (1994)]

OBSERVATION: The conflicting decisions in the *Arnes* cases may have been the result of the failure of the IRS to properly consolidate its actions. The case of John Arnes, if appealed, would be heard by the Ninth Circuit, which has already decided in favor of Mrs. Arnes. In a consolidated case, the Tax Court found a primary and unconditional obligation of the husband to purchase the wife's shares. Therefore, there was a constructive dividend to the husband. [*Hayes*, 101 TC No. 40 (1993)] In yet another case, the husband had no primary liability to purchase the wife's shares, and there was no constructive dividend. [*Blatt*, 102 TC No. 5 (1994)] Thus, the courts seem to decide each case upon its particular merits. The distinguishing feature in the Tax Court decisions is the presence or absence of a primary and unconditional obligation on the part of one shareholder to purchase the stock of another shareholder.

PLANNING TIP: The IRS is willing to rule that there is no constructive distribution, if continuing shareholders are not obligated to purchase the stock being redeemed. [PLR 9412032] Especially when the redemption involves a complete termination of a shareholder's interest, it may be in the best interests of all of the parties to obtain a ruling.

1510.2. Constructive ownership rules. The most important redemption tests require the measurement of a shareholder's percentage of ownership of stock in the corporation, both before and after the redemption. In determining this percentage, the shareholder must be aware of the constructive ownership (also known as *attribution* rules).

The constructive ownership rules of §318 are used to test the pre- and post-exchange ownership. These rules, which are most important in tests of substantial disproportion and complete termination, treat a shareholder as owning what family members and related entities own. There are four general classes of indirect ownership:

- Family attribution
- Entity-to-owner attribution
- Owner-to-entity attribution
- Option attribution

OBSERVATION: There are several sets of constructive ownership rules in the Code. In addition to §318, there are some constructive ownership rules in §267 that relate primarily to the disallowance of losses on sales of property between related persons, and in §544, which directly relate to personal holding companies. Provisions elsewhere in the Code will call upon one of the constructive ownership rules of §267, §318, or §544 for a variety of purposes. Sometimes an operating rule that uses one of these attribution tests will modify the relationships. The different attribution rules also have different specified relationships. For example, brothers and sisters are related parties within the meaning of §267, but not of §318. Partners are treated as related to each other in §544, but not in §318. The tax professional needs to ascertain the constructive ownership rules in use whenever a Code provision refers to direct or indirect ownership.

1510.21. Family attribution. The family attribution rules of §318 are narrowly defined. *Family members* include only the shareholder's spouse, children, grandchildren, and parents. [§318(a)(1)]

EXAMPLE 15 - 10: George and Barbara (husband and wife) each own 50 shares in the GB Corporation. Barbara's brother, Ross, also owns 50 shares. George and Barbara are each treated as owning the other's stock. Barbara and Ross are not treated as owners of each other's shares.

1510.22. Entity-to-owner attribution. The *entity-to-owner* rules attribute shares owned by an entity back to the entity's owner. [§318(a)(2)] For example, stock that is actually owned by a partnership is treated as if it were owned proportionately by its partners. [§318(a)(2)(A)] (This rule has no relevance to the redemption of stock from an S corporation, since a partnership cannot be a shareholder.) If stock is owned by an estate, each beneficiary of the estate is treated as owning a proportionate share of the estate's stock. [§318(a)(2)(A)]

EXAMPLE 15 - 11: Harry's estate owns 100 shares of Harrco. Judy and Ken are equal beneficiaries in Harry's estate. Judy and Ken also each directly own 100 shares of Harrco. Judy and Ken are each treated as owning 150 shares in Harrco.

Stock actually owned by a trust is treated as being owned proportionately by its beneficiaries. This rule is not extremely important to most S corporations, since the ability of trusts to own shares is limited. A grantor trust or QSST can have only one current income beneficiary. One of these trusts, however, may have remainder beneficiaries, who would acquire the trust's property upon the death of the current income beneficiary. A grantor trust, however, disregards the remaining beneficiaries, and attributes all of its shares to the deemed owner. [§318(a)(2)(B)(ii)]

15

EXAMPLE 15 - 12: Floyd, age 70, has transferred his shares in Floco to a grantor trust. Upon Floyd's death, his daughter Florence will become the sole beneficiary of the trust. Although Florence has an indirect interest in the trust property, all of the trust's shares are attributed to Floyd.

A testamentary trust, which can own shares for up to 2 years, may have multiple beneficiaries. Similarly, an ESBT may have multiple beneficiaries. When one of these trusts owns shares in a corporation, each beneficiary's actuarial interest determines the portion attributable to the beneficiary. [§318(a)(2)(B)(i)]

When a corporation owns stock in another corporation, the attribution rules become somewhat more complicated. If the corporation that owns the shares in the other corporation is a C corporation, there is no attribution to a shareholder who owns less than 50% of the stock. [§318(a)(2)(C)] A shareholder who owns 50% or more of the stock of a C corporation is treated as owning a proportionate share of what the C corporation owns.

> **EXAMPLE 15 - 13:** Leonard and Michelle, husband and wife, each own 100 shares in LMN Corporation, a C corporation. Nancy, Leonard's sister, also owns 100 shares of LMN. There are no other shareholders in LMN. LMN owns 90 shares in OPQ Corporation. Since Leonard and Michelle are each treated as owning two-thirds of LMN, they are each treated as if they owned 60 shares (two-thirds of 90) of OPQ. Since Nancy is not one of the specified family members, she is not treated as owning any of Leonard's or Michelle's stock. She owns only one-third of LMN and is not treated as owning any shares in OPQ.

If the corporation that owns stock in another corporation is an S corporation, the attribution rules treat the S corporation as a partnership. [§318(a)(5)(E)] Accordingly, minority shareholders of an S corporation will be treated as owning a proportionate amount of stock owned directly by the S corporation.

> **EXAMPLE 15 - 14:** Assume the same facts as in Example 15-13, except that LMN is an S corporation. (Also assume its ownership of OPQ is less than 80% of OPQ's total outstanding stock, so that there is no affiliated group of corporations.) Leonard and Michelle are each treated as owning 60 shares of OPQ. Nancy is treated as owning 30 shares of OPQ.

1510.23. Owner-to-entity attribution. *Owner-to-entity* rules provide that a partnership indirectly owns stock that is actually owned by its partners, and an estate or trust indirectly owns shares that are directly owned by its beneficiaries. [§318(a)(3)] A C corporation indirectly owns stock that is directly held by its majority shareholders. An S corporation indirectly owns any stock held by any of its shareholders.

> **EXAMPLE 15 - 15:** Roger and Susan, husband and wife, each own 100 shares in RST Corporation, a C corporation. Susan's brother, Terry, also owns 100 shares in RST. There are no other shareholders. Roger also owns 200 shares in UVW Corporation, and Terry owns 300 shares in UVW. RST is treated as a constructive owner of Roger's UVW stock. RST, however, is not treated as the owner of Terry's UVW stock, since Terry is not treated as a majority shareholder in RST. If RST were an S corporation, RST would be treated as the constructive owner of Terry's UVW stock.

15

1510.24. Option attribution. A person who holds an option to purchase stock is treated as the constructive owner of that stock. [§318(a)(4)] It does not matter what the option price is or how likely the exercise of that option may be.

1510.25. Reattribution. In general, stock owned constructively by any person is treated as owned constructively by any party related to that person. [§318(a)(5)]

> **EXAMPLE 15 - 16:** Jim owns all of the shares in JR Corporation. Jim lives in a separate property state. His wife Rebecca owns no shares in JR and has no incidents of ownership under local law. For tax purposes, however, Rebecca is treated as the constructive owner of all of JR's stock. JR Corporation owns 50 shares in KS Corporation. Rebecca is treated as the constructive owner of all of the KS shares owned by JR.

There are certain limits on the reattribution:

1. A family member's constructive ownership of another family member's stock cannot make a third family member also the constructive owner of the stock.

   EXAMPLE 15 - 17: Jean owns 100 shares in Jeaco. Her sons, Bob and John, each own 100 shares. Jean is treated as the owner of all 300 shares, since Bob and John are both related to Jean (within the meaning of §318). Bob and John are each treated as the owner of Jean's shares, since Jean is their mother. However, Jean's indirect ownership of Bob's shares is not attributed to John, and her indirect ownership of John's shares is not attributed to Bob. Bob and John would indirectly own only those shares directly owned by their mother. Therefore, Bob and John would each be treated as the owner of 200 shares in Jeaco.

2. Stock held by a partner, a beneficiary of a trust or an estate, or a shareholder in a corporation is not attributed to another person who has an interest in the same entity. If the law permitted such reattribution, it would have the effect of attributing ownership to co-owners in other enterprises. The ownership rules are not intended to be that broadly constructed.

   EXAMPLE 15 - 18: The Curtis estate owns 300 shares of Curco. The estate has two equal beneficiaries, Richard and Margaret. Richard and Margaret are brother and sister and are therefore not considered to be related to each other for purposes of §318. Margaret and Richard each own 50 shares directly in Curco. The estate is treated as the owner of 400 shares, since the ownership of any beneficiary is attributed to an estate. Richard and Margaret are each treated as the owner of 50% of the estate's 300 shares. Richard, however, is not treated as the constructive owner of Margaret's shares and Margaret is not a constructive owner of Richard's shares. Therefore, Richard and Margaret are each treated as the owner of 200 shares in Curco.

1510.3. Substantially disproportionate redemptions. The rule of substantially disproportionate redemption provides that any redemption that meets its criteria is a sale or an exchange, rather than a dividend-type distribution. [§302(b)(2)] To qualify as a substantially disproportionate redemption, the transaction must meet three tests, which are applied immediately after the redemption. At that time:

- The shareholder must own (directly or indirectly) less than 50% of all voting stock.
- The shareholder must control (directly or indirectly) less than 80% of voting power owned prior to redemption.
- The shareholder must own (directly or indirectly) less than 80% of outstanding shares of common stock owned prior to redemption.

In applying these tests, the shareholder must count both actual and constructive ownership. The constructive ownership rules may make a substantially disproportionate redemption difficult for a family-owned corporation to accomplish.

EXAMPLE 15 - 19: Don and Hannah each own 50 voting shares of DH Corporation. There are no other shareholders. DH redeems 25 of Hannah's shares and none of Don's shares. If Hannah does not constructively own any of Don's shares, the redemption is substantially disproportionate, as demonstrated by the following calculation:

Hannah's percentage of ownership before redemption (50/100)	50%
Maximum percentage permitted after redemption (<80% of 50%)	<40%
Hannah's actual stock ownership and voting power after redemption (25/75)	33.3%

If Don and Hannah were related parties, such as husband and wife, father and daughter, or mother and son, Hannah would actually and constructively own 100% of the stock after the redemption. It would not qualify for exchange treatment, and it would be a dividend to the extent of the corporation's AEP.

1510.4. Termination of a shareholder's entire interest. In many cases, the termination of a shareholder's entire interest qualifies as a substantially disproportionate redemption. The special rule for complete termination of interest, however, applies when a shareholder completely divests of his or her holdings but stock is still held by family members. This test is perhaps most useful in family-held corporations where one shareholder wants to completely retire from the business but other family members want to continue to own and operate the corporation.

If a shareholder completely terminates his interest but stock continues to be held by family, the transaction may qualify as a sale or exchange of the stock. [§302(b)(3)] This test waives any family attribution. There are several additional requirements:

- The former shareholder must retain no interest other than as a creditor. The shareholder must terminate any interest as a shareholder, officer, or employee.
  - Recent decisions in this area suggest that no services may be formed for the redeeming corporation; if services have been formed, the former shareholder has retained a forbidden interest. [*Seda*, 82 TC 484; *Perry S. Lewis*, 47 TC 129; *Estate of Lennard*, 61 TC 554; and *William M. Lynch*, 86-2 USTC 9731 (9th Cir.)]
  - Even if there is family hostility between the redeemed shareholder and the other owners, the courts will not waive family attribution. [See *Cerone*, 87 TC 1 (1986), in which the former shareholder's salary was approximately $3,500 after the redemption, and constituted a prohibited interest.]
  - The IRS has ruled that a former shareholder could receive rent from the corporation without retaining a forbidden interest. [PLR 9837022]
- A 10-year "look-back" rule states that no portion of the stock redeemed was acquired from a related party during the last 10 years (per §318). It also provides that no related person (per §318) acquired stock during the last 10 years from the taxpayer whose stock is being redeemed. The test may be waived if the current transfer was not motivated by tax avoidance. [PLR 9837022]
- There is also a 10-year "look forward" rule. The former shareholder must agree not to acquire any forbidden interest except by bequest. This includes an interest in the issuer and its successor, parent, or subsidiary. The shareholder must also agree to hold the statute of limitations open for one year after acquisition of the interest.

15

EXAMPLE 15 - 20: Paul owns all 100 outstanding shares of PJ Corporation. Paul's son John has become active in the business and is serving as a capable general manager. Paul has decided to retire. Paul has $400,000 basis in his shares, which are valued at $1,000,000. PJ's AEP exceed $1,000,000. Paul gives 10 shares to John, and the corporation redeems Paul's remaining shares for $900,000. If Paul retains no interest in the corporation and agrees to the other conditions for complete termination, the exchange will qualify for capital gain treatment, even though Paul would generally be considered the constructive owner of all of John's shares. Since Paul had transferred shares to John as a gift within the past 10 years, the parties should seek a ruling that the transfer was not motivated by tax avoidance.

1510.5. Not essentially equivalent to a dividend. A redemption qualifies as an exchange if it is not essentially equivalent to a dividend. [§302(b)(1)] This is a holdover from the 1939 Code and is difficult to substantiate. The IRS has ruled favorably in several situations where the shareholder was divested of some meaningful degree of control. [Rev. Ruls. 75-502, 1975-2

CB 111; 75-512, 1975-2 CB 112; 76-364, 1976-2 CB 91] When a shareholder has constructive control of the corporation after the redemption, however, this test is not likely to be useful. [*Maclin P. Davis*, 70-1 USTC 9289 (USSC)] Shareholders have been unsuccessful in waiving family attribution rules, even in the event of family hostility. [Rev. Rul. 80-26, 1980-1 CB 66; *Metzger*, 82-2 USTC 9718 (5th Cir.)]

1510.6. Partial liquidations. A distribution to a shareholder is treated as a sale or an exchange if it qualifies as a partial liquidation of the corporation. [§302(b)(4)] The rules, contained in §302(e), limit the application to individual shareholders. (Regulations are issued under Code §346, which contained the partial liquidation rules until a 1982 amendment to the law.)

One type of partial liquidation is the corporate contraction. There is often some uncertainty in a contraction, but it requires that the distribution be pursuant to a plan and the proceeds be distributed in the year of the plan or the year following adoption of the plan. There must be a genuine contraction; for example, a corporation's building was destroyed, and the corporation reduced its operations. [*Joseph W. Imler*, 11 TC 836 (1948)] If a corporation distributes excess working capital, which is not the result of a sudden contraction, the distribution is not a partial liquidation. [Rev. Rul. 60-322, 1960-2 CB 118] The IRS will not issue a favorable ruling unless there is a 20% reduction in gross revenue, net value of assets, and employees. [Rev. Proc. 82-40, 1982-1 CB 175]

Termination of a business is another type of partial liquidation. [§302(e)(2)] To meet this test:

- The corporation must cease to operate one business and must either sell or distribute its assets.
- The corporation must continue to operate one or more businesses.
- Both businesses must have been actively conducted for five years.
- Neither may have been acquired (within last five years) in a taxable transaction.

PLANNING TIP: Corporations may want to structure transactions to avoid partial liquidation treatment. In a partial liquidation, each shareholder is deemed to surrender a portion of his or her stock. The distribution results in a gain if it exceeds the basis attributable to the portion treated as redeemed. A regular distribution, by contrast, allows the shareholder to recover his or her entire stock basis before reporting any gain.

In one recent case, the Tax Court held that a distribution of real property that was operated as a separate trade or business qualified as a partial liquidation. [*White's Ferry, Inc.*, TC Memo 1993-639, 66 TCM 1855] As a practical matter, partial liquidations are infrequent. Therefore, this book contains no examples and no further discussion.

1510.7. Redemptions to pay death taxes. The surviving shareholders in a closely held corporation may be able to use some corporate assets to pay a certain portion of the estate taxes following the death of a shareholder. This special tax rule applies to a decedent's estate or to other persons who receive the stock as a result of a shareholder's death. [§303] If a redemption meets the qualifications of this provision, the redemption is treated as a sale or an exchange, even though the surviving shareholders are still in complete control of the corporation. The requirements are:

- The stock must have been included in the decedent's estate. [§303(a)]
- The stock must exceed 35% of the decedent's gross estate, less debts, expenses, taxes and losses. [§303(b)(2)(A)]

- The person whose stock is redeemed must bear the economic burden of payment of the death taxes, which include federal and state estate taxes and inheritance taxes. [§303(b)(3)]

EXAMPLE 15 - 21: When Earl died, his gross estate, less taxes, debts, expenses, and losses, was $1,000,000. His daughter Jane inherited all of his property. Included in his estate was stock in EJ Corporation that had a value of $500,000 at the date of his death. Earl's death taxes were $200,000, of which $100,000 was attributable to his stock in EJ. Jane may redeem shares for $100,000 and use the money to pay that amount of death taxes. The redemption qualifies as an exchange, even if Jane owns 100% of the stock of EJ.

1515. Effects of a redemption on the corporation.

When a corporation redeems its own stock, it must make appropriate accounting adjustments. If the corporation is an S corporation, it also needs to be concerned with the possibility that the redemption will create a second class of stock, especially if one shareholder is receiving more than his or her proportionate share of the corporation's assets.

1515.1. Possibility of a second class of stock. A redemption of one shareholder's stock means that a person receives a distribution from the corporation that is different from any distribution received by continuing shareholders. Treatment of a redemption as a sale or an exchange should prevent the IRS from asserting that a second class of stock exists, because such a redemption is not considered a distribution. If a redemption fails the sale-or-exchange test, however, §302(d) treats the proceeds as a distribution to which §301 applies. If such a distribution is not equal with respect to all shares, the second-class-of-stock question may be relevant.

Regulations §1.1361-1 provides that redemptions do not create a second class of stock unless the redemption price varies significantly from the fair market value of the stock. The Regulation also provides a safe harbor for book value. [Regs. §1.1361-1(l)(2)(iii)] Under the Regulation, the treatment of a redemption as an exchange or a distribution is immaterial. [PLR 9404020, 9810020]

OBSERVATION: When referring to the use of book value as a safe harbor in redemption agreements, the Final Regulations refer to statements prepared according to generally accepted accounting principles or a book value that is used for any substantial nontax purpose. Thus a cash basis book value would appear to be within the safe harbor, if a lender or bonding company is willing to accept statements prepared by this accounting method.

15

EXAMPLE 15 - 22: Bob and Bill each own 50% of the shares in BB Corporation, an S corporation. In 1992, Bob is in some financial trouble. The corporation redeems 10% of his shares at their book value. The redemption does not qualify as a sale or an exchange under any of the Subchapter C tests. Bob has received a distribution that is not equal to Bill's distributions during the year, but because the corporation redeemed Bob's shares at book value, the distribution does not create a second class of stock.

Before the issuance of the Final Regulation on stock classes, the IRS had ruled that a stock redemption did not create a second class of stock. [PLR 9124009] Therefore, it appears that a redemption of stock will not be treated as indicative of multiple classes of stock unless the value of the stock differs materially from its fair market value or book value. In some cases, however, a redemption may be evidence that the corporation has more than one class of stock.

EXAMPLE 15-23: Suzanne and Amy are nominally equal shareholders in SA Corporation, an S corporation. They have an unrecorded agreement, however, that Suzanne will receive the first $100,000 of profits as a distribution. The agreement has the effect of creating a second class of stock. On August 22, 1992, the corporation redeems all of Suzanne's shares for $120,000. Amy receives no distribution from the corporation. Later in the year, Suzanne buys half of Amy's shares for $20,000. This type of arrangement is tantamount to the corporation having two classes of stock.

PLANNING TIP: If one shareholder in an S corporation needs cash, the corporation may be able to provide an extra distribution by redeeming some of that shareholder's stock. The redemption would not need to meet one of the sale or exchange tests and would not disqualify the corporation from S status. If the total of the corporation's distributions for the tax year exceeded the Accumulated Adjustments Account, part of the redemption, as well as part of the other distributions, might be treated as a dividend.

1515.2. Gain or loss on distributions of property in redemption of stock. As discussed in Chapter 7, at 730.1., a corporation must recognize any gain on the distribution of appreciated property. [§311(b)] A corporation is not allowed to recognize any loss if the distributed property's fair market value is less than the corporation's basis. [§311(a)] These rules apply when property is transferred by the corporation in a stock redemption, in the same manner as when property is surrendered in a routine distribution. The classification of the redemption as an exchange or dividend-type distribution has no effect on this rule. The examples and discussion of property distributions in Chapter 7 have equal relevance to the corporate tax consequences on the distribution of property in a redemption.

1515.3. Effects of the redemption on the corporation's equity accounts. If a redemption fails to meet the tests of a sale or an exchange, the corporation's AAA and other equity accounts will be affected in the exact same manner as any other distribution. [Rev. Rul. 95-14, 1995-6 IRB 29; PLR 9810020] Chapter 7 contains numerous examples of the accounting for distributions.

If a redemption is treated as an exchange, however, Subchapter S provides two rules:

1. The corporation's AAA is reduced by the percentage of outstanding stock redeemed. [§1368(e)(1)(B)]
2. The corporation must make a "proper adjustment" to its AEP. [§1371(c)(2)]

The Code does not define the term *proper adjustment*, in reference to the corporation's AEP. Nor does the Code give any special rules for the calculation of the corporation's AAA at the date of the redemption.

1515.31. General rules for reduction of AAA. The Code gives no guidance on how to calculate the appropriate AAA balance at the time of a redemption. Until June 1992 the IRS had issued no rules for reduction for an AAA due to a stock redemption. Regulations proposed in 1992 followed some old C corporation rules that required an S corporation to separate the current components of AAA from the balance in place at the beginning of the taxable year. [Rev. Ruls. 74-338, 1974-2 CB 101; 74-339, 1974 CB 103] These rules turned out to be extremely complex in some situations, and they were replaced by a simple rule in the Final Regulations.[1] The Final Regulations treat any redemption as if it were the final event in the corporation's taxable year, following all adjustments to the AAA for income losses, deductions, and all nonredemption ("ordinary") distributions. [Regs. §1.1368-2(d)(1)(ii)]

15

[1] See Chapter 15, at 1515.3., in the 1994 edition of the *S Corporation Tax Guide* for a discussion of the rules contained in Proposed Regulations §1.1368-2. These rules receive no discussion in this edition.

Thus the time at which the redemption occurs during a taxable year is generally irrelevant in determining the adjustment to the AAA, unless the corporation closes its books at the date of the redemption.

EXAMPLE 15 - 24: Mary owns 35% and Lars owns 65% of the stock in ML Corporation, an S corporation. The corporation uses the calendar year. On December 31, 1993, ML's AAA balance is $25,000. On May 26, 1994, ML redeems all of Mary's shares, and the redemption qualifies as a complete termination of Mary's interest under §302(b)(3). ML made no ordinary distributions in 1994, and the corporation did not elect to close the books as of the date of the redemption. ML's net income for the entire year of 1994 was $50,000.

The corporation's AAA calculations for 1994 are:

Beginning balance	$25,000	
Current year's income	50,000	
Balance before redemption	75,000	
Portion attributable to shares redeemed (35%)	(26,250)	(75,000 x .35)
Balance after redemption	$48,750	

The reduction of the AAA does not consider the total amount of the redemption proceeds. If the price paid for the stock exceeds the reduction of AAA, the remainder should be accounted for as treasury stock.

EXAMPLE 15 - 25: Refer to Example 15 - 24. Assume that ML gave Mary $75,000 in cash for her shares and that the corporation had no AEP. The appropriate accounting treatment is:

AAA	$26,250
Treasury stock ($75,000 – $26,250)	48,750
Cash	$75,000

If the redemption proceeds are less than the amount that would be charged to the AAA under the general rules, the reduction of the AAA is limited to the amount paid for the stock. The Code does not expressly require this treatment, but the legislative history to the Deficit Reduction Act of 1984 gives this result. [Staff of Joint Committee on Taxation, *General Explanation of the Revenue Provisions of the Tax Reform Act of 1984,* page 181]

EXAMPLE 15 - 26: Refer to Example 15 - 24. Assume that the redemption price was only $20,000. The corporation would reduce its AAA by $20,000.

15

If the corporation also makes ordinary distributions during the year, the ordinary distributions reduce the AAA before the corporation reduces the AAA to reflect the redemption. The timing of the redemption and the ordinary distributions does not matter.

EXAMPLE 15 - 27: Refer to Example 15 - 24. Assume that ML distributed $12,000 to its shareholders on March 1, 1994, and also distributed $3,000 on August 18, 1994. The March and August distributions are treated as coming before the redemption.

Beginning balance	$25,000
Current year's income	50,000
Less ordinary distributions	(15,000)
Balance before redemption	60,000
Portion attributable to shares redeemed (35%)	(21,000)
Balance after redemption	$39,000

If the corporation had a negative AAA in the year of the redemption, it would apply the same proportional reduction to the AAA as it would for a positive balance.

EXAMPLE 15 - 28: Micco, an S corporation, uses the calendar year. On January 1, 1994, its AAA was $40,000. On June 21, 1994, the corporation redeemed 30% of its outstanding shares in a redemption that qualified as an exchange under §302(b)(3). During 1994, the corporation realized a net loss of $75,000 and made no ordinary distributions. The balance in the AAA, at the end of the year but before the redemption, would be negative $35,000. Therefore, the corporation would reduce this negative balance by 30%, or $10,500. The corporation would begin 1994 with a deficit of $23,500 in its AAA.

1515.32. Election to split year. If the redemption terminates a shareholder's interest or results in a sale of at least 20% of the corporation's outstanding shares, the corporation may close its books on the date of the redemption. These rules are discussed in Chapter 6, at 630.2. In order to close the books as of the date of a redemption, the redemption must meet one of two criteria:

- It must qualify as an exchange under §302 or §303 [Regs. §1.1368-1(g)(2)(B)], or
- It must constitute a complete termination of a shareholder's stock interest.[2]

EXAMPLE 15 - 29: Refer to Example 15 - 27. Since the redemption terminated Mary's interest in the corporation, the corporation may close its books as of May 26, 1994. Up to that date, the corporation's net income was $18,000. If the corporation elects to close its books as of May 26, the AAA balance on the date of the redemption would be:

Beginning balance	$25,000
Current year's AAA through May 26	18,000
Less March distribution	(12,000)
Balance at the end of May 26	31,000
Portion attributable to shares redeemed (35%)	(10,850)
Balance after redemption	$20,150

Thus, if an S corporation redeems all of the stock of a shareholder who still retains an indirect interest through the constructive ownership rules of §318, the redemption would not qualify as an exchange under §302, but should be a termination of the person's entire *shareholder* interest. In this case the corporation could elect to split its year under §1377(a)(2). If a redemption did not qualify as an exchange under §302 or §303 and the shareholder retained direct ownership of shares in the corporation, it appears that the corporation could not elect an interim closing.

15

1515.33. Reduction of the corporation's AEP. An S corporation must also reduce its AEP for the percentage of shares redeemed if the redemption qualifies as an exchange. Ordinarily, the corporation will merely reduce the prior year's balance by the percentage of shares redeemed. There are circumstances, however, under which the corporation will need to make a special calculation of its AEP as of the date of a redemption:

- If the corporation had acquired another corporation in a tax-free reorganization before the date of the stock redemption, it would need to add the acquired corporation's AEP to its own prior balance.

[2]Temporary Regulations §18.1377-1 allows the election when any shareholder "terminates his or her entire *shareholder* interest" [emphasis added]. Also see Regulations §1.1377-1(b)(3).

- If the corporation's other distributions during the taxable year (other than the redemption) exceeded the corporation's current and prior AAA, the corporation would chronologically assign its AEP to the various distributions during the year. Any distributions made before the redemption would reduce the corporation's AEP, to the extent that those distributions exceeded their allocable portions of AAA. Any distributions made after the redemption would not affect the AEP balance as of the date of the redemption. [Rev. Rul. 74-339, 1974-2 CB 103]
- If the corporation, with the consent of its shareholders, made an election to distribute AEP before the AAA, the corporation should ascertain whether any nonredemption distributions occurred before the redemption. Under the general rules of Subchapter C, a corporation assigns its AEP to distributions in chronological order. It would appear, therefore, that the S corporation should reduce the AEP balance to reflect any distributions that took place before the redemption.

The Regulations under §1368 do not explicitly coordinate the reduction of AEP with the reduction of AAA. They merely refer to §312(n)(7), which provides the rules for coordinating current and AEP. Since an S corporation does not generate any current earnings and profits, the reduction to an S corporation's AEP would be the same as if the corporation were a C corporation that had zero current earnings and profits.

EXAMPLE 15 - 30: At the beginning of 1994, John owns 40% and Kathy owns 60% of the stock of JK Corporation, a calendar-year S corporation. At the beginning of 1994, the corporation's AAA balance is $50,000 and the balance of AEP is $70,000. During 1994, the corporation has $30,000 of ordinary loss and separately stated items. The corporation makes the following payments to its shareholders in 1994:

- On March 14, 1994, the corporation distributes $60,000 to its shareholders.
- On August 7, 1994, JK redeems half of John's shares in a transaction that qualifies as a substantially disproportionate redemption under 302(b)(2).
- On October 19, 1994, the corporation distributes $40,000 to its shareholders.

The calculation of the AAA would be as follows:

Beginning balance	$50,000
Current year's loss	(30,000)
Balance before distributions	$20,000
Allocated to March 14 distribution [(60,000/100,000) x 20,000]	$12,000
Allocated to October 19 distribution [(40,000/100,000) x 20,000]	8,000
Total	$20,000
Balance after distributions	$ 0

Therefore, there would be no balance in the AAA to allocate to the redemption, since distributions cannot create a negative AAA and the redemption is treated as occurring after all ordinary distributions. The next step is to calculate the effect of the redemption on the corporation's AEP.

Beginning balance	$ 70,000
Less amount distributed on March 14, 1994	(48,000)
Balance at date of redemption	22,000
Effect of redemption (20%)	(4,400)
Balance after redemption	$ 17,600

Thus the distribution on October 19 would be treated as follows:

From AAA	$ 8,000
From AEP	17,600
From paid in capital	14,400
Total	$40,000

The Regulations under §1368 offer no guidance for a corporation that redeems stock at a redemption price less than the proportionate share of the corporation's AAA and AEP. The statute requires an adjustment to both accounts. [§1368(e)(1)(B), §1371(c)(2)] Until the IRS issues some specific directions, it makes sense to allocate the total redemption price proportionately between the AAA and AEP. [Staff of Joint Committee on Taxation, *General Explanation of the Revenue Provisions of the Tax Reform Act of 1984*, page 181]

EXAMPLE 15 - 31: Nikita Corporation is an S corporation that redeems 30% of its outstanding shares in a transaction that qualifies as an exchange under §302. The redemption price was $50,000. At the time of the redemption, the corporation's AAA was $120,000 and its AEP was $105,000. According to the general rules governing reduction of the equity accounts, the corporation would make the following reductions:

AAA (30% of $120,000)	$40,000
AEP (30% of $105,000)	35,000
Total	$75,000

In this situation, however, the total redemption price is less than the $75,000 reduction required under the normal rules. Therefore, the corporation should make the following reductions:

Total redemption proceeds as fraction of normally required reduction:

$50,000/$75,000	$^2/_3$

Application of fraction to AAA and AEP:

AAA [$^2/_3$ of (30% of $120,000)]	$26,667
AEP [$^2/_3$ of (30% of $105,000)]	23,333
Total	$50,000

1515.34. Effect of an AAA bypass election. As discussed in Chapter 7, an S corporation with AEP can elect to distribute its AEP before distributing its AAA. The Regulations do not provide any coordination regarding the effect of a bypass election (or deemed dividend election) on the corporation's accounting for a redemption. The rules of Subchapter C provide no guidance, since a C corporation never faces a situation analogous to a bypass election by an S corporation. It would seem reasonable, however, to adopt the following rules: 15

1. If there are no distributions before the redemption, simply reduce the prior year's balance by the percentage of shares redeemed. Assign the remaining balance of AEP to the distributions later in the year, in chronological order.
2. If any distributions precede the redemption during the taxable year, the steps are somewhat more complicated.
    - Assign the corporation's AEP to distributions that occur before the redemption, in chronological order.

- If these distributions exceed the corporation's AEP as of the end of the prior year, treat the excess of these distributions as distributions from the AAA. Then adjust the AAA balance for the portion of shares redeemed, in the manner prescribed above. There would be no adjustment to the corporation's AEP for the redemption, since that account would have been absorbed by the earlier distributions.
- If these distributions do not exceed the corporation's AEP, reduce the corporation's AEP for these distributions. Then reduce the remaining balance for the percentage of shares redeemed.

> **OBSERVATION:** The steps given above have no direct support from any law, Regulation, Ruling, or other pronouncement. They are consistent with the general philosophy of a bypass election, which places AEP before the AAA in the hierarchy of distributions.

1515.35. Effect of a redemption on PTI. It would appear logical to reduce PTI (see Chapter 7) for the percentage of shares redeemed. The 1982 version of Subchapter S, however, is completely silent on this issue. As of this writing, there are no Regulations or other pronouncements that yield any information. Therefore, it is necessary to turn to the Regulations and rulings under old Subchapter S for guidance.

Under the old rules, a distribution could be made from PTI only if it would otherwise be a dividend. [Regs. §1.1375-4(b)] Therefore, a redemption that fails to meet one of the exchange tests of §302 or §303 would absorb PTI according to the normal ordering rules. A distribution that meets one of the exchange tests, however, would have no effect on any shareholder's PTI account. [Regs. §1.1373-1(d); PLR 7823012] The PTI accounts would remain intact after the redemption. If a shareholder's stock is completely redeemed and that shareholder had a PTI balance, that amount should be closed to paid-in capital.

1515.4. Redemption rules summarized. As the foregoing text demonstrates, the stock redemption rules may be very important for certain S corporations. As a general rule, the importance to the corporation and to the shareholders is a function of the balance in the corporation's AAA and AEP. If a corporation has an extremely large AAA, sufficient to cover both the current redemption and all reasonably foreseeable distributions, the sale or exchange treatment may be immaterial. In some cases, a redemption that does not qualify as a sale or an exchange may even benefit the shareholder, who will be able to recover his or her entire stock basis. The redemption tests may be completely irrelevant if the corporation has no AEP. If the corporation has a relatively low AAA balance, however, and has significant AEP, the redemption tests may be extremely important to both the redeemed shareholder and to the corporation. See Figure 15 - 1 for an illustration the redemption rules as they relate to S corporations.

1515.5. Treatment of redemption expenses. In general, the expenses incurred by a corporation pursuant to a redemption of its stock are nondeductible. [§162(k)(1)] The expenses, such as legal and accounting fees incurred by the corporation, are capitalized as part of the stock acquisition cost. Therefore, they should be treated as a reduction in paid-in capital. Such expenses should not flow through to the shareholders[3] and do not reduce the corporation's AAA. [Regs. §1.1368-2(a)(3)(i)(C)]

If the corporation borrows money to finance the redemption, the interest paid on the loan generally will be deductible. The corporation may obtain its financing from an outside

---

[3] Regulations §1.1367-1(c)(2) requires a reduction in basis for a shareholder's portion of "noncapital, nondeductible expenses."

***Figure 15 - 1:** Application of stock redemption rules to S corporations.*

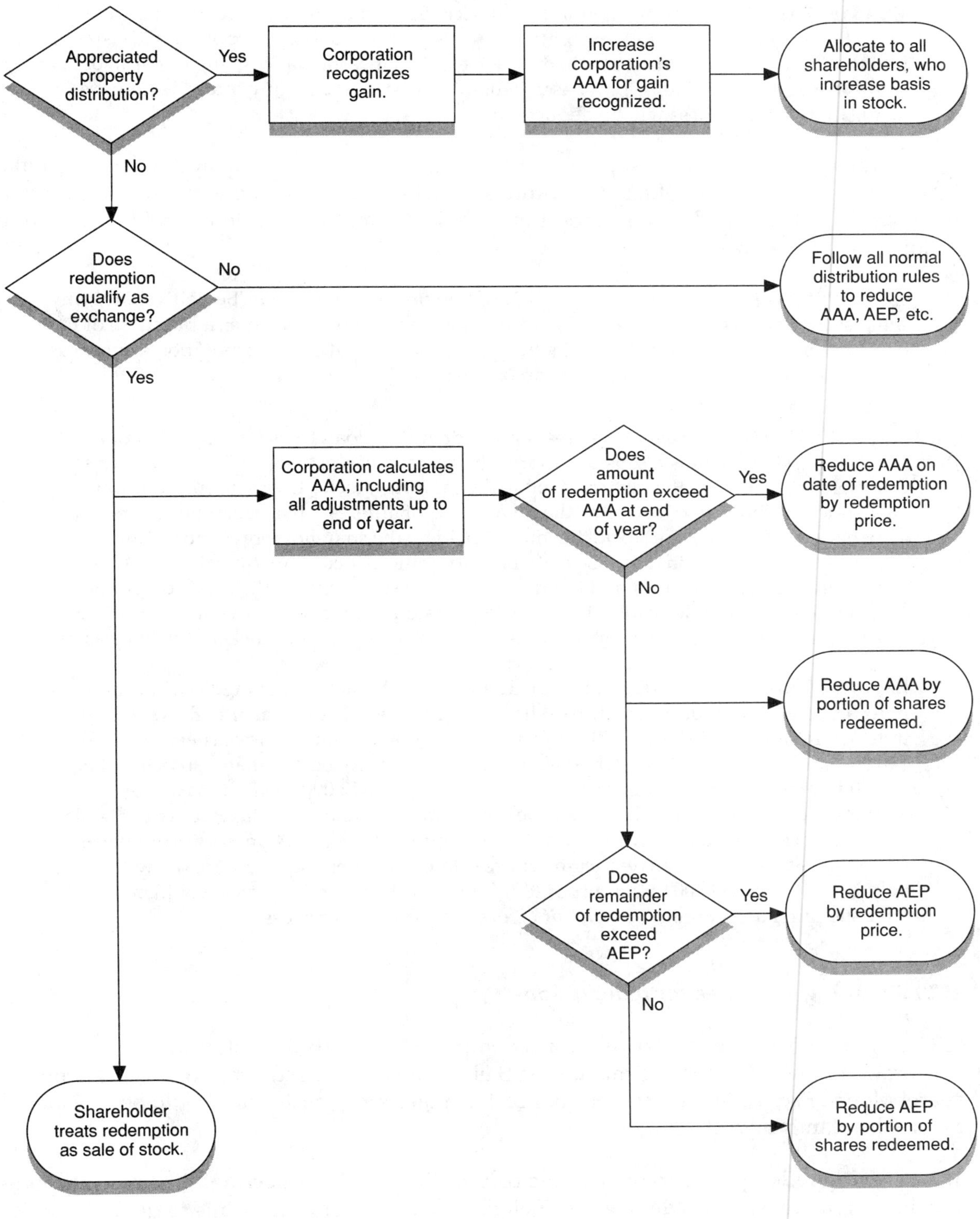

15

lender or from the redeemed shareholder. The IRS has said that interest paid in connection with the purchase of S corporation stock is treated as interest paid on a loan to purchase the assets of the corporation. [Notice 88-20, 1988-1 CB 487; Notice 89-35, 1989-1 CB 917] (See Chapter 16, at 1630.36., for further discussion.)

EXAMPLE 15-32: Eunice owns 80% of the stock of EB Corporation, an S corporation. Beulah owns the other 20%. All of the corporation's assets are related to the corporation's business, and Eunice materially participates in the business activities. Beulah is going to sell all of her shares for $20,000. If Eunice purchases Beulah's shares directly, any interest she pays on acquisition indebtedness will be deductible.

The IRS has held that interest paid by a corporation on a stock redemption is treated like interest paid by the shareholders to acquire stock. [PLR 9116008] Therefore, the corporation treats interest paid on a loan in connection with a redemption as interest paid on a loan to acquire its own assets.

EXAMPLE 15-33: Refer to Example 15-32. If the corporation redeems Beulah's shares, any interest the corporation incurs on the acquisition debt will be treated as a purchase of the corporation's assets. Since the assets are all connected with the corporation's business activity, the interest will be treated as an ordinary deduction.

OBSERVATION: Treating interest on a redemption loan the same as interest on a stock purchase loan is a sensible approach. In many cases, there will be no essential difference between the two methods of acquiring stock. There is one important distinction, however, between the two types of interest. If a shareholder incurs personal debt to acquire stock, the interest paid by the shareholder will not be limited to his or her basis in the stock, if the corporation incurs an overall loss. If the corporation redeems stock and finances the purchase, the interest will be a corporate-level expense. The deductibility of any corporate loss, including the amount of the loss attributable to the interest, is limited to each shareholder's stock and debt basis.

EXAMPLE 15-34: Refer to Examples 15-32 and 15-33. Beulah accepts a $20,000 installment note, bearing 10% annual interest, in exchange for her stock. In the year after the redemption, the corporation incurs a loss of $50,000 from its operations. Eunice's basis in her shares is only $40,000, and Eunice has no debt basis. If the corporation redeems Beulah's shares and pays $2,000 interest to Beulah, the corporation's loss will be $52,000. Beulah may deduct only $40,000, and the remaining $12,000 will be carried forward to the next taxable year. If Beulah had purchased the stock directly from Eunice and paid the $2,000 interest from her own funds, she would be able to deduct the entire interest payment. In addition, she would still be able to deduct $50,000 of the corporation's loss for that year. Her basis would be $60,000 after she purchased Eunice's stock but before the current year's loss.

15

1520. Planning strategies for redemptions.

A C corporation may consider using a redemption to qualify itself for an S election. A C corporation may also consider making an S election before it redeems some stock from its shareholders. Each of these situations has certain planning aspects that should be considered before the plan is undertaken.

1520.1. Using redemptions to qualify the corporation for the S election. When a C corporation has too many shareholders or has ineligible shareholders and wants to qualify itself to be an S corporation, it has two primary methods to achieve this result:

- Current, or desired, eligible shareholders may purchase stock directly from the persons whose stock is to be eliminated.
- The corporation may use its own funds to redeem the stock of the ineligible persons.

If the shareholders whose stock is to be redeemed are individuals, trusts, or partnerships, there are no special tax considerations involved. Normally, these taxpayers will prefer sale or exchange treatment, as opposed to dividend treatment, on the redemption. In these cases, the course of action will depend largely on the availability of funds. The parties should, however, be aware of the effect of the redemption on the corporation's earnings and profits.

EXAMPLE 15 - 35: Jim, Rebecca, Bill, and Melody are four equal, unrelated shareholders in Phoco, a C corporation that intends to qualify itself for S status. Jim is a citizen and resident of Canada, whereas the others are citizens of the United States. Jim is willing to sell all of his Phoco stock, and the parties have all agreed that the fair market value of Jim's stock is $30,000. Rebecca, Bill, and Melody all intend to be equal shareholders in the corporation after purchasing Jim's shares.

The three remaining shareholders may each purchase $10,000 worth of stock from Jim. If the corporation has sufficient liquid assets to purchase all of Jim's shares, or if Jim is willing to accept a note from the corporation, they may structure the transaction as a stock redemption. The redemption will qualify as a substantially disproportionate redemption or as a complete termination of Jim's interest. Therefore, the tax consequences to Jim are identical, whether the deal is a purchase by the other shareholders or a stock redemption.

If the other three shareholders purchase Jim's stock, there will be no effect on the corporation's AEP. If the corporation redeems Jim's stock, however, the corporation will eliminate 25% of its AEP. This plan may work to the corporation's benefit if it anticipates substantial passive investment income.

If the redemption does not qualify as an exchange, the selling shareholder will have dividend income in the amount of the redemption price. However, the entire proceeds of the redemption will reduce the corporation's AEP. If the redemption could eliminate the corporation's AEP, and if the corporation anticipates substantial passive investment income, it may be worthwhile to increase the redemption price and make sure that the redemption fails to meet the exchange tests.

EXAMPLE 15 - 36: Refer to Example 15 - 35. The parties investigate the possible consequences of a dividend to Jim. They decide that Jim would pay approximately $6,000 more in U.S. tax if the transaction were a dividend than if it were an exchange. The corporation has substantial income from equipment leases, and it would have passive investment income problems. The corporation has $36,000 in AEP as of the end of the current year. If the redemption is an exchange, the corporation may eliminate $9,000 of its AEP.

The parties all decide to pay Jim $36,000 for his stock. Each of the shareholders gives Jim an option to purchase 50% of his or her shares. With the option attribution rules, Jim is treated as a 50% shareholder after the redemption, and the redemption is a dividend. The corporation's AEP are eliminated by the redemption of Jim's stock. The attribution rules, which treat Jim as a shareholder, are limited to testing for dividend equivalency of the redemption. These attribution rules do not treat him as a shareholder for any other purpose. Therefore, his indirect ownership would not make the corporation ineligible to be an S corporation.

If the ineligible shareholder is a C corporation, dividend treatment might be preferable to exchange treatment. The corporation may qualify for the dividends-received deduction under §243 and may actually report less taxable income from a dividend than from an exchange. The redeemed corporation's stock basis would be transferred to the shares that are indirectly owned by the corporation but are actually owned by the continuing shareholders.

EXAMPLE 15 - 37: Alder Corporation is owned in equal portions by individual Byron and Chestnut Corporation. Byron owns all of the stock of Chestnut. Byron wants to qualify Alder to be an S corporation. Alder's AEP are $100,000. The fair market value of Alder's stock is $200,000.

Alder redeems all of Chestnut's shares for $100,000. Chestnut's basis is $40,000. Since Chestnut is constructively in control of Alder after the redemption, the transaction will be a dividend to Chestnut. Chestnut has gross income of $100,000, but a dividends-received deduction of $80,000. Byron gets Chestnut's $40,000 basis. Alder is now eligible to be an S corporation and has no AEP.

1520.2. Electing S status before redemption. In some cases, an uninformed C corporation may decide to make an S election before it redeems shares. This strategy may make sense if the corporation anticipates a significant positive AAA in the year of the redemption and the redemption is not likely to be treated as an exchange. There may be pitfalls, however, especially if the corporation plans to distribute some appreciated property in redemption of the stock. Examples 15 - 38 through 15 - 40 illustrate some considerations for a C corporation that intends to redeem stock and is considering making an S election before the redemption.

EXAMPLE 15 - 38: Shareholder Y owns 45% of the stock in YZ Corporation, a C corporation. Y is related to Z, who owns the other 55% of YZ Corporation's outstanding stock. The corporation redeems the stock with property that has fair market value of $45,000 and basis to the corporation of $23,000. Y had a basis of $15,000 in his stock immediately before the redemption. Because Y is related to Z and continues to be employed by the corporation, the redemption does not qualify as an exchange. The redemption occurs on the last day of the corporation's year. On the day before the redemption, the corporation has current earnings and profits of $8,000 and AEP of $40,000. (Assume taxable income equal to current earnings and profits, before tax.) The redemption occurs on the last day of the corporation's year. The corporation made no other dividend distributions in the tax year. The effect on YZ Corporation is:

Taxable income:	
Not including gain on redemption	$ 8,000
Gain on redemption ($45,000 – $23,000)	22,000
	$30,000
Current earnings and profits:	
Taxable income	$30,000
Less tax ($30,000 at 15%)	(4,500)
	$25,500
Accumulated earnings and profits:	
Beginning of year	$40,000
Add current earnings and profits	25,500
	$65,500
Less reduction for distribution	(45,000)
Ending balance	$20,500

Shareholder Y recognizes $45,000 dividend income on the distribution. His basis in his shares attaches to Z's basis, since Y and Z are related.

EXAMPLE 15 - 39: Assume the same facts as in Example 15 - 38, except that Y terminates his interest in YZ. The redemption is treated as an exchange under §302(b)(3). The effects on the corporation would be the same as in Example 15 - 37, except that the final reduction of AEP would be $29,475 (45% of $65,500). Shareholder Y, however, would recover his $15,000 basis and would report $30,000 capital gain. Z's stock basis would not be affected by the transaction.

EXAMPLE 15 - 40: Assume the same facts as in Example 15 - 39, except that the corporation had made an S election at the beginning of the year in which the redemption occurred. Recall that Y's interest in YZ is not terminated. The corporation's taxable income of $30,000 is added to the AAA, rather than to current earnings and profits.

Assume that the $22,000 gain the corporation recognizes on the distribution of property in redemption is taxable as a built-in gain. The corporation's accounting would be:

Taxable income:	
Not including gain on redemption	$ 8,000
Gain on redemption ($45,000 – $23,000)	22,000
Tax on built-in gain (.35 x $22,000)	(7,700)
Pre-distribution AAA	$22,300

The distribution to Y would come under the normal distribution rules for S corporations, as follows:

From AAA	$22,300
From AEP	22,700
	$45,000

The portion of the distribution from the AAA would first be treated as a recovery of Y's basis, computed as follows:

Basis, beginning of year	$15,000
Y's share of corporate income ($22,300 x .45)	10,035
Basis at redemption	$25,035

Since Y's basis exceeds the AAA, none of the distribution per se would be taxable. Y would, however, be taxed on his share of the corporation's income—$10,035—under the usual allocation rules.

Z, the other shareholder, would also be affected by the distribution if the S election were in effect. His share of the corporation's taxable income is $12,265 ($22,300 x .55).

EXAMPLE 15 - 41: Assume the same facts as in Example 15 - 40, except that Y terminates his interest in YZ. The redemption is treated as an exchange under §302(b)(3). The corporation's AAA and built-in gains tax would be computed in the same manner as in Example 15 - 40, up to the point of distribution. At that point, the corporation's accounting would change. It would reduce both the AAA and AEP by 45%. The final balances would be:

	AAA	*AEP*
Before redemption	$ 22,520	$ 40,000
Reduction	(10,035)	(18,000)
Final balance	$ 12,485	$ 22,000

The result to Y would be:

Amount realized	$ 45,000
Less adjusted basis ($15,000 + $10,035)	(25,035)
Capital gain	$ 19,965

The following analysis compares the results of the preceding four examples, assuming a 31% marginal tax rate on ordinary income and a 28% rate on capital gains, for both Y and Z.

15

	Without S Election	*With S Election*
Treated as distribution		
Tax on YZ	$ 4,500	$ 7,700
Tax on Y ($45,000 x .31)	13,950	
[($10,035 + $22,700) x .31]		10,148
Tax on Z	0	
($12,265 x .31)		3,802
Total tax	$18,450	$21,650
Treated as exchange		
Tax on YZ	$ 4,500	$ 7,700
Tax on Y ($30,000 x .28)	8,400	
[($10,035 x .28) + ($19,965 x .31)]		8,999
Tax on Z	0	
($12,485 x .31)		3,870
Total tax	$12,900	$20,569

As the examples indicate, the corporation would be better off without an S election. But there are factors that could change the result—for example:

- The marginal tax rate of the corporation
- Use of appreciated property to effect the redemption
- Use of other than built-in gain property to effect the redemption
- The ability of any or all parties to utilize suspended losses against the resulting gains

1525. Corporate liquidations.

In many transfers of a business, the selling corporation will be liquidated. When the transfer is structured as an asset sale, the shareholders may be left with a corporate shell that has no assets except for consideration received from the buyer. If the corporation is no longer engaged in any business activity and does not intend to enter into any new business, the shareholders may decide to liquidate the corporation and take the property into noncorporate ownership. In other cases, it may be the purchaser who decides to liquidate the target corporation. The transfer of the business may have been structured as a stock sale, and the purchaser wants to combine the assets of the acquired corporation with other business assets. Although a complete discussion of corporate liquidations is beyond the scope of this book, some brief coverage is in order.

1525.1. Complete liquidation defined. For a transaction to constitute a complete liquidation, the corporation must cease to be a going concern. Any remaining activities relate to paying debts and distributing property to shareholders. [Regs. §1.332-2(c)]

The corporation need not be dissolved under state law. Its charter may be retained to protect its name for possible future reactivation. A formal plan is not necessary, but is advisable. Without such a plan, there may be some confusion about the distribution of the corporation's property.

1525.2. Effect of liquidation on corporation—General rules. The corporation that distributes its assets in complete liquidation is treated as having sold all of its assets at fair market value.[4] [§336(a)] If any property is subject to a liability, the corporation is treated as having sold the property for not less than the liability. [§336(b)]

---

[4] This rule reflects a major change made by the Tax Reform Act of 1986 and is generally applicable to liquidations occurring after July 31, 1986. There were different rules under prior law and some transitional rules. The transitional rules are discussed in Chapter 11, at 1120., since they also relate to the built-in gains tax. This book does not cover any of the rules in effect before 1986.

EXAMPLE 15 - 42: Outco has discontinued business and is liquidating. One of its assets has a basis of $5,000 but a fair market value of only $4,000. If the property is not subject to a liability greater than $4,000, the corporation is treated as selling the property for $4,000. It recognizes a loss (subject to restrictions discussed at 1525.22.) of $1,000.

Assume, however, that the property is subject to a liability of $7,000. The corporation is treated as having sold the property for $7,000, and it recognizes a gain of $2,000.

The taxable year of the corporation closes immediately after the distribution of all property in complete liquidation. The IRS has ruled that, for purposes of §1375, a liquidating distribution will rid the corporation of all accumulated earnings and profits. [PLRs 9747035, 9752038] Thus, for its last hypothetical moment of existence the corporation has no accumulated earnings and profits and is not subject to the passive investment income tax for its final year, even if its passive gross receipts exceeded 25% of its total, and it had AEP at the beginning of its final year. See discussion in Chapter 12, at 1230.5.

1525.21. Character of gain of loss. The character of gain or loss is determined as if the property had been sold to the shareholder in a fully taxable transaction. In most cases, the character will be determined by how the corporation used the property. If the property is depreciable to the shareholder, however, any gain is treated as ordinary income to the corporation under §1239. See Chapter 8, at 835.2., for a discussion of §1239.

If a corporation distributes sufficient assets to constitute a going concern, both the corporation and the shareholder will be required to value all assets under the rules of §1060, discussed above. Any intangibles, such as goodwill, must be included in the valuation. In a liquidation, any value to a lease, an employment contract, or a covenant not to compete will be impossible to assign, since the corporation will cease to exist. In one recent liquidation case, the corporation was required to value a leasehold interest that it distributed to its sole shareholder and was required to recognize gain on the value of this interest. [*Buda*, TC Memo 1999-132]

If any of the shareholders at the time of liquidation is a QSST, there is another special rule: Any gain that passes through to the shareholder as a result of the distribution of assets in liquidation is treated as income to the trust, not income to the beneficiary of the trust. [PLR 199905011]

1525.22. Loss disallowance rules. A liquidating distribution is not like other corporate distributions. In most instances, the corporation will recognize both gains and losses on these distributions. A loss can be recognized on a distribution to a majority shareholder, even though a sale of property in any other context would not result in an allowable loss.[5] There are certain limits on losses, however. Certain losses are denied on the distribution of property to majority shareholders, while certain other losses are denied on the distribution of property to any shareholder.

There are two provisions that disallow recognition of a corporate loss on the distribution of property to a majority shareholder: 15

- Any loss on such property if the distribution is not pro rata [§336(d)(1)(A)(i)]
- Any loss sustained on the distribution of disqualified property [§336(d)(1)(A)(ii)]

A majority shareholder is a person who owns more than 50% of the stock of the liquidating corporation, including any constructive ownership by the rules of §267. [§336(d)(1)(A)] See

---

[5] Code §267(a)(1) specifically excludes liquidating distributions from the disallowance of loss. Code §311(a), however, disallows any loss to a corporation that distributes property, if the distribution is not in complete liquidation of the corporation. See Chapter 7, at 730.1., for discussion of the general rules of §311(a) and Chapter 15, at 1515.2., for the application of §311(a) to redemptions.

Chapter 8, at 835., for a discussion of the constructive ownership rules of §267. The Code does not specifically define a distribution that is not pro rata. Apparently the provision applies when a majority shareholder receives more or less than a proportionate interest in the loss property.

EXAMPLE 15 - 43: X owns 60% and Y owns 40% of the XY Corporation. XY's assets consist of $40,000 cash and property with an adjusted basis of $75,000 and fair market value of $60,000. If Y receives the cash and X receives the other property, XY will recognize no loss. If 40% of the cash and property is distributed to Y and the remaining 60% is distributed to X, XY will be allowed loss in full.

Apparently, there could not be a non–pro rata distribution if one person owns all of the stock immediately before the liquidation. The term disqualified property is specifically defined. It includes any property that was received by the corporation in a §351 transfer or as a contribution to capital within five years of the distribution. [§336(d)(1)(B)]

EXAMPLE 15 - 44: Ernie owned 70% of the shares in Ernco, which was liquidated on September 16, 1992. Yarrow owned the other 30%. Ernie and Yarrow are not related parties within the meaning of §267. On October 17, 1987, Ernco had received property in a §351 transaction. On September 16, 1992, Ernco's basis in this property was $200,000 and its fair market value was $165,000.

If Ernco distributes that property to Ernie, the corporation will not be allowed to recognize the loss. It does not matter whether Ernie, Yarrow, or any other former shareholder contributed the property. Nor is it important what the value of the property may have been on the date Ernco received it. If the corporation distributes the property to Yarrow, however, Ernco will be able to deduct the loss on its 1992 tax return.

OBSERVATION: The loss disallowance rule for recently contributed property prohibits a shareholder from infusing the corporation with loss property. A shareholder cannot shelter the distribution of gain property, nor can a double deduction be obtained (e.g., a corporate-level loss on the distribution and a shareholder-level loss on receipt of the contributed loss property in liquidation of his or her stock).

A corporation could run afoul of the provision if a shareholder contributes property to a corporation, particularly one that is sick and dying. This is not a subjective rule; it could apply to an innocent attempt to shore up a corporation, if the contribution is made not more than five years before the corporation liquidates.

PLANNING TIP: If a corporation intends to liquidate, it could recognize a loss on recently contributed property by selling that property rather than distributing it in liquidation. If the sale is made to a controlling shareholder, however, observing the constructive ownership rules of §267, the loss would be disallowed to the corporation.

There is also a rule limiting the corporation's ability to deduct loss on the distribution of certain carryover basis property. [§336(d)(2)(B)] Under this rule, a corporation's loss is limited if the property had been contributed pursuant to a plan to allow loss recognition on the liquidating distribution. This rule is much narrower than the disallowance with respect to disqualified property, in that (1) not all of the loss is disallowed and (2) the property must have been contributed with a purpose of allowing the loss. It is broader than the disqualified property rule, however, in that it limits the loss on distribution to any shareholder, even if the shareholder did not own a majority of the stock before liquidation. It also applies to a sale or an exchange of the property, in addition to a distribution to a shareholder.

Any property that the corporation received in a §351 transfer or as a contribution to capital is treated as if it were contributed pursuant to such a plan-if it was received by the corporation within two years before adoption of the plan to liquidate. [§336(d)(2)(B)] This rule is subjective, however. A corporation may rebut the presumption that such property was acquired with a principal purpose of allowing a loss on liquidation, if the property had a clear and substantial relationship to the corporation's business. [Joint Committee on Taxation, General Explanation of the Tax Reform Act of 1986, page 343] The IRS is authorized to issue Regulations creating a safe harbor from the presumption. [§336(d)(2)(C)] (As of this writing, the IRS has not issued any such Regulations.)

The loss on such property will be allowed to the extent of any economic loss incurred after it was contributed to the corporation. The disallowance extends only to the excess of the corporation's basis in the property over its fair market value at the time of contribution.

> **EXAMPLE 15 - 45:** When Xelow Corporation was liquidated on September 5, 1992, it distributed property to a minority shareholder. The property had been received by Xelow as a contribution to capital in early 1992. The contributor's basis was $150,000, the fair market value at the time of contribution was $125,000, and the fair market value at the time of liquidation was $115,000. The corporation realizes a loss of $35,000 on the distribution, since it still has a basis of $150,000. Unless the property had a clear and substantial relationship to Xelow's business, however, the loss recognized on the liquidating distribution is limited to $10,000, which represents the decline of the property's value after it had been received by the corporation. Xelow's loss would also be limited to $10,000 if the property were sold, rather than distributed, pursuant to the plan of liquidation.

Any property for which the corporation's loss is limited would also meet the definition of disqualified property, and no loss would be allowed to the distributing corporation. The disallowance of loss on disqualified property, however, applies only to a distribution to a majority shareholder.

> **EXAMPLE 15 - 46:** Refer to Example 15 - 45. If Xelow had distributed the property to a majority shareholder, it would recognize no loss.

After the liquidation, the corporation ceases to exist for tax purposes. All of its tax attributes, as well as earnings and profits, Accumulated Adjustments Account (if it was an S corporation), and tax elections simply disappear.

1525.3. Effect on the corporation of distributing installment obligations. A C corporation that distributes installment receivables must recognize any gain for the difference between the fair market value of the receivables and the corporation's adjusted basis.[6] There is, however, a special rule for S corporations.

Under certain circumstances, an S corporation is not required to recognize gain on the distribution of an installment receivable to its shareholders in a liquidating distribution. [§453B(h)] To qualify for the nonrecognition, the installment receivable must have been generated by a sale of the S corporation's assets within the 12-month period ending on the date of the liquidating distribution. In addition, the S corporation must have adopted a plan to liquidate before making the sale that generated the receivable.

15

> **EXAMPLE 15 - 47:** In 1992, Lyco, an S corporation, sold some land on the installment method. The sales price was $300,000, and Lyco's basis in the land was $100,000. In 1993, Lyco received an offer for all of its remaining assets, for which it had a basis of $800,000. Upon receipt of the offer, Lyco adopted a plan to liquidate. It sold all of its remaining property to the purchaser and received an installment obligation for $2,000,000. After the sale of its remaining properties, Lyco's only two assets were the two installment receivables, which it

[6] Neither §336 nor any other provision treats installment receivables any differently from other property distributed in the liquidation by a C corporation.

then distributed to its shareholders. Lyco must recognize all $200,000 gain on the installment obligation it received for the 1992 land sale, but it does not recognize the $1,200,000 gain on the other installment obligation.

There are certain other limitations on the distribution of an installment receivable in liquidation. Any depreciation recapture under §1245 or §1250 may not be reported on the installment method. [§453(i)] The S corporation that sells the depreciable property must report the gain at the time of sale. Such gain would add to the S corporation's basis in the installment receivable and would not be a gain recognized on the distribution of such receivable. This is a general rule regarding the installment method, and it has no unique applications to an installment receivable generated in a complete liquidation. Any gain on depreciable property that is not covered by the depreciation recapture provisions, however, may be reported on the installment method. If the S corporation then distributes the installment receivable in liquidation, the S corporation generally would not recognize the gain on distribution, if the corporation sold the property to a party related to the shareholder. If the installment receivable is distributed to a person who (actually and constructively) owns more than 50% of the S corporation's stock, any of the installment gain attributable to depreciable property is recognized. This corresponds to the sale of depreciable property to a controlling shareholder under §1239. Chapter 8, at 835.2., discusses §1239.

EXAMPLE 15 - 48: Refer to Example 15 - 47. The 1993 installment receivable represented, in part, a gain on a building on which Lyco had claimed straight-line depreciation. The gain on the building was $400,000. Lyco had only one shareholder, who received both installment obligations in liquidation. As stated in Example 15 - 47, Lyco must recognize the gain on the 1992 obligation.

If the buyer of the depreciable property were related to the shareholder, Lyco would recognize $400,000 of the gain on the 1993 obligation.

If the S corporation generated the installment receivable from the sale of inventory, it is important to know how much of the corporation's inventory was sold in that transaction. If the S corporation sold all of its inventory in one bulk sale to one buyer, the S corporation is not required to recognize gain on the distribution of the installment receivable. [§453(h)(1)(B)] If the inventory was sold in partial lots, however, the S corporation must recognize gain on the distribution of the installment receivable.

CAUTION: Two special installment sale provisions can be easily confused. The provision discussed in this portion of the chapter is *§453(h)*. It relates to shareholders who receive certain installment notes as consideration for their stock in a corporate liquidation. This provision applies to shareholders in both C and S corporations. Later in the chapter, at 1525.6., the discussion turns to *§453B(h)*, which is applied at the corporate level and relates only to S corporations. To heighten the confusion, §453B(h) contains cross-references to §453(h).

15

The nonrecognition on the distribution of an installment receivable by an S corporation in complete liquidation is tied directly to the nonrecognition at the shareholder level, discussed below, at 1525.6. The nonrecognition does not cover any of the corporation's built-in gains from the installment receivable, and those gains must be included in the corporation's income in the year of disposition. If any of the gain is from the S corporation's sale of stock or securities, it may be subject to the passive investment income tax. The corporation would be required to report all such passive investment income in the year of the disposition, to the extent such gain exceeds 25% of the corporation's gross receipts.[7]

[7] Code §453B(h) disallows nonrecognition treatment for any taxes imposed by Subchapter S.

The installment receivable rules are extremely important considerations for S corporations contemplating liquidation. Accordingly, these rules receive further discussion at various later parts of this chapter. Special rules, governing certain sales by corporations undergoing liquidation, are discussed at 1525.6. The rules for the taxability of gain or loss to the liquidating S corporation are summarized in Figure 15 - 2.

1525.4. Gain or loss to the shareholders—General rule. A shareholder who receives property from a liquidating distribution reports all gain or loss in the same manner as any other completely taxable sale of his or her stock. [§331] The shareholder's amount realized for the stock is the fair market value of property received from the corporation, less any of the corporation's liabilities taken by the shareholder. The shareholder's gain or loss is generally capital, since stock is usually a capital asset to a shareholder.

Rather narrow exceptions apply if the shareholder is a dealer in securities and holds the S corporation stock in inventory at the time of liquidation. Since S corporations are almost all closely held and few if any shares of S corporations are readily traded, this situation is unlikely. There is also an exception when the corporation is a collapsible corporation, which is almost impossible under current law. [§341]

The IRS has attempted to treat a liquidating gain to a shareholder as ordinary income when the shareholder included his portion of the corporation's net operating loss for the year of liquidation as an ordinary deduction on his return. The court held that the ordinary loss was allowed and reduced stock and debt basis. The receipt of property in complete liquidation resulted in capital gain to the shareholder. [*Klein*, 75 TC 298 (1980). See Chapter 9, at 930.9.]

If the stock is §1244 stock and the shareholder realizes a loss on the liquidation, the loss is an ordinary loss subject to the limitations of §1244. See Chapter 14, at 1430., for a discussion of the rules of §1244.

If all of the liquidating distributions are received in one taxable year, the shareholder is able to compute and must report the exact amount of gain or loss. If the shareholder receives a series of distributions over two or more taxable years, the shareholder uses the cost recovery method for reporting. [Rev. Rul. 68-348, 1968-2 CB 141; Rev. Rul. 85-48, 1985-1 CB 126] Under the cost recovery method, each payment is first treated as a nontaxable return of the shareholder's basis in his stock. Once the shareholder's basis is fully recovered and is reduced to zero, all subsequent receipts are recognized as gain when received. The cost recovery method is applied separately for each block of stock the shareholder owns. Distributions are allocated to each block in proportion to the number of shares in each block, regardless of which shares are surrendered by the shareholder or when they are surrendered. Loss is recognized only after all distributions have been received.

For purposes of computing the gain or loss, the amount realized is the fair market value of all property received, including both tangible and intangible property. Intangible property includes the value of any goodwill where the shareholders continue to operate the business. [Rev. Rul. 66-81, 1966-1 CB 64] In this situation, both the corporation and the shareholder would be required to report the allocation of the fair market value under the rules of §1060.

A shareholder might consider contributing property to the corporation shortly before liquidation. If the property's basis is higher than its fair market value, the result would be to minimize the shareholder's gain or to create or increase a loss on the liquidating distribution. The Code has elaborate rules that disallow the corporate-level loss on property contributed in this manner. However, there are no statutory rules that disallow basis to a shareholder for such a contribution. The IRS could attack such a scheme as a sham transaction, lacking in substance, and recalculate the gain under general doctrines.

In some cases, the amount realized may not be finally determined until some years after the liquidation occurs. For example, the corporation may have had a contingent liability,

Figure 15 - 2: Summary of liquidation rules from the S corporation's perspective.

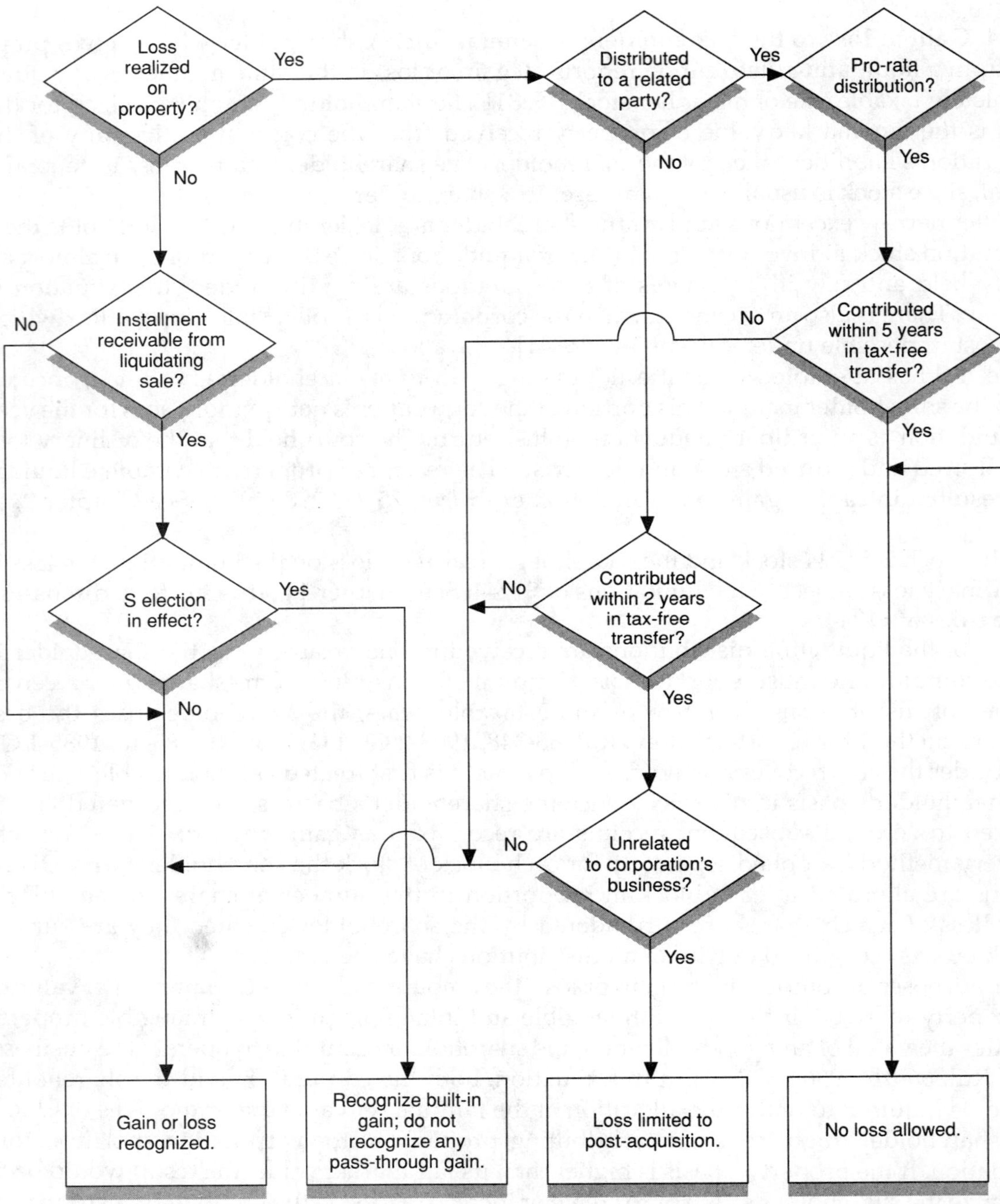

which the shareholder was obligated to pay at some later date. If the shareholder pays that contingent liability in a year *after* the liquidation, the amount of such payment is a capital loss since it relates back to the original transaction. [*F. D. Arrowsmith*, 52-2 USTC 9527 (S.Ct.)]

In general, a person who actually or constructively owns more than 50% of a corporation's stock is not allowed to recognize any loss on a sale of property to the corporation. (See Chapter 8, at 835.1., and Chapter 15, at 1510.14.) However, this rule does not apply to stock transferred by a shareholder in complete liquidation of the corporation. [§267(a)(1)] Therefore, a shareholder who receives property in a complete liquidation recognizes a capital loss if his or her stock basis is less than the fair market value of the property received from the corporation.

If a QSST owns stock at the time of liquidation, any gain attributable to the deemed sale of the stock pursuant to §331 is treated as gain reportable by the trust, and such gain does not pass through to the beneficiary under the QSST rules. [PLR 199905011] This is consistent with Regulations §1.1361-1(j)(8), which states that the QSST election terminates when the trust disposes of stock.

1525.5. Basis of property received by shareholders—General rule. A shareholder who receives property from a corporation in complete liquidation is treated as having received the property in a completely taxable transaction. Therefore, the shareholder's basis is the fair market value of property received. [§334(a)] Mathematically, the computations work out quite nicely: The shareholder's basis is the amount realized from the corporation, plus any liabilities. However, problems arise in two situations:

- When the property received by the shareholder has a fair market value less than the liabilities to which it is subject
- When the shareholder receives an installment obligation from the corporation

The problem of liabilities in excess of the property's fair market value is relatively easy to solve. The Code does not state a specific rule, but the intent of Congress is clear. A corporation is treated as selling the property for not less than the amount of liabilities to which the property is subject. [§336(b)] Congress intends that this same rule be applied to the shareholders. [Joint Committee on Taxation, General Explanation of the Tax Reform Act of 1986, page 339, footnote 77] Thus, a shareholder's basis in property received from the corporation is not less than the liabilities assumed, or taken, by the shareholder.

> **EXAMPLE 15 - 49:** Lossco liquidates and distributes all of its property to its sole shareholder, Lou. The actual fair market value of the property Lou receives is $10,000. Lou takes the property subject to $12,000 of Lossco's liabilities. Lou's basis in the property received from Lossco is $12,000.

The shareholder's holding period for any property received in liquidation begins on the date the property is received. There is no special rule mandating this result, which is the same for any property received in a fully taxable transaction.

1525.6. Special rules for receipt of installment obligations. A shareholder who receives an installment obligation from a corporation in complete liquidation must generally take the obligation into account at its fair market value. However, if the installment receivable was generated in a liquidating sale of assets by the corporation, the shareholder treats the receivable as if it were received for an installment sale of stock. [§453(h)(1)] The shareholder must allocate his or her stock basis between the "issue price" of the installment receivable and any other property received from the corporation in proportion to the relative fair market values.

EXAMPLE 15 - 50: At the time of liquidation, Vasco, Inc., had two remaining assets-cash of $50,000 and a note receivable of $100,000 arising from the sale of land. The note was payable in five installments of $20,000 beginning on December 31, 1993. The land, which had a basis of $40,000, was sold shortly after the plan of liquidation had been adopted. On October 31, 1992, the corporation distributed the cash and note to its sole shareholder, Martha, in complete liquidation. Martha had a basis in her stock of $9,000.

Martha realizes a gain of $141,000 ($50,000 + $100,000 – $9,000). However, Martha is allowed to report the gain allocable to receipt of the note as the note is collected. To determine the gain allocable to receipt of the note, the shareholder's basis is allocated between the note and other amounts received based on relative fair market values.

$$\frac{\text{Cash}}{\text{Total receipts}} \times \text{Basis} = \frac{\$50{,}000}{\$150{,}000} \times \$9{,}000 = \text{\$3,000 basis allocated to cash}$$

$$\frac{\text{Note}}{\text{Total receipts}} \times \text{Basis} = \frac{\$100{,}000}{\$150{,}000} \times \$9{,}000 = \text{\$6,000 basis allocated to cash}$$

Cash received in 1992	$50,000
Basis of cash	(3,000)
Gain recognized in 1992	$47,000

The balance of the gain, $94,000 ($141,000 – $47,000), is reported as the note is collected. The new basis in the note is $6,000, resulting in a new gross profit ratio of 94% ($100,000 – $6,000 = $94,000/$100,000). Therefore, Martha's gain recognized in 1993 and each of the next four years is $18,800 ($20,000 x 94%).

To qualify for the deferral, the installment receivable must meet all of the requirements discussed at 1525.3. The deferral is not available for the portion of the gain represented by an inventory sale, unless the inventory was sold in bulk to one buyer. The portion of the gain attributable to depreciable property is not deferred if the corporation distributes the receivable to a controlling shareholder. The receivable must have been generated after the corporation adopts its plan to liquidate, and it must be distributed in a complete liquidation.

When the shareholder who receives property in liquidation is also a creditor, the installment sale must be received in exchange for the shareholder's stock. Any part of the installment sale that is received in exchange of debt is not subject to the deferral. The planning possibilities for the extinguishment of debt are discussed below, at 1630.32.

Recent Regulations have clarified some the tax treatment of installment receivables qualifying for the special treatment under §453(h). Regulations §1.453-11 deals with the issue price and shareholder's basis. The issue price is determined by discounting the receivable to reflect any deficiency between the interest charged on the obligation and the applicable federal rate, as of the date of distribution. The issue price is then increased for any interest accrued but unpaid while the obligation was held by the corporation. [Regs. §1.453-11(a)(2)(ii)]

The basis of the shares is increased by any indebtedness of the corporation that is transferred to the shareholder as a result of the liquidation. [Regs. §1.453-11(a)(4)] The treatment is also extended to an installment receivable from a liquidated subsidiary which distributed to the parent corporation, and then the parent liquidates. [Regs. §1.453-11(c)(3)]

1525.7. Liquidations of controlled subsidiaries. Liquidation of a subsidiary corporation into its parent is generally a tax-free event. Neither the parent corporation nor the liquidating subsidiary recognizes any gain or loss.[8] To come within the scope of these rules, the parent corporation must own at least 80% of the stock of the subsidiary. At the time of this writing, the

---

[8] Code §332 provides the exemption for the parent corporation, and §337 applies to the subsidiary corporation.

prohibition against affiliated groups has limited the scope of subsidiary-parent liquidations to situations involving momentary ownership, discussed in Chapter 16, at 1630.32. There were two provisions of the Small Business Job Protection Act of 1996 that make this type of liquidation likely to be much more frequently encountered in the future. First, the general prohibition against membership in an affiliated group is removed for S corporations, for taxable years beginning after 1996. [§1361(b), as amended by the Small Business Job Protection Act of 1996] Second, the amendment of §1371(a) by §1310 of the Small Business Job Protection Act of 1996 to remove a phrase stating that "an S corporation shall be treated as an individual when it is a shareholder in another corporation" clarifies that Congress intends that S corporations should be subject to the §332 rules. [H.R. Conf. Rep. 104-737, p. 208]

1525.71. Effects on the parent corporation. When a corporation owns at least 80% of the outstanding shares in another corporation, the liquidation of the subsidiary corporation is (at least primarily) a tax-free transaction. Under §332, the parent corporation recognizes no gain or loss on the receipt of property from the subsidiary corporation in complete liquidation. [§332(a)] The liquidation must result in a complete redemption or cancellation of all of the subsidiary's stock and must meet some specific timing rules. If the plan of liquidation is silent as to the schedule of liquidating events, the liquidation must occur within the same taxable year. [§332(b)(2)] Thus a parent corporation may liquidate a subsidiary merely by distributing all of the subsidiary's assets in cancellation or redemption of all of the subsidiary's outstanding shares, even if there is no formal plan of liquidation, and receive tax-free treatment. There may be a formal plan of liquidation, and the plan may allow up to two years, beyond the taxable year in which the plan is adopted, for the liquidating distributions. In this case, the liquidation will be tax-free under §332. [§332(b)(3)]

The parent corporation must own at least 80% of the subsidiary's stock at the time the plan of liquidation is adopted and at all times thereafter until the liquidation is complete.[9] [§332(b)(1)] Finally, the parent must receive property in exchange for its stock. [§332(a)] Therefore, the rule cannot apply to liquidation of an insolvent corporation. [Regs. §1.332-2(b)] The rule does not apply to a minority shareholder, who is governed by the general liquidation rules of §331.

1525.72. Effects on the liquidated corporation. The distribution of property to the parent corporation does not result in gain or loss to the subsidiary corporation. [§337(a)] Similarly, the liquidating corporation recognizes no gain or loss on the distribution of property to the parent corporation in satisfaction of intercompany debt. [§337(b)(1)]

This rule does not apply to any property distributed to a minority shareholder. In this case, the liquidating subsidiary must recognize gains on the distribution of appreciated property. [§336(a)] The subsidiary, however, is not allowed to recognize a loss on the distribution of property to a minority shareholder. [§336(d)(3)]

1525.73. Applicability to S corporations. When an S corporation liquidates a subsidiary corporation in which it owns at least 80% of the stock, the liquidation is governed by §332 and §337. [§1371(a); also see Small Business Job Protection Act of 1996, §1310, which expressly addresses this issue.]

OBSERVATION: Before the Small Business Job Protection Act of 1996, there was some confusing language in §1371(a) and the IRS vacillated on whether the S corporation was a "corporation" or an "individual" with respect to the liquidation provi-

[9] This provision refers to §1504(a) for the ownership rules. Therefore, the two corporations involved in a subsidiary liquidation must meet the definition of an *affiliated group*. Thus, for years beginning before 1997, it was necessary to secure a waiver of the affiliated group prohibition under the momentary ownership doctrine.

sions. [See PLRs 8818049 and 9323041.] The legislative history to the Small Business Job Protection Act of 1996 demonstrates that Congress intends that an S corporation be treated as a parent corporation when liquidating a subsidiary. [H.R. Conf. Rep. 104-737, p. 208]

In some instances, an S corporation may want the liquidation to be taxable. As discussed at 1525.8., the S corporation may make a §338 election and achieve this result.

1525.74. Basis and other tax attributes. When a liquidation of a subsidiary corporation is governed by §332 and §337, there is a special rule for the basis of property received by the parent corporation in the liquidation. In contrast to the general rule, in which the property's basis is its fair market value at the time of the liquidating distribution, the property received in a §332 liquidation takes a carryover basis. Each item received by the parent corporation retains the basis it had in the hands of the subsidiary before the liquidation. [§334(b)] The IRS has held that all property received by an S corporation in a §332 liquidation is subject to the built-in gains tax for a period of 10 years following the liquidation. [TAM 9245004. This position is, in part, completely consistent with §1374(d)(8).] See Chapter 11, at 1140.2.

According to Regulation §1.1363-2(a)(2),[10] an acquired C corporation that is liquidated under §337 is subject to the LIFO recapture tax, if it had used the LIFO inventory method. The LIFO recapture is added to the corporation's taxable income in its final year of existence. The first installment of the tax is due on the due date of the liquidated corporation's final return. The remaining three installments must be paid on the due dates for the surviving corporation's next three returns. [Regs. §1.1363-2(b)(2)] See Chapter 3, at 320.5., for additional discussion and examples.

In addition, the liquidated subsidiary's tax history continues. [§381(a)(1)] Its earnings and profits, accounting methods, elections, carryovers, and several other tax attributes survive intact.[11] In essence, the tax treatment of a §332 liquidation is almost identical to a tax-free reorganization.

EXAMPLE 15 - 51: Purco, an S corporation, purchased all of the stock of Soldco, a C corporation, on August 6, 1993, for $1,000,000. Purco completely liquidated Soldco on August 6, 1993.

The fair market value of Soldco's assets was $1,000,000, and its aggregate adjusted basis in its assets was $400,000. Soldco's accumulated earnings and profits were $500,000.

Under the IRS's 1992 ruling position, as codified by the Small Business Job Protection Act of 1996, there would be no taxable gain or loss on the receipt of Soldco's property in liquidation.

Under the 1992 ruling position, Soldco would recognize no gain or loss on the distribution of its assets in complete liquidation. Purco's basis in the assets would be $400,000. Also, Purco would now have $500,000 accumulated earnings and profits, in addition to any of its accumulated earnings and profits which already existed before August 6, 1993. The assets Purco received from Soldco would be subject to the built-in gains tax until August 6, 2006.

15

If Purco would rather treat the liquidation as taxable (an unlikely but not impossible situation), it could divest itself of 21% of the Soldco stock before liquidation and thus disqualify Soldco from the application of §337. Alternatively, if it qualified under rules discussed below, it could make a §338 election with respect to Soldco's assets. If Purco were to make the liquidation taxable, Soldco would recognize a taxable gain of $600,000 on the distribution of its assets at their fair market value. In that case, Purco's basis in the assets would be its fair market value of $1,000,000. Purco's earnings and profits and other tax attributes would completely disappear.

---

[10] This rule applies to liquidations that take place after August 18, 1993.

[11] Code §381(c) lists 25 tax attributes that survive §332 liquidations and most tax-free reorganizations.

1525.8. Stock purchase treated as asset purchase. If a parent corporation purchases 80% or more of the stock of a subsidiary in a 12-month period, the purchasing corporation may be able to treat the transaction as a purchase of the subsidiary's assets. Under §338, the acquired corporation is treated as if it were liquidated in a fully taxable transaction on the date the parent corporation completes its stock purchase. The acquired corporation is treated as if it repurchased all of the same assets on the next day. The basis of the assets treated as repurchased is computed using the residual method described above under §1060. The cost of the target stock, the liabilities, and the percentage purchased by the parent corporation are all factored into the new basis. The §338 election is a complicated provision. Under current law, its uses are rare, since liquidations are now completely taxable. See Chapter 11, at 1110., for a discussion of the 1986 repeal of the General Utilities doctrine of corporate liquidations.

1525.81. Purchase requirement. In order to qualify for §338 treatment, a purchasing corporation must acquire 80% of the stock of the target corporation within a 12-month period. [§338(h)(1)] The purchase may be made in one transaction, or it may be several transactions from different sellers. The acquisition must not be any variety of nontaxable exchange, such as a reorganization, a §351 transfer, or a contribution to capital. The stock cannot be purchased from any person or entity that is considered a related party to the purchasing corporation. The rules can become complicated when there are several transactions, and they are even more cumbersome if the purchasing corporation also acquired some stock outside of the 12-month period.

The purchase of 80% of the stock of a target corporation does not in and of itself activate the rules of §338. In general, the purchasing corporation must make an election to treat the acquired corporation as if it were liquidated on the day the purchaser acquired the stock that brings the purchase up to the 80% threshold. [§338(g)]

1525.82. Deemed or actual liquidation. The §338 election treats the subsidiary as if it had sold all of its assets at fair market value on the day of the acquisition of 80% of the stock. The deemed sale is not tax-free under §337. Instead, the subsidiary recognizes all gains or losses. [§338(a)(1)] The election must be filed by the parent corporation within 8 months and 15 days after the end of the month that includes the acquisition date. [§338(g)(1)]

If the purchasing corporation intends to keep the subsidiary alive as a separate entity (which is not permitted for S corporations under current law), the target corporation is treated as having purchased all of its assets on the day after the deemed sale. [§338(a)(2)] The deemed purchase price is the "adjusted-grossed up basis" of the stock purchased by the parent corporation in the 12-month period. When there is a single transaction in which the parent corporation purchases all of the stock, the adjusted grossed-up basis is the purchase price of the stock, plus any liabilities assumed by the parent corporation, including the subsidiary's income tax liability resulting from the deemed sale.[12] [§338(b)]

If the parent corporation actually liquidates the subsidiary, then the basis is computed in the same manner. The only difference is that the parent corporation is treated as purchasing all of the subsidiary's assets on the day following the liquidation. The subsidiary still treats the liquidation as a taxable sale of all of its assets. The purchasing corporation acquires all of the subsidiary's assets at the adjusted grossed-up stock basis. All tax attributes of the target corporation disappear.

A consistency requirement is in force to prevent a purchasing corporation from acquiring several corporations from one selling parent corporation and treating some as liquidated and others as continuing to exist. All corporations purchased within 12 months from the

[12] If the parent has purchased less than 100% of the stock, or has purchased some stock outside the 12-month period, the computations can become cumbersome.

same controlled group are subject to the same §338 election. [§338(f)] If the purchaser does not make an election for the first corporation acquired in this manner, it cannot make the election for any of the other corporations so acquired. A similar rule applies when a purchasing corporation acquires at least 80% of the stock of one member of a controlled group and acquires assets from one or more of the other members within a 12-month period. If the purchasing corporation takes a cost basis in the asset acquisition, it must make a §338 election with respect to the stock acquisition. If it does not desire to do so, it may make a protective carryover basis election with respect to the asset acquisition, in which it takes the same basis as that of the seller. [Temporary Regs. §1.338-4T(f)(6)(iii)]

Since the sale of the assets by the target corporation is completely taxable, the §338 election is rare under current law. There are two uses of the election that may merit consideration. First, if the target corporation has loss carryovers and other favorable tax attributes, the change of ownership may limit the ability of the corporation to receive future tax benefits. (See the brief discussion of these complicated rules at 1640.73.) These tax benefits, however, may be used to reduce the tax liability of the deemed sale pursuant to a §338 election. [§382(h)(1)(C)] The second use of the §338 election that deserves general consideration is the election by the selling parent corporation, discussed below.

1525.83. Special election by buying corporation and sellers under §338(h)(10). A special variation of the §338 election applied only when a parent corporation sells one of its subsidiaries, where the two corporations had been filing consolidated returns. [§338(h)(10)] As is discussed below, this type of transaction now clearly applies when the sellers are shareholders and the sold corporation is an S corporation. The selling parent and the purchasing corporation jointly make the election. [Temporary Regs. §1.338(h)(1)-1T(d)(6)]

The result of a §338(h)(10) election is that the subsidiary is treated as if it were liquidated into the selling parent in a tax-free §337 liquidation. The parent is then treated as if it took a carryover basis from the subsidiary and then sold the assets at fair market value to the purchasing corporation. Consequently, the subsidiary, which actually owns the assets, receives a basis in each of its own assets equal to their aggregate fair market values.

1525.84. Applicability to S corporations. Until recently, there was little guidance on the ability of S corporations to participate in §338 elections. In 1988, the IRS ruled that an S corporation that acquired all of the stock of another corporation could not make a §338 election with respect to the acquired assets. [PLR 8818049] The IRS has reversed this position in some letter rulings, and then the position was codified in the Small Business Job Protection Act of 1996. [H.R. Conf. Rep. 104-737, p. 208, describing the change in §1371(a)]

1. When an S corporation acquires all of the stock of another corporation and the transaction meets all of the §338 requirements, the S corporation can make a §338 election with respect to the acquired corporation or may join with the seller in making an election to treat the transactions as a sale of assets under §338(h)(10). [PLR 9245004 (TAM)] See discussion above at 1525.8.

   Regulations under §338 that were adopted in 1994 also hold that shareholders of a target S corporation can join with the purchaser in making a §338(h)(10) election. [Regs. §§1.1338(h)(10)-1(a), 1.338(h)(10)-1(c)(2)] This election is permitted for all qualifying exchanges that occur on or after January 20, 1994. [Regs. §1.338(i)-1(a)]

   For the corporation to qualify for this election, the stock must be sold to another corporation that is eligible to make a §338 election. The acquiring corporation and the selling shareholders must agree to make the election no later than the fifteenth day of the ninth month after the purchaser acquires the stock that puts it over the 80% threshold. [Regs. §1.338(h)(10)-1(d)(2)] The IRS has granted relief from the filing deadline of the §338(h)(10) election. This relief is granted pursuant to the IRS's discretionary authority under Regulations §301.9100-1. [PLRs 9543035, 9608028, 9711022, 9831008, 9831009, 9832002, 9832025, 9850014, 9853005, 199904016, 199907005, 199909015, 199909030, 199912020, 199917033, 199917043, 199920026, 199922041]

EXAMPLE 15 - 52: Richard, Susan, and Terry were all equal shareholders in Targco. Purco, a C corporation owned by parties unrelated to Richard, Susan, and Terry, offered $1,200,000 for all of Targco's assets. The corporation's basis in its assets was $300,000. Richard, Susan, and Terry each had $100,000 basis in their stock. Susan and Richard were willing to have Targco sell off all its assets, and then they would liquidate Targco. Terry, however, insisted that the transaction be structured as a stock sale. Purco agreed to structure the deal as a stock sale, provided Susan, Richard, and Terry would all agree to join in an election under §338(h)(10).

On April 17, 1994, Richard, Susan, and Terry transfer all of their shares in Targco to Purco. Targco's S election must terminate on April 17, 1994, because it has an ineligible shareholder on that date. The deadline for making the §338(h)(10) election is January 15, 1995, which is the fifteenth day of the ninth month after Purco had acquired 80% of Targco's stock.

2. When the buyer and the selling shareholders make a §338(h)(10) election, the target corporation is treated as if it had sold all of its assets at fair market value on the acquisition date. The selling shareholders must report all of the corporation's gains and losses on their returns. [Regs. §1.338(h)(10)-1(e)(2)(ii)] To qualify for the §338(h)(10) election, the purchaser must acquire all of the stock (or at least 80%) on the day (the acquisition date). The purchaser may not have acquired any stock before the acquisition date. [Regs. §1.338(h)(10)-1(c)(2)] Thus the result is the same as if the S corporation had sold all of its assets on the acquisition date and had terminated its existence at that time. The target corporation will not be treated as a C corporation before the §338 election occurs. [Regs. §1.338(h)(10)-1(e)(2)(iv)]

   When the shareholders report the gain on the deemed sale, they will adjust their stock basis to its fair market value. [Regs. §1.338(h)(10)-1(e)(2)(iii)] Thus there is no gain or loss on the sale of stock, per se, although there may be a gain or loss on the deemed liquidation. [Regs. §1.338(h)(10)-1(e)(2)(iv)] If the selling shareholders retain any stock in the corporation, the basis of that stock becomes its fair market value on the acquisition date. [Regs. §1.338(h)(10)-(e)(2)(iii)]

EXAMPLE 15 - 53: Refer to Example 15 - 52. Targco will report $900,000 as a gain on the sale of its assets on April 17, 1994. Richard, Susan, and Terry will each report $300,000 of that gain as flowing through from the S corporation.

EXAMPLE 15 - 54: Darryl was the owner of all the shares in Darco, an S corporation. On June 12, 1994, he sold all of his shares to a purchasing corporation. On the date of the sale, Darryl's basis was zero, and he had suspended losses of $100,000 from prior years. The corporation has a basis of $250,000 in its assets. The fair market value was $750,000, which was the same as the fair market value of the stock. Thus, under the Regulations, Darryl must report $500,000, the gain recognized by the corporation, on his return. His basis goes from zero to 500,000. Immediately after the deemed sale is the deemed liquidation. At this point, Darco hypothetically has the $750,000 of cash paid by the purchaser. (Actually, the cash went directly to Darryl.) Next Darco is treated as if it paid the $750,000 cash to Darryl in complete liquidation of the corporation. At this point Darryl recognizes $250,000 of additional gain.

OBSERVATION: There is no reference to the §338(h)(10) election in any of the Regulations issued under Subchapter S. Thus there is no guidance on the effect of the reported gain from the deemed asset sale on a shareholder's ability to utilize suspended losses. Future Regulations or other administrative pronouncements will need to clarify these issues, especially as S corporations begin to deal more frequently with controlled subsidiaries after the affiliated group prohibition is gone.

CAUTION: A shareholder who is selling all of his or her stock will probably want to calculate the effects of the §338(h)(10) election on his or her personal tax situation. This election should not affect the total gain or loss that the shareholder would otherwise recognize on a direct sale of stock. It may, however, affect the character of the gain, since ordinary gains and losses realized by the corporation will be reported by the shareholders. Because the rule regarding §338(h)(10) elections by selling shareholders of S corporations is so new, there have as yet been no cases, rulings, or other commentary regarding its uses and pitfalls. Tax professionals should be aware of this new opportunity for planning for the sale of an S corporation and should be on the alert for unforeseen consequences.

1525.85. Extinguishment of tax attributes. Under the general rules of §338, the "new" target corporation is treated as a new corporation for tax purposes. [§338(a)(2)] Thus the earnings and profits, carryovers, and all other tax attributes and elections of the "old" corporation simply disappear. The "new" corporation is then free to make any of its own tax elections. When the old target is actually liquidated into the purchasing corporation, the purchase may make any permissible election with respect to the properties acquired.

1525.9. Reporting requirements. When a corporation adopts a plan to liquidate, it should file Form 966 with the office of the District Director of the IRS where the corporation files its income tax returns. [Regs. §1.6043-1] The requirements are identical for S corporations and C corporations. The form is filed within 30 days after the adoption of the plan to liquidate. The corporation also files a tax return for its final year. Gains and losses on the liquidation distributions are reported on the final Form 1120S (or Form 1120 for C corporations). The corporation also files Form 1099L with both the IRS and its shareholders. That form lists the amount of money and the fair market value of other property distributed to each shareholder. Each shareholder then reports the gain on his or her individual return for the year of the liquidation.

Failure to conform to the filing requirements will endanger the treatment of distributions to the shareholders. It is important to classify distributions as liquidating, rather than other types, if the corporation realizes a loss on distributed property. If a distribution is not in complete liquidation, the corporation will not be allowed to recognize a loss. If a distribution includes an installment obligation, the corporation will be required to recognize all deferred gain, unless the installment obligation qualifies for the special treatment afforded to liquidating distributions of installment obligations.

When there is a §338 election involved, the purchaser files Form 8023. If the buyer and seller are joining in an election under §338(h)(10), they must each file Form 8023A.

1530. Practice aids.

Checklist 15-1 reminds the tax professional of the various factors to consider when a corporation is contemplating a stock redemption.

Checklist 15 - 1: Stock redemption considerations

	Applicable (Yes/No)	*Completed (Date)*
Check for shares to be redeemed		
Advantage or disadvantage of exchange treatment		
AAA and basis		
AEP		
For exchange treatment		
Disproportionate		
Check for constructive ownership		
Family		
Entity		
Option		
Complete termination		
All interests to be severed		
No entity or option attribution		
10-year look back		
10-year look forward agreement		
Partial liquidation		
Contraction of corporation		
Disposition of S year owned business		
Retention of S year owned business		
Not essentially equivalent to dividend		
Check recent rulings for IRS positions		
Redemption to pay death tax		
Percent of estate		
Burden of tax payments		
Reduction to AAA		
Reduction to AEP		
Other equity accounts		
Treasury stock on books		

Copyright © 2000 by Harcourt, Inc. All rights reserved.

ACQUISITIONS AND DISPOSITIONS OF S CORPORATIONS

CONTENTS

1600. Overview.

The change of ownership of a corporation may be brought about by means of several different transactions. In substance, the former owners of the business are transferring their interests to new owners, and such a transfer generally is a fully taxable event with the sellers recognizing all gains or losses and the buyers taking a new cost basis for the properties acquired. There are, however, several different ways to transfer an interest in a business. The tax consequences can vary significantly, depending on how the parties structure the transaction.

Subchapter S provides very little information about the tax consequences of transferring a business. The tax professional will need to be aware of rules of Subchapter C, as well as other provisions of the Internal Revenue Code, regarding the tax consequences of the transfer of the assets of an entire business. When the buyer, the seller, or both are S corporations, the mixture of Subchapter S rules with the other tax provisions can provide for some interesting effects.

1610. Basic transactions covered.

A transfer of the business of an S corporation may take one of three basic structures:

1. A sale of all (or substantially all) of the selling corporation's assets to a purchaser
2. A sale of all of the selling corporation's stock to a purchaser
3. A tax-free reorganization, whereby one corporation acquires another corporation and the shareholders of the acquired corporation receive stock in the acquiring corporation

There are several possible variations for each of these transaction types. Both the buyer and the seller should be aware of the nontax and tax aspects of the form chosen for a transfer of interest. Frequently, the seller and the buyer have adverse interests as to the optimum form of the transaction.

1610.1. General considerations. From the seller's point of view, a cash sale of all of the seller's stock in the corporation, together with complete relief from the corporation's debts, would be the ideal outcome in the transfer of a business.

By contrast, the buyer of that business would prefer to use as little cash as possible, to acquire only the assets which it would use in the continuation of the business, and to have responsibility for payment of only the minimum possible liabilities of the business.

Regarding taxes, the seller might prefer to recognize capital gain, which is generally the result of a stock sale. If the seller desires to defer recognition of gain and is willing to finance the sale, he or she may be able to use the installment method to report the gain from the sale of stock. Therefore, the tax considerations, as well as the general financial ones, encourage a seller to structure the transaction as a stock sale.

The tax considerations of the buyer are adverse to those of the seller. The buyer generally desires a cost basis in the assets of the business, especially any assets that are to be sold in the near future, such as inventory. The buyer might also prefer a cost basis in depreciable property, in order to claim depreciation deductions on the actual cost of the property. A purchase of assets, rather than a purchase of stock, might serve the best interests of the buyer.

If the business has suffered a decline in value, the ideal positions might be reversed. The seller might prefer an asset sale, in order to recognize ordinary losses on the sale of individual assets. A stock sale would result in a capital loss, which is limited in its deductibility. The buyer might prefer to purchase the stock of the corporation, in order to preserve the basis of assets.

1610.2. Specific tax considerations. For each prospective sale, the parties should be aware of the following tax considerations:

1. Gain or loss recognized by the selling corporation
   - Corporate built-in gains tax on disposition
   - Continuation of the seller's S election
2. Gain or loss recognized by the selling shareholders
   - Amount of gain or loss
   - Character of gain or loss
   - Timing of recognition of gain or loss
3. Basis in the acquired property to the purchasers
4. Survival of the tax attributes of the acquired corporation
   - Continued S election
   - Tax elections
   - AAA, earnings and profits, and other considerations

When a business is to be sold, the buyer and seller should each consider their own preferred treatment. Each should be aware of the other's interests, however, in order to negotiate. Example 16 - 1 illustrates the points of negotiation.

EXAMPLE 16 - 1: Buyer, Inc., is contemplating the purchase of the business of Sellco, an S corporation, in 1999. The approximate value of Sellco's business to Buyer is $1,000,000. Sellco's basis in its assets is $500,000, and Sellco's shareholder's basis in the Sellco stock is also $500,000. All of Sellco's assets would produce ordinary income and built-in gains if sold by Sellco. Both Sellco's shareholder and Buyer are in the 39.6% tax bracket for ordinary income and in the 20% bracket for capital gains. The sole consideration paid by Buyer will be cash. If the transaction is a stock sale, Buyer will liquidate Sellco. If the deal is structured as an asset sale, Sellco's shareholder will liquidate Sellco.

A comparison of the two forms of sale, from Sellco's current shareholder's perspective, reveals the following:

Structure as asset sale:

	Taxable Income	*Cash Flow*
Cash received by Sellco		$1,000,000
Corporate gain	$ 500,000	
Built-in gains tax	(175,000)	(175,000)
Corporate income to shareholder	325,000	
Shareholder's basis prior to asset sale	500,000	
Shareholder's basis after sale	825,000	
Net cash to shareholder	825,000	$ 825,000
Gain on distribution	$ 0	
Shareholder's tax on corporation's income ($325,000 x 39.6%)		(128,700)
Cash to shareholder after tax		$ 696,300

16

Structure as stock sale:

	Taxable Income	*Cash Flow*
Cash received by shareholder	$1,000,000	$1,000,000
Less basis in shares	(500,000)	
Capital gain	$ 500,000	
Tax on capital gain		(100,000)
Cash to shareholder after tax		$ 900,000

If Buyer pays $1,000,000 for the assets, it will have a cost basis of the same amount. If Buyer pays $1,000,000 for the stock and then liquidates the corporation, it would need to pay an additional $175,000 of built-in gains tax when Sellco distributes its assets, since Sellco would retain its basis of $500,000. Therefore, the tax treatment to the two parties can be compared.

	Asset Sale	*Stock Sale*
Cash paid by Buyer, including tax liquidation	$1,000,000	$1,175,000
After tax cash to selling shareholder	(696,300)	(860,000)
Combined tax burden	$ 303,700	$ 315,000

Buyer and Sellco's shareholders have considerable room to negotiate. Perhaps Buyer could offer a higher price than $1,000,000 for all of Sellco's assets and leave Sellco's current shareholders with the burden of liquidating Sellco. Or perhaps Sellco's shareholders could offer Buyer all of their stock at less than $1,000,000.

There are many transfers of businesses under each structure. There are also variations, whereby the purchaser buys something other than the stock or the assets held by the corporation from the seller. For example, an employment agreement or consulting contract between the seller of the business and the buyer may alter the tax effects somewhat. Under such an arrangement, one or more of the individual sellers will agree to remain employed by the buyer, who agrees to pay the sellers a certain amount of money for their services.

EXAMPLE 16 - 2: Refer to Example 16 - 1. The parties agree to structure the deal as an asset sale. In order to compromise on the tax benefits, which will accrue to Buyer, Buyer will pay Sellco $800,000 for all of its assets. In addition, Buyer will pay Sellco's shareholder $250,000 as a covenant not to compete. The tax consequences will be:

	Taxable Income	*Cash Flow*
Cash received by Sellco		$800,000
Corporate gain	$300,000	
Built-in gains tax (35%)	(105,000)	(105,000)
Corporate income to shareholder	195,000	
Shareholder's basis prior to asset sale	500,000	
Shareholder's basis after sale	695,000	
Net cash to shareholder	695,000	$695,000
Gain on distribution	$ 0	
Shareholder's tax on corporation's income (39.6% of 195,000)		(77,220)
Cash to shareholder after tax		617,780
Cash received directly from Buyer as covenant		250,000
Tax on value of covenant (39.6% of $250,000)		(99,000)
		$768,780

By this plan, Sellco's shareholder will have more after-tax cash than in a strict asset sale from the corporation and less than in a pure stock sale. Buyer takes assets with a basis of $800,000,

16

with no tax burden of liquidating the corporation. Buyer also receives an amortizable intangible asset, the covenant, with a basis of $250,000. Comparing this compromise position with the other two structures, it is apparent that both parties have compromised approximately equally.

PLANNING TIP: A covenant not to compete can be an important asset for a purchaser of an entire business, for nontax as well as tax reasons. First and foremost, the buyer will want to make sure that the seller has no right to reopen the business in the general vicinity for a definite period of time. When the seller is a corporation, a covenant binding the corporation not to compete may be of dubious value. If the corporation could be easily liquidated, the selling shareholders might be able to start a new corporation, or another business form, and take back much of the business that they had supposedly sold. Thus, it is usually prudent to acquire a covenant not to compete directly from the owners of the selling business. In some cases, where the selling corporation is likely to continue, it may be a good idea to acquire covenants from both the corporation and its owners, although the covenant from the owners is usually the most valuable. For valuation of a convenant not to compete, see *Custom Chrome Inc.*, TC Memo 1998-317.

Prior to the Revenue Reconciliation Act of 1993, buyers of a business would often try to allocate as much of the consideration as possible to a covenant not to compete from the seller. The tax advantage to the buyer was that all payments under the covenant would be deductible. The Revenue Reconciliation Act of 1993, however, changed the tax treatment considerably. Under new Code §197, when a buyer acquires a going concern all intangible assets, including a covenant not to compete, must be amortized over 15 years.

1615. Background rules.

Although this book is devoted to S corporations, certain rules applicable to other entities deserve some coverage. Specifically, a taxable transfer of all of a business from one taxpayer to another has some special reporting considerations. The rules are not unique to S corporations; they apply to all types of taxable entities.

Some of the transactions that might accompany the transfer of interest in a business have unique rules applicable to corporations; for example, a transfer might involve a corporate liquidation or reorganization. The principal rules for these transactions are in Subchapter C, and they apply to all corporations, although there are some special considerations for S corporations.

This portion of the chapter is dedicated to the discussion of the general tax problems of a transfer of a corporate business. Later portions discuss the specific problems of S corporations.

1620. Allocation of consideration for a going concern.

When a taxable transfer of assets includes all of the assets of a going business, there are special rules, contained in §1060, which require specific allocation methods. When making such an allocation, seller and buyer have, at least historically, often been at adverse positions. Sellers have usually preferred to allocate as much of the sales price as possible to capital assets, since sales of capital assets resulted in favorable treatment. Buyers, by contrast, preferred to allocate as much as possible of the purchase price to assets such as inventory. Inventory is expected to be sold shortly, which results in ordinary income or loss. Depreciable assets with relatively short cost recovery periods are also assets for which high basis produces quick tax benefits.

Prior to the Revenue Reconciliation Act of 1993, buyers would typically prefer to allocate as little as possible of the purchase price to goodwill, which could not be amortized or depreciated. Accordingly, they would attempt to allocate purchase price to tangible assets, such as equipment and buildings, which could be depreciated. Buyers would also specifically negotiate for other intangible assets, such as customer lists, which could be amortized. The IRS took a dim view of short-lived intangible assets in a purchase of a going concern and would try to allocate as much of the purchase price as possible to goodwill. The IRS was not always successful. Shortly before the Revenue Reconciliation Act of 1993 was enacted, a taxpayer won a major victory, when the Supreme Court decided that short-lived intangibles could be amortized over their useful lives. [*Newark Morning Ledger*, 93-1 USTC 50,228 (S.Ct.)]

The Revenue Reconciliation Act of 1993 changed the entire strategy. In any asset acquisition that occurs after August 10, 1993 (the date of enactment of the Revenue Reconciliation Act of 1993), the intangible assets received are amortizable over a 15-year period.[1] [§197] This change in the law is extremely beneficial to taxpayers who acquire goodwill. It now gives more rapid deductions for goodwill than on long-lived equipment or buildings. These rules receive additional discussion at 1620.3., below.

> **OBSERVATION:** Before August 1993, buyers usually wanted to allocate as little as possible to goodwill, since it was nondepreciable. The rules of §1060 are designed so that a buyer who pays consideration that exceeds the values of the identifiable assets will be forced to allocate a portion of the cost to goodwill. As a result of the amortization rules of §197, discussed at 1620.3., goodwill now receives more beneficial tax treatment than many other assets. For example, buyers will generally want to allocate more of the purchase cost to goodwill than to land, which is not depreciable, or buildings, which now have a depreciation life of 39 years.
>
> Thus in many situations only current assets, such as receivables and inventory, or short-lived personal property, such as computers and vehicles, are likely to produce greater tax benefit than goodwill, considering the time value of money. In some situations, however, it might still be best to allocate as much of the purchase price as possible to long-lived assets or land. If the long-lived asset is likely to be sold in the near future, the primary tax benefit would be a recovery of basis on the sale.

A seller usually has no adverse impact from the sale of goodwill. Generally, goodwill is a capital asset. Where the goodwill has been generated by the reputation of the company, it is not likely to have any basis. Therefore, most sellers will report capital gain on the sale of goodwill. For individual taxpayers, a capital gain is taxed at a maximum rate of 28%, whereas ordinary income may be taxed at a rate as high as 39.6% after 1992.

When the buyer and the seller agree on the allocation of the price to individual properties, they will generally be bound by the values assigned. In the case of *Danielson*, for example, the parties had structured a transfer to include a covenant by the seller not to compete with the buyer. The seller, having discovered that an amount received for a covenant constitutes ordinary income, later decided to report the transfer as a sale of a capital asset (stock). The court held that, absent duress or material misrepresentation, the parties were bound by the values assigned to each asset transferred. [*Carl Danielson*, 50 TC 782 (1968)]

Under current law, both buyers and sellers are to report the valuation assigned to various classes of assets on their tax returns for the year of the transfer. Code §1060 requires the use of the *residual method* (explained below) for the allocation. The seller and the buyer do not need to agree on the allocation, but they must report whether they agree or disagree.

16

[1] This treatment applies to intangibles acquired after July 25, 1991, and before August 10, 1993, if the purchaser elects such treatment on all intangibles acquired after July 25, 1991. [Revenue Reconciliation Act of 1993, §13261(g)(2)]

When the seller of a going concern is an S corporation, there may be another important consideration. The seller will generally want to give a low value to any assets which are subject to the built-in gains tax, and higher values to properties which are not subject to this tax. On this particular matter, buyer and seller may have no adverse interest.

Misrepresentation of the purchase of a business can lead to imposition of fraud penalties. This happened in one recent case where the cost of an acquired corporation's stock was deducted as "services purchased." [*U.S. v. Fletchall*, 80 AFTR 2d 97-6259] In contrast, costs allocated to a covenant not to compete were respected and were not treated as disguised consideration for stock. [*Thompson*, TC Memo 1997-287]

1620.1. Applicability of §1060. This provision requires that the buyer and seller report the valuation assigned to multiple assets transferred in the same transaction under two conditions, both of which are stated in §1060(c).

- The transaction must include sufficient assets to constitute a complete business [§1060(c)(1)]
- The buyer's basis is determined wholly by reference to the purchase price [§1060(c)(2)]

The first requirement, that the assets constitute a complete trade or business, applies if they meet either one of two conditions:

- If they would constitute an active trade or business for a divisive reorganization, discussed in Chapter 17
- If any goodwill or going-concern value attaches to the assets [Temporary Regs. §1.1060-1T(b)(2); Regs. §1.355-3(b)(2)(ii)]

A facility such as a retail store or a manufacturing plant may or may not constitute a going concern. If it is independently operated and has its own sources of supply and its own customers, it would be treated as a trade or business. If it is operated as a profit center, classification as a trade or business is likely. However, if its sources of supply and the users of its output are completely dictated elsewhere in the company, its status as a separate trade or business is doubtful. For example, real estate operations, unless they are run completely independently, generally are not treated as independent businesses.

The second requirement, that the buyer's basis be determined solely by reference to the consideration paid, is a somewhat backhanded way of stating that the transfer must be completely taxable. The allocation rules are required for complete liquidations of corporations (discussed below) as well as for taxable asset sales. The Code also provides that when some of the assets are transferred in a like-kind exchange but a portion of the transfer is taxable, §1060 applies to the taxable portion of the exchange. [§1060(c)] The rules do not require a reported allocation of price in any of the following situations (i.e., §1060 does not apply):

16

- A proprietor contributes his or her going concern to a partnership in exchange for a partnership interest, since the partnership that receives the property computes its basis in the same way as the contributing partner's basis. [§723]
- A proprietor contributes his or her going concern to a controlled corporation in exchange for stock and/or securities. In this case, the corporation's basis in the acquired property is determined by reference to the shareholder's basis. [§362(a)] Apparently, even if the shareholder receives sufficient boot to make the transaction completely taxable, there is no required reporting under §1060, since the corporation's basis in the property received is still computed by reference to the shareholder's basis.

- A corporation acquires assets from another corporation in a tax-free reorganization. Even if some shareholders of the target corporation receive boot and recognize gain, §1060 does not apply. The basis in any property transferred between corporations in a reorganization is unchanged from that of the prior holder. [§362(a)] This rule exempts reporting under §1060 if the reorganization is a division, discussed in Chapter 15, or an acquisition, discussed in Chapter 17.
- A corporation liquidates it subsidiary, and the subsidiary is not newly purchased. Basis of property received by the parent corporation is the same as the liquidated subsidiary's basis. [§334(b)]

Code §1060 has no rules that are unique to S corporations. Its rules are not affected by the business form of either the seller or the buyer. It covers all of the following situations:

- A proprietor buys another proprietorship and continues to operate as a proprietorship.
- A partnership buys a proprietorship and continues to operate as a partnership.
- A corporation buys a partnership or a proprietorship.
- A proprietorship or partnership buys a going concern from a corporation, whether or not the corporation is liquidated.
- A corporation makes a §338 election for a newly purchased subsidiary.

1620.2. Operating rules for §1060. The purchaser and the seller must each use the residual method of allocating the cost and sales price of the individual properties transferred. The process is a step allocation to five classes of assets. At each step, the amount allocated is the total consideration (less any consideration allocated to a senior class) or the identifiable fair market value of the property within the class, whichever is less. The classes, in order of seniority, are:

Class	*Description*
I	Cash and demand deposits
II	CDs and government and marketable securities
III	All other, except goodwill
IV	Intangible assets, other than goodwill and going-concern value
V	Goodwill and going-concern value

Examples 16 - 3 and 16 - 4 illustrate the allocation method, where the total price paid is greater than the identifiable values of the first four classes of assets.

EXAMPLE 16 - 3: Buyer buys an entire business from Sellco. Before the sale the balance sheet was:

	Basis	*Value*
Assets:		
Cash	$ 150,000	$ 150,000
Marketable securities	125,000	200,000
Accounts receivable	325,000	300,000
Inventory	650,000	800,000
Plant and equipment	800,000	900,000
Undeveloped land	100,000	700,000
	$2,150,000	$3,050,000
Liabilities and Equity:		
Liabilities	$ 500,000	$ 500,000
Equity	1,650,000	2,550,000
	$2,150,000	$3,050,000

16

Buyer assumes all of the liabilities and pays Sellco $3,000,000 in cash. Buyer also pays a business broker $150,000 as a finder's fee. In addition, Buyer purchases a covenant not to compete for $50,000. Sellco has $100,000 expenses of sale. The allocations for Sellco are:

Proceeds (cash from Buyer plus liabilities assumed)		$3,500,000
Less expenses of sale		(100,000)
Amount realized		$3,400,000
Allocation		
To Class I:		
Value	$ 150,000	
Consideration	3,400,000	
Lesser of two amounts		$ 150,000
To Class II:		
Value	$ 200,000	
Consideration (after I)	3,250,000	
Lesser of two amounts		200,000
To Class III:		
Value		
Accounts receivable	$ 300,000	
Inventory	800,000	
Plant and equipment	900,000	
Undeveloped land	700,000	
Total Class III	2,700,000	
Consideration (after II)	3,050,000	
Lesser of two amounts		2,700,000
		350,000
To Class IV:		
Value		
Covenant not to compete	$ 50,000	
Total Class IV	50,000	
Consideration (after III)	350,000	
Lesser of two amounts		50,000
To Class V:		300,000
Total allocation of sales price		$3,400,000

Since the amount allocated to the Class III assets is equal to the fair market value of the total assets in that class, each individual asset is treated as sold at its identified fair market value. Sellco then computes gain or loss on each asset:

Description	*Sales Price*	*Adjusted Basis*	*Gain or (loss)*
Cash	$ 150,000	$ 150,000	$ 0
Marketable securities	200,000	125,000	75,000
Accounts receivable	300,000	325,000	(25,000)
Inventory	800,000	650,000	150,000
Plant and equipment	900,000	800,000	100,000
Undeveloped land	700,000	100,000	600,000
Goodwill	350,000	0	350,000
Total	$3,400,000	$2,150,000	$1,250,000

The character of gain or loss is determined under the usual tax rules. If Sellco is subject to the built-in gains tax, it has the burden of establishing that any of the gains are not built-in gains. The loss on the accounts receivable is an ordinary loss. Sellco has the burden of establishing that the loss is a built-in loss.

EXAMPLE 16 - 4: Buyer allocates its purchase price among the various assets by the same formula. Buyer's total purchase price is different from the amount realized by Sellco, due to the expenses of sale. Whereas Sellco reduced the amount realized for its own expenses of sale, Buyer adds its purchase expenses to the amount paid to Sellco:

Cash and liabilities assumed	$3,500,000
Finder's fee	150,000
Total to be allocated	$3,650,000

Allocation		
To Class I:		
Value	$ 150,000	
Consideration	3,650,000	
Lesser of two amounts		$ 150,000
To Class II:		
Value	$ 200,000	
Consideration (after I)	3,500,000	
Lesser of two amounts		200,000
To Class III:		
Value		
Accounts receivable	$ 300,000	
Inventory	800,000	
Plant and equipment	900,000	
Undeveloped land	700,000	
Total Class III	$ 2,700,000	
Consideration (after II)	$ 3,300,000	
Lesser of two amounts		2,700,000
To Class IV:		
Value		
Covenant not to compete	$ 50,000	
Total Class IV	$ 50,000	
Consideration (after III)	$ 600,000	
Lesser of two amounts		50,000
To Class V:		600,000
Total allocation of basis		$3,650,000

PLANNING TIP: When a seller is an S corporation and some of the property sold is subject to the built-in gains tax, the seller may want to devalue that particular property and assign higher values to other assets. An ideal candidate for increased valuation might be a covenant not to compete. As discussed above, the valuation of a covenant may be suspect, especially if the seller is not realistically in a position to compete. The covenant could be purchased from the selling corporation or from the selling shareholders or from both. The actual seller or sellers of the covenant would recognize ordinary income on receipt. The covenant should not cause any built-in gains tax to the seller, regardless of whether the seller is the corporation or the shareholders. The covenant is an asset that would not exist until the effective date of a sale and would not have been in existence when the selling corporation's S election took effect.

Occasionally, as in a distress sale, a seller is extremely anxious to receive cash. In these cases, the price paid for the whole business is apparently less than the sum of its parts, and the financial accounting treatment is often to record a negative goodwill balance. This concept has no counterpart in tax accounting. Examples 16 - 5 and 16 - 6 demonstrate the allocations required when the total consideration is less than the fair market value of the identifiable properties.

EXAMPLE 16 - 5: Assume the same facts as in Examples 16 - 3 and 16 - 4, except that Sellco is in financial distress and sells the entire company for $1,500,000 in cash, plus the assumption of liabilities. Sellco has $100,000 expenses of sale. There is no covenant not to compete. Buyer also pays a business broker $150,000 as a finder's fee. The allocations for Sellco are:

Proceeds (cash from Buyer plus liabilities assumed)	$2,000,000
Less expenses of sale	(100,000)
Amount realized	$1,900,000

Allocation		
To Class I:		
Value	$ 150,000	
Consideration	1,900,000	
Lesser of two amounts		$ 150,000
To Class II:		
Value	$ 200,000	
Consideration (after I)	1,750,000	
Lesser of two amounts		200,000
To Class III:		
Value		
Accounts receivable	$ 300,000	
Inventory	800,000	
Plant and equipment	900,000	
Undeveloped land	700,000	
Total Class III	$ 2,700,000	
Consideration (after II)	1,550,000	
Lesser of two amounts		1,550,000
To Classes IV and V:		0
Total allocation of sales price		$1,900,000

Sellco then computes gain or loss on each asset. Since the total allocation to Class III was less than the identified fair market value, Sellco must first allocate within that class:

	Market Value	*Percent Total*	*Allocated Price*
Accounts receivable	$ 300,000	.11	$ 170,500
Inventory	800,000	.30	465,000
Plant and equipment	900,000	.33	511,500
Undeveloped land	700,000	.26	403,000
Total	$2,700,000	1.00	$1,550,000

The computation of gain or loss is:

	Sales Price	*Adjusted Basis*	*Gain or (Loss)*
Cash	$ 150,000	$ 150,000	$ 0
Marketable securities	200,000	125,000	75,000
Accounts receivable	170,500	325,000	(154,500)
Inventory	465,000	650,000	(185,000)
Plant and equipment	511,500	800,000	(288,500)
Undeveloped land	403,000	100,000	303,000
Goodwill	0	0	0
Total	$1,900,000	$2,150,000	$ (250,000)

EXAMPLE 16 - 6: Refer to Example 16 - 5. Buyer computes its basis by the same means. As in earlier examples, Buyer's total basis differs from Sellco's amount realized, due to the expenses of the transaction.

Cash and liabilities assumed		$2,000,000
Finder's fee		150,000
Total to be allocated		$2,150,000
Allocation		
To Class I:		
Value	$ 150,000	
Consideration	2,150,000	
Lesser of two amounts		$ 150,000
To Class II:		
Value	$ 200,000	
Consideration (after I)	2,000,000	
Lesser of two amounts		200,000
To Class III:		
Value		
Accounts receivable	$ 300,000	
Inventory	800,000	
Plant and equipment	900,000	
Undeveloped land	700,000	
Total Class III	$2,700,000	
Consideration (after II)	1,800,000	
Lesser of two amounts		1,800,000
To Classes IV and V:		0
Total allocation of basis		$2,150,000

Buyer must assign basis to each asset. Since the total allocation to Class III was less than the identified fair market value, Buyer must also allocate within that class:

	Market Value	*Percent Total*	*Allocated Basis*
Accounts receivable	$ 300,000	.11	$ 198,000
Inventory	800,000	.30	540,000
Plant and equipment	900,000	.33	594,000
Undeveloped land	700,000	.26	468,000
Total	$2,700,000	1.00	$1,800,000

The breadth of Class III will create some strange results for Buyer. For instance, as soon as Buyer collects the accounts receivable, it will have $102,000 ordinary income. Because the undeveloped land might not be sold or used for some time, Buyer could be tempted to assign a much lower value to the land. Note that Sellco is in an adverse position. By using the values as they were stated, it has reported an ordinary loss on the accounts receivable and inventory. Sellco's loss on the plant and equipment would be covered by §1231 and would probably be an ordinary loss. Yet it reports capital gain on the land.

PLANNING TIP: When the total consideration paid for a business is less than the sum of the identifiable parts, there may be some misstatement of value. A buyer would want to examine the assets in Class III carefully and attempt to find any overstatements of value within this class. Current assets, such as inventory and receivables, should be relatively easy to value, since they usually will have been sold or collected by the time the buyer files its tax return for the year of the transaction. It would be helpful to the buyer, but not absolutely crucial, for the seller to agree to the buyer's chosen allocation. The seller might be willing to cooperate in order to expedite the sale.

EXAMPLE 16 - 7: Refer to Example 16 - 6. The buyer has reviewed the transaction and determined that the seller's valuations were misstated. Buyer should insist on a low valuation of the investment land and possible reduction of the value of the plant and equipment, especially any portion that is land or buildings. Assume that Buyer renegotiates, setting the value of the plant and equipment at $500,000 and the investment land at $200,000. The basis Buyer will determine is:

Allocation		
To Class I:		
Value	$ 150,000	
Consideration	2,150,000	
Lesser of two amounts		$ 150,000
To Class II:		
Value	$ 200,000	
Consideration (after I)	2,000,000	
Lesser of two amounts		200,000
To Class III:		
Value		
Accounts receivable	$ 300,000	
Inventory	800,000	
Plant and equipment	500,000	
Undeveloped land	200,000	
Total Class III	1,800,000	
Consideration (after II)	$1,800,000	
Lesser of two amounts		1,800,000
To Classes IV and V:		0
Total allocation of basis		$2,150,000

By valuing the specific assets in this manner, Buyer comes up with a total basis that is exactly the same as the fair market value of each asset. Therefore, Buyer will have no gain when it collects the accounts receivable or sells the inventory.

16

1620.3. Special considerations for intangible assets exchanged. Prior to the Revenue Reconciliation Act of 1993, purchasers devoted considerable energy to avoiding goodwill. Often, the parties would attempt to create numerous intangible assets that could be amortized. [*Annabelle Candy Co.*, 63-1 USTC 9146 (9th Cir.)] The IRS warned that the burden of proof was on the taxpayer to establish that an intangible did have a limited, rather than an indefinite, life. [Rev. Rul. 74-456, 1974-2 CB 65] On occasion, taxpayers were able to sustain their burden of proof, and the courts would allow amortization of intangibles other than goodwill. [*Newark Morning Ledger*, 93-1 USTC 50,228 (S.Ct.)]

The adoption of a uniform provision for amortization of intangibles has probably put an end to much of this controversy, at least when a buyer has acquired assets of a going concern. New Code §197 allows amortization of goodwill and other intangibles over a 15-year period. Many taxpayers will benefit from this provision, since they no longer need to avoid goodwill in order to depreciate a portion of the purchase price. Other taxpayers may suffer when they purchase shorter-lived intangibles. The uniform amortization rules apply the arbitrary 15-year amortization period to all of the following intangible assets, when acquired in connection with a going concern:

1. Goodwill [§197(d)(1)(A)]
2. Going-concern value [§197(d)(1)(B)]
3. Workforce in place [§197(d)(1)(C)(i)]
4. Books, records, information base, including customer list [§197(d)(1)(C)(ii)]
5. Patents, copyrights, formulas, processes, designs, patterns, etc. [§197(d)(1)(C)(iii)]
6. Any customer-based intangible [§197(d)(1)(C)(iv)]
7. Any supplier-based intangible [§197(d)(1)(C)(v)]
8. Value resulting from future acquisitions of goods or services pursuant to relationships with suppliers (contractual or otherwise) [§197(d)(3)]
9. "Any other similar item" [§197(d)(1)(C)(vi)]
10. Any license, permit, etc., granted by government [§197(d)(1)(D)]
11. Covenant not to compete, if entered into in acquisition of a business [§197(d)(1)(E)]
12. Franchise [§197(d)(1)(F)]
13. Trademark [§197(d)(1)(F)]
14. Tradename [§197(d)(1)(F)]

If a buyer acquires any combination of these intangibles in a single transaction, the same 15-year period will apply to each. The buyer cannot deduct any loss on a disposition of any intangible acquired in a single transaction, unless the buyer disposes of the entire business. [§197(f)(1)] For example, if a buyer acquires a covenant not to compete in connection with the acquisition of a going business, the covenant must be amortized over the 15-year period, regardless of its actual duration. If the buyer disposes of any of the intangible assets at a gain, the gain attributable to any amortization deductions claimed is treated as depreciation recapture. [§197(f)(7)] Therefore, it will result in ordinary income and cannot be deferred through the use of the installment method.

OBSERVATION: When an S corporation sells all of its assets, the buyer will probably not care about the allocation to individual intangible assets, since they will all be amortized over the same period. Therefore, in many cases it will make sense to allocate a substantial portion of the purchase price of a business to intangible assets. The seller, however, might want to place relatively high values on assets that are not subject to the built-in gains tax. For example, the seller might still want to allocate a substantial portion of the purchase price to a covenant not to compete, since that asset probably did not exist at the time the S election took effect.

CAUTION: The rules regarding amortization of intangible assets are complex. There are special problems dealing with acquisitions of these assets from related parties, as well as special rules for the acquisition of intangibles in a transaction that does not involve the transfer of a going concern. In general, the rules apply to intangible assets acquired after August 10, 1993, although it is possible to elect such treatment for intangibles acquired after July 25, 1991. Tax professionals will need to assess these provisions thoroughly in planning for the acquisition or disposition of intangible assets.

1620.4. Reporting requirements. Both the buyer and the seller must make, and report, the allocation on Form 8594. The buyer and seller each make their own allocations, which need not agree. However, they must report, whether they agree or disagree. The total amounts reported will not be the same for the buyer and the seller, if there are any expenses of the sale.

Form 8594 generally does not require the listing of specific assets within a class, but only the total amount allocated to each of the four classes. The law now requires that each §197 intangible asset be specifically identified. Form 8594 will need to be changed to reflect this new provision.

Form 8594 is treated as an information return. Failure to file this form when required triggers a penalty under §6721(a) and (b). The penalty for failure to file an information return on the prescribed date is generally $50 per return; in the case of intentional disregard, the penalty becomes the greater of $100 or 10% of the "aggregate amount of items required to be reported" without limitation. [§6721(d)] Since the entire amount of consideration paid in an applicable asset acquisition must be reported on Form 8594, the penalty for intentionally disregarding the filing requirement could be enormous.

If there is a change in consideration, the allocations may change in the future. In this case, the seller will need to amend the sales price and thus restate the gain or loss on each asset. The nature and amount of the gain or loss will be determined by reallocating the revised consideration for the year of sale. The reporting of the revised gain or loss, however, will be included on the seller's return for the year of the change in consideration. The buyer will adjust the basis of any asset still held at the time of the change. Assets disposed of prior to the year of change will be subject to a revised calculation of gain or loss. Any revisions that result in immediate taxable income to the buyer will be reported in the year of the change. There is a supplemental statement of Form 8594 for this purpose. [Temporary Regs. §1.1060-1T(f); Also see *F. D. Arrowsmith*, 52-2 USTC 9527 (S.Ct.)]

The buyer and seller must also report certain other transactions that are related to the transfer of assets. The buyer may enter into a lease or royalty arrangement, a covenant not to compete, or an employment, management, or consulting contract with the seller. The buyer might also enter into such an agreement with a party related to the seller, such as a shareholder of the selling corporation or another corporation or partnership that is under common control with the seller. In such cases, the buyer (but not the seller) is required to report the nature of such an arrangement on Form 8594. If the seller of the assets is a corporation, the buyer must inform the IRS of any dealings of this nature with a person who owns at least 10% (including attribution rules of §318) of the selling corporation's stock. [§1060(e)]

16

1625. Taxable exchange of corporation's assets.

As discussed in the coverage of the basic transactions, earlier in the chapter, at 1610., a seller generally prefers to sell stock, whereas a purchaser generally prefers to purchase assets. In practice, both varieties of transactions occur frequently. Section 1625.1. of the chapter discusses the transfer of assets in a taxable transaction, in particular the ramifications to all parties of a taxable asset transfer.

When the sale of assets is completed, the selling corporation must decide whether to remain in existence or to liquidate. In some cases, one choice will dominate. In others, the decision may be quite difficult. The parties of ultimate concern, of course, are the selling corporation's shareholders. They must first analyze the effects on the corporation of either course of action.

1625.1. Effects of the transfer on the selling corporation. The selling corporation generally recognizes gain or loss on each asset sold in the transfer. The gain or loss may pass through to the shareholders intact, or it may be subject to a corporate-level tax.

1625.11. Allocation of sale price. As discussed above, the selling corporation must determine whether §1060 applies to the transaction. If substantially all of the assets, or at least enough of the assets to constitute a going concern, are transferred to one buyer, §1060 will require the seller to use the residual method. If the assets are fragmented and sold to different buyers, there will be no specifically required allocation. In either case, the sales agreement should be drafted carefully, so that the IRS will respect an arm's-length negotiation.

1625.12. Built-in gains tax considerations. In order to minimize the built-in gains tax, the corporation should carefully review its history. Important points to consider include:

1. If the selling corporation filed its S election in 1987 or 1988, it may qualify as a transitional corporation. In this case it would be subject to the built-in gains tax on ordinary assets, but it may be exempt from the built-in gains tax on some or all of its capital and §1231 gains. It still may be subject to the prior capital gains tax on the capital and §1231 gains, if the sale is made within three taxable years of the S election. See Chapter 11 for discussion of transitional corporations.
2. The selling corporation should also ascertain whether it has acquired any of its assets in a tax-free reorganization within 10 years before the sale. If it has acquired assets in this manner, it will be subject to the built-in gains tax on those assets acquired in the reorganization, but it may be exempt from the tax on other assets.

> **PLANNING TIP:** Whenever a selling corporation is subject to the built-in gains tax on some, but not all, of its assets, it may want to carefully evaluate each property it intends to sell. There may be an opportunity to find value in an intangible asset, such as a covenant not to compete with the buyer, that could not have possibly existed when the S election took effect. Both the buyer and the seller should make sure there is a real value to such an intangible asset.

1625.13. Uses of installment sales. When the selling corporation receives an installment obligation as part of its sales price, there are special considerations. Often the choice to liquidate or to keep the corporation in existence can be significantly affected by the presence or absence of an installment obligation. These problems receive further discussion at 1625.31. There are, however, some special rules that need to be considered at the time of the sale.

Generally, under the installment method of reporting, a seller does not recognize any gain except to the extent that it receives payments on the obligation. [§453(a), §453(c)] There are no special rules dealing with losses on property sold where an installment receivable is part of the consideration, so all losses are recognized in the year of sale. Certain types of gains, however, are not subject to deferred reporting on the installment basis:

- Dispositions of inventory [§453(b)(2)] (There are special rules for residential lots and timeshares in §453(l).)
- Dispositions of depreciable property, to the extent of depreciation recapture under §1245 or §1250[2] [§453(i)]

16

---

[2] This rule also covers any gain characterized as depreciation recapture under §291, which applies to C corporations and to former C corporations for three taxable years. Accumulated amortization deductions for intangible assets acquired after the effective date of new §197 are also treated as depreciation recapture.

- Dispositions to related parties, if the buyer disposes of the property within two years of the transfer[3] [§453(e)]

OBSERVATION: If the selling corporation was subject to the prior capital gains tax, it could use some effective planning to eliminate or minimize this tax. It could terminate a §444 taxable year to make the sale occur in its fourth taxable year as an S corporation. It could also use the installment method to defer the gain to its fourth year as an S corporation.

These techniques do not work with the built-in gains tax. That tax is imposed for 10 *years*, rather than 10 *taxable* years, following the S election. The position of the IRS is that an installment sale of built-in gain property will be subject to the built-in gains tax, even on portions received after the 10-year recognition period expires. [Notice 90-27, 1990-1 CB 336; Regs. §1.1374-10(b)(4). This is one of the few effective dates in the new Regulations before December 27, 1994.] See discussion in Chapter 11, at 1140.31.

The character of gains from the sale of assets is ordinary, capital, or §1231, depending upon the nature of the asset sold. When a seller receives an installment receivable, there must be an allocation of the gain. Although the ordinary income from depreciation recapture will be recognized in the year of sale, other ordinary items may be reported on the installment method, such as cash basis accounts receivable and self-developed copyrights. (Code §1221 specifically excludes these assets from categorization as capital assets.) A bulk sale of inventory to one buyer may also be reported under the installment method, but only if the corporation is liquidated.

If the selling corporation receives an installment obligation as part of its consideration, it can elect to report all gain in the year of sale. Before making this election, the corporation should be careful to ascertain the effects of such an election on its shareholders.

1625.14. Reporting of gains and losses to the shareholders. For the year of sale, the corporation reports all of its gains and losses, according to its normal method of accounting. If the corporation is not liquidated before the end of the year that includes the sale, there is no acceleration of the reporting to the shareholders, and no acceleration of the due date for the selling corporation's Form 1120S.

1625.2. Selling corporation continues after sale. Once the corporation has sold all, or substantially all, of its assets, the shareholders must decide whether to keep the corporation alive or liquidate it. In some situations, there are really no adverse tax consequences to either course of action. When the shareholders' bases in the stock, after the recognized gain or loss at the corporate level, are approximately the same as the fair market value of the corporation's assets, and the corporation's basis in the property it has received is approximately the same as fair market value, liquidation will result in no significant gain or loss to the shareholders.

There are some good reasons, however, why the corporation might not want to liquidate immediately:

- If the corporation has substantial installment obligations, especially obligations received before the sale of substantially all of its assets, liquidation will accelerate gain recognition to the shareholders.

[3] The original sale is recast to require immediate gain recognition. If the property sold to a related person is marketable securities, a disposition by the buyer at any time will cause the first sale to be subject to immediate gain recognition.

- If the corporation still has some property on which it would recognize a loss, especially if the property was received in a §351 transfer or contribution to capital almost (but not quite) five years ago, delaying the liquidation may allow the corporation to recognize the loss. [§336(d)(1)(A)(ii)] See discussion beginning in Chapter 15, at 1525.2.
- If the corporation still owns or has already sold loss property that was received in a §351 transfer or as a contribution to capital, the loss might be disallowed if the corporation liquidates. [§336(d)(2)(B)(ii)] See discussion beginning in Chapter 15, at 1525.2. By keeping the corporation alive, the corporation eventually might be able to recognize the loss, since the disallowance applies only to a liquidating corporation.
- If the corporation has retained some property with a low basis and a high fair market value, other than an installment receivable generated in a liquidating sale, it would recognize gain if it distributed the property in liquidation. By remaining in existence, the corporation and its shareholders could continue to use the property or they could defer gain recognition until the corporation could sell the property at a reasonable price.
- If the corporation has an installment receivable, including a receivable generated in a liquidating sale, immediate liquidation would accelerate the built-in gains tax on any portion of the otherwise deferred gain, if the gain resulted from the sale of built-in gains property.
- If the corporation uses a fiscal year, immediate liquidation would cause the corporation's taxable year to end. This could accelerate reporting of the corporation's income in the year of sale.

On the other hand, it might be a nuisance to keep a corporation alive if all that remain are some investment assets. There may be state or local income or franchise taxes, filing fees, and other costs that could be avoided by liquidating the corporation promptly. The major federal income tax risk of not liquidating the corporation occurs when the corporation has substantial earnings and profits from C corporation years.

1625.21. Passive investment income problems. The problems of passive investment income, discussed in Chapter 12, may present the most formidable obstacle to an S corporation's existence after the sale. The assets held by the corporation after the sale of its business are probably investment assets. The income from these assets could cause the corporation to run afoul of the 25% passive investment income limit. In this case, the corporation could be subject to the passive investment income tax for three years and then lose its S election at the beginning of the fourth year after the sale. At that time, the corporation might become a personal holding company, which must either pay dividends to its shareholders or pay an additional tax of 39.6% on its income.

If the corporation sold all of its property for cash, it would have recognized all gains and losses at the time of the asset sale. Its sole source of income would now, presumably, be investment income from wherever it invested the cash. In this case, the decision whether to liquidate is rather simple. If the corporation has no accumulated earnings and profits from C corporation years, its investment income will not cause any adverse effects. The sole tax consideration will be at the shareholder level. If the shareholders all have bases in stock that are roughly equal to the fair market value of the stock, there will be no appreciable gain at the shareholder level.

However, if the shareholders' bases are more or less than the value of the stock, the liquidation will be a taxable event. If, for example, a shareholder's basis is higher than the value of the stock, and the stock is §1244 stock, the shareholder may recognize an ordinary loss on the liquidation distribution, up to $50,000 (or $100,000 on a joint return). In that instance, liquidation of the corporation will probably provide an immediate tax benefit. See Chapter 14 for a discussion of §1244 stock.

In contrast, if a shareholder's basis is less than the value of the assets that would be distributed in liquidation, the shareholder will recognize a gain. The shareholder might be better off if the corporation continues to exist, but keeping the corporation alive may present passive investment income problems.

If some of the consideration from the asset sale is an installment note, the gross profit from the collections of the installment would not be passive investment income, except to the extent that it resulted from the sale of stock or securities that the purchaser had acquired in the deal. [*J. S. Bradshaw*, 82-2 USTC 9454 (Ct.Cls.)]

The interest received on the installment note would be passive investment income. If interest results from a sale of inventory, there is an exception to treating it as passive investment income. That rule, however, applies only where the inventory is sold in the ordinary course of business; it would not apply to a bulk sale of inventory. [§1362(d)(3)(D)(ii)] There are certain minimum interest requirements that prevent a corporation from keeping the interest rate artificially low. These rules are found in §1274 and §483. Although a complete discussion of these provisions is beyond the scope of this book, a brief summary is in order.

The original issue discount (OID) rules of §1274 require a minimum interest charge on installment notes that are not traded on an established securities market. The minimum interest rate is the applicable federal rate (AFR), which is issued monthly by the IRS. [§1274(b)(2)(B)] For a sale in which the amount financed by the seller does not exceed $2,800,000, the parties may use a statutory rate of 9% compounded semiannually (equivalent to 9.2025% compounded annually) if this rate is lower than the AFR. [§1274(a)] In addition to requiring minimum interest, these rules place both the seller and the buyer on the accrual method. Therefore, an S corporation cannot avoid passive investment income problems in early years by postponing interest payments until later years.

The primary purpose of these rules is to prohibit corporations from converting ordinary income into capital gain and shifting income in certain transactions. Although circumvention of the passive investment income rules for S corporations was not one of the primary motivations behind §1274, the rules are sufficiently broad to give this result.

Certain installment receivables are *not* subject to the OID rules:

- The sale of a farm for $1 million or less by individuals, by a corporation that on the date of the sale is considered a small business corporation under §1244(c)(3) (e.g., has less than $1,000,000 capitalization), or by a partnership that also meets the requirements for small business corporations under §1244(c)(3)
- A sale in which the sum of the payments (principal and interest) under the instrument, the payment under any other debt instrument received in the sale, and the value of any other consideration does not exceed $250,000
- A sale of land among family members to the extent that the sales price does not exceed $500,000

16

- An exchange of a debt instrument for a patent subject to §1235
- A sale for which all of the payments are to be made within six months
- The sale of a principal residence of an individual

If the OID rules do not apply, §483 generally operates to require the taxpayer to charge adequate interest. That provision, however, does not place the parties on the accrual method.

The time of the asset sale is an opportunity to determine the amount of the corporation's accumulated earnings and profits. The selling corporation's shareholders should determine whether the accumulated earnings and profits arose from years when the selling corporation was a C corporation or from when the selling corporation was an S corporation. S corporations do not generate any earnings and profits under current law, but could have generated them under Subchapter S as it existed prior to 1983. If all of the selling corporation's accumulated earnings and profits were generated under prior Subchapter S, it will not be subject to the passive income tax. If any were generated when the selling corporation was a C corporation, the selling corporation may encounter passive income tax or termination problems.

EXAMPLE 16 - 8: Sellco, an S corporation, sold all of its assets to a single buyer for $4,000,000. Sellco received $1,000,000 in cash and an installment receivable with a face amount of $3,000,000 and basis of $300,000. None of the assets sold were stock or securities, and therefore none of the installment gain will be passive investment income. Therefore, Sellco must report 90% of each collection as gain, computed as follows.

(Sales price – basis)/contract price = ($3,000,000 – $300,000)/$3,000,000 = 90%

The installment obligation bears an interest rate of 10% per annum, which meets the AFR at the time of sale. The payments are to be received over 10 years.

If Sellco does not liquidate, its projected receipts will be:

Year	*Principal*	*Basis*	*Gain*	*Interest*
1	$300,000	$30,000	$270,000	$300,000
2	300,000	30,000	270,000	270,000
3	300,000	30,000	270,000	240,000
4	300,000	30,000	270,000	210,000
5	300,000	30,000	270,000	180,000
6	300,000	30,000	270,000	150,000
7	300,000	30,000	270,000	120,000
8	300,000	30,000	270,000	90,000
9	300,000	30,000	270,000	60,000
10	300,000	30,000	270,000	30,000

For the first eight years, Sellco's interest income would exceed 25% of its gross receipts. If Sellco did not distribute its cash, but invested it in portfolio assets, the passive investment income would be even higher. Therefore, if Sellco had any earnings and profits from C corporation years, it would be subject to the passive investment income tax for three years and would lose its S election after the third year. At that point, Sellco would become subject to both the regular corporate tax and the personal holding company tax. Therefore, Sellco should consider liquidation. That could, however, cause immediate tax liability, if Sellco were subject to the built-in gains tax. Liquidation could also accelerate recognition of gain to the shareholder, as discussed below.

An S corporation with passive investment income as its primary source of receipts may want to consider the election to distribute all of its accumulated earnings and profits as dividends. This distribution would exempt the corporation from the passive investment income tax and termination of its S election. The election procedures are specified in §1368(e)(3). The corporation must make the election and attach the consent of its shareholder to the return for the year of the distribution. See Chapter 7, at 740., and the practice aids at 760.

EXAMPLE 16 - 9: Refer to Example 16 - 8. Assume that Sellco's accumulated earnings and profits from C corporation years were $200,000 and that Sellco's sole shareholder was in the 39.6% income tax bracket. If Sellco made a bypass election to distribute earnings and profits, the tax cost to the shareholder would be $79,200 ($200,000 x .396). By making a bypass election, however, Sellco would be permanently exempt from the passive investment income tax and would not risk the loss of its S election after the third year.

1625.22. Built-in gains problems. To the extent that the selling corporation's property was subject to the built-in gains tax, the selling corporation would be liable for the tax at the time of sale. If the selling corporation received an installment obligation from the purchaser, each portion of the reported gain that was a built-in gain would be subject to the tax, but only when the corporation received payment on the obligation. Any installments received after the corporation's 10-year recognition period expires would also be subject to the built in gains tax, according to the current IRS position. [Notice 90-27, 1990-1 CB 336; Regs. §1.1374-10(b)(4). This is one of the few effective dates in the new Regulations before December 27, 1994.] See discussion in Chapter 11, at 1140.3.

EXAMPLE 16 - 10: Refer to Examples 16 - 8 and 16 - 9. Assume that $1,000,000 of the installment gain was a built-in gain. Each year, Sellco would recognize $100,000 of built-in gain and would pay $34,000 in built-in gains tax. Sellco could elect out of the installment method and pay the entire $340,000 of tax in the year of sale. It would be quite unusual for election out of the installment method to be beneficial. If the corporation had any built-in losses or net operating loss carryforwards, it might be appropriate to elect out of installment sale treatment. By doing so, it could assure that its built-in gains were recognized within the recognition period, during which either of these items might save tax.

PLANNING TIP: Even though a corporation is taxable on built-in gains included in installment gains, there are opportunities to use the installment method to the benefit of all parties. The corporation would be forced to recognized its built-in gains immediately upon a disposition of the installment obligation, whereas keeping the corporation alive and paying the tax as it recognizes the gain may ease cash flow problems. In some instances, it may be appropriate for a C corporation to elect S status before liquidation. Thus it could continue to extend payment of the corporate tax over the collection period of the installment receivable.

1625.23. Effects on the selling corporation's shareholders. If the selling corporation remains in existence and does not terminate its S election, it will pass through all of its income and deductions in the normal manner. The shareholders will include their portions of the corporation's items on their returns.

EXAMPLE 16 - 11: Refer to Examples 16 - 8 through 16 - 10. Assume that Sellco does not make the bypass election to distribute its earnings and profits. All of its installment gain is properly treated as capital gain, and $100,000 per year is also a built-in gain. Sellco has one shareholder, who is in the 39.6% tax bracket for ordinary income and the 28% bracket for capital gains. The reporting to the shareholder for the next three years will be:

Year 1		
Interest income		$300,000
Gross receipts	$570,000	
25% of gross receipts	142,500	
Interest in excess of 25% of gross receipts	157,500	
Passive investment income tax (35%)	55,125	(55,125)
Pass through to shareholder		$244,875
Installment gain		$270,000
Recognized built-in gain	$100,000	
Built-in gains tax	35,000	(35,000)
Pass through to shareholder		$235,000
Year 2		
Interest income		$270,000
Gross receipts	$540,000	

25% of gross receipts	135,000	
Interest in excess of 25% of gross receipts	135,000	
Passive investment income tax (35%)	47,250	(47,250)
Pass through to shareholder		$222,750
Installment gain		$270,000
Recognized built-in gain	100,000	
Built-in gains tax	35,000	(35,000)
Pass through to shareholder		$235,000
Year 3		
Interest income		$240,000
Gross receipts	$510,000	
25% of gross receipts	127,500	
Interest in excess of 25% of gross receipts	112,500	
Passive investment income tax (35%)	39,375	(39,375)
Pass through to shareholder		$200,625
Installment gain		$270,000
Recognized built-in gain	100,000	
Built-in gains tax	35,000	(35,000)
Pass through to shareholder		$235,000

In Year 4, Sellco would lose its S election. It would become a personal holding company and would have to either pay the personal holding company tax or distribute its current earnings and profits as a dividend. If the corporation made an annual distribution of its current earnings and profits, the corporation's tax and the shareholder's dividend would be:

Year 4	
Interest income	$210,000
Installment gain	270,000
Taxable Income	480,000
Tax	(163,200)
Current earnings and profits (dividend)	$316,800
Year 5	
Interest income	$180,000
Installment gain	270,000
Taxable Income	450,000
Tax	(153,000)
Current earnings and profits (dividend)	$297,000
Year 6	
Interest income	$150,000
Installment gain	270,000
Taxable Income	420,000
Tax	(142,800)
Current earnings and profits (dividend)	$277,200
Year 7	
Interest income	$120,000

Installment gain	270,000
Taxable Income	390,000
Tax	(132,600)
Current earnings and profits (dividend)	$257,400

Year 8

Interest income	$ 90,000
Installment gain	270,000
Taxable Income	360,000
Tax	(122,400)
Current earnings and profits (dividend)	$237,600

Year 9

Interest income	$ 60,000
Installment gain	270,000
Taxable Income	330,000
Tax	(111,950)
Current earnings and profits (dividend)	$218,050

Year 10

Interest income	$30,000
Installment gain	270,000
Taxable Income	300,000
Tax	(100,250)
Current earnings and profit (dividend)	$199,750

The shareholder's tax in each year would be:

	Taxable Income		*Tax Liability*		
Year	*Capital Gain*	*Ordinary*	*Capital Gain*	*Ordinary*	*Total Tax*
1	$235,000	$244,875	$65,800	$ 96,971	$162,771
2	235,000	222,750	65,800	88,209	154,009
3	235,000	200,625	65,800	79,448	145,248
4		316,800		125,453	125,453
5		297,000		117,612	117,612
6		277,200		109,771	109,771
7		257,400		101,930	101,930
8		237,600		94,090	94,090
9		218,050		86,348	86,348
10		199,750		79,101	79,101

16

The total tax to both the corporation and the shareholder over the 10-year period would be:

Year	*Corporation's Taxes*	*Shareholder Tax*	*Total*
1	$ 90,125	$162,771	$252,896
2	82,250	154,009	236,259
3	74,375	145,248	219,623
4	163,200	125,453	288,653

5	153,000	117,612	270,612
6	142,800	109,771	252,571
7	132,600	101,930	234,530
8	122,400	94,090	216,490
9	111,950	86,348	198,298
10	100,250	79,101	179,351

The bypass election to distribute all earnings and profits could accomplish a substantial tax savings. The corporation would not be subject to the passive investment income tax and would not terminate its S election.

EXAMPLE 16 - 12: Assume the same facts as in Examples 16 - 8 through 16 - 11, except that the corporation made the bypass election to distribute earnings and profits in Year 1. For each of the 10 years, the corporation's income and tax would be:

Year	*Capital Gain*	*Less Built-In Gains Tax*	*Capital Gain to Shareholder*	*Interest*
1	$270,000	$35,000	$235,000	$300,000
2	270,000	35,000	235,000	270,000
3	270,000	35,000	235,000	240,000
4	270,000	35,000	235,000	210,000
5	270,000	35,000	235,000	180,000
6	270,000	35,000	235,000	150,000
7	270,000	35,000	235,000	120,000
8	270,000	35,000	235,000	90,000
9	270,000	35,000	235,000	60,000
10	270,000	35,000	235,000	30,000

The shareholder's tax in each year would be:

	Taxable Income		*Tax Liability*		
Year	*Capital Gain*	*Ordinary*	*Capital Gain*	*Ordinary*	*Total Tax*
1	$235,000	$500,000*	$65,800	$198,000	$263,800
2	235,000	270,000	65,800	106,920	172,720
3	235,000	240,000	65,800	95,040	160,840
4	235,000	210,000	65,800	83,160	148,960
5	235,000	180,000	65,800	71,280	137,080
6	235,000	150,000	65,800	59,400	125,200
7	235,000	120,000	65,800	47,520	113,320
8	235,000	90,000	65,800	35,640	101,440
9	235,000	60,000	65,800	23,760	89,560
10	235,000	30,000	65,800	11,880	77,680

* Ordinary income consists of $300,000 interest income and a $200,000 distribution of earnings and profits from the S corporation.

The total of the corporation and the shareholder's income tax liability for each year would be:

Year	*Corporation's Taxes*	*Shareholder Tax*	*Total*
1	$35,000	$263,800	$298,800
2	35,000	172,720	207,720
3	35,000	160,840	195,840
4	35,000	148,960	183,960
5	35,000	137,080	172,080
6	35,000	125,200	160,200
7	35,000	113,320	148,320

16

8	35,000	101,440	136,440
9	35,000	89,560	124,560
10	35,000	77,680	112,680

A comparison of the annual total tax bill, with and without the bypass election, reveals the following:

Year	*Without Election*	*With Election*	*Savings (Cost)*
1	$252,896	$298,800	$(45,904)
2	236,259	207,720	28,539
3	219,623	195,840	23,783
4	288,653	183,960	104,693
5	270,612	172,080	98,532
6	252,571	160,200	92,371
7	234,530	148,320	86,210
8	216,490	136,440	80,050
9	198,298	124,560	73,738
10	179,351	112,680	66,671

1625.3. Selling corporation liquidates. If a selling corporation liquidates, any gain or loss on its assets will be recognized in the year of the liquidating distribution. There are certain limitations on loss recognition, as well as the special rules discussed above. There are also special rules dealing with the disposition of an installment obligation. Section 453B(h), a corporate-level rule that applies only to S corporations, allows S corporations to escape immediate recognition on the distribution of an installment receivable, if the receivable was generated by a sale pursuant to a plan of complete liquidation.

If the corporation is not subject to the built-in gains tax, this rule is a major advantage of the S corporation over the C corporation. Section 453B(h), however, does not apply to the built-in gains tax, so an S corporation must recognize its taxable built-in gains on the distribution of an installment receivable in liquidation, if the receivable was from the sale of built-in gain property. That will cause an immediate incidence of corporate tax. The built-in gains tax will flow through to the shareholders as a loss.

1625.31. Installment obligations received in exchange for stock. In general, receipt of property from a distribution in complete liquidation is equivalent to a sale of stock by the shareholders. Gain or loss is recognized in full by each shareholder. [§331] The basis of property received is its fair market value. [§334(a)] However, there is a special shareholder-level rule, §453(h), which applies to liquidations of both C corporations and S corporations, for installment receivables distributed to the shareholders. This provision postpones recognition at the shareholder level upon receipt of an installment obligation, if that obligation was generated in a transaction pursuant to a plan of complete liquidation. It requires that each shareholder allocate his or her stock basis between the installment receivable and the other property received from the corporation.

EXAMPLE 16 - 13: Assume the same facts as in Examples 16 - 8 through 16 - 12, except that Sellco decides to liquidate immediately after the sale. The corporation's only assets are cash of $1,000,000 and the installment receivable with a face amount of $3,000,000 and basis of $300,000. Under the general rules for S corporations, Sellco would not recognize any gain on the disposition of the installment receivable. The nonrecognition rule, however, does not apply to the built-in gains tax. Therefore, Sellco's entire $1,000,000 of built-in gains would be taxable immediately. The $350,000 of built-in gains tax would be the only recognition item which would pass through to the shareholder. It would reduce the shareholder's stock basis by the same amount.

Assume that the corporation uses $350,000 of its cash to pay the built-in gains tax. Thus, the corporation would distribute $650,000 of cash and the $3,000,000 installment receivable to the shareholder. The shareholder's basis, which had been $1,000,000, is now $650,000, due to the pass-through of the built-in gains tax.

The shareholder would be required to apportion basis in stock between the installment receivable and the cash as follows:

	Cash	*Percent*	*Installment Receivable*	*Percent*
Amount received	$650,000	17.81	$3,000,000	82.19
Basis	(115,753)		(534,247)	
Gain realized	534,247		2,465,753	
Gain recognized on receipt of property in liquidation	$534,247		$ 0	

The shareholder would treat the installment obligation as an installment sale of stock. The gross profit ratio is computed as follows:

Contract price	$3,000,000
Basis	(534,247)
Gross profit	2,465,753
Divide by face amount	3,000,000
Gross profit ratio	82.19%

Of each $300,000 installment, $53,425 will be a recovery of basis and $246,575 will be a capital gain. The shareholder will report the same ordinary income from the installment sale as the corporation would have if it had not liquidated. Therefore, the shareholder's recognized gain will be:

Year	*Principal*	*Basis*	*Gain*	*Interest*
1	$300,000	$53,425	$246,575	$300,000
2	300,000	53,425	246,575	270,000
3	300,000	53,425	246,575	240,000
4	300,000	53,425	246,575	210,000
5	300,000	53,425	246,575	180,000
6	300,000	53,425	246,575	150,000
7	300,000	53,425	246,575	120,000
8	300,000	53,425	246,575	90,000
9	300,000	53,425	246,575	60,000
10	300,000	53,425	246,575	30,000

The shareholder's tax in each year would be:

	Taxable Income		*Tax Liability*		
Year	*Capital Gain*	*Ordinary*	*Capital Gain*	*Ordinary*	*Total Tax*
1	$430,822*	$ 300,000	$120,630	$118,800	$239,430
2	246,575	270,000	69,041	106,920	175,961
3	246,575	240,000	69,041	95,040	164,081
4	246,575	210,000	69,041	83,160	152,201
5	246,575	180,000	69,041	71,280	140,321
6	246,575	150,000	69,041	59,400	128,441
7	246,575	120,000	69,041	47,520	116,561

8	246,575	90,000	69,041	35,640	104,681
9	246,575	60,000	69,041	23,760	92,801
10	246,575	30,000	69,041	11,880	80,921

*This amount consists of $534,247 gain realized and recognized on the distribution of cash and $246,575 gain recognized on the collection of the installment receivable, less the $350,000 of built-in gains tax, which passes through to the shareholder as a loss.

The total of the corporation's and the shareholder's income tax liability for each year would be:

Year	*Corporation's Taxes*	*Shareholder Tax*	*Total*
1	$350,000	$239,430	$589,430
2	0	175,961	175,961
3	0	164,081	164,081
4	0	152,201	152,201
5	0	140,321	140,321
6	0	128,441	128,441
7	0	116,561	116,561
8	0	104,681	104,681
9	0	92,801	92,801
10	0	80,921	80,921

The shareholder should compare the tax cost of liquidating the corporation with the tax cost of keeping the corporation alive. As demonstrated in Example 16 - 26 and the preceding Examples, the best course of action, if the corporation is to be maintained, is to make the bypass election. Comparing the total tax liabilities in this Example with those shown in Example 16 - 25 (with the bypass election), the results are:

Year	*Retaining Corporation*	*Liquidating Corporation*	*Savings (Cost)*
1	$298,800	$589,430	$(290,630)
2	207,720	175,961	31,759
3	195,840	164,081	31,759
4	183,960	152,201	31,759
5	172,080	140,321	31,759
6	160,200	128,441	31,759
7	148,320	116,561	31,759
8	136,440	104,681	31,759
9	124,560	92,801	31,759
10	112,680	80,921	31,759

OBSERVATION: Note that the Examples make no assumptions about the investment of the $1,000,000 cash received in the year of sale, or about the investment of the after-tax receipts each year. Nor do the examples employ any net present value analysis. Therefore, they cannot be viewed as comprehensive approaches, but only as an aid to the decision to liquidate, remain in existence without a bypass election, or remain in existence with a bypass election.

As the above Examples demonstrate, the decision to liquidate or to maintain the corporation is not always easy. There are several factors that were not included in the Examples. If any of the assumptions had varied, the results could be entirely different. Table 16 - 1 lists some of the more important points the tax professional should consider when helping to determine the corporation's best course.

TABLE 16 - 1: Factors to Consider in Liquidation

Factors Favoring Liquidation	*Factors Favoring Continuation*
1. Corporation would recognize loss on distribution of property.	1. Corporation would recognize gain on distribution of property.
2. Shareholder would recognize loss on surrender of stock.	2. Corporation would get no tax benefit from recognized loss on distribution of property.
3. Corporation's Subchapter C earnings and profits are substantial.	3. Shareholder would recognize gain on surrender of stock.
4. Passive investment income problems would be significant.	4. Shareholder would get no tax benefit from recognized loss on surrender of stock.
5. Recognized built-in gain would be substantial.	5. Corporation's Subchapter C earnings and profits are low or nonexistent.

1625.32. Installment obligations received in exchange for debt. The special nonrecognition rule for receipt of installment obligations applies only to amounts received by a shareholder in exchange for stock. [§453(h)(1)(A)] Therefore, any amounts received in exchange for debt of the corporation would be fully taxable. Since the special nonrecognition rule for shareholders also governs nonrecognition by the corporation, the corporation would also recognize a gain on the distribution of an installment receivable to satisfy indebtedness to a shareholder. A shareholder may consider contributing the corporation's debt back to capital immediately before liquidation. By doing so, the shareholder would receive the entire obligation in exchange for stock, and both the shareholder and the corporation would be subject to the nonrecognition rules of §453(h), which applies to the shareholders, and §453B(h), which applies to the S corporation.

1625.33. Liquidating a distressed corporation. As was discussed in Chapter 6, at 610.6., a bankrupt taxpayer, including an S corporation, realizes no gross income from the discharge of debt. In some cases, however, a shareholder may have guaranteed a corporation's bank loans and may not be able to have the corporation declare bankruptcy without risking his or her personal assets. When a shareholder needs to make payments on loans of a troubled corporation, the shareholder will generally be allowed a loss deduction. The problem to be faced is whether the loss deduction will be an ordinary loss or a capital loss.

Under the *Arrowsmith* rule (see discussion of this case at 1625.4. and in Chapter 14 at 1425.37.), a shareholder who pays off debts of a corporation after the corporation has liquidated will be allowed a capital loss deduction. [*F. D. Arrowsmith*, 52-2 USTC 9527 (S.Ct.)] In some cases, this rule may work extreme hardships.

EXAMPLE 16 - 14: Loren is the sole owner of Lorco, an S corporation. He has personally guaranteed a $500,000 note from Lorco to First Bank. After selling all of its assets, Lorco has only $100,000 to pay the bank loan. Loren has worked out a schedule whereby he will pay the remaining $400,000. Loren plans to liquidate Lorco. If Loren liquidates Lorco and pays the bank, he will be allowed a $400,000 capital loss deduction under the *Arrowsmith* rule. The loss will be deductible to the extent of Loren's capital gains plus $3,000 per year, with any nondeductible loss being carried forward.

In this situation, Lorco had probably suffered substantial ordinary losses, and Loren's basis has already been reduced to zero. Therefore, it is likely that Loren has not yet been able to deduct all of Lorco's ordinary losses. If Loren liquidates Lorco, he will have no opportunity to use his suspended losses in a future year, since the corporation will no longer exist. He would be well advised to pursue one of the following courses of action.

1. Keep Lorco's existence intact until he has paid the bank loan. Each payment will be treated as a contribution to capital and will give him additional stock basis. The added stock basis will enable him to deduct suspended losses. [Rev. Rul. 70-50, 1970-1 CB 178; Rev. Rul. 71-288, 1971-2 CB 319] See Chapter 9, at 920.22., for further discussion.
2. Loren could arrange with the bank to substitute his personal note for the corporation's note, before he liquidates Lorco. He should obtain competent legal advice on whether this action will cause subrogation under state law. If subrogation occurs, he will be allowed full basis. [Rev. Rul. 75-144, 1975-1 CB 277] See Chapter 9, at 920.22. If subrogation does not occur, he may nevertheless be able to claim basis at the time he substitutes the note. [*Gilday, Donald S.*, 43 TCM 1295 (1982)] See discussion in Chapter 9, at 920.34. This immediate increase to basis will allow him to deduct all previously suspended losses, to the extent he now has basis. He may then liquidate Lorco.

1625.4. Collateral effects on the selling shareholders. The selling shareholders should determine if the asset disposition completely terminated an interest in a passive activity. If the asset sale had that effect, the selling shareholders will be allowed to deduct suspended losses, under §469, with respect to those activities. See Chapter 10 for discussion of the passive activity loss rules as they apply to shareholders in S corporations.

If a shareholder's basis, after adjustment for all items in the year of the asset sale, is higher than the value of the stock, prompt liquidation of the corporation might assure §1244 loss deductibility. Waiting three years or more to liquidate could cause the corporation to lose its small business corporation status, due to the absence of an active business. See Chapter 14 for a discussion of §1244.

1625.5. Effects on the purchaser. A taxable asset purchase has few complicated tax ramifications to the purchaser. If the assets constitute a going concern, the purchaser will need to make the allocations required by §1060. Otherwise, the purchaser will have negotiated the price paid for the assets. The purchaser assumes liabilities, or takes property subject to liabilities, only to the extent covered in the purchase contract. It does not acquire any of the seller's tax attributes, such as Accumulated Adjustments Account, accumulated earnings and profits, tax years, or tax elections.

1625.51. Basis in property acquired. The purchaser takes a cost basis in each asset acquired. In negotiating the allocations, the purchaser will want to weigh the consideration toward short-lived assets and away from assets, such as land, for which a tax benefit is either distant or unlikely. The purchaser will not be bound by any of the seller's elections, such as inventory method or depreciation.

1625.52. Other tax attributes. The purchaser will not succeed to any of the seller's attributes, such as the selling corporation's AAA or AEP. If the purchaser is a new corporation, the purchasing shareholders may be able to capitalize the corporation to meet the requirements for §1244 stock. This option would not be available for a purchaser of stock. See Chapter 14 for discussion of §1244.

If the purchaser is an S corporation, none of the assets acquired in a taxable transaction will be subject to the built-in gains tax. Purchased property is not carryover basis property and therefore is not built-in gains property, even if the purchaser acquires the entire business of another corporation.

1625.53. Interest paid to finance purchase. A purchaser of stock in an S corporation may borrow from an outside lender to finance the deal. Alternatively, the seller might finance some or all of the consideration through an installment receivable. The deductibility of the purchaser's interest can be an important problem. In general, a loan used to finance the purchase will be allocated among the various assets, in proportion to fair market value. [Temporary Regs. §1.163-8T] As long as all of the assets are used in the purchaser's trade or business, the interest will be fully deductible and will not require any special reporting. If the purchase involves some investment assets, however, or an interest in a passive activity, the value of those properties as of the date of purchase can affect the interest deduction.

EXAMPLE 16 - 15: Debbie owns all of the shares in Debco, an S corporation. Debco purchases all of the assets from Martco. Debco gives Martco $100,000 cash and an installment obligation of $400,000. The valuation, and types, of assets are as follows:

Portfolio investments	$100,000
Interest in a rental partnership	150,000
Active business assets	250,000
Total	$500,000

In the current year, Debco pays Martco $5,000 of interest. Debco should allocate the interest as follows:

Activity	*Value*	*% Total*	*Interest*	*Reported on*
Portfolio	$100,000	20	$1,000	Form 4952
Passive	150,000	30	1,500	Form 8582
Business	250,000	50	2,500	Schedule E
	$500,000	100	$5,000	

1625.54. Effect on purchasing corporation's S election. When an S corporation agrees to acquire all of the assets of another business, it should make sure that it is not indirectly becoming a member of an affiliated group before its first taxable years beginning after 1996. This situation has occurred when a blanket purchase included a wholly owned subsidiary of the selling corporation. [PLR 9001050] (In that ruling, the acquiring corporation was granted inadvertent termination relief.) It could also occur when the purchasing corporation already owns some stock in a subsidiary corporation and the selling corporation owned enough stock in the same corporation to put the purchasing shareholder at or above 80%. In these cases, there are some courses of action that can preserve the purchaser's S election:

- The seller could liquidate the subsidiary before the sale of assets.
- The seller could keep the subsidiary stock.
- The purchasing corporation's shareholders could purchase at least 20% of the subsidiary's stock directly.

If the buyer is highly leveraged and the seller takes substantial security, the seller's retained interest in the corporation's assets could constitute a second class of stock. Of special concern might be an amount paid to a seller for an employment contract or a covenant not to compete. Under current Regulations, such arrangements would not constitute a second class of stock, unless there is a principal purpose to circumvent the single class of stock rules. [Regs. §1.1361-1(l)(2)(i)] If a seller retains an option to reacquire any shares, there could also be a problem of a second class of stock. In this case, however, the option will not be treated as a second class of stock unless the option would be considered equity under general tax rules and has the avoidance of the single class of stock rule as a principal purpose. [Regs. §1.1361-1(l)(4)(ii)(A)]

1630. Taxable exchange of stock.

A taxable exchange of stock is, in many respects, a much simpler transaction than a taxable asset exchange. The complexities with stock sales usually arise after the transfer of shares. If the purchaser is an eligible shareholder, the corporation's S election may continue. Alternatively, the purchaser may terminate the corporation's S election, or may terminate the corporation's existence by liquidation or merger.

When the purchaser is clearly an ineligible shareholder, the corporation's S election will be terminated as of the date of transfer. When the purchaser is another S corporation, the two had both become ineligible to be S corporations, under the laws in existence prior to the Small Business Job Protection Act of 1996.

> **OBSERVATION:** There are two significant changes that occur after December 31, 1996, as a result of the Small Business Job Protection Act of 1996, that will affect the stock purchase transaction. First, the affiliated group prohibition disappears. Second, the acquired corporation may now be a qualified Subchapter S subsidiary, if the purchasing corporation is an S corporation and acquires 100% of the stock of the target corporation. Under prior law, the IRS would generally allow membership in an affiliated group under the doctrine of momentary ownership. See discussion below at 1630.12.

1630.1. Effects on the selling corporation. The transfer of an S corporation's shares has no effect on the corporation's asset basis, Accumulated Adjustments Account, or accumulated earnings and profits. In this respect, an S corporation is more similar to a C corporation than it is to a partnership. Under partnership rules, basis of assets may be adjusted to reflect a purchasing partner's new cost basis. [§743(b)] The partnership must make an election under §754 to adjust its asset basis. There is, however, no equivalent of this rule for S corporations.

Although the corporation's equity accounts maintained under current law are unchanged as a result of a share transfer, that is not true for previously taxed income (PTI). As discussed in Chapter 7, each shareholder's PTI account is personal and cannot be transferred. Therefore, any PTI account of a selling shareholder is extinguished and should be closed to paid-in capital at the time of the sale.[4]

The corporation's potential for the built-in gains tax is also unchanged as a result of a sale. The assets subject to the tax and the recognition period do not change as a result of the transfer of stock.

One problem that can arise upon the sale of a corporation's shares is limitation of carryforwards under §382. Under that provision, a corporation's net operating loss and other carryforwards may be limited following an ownership change. Code §382 states that the corporation's losses that originated in years before the change (pre-change losses) are limited for years after the change (post-change years).

> **OBSERVATION:** The following discussion of §382 is brief and is intended only to illustrate the general concepts of this provision. The actual workings of these rules can become extremely complicated in practice.

16

An ownership change occurs when the aggregate holdings of persons who individually own 5% or more of the corporation's shares have increased by 50 percentage points in a three-year period. [§382(g)] The amount of any pre-change loss that may be utilized in a post-change year is limited to a percentage of the value of the corporation at the time of transfer.

---

[4] If the selling shareholder is still alive at the transfer, technically the PTI account is suspended. If the selling shareholder reacquires any stock, the PTI account would again be available for distribution to that person.

The percentage is the long-term tax-exempt interest rate, which is published monthly by the IRS. [§382(b)(1)]

> **EXAMPLE 16 - 16:** Mr. Burns purchased all of the stock of Loss Corporation for $1,000,000. Loss Corporation had a net operating loss (NOL) carryover of $1,000,000. Since there was a complete change of ownership, the limitation on the NOL carryover applies. In computing the limitation, the value of the loss corporation is assumed to be equal to the amount paid by Burns—$1,000,000. Assuming that at the time of the purchase the long-term tax-exempt rate was 6%, the maximum amount of NOL carryover that can be used in any year is $60,000 ($1,000,000 x 6%). Thus, assuming the corporation becomes profitable under the new ownership and generates $100,000 of taxable income, only $40,000 would be taxable, since $60,000 of the corporation's NOL can be used. In effect, the new corporation earned $60,000 of taxable income that was not subject to tax, the same as if Mr. Burns had invested $1,000,000 in tax-exempt securities yielding 6%. Note that the maximum loss the corporation could use before it expired is $900,000 (15 years x $60,000). Therefore, $100,000 of the $1,000,000 carryover would be wasted.

The loss limitation may also apply to certain recognized built-in losses that occur after the ownership change. Such losses are conceptually similar to the recognized built-in losses discussed in Chapter 11, under the built-in gains tax. In order for this limitation to apply, there must be a net unrealized built-in loss at the time of the ownership change. The net unrealized built-in loss is the amount by which the unrealized built-in losses exceed the net unrealized built-in gains. In addition, the net unrealized built-in loss must be at least 15% of the value of the corporation at the date of the ownership change (or $10,000,000, if that amount is less than 15% of the corporation's value). [§382(h)(3)(B)]

The limit on loss utilization is relaxed for a corporation that has a net unrealized built-in gain at the time of ownership change. [§382(h)(1)(A)(i)] The net unrealized built-in gain must be at least 15% of the value of the corporation at the time of change, or $10,000,000, whichever is less. [§382(h)(3)(B)] The corporation is allowed to recognize a net operating loss from a pre-change year to the extent of any recognized built-in gain, in addition to the long-term tax-exempt interest rate, times the value of the corporation at the date of change. [§382(h)(7)(A)]

Any recognized built-in loss that is limited, or any recognized built-in gain that relaxes the limitation, must be taken into account within the corporation's recognition period. For §382, the recognition period is five years from the date of ownership change.

The applicability of §382 to S corporations is dubious, for two reasons:

- S corporations measure taxable income in the same manner as individuals. [§1363(b)] Code §382 applies only to corporations, and not to individuals.
- S corporations normally do not generate net operating loss carryovers, since losses pass through to the shareholders.

> **OBSERVATION:** When an S corporation is subject to the built-in gains tax or passive investment income tax, it must use the corporate rules in computing its taxable income. See discussions in Chapters 11 and 12. For these computations, Regulations §1.1374-5(a) imposes §382 limits on S corporations.

In one recent ruling, a corporation purchased all of the stock of an S corporation. The agreement contained a contingent price, or "earnout" clause, whereby some selling shareholders would receive additional consideration based upon the performance of the target corporation. Other shareholders received additional cash. Therefore, all prices per share were considered to have been made equal to the price obtained by the selling shareholders. The IRS ruled that there was no second class of stock, and the target corporation's S election continued through the date of sale. [PLR 9821006] See Chapter 2, at 225.8.

1630.11. Selling corporation's S election continues. The sale of stock in an S corporation does not terminate the corporation's S election, as long as the purchasers are eligible shareholders. Under current law, there is no requirement that the new shareholders file a new S election or consent to the continuation of the corporation's existing election.[5]

There are few complications when the seller's S election continues. Aside from the general considerations discussed above, the only real problem is the allocation of income between the selling shareholders and the buying shareholders. As discussed in Chapter 6, at 630.2., the general rule is that all items must be prorated on a daily basis and allocated to the shareholders in proportion to their weighted-average ownership. [§1377(a)(1)] As an alternative, the corporation, with the consent of its shareholders, may elect to close its books as of the date of sale. [§1377(a)(2)] The corporation then allocates all items, up to and including the date of sale, to the selling shareholders. [Regs. §1.1367-1(d)(3)] All of the later items are allocated to the purchasing shareholders. For taxable years beginning before 1997, all shareholders must consent to the rule. Thereafter, only the shareholders whose allocations would be affected by the allocation must consent. [§1377(a)(2)(B)]

The sale of stock in an S corporation does not terminate the corporation's taxable year. Therefore, both the selling and buying shareholders report their shares of the corporation's items in the year in which the taxable year of the corporation ends. The only means by which the reporting is accelerated is if the corporation's year terminates. An election to treat the year of sale as two taxable years for allocation of income has no effect on the reporting date.

> **EXAMPLE 16 - 17:** Targo is an S corporation that had elected a §444 year ending September 30. On November 2, 1992, Selma, the sole shareholder, sold all of her stock to Byron. Unless the corporation's year terminates prematurely, both Selma and Byron will report their shares of income from the corporation in 1993, regardless of whether the corporation prorates its income across its entire year or closes the books on November 2, 1992.
>
> If Byron causes the corporation to terminate its §444 year, however, Targo would have a short year ending December 31, 1992. Both shareholders would report their portions of income from that short year on their 1992 tax returns.

1630.12. Momentary ownership. When an S corporation's stock is acquired by an ineligible shareholder, the corporation's election should terminate immediately. The IRS, however, has waived the violation of eligibility when a shareholder's ownership of an S corporation is extremely brief and is only a temporary step in a series of transactions. There are numerous rulings that have allowed ineligible persons to momentarily own shares in S corporations, without endangering the corporation's S election, in several contexts:

- Incorporation of a partnership, where the partnership is the first owner of the corporation's stock [PLR 8926016] (See discussion in Chapter 14, at 1415.9.)
- Divisive reorganizations, where a parent corporation owns stock briefly [Rev. Rul. 71-266, 1971-1 CB 262; Rev. Rul. 70-232, 1970-1 CB 177; Rev. Rul. 64-94, 1964-1 CB (Part 1) 317, GCM 39768; Rev. Rul. 72-320, 1972-1 CB 270, GCM 37677 (1978); Rev. Rul. 79-52, 1979-1 CB 283. Also see PLRs 8735061, 8801026, 8806031, 8806036, 8807037, 8810045, 8847084, 8909022, 8922004, 8934020, 8940052, 8932020, 8939015, 8950019, 9011044, 9116026, 9116027, 9117054, 9117057, 9117062, 9123059, 9124049, 9139012, 9143021, 9147047, 9140054, 9147043, 9151008, and 9152029. See discussion in Chapter 17, at 1735.31.]

16

> **OBSERVATION:** These transactions required that the original corporation set up a wholly owned subsidiary, which meant that the corporation was a member of an affiliated group of corporations. For taxable years beginning before 1997, this affilia-

[5] There was a requirement for consent by new shareholders before the Subchapter S Revision Act of 1982.

tion violated the eligibility rules for the S election. Thus it was necessary under prior law for the IRS to waive momentary ownership in order to keep the parent corporation's S election intact. This particular problem has disappeared with the Small Business Job Protection Act of 1996, for taxable years beginning after 1996. However, it may still be necessary for the IRS to waive momentary ownership, so that the subsidiary corporation may qualify for S status.

- Acquisitive reorganizations, where the target corporation briefly owns stock in the acquiring corporation. (See discussion in Chapter 17, beginning at 1710.)

OBSERVATION: For taxable years beginning before 1997, this affiliation violated the eligibility rules for the S election. Thus it was necessary under prior law for the IRS to waive momentary ownership in order to keep the acquiring corporation's S election intact. This particular problem has disappeared with the Small Business Job Protection Act of 1996, for taxable years beginning after 1996.

Momentary ownership has important ramifications to the purchasing corporation, when the purchaser is also an S corporation. Under pre-1997 law, the IRS frequently waived the affiliated group prohibition to the purchaser when it acquired a subsidiary and promptly liquidated or merged the acquired corporation. [PLRs 8228099, 8338030, 8439013, 8504028, 9745004] For post-1996 years, the affiliation no longer endangers the purchasing corporation's S election.

Although the acquired corporation's existence, and therefore its S election, will terminate when it is liquidated into the purchaser, there is some question as to whether its S election would remain in effect through the liquidation. If the IRS is willing to overlook momentary ownership and keep the corporation's S election in force, the gains and losses on the liquidating distribution could be allocated in one of three ways:

- The gains and losses on the liquidating distribution could be combined with the corporation's other taxable income for its final year, and be prorated between the selling shareholders and the purchaser. [§1377(a)(1)]
- The selling shareholders and the purchaser could consent to an election to close the books on the day before selling shareholders sold their stock. [§1377(a)(2)] This allocation would force the incidence of tax on the purchaser, which would be the sole shareholder on the day of the liquidation.
- The selling shareholders could revoke the corporation's S election on the day before the sale. The selling corporation would then have one day as a C corporation. Any tax on the liquidating distribution would be borne by the selling corporation as a C corporation, with the ultimate payment of the tax liability imposed on the purchasing corporation, its sole shareholder at the time of liquidation. Since there is a sale of more than 50% of the selling corporation's stock, the corporation could not use pro rata allocation in its final year. [§1362(e)(6)(C) and (D)] See discussion in Chapter 13, at 1335.4.

As of this writing, there have been no rulings or other announcements that allow or forbid any of these three alternatives. The third option, terminating the S election before the liquidation, can be accomplished by an election under §1362. It is the only certain result until rulings, Regulations, or other pronouncements approve one of the other allocation methods.

PLANNING TIP: The purchaser and seller should negotiate the incidence of tax liability resulting from the sale and liquidation of an S corporation. If they do not want to seek a ruling, the selling shareholders may want to terminate the S election immediately before the sale.

1630.13. Selling corporation's S election terminates. When a corporation's S election terminates in the year of a stock sale, the corporation will generally be required to close its books as of the date of termination. See Chapter 13, at 1345., for discussion and examples.

1630.14. Selling corporation is liquidated. Liquidation of a corporation terminates the corporation's taxable year. If the S election is in effect through the final day of the corporation's existence, all of the income, losses, and other items for the year are allocated between the sellers and the buyers in the normal manner. The buyers and sellers may be able to time the transactions carefully for the desired tax treatment.

> **EXAMPLE 16 - 18:** Liqco was a calendar-year S corporation. All of the shares were owned by Leon until October 26, 1995. On that date, Leon sold all of his shares to Melanie, a U.S. citizen, for $500,000. Melanie promptly liquidated Liqco. Leon's basis, on January 1, 1995, was $100,000. From January 1, 1995, through October 25, 1995, Liqco operated at a break-even, with no net income or loss. On liquidation, Liqco recognized net gains of $300,000.
>
> If the liquidation took place on October 26, 1995, the gain would pass through to Leon, under the rule prescribed in the Regulations. [Regs. §1.1367-1(d)(3)] An election to split the year into two portions would have no effect, since there is no income after October 26, 1995. If the liquidation took place on October 27, 1995, the parties could agree to close the books or to prorate the corporation's income for the entire year.
>
> In this example, both shareholders could benefit from allocating the income entirely to Leon. Leon would report a $400,000 gain on the sale of his stock, if he had no basis adjustment. The flow-through of $300,000 to Leon will increase his stock basis to $400,000 at the time of sale, resulting in a gain of only $100,000.

1630.15. Selling corporation is merged. Another alternative would be for a purchasing corporation or its shareholders to acquire the stock of the target corporation from the shareholders and immediately merge the two corporations. If the consideration is cash, or property other than stock in the purchasing corporation, a merger will not be treated as a tax-free reorganization, since it would lack continuity of proprietary interest. See discussion of tax-free reorganizations, in Chapter 17 beginning at 1710.

This acquisition technique, known as a "cash merger," would be fully taxable to the selling corporation's shareholders. It should result in a fair market value basis for all assets acquired from the extinguished corporation. [*Yoc Heating*, 61 TC 168 (1973)]

1630.16. Effect of a §338(h)(10) election. The §338(h)(10) election is discussed in Chapter 15, at 1525.83. This transfer clearly treats the acquired corporation as if the S election had been in effect through the deemed sale and liquidation. [Regs. §1.338(h)(10)-1(e)(2)(iv)] Thus the gains and losses from the deemed sale would pass through to the selling shareholders on the date of the deemed sale.

> **EXAMPLE 16 - 19:** Assume the same facts in Example 16-18, except that Leon sold all of the Liqco stock to a corporation. Absent a §338(h)(10) election, all of the income and deduction items occurring on October 26, 1995, will be assigned to the C corporation portion of the year. Moreover, Liqco must close the books on October 25, 1995, and cannot allocate any of the October 26 items back to Leon. See Chapter 13, at 1335.4., for discussion of mandatory closings in S termination years. If Leon and the purchaser join in a §338(h)(10) election, all of the October 26 items will be treated as occurring while the S election is still in effect, and they would pass through to Leon in their entirety.

1630.2. Effects on the selling shareholders. A stock sale is usually the simplest form of transfer for the selling shareholders. They generally report capital gain or loss from the sale of stock. The shareholders' stock bases would be adjusted for any of the corporation's income up to the date of the sale. If the corporation's S election survived (for which the parties should seek a letter ruling), the selling shareholders' bases would include their portion of income or loss allocated from the corporation up to the date of sale.

As discussed above, each shareholder reports his or her share of the corporation's items as of the end of the corporation's taxable year. In some cases, the income or loss may be reported in a year later than the sale. See Chapter 6, at 630.5., for discussion and examples. On occasion, it may be necessary to determine the actual date of the sale transaction, especially when there are multiple steps in the transaction. The beneficial owner—who participates in the risks and rewards of ownership—must include the income to the date of sale. [See *McMichael v. U.S.*, 82 AFTR 2d 98-5158 (DC-FL, 1998)]

If the selling shareholders receive installment obligations from the purchaser, they should be able to report capital gains using the installment method. There would be no depreciation recapture or other immediate recognition of gain on the sale.

If the sale results in a loss to any shareholder, the loss may qualify for ordinary treatment under §1244. See Chapter 14 for a discussion of the allowance of such losses to S corporation shareholders.

1630.21. Treatment of losses under Subchapter S. As discussed in Chapter 6, a shareholder's deduction for losses is limited to his or her basis in the S corporation's stock and debt. In most circumstances, the basis is determined at the end of the corporation's taxable year, after adjusting the shareholder's basis for any income items of the current year.

In the year of a sale, however, the shareholder's loss is limited to his or her basis on the last date as a shareholder. [Regs. §1.1367-1(d)(1) and §1.1367-2(b)(2)] If such losses exceed the shareholder's basis as of that date, there probably will be no further opportunity for a tax benefit. As discussed in Chapter 6, the sale of a shareholder's stock does not release any previously suspended losses.

1630.22. Interaction with the at-risk rules. If a shareholder had losses that did not exceed basis but were limited to the amount at risk, a sale of the stock will usually create a gain. In this case, the gain from the sale of an interest in an activity is treated as income from the activity. [Proposed Regs. §§1.465-12(a) and 1.465-66(a)] See Chapter 10 for discussion of the at-risk rules.

1630.23. Interaction with passive activity loss rules. A sale of stock in an S corporation may or may not result in a complete disposition of a shareholder's interest in a passive activity. If the shareholder still has an interest in the corporation's activities through other forms of ownership, then the gain or loss on the sale would be passive activity income or loss.

> **EXAMPLE 16 - 20:** Sally sold all of her shares in Salco, an S corporation, on October 17, 1992. Salco owned an interest in a rental partnership. Sally also owned a limited partnership interest in the same partnership. She did not dispose of her limited partnership interest in 1992; therefore, any gain or loss on the sale of her Salco stock is passive income or passive loss, to the extent such gain or loss is attributable to her indirect interest in the rental partnership.

When an S corporation has interests in more than one passive activity, the gain or loss on the shareholder's sale of stock must be allocated among the activities owned by the corporation. [Temporary Regs. §1.469-2T(e)(3)(ii)(A)] At that point, the shareholder must determine if there is an overall gain or an overall loss on the disposition of the stock.

16

If the disposition of stock results in an overall gain to the selling shareholder, he or she must allocate all of the gain to net gain activities, as follows:

- On each activity, compute t2he hypothetical gain as if the S corporation had sold all of the property used in the activity on disposition date.

- Compute the total hypothetical gain as if the S corporation had sold all activities on which gains would have been recognized on same date.
- Disregard any activity on which a loss would be realized.
- Divide each individual hypothetical gain by the total hypothetical gain.
- Apply the portion allocated to each hypothetical gain to the shareholder's recognized gain on the sale of stock. [Temporary Regs. §1.469-2T(e)(3)(ii)(B)(1)]

However, if the disposition of stock results in an overall loss to the selling shareholder, he or she must allocate all of the loss to net loss activities, as follows:

- On each activity, compute the hypothetical loss as if the S corporation had sold all of the property used in the activity on the disposition date.
- Compute the total hypothetical loss as if the S corporation had sold all activities on which losses would have been recognized on the same date.
- Disregard any activity on which a gain would be realized.
- Divide each individual hypothetical loss by the total hypothetical loss.
- Apply the portion allocated to each hypothetical loss to the shareholder's recognized loss on the sale of stock. [Temporary Regs. §1.469-2T(e)(3)(ii)(B)(2)]

If one of the allocations stated above cannot be determined, the shareholder must allocate gain or loss based on relative fair market value of each corporate activity. [Temporary Regs. §1.469-2T(e)(3)(ii)(B)(3)]

1630.24. Installment reporting problems. Generally, a shareholder who sells stock in an S corporation, and receives an obligation from the purchaser as part of the consideration, may report the sale on the installment method. Under this method of accounting, the seller reports gain as the installments are collected. [§453] Such treatment is usually advantageous, since it defers tax on the gain until the installments are collected. In the event that any seller desires immediate reporting of the gain, the seller may elect to report all gain in the year of sale. [§453(d)] If the sale results in a loss, the installment method does not apply, and the loss is reported in full in the year of sale.

There are some special rules that may be of interest to sellers of S corporation stock:

- If the obligations received from the purchaser are in registered form, or are readily tradable on an established securities market, the seller may not use the installment method. [§453(f)(3), (4), (5)]
- If the stock is sold to a related party (within the meaning of §318(a)[6] [§453(f)(1)(a)] or of §267(b)), the gain on the sale is accelerated if the buyer disposes of the stock within two years. [§453(e), §453(f)(1)] (See Chapter 8, at 835.1.)
- If the stock sold is traded on an established securities market, the installment method is not available. [§453(k)(2)] This rule usually will not affect the seller of stock in an S corporation, because of the ownership restrictions. [TAM 9306001, 9306003] It may, however, deny installment reporting if the sale is made at the same time the corporation is taken public.

16

If the seller disposes of the installment receivable, the gain is accelerated. [§453B(a)] The disposition does not accelerate the gain if it is due to the holder's death [§453B(c)] or if it is transferred to the seller's spouse. [§453B(g)] Similarly, if the holder transfers the obligation to a former spouse, incident to a divorce, the gain is not accelerated. [§453B(g)]

---

[6] See Chapter 15, at 1510.2. An option holder is not treated as a related party for purposes of the installment sale provisions.

Until 1995, there was some confusion when the owner of the stock is a QSST and the stock is sold on the installment method. The IRS has ruled that all gains on the sales of stock are to be taxed to the current income beneficiary, just as if the gain had passed through to the trust from the S corporation. [Rev. Rul. 92-84, 1992 CB 216] Fortunately, Regulations §1.1361-1(j)(8) states that a trust is no longer a QSST when it no longer holds shares in an S corporation. Thus the gain on the sale will be taxed to the trust. Most likely, the gain will not even be trust accounting income, and could not be distributed to the beneficiaries. The IRS has extended this treatment to gains recognized on corporate liquidations. [See PLR 199905011.] See Chapter 15.

1630.25. Effect of a §338(h)(10) election. As was discussed above, a §338(h)(10) election treats the target corporation as if it had sold all of its assets to the purchaser on the acquisition date. Thus the gains and losses would be determined at the corporate level. Some may be capital, whereas others are ordinary or classified under §1231.

If a QSST owns stock at the time of a §338(h)(10) election, then the trust treats the gain as gain from the disposition of stock, within the meaning of Regulations §1.1361-1(j)(8). Thus, the IRS has ruled that such gain is taxable to the trust, and not to the beneficiary of the trust. [PLRs 9828006, 199920007]

1630.26. Other gain recharacterization problems. The sale of stock in an S corporation typically results in capital gain to the seller. At one time, the IRS tried to recharacterize gain as ordinary, to the extent that a shareholder had deducted ordinary losses in arriving at his adjusted basis as of the date of sale. The court held, however, that the gain was capital. [*Klein*, 75 TC 298 (1980). See Chapter 9, at 930.9.]

Recently, the IRS has decided to try again to recharacterize at least some of the gain from the disposition of S stock as ordinary income, in limited circumstances. On a taxable disposition of stock, a shareholder must report ordinary income to the extent of his or her share of natural resource recapture property under §1254. [Regs. §1.1254-4.] This ordinary income is limited to the amount of ordinary income that the shareholder would have reported if the corporation had disposed of the natural resource property on the date of the shareholder's disposition of his or her stock. This rule applies to development costs deducted by the corporation on mineral property, or on mining costs that pass through to the shareholders under §1363(c). See Chapter 6, at 610.1., for elections made at the shareholder level with respect to natural resource property.

This rule applies only to the shareholder who received the tax benefit of the deduction when the costs were initially incurred. Thus, this rule does not apply to a subsequent shareholder who received the stock by death of another shareholder or by purchase. [Regs. §1.1254-4(e).] The ordinary income characterization is applicable to dispositions of stock occurring on or after October 10, 1996. [Regs. §1.1254-6]

1630.3. Effects on the purchaser. The concerns of the purchaser are primarily the basis and tax attributes acquired in the transaction. In addition, the purchaser may want to continue the selling corporation's S election. The discussion that began above describes some of the concerns of the liquidating corporation. This portion of the chapter discusses some of the alternative methods of dealing with the corporation after the transfer.

1630.31. Selling corporation is retained intact. If the purchaser is eligible to be an S corporation shareholder, he or she (or they) will receive a cost basis in the shares. There is, however, no adjustment to the corporation's basis in its assets. Therefore, if the corporation is liquidated in the future, the corporation will still have the same taxability as it would if it had been liquidated by the seller.

In any year beginning before 1997, if the intended purchaser is a corporation, it may be best to structure the deal as a purchase by the purchaser's shareholders, rather than by the corporation itself. In this manner, the acquired corporation's S election could remain intact.

OBSERVATION: After 1996, it may be possible for an S corporation to acquire another S corporation and convert the newly acquired corporation from a stand-alone S corporation to a qualified Subchapter S subsidiary. At the time of this writing, there is no guidance as to whether this type of transaction is permitted, let alone what procedures are necessary to effect the change in status. Practitioners will need to be on the lookout for Internal Revenue Service announcements governing these matters.

Alternatively, the purchasing corporation could acquire less than 80% of the stock, with its shareholders acquiring the balance of the shares. The acquired corporation's S election is terminated, since it has an ineligible shareholder. The purchasing corporation's S election could remain in effect.

If the acquired corporation remains in existence, all of its tax attributes (except for its PTI) would survive intact. These attributes may include some favorable items, such as its Accumulated Adjustments Account, a fiscal year, or a pre-1987 S election. Some unfavorable attributes, such as low basis in property, may survive the acquisition as well.

Stock acquired by purchase would not be §1244 stock to the new owners. If §1244 treatment is desired (as would be the case with a risky enterprise), the purchaser may want to use an alternative structure such as a merger, discussed below.

1630.32. Momentary ownership. For all taxable years beginning before 1997, the prohibition against membership in an affiliated group was in effect. This portion of the chapter relates to those years, and the situations discussed herein relate to the need for waiver of momentary ownership of a subsidiary corporation by an S corporation.

When an S corporation intended to purchase the stock of another corporation, it needed to be wary of the possibility of creating an affiliated group. As discussed in Chapter 2, an S corporation could not own 80% or more of the shares in another corporation in taxable years beginning before 1997. Therefore, a purchase of stock of any corporation (whether the target corporation is a C corporation or an S corporation) could result in a termination of the purchaser's S election.

In several situations, the IRS ruled that an S corporation could momentarily own 80% or more of the stock of another corporation, if the acquired corporation was promptly liquidated or merged, or if the acquiring corporation immediately divested itself of at least 20% of the stock of the acquired corporation. In 1972, the IRS ruled that an S corporation could form a subsidiary in order to accomplish a divisive D reorganization. [Rev. Rul. 72-320, 1972-1 CB 270] See discussion in Chapter 17, at 1720.6. A key element in this ruling was that the parent corporation never contemplated continued ownership of the subsidiary.

In 1973, the IRS issued a similar ruling in a different context. Revenue Ruling 73-496 allowed an affiliation where the acquired corporation was completely liquidated within 30 days of its acquisition. [Rev. Rul. 73-496, 1973-2 CB 313] By issuing a ruling that allowed affiliations for 30 days, the IRS eased the means by which an S corporation could acquire the assets of another corporation.

The blanket waiver of 30 days' ownership came under an ironic attack, however, in 1986. In the case of *Haley Bros. Construction Corp.*, an S corporation had acquired all of the stock of a troubled corporation. The acquired corporation immediately ceased conducting any active business. It gradually disposed of its assets, but it was not liquidated for approximately two years. [*Haley Bros. Construction Corp.*, 87 TC 498 (1986)] Upon examination of the parent corporation, the IRS terminated the S election for the year of the acquisition and for all subsequent years.[7] The taxpayer disagreed with the IRS and argued that the 30-day rule was too narrow. The Tax Court upheld the IRS's disallowance of the S election, but it also went one

---

[7] Under pre-Subchapter S Revision Act of 1982 rules, disqualification of a corporation for S status was effective on the first day of the year of the disqualifying event.

step further: The Tax Court disagreed with the momentary ownership rule. In dicta, which did not effect the decision per se, the Tax Court stated that the IRS had no power to allow a temporary affiliation of 30 days. The Tax Court did not state, however, that the IRS should not waive momentary ownership if the divestiture is immediate. The IRS has continued to issue favorable rulings when the acquiring corporation liquidates or merges the acquired corporation on the same day it acquires the stock. [PLRs 8818049, 8228099, 8338030, 8439013, 8504028]

PLANNING TIP: For taxable years beginning after 1996, an S corporation can own any amount of stock in other corporations. In order for the subsidiary corporation to also be treated as a qualified Subchapter S subsidiary, however, the parent S corporation must own exactly 100% of the stock. There may be some situations arising after 1996 in which the parent corporation is not able to complete the entire acquisition in one transaction. In these cases, the logic of the old momentary ownership rulings should help S corporations apply for temporary waivers of the 100% ownership requirement, so that acquired subsidiaries will not lose their status as S corporations merely because of a slight delay in an acquisition.

1630.33. Selling corporation's S election terminates. In many cases, the purchaser has no desire or ability to continue the acquired corporation's S election. In this situation, the purchase of the acquired corporation's shares may constitute a termination of the S election. If the acquired corporation is retained intact, the basis of assets, as well as most other tax attributes, will be unchanged. The parties may need to be concerned with the identification of the S termination year, as well as the allocation of the corporation's items within that year.

If the purchasing corporation has a consolidated return election in effect, the acquired corporation's taxable year will end on the date of acquisition. [Regs. §1.1502-76(b)(2)] Whenever there is a change of more than 50% stock ownership in a termination year, the corporation must close its books on the final day of the S short year and allocate the items in the S short year to the selling shareholders. See Chapter 13 for discussion of these issues.

OBSERVATION: Under current (1999) Regulations, an S corporation is faced with a rather strange situation when it is acquired by a group of corporations filing a consolidated return. The corporation's S election will terminate on the day before the acquisition, but the corporation cannot join a consolidated return until the day after the acquisition. Thus, on the acquisition day, the corporation is a stand-alone C corporation. Proposed amendments to Regulations §1.1502-76(b)(1)(ii)(A)(2) and Regulations §1.1362-3(a) would accelerate the corporation's admission into the consolidated group and would eliminate this one-day year.

After the S election terminates, there will be a post-termination transition period, also discussed in Chapter 13. During that period, cash distributions will come first from the Accumulated Adjustments Account, to the extent of its balance on the final day of the S short year. [§1371(e)] The IRS has limited this treatment of distributions made to persons who were shareholders in the corporation before the S election terminated. [Proposed Regs. §1.1377-2(b)]

1630.34. Selling corporation is liquidated. If the selling corporation is liquidated immediately after the sale of the stock, it will be subject to all of the tax rules discussed above, under 1625. Especially important may be the nonrecognition of losses on property acquired by the liquidating corporation as contributions within the past five years (see the discussion above). The loss is not allowed merely because the corporation's shares change hands.

EXAMPLE 16 - 21: Celco was a corporation that received property from its sole shareholder, Cecilia, as a contribution to capital on June 23, 1989. Celco's basis in the property was

> $450,000. In 1992, Cecilia sold all of her stock to Ricardo, an unrelated person. In 1992, Ricardo liquidated Celco. The basis in the property at the time of liquidation was still $450,000, but its fair market value had dropped to $300,000. Under the loss disallowance rules, Celco could not recognize the loss on the distribution of the property to Ricardo, even though he was not the shareholder who contributed the property.

It is unlikely that the new shareholder will recognize any gain or loss, since the basis to that shareholder will be the fair market value of the assets, as evidenced by the recent purchase price.

If the purchaser is a C corporation, liquidation of the acquired subsidiary may be a tax-free transaction under §337. If a liquidation occurs shortly after the acquisition, however, the subsidiary will recognize all gains and losses, pursuant to §338. A discussion of these rules can be found in Chapter 15, at 1525.8.

The current law is that liquidation of a subsidiary by an S corporation, if the S corporation owns 80% or more of the stock, is tax-free to the parent under §332 and is tax-free to the subsidiary under §337. [§1371(a). See H.R. Conf. Rep. 104-737, p. 208.]

The buyer could cause the liquidation to be taxable by making a §338 election, or the buyer and seller could jointly agree to an election under §338(h)(10). See discussion in Chapter 15, at 1525.81. and 1525.84. Another popular technique for making a taxable acquisition is the cash merger, discussed in the next part of this chapter.

1630.35. Selling and buying corporations merge. An acquiring corporation, or its shareholders, may acquire a target corporation and then merge the two corporations. Many mergers are structured as tax-free reorganizations, which are discussed in Chapter 17. However, if the consideration given to the selling corporation's shareholders is primarily cash, or any property other than stock in the purchasing corporation, the merger will lack the continuity of interest necessary for treatment as a tax-free reorganization. In this situation, the entire series of transactions, known as a *cash merger*, may be treated as a purchase of the acquired corporation's assets. [*Yoc Heating*, 61 TC 168 (1973)] After the acquisition, the parties may have some flexibility in determining the identity of the surviving corporation. When the purchasing corporation emerges as the surviving entity, the merger may be called a *forward merger*. If the acquiring corporation is merged into the selling corporation, the result is known as a *reverse merger*.

The acquired corporation's tax attributes should disappear, and the assets would be given a basis of fair market value at the time of the purchase. The structure as a forward or reverse merger should not affect this result. There are some considerations, however, that will usually favor the forward merger. For example:

- If the shareholders are concerned with §1244 treatment, a reverse merger would not result in §1244 stock to the new owners. See Chapter 14. A forward merger, however, could produce §1244 stock, if the stock in the surviving corporation were acquired by a contribution from the current shareholders.
- If the shareholders of the acquiring corporation have any suspended losses in excess of basis, they would clearly be able to deduct those losses against future income of the same corporation. The suspended losses from one corporation are not clearly deductible against future income of a different corporation.

In some cases, however, selection of the surviving corporation may require further analysis. For example, if either corporation has a desirable tax attribute, such as a natural business year end, it may be beneficial to have that corporation survive the merger. If either corporation has terminated an S election within the past five years, the corporation with a current S election may also be the most desirable survivor.

1630.36. Treatment of purchaser's interest expense. The treatment of interest on a loan used to purchase stock in a corporation can vary depending on the tax status of the corporation and the purchaser's relation to the corporation. According to general tax rules, the loan proceeds must be traced to their use. [Temporary Regs. §1.163-8T] When the seller of property finances the purchase, as in an installment sale of stock, the interest will be traced directly to the stock purchase. If the purchaser is an individual, it may be extremely important to preserve the acquired corporation's S election.

When an individual borrows money to purchase stock in a C corporation, the interest is treated as investment interest. [Temporary Regs. §1.163-8T] Such interest is deductible only to the extent of the individual's net investment income. [§163(d)] If the purchaser has sufficient investment income to offset the interest paid, the deduction will be allowed in full. It is, however, an itemized deduction.

In one case under prior law, a purchaser was able to persuade the Tax Court that his motive in purchasing stock was related to his employment, rather than to an investment. [*Chester W. Chanhofer*, TC Memo 1986-166] In this case, the purchaser was a manager for a beer distributor and was going to lose his job if the business was sold. Instead of losing his job, the manager borrowed money and purchased all the shares of the company. According to the Tax Court, the buyer did not have an investment motive in buying the stock, particularly in view of the high price he paid for the stock, its limited marketability, and other licensing restrictions. Rather, the purchase was motivated by the fact that he did not want to lose his job. As a result, the Tax Court held that the interest was fully deductible as business interest.

> **OBSERVATION:** The taxpayer's victory in the case of Chanhofer was unique to the treatment of interest prior to the Tax Reform Act of 1986. Under current law, such interest may not be deductible, since interest incurred in the taxpayer's employee capacity is considered nondeductible personal interest. [§163(h)(2)(A)]

When the purchaser is able to retain the S election, however, the interest on acquisition indebtedness is traced to the corporation's assets. The authority for this is somewhat obscure, the result of several IRS Notices. In 1988, the IRS issued Notice 88-20, which requires that the debt proceeds be allocated to entity's assets in any reasonable manner. [Notice 88-20, 1988-1 CB 487] That Notice suggests that the fair market value of the corporation's assets is a reasonable manner of allocation. That Notice, however, applies only to debt taken out before 1988.

In 1989, the IRS issued another Notice, which continues the rules of Notice 88-20 until and unless a new rule is adopted. [Notice 89-35, 1989-1 CB 917] Therefore, the interest paid on acquisition indebtedness receives much better treatment if the acquired corporation is an S corporation rather than a C corporation.

> **EXAMPLE 16 - 22:** Dr. Z is offered the opportunity to purchase shares in the ABC Clinic, Inc. He will need to borrow $250,000. His first-year interest expense will be $30,000. If the clinic is a C corporation, Dr. Z will be subject to the investment interest limit on the $30,000 interest. If it is an S corporation, he will be allowed an above-the-line trade or business deduction for the interest.

16

The reporting of the interest on the borrower's tax return corresponds with the buyer's relationship to the S corporation's assets. Notice 88-20 gives specific instructions for reporting the deduction:

- Interest on debt allocated to active business assets is reported on Schedule E, on a separate line in column a, noted as "business interest."
- Interest on debt allocated to passive activity assets is reported on the Form 8582 worksheet, in accordance with the activity's classification. Any deductible portion is then reported on Schedule E.

- Interest on debt allocated to portfolio assets goes to Form 4952 or directly to Schedule A as investment interest.

EXAMPLE 16 - 23: George borrows $100,000 to purchase all of the stock of G Corporation, an S corporation. The corporation has total assets of $500,000, as follows: $100,000 of the assets are portfolio investments, $150,000 is a rental activity, and the remaining $250,000 are assets used in the corporation's business, in which George materially participates. George pays $5,000 of interest on the debt used to buy the stock. He must allocate the $5,000 as follows:

Activity	*Value*	*% Total*	*Interest*	*Reported on*
Portfolio	$100,000	20	$1,000	Form 4952
Passive	150,000	30	1,500	Form 8582
Business	250,000	50	2,500	Schedule E
	$500,000	100	$5,000	

If a shareholder borrows money and then lends it to the corporation, the treatment is somewhat different. In this case, the interest paid by the shareholder would be investment interest. A carefully constructed loan from the shareholder to the S corporation, however, should ensure that there is no significant tax detriment. Any interest received by the shareholder from the corporation would be investment income. Therefore, if the shareholder charges at least as much interest as he or she must pay, the interest paid would be fully deductible.

If a shareholder has purchased stock in a C corporation, it may be beneficial to make an S election as soon as possible. The IRS has expanded the treatment of interest to allow a trade or business deduction for interest paid on a debt used to acquire C corporation stock, after the corporation's S election took effect. [PLR 9040066] The IRS has also allowed acquisition interest to continue to be treated as trade or business interest when a QSST was liquidated. The trust transferred the S corporation stock to the beneficiary, who assumed the purchase money note. The beneficiary was able to deduct the interest expense under the rules of Notice 88-20. [PLRs 9804031, 9804029, 9804028, 9804027, 9804026]

1630.37. Effect of a §338(h)(10) election. The purchaser is treated as acquiring all of the assets on the opening of business on the day after acquisition date. The purchase price, and thus the basis of the assets acquired, is the Modified Adjusted Deemed Sale Price (MADSP).

The MADSP is calculated as if the price paid for the stock on the acquisition date were representative of the entire owner's equity of the corporation (the "grossed-up" stock basis to the purchaser). It is adjusted for any liabilities that remain with the target corporation, as well as any liabilities that might be created as a result of the transfer. [Regs. §1.338(h)(10)-1(f)(2)] The most likely liability created as a result of the transfer is a built-in gains tax at the corporate level. There can be other liabilities that are triggered on the sale or exchange of a corporation's stock, such as deferred compensation arrangements with key employees.

16

EXAMPLE 16 - 24: Purco offered $900,000 for 90% of the stock of Targco, an S corporation. Targco had $200,000 of liabilities. The MADSP of Targco's assets would be:

Grossed-up stock basis $900,000/.9	$1,000,000
Add liabilities	200,000
MADSP	$1,200,000

The MADSP would be allocated according to the residual method described earlier in this chapter. Thus the gain or loss would be measured for each asset according to the character (capital, ordinary, §123, etc.) of each.

1630.38. Effect of a QSub election. The purchaser may be able to make a QSub election for the target. The Proposed Regulations issued in 1998 are specific on the timing of events with respect to this election under varying purchase transactions. See Chapter 5, at 550., for discussion of the election mechanics, and timing rules. In general, if an S corporation acquires all of the stock of the target corporation, it may make an election as of the acquisition date. It has a grace period of 2 months and 15 days to make this election. [Proposed Regs. §1.1361-3(a)(3)] The target corporation is then treated as being liquidated under general tax principles on the effective date of the election. See Chapter 15, at 1525.7., for the general liquidation rules for controlled subsidiaries. The election need not be made for the first day on which the target corporation is eligible for QSub treatment.

When the QSub election follows a §338 election, some special rules apply. If the purchasing corporation makes a regular election—not a §338(h)(10) election—for the target, the QSub election may take effect the day after the acquisition date, but not before. The target corporation will need to file its return as a C corporation for the year ending on the date of the deemed sale. [Proposed Regs. §1.1361-4(b)(3)]

> **EXAMPLE 16 - 25:** Bobco acquired all of the stock of Carco on July 22, 1998, made a §338 election, and immediately elected to treat Carco as a QSub. If Carco had been a C corporation before the acquisition, it would file a tax return for its taxable year ending July 22, 1998. It would then be treated as a new corporation commencing business on July 23, 1998. If Bobco filed the proper QSub election on or before October 7, 1998 (2 months and 15 days after July 22, 1998), the "new" Carco would be a QSub from its inception. If Bobco did not file the QSub election in time for Carco to be a QSub on July 23, 1998, the "new" Carco would be a C corporation, wholly owned by Bobco, until the QSub election took effect.

If the target corporation had been an S corporation up to the point of acquisition by the acquiring corporation, the target would undergo two changes if the acquiring corporation makes a §338 election. The first change is conversion of the "old" target to a C corporation, and the second change is formation of the "new" target as a QSub. If the QSub election is not effective immediately after the acquisition, the target may have four separate identities in a relatively short period of time.

> **EXAMPLE 16 - 26:** Jayco acquired all of the stock of Simco on July 22, 1998, made a §338 election, and immediately elected to treat Simco as a QSub. If Simco had been an S corporation before the acquisition, it would file a tax return for its taxable year ending July 22, 1998. That return would be for an S termination year, and the entity would be treated as an S corporation for the portion of the year up to July 21 and as a C corporation starting the next day. See Chapter 13 for the operating rules. The disposition of all property in the deemed liquidating sale would be reported on a one-day C corporation return.
>
> If Jayco filed the proper QSub election on or before October 7, 1998 (2 months and 15 days after July 22, 1998), the "new" Simco would be a QSub from its inception. If Jayco did not file the QSub election in time for Simco to be a QSub on July 23, 1998, "new" Simco would be a C corporation, wholly owned by Jayco, until the QSub election took effect.

If the target were an S corporation and the acquiring corporation joined with the sellers to make a §338(h)(10) election, the outcome would be different. The old corporation would continue as an S corporation through the acquisition date, and the new corporation could then be a QSub from its inception.

> **EXAMPLE 16 - 27:** Assume the same facts as in Example 16 - 26, except that Jayco and the selling shareholders of Simco join in an election under §338(h)(10). If Jayco then files a QSub election to take effect the next day, "old" Simco is an S corporation through July 22, 1998, and new Simco is a QSub beginning July 23, 1998.

Note that a §338 election would clean the target of any taint as a former S corporation. Since the target would become a brand new corporation on the acquisition date, there would be no waiting period or need for a ruling from the IRS to allow the QSub election if the target had lost its S corporation status or QSub status within the preceding five years.

1635. Practice aids.

The practice aids in this chapter include one tax form and several checklists. Tax Form 16-1 is a copy of Form 8594, which must be filed by both the purchaser and the seller in any "applicable asset acquisition," discussed at 1620. The form is not difficult to fill out. Except for intangible assets other than goodwill, there is no requirement to list the specific assets in each of the four categories. As is discussed at 1620.4., the penalties for failure to file this form may be quite severe. Accordingly, a tax advisor to either the buyer or the seller should insist that his or her client file this form whenever it is likely that a transaction meets one of the definitions within §1060.

The checklists in this chapter are arranged into two general groups. Checklists 16-1 through 16-4 are oriented toward the seller of the business; the remaining checklists are prepared from the buyer's perspective. Checklist 16-1 is a brief overview of the alternative forms of disposition, with a cross-reference to the more detailed checklists unique to each form of disposition.

Checklist 16-5 is a brief overview of alternatives available to the purchaser. Each major alternative is cross-referenced to its own checklist.

These practice aids should serve as reminders to the tax advisors to both parties of a business exchange. The parties also should be aware of any problems that might arise under local law, and they should consult competent counsel to assure that the transaction works smoothly.

Checklist 16-1: Business sale

Form of transaction	*Action*	*Yes*	*No*	*N/A*
Stock sale	Complete Checklist 16-2			
Asset sale	Complete Checklist 16-3			
Tax-free reorganization	Complete Checklist 17-1			

Evaluation of alternatives:

Checklist 16-2: Stock sale

16

	Applicable (Yes/No)	*Completed (Date)*
Anticipated stock basis at disposition		
Gain or loss to date of sale		
Consider revoking S status before sale		
Agreement to elect to terminate year under §1377(a)(2)		

Copyright © 2000 by Harcourt, Inc. All rights reserved.

Warranties from buyer		
Any early termination of fiscal year?		
Gain or loss on stock sale		
Any §1244 loss? (See checklist in Chapter 14.)		
Sales outside corporate shell (covenant, employment agreement, etc.)		
Determine any relationship to purchaser		
Disallowance of loss		
Agreements with any related buyer for goodwill to deal with anti-churning problems		
Installment sale terms		

	Applicable (Yes/No)	*Completed (Date)*
Transfer of shares to family members or QSST before sale		
Consider §338(h)(10) election		
Joint and several tax liability		
Effect of disappearing stock basis		
Character of gain or loss		

Checklist 16-3: Asset sale

	Applicable (Yes/No)	*Completed (Date)*
Identification of all assets to be sold		
Identification of liabilities to be assumed		
Valuation problems		
Built-in gains tax exposure		
Nature of assets to be retained		
Need to file Form 8594		
Exposure to passive investment income tax		
Character of income if not liquidated		
Amount of Subchapter C EP		
Cost of bypass election		
Cost to liquidate		
Corporate-level gain or loss		
Built-in gains problems		

Copyright © 2000 by Harcourt, Inc. All rights reserved.

Installment receivables		
Applicability of §4538(h)		
File Form 966		
Shareholder-level gain or loss		
Applicability of §453(h)		
§1244 loss		
Basis in property received		
If retained assets constitute going business, file second Form 8594		

Checklist 16-4: Business purchase

Form of transaction	*Action*	*Yes*	*No*	*N/A*
Stock purchase	Complete Checklist 16-5			
Asset purchase	Complete Checklist 16-6			
Tax-free reorganization	Complete Checklist 17-2			

Evaluation of alternatives:

Checklist 16-5: Stock purchase

	Applicable (Yes/No)	*Completed (Date)*
Identity of purchaser (corporation, direct purchase by shareholders, etc.)		
Continued eligibility of target corporation for S status		
Continued eligibility of purchasing corporation for S status		
Agreement to elect to terminate target year under §1377(a)(2)		
Warranties from seller		
Immediate liquidation of target		
Tax-free under §332, §337		
§338 election		
Need to file Form 8594		
§338(h)(10) election with seller		
Joint and several tax liability		

Copyright © 2000 by Harcourt, Inc. All rights reserved.

Ruling waiving momentary ownership (if completed before 1997)	________	________
Assets outside corporate shell (covenant, employment agreement, etc.)	________	________
Determine any relationship to seller	________	________
Disallowance of loss	________	________
Agreements with any related seller for goodwill to deal with anti-churning problems	________	________
Transfer of shares to family members or QSST after purchase	________	________

Checklist 16-6: Asset purchase

	Applicable (Yes/No)	*Completed (Date)*
Identification of all assets to be acquired	________	________
Identification of liabilities to be assumed	________	________
Indemnification form seller	________	________
Valuation problems	________	________
Need to file Form 8594	________	________
Allocate basis by residual method	________	________
Treatment of covenants and employment agreements	________	________
Check for anti-churning rules on goodwill, if related to seller	________	________

16

Copyright © 2000 by Harcourt, Inc. All rights reserved.

Tax Form 16-1: Form 8594, page 1

Form **8594** (Rev. July 1998) Department of the Treasury Internal Revenue Service	**Asset Acquisition Statement Under Section 1060** ▶ **Attach to your Federal income tax return.**	OMB No. 1545-1021 Attachment Sequence No. **61**

Name as shown on return	Identification number as shown on return

Check the box that identifies you: ☐ Buyer ☐ Seller

Part I **General Information–** To be completed by all filers.

1 Name of other party to the transaction	Other party's identification number
Address (number, street, and room or suite no.)	
City or town, state, and ZIP code	
2 Date of sale	3 Total sales price

Part II **Assets Transferred–** To be completed by all filers of an original statement.

4 Assets	Aggregate Fair Market Value (Actual Amount for Class I)	Allocation of Sales Price
Class I	$	$
Class II	$	$
Class III	$	$
Classes IV and V	$	$
Total	$	$

5 Did the buyer and seller provide for an allocation of the sales price in the sales contract or in another written document signed by both parties? . . . . ☐ Yes ☐ No

If "Yes," are the aggregate fair market values listed for each of asset Classes I, II, III, IV and V the amounts agreed upon in your sales contract or in a separate written document? . . . . ☐ Yes ☐ No

6 In connection with the purchase of the group of assets, did the buyer also purchase a license or a covenant not to compete, or enter into a lease agreement, employment contract, management contract, or similar arrangement with the seller (or managers, directors, owners, or employees of the seller)? . . . . ☐ Yes ☐ No

If "Yes," specify (a) the type of agreement, and (b) the maximum amount of consideration (not including interest) paid or to be paid under the agreement. See the instructions for line 6.

For Paperwork Reduction Act Notice, see instructions. Cat. No. 63768Z Form **8594** (Rev. 7-98)

Tax Form 16-1: Form 8594, page 2

Form 8594 (Rev. 7-98) Page **2**

Part III **Supplemental Statement–** To be completed only if amending an original statement or previously filed supplemental statement because of an increase or decrease in consideration.

7 Assets	Allocation of Sales Price as Previously Reported	Increase or (Decrease)	Redetermined Allocation of Sales Price
Class I	$	$	$
Class II	$	$	$
Class III	$	$	$
Classes IV and V	$	$	$
Total	$		$

8 Reason(s) for increase or decrease. Attach additional sheets if more space is needed.

9 Tax year and tax return form number with which the original Form 8594 and any supplemental statements were filed.

TAX-FREE REORGANIZATIONS

Contents

17

1700. Overview.

When a shareholder of one corporation receives stock in another corporation, generally there is a taxable exchange. The fair market value of the stock received, less the adjusted basis of the stock surrendered, is a gain or loss recognized. However, if stock in a corporation that is a party to a reorganization is exchanged for stock in another (or the same) corporation that is also a party to the same reorganization, the shareholder recognizes no gain or loss. [§354(a)] A corporation that transfers property to another corporation in exchange for stock in the receiving corporation must also generally recognize gain or loss on the transfer. If the two corporations are parties to the same reorganization, however, neither corporation recognizes gain or loss. [§361]

Because the tax consequences of a reorganization are significant, it is necessary to find a definition of what constitutes a reorganization. The Code gives §368(a)(1) the exclusive authority to define *reorganizations*. That provision lists seven different transactions.

1710. Transactions qualifying as reorganizations.

Only a few transactions are classified as tax-free reorganizations. They are all described in §368.[1] For a transaction to qualify as a tax-free reorganization, it must meet one of these criteria. No other transfer of property is a tax-free reorganization. The basic patterns have each received commonly used nicknames, which correspond to the subparagraph in §368(a)(1). Table 17 - 1 lists the basic types of reorganizations, together with the statutory reference and the commonly used name of each.

The Code also permits variations on some of these patterns. For example, in a Type B or Type C reorganization, the corporation that acquires the target corporation may use its own stock or the stock of its parent corporation. Such variations are also permitted in a Type A reorganization, although there are specific statutory limits on the amount of property acquired and consideration given. [§368(a)(2)(D), §368(a)(2)(E)]

1715. Applicability to S corporations.

Under the general rules of Subchapter S, an S corporation is subject to all rules of Subchapter C, unless the rules are inconsistent with Subchapter S. [§1371(a)(1)] Accordingly, the IRS has held that S corporations can engage in tax-free reorganizations. [GCM 39768 (1998)] Many

TABLE 17 - 1: Basic Statutory Reorganizations

Reference	*Description*	*Short Name*
§368(a)(1)(A)	Statutory Mergers and Consolidations	Type A
§368(a)(1)(B)	Acquisition of Stock for Voting Stock	Type B
§368(a)(1)(C)	Acquisition of Property for Voting Stock	Type C
§368(a)(1)(D)	Transfer of Assets to Controlled Corporations	Type D
§368(a)(1)(E)	Recapitalizations	Type E
§368(a)(1)(F)	Changes in Identity, Form, Place	Type F
§368(a)(1)(G)	Insolvency Reorganizations	Type G

[1] Code §367 describes some reorganization transactions, in the multinational context. Those rules are not discussed in this book.

earlier rulings also support this position. As the next portion of the text demonstrates, however, several of the reorganization transactions contain violations of the Subchapter S eligibility requirements. Although an S corporation may be able to engage in these transactions, it will lose its S election.

1720. Description of reorganizations.

Each of the basic reorganization types, as well as the permitted variations thereon, can encompass extremely complicated transactions. A limited discussion of each type, as it relates to S corporations, follows.

> **OBSERVATION:** The reorganization provisions are extremely complex. The material that follows gives a brief discussion of the different transactions. It is intended only to give sufficient background to alert the reader to the special problems of S corporations that undertake reorganizations. Tax professionals who do not regularly participate in these transactions should research all existing authority carefully before advising clients on these matters. State and local law may have significant impact on certain reorganizations, and competent legal counsel should always be involved from the outset. Frequently, the parties to the reorganization are best served by obtaining a private letter ruling from the IRS, so that the transaction will not be challenged later. The IRS issues rulings frequently, and the tax professional should read recent rulings in order to ascertain current policy.

1720.1. Type A straight merger or consolidation. The Type A reorganization is a statutory merger or consolidation. A statutory merger occurs when one corporation is absorbed by another. The extinguished corporation, often called the target, transfers all of its attributes, including assets, liabilities, and all other tax and nontax rights and responsibilities, to the acquiring corporation, often known as the survivor or purchaser. When the target corporation merges directly into the acquiring corporation, the transaction may be known as a straight merger, in contrast to some variations, discussed below. Figures 17 - 1 through 17 - 6 show the status of the various parties before, during, and after the reorganization.

As Figure 17 - 1 demonstrates, the acquiring and target corporations are separate corporations before the merger. The figure shows separate groups of shareholders, but they need not actually be separate persons. In many cases, a parent corporation is merged into a subsidiary, a subsidiary corporation is merged into a parent, or brother–sister corporations whose shareholders are the same persons or entities are merged to become one corporation.

Figure 17 - 1: Corporations and shareholders before merger.

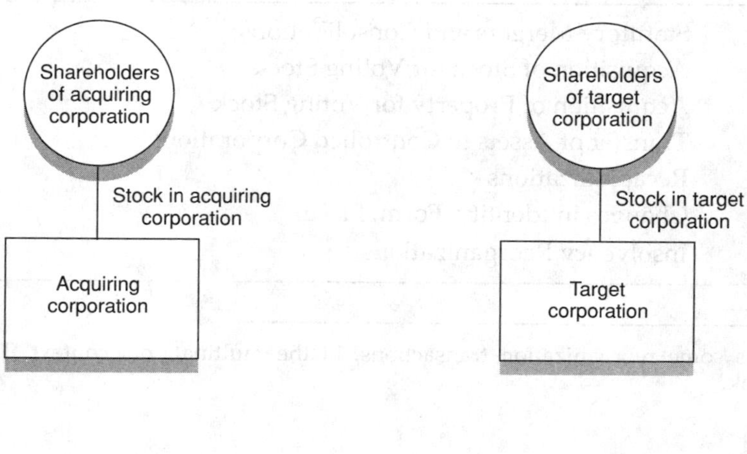

17

Figure 17 - 2: Merger transaction.

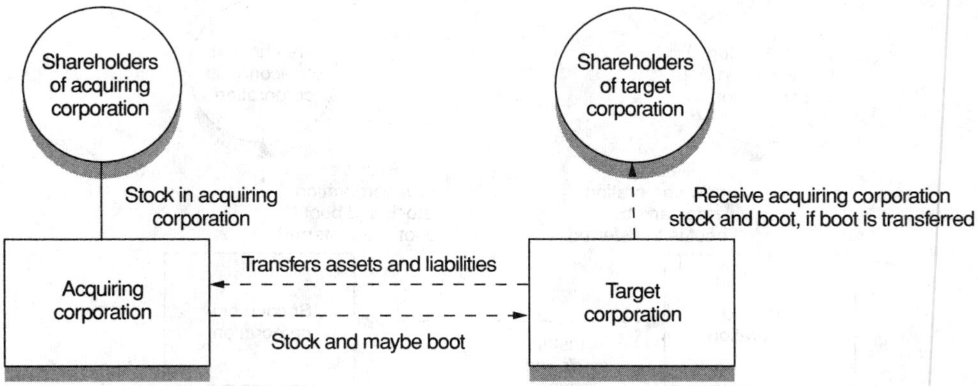

Figure 17 - 2 shows the merger transaction. The target corporation transfers all of its assets, liabilities, and any other rights and obligations to the acquiring corporation. The transfer is effected by operation of law. The merger must conform to the laws of the state or states in which the corporations are located. Typically, the shareholders of both corporations must approve the mergers. Dissenting shareholders must be compensated, and they may demand a judicial appraisal of the value of their shares.

After the merger has been completed, the former shareholders of both of the former corporations are shareholders in the surviving corporation. The surviving corporation has its own assets, liabilities, and other attributes, in addition to those of the extinguished corporation, to the extent that local law so provides (Figure 17 - 3). As later discussion indicates, the identity, in form, of the corporation that is to survive the merger may be important.

There are two variations on the Type A merger. These are known as triangular mergers, and they are discussed below at 1720.2. and 1720.3.

A consolidation is used less frequently than a merger. Figure 17 - 4 illustrates the process of consolidation, whereby the shareholders of all of the old corporations' shares exchange their shares for stock in the new corporation.

Figure 17 - 5 depicts the relationship of the old corporations' shareholders to the new corporation after the consolidation. As Figure 17 - 5 demonstrates, the former shareholders of the old corporations own stock in the new corporation.

One of the appealing aspects of the Type A straight merger or consolidation is the flexibility of permissible consideration. The Code sets no minimum limit on the target

Figure 17 - 3: Surviving corporation and shareholders after merger.

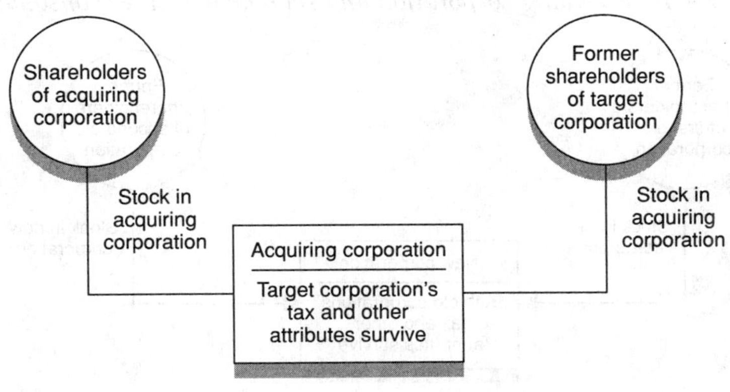

Figure 17 - 4: Consolidation transaction.

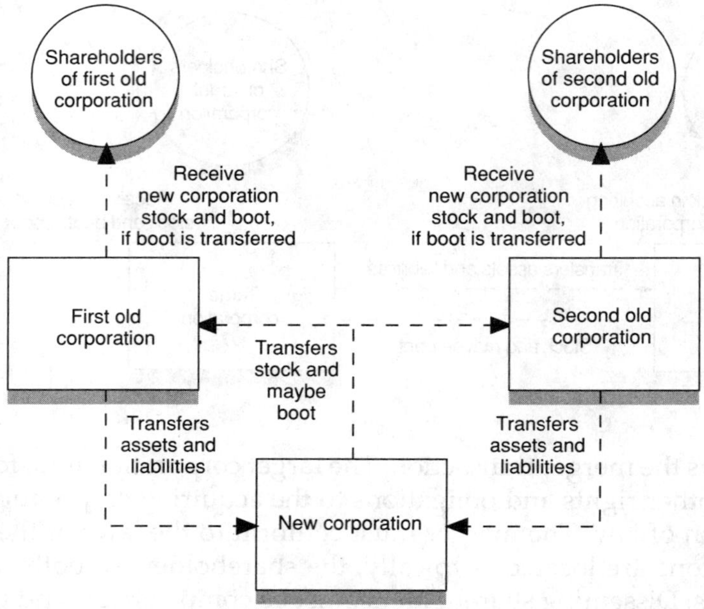

corporation's shares that must be exchanged for purchaser's stock, in contrast to some of the reorganizations discussed later. Nor is there an express limit on the amount of other consideration (boot) that can be received by the target corporation's former shareholders. The IRS position on issuing a favorable ruling is that up to 50% of the total consideration given in a straight merger or consolidation may be in the form of boot. [Rev. Proc. 77-37, 1977-2 CB 568]

PLANNING TIP: An S corporation may be the target corporation or the surviving corporation in a straight merger or consolidation, as long as it meets all of the Subchapter S eligibility requirements. Rulings on Type A reorganizations held that the S election of the surviving corporation continued in effect following a merger of a C corporation into an S corporation. [PLRs 8825056, 8937051, 9011042, 9115029, 9115059, 9117055] There have also been rulings approving the merger of one S corporation into another S corporation. [PLR 8912045]

Figure 17 - 5: Surviving corporation and shareholders after consolidation.

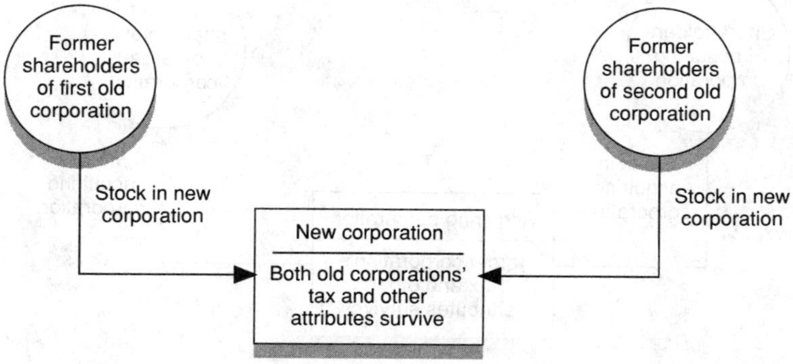

17

The IRS National Office will not rule on a proposed transaction's status as a merger. [Rev. Proc. 93-3, 1993-1 IRB 71] A taxpayer may request a determination from the District Director in order to have a transaction respected as a merger.

1720.2. Type A forward triangular merger. Type A reorganizations are frequently used, with the merger being far more popular than the consolidation. One potential problem with a merger, however, is the liability for any claims against the acquired corporation, now that its existence is terminated. The acquiring corporation should conduct a thorough examination of the target corporation's affairs before it consummates the merger. It is also wise to obtain representations and indemnity from the shareholders of the target corporation. These problems are beyond the realm of the tax professional. It would be foolhardy, even if possible, to attempt a merger without the advice of competent legal counsel.

The acquiring corporation may intend to operate the acquired corporation as a subsidiary. Accordingly, after the merger it may transfer all of the acquired corporation's assets and liabilities into a subsidiary corporation. The transfer would generally be nontaxable under §351. An alternative approach is to have the target corporation merge into a subsidiary of the acquiring corporation, rather than into the acquiring corporation itself. By doing so, the acquiring corporation could possibly limit its risk from hidden claimants against the target corporation. It could also avoid the necessity of having all of its own shareholders approve the merger. Both of these problems are beyond the domain of the tax practitioner, and they may vary with local law. The merger of a target corporation into a subsidiary of the acquiring corporation has become popular in recent years. It is essentially the same as any other Type A merger, except that the shareholders of the target corporation receive stock in the parent of the corporation that survives the merger, rather than in the surviving corporation itself. This transaction is expressly permitted as a tax-free reorganization by §368(a)(2)(D). The popular terms are Type A triangular merger and forward triangular merger. Figures 17 - 6 through 17 - 8 illustrate this transaction. As Figure 17 - 6 demonstrates, the parties before the reorganization are the same as those before a Type A merger, except that a subsidiary of the acquiring corporation is now a party to the reorganization.

Figure 17 - 6: *Corporations and shareholders before forward triangular merger.*

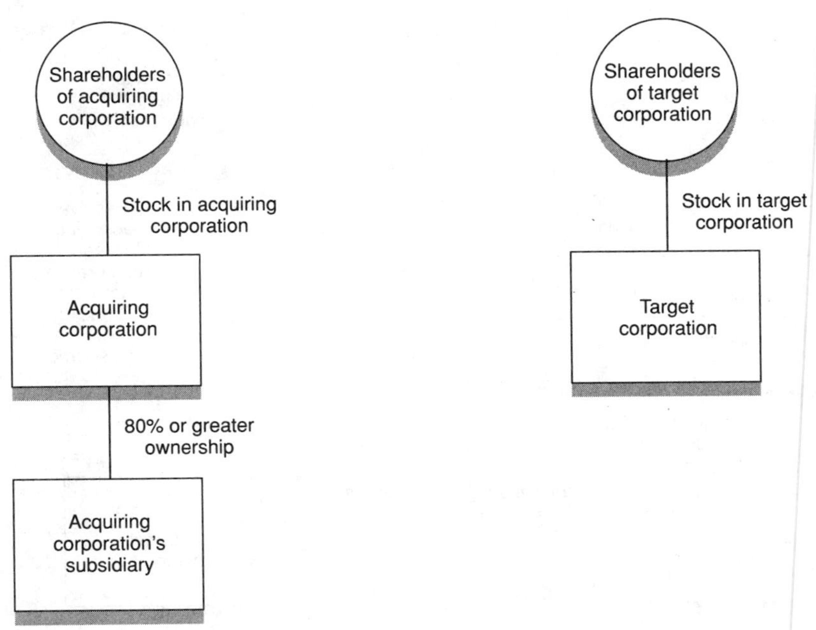

17

As shown in Figure 17 - 7, the target corporation transfers its assets and liabilities to the subsidiary. The transfer happens by operation of law, since this transaction is a statutory merger.

After the triangular merger, the acquiring corporation's subsidiary survives. The surviving corporation has its own assets, liabilities, and other attributes, as well as those of the extinguished corporation, to the extent that local law so provides. Figure 17 - 8 shows the position of the parties after the triangular merger. When compared to the straight merger, there are certain advantages. First, the triangular merger may facilitate shareholder approval, from the purchasing corporation's point of view. Typically, the subsidiary that survives the actual merger has only one shareholder—the parent corporation. Second, all hidden claims against the target corporation are transferred by law to the subsidiary corporation, rather than to the parent. Third, the businesses may not be able to be merged, because of some nontax regulatory constraint.

There are, however, two limits on the triangular merger that are not present in a straight merger. First, the surviving corporation (the subsidiary) may not transfer any of its own stock, but only stock of its parent corporation. This rule prevents the shareholders of the target corporation from getting their old corporation back by receiving some issue of preferred stock in the subsidiary.

Second, the surviving corporation must acquire, and keep, substantially all of the properties of the target corporation. Although the phrase "substantially all" is included in the statute, it is not defined. The position of the IRS is that the surviving corporation must acquire at least 70% of the fair market value of the gross assets and 90% of the owner's equity of the target. [Rev. Proc. 77-37, 1977-2 CB 568]

> **PLANNING TIP:** A triangular merger involves the permanent establishment of an affiliated group. Beginning in 1997, however, this type of reorganization may be extremely useful to S corporations that intend to acquire subsidiary corporations, including qualified Subchapter S subsidiaries. If a target corporation is merged into a QSub, however, the merger should be treated as a straight merger, rather than a

Figure 17 - 7: Forward triangular merger transaction.

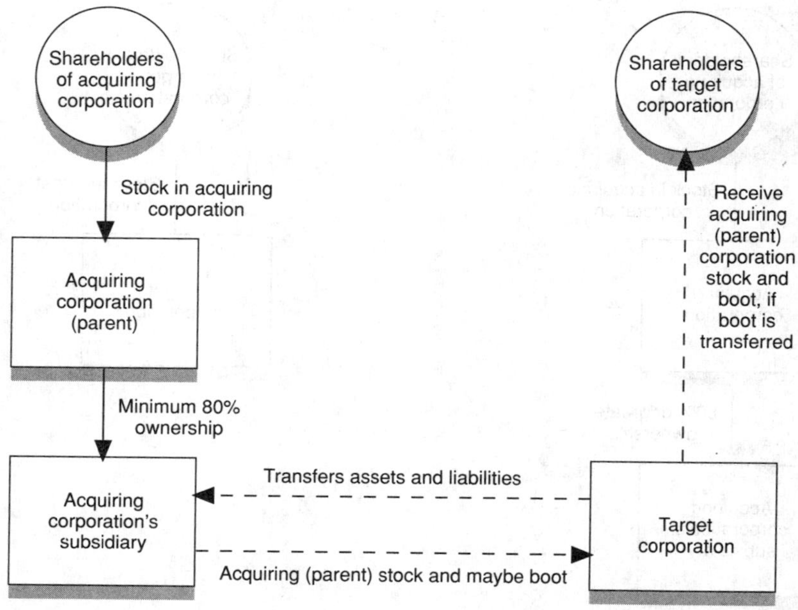

17

Figure 17 - 8: *Surviving corporations and shareholders after forward triangular merger.*

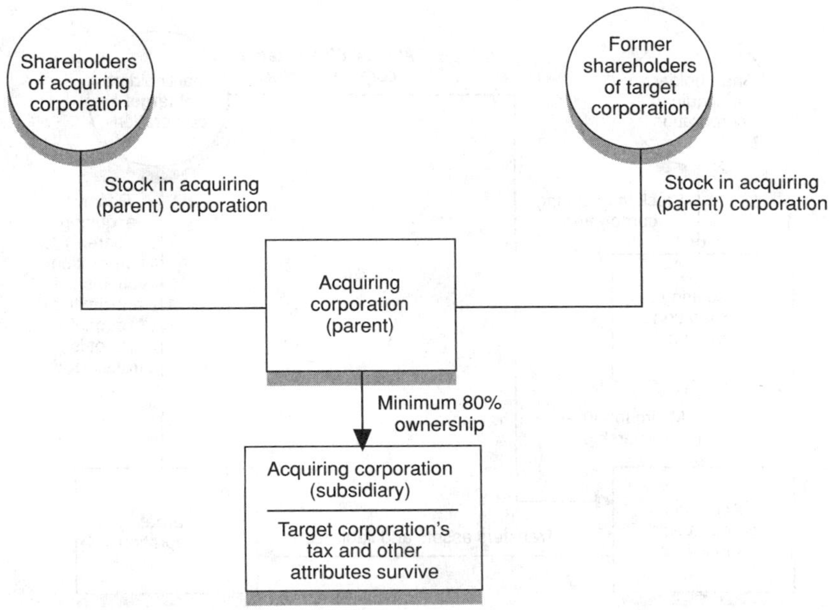

triangular merger, due to the nonentity status of the QSub. There may be some different considerations, however, for banks and bank holding companies, whereby the QSub may be treated as a separate corporation for some purposes.

EXAMPLE 17 - 1: An S corporation establishes a wholly owned subsidiary for the purpose of acquiring a target corporation. Within 75 days after the subsidiary is established, the parent S corporation files an election to treat the target as a QSub. See Chapter 5, at 545. The deemed liquidation of the subsidiary takes place on the merger date. The subsidiary would be ignored for federal tax purposes. Thus the tax treatment of the arrangement would be a merger of target corporation into parent.

1720.3. Type A reverse triangular merger. A variation on the triangular merger occurs when a subsidiary of the purchasing corporation is merged into the target corporation. What primarily distinguishes this transaction, known as the reverse triangular merger, from the forward triangular is that the target corporation's identity survives. This may be advantageous when the target corporation has certain nontax attributes that are not easily transferable. The status of the parties before a reverse triangular reorganization is exactly the same as before a forward triangular merger, as shown earlier in Figure 17 - 6.

The steps are essentially the same as those in a forward triangular merger, with one significant exception. Instead of merging the target corporation into the subsidiary, the subsidiary is merged into the target. The target then emerges as a subsidiary of the purchasing parent corporation. Figure 17 - 9 illustrates the merger, and Figure 17 - 10 shows the status of the parties after the reorganization.

The reverse triangular merger has a significant advantage over the straight and forward triangular mergers, if it is important for the target corporation to survive as an entity. Some restrictions do apply to this form of transaction, however. First, as was the case with the forward triangular merger, the target corporation must retain substantially all of the property it owned before the merger. Second, the former shareholders of the target must receive voting stock of the purchasing corporation (parent) in exchange for at least 80% of the

17

Figure 17 - 9: Reverse triangular merger transaction.

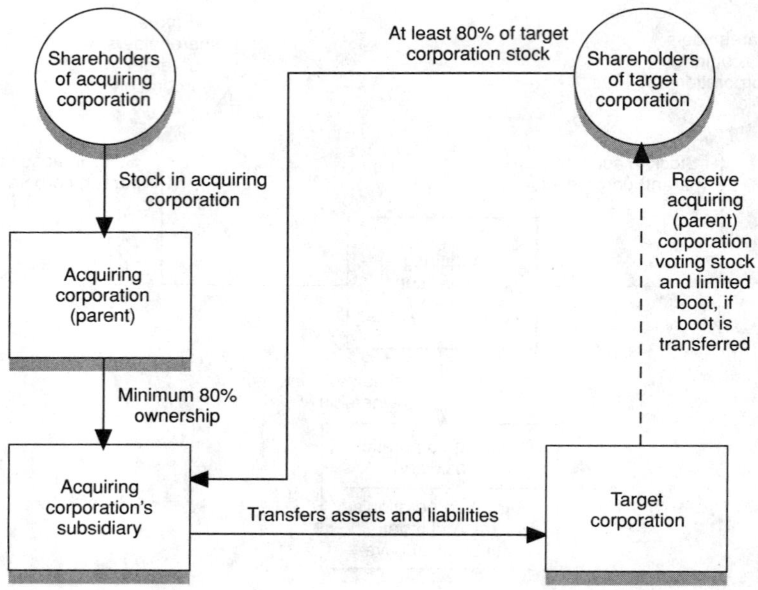

Figure 17 - 10: Surviving corporations and shareholders after reverse triangular merger.

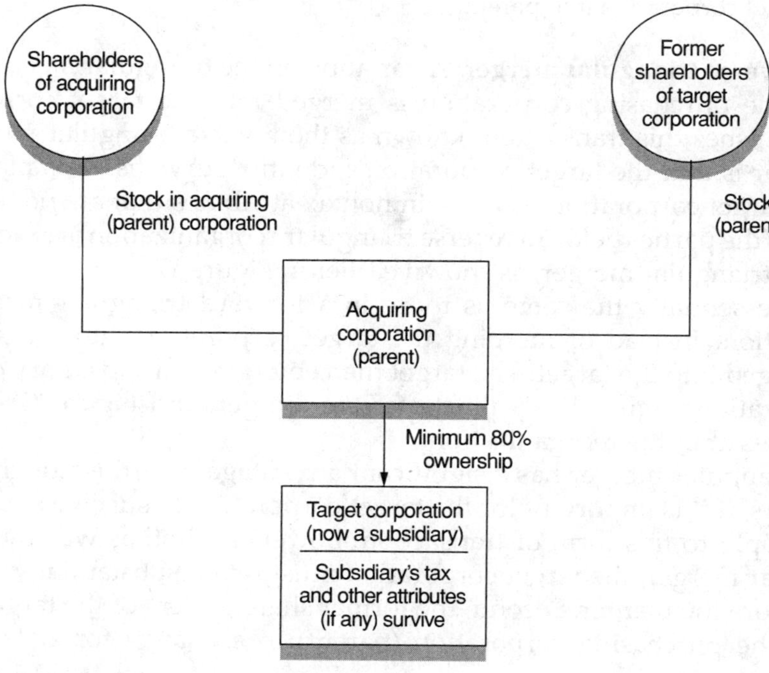

17

target's outstanding stock. [§368(a)(2)(E)] The purchasing corporation may transfer boot to the shareholders, but the boot is extremely limited. If the purchasing corporation already owned shares in the target corporation, it cannot count the previously owned shares towards the 80% requirement. In other words, if the purchasing corporation owned exactly 20% of the target, it would need to acquire all remaining shares in the transaction, solely in exchange for its own voting stock.

PLANNING TIP: Like a forward triangular merger, a reverse triangular merger involves the permanent establishment of an affiliated group. Therefore, if either the target corporation or the acquiring corporation was an S corporation before the reorganization, it will lose its S status at the time of the reorganization, if the reorganization occurs before 1997. Like the forward triangular reorganization, discussed above, the reverse triangular merger may become a popular acquisition technique for acquisitions after 1996. Also like the forward triangular merger, a merger of a QSub into the target would probably be treated as a merger of the target into the parent corporation. Thus, it may be possible to accomplish the nontax objectives of the forward triangular merger without experiencing the restrictions on the use of boot, or without needing to retain substantially all of the assets of the target corporation. Both of these are more restrictive with the reverse triangular merger than they are with the straight merger.

EXAMPLE 17 - 2: An S corporation establishes a wholly owned subsidiary for the purpose of acquiring a target corporation. The subsidiary merges into the target corporation and the target corporation's shareholders receive parent corporation stock. Within 2 months and 15 days after the merger, the parent S corporation files an election to treat the target as a QSub. See Chapter 5, at 545. The deemed liquidation of the target takes place on the merger date. The target (now a subsidiary) would be ignored for federal tax purposes. Thus the tax treatment of the arrangement would be a merger of target corporation into parent.

1720.4. Type B stock-for-stock reorganization. The stock-for-stock transfer, described in §368(a)(1)(B), is the simplest form of reorganization. The shareholders of the target corporation simply exchange their shares for voting stock in the purchasing corporation. In contrast to the Type A reorganization, including its triangular variations, the acquiring corporation may give no consideration other than its voting stock. The only exception occurs when cash is issued for fractional shares. [Rev. Proc. 77-37, 1977-2 CB 568] The IRS may closely scrutinize any transactions between the acquiring corporation and the target corporation's shareholders, such as employment contracts and other arrangements, to determine if the acquiring corporation is indirectly paying any other consideration for target's shares. [Rev. Proc. 77-37, 1977-2 CB 568] The only variation, the triangular B reorganization, allows a subsidiary of a parent corporation to acquire the stock of the target corporation and use the parent corporation's voting stock as consideration.

The status of the parties before the reorganization is the same as that shown above in Figure 17 - 1. The actual transaction is shown in Figure 17 - 11. The acquiring corporation must issue sufficient voting stock in the reorganization so that after the transaction the acquiring corporation has 80% of the stock of the target corporation. It does not, however, need to acquire the 80% control in the exchange. For instance, the acquiring corporation could already own 25% of the target corporation's stock. In the reorganization, if it acquires at least 55% of the total outstanding shares, it will own 80% after the reorganization and meet the control requirement. Contrast this rule with that of the reverse triangular reorganization, which requires that the acquiring corporation receive 80% of the target corporation stock in the reorganization.

After the Type B reorganization, the target corporation is a subsidiary of the acquiring corporation. As Figure 17 - 12 illustrates, the situation after the transfer is exactly the same as

Figure 17 - 11: Type B reorganization transaction.

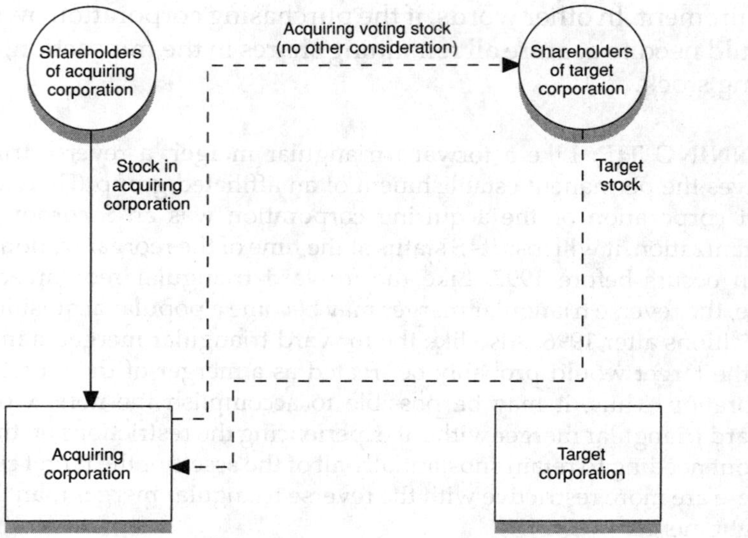

Figure 17 - 12: Surviving corporations and shareholders after type B reorganization transaction.

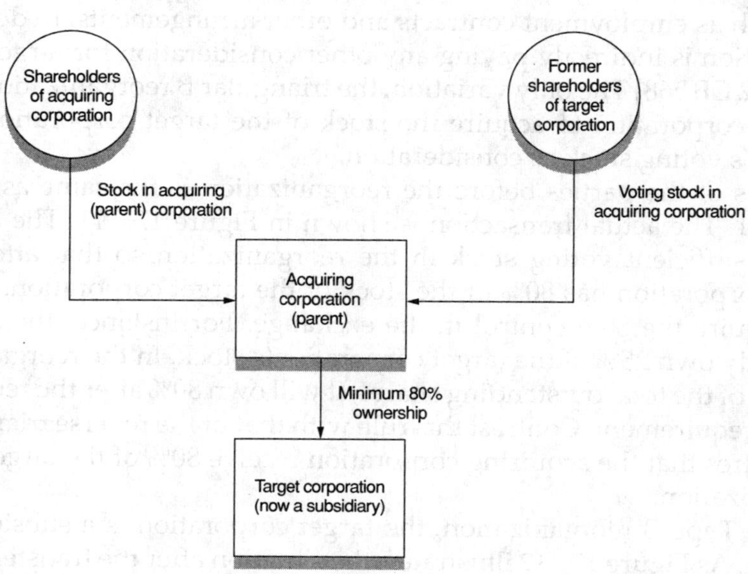

17

that of a reverse triangular Type A merger. There is one major distinction, however. Whereas the reverse triangular rules require that the target corporation retain substantially all of its assets, a Type B reorganization no similar requirement. Therefore, the target corporation may dispose of any assets the acquiring corporation does not want.

PLANNING TIP: A Type B reorganization involves the permanent establishment of an affiliated group, as does a forward or reverse triangular merger. Therefore, if either the target corporation or the acquiring corporation was an S corporation before the reorganization, it will lose its S status at the time of the reorganization, if the reorganization occurs before the beginning of 1997. After 1996 the Type B reorganization may become a popular acquisition technique for S corporations.

1720.5. Type C stock-for-asset reorganization. The Type C reorganization, often called a practical merger, is economically similar to a Type A merger. The target corporation transfers substantially all of its assets to the acquiring corporation in exchange for voting stock of the acquiring corporation. The major difference in the transaction is that the transfer of assets occurs by express agreement, rather than by statutory merger. The status of all parties before the reorganization is exactly the same as before a Type A reorganization, as was shown in Figure 17 - 1.

The reorganization, shown in Figure 17 - 13, transfers assets from the target to the acquiring corporation and transfers voting stock from the acquiring to the target.

Usually, the acquiring corporation needs to assume the target's liabilities or take property subject to the target's liabilities. In most cases, the assumption of the target's liabilities is not treated as payment of boot from the acquiring corporation to the target.

EXAMPLE 17 - 3: Target Corporation has assets with a fair market value of $100,000 and liabilities of $13,000. Acquiring Corporation assumes all the liabilities and transfers $87,000 of its own stock. Although the assumption of debt is normally treated as the transfer of boot, in this case the liabilities are ignored.

***Figure 17 - 13:** Type C reorganization transaction.*

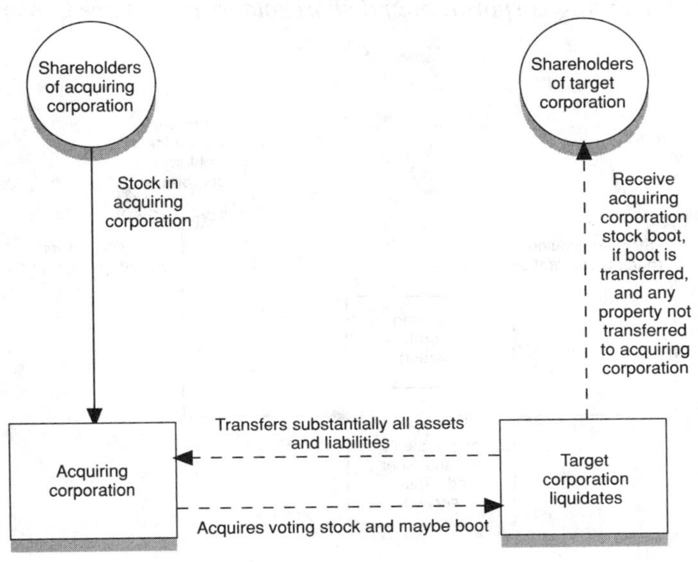

17

There can be a serious problem, however, if the acquiring corporation transfers any property other than its voting stock. If it does so, the assumption of liabilities is considered boot. An acquiring corporation is allowed to use some boot in a Type C reorganization, but if it does it must acquire at least 80% of the target corporation's assets for voting stock. [§368(a)(2)(B)] Therefore, as a practical matter, the only consideration that the target may receive is voting stock of the acquiring corporation, plus liabilities taken by the target corporation.

> **EXAMPLE 17 - 4:** Target Corporation has assets with a fair market value of $100,000 and liabilities of $13,000. Acquiring Corporation assumes all the liabilities. Acquiring Corporation can transfer only $7,000 of cash, since the maximum amount of boot is limited to 20% of the value of the assets ($100,000 x 20% = $20,000 – liabilities assumed of $13,000).

Figure 17 - 14 illustrates the position of the parties immediately after the transfer. The target corporation holds voting stock of the acquiring corporation, as well as any property that was not transferred in the reorganization.

Within a year of the transfer, the target corporation must be completely liquidated. The target corporation recognizes no gain on the distribution of the voting stock it received in the reorganization. It recognizes gains, but not losses, on the distribution of any property it had retained. [§361(c)(2)] After the reorganization, the acquiring corporation must retain substantially all of the properties of the target, as they existed before the reorganization. In this case, "substantially" all means 70% of the gross assets and 90% of the net assets. [Rev. Proc. 77-37, 1977-2 CB 568]

> **PLANNING TIP:** An S corporation should be able to engage in a Type C reorganization and retain its S status. The IRS has indicated that the corporation should waive momentary ownership, which occurs from the time the acquiring corporation transfers its stock to the target corporation until the target corporation distributes such stock to its shareholders in complete liquidation. [GCM 39768 (1988)] The IRS has also ruled, on stock for asset transfers that qualify as Type D nondivisive reorganizations, that the target corporation's momentary ownership of the acquiring corporation's stock did not terminate the acquiring corporation's S election, even though the target corporation was an ineligible shareholder. A nondivisive Type D reorganization may

Figure 17 - 14: *Surviving corporation and shareholders after Type C reorganization.*

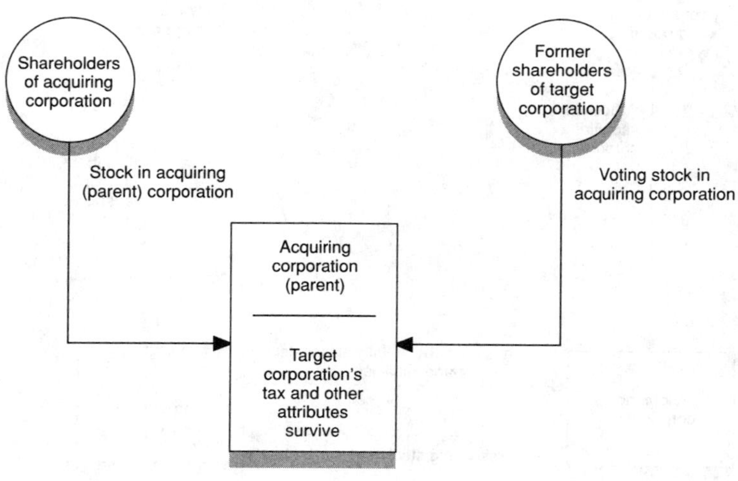

17

take the exact same form as a Type C reorganization, except that former shareholders of the target corporation are in control of the acquiring corporation immediately after the reorganization. As of this writing, however, there is little evidence that any S corporations are using this form of reorganization.

1720.6. Type D transfer of assets to controlled corporation. The Type D reorganization involves the transfer of part or all of a parent corporation's assets to one or more subsidiaries. After the transfer of assets, the parent corporation distributes the stock in the subsidiary or subsidiaries to its shareholders. This reorganization has two fundamental variations: divisive and nondivisive. The divisive reorganization, by far the more widely used of the two, is discussed later in this chapter.

A nondivisive Type D reorganization offers only limited tax-planning opportunities. In most cases a Type F or Type A reorganization will accomplish the same objectives. In some instances, however, the nondivisive Type D reorganization can be a valuable tool. For example, a bank may prefer to deal with an entirely new corporate shell in financing a leveraged buyout. The IRS has held that a new corporation resulting from a nondivisive D reorganization could make an S election for its first year. [PLR 9401001]

OBSERVATION: The nondivisive Type D reorganization may resemble a Type F reorganization, discussed below, when the old corporation transfers all of its assets to a new corporation. One difference is that the new corporation will begin a new tax year as of the date of its formation. A new corporation resulting from a Type F reorganization, however, does not start a taxable year. Therefore, it could be an advantage to structure a transfer as a Type D reorganization if the corporation has not had an S election in effect and wishes to make an immediate S election. A nondivisive reorganization has most of the same consequences as an acquisitive reorganization. Thus the old corporation's earnings, profits, and other tax attributes will carry intact to the new corporation. [§381(a), §354(b)(1)]

A nondivisive reorganization has most of the same consequences as an acquisitive reorganization. Thus, the old corporation's earnings, profits, and other tax attributes will carry intact to the new corporation. [§381(a), §354(b)(1)] The nondivisive Type D reorganization may also provide a trap for certain liquidations that are followed immediately by contributions to new corporations.

EXAMPLE 17 - 5: Slippery Corporation has two shareholders, Herman and Wanda, who are also husband and wife. Slippery has some liquid assets, low AAA, high accumulated earnings and profits, and real property that has declined significantly in value. Each of the shareholders has high basis in stock. Slippery liquidates by distributing the liquid assets and the depreciated real property. Slippery recognizes a loss on the property, which is distributed pro rata and which neither shareholder contributed to in the last five years. The shareholders report their portions of the loss on their personal tax returns. They also each report a loss on the disposition of stock.

The two shareholders then contribute the real property, but not the liquid assets, to a new corporation. Apparently, they have been allowed to recognize a loss and continue corporate operations as before. If the IRS were to invoke the step transaction doctrine, it could treat the entire series of transactions as a nondivisive Type D reorganization. By doing so, the IRS would disallow all losses on the purported liquidation. The liquid assets, which the shareholders kept, would be treated as boot received in the reorganization. Due to the corporation's high accumulated earnings and profits, and the continuity of ownership, the boot would probably be treated as a dividend.

A purported Type C reorganization may also be reclassified as a nondivisive Type D reorganization, if the shareholders of the target corporation hold more than 50% of the surviving entity.[2] There is little practical difference between the two forms, except for the treatment of certain liabilities.

The IRS has held that the momentary ownership of the acquiring corporation's stock by the target corporation in the process of a nondivisive Type D reorganization did not terminate the acquiring corporation's S election. [PLRs 9331018, 9335013, 9401020, 9721010] The IRS has also held that the target corporation in a nondivisive Type D reorganization was able to keep its S election in place until it was dissolved. [PLR 9335013]

> **PLANNING TIP:** The divisive D reorganization is extremely useful to S corporations. The nondivisive D reorganization is also a useful acquisition technique in limited circumstances. One of the most appealing aspects of the nondivisive Type D reorganization is that it starts a new taxable year, which may allow a corporation to make an S election on a date that would not have been the beginning of the year for the predecessor corporation.

1720.7. Type E recapitalization. Unlike the other types of reorganizations, the Type E recapitalization involves only one corporation. Its primary use is to exchange stock for stock, or securities for securities. There are two possible uses in the context of S corporations. First, a C corporation that has multiple classes of stock may undergo a recapitalization to qualify for S status. Holders of preferred stock can exchange their shares for common stock. Second, a recapitalization might be useful if a shareholder wants to sell or give away some equity but not relinquish control. A shareholder might accomplish this objective by exchanging some, but not all, of his or her voting stock for nonvoting stock. He or she could then keep the voting stock and relinquish the nonvoting stock.

> **PLANNING TIP:** The most esoteric use of the Type E reorganization is the estate tax freeze, in which a common stockholder exchanges some of his or her shares for preferred stock. The preferred stock, which usually has a fixed dividend rate, has a stable value. The common stock, which is given to younger generations, absorbs all of the future appreciation, which is not included in the original holder's estate. This planning device has some serious complications and is subject to some valuation problems addressed in Chapter 14 of the Internal Revenue Code (§2701 and following). Since it involves preferred stock, it has no application to S corporations.

1720.8. Type F reorganization. This reorganization is a mere change in form, identity, or place of organization of a single operating corporation. In form, one corporation transfers all of its assets to a new corporation, after which the old corporation is dissolved. This technique has been used most frequently to move a corporation to another state. It can also serve to rid a corporation of an undesirable charter. It has little federal tax-planning use. The principal federal tax advantage is that the corporation may find a new identity and actually transfer all of its assets without any imposition of tax. Like a nondivisive Type D reorganization, a Type F reorganization can happen by accident.

There is, in essence, a fiction that a Type F reorganization does not change the substance of a corporation's existence. For example, all of the former corporation's tax attributes carry over to the new corporation. [Rev. Rul. 57-276, 1957-1 CB 126] The old corporation's S election continues in effect, so there is no need to file a new Form 2553. [PLR 9749007] The new corporation uses the same identification number as the old corporation. [Rev. Rul.

[2] For nondivisive Type D reorganizations only, the former shareholders of the extinguished corporation need only have 50% control of the surviving corporation. [See §368(a)(2)(H).]

73-526, 1973-2 CB 404] There is no change in the taxable year, and the IRS has held that the new corporation continues to use the same fiscal year under §444. [PLR 9304023][3]

EXAMPLE 17 - 6: Lateco was incorporated in Illinois on April 1, 1992. It neglected to make an S election before June 15, 1992, but it had not begun substantial operations by that time. Its shareholders form another Illinois corporation, Fastco, on July 31, 1992, and Fastco files an immediate S election. On August 1, 1992, Lateco merges into Fastco in accordance with Illinois merger law. If Fastco is treated as a new corporation for federal tax purposes, its S election will take effect on July 31, 1992. If the merger is considered a Type F reorganization, however, Fastco and Lateco will be treated as a single corporation whose taxable year began on April 1, 1992. The S election filed on July 31, 1992, could not take effect until the next taxable year.

PLANNING TIP: One published ruling [Rev. Rul. 64-250, 1964-2 CB 333] and several private letter rulings [PLRs 9001021, 9118029, 9123049, 9548032] have been issued that permit S corporations to use Type F reorganizations. S corporations occasionally use Type F reorganizations, primarily to transfer their operations to a more favorable political climate.

1720.9. Type G bankruptcy reorganization. This transaction can be used only during a receivership, foreclosure, or similar proceeding under the Bankruptcy Act. This reorganization resembles a Type D, except that the control requirement is satisfied if creditors of the transferor are in control of the transferee. The old corporation transfers some or all of its assets to one or more subsidiaries, then transfers the stock of those corporations to creditors. As of this writing, there appears to be little applicability to S corporations. In one recent ruling a bankrupt S corporation transferred assets to another corporation in a Type G reorganization. The newly formed corporation was to be a C corporation, but the transfer and momentary affiliation did not terminate the bankrupt corporation's S election. [PLR 9629016]

1725. General reorganization rules.

A reorganization is tax-free in theory, because the shareholders of the target corporation have not liquidated their interest (i.e., cashed in) but rather have continued their investment, albeit through a new entity. Accordingly, both the ownership interests of the former shareholders and the business of the target corporation must survive the reorganization. In addition, there must be a business purpose, or the IRS can recharacterize the entire transaction.[4]

1725.1. Continuity of ownership. There must be continuity of interest before the exchanges that are part of the reorganization qualify for tax-free treatment. In many reorganizations, the permissible consideration is specified in the law. For the Type A merger, the Type A consolidation, the Type A forward triangular merger, and the Type F reorganization, however, the Code provides no express requirements for consideration. The IRS position is that it will rule favorably on this issue if at least 50% of the total consideration given for shares in the target corporation is stock in the surviving corporation (or parent corporation in the forward triangular merger). [Rev. Proc. 77-37, 1977-2 CB 568] The focus is on the consideration given to target shareholders in the aggregate, and not on what is received by any individual.

---

[3] The corporation in this ruling was not an S corporation, but was a personal service corporation, subject to the same taxable-year restrictions as an S corporation.

[4] See *Gregory v. Helvering*, 35-1 USTC 9043 (S.Ct.) for discussion of a transaction that met all of the reorganization requirements in form, but lacked a business purpose.

EXAMPLE 17 - 7: Rancho Corporation is owned in equal portions by Bernardo, Claudine, Dee, and Everett. The value of each shareholder's stock is $100,000. Poway Corporation intends to acquire Bernardo in a Type A straight merger. The following mixtures of stock and boot are acceptable for ruling purpose:

- Half stock and half boot to each shareholder
- All stock to two shareholders and all boot to the other two
- All stock to one shareholder, all boot to another shareholder, and half stock, half boot to the other two shareholders
- Any blend of any of the above packages, as long as the total consideration consists of at least 50% stock

The Supreme Court has held that a tax-free reorganization occurred when the shareholders of a target corporation received approximately 38% stock and 62% boot. [*John A. Nelson Co. v. Helvering*, 36-1 USTC 9019 (S.Ct.)] A merger with this mixture of consideration should withstand a court test, although it will probably not be able to obtain a favorable ruling.

The IRS has ruled that a transfer of stock in corporations to be merged to grantor trusts does not violate the continuity of interest condition of a tax-free reorganization. Therefore, a shareholder in an S corporation may transfer his or her stock in a target corporation to a grantor trust either before or after a merger without endangering the substance of the merger. [PLR 9410046] Note, however, that a transfer to a QSST could possibly endanger the merger status, due to a lack of continuity of interest.

1725.2. Continuity of business. Another principle that underlies the tax-free treatment of reorganizations is that the business continues, although in a modified form. A reorganization is tax-free only if it meets the continuity of business enterprise requirement. To meet this requirement, the acquiring corporation must either continue the target corporation's historic business or use a significant portion of the target corporation's assets in a business.

1725.3. Business purpose. There must be a business purpose for the transaction. Even if a transaction appears to meet one of the allowable forms of a reorganization, the IRS can treat the transaction as taxable if it serves no business purpose. Accordingly, obtaining a private letter ruling is often advisable, to assure that a transfer will be honored as a tax-free reorganization.

1730. Acquisitive reorganizations.

The acquisitive reorganizations differ entirely in their substance from the divisive reorganizations. The two types of reorganization sometimes bear little resemblance to each other in form. They have similar results, in that the shareholders of the acquired ("target") corporation receive shares of the purchasing corporation or, in some cases, shares of the parent of the acquiring corporation. Depending upon the specific type of transaction, boot may or may not be permitted in the exchange.

1730.1. Treatment of the shareholders of the target corporation. The parties to the reorganization are, in most cases, the acquiring corporation, the target corporation, and the shareholders of the target corporation. As a practical matter, the shareholders of the surviving corporation have not engaged in any distinct exchange and are not parties to the reorganization. The focal point of reorganization negotiations is often the tax treatment of the target corporation's shareholders. It is their tax burden, or lack thereof, that affects the price paid by the acquiring corporation. In many cases, the target shareholders will insist that the acquiring corporation obtain a favorable ruling before going through with the deal.

1730.11. Gain or loss recognized on the exchange. Shareholders who receive only stock in the exchange recognize no gain or loss on the disposition of their target corporation shares. [§354(a)(1)] The same rule applies to holders of securities in target corporation who receive securities in the surviving corporation.

A security is a debt instrument with a maturity date that is more than 10 years from the date of issue. [*Camp Wolters Enterprises, Inc. v. Commissioner*, 56-1 USTC 9314 (5th Cir.)] If the face amount of the securities received exceeds the face amount of those surrendered, the excess principal received is treated as boot. [§354(a)(2)(A)] A person who receives stock of the acquiring corporation in exchange for securities of the target corporation would come under the general nonrecognition rule.

> **EXAMPLE 17 - 8:** Fred owned a Targco security with a maturity value of $8,000. Targco was merged into Survco, and Fred received a Survco security with a face amount of $10,000. If the Survco security's interest rate was such that its fair market value was $10,000, Fred would have received boot of $2,000. However, if the interest rate on the Survco security was higher or lower than the current market rate of interest for a security with similar risk, the amount of boot could be different.
>
> Assume that the interest rate on the Survco security was considerably higher than the market rate and that the Survco security's fair market value was $11,000. Fred would make the following calculation:
>
> | | | |
> |---|---|---|
> | Treated as nonrecognition property: | | |
> | Face amount | $8,000 | |
> | Fair market value | | $8,800 |
> | Treated as boot: | | |
> | Face amount | $2,000 | |
> | Fair market value | | $2,200 |
>
> Fred's boot received in this exchange is $2,200, the fair market value of the excess principal amount of securities received over securities surrendered.

Shareholders who receive boot must recognize gain, to the lesser extent of the gain realized on the exchange or the fair market value of the boot received. This rule is analogous to the boot rule of §351, discussed in Chapter 14. No shareholder who participates in the reorganization may recognize any loss.

1730.12. Treatment of boot received in a reorganization. In a §351 exchange, gain recognized due to boot is usually capital gain. In a reorganization, by contrast, the gain recognized is treated as a dividend, if it has the effect of the distribution of a dividend. [§356(a)(2)] The Code does not explain what this phrase means, but Revenue Rulings provide some guidance: The boot is treated as if it were received in a stock redemption. [Rev. Rul. 74-515, 1974-2 CB 118; Rev. Rul. 74-516, 1974-2 CB 121] Therefore, if the redemption passes any one of the exchange tests of §302 or §303 (see discussion in Chapter 15), the shareholder will recognize capital gain. If the redemption does not meet one of the exchange tests, however, it is a distribution to which §301 applies. That rule, which applies to C corporations, treats a distribution as a dividend to the extent of the corporation's current and accumulated earnings and profits.

When the corporation involved is an S corporation, however, Subchapter S preempts the treatment of a distribution that would otherwise be subject to §301. [§1368(a)] The distribution is a reduction of basis to the extent of the shareholder's stock basis or the corporation's Accumulated Adjustments Account. (See Chapter 7, at 715.1. and 720.1., for discussion.) Therefore, a shareholder who receives boot in a reorganization involving an S corporation should treat the distribution of boot as a capital gain, at least to the extent of the corporation's Accumulated Adjustments Account.

Looking strictly to the S corporation distribution rules, it might appear that a shareholder could merely reduce basis for boot received, rather than report any gain, since this would be the case in a normal distribution. In a reorganization, however, the gain recognition is required by §354.

One problem faced recently by the Supreme Court is the identity of the corporation that actually distributes the boot. Since the distribution of boot occurs simultaneously with the transfer of stock, the situation may be less than clear.

EXAMPLE 17 - 9: Zarco has one shareholder, Zack. Tayco acquires Zarco in a statutory merger. Tayco transfers $600,000 of its stock, along with $400,000 of cash, to Zack. After the merger, Zack owns 20% of the outstanding stock in Tayco. If the boot is treated as a redemption of Zarco stock immediately before the merger, Zack would have been a 100% shareholder after the redemption, and the distribution would be the equivalent of a dividend. If, however, the boot were treated as a redemption of Tayco stock after the merger, Zack's boot would pass the test as a substantially disproportionate redemption. (See discussion of §302(b)(2) in Chapter 15, at 1510.3.)

The Supreme Court has decided that, when boot is given in connection with a reorganization, the hypothetical stock redemption occurs after the merger. [*Donald E. Clark*, 89-1 USTC 9230 (S.Ct.)] As a general rule, the Supreme Court's decision eases the desired treatment when the corporations involved are C corporations.

EXAMPLE 17 - 10: Refer to Example 17 - 9. Zack would be treated as if he had received $1,000,000 worth of Tayco stock, of which Tayco then redeemed 40%. Zack's boot would pass the test as a substantially disproportionate redemption, according to the Supreme Court. Zack would recognize a capital gain of $400,000.

When the corporations involved are S corporations, the timing of the deemed redemption is less important. As a matter of fact, shareholders who are giving up stock in an S corporation may even find it to their benefit to receive a distribution before the merger.

EXAMPLE 17 - 11: Refer to Example 17 - 9. Assume that Zarco was an S corporation with an Accumulated Adjustments Account balance of $400,000 before the merger. Also assume that Zack's basis in his stock was $500,000. If Zack were to take a distribution from Zarco before the merger and receive $600,000 in Tayco stock and no other consideration from Tayco, the economic situation would be the same for all parties. Zack's tax situation, however, would be much better. He would reduce his stock basis to $100,000 immediately before the merger. He would receive no boot in the merger and would report no gain.

1730.13. Basis of stock and securities received. Shareholders take a substituted basis for stock received. [§358] This same rule applies upon receipt of stock in a §351 exchange, as discussed in Chapter 14.

EXAMPLE 17 - 12: Refer to example 17 - 11. Zack's basis in his Tayco stock is $100,000, the same as his basis had been in his Zarco stock.

17

Each shareholder increases basis for gain recognized, regardless of its characterization as capital gain or a dividend. The shareholder then reduces stock basis for the fair market value of the boot received.

EXAMPLE 17 - 13: Refer to Example 17 - 11, in which Zack received $400,000 of boot and reported $400,000 of gain. Assuming that Zack's basis in his Zarco stock was $500,000 before the reorganization, his basis in his Tayco stock would also be $500,000.

Basis before reorganization	$500,000
Add gain recognized	400,000
Less boot received	(400,000)
Basis in stock received	$500,000

1730.14. Survival of other shareholder attributes. It is reasonably clear that if a shareholder's losses exceeded basis before a reorganization, and the corporation that gave rise to those losses survived, the shareholder could use future income from the same corporation to deduct the suspended losses.

Before the IRS issued Proposed Regulations §1.1366-2(c) in 1998, there was no direct authority that would allow a shareholder who had losses in an extinguished corporation to deduct those losses against future income from the surviving corporation. However, the position in that Proposed Regulation is that a shareholder may use income from a post-reorganization corporation to offset losses in excess of basis from an extinguished corporation.

> **EXAMPLE 17 - 14:** Heather owns all of the shares of Heaco, an S corporation. She also owns all of the shares in Therco, another S corporation. Heaco has been consistently producing taxable income, whereas Therco has sustained losses. Heather has no basis in her Therco shares and has suspended losses of $85,000. Since she is reporting taxable income from Heaco and has been unable to deduct losses from Therco, she has decided to merge the two corporations. If Therco emerges as the surviving corporation, she will clearly be able to use any future income from the corporation to deduct her suspended losses. If Heaco survives, she should also be able to deduct the old Therco losses.

The Proposed Regulations governing the at-risk rules provide an unusual rule when an activity with suspended losses is surrendered in a nontaxable transaction, such as a reorganization. Any suspended loss attaches to the basis in the replacement property. [Proposed Regs. §1.465-67(b)] Suspended passive activity losses receive somewhat different treatment: They are suspended at the shareholder level. A tax-free reorganization would not constitute a taxable disposition and would not allow the shareholder to deduct such losses in the year of the stock transfer. A future disposition of the newly acquired stock, however, should allow the shareholder to deduct all previously suspended passive activity losses. See 1025.11 for discussion of passive activity losses at disposition and 1330.2 for discussion of how the losses are treated when the S election is revoked.

1730.15. Survival of other shareholder attributes after reorganization and QSub election. The IRS has issued Proposed Regulations that clarify the shareholder treatment of prior suspended losses if the target corporation is the subject of a QSub election. The Proposed Regulations state that, in this situation, a shareholder of the target corporation who has unused losses from the target may use the purchaser's post-acquisition basis to deduct the old losses. [Proposed Regs. §1.1361-4(c)]. This treatment is allowed if the target corporation becomes a QSub immediately after acquisition.

> **EXAMPLE 17 - 14a:** Refer to Example 17 - 14. If Heaco acquires Therco in a Type B or Type A reverse triangular merger, Therco's identity would be preserved for nontax purposes. Then Heaco immediately (within 2 months and 15 days) elects to treat Therco as a QSub, on the acquisition date. Heather could then continue to deduct her Therco losses to the extent of her basis in Heaco.

17

1730.16. Reorganizations and §1244 stock. A tax-free reorganization has no effect on the status of §1244 stock, if the stock was issued directly to the shareholders in exchange for property and the corporation that issued the stock survives the reorganization. If, however, the corporation that issued the §1244 stock was terminated in the reorganization, the former holders would not be entitled to a §1244 loss on the disposition of stock received. Even if the former shareholders of the extinguished corporation acquired their stock directly from the surviving corporation, they would not receive §1244 stock—because the stock must be received from the issuing corporation in exchange for property other than stock and securities. [§1244(c)(1)(B)] The only reorganizations in which a holder may receive §1244 stock are Type E recapitalizations and Type F changes in name. [§1244(d)(2); Regs. §1.1244(d)-2(c), §1.1244(d)(3)] See Chapter 14, at 1430., for discussion of §1244.

1730.2. Treatment of target corporation. The target corporation recognizes no gain or loss on the transfer of its property in a merger. A target corporation may be able to realize gain in a Type C or Type D reorganization, but the gain is shifted to the shareholders upon the distribution of any boot received by the target corporation. Liabilities assumed by the acquiring corporation are not treated as boot, except in the case of a Type D reorganization. [§357(a), §357(c)(1)(B)] Similarly, the target corporation recognizes no gain or loss when it distributes acquiring corporation stock to its shareholders. [§361(c)(1)]

The target corporation's existence terminates when it is acquired in a Type A straight merger, a forward triangular merger, or a consolidation. The target corporation's existence continues indefinitely in a Type B reorganization or a Type A reverse triangular merger. A distributing corporation's existence is terminated in a nondivisive Type D reorganization or a divisive D reorganization that is a split-up. (See at 1735.11. for discussion of this rarely used transaction.) There is no target corporation, and therefore no termination of a year, in a Type E or Type F reorganization. In a Type C reorganization, the target corporation's tax history disappears at the time of the transfer of assets to the acquiring corporation, and its existence terminates when it distributes all of its property to its shareholders in complete liquidation.

In a Type A reorganization, when the target is an S corporation its S election continues until the corporation's existence terminates. [Rev. Rul. 64-94, 1964-1 Part 1 CB 317; Rev. Rul. 69-566, 1969-2 CB 165; Rev. Rul. 79-52, 1979-1 CB 283; PLRs 8534077, 8351110, 9350003, 9410022] Therefore, there is no S termination year as discussed in Chapter 13. The corporation's final tax year ends on the date of the merger and may cause acceleration of reporting its final year's income or loss to the shareholders. [§381(b)(1)]

> **EXAMPLE 17 - 15:** Fisco was an S corporation that used a natural business year-end of June 30. On October 1, 1995, Fisco merged into Calco. Fisco's shareholders use the calendar year. For 1995, Fisco's shareholders must report the corporation's income for the taxable year ended June 30, 1995. They must also report Fisco's income for the short year that ends on September 30, 1995.

For reorganizations that occur after August 18, 1993, the LIFO recapture rules may apply, if the target corporation was a C corporation that used the LIFO inventory method. [Regs. §1.1363-2(a)(2)] In this situation, the target corporation must include its LIFO recapture in its taxable income in its final year of existence. The first installment of the tax is due on the due date of the liquidated corporation's final return. [Regs. §1.1363-2(b)] The remaining three installments must be paid on the due dates for the surviving corporation's next three returns. [Regs. §1.1363-2(b)(2)] See Chapter 3, at 320.5., for additional discussion and examples.

1730.3. Treatment of acquiring corporation. The acquiring corporation recognizes no gain or loss on the distribution of its stock or securities. Similarly, in a triangular reorganization, the acquiring corporation recognizes no gain or loss on the distribution of its parent corporation's stock or securities.

All of the assets received from the target corporation keep the same pre-reorganization basis. [§362] There is no adjustment, even if the target corporation's shareholders receive boot and recognize gain in the reorganization.[5] Since the basis to the acquiring corporation has no relationship to the value of property exchanged, §1060 does not govern asset basis.

As a general rule, the acquiring corporation's taxable year does not end on the date of the reorganization. It includes all of its own income or loss from the portion of the taxable year before the reorganization on its tax return, as well as the income of the new combined enterprise after the reorganization.

The surviving corporation preserves many of the extinguished corporation's tax attributes. For example, the extinguished corporation's loss carryovers, methods of accounting, inventory, and depreciation elections will all survive a reorganization, as will any deferred gains from installment sales or involuntary conversions that occurred before the reorganization. [§381(c)]

1730.31. Earnings and profits after the reorganization. By statute, the accumulated earnings and profits of an acquired corporation remain intact after a tax-free reorganization. If both corporations have positive balances, or if both corporations have deficits, the two accounts are merely combined. [§381(c)(2)(A)] This is a routine ruling item. [Cf. PLRs 9721010, 9851040, 9833006.]

To ensure that one corporation with positive earnings and profits cannot eliminate its earnings and profits by combining with another corporation that has a deficit, §381(c)(2) creates a special rule: If either the acquiring corporation or the target corporation has a deficit in accumulated earnings and profits and the other corporation has a positive balance, the two are not combined. [§381(c)(2)(B)]

> **EXAMPLE 17 - 16:** Negco and Posco merged in a Type A straight merger. As of the date of the merger, Negco's accumulated earnings and profits had a deficit of $50,000, whereas Posco had a positive earnings and profits balance of $65,000. Immediately after the merger, the surviving corporation has two accumulated earnings and profits accounts, one with a positive $65,000 balance and the other with a negative $50,000 balance. The identity of the surviving corporation would have no impact on these balances.

If the surviving corporation is a C corporation, it reduces a deficit account by its future earnings and profits. If the survivor is an S corporation, however, the two balances would coexist for the foreseeable future. An election to bypass AAA could reduce the positive balance. Apparently, however, if the corporation intended to rid itself of all its earnings and profits, it would need to distribute the entire positive balance. The negative balance would remain intact.

> **EXAMPLE 17 - 17:** Refer to Example 17 - 16. In a year after the merger, the new corporation faces passive investment income problems. Therefore, it intends to distribute out all of its earnings and profits. The distribution would need to exhaust the entire $65,000 positive balance carried over from Posco. The $50,000 deficit from Negco would remain on the books indefinitely.

1730.32. Accumulated Adjustments Account after the reorganization. The IRS has held in several letter rulings that the Accumulated Adjustments Account (AAA) of a merged corporation survives the reorganization and is available for distributions to shareholders in the surviving corporation. [PLRs 9002051, 9115029, 9115059, 9117055] In 1992, the IRS formalized this position in Proposed Regulations. [Proposed Regs. §1.1368-2(d)(2)] The letter rulings and Proposed Regulations gave no rules to apply when, in a pre-reorganization, one corporation has a positive AAA balance and the other corporation has a negative AAA balance. The Final Regulations take the position that all pre-reorganization AAA balances,

---

[5] A limited exception applies to certain Type D reorganizations.

whether positive, negative, or mixed, are combined into a single account after the reorganization. [Regs. §1.1368-2(d)(2)] Therefore, if two S corporations merge, or combine in a Type C or Type D reorganization, a positive balance in the AAA of one of the corporations offsets a negative balance in the AAA of another corporations.

> **OBSERVATION:** If an S corporation that has a positive AAA intends to combine with an S corporation that has a negative AAA, the parties should plan any distributions carefully before consummating the reorganization. If the corporation with the positive AAA distributes cash or other property before the reorganization, the shareholders will get the benefit of the entire positive AAA. If the distribution occurs after the reorganization and the amount distributed exceeds the post-combination AAA, the shareholders may report dividend income, which could have been avoided if the distribution had occurred before the reorganization.

1730.33. Limitations on survival of attributes. As discussed earlier, §382 limits the ability of C corporations to recognize loss carryforwards and built-in losses following a change in ownership. The same provision applies to a corporation surviving a reorganization, if shareholders of a corporation as it existed before the reorganization have changed their ownership percentages. In the case of a reorganization, the term used for the ownership change is *equity structure shift*. If shareholders who individually owned 5% or more of the corporation's stock before the reorganization alter their percentage in the surviving corporation so that it falls below 50 percentage points ownership in the survivor, an equity structure shift activates the loss limitations.

> **EXAMPLE 17 - 18:** Lossco and Gainco merge on October 19, 1992. Before the reorganization, Louise had owned all of Lossco and Gavin had owned all of the shares of Gainco. After the merger, Louise owns 45% of the surviving corporation and Gavin owns 55%. Any pre-merger losses of Lossco would be limited after the reorganization, since Louise's ownership has fallen from 100% to 45%, a change that exceeds 50 percentage points. Any pre-reorganization losses of Gainco would not be limited by §382, since Gavin's ownership declined by only 45 percentage points. It is immaterial for this purpose whether Gainco or Lossco survived the reorganization. (This Example assumes that there were no other ownership changes in either corporation within the three-year period preceding the reorganization.)

Code §384, a parallel statute to §382, limits the ability of a surviving corporation to utilize preexisting gains of an acquired corporation against preexisting losses of the surviving corporation. Neither §382 nor §384 appears to have any direct applicability to S corporations, which measure their taxable incomes by individual rules. Both §382 and §384 apply solely to corporations and not to individuals. However, the IRS could probably apply the limits of §382 or §384 to an S corporation's measurement of taxable income for the built-in gains tax or passive investment income tax.[6]

The IRS has held, in Regulations §1.1374-5(b) and Regulations §1.1374-8(a), that the limitations of §382 apply to S corporations in the calculation of built-in gains tax. See Chapter 11, at 1145.2., for more detailed discussion.

There is another disallowance rule that may apply to restrict pre-acquisition losses of S corporations following a change in ownership. Code §269 empowers the IRS to disallow any tax benefit that results from an acquisition in which tax avoidance was the principal purpose of the transaction. Application of this rule to an S corporation is unlikely, since shareholders cannot transfer any suspended losses to other persons.

---

[6] In Proposed Regulations §1.1374-2(d), the IRS has taken the position that §382 and §384 apply to S corporations for purposes of the built-in gains tax. See discussion in Chapter 11, at 1110.81.

1730.34. Effect of a reorganization on built-in gains. As Chapter 11 discussed extensively, an S corporation that acquires a C corporation in a reorganization is subject to the built-in gains tax on the assets acquired from the C corporation. [§1374(d)(8)] The Code gives the IRS authority to prescribe legislative Regulations on this issue. [§1374(d)(8)(A)] The Regulations issued under §1374 in 1992 require segregation of the assets acquired by an S corporation in a tax-free reorganization or §332 liquidation from its other assets. [Regs. §1.1374-8] The IRS has consistently ruled that the assets so acquired are subject to the built-in gains tax for 10 years following the acquisition. [PLRs 9011042, 9245004 (TAM), 9309031, 9309033]

The current policy, in essence, is that a corporation that survives a reorganization is subject to no less, and no more, of the built-in gains tax than would have been the case if the reorganization had not taken place. In several of the rulings, which took place in the context of divisive reorganizations, the IRS held that an S corporation that arose from an S election filed before 1987 would not be subject to any built-in gains tax. [PLRs 8806031, 8826015, 8922004, 9117062, 9139012, 9712022] Corporations that filed S elections in 1987 and 1988, but were subject to the transitional rule (as discussed in Chapter 11), were partially exempt from the built-in gains tax. [PLR 9140054]

In one ruling involving a merger, an S corporation acquired two other S corporations and two C corporations in simultaneous mergers. The surviving corporation had filed its election before 1987 and was not subject to the built-in gains tax on any of its assets. The two extinguished S corporations had filed S elections in 1987, but were not entitled to transitional relief. They were subject to the built-in gains tax on the assets they possessed on the date their S elections took effect for the 10-year period following the S elections. [PLR 9117055]

EXAMPLE 17-19: Bigco, an S corporation, acquired all the assets of Littleco, a C corporation, on October 19, 1992. Bigco also acquired all of the assets of Smallco, an S corporation, on the same date. Both acquisitions qualified as Type A mergers. Bigco had always been an S corporation. Smallco was a former C corporation and had an S election in effect from January 1, 1990, until the date of the merger. Pursuant to the statutory language of §1374(d)(8) and the IRS ruling policy, the built-in gains treatment of Bigco after the reorganization should be as follows:

1. Assets held by Bigco on or before October 19, 1992: The corporation should be completely exempt from the built-in gains tax on the disposition of any of these assets.
2. Assets acquired from Littleco: Bigco will be subject to the built-in gains tax on any dispositions of these assets before October 19, 2002. Littleco should compute a hypothetical net unrealized built-in gain as of October 19, 1992, which could limit the built-in gains tax exposure to this amount. This position appears reasonable, but Bigco should seek a ruling to obtain this result.
3. Assets acquired from Smallco: Bigco should be subject to the built-in gains tax on property it received from Smallco, for any disposition occurring before January 1, 2000, the date that Smallco's recognition period would have expired if Smallco had remained in existence. The exposure, however, should be limited to Smallco's net unrealized built-in gains after adjustment for any of Smallco's net recognized built-in gains between January 1, 1990, and October 19, 1992.

OBSERVATION: Any S corporation that acquires property from another corporation in a tax-free reorganization should be prepared to rebut the built-in gains presumption on all dispositions of property for 10 years following the reorganization. Since the corporation is subject to the built-in gains tax, even if only on a portion of its total assets, the presumption of built-in gains will apply.

17

A transfer of assets in a Type F reorganization deserves some attention. In this form of reorganization, the new corporation is treated as a continuation of the old corporation for all tax purposes. The IRS has held that the S election of the old corporation continued, that the Accumulated Adjustments Account of the old corporation continued, that there was no LIFO recapture, and that the built-in gains tax applied to the new corporation only to the extent that it would have applied to the old corporation. [PLRs 9118029, 9123049] LIFO recapture would be required in a Type F reorganization if the extinguished corporation was a C corporation that used LIFO and the new corporation is an S corporation. [Regs. §1.1363-2(a)(2). This rule applies to liquidations that take place after August 18, 1993.]

1730.35. Eligibility for S status after a tax-free reorganization. In many of the rulings cited earlier in this chapter, the IRS held that a surviving S corporation's election did not terminate as a result of a Type A, Type D, or Type F reorganization. However, there can be a question about eligibility for an S election if the surviving corporation is a C corporation that now intends to make an S election. In most cases, if the corporation to be acquired already has an S election in effect, that corporation should be chosen as the corporation to survive the reorganization. The S election will continue unabated and will not require the consent of any shareholders.

If the C corporation survives the merger, it will need to make a new S election [PLR 9731028]. If it can do so effective on the first day of the year that includes the merger, no great harm will be done. If, however, an S election does not take effect until the year after the merger, the results could be dramatic.

> **EXAMPLE 17 - 20:** Cee Corporation, a C corporation, intends to acquire Ess Corporation, an S corporation, in a statutory merger. Ess filed its S election before 1987 and is exempt from the built-in gains tax. At the time of the merger, Ess's basis in its assets is $1,000,000, of which the fair market value is $10,000,000. If Ess survives the merger, the potential built-in gains tax will be limited to the assets transferred from Cee. If Cee survives the merger, however, and is unable to make an S election until the next year, all of its assets, including those acquired from Ess, will be subject to the built-in gains tax.

In other cases, a corporation may have terminated its S election within five years of the merger. It will not be able to make a new election within the five-year period, unless more than 50% of its shares have changed hands since the year of the earlier termination. If a target corporation already has an S election in effect or is able to make an S election that takes effect before the merger, there will be no waiting period.

1730.36. Merger of an S corporation into a limited liability company. Some states permit merger of a corporation into a limited liability company. The tax consequences will depend in part upon the classification of the limited liability company for federal tax purposes. If the limited liability company is treated as a corporation (by electing out of its default status under Regulations §301.7701-3), the merger should be a tax-free reorganization. If the limited liability company is treated as a partnership, the former corporation should be treated as if it liquidated.

In one recent ruling, an S corporation merged into a limited liability company and the limited liability company was classified as a partnership for tax purposes. The merger was treated as a liquidation of the corporation. [PLR 9543017] In another situation an S corporation merged into a limited liability company and the limited liability company was classified as an association for federal tax purposes. In this case the merger was treated as a Type F reorganization. [PLR 9636007]

1735. Divisive reorganizations.

In a divisive reorganization, one corporation is split into two (or more) corporations. Neither the old corporation, the new corporation (or corporations), nor any shareholder recognizes any gain or loss on the transaction. In some cases, the shareholders of the old corporation retain their proportionate ownership in all of the corporations. In other cases, some shareholders retain their ownership of the old corporation and other shareholders surrender stock in the old corporation to receive shares in the new corporation.

The steps involved are as follows:

1. Transfer of assets from the corporation to a subsidiary
2. Distribution of subsidiary stock from the parent corporation to its shareholders

Although the steps are relatively simple, a transaction of this nature may also be characterized as a property dividend. A property dividend is a completely taxable event, but a divisive reorganization is nontaxable. Therefore, it is extremely important to distinguish between the two functionally similar transactions.

> **EXAMPLE 17 - 21:** ABC Corporation forms Newco, a new subsidiary. It transfers property to Newco in exchange for all of Newco's stock. It then distributes all of Newco's stock to its shareholders. If this transaction is not a reorganization, it will be a property distribution. ABC would not recognize any gain or loss on the transfer of property into Newco, because it would qualify as a tax-free transfer under §351. It would, however, recognize gain on the distribution of the Newco stock to its shareholders. The shareholders would treat the fair market value of the Newco stock as a dividend. If this transfer qualified as a reorganization, neither ABC nor its shareholders would recognize any gain.

1735.1. General divisive reorganization rules. Many reorganizations involve the acquisition of one corporation by another. One type of reorganization, however, is used to divide a corporation into two or more entities. This type of reorganization is known as a divisive D reorganization, due to its source, which is §368(a)(1)(D). Under this type of reorganization, a corporation may transfer part of its assets to a newly formed corporation in exchange for a controlling (80%) stock ownership interest. The parent corporation then transfers its stock in the subsidiary to its (parent's) shareholders.

The transfer of property to a subsidiary does not need one of the reorganization provisions to attain tax-free status. That step of the transaction would normally qualify under §351, as discussed in Chapter 14. The real focus of the reorganization provisions is to exempt the transfer of the subsidiary stock from the parent corporation to its shareholders from taxation.

1735.11. Qualifying transactions. There are three varieties of the divisive D reorganization:

- A spin-off
- A split-off
- A split-up

A *spin-off* occurs when shareholders in the old corporation now own shares in both corporations. This typically happens when the shareholders want to remain in business together but divide the business into smaller portions. Limitation of liability and insurance savings are often good business purposes, as well as providing in interest to a key employee [PLR 9826045]. In Figure 17 - 15, which illustrates the first step in a spin-off, the existing corporation transfers property to a subsidiary in exchange for stock.

When the old corporation completes the transfer of assets to the new corporation in exchange for stock, it distributes all of its stock in the new corporation to the shareholders. The transfer is usually pro rata. The transfer of the stock in the new corporation to the shareholders of the old corporation is illustrated in Figure 17 - 16.

When the transfers are complete, the two corporations have become brother–sister corporations. Figure 17-17 illustrates the status of the parties after the reorganization is complete.

Figure 17 - 15: *First step in spin-off.*

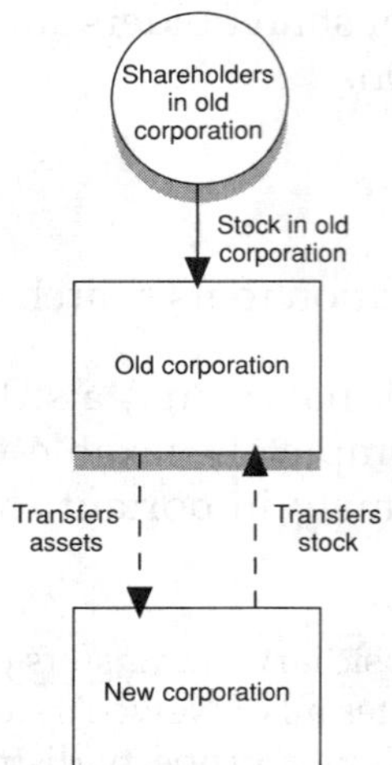

Figure 17 - 16: *Second step in spin-off.*

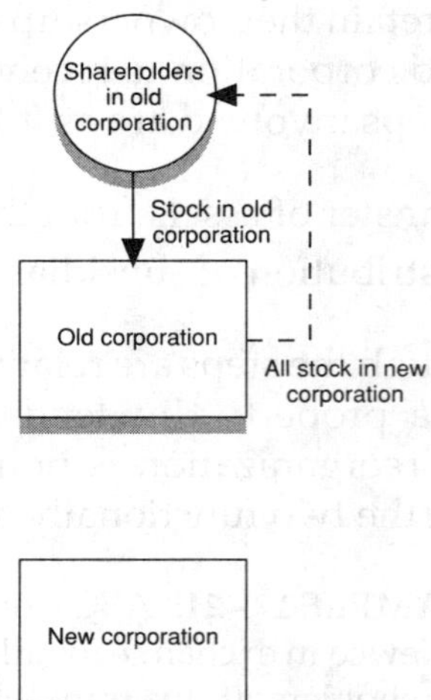

A *split-off* occurs when shareholders want to alter their business relationships. Sometimes this involves new persons joining in the ownership of part of the business; in other cases, the shareholders want to go their separate ways. Figures 17 - 18 through 17 - 20 show the progress of a split-off transaction. In these illustrations it is assumed that two groups of shareholders are dividing the business into separate corporations with separate ownership of each. In the first step, as shown in Figure 17 - 18, the two groups of shareholders own stock in the old corporation. As in a spin-off, the old corporation transfers property to a subsidiary in exchange for a controlling interest in the stock of the subsidiary.

Figure 17 - 19 makes it clear that the major difference between a spin-off and a split-off is in the second step of the transaction. At this stage, some of the shareholders of the old corporation surrender stock in the old corporation and receive stock in the new corporation in its place.

When the split-off is complete, each corporation has its own group of shareholders. Figure 17 - 20 illustrates the relationship of the parties after the split-off is complete.

Figures 17 - 15 through 17 - 20 illustrate the simplest forms of the spin-off and the split-off. Actually, there are many variations, whereby some shareholders divest themselves of their entire interest in one or more of the businesses and others change their percentages of ownership.

One other transaction is covered by §355: the *split-up*, in which the existing corporation transfers all of its assets into two or more subsidiaries, distributes the stock of the subsidiaries, and goes out of existence. The economic consequences are usually the same as for a split-off. A split-up could be used when a corporation wants to divide itself into two or more corporations and simultaneously change its place of incorporation.

Figure 17 - 17: *Relationships after spin-off.*

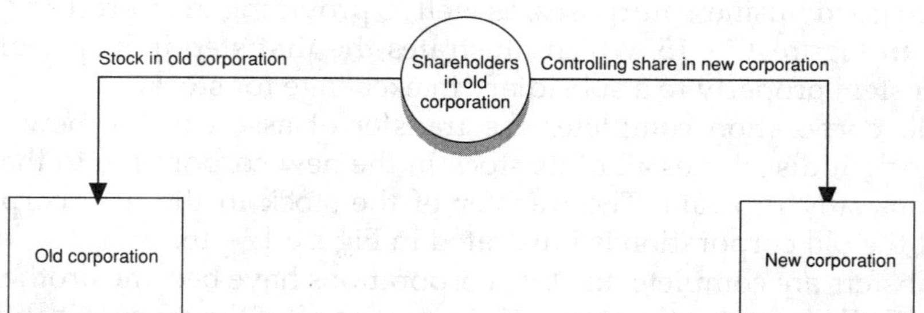

Figure 17 - 18: First step in split-off.

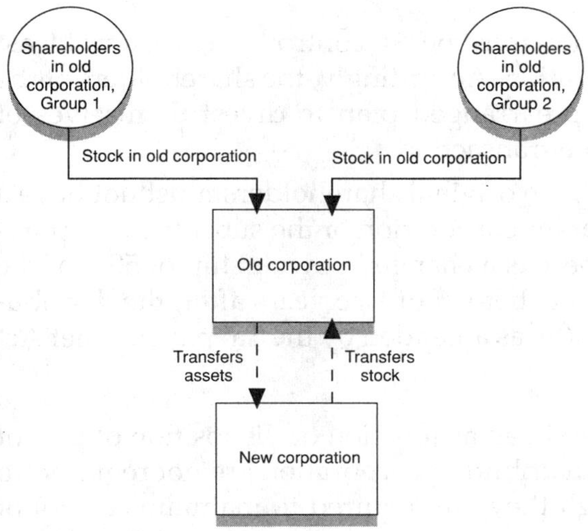

Figure 17 - 19: Second step in split-off.

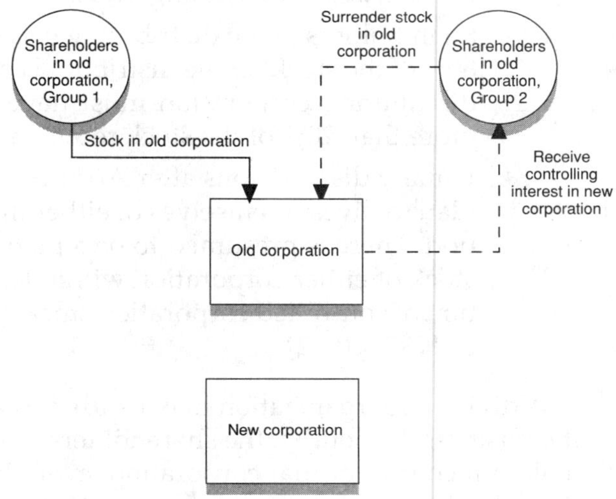

PLANNING TIP: A corporation that plans to use a divisive reorganization before a sale of part of the business must be careful in the transfer of assets to the new subsidiary. The shareholders of the old corporation must continue to control the new corporation, but they do not need to retain their interest in the old corporation. The portion of the business that they intend to sell should be retained in the old corporation, and the portion that they intend to keep should be transferred to the new corporation.

1735.12. Operative provisions of §355. Code §355 provides the exclusive tests for a tax-free division of a corporation. Its requirements can become quite complicated, and a complete discussion of these rules is beyond the scope of this book. But for a transaction to qualify as a divisive reorganization, some essential tests must be noted here:

- The distributing (parent) corporation must have conducted two or more active trades or businesses for at least five years. Furthermore, the corporation may not have acquired either an active trade or an active business in a taxable transaction within the last five years. Each corporation that exists after the transaction must hold at least one of such businesses. [§355(b)]
- The transaction must not be a "device" for distributing earnings and profits. [§355(a)(1)(B)] The IRS interprets this rule as a requirement that the transaction must have a valid non-tax business purpose. [Regs. §1.355-2] The Regulations under §355 contain extensive discussion and examples of the business purpose. As a practical

Figure 17 - 20: Relationships after split-off.

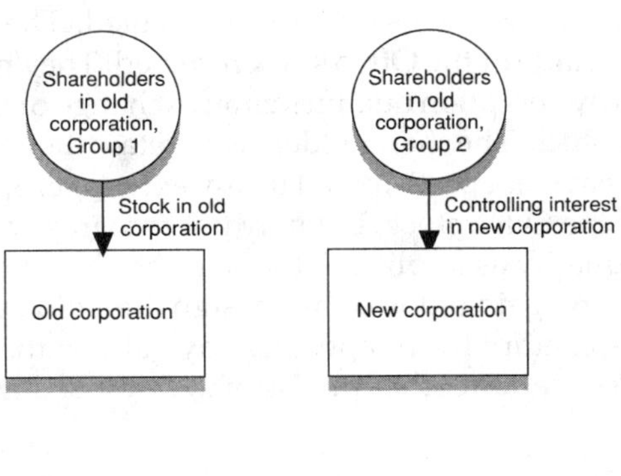

matter, to undertake a corporate division without a favorable ruling from the IRS is probably extremely dangerous.

- Shareholders of the distributing corporation must be "in control" (must own at least 80% of the stock) of the distributed corporation. Accordingly, the shareholders of the distributing corporation must have no prearranged plan to divest themselves of more than 20% of the stock received in the transaction.
- For any distributions after April 16, 1997, the original shareholders must not have a plan to divest themselves of either the parent corporation or the subsidiary corporation. There is presumed to be a plan if there is a change in ownership of 50% of the stock of either corporation within two years before, or two years after, the distribution of controlled corporation stock. [§355(e), as amended by the Taxpayer Relief Act of 1997, §1012]

A divisive reorganization may be used as a step in an acquisition or disposition of part of the business. Generally, the shareholders of the distributing corporation are not required to maintain control of that corporation, even though they are required to maintain control of the subsidiary corporation whose stock they receive in the transaction. (See PLR 9404014, where there was a divisive D reorganization followed by an acquisitive B reorganization of the distributing corporation.) The distributed corporation may also engage in other reorganization transactions following the division, so long as the historic shareholders do not divest of their control. For instance, a corporation created in a divisive reorganization was allowed to acquire another corporation by merger immediately following the divisive reorganization. [PLR 9338037]

1735.13. Tax-free treatment to the shareholders. The shareholders who receive stock in a qualifying division do not report any gain, loss, or income. [§354(a)] They merely assign basis to the shares received. This rule applies to a spin-off, as well as to a split-off and a split-up.

EXAMPLE 17 - 22: Spinco, Inc., creates a wholly owned subsidiary, Offco. Spinco distributes all of its Offco shares to its own shareholders. Each shareholder of Spinco receives one share in Offco for each share in Spinco. No shareholders surrender any Spinco stock. If the transaction does not qualify as a tax-free reorganization, each Spinco shareholder has a dividend equal to the fair market value of the Offco stock received. In addition, Spinco must report any gain if the fair market value of the Offco stock exceeds Spinco's basis in the stock.

If the transaction does qualify as a spin-off, the shareholders will report no dividend income. The shareholders will allocate their former Spinco basis between the Spinco stock retained and the Offco stock received, proportionate to the fair market value of each corporation's stock. Spinco may also be exempt from reporting any gain on the disposition of the Offco stock, although it must meet certain other provisions, discussed below.

EXAMPLE 17 - 23: Assume the same facts as in Example 17 - 22, except that some of Spinco's shareholders surrender their Spinco stock in exchange for Offco stock. Spinco's other shareholders retain their shares in Spinco and receive no stock in Offco. If the transaction does not qualify as a split-off, the shareholders who receive Offco stock in exchange for their Spinco stock will be treated as if their Spinco stock was redeemed. The amount realized on the exchange is the fair market value of the Offco stock received. They must then apply the stock redemption test to see if the redemption qualifies as an exchange or is treated as a distribution with respect to their Spinco stock. The shareholders who retain their Spinco stock will not have a taxable event, since they have not participated in any exchange. Spinco must recognize any gain on the distribution of the Offco stock, but may not recognize any loss.

If the transaction does qualify as a split-off, the shareholders who exchange their Spinco stock for Offco stock report no gain or loss. They assign their old Spinco basis to their Offco shares. Spinco may also be exempt from reporting any gain on the disposition of the Offco stock, although it must meet certain other provisions, discussed at 1735.12.

1735.14. Basis, holding period, and other attributes of stock received. As mentioned above, the recipients of stock in a spin-off, split-off, or split-up apportion basis to the shares received. When a shareholder actually surrenders shares, as in a split-off or a split-up, the basis of shares surrendered becomes the basis of shares received. [§358(a)]

> **EXAMPLE 17 - 24:** Joe and Jenny are two equal shareholders in JJ Corporation. They decide to split the business into two separate corporations. In a qualifying split-off, JJ transfers half of its assets to JN Corporation, a newly formed subsidiary. JJ distributes all of its shares in JN to Jenny, who surrenders all of her stock in JJ. Jenny's basis in her JN stock is the same as her basis in her JJ stock. Joe has not participated in an exchange, and he keeps his basis intact in his JJ shares.

In a spin-off, there may be no actual exchange. In that case, the shareholders allocate basis as if they had all surrendered their old stock and received back the old stock and the new stock simultaneously. [§358(c)] Each shareholder then allocates basis between the old stock and the new stock. [§358(b)] The allocation is made according to the relative fair market values of the stock held in the various corporations after the spin-off. [Regs. §1.358-2(a)(2)]

> **EXAMPLE 17 - 25:** Karl held shares in Karko. His basis was $1,000. Karko distributed stock in Varco to Karl in a spin-off. Karl surrendered no Karko stock. At the time of the spin-off, the fair market value of the Karko stock was $4,000 and the fair market value of the Varco stock was $1,000. Karl allocated his basis as follows:

Stock retained in Karko [($4,000/$5,000) x $1,000]	$ 800
Stock received in Varco [($1,000/$5,000) x $1,000]	200
Total basis	$1,000

The holding period of any stock received includes the holding period of the stock by which the basis was determined. [§1223(1)] If any stock held in the old corporation was §1244 stock to the holder, the stock retained in the same corporation keeps its §1244 attribute. The new stock received, however, is not §1244 stock. [Regs. §1.1244(c)-1(d)(2)] See Chapter 14.

1735.15. Receipt of securities in a split-off or a split-up. A security holder who gives up securities in connection with a split-off or a split-up may receive securities in a new corporation as nonrecognition property. Although the Code does not define a *security*, case law has held that a 10-year debt does qualify as a security. [*Camp Wolters Enterprises, Inc., v. Commissioner*, 56-1 USTC 9314 (5th Cir.)] To qualify as nonrecognition property, however, the securities received, as well as those surrendered, must be from corporations that are parties to the reorganization. If the face amount of the securities received exceeds the face amount of those surrendered, the excess principal received is treated as boot. [§356(d)(2)(C)]

1735.16. Boot received by shareholders. If any shareholder receives any property other than stock in a controlled corporation in an otherwise tax-free corporate division, he or she must report gain. [§356(a)(1)] The gain may be a dividend or a capital gain, depending on the shareholder's continued relationship with the distributing corporation. [§356(a)(2)] (The Regulations under §356 require testing for dividend equivalency in the same manner as a stock redemption.) In a spin-off, any shareholder who receives boot would normally report the gain from the boot as a dividend, to the extent of the distributing corporation's earnings and profits. A shareholder who receives boot in a split-off after surrendering all of his or her shares in the distributing corporation may report a dividend, if the shareholder's surrender of distributing corporation's stock passes one of the redemption tests for sale or exchange treatment discussed earlier in this chapter.

No shareholder may report a loss due to the receipt of any property in a tax-free corporate division. [§356(c)] The topic of boot received in connection with a tax-free reorganization is discussed earlier in this chapter.

1735.17. Taxability of the distributing corporation. The distributing corporation actually makes two transfers:

1. *Transfer of property to the controlled corporation.* The distributing corporation usually recognizes no gain on this transfer, unless the basis of property transferred to the distributing corporation is less than the amount of the liabilities taken by the controlled corporation. See Chapter 14 for a discussion of the transfer of liabilities under §351.
2. *Transfer of the shares of the controlled corporation to the shareholders.* In general, the distributing corporation recognizes no gain or loss on this step. There is one important exception, however: If the distributing corporation gives any shares to a person who, by purchase, has acquired a 50% or greater interest in the distributing corporation within the past five years, the distributing corporation must recognize gain, but not loss, on the transfer to that shareholder. [§355(d)]

1735.18. Effect on the distributing corporation's earnings and profits. In general, a corporation's earnings and profits, as they existed at the time of a reorganization, are allocated to the surviving corporation or corporations. [§381(c)(2)(A)] In the case of a spin-off, split-off, or split-up, however, there are at least two corporations to share in the earnings and profits as they existed before the reorganization. The Regulations provide that the earnings and profits are allocated among the surviving corporations proportionate to the fair market value of assets transferred. [Regs. §1.312-10(a)] The proportion allocated to each corporation is the fair market value of assets, less the liabilities allocated to each corporation, divided by the fair market value of all assets, less all liabilities, as they existed immediately before the division. A deficit in earnings and profits is not allocated to any of the new corporations; it remains with the distributing corporation. [Regs. §1.312-10(c)]

1735.2. Applicability to S corporations. An S corporation is subject to all of the Subchapter C rules regarding tax-free reorganizations. Before 1997, this presented a serious potential drawback. The distributing corporation had to own at least 80% of the controlled corporation immediately before the distribution. Therefore, the two corporations had to be members of an affiliated group between the time of the transfer of property by the distributing corporation to the controlled corporation and the transfer of the controlled organization's shares to the distributing organization's shareholders. Such connection with an affiliated group was prohibited by §1361(b)(2)(A). Thus the distributing corporation either lost its S election or was requested to secure a temporary waiver of disqualification from the IRS.

The Senate Finance Committee reports on the Small Business Job Protection Act of 1996 indicate that Congress understood the legitimate need of business owners "to separate different trades or businesses in different corporate entities." [R.R. Rep 104-586, p. 271] At times, such needs are best served by parent–subsidiary or brother–sister arrangements. Thus, for taxable years beginning after December 31, 1996, an S corporation is permitted to own 80% or more of the stock of a C corporation. The distributing corporation in a divisive reorganization is no longer required to obtain a waiver from the IRS to avoid losing its S election.

17

Further, the new rules allow an S corporation to own a "qualified subchapter S subsidiary." (See discussion in Chapter 14, at 1435.4.) Because this type of entity is new, it is not certain how the new rules will affect a corporation planning a divisive reorganization. Anyone contemplating such a transaction should be alert for IRS instructions in this area.

The new provisions related to stock ownership by S corporations merely put into law long-standing IRS policy. In the past, the IRS has consistently ruled that S corporations can engage in divisive D reorganizations [PLRs 9821054, 9823052, 9823039]. See below, at 1735.21. and 1735.22., for further discussion of the IRS's previous position.

1735.21. Momentary ownership problems. Before 1997, S corporations could not own 80% or more of the stock of another corporation. That same 80% is the minimum control necessary to make a subsidiary an eligible candidate for a divisive reorganization. On the surface, these two mutually exclusive rules would make it impossible for an S corporation to participate in a divisive reorganization. The IRS frequently ruled that S corporations could be parties to divisive reorganizations, under the doctrine of momentary ownership. [Rev. Rul. 71-266, 1971-1 CB 262; Rev. Rul. 70-232, 1970-1 CB 177; Rev. Rul. 64-94, 1964-1 CB (Part 1) 317, GCM 39768 (1988); Rev. Rul. 72-320, 1972-1 CB 270, GCM 37677 (1978); Rev. Rul. 79-52, 1979-1 CB 283; PLRs 9739014, 9746047]

1735.22. Eligibility of new corporation for S status. Since 1997, affiliation is no longer an issue. There still may be a problem with the subsidiary corporation created to effect the division, however. Although an S corporation can be the 100% shareholder of a qualified Subchapter S subsidiary, it cannot be a shareholder in another S corporation, per se. Thus there may be a question as to whether the new corporation will be eligible to be an S corporation in its first taxable year. Under prior law, the IRS allowed the initial ownership of the new corporation to be disregarded, so the new corporation was eligible to be an S corporation from its inception, and the distributing corporation did consent to the new corporation's S election. [PLRs 9140054, 9338037, 9338038, 9340006, 9344022, 9344034, 9350002, 9350039, 9351038, 9402029, 9403031, 9404014, 9414016, 9712022, 9713020, 9730014, 9730015, 9730016, 9730025]

The IRS has waived the waiting period for a former QSub whose shares were distributed to shareholders of its former parent in a divisive reorganization. [PLR 9823016] In addition, the Proposed Regulations governing QSub corporations allow free conversion between S corporation status and QSub status if there is no intervening time in which the corporation is a C corporation. [Proposed Regs. §1.1361-5(d)(2)]

1735.23. Allocation of equity accounts. As discussed above, a C corporation must allocate its earnings and profits to the corporations that exist after a divisive reorganization. The IRS has held that an S corporation's AEP must be allocated between the distributing corporation and the controlled corporation on the basis of the fair market value of assets held by the corporations immediately after the reorganization. [Regs. §1.312-10(a); PLRs 8806036, 8810045, 9302020, 9303021, 9306017, 9310038, 9312019, 9312025, 9318024, 9319016, 9319018, 9319041, 9320009, 9321006] Until 1992 [Regs. §1.1368-2(d)(3)], however, the IRS had been silent on the allocation of the distributing corporation's AAA in a divisive reorganization.

In 1994, the IRS issued Regulations that deal with the allocation of AAA between the corporations in a divisive reorganization. The Regulations provide no new and different rules for S corporations, but they refer to the method used to allocate earnings and profits. [Regs. §1.1368-2(d)(3)] Therefore, an S corporation that engages in a divisive reorganization must allocate both its AAA and its AEP between the surviving corporations in proportion to the fair market value of assets held by each. [Regs. §1.312-10(a)] Apparently, a negative AAA balance is not allocated between the surviving corporations, but would remain with the original corporation.[7]

---

[7] Regulations §1.1368-2(d)(3) refers to Regulations §1.312-10(a) for the manner of allocation. Regulations §1.312-10(a) holds that a negative balance in earnings and profits remains with the original corporation.

The Regulations do not expressly provide a means for determining the AAA balance that exists at the time of a division. Presumably, the most logical approach would be to follow the same rules as those used to calculate a corporation's AAA at the time of a stock redemption, with two exceptions:

1. If the calculation resulted in a negative AAA balance at the time of the division, it would not be allocated between the two corporations.
2. The parent should be required to calculate its AAA as of the date of division by closing its books on that date. In other words, post-division activity of the parent should not have any effect on the AAA allocated at the time of the division.

EXAMPLE 17 - 26: MJK Corporation is an S corporation that uses the calendar year. On September 21, 1992, the corporation transferred 35% of its assets (fair market value) to Tenco, a newly formed subsidiary, in exchange for all of Tenco's shares, which MJK immediately distributed to its shareholders. MJK had secured a ruling from the IRS that allowed it to momentarily own all of Tenco's stock and that approved the status of the transactions as a spin-off. The assets transferred to Tenco had a basis of $150,000 and were subject to liabilities of $40,000.

On December 31, 1991, MJK had a balance of $60,000 in its AAA and $80,000 in its AEP. Between January 1, 1992, and September 21, 1992, MJK's taxable income was $45,000, and the corporation distributed $55,000 to its shareholders. The corporation did not make an election to distribute AEP before AAA in 1992. On September 21, 1992, the corporation's equity account balances were:

AAA	
Balance on 12/31/91	$60,000
Income through 9/21/92	45,000
Distributions through 9/21/92	(55,000)
Balance on 9/21/92	$50,000
AEP	$80,000

The allocation of equity accounts between MJK and Tenco would be:

	AAA	*AEP*
Allocated to Tenco (35%)	$17,500	$28,000
Retained by MJK	32,500	52,000
Total	$50,000	$80,000

Before the publication of Proposed Regulations §1.1368-2, the IRS allocated the old corporation's AAA in the same manner as the corporation's accumulated earnings and profits. [PLR 9321006] Between the issuance of Proposed Regulations §1.1368-2 and the adoption of Final Regulations §1.1368-2, the IRS would not rule consistently on this issue. In one ruling, the IRS specifically declined to rule on the allocation. [PLR 9306017] In many recent rulings, the IRS was silent on the allocation. [PLRs 9302020, 9303021, 9310038, 9312019, 9312025, 9318024, 9319016, 9319018, 9319041, 9320009] In one ruling, the entire problem of

allocations was not even mentioned. [PLR 9304006] The Final Regulation on the matter, however, provides sufficient authority to allocate AAA based on the relative fair market values of assets transferred to, or retained by, the various corporations. Apparently there is no allocation of a shareholder's PTI account in a tax-free division, since PTI is reduced only by distributions that would otherwise be treated as dividends. (See discussion in Chapter 15, at 1515.35., and in Regulations §1.1375-4(b).) The IRS has held that the PTI of the distributing corporation stays with that particular corporation and no portion is assigned to the controlled corporation. [PLR 8810045] If a shareholder who has a PTI account surrenders all of his or her stock in a split-off, the shareholder's PTI account should be closed to paid-in capital.

1735.24. Accounting for the transactions. The allocation of equity accounts is based on the fair market value of the assets, whereas the allocation of assets is made according to the tax basis. As a consequence, the accounting for the transactions is somewhat confusing. The formation of the subsidiary, at the moment in which it is entirely owned by the parent corporation, is relatively straightforward. In this entry, the parent corporation merely accounts for the transfer of assets and liabilities. The accounting for the distribution of the stock in the subsidiary to the shareholders requires a second entry, in which the parent corporation should reduce its capital stock, AAA, earnings and profits, and book retained earnings to reflect the distribution. The adjustment to book retained earnings would have no tax significance, per se, but is needed to keep the parent corporation's accounts in balance. Example 17 - 27 illustrates the accounting entries for both corporations to reflect the spin-off.

EXAMPLE 17 - 27: Refer to Example 17 - 26. Also assume that MJK's capital stock account on September 21, 1992, was $20,000 and that MJK had no paid-in capital. MJK would account for the spin-off in the following manner.

1. Accounting for formation of Tenco.

Liabilities transferred to Tenco	$40,000	
Investment in Tenco	110,000	
Assets transferred to Tenco		$150,000

2. Accounting for the distribution of Tenco stock to the shareholders.

AAA	$17,500	
AEP (retained earnings)	28,000	
Capital stock (35%)	7,000	
Book retained earnings	57,500	
Investment in Tenco		$110,000

Note that the reduction of book retained earnings is necessary to keep the entry in balance. From this point forward, there will be a permanent difference in MJK's book and tax retained earnings accounts. Tenco's accounting for the transaction would be:

Assets	$150,000	
Liabilities		$40,000
AAA	17,500	
AEP (retained earnings)		28,000
Capital stock		7,000
Paid-in capital	57,500	

OBSERVATION: The rules for allocation of equity accounts do not depend on whether the new corporation makes an S election. Therefore, it appears that the old corporation's AAA is assigned proportionately to the new corporation, even if the new corporation does not make an S election. Presumably, if the new corporation does not make an S election it would have a post-termination transition period in which it could distribute its allocable portion of the old corporation's AAA. A letter ruling from the IRS would be advisable if the new corporation wanted to achieve this result.

1735.25. Built-in gains problems after the division. As discussed in Chapter 11, an S corporation that receives property in a tax-free reorganization may be subject to the built-in gains tax on the property it receives. [§1374(d)(8)] The rule should apply to both divisive reorganizations and acquisitive reorganizations. The built-in gains taint, however, covers only those assets received from a C corporation. The IRS has held in several letter rulings that the new corporation resulting from a division is subject to no more, and no less, potential built-in gains tax than would have been the case if the assets had remained with the parent corporation.When the distributing corporation was already subject to the built-in gains tax, the new corporation will also be subject to the tax. The new corporation's recognition period is measured from the date on which the old corporation's S election took effect. [PLRs 9321006, 9338037, 9338038, 9344022, 9414016, 9441024, 9539017, 199907023, 199908010, 199913002] In one ruling the IRS declined to issue an opinion on the built-in gains problems.[8] [PLR 9319041]

EXAMPLE 17 - 28: Oneco was a C corporation through 1990. Its S election took effect for its taxable year beginning January 1, 1991. On August 4, 1997, Oneco formed a wholly owned subsidiary, Twoco. It transferred property to Twoco and immediately distributed all of the Twoco stock to Oneco shareholders in a transaction that qualified as a divisive reorganization. Twoco elected S status for its taxable years beginning August 4, 1997. The IRS will likely rule that Twoco's recognition period for the assets it acquired from Oneco will end on December 31, 2000, exactly 10 years after Oneco's S election took effect.

If the old corporation filed its S election before 1987 (when the Tax Reform Act of 1986 went into effect) and then transferred property to a new corporation in a divisive reorganization, the new corporation is not subject to the built-in gains tax. [PLRs 8806031, 8826015, 8922004, 9117062, 9139012, 9306017, 9310038, 9318024, 9319016, 9319018, 9437017, 9543039, 9544016, 199915031] The IRS has held that when the parent corporation filed its S election in 1987 and qualified for partial relief from the built-in gains tax, the newly formed corporation would be entitled to the same relief. [Tax Reform Act of 1986, §633] (See discussion in Chapter 11.) Accordingly, the subsidiary formed in the reorganization, which filed an immediate S election, was subject to the built-in gains tax, but only on the ordinary assets. Since the parent would not be subject to the built-in gains tax on any of its capital or §1231 assets, those properties that had been transferred to the new corporation were not subject to the built-in gains tax. [PLR 9140054] In addition, the new corporation's recognition period was measured from the date on which the old corporation's S election took effect.

EXAMPLE 17 - 29: Oldco has been an S corporation since its inception. Oldco secures a favorable ruling allowing a divisive reorganization. Oldco transfers property to Newco in exchange for all of Newco's stock. On the same day that Oldco transfers all of the Newco stock to Oldco shareholders, Newco files an S election. Newco will not be subject to the built-in gains tax, since it has not acquired any property from a C corporation in a tax-free reorganization.

EXAMPLE 17 - 30: Assume the same facts as in Example 17 - 29, except that Oldco filed its S election in 1988 to take effect on January 1, 1989. Pursuant to the transitional rules under §633 of the Tax Reform Act of 1986, Oldco was exempt from the built-in gains tax on all of its capital and §1231 assets. Newco will be exempt from the built-in gains tax on the capital and §1231 assets it receives from Oldco. Newco will be subject to the built-in gains tax on any ordinary gains, to the extent they would have been subject to the built-in gains tax if they had been retained by Oldco. The parties should be able to get the IRS to rule that Newco's

[8] The ruling does not state why there was no opinion on this issue. Perhaps the taxpayer did not request a ruling on this point or did not provide sufficient information to the IRS.

recognition period will end on December 31, 1998, the same day Oldco's recognition period expires.

OBSERVATION: When an S corporation that is subject to the built-in gains tax is divided in a reorganization, the built-in gains taint stays with each corporation. Although none of the rulings indicates the allocation method used between the two corporations, it is probably based on the specific assets transferred. Thus, the corporation should take care not to give all assets with built-in gains to one corporation and all assets with built-in losses to another corporation. The corporation with the loss assets would probably never be subject to the tax. The corporation with the gain property might have no built-in losses to offset its taxable built-in gains. None of the rulings to date has given any indication as to how the pre-reorganization net unrealized built-in gain is to be allocated among the surviving corporations.

1735.26. Other issues following division. As discussed above, each shareholder who receives stock as a result of a divisive reorganization assigns a substituted basis to the shares received. Certain other attributes, however, have no statutory rules. For example, a shareholder may have had losses in excess of basis before the reorganization. If a shareholder in the distributing corporation surrenders stock for which he or she had losses in excess of basis, there may be a concern about the ability to use income from the new corporation against losses in excess of basis of the old corporation. The Code literally treats a loss in excess of basis as a loss incurred by the corporation in the succeeding taxable year with respect to that shareholder. [§1366(d)(2)] In Proposed Regulations, the IRS allows a shareholder who has suspended losses on an extinguished corporation to use post-reorganization income to free the suspended losses. [Proposed Regs. §1.1366-2(c)]

EXAMPLE 17 - 31: Leroy was a shareholder in Losco, an S corporation. In 1999, Leroy's portion of Losco's loss exceeded his basis in Losco stock and debt. In 2000, Losco engaged in a divisive reorganization in which Leroy exchanged all of his Losco stock for shares in Newco. In 2000, Newco reports taxable income. Proposed Regulation §1.1366-2(c) allows Leroy to deduct his 1999 Losco loss against the 2000 income of Newco.

If the distributing corporation has changed its method of accounting within the three years prior to the division, it may have an unamortized adjustment under §481. The IRS has ruled that there was no acceleration of this adjustment at the time of a split-off, because the corporation was continuing its prior trade or business. However, there was no allocation of the adjustment to the new corporation, and the original corporation was required to continue to report all of this adjustment on its own returns. [PLR 9843016]

1735.27. Alternative to a spin-off. The brief discussion of divisive reorganizations contained in this book does not begin to cover all of the complexities involved in obtaining a ruling on a divisive reorganization. Since the transactions are so similar in substance to a dividend or stock redemption, undertaking one of these reorganizations without a letter ruling is extremely risky. As an alternative, an S corporation that wants to divide its business may consider another approach. For example:

1. An S corporation may transfer some of its assets to a subsidiary corporation in which it owns less than 80%. If it coordinates its property transfers with those of other shareholders in the subsidiary corporation, the transaction may be tax-free under §351. See Chapter 14 for discussion. The principal advantage over a divisive reorganization is that this transaction does not need to meet the tests of separate trade or business, or any of the other qualifications discussed at 1735.12.

17

Previously, one of the principal disadvantages of this option was that the newly formed corporation had to a C corporation from its inception, since the S corporation held at least some of the stock. The shareholders would not be able to exchange stock in the S corporation for stock in the new corporation without a complete round of taxation. Therefore, this structure was not a good substitute for a split-off or split-up. It is uncertain how the provisions of the Small Business Job Protection Act of 1996 will affect this type of transaction. Practitioners must be alert to developments in this area.

2. An S corporation may transfer assets to a partnership. In one recent ruling, an S corporation transferred some of its assets to a partnership whose other partners were all shareholders in the S corporation. [PLR 9238034] The IRS ruled that it would not disregard the existence of the S corporation and the partnerships as separate entities. (See discussion of Revenue Ruling 94-43, 1994-27 IRB 8, in Chapter 14 at 1435.1.) In many states, the "partnership" could be structured as a limited liability company, so that no member would have unlimited personal liability for any debts of the business.

   Structuring the transaction in this manner avoids the need to comply with the §355 tests, as discussed at 1735.12. It may introduce some complexities of its own, since the partnership will need to comply with all of the partnership rules for allocation of income and deductions.

1735.3. Disposal of existing subsidiary. A corporate division under §355 can be accomplished without a reorganization, per se. If the parent corporation owns at least 80% of the subsidiary and distributes at least 80% of the subsidiary stock to its shareholders, there is no gain or loss recognized, in the same manner as a reorganization. The transaction must meet all of the requirements of §355.

To date, there has been no history of this transaction involving S corporations, since the basic structure is that of an affiliated group of corporations. Recall that S corporations could not be members of an affiliated group before 1997.

1735.31. Subsidiary C corporation. It would seem reasonable that an S corporation could dispose of a subsidiary C corporation under §355 without treating the transaction as a reorganization. If the transaction did not meet the requirements of §355, the S corporation would treat the distribution as a property distribution. If the parent S corporation had no earnings and profits, and the shareholders had sufficient basis, there might be no reason for the transaction to qualify under §355, since the distribution would not be taxable to the shareholders under §1368. If the value of the subsidiary stock exceeded its basis to the parent corporation, however, the parent corporation would be required to recognize gain under §311(b). The parent corporation would not be able to recognize any loss. [§311(a)]. See Chapter 7. If the transaction qualified under §355, the parent corporation would recognize no gain or loss on the distribution of subsidiary stock to its shareholders.

1735.32. Qualified Subchapter S Subsidiary. Any disposition of stock in a QSub would need to be treated as a reorganization in order to qualify under §355. Since the QSub was treated as a nonentity during its term as a QSub, apparently it would be treated as an entirely new corporation for the §355 rules.

17

> **CAUTION:** The statute prohibits a former QSub from becoming a QSub of a standalone S corporation for five years following termination of its QSub status. However, Proposed Regulations allow a former QSub to immediately become an S corporation or a QSub of another S corporation. See Chapter 5, at 525.7. Also see the rulings discussed above at 1735.22.

1735.4. Limits on using a division to qualify for the S election. A corporation may use a tax-free division without a reorganization. A reorganization is necessary only when the corporation transfers property to another corporation and then distributes the controlled corporation's stock to the parent corporation's shareholders. A corporation may be able to transfer shares of an existing subsidiary, in which the parent already owns at least 80% of the stock, in a spin-off, split-off, or split-up. At first glance, this strategy might appear to be an ideal approach to qualify a C corporation for an S election, especially if its ownership of the subsidiary corporation is its only violation of the S corporation eligibility rules. The IRS, however, has required various C corporations to represent that neither the distributing corporation nor the controlled corporation will make an S election if the corporations that exist before the division are not already eligible for S corporation status. [PLRs 9037051, 9038043, 9039028, 9041077, 9137028, 9304018, 9305005, 9307016, 9307020, 9308026, 9335018, 9336023, 9337031, 9338019, 9341027, 9343022, 9344033, 9345043, 9346016, 9346017, 9347023, 9351020, 9409032, 9410043, 9410046, 9414037, 9414049, 9420020, 9420021, 9420022, 9420023, 9420024, 9427010, 9732026, 9732027, 9733012, 9733018, 9734033, 9736027, 9738017, 9739014, 9739019, 9745012, 9750049, 9750065, 9752027, 9752060, 9801032, 9804009, 9804034, 9804037, 9805033, 9810010, 9810012, 9814041, 9818015, 9818016, 9818017, 9819044, 9819035, 9826044, 9823040, 9823046, 9833006, 9843016, 9851040]

1740. Practice aids.

This chapter contains three checklists as practice aids. Checklist 17 - 1 (relating to the target corporation) and Checklist 17 - 3 (relating to the surviving corporation) should be useful guides in planning an acquisitive reorganization. Checklist 17 - 3 provides a similar list of reminders in anticipation of a divisive reorganization.

Checklist 17-1: Reorganization—Target

	Yes	*No*	*N/A*
Form of reorganization	______	______	______
Business purpose	______	______	______
State merger laws reviewed (if applicable)	______	______	______
Continuity of business	______	______	______
Selection of surviving corporation	______	______	______
§1244 stock	______	______	______
Basis	______	______	______
Suspended shareholder losses	______	______	______
Current S election	______	______	______
Fiscal year	______	______	______
Suspended shareholder losses	______	______	______
Amount of boot to be received	______	______	______
Compliance with Rev. Proc. 77-37	______	______	______
Compliance with Nelson rule	______	______	______
Treatment of boot	______	______	______
Redemption equivalency test	______	______	______
Amount of AAA	______	______	______
Amount of AEP	______	______	______
S election intact through merger date	______	______	______
Momentary ownership waiver (if completed before 1997)	______	______	______
Qualification of survivor as S corporation	______	______	______

17

Copyright © 2000 by Harcourt, Inc. All rights reserved.

Checklist 17-2: Reorganization—Survivor

	Yes	*No*	*N/A*
Form of reorganization			
Business purpose			
State merger laws reviewed (if applicable)			
Continuity of business			
Selection of surviving corporation			
§1244 stock			
Basis			
Suspended shareholder losses			
Current S election			
Fiscal year			
Suspended shareholder losses			
Amount of boot to be paid			
Amount permitted by type			
Compliance with Rev. Proc. 77-37			
Compliance with Nelson rule			
Treatment of boot			
Redemption equivalency test			
Effect on AAA			
Effect on AEP			
S election intact after reorganization date			
Surviving corporation meets all eligibility requirements (See checklists in Chapter 2.)			
Post-reorganization AAA			
Post-reorganization AEP			
Post-reorganization PTI			
Post-reorganization built-in gains exposure			
Need for separate asset ledgers			

17

Copyright © 2000 by Harcourt, Inc. All rights reserved.

Checklist 17-3: Divisive reorganization considerations

	Applicable (Yes/No)	*Completed (Date)*
Form of transaction		
Spin-off		
Split-off		

	Applicable (Yes/No)	*Completed (Date)*
Split up		
Disposition of 5-year owned business		
Retention of 5-year owned business		
Business purpose		
Request ruling for momentary ownership waiver (to assure new corporation's eligibility)		
Allocate AAA		
Allocate AEP		
Trace built-in gains property		
S election for new corporation		

17

Copyright © 2000 by Harcourt, Inc. All rights reserved.

ESTATE PLANNING CONSIDERATIONS

Contents

1800. Overview.

All individuals with substantial wealth need to be concerned about their financial affairs at the time of death. Individuals who do not expect to have more than $625,000[1] to leave their heirs probably will not have any substantial worries about estate taxes, but any individual who anticipates that his or her estate may exceed that amount should plan carefully. The objective is to leave the maximum possible amount of wealth to one's family, or other chosen beneficiaries, and reduce the amount that will go to taxes.

This chapter discusses the tax planning environment of the shareholder in an S corporation, with some coverage of estate planning considerations in general, and also provides a brief overview of the federal estate and gift tax system. Mainly, however, it covers techniques that may enhance the value of the S corporation interest when it passes from a shareholder to his or her heirs upon the shareholder's death.

Preserving the wealth of the current owner of stock in an S corporation is the foremost concern of this chapter. Certainly, estate and gift taxes are not always the primary concern; prudent investment, diversification, insurance protection, and other factors may be much more important than the taxes themselves. These factors, however, are of secondary importance in this book. This chapter, like the rest of the *S Corporation Taxation Guide*, is concerned with helping the S corporation shareholder comply with, and plan for, federal tax problems.

The chapter assumes that an S corporation is the client's primary source of wealth, or is at least so significant a source that it merits careful attention. The chapter also assumes that the client wants to retain an interest in the S corporation throughout his or her lifetime or wants to transfer his or her interest in the S corporation to other family members. Upon his or her death, the client may want the shares to go to family members or to other persons or entities. If the shares go to other persons or entities, presumably the client wants the family to receive adequate compensation in liquid assets.

If these are not the shareholder's objectives, he or she should consider disposing of his or her interest through one of the techniques discussed in Chapters 15 and 16. The transactions explored in those chapters could be relevant for any person who has decided to get out of a particular business.

> **CAUTION:** Several of the strategies discussed in this chapter require the use of insurance polices. This book does not purport to discuss the economic considerations involved in purchasing insurance; nor does it endorse any type of policy or any provider.

1810. Family financial planning objectives, in general.

The family financial planning objectives of a shareholder in an S corporation are quite simple: The current shareholder wants to be able to enjoy as much wealth as possible during his or her lifetime, while planning to leave as much wealth as possible to the desired successors. Usually, those successors are the shareholder's spouse and children, although there may be others; religious and educational institutions often receive bequests, or if a person has no close family, charitable organizations may receive the entire estate. In this chapter, however, it is assumed that the shareholder is concerned primarily with the welfare of a surviving spouse and children.

---

[1] As of this writing, individuals who leave less than $600,000 at death are unlikely to have significant estate tax problems. This amount is explained at 1725.23.

The tax professional should first be aware of the client's wishes. No matter how carefully it is drawn up, a tax plan that gets the wealth to the wrong place is unlikely to satisfy a client. Accordingly, the tax advisor must be familiar with the client's circumstances. Some plans are appropriate for a more traditional family structure, where the primary wage earner owns a business that provides a substantial portion of the family's income, and his or her main concern is the well-being of a spouse and young children. If a client has a spouse or children who intend to operate the business after the client's death, the plan may be different. Still another plan would be required for a client who has children from multiple marriages.

The client's age also may dictate key aspects of the estate plan. A client who is at or near retirement may want to get out of the business entirely. He or she may want to liquidate all business holdings, or may want to turn the business over to family members. If no family members have the disposition or the ability to operate the business successfully, the shareholder will probably want the business to be sold at the time of his or her death and the family left with liquid assets sufficient to provide for their well-being.

An estate plan typically involves determining which transfers will wait until the planner's death, and which transfers will take place during his or her lifetime. Certain nontax considerations, such as transferring property to specified heirs or avoiding probate, may dominate the decision, and this book focuses upon the federal tax consequences of those considerations. A gratuitous transfer of wealth involves a federal transfer tax; property that a person owned at the time of his or her death is subject to the federal estate tax; property transferred by gift is subject to the federal gift tax. This chapter will address certain planning devices that are designed to reduce the burden of these taxes.

Sometimes transfers take place directly. For example, a parent might give shares in an S corporation directly to his or her children, or leave property directly to a spouse. Or the transfer may be made indirectly, through a trust. Transfer of property via a trust is necessary in certain circumstances—for example, when the beneficiary is young or is mentally disabled. In other situations, the current owner of the property might not want a young or irresponsible person to have complete control over the property. Used properly, a trust can help to achieve many family financial planning objectives, so trusts are extremely important devices in estate and gift planning.

The income and estate tax problems involving trusts form a complex field in their own right. Again, this chapter points out the planning opportunities and pitfalls of trusts unique to S corporations. As discussed in Chapter 2, there are restrictions on the types of persons and entities eligible to hold shares in S corporations. Chapter 13 describes numerous situations in which improper use of trusts has resulted in inadvertent termination of the S election. Therefore, Chapter 18 will show how the shareholder can maintain the corporation's S status when using a trust to transfer shares to another person.

1810.1. Transfer of control to family members. The tax advisor probably has no more important task than to ascertain the client's desire for control of the business. Often, the owner or part owner of a closely held business wants to retain as much control as possible until he or she leaves the business entirely.

The current shareholder may dream of building an empire and having his or her children continue to build on those beginnings. In other businesses the shareholder may have no such ambitions, but the family may want to continue the business. The family farm that passes from generation to generation has been popular in American tradition and folklore, but this approach frequently does not succeed outside of agriculture. Younger family members may not have the training, disposition, or desire to continue a family business successfully after the death of the founder. It is extremely rare for a founder's business to survive and prosper in the hands of the third generation.

When it really is in everyone's best interest to transfer the closely held business to a younger generation, there are additional considerations. For example, not all of the younger generation may want to participate in the business, or the older generation may want to provide for all of the children but leave only certain members a direct interest in the business. The parents can devise a plan whereby those children who want to participate are given control of the business, while other children receive property unrelated to the business. It is also possible to give the children who are actively involved in the business a voting equity interest and give the other children passive interests, such as nonvoting stock and debt securities.

Any estate plan should anticipate, and attempt to minimize, hostility that may result from inequitable treatment of the heirs. Equitable treatment, however, does not necessarily mean equal division of wealth.

EXAMPLE 18 - 1: George, who has built a successful business during his lifetime and is nearing retirement age, has the following estate planning considerations:

- His primary concern is support of his wife, Edith. Edith has no professional training and no independent source of income. She has never been involved in George's business, and she is 70 years old. She is in good health and has a long life expectancy.
- His daughter Caroline has married a successful businessman. She and her family have a modest but comfortable life-style. They are not likely to accumulate any significant wealth.
- His son Robert is a successful attorney. Robert married a millionaire, and the couple have also been extremely successful investors. Their life-style vastly exceeds that of George and Edith.
- His son Scott has been active in the business. Both George and Scott would like for Scott to take over the business upon George's retirement or death. Scott has no other sources of income. He has no professional training, and he would have difficulty finding other employment that would support him.
- His daughter Kelly is mentally retarded. She is 45 years old and lives with her parents. She will never be able to provide a living for herself, and she will need to be institutionalized when George and Edith are no longer able to care for her.
- George and Edith's children are not close, but they are not openly hostile to one another. Robert and Caroline have serious doubts about Scott's ability to manage the business.
- George's principal wealth is his investment in the business. He believes that Edith will probably consume all of his other assets during her lifetime.

If George were to leave equal interests in the business to his wife and four children, the result could be a family feud. If Robert and Caroline are given powers to vote on business matters, their lack of confidence in Scott could become a self-fulfilling prophecy. By interfering with important business decisions, they could seriously damage, or even destroy, the entire business. Therefore, it might be best, from an economic point of view, to leave the entire business to Scott. Alternatively, it might be best to sell the entire business and leave Edith and the children with liquid assets.

The next problem is the division of property. Kelly appears to have the most substantial needs of any of the children. By contrast, Robert's wealth exceeds that of all other family members combined. George does not want to alienate any of his children.

Example 18 - 1 illustrates some difficult estate planning problems. First, the children do not have equal needs. The parents may be tempted to leave all of the wealth to the person with the greatest need. Unequal division of family wealth, however, may alienate other family members. Contested wills and family feuds are a reality in estate planning, and they must be dealt with.

Another problem demonstrated in Example 18 - 1 is the disposition of the closely held business. It is not entirely clear whether the business should be left to all the children or what rights they should all be given in its operation. In some circumstances it is best to sell the entire business, so that the proceeds may be used to give all family members liquid assets to take care of their needs.

This chapter offers no suggestions on the psychology of family relationships, but concentrates on the tax aspects of the courses of action that have already been determined. In particular, it focuses on the techniques used to mix two important objectives:

- Allowing members of the older generation to maintain control of the business throughout their lifetimes
- Getting the appreciating assets to other family members at the lowest possible transfer tax rate

1810.2. Continuity of control. It is not unusual for the founder, or the current owner, of a business to want to maintain effective control throughout his or her lifetime. This is one of the appealing aspects of keeping all property until death. There are, however, ways to give away wealth but retain control. A corporation may issue voting and nonvoting stock, with the voting stock having a rather low percentage of value. Then the current owner can retain all of the voting stock and shift nonvoting stock to other family members. A good deal of wealth can be transferred in this manner.

If the corporation has only one class of stock outstanding, it should not be difficult to issue massive amounts of new nonvoting stock, especially while all of the shares are still in the hands of the current owner. For example, the corporation could declare a stock dividend, which generally would be nontaxable. [§305(a)]

> **EXAMPLE 18 - 2:** Tom owns all of the stock in Tomco, Inc. At present, Tomco has 1,000 common voting shares outstanding and no other stock authorized or issued. Tomco declares a dividend of 10 nonvoting shares on each voting share. Thus, Tomco issues 10,000 nonvoting shares to Tom.

An alternative approach would be for the current shareholder to exchange some of his or her voting stock for nonvoting stock. The transfer should be a tax-free reorganization under §368(a)(1)(E).

1810.3. Direction of wealth to successors. There are two primary methods for transferring wealth to a shareholder's survivors. The first, and simpler, way is merely to hold on to all property until death, and then transfer by will. The second involves giving certain property as gifts before death. Each of these methods receives considerable discussion below, at 1815.2.

The transfers can be handled directly or indirectly. An indirect transfer usually involves a trust, which is useful for avoiding probate and may provide other nontax benefits.

> **EXAMPLE 18 - 3:** Bob and Florence, husband and wife, have two children, Donna and Marjorie. Bob has three children from an earlier marriage. Bob is the controlling shareholder in Sharpco, an S corporation. Bob's children from his first marriage are all actively involved in Sharpco. Bob wants these children to own all of his Sharpco stock after his death. He is concerned that the children from the first marriage will not be able to agree with his current wife on an equitable division of property. Therefore, he transfers his stock in Sharpco to a trust for the benefit of the older children.

Other persons—in particular, other shareholders—may be affected by a shareholder's estate plan. The relationships among entrepreneurs have some parallels to the family situation. For example, one person may have talents so critical to the business that it would be best to dissolve the entire enterprise upon that person's death or disability. Alternatively, other shareholders may be willing and able to take over the business upon the death or retirement of that key shareholder. This chapter explores some alternatives with respect to these unrelated parties.

1810.4. Transfer to other owners. It is possible that a shareholder intends to transfer his or her business interest gratuitously to unrelated co-owners, but this relationship is unusual. It is more likely that the person wants to transfer business interests to unrelated parties in exchange for valuable consideration that will benefit his or her family. A shareholder who wants to provide his or her family with liquid assets from the business will want to consider two aspects of the arrangement with the other shareholders:

- There should be a binding agreement that forces the corporation, or the other shareholders, to promptly liquidate the interests of any deceased shareholder. Without this arrangement in force, the parties run the risk of the interests losing substantial value. For instance, if the surviving shareholders are not competent to run the business, it could be worthless shortly after the key shareholder's death, and his or her family could be left with nothing.
- There should be some means to fund the agreement. Typically, this funding is accomplished with life insurance.

The primary concern in this arrangement is for the corporation to perform its obligations after the current shareholder's death. Therefore, it is wise to draw up contractual arrangements, in order to arrive at equitable valuation and to insure that the other owners will have the liquidity necessary to complete their parts of the bargain. The two primary forms for accomplishing this are the cross-purchase agreement and the redemption agreement. Both receive considerable discussion below, at 1835.

1810.5. Transfer of some components to family. In many cases a variety of assets are kept under one corporate shell. If a business is incorporated and grows, it may make a good deal of business sense to use corporate retentions to purchase new assets. Historically, many closely held businesses operated as C corporations. As these businesses sought to diversify, they often used corporate funds to acquire new businesses. The only alternative may have been to pay out earnings to shareholders in the form of dividends, so that the shareholders could diversify their holdings. From a tax viewpoint, the savings were substantial if the corporation invested in the diverse activities. As a consequence, many closely held C corporations are made up of several unrelated businesses. It is difficult to divide up a business without incurring a substantial tax burden.

There may, however, be several advantages to keeping separate business operations in separate enterprises. First, this scheme may help insulate certain business assets from claims by creditors of other components of the business. Second, there are some advantages to keeping each corporation "lean and mean." A singular business might be easier to dispose of in a liquidation or a reorganization. Thus an S corporation may want to make distributions to its shareholders, who in turn would use the distributed cash to purchase new business assets and hold them in different entities.

One advantage would occur in estate planning, where the older generation might want to transfer certain assets, such as real estate, to the family but allow the S corporation to be acquired by nonfamily persons who are competent and willing to operate the business. There can be certain tax advantages to keeping some assets, such as real estate, in a partnership rather than in a corporation. Upon the death of any partner, the successors might receive a basis increase in their portions of appreciated assets. [§754, §743(b), §755] Unfortunately, this technique, known as a *§754 election*, is not available to any corporation, including an S corporation.

EXAMPLE 18 - 4: Terrence owns some appreciated real estate. As of April 12, 1995, his adjusted basis is $100,000 and the fair market value is $1,000,000. He wants to transfer part ownership in this property to his children. He knows that if he makes a gift of part interests, the children's basis will be the same as his. [§1015] If he transfers the property to a corporation or a partnership, the entity's basis will be $100,000. [§362, §723] There are some essential differences between the two entities that will become important at the time of his death.

First, assume that he transfers the real estate to a corporation, and retains 90% of the stock. It would make no difference if the corporation were a C corporation or an S corporation. Also assume that the real estate was worth $1,000,000 at the time of his death. The estate tax value of his stock will be $900,000. The basis of the property to the corporation will be $100,000 until the property is sold. If the corporation liquidates after his death, the corporation must recognize the gain on the real estate at the time of liquidation. [§336(a)]

If he transfers the property to a partnership and retains a 90% interest in the partnership, he might get a better result. The estate tax value of his partnership interest will still be $900,000., but his family will own all of his interest after his death. If the partnership makes a §754 election, the basis of the real estate will be stepped up. [§754, §743(b), §755]

The best time to plan the selective transfer of different business components is when the various activities are acquired. For example, good tax planning would dictate that real estate and other volatile items should rarely, if ever, be held by a corporation. It is more difficult to get property out of a corporation than to place it in a partnership initially and keep it in the partnership.

Another consideration for the different business activities is to use a separate corporate shell for each activity. In this way an activity may be sold, or the different activities may be split among family members, without the need to go through a divisive reorganization, discussed in Chapter 17.

1815. Transfer taxes, in general.

A transfer of wealth by gift or estate is subject to the transfer taxes imposed by Chapters 11 and 12 of the Internal Revenue Code (IRC). The taxes are based on the fair market value of the property so transferred. Any property transferred as a result of the death of the previous owner is subject to the estate tax imposed by IRC Chapter 11. [§§2001–2209] A transfer by gift results in an imposition of tax under IRC Chapter 12. [§§2501–2524]

Although the estate and gift taxes are contained in different chapters of the Internal Revenue Code, they are closely coordinated with each other and are subject to one rate schedule. The gift tax is based on the cumulative gifts made by a person during his or her lifetime. The estate tax is imposed on the value of property transferred at death, but the rate is affected by the decedent's taxable gifts made during his or her lifetime, as well as by the value of property in the decedent's estate.

The rates range from a nominal base rate of 18% of the taxable transfer to a nominal top rate of 55%. [§2001(c)(1)] These nominal rates, however, may be misrepresentative of the actual tax imposed. The lowest rates are rarely imposed as an actual tax, due to a unified credit that is allowed to offset estate and gift taxes up to $192,800, which is equivalent to the tax on a taxable estate of $600,000. The Taxpayer Relief Act of 1997 phased in an increase to this credit which will be $345,800 after 2005, equivalent to the tax on a taxable estate of $1,000,000. [§2010] The top bracket of 55% is imposed on certain transfers, but cumulative transfers between $10,000,000 and $21,040,000 are subject to a 5% surcharge, which makes the effective marginal rate 60% for transfers within this range.

At one time it was possible to avoid one generation of the tax by skipping a generation. Thus a grandparent would leave property directly to his or her grandchildren, giving the middle generation a life estate. This opportunity for tax savings has been reduced by imposition of the Generation-Skipping Tax (GST). The rules for this tax are found in Chapter 13 of the Internal Revenue Code. [§§2601–2663]

This book does not attempt to explain any of these taxes. For that purpose, other treatises and journals are available. This book assumes that transferors will want to use gifts and estates to minimize the transfer taxes, and thus ensure that the family or other desired beneficiaries of an S corporation shareholder end up with the greatest possible amount of wealth after the current shareholder's death. Thus this chapter focuses on certain selected techniques to preserve wealth through reduction of taxes.

1815.1. The federal estate tax. The federal estate tax is imposed on transfers that take place at death. [§2001(a)] The tax is imposed on the value of all property owned by the decedent (the "gross estate"), less allowable deductions. The result is the taxable estate. [§2001(c)] The allowable deductions include the decedent's debts, certain funeral and final medical expenses, bequests to charity, and bequests to a surviving spouse.

A decedent's gross estate includes all property owned outright at the date of death, as well as certain property owned indirectly by the decedent. The indirect ownership of most concern for S corporation stock is property held by a grantor trust. Chapter 2, at 215.31, explains the income tax definitions and requirements for this trust.

1815.2. The federal gift tax. The federal gift tax is imposed on gratuitous transfers by gift. As is the case with the estate tax, the starting point of the federal gift tax is the fair market value of the property transferred. Rules similar to those of the estate tax apply to transfers of indirect interests and to other incidents of less than complete ownership. The gift tax also contains deductions for transfers to a spouse and gifts to charity. As is also the case with the estate tax, a transferor is allowed a 100% deduction for a gift to a spouse or charity.

Some aspects of the gift tax have no parallel within the estate tax. First, a gift must be complete. That is, the donor must not have retained sufficient incidents of ownership that he or she continues to be the owner for tax purposes. For example, transfers to a grantor trust usually are incomplete and thus not subject to the gift tax. The property held by the trust will be included in the decedent's gross estate for tax purposes.

> **OBSERVATION:** The income tax and gift tax definitions of a *completed transfer* are not entirely identical when the transfer is made to a trust. One important power that a grantor may retain causes the trust to be a grantor trust for income tax purposes, but does not prevent the transfer from being complete for gift tax purposes. That power is the ability of the grantor to substitute property of equal value in a nonfiduciary capacity. This means a transfer could be subjected to the gift tax at the time the property is transferred to the trust, and thus the value would be removed from the transferor's estate. The trust would be treated as a grantor trust for income tax purposes, however, and would be an eligible shareholder throughout the grantor's lifetime. See additional discussion at 1830.32., below.

Certain gifts are subject to an annual exclusion of $10,000 per donee. [§2503(b)] This exclusion applies to each year's gifts from a donor to each donee. The exclusion is limited to a present interest, in which the donee has the immediate right to unrestricted enjoyment of the property.

> **EXAMPLE 18 - 5:** In 1995, Robert gives $10,000 to his son Bobby (age 22) and $10,000 to his daughter Molly (age 18). Both gifts are in cash and are made directly to the children. These gifts are excluded from Robert's taxable gifts for the year.

The exclusion applies even where the total amount of gifts to each donee exceeds the $10,000 threshold. Thus it is possible to give additional amounts to a person without making the first $10,000 taxable.

EXAMPLE 18 - 6: Assume the same facts as in Example 18 - 5, except that Robert gives $11,000 to each of his children in 1995. Robert would have made a taxable gift of $1,000 to each child.

Since the exclusion applies only to present interests, as opposed to future interests, these terms deserve brief explanation. A *future interest* is one in which the donee does not have an immediate right to the enjoyment of the property. [Regs. §25.2503-3(a)] A *present interest* exists when the donee has the right to immediate use of the property.

EXAMPLE 18 - 7: Assume the same facts as in Example 18-5, except that the gifts are made in trust, and neither Bobby nor Molly can withdraw the property until age 25. Robert would have made a taxable gift of $10,000 to each child.

Another aspect of the gift tax that deserves brief mention is the opportunity for gift splitting. This applies to married donors who make gifts of separately owned property. Each spouse may elect to treat himself or herself as the donor of one-half of the property's value. [§2513(A)] Thus married donors can effectively double the unified credit, the graduated rate schedule, and the annual exclusion.

EXAMPLE 18 - 8: In 1995, Robert gives $20,000 to his son Bobby (age 22) and $20,000 to his daughter Molly (age 18). Both gifts are in cash and are made directly to the children. The cash was not jointly held between Robert and his wife. Robert and his wife can each elect to be treated as the donor of one-half of the property. Thus the transfers may be excluded from the gift tax entirely.

As is discussed in Chapter 2, at 215.32., a transfer of stock to a trust may be a present interest if the beneficiary has the power to withdraw the contribution within a reasonable time. [*Crummey v. Comm'r*, 397 F.2d 82 (9th Cir. 1968). See also Rev. Rul. 73-405, 1973-2 CB 321.] This temporary power to withdraw trust property is often termed a "Crummey Power." The power to direct a trust to distribute income or property to oneself, or to accumulate income or property, is one of the powers that cause a trust to be treated as a grantor trust. [§677(a)] Similarly, the relinquishment of this power is one of the indicators of a grantor trust. When this power has been held by a person other than the grantor, the person who held the power is treated as a grantor. [§678(a)(2).] Thus it is possible to qualify a trust for S corporation shareholder status and simultaneously provide the annual exclusion.

CAUTION: As of this writing, the Clinton administration has proposed that Crummey trusts should be curtailed or eliminated, although no legislation has been introduced to that effect. The reader should be on the lookout for developments in this area in the near future, and may want to accelerate plans to make contributions to trusts in order to qualify under the Crummey rule.

1820. Special problems of the closely held business.

The closely held business has several unique aspects to consider in developing an estate plan. First and foremost is valuation, since all transfer taxes are based on the fair market value of the value transferred. Some special valuation rules apply, as well as some stock redemption opportunities. Finally, a lengthy estate tax payment extension can be obtained for the successor to a closely held business.

1820.1. Valuing the closely held business. In general, the value of any property on a given date, such as the date of gift or the date of death, is "the price at which the property would change hands between a willing buyer and a willing seller, neither being under any compulsion to buy or sell, and both having reasonable knowledge of relevant facts." [Regs. §20.2031-

1(b)] Although the theoretical validity of this statement is unassailable, it is often difficult to apply when there is no arm's-length transfer of the property on a specific date. Thus it is usually necessary to have property appraised at the date of gift or death.

In the case of a closely held business, the IRS has given eight factors that must be considered:

1. The book value of the stock and the financial condition of the company
2. The earning capacity of the company
3. The dividend-paying capacity of the company
4. The company's goodwill or other intangible value
5. The economic outlook in general, and the outlook of the industry
6. The nature and history of the business
7. Sales of the stock, and the size of the block in question
8. The market price of traded stocks of corporations in the same or similar lines of business [Rev. Rul. 59-60, 1959-1 CB 442]

As objective as these standards may seem, they offer only general guidelines. There is no formula for mixing or weighting the different factors. Appraisals are often contested by the IRS. There are undoubtedly numerous settlements within the administrative process, for which there are no available public records. Occasionally, however, the values are determined in the courts.

1820.11. Discount valuation problems. When a business is fragmented as a result of gift or death, each new owner may have received less value than a mere percentage of the value of the business. For instance, a block of stock that represents only a minority interest may not be as valuable as the same block of shares held by a person with a controlling interest.

> **EXAMPLE 18 - 9:** Curtis held all of the stock of Curco, Inc., before his death. At the time of his death the stock could have been sold for approximately $3,000,000. He left equal blocks of stock to his three children. The value of this stock to each of the children may be substantially less than $1,000,000, since none of the three children can independently control the corporation's actions. If the estate acquired all of the stock upon Curtis's death, there would be no minority discount. Accordingly, Curtis would be well advised to make lifetime gifts of minority interest to the children.

At times, the IRS has been reluctant to accept minority valuation discounts. However, taxpayers have often prevailed when they argued their cases in court. There are also other discounts for the stock of a closely held corporation. The IRS specifically acknowledges a discount for blockage or nonmarketability. [Regs. §20.2031-2(e)] Under this rationale, taxpayers have been able to secure 35% discounts for nonmarketability and fragmentation. [*Estate of Dougherty*, 59 TCM 772 (1990); *Estate of Newhouse*, 94 TC 193 (1990)] Also see the case of *Paul E. Brown*, TC Memo, 1997-195, where the IRS valued a majority interest at $111,000 per share, but a minority interest at $76,400 per share.

In some cases, courts have allowed lesser discounts. [*Estate of Murphy*, TC Memo 1990-472 (20%); *Estate of Bennett*, TC Memo 1993-94 (15%)] The Newhouse discount was due to a minority interest, whereas the Bennett discount was allowed for lack of marketability. In some instances, a taxpayer may be able to apply both discounts successfully. In PLR 9050004, the IRS allowed a minority discount. However, the discount served to reduce the marital deduction allowed to the estate. Also see *Hall*, 92 TC 312, and *Gallun*, TC Memo 74-284.

In *Bright*, 81-2 USTC 13,436 ((5th. Cir.), a husband and wife owned 55% of the stock of a closely held corporation. When the wife died, her 27.5% interest passed to a trust for the benefit of their children. Her widower was the trustee. The estate claimed a discount for the minority interest. The IRS, claiming that the same person controlled 55% of the stock, argued that the minority discount was not applicable. The IRS imputed a premium for voting control and valued the entire 55% as one unit, with half of the value being Mrs. Bright's share. However, the court respected the separateness of the two blocks of stock and let the minority discount stand. Similarly, in *Carr*, TC Memo 1985-19, 49 TCM 507 (1985), a couple was allowed to claim a 25% discount for gift of some stock to children, when the family controlled 100% of the outstanding shares. Also see Revenue Ruling 93-12, 1993-1 CB 202, and TAM 9449001, in which the IRS has given up on applying attribution rules for this purpose.

> **OBSERVATION:** Whenever a family business is fragmented or the decedent owned less than a controlling interest, the estate should discount the value of the shares. Based on the cases cited above, a 35% discount should usually be arguable. See *Estate of Arthur F. Little, Jr.*, TC Memo 1982-26, 43 TCM 319, in which the discounts for sales restrictions, irrevocable voting proxy, and escrow totaled 35%, where there was not even a minority discount, per se.

A recent case combined minority and blockage discounts to reduce value by approximately 49% of the proportionate asset value of a closely held corporation. [*Estate of Artemus D. Davis*, 110 TC No. 35] One factor considered by the court is that the corporation would be subject to the built-in gains tax if it sold assets, and that tax would provide a blockage discount. Interestingly enough, the corporation in question was not an S corporation, but the parties all agreed that the value would be enhanced by making an S election.

> **CAUTION:** As of this writing, the Clinton administration has proposed that the blockage and minority valuation discounts, along with the Crummey trusts, should be curtailed or eliminated, although no legislation has been introduced to that effect. The reader should be on the lookout for developments in this area in the near future, and may want to accelerate plans to transfer property in advance of any new legislation.

1820.12. Special-use valuation of certain real estate. In general, property is valued according to its highest and best use. In some cases, this can work a hardship when property that is actually used in a family farm or other small business might have more value if it were sold to become a subdivision or a shopping center. Accordingly, Congress has enacted a rule that allows valuation of certain property based on its actual use, rather than its highest and best use. [§2032A]

The rules covering the special-use valuation are intricate, to say the least, and this book contains only a brief summary. To qualify for special-use valuation, the property must pass from the decedent to a "qualified heir" (member of the decedent's family). At least 50% of the decedent's adjusted gross estate must consist of real and personal property used in a qualified trade or business. At least 25% of the decedent's adjusted gross estate must be the real property in question. The qualified heir must use the property in a qualified trade or business after death. If there is a disposition of the property, or conversion to a nonqualified use within 10 years, the estate must recapture a certain portion of the tax savings.

There are special rules for valuation of farm property, and other rules for the valuation of other real property used in a nonfarm trade or business. The rules apply to property held directly by the decedent or to property held by a corporation, a partnership, or another entity in which the decedent had an interest. The decedent's interest must have been sufficient to qualify for the deferred estate tax payment under §6166, discussed below at 1820.3.

> **OBSERVATION:** Most S corporations will meet the appropriate qualifications for §6166, if the corporation is a significant portion of the decedent's adjusted gross

estate. Therefore, when a significant portion of an S corporation's property consists of a farm or other qualified real property, the estate should examine the possibility that special-use valuation is appropriate.

1820.13. Family-owned business exclusion. In 1997, Congress enacted another provision aimed at reducing estate tax on the transfer of family-owned businesses. [§2033A] This provision has the effect of exempting up to $1,300,000 of a family-owned business from the estate tax. It is not an additional exclusion, but works in conjunction with the unified credit. Thus when the credit is fully phased in for an exemption equivalent of $1,000,000, the family-owned business exclusion will be $300,000. In years before 2006, when the credit is lower, this exclusion will be correspondingly higher. This rule applies to the estate of a person who dies after December 31, 1997. It is a long and complex provision, with rules regarding ownership and continued use.

1820.2. Using business assets to pay taxes. When a shareholder in an S corporation dies, it can be a good strategy to use some of the assets of the business, rather than personal assets held by the family, to pay the decedent's estate tax. Typically, this is accomplished using a stock redemption. As is discussed in Chapter 15, a stock redemption may be treated as an exchange or as a distribution. If the S corporation in question has little or no accumulated earnings and profits, or a large AAA, in relation to the value of the stock that is to be redeemed after the death of the shareholder, it may make little difference how the exchange is treated, at least in the short run.

If the corporation has significant accumulated earnings and profits, and little or no AAA, the characterization of the redemption is important. Characterizing it as an exchange has two benefits in these situations:

1. The estate or other survivor will report the exchange as a capital gain or loss. The gain or loss, however, is measured from the value of the stock on the date of the decedent's death, which determines the adjusted basis of the stock to the new owner. Therefore, the taxable gain or loss on this exchange is likely to be zero.
2. A redemption that is treated as an exchange will reduce the corporation's AAA and AEP proportionately. (See Chapter 15, at 1515.3., for further discussion.) A redemption characterized as a distribution will reduce AAA to the extent thereof, after the corporation has accounted for its nonredemption distributions. The remaining shareholders may not have any AAA available for future distributions after the redemption.

As was discussed in Chapter 15, at 1510.1., there are several criteria that can characterize a redemption as an exchange. The most important of these, in the estate planning context, are (1) the complete termination of a shareholder's interest and (2) a redemption to pay death taxes. If the estate and other family members hold only a minority interest in the stock, the substantially disproportionate redemption also may be useful. The redemption rules of interest in this chapter apply to C corporations and S corporations equally.

1820.21. Complete termination of estate's interest. An estate may waive family attribution rules if it completely terminates its interest in a corporation. After the redemption, the estate and all beneficiaries of the estate must be completely divested of all of their shares. This situation works well for a family corporation, but only if the surviving shareholders are not beneficiaries of the estate and vice versa.

18

EXAMPLE 18 - 10: Richard was a shareholder in Simco. His daughter, Ella, also owned shares. Richard died, leaving his entire estate to his wife, Caroline. Simco redeems all of Richard's stock from his estate. After the redemption Caroline owns no stock in Simco. Ella is now the 100% shareholder in Simco. Richard's estate may waive family attribution, since its only beneficiary, Caroline, does not own any shares directly after the redemption. Therefore, the redemption would qualify as an exchange under §302(b)(3).

1820.22. Redemptions to pay death taxes. When more than 35% of a decedent's adjusted gross estate consists of stock in a closely held corporation, the corporation may redeem a certain portion of the stock without having to pass any of the exchange tests of §302. The enabling provision is §303, which is discussed briefly in Chapter 15, at 1510.7. As that discussion demonstrates, the stock in the S corporation must have exceeded 35% of the value of the decedent's adjusted gross estate. If a decedent owned two or more small business interests, the estate may aggregate the stock of all corporations in which the decedent held more than 20%.

> **EXAMPLE 18 - 11:** This year David died, leaving assets of $5,400,000, including a 30% interest in Beat Corporation worth $1,000,000 and a 90% interest in Bash Corporation worth $500,000. Administrative expenses and debts against the estate totaled $1,400,000. David's adjusted gross estate is $4,000,000 ($5,400,000 – $1,400,000). To qualify for §303 treatment, the stock of Beat or Bash must have a value greater than $1,400,000 (35% x $4,000,000). Although the stock of neither corporation qualifies alone, the two stocks may be aggregated and treated as one for purposes of the 35% test. Aggregation is permitted because at least 20% of the value of each stock is included in the gross estate. Since the aggregate value of Beat and Bash—$1,500,000—exceeds the 35% threshold of $1,400,000, a redemption of either would qualify under §303.

A §303 redemption has another side benefit to continuing shareholders. When a redemption is treated as an exchange under either §302 or §303, the corporation reduces its AAA proportionately in accordance with the percentage of shares redeemed. See Chapter 15, at 1515.3. If the redemption does not qualify as an exchange, the corporation must reduce its AAA (not below zero) for the entire redemption proceeds. [Rev. Rul. 95-14, 1995-6 IRB 29]

1820.3. Deferred payment of estate tax. In general, estate taxes are payable 9½ months after death. This may leave the estate little time to obtain the liquid assets necessary to pay the tax. Congress realized that this problem could work undue hardship on a family-owned business, so §6166 was enacted to allow certain estates a lengthy extension period to pay the tax attributable to interests in closely held businesses.

For the estate to qualify for the deferral, more than 35% of the adjusted gross estate must consist of interest in the closely held business. This business could be a proprietorship, a closely held corporation, or a closely held partnership. Stock in a corporation qualifies for the test if at least 20% of the value of the outstanding stock is included in the decedent's adjusted gross estate, or if the corporation had no more than 15 shareholders. The value of the stock, however, is limited to the value of the portion of the corporation that is engaged in an active trade or business. In other words, passive investment assets do not qualify.

In testing for the 15-shareholder limit, the family attribution rules of §267 are applied. For this purpose, therefore, stock held by a decedent's spouse, ancestors, and descendants is treated as held by one owner. If no one interest qualifies independently, the interests may be aggregated. Aggregation is permitted for any interest in which the decedent owned at least 20% of the total value.

> **OBSERVATION:** The rules for the deferral under §6166 are much like the rules for stock redemptions under §303. In practice, most estates will qualify for both benefits if they qualify for either.

The deferral is limited to the closely held business's contribution to the estate tax, or the percentage of the adjusted gross estate that consists of qualifying interests. The deferral is generous, and it requires no principal payments for five years. At that time, the tax is payable in ten equal annual installments. Interest is payable annually on the balance owed. The first five years require payment of interest only, and each remaining installment includes 10% of the principal balance plus interest on the unpaid balance. The interest on the first $345,800 of tax (tax on $1,000,000) is computed at 4%. Additional interest is charged at the rate applicable to underpayments of tax.

EXAMPLE 18 - 12: Boris died in 1995. His adjusted gross estate was $4,000,000, which included $1,600,000 of stock in Boco, an S corporation that had only five shareholders. All of Boco's assets were used in an active trade or business.

Boris's estate tax was $1,800,000, after adjustment for taxable gifts and reduction for the unified credit. Boris's estate would be allowed deferral for the following portion of the estate tax:

Total estate tax	$1,800,000
Percent attributable to Boco ($1,600,000/$4,000,000)	40%
Qualifying for deferral	$ 720,000

A business interest held indirectly through a partnership or an S corporation may qualify for the deferred payment. In PLR 9644053, the IRS declined to rule directly on the issue, but restated the attribution rules. The attribution rules do apply for determining the number of owners of a business, but there are no attribution rules for the 35% (or 20%) of adjusted gross estate tests.

1825. Special considerations for S corporations.

Most of the planning devices discussed in this chapter are applicable to closely held businesses in any form. When the business is an S corporation, all of the eligibility rules discussed in Chapter 2 are important. The estate planner should ensure continuing eligibility of the corporation for S status; as part of this, the corporation must be careful not to violate the ownership or class-of-stock rules. For instance, a plan that involves transfers to family members may result in too many shareholders. Also, if any family members are not U.S. citizens or residents, transfer of shares to these persons would terminate the S election.

Similarly, a shareholder who has so many desired heirs that transfer to all of them would exceed the shareholder limit must be careful. A divisive reorganization, discussed in Chapter 17, might allow the current shareholder to separate his or her business interests and leave stock in the two or more resulting corporations to different persons. As is discussed in Chapter 17, however, there must be a valid nontax business purpose for a divisive reorganization.

If a shareholder cannot leave stock to all of his or her desired heirs, it is possible to leave stock to some and corporate debentures to others. The corporation should evaluate carefully the risk of reclassification of debt as equity under §385. The straight-debt safe harbor, discussed in Chapter 2, could prevent disqualification of the corporation's S status, but only if the holder of the debt is a U.S. citizen or resident.

1825.1. Postmortem estate planning. Special considerations arise for closely held corporations immediately after the death of a shareholder. This part of the chapter deals with the possibility of an S election by a former C corporation, and also with the eligibility requirements for maintaining the status of an S corporation.

1825.11. S election for year of death. If a shareholder is terminally ill, it may makes sense for a C corporation to file an S election, for the following reason. If the corporation is a C corporation and holds insurance on the shareholder's life, the insurance proceeds will be treated as part of the corporation's adjusted current earnings (ACE) and cause the alternative minimum tax to be imposed on the corporation in the year it receives the proceeds. [§56(g)]

An S corporation, however, is exempt from the corporate alternative minimum tax. [§1363(a)] Also, an S corporation uses the individual tax rules in computing its taxable income [§1363(b)], so an S corporation does not compute ACE—and the insurance proceeds are not subject to alternative minimum tax at either the corporate or the shareholder level. If a shareholder dies within the first 2 months and 15 days of the corporation's taxable year, the executor may be able to elect S status effective as of the first day of the corporation's taxable year.

EXAMPLE 18 - 13: Richard was the 100% owner of Richco, a C corporation, until his death in February 1995. Richco owned a $1,000,000 policy on Richard's life. Richco used the calendar year for tax purposes. Richco was a service corporation, which cannot continue after Richard's death. Its taxable income for 1995 will be zero, after deducting reasonable compensation to Richard. If the corporation does not elect S status for 1995, it will have adjusted current earnings of $1,000,000 when it collects the life insurance. This will result in an ACE adjustment of $750,000, with an alternative minimum tax of $150,000.

If the corporation elects S status, there will be no ACE adjustment. Moreover, the insurance will not be a built-in gain, since Richard was still alive on the conversion date. Nor will the insurance be passive investment income, so the savings will be substantial.

OBSERVATION: The Taxpayer Relief Act of 1997 provides an exemption for certain C corporations from the alternative minimum tax. A C corporation is exempt from this tax for taxable years beginning after 1997 if its gross receipts did not exceed $5,000,000 for its first taxable years beginning after 1996. It will continue to qualify for this exemption unless its average annual gross receipts for its most recent three years exceed $7,500,000. [§55(e)]

An S election for the final year will probably not cause any great loss of tax benefits due to the restrictions on fringe benefits. For example, the medical insurance and medical reimbursement plans will pass through to the shareholders, who will now be the decedent and the estate. These expenses could be prorated across the entire S corporation year or allocated to the shareholders based on an interim closing. See Chapter 6, at 630.

As discussed in Chapter 5, the corporation and the estate or other survivors will want to comply with the election requirements. Typically, the executor must sign on behalf of two shareholders—the decedent and the estate. The election will also need to be signed by a corporate officer, who may or may not be the decedent's executor. Finally, for the election to be valid the corporation will need the consent of any other shareholders.

Note that this technique will *not* work when a shareholder dies after more than 2 months and 15 days of the corporation's taxable year have elapsed. Thus it may make sense for a corporation to make an S election in anticipation of the death of a shareholder. This will be especially important when the corporation carries substantial insurance on one or more shareholders who are terminally ill or extremely elderly.

OBSERVATION: If a decedent dies more than 2 months and 15 days after the beginning of a C corporation's taxable year, it will be impossible for the corporation, per se, to elect S status for the year of death. It may, however, be possible to merge the existing C corporation into an S corporation before the insurance proceeds are disbursed. If the C corporation used the cash method of accounting, it would never receive the proceeds. The surviving S corporation would be exempt from ACE.

1825.12. Maintaining S corporation eligibility after death. When the corporation has an S election in effect at the time of a shareholder's death, it should observe all of the eligibility requirements scrupulously. As discussed in Chapter 2, it must ensure that the number of shareholders does not exceed the maximum, that there are no ineligible shareholders, and that it has only one class of stock. The most troublesome of these requirements has been eligible shareholders, especially when trusts are involved. See Chapter 13, at 1350., for discussion of the numerous inadvertent termination relief rulings granted on this issue. For that reason, the next portion of this chapter deals with the uses of trusts, in the context of the S corporation limitations.

1825.2. Uses of trusts in the estate plan. Trusts are useful vehicles for the administration of a person's wealth. A popular device, now known as the "living trust," enables a person to transfer certain property to a trust during his or her lifetime. Often the person retains the power to revoke the trust or to have trust property revert at any time. In this instance, the trust will be a grantor trust, discussed in Chapter 2, at 215.31.

Also as discussed in Chapter 2, a domestic trust will be a qualified shareholder if it is a grantor trust, a QSST, or an Electing Small Business Trust after 1996. One of the conditions of eligibility for these trusts, however, is that the grantor or beneficiary be a U.S. citizen or resident. Therefore, a shareholder cannot use a trust to transfer stock indirectly to a nonresident alien, without terminating the corporation's S status.

> **OBSERVATION:** At the time of this writing there is no clear guidance on whether a beneficiary in an Electing Small Business Trust must be a U.S. citizen or resident. Readers will need to be on the alert for announcements on this matter.

1825.21. Transfers to *inter vivos* trusts. Transfer of property to a trust is an integral part of many estate plans. One primary objective of this transaction is to ensure passage of title to the property at the time of the grantor's death. Another objective is the ability to ensure competent management of the assets, especially if the intended beneficiary is not likely to manage the property prudently. There may also be some tax-saving objectives. Generally, a trust is treated as a taxable entity separate from either the grantor or the beneficiaries. Accordingly, the trust is entitled to a graduated rate structure on its own income. It is also entitled to a personal exemption. When a trust distributes income to a beneficiary, the trust is allowed a deduction for the distribution.

Compared to those of individual tax structures, the rate brackets and the exemption allowed to trusts are quite low. Therefore, trusts cannot be used to shelter a great deal of income from high rates, but it is possible to effect some moderate tax savings. When the income from the transferred property is split between the trust and the beneficiary, the savings from the use of multiple tax entities may be significant. There are some strict limits, however. If the beneficiary is under age 14, the beneficiary must use the grantor's marginal rate bracket for all taxable income over $600. [§1(i)] The beneficiary may also be subject to some other limitations on the calculation of taxable income. A beneficiary who is a dependent of another taxpayer may not claim a personal exemption on his or her own tax return. [§151(d)(2)] In addition, for a beneficiary who is the dependent of another taxpayer, the standard deduction is limited to the beneficiary's earned income (subject to the statutory limit for the beneficiary's filing status) or $600, whichever is greater.[2] Income distributed from a trust to a beneficiary is unearned income. If the beneficiary is not a dependent of another taxpayer, there are no special limitations on that person's tax rates, standard deduction, or personal exemptions.

[2] Code §63(c)(5). The statutory amount is $500 but is indexed for inflation. The inflation-adjusted amount for 1993 is $600.

The Electing Small Business Trust provides no potential for income tax savings. The trust must pay its income tax at the highest rate imposed on individuals, estates, and trusts, and the trust has an alternative minimum tax exemption of zero. The trust must include all flowthrough items from the S corporation on its own return, as well as any gain or loss from the disposition of its S corporation stock. The trust cannot claim a distribution deduction or use any other means to shift its taxable income to any beneficiary. [§641(d)]

When the property transferred to a trust is S corporation stock, the income tax savings are further reduced. The trust must be a grantor or beneficiary-controlled trust, a QSST, or an Electing Small Business Trust, as described in Chapter 2. If the trust is a grantor, beneficiary-controlled, or QSST, no portion of the income may be taxed to the trust. A grantor trust passes all of its taxable income through to the grantor, who computes his or her tax as if the trust did not exist. The same rules hold for a beneficiary-controlled trust. When the beneficiary of a QSST makes the proper QSST election, he or she has consented to be treated as the direct owner of the S corporation stock for tax purposes. Therefore, the income-shifting potential of any trust that qualifies as a shareholder in an S corporation is no greater than that which would be available through an outright gift.

The IRS does grant inadvertent termination relief to S corporations, however. Chapter 13, at 1350., lists numerous rulings where the event causing termination was the transfer of S corporation stock to a trust. In these cases, the S election usually was lost for one of two main reasons:

- The trust contained provisions that make it ineligible to be a shareholder in an S corporation.
- The trust had all of the provisions necessary to qualify it as a QSST, but the beneficiary failed to file a proper and timely QSST election.

It is imperative, therefore, that any transfer of S corporation stock in trust be made to a trust that qualifies as a shareholder. The rules regarding trust qualification are discussed in considerable detail in Chapter 2, at 215.3. Some recent developments indicate that caution is in order when designing a trust instrument. For example:

- A trust with the right to accumulate income cannot be a QSST until this right expires, in any year beginning before 1997. [PLR 8921013] If the trust qualifies as a grantor trust or a deemed grantor trust, however, it will be an eligible shareholder. For taxable years beginning after 1996, however, an Electing Small Business Trust, which may accumulate or distribute income, is an eligible shareholder.
- A trust with power to add an after-born grandchild is not a QSST. [Rev. Rul. 89-45, 1989-14 IRB 15] Again, such a trust could qualify as a shareholder if it is treated as a grantor trust or a deemed grantor trust. After 1996, this power may be appropriate for an Electing Small Business Trust.
- A charitable remainder trust did not qualify as a shareholder in an S corporation. [Rev. Rul. 92-48, 1992-1 CB 301; PLR 8922014] The IRS has held that such a trust cannot qualify as a shareholder, even if it also meets the definition of a grantor trust.

CAUTION: The rules regarding the Electing Small Business Trust (ESBT), an allowable shareholder after 1996, permit a charity to be a contingent beneficiary if it is not a potential current income beneficiary. For an S corporation's taxable years beginning after 1997, a charity can be a potential current income beneficiary of the ESBT. A charitable remainder trust, however, cannot be a shareholder, even if it otherwise would qualify as an ESBT. [§1361(e)(1)(B)(iii)]

18

- A trust that reserves the power to change beneficiaries only if the trust no longer holds shares in an S corporation is not a qualified Subchapter S trust. [Rev. Rul. 89-55, 1989-

15 IRB 14] This type of trust power is quite appropriate for an Electing Small Business Trust. In this type of trust the trustee may have the discretion to distribute income or corpus to multiple beneficiaries, or to accumulate income.

- For a trustee to have the power to apportion income in the event the trust no longer holds S corporation stock disqualifies the trust as a QSST. [Rev. Rul. 89-55, 1989-15 IRB 14] Again, an Electing Small Business Trust would be an ideal vehicle to accomplish this goal after 1996.
- A custodial account of an insurance company was not an eligible shareholder. [PLR 8847016]
- Ideally, a trust would be treated as a grantor trust during the grantor's lifetime, yet the trust corpus would be excluded from the grantor's gross estate. The grantor can reserve certain powers that will cause this to happen. See the discussion of GRATs at 1830.32. In another situation a trustee, who was a nonadverse party to the grantor, retained the power to change beneficiaries. This power was sufficient to treat the trust as a grantor trust during the grantor's lifetime, yet was not sufficient to include the trust corpus in the grantor's gross estate. [PLRs 9709001, 9710006]

1825.22. Transfers to testamentary trusts. A testamentary trust—that is, a trust that comes into existence through the operation of the decedent's will—can hold shares in an S corporation for 60 days in S corporations' taxable years beginning before 1997. For any taxable years beginning after 1996, the period is for two years.

If the trust instrument gives the beneficiary sufficient powers to treat the trust as beneficiary-controlled, it will be able to hold the shares indefinitely, assuming that the beneficiary is an eligible shareholder.

Alternatively, if a testamentary trust meets the requirements of a QSST, it can be an eligible shareholder, provided the beneficiary makes the proper QSST election. [PLRs 9348036, 9422041] See Chapter 2, at 215.34., for further discussion.

> **CAUTION:** If a testamentary trust does not qualify as a grantor trust and cannot be a QSST, the executor of the estate should take timely action. In some cases, it may be possible to delay transfer to a trust until the instrument has been modified. Another technique is to use a stock redemption. A redemption within 2 years (60 days in taxable years beginning before 1997) after the trust receives the stock will avoid disqualification. It could also prevent disqualification if the decedent had held the shares indirectly through a grantor trust.

On occasion, a trust may be reformed retroactively in order to qualify as an eligible S corporation shareholder. The IRS has ruled that it will not retroactively qualify a trust that has been reformed [Rev. Rul. 93-79, 1993-36 IRB 5], so retroactively amending a trust to become a QSST after it has received shares will not prevent the corporation from losing its S status. In this situation, the only way to keep the S election in place is to apply for inadvertent termination relief. See discussion in Chapter 13, at 1350.

1825.23. Marital deductions and Q-TIP elections. There are some special rules for property left to the surviving spouse. The unlimited marital deduction is appealing, but it has its drawbacks. When property has been left to a surviving spouse, and it qualified for the marital deduction on the estate of the first spouse to die, the same property must be included in the estate of the second spouse to die. The unlimited marital deduction also offers no tax saving for the amount of the estate that would be untaxed due to the unified credit. As a consequence, credit shelter trusts also play an important rule in the estate plan.

Marital deductions. The use of trusts in estate planning is especially important for married persons, since the rights of the different beneficiaries can be closely defined in the governing instrument of the trust. Usually, the testator wants to take care of his or her surviving spouse, with the remaining property going to the children and grandchildren upon the death of the surviving spouse. To lessen the transfer tax imposed on property passing to widows and widowers, the Code provides that any property that passes to a surviving spouse is subject to the marital estate tax deduction and thus is not included in the taxable estate of the spouse who dies first. In general, the surviving spouse must receive a complete interest in the property, so a life estate to a surviving spouse with remainder interests to the children or other beneficiaries will not qualify for the marital deduction.

If the value of a surviving spouse's estate is not likely to be more than the exemption equivalent ($600,000 in 1997, increasing gradually to $1,000,000 by 2006) of the unified credit, leaving all property to a surviving spouse is a reasonably good tax plan. In larger estates, however, this strategy may not make sense in the long run.

> **EXAMPLE 18 - 14:** When Wally died in 1995, his adjusted gross estate was exactly $1,200,000. If Wally left all of his property to his wife Ellie, there would be no tax on his estate. If he left only half of his property to Ellie, there still would be no tax on his estate. Half of his property, $600,000, would be deducted as a bequest to a surviving spouse, and the remaining $600,000 would be his taxable estate. The tax on the latter $600,000, however, would be eliminated by the unified credit of $192,800.
>
> It appears to make no difference whether Wally left all or half of his property to Ellie. At the time of Ellie's death, however, there would be a noticeable difference. Assuming that Ellie is able to live on the income from the bequest and that her property is still worth $1,200,000 at her death, she would have no marital deduction. She would be allowed a unified credit of $192,800, which would eliminate the tax on half of her estate, but the remainder would be subject to the estate tax. If she owned only half of the property from Wally's estate, her unified credit would eliminate the tax on the property she owned at the time of her death.

One way to in effect split an estate, yet give the surviving spouse all of the income from all of the property, is to use two trusts. The first trust is called the marital trust (also known as the widow's trust or the "A" trust). The surviving spouse owns an outright interest in this property, and thus this trust is a deemed grantor trust, as discussed in Chapter 2. The second trust is called the family trust (or bypass trust or credit trust or "B" trust or credit shelter). The surviving spouse has the right to income from this trust for his or her lifetime, and the trustee may invade corpus for the surviving spouse's benefit, if need be. The surviving spouse, however, has no power to change the remainder beneficiary or to give away the corpus of the family trust.

In this two-trust scenario, the property in the marital trust qualifies for the marital deduction in the estate of the first spouse to die, and it is included in the estate of the second spouse. The property in the family trust is included in the estate of the first spouse to die, but it is excluded from the second spouse's estate.

> **OBSERVATION:** When using trusts, the estate planner must be concerned with the continued eligibility of the corporation for S status. In general, the powers given to the surviving spouse in the marital trust are sufficient to cause that trust to be an eligible shareholder, without the survivor needing to make a QSST election. The family trust may be more difficult to work with. Unless this trust meets all of the qualifications for a QSST, and the income beneficiary files the proper election, within 2 months and 15 days after the date the trust is funded, this trust will not be a qualified shareholder unless it meets the definition of an **Electing Small Business Trust** after 1996.

Chapter 13 devotes considerable discussion to the inadvertent termination rulings that have arisen due to faulty trusts or the lack of a timely QSST election by a survivor. See Chapter 13, at 1350.

Q-TIP elections. A popular estate planning device is the Qualified Terminable Interest Property (Q-TIP) trust. This trust gives the surviving spouse a life interest in the property transferred to the trust. The executor of the decedent's estate may elect to treat this property as subject to the marital estate tax deduction or as not subject to that deduction. If the Q-TIP does not qualify for the marital deduction of the first spouse to die, it will not be included in the gross estate of the second spouse. If the property does qualify for the marital deduction in the estate of the first spouse, it must be included in the gross estate of the second spouse. [See PLR 9348036.]

OBSERVATION: Generally, the Q-TIP trust will meet the requirements of a QSST and thus be an eligible shareholder (provided the surviving spouse is a U.S. citizen or resident). A bypass trust may be established to take advantage of the first decedent's unified credit. The bypass trust can be designed to accumulate income, to the extent that the income exceeds the surviving spouse's needs, but the power to accumulate will violate the QSST conditions. The following suggestions may be useful:

1. Put all of the S corporation's shares into the Q-TIP, which will be an eligible S corporation shareholder. Fund the bypass trust with other property.
2. If the bypass trust is created at death, it can be a shareholder for 2 years (60 days in taxable years beginning before 1997), unless the trust qualifies as an Electing Small Business Trust. This leaves the following opportunities:
   - Give the trustee power to distribute the S corporation shares to other persons or QSSTs.
   - Design the trust to qualify as an Electing Small Business Trust. Watch for any election procedures, which are unknown at the time of this writing.
   - Have the corporation redeem the shares from the bypass trust within 2 years (60 days in taxable years beginning before 1997). The redemption may or may not qualify as a sale or an exchange.
     - —If the bypass is a residuary trust and the S corporation stock was more than 35% of the decedent's adjusted gross estate, the redemption will receive sale or exchange treatment under §303. Since the redemption price will be the same as the trust's basis, the trust will recognize no gain or loss.
     - —If the redemption does not qualify under §303, it may qualify under §302(b)(3) as a complete termination of the trust's interest. The trust may waive family attribution rules only if the trust's beneficiary holds no other stock. This would not be the case if the Q-TIP also holds stock.
     - —If the redemption does not qualify as a sale or exchange, it will be a distribution in respect of stock. The distributee will not be taxed if the corporation has no accumulated earnings and profits, or if it has sufficient Accumulated Adjustments Account to cover the entire redemption. The Accumulated Adjustments Account must be allocated among all of the distributions made by the corporation during its taxable year.
     - —The redemption can be funded with life insurance held by the corporation. The proceeds will be exempt from tax, but they will not add to the Accumulated Adjustments Account, if the corporation has accumulated earnings and profits.
3. If the decedent established the trust before his or her death, the bypass trust may be an eligible shareholder for two years following death. The trust must have been a grantor trust during the decedent's lifetime, and the entire corpus must have been included in his

or her estate. If less than the entire corpus was not included in the decedent's gross estate, the eligibility period is only 60 days, for the S corporation's taxable years beginning before 1997. See discussion at 1830.32. for an explanation of the grantor retained annuity trust, whereby a trust would be considered a grantor trust for income tax purposes but would exclude some corpus from the grantor's gross estate.

EXAMPLE 18 - 15: Mr. J has an estate of $1,200,000. The value of his stock in Jayco, an S corporation, will be approximately $600,000. In developing his estate plan, he wants to provide for his wife, who has no other property. He establishes two grantor trusts. One trust has nothing but S corporation stock; it will be the Q-TIP. The other trust has 50% Jayco stock and 50% other assets; it will be the bypass trust. Throughout his lifetime Mr. J owns the stock directly. The two trusts are created at his death. The Q-TIP qualifies as a shareholder, but Mrs. J, the beneficial owner, must make the QSST election within 2 months and 15 days of Mr. J's death. The bypass trust qualifies as a shareholder, but only for 2 years (60 days in S corporations' taxable years beginning before 1997). If the shares are distributed to Mrs. J, the bypass trust will have only $400,000 to accumulate. If the corporation wants to redeem the stock, it will have only 2 years (60 days in S corporations' taxable years beginning before 1997) to accumulate the liquid assets or distribute a note in redemption of stock.

If Mr. J had established both trusts as grantor trusts before his death, the bypass trust would be a qualified shareholder for two years. In addition, if the corporation had taken out a policy on Mr. J's life, it would have the liquidity to redeem the shares from the bypass trust.

1825.3. Classes of stock, and equity accounts. Although an S corporation cannot issue preferred stock in order to reduce the value of an older family member's estate, there are some devices that may partially achieve this objective without violating the single-class-of-stock rule. The estate planner should be wary, however, of diminishing the value of the decedent's stock to the point where the estate will be unable to take advantage of the deferred payment rules, the special redemption rules under §303, or, in some cases, the special valuation of real estate held in the corporation. See discussion at 1820.12.

A good estate planner should be aware of the mix of equity accounts, especially if the S corporation shareholder has significant amounts of PTI. With careful planning, it may be possible to affect the distributions to the generations remaining after the transfers.

1825.31. Voting rights. As is discussed in Chapter 2, at 225.2., an S corporation may issue voting and nonvoting stock without violating the single-class-of-stock rule. It is not unusual for an older family member to want to retain control of a corporation even though he or she is giving equity interest to a younger generation. If the corporation does not have any nonvoting shares outstanding when the older generation develops the estate plan, it should consider issuing some nonvoting shares.

This plan is easiest to work out in a family corporation when there is only one shareholder. It is also possible in a multiple-shareholder corporation, but the corporation should be careful to maintain the single class of stock—by treating all of the current shareholders equally.

Before the older generation develops the estate plan, the corporation should make sure that a substantial number of outstanding shares are nonvoting. If there are no nonvoting shares outstanding, the corporation may want to consider a nontaxable stock distribution or a recapitalization.

A nontaxable stock distribution occurs when all shareholders receive proportionate amounts of new stock. [§305(a)] In this situation, each shareholder allocates his or her basis in the pre-distribution shares to the post-distribution shares. [§307]

18

EXAMPLE 18 - 16: Bob and John are two unrelated and equal shareholders in Bojo Corporation. As of April 9, 1995, each shareholder owns 100 shares, all of which have voting rights. Bob intends to give most of his shares away, but Bob and John want to maintain equal voting power. The corporation distributes 1,000 new nonvoting shares to each shareholder, and the action is treated as a nontaxable stock distribution under §305(a). Bob can then begin to give his 1,000 nonvoting shares to members of his family, yet the two original shareholders will retain their equal voting rights.

1825.32. Equity-flavored compensation. Equity-flavored compensation, discussed in Chapter 2, is another indirect way to shift wealth to family members or to other employees. The vehicle may be stock bonus plans, stock options, stock appreciation rights, phantom stock plans, or any similar device that reduces the residual value of the older generation's equity interest in the corporation.

EXAMPLE 18 - 17: Seaward Corporation is an S corporation. At present, Paul owns all of the stock, which has a value of $1,000,000. Paul's daughter, Judy, is an employee of Seaward. Paul has other children who are not involved in the corporation, and he is concerned about gift tax consequences and family relations if he begins to give stock to Judy. Accordingly, Paul devises a plan to grant Judy some shares and options in the corporation as part of her annual compensation package. Judy will gradually acquire an increased interest in the corporation, and thereby shift a certain percentage of equity from Paul's estate.

When using stock grants and options, the corporation must be aware of the tax burden that will be borne by employees when they receive compensation. A package that is too generous in noncash items and gives the employee little or no cash may leave the employee financially strapped to pay the taxes.

OBSERVATION: An employee stock ownership plan can provide certain tax benefits to a shareholder who wants to turn ownership over to employees but retain voting control of a corporation. The ESOP is eligible to hold shares in an S corporation after 1997.

1825.33. Distributions of previously taxed income. A corporation with an S election that has been in effect since 1982 or earlier may have accumulated some previously taxed income (PTI). As discussed in Chapter 7, at 725., this layer of equity is a tax-free reduction of basis to the shareholder who receives it. In this respect, a distribution of PTI is similar to a distribution from the corporation's AAA. One major distinction between PTI and AAA, however, is that PTI may be distributed only to the shareholder who originally included the accumulation in income.

It is likely, in a family S corporation, that PTI accounts are held by older members of the family. If the holder of the PTI account dies, any undistributed balance will be closed out to paid-in capital, and it will not be available for distribution until the corporation has exhausted its accumulated earnings and profits. For this reason, it might be a good idea to have the corporation exhaust its PTI account as soon as possible. Perhaps the best means for doing so is to make an election to bypass the AAA, as discussed in Chapter 7, at 740. The bypass election makes PTI the first source of distributions, but only to the shareholder who owns the PTI account. Thus, when the AAA bypass election is in effect, the first source of distributions to a shareholder who does not have a PTI balance is the corporation's AEP. The corporation must be careful to watch the timing and amount of distributions, as well as the distribution elections, at or near the time of a plan to shift stock ownership.

EXAMPLE 18 - 18: In late 1995, Jeanne is the sole shareholder in Mobile Corporation, an S corporation. She is nearing retirement age, and she plans to give half of her stock to her son, Jay. At the end of 1995, the corporation has AEP of $350,000 and a PTI balance of $400,000, all of which is attributable to Jeanne. Mobile estimates that its AAA, after 1995 income, will be $200,000. Note that Jeanne has the entire AAA and the entire PTI balance, for a total of $600,000, before any distribution would be a dividend from AEP.

Also note that any other shareholder would have only $200,000 of distributions available before the distributions would be treated as dividends, since no other shareholder can gain access to Jeanne's PTI. Therefore, it would be a good idea for the corporation to distribute exactly \$400,000 to Jeanne, make no other distribution in the same year, and make a bypass election under §1368(e)(3). These steps would help achieve two goals:

1. The \$400,000 distribution—whether in the form of cash, other property, or a corporate obligation—would reduce the value of the corporation and shift Jeanne's property from an appreciating asset to an asset with more stable values.
2. The bypass election would have no adverse effects on Jeanne, but it would leave the entire AAA balance for future distributions to both Jeanne and Jay.

If the corporation needed to make other distributions during the year, it could still give Jeanne an extra \$400,000 by redeeming \$400,000 worth of her stock. See discussion at 1820.2.

1825.4. Charitable planning. A shareholder may want to leave property to charity. Often it is best to accomplish this with lifetime gifts, in order to take advantage of the income tax deduction as well as the gift tax deduction. If the donor does not want to part with the property before death, he or she may contribute property to a charitable remainder trust. The essence of this type of trust is that the donor retains a life interest in property that will pass to the designated charity at the donor's death. The charitable donation is measured as the value of the property, less the value assigned to the retained life interest.

Under prior law, a charitable organization is ineligible to hold shares in an S corporation. The IRS has also held that a charitable remainder trust did not qualify as a shareholder in an S corporation. [Rev. Rul. 92-48, 1992-1 CB 301; PLR 8922014]

> **OBSERVATION:** The Small Business Job Protection Act of 1996 added charities to the types of eligible shareholders. Note that this change takes effect for taxable years beginning after 1997, one year later than most amendments contained in that Act. Also note that, from the charity's point of view, S corporation stock may not be a terribly attractive investment. All of the income that passes through from the S corporation to the charity will be taxed to the charity as unrelated business taxable income (UBTI). Apparently, this characterization even applies to income, such as interest and dividends, that would not be treated as UBTI if received directly by the charity.

A charitably inclined person should be sure to leave other property to the charity before 1998, so that the S election will not terminate. One type of property a charity could hold is debts from the corporation to the shareholder. There could be a special benefit to giving these gifts during life, since they would be capital assets and the donor could deduct the fair market value of the debentures. See discussion in Chapter 10, at 1040.

A transfer of property other than stock during the donor's lifetime may also help the estate qualify for the special rules for stock redemptions, deferred payment of tax, and special valuation of real estate. By ridding the estate of other property, the donor might be able to comply with the percentage requirements to use these special opportunities.

> **OBSERVATION:** A transfer of corporate debts from a shareholder to a charity does not disqualify these debts from the straight-debt safe harbor rules of §1361(c)(5)(A). One of the requirements of the safe harbor is that the holder be eligible to be an S corporation shareholder or person regularly engaged in the trade or business of lending. Charities are eligible shareholders after 1997. See Chapter 2, at 215.4.

1830. Planning for the family to retain the business.

The rules and planning techniques discussed in this portion of the chapter assume that it is in the best interests of all of the survivors that the family remain in control of the business. If this is not the case, the emphasis should be on expeditious disposition of the business, discussed at 1835., below. Even if the current intention is for the business to remain under family control, it may be wise to devise alternate plans for disposition.

1830.1. Tax reduction. The planning strategies employed to reduce taxes have changed as dramatically as the Internal Revenue Code itself. For example, the planning strategies employed when the top rate of income tax was 70% may not be valid in an era when the top rate does not exceed 40%. Other changes have perhaps been more dramatic than the changes in rates themselves. For instance, there used to be significant tax savings associated with the use of trusts. The rate schedule imposed on estates and trusts now, however, reaches the 39.6% bracket at taxable income of approximately $7,500.

When contemplating the transfer of shares in an S corporation, the shareholder must remember to focus on both the income taxes and the transfer taxes that will be imposed on the shareholder and his or her family. Changes in the tax law, especially some provisions of the Tax Reform Act of 1986, have left few strategies for reducing the aggregate family income taxes. Some estate and gift planning opportunities have also been reduced or eliminated by recent tax law changes. This section explores some of the fundamental strategies that remain.

1830.11. Income tax reduction. A gift of S corporation stock is not a taxable event, per se. [§102] Thus, neither the donor nor the donee has any immediate income or loss as a result of the transfer. The subsequent income or loss, however, is shifted to the donee.

Historically, the older generation of the family was in a higher income tax bracket than the younger generation, and a gift of income-producing property from parents to children usually resulted in some income tax savings. Additional savings could be accomplished by putting property into trust, since a trust could be subject to its own graduated income tax rate schedule. One important aspect of this strategy was to design the trust so it would not be a grantor trust, with the income passing through to the grantor. In many cases, trusts also were designed so that they would not be treated as deemed grantor trusts—in order to keep the trust's income separate from that of its beneficiaries.

Recent changes in the law, however, have caused a reversal in this strategy. With the graduated rates on trusts being so steep, often no tax is saved, even when taxpayers are in the highest income tax bracket, by having the trust taxable on its own income. Thus treatment of a trust as a grantor, or deemed grantor, trust now causes little or no additional taxes.

From the estate planning point of view, the recent changes in trust taxation have removed a major disadvantage for the S corporation. At one time, the limitations on trusts as shareholders in S corporations put this business form at a disadvantage. Under current law, however, since the disadvantage of a grantor trust has largely disappeared, the S corporation now stands on equal footing with the C corporation, or one of the partnership forms, when the trust is an integral part of the estate plan.

Another significant reduction in the tax benefits from income splitting came in 1986 with the introduction of the "kiddie tax," whereby children under age 14 now must pay income tax at the parents' marginal rate (or at the higher marginal rate of either parent, when the parents are not married). Dependent children also have a limited standard deduction that may be used against unearned income, and dependents of other taxpayers are not allowed to claim their own personal exemptions.

A final limitation in the ability to reduce income taxes by spreading stock ownership among family members is the family S corporation rule of §1366(e). As is discussed in Chapter 8, at 820.31., an S corporation must compensate service-providing family members adequately, if services are a material income-producing factor.

In spite of all of these limitations, it is still possible, with careful planning, to achieve some modest income tax savings. One of the best strategies may be to employ children in the corporation's business. The wage income of the children will not be subject to the kiddie tax, and it may be offset by a full standard deduction. In addition, the wage income may be sufficient for children to no longer be claimed as exemptions on their parents' tax returns. See discussion at 1830.36, and in Chapter 8, at 820.2., for some of the risks associated with this strategy.

1830.12. Transfer tax reduction, in general. Some of the most important estate tax planning involves charitable and marital bequests. A person could eliminate the tax on his or her estate entirely by leaving all property to charity, to his or her surviving spouse, or to a mix of the two. This strategy may prove shortsighted if a second generation involved. See the discussion of marital bequests and Q-TIPs, at 1825.23.

Estate and gift taxes may be reduced through lifetime transfers. Although the estate and gift tax rates are identical, and the estate tax is based on the taxable estate plus the cumulative gifts, significant tax savings are available through the use of gifts. For example, the annual exclusion can shield considerable wealth if there are enough donees and if the transfers take place each year. Gift splitting is also useful when either the husband or the wife, but not both, is the primary donor. [§2513(a)(1)]

EXAMPLE 18 - 19: Barry owns all of the stock of Barico, which has a current value of $1,000,000. He has substantial wealth, and he has already used up his unified credit. He is in the 45% marginal estate and gift tax bracket. He gives $100,000 worth of stock to each of his five children. He splits the gifts with his wife, Carrie, who is also in the 45% estate and gift tax bracket and who has also used up her unified credit. Thus Barry gives away 50% of his stock in the current year. His taxable gift (including Carrie's portion) will be $80,000 to each child, after the annual exclusion. Thus he and Carrie have total taxable gifts of $400,000 for the current year, and they pay tax of $180,000 ($400,000 x .45). If the stock did not appreciate and Barry left it to his children in his estate, the taxable transfer of the stock itself would be $500,000, which may push Barry's estate into an even higher tax bracket.

A second savings afforded by gifts occurs when the gifted property appreciates before death. The taxable gift is based on the property's value at the date of gift, rather than on its fair market value at the date of the decedent's death.

EXAMPLE 18 - 20: Refer to Example 18 - 19. Assume that Barry lived for five more years after he made the gift and that the stock appreciated by 20% over that period. The stock given to the children would be worth $600,000 at Barry's death, and it would increase the taxable estate accordingly if he had retained the stock until his death.

Another gift savings results when the donor has used all of his or her unified credit and the gifts are subject to current tax. The taxable gifts are based only on the amount of value transferred to the donees, and not on the property available for transfer. The estate tax, by contrast, is imposed on all of the decedent's pre-tax wealth.

EXAMPLE 18 - 21: Refer to Examples 18 - 19 and 18 - 20. If Barry had held the stock until his death, the $180,000 he had previously paid in gift tax (compounded by the earnings on the money) also would have been included in the taxable estate. Thus, even if Barry had held the $180,000 in a no-interest account for the five years, his taxable estate would include the $600,000 value of the stock and the $180,000 he had paid in tax. The taxable value would be $780,000, resulting in a tax considerably higher than $180,000.

OBSERVATION: None of these examples expressly considers reduction of value for a minority discount, discussed at 1820.11. Presumably, the discounts would apply equally to a gift or a transfer at death.

To reduce the tax savings from "deathbed transfers," a decedent's gross estate includes the gift tax payable on any gifts made within three years of death. Thus, the savings of a gift are not nearly as substantial if the donor does not live for at least three years after giving the gift.

Other problems involved with gifts may outweigh the potential tax savings. Often, the older generation is unwilling to part completely with dominion and control over the property. In the case of an S corporation, this problem can be alleviated by giving nonvoting stock and retaining voting stock, but the problem does not disappear entirely. The older generation may fear expensive medical costs and other problems of old age, and be reluctant to part with any wealth. Similarly, the older generation may not completely trust the younger generation's abilities to handle the property.

In addition, the tax savings may backfire. For example, if property declines in value before death, an early gift—when the value is still high—may actually cost more tax than if the property were held until death. A gift plan that concentrates on small business assets, with the older generation retaining other property, may also result in a loss of tax saving under §303 or §6166, or both. Similarly, a transfer by gift may reduce or eliminate the potential tax savings from special-use valuation of farm property and other real estate.

In the final analysis, a gift is a bet that the property will appreciate. Like any other bet, it may be a gamble. The gift strategy may work quite well in connection with the slow freeze techniques discussed below.

1830.2. Basis after death. The basis rules mitigate the strategy of gift giving. If property is held until death, the decedent's successor in interest will receive a step-up (or a step-down) in basis of shares transferred by reason of death. [§1014] Thus, if property has appreciated during the older generation's lifetime, it may be better from an income tax planning point of view to leave the property in the estate.

By contrast, the donor's basis carries to the donee if property is transferred by gift. There are limited adjustments for gift tax attributable to appreciation. [§1015] See Chapter 9, at 910.2., for a brief discussion of these basis rules. Also see Chapter 6, at 630.22.

EXAMPLE 18 - 22: Refer to Examples 18 - 19 and 18 - 20. Assume that Barry's basis in the stock was $250,000 before the gift. If he transfers the property to the children, the basis will be $250,000, plus half of the gift tax (attributable to 50% appreciation in Barry's hands before the gift). Thus each child would have a basis of $50,000 in his or her block of stock. If the value rose to $600,000 at the time of Barry's death, and if the stock were transferred at death, each child would have a basis of $120,000 in the stock received. This example does not consider any minority discounts that might be used to value the stock.

OBSERVATION: The rules for S corporations differ considerably from those for partnerships with respect to property held inside the business. In an S corporation, there is no adjustment to basis of assets held inside the corporate shell. (The §754 election for partnerships does not cover S corporations.) Accordingly, it may be prudent to keep real estate out of the corporation or to distribute real estate to older shareholders before death. Until August 21, 1996, there was no income in respect of a decedent (IRD) for receivables and other property held by an S corporation at the time of transfer by death. The change in the law has no effect on the amount of taxable income reported by the S corporation or its shareholders. It does cause a reduction of basis for inherited stock of an S corporation in which there is IRD. Thus a shareholder who sustains losses, receives large distributions, or sells his or her stock might be disadvantaged as a result of the new law. By contrast, a shareholder may get a deduction on his or her income tax return for estate taxes attributable to the IRD. See Chapter 6, at 630.71., for a discussion of these rules.

1830.3. Freezing the value of the older generation's interest. In the 1980s, a technique known as the "estate tax freeze" became popular, primarily in closely held corporations and partnerships. In theory, it was a relatively simple technique for converting the older generation's interest into a form that was limited in value, but that allowed the older family member to retain control of the business throughout his or her lifetime.

The most straightforward use of the freeze was in the context of a closely held C corporation.

The older family member would cause the corporation to issue voting preferred stock and nonvoting common stock. The older member would retain the preferred stock and give the common stock to the younger members. Typically, the preferred stock would receive a fixed dividend per share, with no additional participation in the corporation's profits. Thus the value of the preferred stock would not grow as the residual value of the company increased.

EXAMPLE 18 - 23: Richard is the sole shareholder of Richco, a C corporation. He plans to leave his stock to his daughters, Tricia and Julie. At present, the value of all of Richco's common stock is approximately $1,000,000. Richard expects the value of the stock to double every five years. Thus, if Richard lived for five more years, the value of the stock would be $2,000,000. If he retained all of his interest in the corporation and lived for five more years, the value of the stock in his gross estate would be $2,000,000.

Richard could apply the freeze technique by recapitalizing the corporation and taking out preferred stock with a par value of $1,000,000 and common stock of negligible value. The preferred stock would be voting and the common stock would be nonvoting. The preferred stock would carry a dividend of 6% of par, or $60,000 per year, and would be redeemable at par upon liquidation of the corporation. Under these conditions, the value of the preferred stock would likely never be more or less than its current $1,000,000.

At present, the value of the common stock is negligible. Thus Richard could give the stock to his daughters without incurring any gift tax and without exhausting any of his unified credit. The common stock would not be included in his gross estate, so his gross estate would be reduced by $1,000,000 over the next five years, compared to what it would have been without the freeze. Without the freeze, the entire $2,000,000 value of the business would have been included in Richard's estate.

The IRS leveled numerous attacks on the freeze. For instance, the IRS declined to rule on recapitalizations as tax-free reorganizations. Thus the planner could not be assured that the exchange of voting common for voting preferred and nonvoting common was a tax-free reorganization. Also, a freeze presented serious valuation problems. If the IRS determined that the value of the preferred stock received in the exchange exceeded the value of the common stock surrendered, the shareholder would have received a dividend for the excess value. On the other hand, if the value of the preferred stock was less than the value of the surrendered common stock, the shareholder would have given away a valuable gift, with the accompanying gift tax consequences.

EXAMPLE 18 - 24: Refer to Example 18 - 23. Assume that the IRS revalued Richco's preferred stock at $1,100,000. Richard would have received a dividend of $100,000—the difference between the value of the stock received and the value of the stock surrendered.

Alternatively, assume that the IRS valued the preferred stock at $750,000. The common stock, which Richard gave to Tricia and Julie, would be valued at $250,000. Therefore, Richard would be liable for a gift tax, or at least would have exhausted some of his unified credit.

In 1987, Congress enacted §2036(c), which repealed freezes. Under this provision, a transfer of a "disproportionately large share of the potential appreciation" by a person who retained an interest in the income of the business was disregarded for estate and gift tax purposes. Any residual equity given away was included in the transferor's estate. This rule is effective for transfers occurring after December 17, 1987.

EXAMPLE 18 - 25: Refer to Example 18 - 24. Assume that Richard made the gift to his daughters on December 20, 1987, that Richard lived for ten more years, and that the value of the company was $4,000,000 on the date of his death. The entire $4,000,000 would be included in Richard's gross estate.

The freeze repeal had far-reaching effects and was extremely unpopular. So, in 1990, the repeal was repealed. [Revenue Reconciliation Act of 1990, §11601(a)] In its place, Congress enacted some special valuation rules [§§2701-2704] that apply to gifts of interest in closely held businesses. In general, these rules are very restrictive with respect to the value of retained senior equity interest, such as preferred stock. For detailed rules regarding the necessary clauses, see Regulations §25.2702-3(b)(3).

They adopt the following residual approach to valuing a gift of an equity interest to a family member:

	Value of the entire business
–	Value of retained interest
=	Value of gift

Thus, the 1990 valuation rules tend to not include value of previously transferred interests in a person's estate. To the contrary, the rules adopted in 1990 tend to place greater value on the current gifts. This is accomplished by imputing a low value to retained equity interests.

1830.31. General inapplicability of freeze to S corporations. Because the classic freeze technique involves the use of preferred stock, it has been considered unavailable to S corporations. There are some techniques, however, that S corporations can use, with the possibility of a substantial reduction in estate tax liability.

1830.32. Use of a grantor retained annuity trust (GRAT). One power that deserves special mention is the grantor's retention of a right to substitute property of equal value to the S corporation stock in a nonfiduciary capacity. This power is specified as a power that causes a trust to be a grantor trust. [§675(4); PLRs 9337011, 9645013, 9648045, 9707005] It does not, however, exempt the transfer of the stock into trust from the federal gift tax. Thus a grantor may transfer S corporation stock into a grantor-retained annuity trust (GRAT) without endangering the corporation's S election.

A GRAT is a trust set up for a term of years. The grantor retains the right to receive an annuity from the trust. The annuity can be a fixed annual percentage of the initial value of property transferred to the trust, or it can be a fixed percent of the trust's assets, as revalued each year. The remainder interest is held by another person, such as a child of the grantor. If the grantor dies during the term of the trust, the value of the property is included in his or her gross estate. If the grantor outlives the term of the trust, he or she has no interest in the property when the trust terminates, and therefore it is not included in the gross estate.

The tax savings from a GRAT result from two causes:

- The property is valued as of the date of the initial transfer to the trust. Post-gift appreciation is never subject to the transfer tax.
- The transferor retains a fractional interest in the property at the time of the transfer. The portion of the transfer that is taxable is only the portion attributable to the remainder interest.

A recent private letter ruling [PLR 9337011] illustrates the creative use of a trust to freeze the value of a grantor's estate. A taxpayer who owned stock in an S corporation outright transferred the stock to a trust. The grantor retained the power to substitute property equal to the fair market value of the S corporation stock into the trust in a nonfiduciary capacity. In other words, no other person could prevent the grantor from repurchasing the stock. The grantor retained no other powers, however, that would cause the trust to be a grantor trust.

This power has two interesting effects. First, it is not a sufficient retained interest for the transfer to be treated as a completed gift. That is to say, the value of the stock is subject to the gift tax (less the value of the interest retained by the grantor), and the stock will not be included in the grantor's gross estate if the grantor outlives the term of the trust. However, this power does treat the grantor as the owner of trust property for income tax purposes. [§675(4)] Consequently, the trust meets the definition of *eligible shareholder* in an S corporation. This technique has been used to allow a shareholder to create a grantor retained annuity trust (GRAT) without endangering the corporation's S election. [PLRs 9352004, 9548013]

After the death of the grantor, the S election may be endangered, depending upon the nature of the trust. If the trust distributes all of its property to eligible shareholders, there is no problem, unless the distribution causes the total number of shareholders to exceed the limit. If the trust now meets the definition of a QSST or an Electing Small Business Trust (after 1996), the trust will continue to be an eligible shareholder indefinitely. If the trust does not meet one of these qualifications, it must divest itself of the S corporation stock within two years of the grantor's death (within 60 days if the grantor died before November 2, 1996). See Chapter 2, at 215.3., for discussion.

One problem with a grantor trust is that all of the taxable income realized by the trust passes through directly to the grantor. In some cases, the grantor may need to get the cash to pay the tax on the income received by the trust. Some trusts have been drafted with a "reimbursement clause" that allows the trust to reimburse the grantor for the taxes attributable to trust income. The IRS has held that a reimbursement clause is not valued as a retained interest, and thus does not reduce the gift to the remainder beneficiaries. These arrangements can keep the grantor from illiquidity. The disadvantage of the reimbursement is that it gives assets back to the grantor, rather than passing them through to the remainder beneficiaries at the time of the grantor's death.

A recent ruling illustrates a well-designed trust arrangement that serves several purposes:

- The trust is a GRAT and qualifies as a shareholder throughout the annuity term.
- At the expiration of the annuity term, the trust will distribute part of its stock to a spousal trust and part to a family trust. Each of these trusts will qualify as a QSST, provided the beneficiary files a proper election.
- Both trusts will terminate upon the grantor's death, and the stock from both will be transferred to a trust for the grantor's widow. This trust will also be a QSST, assuming the widow files a proper QSST election. [PLR 9648045]

1830.33. Use of a stock dividend to effect a slow freeze. As was illustrated above, a stock freeze typically involves the use of preferred stock, and thus it is not available to S corporation shareholders. The slow freeze technique, however, can accomplish much the same result over a longer period of time. The basic operation of the slow freeze uses stock distributions to younger family members coupled with distributions of cash, other property, or notes to older shareholders.

For the S corporation, the first concern of this technique is to maintain a single class of stock. Thus, the distributions should be proportionate in value per share; there is no expressed or implied rule that each distribution must be in the same form of property.

> **EXAMPLE 18 - 26:** AB Corporation, an S corporation, has two shareholders, Allen and Brenda. On January 1, 1995, each shareholder owns 5,000 shares (50% of the outstanding stock). Allen would like to increase his percentage ownership, and Brenda would rather receive cash or a corporate obligation. On January 1, 1995, the fair market value of all of the stock is $1,000,000, or $100 per share. The corporation decides to distribute $100,000 to each person. Allen will receive 1,000 new shares, and Brenda will receive $100,000 cash.
>
> The two distributions are equal in value, so they create no possibility of two classes of stock. As a result of this distribution, Allen now owns 6,000 shares and Brenda owns 5,000 shares.

A stock dividend may or may not be taxable if paid by a C corporation. Under general rules, a stock distribution is nontaxable and requires a basis allocation. [§305(a)] There are a number of important exceptions to this rule, however. If a shareholder has the choice of receiving stock or receiving property (including cash), the distribution will be treated as a taxable distribution, subject to §301. [§305(b)(1)] Generally, a distribution that results in some shareholders receiving property and other shareholders increasing their ownership generally is taxable as well. [§305(b)(2)]

A taxable stock distribution becomes subject to §301—which treats a distribution as a dividend, subject to the paying corporation's current and accumulated earnings and profits. When the paying corporation has an S election in effect, however, §301 is preempted by §1368. (See Chapter 7, at 700.25., for a more detailed explanation.) Thus a stock distribution that is not subject to §305(a) is subject to §301, which is in turn subject to §1368 if the corporation is an S corporation. The shareholder who receives the stock distribution will account for the distribution at the fair market value and, if the corporation has no accumulated earnings and profits, the distribution will be a reduction in basis of the shareholder's other stock. If the corporation has accumulated earnings and profits, the distribution will be subject to the usual hierarchy of AAA, PTI, AEP, and other equity, as explained in Chapter 7.

EXAMPLE 18 - 27: Refer to Example 18 - 26. Assume that the corporation has no accumulated earnings and profits. If Allen's basis (measured at the end of the corporation's taxable year before the distribution) was at least $100,000, Allen would reduce his basis in the original 5,000 shares by $100,000 (the fair market value of the shares received in the distribution) and would assign basis of $100,000 to the new shares. If Allen's basis in the 5,000 shares was less than $100,000, he would reduce the basis of those shares to zero and report a gain from the receipt of the new shares. His basis in the new shares would be $100,000.

Alternatively, assume that the corporation's AAA was less than the total distribution of $200,000 and that the corporation has accumulated earnings and profits. The corporation would reduce its AAA to zero, and each shareholder would treat the distribution from the AAA as a reduction of basis. Each shareholder would report a dividend, to the extent that the fair market value of the distribution exceeded the portion allocated to AAA, but did not exceed a proportionate share of the corporation's accumulated earnings and profits. See Chapter 7 for a comprehensive discussion.

As the foregoing example illustrates, this distribution scheme has two effects. First, it directly decreases the value of the entire corporation, due to the distribution of cash or other property to one shareholder. Second, it decreases the percentage ownership of the shareholder who receives the cash or other property. There are some complications with respect to valuation of the stock.

EXAMPLE 18 - 28: Refer to Example 18 - 26. Assume that the corporation has no accumulated earnings and profits and that each shareholder's basis had been sufficient to absorb the entire distribution. The value of the entire stock would be reduced by the $100,000 cash distributed to Brenda. As a result of these distributions, the ownership would change in the following manner:

Allen	
Before distribution [(5,000/10,000) x 1,000,000]	$500,000
After distribution [(6,000/11,000) x 900,000]	490,909
Brenda	
Before distribution [(5,000/10,000) x 1,000,000]	$500,000
After distribution [(5,000/11,000) x 900,000]	409,091

As these amounts illustrate, the value of the distribution to Brenda is $100,000, but the value to Allen is somewhat less. Therefore, this scheme poses the possibility of a second class

18

of stock. Therefore, a simple algebraic formula can assure that the two distributions are exactly equal:

	Value of all shares before distribution
–	Value of property to be distributed
=	Value of corporation after distribution

$$\frac{\text{Value of property distribution}}{\text{Value of corporation after distribution}} \times \text{No. shares pre-distribution} \times \frac{\text{\% stock owned by stock distributee}}{\text{\% stock owned by property distributee}} = \text{No. shares to be issued}$$

EXAMPLE 18 - 29: Refer to Example 18 - 28. The exact number of new shares to be issued to Allen would be computed as follows:

Value of shares before distribution		$ 1,000,000
Less property to be distributed to Brenda		(100,000)
Value after distribution		$ 900,000
Value of property distribution		$ 100,000
Divided by value of corporation after distribution	÷	900,000
Times pre-distribution shares	x	10,000
Times Allen's shares/Brenda's shares (5,000/5,000)	x	1
New shares to be issued		1,111.11

The slow freeze does not provide dramatic results in a short period of time. Given a few years, however, it can shift a substantial amount of the growth equity from one shareholder to another.

EXAMPLE 18 - 30: Continue with Example 18 - 29. Assume that, as of January 1, 1996, the value of the stock has risen back to $1,000,000 and the corporation intends to distribute additional stock to Allen and $100,000 to Brenda. Note the change in percentage ownership:

Value of shares before distribution		$ 1,000,000
Less property to be distributed to Brenda		(100,000)
Value after distribution		$ 900,000
Value of property distribution		$ 100,000
Divided by value of corporation after distribution	÷	900,000
Times pre-distribution shares	x	11,111.11
Times Allen's shares/Brenda's shares (6,111.11/5,000)	x	1.22
New shares to be issued		1,506.17

After this distribution, Allen would own 7,617.28 shares (6,111.11+1506.17) and Brenda would own only 5,000. If the value of the corporation increased substantially over the next few years, Brenda could shift a substantial portion of the growth to Allen, without incurring any transfer tax liability.

18

The above examples imply that Brenda is of an older generation than Allen and that she probably intends to leave all of her stock to Allen upon her death. The examples also imply that all of the outstanding shares as of January 1, 1995, were voting. Brenda might be concerned with maintaining her 50% voting power throughout her life. The gradual erosion of her ownership might alter this desired ration, unless the new shares issued to Allen are nonvoting. Fortunately, voting differences do not create a second class of stock (see Chapter 2, at 225.2., for further discussion), so the new shares issued each year to Allen could be nonvoting. The shift of value to Allen need not erode Brenda's voting power.

1830.34. Slow freeze using a stock redemption. An S corporation could use a stock redemption to help effect a transfer from one generation to another. As is discussed in Chapter 2, a redemption may indicate a second class of stock, and thus it must be approached with caution. According to the Regulations, a redemption will not indicate a second class of stock if the redemption price is set to the fair market value of the stock. Book value is a safe harbor, and thus any redemption price between book value and fair market value will not be evidence that the corporation has more than one class of stock. [Regs. §1.1361-1(l)(2)(iii)]

The redemption approach offers certain advantages over the stock distribution. First, if the redemption price meets the fair market value or book value safe-harbor tests, the distribution is not required to be proportionate to the shares held by each shareholder.

> **EXAMPLE 18 - 31:** Assume the same facts as in Examples 18 - 26 through 18 - 29, except that Brenda wants to redeem some of her stock. Assume that, in 1995, she is willing to surrender up to $100,000 worth of stock in exchange for cash. Allen will exchange nothing. Example 18 - 26 indicates that each share is worth $100 before the distribution. In lieu of giving Allen a stock distribution, the corporation could redeem 1,000 of Brenda's shares for $100,000. Thereafter, Allen would continue to own 5,000 shares, out of 9,000 outstanding after the redemption.

As was discussed in Chapter 15, at 1510., there are several tests to determine whether a redemption is a sale of stock or a distribution subject to §301 and §1368. Regarding the magnitude of the planned redemption, if the corporation has little or no accumulated earnings and profits, or if it has a substantial AAA, no tax benefit should be gained from treating a redemption as a sale as opposed to a distribution. If the AAA is small in relation to the planned redemption, however, it could create a dividend to the shareholder receiving the property, the shareholder receiving the taxable stock distribution, or both.

1830.35. Simultaneous redemption and distribution. If used in connection with the slow freeze technique discussed above, this combination could accelerate the rate of change from that demonstrated above. A stock dividend to the younger generation, coupled with redemptions of the older generation's stock, could be an annual event, as the corporation obtains cash; or it could be a one-shot transaction, designed to jump-start the slow freeze process.

The combinations of stock redemptions and stock dividends are practically infinite. This technique could be tailored to the unique circumstances of each S corporation.

1830.36. Other means of transferring value. There are several other means of transferring a percentage of the corporation's shares to other shareholders. In the case of family members, the older generation may want to give shares to younger family members.

Children could receive stock as compensation for services performed for the corporation. Under §83, the children could be taxed on the value of the stock when substantial restrictions (if any) expire. Usually, the children should receive sufficient cash to pay any income taxes on the stock received. Issuing additional stock to the children would cause the residual value of stock held by the parent to gradually diminish. The compensation arrangement should not be subject to gift tax, if the compensation is a bona fide arrangement. The value of the stock should be deductible to the corporation and thus should reduce the income taxes to all shareholders proportionately.

18

> **CAUTION:** Compensation to children may be disallowed if it is excessive. [See *Westbrook*, TC Memo 1993-634, 66 TCM 1823, aff'd *Westbrook v. CIR*, 68 F.3d 868, 76 AFTR 2d 95-7397, 95-2 USTC, 50,587 (5th. Cir.), discussed in Chapter 8, at 820.2.] In

addition to disallowing a deduction for compensation, the IRS could also assess gift tax on the parents.

Children, or other key employees, could receive phantom stock or stock appreciation rights as part of their retirement packages. This strategy, discussed in Chapter 2, at 225.55., could erode the residual value of the common stock by giving these persons a claim on corporate property.

OBSERVATION: Any of the slow freeze techniques discussed in this chapter may be used in combination with any of the other techniques. A combination of stock distributions, stock redemptions, stock issued as compensation, and phantom stock plans may combine to provide dramatic transfers from one generation to another within a few years.

One of the most aggressive strategies for transferring an S corporation with a minimum of estate and gift tax was challenged in the case of *Estate of Paul E. Brown*, TC Memo 1997-195. Paul Brown, part owner of the Cincinnati Bengals football team (an S corporation) owned one share of 231 shares outstanding at the time of his death. The remaining 230 shares were held by John Sawyer, Brown's attorney. Several years before his death, Brown had sold all but one of his shares to Sawyer for $30,000 per share, yet Brown remained voting trustee on all outstanding shares. The principal consideration given to Brown by Sawyer was a promissory note. At the same time, Sawyer granted an option to Brown's two sons to buy all but one of his shares for $25,000 per share. They paid Sawyer $1 for the option, which could not be exercised for ten years. A portion of the purchase price would be cancellation of the promissory note that Sawyer owed due to his purchase of Paul Brown's shares. Brown's sons exercised their options when the value of each share was approximately $100,000. The IRS claimed that Brown's estate should include all of the shares subject to the options. The estate prevailed, however, and was treated as owning only one share.

CAUTION: The strategy employed in the *Brown* case was extremely aggressive. The friendship and trust of the parties involved make the arm's length dealing tenuous at best. They secured a deal whereby Sawyer was entitled to all of the distributions from the S corporation for ten years, yet all the appreciation remained in the hands of the Brown family, without there being a second class of stock. There was relatively little cash involved in any of the transactions. The IRS is certain to challenge similar arrangements.

1835. Planning for the estate to dispose of the business.

If the family does not intend to continue the business after the death of the current shareholder, there should be some plan for disposition. If there are no other shareholders, a business broker or financial advisor can probably help the family get the best possible price. If there are other shareholders, some sort of buyout agreement should be in effect. Also, the corporation should have a formula for valuing the stock at the death of any shareholder and a means for the estate or survivors to enforce the agreement.

The agreement should come into effect as soon as possible after the death of a shareholder, in order to avoid protracted arguments and litigation. If the buyout arrangement is unreasonable, the surviving shareholders may have little incentive to settle up with the decedent's estate promptly.

One possible result of the delays and haggling from an incomplete or poorly drafted agreement is that the continuing shareholders might drive down the value of the business by imprudent actions or mere incompetence. In that case, there might be little value left by the time the buyout is completed.

Often, an arrangement to sell a business to existing co-owners is accomplished by one of two techniques:

- A cross-purchase agreement, whereby each shareholder agrees to purchase a portion of the stock from the deceased shareholder's estate or other successor
- A redemption agreement, by which the corporation is obligated to redeem a shareholder's stock from his or her estate or other heirs at the time of his or her death

OBSERVATION: A buyout agreement should be in place in anticipation of death, divorce, or irreconcilable differences among the shareholders. The ideal time to establish the agreement is in the initial phases of the business, when all parties are still compatible. Later, disagreements among the shareholders may make it much more difficult to arrive at an equitable agreement.

1835.1. The cross-purchase agreement. Each of these arrangements—the cross-purchase and the redemption—has its advantages and its disadvantages. The cross-purchase agreement is probably the simpler, in substance, but carries certain risks. First, and foremost, each shareholder will be obligated to purchase stock from the estate of a deceased shareholder. If the surviving shareholder does not have sufficient assets to complete the purchase, litigation, bankruptcy, and other problems could result. Thus it is in the interests of all parties that each participant in a cross-purchase agreement have the wherewithal to meet his or her obligation. Unless the parties are independently wealthy, the most common arrangement is for each shareholder to carry a life insurance policy on the other shareholders in order to fund the cross-purchase agreement.

EXAMPLE 18 - 32: Bob and John are the 50% shareholders in BJ Corporation, an S corporation. They are not related to each other, and neither has any family members involved in the business. Each one would want to take control of the entire corporation upon the death of the other. Both Bob and John have families, and they want their families to receive the value of their stock. They value the entire corporation at $2,000,000. Each shareholder takes out a life insurance policy for $1,000,000 on the other to finance the cross-purchase agreement.

Advantages of the cross-purchase agreement include the following:

- If the agreement is funded by life insurance, the surviving shareholder will have sufficient liquid assets to settle his or her obligation to the estate or family of the deceased shareholder.
- When a shareholder dies, the insurance will not be included in his or her gross estate. Thus it will be exempt from the estate tax, unless the insured had transferred incidents of ownership in the policy to the current holder within three years of the insured's death.
- The surviving shareholder will have no gross income from the maturation of the policy. [§101(a)(1)]
- The surviving shareholder's basis in the stock acquired from the decedent will be its agreed-upon value, or cost.

EXAMPLE 18 - 33: Refer to Example 18 - 32. Assume that neither shareholder can afford to purchase the other's stock, unless the agreement is funded by life insurance. So John takes out a policy for $1,000,000 on Bob's life and vice versa. Then Bob dies. John collects $1,000,000 from the insurance company and uses those funds to purchase all of Bob's shares from his estate.

John reports no taxable income on the proceeds. He takes a cost basis of $1,000,000 in the shares he acquired from Bob's estate. This basis will be available for losses or distributions.

There are also some disadvantages to the cross-purchase agreement. For instance:

- Each shareholder who buys a policy will be charged premiums that reflect the age and health of the other shareholder.
- If a policy lapses due to nonpayment of premiums, the family of the insured shareholder will be at risk.
- If there are more than two shareholders, and not all percentages are equal, differences arise in the number and amount of policies that each shareholder needs in order to cover his or her potential liability to purchase the stock of any other shareholders who might die.

EXAMPLE 18 - 34: Refer to Example 18 - 32. Assume that Bob is 70 years old and in ill health, while John is 50 years old and in excellent health. John must carry a policy on Bob's life, and he will be charged a premium based on Bob's age and health. John must pay substantially higher premiums than Bob, whose premiums are based on John's age and health.

If John fails to pay the premiums and Bob dies first, John might not be able to comply with the cross-purchase agreement, and Bob's family would suffer from John's failure to live up to the agreement.

If surviving shareholders decide to have the corporation redeem the stock of a deceased shareholder, the redemption could be treated as a constructive distribution to the surviving shareholders, since the corporation's purchase of the stock would relieve the surviving shareholders of personal obligations. As was discussed in Chapter 15, at 1510.15., a stock redemption may be a distribution to the continuing shareholder, if the continuing shareholder was primarily and unconditionally obligated to purchase the stock.

EXAMPLE 18 - 35: Refer to Example 18 - 32. Assume that Bob died and that the corporation had sufficient funds to settle up with Bob's estate for the entire $1,000,000. The corporation redeemed all of Bob's stock from his estate. The corporation might have relieved John of a $1,000,000 personal obligation. Thus, part of the $1,000,000 might be a dividend to John, if the corporation had sufficient earnings and profits, or might be a gain, if John's pre-distribution basis had been less than $1,000,000.

A final advantage of the cross-purchase arrangement occurs when the redemption price bears no resemblance to the fair market value of the stock as of purchase date. As is discussed in Chapter 2, at 225.34., a stock redemption agreement may be evidence of a second class of stock, unless the redemption price is at fair market value, book value, or some point in between. [Regs. §1.1361-1(l)(2)(iii)] In a cross-purchase agreement, there is no dealing between the corporation and any shareholder, so it is extremely unlikely that a cross-purchase arrangement could be evidence of more than one class of stock. See *Estate of Paul E. Brown*, TC Memo 1997-195, discussed at 1830.36.

1835.2. The stock redemption agreement. Some of the risks of a cross-purchase agreement can be eliminated through a stock redemption agreement. Under this alternative, the corporation is obligated to redeem the shares of any shareholder who dies. If the arrangement will require substantial liquid assets, the corporation must purchase a life insurance policy on each shareholder. A redemption agreement has the following advantages over a cross-purchase arrangement:

- The differences in premiums due to the age and health of the various shareholders are borne by the corporation, and thus they are allocated ratably among all shareholders.

- The payment of premiums is the responsibility of the corporation, although all of the shareholders should have the knowledge and ability to ensure that no policy lapses.
- The corporation will need to hold only one policy on the life of each shareholder. Especially if there are more than two shareholders and the percentage holdings vary significantly, this aspect can make a redemption agreement much more manageable and enforceable than a cross-purchase agreement.

EXAMPLE 18 - 36: A corporation has eight shareholders, of varying ages and health conditions. If the shareholders undertook a cross-purchase agreement, each shareholder would need to carry a life insurance policy on each of the other seven shareholders, requiring 56 policies to fund the agreement. A redemption agreement, by contrast, would require only eight policies, one on the life of each shareholder, and all shareholders would bear the cost of insuring older shareholders, or those in ill health, proportionately.

- If the shareholders were not primarily and unconditionally obligated to purchase the stock, the redemption of a deceased shareholder's stock will not be treated as a constructive distribution to the surviving shareholders. See Chapter 15, at 1510.15.

There are also certain disadvantages of a redemption agreement as opposed to a cross-purchase agreement. Some of the more significant drawbacks follow:

- The surviving shareholders will not receive a cost basis in the stock of a deceased shareholder, since the survivors do not directly acquire any new shares.
- If the agreement is funded by insurance and the corporation is a C corporation, the insurance proceeds will add to the corporation's current earnings and profits. The proceeds will also be included in the corporation's adjusted current earnings, and they may create alternative minimum tax liability at the corporate level.
- If the agreement is funded by insurance and the corporation is an S corporation, the insurance proceeds will not add to the AAA. This means that if the corporation has AEP, the surviving shareholders will not be able to receive any of the insurance proceeds as distributions until the corporation's AEP are exhausted.
- The surviving shareholders will be allocated portions of the tax-exempt income from the insurance, and they will receive a proportional step-up in basis.
- The redemption gives rise to no tax benefits at the corporate level. The corporation must account for the entire proceeds as treasury stock. As is discussed in Chapter 15, at 1515., the redemption proceeds must be allocated among the corporation's AAA, AEP, and paid-in capital.

EXAMPLE 18 - 37: Deaco, an S corporation, had three equal shareholders until one of the parties died. A redemption agreement was in effect, whereby the corporation would buy back all shares from the estate of the deceased shareholder. Immediately before the death of the shareholder, the corporation had an AAA balance of $30,000 and AEP of $120,000. The corporation held a $500,000 insurance policy on the life of each shareholder. When the shareholder died and the corporation collected the policy, the proceeds added to the OAA. When the corporation redeemed the stock, it reduced both the AAA and the AEP by one-third. See discussion in Chapter 15, at 1515.3. Thus, immediately after the redemption, the corporation's equity accounts were:

AAA	$ 20,000
AEP	80,000
OAA	500,000

Some additional risks are associated with the redemption agreement, although these usually can be surmounted:

- The redemption may be a disproportionate distribution and may create a second class of stock. (See Chapter 2, at 225.) However, there is no danger of a second class of stock if the redemption price is between book value and a reasonable determination of fair market value. (See Regulations §1.1361-1(l)(2)(iii) and discussions in Chapter 2, at 225.34., and Chapter 15, at 1515.1.)
- If the redemption does not comply with one of the transactions described in §302(b) or §303, it may be a taxable dividend to the deceased shareholder's successor. (See discussion in Chapter 15, at 1510.1.) This could occur if the corporation had low or no AAA, high AEP, and the shareholder's basis was less than fair market value, due to the presence of substantial income in respect of a decedent inside the corporation. (See Chapter 6, at 630.71.)

As is discussed at length in Chapter 2, at 225., and in Chapter 13, at 1350., there are numerous problems and rulings dealing with the status of trusts as holders of S corporation stock. The tax advisor of an S corporation must pay careful attention whenever a trust enters into the plan. The IRS has ruled, for example, that the right to have nonvoting stock redeemed upon the beneficiary's death did not prevent a trust from being a QSST. [PLR 8911012]

> **CAUTION:** If the shareholders have decided to use a cross-purchase agreement, and then they want to use a stock redemption, there could be constructive distributions to the continuing shareholders. See discussion in Chapter 15, at 1510.15. It might be best to have the initial agreement be that the corporation has the right of first refusal to redeem the stock of any deceased shareholder. If the corporation does not exercise this right, then the remaining shareholders may proceed with the cross-purchase arrangement. If the corporation does complete the redemption, the corporation will not have relieved any shareholder of a primary and unconditional obligation to purchase stock. This arrangement minimizes the danger that a redemption will be treated as a constructive distribution.

A redemption may provide an opportunity for a shareholder to take a disproportionate distribution, without creating the danger of a second class of stock. The Regulations require only that the redemption meet the fair market value or book value test, and there is no rule that a redemption that does not meet one of the §302 or §303 tests creates a second class of stock. Thus, a redemption of an older generation's stock for cash will simultaneously reduce the value of all of the stock and reduce the percentage held by that generation. Such a redemption could be used in the same year as a bypass election, in order to rid the corporation of PTI.

1835.3. The insurance partnership. A recent private letter ruling illustrates an interesting technique for avoiding some of the drawbacks of the redemption and cross-purchase arrangements. A closely held corporation held insurance on its shareholders' lives. The corporation transferred the policies to a partnership it had formed along with the shareholders. The corporation requested a ruling that the partnership be respected as a valid partnership and that the receipt of insurance proceeds be tax-exempt income to the partnership. The IRS granted both requests. [PLR 9309021]

The partnership can offer some of the advantages of both the redemption and the cross-purchase arrangement. The partnership is not taxed on any income. The collection of the insurance proceeds at the partnership level will add to each partner's basis in the partnership interest, in proportion to his or her profit-sharing allocation. The distribution of the cash from the partnership to the partner is tax-free to the extent of each partner's basis in his or her partnership interest. Since the partnership is insuring the cross-purchase agreement, it needs to hold only one policy on the life of each shareholder. The insurance partnership offers the same simplicity as a redemption agreement, with no threat of double taxation to any of the partners.

> **CAUTION:** One of the important aspects of PLR 9309021 is that the IRS ruled that there was in fact a valid partnership. Recently, the IRS has issued Regulations §1.701-2, a partnership anti-abuse rule. The thrust of the new Regulation is that the IRS may disregard the existence of a partnership if it is used to obtain a tax result contrary to that intended by the Code. There is no indication in the Regulation that it is intended to overturn the result obtained in PLR 9309021. In light of the new Regulation, however, it might be a good idea to contact the IRS to see if it is still possible to obtain a favorable ruling on this issue.

Life insurance trusts. A trust is useful for holding life insurance and keeping the insurance proceeds out of a person's gross estate. The IRS has ruled that a split dollar life insurance agreement between a trust (which was not a shareholder) and an S corporation did not constitute a second class of stock. Moreover, the instance, which was on the life of the majority shareholder, would not be included in the shareholder's estate. [PLR 9651017. See PLR 9709027 for a similar result.] See Chapter 2, at 225.56., for a description of the split dollar life insurance arrangement.

1835.4. Other insurance problems. If insurance is used to fund a cross-purchase arrangement or a redemption arrangement, the premiums will be nondeductible expenses. [§264(a)(1)] There is no legal plan to avoid this problem, since the rule is firmly entrenched in the statute. The estate planner might want to consider the best way to allocate the nondeductible expenditures, however. A redemption agreement would allocate the nondeductible premiums to the shareholders in proportion to their varying stock interests each year, in the same manner as any other corporate expenditure or loss. Each shareholder would treat his or her portion of the insurance premiums as a nondeductible reduction of stock basis. (In some cases, this nondeductible expense may reduce debt basis. See Chapter 6 for further discussion of the elective treatment of nondeductible expenses.)

A cross-purchase arrangement requires that each shareholder directly bear the burden of nondeductible life insurance policies on all of his or her fellow shareholders. Since the ages and health conditions of the shareholders may vary considerably, the highest costs will be borne by the youngest shareholders and those in the best health. The corporation may be able to reimburse the shareholders indirectly for their costs in incurring the premiums, through distributions, salaries, or other payments, as discussed in Chapter 8. These arrangements might require some contrivances, since the payments will be related only coincidentally (if at all) to the services that the shareholders provide to the corporation. If the corporation makes distributions to each shareholder in proportion to his or her financial burden in carrying the policies on other shareholders, it is unlikely that the distributions will be made in proportion to stock ownership. There is a real danger that this type of reimbursement will create a second class of stock.

> **OBSERVATION:** An S corporation may take the position that a cross-purchase arrangement is a reasonable business activity for the corporation, and that the cost of the entire arrangement is a legitimate business expense, even though the cost of maintaining the insurance polices cannot be deducted by the corporation or by any shareholder. As a legitimate corporate expense, the premiums should be borne by the various shareholders in proportion to stock ownership, and the shareholders should share equally in the responsibility of keeping all policies current. The corporation would maintain the policies, although they would be carried in the names of the shareholders. The corporation could then treat the premium payments as distributions to the various shareholders.

EXAMPLE 18 - 38: Jaco Corporation has 15 shareholders of varying ages. The shareholders agree to a cross-purchase arrangement. Upon the death of any shareholder, the remaining shareholders agree to purchase the stock from the deceased shareholder's estate in proportion to their holdings. Each shareholder owns an interest in one policy on the life of every other shareholder. The corporation pays the annual premiums on all of the polices and treats the payment as if it were a cash distribution to each shareholder in proportion to his or her stock ownership.

CAUTION: The approach illustrated in Example 18 - 38 has never been officially permitted or prohibited. The IRS could treat the corporation as if it had made distributions in proportion to the benefit received by each shareholder and adjust the distributions accordingly. In that case, the IRS could find that there is more than one class of stock. Under Regulations §1.1361-1, however, the danger should result only if the arrangement consists of a "binding agreement" to alter shareholders' rights. It would appear that the only purpose of this arrangement is to fund orderly succession, with no intent to create a second class of stock. Therefore, the arrangement should not be readily susceptible to challenge. In a parallel, but not identical, situation, the Regulations hold that payment of unequal premiums on accident and health insurance for the benefit of shareholder-employees does not create a second class of stock. [Regs. §1.1361-1(l)(2)(v), Example 4] Perhaps a corporation that intends to use this strategy should obtain a ruling, or at least contact the National Office of the IRS to assess the position.

Another approach a corporation might use is the split-dollar life insurance plan, discussed briefly in Chapter 2, at 225.56. Under this arrangement, the corporation takes out a whole life policy on the shareholder. The corporation pays the premium and retains ownership of the policy. The shareholder's family or estate, however, is entitled to the death benefit. In the early years, when the premium exceeds the buildup in the cash-surrender value of the policy, the shareholder reimburses the corporation for the cost of the insurance protection. In later years, when the buildup in the cash value exceeds the cost of the insurance protection, the shareholder does not reimburse the corporation, since at this point the insurance cost is essentially free. The corporation always retains ownership of the cash value of the policy, and it may use that value to fund a redemption agreement or distribute the proceeds to the shareholders to fund a cross-purchase agreement. As is discussed in Chapter 2, the IRS frequently rules that split-dollar life insurance policies do not indicate a second class of stock. Therefore, an S corporation should not be overly concerned that split-dollar policies will endanger its S election.

CAUTION: Although the use of split-dollar life insurance policies is an established business practice and will not endanger the corporation's S election, the corporation should obtain competent financial advice on insurance matters. A recent variation on the split-dollar plan is the so-called "private pension," which has been offered by various insurers. The private pension is essentially a leveraged split-dollar policy, in which the corporation borrows the cash value to pay the annual premiums. Insurers may claim that the interest paid on the policy loans is a deductible expense, and this claim may have some merit if the policy owner is a C corporation, since the tax law generally allows C corporations to deduct all interest expense—although the IRS could take a position that the interest is indirectly connected to tax-exempt income and is nondeductible under §265(a)(2). If the owner of the policy is an S corporation, it would be an extremely aggressive position to deduct the interest on a policy loan. As is discussed in Chapter 6, an S corporation must use the rules applicable to individual taxpayers in computing taxable income. Individuals are subject to the tracing rules of Regulations §1.163-8T, discussed in Chapter 8. It may be arguable that interest on a policy loan could be deducted as investment interest, subject to the limitations therein. See Chapter 10. Even this position might be viewed as aggressive, and the IRS could recharacterize the interest as personal interest, which is nondeductible to individuals.

1840. Practice aids.

The practice aids on the following pages of this chapter consist of premortem and postmortem succession planning checklists. The reader should also refer to practice aids located at the ends of other chapters. Particularly important are the shareholder agreements checklist in Chapter 8, the trust checklists in Chapter 2, and certain election checklists in Chapters 7 and 13. Checklists 18-1 and 18-2 are aimed at the corporation, and Checklist 18-3 is designed to be completed for each shareholder.

Checklist 18-1: Premortem corporate succession plan

To be complete each year, or as plans change

	Applicable (Yes/No)	*Completed (Date)*
Any trusts holding shares?		
Already in existence		
Contemplated		
Complete for each trust:		
Grantor or deemed grantor (See Checklist 2-2.)		
QSST (See Checklist 2-2.)		
Fix responsibility for filing timely QSST election (See Sample Letter 5-5.)		
File under Rev. Proc. 98-55, if necessary (See Sample Letter 13-3.)		
ESBT (See Checklist 2-2.)		
Fix responsibility for filing timely ESBT election (See Sample Letter 5-6.)		
File under Rev. Proc. 98-55, if necessary (See Sample Letter 13.4.)		
Buy–sell agreements		
Binding on all shareholders		
Valuation formula		
Cross-purchase		
Redemption		
Funding		
Term insurance		
Whole life		
Split-dollar life		
Other (Describe)		
Review class-of-stock requirements (See Checklist 2-3.)		
Transfer restrictions (See Checklist 8-1.)		
Binding on all shares		
Null and void under local if ineligible shareholder		
Null and void under local law if shareholder limit exceeded		
Nonvoting stock (for gifts, bonuses, etc.)		
Outstanding		
Authorized		
Stock bonus to younger generation		
Bypass election to exhaust AAA (See Sample Letter 7-1.)		
Bypass election to exhaust PTI (See Sample Letter 7-2.)		

Copyright © 2000 by Harcourt, Inc. All rights reserved.

Checklist 18-2: Postmortem corporate succession plan

To be completed immediately upon death of any shareholder

	Applicable (Yes/No)	*Completed (Date)*
Ascertain ownership of all shares (See Checklist 2-1 for eligibility.)		
Estate		
Grantor trust of decedent (CAUTION: 2-year or 60-day qualification)		
Check for qualification as QSST, deemed grantor trust, or Electing Small Business Trust		
If QSST, file election promptly		
QSST election (Sample Letter 5-5)		
File under Rev. Proc. 98-55, if necessary (See Sample Letter 13-3.)		
If Electing Small Business Trust, file election within deadline		
Grantor trust of decedent (CAUTION: 2-year or 60-day qualification)		
Contact decedent's executor or counsel		
Testamentary trust		
Ascertain qualification as deemed-grantor trust		
Ascertain qualification as QSST		
QSST election (See Sample Letter 5-5)		
File under Rev. Proc. 98-55, if necessary (See Sample Letter 13-3.)		
IF NOT DEEMED GRANTOR TRUST, QSST, OR ELECTING SMALL BUSINESS TRUST (AFTER 1996), MAXIMUM 60-DAY HOLDING PERIOD (2 YEARS AFTER 1996)		
Termination elections under §1377(a)(2)		
All consents on file		
Decedent or executor		
Other shareholders		
Date of death		
Date trust funded		
Date trust divested		
Other transfers		
Complete required election statement with tax return (See Sample Letter 6-2.)		
Execution of buy–sell		
Valuation		
Cross-purchase		

18

Copyright © 2000 by Harcourt, Inc. All rights reserved.

	Applicable (Yes/No)	Completed (Date)
Stock redemption (Checklist 15-1)		
Qualify as exchange under §302		
Qualify as exchange under §303		
Desired treatment as distribution		
Other (Describe)		

Checklist 18-3: Premortem shareholder succession plan

To be completed each year, or as plans change

	Applicable (Yes/No)	Completed (Date)
Transfers to trust		
Inter vivos		
Testamentary		
Qualify as grantor trust		
Qualify as QSST		
QSST election, Sample letter 5-5		
File under Rev. Proc. 98-55, if necessary (See Sample Letter 13-3.)		
Qualify as Electing Small Business Trust after 1996		
Party to cross-purchase?		
Ability to fund		
Amend to redemption agreement with right of first refusal		
Gifts		
Nonvoting stock		
Annual exclusion		

18

Copyright © 2000 by Harcourt, Inc. All rights reserved.

STATUTORY AND REGULATORY AUTHORITY

The following pages contain all the Code sections referred to in the Summary of Authority sections dispersed throughout the book. Practitioners can now find cited Code sections more easily, and the relevant sections now appear in context.

CHAPTER 1

STATUTORY AUTHORITY: CODE SECTION 1361(a)

(a) S corporation defined—

(1) In general.—For purposes of this title, the term "S Corporation" means, with respect to any taxable year, a small business corporation for which an election under section 1362(a) is in effect for such year.

(2) C Corporation.—For purposes of this title, the term "C Corporation" means, with respect to any taxable year, a corporation which is not an S corporation for such year.

STATUTORY AUTHORITY: CODE SECTION 1363(a)

(a) General Rule.—Except as otherwise provided in this Subchapter, an S corporation shall not be subject to the taxes imposed by this chapter.

CHAPTER 2

STATUTORY AUTHORITY: CODE SECTION 1361(b) TAXABLE YEARS BEGINNING AFTER DECEMBER 31, 1996

(b) Small business corporation.—

(1) In general.—For purposes of this Subchapter, the term "small business corporation" means a domestic corporation which is not an ineligible corporation and which does not—

(A) have more than 75 shareholders,

(B) have as a shareholder a person (other than an estate and other than a trust described in subsection (c)(2)) or an organization described in subsection (c)(7) who is not an individual,

(C) have a nonresident alien as a shareholder, and

(D) have more than 1 class of stock.

(2) Ineligible corporation defined.—For purposes of paragraph (1), the term "ineligible corporation" means any corporation which is—

(A) a financial institution which uses the reserve method of accounting for bad debts described in section 585

(B) an insurance company subject to tax under Subchapter L,

(C) a corporation to which an election under section 936 applies, or

(D) a DISC or former DISC

STATUTORY AUTHORITY: CODE SECTION 1361(b)(1) (AS AMENDED BY THE SMALL BUSINESS JOB PROTECTION ACT OF 1996)

(1) In general.—For purposes of this Subchapter, the term "small business corporation" means a domestic corporation...which does not—

(B) have as a shareholder a person (other than an estate and other than a trust described in subsection (c)(2)), or an organization described in subsection (c)(7), who is not an individual,

(C) have a nonresident alien as a shareholder.

STATUTORY AUTHORITY: CODE SECTION 1361(b)(1)(D)

(1) In general.—For purposes of this Subchapter, the term "small business corporation" means a domestic corporation which is not an ineligible corporation and which does not—

***

(D) have more than 1 class of stock.

STATUTORY AUTHORITY: CODE SECTION 1361(c)(1)

(1) Husband and wife treated as 1 shareholder.—For purposes of subsection (b)(1)(A), a husband and wife (and their estates) shall be treated as 1 shareholder.

STATUTORY AUTHORITY: CODE SECTION 1361(c)(4)

(4) Differences in voting rights disregarded.—For purposes of subsection (b)(1)(D), a corporation shall not be treated as having more than 1 class of stock solely because there are differences in voting rights among the shares of common stock.

STATUTORY AUTHORITY: CODE SECTION 1361(c)(6)

(6) Certain Exempt Organizations Permitted As Shareholders.—For purposes of subsection (b)(1)(B), an organization which is—

(A) described in section 401(a) or 501(c)(3), and
(B) exempt from taxation under section 501(a),
may be a shareholder in an S corporation.

STATUTORY AUTHORITY: CODE SECTION 1361(d)

(d) SPECIAL RULE FOR QUALIFIED SUBCHAPTER S TRUST.—

(1) In General.—In the case of a qualified Subchapter S trust with respect to which a beneficiary makes an election under paragraph (2)—

(A) Such trust shall be treated as a trust described in subsection (c)(2)(A)(i), and

(B) For purposes of section 678(a), the beneficiary of such trust shall be treated as the owner of that portion of the trust which consists of stock in an S corporation

(2) Election.— . . .

STATUTORY AUTHORITY: CODE SECTION 1361(d)(3)

(3) Qualified subchapter S trust.—For purposes of this subsection, the term "qualified subchapter S trust" means a trust—

(A) The terms of which require that—

(i) during the life of the current income beneficiary there shall be only 1 income beneficiary of the trust,

(ii) any corpus distributed during the life of the current income beneficiary may be distributed only to such beneficiary,

(iii) the income interest of the current income beneficiary in the trust shall terminate on the earlier of such beneficiary's death or the termination of the trust, and

(iv) upon the termination of the trust during the life of the current income beneficiary, the trust shall distribute all of its assets to such beneficiary, and

(B) all of the income (within the meaning of section 643(b)) of which is distributed (or required to be distributed) currently to 1 individual who is a citizen or resident of the United States.

A substantially separate and independent share of a trust treated as a separate trust under section 663(c) shall be treated as a separate trust for purposes of this subsection and subsection (c).

STATUTORY AUTHORITY: CODE SECTION 1361(e)

(e) Electing Small Business Trust Defined.—

(1) Electing Small Business Trust.—For purposes of this section—

(A) In General.—Except as provided in subparagraph (B), the term 'electing small business trust' means any trust if—

(i) such trust does not have as a beneficiary any person other than

(I) an individual,

(II) an estate, or

(III) an organization described in paragraph (2), (3), (4), or (5) of section 170(c),

(ii) no interest in such trust was acquired by purchase, and

(iii) an election under this subsection applies to such trust.

(B) Certain Trusts Not Eligible.—The term 'electing small business trust' shall not include—

(i) any qualified subchapter S trust (as defined in subsection (d)(3)) if an election under subsection (d)(2) applies to any corporation the stock of which is held by such trust,

(ii) any trust exempt from tax under this subtitle, and

(iii) any charitable remainder annuity trust or charitable remainder unitrust (as defined in section 664(d)).'

(C) Purchase.—For purposes of subparagraph (A), the term 'purchase' means any acquisition if the basis of the property acquired is determined under section 1012.

(2) Potential Current Beneficiary.—For purposes of this section, the term 'potential current beneficiary' means, with respect to any period, any person who at any time during such period is entitled to, or at the discretion of any person may receive, a distribution from the principal or income of the trust. If a trust disposes of all of the stock which it holds in an S corporation, then, with respect to such corporation, the term 'potential current beneficiary' does not include any person who first met the requirements of the preceding sentence during the 60-day period ending on the date of such disposition.

(3) Election.—An election under this subsection shall be made by the trustee. Any such election shall apply to the taxable year of the trust for which made and all subsequent taxable years of such trust unless revoked with the consent of the Secretary.

(4) Cross Reference.—For special treatment of electing small business trusts, see section 641(c).

CHAPTER 3

STATUTORY AUTHORITY: CODE SECTION 1363(d)(1)

(d) RECAPTURE OF LIFO BENEFITS

(1) In general. —If —

(A) an S corporation was a C corporation for the last taxable year before the first taxable year for which the election under section 1362(a) was effective, and

(B) the corporation inventoried goods under the LIFO method for such last taxable year, the LIFO recapture amount shall be included in the gross income of the corporation for such last taxable year (and appropriate adjustments to the basis of inventory shall be made to take into account the amount included in gross income under this paragraph).

STATUTORY AUTHORITY: CODE SECTION 1363(d)(2)

(2) Additional tax payable in installments.—

(A) In general.—Any increase in the tax imposed by this chapter by reason of this subsection shall be payable in 4 equal installments.

(B) Date for payment of installments.—The first installment under subparagraph (A) shall be paid on or before the due date (determined without regard to extensions) for the return of the tax imposed by this chapter for the last taxable year for which the corporation was a C corporation and the three succeeding installments shall be paid on or before the due date (as so determined) for the corporation's return for the 3 succeeding taxable years.

(C) No interest for period of extension.—Notwithstanding section 6601(b), for purposes of section 6601, the date prescribed for the payment of each installment under this paragraph shall be determined under this paragraph.

STATUTORY AUTHORITY: CODE SECTION 1363(d)(3) AND (4)

(3) LIFO recapture amount.—For purposes of this subsection the term "LIFO recapture amount" means the amount (if any) by which—

(A) the inventory amount of the inventory aset (sic) under the first-in, first-out method authorized by section 471, exceeds

(B) the inventory amount of such assets under the LIFO method.

For purposes of the preceding sentence, inventory amounts shall be determined as of the close of the last taxable year referred to in paragraph (1). . . .

(4) OTHER DEFINITIONS.—For purposes of this subsection—

(A) LIFO method.—The term "LIFO method" means the method authorized by section 472.

(B) Inventory assets.—The term "inventory assets" means stock in trade of the corporation, or other property of a kind which would properly be included in the inventory of the corporation if on hand at the close of the taxable year.

(C) Method of determining inventory amount.—The inventory amount of assets under a method authorized by section 471 shall be determined—

(i) if the corporation uses the retail method of valuing inventories under section 472, by using such method, or

(ii) if clause (i) does not apply, by using cost or market, whichever is lower.

CHAPTER 4

AUTHORITY: REGULATIONS SECTION 1.444-2T(b)(1) AND (2)

(b) Definition of a member of a tiered structure—

(1) In general. A partnership, S corporation, or personal service corporation is considered a member of a tiered structure if—

(i) The partnership, S corporation, or personal service corporation directly owns any portion of a deferral entity, or

(ii) A deferral entity directly owns any portion of the partnership, S corporation, or personal service corporation.

However, see paragraph (c) of this section for certain de minimis rules, and see paragraph (b)(3) of this section for an anti-abuse rule. In addition, for purposes of this section, a beneficiary of a trust shall be considered to own an interest in the trust.

(2) Deferral entity—

(i) In general. For purposes of this section, the term "deferral entity" means an entity that is a partnership, S corporation, personal service corporation, or trust. . . .

(ii) Grantor trusts. The term "deferral entity" does not include a trust (or a portion of a trust) which is treated as owned by the grantor or beneficiary under Subpart E, part I, subchapter J, chapter 1, of the Code (relating to grantor trusts), including a trust that is treated as a grantor trust pursuant to section 1361(d)(1)(A) of the Code (relating to qualified subchapter S trusts). Thus, any taxpayer treated under subpart E as owning a portion of a trust shall be treated as owning the assets of the trust attributable to that ownership.

AUTHORITY: REGULATIONS SECTION 1.444-2T(b)(3)

(3) Anti-abuse rule. Notwithstanding paragraph (b)(1) of this section, a partnership, S corporation, or personal service corporation is considered a member of a tiered structure if the partnership, S corporation, personal service corporation, or related taxpayers have organized or reorganized their ownership structure or operations for the principal purpose of obtaining a significant unintended tax benefit from making or continuing a section 444 election. For purposes of the preceding sentence, a significant unintended tax benefit results when a partnership, S corporation, or personal service corpo-

ration makes a section 444 election and, as a result, a taxpayer (not limited to the entity making the election) obtains a significant deferral of income substantially all of which is not eliminated by a required payment under section 7519. See examples (15) through (19) in paragraph (f) of this section.

AUTHORITY: REGULATIONS SECTION 1.7519-1T(b)(5)(i)

(i) In general. Except as provided in paragraph (b)(5)(v) of this section (relating to short base years), the net base-year income of a partnership or S corporation is the sum of—
- (A) The deferral ratio multiplied by the partnership's or S corporation's net income for the base year, plus—
- (B) The excess (if any) of—
  - (1) The deferral ratio multiplied by the aggregate amount of applicable payments made by the partnership or S corporation during the base year, over
  - (2) The aggregate amount of such applicable payments made during the deferral period of the base year.

STATUTORY AUTHORITY: CODE SECTION 444(a) and (e)

(a) General rule.—Except as otherwise provided in this section, a partnership, S corporation, or personal service corporation may elect to have a taxable year other than the required taxable year.

***

(e) Required taxable year.—For purposes of this section the term "required taxable year" means the taxable year determined under section 706(b), 1378, or 441(i) without taking into account any taxable year which is allowable by reason of a business purpose. Solely for purposes of the preceding sentence, sections 706(b), 1378, and 441(i) shall be treated as in effect for taxable years beginning before January 1, 1987.

STATUTORY AUTHORITY: CODE SECTION 444(a)(4)

(4) Deferral period.—For purposes of this subsection, except as provided in the regulations, the term "deferral period" means, with respect to any taxable year of the entity, the months between—
- (A) the beginning of such year, and
- (B) the close of the 1st required taxable year ending within such year.

STATUTORY AUTHORITY: CODE SECTION 444(b)

(b) Limitations on taxable years which may be elected.—
- (1) In general.—Except as provided in paragraphs (2) and (3), an election may be made under subsection (a) only if the deferral period of the taxable year elected is not longer than 3 months.
- (2) Changes in taxable year.—Except as provided in paragraph (3), in the case of an entity changing a taxable year, an election may be made under subsection (a) only if the deferral period of the taxable year elected is not longer than the shorter of—
  - (A) 3 months, or
  - (B) the deferral period of the taxable year which is being changed. [Retained]

STATUTORY AUTHORITY: CODE SECTION 444(c) and (d)

(c) Effect of election.—If an entity makes an election under subsection (a), then—
- (1) in the case of a partnership or S corporation, such entity shall make the payments required by section 7519, and
- (2) in the case of a personal service corporation, such corporation shall be subject to the deduction limitations of section 280H.

(d) Elections.—
- (1) Person making election.—An election under subsection (a) shall be made by the partnership, S corporation, or personal service corporation.
- (2) Period of election.—
  - (A) In general. Any election under subsection (a) shall remain in effect until the partnership, S corporation, or personal service corporation changes its taxable year or otherwise terminates such election. Any change to a required tax year may be made without the consent of the Secretary.

STATUTORY AUTHORITY: CODE SECTION 444(d)(3)

(3) Tiered structures, etc.—
- (A) In general—Except as otherwise provided in this paragraph—
  - (i) no election may be [made] under subsection (a) with respect to any entity which is part of a tiered structure, and
  - (ii) an election under subsection (a) with respect to any entity shall be terminated if such entity becomes part of a tiered structure.
- (B) Exceptions for structures consisting of certain entities with same taxable year.—Subparagraph (A) shall not apply to any tiered structure which consists only of partnerships or S corporations (or both) all of which have the same taxable year.

STATUTORY AUTHORITY: CODE SECTION 1378

(a) General Rule.—For purposes of this subtitle, the taxable year of an S corporation shall be a permitted year.

(b) Permitted Year Defined.—For purposes of this section, the term "permitted year" means a taxable year which—
   (1) is a year ending December 31, or
   (2) is any other accounting period for which the corporation establishes a business purpose to the satisfaction of the Secretary.

For purposes of paragraph (2), any deferral of income to shareholders shall not be treated as a business purpose.

CHAPTER 5

STATUTORY AUTHORITY: SECTION 1317(b) THE SMALL BUSINESS JOB PROTECTION ACT OF 1996

(b) Treatment of Certain Elections Under Prior Law.—For purposes of section 1362(g) of the Internal Revenue Code of 1986 (relating to election after termination), any termination under Section 1362(d) of such Code in a taxable year beginning before January 1, 1997, shall not be taken into account.

STATUTORY AUTHORITY: CODE SECTION 1361(e)(3)

(3) Election—A election under this subsection shall be made by the trustee. Any such election shall apply to the taxable year of the trust for which made and all subsequent taxable years of such trust unless revoked with the consent of the Secretary.

STATUTORY AUTHORITY: CODE SECTION 1362(a)(2)

(2) All Shareholders Must Consent to Election.—An election under this subsection shall be valid only if all persons who are shareholders in such corporation on the day on which such election is made consent to such election.

STATUTORY AUTHORITY: CODE SECTION 1362(b)

(b) When Made.—
   (1) In General.—An election under subsection (a) may be made by a small business corporation for any taxable year—
      (A) at any time during the preceding taxable year, or
      (B) at any time during the taxable year and on or before the 15th day of the 3rd month of the taxable year.

STATUTORY AUTHORITY: CODE SECTION 1362(b)(4)

(4) Taxable Years of 2½ Months or Less.—For purposes of this subsection, an election for a taxable year made not later than 2 months and 15 days after the first day of the taxable year shall be treated as timely made during such year.

STATUTORY AUTHORITY: CODE SECTION 1362(b)(5)

(5) Authority to treat late elections, etc., as timely.—If—
   (A) an election under subsection (a) is made for any taxable year (determined without regard to paragraph (3)) after the date prescribed by this subsection for making such election for such taxable year or no such election is made for any taxable year, and
   (B) the Secretary determines that there was reasonable cause for the failure to timely make such election,

   the Secretary may treat such an election as timely made for such taxable year (and paragraph (3) shall not apply).

STATUTORY AUTHORITY: CODE SECTION 1362(f)

(f) Inadvertent Invalid Elections Or Terminations.—If—
   (1) an election under subsection (a) by any corporation—
      (A) was not effective for the taxable year for which made (determined without regard to subsection (b)(2)) by reason of a failure to meet the requirements of section 1361(b) or to obtain shareholder consents, or
      (B) was terminated under paragraph (2) or (3) of subsection (d),
   (2) the Secretary determines that the circumstances resulting in such ineffectiveness or termination were inadvertent,
   (3) no later than a reasonable period of time after discovery of the circumstances resulting in such ineffectiveness or termination, steps were taken—
      (A) so that the corporation is a small business corporation, or
      (B) to acquire the required shareholder consents, and
   (4) the corporation, and each person who was a shareholder in the corporation at any time during the period specified pursuant to this subsection, agrees to make such adjustments (consistent with the treatment of the corporation as an S corporation) as may be required by the Secretary with respect to such period,

then, notwithstanding the circumstances resulting in such ineffectiveness or termination, such corporation shall be treated as an S corporation during the period specified by the Secretary.

STATUTORY AUTHORITY: CODE SECTION 1362(g)

(g) Election After Termination.—If a small business corporation has made an election under subsection (a) and if such election has been terminated under subsection (d), such corporation (and any successor corporation) shall not be eligible to make an election under subsection (a) for any taxable year before its 5th taxable year that begins after the 1st taxable year for which such termination is effective, unless the Secretary consents to such election.

CHAPTER 6

STATUTORY AUTHORITY: CODE SECTION 703(a)(2)

(2) the following deductions shall not be allowed to the partnership:
- (A) the deductions for personal exemptions provided in section 151,
- (B) the deduction for taxes provided in section 164(a) with respect to taxes, described in section 901, paid or accrued to foreign countries and to possessions of the United States,
- (C) the deduction for charitable contributions provided in section 170,
- (D) the net operating loss deduction provided in section 172,
- (E) the additional itemized deductions for individuals provided in part VII of subchapter B (sec. 211 and following), and
- (F) the deduction for depletion under section 611 with respect to oil and gas wells.

STATUTORY AUTHORITY: CODE SECTION 1363(a) AND (b)

§1363. EFFECT OF ELECTION ON CORPORATION

(a) General rule.—Except as otherwise provided in this Subchapter, an S corporation shall not be subject to the taxes imposed by this chapter.

(b) Computation of corporation's taxable income.—The taxable income of an S corporation shall be computed in the same manner as in the case of an individual, except that—
- (1) the items described in section 1366(a)(1)(A) shall be separately stated,
- (2) the deductions referred to in section 703(a)(2) shall not be allowed to the corporation,
- (3) section 248 shall apply, and
- (4) section 291 shall apply if the S corporation (or any predecessor) was a C corporation for any of the 3 immediately preceding tax years.

STATUTORY AUTHORITY: CODE SECTION 1363(c)(1)

(1) In general.—Except as provided in paragraph (2), any election affecting the computation of items derived from an S corporation shall be made by the corporation.

STATUTORY AUTHORITY: CODE SECTION 1363(c)(2)

(2) Exceptions.—In the case of an S corporation, elections under the following provisions shall be made by each shareholder separately—
- (A) section 617 (relating to deduction and recapture of certain mining exploration expenditures), and
- (B) section 901 (relating to taxes of foreign countries and possessions of the United States.

STATUTORY AUTHORITY: CODE SECTION 1366(a)(1)

(1) In general.—In determining the tax under this chapter of a shareholder for the shareholder's taxable year in which the taxable year of the S corporation ends (or the final taxable year of a shareholder who dies before the end of the corporation's taxable year), there shall be taken into account the shareholder's pro-rata share of the corporation's— . . .

STATUTORY AUTHORITY: CODE SECTION 1366(a)(1)(A) AND (B)

(A) items of income (including any tax-exempt income), loss, deduction, or credit the separate treatment of which could affect the liability for tax of any shareholder, and

(B) nonseparately computed income or loss.

STATUTORY AUTHORITY: CODE SECTION 1366(d)(1)

(1) Cannot exceed shareholder's basis in stock and debt.—The aggregate amount of losses and deductions taken into account by a shareholder under subsection (a) for any taxable year shall not exceed the sum of—
- (A) the adjusted basis of the shareholder's stock in the S corporation (determined with regard to paragraph (1) of section 1367(a) for the taxable year), and
- (B) the shareholder's adjusted basis of any indebtedness of the S corporation (determined without regard to any adjustment under paragraph (2) of section 1367(b) for the taxable year).

STATUTORY AUTHORITY: CODE SECTIONS 1366(d)(1) AND 1367(a)(1)

1366(d)(1) Cannot exceed shareholder's basis in stock and debt.—The aggregate amount of losses and deductions taken into account by a shareholder under subsection (a) for any taxable year shall not exceed the sum of
- (A) the adjusted basis of the shareholder's stock in the S corporation (determined with regard to paragraph (1) of section 1367(a) for the taxable year), and . . .

***

1367(a)(1) Increases in basis.—The basis of each shareholder's stock in an S corporation shall be increased for any period by the sum of the following items determined with respect to that shareholder for that period:

(A) the items of income described in subparagraph (a) of section 1366(a)(1),
(B) any nonseparately computed income determined under subparagraph (B) of section 1366(a)(1), and
(C) the excess of the deductions for depletion over the basis of the property subject to depletion.

STATUTORY AUTHORITY: CODE SECTION 1366(d)(2)

(2) Indefinite carryover of disallowed losses and deductions.—Any loss or deduction that is disallowed for any taxable year by reason of paragraph (1) shall be treated as incurred by the corporation in the succeeding taxable year with respect to that shareholder.

STATUTORY AUTHORITY: CODE SECTION 1367(b)(4)

(4) Adjustments In Case of Inherited Stock.—[Effective for stock transferred due to death after August 20, 1996]
(A) In General.—If any person acquires stock in an S corporation by reason of the death of a decedent or by bequest, devise, or inheritance, section 691 shall be applied with respect to any item of income of the S corporation in the same manner as if the decedent had held directly his pro rata share of such item.
(B) Adjustments To Basis.—The basis determined under section 1014 of any stock in an S corporation shall be reduced by the portion of the value of the stock which is attributable to items constituting income in respect of the decedent.

STATUTORY AUTHORITY: CODE SECTION 1371(b)(2)

(2) No carryover from S year.—No carryforward, and no carryback, shall arise at the corporate level for a taxable year for which a corporation is an S corporation.

STATUTORY AUTHORITY: CODE SECTION 1371(b)(3)

(3) Treatment of S year as elapsed year.—Nothing in paragraphs (1) and (2) shall prevent treating a taxable year for which a corporation is an S corporation as a taxable year for purposes of determining the number of taxable years to which an item may be carried back or carried forward.

STATUTORY AUTHORITY: CODE SECTION 1377(a)(1)

(1) In General.—Except as provided in paragraph (2), each shareholder's pro rata share of any item for any taxable year shall be the sum of the amounts determined with respect to the shareholder—
(A) by assigning an equal portion of such item to each day of the taxable year, and
(B) then by dividing that portion pro rata among the shares outstanding on such day.

STATUTORY AUTHORITY: CODE SECTION 1377(a)(2), IN EFFECT FOR S CORPORATION TAXABLE YEARS BEGINNING ON OR AFTER JANUARY 1, 1997

(2) Election To Terminate Year.—
(A) In general.—Under Regulations prescribed by the Secretary, if any shareholder terminates the shareholder's interest in the corporation during the taxable year and all affected shareholders and the corporation agree to the application of this paragraph, paragraph (1) shall be applied to the affected shareholders as if the taxable year consisted of 2 taxable years the first of which ends on the date of the termination.
(B) Affected shareholders.—For purposes of subparagraph (A), the term "affected shareholders" means the shareholder whose interest is terminated and all shareholders to whom such shareholder has transferred shares during the taxable year. If such shareholder has transferred shares to the corporation, the term "affected shareholders" shall include all persons who are shareholders during the taxable year.

CHAPTER 7

STATUTORY AUTHORITY: CODE SECTION 1368(a)

(a) GENERAL RULE.—A distribution of property made by an S corporation with respect to its stock to which (but for this subsection) section 301(c) would apply shall be treated in the manner provided in subsection (b) or (c), whichever applies.

STATUTORY AUTHORITY: CODE SECTION 1368(b)

(b) S corporation having no earnings and profits.—In the case of a distribution described in subsection (a) by an S corporation which has no accumulated earnings and profits—
(1) Amount applied against basis.—The distribution shall not be included in gross income to the extent that it does not exceed the adjusted basis of the stock.
(2) Amount in excess of basis.—If the amount of the distribution exceeds the adjusted basis of the stock, such excess shall be treated as a gain from the sale or exchange of property.

STATUTORY AUTHORITY: CODE SECTION 1368(c)

(c) S CORPORATION HAVING EARNINGS AND PROFITS.—In the case of a distribution described in subsection (a) by an S corporation which has accumulated earnings and profits—

(1) Accumulated Adjustments Account.—That portion of the distribution which does not exceed the AAA shall be treated in the manner provided by subsection (b).

(2) Dividend.—That portion of the distribution which remains after the application of paragraph (1) shall be treated as a dividend to the extent it does not exceed the accumulated earnings and profits of the S corporation.

(3) Treatment of remainder.—Any portion of the distribution remaining after the application of paragraph (2) of this subsection shall be treated in the manner provided in subsection (b).

STATUTORY AUTHORITY: CODE SECTION 1368(e)(1)

(e) DEFINITIONS AND SPECIAL RULES.—For purposes of this section—

(1) Accumulated Adjustments Account—

(A) In general.—Except as provided in subparagraph (B), the term "Accumulated Adjustments Account" means an account of the S corporation which is adjusted for the S period in a manner similar to the adjustments under section 1367 (except that no adjustment shall be made for income (and related expenses) which is exempt from tax under this title and the phrase "(but not below zero)" shall be disregarded in section 1367(b)(2)(A) and no adjustment shall be made for Federal taxes attributable to any taxable year in which the corporation was a C corporation.

(B) Amount of adjustment in the case of redemptions.—In the case of any redemption which is treated as an exchange under section 302(a) or 303(a), the adjustment in the Accumulated Adjustments Account shall be an amount which bears the same ratio to the balance in such account as the number of shares redeemed in such redemption bears to the number of shares in stock in the corporation immediately before such redemption.

(2) S period.—The term "S period" means the most recent continuous period during which the corporation has been an S corporation. Such period shall not include any taxable year beginning before January 1, 1983.

STATUTORY AUTHORITY: CODE SECTION 1368(e)(3)

(A) In general.—An S corporation may, with the consent of all of its affected shareholders, elect to have paragraph (1) of subsection (c) [AAA before AEP] not apply to all distributions made during the taxable year for which the election is made.

(B) Affected shareholder.—For purposes of subparagraph (A), the term "affected shareholder" means any shareholder to whom a distribution is made by the S corporation during the taxable year.

STATUTORY AUTHORITY: CODE SECTION 1371(a)

(a) Application Of Subchapter C Rules.—Except as otherwise provided in this title, and except to the extent inconsistent with this subchapter, subchapter C shall apply to an S corporation and its shareholders.

STATUTORY AUTHORITY: CODE SECTION 1371(c)(1)

(c) EARNINGS AND PROFITS—

(1) In general.—Except as provided in paragraphs (2) and (3) and subsection (d)(3), no adjustment shall be made to the earnings and profits of an S corporation.

STATUTORY AUTHORITY: CODE SECTION 1379(c)

(c) DISTRIBUTIONS OF UNDISTRIBUTED TAXABLE INCOME.—If a corporation was an electing small business corporation for the last preenactment year, subsections (f) and (d) of section 1375 (as in effect before the enactment of the Subchapter of S Revision Act of 1982) shall continue to apply with respect to distributions of undistributed taxable income for any taxable year beginning before January 1, 1983.

CHAPTER 8

STATUTORY AUTHORITY: CODE SECTION 1372(a) AND (b)

(a) General rule.—For purposes of applying the provisions of this subtitle that relate to employee fringe benefits—

(1) the S corporation shall be treated as a partnership, and,

(2) any 2-percent shareholder of the S corporation shall be treated as a partner of such partnership.

(b) 2 percent shareholder defined.—For purposes of this section, the term "2-percent shareholder" any person who owns (or is considered as owning within the meaning of section 318) on any day during the taxable year of the S corporation more than 2 percent of the outstanding stock of such corporation or stock possessing more than 2 percent of the total combined voting power of all stock of such corporation.

CHAPTER 9

STATUTORY AUTHORITY: CODE SECTION 1366(d)(1)

(1) Cannot exceed shareholder's basis in stock and debt.—The aggregate amount of losses and deductions taken into account by a shareholder under subsection (a) for any taxable year shall not exceed the sum of—

(A) the adjusted basis of the shareholder's stock in the S corporation (determined with regard to paragraph (1) of section 1367(a) for the taxable year), and

(B) the shareholder's adjusted basis of any indebtedness of the S corporation to the shareholder (determined without regard to any adjustment under paragraph (2) of section 1367(b) for the taxable year).

STATUTORY AUTHORITY: CODE SECTION 1367(a)

(a) GENERAL RULE—

(1) Increases in basis.—The basis of each shareholder's stock in an S corporation shall be increased for any period by the sum of the following items determined with respect to that shareholder for that period:

(A) the items of income described in subparagraph (a) of section 1366(a)(1),

(B) any nonseparately computed income determined under subparagraph (B) of section 1366(a)(1), and

(C) the excess of the deductions for depletion over the basis of the property subject to depletion.

(2) Decreases in basis.—The basis of each shareholder's stock in an S corporation shall be decreased for any period (but not below zero) by the sum of the following items determined with respect to the shareholder for such period:

(A) distributions by the corporation which were not includible in the income of the shareholder by reason of section 1368,

(B) the items of loss and deduction described in subparagraph (A) of section 1366(a)(1),

(C) any nonseparately computed loss determined under subparagraph (B) of section 1366(a)(1),

(D) any expense of the corporation not deductible in computing its taxable income and not properly chargeable to capital account, and

(E) the amount of the shareholder's deduction for depletion for any oil and gas property held by the S corporation to the extent such deduction does not exceed the proportionate share of the adjusted basis of such property allocated to such shareholder under section 613A(c)(13)(B).

STATUTORY AUTHORITY: CODE SECTION 1367(b)(2)(A)

(2) Adjustments in basis of indebtedness.—

(A) Reduction of basis.—If for any taxable year the amounts specified in subparagraphs (B), (C), (D) and (E) of subsection (a)(2) exceed the amount that reduces the shareholder's basis to zero, any excess shall be applied to reduce (but not below zero) the shareholder's basis in any indebtedness of the S corporation to the shareholder.

STATUTORY AUTHORITY: CODE SECTION 1367(b)(2)(B)

(B) Restoration of basis.—If for any taxable year beginning after December 31, 1982, there is a reduction under subparagraph (A) in the shareholder's basis in the indebtedness of an S corporation to a shareholder, any net increase (after the application of paragraphs (1) and (2) of subsection (a)) for any subsequent taxable year shall be applied to restore such reduction in basis before any of it may be used to increase the shareholder's basis in the stock of the S corporation.

STATUTORY AUTHORITY: CODE SECTION 1374(c)(2) AS IN EFFECT BEFORE REPEAL BY THE SUBCHAPTER S REVISION ACT OF 1982

. . . A shareholder's portion of the net operating loss of an electing small business corporation shall not exceed . . . the adjusted basis . . . of any indebtedness to the shareholder . . .

CHAPTER 10

AUTHORITY: REGULATIONS SECTION 1.469-5T(f)(4)

. . . Contemporaneous daily time reports, logs, or similar documents are not required if the extent of such participation may be established by other reasonable means. Reasonable means for purposes of this paragraph may include but are not limited to the identification of services performed over a period of time and the approximate number of hours spent performing such services during such period, based on appointment books, calendars, or narrative summaries.

STATUTORY AUTHORITY: CODE SECTION 465(a)(1)

(a) Limitations to Amount at Risk.—

(1) In general.—In the case of—

(A) an individual, and

(B) a C corporation with respect to which the stock ownership requirement of paragraph (2) of section 542(a) is met,

engaged in an activity to which this section applies, any loss from such activity for the taxable year shall be allowed only to the extent of the aggregate amount with respect to which the taxpayer is at risk (within the meaning of subsection (b) for such activity at the close of the taxable year.

STATUTORY AUTHORITY: CODE SECTION 465(a)(2)

(2) Deduction in succeeding year.—Any loss from an activity to which this section applies not allowed under this section for the taxable year shall be treated as a deduction allocable to such activity in the first succeeding taxable year.

STATUTORY AUTHORITY: CODE SECTION 469

(a) Disallowance.—
- (1) In general.—If for any taxable year the taxpayer is described in paragraph (2), neither—
  - (A) The passive activity loss, nor
  - (B) The passive activity credit, for the taxable year shall be allowed.
- (2) Persons described.—The following are described in this paragraph:
  - (A) Any individual, estate, or trust,
  - (B) Any closely held C corporation, and
  - (C) Any personal service corporation.

STATUTORY AUTHORITY: CODE SECTION 469(l)

(l) Regulations.—The Secretary shall prescribe such regulations as may be necessary or appropriate to carry out provisions of this section, including regulations—
- (1) which specify what constitutes an activity, material participation, or active participation for purposes of this section, . . .

CHAPTER 11

STATUTORY AUTHORITY: TAX REFORM ACT OF 1986, SECTION 633(b)(1)

(b) Built-in gains of S corporations.—
- (1) In general.—The amendments made by 632 (other than subsection (b) thereof) shall apply to taxable years beginning after December 31, 1986, but only in cases where the return for the taxable year is filed pursuant to an S election made after December 31, 1986.

STATUTORY AUTHORITY: CODE SECTION 1363(a)

(a) General rule. Except as otherwise provided in this subchapter, an S corporation shall not be subject to the taxes imposed by this chapter.

STATUTORY AUTHORITY: CODE SECTION 1366(f)(2)

(2) Treatment of tax imposed on built-in gains.—If any tax is imposed under section 1374 for any taxable year on an S corporation, for purposes of subsection (a), the amount so imposed shall be treated as a loss sustained by the S corporation during such taxable year. The character of such loss shall be determined by allocating the loss proportionately among the recognized built-in gains giving rise to such tax.

STATUTORY AUTHORITY: CODE SECTION 1371(d)

(d) Coordination with investment tax credit recapture.—
- (1) No recapture by reason of election. Any election under section 1362 shall be treated as a mere change in the form of conducting a trade or business for purposes of the second sentence of section 50(a)(4).
- (2) Corporation continues to be liable.—Notwithstanding an election under section 1362, an S corporation shall continue to be liable for any increase in tax under section 49(b) or 50(a) attributable to credits allowed for taxable years for which such corporation was not an S corporation.
- (3) Adjustment to earnings and profits for amount of recapture.—Paragraph (1) of subsection (c) shall not apply to any increase in tax under section 49(b) or 50(a) for which the S corporation is liable.

STATUTORY AUTHORITY: CODE SECTION 1374(a)

(a) General Rule.—If for any taxable year beginning in the recognition period an S corporation has a net recognized built-in gain, there is hereby imposed a tax (computed under subsection (b)) on the income of such corporation for such taxable year.

STATUTORY AUTHORITY: CODE SECTION 1374(b)(1)

(1) In General.—The amount of tax imposed by subsection (a) shall be computed by applying the highest rate of tax specified in section 11(b) to the net recognized built in gain of the S corporation for the taxable year.

STATUTORY AUTHORITY: CODE SECTION 1374(b)(2)

(2) Net Operating Loss Carryforwards from C Years Allowed.—Notwithstanding section 1371(b)(1), any net operating loss carryforward arising in a taxable year for which the corporation was a C corporation shall be allowed for purposes of this section as a deduction against the net recognized built-in gain of the S corporation for the taxable year. For purposes of determining the amount of any such loss which may be carried to subsequent taxable years, the amount of the net recognized built-in gain shall be treated as taxable income. Rules similar to the rules of the preceding sentence of this paragraph shall apply in the case of a capital loss carryforward arising in a taxable year for which the corporation was a C corporation.

STATUTORY AUTHORITY:
CODE SECTION 1374(b)(3)

(3) Credits.—
(A) In General.—Except as provided in subparagraph (B), no credit shall be allowable under part IV of subchapter A of this chapter (other than under section 34) against the tax imposed by subsection (a).
(B) Business Credit Carryforwards From C Years Allowed.—Notwithstanding section 1371(b)(1), any business credit carryforward under section 39 arising in a taxable year for which the corporation was a C corporation shall be allowed as a credit against the tax imposed by subsection (a) in the same manner as if it were imposed by section 11. A similar rule shall apply in the case of the minimum tax credit under section 53 to the extent attributable to taxable years for which the corporation was a C corporation.

STATUTORY AUTHORITY:
CODE SECTION 1374(c)(1)

(1) Corporations Which Were Always S Corporations. Subsection (a) shall not apply to any corporation if an election under section 1362(a) has been in effect with respect to such corporation for each of its taxable years. Except as provided in regulations, an S corporation and any predecessor corporation shall be treated as 1 corporation for purposes of the preceding sentence.

STATUTORY AUTHORITY:
CODE SECTION 1374(c)(2)

(2) Limitation on Amount of Net Recognized Built-In Gains.—The amount of the net recognized built-in gains taken into account under this section for any taxable year shall not exceed the excess (if any) of—
(A) the net unrealized built-in gain, over
(B) the net recognized built-in gain for prior taxable years beginning in the recognition period.

STATUTORY AUTHORITY:
CODE SECTION 1374(d)(1)

(1) Net Unrealized Built-In Gain.—The term "net unrealized built-in gain" means the amount (if any) by which—
(A) the fair market value of the assets of S corporation as of the beginning of its 1st taxable year for which an election under section 1362(a) is in effect, exceeds
(B) the aggregate adjusted bases of such assets at such time.

STATUTORY AUTHORITY:
CODE SECTION 1374(d)(2)(A)(i)

(2) NET RECOGNIZED BUILT-IN GAIN.—
(A) The term "net recognized built-in gain" means, with respect to any taxable year in the recognition period, the lesser of—
(i) the amount which would be the taxable income of the S corporation for such taxable year if (except as provided in subsection (b)(2)) only recognized built-in gains and recognized built-in losses were taken into account, or
(ii) * * * [discussed below]

STATUTORY AUTHORITY:
CODE SECTION 1374(d)(2)(A)(ii)

(2) NET RECOGNIZED BUILT-IN GAIN.—
(A) The term "net recognized built-in gain" means, with respect to any taxable year in the recognition period, the lesser of—
(i) * * * [discussed above]
(ii) such corporation's taxable income for such taxable year (determined as provided in section 1375(b)(1)(B)).

STATUTORY AUTHORITY:
CODE SECTION 1374(d)(2)(B)

(B) CARRYOVER.—If, for any taxable year, the amount referred to in clause (i) of subparagraph (A) exceeds the amount referred to in clause (ii) of subparagraph (A), such excess shall be treated as a recognized built-in gain in the succeeding taxable year. The preceding sentence shall apply only in the case of a corporation treated as an S corporation by reason of an election made on or after March 31, 1988.

STATUTORY AUTHORITY:
CODE SECTION 1374(d)(3)

(3) RECOGNIZED BUILT-IN GAIN.—The term "recognized built-in gain" means any gain recognized during the recognition period on the disposition of any asset except to the extent that the S corporation establishes that—
(A) such asset was not held by the S corporation as of the beginning of the 1st taxable year for which it was an S corporation, or
(B) such gain exceeds the excess (if any) of—
(i) the fair market value of such asset as of the beginning of such 1st taxable year, over
(ii) the adjusted basis of the asset as of such time.

STATUTORY AUTHORITY:
CODE SECTION 1374(d)(4)

(4) RECOGNIZED BUILT-IN LOSSES.—The term "recognized built-in loss" means any loss recognized during the recognition period on the disposition of any asset to the extent that the S corporation establishes that—
(A) such asset was held by the S corporation as of the beginning of the 1st taxable year referred to in paragraph (3), and
(B) such loss does not exceed the excess of—
(i) the adjusted basis of such asset as of the beginning of such 1st taxable year, over
(ii) the fair market value of such asset as of such time.

STATUTORY AUTHORITY: CODE SECTION 1374(d)(5)(A)

(5) TREATMENT OF CERTAIN BUILT-IN ITEMS.—

(A) INCOME ITEMS.—Any item of income which is properly taken into account during the recognition period but which is attributable to periods before the 1st taxable year for which the corporation was an S corporation shall be treated as a recognized built-in gain for the taxable year in which it is properly taken into account.

STATUTORY AUTHORITY: CODE SECTION 1374(d)(5)(B)

(5) Treatment of certain built-in items.—

(A) Income Items. * * * [discussed above]

(B) Deduction Items.—Any amount which is allowable as a deduction during the recognition period (determined without regard to any carryover) but which is attributable to periods before the 1st taxable year referred to in subparagraph (A) shall be treated as a recognized built-in loss for the taxable year for which it is allowable as a deduction.

STATUTORY AUTHORITY: CODE SECTION 1374(d)(5)(C)

(5) Treatment of certain built-in items.—

(A) Income Items. * * * [discussed above]

(B) Deduction Items. * * * [discussed above]

(C) Adjustment to net unrealized built-in gain.—The amount of the net unrealized built-in gain shall be properly adjusted for amounts which would be treated as recognized built-in gains or losses under this paragraph if such amounts were properly taken into account (or allowed as a deduction) during the recognition period.

STATUTORY AUTHORITY: CODE SECTION 1374(d)(6)

(6) TREATMENT OF CERTAIN PROPERTY.—If the adjusted basis of any asset is determined (in whole or in part) by reference to the adjusted basis of any other asset held by the S corporation as of the beginning of the 1st taxable year referred to in paragraph (3)—

(A) such asset shall be treated as held by the S corporation as of the beginning of such 1st taxable year, and

(B) any determination under paragraph (3)(B) or (4)(B) with respect to such asset shall be made by reference to the fair market value and adjusted basis of such other asset as of the beginning of such 1st taxable year.

STATUTORY AUTHORITY: CODE SECTION 1374(d)(7)

(7) RECOGNITION PERIOD.—The term "recognition period" means the 10-year period beginning with the 1st day of the 1st taxable year for which the corporation was an S corporation.

STATUTORY AUTHORITY: CODE SECTION 1374(d)(8)

(8) Treatment of transfer of assets from C corporation to S corporation.—

(A) In general.—Except to the extent provided in regulations, if—

(i) an S corporation acquires any asset, and

(ii) the S corporation's basis in such asset is determined (in whole or in part) by reference to the basis of such asset (or any other property) in the hands of a C corporation, then a tax is hereby imposed on any net recognized built-in gain attributable to any such assets for any taxable year beginning in the recognition period. The amount of such tax shall be determined under the rules of this section as modified by subparagraph (B).

(B) Modifications.—For purposes of this paragraph, the modifications of this subparagraph are as follows:

(i) In general.—The preceding paragraphs of this subsection shall be applied by taking into account the day on which the assets were acquired by the S corporation in lieu of the beginning of the 1st taxable year for which the corporation was an S corporation.

(ii) Subsection (c)(1) not to apply.—Subsection (c)(1) shall not apply.

STATUTORY AUTHORITY: CODE SECTION 1374(d)(9)

(9) Reference To 1st Taxable Year.—Any reference in this section to the 1st taxable year for which the corporation was an S corporation shall be treated as a reference to the 1st taxable year for which the corporation was an S corporation pursuant to its most recent election under section 1362.

STATUTORY AUTHORITY: CODE SECTION 1374(e)

(e) Regulations. The Secretary shall prescribe such regulations as may be necessary to carry out the purposes of this section including regulations providing for the appropriate treatment of successor corporations.

STATUTORY AUTHORITY: CODE SECTION 1375(b)(1)(B)

(B) LIMITATION.—The amount of the excess net passive income for any taxable year shall not exceed the amount of the corporation's taxable income for such taxable year as determined under section 63(a)—

(i) without regard to the deductions allowed by part VIII of subchapter B (other than the deduction allowed by section 248, relating to organization expenditures), and

(ii) without regard to the deduction under section 172.

CHAPTER 12

AUTHORITY: REGULATIONS SECTION 1.1362-2(c)(5)(ii)(A)(1)

(A) Royalties—

(1) In general. "Royalties" means all royalties, including mineral, oil, and gas royalties, and amounts received for the privilege of using patents, copyrights, secret processes and formulas, good will, trademarks, tradebrands, franchises, and other like property. The gross amount of royalties is not reduced by any part of the cost of the rights under which they are received or by any amount allowable as a deduction in computing taxable income.

AUTHORITY: REGULATIONS SECTION 1.1362-2(c)(5)(ii)(A)(2)

(2) Royalties derived in the ordinary course of a trade or business. "Royalties" does not include royalties derived in the ordinary course of a trade or business of licensing property. Royalties received by a corporation are derived in the ordinary course of a trade or business of licensing property only if, based on all the facts and circumstances, the corporation—

(i) Created the property or

(ii) Performed significant services or incurred substantial costs with respect to the development or marketing of the property.

AUTHORITY: REGULATIONS SECTION 1.1362-2(c)(5)(ii)(A)(3)

(3) Copyright, mineral, oil and gas, and active business computer software royalties. "Royalties" does not include copyright royalties as defined under section 543(a)(4); mineral, oil and gas royalties as defined under section 543(a)(3); amounts received upon disposal of timber, coal, or domestic iron ore with respect to which the special rules of section 631(b) and (c) apply; and active business computer software royalties as defined under section 543(d) (without regard to paragraph (d)(5)).

AUTHORITY: REGULATIONS SECTION 1.1362-2(c)(5)(ii)(B)

(B) Rents—

(1) In general. "Rents" means amounts received for the use of, or right to use, property (whether real or personal) of the corporation.

(2) Rents derived in the active trade or business of renting property. "Rents" does not include rents derived in the active trade or business of renting property. Rents received by a corporation are derived in an active trade or business of renting property only if, based on all the facts and circumstances, the corporation provides significant services or incurs substantial costs in the rental business. Generally, significant services are not rendered and substantial costs are not incurred in connection with net leases. Whether significant services are performed or substantial costs are incurred in the rental business is determined based upon all the facts and circumstances including, but not limited to, the number of persons employed to provide the services and the types and amounts of costs and expenses incurred (other than depreciation).

(3) Produced film rents. "Rents" does not include produced film rents as defined under section 543(a)(5).

(4) Income from leasing self-produced tangible property. "Rents" does not include compensation, however designated, for the use of, or right to use, any real or tangible personal property developed, manufactured, or produced by the taxpayer, if during the taxable year the taxpayer is engaged in substantial development, manufacturing, or production of real or tangible personal property of the same type.

AUTHORITY: REGULATIONS SECTION 1.1362-4(c)

(c) Corporation's request for determination of an inadvertent termination. A corporation that believes its election was terminated inadvertently may request a determination of inadvertent termination from the Commissioner. The request is made in the form of a ruling request and should set forth all relevant facts pertaining to the event including, but not limited to, the facts described in paragraph (b) of this section, the date of the corporation's election under section 1362(a), a detailed explanation of the event causing termination, when and how the event was discovered, and the steps taken to return the corporation to small business corporation status.

AUTHORITY: REGULATIONS SECTION 1.1362-4(f)

(f) Status of corporation. The status of the corporation after the terminating event and before the determination of inadvertence is determined by the Commissioner. Inadvertent termination relief may be granted retroactive for all years for which the terminating event was effective, in which case the corporation is treated as if its election had not terminated. Alternatively, relief may be granted only for the period in which the corporation again became eligible for subchapter S treatment, in which case the corporation is treated as a C corporation during the period for which the corporation was not eligible to be an S corporation.

AUTHORITY: REGULATIONS SECTION 1.1375-1(c)(2)

(2) Coordination with section 1374. If any gain —

(i) Is taken into account in determining passive income for purposes of this section, and

(ii) Is taken into account under section 1374, the amount of such gain taken into account under section 1374(b) and §1.1374-1(b)(1) and (2) in determining the amount of tax shall be reduced by the portion of the excess net passive income for the taxable year which is attributable (on a pro rata basis) to such gain. For purposes of the preceding sentence, the

portion of excess net passive income for the taxable year which is attributable to such capital gain is equal to the amount determined by multiplying the excess net passive income by the following fraction:
(NCG – E)/ NPI
Where:
NCG = net capital gain
NPI = net passive income
E = expense attributable to net capital gain

AUTHORITY: REGULATIONS SECTION 1.1375-1(d)(2)

(2) Corporation's request for a waiver. A request for waiver of the tax imposed by section 1375 shall be made in writing to the district director request (sic) and shall contain all relevant facts to establish that the requirements of paragraph (d)(1) of this section are met. Such request shall contain a description of how and on what date the S corporation in good faith and using due diligence determined that it had no Subchapter C earnings and profits at the close of the taxable year, a description of how and on what date it was determined that the S corporation had Subchapter C earnings and profits at the close of the year and a description (including dates) of any steps taken to distribute such earnings and profits. If the earnings and profits have not yet been distributed, the request shall contain a timetable for distribution and an explanation of why such timetable is reasonable. On the date the waiver is to become effective, all Subchapter C earnings and profits must have been distributed.

STATUTORY AUTHORITY: CODE SECTION 1362(d)(3)

(3) Where Passive Investment Income Exceeds 25 Percent of Gross Receipts for 3 Consecutive Taxable Years and Corporation Has Accumulated Earnings and Profits.—
(A) Termination.—
- (i) In General.—An election under subsection (a) shall be terminated whenever the corporation—
  - (I) has accumulated earnings and profits at the close of each of 3 consecutive taxable years, and
  - (II) has gross receipts for each of such taxable years more than 25 percent of which are passive investment income.
- (ii) When Effective.—Any termination under this paragraph shall be effective on and after the first day of the first taxable year beginning after the third consecutive taxable year referred to in clause (i).
- (iii) Years Taken into Account.—A prior taxable year shall not be taken into account under clause (i) unless—
  - (I) such taxable year began after December 31, 1981, and
  - (II) the corporation was an S corporation for such taxable year.

STATUTORY AUTHORITY: CODE SECTION 1362(d)(3)(C)

(C) Passive Investment Income Defined.—For purposes of this paragraph—
- (i) In General.—Except as otherwise provided in this subparagraph, the term "passive investment income" means gross receipts derived from royalties, rents, dividends, interest, annuities, and sales or exchanges of stock or securities (gross receipts from such sales or exchanges being taken into account for purposes of this paragraph only to the extent of gains therefrom).
- (ii) Exception for Interest on Notes from Sales of Inventory.—The term "passive investment income" shall not include interest on any obligation acquired in the ordinary course of the corporation's trade or business from its sale of property described in section 1221(1).
- (iii) Treatment of Certain Lending or Finance Companies.—If the S corporation meets the requirements of section 542(c)(6) for the taxable year, the term "passive investment income" shall not include gross receipts for the taxable year which are derived directly from the active and regular conduct of a lending or finance business (as defined in section 542(d)(1)).
- (iv) Treatment of Certain Liquidations.—Gross receipts derived from sales or exchanges of stock or securities shall not include amounts received by an S corporation which are treated under section 331 (relating to corporate liquidations) as payments in exchange for stock where the S corporation owned more than 50 percent of each class of stock of the liquidating corporation.

STATUTORY AUTHORITY: CODE SECTION 1362(d)(3)(C)(i)

(i) In General.—Except as otherwise provided in this subparagraph, the term "passive investment income" means gross receipts derived from royalties, rents, dividends, interest, annuities, and sales or exchanges of stock or securities (gross receipts from such sales or exchanges being taken into account for purposes of this paragraph only to the extent of gains therefrom).

STATUTORY AUTHORITY: CODE SECTION 1366(f)(3)

(3) Reduction in pass-thru [sic] for tax imposed on excess net passive income.—If any tax is imposed under section 1375 for any taxable year on an S corporation, for purposes of subsection (a), each item of passive investment income shall be reduced by an amount which bears the same ratio to the amount of such tax as—
(A) the amount of such item, bears to
(B) the total passive investment income for the taxable year.

**STATUTORY AUTHORITY:
CODE SECTION 1375(a)**

(a) General Rule.—If for the taxable year an S corporation has—

(1) accumulated earnings and profits at the close of such taxable year, and

(2) gross receipts more than 25 percent of which are passive investment income, then there is hereby imposed a tax on the income of such corporation for such taxable year. Such tax shall be computed by multiplying the excess net passive income by the highest rate of tax specified in section 11(b).

**STATUTORY AUTHORITY:
CODE SECTION 1375(b)(1)**

(b) Definitions.—For purposes of this section—

(1) Excess Net Passive Income.—

(A) In General.—Except as provided in subparagraph (B), the term "excess net passive income" means an amount which bears the same ratio to the net passive income for the taxable year as—

(i) the amount by which the passive investment income for the taxable year exceeds 25 percent of the gross receipts for the taxable year, bears to

(ii) the passive investment income for the taxable year.

**STATUTORY AUTHORITY:
CODE SECTION 1375(b)(1)(B)**

(B) LIMITATION.—The amount of the excess net passive income for any taxable year shall not exceed the amount of the corporation's taxable income for such taxable year as determined under section 63(a)—

(i) without regard to the deductions allowed by part VIII of subchapter B (other than the deduction allowed by section 248, relating to organization expenditures), and

(ii) without regard to the deduction under section 172.

**STATUTORY AUTHORITY:
CODE SECTION 1375(b)(2)**

(2) Net Passive Income.—The term "net passive income" means—

(A) passive investment income, reduced by

(B) the deductions allowable under this chapter that are directly connected with the production of such income (other than deductions allowable under section 172 and part VIII of subchapter B).

**STATUTORY AUTHORITY:
CODE SECTION 1375(b)(4)**

(4) COORDINATION WITH SECTION 1374.—Notwithstanding paragraph (3), the amount of passive investment income shall be determined by not taking into account any recognized built-in gain or loss of the S corporation for any taxable year in the recognition period. Terms used in the preceding sentence shall have the same respective meanings as when used in section 1374.

**STATUTORY AUTHORITY:
CODE SECTION 1375(c)**

(c) CREDITS NOT ALLOWABLE.—No credit shall be allowed under part IV of subchapter A of this chapter (other than section 34) against the tax imposed by subsection (a).

**STATUTORY AUTHORITY:
CODE SECTION 1375(d)**

(d) Waiver of Tax in Certain Cases.—If the S corporation establishes to the satisfaction of the Secretary that—

(1) it determined in good faith that it had no subchapter C [sic] earnings and profits at the close of a taxable year, and

(2) during a reasonable period of time after it was determined that it did have subchapter C earnings and profits at the close of such taxable year such earnings and profits were distributed, the Secretary may waive the tax imposed by subsection (a) for such taxable year.

CHAPTER 13

**AUTHORITY: REGULATIONS
SECTION 1.1362-3(c)(1)**

(1) S corporation that is a partner in a partnership. For purposes of section 706(c) only, the termination of the election of an S corporation that is a partner in a partnership during any portion of the S short year under §1.1362-2(a) or (b), is treated as a sale or exchange of the corporation's entire interest in the partnership on the last day of the S short year, if—

(i) The pro rata allocation rules do not apply to the corporation; and

(ii) Any taxable year of the partnership ends with or within the C short year.

**AUTHORITY: REGULATIONS
SECTION 1.1362-3(c)(6)**

(6) Year in which income from S short year is includible. A shareholder must include in taxable income the shareholder's pro rata share of the items described in section 1366(a) for the S short year for the year with or within which the S termination year ends.

**AUTHORITY: REGULATIONS
SECTION 1.1362-4(c)**

(c) Corporation's request for determination of an inadvertent termination. A corporation that believes its election was terminated inadvertently may request a determination of inadvertent termination from the Commissioner. The request is made in the form of a ruling request and should set forth all relevant facts pertaining to the event including, but not limited to, the facts described in paragraph (b) of this section, the date of the corporation's election under section 1362(a), a detailed explanation of the event causing termination, when and how the event was discovered, and the steps taken to return the corporation to small business corporation status.

AUTHORITY: REGULATIONS SECTION 1.1362-4(f)

(f) Status of corporation. The status of the corporation after the terminating event and before the determination of inadvertence is determined by the Commissioner. Inadvertent termination relief may be granted retroactive for all years for which the terminating event was effective, in which case the corporation is treated as if its election had not terminated. Alternatively, relief may be granted only for the period in which the corporation again became eligible for subchapter S treatment, in which case the corporation is treated as a C corporation during the period for which the corporation was not eligible to be an S corporation.

STATUTORY AUTHORITY: CODE SECTION 1362(d)(1)

(d) TERMINATION.—
- (1) By Revocation.—
  - (A) In General.—An election under subsection (a) may be terminated by revocation.
  - (B) More than One-Half of Shares Must Consent to Revocation.—An election may be revoked only if shareholders holding more than one-half of the shares of stock of the corporation on the day on which the revocation is made consent to the revocation.
  - (C) When Effective.—Except as provided in subparagraph (D)—
    - (i) a revocation made during the taxable year and on or before the 15th day of the 3rd month thereof shall be effective on the 1st day of such taxable year, and
    - (ii) a revocation made during the taxable year but after such 15th day shall be effective on the 1st day of the following taxable year.
  - (D) Revocation May Specify Prospective Date.—If the revocation specifies a date for revocation which is on or after the day on which the revocation is made, the revocation shall be effective on and after the date so specified.

STATUTORY AUTHORITY: CODE SECTION 1362(d)(2)

(2) By Corporation Ceasing to be Small Business Corporation.—
- (A) In General.—An election under subsection (a) shall be terminated whenever (at any time on or after the 1st day of the 1st taxable year for which the corporation is an S corporation) such corporation ceases to be a small business corporation.
- (B) When Effective.—Any termination under this paragraph shall be effective on and after the date of cessation.

STATUTORY AUTHORITY: CODE SECTION 1362(e)

(2) Pro Rata Allocation.—Except as provided in paragraph (3) and subparagraphs (C) and (D) of paragraph (6), the determination of which items are to be taken into account for each of the short taxable years referred to in paragraph (1) shall be made—
- (A) first by determining for the S termination year—
  - (i) the amount of each of the items of income, loss, deduction, or credit described in section 1366(a)(1)(A), and
  - (ii) the amount of the nonseparately computed income or loss, and
- (B) then by assigning an equal portion of each amount determined under subparagraph (A) to each day of the S termination year.

STATUTORY AUTHORITY: CODE SECTION 1362(e)(1)

Treatment of S Termination Year.—

(1) In General.—In the case of an S termination year, for purposes of this title—
- (A) S Short Year.—The portion of such year ending before the 1st day for which the termination is effective shall be treated as a short taxable year for which the corporation is an S corporation.
- (B) C Short Year.—The portion of such year beginning on such 1st day shall be treated as a short taxable year for which the corporation is a C corporation.

STATUTORY AUTHORITY: CODE SECTION 1362(e)(3)

(3) Election to Have Items Assigned to Each Short Taxable Year Under Normal Tax Accounting Rules.—
- (A) In General.—A corporation may elect to have paragraph (2) not apply.
- (B) Shareholders Must Consent to Election.—An election under this subsection shall be valid only if all persons who are shareholders in the corporation at any time during the S short year and all persons who are shareholders in the corporation on the first day of the C short year consent to such election.

STATUTORY AUTHORITY: CODE SECTION 1362(e)(4)

(4) S Termination Year.—For purposes of this subsection, the term "S termination year" means any taxable year of a corporation (determined without regard to this subsection) in which a termination of an election made under subsection (a) takes effect (other than on the 1st day thereof).

STATUTORY AUTHORITY: CODE SECTION 1362(e)(5)

(5) Tax for C Short Year Determined on Annualized Basis.—

(A) In General.—The taxable income for the short year described in subparagraph (B) of paragraph (1) shall be placed on an annual basis by multiplying the taxable income for such short year by the number of days in the S termination year and by dividing the result by the number of days in the short year. The tax shall be the same part of the tax computed on the annual basis as the number of days in such short year is of the number of days in the S termination year.

(B) Section 443(d)(2) [sic] to Apply.—Subsection (d) of section 443 shall apply to the short taxable year described in subparagraph (B) of paragraph (1).

STATUTORY AUTHORITY: CODE SECTION 1362(e)(6)(A)

(A) Short Years Treated as 1 Year for Carryover Purposes.—The short taxable year described in subparagraph (A) of paragraph (1) [the S termination year] shall not be taken into account for purposes of determining the number of taxable years to which any item may be carried back or carried forward by the corporation.

(B) Due Date for S Year.—The due date for filing the return for the short taxable year described in subparagraph (A) of paragraph (1) [the S short year] shall be the same as the due date for filing the return for the short taxable year described in subparagraph (B) of paragraph (1) [the C short year] (including extensions thereof).

STATUTORY AUTHORITY: CODE SECTION 1362(e)(6)(C) AND (D)

(C) Paragraph (2) [pro rata method] Not to Apply to Items Resulting from Section 338.—Paragraph (2) shall not apply with respect to any item resulting from the application of section 338.

(D) Pro Rata Allocation for S Termination Year Not to Apply if 50-Percent Change in Ownership.—Paragraph (2) shall not apply to an S termination year if there is a sale or exchange of 50 percent or more of the stock in such corporation during such year.

STATUTORY AUTHORITY: CODE SECTION 1362(f) AS AMENDED BY THE SMALL BUSINESS JOB PROTECTION ACT OF 1996

(f) Inadvertent Invalid Elections Or Terminations.—If—

(1) an election under subsection (a) by any corporation—

(A) was not effective for the taxable year for which made (determined without regard to subsection (b)(2)) by reason of a failure to meet the requirements of section 1361(b) or to obtain shareholder consents, or

(B) was terminated under paragraph (2) or (3) of subsection (d),

(2) the Secretary determines that the circumstances resulting in such ineffectiveness or termination were inadvertent,

(3) no later than a reasonable period of time after discovery of the circumstances resulting in such ineffectiveness or termination, steps were taken—

(A) so that the corporation is a small business corporation, or

(B) to acquire the required shareholder consents, and

(4) the corporation, and each person who was a shareholder in the corporation at any time during the period specified pursuant to this subsection, agrees to make such adjustments (consistent with the treatment of the corporation as an S corporation) as may be required by the Secretary with respect to such period,

then, notwithstanding the circumstances resulting in such ineffectiveness or termination, such corporation shall be treated as an S corporation during the period specified by the Secretary.

STATUTORY AUTHORITY: CODE SECTION 1366(d)(3)

(3) Carryover of disallowed losses and deductions to post-termination transition period.—

(A) In general.—If for the last taxable year of a corporation for which it was an S corporation a loss or deduction was disallowed by reason of paragraph (1), such loss or deduction shall be treated as incurred by the shareholder on the last day of any post-termination transition period.

(B) Cannot exceed shareholder's basis in stock.—The aggregate amount of losses and deductions taken into account by a shareholder under subparagraph (A) shall not exceed the adjusted basis of the shareholder's stock in the corporation (determined at the close of the last day of the post-termination transition period and without regard to this paragraph).

(C) Adjustment in basis of stock.—The shareholder's basis in the stock of the corporation shall be reduced by the amount allowed as a deduction by reason of this paragraph.

(D) At-risk limitations.—To the extent that any increase in adjusted basis described in sub¶ (B) would have increased the shareholder's amount at risk under §465 if such increase had accused on the day preceding the commencement of the post-termination transition period, rules similar to the rules described in sub¶s (A) through (C) shall apply to any losses disallowed by reason of §465(a).

STATUTORY AUTHORITY: CODE SECTION 1371(e)

(e) Cash distributions during post-termination transition period.—

(1) In general.—Any distribution of money by a corporation with respect to its stock during a

post-termination transition period shall be applied against and reduce the adjusted basis of the stock, to the extent that the amount of the distribution does not exceed the Accumulated Adjustments Account (within the meaning of section 1368(e)).

(2) Election to distribute earnings first.—An S corporation may elect to have paragraph (1) not apply to all distributions made during a post-termination transition period described in section 1377(b)(1)(A). Such election shall not be effective unless all shareholders of the S corporation to whom distributions are made by the S corporation during the post-termination transition period consent to such election.

STATUTORY AUTHORITY: CODE SECTION 1377(b)

(b) Post-Termination Transition Period.—

(1) In General.—For purposes of this subchapter, the term "post-termination transition period" means—

(A) the period beginning on the day after the last day of the corporation's last taxable year as an S corporation and ending on the later of—

(i) the day which is 1 year after such last day, or

(ii) the due date for filing the return for such last year as an S corporation (including extensions)

(B) the 120-day period beginning on the date of any determination pursuant to an audit of the taxpayer which follows the termination of the corporation's election and which adjusts a subchapter S item of income, loss, or deduction of the corporation arising during the S period (as deferred in section 1368(e)(2)), and

(C) the 120-day period beginning on the date of a determination that the corporation's election under section 1362(a) had terminated for a previous taxable year.

(2) Determination Defined.—For purposes of paragraph (1), the term "determination" means—

(A) a determination as defined in section 1313(a), or

(B) an agreement between the corporation and the Secretary that the corporation failed to qualify as an S corporation.

CHAPTER 14

AUTHORITY: REGULATIONS SECTION 1.1361-1(l)(4)(ii)(A)

(A) In general. Except as provided in paragraph (l)(4)(i) of this section, any instrument, obligation, or arrangement issued by a corporation (other than outstanding shares of stock described in paragraph (l)(3) of this section), regardless of whether designated as debt, is treated as a second class of stock of the corporation—

(1) if the instrument, obligation, or arrangement constitutes equity or otherwise results in the holder being treated as the owner of stock under general principles of Federal tax law, and

(2) A principal purpose of issuing or entering into the instrument, obligation, or arrangement is to circumvent the rights to distribution or liquidation proceeds conferred by the outstanding shares of stock or to circumvent the limitation on eligible shareholders contained in paragraph (b)(1) of this section.

STATUTORY AUTHORITY: CODE SECTION 351(a)

(a) General Rule.—No gain or loss shall be recognized if property is transferred to a corporation by one or more persons solely in exchange for stock in such corporation and immediately after the exchange such person or persons are in control (as defined in section 368(c)) of the corporation.

STATUTORY AUTHORITY: CODE SECTION 385

385. TREATMENT OF CERTAIN INTERESTS IN CORPORATIONS AS STOCK OR INDEBTEDNESS.

(a) Authority To Prescribe Regulations.—The Secretary is authorized to prescribe such regulations as may be necessary or appropriate to determine whether an interest in a corporation is to be treated for purposes of this title as stock or indebtedness (or as in part stock and in part indebtedness).

(b) Factors.—The regulations prescribed under this section shall set forth factors which are to be taken into account in determining with respect to a particular factual situation whether a debtor–creditor relationship exists or a corporation–shareholder relationship exists. The factors so set forth in the regulations may include among other factors:

(1) whether there is a written unconditional promise to pay on demand or on a specified date a sum certain in money in return for an adequate consideration in money or money's worth, and to pay a fixed rate of interest,

(2) whether there is subordination to or preference over any indebtedness of the corporation,

(3) the ratio of debt to equity of the corporation,

(4) whether there is convertibility into the stock of the corporation, and

(5) the relationship between holdings of stock in the corporation and holdings of the interest in question.

STATUTORY AUTHORITY: CODE SECTION 1244(a)

1244. Losses on Small Business Stock.

(a) General rule.—In the case of an individual, a loss on section 1244 stock issued to such individual or to a partnership which would (but for this section) be treated as a loss from the sale or exchange of a capital asset shall, to the extent provided in this section, be treated as an ordinary loss.

STATUTORY AUTHORITY: CODE SECTION 1244(b)

(b) Maximum amount for any taxable year.—For any taxable year the aggregate amount treated by the taxpayer by reason of this section as an ordinary loss shall not exceed—

(1) $50,000, or

(2) $100,000, in the case of a husband and wife filing a joint return for such year under section 6013.

STATUTORY AUTHORITY: CODE SECTION 1244(c)

(c) Section 1244 stock defined.—

(1) In general.—For purposes of this section, the term "section 1244 stock" means stock in a domestic corporation if—

(A) at the time such stock is [sic] issued, such corporation was a small business corporation,

(B) such stock was issued by such corporation for money or other property (other than stock and securities), and

(C) such corporation, during the period of its 5 most recent taxable years ending before the date the loss on such stock was sustained, derived not more than 50 percent of its aggregate gross receipts from sources other than royalties, rents, dividends, interests [sic], annuities, and sales or exchanges of stocks or securities.

STATUTORY AUTHORITY: CODE SECTION 1371(a)

(a) Application Of Subchapter C Rules. Except as otherwise provided in this title, and except to the extent inconsistent with this subchapter, subchapter C shall apply to an S corporation and its shareholders.

FINDING LISTS

CODE SECTIONS CITED

FINDING LISTS

FINDING LISTS

REGULATIONS CITED

Final Regulations

Proposed Regulations

Temporary Regulations

FINDING LISTS

REVENUE PROCEDURES CITED

FINDING LISTS

REVENUE RULINGS CITED

PRIVATE LETTER RULINGS AND TECHNICAL ADVICE MEMORANDA CITED

FINDING LISTS

CASED CITED

E

F

G

H

I

J

K

L

M

N

O

P

R

S

T

U

W

Y

Z

FINDING LISTS

MISCELLANEOUS CITATIONS

ACTS OF CONGRESS

FORMS

NOTICES

ANNOUNCEMENTS

FINDING LISTS

OTHER

MILLER

2000 S CORPORATION TAXATION GUIDE

CPE Program

TAKE YOUR CPE TEST ONLINE! www.hbpp.com

Harcourt Professional Publishing

SAN DIEGO NEW YORK CHICAGO LONDON

CPE REQUIREMENTS.
PLEASE READ THIS.

CPE requirements and course acceptability vary from state to state. Your state board is the final authority for the number of credit hours allowed for a particular program, as well as the classification of courses, under its specific licensing requirement. Contact your state board of accountancy for information concerning your state's requirements for the number of CPE credit hours you must earn, and the acceptable fields of study. This course is not currently registered under the Florida QA Service.

NASBA
NATIONAL REGISTRY OF
CPE
SPONSORS

Harcourt Professional Publishing is registered with the National Association of State Boards of Accountancy (NASBA) as a sponsor of continuing professional education on the National Registry of CPE Sponsors. State boards of accountancy have final authority on the acceptance of individual courses. Complaints regarding registered sponsors may be addressed to the National Registry of CPE Sponsors, 150 Fourth Avenue North, Nashville, TN, 37219-2417. Telephone: 615-880-4200.

INTRODUCTION

Thank you for choosing this self-study CPE course from Harcourt Professional Publishing. Our goal is to provide you with the clearest, most concise, and most up-to-date accounting, auditing, and tax information to help further your professional development, as well as the most convenient method to help you satisfy your continuing professional education obligations.

This course is intended to be used in conjunction with your 2000 *S Corporation Taxation Guide*. This course has the following characteristics:

Prerequisites: Basic knowledge of Taxation

Recommended CPE credits: 10 hours

Level of Knowledge: Intermediate—Builds on a basic level of understanding in order to relate fundamental principles or skills to practical situations and extend them to a broader range of applications. This level is for participants with some exposure to the subject.

Field of Study: Taxation

In accordance with the standards of the National Registry of CPE Sponsors, each credit hour awarded for this program is based on 100 minutes of average completion time. Credit hours are recommended in accordance with the Statement on Standards for Formal Continuing Professional Education (CPE) Programs, published by the AICPA. This exam costs $64.00. Payment options are shown on the answer sheet on page 933.

Please allow 2 to 3 weeks (from the date of our receipt of the exam) for grading. A passing score is 70 percent or above. Participants who pass the test will receive a Certificate of Completion to acknowledge their achievement. The self-study CPE Program offered in conjunction with 2000 *S Corporation Taxation Guide* will expire on December 31, 2001. Participants may submit completed tests for the program until that date.

To receive credit, complete the course according to the instructions below.

The CPE test is graded within two weeks of its receipt. A passing score is 70 percent or above. Participants who pass the test will receive a Certificate of Completion to acknowledge their achievement. The self-study CPE Program offered in conjunction with the 2000 *S Corporation Taxation Guide* will expire on December 31, 2000. Participants may submit completed tests for the program until that date.

INSTRUCTIONS FOR TAKING THIS COURSE

This course consists of chapter learning objectives, reading assignments, review questions and suggested solutions, and an examination. Complete each step listed below:

1. Review the chapter learning objectives.
2. Read the assigned material in the 2000 *S Corporation Taxation Guide.*
3. After completing all assigned chapters, take the examination, writing each answer on the appropriate line on the answer sheet.

4. When you have completed the examination, remove the answer sheet, place it in a stamped envelope, and send it to the following address:

   S Corporation Taxation Guide CPE Coordinator
   Harcourt Professional Publishing
   525 B Street, Suite 1900
   San Diego, CA 92101

Be sure to indicate your method of payment on the answer sheet.

PART 1
PREPARATION AND THE ELECTION

CHAPTER 1

Learning Objective: After completing this chapter, you will be able to:

- Determine if a corporation meets the requirements to be able to elect S corporation status.
- Identify the advantages and disadvantages of S corporation status compared to C corporations and partnerships.

Reading Assignment: Chapter 1 (Background and Environment) of the 2000 *S Corporation Taxation Guide.*

Review Question

1. What requirements must a corporation meet to qualify for the S election?

CHAPTER 2

Learning Objective: After completing this chapter, you will be able to:

- Identify the types of corporations that may elect S corporation status.
- Identify who would be an eligible shareholder for the purposes of making an S election.

Reading Assignment: Chapter 2 (Eligibility for the S Election) of the 2000 *S Corporation Taxation Guide.*

Review Question

2. Pine corporation has 76 shareholders on June 30, 1997, including John and Anita who are married to each other.
   a. If the corporation meets the other requirements, can it elect S corporation status?
   b. Assume that John and Anita both own shares in X corporation. Can the corporation continue its S status if John and Anita are divorced?
   c. John dies and the shares are transferred to his estate. Does the corporation remain eligible for S corporation status?
   d. Assume the same facts as in c. above. John's estate distributes the shares to John's daughter. Does the corporation remain eligible for S status?

CHAPTER 3

Learning Objective: After completing this chapter, you will be able to:

- Calculate the LIFO recapture amount and the resulting LIFO recapture tax.
- Compute the amount of a corporation's accumulated earnings and profits.
- Understand the implications of accumulated earnings and profits for S corporation operations.

Reading Assignment: Chapter 3 (C Corporations Considering the S Election: Advantages, Disadvantages, and Solutions) of the 2000 *S Corporation Taxation Guide.*

Review Question

3. What are the steps to be taken in calculating the LIFO recapture amount?

CHAPTER 4

Learning Objective: After completing this chapter, you will be able to:

- Determine the fiscal year that an S corporation may use.
- Calculate any required payments, when necessary, if a fiscal year is used.

Reading Assignment: Chapter 4 (Tax Years of S Corporations) of the 2000 *S Corporation Taxation Guide.*

Review Question

4. What taxable-period options are available for use by S corporations?

CHAPTER 5

Learning Objective: After completing this chapter, you will be able to:

- Properly file the S election on Form 2553 together with shareholder consents.
- Determine the election filing date necessary to secure the desired effective date.
- Determine how to remedy defective S corporation elections.

Reading Assignment: Chapter 5 (Corporate and Shareholder Elections) of the 2000 *S Corporation Taxation Guide.*

Review Question

5. Patsy and Karen are starting a business. They want to incorporate and have the corporation immediately elect S status. The state issues its corporate charter for the corporation on June 5, and shares are issued to the shareholders on that date. The corporation acquires assets and begins doing business on June 15.
   a. When does the S election become effective if the election form, Form 2553, is filed on June 1?
   b. What is the deadline for filing Form 2553 if the S election and incorporation are to incur simultaneously?
   c. Can a corporation request an extension of time to file Form 2553?
   d. Can a corporation request an extension of time to file shareholder consents?

PART II
OPERATING THE S CORPORATION

CHAPTER 6

Learning Objective: After completing this chapter, you will be able to:

- Calculate an S corporation's corporate-level income or loss.
- Allocate an S corporation's income, deductions, credits, and other corporate-level items to its shareholders.

Reading Assignment: Chapter 6 (Income Measurement and Reporting) of the 2000 *S Corporation Taxation Guide.*

Review Question

6. Ben and Marsha each own 50% of an S corporation. At exactly mid-year, Ben sells all of his shares in the corporation to Marsha. At the date of sale, the corporation shows net income of $7,000. During the second half of the year, the corporation shows net income of $13,000. The corporation's combined income on its Form 1120S for the year is $20,000, and there are no separately stated items. If no election is made, how is the income allocated to Ben and Marsha?

CHAPTER 7

Learning Objective: After completing this chapter, you will be able to:

- Determine the tax treatment of distributions from an S corporation that does not have accumulated earnings and profits (AEP).
- Determine the tax treatment of distributions from an S corporation when AEP is present.
- Determine the tax treatment of property distributions from an S corporation.

Reading Assignment: Chapter 7 (Distributions of Income) of the 2000 *S Corporation Taxation Guide.*

Review Question

7. Reed is the sole shareholder in an S corporation. The corporation has an AAA balance of $4,000 at the beginning of the current year and has $10,000 of AEP that it accumulated when it was a C corporation. Reed's stock basis at the beginning of the year is $15,000. At year end, the corporation's Form 1120S shows $20,000 of bottom-line income. The corporation made distributions of $28,000 to Reed during the year.
   a. What is the corporation's balances in AAA and AEP at year end?
   b. What is the taxable nature of the distribution to Reed?
   c. What is Reed's basis in stock at year end?

CHAPTER 8

Learning Objective: After completing this chapter, you will be able to:

- Determine the proper tax treatment of accrued expenses to shareholders.
- Understand the tax implications present in the handling of shareholder compensation and fringe benefits and the business expenses of shareholder-employees.

Reading Assignment: Chapter 8 (Corporate–Shareholder Transactions) of the 2000 *S Corporation Taxation Guide.*

Review Question

8. XYZ Corporation has three equal, unrelated shareholders who use the cash method of accounting. XYZ uses a calendar year and the accrual method of accounting. On December 31, 1998, the corporation accrues bonuses to the three shareholders. The bonuses meet all of the other tests for deductibility. If XYZ Corporation is an S corporation, may it claim a deduction for the bonuses in 1998?

CHAPTER 9

Learning Objective: After completing this chapter, you will be able to:

- Calculate a shareholder's basis in S corporation stock and debt.
- Recognize debt that will provide a shareholder basis in an S corporation.

Reading Assignment: Chapter 9 (Shareholder Stock Basis and Debt Basis) of the 2000 *S Corporation Taxation Guide.*

Review Question

9. Jim is the sole shareholder in an S corporation. At the beginning of the current year, Jim's stock basis was $16,000. He has no debt basis. During the year, Jim made a $3,000 contribution to the corporation's capital. The corporation shows the following items on its Form 1120S for the year:

Separately stated (bottom line) income	14,000
Long-term capital gain	3,000
Loss from rental of real estate	5,000
Charitable contributions	1,500
Distributions to Jim	17,000

a. What is Jim's stock basis at the end of the year?
b. What is the taxable nature of the distributions received by Jim during the year?

CHAPTER 10

Learning Objective: After completing this chapter, you will be able to:

- Identify S corporation losses and deductions that are subject to limitation at the corporate level.
- Apply the at-risk and passive activity rules to determine the deductibility of an S corporation's losses at the shareholder level.

Reading Assignment: Chapter 10 (Integration of Loss Limits) of the 2000 *S Corporation Taxation Guide.*

Review Question

10. Steve's basis in his S corporation's stock and debt before he deducts any current-year losses is $7,000. His share of S corporation losses for the current year is $9,000. Steve's amount at risk is only $4,000. How will John treat his S corporation loss?

PART III
CORPORATE-LEVEL TAXES AND TERMINATION

CHAPTER 11

Learning Objective: After completing this chapter, you will be able to:

- Identify situations where the built-in gains tax would apply to a corporation that is contemplating an S election.
- Apply the rules relating to the tax on built-in gains to existing S corporations.
- Formulate tax-planning strategies to avoid or reduce the built-in gains tax.

Reading Assignment: Chapter 11 (Taxes on Property Dispositions) of the 2000 *S Corporation Taxation Guide.*

Review Question

11. Milco Corporation was a cash-basis C corporation that filed its S election to become effective at the beginning of the current year. The corporation had no unused loss or credit carryovers. An appraisal of the corporation's assets showed that the amounts on the corporation's balance sheet were correct. At the date the S election became effective, its balance sheet showed the following:

	Adjusted Basis	*Fair Market Value*
Accounts Receivable	-0-	$150,000
Fixed Assets	130,000	120,000
Total Assets	$130,000	$270,000
Accounts Payable	$-0-	$ 60,000

Milco Corporation collects the accounts receivable and pays the accounts payable in the first year it operates as an S corporation. No assets are sold or distributed during the year. The corporation's taxable income for the year (computed using modified C corporation rules) is $100,000. Does collection of the accounts receivable and payment of the accounts payable affect the built-in gains calculations? Why or why not?

CHAPTER 12

Learning Objective: After completing this chapter, you will be able to:

- Identify the types of income that are passive investment income and calculate the tax on excess net passive income.
- Protect the S election against an inadvertent termination caused by excess net passive income.

Reading Assignment: Chapter 12 (Passive Investment Income) of the 2000 *S Corporation Taxation Guide.*

Review Question

12. What types of income are classified, in general, as passive investment income?

CHAPTER 13

Learning Objective: After completing this chapter, you will be able to:

- Determine how to voluntarily terminate an S election and recognize occurrences that will result in an involuntary termination of an election.
- Properly allocate S corporation items in the year that the S election is terminated.
- Determine how and when to request inadvertent termination relief from the IRS.

Reading Assignment: Chapter 13 (Termination of the S Election) of the 2000 *S Corporation Taxation Guide.*

Review Question

13. An S corporation reports on a calendar year and files a revocation of its S election on March 1 of the current year.
    a. When does the revocation become effective if the revocation statement stipulates that it is retroactively effective to January 1 of the current year?
    b. When does the revocation become effective if the revocation statement stipulates that it is retroactively effective to March 10 of the current year?

PART IV
RELATIONSHIP TO OTHER TAX AND ACCOUNTING RULES

CHAPTER 14

Learning Objective: After completing this chapter, you will be able to:

- Advise clients on how to contribute property to an S corporation in a nontaxable transaction.
- Determine how to recognize an ordinary loss deduction when a shareholder suffers a loss on §1244 stock.
- Determine how to integrate a S corporation within a larger group of closely held businesses.

Reading Assignment: Chapter 14 (Capital Structure of the S Corporation) of the 2000 *S Corporation Taxation Guide.*

Review Question

14. Laura and Edward are forming an S corporation. Laura contributes property worth $35,000, which had a basis of $25,000, in exchange for 50% of the corporation's stock. Edward contributes property worth $35,000, which had a basis of $30,000, in exchange for 50% of the stock.
    a. Does Laura recognize gain in the transfer of the property in exchange for stock?
    b. Does Edward recognize any loss on the exchange?
    c. What is the corporation's basis in the property it receives from the shareholders?

Chapter 15

Learning Objective: After completing this chapter, you will be able to:

- Recognize various means of obtaining favorable tax treatment when an S corporation redeems its stock.
- Recognize various means of obtaining favorable tax treatment when there is a contraction of an S corporation's operations through a stock redemption or a divisive reorganization.

Reading Assignment: Chapter 15 (Contractions of the S Corporation) of the 2000 *S Corporation Taxation Guide.*

Review Question

15. Robert and Roxanne each own 100 shares of R&R Corporation stock. There are no other shareholders. R&R Corporation redeems 50 of Roxanne's shares and none of Robert's shares.
    a. If Roxanne does not constructively own any of Robert's shares, how will the transaction be regarded for tax purposes?
    b. If Robert and Roxanne were related parties, such as husband and wife or mother and son, would you arrive at a different answer?

Chapter 16

Learning Objective: After completing this chapter, you will be able to:

- Determine the proper tax treatment when an S corporation liquidates.
- Determine the effect upon the S corporation and its shareholders when there is a sale of the stock or the assets of the corporation.

Reading Assignment: Chapter 16 (Acquisitions and Dispositions of S Corporations) of the 2000 *S Corporation Taxation Guide.*

Review Question

16. A C corporation has discontinued business and is liquidating. What is necessary for a transaction to constitute a complete liquidation?

Chapter 17

Learning Objective: After completing this chapter, you will be able to:

- Identify and implement the various types of tax-free reorganizations.
- Determine the impact of a tax-free reorganization upon an S corporation.

Reading Assignment: Chapter 17 (Tax-Free Reorganizations) of the 2000 *S Corporation Taxation Guide.*

Review Question

17. What are the requirements for a tax-free reorganization?

CHAPTER 18

Learning Objective: After completing this chapter, you will be able to:

- Recognize the potential federal inheritance and gift tax problems presented by a decedent's ownership of an S corporation.
- Plan for the maintenance of an S corporation's eligibility after the death of a shareholder.

Reading Assignment: Chapter 18 (Estate Planning Considerations) of the 2000 *S Corporation Taxation Guide.*

Review Question

18. Oldco, Inc., has had an S election in effect since 1979. The company has accumulated a large amount of previously taxed income (PTI). What is the effect on the corporation if a holder of the PTI account dies?

SUGGESTED SOLUTIONS TO REVIEW QUESTIONS

1. After December 31, 1996, corporations eligible to make an S election must meet the following requirements:
   - The corporation must be a domestic corporation.
   - The corporation must have no more than 75 shareholders.
   - Each shareholder must be an individual U.S. citizen or resident, an estate, or one of an expanded group of trusts specifically designed to qualified as shareholders in S corporation.
   - The corporation must have only a single class of stock.
   - The corporation may be a member of an affiliated group of corporations with certain restrictions.

2. As follows:
   a. Yes. Even though the corporation has 36 shareholders, a married couple is counted as one shareholder, so the corporation is considered to have 35 shareholders and is eligible for S status.
   b. No. When the divorce was final, the corporation would have 36 shareholders and would not be able to operate as an S corporation.
   c. Yes. A shareholder's estate is an eligible shareholder.
   d. No. Only married couples are counted as one shareholder. When the shares are transferred to John's daughter, the corporation will have 76 shareholders, and will no longer qualify as an S corporation.

3. Calculation of the LIFO recapture amount involves the following steps:
   a. Determine the corporation's FIFO cost from the corporation's books and records.
   b. Adjust FIFO costs for any uniform capitalization adjustments.
   c. Compare FIFO costs with market value.
   d. Determine LIFO cost with appropriate uniform capitalization adjustments.
   e. Compare the lower of FIFO costs or market with LIFO cost. The difference is the LIFO amount.

4. An S corporation must use a "permitted year" for its taxable income and other information. The options available to an S corporation are:
   a. The calendar year
   b. A fiscal year if it has a majority of shareholders using the same year
   c. A natural business year
   d. A newly elected fiscal year under Revenue Code §444
   e. A grandfathered fiscal year under Revenue Code §444

5. a. The election never becomes effective because the company had not yet become a corporation, and a company must exist as a corporation before it can file a valid election. In this case, the corporation came into existence on June 5 when the state charter was issued.
   b. The deadline is September 20. The election can be retroactive if it is filed within two months and 15 days after the beginning of the year in which it is to take effect. In this case the count begins on June 5 and ends on September 20.

c. No purpose is served in requesting an extension of time in which to file Form 2553, because the IRS has no authority to grant such an extension.

d. The IRS may grant extensions of time in which to file shareholder consents, if there is reasonable cause for delay. The consent must be filed within the period granted by the IRS, and it must be accompanied by consent statements of the shareholders who have not previously consented to the election.

6. Normally, S corporation income, deductions, credits, and any other corporate-level items are allocated to shareholders on a pro rata (per share, per day) basis. In this case, Ben would be allocated income of $5,000 ($20,000 x 50% stock ownership x 50% of the year). Marsha would be allocated income of $15,000; that is, $5,000 ($20,000 x 50% stock ownership x 50% of the year) plus $10,000 ($20,000 x 100% stock ownership x 50% of the year).

7. As follows:

a. The corporation's AAA and AEP balances are determined as follows:

	AAA	*AEP*
Balance, beginning of year	$ 4,000	$10,000
Corporate income	20,000	-0-
Distributions	(24,000)	(4,000)
Balance, end of year	-0-	$6,000

b. Reed treats the distribution as follows:

Nontaxable income to the extent of AAA	$24,000
Taxable dividend income from AEP	4,000
Total distributions	$28,000

c. Reed's basis in stock is determined as follows:

Basis, beginning of year	$15,000
Corporate income	20,000
Distributions from AAA	(24,000)
Basis, end of year	$ 11,000

(Note that distributions of AEP are taxable dividends and do not reduce shareholder's basis.)

8. If XYZ Corporation is an S corporation, it cannot deduct the bonuses until it pays the shareholders. An S corporation may not deduct a payment to a person who actively or constructively owns any of the corporation's shares, until the day the shareholder takes the amount into income. If the corporation had been a C corporation, it may deduct the bonuses in 1996, since none of the shareholders owns more than 50% of the stock in the corporation.

9. a. Basis is adjusted by contributions to capital. It is also adjusted for corporate items of income, loss, and deduction. Basis is then decreased by distributions. Jim's stock basis is $11,500, computed as follows:

CPE PROGRAM

Basis, beginning of year	$16,000
Contribution to Capital	3,000
Separately Stated Income	14,000
Long-term capital gain	3,000
Loss from rental real estates	(5,000)
Charitable contributions	(1,500)
Distributions	(17,000)
Basis, end of year	$12,500

b. Since Jim has stock basis in excess of the amount distributed during the year, the $17,000 distribution reduces stock basis and is not taxable.

10. Steve's loss from his S corporation stock and debt will be limited both by his lack of basis and by the amount at risk. His S corporation loss will be treated as follows:

Loss before basis limits	$9,000
Limit to basis	(7,000)
Carryforward until basis is increased	$2,000
Loss after basis limitation	$7,000
Limit to amount at risk	(4,000)
Carryforward until amount at risk increased	$3,000

11. The collection of cash-basis accounts receivable that were outstanding on the date the S election became effective generates built-in gains. This is because recognized income is built-in gain if the item of income is economically accrued before the S election took effect, and it must be recognized as income during the corporation's recognition period. Cash-basis accounts payable affect the built-in gains calculation because an S corporation can treat a deduction as a recognized built-in loss if the deduction is attributable to a year before the S election took effect.

12. The Internal Revenue Code provides some definitions of *passive income* in §1362(d)(3). Briefly, the sources of passive income are interest, dividends, rents, royalties, and gains from the sale of stock or securities. Income that normally would be considered passive investment income may not be passive if certain conditions are met. For example, rent is not passive investment income if it is received in the ordinary course of an active trade or business or renting property.

13. a. The revocation is effective on January 1 of the current year. A revocation can be retroactive to the first day of the year in which the revocation is filed, if the revocation is filed within two months and 15 days of the first day of the corporation's tax year.

    b. The revocation is effective on March 10. The revocation can be effective for any prospective date, so long as that date is after the date on which the revocation is filed.

14. As follows:

    a. No. Laura recognizes no gain, because this transaction qualifies as a nontaxable exchange. The property was exchanged solely for stock, and the contributing shareholders have control of the corporation after the transfer.

b. No. Edward cannot recognize a loss, because shareholders do not recognize either gain or loss on a nontaxable exchange of property for stock.

c. The corporation has a basis of $25,000 in the property received from Laura and a basis of $30,000 in the property received from Edward. Basis at the corporate level is the same as the basis of the property transferred to the corporation increased by any gain recognized by the transferor shareholder.

15. a. Since Roxanne does not own any of Robert's shares, the transaction is treated as a stock redemption rather than as a distribution. The redemption is substantially disproportionate, as demonstrated by the following calculations:

Roxanne's percentage of ownership before redemption (100/200)	50%
Maximum percentage permitted after redemption (<80% of 50%)	<40%
Roxanne's actual stock ownership percentage and voting power after redemption (50/150)	33.3%

b. If Roxanne and Robert were related parties, Roxanne would constructively own 100% of the stock after the redemption. The transaction would not qualify for exchange treatment and would be a dividend to the extent of the corporation's AEP.

16. For a transaction to constitute a complete liquidation, the corporation must cease to be a going concern. A formal plan of liquidation is not necessary, but would be advisable. Without such a plan, there may be some confusion about the distribution of the corporation's property.

17. The three requirements for a tax-free reorganization are:
    - Continuity of ownership
    - Continuity of business
    - Business purpose

18. Previously taxed income (PTI) represents a layer of equity that is a tax reduction of basis to the shareholder who receives it. If a holder of a PTI account dies, any undistributed balance will be closed to paid-in capital and will not be available for distribution until the corporation has exhausted its accumulated earnings and profits.

EXAMINATION

1. Which of the following items, if any, increases the stock basis of an S corporation shareholder?
   a. Tax-exempt insurance proceeds
   b. Depletion not in excess of basis
   c. Expenses related to tax exempt interest
   d. A distribution from earnings and profits
   e. None of the above
2. Which, if any, of the following items has no effect on the AAA and the stock basis of an S corporation shareholder?
   a. Taxable income items
   b. A shareholder loan
   c. A capital gain
   d. Depletion in excess of basis
   e. All of the above modify AAA and stock basis.
3. A C corporation elects S status. The corporation may be subject to built-in gains tax on which of the following assets?
   a. Capital gain assets
   b. Goodwill
   c. Accounts receivable
   d. All of the above
4. Which of the following statements is true?
   a. The depletion allowance is computed separately for each shareholder.
   b. The basic research credit is available to an S corporation.
   c. All states now recognize the S election.
   d. A shareholder's portion of the self-employment income is subject to the self-employment tax.
   e. All of the above
5. A S corporation may lose its S tax status:
   a. Only at the option of the Internal Revenue Service.
   b. If the corporation has a passive loss during the year.
   c. If any of the shareholders dies and the estate owns the stock.
   d. If any one of the shareholders transfers the stock to a nonqualified trust.
   e. None of the above eliminates the S election.
6. During the year, an S corporation incurs a $75,000 operating loss. Patsy, the sole shareholder, has a $65,000 stock basis, and there is a $70,000 balance in AAA at the beginning of the year. Which of the following statements is correct?
   a. Patsy may show a $70,000 loss deduction on her Form 1040.
   b. At the end of the year there is a zero balance in both Patsy's stock basis and the AAA.

c. At the end of the year, Patsy has a zero basis in her stock and there is a negative $5,000 balance in the AAA.

d. Patsy may deduct $70,000 of the loss.

e. None of the above statements is correct.

7. During 1998 Echelon, Inc., a S corporation, incurs the following transactions:

Net income from operations	$99,000
Interest income from savings accounts	4,000
Long-term capital gain from the sale of securities	11,000
Short-term capital loss from sale of securities	6,000

Echelon, Inc., maintains a valid S election and does not distribute any dividends to its sold shareholder, Donna. As a result Donna must recognize:

a. Ordinary income of $103,000 and a long-term capital gain of $5,000.

b. Ordinary income of $103,000, long-term capital gain of $11,000, and a short-term capital loss of $6,000.

c. Ordinary income of $108,000.

d. None of the above.

8. Which of the following statements is false with regard to an S corporation?

a. Stock basis may not go below zero.

b. AAA may not go below zero.

c. NOL are allocated on a daily basis to all shareholders.

d. AAA may be greater than stock basis.

e. None of the above statements is false.

9. Which item is not stated separately on a S corporation's Schedule K?

a. Section 1250 income

b. Section 1231 gain

c. Dividend income

d. Charitable contributions

e. None of the above

10. Which transaction affects the Other Adjustments Account (OAA) on an S corporation's Schedule M-2?

a. Payroll tax penalties

b. Unreasonable compensation audit adjustment made by IRS

c. Life insurance proceeds (nontaxable to the recipient S corporation)

d. Taxable interest

e. None of the above affects the OAA.

11. Karen has been the sole shareholder of a calendar-year S corporation since 1982. At the end of 1998, her stock basis is $15,500, and she receives a distribution of $17,000. Corporate-level accounts are as follows:

AAA	$6,000
PTI	9,000
Accumulated E & P	600

CPE PROGRAM

How is Karen taxed on the distribution?

a. A $600 taxable dividend and a $1,000 long-term capital gain

b. A $600 taxable dividend and a $1,500 long-term capital gain

c. Tax-free income of $15,400 and a $600 taxable dividend

d. None of the above

12. Graphic, Inc., an S corporation, distributes a machine to Delma, a majority shareholder. This asset has an adjusted basis of $30,000, but a fair-market value of $70,000. Accumulated cost recovery deductions amounted to $22,000.00. Graphics, Inc., recognizes a gain of:

    a. $0.

    b. $18,000.

    c. $22,000.

    d. $40,000.

    e. None of the above.

13. A shareholder's basis in his or her stock in an S corporation is:

    a. Decreased by a pass-through of losses.

    b. Decreased by nonseparately computed taxable income.

    c. Increased by a distribution of pre-1983 PTI.

    d. All of the above.

    e. None of the above.

14. A cash-basis S corporation may minimize any built-in gain tax liability by:

    a. Maximizing built-in losses at conversion date.

    b. Minimizing built-in gain at conversion date.

    c. Accruing compensation costs.

    d. All of the above techniques are effective.

    e. None of the above techniques is effective.

15. What event will not terminate an S election?

    a. Receipt of passive income

    b. Shares of stock given to a nonresident alien

    c. Shares of stock given to a C corporation

    d. Issuance of a second class of stock

    e. All of the above terminate an S election.

16. An S corporation must possess the following characteristic(s):

    a. No more than 75 shareholders

    b. Corporation organized in the United States

    c. Only one class of stock

    d. All of the above are required of an S corporation.

    e. None of the above is required of an S corporation.

17. Which of the following, if any, can be eligible shareholders of a S corporation?

    a. A resident alien

    b. A partnership

    c. A foreign corporation

d. A nonqualifying trust
e. None of the above can own stock in an S corporation.

18. Excess net passive income of an S corporation is $40,000 and taxable income is 30,000. Assuming that there is $50,000 of accumulated earnings and profits from a C corporation year, what would the passive income penalty tax be?
    a. $0
    b. $4,500
    c. $10,500
    d. $14,000
    e. None of the above
19. Which of the following items, if any, has no effect of an S corporation's AAA?
    a. Purchase of 100 shares of stock by a shareholder
    b. A capital loss
    c. Tax-exempt interest income
    d. A distribution from current-year earnings
    e. None of the above
20. Ross Corporation converts to S corporation status for 1998. Ross used the LIFO inventory method in 1997 and had a LIFO inventory of $120,000 (FIFO value $210,000). How much tax must be added to the 1997 corporate tax liability, assuming that Ross Corporation is subject to a 35% marginal tax rate?
    a. $0
    b. $7,875
    c. $31,500
    d. $90,000
    e. None of the above
21. *True or false:* An S corporation may own 82% of a subsidiary corporation.
22. *True or false:* An S corporation may not be a partner in a limited partnership.
23. *True or false:* Any shareholder who owned stock at the beginning of the tax year for which an S election is effective (but who is no longer a shareholder on the date of the election) must consent to the S election.
24. *True or false:* Foreign taxes and the deduction for amortization of organization expenses are allowable as deductions for S corporations.
25. *True or false:* A S corporation that acquires a C corporation in a reorganization is not subject to the built-in gains tax of the assets acquired from the C corporation.
26. *True or false:* If the Internal Revenue Service audits an S corporation, the statute of limitations for any shareholder adjustment runs from the S corporation's tax return filing date.
27. *True or false:* An S corporation is not required to make estimated tax payments.
28. *True or false*: The phrase "passive investment income" as used in Subchapter S closely parallels the definitions of *passive income* and *investment income* as they pertain to individuals.
29. *True or false:* A shareholder of a former S corporation may restore basis and claimed suspended losses by loaning money to the corporation during the post-termination transition period.

CPE PROGRAM

30. *True or false:* The S election can be voluntarily revoked retroactively only if the revocation statement is filed within two months and 15 days of the beginning of the corporation's tax year.
31. *True or false*: The environmental excise tax is imposed upon the AMT income of an S corporation.
32. *True or false*: A S corporation may not maintain qualified pension and profit-sharing plans on behalf of shareholders who are also employees.
33. *True or False:* The sale of an S corporation's stock does not terminate the corporation's S election, as long as the purchasers are eligible shareholders.
34. *True or false*: The LIFO recapture tax is based on the corporation's sales of inventory during its first S corporation year.
35. *True or false:* If the holder of a PTI account dies, any undistributed balance in the PTI account will be available for distribution to the decedent's beneficiary after the corporation has exhausted its accumulated earnings and profits.
36. *True or false:* Salaries paid to an S corporation shareholder are subject to FICA taxes but not to FUTA taxes.
37. *True or false:* A recognized gain on the sale of S corporation's assets may not be a built-in gain if the gain is attributable to appreciation that occurred after the S corporation election was effective.
38. *True or false:* An S corporation that has a large balance in accumulated earnings and profits may be subject to the accumulated earning tax.
39. *True or false*: The deduction allowable under Internal Revenue Code §179 is a separately reported item on an S corporation's Schedule K.
40. *True or false*: If an S corporation has issued some shares of its common stock with voting rights and some shares without voting rights, the corporation will be considered to have more than one class of stock.

2000 S CORPORATION TAX GUIDE CPE PROGRAM

Please record your CPE answers in the space provided on the right. Mail completed page (photocopies accepted) in a stamped envelope to:

☞ *S Corporation Tax Guide* CPE Coordinator
Harcourt Professional Publishing
525 B Street, Suite 1900
San Diego, CA 92101-4495

Name ______________________________

Firm Name ______________________________

Address ______________________________

____

Phone (______) ______________________________

CPA License # ______________________________

ISBN: 0-15-607123-1

TO ORDER: **Call Toll-Free 1-800-831-7799**

METHOD OF PAYMENT

❑ **Payment enclosed ($64.00).**
(Make checks payable to **Harcourt, Inc.**)
Please add appropriate sales tax.
Be sure to sign your order below.

Charge my:
❑ MasterCard ❑ Visa ❑ American Express

Account number ______________________________

Expiration date ______________________________
Please sign below for all credit card orders.

❑ **Bill me.**
Be sure to sign your order below.

Signature ______________________________

1. Ⓐ Ⓑ Ⓒ Ⓓ / Ⓣ Ⓕ
2. Ⓐ Ⓑ Ⓒ Ⓓ / Ⓣ Ⓕ
3. Ⓐ Ⓑ Ⓒ Ⓓ / Ⓣ Ⓕ
4. Ⓐ Ⓑ Ⓒ Ⓓ / Ⓣ Ⓕ
5. Ⓐ Ⓑ Ⓒ Ⓓ / Ⓣ Ⓕ
6. Ⓐ Ⓑ Ⓒ Ⓓ / Ⓣ Ⓕ
7. Ⓐ Ⓑ Ⓒ Ⓓ / Ⓣ Ⓕ
8. Ⓐ Ⓑ Ⓒ Ⓓ / Ⓣ Ⓕ
9. Ⓐ Ⓑ Ⓒ Ⓓ / Ⓣ Ⓕ
10. Ⓐ Ⓑ Ⓒ Ⓓ / Ⓣ Ⓕ
11. Ⓐ Ⓑ Ⓒ Ⓓ / Ⓣ Ⓕ
12. Ⓐ Ⓑ Ⓒ Ⓓ / Ⓣ Ⓕ
13. Ⓐ Ⓑ Ⓒ Ⓓ / Ⓣ Ⓕ
14. Ⓐ Ⓑ Ⓒ Ⓓ / Ⓣ Ⓕ
15. Ⓐ Ⓑ Ⓒ Ⓓ / Ⓣ Ⓕ
16. Ⓐ Ⓑ Ⓒ Ⓓ / Ⓣ Ⓕ
17. Ⓐ Ⓑ Ⓒ Ⓓ / Ⓣ Ⓕ
18. Ⓐ Ⓑ Ⓒ Ⓓ / Ⓣ Ⓕ
19. Ⓐ Ⓑ Ⓒ Ⓓ / Ⓣ Ⓕ
20. Ⓐ Ⓑ Ⓒ Ⓓ / Ⓣ Ⓕ
21. Ⓐ Ⓑ Ⓒ Ⓓ / Ⓣ Ⓕ
22. Ⓐ Ⓑ Ⓒ Ⓓ / Ⓣ Ⓕ
23. Ⓐ Ⓑ Ⓒ Ⓓ / Ⓣ Ⓕ
24. Ⓐ Ⓑ c Ⓓ / Ⓣ Ⓕ
25. Ⓐ Ⓑ Ⓒ Ⓓ / Ⓣ Ⓕ
26. Ⓐ Ⓑ Ⓒ Ⓓ / Ⓣ Ⓕ
27. Ⓐ Ⓑ Ⓒ Ⓓ / Ⓣ Ⓕ
28. Ⓐ Ⓑ Ⓒ Ⓓ / Ⓣ Ⓕ
29. Ⓐ Ⓑ Ⓒ Ⓓ / Ⓣ Ⓕ
30. Ⓐ Ⓑ Ⓒ Ⓓ / Ⓣ Ⓕ
31. Ⓐ Ⓑ Ⓒ Ⓓ / Ⓣ Ⓕ
32. Ⓐ Ⓑ Ⓒ Ⓓ / Ⓣ Ⓕ
33. Ⓐ Ⓑ Ⓒ Ⓓ / Ⓣ Ⓕ
34. Ⓐ Ⓑ Ⓒ Ⓓ / Ⓣ Ⓕ
35. Ⓐ Ⓑ Ⓒ Ⓓ / Ⓣ Ⓕ
36. Ⓐ Ⓑ Ⓒ Ⓓ / Ⓣ Ⓕ
37. Ⓐ Ⓑ Ⓒ Ⓓ / Ⓣ Ⓕ
38. Ⓐ Ⓑ Ⓒ Ⓓ / Ⓣ Ⓕ
39. Ⓐ Ⓑ Ⓒ Ⓓ / Ⓣ Ⓕ
40. Ⓐ Ⓑ Ⓒ Ⓓ / Ⓣ Ⓕ

Copyright © 2000 Harcourt, Inc. All rights reserved.

2000 S CORPORATION TAX GUIDE
CPE SURVEY

	Y	N
1. Were you informed in advance of the:		
a. objectives of the course?	❑	❑
b. experience level needed to complete the course?	❑	❑
c. program content?	❑	❑
d. nature and extent of advance preparation necessary?	❑	❑
e. teaching method?	❑	❑
f. number of CPE credit hours?	❑	❑
2. Do you agree with the publisher's assessment of:		
a. objectives of the course?	❑	❑
b. experience level needed to complete the course?	❑	❑
c. program content?	❑	❑
d. nature and extent of advance preparation necessary?	❑	❑
e. teaching method?	❑	❑
f. number of CPE credit hours?	❑	❑
3. Was the material relevant?	❑	❑
4. Was the presentation of the material effective?	❑	❑
5. Did the program increase your professional competence?	❑	❑
6. Was the program content timely and effective?	❑	❑

Your comments: ______________________________

____

____

____

____

____

____

Copyright © 2000 Harcourt, Inc. All rights reserved.

INDEX

INDEX

C

INDEX

INDEX

INDEX

INDEX

INDEX

INDEX

INDEX

INDEX

INDEX

HARCOURT SOFTWARE LICENSE AGREEMENT

READ THE TERMS AND CONDITIONS OF THIS LICENSE AGREEMENT CAREFULLY BEFORE INSTALLING THE SOFTWARE (THE "PROGRAM") TO ACCOMPANY *S CORPORATION TAXATION GUIDE* (THE "BOOK"). THE PROGRAM IS COPYRIGHTED AND LICENSED (NOT SOLD). BY INSTALLING THE PROGRAM, YOU ARE ACCEPTING AND AGREEING TO THE TERMS OF THIS LICENSE AGREEMENT. IF YOU ARE NOT WILLING TO BE BOUND BY THE TERMS OF THIS LICENSE AGREEMENT, YOU SHOULD PROMPTLY RETURN THE PACKAGE IN RESELLABLE CONDITION AND YOU WILL RECEIVE A REFUND OF YOUR MONEY. THIS LICENSE AGREEMENT REPRESENTS THE ENTIRE AGREEMENT CONCERNING THE PROGRAM BETWEEN YOU AND HARCOURT, INC. (REFERRED TO AS "LICENSOR"), AND IT SUPERSEDES ANY PRIOR PROPOSAL, REPRESENTATION, OR UNDERSTANDING BETWEEN THE PARTIES.

1. License Grant. Licensor hereby grants to you, and you accept, a nonexclusive license to use the Program CD-ROM and the computer programs contained therein in machine-readable, object code form only (collectively referred to as the "Software"), and the accompanying User Documentation, only as authorized in this License Agreement. The Software may be used only on a single computer owned, leased, or otherwise controlled by you; or in the event of the inoperability of that computer, on a backup computer selected by you. Neither concurrent use on two or more computers nor use in a local area network or other network is permitted without separate authorization and the possible payment of other license fees. You agree that you will not assign, sublease, transfer, pledge, lease, rent, or share your rights under the License Agreement. You agree that you may not reverse engineer, decompile dissemble, or otherwise adapt, modify, or translate the Software.

Upon loading the Software into your computer, you may retain the Program CD-ROM for backup purposes. In addition, you may make one copy of the Software on a set of diskettes (or other storage medium) for the purpose of backup in the event the Program Diskettes are damaged or destroyed. You may make one copy of any additional User Documentation (such as the README.TXT file or the "About the Computer Disc" section of the Book) for backup purposes. Any such copies of the Software or the User Documentation shall include Licensor's copyright and other proprietary notices. Except as authorized under this paragraph, no copies of the program or any portions thereof may be made by you or any person under your authority or control.

2. Licensor's Rights. You acknowledge and agree that the Software and the User Documentation are proprietary products of Licensor protected under U.S. copyright law. You further acknowledge and agree that all right, title, and interest in and to the Program, including associated intellectual property rights, are and shall remain with Licensor. This License Agreement does not convey to you an interest in or to the Program, including associated intellectual property rights, are and shall remain with Licensor. This License Agreement does not convey to you an interest in or to the Program, but only a limited right of use revocable in accordance with the terms of the License Agreement.

3. License Fees. The license fees paid by you are paid in consideration of the licenses granted under this License Agreement.

4. Term. This License Agreement is effective upon your installing this software and shall continue until terminated. You may terminate this License Agreement at any time by returning the Program and all copies thereof and extracts therefrom to Licensor. Licensor may terminate this License Agreement upon the breach by you of any term hereof. Upon such termination by Licensor, you agree to return to Licensor the Program and all copies and portions thereof.

5. Limited Warranty. Licensor warrants, for our benefit alone, for a period of 90 days from the date of commencement of this License Agreement (referred to as the "Warranty Period") that the Program CD-ROM in which the Software is contained is free from defects in material and workmanship. If during the Warranty Period, a defect appears in the Program diskettes, you may return the Program to Licensor for either replacement or, at Licensor's option, refund of amounts paid by you under this License Agreement. You agree that the foregoing constitutes your sole and exclusive remedy for breach by Licensor of any warranties made under this Agreement. EXCEPT FOR THE WARRANTIES SET FORTH ABOVE, THE PROGRAM, AND THE SOFTWARE CONTAINED THEREIN, ARE LICENSED "AS IS," AND LICENSOR DISCLAIMS ANY AND ALL OTHER WARRANTIES, WHETHER EXPRESS OR IMPLIED, INCLUDING, WITHOUT LIMITATION, ANY IMPLIED WARRANTIES OF MERCHANTABILITY OR FITNESS FOR A PARTICULAR PURPOSE.

6. Limitation of Liability. Licensor's cumulative liability to you or any other party for any loss or damages resulting from any claims, demands, or actions arising out of or relating to this Agreement shall not exceed the license free paid to Licensor for the use of the Program. IN NO EVENT SHALL LICENSOR BE LIABLE FOR ANY INDIRECT, INCIDENTAL, CONSEQUENTIAL, SPECIAL, OR EXEMPLARY DAMAGES (INCLUDING, BUT NOT LIMITED TO, LOSS OF DATA, BUSINESS INTERRUPTION, OR LOST PROFITS) EVEN IF LICENSOR HAS BEEN ADVISED OF THE POSSIBILITY OF SUCH DAMAGES.

7. Miscellaneous. This License Agreement shall be construed and governed in accordance with the laws of the State of California. Should any term of this License Agreement be declared void or unenforceable by any court of competent jurisdiction, such declaration shall have no effect on the remaining terms hereof. The failure of either party to enforce any rights granted hereunder or to take action against the other party in the event of any breach hereunder shall not be deemed a waiver by that party as to subsequent enforcement of rights or subsequent actions in the event of future breaches.